DATE DUE	RETURNED

HANDBOOK OF RESEARCH ON INTERNATIONAL ENTREPRENEURSHIP

Handbook of Research on International Entrepreneurship

165701

Edited by

Léo-Paul Dana

College of Business and Economics, University of Canterbury, New Zealand

Senior Advisor, World Association for Small and Medium Enterprises

and

Founding Editor, Journal of International Entrepreneurship

Edward Elgar
Cheltenham, UK • Northampton, MA, USA

Published by
Edward Elgar Publishing Limited
Glensanda House
Montpellier Parade
Cheltenham
Glos GL50 1UA
UK

Edward Elgar Publishing, Inc.
136 West Street
Suite 202
Northampton
Massachusetts 01060
USA

A catalogue record for this book
is available from the British Library

Library of Congress Cataloguing in Publication Data

Handbook of research on international entrepreneurship / edited by Léo-Paul Dana.
    p. cm.
    1. International business enterprises–Research–Handbooks, manuals, etc.
    2. Entrepreneurship–Research–Handbooks, manuals, etc.   I. Dana, Léo-Paul.

HD2755.5.H372   2004
338'.04–dc22   2003049348

ISBN 1 84376 069 X (cased)

Printed and Bound in Great Britain by MPG Books Ltd, Bodmin, Cornwall

Contents

Foreword

Entrepreneurship has become recognized as a major force in the global economy and, as internationalization issues become increasingly important to business, there is a growing need to research and understand when, how and why entrepreneurs internationalize their firms. Academic institutions around the world, including Georgia State University, Imperial College, Strathclyde University and the University of Adelaide, have been introducing courses about international entrepreneurship, yet the literature is still emerging, and what exists is quite dispersed. It is, therefore, an honour for me to write the Foreword to the world's first handbook about research on international entrepreneurship. I am sure that this book will be a stimulating and useful volume for researchers, doctoral students and other readers everywhere.

In what is itself a testament to the international nature of business, the editor of this volume, working from the University of Canterbury, in New Zealand, has commissioned chapters from leading researchers around the world. As a result, this reference book presents a wide variety of reflections, concepts and perspectives of international entrepreneurship. It includes recent research conducted by international consultant and McGill University professor Nancy Adler, Paul Beamish (former editor of the prestigious *Journal of International Business Studies*), Robert Brockhaus Sr (delegate to the White House Conference on Small Business), Frank Hoy (former editor of the highly respected journal *Entrepreneurship: Theory & Practice*), Richard W. Wright (founder of the International Business Department at McGill University, and currently the E. Claiborne Robins Distinguished Chair in Business at the University of Richmond) and geographer Henry Yeung.

These notable researchers have a common dedication to rigorous methodologies and vigorous research. Together, in this volume, the researchers have assembled and presented a cross-section of tested methods and innovative approaches. These contributions are an inspiration to younger researchers, and this bids fair to set the tone, and level of intellectual rigour and vigour, for future research in the emerging field of international entrepreneurship. I am delighted that the University of Canterbury, through the work of Léo-Paul Dana, is associated with this endeavour and with this volume.

Professor Bob Kirk
Acting Vice-Chancellor, University of Canterbury, New Zealand
October 15, 2002

Preface

Not long ago, international business was predominantly the domain of large firms, with smaller firms tending to remain local or regional; internationalization was an expansion option of interest to some enterprises, but seldom was it a competitive necessity. Many owner–managers opted to avoid the uncertainties of competing in foreign markets, and simply kept their firms small and local. Traditional internationalization theories, therefore, focused mainly on large multinational corporations, and were less pertinent to entrepreneurs and their smaller firms. Large multinational corporations were the primary unit of interest in international business studies, and international business journals rightly focused on research about multinational corporations. Meanwhile, other journals focused on entrepreneurs and their relatively small enterprises. Entrepreneurship studies tended to examine decision makers in one environment – a domestic setting for mainstream entrepreneurs or a host society for immigrants; entrepreneurial behaviour was often explained as a function of the entrepreneur's personality, rather than as a function of the environment.

Nowadays, technology facilitates internationalization. International business includes the activities of smaller-scale entrepreneurs, and this is not limited to exporting. While there are opportunities for entrepreneurs who internationalize, serious threats face those who ignore the international arena: with the liberalization of trade and improved telecommunications, international competitors threaten domestic firms in formerly protected markets.

Globalization is thus transforming the competitive environment of small and large players alike. As a result, internationalization issues will continue to be increasingly important to business. There is a growing need to understand internationalization in the context of entrepreneurship, as well as large multinationals; knowledge of how, when and why firms internationalize has become an important topic for research. This has given rise to a new field of research, International Entrepreneurship.

The first McGill conference on International Entrepreneurship took place at McGill University, on 25–8 September, 1998; Zoltan Acs and I were keynote speakers. Out of the conference came several journal articles, as well as Richard W. Wright's reference volume, *International Entrepreneurship: Globalization of Emerging Businesses*, published in 1999 by JAI Press. The success of the first conference led to interest in a follow-up. I therefore took it upon myself to organize the second conference, focusing on the internationalization issues of entrepreneurship. This conference was held at the legendary Goodwood Park Hotel, in Singapore, on 15–18 August 1999; keynote speakers were Zoltan Acs and Richard Wright. Some papers were selected for inclusion in a special issue of the *Journal of Euromarketing*, simultaneously published as a book, for which I served as editor. Also, the March 2001 issue of *Small Business Economics* was dedicated to internationalization; this included the prize-winning papers of the conference that I had hosted in Singapore. In April 2001, I first proposed the idea of creating a dedicated journal, and this led to the launch of the *Journal of International Entrepreneurship.*

In September 2001, I was keynote speaker at the McGill Conference on International Entrepreneurship, at Strathclyde; it was there that Francine Sullivan, commissioning editor for Edward Elgar, kindly approached me to edit this *Handbook of Research on International Entrepreneurship*. Shortly thereafter, international entrepreneur Mr Edward Elgar came to New Zealand, and we discussed this project, which – thanks to the support of academic leaders – is now a reality.

It has been an honour to serve as editor for this volume. As institutions of higher learning, around the world, introduce courses about international entrepreneurship, and as relevant research is on the rise, this reference book is indeed very timely.

Léo-Paul Dana

Contributors

Nancy J. Adler is Professor of International Management at the Faculty of Management, McGill University in Montreal, Canada. She received her BA in economics, followed by her MBA and PhD in management from the University of California at Los Angeles (UCLA). Dr Adler conducts research and consults on global leadership, cross-cultural management and women as global managers and leaders. She has authored over 100 articles, produced the film *A Portable Life*, and published the books *International Dimensions of Organisational Behavior* (4th edn, 2002), *Women in Management Worldwide* and *Competitive Frontiers: Women Managers in a Global Economy*. Her newest book is *From Boston to Beijing: Managing with a Worldview*. Dr Adler is a consultant to private corporations and government organizations on projects in Asia, Europe, North and South America and the Middle East. She has taught Chinese executives in the People's Republic of China, held the Citicorp Visiting Doctoral Professorship at the University of Hong Kong and taught executive seminars at INSEAD in France, Oxford University in England and Bocconi University in Italy. She received McGill University's first Distinguished Teaching Award in Management and was one of only a few professors to receive it a second time. Dr Adler has served on the Board of Governors of the American Society for Training and Development (ASTD), the Canadian Social Science Advisory Committee to UNESCO, the Strategic Grants Committee of the Social Sciences and Humanities Research Council, and the Executive Committees of the Pacific Asian Consortium for International Business, Education and Research, the International Personnel Association and the Society for Human Resource Management's International Institute, as well as having held leadership positions in the Academy of International Business (AIB), the Society for Intercultural Education, Training and Research (SIETAR), and the Academy of Management. She received ASTD's International Leadership Award, SIETAR's Outstanding Senior Interculturalist Award, the YWCA's Femme de Mérite (Woman of Distinction) Award, and the Sage Award for scholarly contributions to management. She was selected as a 3M Teaching Fellow honouring her as one of Canada's top university professors, and was elected to both the Fellows of the Academy of International Business and the Academy of Management Fellows.

Ilan Alon teaches International Business at Crummer Graduate School of Business, Rollins College. He is the author and co-editor of seven books and over 60 articles and chapters published in refereed journals, books and conferences. Dr Alon's research focuses on international business, franchising and political risk assessment.

Paul W. Beamish is Associate Dean – Research, as well as Professor of International Business at the Richard Ivey School of Business, University of Western Ontario, in London, Canada. He is the author or co-author of 36 books and over 80 articles or contributed chapters. His books are in the areas of international management, strategic management, international entrepreneurship and, especially, joint ventures and alliances. His articles have appeared in the three Academy of Management journals, *SMJ*, *Journal of International Business Studies*, *Journal of Small Business Management* and elsewhere. He has received best research awards from the Academy of Management, the Academy of International Business and the Administrative Sciences Association of Canada (ASAC). He served as editor-in-chief of the *Journal of International Business Studies* from 1993 to 1997. His consulting, management training and joint venture facilitation activities have been in both the private and the public sector. He has worked for such organizations as The Canadian Foreign Service Institute, Dupont, Harvard Institute for International Development, Hayes-Dana, Labatt, Nortel Networks, Schneider and Valmet. Beamish has authored nearly 80 case studies, primarily in the international strategy area. These have appeared in *Asian Case Research Journal*, *Case Research Journal* and in over 50 books.

Jim Bell is Professor of International Business Entrepreneurship at the University of Ulster, Magee College, Northern Ireland and gained his PhD in Marketing from the University of Strathclyde, Scotland. He lectures in international marketing and has research interests in the internationalization of knowledge-based SMEs and international marketing/business education. He has published widely in both these areas. He has been visiting Professor of Marketing at the University of Nebraska Omaha, visiting Professor of International Business at Creighton University and Associate Professor of Marketing at the University of Otago in New Zealand. He also spent five years in industry, holding several international management positions, has undertaken international research projects for firms in various countries, and has been involved in export training programmes in Eastern Europe. Professor Bell is on the Editorial Advisory Board of the *Journal of International Entrepreneurship*.

The late **Anders Blomstermo** (formerly Majkgård) was formerly Associate Professor at the Department of Business Studies, Uppsala University, in

Sweden. Blomstermo had previously been published in the *Journal of International Business Studies*, the *Journal of Business-to-Business Marketing* and the *Journal of Services Marketing*, among others

Robert H. Brockhaus, Sr, assumed the position of Director of the Jefferson Smurfit Center for Entrepreneurial Studies at Saint Louis University in 1987. In February 1991, he was installed as the Coleman Foundation Chair in Entrepreneurship. He is the past State Director for Missouri Small Business Development Centers, past national chairperson of the Academy of Management's Entrepreneurship division, past President of the National Small Business Institute Directors' Association, past International President of the International Council for Small Business and was an elected delegate to the 1986 and 1995 White House Conference on Small Business. He is also a Fellow of three different academic entrepreneurship organizations – the only person so honoured. Dr Brockhaus is listed in *Who's Who in the World, Who's Who in America, Who's Who in Finance and Industry, International Who's Who in Education, International Businessmen Who's Who*, as well as over 15 other biographical sources of distinction. He has been invited speaker in Australia, Brazil, Canada, China, England, Egypt, Finland, Germany, Japan, Korea, Lebanon, Mexico, New Zealand, Singapore, South Africa and Switzerland, as well as throughout the United States.

Peter Brown spent over ten years actively engaged in international business and export market development prior to joining the University of Otago, Dunedin, New Zealand, as a lecturer in International Marketing. Peter's research interests include small firm internationalization, entrepreneurship and industrial cluster development. Peter is currently working with the Dunedin City Council in a senior management role responsible for marketing and economic development, actively implementing some of the results of his research in clusters and small firm internationalization.

Candida G. Brush is Policy Director of the Council for Women's Entrepreneurship and Leadership (CWEL), and Research Director for the Entrepreneurial Management Institute at Boston University. She was a Research Affiliate to Jonkoping International Business School, Jonkoping, Sweden. She received her DBA from Boston University, her MBA from Boston College and a BA from the University of Colorado. She is the author of two books, *International Entrepreneurship: The Effect of Age on Motives for Internationalization* and *The Woman Entrepreneur: Starting, Financing and Managing a Successful New Business* (1986) and has written 11 book chapters and more than 45 articles published in scholarly journals such as the *Journal of Business Venturing, Strategic Management Journal*,

Entrepreneurship: Theory and Practice, Academy of Management Executive, Journal of Small Business Management and the *Journal of Business Research.* She has authored papers for the Organisation for Economic Cooperation and Development (OECD) and International Labour Organisation (ILO). She is the 2001 recipient of the Entrepreneurship Mentor Award, given by the National Academy of Management Entrepreneurship Division, and co-authored a paper receiving the SBIDA best conceptual paper for 2002. Dr Brush was one of 18 researchers selected to participate in the 1995 White House Conference Research Project: The Future of Small Business and Entrepreneurship into the Year 2010, and was recognized by INC Magazine in 1995 as one of the top 16 researchers in Entrepreneurship in the United States. She served on the Defense Department Advisory Committee on Women in the Services (DACOWITS) an advisory committee to the Department of Defense, is a member of Fleet-Boston's Advisory Board, The Women Entrepreneur's Connection, and served on the Research Advisory Committee for the National Foundation of Women Business Owners. Her research investigates the influence of gender in business start-up, and resource acquisition and strategies in emerging ventures. Most recently with four other researchers, she was funded by the Kauffman Center for Entrepreneurial Leadership, US Small Business Administration, the National Women's Business Council and ESBI (Sweden) to investigate women's access to equity capital, for research referred to as the Diana Project.

Ian Callaghan is at the University of Ulster at Jordanstown in Northern Ireland. His teaching and research interests lie in the areas of management development/education and SME networking. He has published articles in the area of entrepreneurial tendencies of decision makers in small Irish family-owned firms and on intrapreneurial behaviour within larger organizations.

Sylvie K. Chetty is Associate Professor in Marketing in the Department of Commerce, Massey University, Auckland, New Zealand and a visiting researcher at Uppsala University, Sweden. Her research interests are in internationalization, export performance and the business network approach. She has published in such journals as *International Marketing Review, International Business Review, European Journal of Marketing, International Small Business Journal* and the *Journal of Strategic Marketing.*

Chew Soon Beng is Professor of Economics and Industrial Relations and Director of Managerial Economics at the Nanyang Business School, Nanyang Technological University, Singapore. His publications include

Small Firms in Singapore (1988) and *Employment-driven Industrial Relations Regimes: The Case of Singapore* and journal articles in *China Economic Review* and *International Journal of Entrepreneurship and Innovation Management.* Professor Chew is on the Editorial Advisory Board of the *Journal of International Entrepreneurship.*

Rosalind Chew is Associate Professor of the Division of Strategy, Management and Organisation, at the Nanyang Business School, Nanyang Technological University, Singapore. Her publications include *Workers' Perceptions on Wage Determination in Singapore* (1990) and *Wage Policies in Singapore: A Key to Competitiveness* (1996), and journal articles in *Computational Journal* and *International Journal of Manpower.*

Youngjun Choi is a PhD candidate in Strategic Management at J. Mack Robinson College of Business at Georgia State University, Atlanta, GA. Before entering the doctoral programme, he worked as an associate staff member in the planning group of Samsung, and was a strategic planning consultant to small and medium sized companies in Korea. His research interests include global strategies of entrepreneurial firms, the leveraging of knowledge in new ventures, and the effect of industry variables on new venture performance. He obtained his MBA and BBA degrees from Seoul National University, in Seoul, South Korea.

Peggy Cloninger is at the University of Houston-Victoria. Her research activities focus on integrating international, entrepreneurship and social issues into strategic management. She was awarded a Kauffman Center for Entrepreneurial Leadership Grant for her dissertation research examining the influence of service characteristics on the performance of domestic and international US new ventures in the environmental industry. A previous paper, 'Encouraging Ethical Behavior: An Open Systems Approach to Modeling the Influences of Social Controls', was selected by The International Association for Business and Society (I.A.B.S.) for a best papers volume. Dr Cloninger frequently serves as a volunteer at national and international meetings.

Boyd D. Cohen is currently Professor of Strategy and Entrepreneurship at the University of Victoria in British Columbia, Canada. Prior to joining the University of Victoria, Boyd was a professor of entrepreneurship at the Instituto de Empresa in Madrid, Spain. He has taught various entrepreneurship and strategic management courses in undergraduate and MBA programmes. Boyd has focused most of his research on initial public offerings (IPOs), and more recently began studying the internationalization efforts of European entrepreneurial firms. He has several publications, including various book chapters and multiple publications in *Frontiers of Entrepreneurship Research*. He is the coordinator for the 1st Conference on International Entrepreneurship in a European Context (CIEEC), in Madrid, Spain, in March 2003. Boyd also has an extensive consulting background, including three years with Accenture prior to entering academia.

Dave Crick is Professor of Marketing and International Entrepreneurship in the Business School, University of Central England, UK. After six years working in the defence industry, he taught at the University of Strathclyde, the University of Leicester and the De Montfort University before taking up his present position. He has published a number of conference papers at the marketing/entrepreneurship interface and in journals such as *Entrepreneurship & Regional Development*, *International Business Review*, *International Marketing Review*, *Journal of Business Venturing*, *Journal of International Marketing*, *Journal of Small Business Management* and *Small Business Economics*. Professor Crick is on the Editorial Advisory Board of the *Journal of International Entrepreneurship*.

Léo-Paul Dana was formerly Deputy Director of the International Business MBA Programme at Singapore's Nanyang Business School. He also served on the faculties of McGill University and INSEAD. He holds BA and MBA degrees from McGill University, and a PhD from the Ecole des Hautes Etudes Commerciales. He is the author of 100 articles in refereed journals and 15 books, including the best-selling text *Entrepreneurship in Pacific Asia* (1999), *Economies of the Eastern Mediterranean Region* (2000) and *When Economies Change Paths: Models of Transition in China, the Central Asian Republics, Myanmar, and the Nations of Former Indochine Française* (2002). His biography appears annually in the *Canadian Who's Who* (University of Toronto Press), and in *One Thousand Great Scholars* (Cambridge), as well as in the *Who's Who in the World*. He serves as Senior Advisor to the World Association for Small and Medium Enterprises, and as an editorial board member of several journals. Based at the University of Canterbury in New Zealand, he is the founding editor of the *Journal of International Entrepreneurship*.

Laurel J. Delaney is a renowned global small business expert and founder of Global TradeSource Ltd. She has written *Start and Run a Profitable Exporting Business* (Self-Counsel Press Inc.), which offers savvy yet practical global marketing advice. She serves on the Editorial Advisory Board of the *Journal of International Entrepreneurship*.

David Demick is Senior Lecturer in Marketing at the University of Ulster at Jordanstown, in Northern Ireland. His teaching specialization and research interests are in the areas of international export marketing, marketing communications and business education/technology transfer. David has extensive export sales and marketing experience involving over 15 years working with large multinational companies and exporting SMEs. He has undertaken export development and technology transfer programmes in Hungary and Moldova and has been a senior adviser on Marketing and Export development to LEDU (the Northern Ireland small business agency) and on the Advanced Export Development Programme funded by Irish government bodies.

Pavlos Dimitratos is Research Fellow in International Business at the Strathclyde International Business Unit, Department of Marketing, University of Strathclyde. His current research interests include international entrepreneurship and international business strategy and management. He has published in the *Journal of International Entrepreneurship* and *Intereconomics*, contributed to many edited volumes and co-edited a text on international entrepreneurship. Pavlos Dimitratos is Associate Editor of the *Journal of International Entrepreneurship*.

Tiit Elenurm holds the professorship in entrepreneurship at the Estonian Business School. He received his PhD in 1980. He has been visiting researcher at the Helsinki School of Economics and Business Administration and at the London School of Economics. Present research interests of Tiit Elenurm are linked to management of change, international transfer of management knowledge, developing international business, knowledge management and learning organizations in Estonia. In the role of Chairman of the Council of the EBS Executive Training Centre, his aim is to develop synergy between management training, consulting and research activities. Tiit Elenurm is author of 77 scientific publications in the field of organization and management.

Kent Eriksson is Professor at the Centre for Banking and Finance at Södertörn University College, Sweden. He has published several articles in journals such as the *Journal of International Business Studies*, *Strategic Management Journal*, *International Business Review* and *Management International Review*.

Hamid Etemad is Professor of Marketing and International Business at the Faculty of Management, McGill University. A graduate of the University of California, Berkeley, he holds an MEng, an MSc, an MBA and a PhD.

His research interests are in exporting, marketing, economic development, industrial strategy, globalization and technology. Formerly Associate Dean and Director of the McGill MBA Programme, he has also served as President of the Administrative Sciences Association of Canada. Professor Etemad serves on the Editorial Advisory Board of the *Journal of International Entrepreneurship.*

Alain Fayolle is a professor at the INP Grenoble. He is director of a research unit, EPI (Entrepreneurship and Process of Innovation), which specialises in the study of the entrepreneurial processes in a technological and innovative context. From 1991 to 2001, Alain was a full professor at EM Lyon (a leading business school in France) teaching and doing research in the field of entrepreneurship. Alain has higher education degrees in engineering and management. His current research work focuses on the theoretical and methodological issues in studying the entrepreneurial processes and also on some questions related to entrepreneurship education and teaching in France and worldwide. He has published several books and around 30 articles in academic journals. Professor Fayolle serves on the Editorial Advisory Board of the *Journal of International Entrepreneurship.*

Louis Jacques Filion is Maclean Hunter Professor of Entrepreneurship at HEC, the University of Montreal Business School. His academic background includes a BA in Classics (1966), an honours BA in Political Science (1968), an International MA (1974), an MBA (1976) and a PhD (1988). In the course of his career, Dr Filion has started and managed a number of small businesses. His professional experience in management covers the fields of accounting, human resources, operations and marketing. He was a manager with Reynolds Metals and a management consultant with Ernst & Young. In 1981, he joined the Université du Québec à Trois-Rivières, where he remained until 1993, when he became professor of entrepreneurship at HEC-Montreal. He has more than 100 publications to his credit, and has lectured in more than 40 countries. He was past president of the Canadian Council for Small Business and Entrepreneurship (CCSBE-CCPME). His research is concerned with the activity systems of entrepreneurs and the self-employed, small business strategy, epistemology and administrative science research methodologies. He has a special interest in entrepreneurial vision.

Callum J. Floyd completed his master's and PhD degrees at the University of Canterbury. His PhD thesis, titled 'An Organisation Theory Perspective on Choice of Franchising Form', examined choice of franchising forms in seven New Zealand franchise organizations.

Maria Forsman is an economist conducting research at the Swedish School of Economics and Business Administration in Vasa, Finland. Her research interests include knowledge management, business networks and internationalization/deinternationalization processes.

Howard H. Frederick is an American–New Zealander and Stanford graduate with broad European and Latin American experience. He is recognized as an authority in the field of global communications, economic development and new technologies. He is the author of New Zealand's Knowledge Economy Report (1999) and Global Entrepreneurship Monitor New Zealand 2002 and 2001, as well as of numerous journal articles and books. One of New Zealand's leading advocates for the knowledge economy path to development, he is New Zealand's only Professor of Innovation & Entrepreneurship, based at the UNITEC Faculty of Business in Auckland. Before moving to New Zealand, he taught at such universities as Ohio University, University of California, American University and Emerson College. From Emerson College he was shoulder-tapped by the Minister of Economics of the Free State of Saxony to head the Saxony Telematics Development Corporation in eastern Germany, until moving to New Zealand. Current research interests include the impact of technology on national economic development; innovation and entrepreneurship in New Zealand; comparative knowledge societies; global entrepreneurship benchmarking; international communication; e-business implementation; global Internet policy; and business incubation.

Mika Gabrielsson is Professor of International Business at the Helsinki School of Economics, in Finland. His teaching covers areas such as export, international marketing and global marketing, and research interests include, among others, international sales channel strategies and rapid globalization. Before joining the academic world he held several senior positions in purchasing and marketing of global high-tech companies.

Bella L. Galperin received her PhD in International Management from Concordia University, in Canada. She is currently with the International Business Department at Rollins College. Her research areas are cross-cultural management, workplace deviance, innovation and entrepreneurship. Fluent in several languages, she has presented her research findings at a number of professional meetings in Canada, the Caribbean, Israel, Mexico, Poland, Turkey and the United States. She also served as Division Chair, Programme Chair and Academic Reviewer for the International Business Division of the Administrative Sciences Association of Canada. She has worked as a consultant in the telecommunications, pharmaceutical and clothing industries.

Mary Ellen Gordon has bachelor's and MBA degrees from Babson College, and a PhD from the University of Massachusetts at Amherst. Formerly a senior lecturer in marketing in the Department of Management at the University of Canterbury, she is currently managing director of Market Truths, a market research and analysis organization in New Zealand.

J. Patrick Gunning is Professor of Economics at Feng Chia University in Taiwan. He has published books on Austrian economics and public choice. He has also published numerous articles on entrepreneurship, with special attention to its role in the history of economic thought and Austrian economics.

Graham Hall is currently director of Research Degrees at Manchester Business School. He is author or editor of five books, including *Surviving and Prospering in the Small Firm Sector* and *The Internationalisation of SMEs* (both Routledge) and has published in such journals as the *Strategic Management Journal*, the *Journal of Management Studies*, *The European Economic Review*, *Small Business Economics* and the *Journal of Business Finance and Accounting*. He is consultant to a number of companies and has advised the government on small firm policy.

Robert (Bob) T. Hamilton is Professor of Management at the University of Canterbury in Christchurch where he has also served as Faculty Dean. His research interests range from the nature and timing of growth in small firms to the international performance of industries. During the preparation of his contribution to the present volume, he was a 2002 Visiting Slater Fellow at University College, University of Durham, England. He serves on the Editorial Advisory Board of the *Journal of International Entrepreneurship*.

Celia Harvey is a consultant at Marketwise.

Susanna Hinttu graduated from the University of Helsinki, Finland in 1993. After almost 10 years in various positions at three different universities, Susanna Hinttu is currently pursuing her PhD studies at the Swedish School of Economics and Business Administration in Vasa, Finland. Her research interests include social networks, international business and partner selection.

Frank Hoy is Director of the Centers for Entrepreneurial Development, Advancement, Research and Support (CEDARS) at the University of Texas at El Paso (UTEP). He is Professor of Management and Entrepreneurship and holds the endowed Chair for the Study of Trade in the

Americas. From 1991 to 2001, Dr Hoy served as dean of the College of Business Administration at UTEP. He earned his PhD at Texas A&M University, where he developed a small business outreach programme for the Texas Agricultural Extension Service. Subsequently, he became director of the Small Business Development Center for the State of Georgia. He moved from the University of Georgia to Georgia State University in 1988 as the Carl R. Zwerner Professor of Family-Owned Businesses. Dr Hoy's research concentrations are entrepreneurship and economic development, franchising, family business, strategic alliances and social entrepreneurship. He is a past editor of *Entrepreneurship: Theory and Practice* and is currently the editor for Latin America of the *Journal of World Business*. His most recent book is *Franchising: An International Perspective*, co-edited with John Stanworth of the University of Westminster.

A. Bakr Ibrahim is the Canadian Imperial Bank of Commerce Endowed Distinguished Professor of Entrepreneurship and Family Business, Director of the Centre for Small Business and Entrepreneurial Studies and Associate Dean, John Molson School of Business, Concordia University, Montreal, Canada. Professor Ibrahim is the author of *Entrepreneurship and Small Business Management*, 4th edn, *Strategic Management*, *Family Business Management*, *Canadian Entrepreneurial Studies* and *Risk Evaluation of Small Knowledge-Based Firms*. Dr Ibrahim has published numerous articles on entrepreneurship, strategy and family business. He has served as a consultant to businesses and government organizations worldwide.

Bob Kirk was appointed Acting Vice-Chancellor of the University of Canterbury in September 2002. Prior to that he was Deputy Vice-Chancellor from December 2000. For two years prior to that he held the position of Pro-Vice Chancellor Research. Key aspects of research support in the university, most notably involvement with the Research Committee, the Research Office and with Gateway Antarctica Centre, will continue in the new role. Professor Kirk chairs the Academic Staff Committee and his portfolio also includes work in quality assurance and risk management. He chaired the Academic Audit Steering Committee in 2000. Professor Kirk was appointed to the Chair of Geography in 1994. He continues a teaching role in Geography and heads a substantial research group.

Soren Kock is Professor in Management at the Swedish School of Economics and Business Administration in Vasa, Finland. He has published in a number of international journals. His research interests include business networks, international business, cooperation, competition, co-opetition, purchasing and market orientation.

Spyros Lioukas is Professor of Business Strategy at the Department of Management and Technology, Athens University of Economics and Business. At the time of writing his contribution to the present volume, he was the Greek Ambassador to the OECD. His current research interests include business strategy and internationalization as well as entrepreneurship and regulation. He has published in the *Journal of Industrial Economics, Management Science, Organization Science* and *Strategic Management Journal*, among others. He serves on the Editorial Advisory Board of the *Journal of International Entrepreneurship.*

Jane W. Lu is an Assistant Professor in the Department of Business Policy, National University of Singapore. Her research focuses on the intersection between network theory, institutional theory, international strategy and international entrepreneurship. Her research has been published in leading academic journals such as *Strategic Management Journal* and *Journal of International Business Studies.*

Reijo Luostarinen is Professor and Director of the International Business Study and Research Programme at the Helsinki School of Economics. He has lectured in many countries, on four different continents. He has published widely, especially in internationalization/globalization processes and strategies of firms and is involved in training and consulting for multinational companies, governments and international organizations. He has also been a vice-rector of the HSE and is a chairman of the board of three MNCs and a strategy adviser for many internationalizing companies. Dr Luostarinen is a member of the editorial board of six international journals, including the *Journal of International Entrepreneurship*, and a member of many academic foundations. He has also served as a president for the European International Business Academy. Professor Luostarinen serves on the Editorial Advisory Board of the *Journal of International Entrepreneurship.*

Tatiana S. Manolova is a doctoral candidate in Strategy and Policy at Boston University's School of Management. Her current research interests include international entrepreneurship, competitive strategies for small multinationals, and organizational formation and transformation in transitional economies. Recent articles were published in the *International Small Business Journal* and the *Journal of Small Business Strategy.*

Harry Matlay is Reader in SME Development at the University of Central England Business School, in Birmingham, and editor of the *Journal of Small Business and Enterprise Development* (UK). He specializes in training and human resource development and contributes to the research and teaching activities of several centres. Harry Matlay is Book Review Editor of the *Journal of International Entrepreneurship*.

Rod B. McNaughton is Eyton Chair in Entrepreneurship and Director of the Institute for Innovation Research at the University of Waterloo, Canada. His speciality is international marketing strategy, with a focus on the internationalization of small knowledge-intensive firms. He has published widely on choosing international channels of distribution, exporting and export policy, market orientation and value creation, strategic alliances, foreign direct investment and the venture capital industry. Rod previously held a Chair in Marketing at the University of Otago School of Business. He serves on the Editorial Advisory Board of the *Journal of International Entrepreneurship*.

Peter J. Mellalieu is Associate Professor of Business Creativity and Strategy at UNITEC Institute of Technology in Auckland, where he is also Director of the Master of Business Innovation and Entrepreneurship programme. His research interests include longitudinal case studies of global entrepreneurship and the management of innovation strategy.

John Milton-Smith. After graduating from Sydney and Monash universities, Professor Milton-Smith took his doctorate from Cambridge in 1974. While completing his earlier studies on a part-time basis, he held various senior positions in international trade, marketing and management consulting. Following appointments as Dean of Business at RMIT, Victoria College and The Gippsland Institute of Advanced Education, he joined Curtin University of Technology in 1990. Professor Milton-Smith took up his appointment as Professor of Management, Curtin Business School, in 2002, after previously serving as Deputy Vice-Chancellor, Curtin International and Executive Director of the John Curtin Centre (1998–2002) and Deputy Vice Chancellor, Curtin Business School (1990–1997). During 1983–84 he was Visiting Professor in Management at the National University of Singapore and a Visiting Lecturer at several Japanese universities. While living in Singapore he undertook consultancy and training projects for the National Productivity Board, the Singapore Institute of Management and several major companies. Professor Milton-Smith has subsequently been appointed to visiting professorships at leading business schools, including CEIBS, Shanghai, China, in 2001 and EM Lyon, France, in 2002.

Jay Mitra is Director of the Enterprise Research and Development Centre, University of Central England Business School, in Birmingham. He holds a Chair in Enterprise and Economic Development and is the Course Director of the MBA Entrepreneurship Pathway and the novel MSc in Entrepreneurship Programme.

V. Nilakant is a senior lecturer at the department of management, University of Canterbury in New Zealand. He obtained his PhD from Case Western Reserve University. His areas of specialization are organization theory, organizational change and strategic human resource management. His publications include *Managing Organisational Change* (1998) and papers in *Organization Studies*, the *Journal of Management Studies, Human Systems Management* and the *International Small Business Journal*.

Niina Nummela is currently acting as a professor of international business at the Turku School of Economics and Business Administration, Finland. She has researched and published in the area of small business management, cooperation and internationalization.

Jean-Jacques Obrecht is Professor Emeritus, Robert Schuman University, Stragbourg, France. He was formerly Professor of Management at the Faculty of Economics and Management of Louis Pasteur University, Strasbourg, and at the Institute of Business Administration of Robert Schuman University. He held the position of director at that institute until he retired in 1998. He has been the initiator and director of several small business management and entrepreneurship education and training programmes in both universities. At present he is collaborating with the Center for Scientific Studies Applied to Management (C.E.S.A.G.) of Robert Schuman University. He is also involved in the development of a doctoral programme in management science at the National Institute for Accounting and Business Administration (I.N.S.C.A.E.), Antananarivo, Madagascar. Professor Obrecht has published articles and presented papers at international conferences in strategic management of SMEs, ethics and entrepreneurship, especially in an international perspective. As chairman of the 39th Annual World Conference of the International Council for Small Business in June 1994, he published the proceedings of that conference: *Small Business and its Contribution to Regional and International Development*. He was president of the European Council for Small Business from 1991 to 1993. He is still a member of several academic associations and scientific committees of management journals, dedicated to small business and entrepreneurship.

Aidan O'Reilly was formerly Pro-Vice Chancellor and Provost of the University of Ulster and Dean of the Faculty of Business and Management.

He has been Visiting Professor at University College Cork and Dublin Institute of Technology. Aside from his academic activities, he is a former chairman of several Northern Ireland organizations, including Gallaher (NI) and International Business Initiatives (NI), and a director of Calor Gas and Downtown Radio. He has also acted as an export marketing adviser to the United Nations and governments in Africa and the Far East. Currently, he is chairman of Aidan O'Reilly Associates (Belfast and Dublin), a consultancy firm dedicated to improving the international sales and marketing activities of small Irish companies.

Shameen Prashantham, a former Internet editor of *International Marketing Review*, is a researcher at Strathclyde International Business Unit, Department of Marketing, University of Strathclyde in Glasgow, Scotland. His research deals with the impact of the Internet on the internationalization of small knowledge-intensive firms in a developing economy context. He has an MSc with Distinction in International Marketing from the University of Strathclyde, where he won the CIM Prize for Best Academic Performance on the course and a BA with Distinction in Economics from Loyola College, University of Madras, where he won the gold medal. His prior professional experience includes stints in management consulting and advertising firms in the UK and India, while in advertising he worked on the Sun Microsystems account in Bangalore.

Leigh Sear is Research Manager with the Foundation for SME Development, which is part of Durham Business School at the University of Durham. His current interests include small business support structures and governance, social enterprise and entrepreneurship, young people and entrepreneurship and new market development and exporting. Leigh is Book Reviews Editor for the *Journal of International Entrepreneurial Behaviour and Research* and chairs the Research Advisory Group of the Small Firms Enterprise Development Initiative in the United Kingdom.

D. Deo Sharma was until recently Professor at the Department of Marketing of Copenhagen Business School in Denmark. He is now at the Stockholm School of Economics in Sweden. He has published articles on firms' internationalization process in numerous journals, including the *Journal of International Business Studies*, *Journal of Business-to-Business Marketing*, *Journal of Services Marketing* and *International Studies of Management & Organisation*. He serves on the Editorial Advisory Board of the *Journal of International Entrepreneurship*.

Gurvinder S. Shergill is with the Department of Commerce at Massey University, in Auckland, New Zealand. His current research interests are in the areas of marketing strategy, market orientation and financial performance, CRM and financial performance, marketing research, diversification strategy and financial performance. He has published in such journals as the *Journal of Management Studies, Managerial and Decision Economics, New Zealand Economic Papers* and *Pacific Accounting Review,* and he is co-author of *The Logic of New Zealand Business.*

Martine Spence teaches marketing at the School of Management of the University of Ottawa. She has also taught courses in entrepreneurship, international marketing and management strategy in the United Kingdom, France and Montreal. Her principal areas of research interests are in the internationalization process of small businesses and related public policies and various aspects of high-technology entrepreneurship. Her work has been presented at a number of international conferences and published in refereed journals. Prior to academic life, she advised small business owners on start-up and international expansion.

John Thompson is Roger M. Bale Professor of Entrepreneurship at the University of Huddersfield, UK, where he was previously Head of the Department of Management. He is a Visiting Professor at the University of Kuopio in Finland and at UNITEC, Auckland, NZ. His main research interest is the identification of entrepreneurial talent: his current work with Dr Bill Bolton has resulted in two ground-breaking books. He is also interested in fostering and supporting social enterprises.

Ciwen Tu is a final year doctoral student at Manchester Business School. Her thesis centres on various aspects of internationalization, in particular the reasons why some firms seek business overseas, whilst others, facing similar domestic market conditions, do not.

Claudio Vignali is the 'Arnold Ziff' Chair in Retailing at Leeds Metropolitan University. A visiting professor at La Sapienza University of Rome, the faculty of Economics at the University of Zagreb and also at the University of Applied Science Vorarlsberg, in Austria, his main research themes are matrix marketing and action research areas, in which he has published widely. He is case study editor of the *British Food Journal* and joint editor of *Management Case Quarterly.* He also serves on the Editorial Advisory Board of the *Journal of International Entrepreneurship.*

Thierry Volery is Professor of Entrepreneurship and Director of the Swiss Research Institute for Entrepreneurship and Small Business at the

University of St. Gallen, Switzerland. He is also actively involved in various training and coaching programmes for entrepreneurs offered by the Institute. From September 1999 until March 2001, he was Professor of Entrepreneurship and Management at the EM Lyon business school, in France. From 1996 until 1999, he was a senior lecturer in entrepreneurship and international business at Curtin University of Technology in Perth, Western Australia. He is also Visiting Professor at the China Europe International Business School (CEIBS) in Shanghai. He holds a doctorate in business economics and social sciences from the University of Fribourg, Switzerland. His research interests include entrepreneurship in the Asia–Pacific region, corporate venturing and strategic alliances.

Lawrence S. Welch is Professor of International Marketing at Mt Eliza Business School and at the University of Queensland, in Australia. Professor Welch has published extensively on issues pertaining to internationalization and international business operation methods and is a member of the editorial boards of a number of international business journals. His research has involved extensive collaboration with Nordic colleagues over more than two decades. Also he has spent long periods teaching in Nordic business schools, particularly at the Norwegian School of Management BI, Helsinki School of Economics and Business Administration and Copenhagen Business School. He serves on the Editorial Advisory Board of the *Journal of International Entrepreneurship.*

Dianne H.B. Welsh holds the John J. Kahl, Sr Chair in Entrepreneurship at John Carroll University in suburban Cleveland, Ohio. She is also the Academic Director of the University's Muldoon Center for Entrepreneurship. She earned her PhD in Business Administration from the University of Nebraska. Dianne has owned two of her own businesses and has served on numerous boards at the local, state and national levels. She was a Presidential Appointee to the Board of Visitors (Trustees) of the United States Air Force Academy, and served as a member of the Defense Department Advisory Committee on Women in the Service (DACOWITS). Dianne is the Program Chair-Elect of the US Association of Small Business & Entrepreneurship (USASBE), and serves on the Executive Board of the Entrepreneurship Division of the Academy of Management. She has published widely in academic and business journals. Most recently she is the co-editor of the first comprehensive volumes on global franchising. These include two volumes on international franchising in emerging markets published in 2001, and two volumes on industrialized markets published in 2002. She is also President of Welsh International, LLC, a strategic planning firm specializing in entrepreneurial leadership and employee reward systems.

Heather I.M. Wilson is with the Department of International Business at the University of Auckland, New Zealand. Her teaching and research interests include entrepreneurship, innovation, internationalization and networks. She has published in such journals as *Technovation, The Journal of High Technology Management Research* and *International Business Review*. She has also contributed numerous chapters to edited books in international business, strategic management and entrepreneurship.

Len Tiu Wright was previously at the universities of Loughborough, Birmingham and Keele before joining De Montfort University in the UK as a Research Professor. She is co-author of *The Marketing Research Process*, which is now in its fifth edition. She has been employed in a variety of industries and has researched widely in Japan, South East Asia, Europe and North America. Her papers have appeared in academic journals and international conferences for over a decade. Some of these have been given best paper conference awards. Len Tiu has guest edited for a number of academic journals in the UK and abroad. She is the editor of *Qualitative Market Research – An International Journal.*

Richard W. Wright holds the E. Claiborne Robins Distinguished Chair in Business at the Robins School of Business, University of Richmond. Prior to joining the faculty at UR, he was Director of International Business Studies on the Faculty of Management at McGill University, Canada. He serves also as a frequent visitor at other leading management schools around the world. Dr Wright holds a BA degree from Dartmouth College, an MBA from the Amos Tuck School of Business Administration and a doctorate in international management from Indiana University. A citizen of three countries (Canada, the United States and Panama), he worked in the United States diplomatic service and in private business before entering academia. He is president of Wright Consulting Services, an international management consulting and training firm. A prolific writer Dr Wright is the author of 11 books and many journal articles. A co-founder of the McGill Conferences on International Entrepreneurship, his current research and consulting interests focus on the new opportunities and challenges facing small, entrepreneurial firms in the global economy. Professor Wright serves on the Editorial Advisory Board of the *Journal of International Entrepreneurship.*

Henry Wai-chung Yeung is with the Department of Geography of the National University of Singapore. He is a recipient of the National

University of Singapore Outstanding University Researcher Award (1998) and Institute of British Geographers Economic Geography Research Group Best Published Paper Award (1998). He was awarded the Commonwealth Fellowship and the Fulbright Foreign Research Award to spend a sabbatical leave (2002–3) at the University of Manchester and the University of Washington at Seattle. His research interests cover broadly theories and the geography of transnational corporations, Asian firms and their overseas operations and Chinese business networks in the Asia–Pacific region. Professor Yeung has published widely on transnational corporations from developing countries, in particular Hong Kong, Singapore and other Asian Newly Industrialized Economies. He is the author of *Transnational Corporations and Business Networks: Hong Kong Firms in the ASEAN Region* (1998), *Entrepreneurship and the Internationalisation of Asian Firms: An Institutional Perspective* (Edward Elgar, Cheltenham, 2002) and *Chinese Capitalism in a Globalising Era*. He is also the editor of *The Globalisation of Business Firms from Emerging Markets* (Edward Elgar, Cheltenham, 1999) and co-editor of *Globalisation and the Asia Pacific: Contested Territories* (1999), *The Globalisation of Chinese Business Firms* (2000) and *Remaking the Global Economy: Economic Geographical Perspectives* (2003). He has over 50 research papers in internationally refereed journals. He is the co-editor of *Environment and Planning*, associate editor of *Economic Geography*, Asia–Pacific editor of *Global Networks* and business manager of the *Singapore Journal of Tropical Geography*. He sits on the editorial boards of seven other international journals, including the *Asia Pacific Journal of Management*, *European Urban and Regional Studies*, the *Journal of Economic Geography* and the *Review of International Political Economy*.

Ji Feng Yu is at the J. Mack Robinson College of Business at Georgia State University, in Atlanta, Georgia. He received his undergraduate and graduate degrees in financial management from Shanghai University of Finance and Economics. His research interests are international entrepreneurship, corporate governance and e-business.

Shaker A. Zahra is Paul T. Babson Chair of Entrepreneurship at Babson College. His teaching and research centre on the role of technology in global competition, technology business entrepreneurship, corporate entrepreneurship and international entrepreneurship. His research has appeared in the *Academy of Management Journal*, *Academy of Management Review*, *Academy of Management Executive*, *Strategic Management Journal*, *Information Science Research*, *Journal of Management*, *Journal of Management Studies*, *Decision Sciences* and *Journal of Business Venturing*, among others. He is also the (co-)author/(co-)editor of five books. His research has received several awards for excellence, including one from the *Academy of Management Journal* and another from the *Journal of Management*. Professor Zahra has also received awards for excellence in teaching and service, and serves on the Editorial Advisory Board of the *Journal of International Entrepreneurship*.

PART ONE

REFLECTIONS

1 Emerging paradigms of international entrepreneurship*
Léo-Paul Dana and Richard W. Wright

The global business environment is changing dramatically. Traditionally competition in international markets was the realm of large companies, while smaller businesses remained local or regional in scope. However the removal of government-imposed barriers that segregated and protected domestic markets, and recent technological advances in manufacturing, transportation and telecommunications allow even the smallest firms access to customers, suppliers and collaborators around the world. Small companies and/or entrepreneurial enterprises, both domestically and internationally, are increasingly fuelling economic growth and innovation. Reynolds (1997) noted that the recent expansion of markets has not been associated with an expanded role for larger firms. Instead, smaller firms are filling niche roles (Buckley, 1997).

Globalization is having a dramatic impact on the opportunities and challenges facing small businesses. Two changes, in particular, are revolutionizing the management policies and competitive strategies of large and small firms alike. One is the demise of the nation-state as the primary macroeconomic player, or the principal unit around which international economic activity is organized and conducted. The other is the demise of the standalone firm as the primary microeconomic player, or the basic unit of competition. We will elaborate in this chapter on each of these transformations, and then discuss their particular impact on small and medium-sized enterprises (SMEs).

Demise of the nation-state as the primary macroeconomic player
For centuries, the nation-state was the basic unit around which international economic activity was planned, organized and conducted, regardless of the origin of firms. Even business activities that appear highly 'international', such as traditional foreign direct investment (FDI), have been

* This chapter is based on the keynote lecture presented by Léo-Paul Dana at the McGill University Conference on International Entrepreneurship, in Montreal, Canada, 15 September 2002, and on a lecture by Richard W. Wright at the Indiana University Conference on International Business, in Bloomington, Indiana, 23–4 October 2002. The ideas are elaborated in a paper by the same authors, appearing in the *Journal of International Entrepreneurship*, 1(1), March 2003.

moulded strongly by the boundaries of nation-states. The *multidomestic* model of FDI, for example, which has typified foreign investment by European multinationals such as Ericsson, Nestlé, Philips and Unilever, manages highly autonomous subsidiaries, each conforming to local or national environments. The so-called 'international' model, characteristic of the foreign involvement of many American multinationals (including Procter & Gamble) is a more ethnocentric arrangement, in which products and technology are generated mainly by the parent company, but with national subsidiaries in each major (national) market to produce the parent's products for that market. Many Japanese firms, including Komatsu, Matsushita, Sony and Toyota, have followed a more *global* approach. In this model, production may be centralized (often at home) to achieve large production runs of standardized products, but the parent firm still retains a highly national orientation, in its structure and control. Traditional practice and traditional theories thus conform to the prevailing paradigm of the times, reflecting a macroeconomic environment in which international economic activity is moulded and constrained largely by the power of individual nation-states.

The trend towards supranational powers
The traditional models of business involvement, in which business activity is organized largely around the segmentation of factor and product markets into distinct nation-states, is giving way to a new paradigm in which the firm, regardless of where the parent company happens to be based, will obtain various elements of value added from wherever in the world they may be most efficiently obtained, combine or assemble them in whatever location may be the most cost-effective, and then distribute them to wherever appropriate demand conditions exist, almost without regard to national boundaries.

We see examples throughout the world of the decline in the segmentation of product and factor markets by individual nations as power evolves from nation-states to higher, supranational units. This occurs in regional trade agreements such as the European Union (EU), where increasing degrees of power are shifting from the individual member nation-states to the pan-European level, as well as in broader international agreements such as the World Trade Organisation (WTO).

This diminution of national power, and its transfer to supranational or global levels, has profound implications for small businesses and entrepreneurial firms. Primarily, smaller firms now have access to worldwide markets, which most could only have dreamed of a decade ago, as long as they can gain access to the requisite resources. Later in this chapter we will discuss how smaller firms may use collaborative arrangements, especially with larger firms, to springboard themselves into this new, largely border-less world.

The upward evolution of national powers to higher levels also means that firms everywhere now face global competition, without the domestic-market protection formerly afforded by national governments. Even if a small firm prefers not to enter international markets, it must achieve world-scale efficiencies in order to remain competitive and viable in today's open markets. New avenues by which SMEs may achieve these new efficiencies are discussed and illustrated below.

The integration of product and factor markets implies further that any firm operating outside its domestic environment, or even one seeking to obtain world-scale efficiencies without leaving its domestic market, will increasingly need to interface with suppliers and customers in other national cultures. The firm can no longer operate solely within its domestic environment, nor can it decentralize its activities into discreet national profit centres, in which managers often need be sensitive to a single local economy or culture. Therefore managers of large and small firms alike will need intercultural awareness and skills as never before.

The trend towards localization of powers
While economic power and sovereignty are clearly seen evolving from national to supranational levels, we are simultaneously witnessing another important, albeit less obvious, diminution of the traditional powers of nation-states in the opposite direction; there is also a significant power shift from nation-states to local or regional levels. This is especially true in the realm of political and cultural sovereignty.

This trend toward the fragmentation or devolution of powers is most dramatically evident in the abrupt disintegration of the Soviet Union and the former Yugoslav federation. However, devolution of national powers on a more gradual and rational basis is evident elsewhere, most obviously in Western Europe.

- In the United Kingdom, significant new legislative and cultural powers are being decentralized to Scotland and Wales.
- In Spain, the linguistic and cultural assertiveness of regions such as Catalonia, the Basque Region and Galicia are becoming far more pronounced than before.
- Despite the unification of East and West Germany, much greater local autonomy is devolving to the individual German *Länder*, or states.
- Even in France, long considered a bastion of centralized power in the nation-state, a new, semi-autonomous status has been granted to

Corsica; and there is a notable resurgence of regional languages and culture, such as Languedoc or Provençal in the south and Breton in the west.

- In Canada, the Province of Quebec is enjoying greater autonomy than ever before.

It is our belief that local and regional cultural distinctions are becoming more pronounced in the globalized economy, rather than less so. While the consolidation of economic power at increasingly high, supranational levels may enable internationally oriented firms to achieve new productive efficiencies, the growing devolution of cultural and political sovereignty to local and regional jurisdictions means that large firms may need to rely increasingly on smaller, localized firms to achieve the cultural sensitivities they need for local adaptation, thus providing new niche opportunities for SMEs.

Demise of the firm as the primary microeconomic player
The profound change occurring at the microeconomic level is the demise of the company as the primary unit of competition. Management has long viewed the company as a 'black box', a self-contained unit with clearly defined parameters, within which the various management functions take place. Emphasis has been on internalizing value-added functions, to bring them more fully within the control of the firm's management, and on building walls around the firm to help secure the retention of its internal proprietary advantages from competitors. In the new paradigm, however, firms – large and small alike – are often incapable of acquiring and retaining control of the full range of value-added functions on their own. Increasingly, we see firms forming collaborative alliances with other firms, even with potential or actual competitors in the same industry.

Traditional internationalization models
Traditional approaches to internationalization focused on a unipolar and hierarchic distribution of power and control. Internalization Theory (Buckley and Casson, 1976; Morck and Yeung, 1991, 1992; Rugman, 1979, 1981; Teece, 1985) taught us that, by investing in its own foreign subsidiaries, a firm could expand operations, while maintaining control at head office. Likewise, the Eclectic Paradigm (Dunning, 1973, 1977, 1980, 1988) focused on ownership-specific advantages and location-specific advantages that a firm can enjoy, while maintaining centralized control.

A unipolar scenario is also implicit in the Stage Models of Incremental Internationalization (Bartlett and Ghoshal, 1989; Bilkey, 1978; Bilkey and

Tesar, 1977; Buckley, Newbould and Thurwell, 1988; Cavusgil, 1980, 1984; Cavusgil and Nevin, 1981; Johanson and Vahlne, 1977, 1990; Johanson and Wiedersheim-Paul, 1975; Leonidou and Katsikeas, 1996; and Newbould, Buckley and Thurwell, 1978). Internationalization could be achieved without giving up power and control: the internationalizing firm could maintain its unipolar distribution of power and control, albeit at a heavy capital cost. Internationalization, under this model, was expensive because ownership and unipolar (centralized) decision making led to huge, integrated factory complexes. Iron ore entered a plant from one end, and automobiles drove out of the other. Nowadays even Ford has decentralized operations into a multipolar structure. The factory where 100000 employees used to produce 1200 cars a day is down to 3000 employees making 800 cars a day, and this brings us to a new paradigm of international business through networks.

Network models
An alternative to the unipolar paradigm of internationalization assumes a multipolar distribution of power and control. Rather than focusing on the internationalization of an individual centralized firm with a unipolar distribution of power and control, we can focus on a multipolar network of firms. Power and control are divided among independent firms that cooperate voluntarily for increased efficiency and profit. Networks result in the demise of the stand-alone firm (with a hierarchic distribution of power and control) as the principal unit of business competition. Literature pertaining to this networking perspective includes Acs and Dana (2001); Axelsson and Easton (1992); Bodur and Madsen (1993); Brüderl and Preisendörfer (1998); Chetty and Blackenburg-Holm (2000); Coviello and Munro (1995, 1997); Dana (2001); Etemad, Wright and Dana (2001); Fontes and Coombs (1997); Gomes-Casseres (1996); Gynawali and Madhavan (2001); Holmlund and Kock (1998); Johanson and Mattsson (1988, 1992); Johanson and Vahlne (1992); Sharma (1992); Sharma and Johanson (1987); Welch (1992); Welch and Luostarinen (1988, 1993); Welch and Welch (1996); Wilkinson, Mattsson, and Easton (2000). In addition, Stabell and Fjeldstad (1998) discuss reciprocal interdependence. Rather than focus on the individual firm, we can focus on a multipolar system of alliances.

Examples of this move toward global alliances among large firms abound, from a variety of industries. In the airline industry, for example, Northwest and KLM used to be true competitors. Each tried to take away market share from the other; each used to advertise to encourage consumers to *select one over the other*. Marketing by one firm actually hurt the other firm: it was a zero sum game with a limited pie. Today the former rivals engage in symbiotic marketing. By acting together, the two firms increase the attractiveness of flying either airline. In other words, it is no longer a zero sum game. We are no longer dealing with two isolated unipolar firms, but with a multipolar network, in this case an integrated inter-line product. People who otherwise would not fly decide to fly, thanks to the new convenience. In other words, symbiotic management yields an enlarged pie. It is possible, therefore, to play a non-zero sum game (Casti and Karlqvist, 1995; Jarillo, 1993; Webster, 1992; Zineldin, 1998). Leading alliances in the airline sector include the Star Alliance (14 airlines) and Oneworld (eight airlines).

Similar alliances among major firms in other industries are very numerous. Examples include the following:

- an alliance among IBM (USA), Toshiba (Japan) and Siemens (Germany) in electronics;
- another alliance in electronics among ATT (USA), Philips (Netherlands) and Olivetti (Italy);
- an automotive alliance among Ford (USA), Mazda (Japan), Jaguar (UK) and Volvo (Sweden);
- another automotive alliance among GM (USA), Toyota (Japan), Daewoo (South Korea) and Saab (Sweden);
- a network of alliances between Millennium Pharmaceuticals (USA) and nearly 700 partners. For a discussion of alliances in this industry, see Pangarkar and Klein (1998).

The new paradigm of multipolar competition

Relationships of one form or another have always been at the core of competitiveness. Increasingly, however, firms are finding that networks of relationships need not necessarily be 'internalized' or controlled by direct ownership and internal hierarchies to be effective. What we are witnessing today is a shift in paradigm from traditional forms of collaboration, in which the locus of control lies in formal control through ownership and internal hierarchy, to newer forms of collaboration in which control emanates from interdependence and mutuality of benefit. This represents a significant departure from the past tradition. In the newly-emerging competitive paradigm, the unit of competition is no longer the individual firm but, rather, networks of firms collaborating interdependently for higher mutual benefit than their respective independent operations can yield. In this network-centred system, SMEs can focus on a set of capabilities, competencies, knowledge and skills much needed by the network, in order to generate higher benefits both to themselves and to their network partners than any of them could realize by operating independently. Each member of such networks, often regardless of size, can specialize on a different part of the value chain, which may be located in different parts of the world.

A rich literature has been developed on collaboration among large firms. Among the many contributions are Doz and Hamel (1997), Forrest (1992), Gomes-Casseres (1994, 1996), Kanter (1994), Parkhe (1997), Stafford (1994) and the three-volume series edited by Beamish and Killing (1998).

For small firms, perhaps even more than for large ones, partnering with other firms through various forms of collaborative arrangements is becoming imperative. In the first place, SMEs often lack the resources for gradual, 'stages' progression into the international arena over time, particularly within a time frame needed to exploit increasingly short-lived proprietary advantages. In the second place, they need to achieve world-scale efficiencies even if they are not entering world markets, to withstand new competition from abroad.

As a consequence of these new imperatives, small firms are benefiting increasingly from interaction with other small firms in networks of entrepreneurs. This is documented by Bartels (2000), Chetty and Blackenburg-Holm (2000), Coviello and Munro (1995, 1997), Holmlund and Kock (1998), Perrow (1992), Sadler and Chetty (2000) and Welch *et al.* (2000).

Even more significant, in our view, is the growing trend towards symbiotic collaboration between small and large firms, which allows the product of smaller firms to reach global markets more quickly than through independent expansion (Harrison, 1997). Bonaccorsi (1992) and Etemad, Wright and Dana (2001) have explained how small businesses can rely on large firms for parts of their internationalization activities, fusing elements of international business with small business/entrepreneurship. Performing specialized functions for large firms allows small firms to steepen their own learning curve, and to internalize sufficient expertise to become competitive at the global level.

Thus internationalization increasingly involves symbiotic relationships among large and small firms. Networks of small and large firms can enhance the competitiveness of both types of organizations. By supplying a portion of the high-volume needs of bigger firms, small firms can specialize, achieving their own economies of scale. As these smaller firms become more competitive, capturing scale economies not possible without large-firm link-ups, the large firms in turn gain competitiveness by integrating those economies into their own value chains. The large firms also gain flexibility and economies of scope by gaining access to a number of highly specialized small firms, each producing a small range of components at very substantial scale economies. A further benefit to large firms linking up with smaller ones is the enhanced ability to tailor products or processes to fit local demand or content requirements.

New opportunities and new challenges

Our discussion has emphasized the trend towards larger units both at the macroeconomic level and at the microeconomic level. Both the state and the firm have yielded control, in exchange for the advantages inherent in being a part of a larger entity. Simultaneously, at both the macro and micro levels, there is a trend towards greater specialization and local expertise. Governments feel increasing pressure to delegate political and cultural powers to local jurisdictions, while firms benefit from increased focus and specialization in their business activities.

In this emerging global environment, entrepreneurs and small-business managers face unprecedented opportunities and complexities. On the one hand, networks allow even small firms to compensate for their deficiencies in size and factor endowments by linking existing resources in networks that allow for an acceleration of growth and international activities, without the heavy commitment of capital and other resources that were required in former times. In addition, outsourcing allows for delegated management. A paradox, however, is that, while networking gives rise to opportunities for delegating management, it is efficient only when an appropriate management framework is in place (Dyer, Kale and Singh, 2001; Pangarkar and Klein, 2001). This translates into increased managerial complexity, in order to benefit from less complex management! Resource complementarity can be a powerful competitive resource, but only when managed appropriately.

Why is network management so complex? Simply because there are more alternatives. Under a unipolar structure, a firm could often focus on a single, integrated strategy for its international expansion. In networks, differentiated strategies may be needed for dissimilar situations, such as (a) dealing with a small firm in the same network, (b) dealing with a large firm in the same network, (c) dealing with a small firm in a different network, (d) dealing with a large firm in a different network, and (e) dealing with a different network, and perhaps joining it.

To operate effectively in this new competitive paradigm, small-business managers will need new skills and competencies. The integration of product and factor markets implies that any firm operating outside its domestic environment, or even one seeking to obtain world-scale efficiencies without leaving its domestic market, will need to interface with suppliers and customers in other national cultures. The firm can no longer operate solely within its domestic environment, nor can it decentralize its activities into discreet national profit centers in which managers can be sensitive to a single local economy or culture. As a consequence, managers will need greater awareness than ever before of business practices and cultural norms in other countries, whether their firms seek to 'go international' or to remain essentially at home. The need for cross-cultural awareness and skills assumes far more importance today than before, not just for managers of internationally oriented firms, but for all managers.

New skills will be needed also to manage relationships – with suppliers, with customers and with other firms. Entirely new skills are needed to manage relationships and networks: defining individual and joint objectives among collaborating companies, evaluating network performance, interfacing different management cultures, monitoring cross-flows of information, and so on. Entrepreneurs will need to develop their ability to identify network-based opportunities for acquiring the specialized resources needed to compete in today's global marketplace, and to understand their own strategic value in the context of networks as an interdependent, as opposed to an independent, entity.

Summary and conclusions
The strategic alternatives facing small firms have changed, and businesses must recognize that spatial constraints, based on the geography of nation-states, are no longer significant barriers to internationalization. This chapter has explained how the demise of nation-states and individual firms has led to international multipolar business networks. We have discussed collaborative imperatives as they relate to SMEs, and we have provided a summary of ideas about networks and value chains.

Management implications
These sea changes in the global business environment have far-reaching implications for business managers, public policy formulators, and researchers alike. Changes at the macroeconomic level will necessitate strategic changes at the microeconomic level. While differences in resource endowments can be compensated by symbiotic management and network membership, networking also increases managerial complexity. To cope with increased managerial complexity, firms will need multi-prong strategies to handle the different sets of scenarios introduced above: symbiotic management with an ally in the same network, competing with a rival in a different network, and dealing with a different network, and perhaps joining it.

The economic environment facing organizations is becoming increasingly dynamic and complex, transcending traditional geographic and political boundaries. SMEs must face the reality that they must now compete on a global stage, regardless of where they are based. For some entrepreneurs and small-business managers, this reality may be a daunting one, because traditionally organizations have focused on unipolar management, in which resources and control were retained largely within the individual company. SMEs are no longer faced with insurmountable barriers to internationalization, perpetuated by larger and more established firms. Business organizations, both large and small, are moving towards a multipolar distribution of power and control, focused on the development of networks, often spanning the boundaries of traditional nation-states. While this provides new opportunities for SME managers, it also adds new complexity to their tasks. The 'old and the proven' methods may no longer work, as the conventional economics of competition, mainly based on the models of the firm-based economy, is largely incapable of capturing the newly emerging paradigm of global competition based on relationships, customization and collaborative alliances.

Entrepreneurs and small-business managers will need dramatically different strategies to compete successfully in the multipolar world economy. They will need world-class efficiency in order to survive, and for many the means to achieving that efficiency is by symbiotic networks. Above all, they must reorient themselves and their firms from their traditional models of competition of the firm-centred economy, based on centralized control and stand-alone competition, towards competing through networks and collaboration.

Recommendations for future research
Given the above discussion, we suggest that future research on entrepreneurship and international business should reflect the context of networks rather than focusing solely on the firm or the individual entrepreneur. Specifically, we encourage the following:

- clarification of the domain of international entrepreneurship, relevant theories and constructs;
- more research on the interrelationship and coordination of public support for entrepreneur initiatives at various levels of government, including national, supranational and local/regional;
- research reflecting the context of networks, rather than focusing solely on the firm or the individual entrepreneur; and
- research on the way knowledge and other proprietary assets are transferred within a decentralized, multipolar network – a far more complex phenomenon than in traditional, centralized firms, where such transfers were a one-step process from head office to peripheral station, or vice versa.

References

Acs, Zoltan J. and Léo-Paul Dana (2001), 'Contrasting Two Models of Wealth Redistribution', *Small Business Economics* 16 (2), March, pp. 63–74.

Axelsson, Bjorn and Geoff Easton (eds) (1992), *Industrial Networks: A New View of Reality*, London: Routledge.

Bartels, Frank L. (2000), 'International Competition and Global Cooperation', in Léo-Paul Dana (ed.), *Global Marketing Cooperation and Networks*, Binghamton, NY: International Business Press, pp. 85–98.

Bartlett, Christopher A. and Sumatra Ghoshal (1989), *Managing Across Borders: The Transnational Solution*, Boston: Harvard Business School Press.

Beamish, Paul W. and J. Peter Killing (eds) (1998), *Cooperative Strategies: European Perspectives/Asian Pacific Perspectives/North American Perspectives*, San Francisco: The New Lexington Press.

Bilkey, Warren J. (1978), 'An Attempted Integration of the Literature on the Export Behavior of Firms', *Journal of International Business Studies* 9 (1), pp. 33–46.

Bilkey, Warren J. and George Tesar (1977), 'The Export Behavior of Smaller Sized Wisconsin Manufacturing Firms', *Journal of International Business Studies* 8 (1), Spring/Summer, pp. 93–8.

Bodur, Muzaffer and Tage Koed Madsen (1993), 'Danish Foreign Direct Investments in Turkey', *European Business Review* 93 (5), pp. 28–43.

Bonaccorsi, Andrea (1992), 'On the Relationship between Firm Size and Export Intensity', *Journal of International Business Studies* 26 (4), pp. 605–35.

Brüderl, Josef and Peter Preisendörfer (1998), 'Network Support and the Success of Newly Founded Businesses', *Small Business Economics* 10 (3), pp. 213–25.

Buckley, Peter J. (1997), 'International Technology Transfer by Small and Medium-Sized Enterprises', *Small Business Economics* 9, pp. 67–78.

Buckley, Peter J. and Mark Casson (1976), *The Future of the Multinational Enterprise,* London: Macmillan.

Buckley, Peter J., Gerald D. Newbould and Jane C. Thurwell (1988), *Foreign Direct Investment by Smaller UK Firms*, London: Macmillan.

Casti, John L. and Anders Karlqvist (eds) (1995), *Cooperation and Conflict in General Evolutionary Process*, New York: Wiley.

Cavusgil, S. Tamer (1980), 'On the Internationalisation Process of Firms', *European Research* 8, pp. 273–81.

Cavusgil, S. Tamer (1984), 'Differences among Exporting Firms Based on Their Degree of Internationalisation', *Journal of Business Research* 12 (2), pp. 195–208.

Cavusgil, S. Tamer and John R. Nevin (1981), 'International Determinants of Export Marketing Behavior', *Journal of Marketing Research* 28, pp. 114–19.

Chetty, Sylvie and Désirée Blackenburg-Holm (2000), 'Internationalisation of Small to Medium-sized Manufacturing Firms: A Network Approach', *International Business Review* 9, pp. 77–93.

Coviello, Nicole E. and Hugh J. Munro (1995), 'Growing the Entrepreneurial Firm: Networking for International Market Development', *European Journal of Marketing* 29 (7), pp. 49–61.

Coviello, Nicole E. and Hugh J. Munro (1997), 'Network Relationships and the Internationalisation Process of Small Software Firms', *International Business Review* 6 (2), pp. 1–26.

Dana, Léo-Paul (2001), 'Networks, Internationalization and Policy', *Small Business Economics* 16 (2), March, pp. 57–62.

Doz, Yves and Gary Hamel (1997), 'The Use of Alliances in Implementing Technology Strategies', in Michael L. Tushman and Philip Anderson (eds), *Managing Strategic Innovation and Change*, Oxford: Oxford University Press.

Dunning, John H. (1973), 'The Determinants of International Production', *Oxford Economic Papers*, November, pp. 289–336.

Dunning, John H. (1977), 'Trade, Location of Economic Activity and MNE: A Search for an Eclectic Approach', *The International Allocation of Economic Activity: Proceedings of a Nobel Symposium Held at Stockholm*, London: Macmillan, pp. 395–418.

Dunning, John H. (1980), 'Toward an Eclectic Theory of International Production: Empirical Tests', *Journal of International Business Studies* 11 (1), pp. 9–31.

Dunning, John H. (1988), 'The Eclectic Paradigm of International Production: A Restatement and Some Possible Extensions', *Journal of International Business Studies* 19, Spring, pp. 1–31.

Dyer, Jeffrey, Prashant Kale and Harbir Singh (2001), 'How to Make Strategic Alliances Work', *MIT Sloan Management Review* 42 (4), Summer, pp. 37–43.

Etemad, Hamid, Richard W. Wright and Léo-Paul Dana (2001), 'Symbiotic International Business Networks: Collaboration Between Small and Large Firms', *Thunderbird International Business Review*, 43 (4), pp. 481–99.

Fontes, Margarita and Rod Coombs (1997), 'The Coincidence of Technology and Market Objectives in the Internationalisation of New Technology-Based Firms', *International Small Business Journal* 15 (4), pp. 14–35.

Forrest, Janet E. (1992), 'Management Aspects of Strategic Partnering', *Journal of General Management*, 17 (4), pp. 25–40.

Gomes-Casseres, Benjamin (1994), 'Group Versus Group: How Alliance Networks Compete', *Harvard Business Review* 72, July–August, pp. 62–74.

Gomes-Casseres, Benjamin (1996), *The Alliance Revolution: The New Shape of Business Rivalry*, Cambridge, MA: Harvard University Press.

Gynawali, Devi R. and Ravindranath Madhavan (2001), 'Network Structure and Competitive Dynamics: A Structural Embeddedness Perspective', *Academy of Management Review* 26 (3), July, pp. 431–45.

Harrison, Bennett (1997), *Lean and Mean*, New York: Gilford.

Holmlund, Maria and Soren Kock (1998), 'Relationships and the Internationalisation of Finnish Small and Medium-sized Companies', *International Small Business Journal,* 16 (4), pp. 46–63.

Jarillo, Carlos J. (1993), *Strategic Networks – Creating the Borderless Organization*, Oxford: Butterworth-Heinemann.

Johanson, Jan and Lars-Gunnar Mattsson (1988), 'Internationalisation in Industrial Systems – a Network Approach', in N. Hood and Jan-Erik Vahlne (eds), *Strategies in Global Competition*, London: Croom Helm, pp. 287–314.

Johanson, Jan and Lars-Gunnar Mattsson (1992), 'Network Positions and Strategic Action – An Analytical Framework', in Bjorn Axelsson and Geoff Easton (eds), *Industrial Networks: A New View of Reality*, London: Routledge, pp. 205–17.

Johanson, Jan and Jan-Erik Vahlne (1977), 'The Internationalization Process of the Firm – A Model of Knowledge Development and Increasing Foreign Market Commitments', *Journal of International Business Studies* 8 (1), Spring/Summer, pp. 23–32.

Johanson, Jan and Jan-Erik Vahlne (1990), 'The Mechanism of Internationalisation', *International Marketing Review* 7 (4), pp. 11–24.

Johanson, Jan and Jan-Erik Vahlne (1992), 'Management of Foreign Market Entry', *Scandinavian International Business Review* 1(3), pp. 9–27.

Johanson, Jan and Finn Wiedersheim-Paul (1975), 'The Internationalisation of the Firm: Four Swedish Cases', *Journal of International Management Studies* 12 (3), October, pp. 305–22.

Kanter, Rosabeth Moss (1994), 'Collaborative Advantage: The Art of Alliances', *Harvard Business Review* 72, July–August, pp. 96–108.

Leonidou, Leonidas C. and Constantine S. Katsikeas (1996), 'The Export Development Process', *Journal of International Business Studies* 27 (3), pp. 517–51.

Morck, Randal and Bernard Yeung (1991), 'Why Investors Value Multinationality', *Journal of Business* 64 (2), pp. 165–87.

Morck, Randal and Bernard Yeung, (1992), 'Internalization: An Event Study Test', *Journal of International Economics* 33, pp. 41–56.

Newbould, Gerald D., Peter J. Buckley and Jane C. Thurwell (1978), *Going International – The Enterprise of Smaller Companies Overseas*, New York: John Wiley and Sons.

Pangarkar, Nitin and Saul Klein (1998), 'Bandwagon Pressures and Interfirm Alliances in the Global Pharmaceutical Industry', *Journal of International Marketing* 6 (2), pp. 54–73.

Pangarkar, Nitin and Saul Klein (2001), 'The Impacts of Alliance Purpose and Partner Similarity on Alliance Governance', *British Journal of Management* 12, pp. 341–53.

Parkhe, Arvind (1997), 'Strategic Alliance Structuring: A Game Theoretic and Transaction Cost Examination of Inter-firm Cooperation', *Academy of Management Journal*, 36 (4), pp. 794–829.

Perrow, Charles (1992), 'Small Firm Networks', in Nitin Nohria and Robert G. Eccles (eds), *Networks and Organizations: Structure, Form, and Action*, Boston: Harvard Business School Press, pp. 445–70.

Reynolds, Paul D. (1997), 'New and Small Firms in Expanding Markets', *Small Business Economics* 9 (1), pp. 79–84.

Rugman, Alan M. (1979), *International Diversification and the Multinational Enterprise*, Farborough: Lexington.

Rugman, Alan M. (1981), *Inside the Multinationals: The Economics of Internal Markets*, New York: Columbia University Press.

Sadler, Aaron and Sylvie Chetty (2000), 'The Impact of Networks on New Zealand', in Léo-Paul Dana (ed.), *Global Marketing Co-Operation and Networks*, Binghamton, New York: International Business Press, pp. 37–58.

Sharma, D.D. (1992), 'International Business Research: Issues and Trends', *Scandinavian International Business Review* 1 (3), pp. 3–8.

Sharma, D.D. and Jan Johanson (1987), 'Technical Consultancy in Internationalisation', *International Marketing Review*, Winter, pp. 20–29.

Stabell, Charles and Øystein Fjeldstad (1998), 'Configuring Value for Competitive Advantage: On Chains, Shops and Networks', *Strategic Management Journal* 19, pp. 413–37.

Stafford, Edwin R. (1994), 'Using Co-operative Strategies to Make Alliances Work', *Long-Range Planning*, 27 (3), pp. 64–74.

Teece, David J. (1985), 'Multinational Enterprise, Internal Governance and Economic Organization', *American Economic Review* 75, pp. 233–8.

Webster, Frederick E. (1992), 'The Changing Role of Marketing in the Corporation', *Journal of Marketing* 56, October, pp. 1–17.

Welch, Denice and Lawrence S. Welch (1996), 'Internationalization Process and Networks: A Strategic Management Perspective', *Journal of International Marketing* 4 (3), pp. 11–28.

Welch, Denice, Lawrence Welch, Ian Wilkinson and Louise Young (2000), 'An Export Grouping Scheme', in Léo-Paul Dana (ed.), *Global Marketing Co-operation and Networks*, Binghamton, New York: International Business Press, pp. 59–84.

Welch, Lawrence S. (1992), 'The Use of Alliances by Small Firms in Achieving Inter-nationalisation', *Scandinavian International Business Review* 1 (2), pp. 21–37.

Welch, Lawrence S. and Reijo K. Luostarinen (1988), 'Internationalisation: Evolution of a Concept', *Journal of General Management* 14 (2), Winter, pp. 34–55.

Welch, Lawrence S. and Reijo K. Luostarinen (1993), 'Inward–Outward Connections in Internationalization', *Journal of International Marketing* 1 (1), pp. 44–56.

Wilkinson, Ian F., Lars-Gunnar Mattsson and Geoff Easton (2000), 'International Competitiveness and Trade Promotion Policy from a Network Perspective', *Journal of World Business* 35 (3), Fall, pp. 275–99.

Zineldin, Mosad Amin (1998), 'Toward an Ecological Collaborative Relationship Management: A "Co-opetive" Perspective', *European Journal of Marketing* 32 (11/12), pp. 1138–64.

2 An accidental international foray
Frank Hoy

In 1984, the *Academy of Management Review* published 'Differentiating Entrepreneurs from Small Business Owners: A Conceptualization', by James Carland, Frank Hoy, William Boulton and JoAnn Carland. This article has become one of the most frequently cited articles in the entrepreneurship literature. The idea for the article originated with the observations made by Carland and myself when assisting small business owners through the Small Business Development Center of the State of Georgia in the United States. It became evident to us that the majority of our clientele were low growth or no growth ventures, while a minority had the potential and were being managed to achieve rapid growth. The latter were on track to be the wealth and job creators, ventures that are referred to as 'Gazelles'. Carland made the differentiation of these two groups the subject of his dissertation, from which the *Academy of Management Review* article was derived.

Searching for the entrepreneur

The *Academy of Management Review* article was an extension of a research stream that began with my dissertation studies at Texas A&M University. Funded by the United States Department of Agriculture, I conducted an investigation of the decision-making styles of small business owners in rural communities. The study provided information for justifying and designing a university-based network of experts to help small business owners survive and grow in order to maintain and create jobs in rural communities. A survey of 150 business owners generated data, not only about their decision styles, but also about the effectiveness and efficiency of their firms and about their personal characteristics. The research methodology was an early application of multiple triangulation, applying four distinct effectiveness models and obtaining both qualitative and quantitative measurements to the phenomena observed. The findings resulted in articles contributing to the knowledge of rural entrepreneurs (Hoy and Vaught, 1980), organizational effectiveness (Hoy and Hellriegel, 1982; Hoy, Van Fleet and Yetley, 1984) and economic development (Hoy, 1983). Many of the owner characteristics observed were summarized in Vaught and Hoy (1981). Among the key findings we reported were the following.

- Rural entrepreneurs felt that the major obstacles they faced were beyond their control, i.e. the availability of qualified labor, the work ethic of a younger generation, inability to obtain capital, and government regulation, especially the paperwork burden.
- A majority of small business owners were found to be task-oriented, paying close attention to detail. There was little evidence of the 'entrepreneurial vision' associated with innovation, growth or wealth creation.
- The selection of an organizational effectiveness model influences the identification of variables leading to success. In the dissertation study, one model (Pickle and Friedlander, 1967) was determined to be more applicable to small businesses than others examined.
- Providing assistance to small business owners should include fitting the counseling to their learning and decision-making styles as well as providing substantive advice.

In retrospect, the most severe limitation of the sample was its heterogeneity. Although restricted to rural communities and to two industrial classifications, retail and manufacturing, the within-sample variance of industry conditions may have affected interpretation.

These articles, combined with multiple papers presented at various regional and national conferences, represented an attempt through field research and literature reviews to identify characteristics that were consistent among owners of growth-oriented and growth-achieving entrepreneurs. This work was being conducted in an era in which the search for personality, psychological and environmental characteristics of the entrepreneur dominated the field (Hornaday and Churchill, 1987). As director of an economic development organization as well as an academic, I was especially interested in formulating programs to foster or nurture characteristics that would lead to successful business ownership.

The Carland dissertation from which the *AMR* conceptual piece was extracted was the source of empirical support for differentiating entrepreneurs from small business owners. The evidence was published in Carland *et al.* (1988). By that time, an event had occurred that jolted me from my focus on U.S.-based small and entrepreneurial ventures.

Foreign voices
Shortly after its publication, a critique of the Carland *et al.* (1984) article was published in the *International Small Business Journal* (Birley, 1984). The author, a well-established scholar in the field of entrepreneurship, applauded the thesis of the *AMR* article, but faulted its provincial approach to the literature. She properly observed that the conceptualization completely ignored

the rich bodies of literature external to the United States. Having been a regular participant at conferences attended by academics from other countries, I was aware that the study of entrepreneurship was not solely a North American phenomenon. What I and my co-authors had ignored, however, were the many journals and proceedings that were being produced worldwide, adding important pieces to the puzzle that we were calling entrepreneurship.

Shortly after reading this review, I was a member of a group of economic development specialists invited to Brazil to conduct training programs on establishing and managing consulting and assistance centers for small business owners. Other than visits to the adjacent neighbors of the USA, that is Canada and Mexico, this was my first foreign visit since entering academia. The training sessions quickly evolved into mutual exchanges of information. We learned as much as we taught. On both sides, some of the information was transferable, while some was contextually specific. One of the economic development strategies I witnessed and which influenced the practices of the Small Business Development Center of Georgia was described in a paper published in the proceedings of the National Rural Entrepreneurship Symposium (Hoy, 1987).

The Brazil trip was followed in less than two months by my attendance at the Small Firms Policy and Research Conference in Scotland, where I presented another paper describing lessons learned from US-based entrepreneurship and economic development programs. This conference provided my first in-depth exposure to the variety and quality of research being conducted in Europe. It was enlightening to be informed that many of the conferees considered that American researchers, while adept in their methods, were addressing issues of little significance.

These events and experiences influenced my subsequent research directions, leading me to expand my reading of international entrepreneurship and other literature, to engage in collaborative research with colleagues from other countries, to test concepts through field research in international and multicultural contexts, and to encourage other scholars to acquire international experience. Because I was serving as a government official responsible for an entrepreneurship development program in the 1980s, the internationalization of my research initially occurred in the economic development arena, particularly regarding program evaluation.

Implementing and assessing economic development programs

As an economic development program director with academic roots, I began assessing the impacts of various programs and reporting the results in the early 1980s. There were multiple purposes for these evaluations. The first was to gain information for program improvement. Second, on the assumption that the outreach programs were achieving their missions and obtaining returns on taxpayer investments, we anticipated the need for documentation to justify their continuation and possible expansion. Third, research findings could support sharing best practices with colleagues. Initial studies assessed an innovative cooperative education program that placed students in paid work assignments in small firms (Case and Hoy, 1981), university-based management development programs (Hoy, Buchanan and Vaught, 1981) and the relative performance of counseling by students versus extension consultants (Hoy, 1982). A particularly productive line of research focused on the counseling provided by Small Business Development centers across the United States, led by then-doctoral student, James Chrisman (Chrisman, Nelson and Hoy, 1984; Chrisman *et al.*, 1985). Chrisman has pursued investigations of this topic to the present.

The methodology for these studies originated with Richard Robinson's dissertation (Robinson, 1980). Chrisman adapted the Robinson methodology, modifying it over the years with attention both to academic rigor and to the interests of stakeholders. Public policy officials periodically altered their perspectives of the desired outcomes for the programs, at times focusing on tax revenue generated, at other times cost effectiveness, at still others on job creation, and so forth. Additionally, we remained attuned to the refinement of methodologies from other studies. One example was a study commissioned by the United States Small Business Administration and conducted by Centaur Associates (1983). These studies became widely cited and were used as models for other researchers. They were also subjected to intense scrutiny and criticism, which continues to this day (the debate was launched by Elstrott, with a reply by Chrisman *et al.*, both in 1987). The respondents themselves reported the results rather than relying on objective externally verified data. We ensured a conservative assessment of growth measures by inferring causality only in the cases of long-term counseling and by not omitting cases in which counselors had recommended downsizing or termination. The Chrisman *et al.* methodology was defended by Davis (1985) applying an economic argument in support of public sector intervention in the marketplace.

Presentations incorporating the internationalization of this research stream began in 1988 at conferences in California, England and Northern Ireland. In these venues, we examined the US experiences in comparison with efforts under way by universities and government agencies in other countries. In 1991, I was appointed to a commission established by the United States Congress to support governments in Central Europe in creating small business assistance programs. Through this assignment, we were able to apply the American model, modify it through country-specific field research, implement outreach programs in three nations and evaluate each for effectiveness. The design of these projects and their assessments are contained in *Moving to Sustainability: How to Keep Small Business Development Centers Alive* (Fogel, Harrison and Hoy, 1995).

In this book we explained the motivation for American assistance to Central Europe; that is, how it originated with requests from the leaders of the emerging democracies to a congressional delegation. We then outlined the US model, followed by a more detailed discussion of how that model was adapted to various localities. Outcomes assessments were conducted initially through case analyses, followed by data collection for quantitative assessments. Working from the evaluation research designs of Chrisman, Hoy and others, the studies in Central Europe were expanded to cover variables of regional and national importance, such as networking (especially establishing alliances) and obtaining capital.

Other research agendas have superseded my involvement in the program evaluation studies. There is intrinsic value to the field of this research, however. Much of the stimulus for entrepreneurship education and research can be traced back to Birch's seminal work in *The Job Generation Process* (1979). Tracking job creation in the US economy between 1969 and 1976, Birch concluded that firms with 20 or fewer employees were responsible for 60% of the new jobs generated in the country. Public policy makers and universities awakened to the need to pay more attention to a sector that had long been taken for granted or considered unimportant in the macro economy. Programs to foster entrepreneurs and small businesses were launched with taxpayer dollars.

The collapse of the Soviet Union and the emergence of market economies worldwide had a similar effect. Among the many repercussions of the political upheavals has been a global demand for entrepreneurship education, training, assistance programs and research. Those of us who were active researchers in the entrepreneurship and small business arenas in the 1970s and 1980s suddenly found ourselves consulting governments and academic institutions in the former Soviet republics and satellites and in third world nations.

A critical role of academics is to conduct high-quality, objective research. Entrepreneurship scholars are best positioned to design and engage in the evaluative investigations to determine whether such programs should be continued and, if so, how they can be improved. We recognized in the various international efforts that it would be chauvinistic to assume that North American or Western European models could be imposed on other cultures and economies. As a result, the implementation of assistance programs would typically be accompanied by a program evaluation component.

A few examples of work that I have continued to conduct on program assessment and on economic development include a chapter in a book prepared by the United States Department of Agriculture's Economic Research Service (Hoy, 1996) and papers and an article on the ability of small business owners to obtain capital (Schauer and Hoy, 2001). We produce internal assessments of entrepreneurship outreach programs that have been established at the University of Texas at El Paso. These include the Small Business Executive Education Program, the Center for Women in Business, and the Secondary Education Entrepreneurship Program. These programs have also resulted in a book that contains teaching cases on entrepreneurship and cross-border trade (Hoy and Sprinkle, 1999). In particular, I have more recently emphasized research in two other entrepreneurship-related areas in which we also have established outreach programs that seek to foster business formation, survival and growth: family business and franchising.

Family business
In 1988, I accepted an appointment as the Carl R. Zwerner Professor of Family-Owned Businesses at Georgia State University. A major factor in my being offered the position was my experience in studying and counseling small businesses, the vast majority of which can be defined as family businesses. Most typically have multiple family members working in the firm and/or as investors in or lenders to the firm. This specialization spawned a research stream on entrepreneurship and family business which, as with economic development, soon took on international dimensions.

A major outlet for family business research results is the Family Firm Institute (FFI) through the annual conference and journal that it sponsors. FFI is a United States-based organization for firms and professionals who specialize in providing services to family-owned and managed enterprises. FFI has published *Family Business Review* (*FBR*) since the 1980s. Issues of *FBR* are a compilation of scholarly research studies, interviews, book reviews and classic articles addressing family business issues. Taking advantage of our access to business owners in Poland during our economic development work in Central Europe, my co-authors, Gerald Hills and Harold Welsch, and I were able to collect survey data comparing newly emerging family businesses with non-family businesses. In an article we published in *FBR* in 1995, we found that family issues failed to emerge as significant influences on the start-up process. Our unique opportunity to examine a large number of emerging firms in a previously controlled economy allowed us to avoid the usual pitfalls associated with intervening and moderating variables.

In 1990, I was responsible for integrating an academic research track into the annual FFI meeting. We were careful to encourage and select papers that would present practical implications for the FFI membership in their work with family businesses. In that vein, a proceedings paper co-authored with the members of the Atlanta Family Business Study Group, an FFI affiliate, described a case study in which experts from a variety of disciplines worked on the complex issues faced by a small family firm (Hoy *et al.*, 1990). This case study led directly to the formation of multidisciplinary consulting groups that offered greater expertise and more comprehensive services to client firms. Involvement with the FFI also contributed to the formalization of an alliance between the University of Texas at El Paso and the University of Jyväskylä in Finland for family business education, leading to multiple joint research projects.

Academic gatekeeping

One aspect of scholarly research often under-appreciated and sometimes unrecognized is the role of the academic gatekeeper. This is the professional service provided by a scholar through peer review and acceptance. In performing this service, the academic can set a bar for research quality and quantity. He or she can encourage or discourage particular research topics and methodologies. The gatekeeper can invite submissions on themes and solicit contributions from authors based on their reputations and interests. Thus emphases in a field can be influenced by those who control access to publication and presentation outlets.

By chairing the research track for the Family Firm Institute, I was able to encourage the participation of selected entrepreneurship scholars in the family business arena. Earlier, as chair of the Entrepreneurship Division of the Academy of Management, I ensured that family business was encompassed in the domain statement of the division. Subsequently I was appointed editor of *Entrepreneurship Theory & Practice* (1991–4). I commissioned a special issue of the journal focused on family business. In the opening article of that issue, Trudy Verser and I (1994) attempted to define the overlap of the fields of entrepreneurship and family business, drawing on both bodies of literature. This article has become a standard starting point for those who wish to examine family business, entrepreneurship and strategy.

Gatekeeping occurs in a variety of ways under a variety of circumstances. It can be accomplished through service as a conference program chair. As program chair for the International Council for Small Business in 1993, I selected a 'free trade' theme, encouraging theme-related submissions and speakers. As host for an annual Gateway Conference Series program, I promoted the impact of the North American Free Trade Agreement as the central topic for discussion, inviting the then president of the Academy of Management, Michael Hitt, to be keynote speaker. This led to several research articles on international entrepreneurship by Hitt (for example, Hitt and Bartkus, 1997).

The gatekeeping role has continued in association with two additional journals. As of this writing, I am editor for Latin America of the *Journal of World Business*. In this capacity, I solicit scholarly, but practitioner-oriented, research on international strategic management, marketing and human research management. At present, I am negotiating to publish a special issue on international entrepreneurship for the journal. In the 1990s, I co-edited two issues of the *Journal of Business Venturing* with Scott Shane that addressed the entrepreneurship/franchising interface. Although they were primarily focused on the US market, we included studies on international franchising, particularly looking at activity associated with the North American Free Trade Agreement (NAFTA).

Franchising

My interest in franchising was stimulated by multiple factors:

- co-sponsorship of an SBA-funded franchise training program for military veterans;
- involvement of family members in a franchise operation in Mexico;
- moving to a minority–majority city (El Paso, Texas is approximately 70% Hispanic, now with the largest minority group in the United States) at the time the International Franchise Association announced the formation of an initiative to encourage franchisors to engage more minorities in franchising; and
- launching a franchise center at the university which earned several national and regional awards.

Creating the Franchise Center in 1994 was perhaps the foremost factor in my activating a research agenda. To service students and the business community, I needed to be well-versed in the literature and through field research.

Just as with the Hoy and Verser (1994) article that proposed a framework for describing the interconnectedness of family business and entrepreneurship, my initial study of franchising concentrated on the nexus of its domain with entrepreneurship. In an article published in the *International Small Business Journal* (Hoy, 1994), I examined the inherent conflict between franchisor and franchisee brought about by the struggle over autonomy and control. Applying Bull and Willard's theory of entrepreneurship (1993), I explained how the tension in such a relationship is predictable and must be dealt with proactively. In the same year, my son and I presented a paper at the Babson Entrepreneurship Research Conference describing his experience in international franchising (Hoy and Hoy, 1994).

As mentioned previously, between 1996 and 1998, Scott Shane and I co-edited two special issues for the *Journal of Business Venturing* on franchising. Again these were designed to highlight the interrelationship between franchising and entrepreneurship. In the first issue, we concentrated on the entrepreneurial behaviors of both franchisors and franchisees, giving particular attention to international issues, including research in the United Kingdom and on international franchising. In the second issue, we examined franchise networks as entrepreneurial venture forms. Drawing on Hoy (1995), we chose articles that added to our knowledge of growth and wealth creation. One article addressed the impact of NAFTA on franchising.

In 1998, I was invited to London to present research findings to representatives of the British Franchise Association on franchise legislation and regulation in the United States. Their interest stemmed from discussions on regulating franchising taking place among European Union member countries. My study was published in the proceedings of the International Franchise Research Centre Strategy Seminar. Subsequently, the organizer of the seminar, John Stanworth, and I have collaborated on an edited book of readings on franchise research. We observed that many of the seminal studies in the franchise literature are becoming more difficult to get hold of over time. They are being cited in secondary references rather than as original work. Such behavior invites distortion. We sought, therefore, to compile a set of 'must read' contributions to the field. This book, *Franchising: An International Perspective*, became available to franchise scholars and students in 2003.

Lessons learned
My unintended but much valued international odyssey has taught me a few lessons. First and foremost is that professors in general, business professors in particular, and entrepreneurship professors specifically, are not providing students, colleagues and practitioners with a full service if they have not internationalized their research and teaching. This statement is so obvious that justification would be redundant and condescending. Other lessons include the following:

- economic upheaval fosters interest in entrepreneurship. As mentioned above, the failure of communism as a viable economic system stimulated global awareness of the need for entrepreneurial behavior. The Asian Flu, financial crises in Mexico and Argentina, re-engineering and downsizing of multinational corporations have all caused individuals and governments to question whether working in large corporations is any less risky than starting a new venture;

- attendance at professional conferences in which individuals from multiple countries participate. The Babson/Kauffman Entrepreneurship Research Conference and the International Council for Small Business come to mind. These venues encourage the exchange of ideas among scholars and the sense of comfort that one gains from getting to know one's peers. Joint research projects, visiting professor opportunities, consulting assignments and other international arrangements accrue to those who invest their talents in these programs;

- to better appreciate another country's culture and economy, visits should be made to the country for extended periods of time. Business schools frequently employ foreign-born faculty to add to the diversity as well as expertise of their programs. Opportunities for visiting professorships abound. Faculty return from such assignments with a wealth of anecdotes and, it is hoped, collaborative relationships for research projects;

- it is important to recognize that not all academic environments support international research and education, particularly in regard to travel support. In such cases, it is important to advocate such activity and to promote success stories that highlight the benefits reaped by internationalization. It should be easy to demonstrate benefits that outweigh costs.

Looking ahead to creative destruction

What will the future hold for international entrepreneurship research? Are the patterns followed by other disciplines predictive for entrepreneurship? Or, as with the field we study, will we see creative destruction and unexpected innovation? One way to consider the future might be through a set of prospective continua (Figure 2.1). The domain of entrepreneurship has been narrowly defined by some, often restricted to the characteristics of the entrepreneur or the act of starting a venture. Over the years, more and more topics have been encompassed by the label. Will we see increased fragmentation or will researchers engage in more in-depth investigations of a small number of subjects that appear especially productive? My guess is that both will occur, simultaneously. Seminal contributions will engender more research on some topics by talented scholars. The expanding participation of academics in the field will also lead to splintering based on personal interest, access to data, country and culture-specific issues, and other forces. To be able to communicate across national boundaries, scholars will need to be explicit in their definitions and in their research designs.

As many academic disciplines mature, successful authors frequently become more and more specialized in narrower and narrower subject

Research Streams

|———————————————————————————|

Fragmented   Consolidated

Research Topics

|———————————————————————————|

Esoteric   Practical

Degree of Internationalization

|———————————————————————————|

Domestic   Global

Rate of Change

|———————————————————————————|

Incremental   Discontinuous

Applications of Technology

|———————————————————————————|

Tool   Driving force

Figure 2.1   Prospective continua

matter. Eventually they may produce work that is of direct interest only to a small number of academic colleagues. Alternatively, publishing for practitioners may gain a wider audience, but not necessarily credit within academe. To obtain acceptance from faculty in other disciplines, we may see highly talented researchers publish esoteric papers. On the basis of personal observation, however, I expect the field of entrepreneurship to attract a disproportionate share of academics who will choose to keep a foot in practice, conducting and publishing applied research.

Much of what is purported to be international research in the entrepreneurship literature (as well as in other disciplines) consists simply of studies done by one or more academics on entrepreneurship-related variables in countries other than their own. I anticipate that we will move away from this end of the continuum, although I continue to see manuscripts of this type submitted to the *Journal of World Business*. We are much in need of studies that examine cross-border activity. Typical entrepreneurial initiatives into international trade are to adjacent countries with similar cultures and languages. Global studies are appealing and may attract more attention than they warrant in terms of actual economic behavior.

Entrepreneurship, as a field of study, is, at best, in its adolescence. International entrepreneurship is even younger and less explored. Will we learn through incremental contributions, derived from domestic studies, or from models developed within other disciplines, such as marketing, strategic management, international economics and finance? I offer no prediction here, but hope that there will be breakthroughs resulting in discontinuous advances in our knowledge.

Finally, is reflective study being made obsolete by rapidly changing technology? Will we find new technologies to be useful tools aiding our research efforts? Or will technology itself drive our investigations, determining what phenomena we study and how we study them? Will educational technologies change the nature of our profession to such an extent that alternative career paths will be created to meet future knowledge needs? Technology has truly resulted in a shrinking planet. International studies will be easier to conduct, but will this come at the expense of direct international experience?

References

Birch, D.L. (1979), 'The job generation process', research report for the Economic Development Administration of the U.S. Department of Commerce, Cambridge, MA.

Birley, S. (1984), Abstract commentary on Carland *et al.* article, *International Small Business Journal*, 3: 71–2.

Bull, I. and G.E. Willard (1993), 'Towards a theory of entrepreneurship', *Journal of Business Venturing*, 8: 183–95.

Carland, J.W., Jr., J.C. Carland, F. Hoy and W.R. Boulton (1988), 'Distinctions between entrepreneurial and small business ventures', *International Journal of Management*, 5: 98–103.

Carland, J.W., Jr., F. Hoy, W.R. Boulton and J.C. Carland (1984), 'Differentiating entrepreneurs from small business owners: A conceptualization', *Academy of Management Review*, 9: 354–9.

Case, C.R. and F. Hoy (1981), 'Small Business Placements: The extra effort pays off', *Journal of Cooperative Education*, 17: 78–84.

Centaur Associates, Inc. (1983), 'An evaluation of the economic impact of the Small Business Development Center program', U.S. Small Business Administration, Washington, DC.

Chrisman, J.J., R.R. Nelson and F. Hoy (1984), 'Empirical evidence for a contradiction in terms: Cost efficient public sector management', *Proceedings*, Boston, MA: Academy of Management.

Chrisman, J.J., F. Hoy, R.R. Nelson and R.B. Robinson, Jr. (1985), 'The impact of SBDC consulting activities', *Journal of Small Business Management*, 23: 1–11.

Chrisman, J.J., F. Hoy, R.B. Robinson, Jr. and R.R. Nelson (1987), 'Evaluating the impact of SBDC consulting: A reply to Elstrott', *Journal of Small Business Management*, 25: 72–5.

Davis, J. (1985), 'Journal Scan of Chrisman et al. research paper', *New Management*, 2: 64.

Elstrott, J.B. (1987), 'Procedure for improving the evaluation of SBDC consulting activities', *Journal of Small Business Management*, 25:67–71.

Fogel, D.S., M.E. Harrison and F. Hoy (eds) (1995), *Moving to Sustainability: How to Keep Small Business Development Centers Alive*, Aldershot: Avebury.

Hitt, M.A. and B.R. Bartkus (1997), 'International entrepreneurship', in J.A. Katz (ed.), *Advances in Entrepreneurship, Firm Emergence and Growth*, vol. 3, Greenwich, CT: JAI Press, pp. 7–30.

Hornaday, J.A. and N.C. Churchill (1987), 'Current trends in entrepreneurship research', in N.C. Churchill, J.A. Hornaday, B.A. Kirchhoff, O.J. Krasner and K.H. Vesper (eds), *Frontiers of Entrepreneurship Research*, Wellesley, MA: Babson College, pp. 1–21.

Hoy, F. (1982), 'Intervention in new ventures through the SBI versus the SBDC', *Frontiers of Entrepreneurship Research*, Wellesley, MA: Babson College, pp. 506–15.

Hoy, F. (1983), 'A program for rural development from inception through implementation', *Journal of the Community Development Society*, 14: 33–49.

Hoy, F. (1987), 'Who are the rural entrepreneurs?', *Proceedings*, National Rural Entrepreneurship Symposium, Knoxville, TN: Southern Rural Development Center.

Hoy, F. (1994), 'The dark side of franchising or appreciating flaws in an imperfect world', *International Small Business Journal*, 12: 26–38.

Hoy, F. (1995), 'Researching the entrepreneurial venture', in J.A. Katz and R.H. Brockhaus, Sr. (eds), *Advances in Entrepreneurship, Firm Emergence, and Growth*, Vol. 2, Greenwich, CT: JAI Press.

Hoy, F. (1996), 'Entrepreneurship: A Strategy for Rural Development', in T.D. Rawley, D.W. Sears, G. L. Nelson, J.N. Reid and M.J. Yetley (eds), *Rural Development Research*, Westport, CT: Greenwood press.

Hoy, F. (1998), 'Franchising and government initiatives', *Breaking Out of the Home Market*, proceedings of the International Franchise Research Centre Strategy Seminar, London.

Hoy, F. and D. Hellriegel (1982), 'The Kilmann and Herden model of organizational effectiveness criteria for small business managers', *Academy of Management Journal*, 25: 308–22.

Hoy, F. and E.M. Hoy (1994), 'Double your trouble through international franchising: Arby's goes to Mexico', *Frontiers of Entrepreneurship Research*, Wellesley, MA: Babson College.

Hoy, F. and S. Shane (1998), 'Franchising as an entrepreneurial venture form', *Journal of Business Venturing*, 13: 91–4.

Hoy, F. and R.L. Sprinkle (eds) (1999), *Regional Case Studies in International Trade and Strategic Policy*, Dubuque, IA: Kendall/Hunt.

Hoy, F. and B.C. Vaught (1980), 'The rural entrepreneur: A study in frustration', *Journal of Small Business Management*, 18: 19–24.

Hoy, F. and T.G. Verser (1994), 'Emerging business, emerging field: Entrepreneurship and the family firm', *Entrepreneurship Theory and Practice*, 19: 9–23.

Hoy, F., W.W. Buchanan and B.C. Vaught (1981), 'Are your management development programs working?', *Personnel Journal*, 60: 953–7.

Hoy, F. and D. Stanworth (eds) (2003), *Franchising: An International Perspective*, London: Routledge.

Hoy, F., D.D. Van Fleet and M.J. Yetley (1984), 'Comparative organizational effectiveness research leading to an intervention strategy', *Journal of Management Studies*, 21: 443–62.

Hoy, F., L.D. Isaacs, H. Neiman, D.A Schwerzler and P.P. Sidwell (1990), 'A multi-disciplinary application of intervention theory in a family firm', *Proceedings*, Atlanta, GA: Family Firm Institute.

Pickle, H. and F. Friedlander (1967), 'Seven societal criteria of organizational success', *Personnel Psychology*, 20: 165–78.

Robinson, R.B., Jr. (1980), 'An empirical investigation of the impact of SBDC-strategic planning consultation upon the short-term effectiveness of small businesses in Georgia', doctoral dissertation, University of Georgia.

Schauer, D. and F. Hoy (2001), 'A continuing search for relevance in small business and entrepreneurship research', *Academy of Entrepreneurship Journal*, 7: 11–21.

Shane, S. and F. Hoy (1996), 'Franchising: A gateway to cooperative entrepreneurship', *Journal of Business Venturing*, 11: 325–7.

Vaught, B.C. and F. Hoy (1981), 'Have you got what it takes to run your own business?', *Business*, 31: 2–8.

Welsch, H., G. Hills and F. Hoy (1995), 'Family impacts on emerging ventures in Poland', *Family Business Review*, 8: 293–300.

3 Women in international entrepreneurship
*Nancy J. Adler**

I used to question what executive coaches brought to entrepreneurial clients that the entrepreneurs had not already learned from their own experience.[1] I now understand that the answer is perspective – a perspective beyond their own experience or that of their own company or culture. Given my background, I almost always have the opportunity to reframe issues from a broader, global perspective. More frequently, today, I have the opportunity to reframe business realities that have previously been appreciated primarily from a man's point of view into possibilities as seen from both women's and men's perspectives. Part of bringing a broader perspective is offering a context of meaning beyond each entrepreneur's specific position, company and industry. By quietly asking questions that are beyond the bottom line, coaching dialogues offer opportunities to entrepreneurs to consider more consciously the types of contributions they are making to their company and to choose the kinds of contributions they would like to be making to society. Such questions as these often appear unbusinesslike, and therefore illegitimate, when taken out of the privacy of the coaching dialogue:

- What does success mean to you?
- In which ways is your work benefiting society?
- Why would your children be proudest to tell their children about what you have accomplished?

In the public glare of business-as-usual, such questions frequently fail to appear sufficiently pragmatic to warrant an entrepreneur's time. And yet the conversations, reflection and learning that such questions generate often bring soul, along with deep motivation, back into the pragmatism of professionalism and financial success. Context, deep meaning and soul are without counterparts in the pragmatism of successful careers, successful businesses, successful lives and successful societies.

---

* This chapter is based on earlier discussions in Nancy J. Adler's *Coaching Global Executives: Women Succeeding a World Beyond Here* (2000).

Global entrepreneurs: no longer men alone[2]

While few people question anymore that the world of business has gone global, most assumptions about building a global business and succeeding as a global entrepreneur remain based on the experience of men. Many of the most fundamental assumptions about executive success remain paro-chial, limited not only to the experience of men, but often to the experience of men working within their own home country.

Male-based assumptions, however, are no longer appropriate for the twenty-first century. A disproportionate number of women have founded and are now leading entrepreneurial enterprises. According to the US Small Business Administration, for example, women currently own one-third of all American businesses (Kelly, 1996). Across the United States, 'enterprising women are forming businesses at twice the rate of men. At this pace, by the beginning of the twenty-first century, women will [soon] own half the businesses in the United States. There is a revolution reshaping the business landscape' (Jung, 1997). In just the past decade, women-owned US business growth outpaced overall business growth [in the United States] two to one (National Foundation for Women Business Owners, 1996). Over the same period, 'the number of American women-owned businesses . . . skyrocketed by 78 percent' (Grey, 1998). In just a five-year period in the last decade of the twentieth century, the number of women-owned businesses in the United States grew by more than 25 percent to over 8 million (National Foundation for Women Business Owners, 1996).

Similarly, Canada, with a population one-tenth that of the United States, has over 700 000 women-led firms, and the number is increasing at twice the national average: at 20 percent versus 9 percent for all Canadian businesses ('Myths and Realities', 1995; 'Growth of women-led businesses in Canada echoes increases in the U.S.', 1996). Women already represent 'approxi-mately one-third of all business owners [in Canada] . . . and trends indicate that by the year 2010 this number will rise to 50 percent' ('Women wanted', 1996). 'The growth of women-owned firms both in the U.S. and Canada continues to outpace overall business growth by approximately [two to one]' ('Leading women entrepreneurs of the world and women to watch', 1997).

Is the situation for women entrepreneurs different outside North America? No, the increasing number of women entrepreneurs is a growing international trend, not just a North American one ('Women entrepreneurs are a growing international trend', 1997). 'The number of women-owned enterprises is growing faster than the economy-at-large in many countries' (ibid.). 'Across the world, women-owned firms typically comprise between one-quarter and one-third of the business population' (Trieloff, 1998). In Poland, for example, 'the number of women starting their own businesses almost doubled between 1989 and 1991 . . . and the percentage of women among all entrepreneurs [rose] from 27.5% in 1989 to 33% [a 20% increase] over the same three-year period, (Mroczkowski, 1995). Polish women continue to start businesses at a higher rate than do Polish men (ibid.).

Such rapid increases are not confined to transitional economies such as Poland. In economically advantaged countries the pattern is similar. In Germany, for example, 'one-third of all . . . start-ups are now women-owned, up from 10 percent' just two decades earlier (Dwyer *et al.*, 1996: 42).

Moreover, some of the world's poorest women are now being recognized as good entrepreneurs. The Bangladesh-based Grameen Bank, for example, began making microloans two decades ago, mostly to penurious women to start small businesses and cooperatives. By the mid-l990s, the Grameen Bank had loaned over $1 billion to two million people, mostly women. Today, nearly half of their long-term borrowers no longer live in poverty. Replicated in many parts of the world, the Grameen Bank model has an almost unheard of 95 percent repayment rate ('Women and Poverty', 1995).

Worldwide, the number of women entrepreneurs is neither small nor shrinking. Based on current trends, the only valid prediction is that the proportion of women entrepreneurs will increase significantly in the twenty-first century.

Coaching entrepreneurs: are women different?[3]

If business leaders continued to believe current parochial assumptions about business success, few, if any, women would venture out into the world beyond their national borders, and even fewer would succeed once there. As the twenty-first century begins, one of my roles has become coaching executive women to succeed in the global economy by going beyond the myths and erroneous assumptions of history.

Because so few women worked as international managers in the twentieth century, let alone as global executives, ignorance and misleading myths abound (Adler, 1987, 1999). Not surprisingly, many women, especially in such Anglo cultures as the United States, have been led to believe that they must emulate men to succeed.[4] Fearing to differentiate themselves in any way from their successful male predecessors and contemporaries, many women resist openly challenging the abundant myths describing the barriers women supposedly face when attempting to conduct business abroad. One of the most valuable aspects of executive coaching, therefore, has become the private space it creates for women entrepreneurs and executives to ask societally unacceptable, and therefore publicly unaskable, questions, such as the following:

- 'Is it true that as a woman entrepreneur I cannot succeed in the Middle East?'

- 'Will I insult their culture if I lead our company's team in Saudi Arabia?'
- 'How true is it that our company's expansion into South Asia will be jeopardized if I head the project?'
- 'Even if I succeed in getting an invitation to visit potential suppliers in Korea, will I fail once I'm there? I've heard that Korean businessmen just ignore women; that they would never take a business woman seriously.'
- 'Will our joint venture partners be annoyed when they discover that my company is led by a woman?'
- 'Will men in Latin America really think that I'm some kind of sexual plaything? What do I need to do to get Latin men to respect me?'

As I listen to women telling their stories and asking their unaskable questions, my most frequent response is 'Why?' Why do you think that that might happen to you? How can you go beyond all the negative scenarios of what you and many of your colleagues imagine might occur? Why do you think foreigners will show more prejudice against you than do some of the executives you have already successfully dealt with here at home? How can you go beyond history's erroneous assumptions to create your own reality? In the privacy of executive coaching dialogues we laugh, question and explore a world that has literally been foreign to all too many women and companies. In the process, we lay to rest the misleading belief that women entrepreneurs cannot succeed abroad, or that, if they do succeed, they must act like men. Let us explore a few of the more common myths.

Myth one   Global experience and global business is not that important
Kristi is an entrepreneur who founded and currently leads a growing industrial products firm. She has two teenagers at home, both in high school. Kristi recently turned down an opportunity to begin expanding into the European market because she believed it would mean relocating to Frankfurt for at least the next couple of years. Annoyed with her unwillingness to move abroad, the chairman of Kristi's board told her that he could not support any further expansion of the firm if she was not mobile enough to 'go global'. He emphasized that her business would plateau if she did not relocate abroad to develop the European market. Whereas Kristi does not challenge the need to take the business global at some time, she does challenge the importance of going right now, while her children are still teenagers. She sees no need for her either to gain international experience or to start the firm's global expansion right now.

My response to Kristi's angry phone call is a resounding 'No! Business has gone global. Recommending international expansion and experience reflects neither sexism nor insensitivity to your children, nor a new variant of the "glass ceiling". The chairman of your board is right. If you choose not to expand internationally, it is *you* who are choosing to remain limited by parochialism. No man or woman should be supported as a senior executive of a major twenty-first century firm without having gained a deep understanding and appreciation of global business dynamics. Unless your aim is to progress backwards through history and to attempt to have a parochial nineteenth- or twentieth-century business, you don't dare consider limiting your experience to domestic stay-at-home opportunities.'

Kristi, did not like hearing what I said, but she believed me. As an executive coach, an outsider, she knows that I am on her side and that I will tell her the truth – even if it is an inconvenient truth that she would rather not hear. Recognizing the truth, however, does not imply resignation to business growth stopped by a seemingly impenetrable global glass ceiling. The outwardly paradoxical question I raised with Kristi is, 'How can you begin expanding your firm internationally, and thereby gain valuable international experience, and still keep your commitment to not moving during your children's formative high school years?' Asking such paradoxical questions as 'How can you both move abroad and not move abroad?' and then helping executives resolve them is a significant part of executive coaching.

Myth two   Given my family commitments, I cannot take my business global

In reflecting on her situation, Kristi realized that living abroad, while a very powerful way to demonstrate commitment to foreign clients and to gain international experience, was not the only option open to her. As we brainstormed options, she discovered that she could increase her global experience substantially by increasing her international business travel, and by creating short-term opportunities of no more than two to three months in Europe and Asia, coinciding with the time that her two teenagers went away each summer to camp. For Kristi, as well as for many other women who are both executives and mothers, the problem is the form in which international experience has traditionally been offered (long-term commitments to living abroad), not the need for global exposure itself. The trap for Kristi would have been to reject international experience, and therefore her firm's international expansion, because it was 'packaged' in its traditional, and to her unacceptable, form, as a three to five year relocation. The trap for me as a coach would have been to accept Kristi's board's definitions of reality rather than helping her to think beyond the mythology surrounding companies' increasingly anachronistic requirements. As Kristi's subsequent discussions with her chairman revealed, living abroad for significant periods of time, as a developmental strategy, was a better fit for the company's needs in the past when business strategy required key executives to have an in-depth knowledge of one particular foreign culture. By contrast, today's globally integrated business strategies require key executives to understand multiple cultures and their interaction. The very option that Kristi was considering for herself – shorter-term exposure to multiple countries – is actually becoming preferable in many cases to companies' traditional emphasis on a single, longer-term expatriate assignment.

Myth three   For global entrepreneurs, being a woman is a disadvantage

This pervasive and erroneous myth seems to find its way into the thinking of the vast majority of today's executives, both male and female. Arianne, the founder and CEO of a small consulting firm, was offered an opportunity to expand her firm's business into Asia. The expansion would involve creating a regional headquarters in Japan and immediately commencing operations in, among other countries, Pakistan. The expansion would therefore require extensive travel to this Islamic country. Arianne felt simultaneously excited and cautious. Would she, as a woman, be able to succeed in Japan and Pakistan, both countries reputed to be hostile to women executives? She worried that, if she openly raised her fears with her board, they would change their minds and not support the expansion; that, similar to so many other companies, the board would assume that it could not send women abroad. To make sure that she did not ruin the possibility of expanding into Asia, or the opportunity to send other women abroad in the future, she chose not to raise her concerns inside the company but rather relied on the confidentiality inherent in the executive coaching relationship.

Myth four   Certain cultures make it impossible for women executives to succeed

Arianne's initial fear was that no woman could succeed in Japan or Pakistan. Her real fear was that, if she accepted the position, she would be setting herself and her company up for failure. When I asked her why she believed she would fail in either of these two Asian countries, she immediately cited the cultural limitations placed on most women in Japan as well as those working in Islamic countries. As Arianne reflected, 'The scarcity of Japanese and Pakistani women executives says it all. Think how few Japanese and Pakistani women executives you know. Not many!' Unconsciously, yet understandably, Arianne had fallen into the *Gaijin* trap (Adler, 1987). She had assumed that, as a woman, she would be treated similarly to the local Japanese and Pakistani women, few of whom are given the cultural latitude to succeed as business executives. Her mistake was not in her statistics: she is right that there are extremely few women executives in either country. Rather her mistake was in overemphasizing the salience of being a woman.

On the basis of the actual experience of women executives who have worked abroad, we know that Western women are treated as foreigners who happen to be women. They are not treated in the same way as local women. While both the Japanese and the Pakistanis limit the roles that local women can take in business, neither culture confuses foreign women with local women. Arianne's freedom to succeed lies in the fact that she is visibly foreign. The trap for Arianne would be to assume that the Japanese could not tell that she is not Japanese (or that the Pakistanis could not tell that she is not Pakistani); they can. To get accurate tips on how to succeed in such cultures, I suggested that Arianne restrict her advice gathering to conversations with other Western women who had worked as entrepreneurs or for major multinationals in Japan and Pakistan. From them she could learn the nuances of showing respect for each culture without limiting her potential success. I strongly advised that she disregard suggestions made by both men and women who had not had direct experience with women working in the particular countries in which she would be working. Without direct experience, even the best intentioned colleagues unconsciously pass on myths disguised as advice. The only thing that eradicates the myth that women cannot succeed abroad and, simultaneously, the fear that such myths engender in both women entrepreneurs and the companies they lead, is learning about the actual experience of foreign women executives who have worked abroad, the majority of whom unquestionably succeed (see Adler, 1994).

In the next couple of weeks, Arianne talked with many women executives who had worked throughout Asia, coming back to me frequently to ask whether their suggestions would really be advisable for her. Among her many questions, Arianne asked if it was true that women executives did not have to stay up drinking until late into the night in order to do business with Japanese firms. My answer, 'Absolutely true.' Whereas behavior among men in Japan is fairly codified and almost always includes a lot of business entertainment and drinking, the newness of women conducting significant business in Japan means that male/female business behavior has yet to become codified. Given the ambiguity, women at this point in history have more latitude than do men to conduct business in ways that feel most comfortable to them. As one highly successful American woman executive, who had been based in Tokyo for years, laughingly related to me, 'Among all of my male colleagues, I am the only one who has consistently maintained relationships with Japanese clients without needing to put my liver in jeopardy! I can get away with conducting business over lunch and a Perrier; the men can't.'

**Myth five   Public is public, and private is private: to be taken seriously,
women who are entrepreneurs must hide their dual roles as wife
and mother**

The myth, albeit false, is that foreigners will not take a businesswoman
seriously unless she is 100 percent focused on work. American women,
who come from one of the most task-oriented cultures in the world, often
fall into the trap of emulating American businessmen. They try to focus
almost exclusively on business, to the detriment of both their worldwide
business success and their private life. Perhaps one particularly successful
businesswoman's experience says it all. On a business trip to Hong Kong,
Jill, an entrepreneur leading a global telecommunications equipment
service firm, was negotiating her first major contract with a consortium of
Thai, Malaysian and Chinese companies. The negotiations were not going
very well and looked to be in jeopardy of failure. At a particularly tense
moment in the deliberations, Jill glanced at her watch, stood up and apol-
ogized for needing to take a 10-minute break. While receiving quizzical
looks from the group of businessmen, she explained that it was bedtime
for her 7-year-old daughter back home in San José, and that she always
called to say good-night to her daughter, no matter where in the world she
was.

Returning 10 minutes later, Jill was surprised to discover that the tension
around the negotiating table had melted. As she entered the room, the
Thai executive asked how her daughter was doing. Then the lead Chinese
negotiator asked Jill if she had a picture of her daughter. Other negotia-
tors said how difficult they imagined it must be for a mother to be so far
away from her daughter. After this brief exchange of warm interest and
concern, the negotiations continued, now clearly with a focus on efficiently
finding a mutually beneficial agreement. At noon the following day, the
negotiation that had appeared irreversibly stuck came to a successful conclusion.

Most women from Anglo-Saxon cultures, and especially those from the
United States, have been coached by their colleagues to separate their
private life from their professional life.[5] To succeed abroad, however, these
same women need to unlearn the advice that their Anglo-Saxon colleagues
have given them. Unlike the task orientation of Anglo-Saxon countries,
most countries emphasize relationship building. In countries such as
China, Malaysia and Thailand, people will only conduct business with
people whom they know, like and trust. Revealing who you are as a whole
person, including unmasking some aspects of your private life, allows colleagues from relationship-building cultures to get to know you and, therefore, to want to do business with you. It is not that people from
relationship-oriented cultures are not concerned about getting the task

accomplished; they are. It is just that relationship must precede task. Jill's relationship with her daughter added the dimension of wholeness that she needed to succeed.[6]

Today Jill laughs at the number of her women friends who are also global executives who carry pictures of their children very visibly in their business card cases. Why? Because, from the first moment of contact, clients know that they are a whole person: a wife, mother and businesswoman. As Jill's story spread, rumors began circulating that even single women were borrowing pictures of Jill's children to ensure their success abroad.

Executive coaching: reaching beyond the myths of history

Entrepreneurship can be a lonely profession. The privacy of coaching sessions makes it easier for executives to say, 'I'm not certain . . . I just don't know.' Privacy and supportive advocacy legitimize moments of not knowing. Premature certainty and commitment extinguishes innovative possibilities. For both women and men, coaching dialogues foster a depth of questioning that allows executives to escape the bounded thinking of their own professional, organizational and national cultures. For women, coaching sessions encourage exploring alternatives that reach beyond the accepted 'wisdom' gained by successful men working worldwide with other men. One woman who leads a US$400 million business quietly and painfully revealed that her success, while impressive by any publicly visible business or career standard, felt like a betrayal of her soul. While she did not want to let go of her status in the business world, she also knew that she had to do something to reclaim the part of herself that she had ignored for the last 25 years. At their very best, coaching sessions provide the time, space and learning opportunities that allow entrepreneurial executives to offer profound and wise counsel to themselves.

The future: suggestions for research

If future women entrepreneurs are to have access to the success that they and their businesses deserve, we will need to have more research to inform them, both in their public discussions and in their private coaching dialogues. Research is needed to differentiate between the impact of being a woman manager and being a woman entrepreneur or corporate executive.[7] Research is needed to document reactions, both positive and negative, to women entrepreneurs leading their firm's efforts in various countries and cultures around the world. Research is also needed to benchmark the most innovative ways that companies and individuals are balancing professional and private life demands, especially when the careers involve global commitments. As the research advances, the myths will fade into history.

Notes

1. For an in-depth discussion of approaches and benefits to coaching executives, see *Coaching for Leadership,* edited by Marshall Goldsmith, Lawrence Lyons and Alyssa Freas, San Francisco: Jossey-Bass , 2000.
2. An earlier version of the discussion of the increasing number of women entrepreneurs worldwide was published by Adler (1999), 'Global Entrepreneurs: Women, Myths, and History' (original research conducted by Sara Green, McGill University, Montreal).
3. For a more in-depth discussion of women's global leadership and international management careers, see *Competitive Frontiers: Women Managers in a Global Economy*, edited by Nancy J. Adler and Dafna N. Izraeli (Cambridge, Mass.: Blackwell, 1994); *International Dimensions of Organizational Behavior* by Adler (Southwestern, 1997); 'Global Leaders: A Dialogue with Future History', *International Management* (1997), by Adler.
4. For a discussion of the pressure on women to conform, which appears most pronounced in Anglo countries such as the United States, England, Australia and the English-speaking parts of Canada, see Nancy J. Adler's 'Women Joining Men as Global Leaders in the New Economy' (2002).
5. In anthropological terms, the United States is seen as a specific culture, while most Asian cultures are diffused cultures. Specific cultures separate private and professional life, whereas diffused cultures integrate all aspects of life.
6. For a discussion of relationship versus task-oriented cultures, see Chapters 1 and 2 of Nancy J. Adler's *International Dimensions of Organizational Behavior*, 4th edition, Cincinnati, Ohio: South Western, 2002.
7. For a discussion of women leaders (versus women managers), see Adler's 'Global Leadership: Women Leaders' (1997).

References

Adler, Nancy J. (1987), 'Pacific Basin Managers: A Gaijin, Not a Woman', *Human Resource Management*, 26 (2), pp. 169–92.
Adler, Nancy J. (1994), 'Competitive Frontiers: Women Managing Across Borders', in Nancy J. Adler and Dafna N. Izraeli, *Competitive Frontiers: Women Managers in a Global Economy*, Cambridge, Mass.: Blackwell, pp. 22–40.
Adler, Nancy J. (1997), 'Global Leaders: A Dialogue with Future History', *International Management*, 1 (2), pp. 21–33.
Adler, Nancy J. (1997), 'Global Leadership: Women Leaders', *Management International Review*, 37 (1), pp. 171–96.
Adler, Nancy J. (1999), 'Global Entrepreneurs: Women, Myths, and History', *Global Focus*, 11 (4), pp. 125–34.
Adler, Nancy J. (2000), 'Coaching Global Executives: Women Succeeding in a World Beyond Here', in Marshall Goldsmith, Lawrence Lyons and Alyssa Freas (eds), *Coaching for Leadership*, San Francisco, Calif.: Jossey-Bass, pp. 359–68.
Adler, Nancy J. (2002), *International Dimensions of Organizational Behavior*, 4th edn, Cincinnati, Ohio: South-Western.
Adler, Nancy J. (2002), 'Women Joining Men as Global Leaders in the New Economy', in Martin Gannon and Karen Newman (eds), *Handbook of Cross-Cultural Management*, Oxford: Basil Blackwell, pp. 236–49.
Adler, Nancy J. and Dafna N. Izraeli (eds) (1994) *Competitive Frontiers: Women Managers in a Global Economy*, Cambridge, Mass.: Blackwell.
Dwyer, P., M. Johnston and K.L. Miller (1996), 'Europe's corporate women', *Business Week*, 15 April, pp. 40–1.
Goldsmith, Marshall, Lawrence Lyons and Alyssa Freas (eds) (2000), *Coaching for Leadership*, San Francisco, Calif.: Jossey-Bass.
Grey, B. (1998), 'Working woman magazine names top 500 women-owned businesses' (available from *www.Womenconnect.com/business*, accessed 9 April 1998, p. 36).

'Growth of women-led businesses in Canada echoes increases in the U.S.' (1996), National Foundation of Women Business Owners, Washington, DC, 23 August p. 1.

Jung, M. (1997), 'California: Enterprising women move ahead', *Women's Resource & Yellow Pages* (available from *www.workingwomen.com/articles/zjung.htm*).

Kelly, C. (1996), '50 world-class executives', *Worldbusiness*, 2 (2), pp. 21.

Kelly, C. (1997), 'Leading women entrepreneurs of the world and women to watch', National Foundation for Women Business Owners, Washington, DC, p. 45.

Mroczkowski, T. (1995), 'Shaping the environment for private business in Poland: What has been achieved? What remains to be done?', *Law and Policy In International Business*, 56 (June), p. 56.

'Myths and realities: The economic power of women-led firms in Canada' (1995), Bank of Montreal Institute for Small Business and Dun Bradstreet Information Services, Montreal.

Trieloff, B. (1998), 'Succeeding in new markets through diversity', *Women in Management*, 8 (3), p. 3.

'Women and poverty' (1995), Fourth United Nations Conference on Women: Women and Poverty, Beijing (available at Women's Connection Online, 6 September 1995, p. 2).

'Women business owners employ 1 in 4 U.S. workers' (1996), National Foundation for Women Business Owners, Washington, DC, 27 March, pp. 1–2.

'Women entrepreneurs are a growing international trend' (1997), National Foundation for Women Business Owners, Washington, DC, March, p. 1.

'Women wanted' (1996), *The Province (Vancouver)*, 11 April, p. A35.

4 Women, age and money: international entrepreneurship theory in the work of Candida G. Brush

Candida G. Brush and Tatiana S. Manolova

Candida G. Brush is one of the leading scholars in the area of international entrepreneurship. Her numerous contributions to the field include one of the earliest attempts to define the domain of the phenomenon, pioneering work on the effects of firm age on internationalization, as well as an impressive body of research exploring gender effects on new venture creation worldwide. Her recent work investigates gender-based differences in the access to venture capital as part of the DIANA project (Diana Project, 2001),[1] and studies the effects of international sources capital on the growth trajectories of entrepreneurial new ventures.

This chapter is based on a comprehensive literature review of Candida G. Brush's research in the area of international entrepreneurship. Three main themes of Brush's research are presented: the internationalization of new and small ventures, comparative entrepreneurship and equity financing effects on entrepreneurial growth. The literature review is complemented by a recent (2002) semi-structured interview with the author, in which she discusses the motivations for and the evolution of her research interests. She also provides a perspective on the future research agenda in the field of international entrepreneurship.

The chapter is structured as follows. It starts with an account, in Brush's own words, of what triggered her interest in international entrepreneurship. In the following sections, the main themes of her work in the area of international entrepreneurship are presented. The literature review is enriched with excerpts from the interview in which she provides insights on the evolution of her research interests. The chapter concludes with the final section of the interview, in which Brush shares her perspective on future research in the area of international entrepreneurship. In addition, the references at the end of the chapter provide a complete list (as of June 2002) of Brush's work in the area of international entrepreneurship, compiled from a variety of sources and validated with the author.

Early research interest in international entrepreneurship
Professor Brush's research interest in the area of international entrepreneurship dates back to the early 1990s, when the field itself was emerging

around the pioneering work of McDougall (1989) and McDougall and Oviatt (1991). Case based research suggested international new ventures were becoming a growing and important type of new venture start-up (McDougall and Oviatt, 1991; Jolly, Alahunta and Jeannet, 1992). International new ventures were defined as business organizations which, from inception, seek to derive significant competitive advantage from the use of resources and the sale of output in multiple countries (McDougall, Shane and Oviatt, 1994). McDougall *et al.* noted that theories from international business research failed to explain the formation of this type of organization and called for more theoretical and empirical research to explain the phenomenon of international new ventures.

At the same time, research on entrepreneurship in emerging markets, especially the former centrally planned economies (for example Nee, 1992; Hisrich and Grachev, 1993), demonstrated the salience of the entrepreneurship phenomenon on a global scale. These findings offered opportunities for comparative research across multiple national and cultural contexts.

As Brush suggests in her interview, these were among the main factors that triggered her interest in international entrepreneurship.

What triggered your interest in international entrepreneurship?
The main reason I decided to study international entrepreneurship was that as a doctoral student, I was encouraged to study something other than women's entrepreneurship. (I had done a lot of research on women's entrepreneurship before entering the doctoral program, and so I decided that I would stick with entrepreneurship and combine that with small companies internationalizing. I am not sure how the international part came in. I think it might have been through Dr Robert Hisrich – Dr Hisrich was my former co-author for research on women's entrepreneurship[2] and had spent six months doing research and teaching in Hungary.[3] After hearing about his experiences and the entrepreneurial economy developing in Eastern Europe (this would have been 1990 and they had programs that were starting to develop), I decided that it would be interesting to study what US small firms did to internationalize. I did a major literature review of entrepreneurship and international business studies. About the same time Dr Patricia McDougall and Dr Ben Oviatt were starting to explore global start-ups using case studies.[4] So it was the combination of three things: I was encouraged to study something new, Dr Hisrich's work in Hungary, and Dr McDougall and Dr Oviatt's work on global start-ups.

The reason I decided to study age in my dissertation was an interesting story, a real anecdote. I had rented an office outside my house because I needed a quiet place to work on my dissertation away from my young children. I mired myself in all of the Export Marketing and International Business literatures. For about three months I checked books out of the library, read them and returned them, trying to figure out what the research question for my dissertation was going to be. One day I went down to pay my rent and the man I was leasing the office from said, 'What are you working on?', and I said, 'Well, I am trying to figure out what to do for my dissertation. I am trying to develop something that involves entrepreneurial companies.' In the middle of our conversation the phone rang, and it turned out he had a brand new start-up company that was already global in scope. While I was listening to this phone conversation, I started thinking, 'Here he is, in Barnstable, Massachusetts, and his business has customers and a partner in Ireland, and customers and a partner in Germany.' It just dawned on me that that I should investigate the role of age in the internationalization of small firms. I went back to my literature review and it showed that the vast majority of previous work examined size, but not age. That's how I ended up examining age as opposed to size. Up until my dissertation there wasn't really any significant study that looked at the effect of age on internationalization in small firms. In my dissertation I analysed the data for both size and age, and age explained more than size. This was an interesting finding, because all the previous literature had looked at size.

In her dissertation (Brush, 1992), later published as a book by Garland (Brush, 1995) Brush integrated perspectives from entrepreneurship and three streams of international business literature and developed four hypotheses related to the motivations for internationalization and the internationalization strategies of small businesses. The hypotheses were then tested on a representative national sample of small manufacturers (n=134). The study outlined thee major findings. First, the primary motive for internationalization of small businesses was found to be serendipitous; that is, the majority of businesses in the sample did not have a written formal business plan to internationalize, but rather responded to opportunities, such as unsolicited inquiries from abroad. Second, age at internationalization was not found to be important for the success of the small venture; that is, businesses selling abroad when young were not performing more poorly than those going abroad at an older age. Third, age at internationalization was found to be characterized by different motives and international strategies. That is, at a younger age, managerial factors motivated the decision to internationalize, whereas at an older age it was firm-level factors that motivated the decision.

This last finding of the dissertation research has had a major influence on the future development of the international entrepreneurship field. The age variation among internationalized small businesses suggested there were indeed a lot of small companies which internationalized at an early age, an important finding for the emerging international entrepreneurship field. In addition, the age dependence of motivations and strategies was further developed by a number of scholars, including, among others, P. Harveston and B. Kedia's (2000) work on differences between born global and gradually globalizing firms and Autio, Sapienza and Almeida's (2000) work on the effects of age at entry on international growth.

DeWning the domain of international entrepreneurship
A significant thrust of the research effort in the early stages of development of the international entrepreneurship field was directed at defining the

domain of international entrepreneurship. In a symposium at the 1991
Academy of Management meeting, McDougall, Oviatt and Brush (1991)
presented their view of the domain of scholarly research on business organizations. This conceptualization is presented in Figure 4.1.[5]

According to these scholars, there had been a substantial body of
research in quadrants I, III, and IV. Research in quadrant I had been the
preserve of entrepreneurship scholars, and quadrant IV had been the preserve of international business scholars. Multiple functional areas had
focused on quadrant III. Quadrant II, a more sparsely studied area, represented international entrepreneurship (McDougall and Oviatt, 1999: 292).
International entrepreneurship was, therefore, defined as 'the development
of international new ventures or start-ups that, from their inception,
engage in international business, thus viewing their operating domain as
international from the initial stages of the firm's operation' (McDougall,
1989).

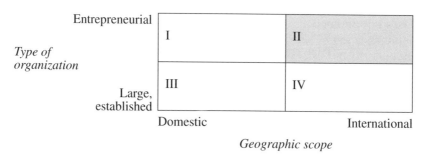

Source: Adopted from McDougall, Oviatt and Brush (1991), published in McDougall and
Oviatt (1999: 292).

Figure 4.1   The domain of academic literature on organizations

In a subsequent theory development piece, Brush (1993b) elaborated on
the conceptualization and boundaries of the domain of international
entrepreneurship. She examined narrow and broad definitions from international business and entrepreneurship literatures based on units of analysis, context of analysis, definitions and activities of interest. The paper
specified the domain of international entrepreneurship based on two
conditions, one from each parent discipline. Consistent with international
business, research should involve two or more countries or compare international activities in two or more countries. Following entrepreneurship,
there should be allowance for multiple units of analysis. Further elaborat-
ing on this intersection, both fields were characterized by 'levels of involvement', providing guidelines for researchers to position their studies.

On the basis of this definition of the domain of international entrepreneurship, Brush traces the evolution and positioning of her own research:

> There are three streams to my international research. First, I study the resources and strategies influencing internationalization and small firm performance. This is an extension of the dissertation research using primarily the resource-based view of the firm. The second stream studies and compares women entrepreneurs in different countries – this is a topic that falls broadly within the entrepreneurship domain. The third area is part of the Diana Project which investigates women seeking capital and the venture capital industry in multiple countries. Within this stream, we are interested in the role of human capital, social networks and institutional barriers that lead to successful acquisition of equity capital and growth of women-led ventures.

Figure 4.2 presents a visual positioning of the three research themes, following Brush's own definition of the domain of international entrepreneurship research. The next sections of the paper highlight these themes. Table 4.1 offers a summary of Brush's studies, including methodology employed and major findings.

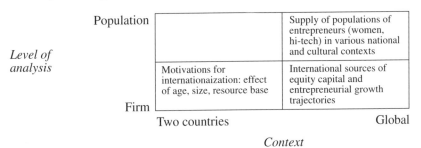

Figure 4.2   The domain of international entrepreneurship in Candida G. Brush's research

Theme one: internationalization of new and small ventures

> I originally considered looking at the small firm strategy–performance linkage in my dissertation, but my committee suggested that it would be more reasonable to examine motivations first. At that point I was interested in the start-up processes, which were more consistent with motives, so I focused on that relationship. I examined the strategy–performance linkage in a subsequent paper.[6] A recent paper also analyzed resources and how these impacted strategy and performance. Instead of looking at what causes internationalization, the motives, I looked at the strategy and performance literature, the overall framework.[7]

The first theme in Brush's research in the area of international entrepreneurship is an extension of her dissertation work. In a subsequent piece

(Brush, 1996) she looked at the effects of age at market entry on internationalization strategies and performance. The study results showed that early and late export entry were associated with different patterns of internationalization strategy. Early entry was associated with greater percentage of total products sold abroad in year one (or breadth of market scope), goals of survival, overcoming problems and obtaining new sources of capital. Further, early entrants held a broad international perspective, or view that small companies were geographically unlimited and needed to be quick to take advantage of international opportunities. In contrast, late entry was associated with greater service to markets which were geographically close, a goal of establishing long-term business relationships, and a narrow international perspective or view that selling abroad was risky for small businesses, and therefore must be planned incrementally (Brush, 1996: 60). In addition, although age at entry appeared to be marginally associated with performance levels, a within-group comparison of early and late internationalizers suggested that, depending on age at entry, different strategies were associated with better or worse performance.

Timing of foreign market entry has since received significant research attention. It has been studied, among others, as the outcome of the level of international experience of entrepreneurial founding teams (Reuber and Fischer, 1997), as the outcome of the stage of development and resource profile of the firm in a resource-based framework (Burgel *et al.*, 2001) or as the determinant of the international growth strategy of entrepreneurial new ventures from an organizational learning perspective (Autio *et al.*, 2000). Brush's study is among the first to highlight the age dependence in the patterns and performance outcomes of internationalization.

Brush's further work in the area of new and small firm internationalization evolved from examination of the effects of firm demographics (age versus size) to an in-depth exploration of the effect of the new and small firm's resource profile on internationalization strategies. Theoretically grounded in the resource-based view of the firm, this line of research (Edelman *et al.*, 1998; Brush, Edelman and Manolova, 2002) looked at the impact of five types of resources (human, social, organizational, financial, and physical) on the scope and scale of internationalization in a stratified sample (n=128) of small US-based firms from three technological sectors (primary, secondary, and tertiary). Results indicated resource profiles distinguished between internationalized and non-internationalized firms, and human resources were the most important in pursuing an internationalization strategy.

Building on the latter finding, Brush's further work explored the effect of several dimensions of human capital as a predictor of internationalization (Manolova *et al.*, 2000, 2002). In particular, four dimensions of human

Table 4.1 *Three international entrepreneurship themes in Candida G. Brush's research*

Study	Research questions	Methodology	Independent variables	Dependent variables	Major findings
Theme 1: The internationalization of new and small firms					
Brush, 1993b	What is the domain of international entrepreneurship?	A theory development paper which examines narrow and broad definitions of international entrepreneurship, based on units of analysis, definitions, activities and research context		Motivations for internationalization	Researchers must adopt a comparative or multi-country approach, but may be flexible in units of analysis
Brush, 1992; 1993a; 1995	Do reasons for internationalization vary significantly by age of small business?	Cross-sectional survey design, n = 134	Firm age, management, firm level, industry, regional and host market factors	Motivations for internationalization	Internationalization in small businesses is serendipitous; motives differ by age of internationalization; age at internationalization is associated with different strategies
Brush, 1993c; 1996	Does the timing of internationalization affect strategy and performance?	Cross sectional survey design, n = 134	Firm age	Internationalization strategies (degree of internationalization, goals and focus, international perspective), firm performance (growth in sales and employees)	Different patterns of international strategy are associated with early and late export entry and, depending on the time of entry, certain strategies are associated with higher performance
Edelman, Brush & Manolova, 1998; Brush, Edelman & Manolova, 2002; Manolova, Brush & Edelman, 2000; 2002	Does the resource base of the firm determine small firm internationalization?	Stratified cross-sectional survey design, n = 128	Firm resource stocks (human, social, technology, organizational, and financial)	Patterns of internationalization (scope and scale)	Internationalized small companies have a better developed resource base; different resource profiles are associated with different internationalization strategies; some dimensions of human capital are more important than others in internationalization

Table 4.1 (continued)

Theme 2: Comparative entrepreneurship

Lerner, Brush & Hisrich, 1997; 1995	What individual factors influence performance of Israeli women-business owners?	A cross-sectional survey, n=220	Five dimensions of individual factors	Business performance (sales, income, profitability, number of employees)	Performance is related to previous business experience, business skills, achievement motivation and affiliation to a single network. Involvement in multiple networks is negatively related to profitability
Khavul, Brush, Kalish & Lerner, 1998a, 1998b	What is the impact of public policies on the Israeli high-tech entrepreneurship?	35 field interviews	Role of mezzo (incubator) environment created through public policy	Resource creation and knowledge transfer in high-technology innovative Israeli start-ups	Business plans/planning, market direction, team building are major benefits of incubators; incubator entrepreneurs differ from others by having strong weak ties and trust.
Brush, 1998	What is the resource base of women-created ventures?	An advocacy paper which develops a model of gender influences on the venture creation process drawing on the resource-based view of the firm			The paper makes public policy recommendations in terms of improved academic research, relevant educational materials and greater visibility of successful women entrepreneurs
Brush, 1999	What are the drivers and economic implications of women's entrepreneurship?	An overview of the phenomenon of women's entrepreneurship which develops an alternative model of organizational practices found in women-owned businesses			The paper suggests that women create different organizational practices, structures, cultures and policies and can be the organizational change leaders in the future

Theme 3: International equity capital and entrepreneurial growth trajectories

Brush, 2002; Greene, Brush, Hart & Saparito, 1999; 2001	Is gender a factor in venture capital financing decisions?	Analysis of NVCA longitu-dinal archival data (30 yrs, n = 16 412 records.	Exploratory analysis, descriptive statistics	There is a gender gap between the growth of women-led businesses and venture capital equity financing. Theoretical approaches which could explain the disparity include the structural barriers, the human capital and the strategic choice approaches
Brush, Carter, Gatewood, Greene & Hart, 2000	What are the factors affecting capital access for women?	3 group cross-sectional surveys of NFWBO women who sought equity capital	Comparison of those who sought and got equity, sought and did not receive, and did not seek, using cross tabs and ANOVA	Those receiving equity have financial expertise, use more advice (social network) and have businesses in internet/info technology. Those not seeking are 'life-style' ventures. Women seeking equity had growth goals
Brush, Carter, Gatewood, Greene & Hart, 2002	How true are the prevailing explana-tions for the gap between the growth of women owned businesses and the lack of venture capital equity financing?	A research report on the relationship between women business owners and equity capital.		Results from analysis of longitudinal data dispel the myths that women are not seeking or qualified for venture capital financing.

Note: NVCA = National Venture Capital Association. NFWBO = National Federation of Women Business Owners.

49

capital were compared across internationalized and non-internationalized small firms: international orientation, international business skills, perceptions of the environment and demographic characteristics. Results suggested environmental perceptions and self-assessed strengths in international business skills significantly differentiated internationalized from non-internationalized small ventures. In addition, human capital configurations varied significantly with business sector.

To summarize, Candida Brush's work on the internationalization of new and small companies makes three major contributions to the evolving field of international entrepreneurship. First, it suggests internationalization strategies and performance are age-dependent. Second, it goes beyond the broad firm-level demographics such as size (traditionally used as a proxy for resource base) and age (traditionally used as a proxy for experience) to investigate the impact of specific resources and resource configurations on new and small firm internationalization. In doing this, her work makes its third major contribution: it brings the resource-based perspective as a suitable theoretical anchor to the study of new and small firm internationalization. This perspective has since been fruitfully used in the study of international entrepreneurship in other national settings such as the United Kingdom and Germany (see, for example, Westhead, Wright and Ucbasaran, 2001; Burgel *et al.*, 2001).

Theme two: comparative entrepreneurship

I don't consider my research to follow what might be considered as the narrow definition of international entrepreneurship. The narrow definition of international entrepreneurship requires that the research involve two countries. I have investigated what causes entrepreneurship worldwide, which would be a broader definition of international entrepreneurship – looking at what happens in Sweden or elsewhere. The ILO piece[8] is an example. It was an invited advocacy paper which studied the contributions of women entrepreneurs in improving the economies of different countries. I considered the role of human capital, strategic choice and other factors that contributed to women's ability to succeed. The ILO paper and my OECD work[9] are really about economic development because they consider how women are engaged in the entrepreneurial process across countries. In other words, this work looks at the supply side of entrepreneurship in an international setting. My unit of analysis was primarily the firm, with the dependent variable being growth, survival or performance.

The second theme in Candida Brush's research in international entrepreneurship follows what McDougall and Oviatt (1999) recognize as one of seven important directions for research in international entrepreneurship. More specifically, these authors ask, 'Do the environmental conditions, venture activities, and entrepreneurs' characteristics that distinguish successful from unsuccessful entrepreneurial firms differ among regions of the world, nations, or subnational cultures? If so, what are those differences?' (ibid.: 301).

One line of Brush's research in this area looks at women's entrepreneurship in different national, economic and cultural contexts. This work builds on her established body of research on US women-led businesses, a theme that Brush has explored for more than 20 years (see, for example, Hisrich and Brush, 1986). Thus the study of 220 Israeli women-owned businesses (Lerner *et al.*, 1995, 1997) used a survey instrument originally developed by Hisrich and Brush to study six categories of factors (social learning, human capital, motivations and goals, networks, demographics and environmental factors) on business performance. The study supported previous research from the United States and Europe which found that performance is related to previous industry experience, business skills and achievement motivations. However, the differential effects of network affiliations were significantly more important for women entrepreneurs in Israel. Affiliation with a single network was found to be highly related to profitability, whereas involvement in multiple networks was detrimental to both revenues and the number of employees (Lerner *et al.*, 1997: 316). Another study on the environment for entrepreneurship in Israel suggested government-supported incubators had a significant impact on the development of the high-technology sector in the country (Khavul *et al.*, 1998a, 1998b).

A second line of research develops models of gender differences in new venture creation and organizational practices, based on the resource-based view of the firm (Brush, 1998, 1999). The theoretical development is supported by evidence from a wide variety of national and economic contexts, including the USA, the Netherlands, Spain, Australia, Japan, sub-Saharan Africa and Latin America. Important public policy recommendations include the need to support research, education and recognition of successful women's entrepreneurship. Brush strongly advocates the need for a change in public policy across all OECD countries to enhance the possibilities for women to create new ventures (Brush, 1998: 161). Similarly, in the advocacy paper prepared for the International Labour Organisation (Brush, 1999), Candida Brush suggests that the domain of entrepreneurship is no longer a male preserve since women are starting and growing businesses worldwide. There is a lot to be learned from observing their organizational practices, structures, cultures and policies. In fact, Brush suggests that women-owned businesses can be the change agents for the 21st century.

The comparative entrepreneurship research theme is important for two main reasons. First, it enriches our understanding of the processes and outcomes by which women-led businesses come into being in different social, economic and political environments. It fleshes out the similarities and differences in women's entrepreneurship around the world and is a useful reference point for further comparative studies. Second, this work has highly relevant public policy implications as it highlights the importance of women-led entrepreneurship and makes specific recommendations which can help support new venture creation by women worldwide.

Theme three: international sources of equity capital and entrepreneurial growth trajectories

Today I describe my research focus to be the emergence and growth of new ventures or how new organizations acquire resources (in particular, equity financing) to achieve high potential. This is a topic of global interest. The major fuel for high growth ventures is equity capital, and this is of course a world-wide phenomenon. The Diana Project was conceived three years ago, and the catalyst for our research was the fact that US women-owned businesses were receiving less than five percent of all equity investments even though they comprised more than thirty-seven percent of all businesses. We have systematically examined the influence of human and social capital, structural barriers and strategic choice as possible explanations for this disparity. We conducted a multi-phased longitudinal study, starting with an analysis of all investments in US businesses over thirty years, analyzed by gender of the owner; a panel study of the influences of human, social and financial capital on growth trajectories of high tech women-led firms; an analysis of nine hundred applicants to the Springboard Venture Forums; and an analysis of women's participation in the venture capital industry. Not only is our study the first considering women as seekers of capital, but it is also the first examining women as venture capitalists.

Financing of women-led firms in other countries is similarly understudied. Our initial paper from the Diana Project included some comparative data.[10] Since then, we've collected data on women-led businesses in the UK that were funded by venture capital, completed an annotated bibliography of more than three hundred articles about women's entrepreneurship and venture capital that includes several international journals, and we plan to set up a multi-country research project to examine women's access to equity capital and women's participation in the venture capital industry in other countries.[11]

There are fewer opportunities for women to create and grow businesses in other countries. For example, in Japan for a woman to get venture capital would be almost unheard of. And the same is true for many other European countries. Hence our future work will examine the other countries besides the U.S.

An emerging line of Brush's research is associated with the DIANA project, a multi-university, multi-stage project which studies women business owners and their business growth activities.[12] A recent report of the first results investigates how substantive eight popular myths are in explaining the disparity between the number and contributions of women-led businesses and the tiny amount of equity financing received by these businesses.

Some of the stereotypical explanations for this gap are, for example, that women do not want to own high-growth businesses, or they are not adequately qualified, or that they do not submit business plans to equity providers. Empirical evidence disproves all of the reigning explanations, or 'popular myths', explaining the disproportionately low levels of venture capital equity financing for women-led ventures (Greene *et al.*, 2001; Brush, 2002).

Further work on gender-based issues in venture capital funding (Greene *et al.*, 1999, 2001) analyzes evidence from several countries to highlight the gravity of the gap between the scale of women-led businesses and the level of venture funding availability for these ventures. One important finding of this research is, in particular, the fact that the authors were unable to identify a single study in venture capital from Europe that included or analyzed funding of women-led ventures (Greene *et al.*, 2001: 80). Apparently this presents an important research opportunity and a research question highly relevant to both entrepreneurs, venture capitalists and public policy makers.

Future research agenda in the area of international entrepreneurship
In the final part of the interview, Brush offered her perspective on the research agenda in the area of international entrepreneurship. From a theory development perspective, she called for clarification of the domain of international entrepreneurship and specification of the relevant theories and constructs. She also suggested integration of new levels of analysis into the international entrepreneurship framework, for example the emergence of global industries. From a comparative entrepreneurship perspective, she called for more research on the variation of public support for private entrepreneurial initiatives, including, for example, comparative studies of incubator effects on national rates of entrepreneurship.

What are the interesting questions in international entrepreneurship today?
I would say that a valuable contribution would be a paper that clearly defines 'What is international entrepreneurship?' How do you define the domain differently from just entrepreneurship per se, international business, international marketing or economic development? What are the boundaries of the domain? What is the domain? Should the unit of analysis only be the firm? What elements of entrepreneurship are central to the domain (e.g. innovation? Growth? Risk-taking?) Is it required that research include at least two countries? For example, if a US small company has global suppliers, is this international entrepreneurship? If a family business serves multiple countries, is this international entrepreneurship? Or, because nearly every start-up has an internet or web presence that can be accessed world wide, does this mean that every start-up is an international entrepreneurial venture? You could argue the answer is 'yes': if I go to a website that happens to be in China when I am starting a business, I could be an international entrepreneur. So the domain both conceptually and empirically is messy. Another paper I would like to read would be about theories and

concepts crucial to understanding international entrepreneurship: the motivations, strategies and outcomes of international entrepreneurship. Perhaps an extension to McDougall and Oviatt's work would be very interesting.

Another promising area is the emergence of global industries. I think that is an interesting international entrepreneurship question. What contributes to the success of global industries? How do they emerge? Are there different patterns? One of the examples that comes to mind is the clinical testing industry. How do industries emerge that happen to be global in nature or, if you will, how do international entrepreneurial industries emerge?

Finally, another interesting area might be an extension of public policy influences on entrepreneurial enterprises, following the work of Susanna Khavul on the role of business incubators. What is the role of private or public incubators in the successful emergence and growth of international entrepreneurial start-ups?[13] Looking at the phenomenon from a comparative dimension would be very interesting, because it would have extremely relevant public policy implications.

These are my three areas for future study.

Concluding remarks

The work of Candida Brush has left a lasting imprint on the development of the international entrepreneurship field. Not only is her study of age effects on small firms' motivations for internationalization one of the pioneering works in the field, but her subsequent work contributed to the introduction of appropriate theoretical perspectives to enhance the understanding of the international entrepreneurship phenomenon. In a field sometimes deplored as 'atheoretical', her research grounded in the resource based view of the firm offers a theoretical anchor which helps explain and predict the variance in new and small international ventures' strategies and performance. In addition, her work on women and high-technology entrepreneurs pushed back the boundaries of the field by including salient comparative points of reference. Her emerging research agenda also holds the promise of creatively intertwining the international dimension with the study of entrepreneurial growth trajectories and high potential organizations.

In summary, Candida G. Brush's research has been at the forefront of scholarly discovery because her research domain has emerged at the intersection of the fields of entrepreneurship, strategy and international business. As she says, 'this is where the interesting questions are'. Her work is thus well positioned to make numerous further contributions to the evolving domain of international entrepreneurship in years to come.

Notes

1. The Diana Project is a multi-year, multidisciplinary investigation of growth-oriented women-led ventures. Project principles are Nancy Carter, Patricia Greene, Elizabeth Gatewood, Myra Hart and Candida Brush.

2. Brush refers to her research with Hisrich on women entrepreneurs (see, for example, Hisrich and Brush, 1986).
3. Brush refers to Hisrich's research on entrepreneurship in transitional economies (see, for example, Hisrich and Grachev, 1993).
4. Reference is made to McDougall and Oviatt's early case based research (see, for example, McDougall and Oviatt, 1991).
5. Adopted from McDougall and Oviatt (1999).
6. Brush (1996).
7. Reference is made to Edelman *et al.* (1998), Manolova *et al.* (2000, 2002), Brush, Carter, Gatewood, Greene and Hart (2002).
8. Reference is made to Brush (1999).
9. Reference is made to Brush (1998).
10. Reference is made to Greene *et al.* (2001).
11. This annotated bibliography will be forthcoming in Fall 2002 as a CD and in electronic format from ESBRI, Sweden.
12. The DIANA project combines comprehensive studies of both the demand side (more than 2500 applications for venture financing made by women-led businesses) and the supply side (data from the National Venture Capital Association over the 1957–98 period), as well as a proprietary data set on women in the venture capital industry) (Brush *et al.*, 2000).
13. Reference is made to Khavul (2001).

References

Autio, E., H.J. Sapienza and J.G. Almeida (2000), 'Effects of age at entry, knowledge intensity, and imitability on international growth', *Academy of Management Journal*, 43(5), 909–24.

Brush, C.G. (1991), 'Entrepreneurial firms that are born international', panel presentation at the Symposium on Global Start-Ups: Entrepreneurial Firms that are Born International, Academy of Management annual meeting, Miami, Fl, August.

Brush, Candida G. (1992), 'Factors motivating the small firm to internationalize: The effects of firm age', unpublished doctoral dissertation, Boston University.

Brush, C.G. (1993a), 'International entrepreneurship: Motives for internationalization and the effect of firm age', paper presented at the Academy of Management annual meeting, Atlanta, GA, August.

Brush, C.G. (1993b), 'Defining the domain of international entrepreneurship', panel presentation at the pre-conference workshops, Academy of Management annual meeting, Atlanta, GA, August.

Brush, C.G., (1993c), 'International entrepreneurship: Motives and the effect of age at internationalization on performance', paper presented at the Babson College Conference on Entrepreneurship Research, Houston, TX, March.

Brush, Candida G. (1995), *International Entrepreneurship: The Effect of Firm Age on Motives for Internationalization*, New York: Garland Publishers.

Brush, C.G. (1996), 'Export entry in small companies: Effects of timing on strategy and performance', *Journal of Small Business Strategy*, 7(3), 53–68.

Brush, Candida, G. (1998), 'A Resource Perspective of Women's Entrepreneurship: Research, Relevance and Recognition', *Proceedings of the Organisation for Economic Cooperation and Development on Women Entrepreneurs in Small and Medium Sized Enterprises: A Major Force in Innovation and Job Creation*, Paris: OECD, pp. 155–68.

Brush, Candida G. (1999), 'Women's Entrepreneurship', *International Small Enterprise Programme*, Zurich: The International Labour Organisation, pp. 141–50.

Brush, Candida G. (2002), 'Venture Capital Access in the New Economy: Is Gender an Issue?', in David Hart (ed.), *The Emergence of Entrepreneurship Policy: Governance, Start-ups, and Growth in the Knowledge Economy*, London: Cambridge University Press.

Brush, C.G., L.F. Edelman and T.S. Manolova (2002), 'The impact of resources on small firm internationalization', *Journal of Small Business Strategy*, 13 (1), 1–17.

Brush, Candida G., Nancy Carter, Elizabeth Gatewood, Patricia G. Greene and Myra M. Hart (2000), 'Women and equity capital: An exploration of factors affecting capital access', in Candida G. Brush, Per Davidsson, Patricia G. Greene, Paul G. Reynolds and Harry H. Sapienza (eds), *Frontiers of Entrepreneurship Research, Proceedings of the Babson Entrepreneurship Research Conference*, Babson Park, MA: Arthur M. Blank Center for Entrepreneurship at Babson College.

Brush, C.G., N. Carter, E. Gatewood, P.G. Greene and M.M. Hart (2002), *The Diana Project. Women Business Owners and Equity Capital: The Myths Dispelled*, Kansas City, MS: Kauffman Center for Entrepreneurial Research.

Burgel, O., A. Fier, G. Licht and G. Murray (2001), 'Timing of international market entry of UK and German high-tech start ups', paper presented at the Babson Entrepreneurship Research Conference, Jonkoping, Sweden, June.

Edelman, L., C.G. Brush and T.S. Manolova (1998), 'Internationalization of small firms: Which resources matter?', paper presented at the Academy of Management annual meeting, San Diego, CA, 11 August.

Greene, Patricia P., Candida G. Brush, Myra M. Hart and Patrick Saparito (1999), 'An Exploration of the Venture Capital Industry: Is Gender an Issue?', in William Bygrave, Nancy Carter, Colin Mason, Dale Meyer, Sophie Manigart and Kelly Shaver (eds), *Frontiers of Entrepreneurship Research, Proceedings of the Babson Entrepreneurship Research Conference*, Babson Park, MA: Arthur M. Blank Center for Entrepreneurship at Babson College.

Greene, P.G., C.G. Brush, M. Hart and P. Saparito (2001), 'Patterns of venture capital funding: Is gender a factor?', *Venture Capital*, 3(1), 63–83.

Harveston, P.D. and B.L. Kedia (2000), 'Internationalization of born global and gradual globalizing firms: The impact of firm strategy, technology intensity and international entrepreneurial orientation', paper presented at the Academy of Management annual meeting, Toronto, Canada, 7 August.

Hisrich, R.D. and M.V. Grachev (1993), 'The Russian entrepreneur', *Journal of Business Venturing*, 8(6), 487–98.

Hisrich, Robert D. and Candida G. Brush (1986), *The Woman Entrepreneur: Starting, Financing and Managing a Successful New Business*, Boston, MA: Lexington Books.

Jolly, V.K., M. Alahunta and J.-P. Jeannet (1992), 'Challenging the incumbents: How high technology start-ups compete globally', *Journal of Strategic Change*, 1, 71–82.

Khavul, Susanna (2001), 'Money and Knowledge: Sources of Seed Capital and the Performance of High Technology Start Ups', unpublished doctoral dissertation, Boston University.

Khavul, Susanna, Candida G. Brush, Shlomo Kalish, and Miri Lerner (1998a), 'Public Policy and Private Initiatives in the Incubation of Israeli High Tech Entrepreneurial Firms', in William D. Bygrave, Nancy Carter, Colin Mason, Dale Meyer, Sophie Manigart and Kelly Shaver (eds), *Frontiers of Entrepreneurship Research, Proceedings of the Babson Entrepreneurship Research Conference*, Babson Park, MA: Arthur M. Blank Center for Entrepreneurship at Babson College, pp. 330–44.

Khavul, S., C.G. Brush, S. Kalish and M. Lerner (1998b), 'Public policy and private initiatives: Incubator effects on Israeli high technology entrepreneurial firms', paper presented at the ABI Informs annual meeting, July.

Lerner, Miri, Candida G. Brush and Robert Hisrich (1995), 'Factors Affecting the Performance of Israeli Women Entrepreneurs: An Examination of Alternative Perspectives', in William D. Bygrave, Barbara Bird, Sue Birley, Neil Churchill, Michael Hay, Robert Keeley and William E. Wettzel, Jr. (eds), *Frontiers of Entrepreneurship Research, Proceedings of the Babson Entrepreneurship Research Conference*, Babson Park, MA: Arthur M. Blank Center for Entrepreneurship at Babson College.

Lerner, M., C.G. Brush and R. Hisrich (1997), 'Israeli women entrepreneurs: An examination of factors affecting performance', *Journal of Business Venturing*, 12(4), 315–34.

Manolova, T.S., C.G. Brush and L.F. Edelman (2000), 'Internationalization of small companies: Personal factors revisited', paper presented at the Academy of Management annual meeting, Toronto, Canada, 7 August.

Manolova, T.S., C.G. Brush and L.F. Edelman (2002), 'Internationalization of small companies: Personal factors revisited', *International Small Business Journal*, 20(1), 3–23.

McDougall, P.P. (1989), 'International versus domestic entrepreneurship: New venture strategic behavior and industry structure', *Journal of Business Venturing*, 4(6), 387–400.

McDougall, P.P. and B.M. Oviatt (1991), 'Global start-ups: New ventures without geographical limits', *The Entrepreneurship Forum* (Winter), 1–5.

McDougall, Patricia P. and Benjamin M. Oviatt (1999), 'International Entrepreneurship Literature in the 1990s and Directions for Future Research', in Donald L. Sexton and Raymond W. Smilor (eds), *Entrepreneurship 2000*, Chicago, IL: Upstart Publishing Company, pp. 291–320.

McDougall, P.P., B.M. Oviatt and C.G. Brush (1991), 'A symposium on global start-ups: Entrepreneurial firms that are born international', presentation at the Academy of Management annual meeting, Miami, FL, 11–14 August.

McDougall, P.P., S. Shane and B.M. Oviatt (1994), 'Explaining the formation of international new ventures: The limits of theories from international business research', *Journal of Business Venturing*, 9, 469–87.

Nee, V. (1992), 'Organizational dynamics of market transformation: Hybrid forms, property rights and mixed economy in China', *Administrative Science Quarterly*, 37, 1–27.

Reuber, A.R. and E. Fischer (1997), 'The influence of the management team's international experience on the international behavior of SMEs', *Journal of International Business Studies*, 28(4), 807–25.

The Diana Project: Women Business Owners and Equity Capital – The Myths Dispelled, 2001 Insight Report, Kansas City, MO: The Kauffman Center for Entrepreneurial Leadership.

Westhead, P., M. Wright and D. Ucbasaran (2001), 'The internationalization of new and small firms: A resource-based view', *Journal of Business Venturing*, 16(4), 333–58.

5 The new globetrotters
Laurel J. Delaney

In my research, I have found that two significant business developments are taking place in the global economy of the 21st century. One is the explosion of women-owned businesses (Jalbert, 2000). The second is international trade (ibid.). Putting these two business developments together creates a powerful force with which to reckon. This force contributes to economic growth, development and prosperity in our world. These imperatives are producing a new business dynamic around the world (Taylor and Webber, 1996). I strongly believe the timing has never been better for businesswomen to get out of their own backyards and move from local, regional or niche-market-players into global players. It is my desire through my work to become a resource, strength and a supportive person for professional women to ensure they stand out as much-needed role models for what it takes to go forward, venture and succeed (Ericksen & Ernst & Young LLP, 1999).

If a businesswoman sees that the important people in her life believe in her idea, then that person begins to believe more strongly in herself (Anna *et al.*, 2000). I yearn for all companies to become more aware of their human capital, especially women, and to recognize their contribution to the world of business. This ensures that no (wo)man feels left out as she develops a clear sense of her own capabilities (Kuemmerle, 2002) and works towards living life on her own terms.

The potential is infinite
Today women are starting businesses at twice the rate of men and becoming major forces both in the traditional and the new global e-business marketplace (Cheskin Research, 2000). A snapshot of the facts indicates that women make up half of the world's human resources. There are 9.1 million women-owned American businesses alone, employing over 27.5 million people and contributing nearly $4 trillion in sales annually to the economy (Smilor, 2001). These businesses are increasing at a rate that is nearly twice that of the national average (Center for Women's Business Research, 2002). Over one in

---

* This chapter presents an overview of Laurel Delaney's work in the area of women in international entrepreneurship. It is adapted, in part, from a book Ms. Delaney is currently working on, *Women Entrepreneurs Take On The World, Not For Women Only*.

18 adult women in the USA, or 5.7 percent, is a business owner (ibid.). There is perhaps no greater initiative a country can take to accelerate its pace of entrepreneurial activity than to encourage more of its women to participate (Autio *et al.*, 2001). Furthermore observations have been made that American women are just as capable as men in the world of business (Axtell, 1993).

Between one-quarter and one-third of the world's businesses are owned by women. In fact, according to the Small Business Administration, the number of women-owned businesses increased by 90 percent in the last decade. Further, small firms with fewer than 10 people tend to hire more women than larger firms (Korn/Ferry International, 2001). As of 2000, only about 13 percent of women-owned businesses were involved in the global marketplace, despite the fact that the global market presents a huge opportunity for women to advance their careers and make an impact on the world of business (Barnett, 2001; Center for Women's Business Research, 1995).

Just like me, some women business owners are already participating in the global marketplace. In fact, women account for 30 percent of the businesses that export more than half of their products, and their potential to impact the worldwide market has not gone unnoticed (Center for Women's Business Research, 1995).

'Women-owned firms participating in the global marketplace grow more rapidly than women-owned businesses that are primarily domestic', former Small Business Administration (SBA) administrator Aida Alvarez said. 'They are more apt to develop a new product or service and expand domestically. At the SBA, we have several programs in place to help women-owned businesses take advantage of the outstanding opportunities available through international trade.'

Internationalization
In a statistical report released last year, the US SBA Office of International Trade indicated that 'America's small businesses are big players in international trade, and their role is growing rapidly.' Export data analysis shows that 97 percent of US companies that export are small businesses (Keating, 2001) and women own 40 percent of all small businesses (United States Case Study, 2000).

Other studies I have examined also make the case for small businesses and women-owned businesses as exporters. Consider, for instance, a case study regarding successful public and private initiatives for fostering entrepreneurship among women that was prepared by the National Women's Business Council's Interagency Committee on Women's Business Enterprise for the 2000 Organization for Economic Cooperation and Development Conference (United States Case Study, 2000). That study noted the significant role women have played in recent economic prosperity and affirmed that 'countries with high levels of economic activity and with the highest start-up business rates are the ones where women are well-engaged in entrepreneurial activity'. The authors also noted that small businesses owned by women and minorities are focusing more intense efforts on exporting than are small businesses owned by non-minority men. The days of purely domestic markets are gone forever (Collins and Lazier, 1992).

A recent report issued by the Small Business Survival Committee made this point: 'Small and mid-sized businesses, entrepreneurs, and many U.S. workers are seen as falling short of what it takes to make it in the rough and tumble global marketplace. The thinly veiled assertion is that these folks cannot cut it; they need coddling and protection. Of course, the notion that U.S. entrepreneurs, smaller enterprises and workers cannot compete internationally is as false as it is insulting' (Keating, 2001).

When I explored further, a Canadian study, 'Beyond Borders: Canadian businesswomen in international trade' (Rayman,1999), reveals that most women entrepreneurs start to enter foreign markets soon after start-up. In fact, nearly 55 percent of business owners take their first active step towards exporting (for example, gathering information on a foreign market) within two years of start-up. This finding reflects a global trend towards a narrower time gap between start-up and international activities and is true of both those who already are active exporters and those who are still in the planning stages for exporting. It also indicates that women business owners are cognizant of the global economy and its potential consequences for their firms.

Preparation time for entering a first foreign market is minimal, reflecting the opportunistic nature of many first-time exporters. The average elapsed time between the first step towards exporting and the jump of actually making a foreign sale is less than four months. It is important to note also that, in my key findings, there are no statistically significant differences in the time it takes product-based firms and service-based firms to enter foreign markets. On average, firms tend to enter close proximity overseas markets (for example, a Canadian company exporting to the USA (or a US company exporting to Mexico) one year earlier than they enter other foreign markets (Rayman, 1999).

Why internationalize?
There are a number of realistic incentives for women to take their businesses global. They include increasing sales; generating economies of scale in production; raising profitability; insulating seasonal domestic sales by finding new foreign markets; creating jobs; encouraging the exchange of views, ideas and information; establishing educational programs, confer-

ences and other activities to advance women; and promoting professional growth, mentoring, education and leadership among women.

If these incentives are not enough, I always emphasize: how about pure and simple business survival? We all know that business is about beating the competition, or keeping up at the very least. These days, you have got a lot more to worry about than your competition on the other side of town. No matter what your product or service, you are now operating in a worldwide market, which means you have competition all over the world. Fortunately small businesses can not only compete on a more level playing field, but can also enter international markets with less financial risk (Oliver, 2000).

More and more of those competitors are managing worldwide operations, and they are working hard to increase their share of the pie. The question I ask is: 'Are you?' The best and maybe even the only way to stay competitive with this new breed of global business manager is to become one yourself. In running my international business, I found you must act as if you were born to go global (Kanter, 1995).

Furthermore one must consider how a business helps fuel a country's economic engine. If all of us, including business women, fail to keep pace with the changing world and globalize, that engine will run out of steam. Where will we be if that happens?

Begin with the basics
To survive in today's world, one must seriously consider the step of internationalization. What distinguishes the world-class from the merely good is the ability to be a global center of thinking, making or trading (Kanter, 1995). Once you decide going global is for you, you need to stop thinking that it is a fantasy and begin to make it an integral part of your business plan.

Going global is for life. I tend to look at the basics and examine the 'inside job' of understanding what it takes to go global. First, you have to learn how to navigate your business through uncharted waters worldwide. To do that, you need to develop the right mindset, establish special character traits, map out a global strategy and just flat-out take the initiative to take on the world. Secondly, you must stop acting by the old rules and start creating new ones. The question becomes, 'What in the world are you doing with your business today?' Lastly, the single most important element in implementing a successful global launch is you. Only you can unleash your potential to build a dream global empire.

Twelve keys to developing a global entrepreneurial mindset
When I began my global consulting company, I did not think I had a unique perspective on the business world. I felt sure I could make all kinds of

things happen if I just kept at it and I did not think being a woman would create any obstacles. I started the company because I needed to do something on my own or be my own boss (Moore, 2000). I wanted personal freedom, more opportunity for creative expression and the excitement of encountering diverse cultures. And I longed to reinforce that important element of the free agent work ethic of putting myself on the line (Pink, 2001). I had been trained in the basics of exporting at my former job, and I wanted to put this know-how to work on a larger scale that would offer daily challenges and boundless potential for growth. Now, after running the company for over 15 years, I remember the remarks people used to make when I would tell them how I built my business. They would exclaim, 'I cannot believe you did that!' or 'and then what happened?'

I have never been lacking in guts and I have always been eager to take on the world, so that is why I decided to reach out to others to enable them to go global too. My temperament and my early export experience gave me a habit of thinking about the global marketplace in a big, broad way that continues to shape my operations today. I have never been intimidated by flying alone to conduct business in distant places, nor am I afraid to call up presidents of major companies to talk to them about what I do. I remember sending a fax to the founder of Sony Corporation to see if I could meet him during my next trip to Japan to introduce myself and talk to him about sourcing American products for Sony. I thought it was important that he knew me. It was just an idea, and my attitude was and still is 'why not?'

It has always seemed natural for me to act in these ways. I find it is most satisfying to live according to the rules you create for yourself. I ask you to stop right now and ask yourself this: do these ways of being come naturally to you? Perhaps not yet. But I invite you to take stock of yourself and decide if you are ready to develop the dynamic outlook that will enable you to take on the world.

Entering the global market requires a special way of understanding the world but only for those who are willing to give up their old ways of thinking (Ohmae, 2000). It requires an ability to see things that others do not. It is not a lifestyle; it is a 'mindstyle'. The following are 12 key aspects that I developed reflecting this powerful worldview. These are your prerequisites to taking on the world, and your foundation for starting and running a profitable international business (Delaney, 1998).

1. A global entrepreneur must be comfortable with change. He knows that the world is rapidly changing, and that change always includes the potential for positive developments. International sellers learn to enjoy the challenges of the unknown and to watch for emerging opportunities. Every nanosecond something new is happening in the

world. We must take that into account in our global dealings because it affects the outcome of all our efforts. The more connections you create with other human beings worldwide, the more acute the need to be comfortable with change.

2. A global entrepreneur must continuously welcome new experiences, even crises, for they bring about a positive confrontation between different perspectives. These challenges to your perspective should be used to map out new directions for your creative energies. As a global entrepreneur, you must always seek to improve yourself, your product, your business and your world.

A global entrepreneur is never content with the obvious explanation when she suspects there is more to it than that, never satisfied with one task when she can manage a project, never happy with a project when she can manage an organization. Similarly, global entrepreneurs are constantly scanning the geographical horizon to learn more about potential markets and competitors, new technology and new suppliers. Achieving excellence in any activity is always much, much more fun than doing just okay!

It is good to expect surprises, but even better to seek them out. Even a relatively ordinary life will teach you that the world is full of surprises. When you welcome them, you are light years ahead of those who have been trained to guard against them. In the business world, the fittest will survive and thrive. Evolve, and you will be one of them!

3. A global entrepreneur must be adaptable, take risks and innovate. She must be nimble-minded and take nothing for granted. She must do whatever she can to extend her global reach. Did you know that Americans are generally viewed around the world as narrow-minded, parochial people who insist on having everything 'the way we do it back home', and always seem to be trying to recreate the world in America's image? This is not only bad etiquette but it is bad politics and bad business. If you want to take your place in the global market, you must rid yourself of this attitude immediately.

Your adaptability means that you know how different markets operate, and are sensitive to the cultural values of other countries. If things appear one way today and another tomorrow, you shift gears and work with conditions as you find them. Learn to create your strategy on your feet. That is the only way to do global business. The more you risk, the greater your chances for success or failure, but, either way, you are pushing your limits and extending your reach. Remember, you learn the most from failure, so take what chances you can afford. There always comes a point where you realize there are risks, acknowledge them and then move forward anyway.

Keeping the mind fresh, fertile and open to new perspectives is a must if you want to conduct business effectively worldwide. You must not merely innovate, but transform the way you do business so boldly that you inspire everyone around you. There are endless ways of opening your mind that you can get to work on right now. Visit your library and try some completely different reading. Take long walks in unfamiliar neighbourhoods. Look out at a body of water. See foreign films. Meet people in other professions. Join social groups that attract members of other nationalities. Challenge your own preconceptions about what is and what can be. Do not withdraw when confronted by cultural differences. Instead, hang in there and ask yourself why you feel the way you do. This is real learning. Give yourself a chance to discover your own unexamined values and assumptions, and you will find it a lot easier to accept others' unfamiliar ways.

4. A global entrepreneur must be willing to learn as much as possible about the culture in which he is about to do business. She must pay attention to etiquette and protocol, and behave exactly as interpersonal situations dictate. One day you are a diplomat, the next a leader, sometimes both. When your every move is subject to interpretation, it is best to come equipped with the knowledge that will put you ahead of the game.

    You can start by thinking about what makes you different from your next door neighbour. Then form the habit of doing the same thing on a citywide, nationwide and worldwide scale. Try to understand how and why people from different ethnic and cultural backgrounds think and behave the way they do.

    Then focus your investigations by reading all you can about the culture of a country you plan to visit. For a real jump-start, call up a local foreign consulate and set up a meeting. Explain that you want to know more about their national culture before visiting. You will be amazed at how receptive they are, and how impressed that you would take the time to learn about their ways. In addition, they may offer to assist with your trip in any way they can, and will probably have some excellent books on hand for you to read.

5. A global entrepreneur must have enormous reserves of energy along with patience and the ability to stick with it. It is great to be an aggressive, energetic mover-and-shaker, but just as important to know when to slow down and let a negotiation take its own course. You must be more than a regular go-getter to face the world market. The work you must do is difficult and draining. Real business breakthroughs do not come easily or quickly on the domestic front, and in the global market it is a thousand times more difficult. You must deliver long-term value

in terms of product quality and customer service while building and maintaining the alliances a global market demands, and you must expect it to take a lot of time. You can be a little greedy, which global entrepreneurs tend to be, but do not be impatient. You will not get far with a narrow focus on boosting next quarter's sales figures, or with slick hard-sell tactics. The kind of short-term, bottom-line, quick-return thinking we tend to use in our domestic operations shows a basic lack of understanding about the demands of global business. It is a slow process, and it requires patience.

The ability to stick with it is vital if you are going to maintain the committed effort needed to make things work. Do not quit before you have to, just because you lack the nerve to keep up your efforts when there is no payoff in sight. You must get through the discouraging, nerve-racking times. Your perseverance will give you strength and confidence that carry you through even bolder efforts in the future.

6. A global entrepreneur must be comfortable with himself before he can present himself well in the international arena. You must know yourself well enough to anticipate how you will react in new and difficult circumstances. You must be able to exercise self-control. You must develop inner security by counting yourself as valuable apart from your successes or failures. When you know yourself well, you are able to build connections with others by listening, empathizing and understanding. The people skills that are so essential for cultivating relationships in the global marketplace start with the positive relationship you cultivate with yourself.

Certainly you will make mistakes now and then, but only one is always disastrous: global entrepreneurs must never take the position that they are always right and the other person is wrong. They must remain open-minded, thoughtful and sensitive. People who are personally secure and can allow others to be themselves have by far the best chance of creating the harmonious business relationships that global dealings demand.

7. A global entrepreneur must have passion, enthusiasm, playfulness and curiosity. You need to be alive, alert and exquisitely aware of the world around you. Show your business associates that you value every negotiation as if it is a matter of life or death. Let your body language communicate how intensely you care. Whether standing or seated, keep your posture straight, but lean forward ever so slightly and gesture with your hands to convey urgency. Look your listener straight in the eye. Let them see something in you that they have never experienced in the course of a mundane business transaction and

make them want more of it. Let them see that you are passionate about what you are building together.

Enthusiasm makes your passionate involvement friendly and accessible. Smile, let your eyes light up, let your energy flow through every gesture you make. Make your listener want to bottle up your energy and use it themselves. Or make them want to put up a shield to ward it off! Enthusiasm is contagious and irresistible and tends to draw people to you no matter where in the world you are.

Want to fill yourself with passion and enthusiasm? Remember what it was like to be a kid? Spontaneous, free, not a care in the world? Let some of that powerful playfulness show. Use it carefully because there is obviously a time for play and a time for seriousness. Bringing a judicious helping of childlike joy and high good humor to your business ventures can sometimes make or break an international deal.

Finally, show your eagerness to discover more, to do more, to push the limits of the known. You need curiosity to drive you in search of 'more'. Your passion, enthusiasm and playfulness need somewhere to go. Take the next step, go the extra mile, and wonder what if, what is next, what is possible.

8. A global entrepreneur should have traveled to at least one foreign country and stayed for several weeks with a native family and desire to return. Get on a plane and head for a place you have never been before. When you get there, make yourself at home. If you can do that, you are on your way to becoming a global entrepreneur. If you have not exposed yourself to foreign travel, make yourself a promise to do it soon. And when you have landed yourself somewhere far from home, teach yourself to adjust, interact with the locals, cultivate friendships and ask a lot of questions. This is the best possible training for becoming a global entrepreneur. Many people are reluctant to try it because it is expensive, they do not want to take the time, they do not know anybody in other countries or they are nervous about the unknown. They need to challenge this fear. By making a trip like this, you stand to gain invaluable international experience and, quite likely, will have the most fun you have ever had in your life.

9. A global entrepreneur must value the relationship more than the deal. When cultivating a potential client, never forget that that individual is more important than closing the deal under discussion. You can only do so much to make it happen and then you have to let it happen. If a relationship is meant to be, it will develop itself over time and at its own pace. I find it is analogous to cultivating a garden: in time, and after much care, good things will begin to grow.

You must become a true insider wherever you decide to do business, and the only way to accomplish that is to get to know the person with whom you wish to have a relationship and forget about how much time it takes. To have a genuine relationship with anyone, you must develop a history together or 'grow up together', as it were. You have to deal with someone from time to time over a period of years, and learn to see them clearly. Trust and respect your contact, because otherwise there is no point in continuing the relationship next door, let alone across international borders. If it does not work out, you will survive. And, who knows, you might even meet someone else with whom you can do your best and most inspired business.

10. A global entrepreneur must have all-encompassing perspective. He or she should be able to function well on both a small and a large scale. They should hone in on details, yet always comprehend the big picture, and keep pace with that picture as it changes. One day you will be trying to pin down just why Japanese women like the color pink and the next day you will be sorting out how the drop in the peso will affect your latest acquisition in Mexico. You will need to take in information, see its significance and act on it. Cultivate your perspective and it will keep you at the cutting edge of global business.

11. A global entrepreneur must be an inspired, and inspiring, team builder and leader. The old top-down, hierarchical, 'my way or the highway' business style does not work any more. The challenges of the global economy are best met by a new organizational model: a team of highly gifted professionals brought together by a leader who knows how to act as 'first among equals'. Such a leader must have an eye for talented people who can contribute something unique and irreplaceable to the group, and must know how to provide an environment in which each member feels recognized and valued for their contributions, project after project. The leader must provide direction, encouragement, vision and inspiration so that, together, the group becomes much more than the sum of its parts. If you can find the right people, trust them and help them grow to do great things, you will be on the surest possible ground. The only resource your competitor cannot duplicate is the unique and winning chemistry of your talented team.

12. Above all else, a global entrepreneur must have courage because freedom in this world is born from courage. You can page through a hundred college catalogs and you will not find any adult education courses in courage. Even if you did, you might enroll, read, do all your homework, participate in class discussions and complete the course with an 'A+' without having gained a single iota of courage. To acquire courage, you must put yourself in challenging situations,

either by choice or by accident, and get through them. The one thing to keep in mind is that, since few situations are truly life-or-death, you know you will survive.

Even so, going forward with anything about which you have even the smallest doubt takes courage. Taking the first step on a project which everyone else tells you will be difficult or impossible takes courage. Putting your reputation on the line and making up your mind to deal with the consequences takes courage. Staying true to your vision, and your mission, in the face of criticism and opposition takes courage. But if you can somehow call it up when you need it, your rewards will be extraordinary. Courage crosses all boundaries and knows no barriers. In the complicated, ambiguous world of foreign business, it is essential for the aspiring globalist.

These are the attributes that I have found a global entrepreneur must cultivate and put to work in the international marketplace. They have been effective for me. Gender does not matter. To take on the world, a world in which only the fittest will survive, you must make yourself one of the fittest. This is hard work, and will test your motivation at every turn. Are you ready to take it on? I hope my words have inspired you and, if so, it is time to get started!

How to choose a market
Where in the world should you take your business first? That was the big question I asked myself before I began. You could just wait to be deluged with e-mails from other countries. Better yet, your partner speaks French. How about making France the target for your first market? Wait a minute, did you say you are selling perfume? Do the French need another enticing scent to dab behind their ears? I doubt it, but at least when they tell you so, your partner will understand.

It is a little trickier than that to decide which overseas market is most promising for your product. Sometimes, while you are busy servicing the domestic market, you will get lucky and an inquiry will come through, pointing you directly at an ideal new market. But it is more likely you will need to do your homework to find customers. I believe that conducting market research will tell you where they can be found.

Your first market research project is usually the toughest because it is all unfamiliar terrain. But, take heart, because once you have searched out the data you need to predict how a specific type of product will sell in a specific geographic location, you can use the information repeatedly as a guideline for exports of similar products in the future.

As you build your personal information database on global markets and learn to keep yourself up-to-date on developments in international trade, it will become less of a chore to determine where to take your product. You will find that market research is a powerful tool for exploring, and taking control of, your global territory.

When deciding where to concentrate your sales efforts, choose a market that intrigues you or offers a challenge, and then consider products that you might want to sell there. That is what I have found works best. My first export market was Japan. I felt that if I successfully conducted business there, I could sell anywhere. Later this notion proved to be true because it brought me recognition and respect as a global player as well as an impressive sales record.

Keep in mind that you will be visiting the market you choose frequently and getting to know its people intimately, so, just as you should pick a product that will delight you for years to come, you should plan on exporting to a country that delights and fascinates you. Doing this will give you a good place to start. But remember to use common sense. Do not ignore other countries that offer good prospects for your product, and do not expend too much time and energy on your first-choice market if it turns out to be a poor prospect.

Ten steps to take on the world
In summary, I would like to share with you 10 action-oriented business principles that have been most valuable to me as an internationalist and invite you to take them to heart as your blueprint for taking on the world (Delaney, 2002).

1. Get company-wide commitment. Every person at a company is a vital member of the international team, from the receptionist through customer service, engineering, purchasing, production and shipping. Exporting is not something you work at one day and forget about the next. It is an investment in your company's future that deserves your consistent attention regardless of how well you are doing domestically.
2. Research and map out your export journey. Do your homework and perform a global-readiness assessment, planning your strategy all the way to implementation. Just because your service is needed here in your own country does not indicate that it will be well received in a foreign country. You must always check with either your prospective customer (let them review it at no charge) or a local foreign consulate to see if they can help you determine whether your service makes sense for their host country.
3. Know where you want to go and go there. Know your destination but be willing to make adjustments along the way. Forcing a customer to

buy what you have available with little or no willingness on your part to make improvements is not just insensitive but downright hostile. Global marketing has come a long way since the days of Henry Ford, who said, 'The customer can have a car painted any color that he wants, so long as it is black.'

4. Take that decisive step and follow it up with sensible judgment. Jump in with both feet first but keep them firmly planted on the ground. It gets you back to basics. Pick one service, pick one market and then stick to it. You need to put on your mental blinders and ignore distractions, channel your energies and define the territory in which you are going to play. It takes a lot of discipline to resist the scattershot approach to doing business and stay focused. Yet, after a while, the discipline becomes automatic. The person who makes it is the kind of person who has the persistence to keep trying until he or she succeeds (Weiss, 1997).

5. Keep your ego in check. Do not let the prospect of going global inflate your ego and cause misjudgments.

6. Trust your instincts. If it smells, looks or feels bad, do not try to rationalize otherwise.

7. Treat other people as you want to be treated. People are basically the same worldwide; it does not matter where you are. Awareness and respect of cultural protocol demonstrates honesty and goodwill, and this leads to trust, which in turn leads to mutually profitable relationships.

8. Make personal contact with attentiveness, courtesy, professionalism and consistency. In-person visits are vital to building a relationship with rapport. You cannot afford not to meet prospective customers because, without face-to-face contact, there will be no business. Customers matter, and the personal meeting is the best way to demonstrate your professional commitment.

9. Factor in a two-year lead-time for world market penetration. It takes time and patience.

10. In a global marketplace, welcome the unknown. Do not let the prospect of the unknown frighten you. Rather learn to welcome it, take it apart piece by piece and then slowly digest it all. The rewards can be great.

I do not underestimate the challenge of conducting world business, but I cannot emphasize enough how personally and professionally rewarding it has been for me. I continue to view new products, breakthrough technology, consumer trends and global marketing ideas with an eye to how they will work in the world. I remind myself always of the continual efforts that will be required to keep a foothold for my company and its offerings in this bountiful but competitive territory. If you have the vision, dedication and courage to accept this challenge, I encourage you to begin cultivating a 'garden' of your own, so that you can harvest rich rewards in the years to come (Delaney, 1994).

References

Anna, J., G. Chandler, E. Jansen and N. Mero, (2000), 'Women business owners in traditional and non-traditional industries', *Journal of Business Venturing*, 15, 279–303.

Autio, E., W. Bygrave, S. Camp, M. Hay and P. Reynolds (2001), *Executive Report, Global Entrepreneurship Monitor*, Kansas City, Missouri: Kaufman Foundation.

Axtell, R. (1993), *Do's and taboos around the world*, New York: John Wiley & Sons.

Barnett, J. (2000), 'Women entrepreneurs: The new globetrotters', *Enterprising Women*, November/December, 25–33.

Center for Women's Business Research (1995), 'Women-owned firms are going global', Washington, DC.

Center for Women's Business Research (2001), 'Number of women-owned businesses expected to reach 6.2 million in 2002', Washington, DC.

Center for Women's Business Research (2002), '1 in 18 U.S. women is a business owner', Washington, DC.

Cheskin Research (2000), 'Women entrepreneurs study', Santa Clara University, Center for Innovation & Entrepreneurship, The Center for New Futures, January.

Collins, J. and W. Lazier (1992), *Beyond entrepreneurship: Turning your business into an enduring great company*, Englewood Cliffs, New Jersey: Prentice-Hall.

Delaney, L. (1994), 'An American trader in Japan', *Journal of Japanese Trade & Industry*, 4: 32–8.

Delaney, L. (1998), *Start & run a profitable exporting business*, Bellingham, Washington: Self-Counsel Press.

Delaney, L. (2002), *Insanely global!* (*http://www.ebookmall.com/ebooks/showdetl.cfm?DID= 8&Product_ID=65325*).

Ericksen, G. & Ernst & Young (1999), *Women entrepreneurs only: 12 women entrepreneurs tell the stories of their success*, New York: John Wiley & Sons.

Jalbert, S. (2000), 'Women entrepreneurs in the global economy study', Center for International Enterprise, Washington, DC, March.

Kanter, R.M. (1995), *World class: thriving locally in the global marketplace*, New York: Simon & Schuster.

Keating, R. (2001), 'The importance of moving ahead on the trade front', Small Business Survivor Committee (SBSC), Washington, DC.

Korn/Ferry International Survey (2001), 'What women want in business: A survey of executives and entrepreneurs', in conjunction with Eugene M. Lang Center for Entrepreneurship at Columbia Business School, Fortune Small Business and the Duran Group, New York.

Kuemmerle, W. (2002), 'The Entrepreneur: A Test for the Fainthearted', *Harvard Business Review*, 122–7.

Moore, D.P. (2000), *Careerpreneurs: Lessons from leading women entrepreneurs on building a career without boundaries*, Palo Alto, California: Davies-Black Publishing.

Ohmae, K. (2000), *The invisible continent: Four strategic imperatives of the new economy*, New York: Harper Business.

Oliver, R. (2000), 'The future of small business: Trends for a new century', American Express, IBM, National Small Business United and in cooperation with RISEbusiness, Owen Graduate School of Management at Vanderbilt University, Nashville, Tennessee.

Pink, D. (2001), *Free agent nation: How America's new independent workers are transforming the way we live*, New York: Warner Books.

Rayman, R. (1999). 'Beyond borders: Canadian businesswomen in international trade', Foreign Affairs & International Trade Info Centre, Toronto, Canada.

Shattuck, R. (2000). 'Starting From Scratch', *The American Scholar*, Autumn, 47–56.

Smilor, R. (2001), *Daring visionaries: How entrepreneurs build companies, inspire allegiance, and create wealth*, Holbrook, Massachusetts: Adams Media Corporation.
Taylor, C. and A. Webber (1996), *Going global: Four entrepreneurs map the new world marketplace*, New York: Penguin Books.
United States Case Study (2000), 'Successful public and private sector initiatives fostering the growth of women's business ownership', a report prepared by the National Women's Business Council's Interagency Committee on Women's Business Enterprise in conjunction with the 2000 Organization for Economic Co-operation and Development (OECD) conference on women entrepreneurs in small and medium enterprises, November, Washington, DC.
Weiss, K. (1997), *Building an import/export business*, New York: John Wiley & Sons.

Reference web sites to facilitate internationalization

Basic questions about going global can be answered by visiting a handful of online resources. Here are some tips for educators and their students:

Businesswomen in Trade (*http://www.infoexport.gc.ca/businesswomen/menu-e.asp*)
Country Watch (*http://www.countrywatch.com/*)
Dun & Bradstreet (*http://www.dnb.com/*)
Export Hotline (*http://www.exporthotline.com/*)
Globe Women (*http://www.globewomen.com*)
GlobeTrade.com http://www.globetrade.com
How To Conquer The World (*http://www.howtoconquertheworld.com/*)
International Trade Administration, US Department of Commerce (*http://www.ita.doc.gov/index.html*)
Michigan State University (*http://globaledge.msu.edu/*)
Office of International Trade, US Small Business Administration (*http://www.sbaonline.sba.gov/OIT/*)
Organisation of Women in International Trade (*http://www.owit.org/*)
Stat-USA / Department of Commerce (*http://www.stat-usa.gov/*)
The Federation of International Trade Associations (*http://www.fita.org/index.html*)
The US Commercial Service (*http://www.usatrade.gov/website/website.nsf*)
Trade Compass (*http://www.tradecompass.com/*)
U.S. Department of Commerce & Global Publishers Partnership (*http://www.myexports.com/resource_links/index.html*)
Worldskip (*http://www.worldskip.com*)

6   International entrepreneurship and Chinese business research

Henry Wai-chung Yeung

International entrepreneurship is a relatively new field of academic and policy pursuits, as testified in the chapters by leading scholars in this volume. In this emerging field, research attention has been largely placed on the internationalization of entrepreneurship in relation to new venture formation and the internationalization of small- and medium-sized enterprises (SMEs). In one of the earliest contributions to international entrepreneurship, McDougall (1989; also McDougall *et al.*, 1994; McDougall and Oviatt, 1996, 2000) focused almost exclusively on international new venture firms and compared their strategic behaviour and industry structure with domestic new ventures. Firm-specific and industry-specific factors were presented as the critical dimensions to explain and differentiate firm behaviour. There was neither a theoretical nor an empirical role given to individual entrepreneurs who have propelled the firms into an international arena. This is not surprising because, as recently as 1994, international entrepreneurship was still considered as an 'even newer thrust of research activity' in international business research (Wright and Ricks, 1994: 699). Moon and Peery (1997: 11) also argued that 'Entrepreneurship is very important in international business. There are some noteworthy, new international ventures that, from inception, seek to derive significant competitive advantage from the use of resources and the sale of outputs in multiple countries.'

In this chapter I aim to take the argument further and propose the concept of 'transnational entrepreneurship' as the key to unite two separate fields of management studies: entrepreneurship research and international business research (see Yeung, 2002a, 2002b, for a complete theoretical exposition and detailed empirical analysis). I define transnational entrepreneurship simply as *the exceptional qualities required in the processes of creating and sustaining particular business ventures across national boundaries by social actors*. These social actors are, of course, defined as 'transnational entrepreneurs'. To this effect, I have chosen to use a process definition of transnational entrepreneurship and an agency definition of transnational entrepreneurs. In comparison with 'international entrepreneurship', the term 'transnational entrepreneurship' offers a more precise description of the phenomenon under investigation – entrepreneurs who operate across national boundaries (hence 'transnational').

Consider a businessperson who is confronted by a saturated market in the home country, or another businessperson who stumbles upon an opportunity to expand into foreign markets. It takes great courage and other exceptional qualities, or 'aptitudes', in the words of Schumpeter (1942: 132), for this person to act on these situations and to get things done. This person may be an owner and/or a manager of an evolving transnational corporation (TNC), defined as a firm that operates and controls business enterprises in two or more countries (irrespective of the level of equity ownership). In both cases, the businessperson is bound to be confronted by the inherent difficulties of operating in a foreign land of which he or she has less information, experience and knowledge, and faces a different set of institutional contexts. These difficulties of engaging in international business activities can be overcome, sometimes, by sheer luck. But it is more likely they can only be handled with great initiatives and capabilities embedded in the social actor and his/her repertoire of institutional resources and relations. We may therefore conceptualize these transnational entrepreneurs as businesspersons who take specific proactive action to overcome inherent problems and difficulties associated with international business activities. Their action, however, is both facilitated and constrained by current processes of institutional relations in both home and host countries. These institutional relations may be defined by the social and business networks, in which these transnational entrepreneurs are embedded, political–economic structures, and dominant organizational and cultural practices in the home and host countries.

How then does transnational entrepreneurship work in an empirical sense? How much do we know about the nature and extent of transnational entrepreneurship in different parts of the world? Through the lens of my own research into ethnic Chinese business firms over the past ten years, I seek to argue, in this chapter, for transnational entrepreneurship to become a new horizon of research not only in management studies, but also in the wider social sciences. In the remaining sections, I first trace the genealogy of my research into Chinese business since my doctoral studies, bearing in mind all the inherent problems and biases in post hoc reconstruction of one's research path. I then place this body of literature on Chinese business within the contexts of entrepreneurship and international business studies. The concluding section offers some reflections on the future of Chinese business research.

It all began with transnational entrepreneurship
It all began in late 1992, when I embarked on my doctoral research into the internationalization of Hong Kong firms into the Southeast Asian region.

As an economic-geographer-to-be, I was interested in describing and explaining the geographic expansion of these firms in different host economies. At that time, I was confronted by two major strands of literature that informed my research framework: (1) international business studies of the so-called 'Third World multinationals' and (2) sociological studies of Chinese family business. In engaging this research project, little did I know that I was literally doing transnational entrepreneurship research, an unintended trajectory I have only realized recently. The first strand of literature has its origins in the early work by Wells (1977, 1983) and Lall (1982, 1983) on the internationalization of firms from developing economies, particularly Hong Kong and India (see Yeung, 1999a, for a comprehensive collection of all major papers from 1973 to 1998). While this literature describes the economic factors and business considerations accounting for the emergence of 'Third World multinationals', I found the majority of these studies biased in their underlying assumptions and thin in their theoretical frameworks. In my *Third World Quarterly* paper (Yeung, 1994a), I critiqued the assumption that these emerging firms are 'unconventional' – a terminology in Heenan and Keegan's (1979) classic *Harvard Business Review* paper. In another paper (Yeung, 1994b), I also questioned the lack of well-developed theoretical framework in guiding most research into firms from developing economies.

So much for the international business literature. What about those sociological studies of Chinese family business in East and Southeast Asia? My venture into this second strand of literature subsequently proves to be critical and enriching, perhaps because the literature contains many signposts to the wider social scientific debate on economy and society. Why bother, you might ask, with this seemingly unrelated literature if I was just interested in describing and explaining the internationalization of Hong Kong firms? Why not just rely exclusively on the 'Third World multinationals' literature? One immediate answer is that most Hong Kong firms were, and still are, family-owned and managed. It would be naïve to ignore this sociological literature that purports to explain the nature and organization of Chinese capitalism in East and Southeast Asia. More importantly at that time, I thought I had found something exciting in *theoretical* terms in this literature on Chinese capitalism – what turned out to be the Weberian approach to economic development. In some of these key studies on Chinese capitalism after Max Weber's famous argument for the protestant ethic in the emergence of modern capitalism, a *cultural* approach was offered to explain the exceptionally high level of entrepreneurship among Chinese family firms throughout the East and Southeast Asian region (for example, Redding, 1980, 1990; Hamilton and Biggart, 1988; Wong, 1988a, 1988b; Hamilton, 1991; see Brown, 1995, for a four-volume collection).

This strand of sociological literature certainly compared favourably with the 'Third World multinationals' literature. The former not only identified and described the entrepreneurial tendencies of Chinese family firms, but also explained these tendencies in relation to Chinese culture and familism (family-centred social life). This cultural predisposition towards the family among the 'overseas' Chinese was theorized as the foundation for the social organization and emergence of business networks.

Redding (1990), for example, argued that 'overseas' Chinese capitalism is essentially an economic culture characterized by a unique capacity to cooperate, and the 'overseas' Chinese are united by their deep sense of themselves as ethnic Chinese who have not psychologically left China or some ideal and romanticized notion of Chinese civilization (cf. Wang, 2000). 'Overseas' Chinese capitalism is not based on an elite system (such as in Japan), neither does it rest on an explicit political system (such as the USA), but rather is predicated on a household economy that is well adapted only to its sociocultural milieu. The spirit of 'overseas' Chinese capitalism is therefore a 'set of beliefs and values which lies behind the behavior of Chinese businessmen' (Redding, 1990: 79).

1. Certain values surrounding authority in Chinese culture (for example, Confucianism) foster the stability and adaptiveness of the family firm.
2. Chinese values legitimize a distinct form of cooperation between organizations.
3. Chinese values retain long-term legitimacy because of their grounding in Chinese ethics.
4. Economic exchange and growth is enhanced by intra-organizational stability and inter-organizational cooperation.
5. There is no tight linkage between a set of state-supported institutions and the organizational principles of business.
6. Kinship relationships are very important in Chinese organizations.

In particular, the family provides the central foundation on which Chinese social organization and institutions are constructed. The family becomes the central unit of social thought and worldview among the Chinese, thanks to the teaching of Confucianism that maintains the role of family, compliance and social order. This phenomenon among the 'overseas' Chinese is known as 'familism', which refers to the centrality of the family as a fundamental unit of social and economic organization among the Chinese. Some scholars of Chinese capitalism argued that it is familism that gives the 'overseas' Chinese a sense of 'Chineseness'. This 'culturalist' approach explains the success of 'overseas' Chinese capitalism through the role of familism and the Chinese socialization process.

It was this concern with theorizing business networks of the 'overseas' Chinese that captured my intellectual imagination and firmly established my research trajectory. There is one exception here, though. I did not quite agree with the 'culturalist' explanation of the nature and organization of Chinese family firms and their business networks. In one of my earliest papers on Hong Kong firms in Southeast Asia (Yeung, 1994c), I argued that the *institutional embedding* of these firms in different host economies could be equally, if not more, important in shaping their entrepreneurial activities and networks. Drawing upon the leading work in organizational analysis and economic geography published in the late 1980s and the early 1990s (see Yeung, 1994d, 1998a), I then developed a *business network* approach to explain the internationalization of Hong Kong firms. In this theoretical framework (see Table 6.1), I argued that three forms of networks relations provide the generative mechanisms for transnational operations by entrepreneurial firms: intra-firm, inter-firm and extra-firm. The major attributes of network relations elaborated in this framework are summarized as follows.

1. Networks are necessarily relational: atmosphere, trust and social order/cohesion.
2. Network relations are characterized by 'cooperative competition'.
3. Participation in network relations is motivated by both economic and non-economic goals.
4. Emergent powers are present in network relations, not reducible to individual firms: control, power and strategic advantages.

In operationalizing these theoretical claims in the case of Chinese business firms from Hong Kong, I found that transnational entrepreneurs from Hong Kong did not rely exclusively on family networks to venture into Southeast Asia. Indeed they engaged in a variety of network relations to establish their transnational operations in the host economies. Sometimes they exploited family linkages and friendship ties, a finding supporting the 'culturalist' explanation. In many other circumstances, these Hong Kong entrepreneurs developed network or *guanxi* relationships with other non-Chinese firms and the host economy institutions (such as local authorities and government organizations). This latter finding led me to theorize that transnational entrepreneurship in the Chinese context cannot be reduced to culture per se, but should rather be analysed in relation to different *varieties* of networks and organizations (see details of these arguments in Yeung, 1997a, 1997b, 1998b). Table 6.2 summarizes these diverse network relations facilitating the entrepreneurial activities of Hong Kong firms in Southeast Asia.

Table 6.1 A typology of network relations and the sociospatial organization of firms

Categories	Network relations		
	Intra-firm	Inter-firm	Extra-firm
Nature	• parent–subsidiary relationship • internalized operations: proprietary rights and economies of scale	• firm–firm transactional and institutional relationship • externalized operations: economies of scope and joint production/marketing	• firm–institution politics and relationship: state and non-state • contractual basis: direct business • legal laws and enforcement
Instruments	• integration (horizontal and/or vertical) • coordination (loose v. tight and centralized v. dispersed) • internal arbitration of disputes: labour relations • transfer pricing	• competition and cooperation • contracts and agreements • flexible production systems: just-in-time	• conflicts and negotiations • political bargaining • social regulation • propaganda strategy
Concrete dimensions	• tentative full integration of R&D and production • high quality at reasonable cost • decentralization of production decisions	• close and long-lasting ties between producers and users • networking to reap specialization and coordination gains • long-run and cooperative subcontracting	• power relations more than monetary relations • quest for propriety rights • search for social and political legitimacy
Organizational forms	• quasi-integration • internalization • multi-divisions • family business groups • conglomerates	• joint ventures • subcontracting • cooperative agreements • strategic alliances • licensing and franchising • ethnic and personal networks • technology financing	• government contracts • joint R&D collaboration • institutional relationship, e.g. memberships

Source: Yeung (1994d: Table 3).

Another key finding in my study that challenged the 'culturalist' explanation of Chinese family business and entrepreneurship was that internationalization and globalization allow Chinese family firms to go beyond the culturally predetermined 'limits' to their growth and expansion. Since Wong's (1985) paper in the *British Journal of Sociology*, many Chinese business researchers have taken for granted that the cultural predisposition of Chinese family firms towards the exclusive deployment of family members in top management deterred their growth and expansion, because, as some might say, there are only so many sons (legitimate and illegitimate) a Chinese patriarch can possibly have. If true, this culturally determined argument could have serious implications for transnational entrepreneurship among Chinese businesspeople. My research into Hong Kong firms in Southeast Asia, however, demonstrated clearly that these alleged cultural limits could be overcome by the processes of 'family-ization' and professionalization (Yeung, 1997c, 2000a, 2000b).

To sum up this section, my doctoral research into Hong Kong firms in Southeast Asia had unintentionally uncovered their transnational entrepreneurial tendencies. While rooted in the 'Third World multinationals' literature, my study was much better connected to sociological studies of Chinese capitalism. However my network approach to explaining the internationalization of Hong Kong firms moved significantly beyond the dominant 'culturalist' explanation of Chinese transnational entrepreneurship. It also helped to demystify the inherent cultural limits to the growth and expansion of Chinese family firms, an important argument to be followed up in my more recent theoretical work (see below).

Transnational entrepreneurship in a comparative perspective
Since 1996 I have been working on the regionalization of Singaporean firms into the East and Southeast Asian region. While not entirely different from their counterparts in Hong Kong, Chinese business firms in Singapore – a city–state spearheaded by significant government initatives – tend to be overshadowed by other types of major corporations, namely foreign TNCs and large government-linked companies, in their participation in the Singapore economy. Here a potentially very interesting case for comparison emerges from the very different nature of political economies in both Hong Kong (laissez-faire) and Singapore (state-driven). Key research questions are whether there will be any difference in the nature and extent of transnational entrepreneurship between Chinese business firms from two contrasting institutional contexts, and, if so, how we account for the difference.

To answer these comparative questions, I adopted a three-pronged approach. First, I examined the general patterns and processes of the internationalization of Chinese business firms from Southeast Asia (Yeung,

Table 6.2 Network relations and the sociospatial organization of Hong Kong firms and their Southeast Asian operations

Categories	Network relations		
	Intra-firm	Inter-firm	Extra-firm
Nature	• family business • regional ties • promotion of internal entrepreneurship	• informal and closely-knit coalition among leading businessmen • strengthening of 'institutional thickness' • less reliance on regional ties	• political patronage • cooperative extra-firm relationships
Instruments	• horizontal integration • loose coordination • reliance on trust mechanisms • embeddedness in personal relationships	• informal contacts and agreements • bargaining power through collective representation • intra-firm and extra-firm relationships • cooperative competition	• political bargaining • added competitive advantages • power relationships
Concrete dimensions	• lack of economies of scope and joint marketing with local partner • strong decentralization of production and management	• close and long-lasting ties among shareholders • networking to reap *guanxi* advantages • long-run and cooperative	• search for political legitimacy • local expertise
Organizational forms	• joint venture at the beginning • internalization over time: cooperative partnership or quasi-integration • cooperative ventures in China	• equity joint venture • loose cooperative organizational form • ethnic and personal networks • relocation of corporate HQs	• majority joint venture • government contracts • institutional relationship, e.g. subcontracting

Source: Yeung (1997a: Table 3).

1999b, 1999c, 1999d, 2000c; Tan and Yeung, 2000a, 2000b). The key objective in this series of publications was to ascertain the regional context in which Chinese business firms from Singapore engage in international operations. Here transnational entrepreneurship among Chinese business firms in Southeast Asia must be understood in relation to the changing political–economic regimes of respective 'home' countries of Chinese transnational entrepreneurs. For example, two-way investments between Malaysia and Singapore during the past three decades cannot be accounted for without an appreciation of transnational business networks among many Chinese business families in the two adjacent economies (Yeung, 1998c).

Second, I sought to demystify the negative impact of the recent (1997/8) Asian economic crisis on the emergence of Chinese business in Southeast Asia (Yeung, 1999e, 2000d, 2000e). Situating the crisis within the broader debate on economic globalization, I argued that globalization is a highly contested process. On the one hand, it poses a serious threat to the cultural practice and social organization of Chinese capitalism in Southeast Asia, and has put Chinese business under siege. On the other hand, globalization presents opportunities for such social institutions as Chinese business firms to take advantage of both the pragmatic response of nation states to globalization and the unintended opportunities opened to Chinese capitalists. Clearly, then, the entrepreneurial tendencies of Chinese business firms were important factors that explain why some Southeast Asian firms were much better at weathering the economic crisis than others (see Yeung, 2000f, 2001).

The third and related approach proved to be most significant for my comparative understanding of transnational entrepreneurship in terms of theoretical rigour and implications for empirical analysis. Extending my earlier business networks framework and synthesizing it with the actor network theory (popular in studies of the sociology of science and knowledge), I began to envision a different way to analyse the internationalization of Chinese business firms. Instead of seeing culture as the 'stabilizer' of business relations and entrepreneurial tendencies in Chinese capitalism, I focused on the *network dynamics* embedded in the globalization processes of Chinese business firms (Yeung, 2000c; 2000g). In Olds and Yeung (1999), for example, we explored the relationships between globalizing tendencies and the changing form of Chinese business networks. We discussed how Chinese business networks, traditionally conceptualized as closed and internally shaped owing to a variety of historically and geographically specific factors, are being (re)shaped by an array of actor networks with an *international business* dimension. Groups of actor networks associated with international finance, the international business media and multilateral institutions are engaging with Chinese business networks. Through their capacity to enrol relevant Chinese firms in their actor networks, the international business community is forging changes in some business practices, while reinforcing others.

These increasing linkages and interconnections that are formed with non-Chinese actor networks underlie the dynamics of some of the most powerful Chinese business firms in the globalizing era. These linkages and interconnections also provide new sources of competitive advantage for large-scale Chinese business firms in the global economy, while also enhancing risk and generating new forms of interdependencies. At the most basic of levels, though, the reshaping of Chinese business practices has been driven by the desire of large Chinese firms to gain access to the financial resources that flow through the global financial system (see Shikatani, 1995; Yeung and Soh, 2000). That such a situation should arise is not surprising, given the nature of profits that have been generated from the development process in the Asia–Pacific region over the past two decades (before the onset of the Asian economic crisis). In the context of the reworking of global capitalism and the reshaping of sub-global *capitalisms*, such a relational approach to analysis of economic organization may help shed some light on the Chinese business networks that bind together entrepreneurial actors and institutions over time and space in uneven (albeit evolving) relations of interdependence.

Having explored these interrelated issues in the context of transnational entrepreneurship among Chinese business firms in Southeast Asia, I started to develop an *institutional perspective* on transnational entrepreneurship (Yeung, 2002a, 2002b). Here I argued that significant variations in institutional structures of home countries explain variations in the entrepreneurial endowments and resources of prospective transnational entrepreneurs and intrapreneurs. These structures also form and enforce conventions, values, views, norms, practices and 'rules of the game' to shape the logics governing economic decision making and actions, and market processes. Figure 6.1 maps the institutional structuring of entrepreneurship in specific national business systems. As explained earlier, an entrepreneur must be endowed with at least some resources to be able to act differently in the competitive marketplace. These entrepreneurial endowments and resources are often nationally based in that they are embedded in national business systems and are structured by pre-existing institutional arrangements. This geographical specificity of entrepreneurial endowments and resources explains why some countries tend to produce more entrepreneurs and entrepreneurial activities. But then, why are some entrepreneurs from the same sectors and same home countries more actively and successfully engaged in international business activities than others? As a prelude, such a difference among domestic entrepreneurs from the same sectors and same home countries can be explained by their differential access to transnational institutional structures. How, then, do individual entrepreneurs from the home countries benefit from their entrepreneurial endowments and resources? Figure 6.1 shows that these endowments can be divided into at least five dimensions: information asymmetry; risks and opportunities; finance and capital; experience in business and/or management; and relationships with customers and/or suppliers.

Once embedded in these institutional structures, transnational entrepreneurs and/or intrapreneurs have differential abilities and access to make use of their entrepreneurial endowments and resources for international business activities. Home country institutional structures and business systems significantly shape these endowments and resources. Moreover, whether specific transnational entrepreneurs and/or intrapreneurs succeed in establishing themselves in foreign markets depends on their enrolment in transnational actor networks. These networks and relations tend to span national boundaries and different business systems. They are therefore not peculiar to specific home countries and business systems, and provide specific mechanisms to enable international business operations by transnational entrepreneurs and intrapreneurs. For example, the differential ability to exercise home country endowments due to differential embeddedness in cross-border actor networks can also explain why a transnational entrepreneur from a home country with weaker institutional structures (such as a restricted home market) may perform better in the same host country *vis-à-vis* a transnational entrepreneur from another home country with stronger institutional structures (such as a more competitive home market).

Having set up this theoretical apparatus, I analysed my large database (N=over 200) on the regionalization of Singaporean firms and compared the Singapore case with my earlier findings on Hong Kong (Yeung, 2002b). My central finding once again refuted squarely the 'culturalist' explanation of Chinese entrepreneurship. I found that, despite the cultural and historical–geographical similarities between Hong Kong and Singapore, they have indeed very different dominant forms of economic organization in relation to business organizations, industrial structures, labour organizations and capital markets. These institutional differences are an outcome of the differential role of the state and entrepreneurship in driving economic development. Whereas Hong Kong's postwar economic development can be largely explained by its neoliberal laissez-faire economic ideologies that favour the role of private entrepreneurship in economic development, Singapore seems to have taken a significantly different pathway to economic development. In particular, Singapore's developmental state has taken over the primary responsibility of economic development from

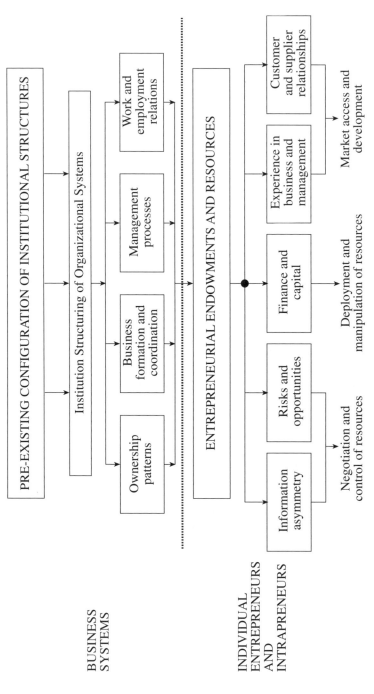

Source: Yeung (2002a: Figure 1).

Figure 6.1 The institutional structuring of entrepreneurship in specific national business systems

private entrepreneurs. The state has therefore become a public entrepreneur in its own right and has invited global corporations to locate their production facilities in Singapore. Put in their different historical contexts, the two city-states have evolved into very different business systems in which pre-existing configurations of institutional structures have a differential impact on entrepreneurial activities. Transnational entrepreneurs and/or intrapreneurs in both city-states therefore enjoy differential access to entrepreneurial endowments and resources.

These institutional differences in home country business systems are directly translated into quantitative and qualitative differences in outward investments and transnational corporations from Hong Kong (HKTNCs) and Singapore (SINTNCs). In Yeung (2002b), I drew upon extensive primary and secondary data to show that outward investments from Hong Kong tend to have a longer history and geographical reach, compared with those from Singapore. This may be explained by the state-directed preoccupation with nation building and domestic economic development in Singapore. There is either insufficient encouragement for outward investments from Singapore or a lack of transnational entrepreneurship to take business across borders. Indeed the two economies have developed very different external presence. In the case of Hong Kong, the domestic economy is dominated by SMEs in most industries and sectors. When these vibrant and entrepreneurial SMEs grow into large firms, they begin to internationalize their operations into Asia and beyond. There is thus a natural process of conversion from private and domestic entrepreneurship to transnational entrepreneurship when these entrepreneurs and intrapreneurs tap into their entrepreneurial endowments and resources.

This process, however, is less evident in Singapore, where the state has taken a lead in domestic economic development, mainly via the establishment of government-linked companies (GLCs). These GLCs were known as state-owned enterprises before major privatization initiatives took place in the late 1980s and early 1990s. The dominant role of GLCs (and global corporations) in Singapore's domestic economy has led to two consequences: first, they account for a large proportion of outward investments from Singapore; second, private entrepreneurs from Singapore have to look elsewhere for new markets for their products and/or services. Their relative lack of access to entrepreneurial endowments and resources in Singapore has effectively forced them to engage in international business activities. These private entrepreneurs do not progress naturally from being domestic to becoming transnational entrepreneurs. Instead they have reluctantly become transnational entrepreneurs because of limited business opportunities in their home country.

Summarized in Table 6.3, my empirical findings show that there are

Table 6.3 Comparison of transnational entrepreneurs and transnational intrapreneurs

Category	Transnational entrepreneurs	Transnational intrapreneurs
Foreign actor networks	• strong personal relationships • family business and linkages	• corporate/client relationships • reputation of established business • introduction from third party institutions
Information asymmetry	• personal networks • past experience • host country partners	• help from established subsidiaries and other institutions (e.g. government agencies) • client networks
Risks and opportunities	• high risks • quick decisions and deployment of resources • personalized business opportunities	• risk minimization strategy • assessment through established corporate procedures • joint or consensual decision making • tapping into client networks
Finance and capital	• severe constraints from home and host country banks • reliance on local partners • reliance on personal or family networks • some successful public listing	• strong support from parent companies • mostly listed in the stock exchanges • little dependence on host country partners or personal networks
Experience in business & management	• significant personal experience in business • more hands-on approach to international operations • more centralization of authority	• mostly corporate management experience • more delegation of authority • more professional management practices
Customer and supplier relationships	• strong personal contacts • personal marketing practices • secured business in some cases	• established brand names and/or client networks • dedicated marketing units or departments • strong home country market shares

Source: Yeung (2002b: Table 6.1).

observable differences between transnational entrepreneurs and intrapreneurs. While many scholars of entrepreneurship argue that entrepreneurship is inborn with an entrepreneur and cannot be taught, there are still important lessons to be learnt from my analysis. In today's globalizing era, many countries and companies are particularly interested in developing entrepreneurship in their people and/or managers in order to compete effectively in the global economy. More specifically, I argue that there are significant differences in the nature and attributes of transnational entrepreneurship between entrepreneurs (owners) and intrapreneurs (managers). These differences are significantly shaped by peculiar home and home business systems. The differences between transnational entrepreneurs and intrapreneurs are therefore highly relevant for our understanding of the underlying factors that condition their entrepreneurial tendencies. Although we cannot be very precise in comparing and explaining their differences, we can at least draw some important implications for policy and research purposes.

Reflections on the future of Chinese business research
In this concluding section, I would like to reflect on the future of Chinese business research, particularly for researchers interested in international/ transnational entrepreneurship. I must reiterate that, while much has been written on Chinese entrepreneurship, particularly from a 'culturalist' perspective, very little has been done to examine how this entrepreneurship, domesticated in very historically and geographically specific contexts, operates across borders. The majority of studies on Chinese business networks argue that the Chinese tend to cultivate personal relationships or *guanxi* to such an extent that they tend to personalize their economic relations through business networks. Although these early studies of Chinese business networks have helped us to understand better Chinese capitalism in East and Southeast Asia, they are largely concerned with the nature of Chinese business in relatively narrow sociocultural and geographic (domestic/host) contexts. Consequently I believe that many (not all) of them tend to suffer from four general weaknesses: static analysis, small family firm bias, lack of attention to capital sourcing and structural determinism.

1.   They tend to see ethnic Chinese business networks as a somewhat static product of cultural adaptation – an inward-oriented defence strategy to survive host country hostility. Once established, such business networks are perceived to exhibit few internal and external transformations, but rather continue to exist as relatively 'closed' (albeit evolving) sociocultural formations, often anchored in one national or regional base.

2. While small family firms continue to receive the majority of attention from academics, few resources have been devoted to the analysis of the growth of conglomerates (with listed arms) that are controlled by the ethnic Chinese.
3. There are few studies on the changing nature of capital sourcing for business expansion. This is a significant weakness in the context of the spread of global production networks driven by transnational corporations throughout the Asia–Pacific region (see Dicken and Yeung, 1999) and the growth of regional equity and bond markets. Such markets are heavily dependent upon the operation of Chinese-controlled conglomerates and they (via digital technologies) provide real-time links between Chinese firms and the skein of global financial centres.
4. These early studies privilege broader structural influences at the expense of real actors in Chinese business. Many characteristics of Chinese business are explained by the institutional structures from which these Chinese business firms emerge. These institutional structures can be the imperial system in China or the discriminatory structures in Southeast Asia. As such, actors in Chinese business are allowed little power and autonomy to negotiate these deterministic structures. It is precisely for these reasons that we need to look at the way actors in 'Chinese' business networks negotiate change in an era of volatile globalization by connecting (or being connected to) actor networks that are embedded within *much wider* geographical and organizational spaces.

What, then, remain as the fruitful avenues for future research into Chinese business firms and transnational entrepreneurship? I believe three mutually constitutive research directions are critical here. First, we need to know more about the nature and extent of Chinese entrepreneurship across borders. While international/transnational entrepreneurship remains an emerging field of management studies in its own right, I believe there is much opportunity for cross-fertilization between research into international/transnational entrepreneurship and research into Chinese entrepreneurship. For one thing, studies of transnational entrepreneurship in the ethnic Chinese context can certainly benefit from the analysis of firm-specific variables that often form the backbone of most international/transnational entrepreneurship research. For another, international/transnational entrepreneurship studies can learn from research into Chinese business how to incorporate sociocultural and institutional contexts into their firm-specific analysis. Either way, I will argue that any analysis of transnational entrepreneurship must incorporate both firm and context specificities.

Second, I believe that, despite some recent musings (for example, Weidenbaum and Hughes, 1996; Hefner, 1998; Chen, 2001), the 'culturalist' approach to Chinese business and entrepreneurship has come to the end of its intellectual life cycle. More recently, Chinese business researchers have seriously contested this Weberian 'culturalist' explanation (for example, Hodder, 1996; Yeung and Olds, 2000a; Gomez and Hsiao, 2001; Yang, 2002). They suggest that the recent interest in and discourse on 'Chinese capitalism' as an alternative paradigm of development is little more than an invention of a new post-socialist and post-revolution discourse on global capitalism. Dirlik (1997: 308) suggested four reasons for the prevailing discourse on Chinese capitalism possibly going wrong.

1. The notion of 'Chineseness' is rather vague and contestable. There are different self-images among the various Chinese populations in East and Southeast Asia. These individuals are presented and treated in analysis as a unidimensional phenomenon: 'the Chinese'. This line of thought is particularly problematic because 'it creates and legitimises the notion of "the Chinese" as a distinct entity which can be explained by the implicit application of laws and forces which are presumed to exist' (Hodder, 1996: 12–13).
2. The Confucian revival in East Asia (for example, Taiwan and Hong Kong) and Southeast Asia (Singapore) represents a 'Weberizing' of Confucianism because the dominant discourse suppresses the 'dark side' of Confucianism (such as authoritarianism and gender insensitivity; see Backman, 1999).
3. Kinship ties are not unique to the Chinese. As argued by Maurice Freedman, some four decades ago (cited in Wong, 1988b: 132), the crucial distinction between Chinese and Western economic behaviour is not that of kin and non-kin, but of the personal and impersonal. Chinese individuals tend to personalize their economic relations, and kinship is just one of the possible bases for this solidarity.
4. Business networks among ethnic Chinese may be a transitional strategy that is more pertinent in some circumstances (such as a hostile host environment).

To produce breakthroughs in Chinese entrepreneurship research, we therefore need to seek alternative explanations embedded in comparative institutional analysis. Here I envisage a much closer connection between research into Chinese entrepreneurship and leading theoretical frameworks in management and entrepreneurship studies (see also Peng *et al.*, 2001).

Third, while much has been written on Chinese family/business firms in their domestic or national settings, much more research attention must be paid to what John Kao (1993) called, a decade ago, the 'worldwide web' of Chinese business. With few exceptions (for example, Hsing, 1998; Yeung and Olds, 2000b; Olds, 2001; Tsang, 2002), most recent volumes on Chinese business remain firmly rooted in specific domestic settings (Douw *et al.*, 1999; Gomez, 1999; Brown, 2000; Chan, 2000; Gomez and Hsiao, 2001). This is clearly surprising in view of the rapid globalization of Chinese business firms. A greater research focus on the globalization of Chinese business firms can contribute to the theoretical debate on theories of transnational corporations. In their processes of globalization, Chinese business firms may behave and be organized differently from their American, European and Japanese counterparts. This may help to revise our current theories of TNCs and foreign direct investment (FDI). Dunning (1995: 463), for example, noted that 'Until the late 1970s, scholars usually considered cooperative forms of organizing economic activity as *alternatives* to hierarchies or markets, rather than as part and parcel of an organizational *system of firms*, in which inter-firm and intra-firm transactions complement each other' (original emphasis).

In this regard, our closer attention to the role of ethnic business networks in the global operations of Chinese business firms and their transferability to other contexts holds some serious promises for the development of new theories in international business and international entrepreneurship studies. In the final analysis, the study of Chinese business and Chinese capitalism must incorporate internationalization and globalization as its key analytical theme. This reorientation of research direction, however, is incomplete without taking on the intellectual and analytical challenge of unpacking the international and transnational entrepreneurship embedded in this particular form of capitalism.

References

Backman, Michael (1999), *Asian Eclipse: Exposing the Dark Side of Business in Asia*, Singapore: John Wiley.

Brown, Rajeswary Ampalavana (ed.) (1995), *Chinese Business Enterprise*, 4 v, London: Routledge.

Brown, Rajeswary Ampalavana (2000), *Chinese Big Business and the Wealth of Asian Nations*, London: Palgrave.

Chan, Kwok Bun (ed.) (2000), *Chinese Business Networks: State, Economy and Culture*, Singapore: Prentice-Hall.

Chen, Ming-Jer (2001), *Inside Chinese Business: A Guide for Managers Worldwide*, Boston, MA: Harvard Business School Press.

Dicken, Peter and Henry Wai-chung Yeung (1999), 'Investing in the future: East and Southeast Asian firms in the global economy', in Kris Olds, Peter Dicken, Philip Kelly, Lily Kong and Henry Wai-chung Yeung (eds), *Globalisation and the Asia–Pacific: Contested Territories*, London: Routledge, pp. 107–28.

Dirlik, Arif (1997) 'Critical reflections on 'Chinese Capitalism as paradim, *Identities*, 3(3), pp. 303–30.

Douw, Leo M., Cen Huang and Michael R. Godley (eds) (1999), *Qiaoxiang Ties: Interdisciplinary Approaches to 'Cultural Capitalism' in South China*, London: Kegan Paul.

Dunning, John H. (1995), 'Reappraising the eclectic paradigm in an age of alliance capitalism', *Journal of International Business Studies*, 26(3), pp. 461–91.

Gomez, Edmund Terence (1999), *Chinese Business in Malaysia: Accumulation, Accommodation and Ascendance*, Richmond, Surrey: Curzon.

Gomez, Edmund Terence and Hsin-Huang Michael Hsiao (eds) (2001), *Chinese Business in South-East Asia: Contesting Cultural Explanations, Researching Entrepreneurship*, Richmond, Surrey: Curzon.

Hamilton, Gary G. (ed.) (1991), *Business Networks and Economic Development in East and South East Asia*, Hong Kong: Centre of Asian Studies, University of Hong Kong.

Hamilton, Gary G. and Nicole Woolsey Biggart (1988), 'Market, culture, and authority: a comparative analysis of management and organization in the Far East', *American Journal of Sociology (Supplement)*, 94, S52–94.

Heenan, David A. and Warren J. Keegan (1979), 'The rise of third world multinationals', *Harvard Business Review*, January–February, pp. 101–9.

Hefner, Robert W. (ed.) (1998), *Market Cultures: Society and Values in the New Asian Capitalisms*, Singapore: Institute of Southeast Asian Studies.

Hodder, Rupert (1996), *Merchant Princes of the East: Cultural Delusions, Economic Success and the Overseas Chinese in Southeast Asia*, Chichester: John Wiley.

Hsing, You-tien (1998), *Making Capitalism in China: The Taiwan Connection*, New York: Oxford University Press.

Kao, John (1993), 'The worldwide web of Chinese business', *Harvard Business Review*, March–April, pp. 24–36.

Lall, Sanjaya (1982), 'The emergence of Third World multinationals: Indian joint ventures overseas', *World Development*, 10, pp. 127–46.

Lall, Sanjaya (1983), *The New Multinationals: The Spread of Third World Enterprises*, Chichester: Wiley.

McDougall, Patricia P. (1989), 'International versus domestic entrepreneurship – new venture strategic behavior and industry structure', *Journal of Business Venturing*, 4(6), pp. 387–400.

McDougall, Patricia P. and Benjamin M. Oviatt (1996), 'New venture internationalisation, strategic change, and performance: a follow-up study', *Journal of Business Venturing*, 11(1), pp. 23–40.

McDougall, Patricia P. and Benjamin M. Oviatt (2000), 'International entrepreneurship: the intersection of two research paths', Special Research Forum, *Academy of Management Journal*, 43(5), pp. 902–906.

McDougall, Patricia P., Scott Shane and Benjamin M. Oviatt (1994), 'Explaining the formation of international new ventures: the limits of theories from international business research', *Journal of Business Venturing*, 9(6), pp. 469–87.

Moon, H. Chang and Newman S. Peery Jr. (1997), 'Entrepreneurship in international business: concept, strategy, and implementation', *Entrepreneurship, Innovation, and Change*, 6(1), pp. 5–20.

Olds, Kris (2001), *Globalisation and Urban Change: Capital, Culture and Pacific Rim Mega Projects*, Oxford: Oxford University Press.

Olds, Kris and Henry Wai-chung Yeung (1999), '(Re)shaping "Chinese" business networks in a globalising era', *Environment and Planning D: Society and Space*, 17(5), pp. 535–55.

Peng, Mike W., Yuan Lu, Oded Shenkar and Denis Y.L. Wang (2001), 'Treasures in the China house – A review of management and organizational research on Greater China', *Journal of Business Research*, 52(2), pp. 95–110.

Redding, S. Gordon (1980), 'Cognition as an aspect of culture and its relation to management process: an exploratory review of the Chinese case', *Journal of Management Studies*, 17(2), pp. 127–48.

Redding, S. Gordon (1990), *The Spirit of Chinese Capitalism*, Berlin: De Gruyter.

Schumpeter, Joseph (1942), *Capitalism, Socialism and Democracy*, New York: Harper and Brothers.

Shikatani, Takuya (1995), 'Corporate finances of overseas Chinese financial groups', *Nomura Research Institute Quarterly*, 4(1), pp. 68–91.

Tan, Chia Zhi and Henry Wai-chung Yeung (2000a), 'The regionalization of Chinese business networks: a study of Singaporean firms in Hainan Province, China', *The Professional Geographer*, 52(3), pp. 437–54.

Tan, Chia-Zhi and Henry Wai-chung Yeung (2000b), 'The internationalisation of Singaporean firms into China: entry modes and investment strategies', in Henry Wai-chung Yeung and Kris Olds (eds), *The Globalisation of Chinese Business Firms*, London: Macmillan, pp. 220–43.

Tsang, Eric W.K. (2002), 'Learning from overseas venturing experience – The case of Chinese family businesses', *Journal of Business Venturing*, 17(1), pp. 21–40.

Wang, Gungwu (2000), *The Chinese Overseas: From Earthbound China to the Quest for Autonomy*, Cambridge, MA: Harvard University Press.

Weidenbaum, Murray and Samuel Hughes (1996), *The Bamboo Network: How Expatriate Chinese Entrepreneurs Are Creating a New Economic Superpower in Asia*, New York: The Free Press.

Wells, Louis T. Jr. (1977), 'The internationalisation of firms from developing countries', in Tamir Agmon and Charles P. Kindleberger (eds), *Multinationals from Small Countries*, Cambridge, MA: MIT Press, pp. 133–56.

Wells, Louis T. Jr. (1983), *Third World Multinationals: The Rise of Foreign Investment from Developing Countries*, Cambridge, MA: MIT Press.

Wong, Siu-lun (1985), 'The Chinese family firm: a model', *British Journal of Sociology*, 36, pp. 58–72.

Wong, Siu-lun (1988a), 'The applicability of Asian family values to other sociocultural settings', in Peter L. Berger and H.H. Michael Hsiao (eds), *In Search of an East Asian Development Model*, New Brunswick, NJ: Transaction, pp. 134–52.

Wong, Siu-lun (1988b), *Emigrant Entrepreneurs: Shanghai Industrialists in Hong Kong*, Hong Kong: Oxford University Press.

Wright, Richard W. and David A. Ricks (1994), 'Trends in international-business research 25 years later', *Journal of International Business Studies*, 25(4), pp. 687–701.

Yang, Mayfair M.H. (2002), 'The resilience of *guanxi* and its new deployments: A critique of some new *guanxi* scholarship', *The China Quarterly*, 170, pp. 459–76.

Yeung, Henry Wai-chung (1994a), 'Third World multinationals revisited: a research critique and future agenda', *Third World Quarterly*, 15(2), pp. 297–317.

Yeung, Henry Wai-chung (1994b), 'Transnational corporations from Asian developing countries: their characteristics and competitive edge', *Journal of Asian Business*, 10(4), pp. 17–58.

Yeung, Henry Wai-chung (1994c), 'Hong Kong firms in the ASEAN region: transnational corporations and foreign direct investment', *Environment and Planning A*, 26(12), pp. 1931–56.

Yeung, Henry Wai-chung (1994d), 'Critical reviews of geographical perspectives on business organisations and the organisation of production: towards a network approach', *Progress in Human Geography*, 18(4), pp. 460–90.

Yeung, Henry Wai-chung (1997a), 'Cooperative strategies and Chinese business networks: a study of Hong Kong transnational corporations in the ASEAN region', in Paul W. Beamish and J. Peter Killing (eds), *Cooperative Strategies: Asia–Pacific Perspectives*, San Francisco, CA: The New Lexington Press, pp. 22–56.

Yeung, Henry Wai-chung (1997b), 'Business networks and transnational corporations: a study of Hong Kong firms in the ASEAN region', *Economic Geography*, 73(1), pp. 1–25.

Yeung, Henry Wai-chung (1997c), 'Limits to the growth of family-owned business? The case of Chinese transnational corporations from Hong Kong', *Proceedings of the Academy of International Business Asia Pacific Area Conference*, University of Hawaii, 19–21 June, pp. 43–8.

Yeung, Henry Wai-chung (1998a), 'The social–spatial constitution of business organisations: a geographical perspective', *Organization*, 5(1), pp. 101–28.

Yeung, Henry Wai-chung (1998b), *Transnational Corporations and Business Networks: Hong Kong Firms in the ASEAN Region*, London: Routledge.

Yeung, Henry Wai-chung (1998c), 'Transnational economic synergy and business networks: the case of two-way investment between Malaysia and Singapore', *Regional Studies*, 32(8), pp. 687–706.

Yeung, Henry Wai-chung (ed.) (1999a), *The Globalisation of Business Firms from Emerging Economies*, 2 vols, Cheltenham, UK and Northampton, MA, USA: Edward Elgar.

Yeung, Henry Wai-chung (1999b), 'Introduction: competing in the global economy', in Henry Wai-chung Yeung (ed.), *The Globalisation of Business Firms from Emerging Economies*, 2 vols, Cheltenham, UK and Northampton, MA, USA: Edward Elgar, pp.xiii–xlvi.

Yeung, Henry Wai-chung (1999c), 'The internationalisation of ethnic Chinese business firms from Southeast Asia: strategies, processes and competitive advantage', *International Journal of Urban and Regional Research*, 23(1), pp. 103–27.

Yeung, Henry Wai-chung (1999d), 'The regionalisation of Chinese entrepreneurs', in Léo Paul Dana (ed.), *International Entrepreneurship*, Singapore: NTU-Entrepreneurship Development Centre, pp. 295–304.

Yeung, Henry Wai-chung (1999e), 'Under siege? Economic globalisation and Chinese business in Southeast Asia', *Economy and Society*, 28(1), pp. 1–29.

Yeung, Henry Wai-chung (2000a), 'Limits to the growth of family-owned business? The case of Chinese transnational corporations from Hong Kong', *Family Business Review*, 13(1), pp. 55–70.

Yeung, Henry Wai-chung (2000b), 'Strategic control and coordination in Chinese business firms', *Journal of Asian Business*, 16(1), pp. 95–123.

Yeung, Henry Wai-chung (2000c), 'The dynamics of the globalisation of Chinese business firms', in Henry Wai-chung Yeung and Kris Olds (eds), *The Globalisation of Chinese Business Firms*, London: Macmillan, pp. 75–104.

Yeung, Henry Wai-chung (2000d), 'A crisis of industrial and business networks in Asia?', *Environment and Planning A*, 32(2), pp. 191–200.

Yeung, Henry Wai-chung (2000e), 'Economic globalisation, crisis, and the emergence of Chinese business communities in Southeast Asia', *International Sociology*, 15(2), pp. 269–90.

Yeung, Henry Wai-chung (2000f), 'Managing crisis in a globalising era: the case of Chinese business firms from Singapore', in David Ip, Constance Lever-Tracy and Noel Tracy (eds), *Chinese Businesses and the Asian Crisis*, Aldershot: Gower, pp. 87–113.

Yeung, Henry Wai-chung (2000g), 'The dynamics of Asian business systems in a globalising era', *Review of International Political Economy*, 7(3), pp. 399–433.

Yeung, Henry Wai-chung (2001), 'Managing traditional Chinese family firms across borders: four generations of entrepreneurship in Eu Yan Sang', in Leo Douw, Cen Huang and David Ip (eds), *Rethinking Chinese Transnational Enterprises: Cultural Affinity and Business Strategies*, Surrey, UK: Curzon, pp. 184–207.

Yeung, Henry Wai-chung (2002a), 'Entrepreneurship in international business: an institutional perspective', *Asia Pacific Journal of Management*, 19(1), pp. 29–61.

Yeung, Henry Wai-chung (2002b), *Entrepreneurship and the Internationalisation of Asian Firms: An Institutional Perspective*, Cheltenham, UK and Northampton, MA, USA: Edward Elgar.

Yeung, Henry Wai-chung (2004), *Chinese Capitalism in a Global Era: Towards Hybrid Capitalism*, Routledge Advances in International Political Economy Series, London: Routledge.

Yeung, Henry Wai-chung and Kris Olds (2000a), 'Globalizing Chinese business firms: where are they coming from, where are they heading?', in Henry Wai-chung Yeung and Kris Olds (eds), *The Globalisation of Chinese Business Firms*, London: Macmillan, pp. 1–28.

Yeung, Henry Wai-chung and Kris Olds (eds) (2000b), *The Globalisation of Chinese Business Firms*, London: Macmillan.

Yeung, Henry Wai-chung and Tse Min Soh (2000), 'Corporate governance and the global reach of Chinese family firms in Singapore', *Seoul Journal of Economics*, 13(3), pp. 301–34.

7 A typology
Hamid Etemad

The existing literature on the growth and internationalization of small and medium-sized enterprises (SMEs) does not consider the presence of multinational enterprises (MNEs) in SMEs' competitive space and disregards their corresponding impact on SMEs' internationalization patterns. Neither does the literature consider the impact of networks (and clusters) of local firms on SMEs, regardless of the size. Nor does it compare their respective effects and impacts on the affected SMEs.

This chapter presents a competitive typology with six layers of competitive intensity at the top of which MNEs, as a network of small and large firms, spread around the world, compete globally with large and small firms regardless of size, location and extent of their internationalization. The extensive MNE subsidiary networks make up the competitive context within which the growth-oriented SMEs, who aspire to internationalize, must compete in the global markets. Local industrial clusters, conceptualized similarly but at the local level and with a lesser competitive advantage than that of the MNEs, occupy the middle layers of the hierarchy in the typology. The typical independent, local, small firms reside in the lowest level of the typology.

The chapter examines a typical subsidiary's evolutionary pattern from the perspective of the competitors, and global competition, in order to suggest counter-strategies for the competing SMEs who aspire to globalize effectively and strategically. Interactions between the inner dynamics of MNEs, learning and regional networks (or clusters) and their respective impacts are combined to formulate these competitive counter-strategies. Globalizing SMEs must deploy similar strategic logic to formulate similar counter-strategies to out-compete the growing and evolving subsidiaries locally and globally in the quest for internationalization.

MNEs and SMEs competed mainly with their own kind in the fragmented market of the past. Regulatory and environmental barriers separated their respective economic space and shielded SMEs from competing directly with MNEs in the same markets (Dana, Etemad and Wright 2001; Etemad 2003a, 2003b; Etemad, Wright and Dana, 2001). As a result, the SME's environment was segregated and assumed to be local. SMEs came close to feeling MNEs' competitive strengths in their indigenous home markets when local subsidiaries appeared on the scene. However, the

SMEs' home market was a foreign market for the MNEs' subsidiary and it suffered from the disadvantage of 'foreignness' (Hymer, 1976) initially.

A host of fundamental developments have changed the above situation and have brought MNEs and SMEs face-to-face in the economic space of the global markets, including the rapid globalization of environments, the tyranny of technological race(s) on a global scale (Dosi, Pavitt and Soeto, 1990), the emergence of local industrial clusters, rapid technological development outside North America (Gerybadze and Reger, 1999), the emergence of multipolar product life cycles (PLCs), the emergence of network and alliance of previously-independent firms from different countries of the world (Enright, 2000) and the vast spread of MNEs resembling learning organizations (Nonaka and Takeuchi, 1995) in network-type structures. Combined, these fundamental patterns of change are transforming the previously isolated local competitive space and integrating them into the global environment. Protective local boundaries are falling, globally competitive institutions are entering the local markets and a level playing field is slowly prevailing. In other words, the rules of the game are changing.

For example, powerful global advertising, financed by massive production and scale and scope economies, is allowing burgeoning global brands to increase consumer awareness of the value they offer and thereby capture market share from local firms. Local brand loyalties limiting competition are being slowly replaced by unbridled competition amongst a few from well-recognized and trusted global brands offering value to shrewd consumers, which are fighting for consumers' purchasing power and loyalties, regardless of language, culture, time and location. Such globally competitive brands and firms maximize their incremental gains to further support the globally recognized brands, which cover a wide range of goods and services that were offered previously by local SMEs.

SMEs find it imperative to become as competitive in their own home markets as these global competitors in order to survive. Competitors in general, and SMEs in particular, find very few firms or markets remain unaffected, ignored or uncontested. Past successes can no longer be expected to repeat themselves. Neither can relative weaknesses (and successes) remain hidden from competition; nor can they be protected by artificial means, including the heavy arm of the home governments. Furthermore, international institutions such as the World Trade Organisation (WTO) rule against unjustified protection and violators pay a heavy price. It is therefore necessary to review the fundamental drivers of change and understand their respective impacts. In short, the globalization of markets has brought a high level of transparency to competition, and all competitors, especially SMEs, must devise more potent strategies to compete effectively in order to survive.

This chapter comprises four sections. In the first, the fundamental patterns of change are reviewed. As MNEs are the strongest players in SMEs' markets, the dynamics of competitiveness enabling their growth in international markets are reviewed next. Regional industrial clusters and MNEs share the network aspects, and are increasingly capable of exerting competitive pressures on independent SMEs. A typology of global competition, with a hierarchy of competitive intensity in six layers, is presented in the third section to study the immediate impacts of these network-type structures in the local marketplace. The implications of this conception of competitive space facing SMEs are examined next followed by the appropriate counter-strategies drawn from them. Conclusions and implications for managers, scholars and public policy formulation are included in the final section.

The fundamental patterns of change
The rapid globalization of the environment
The repeated and increasing waves of free and freer trade and investments have continually dismantled barriers and facilitated the flow of goods, services and knowledge around the globe. They have transformed the global competitive environment to multipolar centres of specialized competencies (Anderson and Johanson, 1996; Forsgren, Holm and Johanson, 1992; Forsgren and Pahlberg, 1992). As a result, some traditional explanations, even theories, are not as applicable as in the past. Consider, for example, the international product life cycle (IPLC), as proposed by Raymond Vernon (1966), which is no longer unipolar (or with very few origins in the industrial markets). The traditional flow of new products beginning at the MNEs' home and radiating to the peripheries, as in a unicentred web, has changed into inverted webs of multipolar origins of competencies, each of which is highly specialized in a part of the total value chain and capable of producing value-loaded products at scale economies for distribution to the rest of the world. They are no longer located only in the USA or dominated by US-based MNEs. Both US and non US-based MNEs, on the other hand, are serving as the nerve centres of their own spider webs and directing investment and knowledge to their own peripheries within their networks, thereby further enhancing intra-firm trade, developments and competitiveness worldwide.

Rapid technological developments outside North America (and in the Triad) and corresponding migration of production and supply chains
Rapid technological developments in Europe and Asia generally parallel a relative reduction in the US position in those technologies, especially when utilized in US-dominated industries. Many products and technologies

created and perfected in North America have experienced higher growth rates outside the USA (and Europe in some cases) and the US position is no longer dominant. Consider for example the following:

- air frames: from the USA to Europe (for example, Air Bus Industries) and moving further east and south, to Japan, China and even Brazil;
- jet engines: from the USA to the UK, France, Italy, Brazil and beyond;
- computers: from the USA to Japan, Korea, Taiwan, People's Republic of China (PRC) and elsewhere;
- household electronic (microwave ovens, high-fidelity equipment, TVs, kitchen appliances and so on): from the USA to Japan, Taiwan, Korea, PRC and their respective supply chains throughout the world;
- chemicals and plastics: from Europe and the USA to PRC, oil-producing countries and others;
- military industries: from the USA and Europe to China, Israel, South Africa and others.

Producers in each of the industries follow their own strategies for increased global market share, thereby transforming the world to markets for products of their inverted network of multipolar centres of excellence, each of which is competing against other networks for an ever-larger share of the global markets. The USA- and Europe-based MNEs no longer dominate the value chain of such products. Rather, globally competitive SMEs enable the value chain of their respective flagship enterprises (Rugman and D'Cruz, 2000) to compete globally.

The emergence of multi-polar IPLCs

Vernon's (1966) theory of the international product life cycle (IPLC) proposed three principal phases in a complete product life cycle. In the initial phase, the innovative ideas originating in US corporate laboratories would lead to new products (or services) marketed to the US markets first before being exported to the European markets and then to other markets in time. Along with further development of European markets, the theory proposed that a European subsidiary would be set up (with the headquarters' investment) to produce the product locally for local consumption and also to export to other countries in the second phase (Vernon, 1966; Norton and Rees, 1979). The next phase comprised a further movement of production to the developing countries as their markets for the product(s) grew sufficiently to justify investment in local production facilities. It was initially intended to satisfy local consumption, and later to export to other countries with a higher cost structure, including the USA and European markets, bringing the IPLC to a complete circle. For example, the US-based MNE which used to export to the rest of the world (ROW) in the first phase would become an importer at the end of the third phase in the IPLC.

It is important to identify the evolutionary path of a few factors in the background and to analyse their impact on IPLC from other perspectives. The first international movement of the initial products from the headquarters to other countries paralleled three significant developments already under way.

First the increased production scale (due to exports) contributed to a reduction of average costs, enabling other lower-income communities to join markets for the product and in turn contribute to further production and scale economies. We refer to this as *scale economies and market development interaction.* As scale economies reduced costs further, lower-income populations were enabled to afford the product at lower prices and thereby further increase the size of the previous market, necessitating further production expansion.

Second, the relative capital and skilled-labour intensity of initial input factors, requiring production in a highly developed location, such as the USA, capable of supplying them, dictated that the site for the initial production (in the first phase of the IPLC) should be the USA. However, as manufacturing processes became simpler, the composition of factor inputs began to change in favour of the factor inputs in developing countries with increased production, thereby forcing production to shift from the USA to these countries. Vernon assumed that the skill and capability levels outside the USA were not high enough to warrant production elsewhere in the early phases of IPLC, in spite of their potentially lower costs. However evolutionary changes in production, mainly due to learning and automation, reduced the capital and skill requirements, allowing production to shift to other countries with lower skills, capabilities and costs than the USA. We refer to this phenomenon as *interaction between production requirements and local capabilities, including factor inputs.*

Third, the inherent processes in IPLC resulted in increasing transfers of knowledge, skills and capabilities from the centre to the periphery (for example, from the US-based headquarters to the local subsidiary elsewhere). Further investment and trade increased the rate of transfer with time. Therefore the birth stage in Vernon's IPLC of new products, which started in the USA, and progressed through phases, transferred more knowledge and capabilities to other subsidiaries. As a result of such transfers within the MNE's network of subsidiaries, more skills, expertise, capabilities and knowledge became available at the peripheries of the network. The periphery would soon be capable of replicating the initial US-based advantage in terms of producing similar, if not more advanced, versions of goods and services initially produced for the industrialized markets. This process further contributed to the faster diffusion of knowledge, technology and other capabilities to other locations outside the USA. We refer to this phenomenon as *transfer of non-location-specific advantage to a subsidiary and its inevitable localization of such advantages (such as resources, skills and capabilities)* in the process. The modern theory of MNEs lends further support to such transformation of resources, skills and capabilities (Dunning, 1980, 1988; Dunning and Rugman, 1985).

Convergence of IPLC and the modern theory of MNEs
The OLI theory of MNEs (Dunning 1980, 1981, 1986, 1988) suggested that the ownership advantage (the 'O' component of the theory, for example the IPLC's initial flows of knowledge, expertise and capabilities to the subsidiary) would be enhanced and integrated with the locally-based advantages (the 'L' component of the theory, such as cheaper local input factors) in the local subsidiary. This combination would naturally evolve with time into a superior advantage than the initial ownership advantage transferred to the local subsidiary in the early stages of its life cycle. Furthermore Dunning (1980, 1988) proposed that the combined (or enriched) advantages would then be internalized (the 'I' component of the theory), that is, made available through internal trade in the internal markets, populated by the MNE's sister-subsidiaries and the headquarters, for their respective use, at privileged prices, with the headquarters' blessings. Operationally this would imply that the headquarters would be importing into the internal market from the local subsidiary at later stages the results of the capabilities and resources that it had initially transferred to the subsidiary in the first phases of the IPLC.

As can easily be seen, Dunning's OLI and Vernon's IPLC converge on the initial transfer of capabilities, expertise and knowledge (constituting the ownership advantage) to the subsidiary, thereby initiating an international life cycle, although their respective motivations for doing so may have differed at the outset.[1] Furthermore they also converge on the concept of reverse- or cross-transfer of the localized (or contextualized for local condition) advantage back to the MNE network. There is, however, a significant difference: Dunning's eclectic theory would 'internalize' the locally enriched advantage for further use in a multitude of sister-subsidiaries (hence further enabling these subsidiaries) while Vernon's would only import back the end products of the enhanced capabilities rather than the upgraded capabilities. In both of these theories, even for the US-initiated products, US headquarters would become a recipient of a different kind (an importer of the enriched advantage or end-product) at the later stages of the IPLC. Both theories agree on multiple subsidiaries possessing the enhanced capabilities and even deploying them to produce related product lines in developing country sites. While such migration of production portrays the evolutionary path of competition towards simple price competition globally, the IPLC should be viewed as a reflection of MNEs' striving for efficiency, cost reduction and increased competitiveness globally, owing to lower costs and prices due to learning, scale and scope economies in a contemporary view of strategy (Nonaka and Takeuchi, 1995).

The inevitable transformation of the subsidiary and the impact on its competitive environment

Once a subsidiary becomes capable of enhancing its ownership-based advantages with the locally-based (or acquired) capabilities, in order to produce for the local market and then to export to the rest of the world, it could act as the headquarters for its specific product mandate (Birkinshaw, 1996; Crookell, 1986; Etemad and Seguin-Dulude, 1986a; Roth and Morrison, 1992) initiating an IPLC of its own, following the footprints of its own headquarters (Etemad and Seguin-Dulude, 1986a, 1986b; Pearce, 1989). Alternatively it could act as a centre of excellence (Forsgren, Holm and Johanson, 1992) or provide specialized centres within differentiated networks (Nohria and Ghoshal, 1997) within the sister subsidiary system.[2] Following a natural IPLC path, it would be exporting to the rest of the world in the early stages of the IPLC, including the more advanced countries (or richer markets). It could also outsource the necessary supplies from the other less advanced countries, thereby reinforcing, if not propagating, its own product mandate (Etemad, 1986) and the corresponding network supply chain as well as marketing and distribution within and outside the sister-subsidiary system. In other words, it behaves as headquarters in its own right and expands its sphere of influence.

The PLC that resembled a spider's web with one central node would soon be transformed into an inverted web with many nodes, each with its own capabilities and expertise, acting as a centre of excellence in a connected web of sister-subsidiaries (and possibly others) as well as in its own respective supply chain network(s). This would in fact truly globalize the original IPLC. This chapter proposes that this conception of an IPLC, within a given multinational enterprise, would force others within and outside the MNE to face the new competitive reality soon and to emulate it (Knickerbocker, 1973) in order to avoid falling behind. Not only would such emulation transform a simple competition into a more sophisticated and strategic one (which could involve multiple players and multiple period gaming, in contrast to a simple game played in one time period in one site), but it would also result in technological speed-up (that is, increased rate of technological change) much beyond what was intended, or implied, by either the IPLC (Vernon, 1966) or the OLI (Dunning, 1980, 1988) theories of global expansion through internationalization. The important aspect to note is that the initial transfer of certain capabilities, knowledge and expertise from the centre to the periphery in a globalized environment would inevitably initiate the creation of multipolar structures, with each centre exerting higher competitive pressures in its own competitive space. The ultimate reversed flow of the enriched and enhanced capabilities to other locations can logically begin a new round of IPLC spiralling upwards over time. Such developments are manifestations of increased competition worldwide, based on the increasing transfers of knowledge and know-how (Huber, 1991; Teece, 1977; Nonaka and Takeuchi, 1955) leading to further intensification of local competition, especially in the host country markets within which these subsidiaries are located.

The spread of MNE-like institutions
The logical extension of the above argument suggests the rise of MNE-like subsidiaries as each simple subsidiary can evolve to resemble headquarters of its own (Hedlund, 1981; Halal, 1994; Malnight, 1996; Birkinshaw, Hood and Jonsson, 1998). In the process of evolving to respond to the local competition in order to meet external demands, such subsidiaries may embark on a strategic game (that resembles multi-location and multi-period gaming as compared to a simple competitive game) exerting considerable upward pressure on all competitors in their shared competitive space, including local SMEs. This will inevitably force local SMEs either to compete at the subsidiary level or to face the eventual risk of elimination from such markets (Etemad, 1986, 1999; Etemad and Seguin-Dulude, 1986b; Birkinshaw, Hood and Jonsson, 1998; Hedlund, 1981; Malnight, 1996). The inescapable implication of this fundamental evolutionary pattern is an equal upward movement in competitive intensity in both the local and the international markets. Stated differently, the common denominator of local competition would be transformed to the lowest level at which a subsidiary, representing a networked entity, would be willing to compete. Once a networked enterprise capable of competing at a higher competitive level appeared on the scene, the competitive intensity would have to rise again to at least that level to avoid massive attrition (Bishop and Crookell, 1986; Jarillo and Martinez, 1990).

The interesting research question is then: what are the distinguishable levels of competition in a given competitive space prior to and after the appearance of subsidiaries and other networked entities? We will develop and present a logical set of benchmarks for distinguishing the various competitive levels for internationalizing SMEs in the next section.

The emergence of the global technological race
The flow of information, knowledge and technology, as well as the supporting investments, described above, may have in fact triggered the continual
introduction of higher flows in general and ever-higher technology (especially in rapidly changing technologies) in particular in most subsidiary
markets, transporting them to a conducive stage for later technological
races (Etemad, 1999; Galunic and Roden, 1998). Prior to entering the
global trading system and receiving continuous injections of such high-
technologies, these markets were based on lower technologies, using simple
price competition to compete for market share. Such further deployment of
high, and higher, technologies would transform their respective cost structure from a relatively low fixed cost and high variable cost to higher fixed
cost and lower variable cost regimes. Such regimes would require increasingly larger scale and faster amortization owing to rapid technological
obsolescence, which would in turn incite a new round of technological races
and increased competition to capture the necessary incremental market
share to support such operations. As a direct result, the competition in high
technology-intensive products and processes would be transforming the
competitive battles supported by technological races into temporal games
(or gaming) with very few winners in each round of IPLC, further stimulating the losers to try to win in the next generations of products and services in order to recoup their previous losses and to survive. The extant
literature of the 'first mover advantage' provides ample evidence to suggest
that competitors view competition involving a high-technology product
market as a multi-period and multi-location competition at the end of
which the first movers are not necessarily the ultimate winners (Liberman
and Montgomery, 1998). Unless local SMEs understand the nature of the
game and the strategy of the game players, they stand a lower chance of
succeeding than otherwise.

The emergence of regional industrial clusters
Two aspects of the regional industrial clusters are germane to the transformation of local competition and global competitiveness.

Strategic evolution in the firm   Ample research suggests that the geographical proximity of firms in a regional cluster facilitates cooperation and alliances (Cohen and Levinthal, 1989). The increased cooperation, based
mainly on social embeddedness (Amit and Schoemaker, 1993), stimulates
a migration from independence to interdependence (Etemad, Wright and
Dana, 2001) and even co-dependence (Acs and Yeung, 1999) and symbiosis (Etemad 2003a, 2003b; Etemad, Wright and Dana, 2001; Dana, Etemad
and Wright, 2001), which in turn encourages joint action, including invest-

ment in research and development, which is the necessary introduction to co-learning, thereby favouring a strategic reorientation in favour of optimization of the joint value chain. Such reorientation may further transform the members of the regional cluster in the direction of increased specialization and in turn re-enforce the initial dependence.

Transformation of the Value Chain   The gradual transformation of joint value chains in the region contributes to the increased competitiveness of both the firms and the region as a whole. Each firm would specialize on a particular part of the value chain for maximum scale economies without sacrificing either product quality or scope economies, which would eventually assist all cooperating firms in a value chain to become more competitive as a result of increased co-dependence stimulating joint actions. The reduced risk resulting from joint action and co-learning, supported by accumulation of trust (Gomes-Casseres, 1996, 1997; Gulati, 1995) based on social embeddedness (Anderson and Johanson, 1996), would transform the firms, if not the cluster, into a coalition resembling, and even acting in a way very similar to, networked firms (Malnight, 1996). As compared to multinationals, the main difference between regionally networked firms and MNEs is the basis of their competitiveness. While it may be locally bound for the former, it is universally applicable and locally enhancing for MNEs, resulting in some competitive edge for the latter over the members of regional industrial clusters. However, the members of the local regional cluster will not be disadvantaged by 'foreignness' (Hymer, 1976) or have to compete against one another. The above discussion suggests that a rich variety of mechanisms are available to firms for increasing their respective competitiveness, as described in the next section of this chapter.

MNEs becoming learning organizations
Although Vernon, Dunning and other scholars, dealing with the growth of MNEs, did not explicitly incorporate learning in their conceptualization, a learning capability (Kogut and Zander, 1992; Nonaka and Takeuchi, 1995) is inherent in the headquarter–subsidiary structure. It is not difficult to point to the obvious incidents of learning in a typical MNE–subsidiary relation as the non-location-specific components of ownership-specific advantages (OSA) which are utilized by a local subsidiary.

Contextualization of production   It is necessary for the subsidiary to learn the ownership specific advantage fully in order to use and adapt it for its local environmental context in the early stages of a subsidiary's life (in Dunning's conceptualization). We refer to this learning as *contextualization* to the local environment or *context-seeking learning for incremental local value creation.* It is equally essential to Vernon's conceptualization for the young subsidiary to learn from the parents in the early stages of IPLC in order to produce the product locally for less than imported prices. In both conceptualizations, the subsidiary has to learn how to create value by adapting the OSA to the local factor inputs, environment and market characteristics.

Cross-Transfer and Exportation   Goods and services traded in the MNE's internal market are demanded, supplied and supported by sister-subsidiaries. In order for the internalization concept in Dunning's theory to function, the subsidiary must learn how (or acquire the capability) to support its transactions with the internal market (both transfers to and from the internal markets) especially in the case of services. This support implies that at least some of the newly gained capabilities at the subsidiary (capabilities learned in the contextualization process) are transferred back to the internal markets. In the second phase of Vernon's IPLC theory, the subsidiary must at least acquire all the necessary expertise to support the local production and the exportation of the products to other markets. We refer to this capability as 'decontextualization', as it is learning to transfer some locally specific resources or capabilities to other locations and markets which do not have the same or similar specificities. Decontextualization entails a thorough examination of a few tasks, including the identification of the local knowledge and the capability components inherent in the locally adapted OSA, their form and composition (explicit, tacit, embedded and so on), which will have to be prepared for a *reverse-transfer* to the internal market or exported to the other subsidiary markets (in Vernon's IPLC).

Decontextualization may alternatively be viewed as global context-seeking learning for incremental value creation in international markets by other subsidiaries through the internal market. In contrast to the headquarters' passive learning (from subsidiaries) mode in IPLC theory, they must be active learners in the OLI theory in order to run efficient and effective internal markets. The internal market must be able to offer an increasingly more advanced set of expertise and capabilities than the headquarters' initial ownership advantage to stay relevant as time marches on. The theory's implication is that the internal markets are time-sensitive. Without a reverse-transfer, there will soon be no demand for the initial headquarters' OSA. In other words, if the enhancements, due to contextualization of OSA, combined with enrichments, due to integration of the subsidiary's local advantage, are not decontextualized and reintroduced into the internal markets, the MNE will face the risk of obsolescence in its initial OSA.

The enhancements and enrichments are therefore the necessary parts of the internal market concept as they provide for the OSA's renewal, which can then be traded in the internal market again.[3] They can be reutilized to establish new subsidiaries, to upgrade the sister-subsidiary's current capabilities or even to build new capabilities as a basis for introducing more advanced generations of goods and services.[4] This process will in turn renew the previous OSA component, enhancing and enriching it through the local subsidiary's local advantage (LSA) to create an integrated and enriched advantage, which constitutes the new tradable internal currency for the internal market. This renewal and enhancement of necessary capabilities over time is in fact due to learning. We suggest that this learning and accumulation of capabilities is similar to the concept of dynamic capabilities (Teece, Pisano and Shuen, 1997).

Levels of competition in a region
The multitude of operational differences in a region suggests a hierarchy of competition and competitiveness in that region. At the bottom of the competitive hierarchy is the independent SME, unable to take advantage of cooperation, co-learning and joint action readily available to networked firms, regardless of the size or attributes of the networks. Mainly because of the possibility of co-learning and joint action, the members of regional industrial clusters appear to be more competitive than the local firms, experiencing a higher level of competition. The young subsidiaries of multinational enterprises in a hostile host country environment, with tentative (or no) links to the local or regional networks would be experiencing a still higher level of competition. Even in the absence of local links and as members of the MNE's network of sister-subsidiaries with access to diversified capabilities and resources, these young subsidiaries must be more competitive than the members of the regional clusters, owing to their access to international resources in addition to their network advantage. Naturally the more mature subsidiaries of multinational enterprises with a host of links to the local and regional cluster, as well as access to their own international networks, should experience a still higher competitive level. Those subsidiaries which are permitted to act as their own headquarters, with their extensive access to the local, regional and international networks of their own supply chains, and possibly others through alliances, can still impose higher competitive standards. The multinational enterprises, with potential linkages to numerous regional industrial clusters, will have to be placed at the top of the competitive hierarchy.

Briefly stated, at least *six broad, yet distinct, levels of competition* can be easily identified, each of which is based on the extent to which a firm can take advantage of cooperation, co-dependence, co-learning, risk sharing, and joint action as a member of formal and informal networks. A firm must be able to identify the prevailing level of competition and compete *at least*

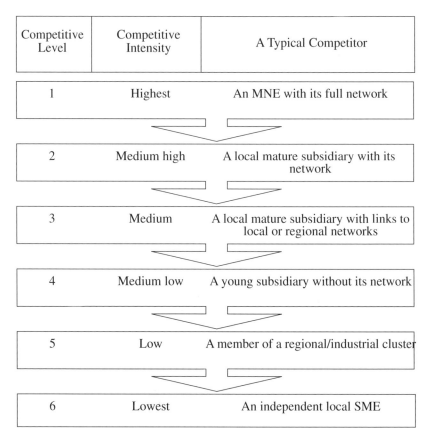

Competitive Level	Competitive Intensity	A Typical Competitor
1	Highest	An MNE with its full network
2	Medium high	A local mature subsidiary with its network
3	Medium	A local mature subsidiary with links to local or regional networks
4	Medium low	A young subsidiary without its network
5	Low	A member of a regional/industrial cluster
6	Lowest	An independent local SME

Figure 7.1   A hierarchy of competitive levels in open global environments

at that level in order to survive in the short term. In highly dynamic environments, competitive logic dictates that firms strive to reach the highest competitive level as soon as possible in order to compete effectively in the mid-to-long term. Increased competitiveness is the necessary condition for fending off the strong local and global competitors capable of competing at higher levels. The typology of competitive levels is presented in a hierarchy, from the highest to the lowest, in Figure 7.1 and the characteristics of these levels are highlighted in Table 7.1.

MNEs' growth and SMEs' globalization
Following the comparison of MNEs' and SMEs' capabilities, as articulated above and highlighted in Figure 7.1 and Table 7.1, we adopt a game-

theoretic framework to examine the evolutionary pattern of competition between SMEs and the subsidiary of MNEs as a subsidiary grows from a young and disadvantaged (for example by foreignness) competitor to a centre of excellence which is much more competitive (Etemad and Seguin-Dulude, 1986a; Birkinshaw, 1997) and capable of competing globally. We use this process to suggest a set of parallel growth strategies for a typical SME wishing to globalize in unavoidable competition with various local subsidiaries in national and international markets. This process can point both to the strategic opportunities and to the threats that form the basis for the subsidiary's (and the MNE's by extension) formulation of competitive strategy. Following a game-theoretic framework for formulation of competitive strategies, it is imperative for globalizing SMEs facing these strong competitors in international markets to understand their strategies in order to at least emulate and even to supersede them. This view of strategy from within the MNEs can then be used as the basis for formulating potent counterstrategies for the local SMEs competing with them in those markets. The process of a subsidiary's evolutionary life cycle can be formally stated in three stages, for each of which a set of counter-strategies is formulated.

The three stages of an SME's counter-strategies in response to the subsidiary's evolutionary growth
The first stage in a subsidiary life cycle is the initial OSA transfer from headquarters or the internal market to a local subsidiary. This transfer of proprietary assets, capabilities, expertise and knowledge provides for the young subsidiary's initial capabilities, helps it to take root in the local market and enables it to compete with the local firms, SMEs and large enterprises alike. The nature of the advantage is assumed to be globally applicable or universal for a typical subsidiary's use anywhere in the world. The young subsidiary may further build on this globally oriented advantage by incorporating the local advantage (LSA) and in the process adapting the advantage for the local environment. This is a transformation of presumed globally oriented (or universally applicable) advantage to a locally adapted (or local responsiveness (Bartlett and Goshal, 1989)) within the subsidiary, which would be at least a value adding process, if not innovative as well. As discussed earlier, we call this a contextualization process. Among the advantages that help the subsidiary in its early stages of its life cycle are the following:

1. the MNE's global scale may lead to lower costs and prices;
2. the lower set-up costs and transfer costs (due to previous experience and learning by doing elsewhere) leading to a lower fixed-cost regime of operations at the subsidiary than an indigenous greenfield start-up;

Table 7.1   The typology of the six levels of competition in open global environments

Competitive levels	Profile of a typical competitor	Typical sources of competitive advantage	The basis of competition
1	An MNE with an extensive worldwide network of sister-subsidiaries, each of which has its own network of buyers and suppliers.	Ownership-specific advantages (OSAs) + locally specific advantage (LSA) + links to its own worldwide network of sister-subsidiaries (WNSS)	MNE advantage and advantages of multiple global networks
2	A local mature subsidiary with its own network of buyers and suppliers	OSA + LSA + links to network of sister-subsidiaries + links to its own network of local buyers and suppliers	Localized MNE advantage and multiple global/regional network advantages
3	A local mature subsidiary with links to the local or regional networks	OSA + LSA + potential links to network of sister-subsidiaries + links to local or regional networks	Localized MNE advantage and advantages of regional networks
4	A young subsidiary of an MNE	OSA + LSA + potential links to network of sister-subsidiaries	Localized MNE advantage
5	A member of a regional/industrial clusters (member of an informal network)	Own + local network advantage (regional/industrial cluster)	Advantages of regional/industrial networks
6	An independent local SME	Own competitive advantage only	Own LSA

3. the local subsidiary may even take advantage of its 'foreignness' and its foreign origin to differentiate itself from its local competitors by emphasizing the affiliation of its products and brands with international quality standards, especially when local markets prefer foreign brands to local goods and services. In fact, a positive response is a predictable reaction by local consumers to lethargic and unresponsive SMEs resulting from protected, fragmentary and/or isolated local markets.

This process is represented in Figure 7.2.

Figure 7.2 *A schematic representation of the consequence of the initial transfer of OSA (OSA @t$_0$) to a subsidiary)*

In Figure 7.2, the OSA transfer to Sub$_1$@$_{t_1}$_ (leads to):
  __ global scale __ costs; and also leads to
  __ set-up costs __ transfer costs __overall cost structure;
  __ long-term costs and prices __ market share;
  __ local responsiveness __ local value;
  __ global scale operations __ costs and prices __ profits;
  __ added value to the transferred OSA @ t$_0$ as time progress (that is, OSA @ t_1> OSA @ t$_0$).

The schematic representation of the initial transfer in Figure 7.2 shows that the young subsidiary may start competing initially on the basis of the transferred OSA to market-differentiated products with higher perceived value at relatively lower prices (that is, advertising as foreign-based design, brand, and so on, at comparable local prices). However, as the local subsidiary slowly grows and comes to resemble the local SMEs, it begins to appropriate the local knowledge, the local content and the local advantage in order to integrate them with its globally oriented OSA, which can give it a much stronger basis for competition than before and also upgrade its OSA-based capabilities in the process.

As market share and local-scale operations (and also MNE's global scale by extension) increase, this subsidiary may begin to expand on its contextualization by further incorporating the local advantage into the already updated OSA, increase its local responsiveness and deliver even higher value to the local markets. After the initial adjustment period, the subsidiary may have already shed its foreignness, and acquired all the local advantages, thereby operating more competitively than its local SME counterparts. Its advantages can be simply stated as own OSA transferred @ t_1, added enrichments and enhancements due to incorporation of the LSA, and access to the OSA enhancements by other sister-subsidiaries, residing in the MNE system elsewhere. Therefore the subsidiary will be able to operate with an increasingly rich set of capabilities *vis-à-vis* the local firms, especially SMEs. This process of enrichment of its own OSA, combined with further enhancements by the MNE system, will give it a highly competitive stance and power with which to compete in the local market.

The learning process necessary to operationalize the initial OSA in the local environment and the further enrichment and enhancement necessary for the increased local responsiveness are bound to instil new capabilities, skills and knowledge in the new subsidiary. These newly gained capabilities, along with enrichment and enhancements over time, can in turn be transferred back to the headquarters and also made available to the existing network of sister-subsidiaries. We refer to these cross-transfers (to the internal markets) as the beginning of another round of learning, enhancement, enrichment and local responsiveness, which would add to the richness and diversity of previous corporate OSA. Such enhanced and improved OSA will in turn update the older OSAs and enable subsidiaries to withstand local competition (which would continually emulate in order to catch up and out-compete them).

The local SMEs' counter-strategy facing subsidiaries in stage 1   The unresolved question for a local SME, facing a growing subsidiary, is how to stop its own market share eroding, stabilize its position and even regain its previous competitive balance. The failure of local firms to stop their collective losses to a typical subsidiary will serve as a signal to other MNEs. The scale of the problem will soon be larger than before. The simple strategy (but not necessarily simple to implement) is to learn from the subsidiaries and at least emulate them. On the basis of the arguments presented previously, this process must initially entail competing on the basis of superior capabilities and learning to enhance and enrich them with time at a rate similar to, and possibly higher than, that of the local subsidiary. This process may require a transfer of knowledge, expertise and capabilities from the others to enable the local SME to catch up and to compete with the young subsidiary. The local enterprise may alternatively join the supply chain of another subsidiary to learn from within and to emulate the subsidiary. SMEs must learn from subsidiaries how to transfer and internalize acquired capabilities and then contextualize them for their own local skill set in order to constitute a similar process for upgrading their own capabilities to form a basis for sustained competition. Although, without access to a parent company, this may not be easy to implement, the characteristics of headquarters are known and can be replicated. SMEs are therefore forced to devise alternative strategies which mimic the MNE system in order to stop market share erosion at home and to expand globally, which may include, but not necessarily be limited to the following:

1. *Increasing the operational scale.* The local enterprises, including SMEs, must begin to increase their scale in order to appropriate scale economies by, for example, exporting to other markets leading to lower costs and lower corresponding prices, which would enable them to compete. This option may include producing as original equipment manufacturer (OEM) or as a supplier to foreign supply-chains. All of the above add to the SME's scale and scope operations and learning capacity, thereby enhancing its operational economies, leading to further competitiveness at home and abroad.

2. *Learning.* Local SMEs must be able to learn from the diversity of other export/local markets and to incorporate them in their skill set in order to offer further distinguishing features for countering the subsidiaries' differentiating strategies. This can be accomplished, for example, by transferring from other markets and internalizing locally, which is similar to the headquarters–subsidiary learning and internalizing processes for achieving higher capabilities with time. This is the necessary process for the SME to further differentiate itself from competing firms at home and abroad by offering a continually higher value package (in terms both of lower prices and of higher differentiating features) to prospective markets.

3. *Networking.* To counter the subsidiary's network advantage, local SMEs may form alliances of their own or join other alliances to benefit from networking and collaborative advantage (Doz, 1996; Kanter, 1984; Ghoshal and Bartlett, 1991; Johanson and Mattson, 1988). Such networking allows the SME to accomplish its competitive objectives through cooperation with, and learning from, others and improving their initial capabilities.

4. *The local clusters.* SMEs may form regional clusters with other local enterprises, including foreign subsidiaries, to share costs, increase the pace of innovation and benefit from joint action (Doz, 1996; Ghoshal and Nohria, 1989; Johanson and Mattson, 1988). The success of

regional clusters, such as those in Silicon Valley in the San Francisco Bay Area, and Route 128 in Boston, point to the increased competitiveness of regional industrial clusters, which initially consisted of local enterprises.

5. *Vicarious learning.* A fifth alternative for SMEs is to capture learning benefits vicariously from others, including suppliers, members of the supply chains, other MNEs and local industrial clusters. This will suggest capturing what Kanter (1984) calls 'collaborative advantage' and it may lead to reconfiguration of their supply chains (Yoshino and Rangan, 1995: 25–40) in order to remain competitive at home. Theoretically, SMEs should be able to emulate the subsidiary's strategy so long as the essence of its learning remains a single-loop type (Gupta and Govindarajan, 1991, 1994; Huber, 1991).

The essence of the above strategy is to start with a reasonable set of capabilities and then become a learning organization for capturing and exploiting improvements with time in terms of both the quantitative (scale economies) and the qualitative (the differentiating features from other competitors and environments) in order to stay up with the competition. The necessary conditions for achieving the improvements are learning from others, including the local subsidiary of MNEs or the members of the regional industrial cluster, as well as learning to internalize them as rapidly as possible. In other words, this will require the local SME to operate interdependently (Etemad, 2003a, 2003b), symbiotically (Etemad, Wright and Dana, 2001; Dana, Etemad and Wright, 2001) and even synergistically (Etemad, 2003a). It would also force the SME to become a fast learning and rapidly exploiting organization.[5] The possibility of learning through internalization has been an implicit feature of MNE structures, as reviewed above, which can help to enhance and enrich capabilities of the local SMEs and to transform the nature of competition between SMEs and the local subsidiary representing global competition.

The second stage in a subsidiary life cycle is reverse-transfer of the enriched and enhanced advantages to the internal markets. This stage begins when the subsidiary prepares to transfer its enhanced advantage back to the MNE system, which will require it to audit its state of capabilities, expertise and knowledge. Some of these capabilities originated at the headquarters as globally oriented expertise, knowledge and capabilities in a variety of forms. This set of capabilities and expertise may be in the form of tacit knowledge and know-how, and embedded expertise transferred to the subsidiary by expatriates, as well as corporate techniques contained in corporate routines and technology.

The audit, for the purposes of reverse-transfer, will force the subsidiary to articulate the current state of its knowledge and capability in terms of its initial OSA, local enhancement, local enrichment and the form in which they are contained. Such audits differentiate improvements from what came from the MNE and also identify their current form and composition (that is, what proportion of which capability is explicit, tacit or embedded). Such assessment of the current contextual form in terms of whether they are explicit, tacit, experiential (carried by employees) or embedded in technology, machinery or in the corporate routines, will determine what and how they will be transferred to the parent company's internal market. This assessment and articulation will in turn allow the subsidiary to examine its own strengths, weaknesses and incremental gains in terms of the current state of the art, especially in relation to that of the local firms. This articulation and assessment may also help the corporate learning process in identifying what learning has been explicit, tacit or embedded, as well as their properties, sources and repositories. Such well articulated knowledge will then further enable the company as a whole to assess how effectively it had learnt previously and also to 'learn how to learn' in the future, both for its own use and for optimal transfer to others. Such audits may in fact instil a learning process in the local subsidiary. It may also set the scene for further improvements and internalization within the local subsidiary under a regular and cohesive set of audit/review policies to further integrate and internalize as a part of a periodical self-assessment routine. The entire accumulation of tacit capabilities, learned in dispersed fashion from different sources and in different time periods, can be routinely combined to make them much more wholesome and thus easier to further re-enhance, redeploy and even to transfer to the other affiliates, when necessary. Continuous re-enhancement may start at the subsidiary or come from the other subsidiaries receiving the technology or the advantage through such cross-transfers.

Thus the essence of stage two is both in the recognition of and the set up for continuous learning/improvement at the subsidiary through the mechanism of articulation for transfer to the others within the MNE system. There is no reason to expect that an independent indigenous firm, including a typical local SME, would audit its capabilities regularly performing a function resembling the internalization process. Internalization appears to be the distinguishing factor between the local subsidiary and the local enterprise. This difference would suggest that all local SMEs, regardless of size and age, should audit their capabilities for ensuring the internalization of the newly acquired knowledge, capability or technology so that they can re-enhance it over time, re-deploy it elsewhere or even transfer the new improvements to the others for appropriating opportunistic benefits (for example, collecting rent and royalties through the licensing of technology).

Furthermore the transfer of technology literature is replete with errors, delays and cost overruns arising from the inability, or reluctance, of the licensor to articulate well in the initial technology transfer. Naturally this will in turn set the scene for a total reluctance, if not confusion, in the licensee to reverse or, cross-transfer, incremental improvements back to the original licensor, as the true origin of improvements may not be very clear. This massive failure of cross-licensing in transferring improvements back to the original licensor is mainly due to the lack of licensees' organized audit and assessment capabilities at the beginning to identify initial short-ages and distinguish incremental improvements over time (from the content of the initial licence) for a reverse-transfer. A successful cross-transfer will necessarily require the identification of the contextual form of the improve-ments to facilitate the mode of transfer. For example, if they are tacit or embedded in a certain context (such as local employees), the context (or a similar context) may have to be transferred to preserve the integrity of the transfer. The schematic representation of stage 1 is depicted in Figure 7.3, while Figure 7.4 captures the transformation and the dynamics of stage 2, which involves at least two interactive learning processes: the learning pro-cesses required to contextualize the original OSA to the local environment and to integrate it with the local advantage (i.e., OSA + LSA, symbolically), and the learning that results from the assessment and articulation processes in order to reverse-transfer the enhanced and enriched advantage to the internal market and the sister subsidiary system. This capability may, in

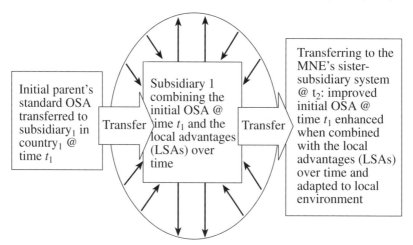

Figure 7.3   A schematic representation of the initial transfer of OSA @ time t_1 to the local subsidiary and subsequent transfers to other sister subsidiaries

turn, force further improvements, learning and add to the combined advantage. These two processes are depicted schematically in Figure 7.4.

The local SMEs' counter-strategy facing subsidiaries in stage 2 As stated earlier, the counter-strategy in this stage is also predicated on a process of learning from, or at least emulating, the local subsidiary. It necessitates that the local SMEs acquire capabilities comparable, if not superior, to those of the local subsidiary at all times. When there are gains involved in the actual work of cross-transferring the enhanced and enriched capabilities back to the headquarters, enabling them to usher in a new round of improvements, the local SMEs must strive to compensate for them as well. If the actual work of cross-transfer results in a compensating return from the internal markets (or other sister-subsidiaries in terms of new innovative products and processes), consequently unleashing more potent competitive forces in the local marketplace than before, the local SME must also be prepared to counter such compensating interjections. This game-theoretic process dictates that local SMEs audit their own capabilities from time to time in relation to all competitors in their competitive space, including mature subsidiaries.

It must be noted that examination and assessment involved in such audits allow the subsidiary to benchmark itself against the prevailing OSA, presumably becoming much more potent with time as a result of cross-transfers to the internal market, and to prepare itself to compete with, if not exceed, the local as well as the global competition. The same logic can apply to the local SME if a similar process is followed. If the local SME can benchmark itself against the local subsidiary and acquire, or develop, the necessary competence in order to compete with the local subsidiary, representing the global competition in the local market, it can compete effectively both locally and internationally.

In contrast to the licensing literature, which discourages repeated licensing because of its potential dissipating impact on proprietary knowledge and know-how, the argument presented above suggests that the actual job of transferring knowledge and know-how develops certain expertise which can facilitate the process of updating, enhancing and enriching the initial capability by, for example, detecting a typical flaw in the current capability. It can also incorporate certain flexibilities for adapting to different environments, and even incremental improvements, with each round of transfers, if not continuously thereafter. The implication of this stage for the local SME is to license proprietary knowledge and know-how from others and cross-license improvements to others for their intrinsic beneficial advantages to the firm itself. Such licensing agreements should preferably be done with the members of the supply chain (or the members of the strategic alliance) which competes with the subsidiary locally or internationally. Alternatively, they can be done within the network of other competing MNEs with which the local SME would cooperate. Such supply chains may include the rival MNE's local subsidiaries. The essence of this set of counter-strategies at this stage is the constant benchmarking necessary for continuous improvements in the SME's capabilities, which in turn allows them to increase the complexity of competition and take the necessary steps, including but not limited to increasing learning and scale economies and improving upon global competitiveness through active membership in alliances and networks.

The third stage in a subsidiary life cycle is reverse-transfer of the enriched and enhanced advantages to the internal markets. As a result of a subsidiary's double-learning loop, it would be able to update and upgrade the initial OSA as well as its capabilities and to climb to a new and higher plateau of resources and capabilities, which could be replicated with each round of transaction with the internal markets. Logically, such a process can even form a basis for a continuous process of improvement through acquiring certain capabilities from the internal markets and supplying the internal market with a more improved, enhanced and enriched version. This process is predicated on the subsidiary functioning as a learning institution. As a learning organization (Gupta and Govindarajan 1991, 1994; Kogut and Zander, 1992), it becomes more advanced and more competitive with time and relative to its competitors with each cycle of transaction with the internal market and other sister-subsidiaries. Consequently, the MNE's system can possess much richer capabilities than the initial OSAs, mainly due to cross-transfer from various subsidiaries. This process also enables the MNE system, as a whole, to climb to much higher plateaux of resources and capabilities. Therefore, at the end of stage 2, and the beginning of stage 3, in a subsidiary's life cycle, a standard MNE capability, expertise and resource (universally applicable to any subsidiary) is enhanced by adaptation to the subsidiary's local environment, enriched by its local advantage, resulting in at least one subsidiary equipped with well adapted capabilities and resources for competing in that environment effectively. A parallel transfer from the internal market to the diverse environments of other countries combined with a reverse-transfer back to the internal market system of the MNE system will add to the system's collective capabilities in both qualitative and quantitative terms, not replicable by other dissimilar systems unless they would simulate and emulate them. Owing to the learned capabilities, the subsidiary can function similarly to the headquarters in transferring the combined and enhanced advantage to another subsidiary, resulting in further learning and feed-back loops, as shown in Figure 7.4.

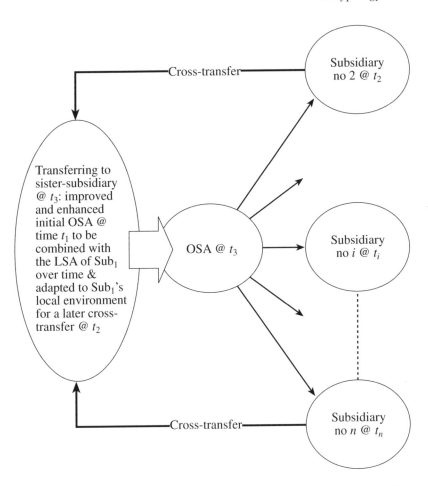

Figure 7.4   MNE's system of continual capability enhancement, transfer and cross-transfer over time

Thus the mature subsidiaries, and the MNE's collective capabilities by extension, will gain diverse capabilities incrementally with each transfer; and each incremental transfer becomes capable of responding to a particular demand, at an increasingly fast rate. The subsidiary can begin to function similarly to and even as its own subsidiary. Repeated transfers and cross-transfers to other members of its network, including sister-subsidiaries, should consequently elevate and expand the scope of the initial capability and continually improve upon and update the previous advantage. The richer variety and diversity in environments within which subsidiaries compete would naturally result in richer capabilities due to the continuous updating, cross-transfer and further transfers (from the internal market when a capability is updated elsewhere).

The local SMEs' counter-strategy facing a mature subsidiary in stage 3
This counter-strategy is again based on learning from and emulating the MNE–subsidiary interactions. Competing SMEs should strive to simulate the MNE–subsidiary's cooperative system and emulate the learning that results from transfer and cross-transfer of capabilities. The former (the cooperative system) facilitates the latter process and the latter reinforces the former process. Combined, these two broad processes enable the subsidiary (and the MNE by extension) to compete more vigorously locally and globally.

As regards the former process, local SMEs can utilize regional industrial clusters as well as the web of alliances to simulate the conditions of cooperative networks to allow them to compete against others. With a game-theoretic framework and terminology, this is analogous to setting up numerous cooperative games within a coalition in order to win a competitive game against a competing coalition. The coalition of the members of a supply/value chain is a typical example which can be based on principles of synergistic and symbiotic relations (Etemad, 2003a, 2003b), which allows for the introduction of deep specialization and scale economies, leading to further competitiveness.

As for the latter process, the process of transfer and cross-transfer among the members of the supply chain or the strategic alliances can replicate the double- or triple-loop learning processes and lead to increasingly high capabilities for the entire coalition. Repeated transfers and cross-transfers of the improvements by each member to the other members would foster and further enhance the learning process (as in MNE–subsidiary cooperation) described above within the coalition and for the purpose of enhancing and enriching each member's capabilities. The strategic content for SMEs facing mature subsidiaries in the third stage of their life cycle can be summarized in two processes:

1. to form or join a coalition, preferably along a supply/value chain, whose objective is to become globally competitive and compete with other cooperative networks, such as the cooperative network on an MNE's sister-subsidiary system, locally and globally; and
2. to engage in a process of cooperative or joint improvements based on repeated transfers and cross-transfers designed to elevate the capabilities of each member as well as the coalition as a whole.

Concluding remarks and implications

Two fundamental assumptions were implicit in the discussion of the chapter. First, the multinational corporations (MNEs) and their sister-subsidiary system are capable of competing locally and globally with a high degree of intensity. Their network structure, combined with a common ownership, gives them a competitive advantage that the local independent SMEs simply lack. The incentives in the sister-subsidiary system and in the internal market structure hold the potential for enhancing, enriching and improving a local subsidiary's resources and capabilities, and those of MNE's ownership advantage (OSA) by extension, continuously and when necessary make them available to local subsidiaries that compete with local enterprises.

Although a local subsidiary may suffer from 'foreignness' disadvantage at the beginning of its life cycle, with the injection of continuous improvements, resulting from transfer and cross-transfers of the enhanced and enriched capabilities back and forth between the internal market and various subsidiaries, the subsidiary can become competitive and could soon exceed the competitive local norms. After the initial threshold period, and with the assistance of the headquarters and the sister-subsidiary system, the local subsidiary can set and maintain much higher competitive standards, levels to which local firms must rise in order to compete and survive.

Second, the globalization of markets has removed barriers, and local firms can no longer take refuge behind the nation state's protective walls. This is forcing even the local small firms to compete with the local subsidiaries at home in all stages of their evolutionary life cycle. In turn, the local subsidiaries are also forced to compete with other, equally powerful, subsidiaries and national firms to preserve their respective market share, if not for survival. For SMEs aspiring to internationalize, this openness in markets has transformed the Richardian notion of local competition to a series of competitive temporal sub-games, each part of a larger and broader global game, played by global players. In other words, the independent, local small firms are involuntarily obliged to play the global game even at home. Such firms suffer from the traditional disadvantages associated with limited resources and size (Etemad 1982, 1999), resulting in diseconomies of scale and low specialization, especially in the absence of collaborative advantage (Kanter, 1984). Even the large local firms cannot benefit from the advantages associated with diversity, specialization and learning to the extent that the local subsidiary of MNEs do in the international markets (Cavusgil, 1980; Dana, Etemad and Wright, 2000; Gupta and Govindarajan, 1991, 1994; Sugiura, 1990). The independent local firms, regardless of size, find it imperative to compete with the local subsidiary which can call upon the MNE's network of sister-subsidiary systems for a range of advantages unavailable to local independent firms. Even the local competition becomes a fight among global coalitions for market share, regardless of size, location and time, in which the local firms are also competing for their respective shares.

Three conclusions can be easy derived from the discussion of this chapter.

Size–scale syndrome

The small independent local firms, by definition, do not have the size to benefit from economies of scale while they continue to produce complete products (Dana and Etemad 1995). If they draw upon highly specialized partners and form a supply chain with their help and collaboration, each member of the supply chain can benefit from common scale economies and even share and transfer some of the benefits of specialization to other members who are lacking them. Such economies may help the chain produce higher value, gain more competitiveness and increase its market share in the local market. The consequent scale economies and collaboration within the supply chain network can offer the entire group, including the local SME, further economic and collaborative benefits enabling it to compete with local subsidiaries much more effectively than without the help of collaborators. The cost of newly-gained competitiveness is increased dependence on, or interdependence (Etemad, Wright and Dana, 2001; Dana, Etemad and Wright, 2001) with, the other members of the supply chain with which the local SME would collaborate. This collaborative arrangement could then be viewed as a coalition capable of emulating networked firms, such as multinationals, even without a governance system based on a common ownership structure.

Collaboration–network advantage

Cooperation and collaboration can span a wide range and are not costless. In addition to the required coordination for managing an efficient supply/ value chain, most production-related decisions, for example, must be made jointly. Joint decision making has been traditionally viewed by entrepreneurial firms as a cost of cooperation, as it impinges on the enterprise's independence. The extent of benefits associated with interdependence of the network members varies according to the degree of cooperation and collaboration among the members of a network. A maximum interdependence may produce the largest synergy and symbiosis between one member and the others in the network (Etemad, 2003a, 2003b). It will also offer the highest economies associated with collaboration, scale and diversity, and thereby help the local SMEs to achieve some, if not most, of the benefits the local subsidiary receives from the MNE systems as a whole.

Learning as a basis of sustained competitiveness
Although further economies of scale, scope and specialization can be gained by increased collaboration within a network, the advantages of learning may not materialize automatically. A receptive environment must be created and proper mechanisms for learning should be introduced for the members of the network to learn from one another and internalize what has been learned within the firm. However the possibility of opportunism always exists, and that should be treated as a partial cost of collaboration. Although the common ownership structure of MNEs minimizes opportunistic behaviour within its system, it is not a justification for the other not to create MNE-like networked structures without common ownership governance structure. Therefore a governance system, mimicking an MNE's form of structure, that can minimize opportunistic behaviour and maximize interdependence at the same time, must be designed and be reinforced strictly to maximize network-related benefits for all members, including local SMEs who aspire to globalize. The members of the supply chain, or value chain network, may not voluntarily transfer the learning benefits to all other members unless the incentives and sanctions safeguard against opportunism similar to typical subsidiary–headquarter interactions within an MNE.

The governance structure must therefore encourage behaviour similar to transfers and reverse-transfers of improved and enhanced capabilities in the sister-subsidiary system of the multinational corporations, which would make the locally acquired benefits available to other subsidiaries when necessary. Without such a support system the local subsidiaries may not sustain their competitive advantage in the face of other hostile global coalitions cooperating to gain competitiveness. As stated earlier, local independent firms must try to take advantage of licensing and cross-licensing to improve upon the state of support technologies from within or outside their network for their mutual benefit. The periodic assessment and benchmarking necessary for proper acquisition of cutting-edge capabilities and cross-transfers of improvements learnt or applied to them by other members of the network may simulate the MNE–subsidiary types of interaction and allow the SMEs to emulate their strategies and match, if not surpass, their competitiveness.

The overriding conclusion of this chapter is that globalization of markets has facilitated MNEs' presence in almost all local markets and the local SMEs have no choice but to compete with the MNEs' local subsidiaries. This chapter derived and proposed a layered competitive framework, comprising a typology of six distinct levels of competition, each populated by firms with different capabilities and resources. This six-layer typology is based on the resource-based view of the firm within a game-theoretic framework drawing on and incorporating the distinct features of Dunning's modern theory of multinationals, Vernon's theory of IPLC, and Nonaka and Takeuchi's learning organizations. In the intensifying global competition, where subsidiaries and local SMEs must compete side-by-side, regardless of their affiliation and size, SMEs could identify the competitive level at which they must, or aspire to, compete and learn from the practitioners of those strategies in order emulate, if not exceed, them. As MNEs' networked structure and local subsidiaries pervade all higher levels of the hierarchy in the proposed competitive typology, their strategies should be viewed as benchmarks for SMEs aspiring to internationalize and compete with them in global markets. In the final analysis, global competition dictates that the local SMEs must shed their traditional fears and adopt new innovative strategies involving networks, synergy, symbiosis and maximum learning to create competitive entities similar to MNE–subsidiary structures.

Notes

1. Dunning (1986) acknowledges the similarity and convergence outlined in this section.
2. Various terminologies have been used to suggest the same or similar concepts. Nohria and Ghoshal (1997), for example, suggested specialization within differentiated networks, Birkinshaw (1996) followed the concept of 'World Product Mandates' and Etemad (1986) extended the subsidiary to its ultimate evolution to resemble the headquarters with respect to its 'Global Product Mandates'; while Jarillo and Martinez (1990) have envisioned still other functions for the subsidiary.
3. Bartlett and Ghoshal (1986) suggest that MNEs can 'tap' their subsidiaries and therefore support the above argument.
4. Bartlett and Ghoshal (1986, 1989) follow a similar thinking in their conception of managing across borders.
5. This was reviewed earlier, in the second section, under a range of topics, including the technological race, time compression and shortening of cycle times.

References

Acs, Z. and B. Yeung (1999), 'Entrepreneurial discovery and the Global Economy', *Global Focus*, **11** (3), 63–72.
Amit, R. and P. Shoemaker (1993), 'Strategic Assets and Organizational Rent', *Strategic Management Journal*, **14**, 33–46.
Anderson, U. and J. Johanson (1996), 'Subsidiary Embeddedness and its Implications for Integration in the MNC', *Proceedings of the European International Business Association*, 235–56.
Bartlett, C.A. and S. Ghoshal (1986), 'Tap Your Subsidiaries for Global Reach', *Harvard Business Review*, **64** (6), 87–94.
Bartlett, C.A. and S. Ghoshal (1989), *Managing Across Borders: The Transnational Solution*, Boston: Harvard Business School Press.
Birkinshaw, J.M. (1996), 'How Subsidiary Mandates are Gained and Lost', *Journal of International Business Studies*, **27**, 567–496.
Birkinshaw, J.M. (1997), 'Entrepreneurship in Multinational Corporations: The Characteristics of Subsidiary Initiatives', *Strategic Management Journal*, **18**, 207–29.
Birkinshaw, J.M., N. Hood and S. Jonsson (1998), 'Building Firm-Specific Advantages in Multinational Corporations: The Role of Subsidiary Initiative', *Strategic Management Journal*, **19** (3), 221–41.

Bishop, P. and H.H. Crookell (1986), 'Specialization in Canadian Subsidiaries', in D.G. McFetridge (ed.), *Canadian Industry in Transition*, Toronto: University of Toronto Press, 305–85.

Cavusgil, S.T. (1980), 'On the Internationalization Process of the Firm', *European Research*, **8**, 273–381.

Cohen, W. and D. Levinthal (1989), 'Innovation and Learning: The Two Faces of R&D', *Economic Journal* (September), 569–96.

Crookell, H.H. (1986), 'Specialization and International Competitiveness', in H. Etemad and L.Seguin-Dulude (eds), *Managing the Multinational Subsidiary*, London: Croom Helm, 102–11.

Dana, L.P. and H. Etemad (1995), 'SMEs Adapting Strategy for NAFTA: A Model for Small and Medium-sized Enterprises', *Journal of Small Business and Entrepreneurship*, **12** (3), July–August, 4–17

Dana, L.P., H. Etemad and R. Wright (2000), 'The Global Reach of Symbiotic Networks', *Journal of Euromarketing*, **9** (2), June, 1–16

Dana, L.P., H. Etemad and R. Wright (2001), 'Symbiotic Interdependence', in D. Welsh and I. Alon (eds), *International Franchising in Emerging Markets*, CCH Publishing, 119–129.

Dosi, G., K. Pavitt and L. Soete (1990), *The Economics of Technical Change and International Trade*, New York: New York University Press.

Doz, Y.L. (1996), 'The Evolution of Cooperation in Strategic Alliances: Initial Conditions or Learning Processes?', *Strategic Management Journal*, **17**, 55–83.

Dunning, J.H. (1980), 'Toward an Eclectic Theory of International Production: Empirical Tests', *Journal of International Business Studies*, **11** (1), 9–31.

Dunning, J.H. (1981), *International Production and the Multinational Enterprise*, London: Allen & Unwin.

Dunning, J.H. (1986), 'The Investment Cycle Revisited', *Weltwirtschaftliches Archiv*, **122**, 667–77.

Dunning, J.H. (1988), 'The Eclectic Paradigm of International Production: A Restatement and Some Possible Extensions', *Journal of International Business Studies*, **19** (1), 1–31.

Dunning J.H. and A. Rugman (1985), 'The Influence of Hymer's Dissertation on the Theory of Foreign Direct Investment', American Economic Review, **75**, 228–32

Enright, M.J. (2000). 'Regional Clusters and Multinational Enterprises', *International Studies of Management and Organization*, **30** (2), Summer, 114–38.

Etemad, H. (1982), 'World Product Manadates in Perspective' in A. Rugman (ed.), *Multinational and Technology Transfer: The Canadian Experience*, New York: Praeger, 108–25.

Etemad, H. (1986), 'Industrial Policy Orientation, Choice of Technology, World Product Mandates and International Trading Companies', in H. Etemad and L. Seguin-Dulude (eds), *Managing the Multinational Subsidiary: Response to Environmental Change and Host Nation R&D Policies*, 112–35.

Etemad, H. (1999), 'Globalization and Small and Medium-Sized Enterprises: Search for Potent Strategies', *Global Focus*, **11** (3), Summer, 85–105.

Etemad, H. (2003a), 'Managing Relations: The Essence of International Entrepreneurship', in H. Etemad and R. Wright (eds), *Globalization and Entrepreneurship: Policy and Strategy Perspectives*, Cheltenham, UK and Northampton, MA, USA: Edward Elgar.

Etemad, H. (2003b), 'Marshalling Relations', in L.P. Dana (ed.), *The Handbook of Research on International Entrepreneurship*, Cheltenham, UK and Northampton, MA, USA: Edward Elgar.

Etemad, H. and L.Seguin-Dulude (1986a), 'The Development of Technology in MNEs: A Cross-Country and Industry Study', in A.E. Safarian and G.Y. Bertin (eds), *Multinationals, Governments and Technology Transfer*, London: Croom Helm.

Etemad, H. and L.Seguin-Dulude (1986b), 'Inventive Activity in MNEs and their World Product Mandated Subsidiaries', in *Managing the Multinational Subsidiary: Response to Environmental Change and Host Nation R&D Policies*, 117–206.

Etemad, H., R. Wright and L.P. Dana (2001), 'Symbiotic International business Networks: Collaboration Between Small and large Firms', *Thunderbird International Business Review*, **43** (4), August, 481–500.

Forsgren, M. and C. Pahlberg (1992), 'Subsidiary Influence and Autonomy in International Firms', *International Business Review*, 1 (3), 41–51.

Forsgren, M., U. Holm and J. Johanson (1992), 'Internationalization of the Second Degree: The Emergence of European Based Centers in Swedish Firms', in S. Young and J. Hamill (eds), *Europe and the Multinationals*, Aldershot, UK and Brookfield, US: Edward Elgar, 235–53.

Galunic, D.C. and S. Roden (1998), 'Resource Recombination in the Firm: Knowledge and Potential for Schumpeterian Innovation', *Strategic Management Journal*, 19 (12), 1193–1201.

Gerybadze, A. and G. Reger (1999), 'Globalization of R&D: recent changes in the management of innovation in transnational corporations', *Research Policy*, 28 (2–3), 251–74.

Ghoshal, S. and C.A. Bartlett (1991), 'The Multinational Corporation as an Inter Organizational Network', *Academy of Management Review*, 15, 603–25.

Ghoshal, S. and N. Nohria (1989), 'Internal Differentiation Within Multinational Corporations', *Strategic Management Journal*, 10, 323–37.

Gomes-Casseres, B. (1996), *The Alliance Revolution: The New Shape of Business Rivalry*, Cambridge, MA: Harvard University Press.

Gomes-Casseres, B. (1997), 'Alliance Strategies of Small Firms', *Small Business Economics*, 9 (1), 33–44.

Gulati, R. (1995), 'Does Familiarity Breed Trust? The Implications of Repeated Ties for Contractual Choice in Alliances', *Academy of Management Review*, 38(1), 85–112.

Gupta, A.K. and V. Govindarajan (1991), 'Knowledge Flows and the Structure of Control Within Multinational Corporations', *Academy of Management Review*, 16, 768–92.

Gupta, A.K. and V. Govindarajan (1994), 'Organizing for Knowledge Within MNCs', *International Business Review*, 3, 443–57.

Hatal, W. (1994), 'From Hierarchy to Enterprise: Internal Markets are the New Foundation of Management', *Academy of Management Executive*, 8 (4), 69–83.

Hedlund, G. (1981), 'Autonomy of Subsidiaries and Formalization of Headquarter–Subsidiary Relationships in Swedish MNEs', in L. Otterbeck (ed.), *The Management of Headquarter–Subsidiary Relationships in Multinational Corporations*, Aldershot: Gower, 25–78.

Huber, G. (1991), 'Organizational Learning: The Contributing Processes and the Literatures', *Organization Science*, 2, 88–115.

Hymer, S.H. (1976), *The International Operations of National Firms: A Study of Direct Foreign Investment*, Cambridge, MA: MIT Press.

Jarillo, J.C. and J.I. Martinez (1990), 'Different Roles for Subsidiaries: The Case of Multinational Corporations in Spain', *Strategic Management Journal*, 11 (7), 501–12.

Johanson, J. and L.G. Mattson (1988), 'Internationalization in Industrial Systems – A Network Approach', in N. Hood and J.E. Vahlne (eds), *Strategies in Global Competition*, London: Croom Helm, 287–314.

Kanter, E.M. (1984), 'Collaborative advantage: The art of alliances', *Harvard Business Review*, July–August, 96–108

Knickerbocker, F.T. (1973), *Oligopolistic Reaction and Multinational Enterprise*, Boston, MA: Harvard University Press.

Kogut, B. and U. Zander (1992), 'Knowledge of the Firm, Combinative Capabilities and the Replication of Technology', *Organization Science*, 3, 383–97.

Liberman, M. and D.B. Montgomery (1998), 'First-Mover (Dis)advantages: Retrospective and Link with the Resource-Based View', *Strategic Management Journal*, 19, 1111–25.

Malnight, T. (1996), 'The Transition from Decentralized to Network-Based MNC Structures: An Evolutionary Perspective', *Journal of International Business Studies*, 27 (1), 43–65.

Nohria, N. and S. Ghoshal (1997), *The Differentiated Networks: Organizing Multinational Corporations for Value Creation*, San Francisco: Jossy-Bass.

Nonaka, I. and H. Takeuchi (1995), *The Knowledge-Creating Company*, New York and Oxford: Oxford University Press.

Norton, R.D. and J. Rees (1979), 'The Product Cycle and the Spatial Decentralization of American Manufacturing', *Regional Studies*, 13, 141–51.

Pearce, R.D. (1989), *The Internationalization of Research and Development by Multinational Enterprises*, New York: St Martin's Press.

Roth, K. and A. Morrison (1992), 'Implementing Global Strategy: Characteristics of Global Subsidiary Mandates', *Journal of International Business Studies*, **23**, 715–36.

Rugman, A. and J. D'Cruz (2000), *Multinationals as Flagship Firms: A New Theory of Regional Business Networks*, Oxford: Oxford University Press.

Rugman, A.M. and S. Douglas (1986), 'The Strategic Management of Multinational and World Product Mandating', in H. Etemad and L. Seguin-Dulude (eds), *Managing the Multinational Subsidiary*, London: Croom Helm, 99–101.

Sugiura, H. (1990), 'How Honda Localizes Its Global Strategy', *Sloan Management Review*, **31** (Fall), 77–82.

Teece, D.J. (1977), 'Technology Transfer by Multinational Firms: The Source Cost of Transferring Technological Know-How', *Economic Journal*, **87** (June), 242–67.

Teece, D. J., G. Pisano and A. Shuen (1997), 'Dynamic Capabilities and Strategic Management', *Strategic Management Journal*, **18** (7), 509–33.

Vernon, R. (1966), 'International Investments and International Trade in the Product Cycle', *Quarterly Journal of Economics*, **80** (2), 190–207.

Yoshino, M. and V.S. Rangan (1995), *Strategic Alliances: An Entrepreneurial Approach to Globalization*, Boston, MA: Harvard Business School Press.

PART TWO

CONCEPTUAL CHAPTERS

8   Internationalization: motive and process
A. Bakr Ibrahim

The recent growth of international business activities by entrepreneurial firms has been phenomenal. The early internationalization of relatively new entrepreneurial ventures has received considerable attention in the literature (Zahra *et al.*, 2000; McDougall and Oviatt, 2000; Hitt *et al.*, 2001; Ibrahim and McGuire, 2001).

Indeed international activity is a key element of entrepreneurship. Research studies suggest that, as part of the entrepreneurial process, most entrepreneurs perceive international opportunities from the first day they start their business (Zacharakis, 1997; Oviatt and McDougall, 1994). The entrepreneurial process includes identifying and assessing the opportunity and marshalling the resources to exploit it (Ibrahim and Ellis, 2002). In other words, entrepreneurs are opportunity-driven regardless of the location – be it domestic or international opportunity. Entrepreneurs' personality traits and backgrounds drive them to scan the environment (local or international) looking for market opportunities. McDougall and Oviatt (2000) define international entrepreneurship as 'the combination of innovative, proactive, and risk-seeking behavior that crosses national borders and is intended to create value in organizations'.

Despite the growing interest of international entrepreneurship, most research studies in international business tend to focus on large multinational enterprises (MNEs) as the traditional unit of analysis (Brush, 1995; Coviello and McAuley, 1999; Oviatt and McDougall, 2000; Ibrahim and McGuire, 2001). While the theoretical contributions offered in the international literature have added much to our understanding of the internationalization motive and process in the context of large organizations, most of these frameworks have proved to be too limited to explain the entrepreneur's internationalization motive and process. A major criticism levelled at these theoretical frameworks is that they are partial as they focus on only one factor. Furthermore entrepreneurship is a complex phenomenon. There are many factors that shape the entrepreneurial mind and motivate the entrepreneur to pursue an international strategy. Thus the objective of this research is twofold: first, to review the theoretical contributions offered in the international business literature and, second, to offer a theoretical framework that integrates both international and entrepreneurship research. Such a framework provides a more realistic explanation of international entrepreneurship.

International business theories

Most theoretical contributions have focused on managerial and economic issues related to the motive and process of internationalization. These include the firm's growth stage, acquisition of knowledge and organizational learning; the product or the industry life cycle; availability of resources; interorganizational linkages and network; and imperfect competition and competitive advantage (Ahroni, 1966; Caves, 1971; Roboch and Simmonds, 1989; Zacharakis, 1997; Oviatt and McDougall, 1994; Coviello and McAuley, 1999; Autio *et al.* 2000).

Process-stage theories of internationalization

A popular school of thought in the international business literature is the notion of stage process. In this approach, internationalization is viewed as an incremental process that occurs gradually as a result of organizational learning. A number of research studies suggest that the internationalization process is shaped over time as the firm's managers gain experience and knowledge of foreign markets (Coviello and McAuley, 1999).

Earlier work by Ahroni (1966), known as the 'global horizon' approach, suggests that the firm's geographical horizons change as part of the firm's growth and evolutionary process. The change is seen as necessary in order for the firm to take advantage of opportunities in other geographical areas. In the early stage of the firm's growth process, the horizon is usually limited to the domestic market. However, as the firm grows, it may expand its horizon and invest in foreign markets to exploit windows of opportunity.

According to the global horizon approach, internal and external factors may provide the firm with the opportunity and motive to go international (Ahroni, 1966, Ibrahim and McGuire, 2001). Internal factors may provide the firm with absolute advantage. The concept of absolute advantage has been a key tenet of international trade theory (Roboch & Simmonds, 1989). The advantage may be the result of superior and unmatched technology such as is the case with Microsoft. External factors such as tax incentives, subsidies and grants offered by foreign governments may also provide the motive for a firm to internationalize.

An extension of the process or stage theories is the life cycle concept. The industry and the product life cycle have been espoused to explain the internationalization motive. According to this approach, the firm follows the various stages of the product of the industry life cycle. In the introduction stage, the product is produced only in the home country, and international activities, if any, may be limited to export. As the product reaches maturity, competition intensifies and the establishment of foreign manufacturing facilities becomes necessary in order for the firm to reduce its cost and compete effectively in foreign markets (O'Farrel *et al.*, 1988; Roboch and Simmonds, 1989).

A major assumption of the stage or process theory is the gradual accumulation of knowledge. In essence, the notion of organizational learning is fundamental to the success of the firm's internationalization strategy. Organizational learning in this context is the process of acquiring and assimilating new knowledge about the foreign market into the firm's pool of knowledge (Autio *et al.*, 2000). Two types of knowledge are critical to the firm's success in the international market: knowledge about the foreign market and entrepreneurial knowledge (ibid.). Zahra *et al.* (2000) suggest a third type of knowledge: technological knowledge. They suggest that the firm's technological learning process is critical to successful internationalization. Zahra *et al.* identify three dimensions of technological learning; breadth, depth and speed. These dimensions are influenced by a number of factors such as international, technological, cultural and geographical diversity. Furthermore technological learning is influenced by the choice of entry mode.

Advocates of the stage or process theories contend that acquisition of knowledge about foreign markets allows the firm to enhance its learning capabilities and thus reduces the uncertainty and risk, often associated with international business, as well as improving its competitive position (Roboch and Simmonds, 1989; Autio *et al.*, 2000).

However, a growing number of research studies have challenged the basic assumption of the process stage theories (Oviatt and McDougall, 1994; O'Farrel *et al.*, 1988; Schrader *et al.*, 2000; Autio and Sapienza, 2000). Some of these studies suggest that the process theory is too limited and provides a partial answer to the entrepreneur's or the firm's internationalization motive and process (Autio and Sapienza, 2000). A major criticism has been directed at the key tenet of the process theory: the notion that the internationalization process is incremental and occurs at a later stage of the firm's growth process. Indeed the theory does not explain the recent phenomenal growth of early internationalization of relatively new knowledge-based entrepreneurial firms. In many of these firms, international activities are initiated during the venture creation process or in the early stage of the venture growth.

This recent phenomenon has led Oviatt and McDougall (1994) to introduce a theory of internationalization of new ventures. The theory basically provides a framework to explain the rapid growth of new entrepreneurial ventures in the international market. Oviatt and McDougall's work confirm early research by O'Farrel *et al.* (1988), which suggests that the internationalization process is rapid and does not occur in an incremental process, as advanced by the process theory. Jones (1999) also suggests that the stage approach is not realistic, as it does not address the issues and characteristics of entrepreneurial small firms. These firms are opportunity-driven and as such they act fast when they see a good prospect.

The network approach
Research studies have also advanced the concept of organizational linkage or network to provide an explanation of the firm's internationalization motive and process (Coviello and McAuley, 1999; Jones, 1999). This approach focuses on the firm's ability to develop linkages with stakeholders such as customers and suppliers. A number of small business network models have been introduced in the literature. For example, Jones (1999) conducted an empirical study of 97 high-tech SMEs and identified three dimensions under which cross-border links are developed. Five types of SMEs were identified, based on their international activities.

Interorganizational linkage and networking provide convincing evidence of the development of strategic alliances and other forms of partnerships in the international market (Steensma *et al.*, 2000). A key objective of these strategic alliances is to spread cost and reduce the risk and uncertainty level involved in foreign markets.

Resource-based theories of internationalization
The entrepreneur's decision to go international has also been attributed to the availability of resources, or lack of them (Burgel and Murray, 1998; Westhead *et al.*, 1998; Almeida *et al.*, 2000; Ibrahim and McGuire, 2001). This approach is based on Penrose's (1980) work, which views the entrepreneurial firm as a collection of resources. These resources include financial, physical, technological and human resources. The more resources the entrepreneurial firm has, the more likely it will engage in international activities (Almeida *et al.*, 2000). Furthermore the choice of an entry mode to a foreign market is driven by the availability of resources (Burgel and Murray, 1998). For example, a small firm with limited resources may choose an export mode, while a firm with more resources is more likely to establish a foreign manufacturing base.

Advocates of the resource-based theory have also advanced a second approach to explain the motive for internationalization: basically entrepreneurs go international because of their limited resources. In other words, entrepreneurs venture into foreign markets in search of critical resources (Westhead *et al.*, 1998; Ibrahim and McGuire, 2001). This explanation is consistent with entrepreneurs' behaviour and characteristics as opportunity-driven.

Foreign direct investment theories
A number of theoretical contributions have been advanced to explain the decision and process of internationalization. These theories argue that the foreign investment decision is based for the most part on economic factors such as the investment level, transaction cost, competitive advan-

tage and location (Caves, 1971; Roboch and Simmonds, 1989; Dunning, 1988; Zacharakis, 1997).

A major theoretical contribution to the foreign direct investment theories comes from the market imperfections approach. This approach is based on the concept of competitive advantage. The firm pursues a foreign investment strategy because it enjoys a competitive advantage over local competitors in the foreign market. In other words, competitive advantage creates an imperfect market (Caves, 1971). Competitive advantage is achieved as a result of technological superiority, product differentiation and product innovation, among other things (Ibrahim, 1993). It is also achieved as a result of an industry oligopolistic structure.

An extension of the market imperfections approach is the international production theory. This theory argues that locational advantage drives the organization to invest in a particular foreign market (Dunning, 1988).

The foreign direct investment decision theories continue to shape much of our business thinking. However these theoretical contributions have proved to be too limited. Foreign direct investment theories seem to focus more on issues related to multinational firms than on small entrepreneurial ventures.

The population ecology approach
The motivation to internationalize has also been attributed to external forces. Advocates of the population ecology approach argue that external forces such as competition drive the entrepreneur to look for other opportunities in foreign markets in order to survive (Westhead *et al.*, 1998).

The decision to internationalize is perhaps the most important decision the entrepreneur will ever make. Many schools of thought have attempted to explain the entrepreneur's motive to internationalize and the process involved. However we believe that no one single contribution can claim to provide a realistic explanation of the internationalization process in the context of small business.

To gain a better insight on the entrepreneur's decision to internationalize, we must understand the entrepreneurial mind and characteristics. Indeed many schools of thought have been offered in the literature on the making of the entrepreneur. Most of these draw a picture of an individual driven by a host of environmental factors and personality traits.

Entrepreneurship research has identified a number of traits associated with entrepreneurs, such as the need for achievement, risk-taking propensity, innovations, locus of control and tolerance of ambiguity (Ibrahim and Ellis, 2002). It has also been argued that the choice of an entrepreneurship career is related to external factors such as culture. Dana (1993) and Shapero (1975) noted that some cultural groups demonstrate more entrepreneurial characteristics than others. The 'push–pull' theory in entrepreneurship argues that the motives for new venture creation are the result of external factors. Studies suggest that an individual is either pulled into entrepreneurship by positive factors in the environment such as new opportunities and potential elements in the industry, or pushed into it by negative elements such as being unable to find a job. Research on entrepreneurship has also revealed that entrepreneurs' previous experience increases the likelihood of success in new venture creation (Ibrahim and Goodwin, 1986). Family background has also been offered in the entrepreneurship literature to explain the individual's motive for starting a business. Kets de Vries (1977) noted that poor and troubled family relations might explain the weak compliance motive and thus the need to be independent in order to avoid authority figures.

In the entrepreneurship literature, entrepreneurs are depicted as those individuals who can identify an opportunity and marshal the resources to exploit it (Stevenson *et al.* 1989; Ibrahim and Ellis, 2002). Thus the entrepreneur's decision to venture to foreign markets should be viewed as part of the entrepreneurial process, to scan the market looking for new opportunities and to marshal the resources to exploit it (Zacharakis, 1997; Oviatt and McDougall, 1994).

It is in this context that we offer our conceptual framework. The entrepreneur's internationalization decision and process are seen as a result of a number of factors related to the entrepreneur's personality traits and background as well as to international business factors, as shown in Figure 8.1.

In essence, we believe entrepreneurs' internationalization decision and process is best understood by integrating theoretical frameworks of both entrepreneurship and international business. Indeed studies by Coviello and McAuley (1999) and Jones (1999) emphasize the need to integrate the various theoretical frameworks in the field in order to offer a more realistic approach to entrepreneurs' internationalization decision and process.

Conclusion

The recent growth of international entrepreneurship is phenomenal. Entrepreneurs are opportunity-driven, therefore internationalization is a key element of the entrepreneurial process. Many theories of internationalization were advanced to explain the firm's internationalization motive and process, but while these theoretical contributions have added much to our knowledge of international business, they tend to be too limited and to focus mostly on multinational business. This research argues that entrepreneurship is a complex phenomenon and therefore any attempt to explain the entrepreneur's motive and process for going international must address the entrepreneur's characteristics and background.

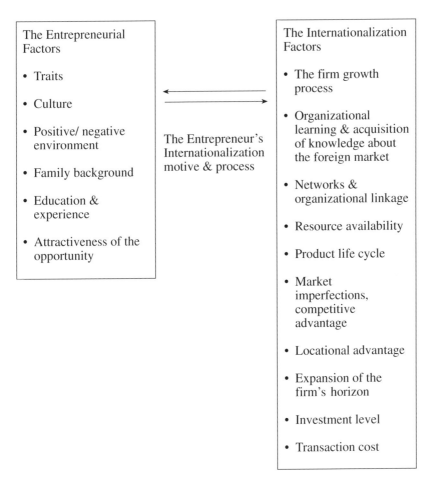

Figure 8.1 The entrepreneur's internationalization motive and process: a theoretical framework

This chapter offers a conceptual framework which integrates the theoretical contributions of both entrepreneurship and international business research. This framework is an attempt to provide a realistic explanation for the entrepreneur's internationalization motive and process.

References

Ahroni, Y. (1966), *The Foreign Investment Decision Process*, Boston: Harvard Business School.

Almeida, J., H. Sapienza and J. Michael (2000), 'Growth through internationalization: Patterns among British firms', *Frontiers of Entrepreneurship Research*, 402.

Autio, E. and Sapienza, H. (2000), 'Comparing process and born global perspectives in the international growth of technology-based new firms', *Frontiers of Entrepreneurship Research*, 413.

Autio, E. Sapienza, H. and Almeida, J. (2000), 'Effect of age at entry, knowledge intensity, and imitability on international growth', *Academy of Management Journal*, 43 (5) 909–24.

Brush, C. (1995), *International Entrepreneurship: The Effect of Firm Age on Motives for Internationalisation*, New York: Garland Publishing.

Burgel, O. and Murray, G. (1998), 'The international activities of British start-up companies in high-technology industries: differences between internationalizers and non-internationalizers', *Frontier of Entrepreneurship Research*, 449.

Caves, R. (1971), *International corporations: The industrial economics of foreign investment*, Cambridge, Mass.: MIT Press.

Coviello, N. and McAuley, A. (1999), 'Internationalisation and the smaller firm: A review of contemporary empirical research', *Management International Review*, 13 (3), 223–56.

Dana, L. (1993), 'An inquiry into culture and entrepreneurship: case studies of business creation among immigrants in Montreal', *Journal of Small Business Entrepreneurship*, Sept., 16–27.

Dunning, J. (1988), 'The eclectic paradigm of international production: A restatement and some possible extensions', *Journal of International Business Studies*, spring, 1–31.

Hitt, M., Ireland, D., Camp, S. and Sexton, D. (2001), 'Guest editor's introduction to the special issue: strategic entrepreneurship', *Strategic Management Journal*, 22, 479–92.

Ibrahim, A.B. (1993), 'Strategy types and firms' performance: An empirical investigation', *Journal of Small Business Strategy*, 5 (1), 13–22.

Ibrahim, A.B. and Ellis,W. (2002), *Entrepreneurship and Small Business Management*, 4th edn, Iowa: Kendall/ Hunt Publishing Company.

Ibrahim, A.B. and Goodwin, R. (1986), 'Perceived causes of success in small business', *Entrepreneurship Theory & Practice*, 11, 41–50.

Ibrahim, A.B. and McGuire, J. (2001), 'Technology transfer strategies for international entrepreneurs', *International Management*, 6 (1), 75–83.

Jones, M. (1999), 'The internationalisation of small high-tech firms', *Journal of international marketing*, 7 (4), 15–41.

Kets de Vries, M. (1977), 'The entrepreneurial personality: a person at the cross roads', *Journal of Management Studies*, XIV, 34–57.

McDougall, P. and Oviatt, B. (2000), 'International entrepreneurship: The intersection of two research paths', *Academy of Management Journal*, 43 (5), 902–6.

O'Farrel, P., Wood, P. and Zheng, Z. (1988), 'Internationalisation by business service SMEs: an inter-industry analysis', *International Small Business Journal*, 16 (2), 13–33.

Oviatt, B. and McDougall, P. (1994), 'Toward a theory of international new ventures', *Journal of International Business Studies*, 25 (1), 45–62.

Penrose, E. (1980), *The Growth of the Firm*, Oxford: Basil Blackwell Publishers.

Roboch, S. and Simmonds, K. (1989), *International Business and Multinational Enterprises*, 4th edn, Homewood, Ill: Irwin.

Shapero, A. (1975), 'The displaced uncomfortable entrepreneur', *Psychology Today*, November.

Shrader, R., Oviatt, B. and McDougall, P. (2000), 'How new ventures exploit trade-offs among international risk factors: lessons for accelerated internationalisation of the 21st century', *Academy of Management Journal*, 43, (6), 1227–47.

Steensma, K., Weaver, L. and Dickson, P. (2000), 'The influence of national culture on the formation of technology alliances by entrepreneurial firms', *Academy of Management Journal*, 43 (5), 951–73.

Stevenson, H., Roberts, M. and Grausbeck, H. (1989), *New Business Ventures and the Entrepreneur*, 3rd edn, Homewood, Ill: Irwin.

Westhead, P., Wright, M. and Ucbasaran, D. (1998), 'The internationalisation of new and small firms', *Frontier of Entrepreneurship Research*, 464.

Zacharakis, A. (1997), 'Entrepreneurial entry into foreign markets: A transaction cost perspective', *Entrepreneurship Theory and Practice*, 21 (3), 23–39.

Zahra, S., Ireland, D. and Hitt, M. (2000), 'International expansion by new venture firms: international diversity, mode of market entry, technological learning, and firm performance', *Academy of Management Journal*, 43, 925–50.

9 International entrepreneurship and internationalization: common threads

Lawrence S. Welch

Entrepreneurship and international entrepreneurship have come into vogue in recent times, alongside an interest in international new ventures or 'born globals' (Andersson, 2000; Madsen and Servais, 1997; McDougall and Oviatt, 2000; Oviatt and McDougall, 1994). In some of this new work, there has been a characterization of research on internationalization, from a process perspective, as being ill-equipped to explain the entrepreneurial strain of international activities, especially when it generates new companies that rapidly move into international operations. For example: 'Researchers at the intersection of entrepreneurship and internationalization have objected that the process view fails to explain entrepreneurial firms that go international early in their existence' (Autio *et al.* 2000: 909). One component of the critique of the process view, and its supposed inability to explain the role of entrepreneurial activities, is that internationalization researchers often are deemed to have ignored the importance of networks as an explanation for companies' moves into the international arena (Coviello and Martin, 1999). However, before such views become accepted as a true statement of thinking about internationalization from a process perspective, it is appropriate to go back to the earlier research on, and evolution of, ideas about internationalization, and to consider these in the light of the developing field of international entrepreneurship.

An important initial question, though, is: what is meant by the term 'international entrepreneurship'? This has been a concern of writers seeking to define, and refine, the field of international entrepreneurship. McDougall and Oviatt (2000: 903) have defined international entrepreneurship as 'a combination of innovative, proactive, and risk-seeking behavior that crosses national borders and is intended to create value in organizations'. This seems to encapsulate the thinking of many of the writers in the field, with an international focus added to the earlier concepts espoused by Schumpeter (1934), who emphasized business entrepreneurship as breaking new ground, in such areas as entering new markets, introducing new products, applying new methods of production and developing new sources of supply; and accepting the increased risks that this entailed. By its very nature, internationalization can seemingly be defined as entrepreneurial in these terms, particularly at the initial step into international operations, but also in the many later steps that are required to sustain internationalization, for example entry into new foreign markets, necessitating exposure to new cultures, different languages and a range of different ways of doing business.

Internationalization as entrepreneurial activity

The argument regarding the inability of the process view of internationalization to explain international entrepreneurial activity centres upon the emphasis on incrementalism, that individuals/companies are constrained by limited information about foreign markets, limited experience of international operations and a general concern not to be exposed to unacceptably high levels of risk and uncertainty. Risk and uncertainty were viewed as being accentuated by the extent to which foreign markets were different from the home market, difference being culturally based and summed up in the term 'psychic distance' (Johanson and Wiedersheim-Paul, 1975; Wiedersheim-Paul, 1972). As a result, it could be expected that, as a way of minimizing exposure to risk, companies would prefer to develop international operations first in countries that were closer in a psychic distance sense. This appeared to be borne out for Swedish firms, judging by a detailed study of four Swedish multinationals' internationalization over an extended period of time (Johanson and Wiedersheim-Paul, 1975). It was evident also in the internationalization patterns of Finnish manufacturing firms, examined around the same time, but on a far broader basis, encompassing close to the population of Finnish manufacturing firms (Luostarinen, 1979).

Early research on internationalization, from the process perspective, stressed the importance of information flows and contact patterns as being, in part, related to psychic distance, with physical distance potentially reinforcing this effect, as in the case of Australia and New Zealand, as they affected communication flows in a broad sense, and therefore the likelihood of relevant information or contact generating the commonly found pattern of unsolicited inquiries or orders leading to export entry (Bilkey and Tesar, 1977; Wiedersheim-Paul *et al.*, 1978). Distance effects on behaviour were seen as being accentuated by a preference for face-to-face contacts in the uncertainty of the international entry situation.

In the face of the constraining effects of a lack of knowledge and experience of international markets faced by many new exporters, it is little wonder that a number of early researchers saw the export start as a departure, as an innovation in business activity (Lee and Brasch, 1978; Johanson *et al.*, 1976). In this respect, the work of Simmonds and Smith (1968) was important in looking at the background of those involved in initiating the first export order by nine British firms. It was found that all had some experience in foreign countries. The nine firms were found to have 'a high degree of risk tolerance, aggressive drive, and profit motivation' (ibid.: 98), that was instrumental in taking them down the export path. Such a characterization appears to bear all the hallmarks of what today might be referred to as an entrepreneurial orientation.

Subsequent research, however, indicated that many of the firms embarking on exporting for the first time were anything but 'entrepreneurial' in orientation in the way they approached the new activity, as evidenced by the importance of unsolicited orders, and as shown in research on the type of internationally relevant activities during the pre-export stage, leading up to the export start (Wiedersheim-Paul *et al.*, 1978). The latter research on Australian companies revealed a wide range in the extent of activity, commitment and drive to achieve internationalization preceding its fulfilment. Some companies exhibited little or no interest in exporting, and almost 'fell' into it as a result of the intervention of outside change agents. Other companies took considerable time, and undertook many steps in the process of preparing for export entry, including foreign market visits, foreign market research and utilizing the government export assistance service. In general there appeared to be strong recognition of the risk involved in the step into exporting by the various companies, whatever the type and extent of background preparation for the move. Nevertheless the responses to this perception varied widely. Many of the companies committed little to the new activity, seeing it as a type of experimentation, thereby minimizing risk exposure, but ensuring that, if outcomes were unacceptable, it would not be difficult to withdraw from exporting, as some of the companies subsequently did. Research on Italian small companies indicates that this is not an unusual approach – in fact, many Italian firms displayed serial export entry and exit behaviour (Bonaccorsi, 1992). Also, during the pre-export stage, a number of Australian companies withdrew from the move towards export entry as a result of what was considered negative feedback from their explorations, such as logistical problems, higher costs than expected (particularly freight) and uncertainty about foreign market demand.

In seeking to understand these responses, researchers had been considering a wide range of explanations and fields of study, including information economics and an interest in the cost of information as a constraining factor on international activity (Carlson, 1973, 1974). From an early stage, though, because of the focus on internationalization as a process, information and knowledge were seen in terms of their effect on the approach of companies to international operations through time, rather than the more rigid comparative statics approach of economics. This generated an interest in the idea of experiential knowledge as earlier espoused by Penrose

(1959): experience of international markets was seen as being important in changing a company's ability to understand and handle increased commitments to international activity. As Carlson (1975: 8) stressed, on the basis of the Uppsala empirical work, 'the accumulation of knowledge of foreign operations seems more or less to follow a learning curve'. Perhaps more importantly, Johanson *et al.* (1976: 37) took these ideas about the role of knowledge a stage further, in effect closing the learning loop: 'an important aspect of experiential knowledge is that it enables us to perceive opportunities for new or enlarged business activities. Knowledge of these opportunities . . . serves as an input in the decision process that will eventually lead to commitment decisions'. Thus a dynamic or process model was being created which was reflected in the seminal article on internationalization by Johanson and Vahlne (1977), that has come to be viewed as the epitome of the so-called 'Uppsala School'. At the same time, it could be said that this early Uppsala work was establishing a link between knowledge and entrepreneurial activity in internationalization: knowledge, or more particularly knowledge change, was presented as a key factor in the preparedness of companies to take on new ventures and new risks – that is, to behave in an entrepreneurial way. Instead the Uppsala model has come to be depicted more in terms of incrementalism in a company's chain of foreign establishments. In general, a preoccupation with the 1977 article on internationalization may well have constrained reference to broader work by Uppsala researchers and others in the field at the time, which could be said to have stretched the process model in ways that aligned it more closely with some of the current approaches to international entrepreneurship. The characterization of the 'Uppsala stages model' as a rigid, deterministic pattern is a myopic view of the work at the time and has all the hallmarks of a convenient 'straw man' (Benito and Welch, 1994).

Behavioural explanations

Early researchers on internationalization were concerned with behavioural explanations of international activity, which were interlaced with the interest in information processes and learning. In this focus they were influenced by, but went beyond, the set of ideas which became known as 'the behavioural theory of the firm' (Cyert and March, 1963). For example, at the heart of Luostarinen's (1979) model of internationalization was a 'behavioural decision-making framework'. In this framework, the behavioural factors of limited perception, restrictive reaction, selective search and confined choice (driven by risk and uncertainty avoidance) were presented as generating so-called 'lateral rigidity' in decision-making processes in the international arena, thereby constraining forward momentum. Organizational learning was viewed as the key to reduction in the degree of lateral rigidity, and thereby facilitating new steps in foreign market operations. Importantly, it was stressed that the learning process might raise rigidity – for instance, by generating negative information about foreign market possibilities. Not surprisingly, there was an early recognition of the implications of these ideas: that such negative feedback might lead to stages of de-internationalization and re-internationalization, that is, far from the deterministic approach often claimed (Welch and Luostarinen, 1988; Welch and Wiedersheim-Paul, 1980a).

A behavioural model was used also to explain pre-export activity and the step into exporting, and the early stages of exporting (Welch and Wiedersheim-Paul, 1980a; Wiedersheim-Paul *et al.*, 1978). In this model there is a strong emphasis on the backgrounds of individual decision makers as drivers of the export entry process. This is in line with some recent approaches to exploring the link between entrepreneurial behaviour and internationalization, stressing the role of individuals. For example, using a study of a small number of Swedish firms, Andersson (2000: 77) concluded that 'entrepreneurs' intentions and persistence in carrying out different strategies are decisive for [the] firms' early internationalization'. Cases emerged from the Australian study of pre-export behaviour in which the decision maker was able to utilize international experience, knowledge and contacts (gained outside the company) to move their company rapidly into international operations: what would be described in current parlance as 'born globals'. For some there was the natural advantage of having been born and having lived in another country so that, after migration to Australia, to export back to the 'home' country was perceived as a relatively simple step. While seemingly highly entrepreneurial, because of the rapidity of the move into exporting, in reality it was seen as a low-risk activity. In contrast, for those with only Australian experience, or even regional experience within Australia, when receiving interest, or an order, from a foreign company, to respond required a large step – developing foreign activities – and was typically seen as a high-risk move (Welch and Wiedersheim-Paul, 1980b). Thus the speed of the move into the international arena was not necessarily an indicator of the extent of entrepreneurship involved in internationalization. Clearly, too, internationalization researchers were seeking to understand and explain examples of the born global phenomenon, emphasizing behavioural and network aspects.

Networks
Some of the recent literature on international entrepreneurial activity has focused on the importance of networks, particularly personal networks, as key explanatory factors (Andersson, 2000; Coviello and Martin, 1999). This is not surprising given that it is through networks that critical information

and contacts relevant to foreign markets are developed and influence on behaviour (Ford, 1990). However this was recognized and stressed in the early work on internationalization. For example, Wiedersheim-Paul *et al.* (1978: 49) commented: 'The export start can be categorized as an orientation process and is therefore especially dependent on face-to-face contacts and other types of informal contacts.' Further Welch and Wiedersheim-Paul (1980b: 9) noted, in the Australian context, that 'as the firm's communication network expands interstate, there is a greater likelihood of it being exposed to export market contacts'. The early thinking about the role of networks was influenced by research in economic geography on 'contact systems', information flows, search behaviour and their links to the spatial aspects of industrial patterns (Pred, 1974; Tornqvist, 1970). Subsequent research, including that in the area of international entrepreneurship, seems to support this role: that the ability to undertake seemingly entrepreneurial activity in the international arena depends, in part, on the quality and accessibility of a firm's (or staff's) networks.

The criticality of the personal networks of key decision makers was illustrated in the case of an Australian asparagus-exporting company, much lauded in the press as an example of a successful, internationally entrepreneurial SME (small/medium-sized enterprise). On the basis of research into the company, McGaughey *et al.* (1997: 179) concluded: 'Much of the ability of the company to initiate and carry through international operations resided in the decision-makers' personal networks.' The company had been established specifically to export asparagus to the Japanese market: a quintessential example of the born global phenomenon. The two owner-founders brought together a background of knowledge, experience and networks in the asparagus farming industry and international trading in food products, which meant that much of the uniqueness of the task of export entry, and thereby perceived risk, was removed. Nevertheless experience and contacts in the Japanese market were lacking, even though a very real market opportunity had been exposed by a visit there. There was a recognition of the gap in supply – local and imports – as a result of the seasonal down period in northern hemisphere production, along with the demanding requirements of the Japanese market with regard to product characteristics. The deficiency in Japanese networks and experience was partially overcome by utilizing the networks of the Australian trade promotion body, Austrade, which had a Japanese office and had for some time been working on programmes to facilitate the development of Australian exports of agricultural products to Japan. The company eventually 'used one main distributor in each of Tokyo and Osaka, as well as some smaller ones from time to time. Assistance in finding these was obtained from Austrade's Japan office' (ibid.: 170).

The risk of the venture was further reduced by the way that the founders were able to organize payments for shipments such that financial exposure was miniscule, with almost no personal financial outlay by the founders. Taken as a whole, this case, which on the surface looked to be an example of a highly entrepreneurial step into the international arena, demonstrated that there is far more involved than the overt act of international entry itself, and that there is a limit to how far individuals/companies may be prepared to leap into the unknown. The incrementalism of the process model could be developed away from the company, in the background experience and networks of individuals, or of those that they are able to tap into, as shown in the early research on international entry (Simmonds and Smith, 1968; Wiedersheim-Paul *et al.*, 1978) and in the later work of Madsen and Servais (1997) and their research model of born globals. Again the meaning of entrepreneurship in internationalization is thrown into question. For example, though awkward, it would appear that to equate the born global phenomenon with entrepreneurship may be far too simplistic.

International franchising
While the bulk of the focus of early research on internationalization was on exporting, which led to foreign direct investment in many cases, research had begun to extend into services and other forms of foreign operation, such as licensing, franchising and management contracts (Sharma, 1983; Tesar, 1977; Walker and Etzel, 1973). International franchising is interesting to consider because it is often viewed as having a strong component of entrepreneurial activity, driving a powerful expansion ethos (Welch, 1990). Many of the franchising chains reflect the desire of individuals to develop and exploit new products, services and business concepts. However research on Australian franchisors demonstrated again that the apparent high degree of entrepreneurship, when placed in the context of international entry, showed a pattern of entry, a process, similar in many respects to that found for exporting companies (ibid.). As with exporters, unsolicited approaches were the primary stimulus for the move into international franchising. Of critical importance, though, in understanding the response to the opportunities presented by such approaches, was the background experience and attitudes of the key decision makers. In a number of cases, individuals had their initial experience of international franchising through acting as franchisees for international franchising chains. As a result, after starting their own franchising chains, the international move was seen as almost a natural progression of their domestic franchising operations. The pre-international stage for the Australian franchisors, in a similar way to exporters', showed a wide range of activities and degrees of preparation for, and commitment to, the international step – from almost accidental

involvement to carefully planned and executed foreign market penetration. In general, franchisors appeared to be undertaking international entry faster than exporters, but it would be difficult to characterize the process as more, or less, entrepreneurial than that for exporters.

Inward–outward internationalization

In the development of ideas about internationalization, inward processes have received relatively limited attention. Nevertheless there was interest in this aspect from the earliest stages, although it is more recently that the issue has been rediscovered and advanced as a result of viewing it from the perspective of potential connections and influences between the inward and outward sides (Haakansson and Wootz, 1975; Korhonen, 1999; Luostarinen, 1970; Welch and Luostarinen, 1993). The issue may be particularly important when considering the entrepreneurial basis of internationalization, given the research which indicates that many firms begin their first international activity on the inward side, as importers, licensees, franchisees (see above) and the like. Indeed, in a large study of Finnish SMEs, it was revealed that more than half internationalized first on the inward side (Korhonen *et al.*, 1996). Clearly this changes how the international entry process should be viewed. For example, a seemingly rapid and entrepreneurial move into exporting may be explained by developments on the inward side, from which an export order could have emanated. This illustrates the importance of investigating preceding processes in seeking to explain international entrepreneurial behaviour. In the case of exporting, the primary entrepreneurial action may lie in the development of international sources of supply, as a prelude to any outward steps. As some of the emerging research indicates, the processes leading from inward to outward operations can be subtle and removed in time within the firm, with limited awareness of their operation (Korhonen, 1999).

Emerging ideas about internationalization

The investigation of inward–outward connections in internationalization is an example of the variety of new work which is broadening and refurbishing ideas about, and reinvigorating conceptual development of, internationalization from a process perspective. Another example is the reconsideration of operation mode development in internationalization, bearing in mind that the early Uppsala work focused on this as a way of depicting the pattern of internationalization (Johanson and Wiedersheim-Paul, 1975). This new work stresses the need to view operation modes as potentially being used in combination, as commonly occurs, in the process of exploiting foreign markets. From this perspective, important changes in foreign market servicing may not involve a simple replacement of one mode with another, but could be handled by mode addition to, or deletion from, a package. Research on Danish companies' activities in south-east Asia indicated that this was a common approach, and had an important impact on the character of these companies' expansion in the region: mode addition could be seen as a contributor to incrementalism in the companies' operations (Petersen and Welch, 2002; Petersen *et al.*, 2001). Burgel and Murray (2000: 33) have commented that 'within the emerging research stream of international entrepreneurship, curiously little attention has been devoted to the empirical analysis of foreign market entry forms'.

It is not the purpose of this chapter to review all of the newer developments in thinking about internationalization, but this limited exploration provides an indication of the type of emerging explanations of different aspects of internationalization. Much of this work would appear to have important implications for understanding the nature of international entrepreneurship.

Conclusion
The discussion of international entrepreneurship and internationalization from a process perspective might well lead to a conclusion that the initial ideas about international entrepreneurship are conceptually rooted in the development of ideas about internationalization, even though the word 'entrepreneurship' was rarely used. Rather than being in conflict, therefore, it can be argued that international entrepreneurship and internationalization have a common heritage and a concern about similar issues. It is clear that there was an early interest in the role of the individual decision maker and the circumstances surrounding what appeared, in some cases, to be large leaps in international operations. Behavioural and network explanations, along with a focus on the way firms dealt with the issue of risk, were all part of the mix in seeking to explain internationalization. The net was cast far wider than the so-called 'Uppsala model', as represented by the seminal article of Johanson and Vahlne (1977), the popularity of which has probably constrained interest in the broader set of ideas which was emerging at the time, and to some extent this remains a problem. Clearly there is much that a broader perspective of the process model of internationalization can contribute to an understanding of international entrepreneurship.

The question of what entrepreneurship means in the context of internationalization remains a difficult issue for both perspectives. Knight (2000) investigates the impact of entrepreneurial orientation on the international behaviour of a sample of SMEs in the USA. He stresses attitude and action components in developing a definition of entrepreneurial orientation: 'it is associated with opportunity seeking, risk taking, and decision action catalyzed by a strong leader or an organization' (ibid.: 18), and is reflected in a more proactive approach to foreign market penetration. Regarding the latter aspect, it was found that 'SMEs that respond to globalization and prepare in advance to enter foreign markets tend to enjoy better performance. Internationalization preparation entails conducting market research, committing resources to international marketing operations, and adapting products to suit conditions overseas' (ibid.: 29–30).

This link between entrepreneurship, proactive international behaviour and performance was of concern in the early work on internationalization, involving the active-to-passive profiling of exporters and pre-exporting companies in their approach to foreign market activities, with an emphasis on assessing what this meant for internationalization performance (Welch and Wiedersheim-Paul, 1980a; Wiedersheim-Paul *et al.*, 1978). However this still leaves us with the question of what entrepreneurship means in this context. Is it a state of mind, defined by action, involving proactive behaviour, requiring the taking of risks without full knowledge? It will always be difficult to draw the line on the extent of proactive preparation for international entry that is consistent with an entrepreneurial orientation. In addition, it could be argued that far greater risk is taken on when firms enter foreign markets without careful preparation and adequate knowledge, or even act contrary to received knowledge. Thus, while an entrepreneurial orientation may lead to a more active and prepared approach to international entry, extent of preparation could never be the definition of it. Also it may reflect a security-conscious, risk reduction approach.

The nature of this conundrum is evident in the early work on exporting. In this research many exporters were found to have become involved in exporting with little or no preparation for the move, displayed limited commitment and, despite achieving export sales, remained passive in their approach to the activity, so that there was almost an inevitability about their ultimate withdrawal from exporting operations: a type of vicious circle had been created (Wiedersheim-Paul *et al.*, 1978). While the fact that such firms took on a new marketing initiative, in the face of limited knowledge and with considerable perceived risk, might seem to justify the 'entrepreneurial' label, the way many of the companies approached the new activity would seem to negate this. The role of external change agents in exposing exporting possibilities and generating interest in them was shown to be important and, to some extent, this replaced internal, company-driven approaches to internationalization, thereby, it could be said, removing a significant part of the entrepreneurial role and ensuring the type of passive responses often found. Even in such cases, though, one cannot assess the outcomes simply on the basis of the seemingly non-entrepreneurial way in which the exporting option was exposed. Some firms did pick up the international opportunity, particularly when the background of key individuals had created a stronger predisposition towards international operations: for example, through international experience. In a similar vein to Knight's (2000) depiction of entrepreneurial orientation in SME internationalization, the early behavioural model of exporting exposes action and attitude components of entrepreneurship, but with a strong emphasis on processes connected to the firm's preceding activities, as well as the background of key individuals.

Clearly the exposure of international market opportunities may occur at an early stage after a company's formation, perhaps leading to a born global player, or much later. Early exposure would appear to be more likely in an environment today where the Internet has created the potential of ready-made connections to global markets, even for small firms. Earlier international entry, however, may not necessarily denote a stronger entrepreneurial orientation amongst exporters.

The examination of entrepreneurship and internationalization through the lens of export entry illustrates something of the complexity of this issue, but also it provides an indication of the contribution which can be made by the process model to the understanding of international entrepreneurship and international new ventures. Indeed that is the message of this chapter: rather than simplistic dismissal of the process model, there is much to learn from it. The more recent research on inward–outward connections in internationalization is an example of the way this potential contribution lies not only in the earlier research which has been the focus of much of this chapter. For many companies, inward internationalization may be the critical arena for entrepreneurial activities which explain eventual outward international activities and related networks.

It must be said, of course, that there is much to be learnt in the reverse direction: involving the movement of ideas from international entrepreneurship to the process model. For example, behavioural explanations of international entry and the focus on key decision makers, explored in early research on internationalization, have tended to be picked up more strongly in some of the international entrepreneurship literature. If not a merging of the fields, there is considerable potential for a stronger two-way flow between them.

References

Andersson, S. (2000), 'The internationalisation of the firm from an entrepreneurial perspective', *International Studies of Management and Organization*, 30 (1), 63–92.

Autio, E., H.J. Sapienza and J.G. Almeida (2000), 'Effects of age at entry, knowledge intensity, and instability on international growth', *Academy of Management Journal*, 43 (5), 909–24.

Benito, G.R.G. and L.S. Welch (1994), 'Foreign Market Servicing: Beyond Choice of Entry Mode', *Journal of International Marketing*, 2(2), 7–27.

Bilkey, W.J. and G. Tesar (1977), 'The export behavior of smaller-sized Wisconsin firms', *Journal of International Business Studies*, 8 (1), 93–8.

148   *Conceptual chapters*

Bonaccorsi, A. (1992), 'On the relationship between firm size and export intensity', *Journal of International Business Studies*, 23 (4), 605–635.

Burgel, O. and G.C. Murray (2000), 'The international market entry choices of start-up companies in high-technology industries', *Journal of International Marketing*, 8 (2), 33–62.

Carlson, S. (1973), 'Investment in knowledge and the cost of information', in *Annales Academiae Regiae Scientarum Upsaliensis*, Stockholm: Almqvist and Wiksell, 15–28.

Carlson, S. (1974), 'International transmission of information and the business firm', *The Annals*, 412 (2), 55–63.

Carlson, S. (1975), *How Foreign Is Foreign Trade?*, Uppsala: Acta Universitatis Upsaliensis, Studia Oeconomiae Negotiorum 11.

Coviello, N.E. and K.A.-M. Martin (1999), 'Internationalisation of service SMEs: an integrated perspective from the engineering consulting sector', *Journal of International Marketing*, 7 (4), 42–66.

Cyert, R.M. and J.G. March (1963), *A Behavioral Theory of the Firm*, Englewood Cliffs, NJ: Prentice-Hall.

Ford, D. (ed.) (1990), *Understanding Business Markets: Interaction, Relationships and Networks*, London: Academic Press.

Haakansson, H. and B. Wootz (1975), 'Supplier selection in an international environment – an experimental study', *Journal of Marketing Research*, 12 (1), 10–16.

Johanson, J. and J.-E. Vahlne (1977), 'The internationalisation process of the firm: a model of knowledge development and increasing foreign market commitments', *Journal of International Business Studies*, 8 (1), 23–32.

Johanson, J. and F. Wiedersheim-Paul (1975), 'The internationalisation of the firm – four Swedish cases', *Journal of Management Studies*, 12 (3): 305–22.

Johanson, J., L.-G. Mattsson, P. Sanden and J.-E. Vahlne (1976), 'The role of knowledge in the internationalisation of business', *Uppsala University 500 years*, Uppsala: Acta Universitatis Upsaliensis.

Knight, G. (2000), 'Entrepreneurship and marketing strategy: the SME under globalization', *Journal of International Marketing*, 8 (2), 12–32.

Korhonen, H. (1999), *Inward–Outward Internationalisation of Small and Medium Enterprises*, Helsinki: Helsinki School of Economics and Business Administration.

Korhonen, H., R. Luostarinen and L.S. Welch (1996), 'Internationalisation of SMEs: Inward–Outward Patterns and Government Policy', *Management International Review*, 36(4), 315–29.

Lee, W.-Y. and J.J. Brasch (1978), 'The adoption of export as an innovative strategy', *Journal of International Business Studies*, 9 (1), 85–93.

Luostarinen, R. (1970), *Foreign Operations of the Firm*, Helsinki: Helsinki School of Economics.

Luostarinen, R. (1979), *Internationalisation of the Firm*, Heksinki: Academiae Oeconomicae Helsingiensis, Helsinki School of Economics.

Madsen, T.K. and P. Servais (1997), 'The internationalisation of born globals: an evolutionary process?', *International Business Review*, 6 (6), 561–83.

McDougall, P.P. and B. Oviatt (2000), 'International entrepreneurship: the intersection of two research paths', *Academy of Management Journal*, 43 (5), 902–6.

McGaughey, S., D. Welch and L. Welch (1997), 'Managerial influences and SME internationalisation', in I. Bjorkman and M. Forsgren (eds), *The Nature of the International Firm*, Copenhagen: Copenhagen Business School Press, 165–88.

Oviatt, B. and P.P. McDougall (1994), 'Toward a theory of international new ventures', *Journal of International Business Studies*, 25 (1), 45–64.

Penrose, E.T. (1959), *The Theory of the Growth of the Firm*, Oxford: Basil Blackwell.

Petersen, B. and L.S. Welch (2002), 'Foreign Operation Mode Combinations and Internationalisation', *Journal of Business Research*, 55 (2), 157–62.

Petersen B., L.S. Welch and K.V. Nielsen (2001), 'Resource Commitment to Foreign Markets: The Establishment Patterns of Danish Firms in South-East Asian Markets', in S. Gray, S.L. McGaughey and W.R. Purcell (eds), *Asia–Pacific Issues in International Business*, Cheltenham, UK and Northampton, MA, USA: Edward Elgar, 7–27.

Pred, A. (1974), 'Industry, information and city systems interdependencies', in F.E.I. Hamilton (ed.), *Spatial Perspectives on Industrial Organization and Decision-Making*, London: John Wiley.

Schumpeter, J.A. (1934), *The Theory of Economic Development*, Cambridge, MA: Harvard University Press.

Sharma, D.D. (1983), *Swedish Firms and Management Contracts*, Uppsala: Acta Universitatis Upsaliensis, Studia Oeconomiae Negotiorum.

Simmonds, K. and H. Smith (1968), 'The first export order: a marketing innovation', *British Journal of Marketing*, 2 (Summer), 93–100.

Tesar, G. (1977), 'Corporate internationalisation strategy through licensing arrangements in industrial marketing', paper presented at the annual meeting of the Academy of Marketing Science, Akron, Ohio, 4–6 May.

Tornqvist, G. (1970), 'Contact systems and regional development', *Lund Studies in Geography*, ser. B 35, Lund: Gleerup.

Walker, B.J. and M.J. Etzel (1973), 'The internationalisation of U.S. franchise systems', *Journal of Marketing*, 37 (2), 38–46.

Welch, L.S. (1990), 'Internationalisation by Australian franchisors', *Asia Pacific Journal of Management*, 7 (2), 101–21.

Welch, L.S. and R. Luostarinen (1988), 'Internationalisation: Evolution of a Concept', *Journal of General Management*, 14(2), 34–55.

Welch, L.S. and R. Luostarinen (1993), 'Inward–Outward Connections in Internationalisation', *Journal of International Marketing*, 1(1), 44–56.

Welch, L.S. and F. Wiedersheim-Paul (1980a), 'Initial exports – a marketing failure?', *Journal of Management Studies*, 17 (3), 333–44.

Welch, L.S. and F. Wiedersheim-Paul (1980b), 'Domestic expansion: internationalisation at home', *Essays in International Business*, 2 (December), 1–31.

Wiedersheim-Paul, F. (1972), *Uncertainty and Economic Distance – Studies in International Business*, Uppsala: Almquist and Wiksell.

Wiedersheim-Paul, F., H.C. Olson and L.S. Welch (1978), 'Pre-export activity: the first step in internationalisation', *Journal of International Business Studies*, 9 (1), 47–58.

10 The praxeological concept of international entrepreneurship

J. Patrick Gunning

The dual aim of this chapter is to summarize the theory of praxeological entrepreneurship that I have been developing in recent research and to show its relevance to international economics. In my 1990 book, I used the term 'new subjectivism' to refer to Ludwig von Mises's *praxeology*, or theory of action (Mises, 1966). I defined entrepreneurship in terms of the method one must use to identify and elucidate the properties of action in the market economy. I wrote that 'Entrepreneurship is that part of economic interaction under the conditions specified in the definition of the market economy that cannot be represented by robots' (Gunning, 1990: 85). To identify and elucidate its properties, one must use the method of contrasting interaction in the market economy with an image of a robot economy, from which such interaction is necessarily absent. I proceeded to derive what I called three fundamental categories of entrepreneurial action: appraisement of factors of production, undertaking and uncertainty bearing. To appraise factors means to identify them and to estimate the 'net benefits of using a prospective factor according to a production plan' (Gunning, 1997: 176). I claimed that economics assumes that every normal human being possesses these categories.

Identifying and elucidating the properties of entrepreneurship is important in economics because it is the first step in dealing with the enormous complexity of the market economy. To identify patterns in this complex, we begin by building simple images of the market economy based on the assumption that everyone is an entrepreneur: that is, that everyone is a normal human actor. In my book, I argued that, to ensure that our images reflect this assumption while at the same time simplifying the complexity of the market economy interaction, we must employ images of 'entrepreneur economies', in which some subjects are robots that operate according to algorithms and others are 'fully integrated entrepreneurs'.

Entrepreneurship and praxeological economics

I briefly summarized this view of entrepreneurship in my 1997 paper. I defined entrepreneurship as

> the willingness to bet one's time and/or money that one's appraisals of factors are superior to the appraisals of others. To fit this definition into the saving–

production-consumption nexus, we must add that the bet contributes in some way to the production of goods to satisfy consumers' wants. (Ibid.: 175–6)

At the end of the paper, I described my previous work by saying that

> I have tried to elaborate and expand these ideas in an effort to construct an image of entrepreneurship that we can trace directly to distinctly human action. I wanted a concept of entrepreneurship that embodies all of the distinctly human action in the market economy. This is the kind of concept that I believe Mises had in mind when he wrote about the function of the entrepreneur. I have called this the new subjectivist concept of the entrepreneur. (Ibid.: 187)

In my more recent manuscripts, I have replaced the label 'new subjectivist' with the term 'praxeological'. Briefly, praxeological entrepreneurship refers to distinctly human action under the conditions of the pure market economy. It refers more specifically to the actions of appraisement, undertaking and uncertainty bearing by individuals who are assumed to possess imagination, creativity and inventiveness. I have also suggested the term 'praxeological economics' to refer to a study of the market economy that makes praxeological entrepreneurship its foundation.

In building its basic theory, praxeological economics, like economics generally, assumes a specific set of market economy conditions: private property rights, free enterprise, a stable money and specialization. With the exception of specialization, these conditions are the same for everyone. For example, private property rights implies that everyone faces the same laws regarding the acquisition and disposition of the items and control over actions defined as property. Free enterprise means that all actors are equally permitted by law to negotiate any business or employment agreement. In the eyes of the law, there are no restrictions on movement from one place to another and the relevant law is identical in all locations.

Thus the starting point of economics is an image of interaction under a kind of ideal law. Under it, people are not treated differently because (1) they were born in one location or another or (2) they are classified as having a particular ethnicity, religion, sex, age and so on. More generally we assume that the laws defining private property rights and free enterprise do not discriminate in favour of particular classes of individuals. We deliberately disregard discriminatory treatment in order to develop images that are simple enough to illustrate the general patterns that are present, to a greater or lesser extent, in all of the more capitalistic societies. Later, having identified the most important patterns, we turn our attention to the task of understanding real capitalist societies. At that stage, we must modify our images to take account of the different legal statuses of different individuals.

In building images of the market economy, praxeological economics also assumes that everyone faces the same monetary regime. We shall have little to say about that assumption in this chapter.

International economics

The subject of international economics is a special field within the broader field of economics. Its focus is not the market economy but the international economy. Praxeological economics defines the difference between these from the standpoint of entrepreneurship. From this standpoint, there are two key differences: (1) different nations have different property rights, free enterprise conditions and monetary regimes; and (2) the property rights and free enterprise conditions (and possibly the freedom to use money in particular ways) differ according to an individual's citizenship status and location. Individuals acting in the role of the entrepreneur who are citizens (and/or who act in one location) are treated differently from those who are not citizens (and/or who act in another location).[1] The focus in this chapter is on the second difference. Before discussing it further, let us briefly review the history of progress from the point of view suggested by the praxeological concept of international entrepreneurship.

A brief history of entrepreneurship-driven progress in the international economy

Those people who are in a position to take advantage of it are in the midst of a period of historically unprecedented growth in technology and potential well-being. The visible evidence of this includes progress in transport in overland carriage, shipping, aviation and space travel; progress in communication from handwriting to computer graphics, from typeset printing to computer graphic design, and from overland mail delivery, to telegraph, to satellite-relayed messages delivered to a computer screen; progress in medicine and, beyond that, in life extension; progress in agricultural productivity; and progress in materials development which facilitated the other types of progress. A catalogue of these achievements is unnecessary. Technological growth is evident to anyone who pays attention to these industries.

Although the inventors and innovators in some nations were definite pioneers in this growth, it spread quickly to those nations whose leaders have allowed their people to interact with the pioneers. The leaders of a nation can do more than merely permit their citizens to gain from advances that have occurred in other nations. If they develop institutions that are conducive to progress, their citizens will be able to become pioneers themselves. Accordingly, after World War II, as the USA opened its trade to several Asian countries, and as an increasing number of nations became part of the global trading club following the General Agreement on Tariffs and Trade (GATT) and the World Trade Organisation (WTO), individuals in an increasing number of countries have made contributions to technological advance. Entrepreneurship has 'globalized'. The imaginative, creative and inventive activities associated with the distinctly human action of individuals in an increasing number of countries have contributed to progress not only in their own countries but also in their trading partners' countries.

This process of globalization has not proceeded along a straight path. As the progressing empires of the early capitalist era set out on their adventures to acquire resources and colonize territories occupied by militarily weaker peoples, their agents encountered a wide variety of different groups. Many of the people lived in small family groups, clans, tribes and small villages. From the standpoint of global technology, their daily activities contributed virtually nothing to the progress and development of their neighbours, including the colonizers. Occasionally the colonizers learned about new products and new methods of production from such people; the indigenous people also learned from the colonizers. Rarely, however, did the indigenous people invent products or methods of production that were totally new to both themselves and the colonizers.

The colonizers sometimes encountered more organized empires, albeit with inferior military might. In this case there was a choice: trade or conquer. When they chose trade, the result was trade between the merchant traders of the technologically advanced empire and either government agents of the newly-discovered empire or individuals whose actions were strictly controlled by the empire's government. Such arrangements proved unstable since it was profitable to circumvent the government's restrictions. Smuggling and other black market activities occurred, which undermined the emperor's power. So the emperor tried to block it. The result was often war. Seldom did the two empires become sufficient 'partners in trade' to enable their citizens to profit reciprocally from the invention in each empire of new products and methods of production.

During the long period of colonization and appropriation by militarily superior empires, the location of national boundaries was continually brought into question. Often the result was war. In other words, the expanding empires competed not only economically but militarily. They battled both the indigenous people and other empires for territory. The result was insecure private property rights and stiff restrictions against foreign free enterprise in the conquered lands. For example, the governments of Europe often sanctioned piracy by their own citizens against the merchant shippers of other empires. And the desire to conquer the territory currently in the possession of rivals, rather than to colonize new territory, was occasionally the primary goal of national leaders.

International conflict was not the only factor that hampered the development of a global trading system during the past 600-or-so years. Capitalism in the empires themselves was often not strong. The most technologically advanced nations only gradually shifted from a set of domestic laws, which helped perpetuate a system of class and privilege, to a system of relatively equally-applied private property rights and free enterprise. Even today, this shift is far from complete and it varies among the more capitalistic countries.

This era of international instability ended abruptly with World War II. In the years that followed the war, two factors played an important role in the development of a global economy. First, the winners of the war, for the most part, came to promote the principle that peace requires respect for national boundaries where they exist and the creation of nations with boundaries where they do not. In the non-communist world, the great empires gradually transformed many of their previous colonies into nations by granting independence and trying to establish and defend distinct national boundaries. Although the communist countries did not participate, the balance of power during the cold war mitigated against 'undue' expansionism by the militarily stronger nations, thereby continuing the acceptance of the distinct national boundaries. Gradually the post-World War II boundaries in the non-communist world came to be respected, for the most part.

Second, the winners promoted relatively free trade and economic interdependence. The Lend Lease programme and the relatively free import policy of the USA enabled previously belligerent nations like Japan and West Germany gradually to emerge from the devastation that they suffered during the war and to become leaders in the new world trading system. The government officials in these nations also developed a strong motivation to continue the new trading system and to take steps to reduce the probability of war. The same was true over the longer period for nations and territories like South Korea, Hong Kong, Taiwan and Singapore. International trading agreements, spearheaded by the victors of World War II, also played an important role. Many of the nations that came into being after the war were incorporated into GATT and the WTO. Some also joined regional trading unions like the European Union. The vast North American region also took large steps towards becoming a trading union. Later, as the Soviet Union collapsed, some of the former members of the Soviet Bloc joined the system. Other countries in the Far East, South America and Africa tried to follow this lead. The result is that many nations moved rapidly from relative isolation to a mode of living that was largely integrated with the economies of other nations. Broadly speaking, there has been a surge of technological progress in those countries that have joined the world trading system. This surge is highlighted by the contrast with countries, excepting those with natural resource wealth, that have not joined and that, for one reason or another, have failed to institute conditions associated with the market economy.

The reason for progress in the countries that (a) have developed an internal system of private property rights and free enterprise and (b) have joined the world trading system is, of course, *distinctly human action*. In other words, it is entrepreneurship. Joining the world trading system has enabled individuals in member countries to enjoy the benefits of entrepreneurship in other member countries and has, broadly speaking, enabled ordinary people in each member country to gain from the widening of competition. From this point of view, it can be said that 'international entrepreneurship' has been the main 'engine of growth' for the global economy just as it is, by definition, the main 'engine of growth' in the pure market economy.

Plan of the chapter
To achieve the goal of showing the relevance of praxeological entrepreneurship to international economics, we must accomplish two sub-tasks: describe the praxeological concept of entrepreneurship and its application to the market economy, and apply the concept to an international setting. The next section of this chapter describes praxeological entrepreneurship and the method used to derive various patterns of economic interaction in the pure market economy. The third section identifies various procedures that can be used to apply the concept of praxeological entrepreneurship to the problems of international economics. It presents an addendum to the principle of comparative advantage, it describes a procedure for analysing a nation's trade barriers, and it shows how to use the concept of praxeological entrepreneurship to compare a two-nation global pure market economy in which nations have different policies towards liability for pollution.

Praxeological entrepreneurship and the method of economics
It is obvious that technological progress is the product of 'distinctly human action'. We do not observe progress of this sort among other species of animals. Nevertheless the mere existence of human beings does not guarantee progress. Today's world still contains functioning hunter–gatherer societies. And there is widespread poverty, occasional starvation, illiteracy and general misery in societies in which the cultures are way beyond the stages of the hunters and gatherers. Being distinctly human is not enough. To achieve the progress that we have observed in recent times, groups must have 'institutions' that make it possible for distinctly human action to have this particular manifestation. In short, technological progress in the global economy has been caused by distinctly human action *and* institutions.

Praxeology (the study of distinctly human action) and economics
Mises used the term 'praxeology' to refer to the logical extension of the work done by the classical and neoclassical economists (Mises, 1966: 1–3). Following Adam Smith, these writers studied the various causes and complements of the wealth of nations. By the end of the nineteenth century, the best economists understood that, to explain the growth of wealth and technological progress, one had to account for the institutions of capitalism. They set out to build models of the essential characteristics, or conditions, of these institutions and of the interaction they believed would occur if they were present. In those models, they assumed that individuals make choices on the basis of self-interest. Mises recognized that the systematic building of such models was something totally new in the field of human knowledge. Moreover he argued that the economic procedure used to understand action under the conditions of capitalism is also the proper one for studying human action and interaction under all sorts of assumed conditions. He proceeded to deepen the methodological underpinnings of economics by substituting the concept of 'action' for that of 'choice in one's self-interest' and by exploring the epistemological status of the 'action' concept. This enabled him to support his contention that economics is a *branch* of a broader, yet-to-develop praxeology. Whereas praxeology deals with action in general, economics deals with action and interaction under the conditions of the market economy.

The task faced by those who aim to develop the science of economics as a branch of praxeology is to rework the images and models of economics based on self-interested choice so that action becomes the foundation of the images. The problem with the concept of 'self-interested choice' is that the builders of models developed on the basis of this assumption too often disregarded the imagination, creativity and inventiveness of human actors. They neglected the fact that economists can only make educated guesses about a small portion of goals of individuals and the alternative means of achieving them that the individuals perceive.

Mises believed that, if economists follow the procedure of praxeological economics, they will have a sounder epistemological foundation and be able to avoid some of the errors associated with using the self-interested choice models. My work on entrepreneurship has been an attempt to develop praxeological economics by identifying the procedure that praxeological economists must use to ensure that imagination, creativity and inventiveness are not neglected.

Entrepreneurship as distinctly human action under market economy conditions
If the task of making praxeology the foundation for economics is to succeed, a term is needed to refer generally to distinctly human action under the

conditions of the market economy. By using the term 'entrepreneurship' for this purpose, I followed the lead not only of Mises but of some major writers in the history of American economic thought, including Hawley (1900), Davenport (1914) and Knight (1921). Mises refers to the entrepreneur as a 'catallactic category' (1966: 251). Davenport and Knight incorporated this concept in a specific procedure that entails building a sequence of images in which entrepreneurship is embodied in a particular way.[2]

The procedure of praxeological economics

If we assume that entrepreneurship is present in all actors, the question arises of how we should deal with two obvious problems. The first is complexity. One of the conditions of the market economy is specialization. With so many varied and specialized individuals acting in the role of the entrepreneur, how can we identify patterns of economic interaction? The second is the fact that some people play a more significant role in causing progress to occur than others. How do we square the assumption that 'everyone is an entrepreneur' with the knowledge that some individuals are more important than others?

These problems are solved by using a specific procedure. In this procedure, we build images of the pure entrepreneur, the pure entrepreneur economy and other entrepreneur economies. Following this, we give examples of entrepreneurship. Good economists have always proceeded in this way. A recognition of the praxeological foundations of economics and the use of the praxeological concept of the entrepreneur helps us understand why.

The pure market economy

The derivation of the role of the entrepreneur begins with pure market economy. We cannot directly observe such an economy. For this reason, we can say that it is an imaginary construct. Reason and experience reveal to us that we must build an image of it in order to comprehend the capitalist system, or capitalism, which we can observe. We conceive of this image by assuming that many of the characteristics of capitalism, as we know it, are absent.

The pure market economy refers to interaction under four hypothetical conditions. The first two are complete private property rights and freedom of enterprise. By complete private property rights we mean that each person has a right to all the benefits of her action and must bear full responsibility for any harm that she does.[3] Both of these conditions apply equally to everyone. There are no privileged individuals or classes. The third condition is the use of money. In the pure market economy, all wants are satisfied indirectly, as it were, through the medium of money. There is no self-production or barter. The fourth condition is specialization, which corresponds to the reason why individuals would choose to satisfy their wants only indirectly by using money. To avoid the complication of taxes, the hypothetical pure market economy contains no government, even though it is assumed that there are private property rights.[4] To avoid the complication of public goods, the image of the pure market economy assumes only private goods; no goods possess the jointness-in-consumption characteristic that we associate with public goods. Finally, for simplicity, we disregard fraud and deception, such as that involved in misleading advertising.

The image of the hypothetical pure market economy was invented (a) to represent the features of capitalism that economists have traditionally regarded as part of their subject matter, and (b) for simplicity. Capitalism (which corresponds to most economists' notion of the market economy) refers to a broader set of characteristics. It includes externalities such as pollution, congestion, personal injury and property crime, which are associated with yet-to-be-defined or costly-to-enforce private property rights; the special problems related to public goods; and the bargaining associated with the development and use of institutions to enforce contracts and property rights. It also includes taxes, self-production and barter, fraud and deception.

Capitalism itself is a limited concept in the sense that it refers to only one aspect of all of the human action and interaction that take place in a society in which capitalism exists. Capitalism does not include pure political activity such as that involved by one group to obtain a transfer of wealth from another group. Nor does it include the use of collective action to appropriate or to help appropriate the wealth of peoples outside the jurisdiction of a nation. The term 'capitalist society' may be used to refer to this broader notion.

Capitalism is a broader and more vague notion than the pure market economy. Indeed it is precisely for this reason that economists start by trying to build an image of the narrower concept of the pure market economy. An economist who aims to evaluate economic policy arguments in a real capitalist economy would have to supplement the theory of the pure market economy with a theory that includes the relevant factors with which this simplistic definition does not deal.

The praxeological concept of the entrepreneur
The key concept in understanding the pure market economy is the praxeological concept of the entrepreneur, which refers to a *role* that represents what we know from intuition and experience to be the undeniable 'category of human action' (Mises, 1966: ch. 4), as it becomes manifest in the hypothetical pure market economy. 'It means: acting man exclusively seen from the aspect of the uncertainty inherent in every action' (ibid.: 253) and

'acting man in regard to the changes occurring in the data of the market' (ibid.: 254). To use this concept, we must begin by identifying the necessary properties of distinctly human action. Then we must devise a means of showing how these properties come to be manifest under the conditions of the market economy. As mentioned in the introduction, entrepreneurship appraises, undertakes and bears uncertainty, and it exhibits the characteristics of imagination, creativity and inventiveness.

The distinguishing advantage of using the praxeological concept of the entrepreneur is greater efficiency of communication. Because economists are normal[5] human actors, they can form identical concepts of distinctly human action. Moreover, because each economist can reason logically about how that action will become manifest under particular conditions, there is no doubt about his ability to know exactly what he means by the praxeological concept of the entrepreneur. The concept of the praxeological entrepreneur is an intuitive notion based on an a priori assumption about normal human beings and upon experience which helps one reason about how human beings would act under the conditions of the pure market economy.

The role of the pure entrepreneur

To help us identify patterns in the pure market economy, we build an image of the pure entrepreneur. To do this we draw a sharp distinction between distinctly human economic interaction and the function-performing behaviour of the consumer–saver, factor supplier and hired manager. The latter roles are said to perform the routine functions that we derive from our definition of economic action. They behave automatically like robots, according to programmes or algorithms. Kirzner uses the term 'Robbinsian economizers' to describe them (Kirzner, 1967: 796–7; 1973: 32–3; see below).

The role of the pure entrepreneur is vastly different. He identifies the items or actions that are candidates for being factors of production, and proceeds to appraise them in anticipation of producing goods that consumers will buy. Next he buys or leases the factors from the factor suppliers, then he proceeds to direct that they be used to produce specific goods for the purpose of sale. In performing these actions, he exercises creativity, imagination and inventiveness.

The pure entrepreneur bears all of the intersubjective uncertainty. In other words, he bears all of what are often referred to as consumer uncertainty, worker uncertainty and the uncertainty connected with lending and ownership of property. He can do this because we assume that he possesses factors or sufficient funds to buy or lease the factors; or, if he borrows money to finance production, we assume that he possesses sufficient guaranty to pay off all of the loans if he makes a loss.

The actions that encompass the role of the pure entrepreneur can only be elucidated by making a contrast between (1) an image in which non-entrepreneurial routine functions of consuming, saving, factor supplying, and producing are performed by robots and (2) what we know from intuition and experience to be how distinctly human actors would perform these functions under the conditions of the pure market economy. (Gunning, 1990: ch. 6; 1997: 174–6). In the older economics literature, the first image was called the static equilibrium. Mises introduced what is probably a better term, the *evenly rotating economy*.[6]

The characteristics of the pure entrepreneur are derived by using intuition and experience to inform us about how distinctly human actors differ from the robot consumers, savers, factor suppliers and producers of the evenly rotating economy. We look first at the evenly rotating economy. Then we ask: how would consumption, saving, factor supply and production take place under the assumption that these robots are, in fact, distinctly human actors? Thus we say that the characteristics of the pure entrepreneur are derived by means of a *contrast* between the robots of the evenly rotating economy and what we can know from intuition and experience about distinctly human action under the conditions of the pure market economy.

Entrepreneur economies
As a role, entrepreneurship is present in every market action, including a household's shopping and a janitor's cleaning. Everyone who makes a distinctly human decision to earn money or to use money with the aim of obtaining goods is acting in the role of the entrepreneur. However, in order to build the simplest image of a pure market economy, we imagine an economy consisting of distinctly human pure entrepreneurs and robot, economizing consumer-savers and factor suppliers. We call such an image the *pure entrepreneur economy*. At least one pure entrepreneur commands the production of each product. And each pure entrepreneur has a perspective sufficiently broad that, if conditions warrant, he can shift his funds from the production of one good to the production of others. Thus each pure entrepreneur is a potential competitor with every other pure entrepreneur.

The pure entrepreneur economy can be conceived as a consequence of the interaction of all distinctly human actors who, together, initially own all of the factors of production in an economy. Some of the actors choose to sell or rent out control over their factors to others and, consequently, give up the rights to control them. Others acquire those rights and thereafter behave as robots. The ones who acquire them become pure entrepreneurs. The pure entrepreneur economy is useful in helping us identify various patterns of the pure market economy. These include competition, the relationship between the prices of goods and the prices of the factors of production, and consumer sovereignty.

We build images of other entrepreneur economies in order to help us understand the division of entrepreneurial tasks. For example, we can build an image of an economy containing wealthy *capitalist entrepreneurs*, who do not themselves decide how the factors will be used but who only guarantee the loans from savers to other producing entrepreneurs, who we assume are penniless. Such an image gives us insight into the role of middleman activity and the division of knowledge. Some entrepreneurs specialize in production (penniless entrepreneurs), others in deciding which lines of business are most profitable (guarantors) and still others (middlemen) in facilitating this specialization by arranging trades and in supplying information. Such an image helps us understand the role of financial institutions and specialists. Other entrepreneur economies are similar. By making the realistic assumption that exchange entails costs of transactions, we can build images of entrepreneur economies in which specialists emerge to economize on these costs and in which the economic organization depends on the nature of such costs and the means of avoiding them.

The international aspects of entrepreneurship
In this section we introduce two ways in which praxeology is relevant to international trade. In the first, we show how it can be used to modify the typical beginning point of international economics: the theory of comparative advantage. In the second, we begin with the theory of a pure global market economy and then show how to determine the effects of various interventions associated with dividing the regions of the global economy into 'nations'. To complete the latter task would require much more space than allotted here. Our main goal is to provide some hints for further investigation.

The theory of comparative advantage
The theory of comparative advantage is designed to deal with trade between two 'nations', where a nation is treated as an individual. The logic of the theory has two steps. The first is to make the assumption that comparative advantage exists. Here we consider only the simple two-good case. In this case, comparative advantage refers to a difference in the ratio of the marginal opportunity costs of supply. The nation with the lowest relative marginal opportunity cost of producing a good has a comparative advantage in producing the next unit of it. We may make the model more complex by assuming production in which each nation possesses different factors of production, but, to maintain the integrity of the theory, we must assume that these factors cannot cross the nation's boundaries.

The second step is to show that, when there is comparative advantage, a rate of exchange between the two goods exists such that, if the two nations trade at this rate, each nation can obtain more of both goods than it could obtain if trade did not occur. This shows that trade has the potential of raising a nation's well-being for the case under consideration. This is the principle of comparative advantage B that *trade according to comparative advantage raises the potential economic welfare of the traders.*

The principle of comparative advantage is a praxeological principle. It assumes that the agents of nations or individual traders have evaluated alternatives and calculated opportunity cost. They do this in the expectation that they can benefit from trade. However the usual models assume only limited scope for imagination, creativity and inventiveness. In making their calculations, the agents are assumed to have only limited interaction. At some point, each is assumed to find out that his opportunity cost differs from that faced by the other and, therefore, that there are potential gains from trade. Consider, for example, a two-good model. Assume that in nation 1, good A has a lower relative opportunity cost mainly because the producer of A has superior knowledge of how to produce it. The model rules out the possibility that the producer of A in nation 2 may learn from the producer in 1 and, as a result, reverse the initial direction of comparative advantage. One might wish to say that we had already ruled this out on the grounds that knowledge is a factor of production, the transfer of which between nations is ruled out by definition. However humans have the ability to at least partly infer, from the consequence of another person's action, the sequence of steps that preceded the consequences. A human being can even partly infer the mental processes that another person used to decide what action to take. When we think about the imagination, creativity and inventiveness entailed in the mental processes needed to make such inferences, we are led to recognize the limited relevance of assumption of factor immobility. One might also wish to rule out such learning owing to the assumption that the goods traded are homogeneous. If the good imported by nation 1 is identical to the domestically produced good, how could a producer in 1 learn anything that he does not already know? However, if we assume complete homogeneity, we again limit the relevance of the theory.[7]

The model does not rule out learning per se. As a model of interaction at a specific time, it disregards for simplicity changes that occur through time. A competent user model could 'dynamicize' the model in order to include changes in technology. What is disregarded is the learning by one agent from the actions of another agent in the other country. To see the importance of this, suppose that during the trading period assumed in such a dynamic model, the producer of A in 2 learns to exactly duplicate nation 1's technology and that the producer of B in 1 learns to exactly duplicate nation 2's technology. Comparative advantage and the rationale for trade would disappear. There would be no further potential for gains from trade according to the principle of comparative advantage. Yet trade will have benefited the agents in both nations. However such benefits cannot be represented by the increased potential output due to trade based on comparative advantage.

By taking more complete account of the praxeological nature of trading actions, we see that free trade may improve the conditions in two nations regardless of the ultimate volume of trade. We are thus in a position to make the following addendum to the theory. *If the governments of two previously non-trading market economies permit free trade in goods, the potential welfare of the trading nations is likely to rise even if, in the longer term, no actual trade occurs. The reason is the potential that individuals in one nation have for learning the methods of production used in another nation.*

An interesting corollary is that a nation may gain from trade even if there is no initial difference in relative marginal opportunity cost. Assume that nation 1 has an absolute advantage in both goods because its technology is more advanced than nation 2's. Nation 2 may gain from importing both goods and enabling its producers to copy the technologies.

Learning need not be confined to mere duplication of production methods. The producer in 2 may combine knowledge that he initially possesses with new knowledge and, as a result, improve the technical efficiency of production over that used in 1. If so, 1 could later gain by importing from 2. Trade would occur even though initial marginal opportunity costs were identical in the two nations.

It seems evident, that if economists took account of the implications of the praxeological approach to international trade, they would want to make major revisions in the fundamental theory. This, in turn, is likely to lead to fundamental revisions in the evaluation of arguments for and against free trade and in policy recommendations. For example, consider a technologically-superior nation that removes its trade barriers with a technologically-inferior nation. Assume that entrepreneurs in the latter nation are adept at copying. It is easy to build a multi-nation model in which the majority of citizens in the advanced nation are made worse off as a consequence of trade. In the extreme, we can imagine a case where the import of one unit of each good would enable individuals in the low-tech nation to exactly duplicate the technology of the high-tech nation and thereby eliminate the latter's gains from trade due to this initial difference.

Methodology for determining the effects of government intervention in international trade
International economics is a branch of general economics. Like general economics, its aim is to provide the reasoning tools required to evaluate

various policy arguments (and, by implication, the ideologies that support them, such as socialism and interventionism). To do this it proceeds from an image of the pure market economy to images of other economies that contain the elements needed to evaluate a particular argument. In the case of international trade, one of the elements is the division of the market economy into nations. Accordingly a necessary step in international economics is the definition of a 'nation' and, correspondingly, of characteristics that distinguish one nation from another. It follows from this that the methodology for doing international economics divides into two parts. The first part is the methodology for doing economics in general. The second is methodology associated with operationalizing the notion of a 'nation' and differences among nations. Since many economists pay very little attention to methodology, it will be helpful to describe both of these problems in turn before proceeding further.

Methodology of general economics   Praxeological economics begins with the theory of the pure market economy. The basic image is the pure entrepreneur economy. We build images of other economies in order to evaluate arguments for or against intervention in the capitalist economy under realistic conditions. Because the pure market economy differs from the reality for which the arguments are constructed, we must make assumptions in order to build relevant images. Consider a few of the more obvious of the assumptions we might make, depending on the particular argument we aim to evaluate.

We can begin by recognizing that a market economy contains specialization and transactions costs. Transactions costs help determine the nature of specialization and lead individuals to choose one form of production and marketing organization over another. We may want to make realistic assumptions about the nature of such specialization and transactions costs. To describe other assumptions, it is helpful to use the word 'capitalism' to refer to the realistic conditions in which a market economy is embedded. Then we can say that the pure market economy differs from capitalism in various ways.

Under capitalism, private property rights are necessarily incomplete. Government agents must identify and define the private property rights that are important and it must employ factors to enforce them. A theory of capitalism must make assumptions about the nature of this incompleteness and about how the assumed structure of private property rights is likely to be incorporated by entrepreneurship into its appraisals and decisions to produce goods.[8] There are also jointness-in-consumption goods that are more or less excludable. Government agents may deal with these by imposing taxes and spending. Capitalism also contains fraud and deception.

Buyers and sellers aim to avoid fraud and we may want to make assumptions about how they do so, including the use of government agents to deter such activities. To evaluate a particular argument, we may have to describe the particular form that specialization in a market economy takes. This form ordinarily depends on the nature of transactions costs. We may have to make assumptions about these. Unlike the pure market economy, capitalist economies ordinarily contain intervention in free enterprise and intervention that destabilizes the money. Although our aim is to evaluate a particular argument for a particular type of intervention, we may find it necessary to add assumptions about other government intervention. Finally the market economy is embedded in a society, a political system and natural environment. We may wish to add assumptions about culture, politics and the natural environment.

The aim of economics is not to build a complete model of either capitalism or a capitalist society. These tasks are impossible to accomplish in their entirety. The main practical use of economic reasoning is to evaluate arguments for and against modifying private property rights or free enterprise in a way that would reduce the role of entrepreneurship, as opposed to that of government agents, in determining the actions that people will take. By analogy, the main use of international economics is to evaluate arguments favouring intervention in a global market economy. One form of intervention is barriers to international trade constructed by agents of national governments. The theory of international trade has been mainly concerned with the evaluation of arguments relating to such barriers.

Methodology of international economics: barriers to trade in the pure global market economy   The procedure we follow in international economics begins with an image of a pure global market economy. In such an economy, each person has the same private property rights and rights to engage in free enterprise as everyone else. There is a single money. The pure global market economy is identical to the pure market economy. We use the modifier 'global' to indicate that we are planning to consider the effects of various barriers that might be imposed in a system where people are divided into nations. Beginning with the pure global market economy, we proceed to conceive of various types of barriers. Reason seems to suggest two possible images of barriers for the next step.

In the first, we assume that every nation except one is part of a pure global market economy. One nation is outside because it imposes an intervention that either restricts its citizens from fully participating in the otherwise pure global market economy, or restricts non-citizens from fully participating in its own, otherwise pure market economy, or both. In the second, we assume that all nations intervene in the pure global market economy in the same way. Using one of these two images as a reference, we proceed to contrast the outcome of a particular intervention with the outcome that we deduce would occur in the absence of the intervention. For example, if we wanted to determine the effects of a tariff, we could assume that a single nation's tariff is the only exception to a pure global market economy. Or we could assume that all nations impose an identical tariff. More complex models would proceed from one of these reference images.

Consider the analysis of a single nation's imposition of a tariff in an otherwise pure global market economy. The approach of praxeological entrepreneurship leads us to ask how the tariff would affect the incentives to appraise factors, produce goods and bear uncertainty, and how it would affect imagination, creativity and inventiveness in these activities. Suppose that the only intervention is the imposition of a tariff by one nation on a single good. Assume that entrepreneurship is blocked from crossing national boundaries.[9] Because the tariff raises the profit of domestic production of the good, domestic entrepreneurship will have a relatively greater incentive to produce the good in the industry protected by the tariff. Foreign entrepreneurship will have a relatively lower incentive to produce it. Relatively less of the tariff-imposing nation's entrepreneurship will be devoted to producing other goods and relatively more of other nations' entrepreneurship will be devoted to these. Since entrepreneurship implies imagination, creativity and inventiveness, we would expect similar shifts in these characteristics. For example, relatively more domestic entrepreneurship will be devoted to identifying new methods of producing the good and relatively less will be devoted to identifying new methods of producing other goods. This implies that domestic entrepreneurship is less likely to make technological advances in the production of other goods.

Finally, since profit depends on being able to predict a future tariff, a flexible tariff policy will provide incentives for entrepreneurs to identify the reasons why government officials impose a tariff and the preconditions that prompt them to do so. If an entrepreneur believes that he can gain from a change in the tariff, he may have an incentive to employ factors for the purpose of rent seeking. If he believes that he will lose from a tariff, he may have an incentive to employ factors for defensive rent seeking. In both cases, entrepreneurs would also have an incentive to use their imagination, creativity and inventiveness to try to identify new methods of succeeding (and of preventing their rivals from succeeding) in their rent-seeking efforts. The imagination, creativity and inventiveness that can be applied to the rent-seeking game ensures that the game between offensive and defensive rent seekers will evolve and that the rent seekers will have a continuing incentive to identify new methods of dealing with their rivals and with government agents.

This example gives a rough indication of the way to analyse the effect of intervention by identifying the incentives faced by entrepreneurship. To explore this principle further, consider a nation that completely blocks foreign entrepreneurs from competing with domestic entrepreneurs in producing a specific final good that is only consumed by consumers in the nation and not in any other nation. We recognize that, in comparison with the pure global market economy, the technological growth of the domestic industry would depend entirely on the imagination, creativity and inventiveness of the domestic entrepreneurs. International entrepreneurs would no longer contribute.[10]

Different liability laws   It is possible to identify patterns by beginning with an image of a two-nation global economy. In this economy, we assume that the government completely prohibits the migration of people and, therefore, of entrepreneurship. Assume that the two nations are identical in all respects except that the court system of the first permits people who are damaged by water pollution to sue the polluter for the total amount of the damages caused to all persons harmed plus costs, while the second does not. Assume further that the courts always make correct judgments. If the costs of making transactions were zero and if we disregard wealth effects, the difference in legal liability would not matter, since a producer would face the same marginal opportunity costs in both nations (by the Coase theorem).[11] If we assume transactions costs, however, producers would adjust their appraisals to account for these. Let us assume that water pollution is caused by a relatively small number of polluters and that it imposes harm on a relatively large number of people. Then the transactions costs would be higher to those who want to buy the right to control pollution under the no-liability rule than they would be to those who want to buy the right to control pollution under the liability rule.

Consider first the entrepreneurship in the liability-for-pollution nation. Entrepreneurship would find it more profitable to appraise and employ factors that could be used to control the emission of water pollution than the entrepreneurs. This is because of the high transactions costs to the potential victims of pollution associated with their efforts to sell the right to control pollution to the polluters. We would also expect new products and methods of production. The products identified as profitable to produce would consist of a smaller proportion of relatively high-polluting products and producers would become more technologically competent in producing products with relatively low-polluting methods of production. Entrepreneurship would also develop new low-polluting methods of production.

Now consider entrepreneurship in the no-liability-for-pollution nation. Entrepreneurship would find it more profitable to appraise and employ factors that could be used to clean the polluted water in order to prevent it from causing substantial damage to users. This is because of the high transactions costs to the potential victims of pollution associated with their efforts to buy the right to control pollution from the polluters. High transactions costs may lead to political rather than economic means of supply, with the attendant rent-seeking and incentive problems. We would also expect new products and methods of production. The products identified as profitable to produce would consist of a larger proportion of relatively high-polluting products, and producers would become more technologically competent in using relatively high-polluting products and methods of production. Entrepreneurship would also develop new high-polluting methods of production and new means of cleaning polluted water for later use.

Conclusion

The idea of the praxeological entrepreneur can be traced to the early part of the 20th century. The idea of a praxeologically-based economics, or praxeological economics, comes from Mises, although economics has been praxeological from the very beginning. Much of the author's work has sought to describe and clarify these ideas and to organize them into a coherent framework for studying the pure market economy and for evaluating arguments relating to government intervention. The early part of this chapter briefly described the general thrust of this work. The later part addressed the issue of how these ideas may be applied in an international setting.

The first application was to the theory of comparative advantage. We pointed out that because the typical model of comparative advantage rules out entrepreneurial learning, it disregards an important source of effects due to trade that have nothing to do with comparative advantage and that would be present even if no comparative advantage existed. For example, if a nation has an absolute disadvantage in producing a good, its producers can learn to reduce and perhaps even reverse that disadvantage. We deduce this on the basis of the assumptions that distinctly human action possesses the characteristics of imagination, creativity, and inventiveness and that these characteristics are used to copy and innovate. We cannot know exactly what contributions a nation's entrepreneurship will make. As economists, we cannot be specialists in every field. Nevertheless, we are confident that in a free enterprise setting, producers will anticipate profit from successful copying and innovating.

Although the textbook theory of comparative advantage represents the outcome of distinctly human action, it disregards the imagination, creativity, and inventiveness of the producers. When appropriate account is taken of this entrepreneurship, we find that free trade is likely to have very different effects than those suggested by the simple theory of comparative advantage. Indeed, our analysis suggests that in order to account for international entrepreneurship, international trade theory is in need of considerable rebuilding.

Praxeological economics also challenges the usual way of deducing the effects of barriers to trade like tariffs. It suggests that the appropriate beginning point is an image of a pure global market economy with no national boundaries. It conceives of the division of that market economy into nations as a market intervention. This suggests two approaches to the subject of international trade theory. In the first we assume the formation of a single nation in an otherwise pure global market economy. To form a nation means to grant citizens legal rights to do business that differ from those granted to non-citizens. In the second we assume that all nations intervene in the same way. In the analysis of the effects of such interventions, praxeological economics emphasizes imagination, creativity, and inventiveness in the identification, discovery and production of factors, techniques, and consumer goods. It also emphasizes the entrepreneurship exercised in the interaction between those affected by the laws and those charged with making and administering them. It thereby deduces that entrepreneurship in rent seeking is an integral part of the evaluation of arguments for intervention in the global market economy.

Notes

1. Different nations also differ in their natural resources, the nature of their specialized factors, and their culture. However different regions in the market economy also contain such differences. Thus these do not constitute key differences between the market economy and the international economy.
2. See Gunning (1993) for a review of Knight on entrepreneurship, and Gunning (1998) for a review of Davenport on the subject.
3. Mises writes: 'Carried through consistently, the right of property would entitle the proprietor to claim all the advantages which the good's employment may generate on the one hand and would burden him with all the disadvantages resulting from its employment on the other hand' (Mises, 1966: 655).
4. Mises defined the pure market economy in the following way:

   It assumes that the operation of the market [exchange of goods and services] is not obstructed by institutional factors. It assumes that the government, the social apparatus of compulsion and coercion, is intent upon preserving the operation of the market [exchange of goods and services], abstains from hindering its functioning, and protects it against encroachments on the part of other people. The market [exchange of goods and services] is free; there is no interference of factors, foreign to the market, with prices, wage rates, and interest rates. (Ibid: 237–8)
5. The term 'normal' is used in order to rule out people who would be classified as human beings by biologists but who either cannot or are as yet unable to act in a way that we know by intuition and experience human beings can act. Examples are the infirm, the mentally handicapped and children. Mises notes that 'the minor family members in the market society . . . are . . . themselves not actors' (*ibid.*: 252).

6. He says: 'Such a rigid system is not peopled with living men making choices liable to error; it is a world of soulless unthinking automatons; it is not a human society, it is an ant hill' (Mises, 1966: 248). Mises's concept was criticized by Cowen and Fink (1985) and the criticism was countered by Gunning (1988).
7. This is especially true if our aim is to build an image that is relevant to the modern world of low-cost communication.
8. Moreover the existence of incomplete private property rights implies some amount of flexibility. In other words, it suggests both that government agents may change the structure of private property rights and that private individuals may invest in establishing private property rights themselves or in strengthening enforcement. Given that this is possible, one would have to add the assumptions that entrepreneurship would have an incentive to produce private property rights and to identify ways to influence the government agents (that is, to seek rent).
9. In a really capitalist society, this can be accomplished imperfectly by blocking travel in and out of the country. Assuming that entrepreneurship cannot cross boundaries, it cannot profit from moving to the tariff-imposing nation if it perceives higher profit. However, an individual in one nation may still be able to learn something about the cognitive processes used by entrepreneurship in another nation by studying the results of its actions and its words, as suggested earlier in the paper. Moreover, physical travel may not be necessary. An entrepreneur in the free enterprise nation may be able to communicate means of profit to entrepreneurship in the tariff-imposing nation in exchange for money or other benefits. These means of circumventing a travel ban, however, are not perfect substitutes for free enterprise.
10. We must qualify this statement by recognizing that effective laws blocking the production of a final product may be difficult not only to enforce but also to make in the first place. For example, a law blocking production may not block assembly of foreign-produced parts. In this case, the effect would be partly to encourage a domestic entrepreneurial shift into the assembly of parts. If the government also blocked assembly, it would have to define the process of assembly by specifying the exact components the assembly of which is prohibited. If it took the other extreme and blocked the import of all factors used to produce the final good, it might hamper the production of other domestic products that use the same factors. To analyse the effects of the law requires a complete specification of what is prohibited and of how the government plans to use its enforcement resources.
11. See Demsetz (1972a, 1972b).

References

Cowen, T. and R. Fink (1985), 'Inconsistent Equilibrium Constructs: The Evenly Rotating Economy of Mises and Rothbard', *American Economic Review*, September.
Davenport, H. (1914), *Economics of Enterprise*, New York: Macmillan.
Demsetz, H. (1972a), 'When Does the Rule of Liability Matter?', *Journal of Legal Studies*, July.
Demsetz, H. (1972b), 'Wealth Distribution and the Ownership of Rights', *Journal of Legal Studies*, July.
Gunning, J. (1988), 'Mises on the Evenly Rotating Economy', *Review of Austrian Economics*, 3.
Gunning, J. (1990), *The New Subjectivist Revolution: An Elucidation and Extension of Ludwig von Mises' Contribution to Economic Theory*, Savage, Maryland: Rowman and Littlefield.
Gunning, J. (1997), 'The Theory of Entrepreneurship in Austrian Economics', in W. Keizer, B. Tieben and R. Van Zijp (eds), *Austrians in Debate*, London: Routledge.
Gunning, J. Patrick (1993), 'Entrepreneurists and Firmists: Knight vs. the Modern Theory of the Firm', *Journal of the History of Economic Thought*, 15: 31–53.
Gunning, J. Patrick. (1998), 'Herbert J. Davenport's Transformation of the Austrian Theory of Value and Cost', in Malcolm Rutherford (ed.), *The Economic Mind in America: Essays in the History of American Economics*, London: Routledge.

Hawley, F. (1900), 'Enterprise and Profit', *Quarterly Journal of Economics*, November.
Kirzner, I.(1967), 'Methodological Individualism, Market Equilibrium, and Market Process', *Il Politico*, 32:787–99.
Kirzner, I. (1973), *Competition and Entrepreneurship*, Chicago: The University of Chicago Press.
Knight, F. (1921), *Risk, Uncertainty, and Profit*, New York: Houghton Mifflin.
von Mises, L. (1966), *Human Action: A Treatise on Economics*, Chicago: Henry Regnery Company.

11 Entrepreneurship and marketing: issues for independent inventors
Len Tiu Wright and Celia Harvey

Introduction

Companies need to develop new products to sustain their growth and long term profitability when existing products reach the maturity stage and face heavy competition while old unprofitable products are phased out. This development of new products is done in a variety of ways, most commonly by developing them in-house with their own research and development (R&D) departments or through joint ventures and strategic alliances with other companies or by sub-contracting to external consultants. Most prior writings in the academic and business literature have a focus upon the needs, methods, failures and successes of organizational priorities and policies in carrying out R&D, R&D interfaces with marketing and sales, and new product development (NPD). While writings in the academic literature in the last two decades concentrate on these areas (e.g. Gupta et al., 1985; Moenaert and Souder, 1990; Cooper, 1984; Wang and Montaguti, 2002), there is comparatively little written about the entrepreneurial role played by independent inventors in the R&D and market development needs of business organizations or in contributing to their NPD. In addition data about the businesses run by independent inventors, apart from those registered at national patent offices, are lost amongst the myriad of statistics concerning small and medium sized enterprises (SMEs). Information about private sector businesses, such as those registered at the UK government's 'Companies House', for small, medium and large companies exist, but there is relatively little up-to-date published information about enterprises concerning inventors. There are writings about small entrepreneurial businesses, the support of family units for enterprises and the proactive responses to problematic business succession that may involve disruptive innovation (Martin et al., 2002; Cui and Choudhury, 2002), although these are also limited in scope.

This chapter contributes to reducing a gap in the literature with research about inventors and the difficulties they face, as they seek to become entrepreneurs by putting their inventions in the marketplace. It is also about the need to reduce the barriers to innovation experienced by inventors-entrepreneurs and the importance of inventions in the technological development of countries in general. Research undertaken with inventors and companies as corporate adopters identifies the risks and barriers to innovation and the lessons that have relevance to independent inventors. Despite the accessibility of the Internet and its potential for e-networking and e-marketing, there are communication problems between inventors, potential adopter organizations and support agencies. Key factors appear to be stereotyping, the 'not invented here' (NIH) syndrome, attitudes to risk and lack of national support. In today's global market, facilitated by the Internet, opportunities exist not only to overcome these barriers but also to access much wider markets. So new strategies are needed for independent inventors to optimise these opportunities and for potential adopter companies to provide channels for inventors to do business with them.

Invention, innovation and entrepreneurial culture
The *Oxford English Reference Dictionary* (1996) defines an *invention* as 'the process of inventing . . . created by thought, devised, a new method originated . . . a contrivance especially for which a patent is granted'. On the other hand an *innovation* 'brings in new methods . . . ideas often followed by making changes'. Therefore, for the purpose of this chapter the word 'inventors' is used as the research was conducted with them (see the later section 'Findings'). The discussion in this chapter about the risks, barriers and support to innovation is important because inventors, having created their unique ideas or methods, face the processes for adaptation or change to get them adopted in the marketplace. These innovation processes are complex because there are interrelated activities and decisions concerning research, development and management from the creation of a product to acceptance in a market (Johnson, 1976).

For a product to be patentable, it must meet the three criteria of being 'original', 'useful' and 'not obvious'. For a new product to be of value to a company, comprehensive protection through the patent system is almost essential. Lack of global patent law will complicate such issues for a long time. Inventors hoping to develop enterprises based on their inventions could face problems in maintaining ownership of intellectual property, especially when ideas and inventions could be copied by other individuals or companies in other countries.

These factors present problems for developing the entrepreneurial culture of countries. The adoption rate of technology plays a major part in enhancing the productivity and international competitiveness of countries (Kitchell, 1997). Therefore, to remain competitive, there is a need not only for the incremental improvements that are more usually associated with R&D, but also for the depth and freshness of the independent inventor's approach.

One *Economist* survey (1999) noted that, compared to the USA, the UK scored highly for its inventiveness and creativity, having seventy-one Nobel prizes for science and medicine. The UK's record of commercial exploitation was seen as woeful. UK companies are not keen to take on ideas from independent inventors, as was seen when the clockwork radio was invented. Risks and costs are inherent in new ideas and the current culture in British industry compared to the USA and Japan appears to be one of low risk and incremental progress. However, Japan's lack of small high technology companies is giving it cause for concern (*The Economist*, 2002), when compared to the successes of America's Silicone Valley or India's nurturing of its high technology enterprises.

International differences in support of innovation exist. Investment in R&D has increased year on year for the countries surveyed by the DTI (*The Economist*, 1999), but the increase was only 5% for Italy and 3% for Britain. This compared most unfavourably against increases in Denmark, Canada and the USA which were in the range of 17%-26%, see Table 11.1. All these are technologically rich countries when compared to the poorer ones in Eastern Europe, Africa and South East Asia. The gap widens when poor countries fall further behind, due to lack of investment in resources and skills in new technologies to innovate or in their business infrastructures to create a culture of enterprise. The opportunities for the independent inventor are obvious and e-information exists to inform the inventor about which countries and companies are more open to innovation. Targeting may be made much more effective through adept interpretation of marketing intelligence.

Table 11.1   International differences in support of innovation

Research & Development: expenditure as % of sales			
Europe		*Other parts of the world*	
UK	2.5	Canada	10.8
Denmark	16.3	Japan	4.8
Finland	10.4	USA	4.9
Germany	4.3		
Italy	2.0		

Source: The Economist, 1999

The strategy of exploiting inventions from independent inventors might work since they may not, through necessity, feel tied to any country or organization, in their search for sponsors for their inventors. Francis Bacon writing in the seventeenth century observed in his paper, 'On Innovation', that 'he who will not apply new remedies must expect new evils, for time is the greatest innovator'. Whilst the final shape of the emerging 'new economy' is still far from certain, what is clear is that the capacity to innovate and to develop the entrepreneurial culture of countries is a crucial factor. Compared to the USA and Japan, Britain has a very low commercial uptake of inventions. This is a recent phenomenon in terms of world history. During the eighteenth century Britain and parts of Europe led the Industrial Revolution. During the nineteenth century the USA increased its leadership for innovations and in the latter part of the twentieth century the Pacific Rim was added to the forefront of technological innovation (Davies, 1995).

For inventors who are small entrepreneurs, the risk of failure remains high. The vast majority of inventions fail to make the market or to achieve acceptance and there are many reasons why. Some simply do not work because of a basic flaw, some do not actually save any time or effort while many are unreliable, expensive or totally impractical. However, hundreds and possibly thousands of potentially profitable ideas are not developed, despite the long lists of patents granted, with some never making it to market. Whatever its source, an invention needs to be financed, developed, protected in law and marketed, often with uncertain outcome. Very small businesses, such as many of the small start-up dot-com companies, have not been successful in returning profits to investors. This extends from the service to the scientific sector, for example, the small biotechnology companies that have been relying on continuous investment for years, but are still not profitable. The costs of training in the use of computers and software or for the design of websites to advertise their inventions add to the costs of patent protection and marketing for inventors-entrepreneurs. The traditional option is for inventors to sell their ideas to 'adopters', that is, to commercial organizations that will stand the costs and risks involved in undertaking the financial assessments, technical development and manufacturing, product launches and continual market developments.

Problems of fit with the organizational culture
The adoption of marketing by many companies has taught them to involve their customers very early on. Marketing research is used to gather data about markets and decision making is formalized in structures and procedures so that the whole chain of decision-taking and value creation through organizational levels and processes can create efficiencies and add value for both customers and employees. The added expertise of product designers, executives, suppliers, buyers and marketing specialists that are a growing part of everyday business and which combine to provide an assessment of marketability are taken for granted by companies. The lack of such net-

works makes it very difficult for independent inventors to share ideas and problems, and to gain a feel of the acceptability of their inventions in the marketplace.

There are two routes commonly taken by independent inventors to get their inventions to market. One route is to find financial backers or companies willing to adopt their inventions and so take on the risks and costs of research and development (R&D), sales and marketing. Another route is for inventors to undertake the work themselves with the associated personal and financial risks that this entails, as in the establishment of the bagless vacuum cleaner's in the marketplace. Business organizations are faced with choices, sometimes difficult ones, about adopting inventions from individuals who may not have a history of operating with their companies. The formation of negative views by companies about the personalities of inventors does not help. Independent inventors, by developing their own jargon and perspectives, might not realize the extent to which there is a lack of fit with the organizational culture of the companies they approach.

These factors present a number of problems for independent inventors, which we now address.

Attitudes of independent inventors towards risks
The majority of independent inventors find themselves working alone. This occurs for many reasons but perhaps most importantly because of the need to retain confidentiality regarding their ideas. Once an idea has been described to someone else, retaining the rights to the intellectual property becomes extremely difficult. UK patent law is very complex and there is not yet any global patent law. Patenting ideas is a very expensive process. Without the protection of patents the inventors are left to trust those to whom they choose to disclose their ideas, or the flimsy cover of confidentiality agreements which again are expensive to fight in the courts if breached. Therefore, inventors face many difficulties in their attempts to move their ideas from the drawing board to the marketplace.

On the other hand, independent inventors must also understand the viewpoint of the R&D departments of companies. Steele (1991) described the Holy Grail of industrial R&D as a major invention or discovery that creates an entirely new kind or level of capability, preferably in the form of a new product or a significant new process. R&D organizations see their primary mission as one of discovering and inventing, but this attitude can easily translate into 'not invented here' (NIH) because inventions made elsewhere can create an 'implicit invidious comparison with internal creativity'. There may be a wish to guard their autonomy against any external encroachment or to defend against a perceived threat from external inventors.

Experience of working in industry

The credibility of inventors is reliant on the inventors' employment and work experience or, at the very least, their demonstrating a basic understanding of the industries and markets of the corporate adopters they wish to approach.

In reality the focus on developing inventions could leave an inventor time for little else, such as marketing or setting up in business as an entrepreneur. Inventors develop their inventions with very limited knowledge of potential markets. Typically, they do not have the investments or the financial, marketing and human resources, unlike organizations with established businesses.

Striking the right balance is important in each independent inventor's assessment of the nature of the corporate adopter's company. It is very difficult for an outsider to evaluate or to appreciate the current strategic position of an adopter's organization. In particular the adopter's attitude towards risk, its receptivity to independents, the level of NIH, the inter-organizational powers and spread of key influencers in the decision-making units, could all be difficult for an inventor to appreciate. Inventors have to overcome this NIH syndrome by demonstrating the creativity, expertise and market potential of their ideas or inventions, even when companies show lack of interest because such inventions were not developed 'in-house' within their own organizational processes. In addition, without a track record for specific expertise in a chosen field, inventors run the risk of being seen as developing inventions without much market knowledge, engineering expertise or business acumen.

Need to be customer-centred

Independent inventors who become too focused on enthusiasm for their own inventions run the risk of not being able to present their inventions in terms of the corporate adopters' needs and capabilities. This is supported by Baggozi and Foxall (1996), who found inventors to be innovative but not adaptable. An unwillingness to be flexible about their ideas could in turn be exacerbated by the corporate adopters' requirement to focus on the needs and demands of their existing customer bases.

Well-educated, free-thinking, confident, but weak in terms of marketing and finance was how Hisrich (1985) described independent inventors. Much evidence, both anecdotal and substantiated, exists about independent inventors lacking the marketing skills required by industry, with their focus on ideas rather than marketing. The belief is that the idea should sell itself and that industry should be only too glad to take the idea on. This belief is far removed from the attitude of industry, which sees the idea as just the beginning of the innovation process. Inventors possess problem-solving and creative skills but need to apply these to the marketing of their inventions.

Independent inventors experience few risks in the innovation process. There may be financial risk in the development of inventions or ideas and a degree of risking their reputations (that is, being seen as cranks), but the risks for corporate adopters are far higher. The costs and risks involved in undertaking financial assessments, technical development and manufacturing, marketing, product launches and continual market development are substantial. There is a high degree of risk for companies in adopting inventions. Beyond the more obvious financial risks of additional research, development, production, marketing and so on, the reputation of a company could be affected. For example, if a company adopts a new product, this may affect all of its sales by changing its image to that of an innovator. If the product is successful, the company's reputation will be enhanced. If, however, the product is a failure, the company's reputation will be damaged and this may result in the demand for other goods being reduced which will increase the cost of the failure (Jensen, 1992). Whether or not a company adopts ideas from independent inventors may well depend on company strategy and the attitude of the buyer towards risk.

A purchase is likely to be perceived as being more important to the buying organization when it involves large sums of money, when the cost of making the wrong decision is high and when there is considerable uncertainty about the outcome of alternative offerings. For this reason considerable and continued marketing effort is required by the inventor.

Image and professionalism
Inventors need to exhibit awareness of marketing principles and specific good practices. Whilst it may not be possible or even desirable for inventors to change some aspects of their own personality, their marketing and communication strategies and tactics often could be improved. The research evidence in the section 'Findings' below, suggests that most approaches to adopter companies by independent inventors could be improved significantly in terms of targeting, preparation and presentation. All of these could be improved relatively easily through online information. The Internet has allowed inventors to have direct access to the marketplace to search for information, ask questions and develop links with potential suppliers and consumers. Inventors can put a stronger case to potential adopter organizations if they have conducted initial research and information about the likelihood of purchases by end-users. Information and intelligence about markets, companies and similar products allow the inventor to present a much more professional case.

First impressions count and inventors who create the wrong image lose credibility, whatever the product idea. Post (1994) identified minor neurotic tendencies as a characteristic common to many inventors. The independent inventor has often been portrayed as something of a mad scientist-type or an uneducated dreamer in search of the Holy Grail (Parker et al., 1996). The result of these negative perceptions is that the independent inventor, in many cases, is not viewed as a serious source of product innovation.

If this stereotype presents a caricature, at least the Internet offers some hope for inventors. Companies that are open to approaches will be able to deal with inventors through an electronic medium in the early stages of the negotiations rather than face to face. Inventors have the opportunity to demonstrate a professional approach, although there may be a risk that another stereotype of e-entrepreneurs exists. The ability to present a professional approach by effective use of the information available is important. Independent inventors work in an entirely different way from commercial organizations and this cultural difference can be perceived by both parties as an insurmountable barrier. Once this barrier is acknowledged, ways may be found to limit its effects or indeed to eliminate them.

CASE EXAMPLE

Research with corporate adopters, inventors and support organizations in the UK

Companies are not structured for innovation. For inventors, developing the right marketing processes and identifying the best people to approach are very difficult tasks (Wright and Nancarrow, 2001). Leavy (1997) examines whether the capacity for innovation and entrepreneurship is primarily a personal or systematic management process. In both traditional and internet business practices, little effort is made to encourage independent inventors and systems are rarely in place to manage worthwhile approaches. The personalities of the key influencers in these organizations will be instrumental in their corporate adopters' approach to independent inventors. Corporate adopters' perceptions of the inventors' understanding of their markets are likely to be negative until the latter produce evidence to overturn this.

Therefore, research was undertaken in the UK to examine:

(1) the perceptions and experiences of corporate adopters about the approaches to them by independent inventors

including the reasons for positive and negative views of the latter;

(2) barriers faced by independent inventors and examples of effective marketing communications to help them to be successful with corporate adopters; and

(3) the help available from support organizations.

Three main groups were selected for research: (a) commercial organizations that were corporate adopters of inventions; (b) independent inventors; and (c) relevant support organizations such as professional bodies, trade associations and government agencies. The research was exploratory by nature so a qualitative approach was applicable.

The method of investigation was by in-depth interviews with seven independent inventors and ten adopter companies incorporating the use of semi-structured questions. Selection of inventors and companies was drawn from the Kompass Directory of UK companies and a total of seventeen was arrived at, of those willing to take part in the research. Communications and correspondence were also carried out with the relevant support organizations to solicit information. Questions concerned the support available in industry and the UK to help independent inventors to put their inventions in the marketplace and to solicit further information about inventors and corporate adopters.

Findings
The research uncovered a list of barriers to innovation. The key issues that had a negative influence on the rate of adoption by 'corporate adopters' were the following:

- the lack of a 'track record' or experience in R&D in the previous employment of independent inventors; and
- problems concerning the inventors' understanding and experience of industry.

Many inventors lacked diverse and business backgrounds, especially in marketing, and did not have the resources necessary to complete the innovation process. Those who lack experience of industry may have difficulty identifying the type of information required by the purchaser, even though consumer information may be quite readily and cheaply available via the Internet. First impressions count and inventors who give the wrong image lose credibility, whatever the product idea.

Inventors could not easily communicate the utility of their inventions, resulting in the corporate adopters being unable to see sufficient applications for public demand.

Professionalism and realism are key requirements, as are technical and commercial credibility together with an understanding or appreciation of the demands and requirements of the corporate adopter's business. Every valuable, creative idea is logical in hindsight. Having the foresight to see the value in advance is a limiting factor which every inventor must overcome in his attempts to sell his or her idea. It is likely that an inventor is unable to anticipate all the applications to which the invention could be put. Whilst products frequently take off in ways its inventors never predicted, no commercial organization will take on a product for which there is no perceived need or demand.

There is a lack of adaptation for the inventors when they do not see their inventions in terms of the corporate adopters' needs and capabilities as they become too focused on the enthusiasm for their own inventions.

The inventors were seen to demonstrate little business acumen or sense of reality about development costs or had not conducted proper research into each company approached, despite research into companies via their individual web sites that were relatively easy to access via the Internet.

Findings with corporate adopters showed that they had skewed perceptions of the image of inventors with the existence of stereotyping relating to rating the 'attractiveness' of inventors in terms of their perceptions of these inventors' interpersonal and communication skills. Strong stereotypical quotes about independent inventors (Attlee, 1999) used by corporate adopters include: 'nutters, eccentrics, they have a passion, unable to work in teams, a little crazed, channelled in their belief in their own inventions, cannot see their own disadvantages or faults, dress badly, don't comb their hair, passionate, enthusiastic and obsessive'.

Problems identified by independent inventors included the following:

- the need to improve problem-solving and creative skills in order to market their inventions;

- getting over to corporate adopters the viability of their marketing strategies;
- while e-research is a cheap and effective method of utilising secondary data to identify appropriate companies, appropriate targeting of companies needed to be refined;
- the specific need to understand or to talk the 'customer-oriented' language of the buyers;
- what types of persuasive communication techniques which could be used; and
- lacking knowledge of useful market data that could be provided by inventors to the companies.

However, while potential customers could be identified and hence market research, both primary and secondary, could be conducted via the internet, the problem was that maintaining confidentiality about the inventions required careful attention.

Overall the research showed that inventors lacked some of the communication skills that could help in their marketing processes. Horevitz and McCarthy (1997) included an explanation from the Greek philosopher, Aristotle. Persuasion is seen to require the deft use of all three 'proofs': the ethos (ethics or credibility); the pathos (passion); and the logos (logic or reason). Inventors who use too much passion or enthusiasm may lack credibility, whilst those who apply too much logic or scientific information to argue their cases may fail to gain the interest of the company through lack of passion. To make it even more difficult for each inventor, the balance of the three 'proofs' will be different for each company and will depend on the personality and requirements of each individual buyer.

Disappointment with the limited support for innovation

The processes which inventors must undergo prior to attempting to sell their inventions are complex. A patent search should be conducted (requiring many hours of expensive and skilled time on an electronic database), followed by a patent application (usually requiring the services of a patent agent who, by law, must be a qualified solicitor), research and building of a prototype (or proof of principle model). All of these stages in the process are expensive and there is no real support mechanism at any stage for a person working independently. The complications of patent law in a global market have already been alluded to. There are agencies that offer to market inventions to industry, but they may receive a bad press. They generally require a full patent before they will market a product and require a fee (typically several thousand pounds in sterling).

Although there are varying levels of financial support between countries, most inventors generally have to be proactive in seeking out sources of assistance to finance their inventions themselves. The UK is no exception. As one invention becomes successful and credibility is established, it becomes easier to obtain financial assistance. For example, in the UK a 'Smart' award, (a grant from the Design Council), can be obtained. There is little effective support available to an independent inventor trying to market his first idea. There is no system for assessing its potential. Relevant trade associations, government institutions and professional bodies in the UK offer very limited advice to inventors who contact them. Most advice revolves around patent, intellectual property and legal issues rather than marketing. Whilst this type of information is now available electronically, these organizations offer virtually no advice on marketing ideas.

Currently, no National Innovation Centre exists in the UK to help develop ideas, but Trevor Baylis, inventor of the clockwork radio, has laid the foundations for an Academy of Inventors' based at the Institute of Mechanical Engineers to assist in the innovation process. In 1991, the House of Lords Select Committee on Science and Technology 'regretted that British companies are often slow to take advantage of technology transfer from Research Councils and Higher Education Institutions' and urged them to improve their responsiveness. The Government White Paper 'Realising our Potential', published in May 1993, set out a series of reforms giving commitment to easier access for small and medium sized enterprises to the innovation support programmes run by the Department of Trade and Industry (DTI). The Enterprise Bill, introduced to the House of Commons in March 2002, put forward a range of measures to enhance enterprise. The Patent Office provides advice on its website for Universities wishing to manage intellectual property. The DTI devised a Science and Innovation Strategy in 2001, but as with most of the support available, this is aimed at industry rather than independent inventors. On an optimistic note though a CBI survey of employers in the UK reported that 33 per cent of small and medium sized enterprises (SMEs) in 2002 were more optimistic about their prospects in the economy compared to 19 per cent in 2001 (BBC 2, 2002).

Opportunities afforded inventors by the Internet as they seek to become entrepreneurs

With scarce resources independent inventors need to be aware of how to make the best use of freely available sites. Independent inventors can actively engage in searches, view advertisements of products and services on-line and use ways of communicating through emails, news/chat lists, via web-based information and retail sites, without the limitations of national borders and the political restrictions of governments.

The Internet has revolutionised the way in which individuals and organizations communicate in an interactive way through the technological medium. The increase in commercial activities that centre on the Internet has led to transformations for commercial organizations, e-businesses and their e-marketing (Hardaker and Graham 2001, Strauss and Frost 2001).

One significant change for inventors-entrepreneurs has been the ability of individuals externally and internally to get in touch with decision-makers at different levels of organizations via emails and so on, thereby facilitating the speed of decision-making. The traditional gatekeeper role in organizations hampered inventors, for as would-be entrepreneurs they frequently had to go through the gatekeeper hurdles of buyers and secretaries in the process of getting through to users and decision-makers in management.

A second important change has been the way in which the Internet has allowed inventors to have direct access to the marketplace to seek information, ask questions, develop links with potential suppliers and with consumers (Wright and Crimp 2000). It helps inventors to put a stronger case to potential adopter organizations if they have initial research and information on the likelihood of purchases by end-users.

A third change has been accessibility to international markets and the way in which organizations and individuals, regardless of distances, are able to develop and maintain their exploratory and contractual relationships with one another on a global basis.

In terms of the differing levels of Internet penetration, as seen from Table 2, Sweden and the USA have compared very favourably with the UK, France, Spain and Germany. Ease of access to emails, search engines and the proliferation of free websites easily accessible from home are benefits of the modern age that entrepreneurial independent inventors can use. The most visited sites in January 2001, in the highest used order, were given as msm.com, yahoo.com, microsoft.com, msm.co.uk, passport.com, yahoo.co.uk, bbc.co.uk and lycos.com (FT Connectis, 2001). Free not-for-profit websites with useful information include those provided by university libraries, for example, the Association of Research Libraries (ARL) comprising over 120 libraries of North American research institutions and the patent offices of the industrialized countries. Other free sites supported by government agencies should be used too.

The Internet affords inventors-entrepreneurs an easily accessible medium or channel to support their marketing communications' initiatives

Table 11.2   E-marketing and innovation

	Internet penetration (% of population)				
UK	France	Spain	Germany	Sweden	USA
35.6	18.4	17.3	29.2	56.4	58.6

	Internet penetration (% of population)				
UK	France	Spain	Germany	Sweden	USA
35.6	18.4	17.3	29.2	56.4	58.6

	Internet penetration from home via PC (% of internet users)				
UK	France	Spain	Germany	Sweden	USA
39.1	32.4	23.3	40	41.5	46.1

Source: FT Connectis, 2001

as it has the potential to be much more cost-effective than the traditional means of advertising in enhancing 'direct-to-consumers' and 'direct responses with businesses'. The popularity of marketing by organizations and individuals on the Internet is seen in the following UK figures. As derived from the Direct Marketing Association and the Advertising Association (Financial Times, 2001) total direct marketing expenditure in the UK rose to £10.1 billions by 2001.

On the export front, the role of government sponsored trade missions has not diminished with the increasing popularity of the Internet in advancing global contacts and communications. Trade missions play an important part in promoting personal links and establishing networks to enhance relationship building between individuals and companies in different countries. In the USA, there are important sites directed at working with American enterprises and business organizations to promote exports and increase economic prosperity. They include those of the Department of Commerce, such as www.*Ita.doc.gov/doctm* and the federal government's *www.usconsulate* and e*xportsource.gc.ca/nonframe/engdoc.3c.html* that have linkages to information on trade organized with the aim of promoting US exports to certain countries. One example of how trade missions are put together to introduce the UK's renewable energy companies to potential partners or clients is at *www.dti.gov.uk/renewabl/trademissions.* Independent inventors and SMEs could, therefore, link into government assistance and access to information with the accessibility and networking opportunities offered by the Internet.

Conclusions

Invention and the fostering of an entrepreneurial culture are important in sustaining the growth of companies and international competitiveness. Independent inventors and UK potential adopter organizations both seem to fail to take full advantage of their inventiveness. As most organizations are structured for stability rather than innovation and strategies are devised years in advance, companies may have to learn to structure for innovation and to adopt a culture that welcomes innovation regardless of its source. In particular, opportunities exist for developing countries to purchase new ideas from any source without the normal R&D costs.

The expertise of product designers, executives, higher education institutions, buyers and marketing specialists could be combined to provide an assessment of marketability for independent inventors. Good links now exist between universities and industry but there is no way for an independent inventor to break into this system and take advantage of academic research or market assessment of the idea. As seen from the case example, potential adopter organizations in the UK are not enthusiastic about approaches from independent inventors. In particular, R&D Departments are prone to NIH syndrome. Companies do not make it easy for inventors to approach them. An infrastructure is needed to make it easier for existing ideas and inventions to reach the marketplace. Clearly, companies in any part of the world need to examine the extent to which they are geared to attract and process approaches by independent inventors.

Inventors need to exhibit greater awareness of marketing principles and specific good practices. They also need to exploit the potential of the Internet in gaining free web based information, making contact with corporate adopters via emails and in gaining government assistance with regard to exports. While it may not be possible or even desirable for inventors to change some aspects of their own personality, their marketing and communication strategies their tactics often could be improved with more care to the presentation and attention to detail. See Appendix A.

The research evidence in the case example suggests that most approaches to adopter companies by independent inventors could be improved significantly in terms of targets, preparation and presentation. Information and intelligence about markets, companies and similar products allow independent inventors to present much more professional cases.

References

Attlee, C.J. (1999), 'The Role of Communication in the Commercial Adoption of Independent Inventions', *University of the West of England*, unpublished MA thesis.
Baggozi, R. and Foxall, G. (1996), 'Construct Validation of a Measure of Adaptive-

Innovative Cognitive Styles in Consumption', *International Journal of Research in Marketing,* 13, (3), 201–213.

BBC 2. (2002), 'Working Lunch' television series, 12.40 pm, Monday 13th May.

Cooper, R.G. (1984), 'New product strategies: what distinguishes the top performers?', *Journal of Product Innovation Management*, 2, 151–164.

Cui, G. and Choudhury, P. (2002), 'Marketplace diversity and cost-effective marketing strategies', *Journal of Consumer Marketing*, 19 (1), 54–73.

Davies, E. (1995), *Inventions,* London: Dorling Kindersley.

Financial Times: FT Connectis Magazine (2001), May, 6.

Financial Times (2001), *Creative Business* survey insert June.

Gupta, A.K., Raj, S.P. and Wilemon, D. (1985), 'R&D and marketing dialogue in high-tech firms', *Industrial Marketing Management*, 14, 289–300.

Hardaker, G. and Graham, G. (2001), *Wired marketing: Energizing Business for e-Commerce*, Chichester: John Wiley and Sons.

Hisrich, R.D. (1985), 'The Inventor: A Potential Source for New Products', *The Mid-Atlantic Journal of Business*, 24 (1), Winter, 67–80.

Horevitz, A. and McCarthy, J. (1997), 'Appraisal Writing, Aristotle and the Art of Persuasion', *Appraisal Journal*, 65 (3), July, 242–246.

Jensen, R. (1992), 'Reputational Spillovers, Innovation, Licensing and Entry', *International Journal of Industrial Organization*, 10 (2), June, 193–212.

Johnson, B.A. (1976), 'Inventions, Innovations and Incentives, The Public Need and the Role of the Inventor', *US Department of Commerce, National Bureau of Standards, Special Publication*, 6.

Kitchell, S. (1997), 'CEO Characteristics and Technological Innovativeness: A Canadian Perspective', *Canadian Journal of Administrative Sciences*, 14 (2), June, 11–125.

Leavy, B. (1997), 'Innovation and the Established Organization', *Journal of General Management*, 22 (3), Spring, 38–52.

Martin, C., Martin, L.M. and Mabbett, A. (2002), 'SME ownership succession – business support and policy implications'. Report commissioned for the UK Small Business Service: *Sheffield, DTI Small Business Service*.

Moenaert, R.K. and Souder, W.E. (1990), 'An information transfer model for integrating marketing and R&D personnel in new product development projects', *Journal of Product Innovation Management*, 7, 91–107.

Narin, F. (1993), 'Technology Indicators and Corporate Strategy', *Review of Business*, Vol 14, (3), Spring, 19–23.

Parker, R.S, Udell, G. and Blades, L. (1996), 'The New Independent Inventor: Implications for Corporate Policy', *Review of Business*, 17 (3), Spring, p 7–11.

Post, F. (1994), 'Creativity and Psychopathology – A Study of 291 World-Famous Men', *British Journal of Psychiatry*, 165, July, 22–34.

Steele, L.W. (1991), 'Needed: New Paradigms for R&D', *Research-Technology-Management*, 34 (4), Jul/Aug, 13–21.

Strauss, J. and R. Frost. (2001), *E-Marketing*, Prentice Hall, New Jersey.

The Economist (1999), 'Innovation in Industry', February 20th, loose survey insert.

The Economist (2002), 'Japan's little firms – Small Mercies', June 8th, 66.

Wang, Q. and Montaguti, E. (2002), 'The R&D-marketing interface and new product entry strategy', *Marketing Intelligence & Planning*, 20 (2), 82–85.

Wright, L.T. and Crimp, M. (2000), *The Marketing Research Process*, FT Prentice Hall.

Wright, L.T. and Nancarrow, C. (2001), 'Improving marketing communication & innovation strategies in the small business context', *Small Business Economics,* 16, 113–123.

Appendix A.   Factors to take into account in the Communications Strategy for Independent Inventors

Planning the Communications Strategy for Independent Inventors	Communications Toolkit for Independent Inventors	What Adopter Organizations Commonly Require
Conduct a basic S.W.O.T. analysis. Decide what environmental forces (e.g. competitive, regulatory, economic, social and technological) would help to create positive arguments for the demand for the ideas, technologies or products.	Carry out preliminary research into organizations that have similar requirements for inventors' ideas, technologies or products. Gauge depth of interest from opinion leaders, trade associations and end user customers, before approaching the adopter organizations to be targeted.	Indications that inventors understand the wider constraints of the external marketing environment in which adopter organizations operate. Appreciation of the types of customer base of adopter organizations.
Solicit for interviews and explain clearly and concisely the purposes of the interviews. Practice interpersonal skills as inventors might be interviewed by a number of people from different departments within the adopter organizations.	Use the correct forms of address with regard to names and job titles. Make contact with the relevant people in adopter organizations to obtain interviews and use the phone, emails, faxes and letters, when appropriate. Use professionally printed and visually attractive documents to give properly explained accounts of specified ideas, technologies or products. Explain uses for the target markets. Give commercially viable arguments.	Recognition by inventors of the requirements or needs of adopters. Would the inventions help to solve production, product, service or market problems?
Use persuasive communications skills to explain the mutual benefits to the corporate adopters.	Be prepared to be realistic in explaining own requirements for the use of the inventions and how the adopter organizations could help.	Compliance with adopters' need for confidentiality and procedures in decision-making.

Appendix A. (continued)

Planning the Communications Strategy for Independent Inventors	Communications Toolkit for Independent Inventors	What Adopter Organizations Commonly Require
	Be amenable in recognising own limitations with regard to questions from corporate adopters. Accept areas of mutual concern. Establish benefits of alliances between inventors and adopters.	
Employ persistence in communications to gain decisions from corporate adopters. Maintain approaches to other corporate adopters.	Apply a follow-up procedure e.g. telephone calls or emails to express appreciation for interviews and after two weeks, to prompt progress about decisions on inventions. Select best offer.	Satisfaction of inventor's competence and ability to work within the requirements of the adopter organizations.

12 Learning, innovation and globalization: the competitive advantage of collaborative entrepreneurship

Harry Matlay and Jay Mitra

Small, innovative firms are best placed to pursue global competitive advantage when they choose to operate within industrial clusters. This chapter investigates entrepreneurship in existing and emerging clusters in the United Kingdom and Italy. The authors argue that cluster-based enterprises not only make optimum use of global markets, strategic alliances and niche opportunities, but also enable wider, regional linkages for the clusters within which they operate (Mitra and Matlay, 2002). Locally defined, strategic connections, linkages and partnerships are the key factors that distinguish clusters from other forms of business collaborations (Beccatini, 1989; Camagni, 1991; Porter, 1998; Enright, 1998; Cooke and Morgan, 1998; Mitra, 2000). The nature of related linkages – between firms, customers, suppliers, distributors, agencies and across sectoral boundaries – influence the scope and purpose of a variety of entrepreneurial activities and determine the effectiveness of organizational competitiveness at local, national and international levels. The scale and intensity of entrepreneurship at each of these levels is perceived to change strategically, as a result of a continuum of learning, as firms weave their distinctive patterns of innovation, growth and competitiveness (Mitra and Matlay, 2000; Cullen and Matlay, 1999; Leonard, 1998).

The quest for sustainable competitive advantage manifests itself in the distinctive and differentiating use of labour and intermediate inputs as well as a propensity for collective learning (Mitra, 2000; Matlay, 2000; Nachum and Keeble, 1999). Research evidence suggests that the learning process is as much a function of entrepreneurship as it is of the innovative dynamics of evolutionary growth and abstractions of 'convergence', 'complexity' and 'paradox' (see, for example, Matlay, 2000; Matlay and Fletcher, 2000). Cumulatively, these features form an integral part of the global process of change, as firms and the regions in which they are located link up with entrepreneurs across the world (Matlay, 1999). Furthermore the process of cluster-based internationalization and globalization tends to reinforce and promote the entrepreneurial and competitive strengths of participating firms (Porter, 1998; Nachum and Keeble, 1999).

The chapter is structured broadly in two parts. Part One critically evaluates relevant theoretical concepts drawn from the extensive literature on innovation, organizational learning and entrepreneurship. It provides a tentative 'learning model' that incorporates the main strategic aspects of firms engaged in cluster-based entrepreneurial processes. Part Two tests this model and contextualizes learning processes within two case studies of clusters, one in a high-technology sector in the UK and the other in a traditional manufacturing sector in Italy. Of particular importance for cluster competitiveness is the emergent notion of learning for innovation. It is suggested that an understanding of relevant learning processes can prove critical to the success of entrepreneurial firms engaged in cluster-type cooperation. Using current research evidence, the authors investigate various forms of entrepreneurial learning at both the level of the firm and that of the cluster. The research results presented in this chapter originate from a current 'Clusters' project funded by the European Commission.

Introduction

In considering the idea and value of learning at the global level, it is appropriate at the outset to outline a number of key assumptions. For the purpose of this chapter, these assumptions could help provide a useful framework for testing various hypotheses on learning and its concomitants, namely innovation and sustainable competitive advantage, with particular reference to small and medium sized enterprises (SMEs). The key assumptions implied in this framework are that:

1. learning for SMEs is closely associated with innovation (in all its forms) because of their need to survive through incremental differentiation or to grow through dynamic change processes;
2. learning at the level of the firm is usually focused on systems, based on either Schumpeterian notions of specialist, science-based research and formalized coordination, the notion of more intensive forms of participation by firms, or collective innovation processes in industrial districts/clusters; and
3. systems of organizational learning and innovation are both location- and culture-specific, suggesting the need for an evolutionary and/or social constructivist approach.

Learning processes, and especially collective or organizational learning, underline different types of innovation. Innovation is often the result of interactions between various disciplines, technologies, people and organizations. Similarly, learning processes underpin innovative activities in organizations of various sizes and sectors of economic activity. Learning can be defined as a process that modifies the state of knowledge at individual and/or organizational level. A change in knowledge may take the form of the adoption of a new belief about causal relationships, the modification of an existing belief, the abandonment of a previously held belief or a change in the degree of confidence with which an individual or individuals within an organization hold a belief or a set of beliefs (Sanchez and Heene, 1997:6). Typically SMEs are better able to innovate when they operate in clusters because it is through the networking process and the management of externalities (key elements in clustering) that they develop new products, processes and/or services. The networking process best manifests itself in particular locations (for example, a geographical region), through strategic connections between different organizations, technologies and skills and in the context of an economically dynamic system.

Innovation systems
The concept of innovation as a 'system' with spatial and sociocultural dimensions involves the study of regional and national systems of innovation, including industrial districts, spatial networks, clusters and other 'focused environments'. A fundamental aspect of the 'systemic view' is that it allows for a strategic connection between 'technological' and 'organizational' innovation (Mitra, 2000). This approach also suggests that the main factors that foster or discourage technological innovation are not limited to the internal jurisdiction of a firm (Cooke and Morgan, 1998). When it occurs, innovation is 'new' to the firm and/or to the market, and even when it is absorbed within an organization it has nevertheless introduced a 'novel' dimension or perspective. Competitive factors of cost reduction, value added and new market opportunities may be the motives behind innovative drives, but successful innovation tends to enhance a firm's activities and/or capabilities (Mitra and Matlay, 2000; Mitra and Matlay, 2002). In this context, a firm has made an additional connection with the market as well as the wider economic environment, sometimes beyond its routine, daily business activities. Additionally the innovation process combines, inter alia, different activities, such as design, research, market investigation, process development, organization restructuring and employee development. The innovation process, therefore, is not complete unless connections are made at the level of skills, functions, technologies, commercial production, markets and other organizations (Mitra, 1999).

The resources and activities of SMEs are often embedded in their regions (Granovetter, 1985; Becattini, 1989) and innovative outcomes can sometimes be seen to be the result of a symbiotic relationship between the strategies of individual firms and the clusters in which they operate.

Regional embeddedness incorporates both social and economic forms and it is often viewed as an important determinant of learning (see, for example, Danson, 1996). In this context firms, communities and the region act collectively as 'learning networks'. Firms cooperate and network together in order to reduce uncertainty and maintain stability within a spatial setting. In the process, they form a 'common set of meanings and agendas' as building blocks for organizational learning (Cullen and Matlay, 1999). Competitive advantage at the level of both the firm and the region rests on the management of the interface between 'related industries'. While public policy can help identify and support such industries, individual firms need to understand, cultivate and promote their unique brand of strategic relationships. It is suggested that such understanding is perhaps best developed through collective learning, based on connected interorganizational activities and strategic goals (Mitra and Matlay, 2000).

Connectivity and the systemic view of innovation
In recent years, Lundvall (1992) and Nelson and Rosenberg (1993) have focused their research on national innovation systems, while Saxenian (1994), Braczyk *et al.* (1998) and Cooke and Morgan (1998), have concentrated their attention on regional innovation systems. Other researchers (for example, Carlsson and Stankiewicz, 1991; Freeman and Soete, 1997) have studied technological innovation systems. The 'systemic' view has as its antecedents the Marshallian (1920, 1923) notion of externalities, where knowledge and its transfer to stakeholders is a factor favouring spatial concentration of industries. The Marshallian idea of 'knowledge spillover' plays an important role in the regionalization of innovation and is significant within both rural and urban areas (Audretsch and Feldman, 1994). Manifesting itself within supply chain relationships, horizontally related firms, transfer of people and their skills, shared pools of knowledge of markets, research and so on, these spillovers are considered to benefit industrialized regions disproportionately. The economic rationale offered for the existence of such localization (or indeed clusters) from Marshall (1920, 1923) onwards to Weber (1929) and Krugman (1991), is to be found in the concept of special benefits coupled with the presence of natural resources, a combination that helps to reduce uncertainties and risks associated with innovation. Knowledge spillovers, inter-firm relationships, utilization of shared resources, a well-developed local skills base and the evolution of the region through tacit and explicit knowledge exchange are typical features of regional clusters. These features also provide a basis for the social and economic 'connectivity' that underlines the operation of firms and clusters.

Clusters: competitive advantage of regions

The definition of clusters as 'groups of firms in the same industry, or in closely related industries that are in close geographical proximity to each other' is meant to include geographically concentrated business, including 'industrial districts' (Enright, 1998: 337). The geographic concentration of interconnected firms is supported by similarly connected suppliers, downstream channels, customers and manufacturers of complementary products, and can also extend to include companies with complementary skills (Porter, 1998). Clusters also include public, government and educational institutions, as well as support services. In practice, linkages and complementarities define cluster boundaries across interconnected institutions and industries (see Porter, 1998). The linkage between regional innovation and clusters lies in the understanding of the successful evolution of competitive groupings whereby their formation, organization and structure are themselves features of an innovation process.

Various clusters have evolved from being 'comparative advantage' players (based on physical resources) to 'competitive advantage' groups (based on learning and knowledge) in order to overcome the loss of their traditional 'locational advantage'. Thus the replacement of waterpower by electricity and wood by coal, and the easy availability of steel, did not prevent the Solingen location from continuing as a successful base for the cutlery industry. It achieved this through its reliance on the particular expertise of its workforce (Enright, 1998). Similarly the disadvantages of a poorer regional economy have not prevented Sialkot in Pakistan from becoming the second largest exporter (after Germany) of surgical instruments in the world (Nadhvi, 1998). In essence, therefore, the ability to identify, accumulate, utilize and recycle learning resources embedded in a location has proved to be the major source of 'competitive advantage' for many regions (Mitra, 2000).

The consequence of innovative evolution has resulted in clusters attracting public and private finance, chambers of commerce and trade associations generating relevant commercial market research, regional government providing industry-specific infrastructure and local educational institutions undertaking industry-specific training and research. Thus, in clusters, the combination of integrated and leveraged activity is often at the heart of innovation and collective learning (Rosenberg, 1982; Malecki, 1991).

Region-specific resources and activities

What would have been regarded as the 'invisible hand' factor that supported the success of specific regions in the past can now be attributed to 'softer' issues. Interestingly, 'softer' issues include competitive technical and managerial expertise, explicit and tacit knowledge, the synergies derived from strong interaction in input–output linkages, collective learning and the 'dynamic socialization' process based on trust, openness, reciprocity and voluntarism (Capello, 1998). Such 'softer' issues have a tangible force only if they are embedded in regional economic activity and prove difficult or impossible to duplicate (Granovetter, 1985; Becattini, 1989).

Pressures, incentives, capabilities and competencies tend to work through collective learning, inter-firm linkages and region-specific resources that support localized activities. Barney (1991) argues that a firm's resource mix can lead it to a position of sustainable competitive advantage if it proves valuable, rare, imperfectly imitable and not subject to substitution. In turn, Enright (1998) claims that, potentially, a region's specific resource mix can offer competitive advantages for the firms that operate within it. Consequently just as, 'with firms, the region's resources will be difficult to imitate if they depend on unique historical conditions, the link between resources and competitive advantage is causally ambiguous or the resources are socially complex' (ibid.: 322).

Region-specific resources can be generated by close linkages among flexible and specialized SMEs, often in the same industry and contributing to the production of a similar product group (Braczyk *et al.*, 1998). The Gremi group's idea of the 'innovative milieu' posits a dynamic model in which the milieu is a complex network of informal relationships in a limited geographical area and enhancing local innovative capability through 'synergetics' and collective learning processes (see Camagni, 1991). The 'territorial ecosystem' of the innovation model, developed by Mitra and Formica (1997), highlights the spatial dimension of networking and learning among regional firms and institutions.

Evolutionary stages of innovation and learning

The region-specific resources model, however, does not necessarily explain how the learning relationships between firms and regions work. What needs to be taken into consideration is the evolution of the innovation process through different development stages of a firm, in particular regions and in association with other businesses operating in the cluster. Innovation through these development stages is closely linked to learning as firms move from one form of organizational practice to another in order to create new and competitive portfolios of products and services.

In recent years, theoretical and empirical studies have identified significant changes in the distinctive characteristics of clusters and industrial districts (IDs). The evolutionary process of most IDs manifests itself in three stages: 'formation', 'development' and 'maturity' (for a detailed analysis, see Carbonara and Mitra, 2001). As they evolve, and especially in the last stage, there is often a modification in the IDs' structural characteristics, including their innovation management processes. These stages in an ID's existence would appear to reflect its own individual evolutionary path, including 'variation', 'selection', 'retention', 'diffusion' and 'struggle for resources' processes that are likely to be specific to each member firm (see Aldrich, 1999).

The early stages are characterized by the reinforcement of a 'craftsman-like' manufacturing system localized in a specific geographic area and by the development of networking processes among firms that carry out an integrated system of production activities in accordance with the 'flexible specialization' model (Piore and Sabel, 1984). During these stages, the technical–operative, tacit and informal knowledge, widespread in the local area, plays a fundamental role in innovative processes and in the industrial development of the IDs. The growth of technical–operative knowledge, supported by processes of 'learning by doing' and 'learning by using', combined with 'dynamic socialization', produces important innovative results (Capello, 1998). This property, known as 'widespread innovative capacity' (WIC), is probably the most important source of competitive advantage for clusters, as long as the competitive environment remains static (Bellandi, 1989). In this context, an adaptive learning process, characterized by incremental improvement of products, services and technologies, enables member firms to generate and sustain competitive advantage. The analysis of different stages of evolution is complicated by factors associated with both the density of inter-firm links and the rapid changes associated with technological developments, such as uncertainty, complexity and the constant need to assess relevant competencies with which to sustain the continuing learning process.

Complexity, uncertainty and innovation
Technological change, inter-firm interaction and alliances, trust and reciprocity are all part of a complex web of issues relating to entrepreneurship. Complexity is heightened by considerable uncertainty in the external environment as well as within individual firms. Complexity and uncertainty are perhaps usefully dealt with when there is a range of entrepreneurial competencies and capabilities within as well as among the firms in a cluster. These facilitate the use of firm-specific and cluster-based complementarities in pursuit of common entrepreneurial activities. Typically 'competence building' (to achieve qualitative change, such as new firm creation or new product/service development) and 'competency leveraging' (applying competencies to market opportunities and/or shared activities) are the most effective actions taken by firms in their drive to generate learning resources. Entrepreneurial competencies can supplement 'firm-specific

assets' (assets exclusive to, and tightly controlled by, a firm) and 'firm-addressable assets' (assets which the firm is able to draw upon through networking within the cluster). Thus the entrepreneur is able to manage 'causal ambiguities' resulting from asymmetrical and ambiguous data gathered from an increasingly uncertain environment.

While 'competency building' and 'firm-specific' assets are part of the internal portfolio of a firm, 'competency leveraging' and 'firm-addressable' assets are externalities that a firm is best able to manage and use through cooperation and interaction with cluster members (Sanchez and Heene, 1997; Bellini *et al.*, 1997). Entrepreneurs, operating in clusters, learn to innovate through a systematic application of these competencies and through the use of these assets. The learning process is continuous and tends to take place even when innovations are not apparent (as in the case of incremental innovations).

Entrepreneurial competency building and leveraging with the use of firm-specific or firm-addressable assets can be viewed as common features of systemic efforts in that they promote the management of routines and outcomes leading to continuous change. Furthermore, they should be perceived as key elements of a 'learning system' for any innovative organization operating in a cluster (Mitra, 2000). While large firms are better placed to internalize such a system and operate independently, SMEs have to rely on external linkages and networks in order to manage learning and innovation processes. The cluster model presented in this chapter incorporates a 'learning system' that is supported by a complex web of connections and interactions between member firms – in both spatial and organizational terms.

Innovation and learning systems

Generation, codification and transfer of knowledge are essential elements of a cluster-based 'learning system'. In a cluster, the system is operational within and across member firms through the dynamic exchange afforded by 'competency building' and 'competency leveraging'. Arguably the cluster environment is conducive to innovation owing to the availability of essential 'attractors' (skills and knowledge base, information access, capability of market conversion of ideas and technological spillover). In this context, learning for innovation is mostly concerned with (a) the creation, adaptation and fusion of new ideas among firms and across the region (generation and competency building), (b) the generation of knowledge through continuous learning (codification and competency leveraging), and (c) the transfer of knowledge from one firm to another or between institutions and firms (transfer and coordination, and the move from firm-specific assets to firm-addressable assets).

Convergence and paradox in clusters

The 'learning system' approach helps us identify other important features of clusters and their learning environment. The first feature of a 'learning system' is that of *convergence*. Longhi and Keeble (1998) have referred to the evidence of clustering found in European high-technology regions during the 1990s. Convergence can manifest itself in sectoral structures in terms of diversification, combination of technologies and the emergence of micro clusters such as biotechnology and information and communication technologies (ICT), Internet applications, image processing and multimedia. Convergence can also be observed in growth processes, through spinoffs (endogenous growth) relative to external, large firm investment, and in the proactive technology transfer policies and training programmes of universities as well as in the development of regional collective enterprises.

The second extended feature is that of *paradox*. Clusters, and SMEs within clusters, are perceived to innovate through the management of paradox (Mitra, 1999). Paradox is evident in the globalization–regionalization tensions inherent in most entrepreneurial clusters. Successful clusters, such as those in the Silicon Valley, Emilia Romagna and Basle, tend to balance regional productive excellence with international market positioning. Empirical studies (Keeble *et al.*, 1997, in Cambridge and Oxford; Mitra and Formica, 1997, in London) have found that entrepreneurial firms with above average international links have higher local linkage intensities and frequencies than their nationally oriented counterparts. Paradox is also evident in the entrepreneurial need to mass-customize products/services while concentrating on core competencies. Similarly paradox is manifest in the existence of both traditional and high technology-based industries within the same entrepreneurial cluster. Interestingly, radically different levels of industrial/sectoral and technological convergence can result in both increasing and diminishing returns (depending on the industry) within the same cluster environment.

The learning process involved in the building and use of competencies and firm-specific assets can assist entrepreneurs in identifying issues of convergence and paradox, and in managing the complexity and uncertainty of their environment. It is suggested that every attempt at developing a new product, a new process and a new market opportunity is a function of this learning process. Figure 12.1 illustrates the 'learning system' approach to cluster-based innovation.

Evolutionary trajectories of high-technology SME clusters

In considering the different levels of 'connectivity' in industrial clusters, two examples, one from the UK and the other from Italy, are used to illus-

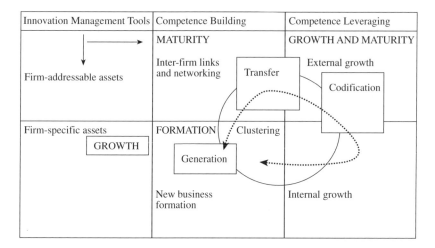

Innovation Management Tools	Competence Building	Competence Leveraging

Source: adapted from Mitra (1999) and Bellini *et al.* (1997).

Figure 12.1   The learning system approach to SME clustering and innovation

trate the nature, scope and type of connections enabling innovation in clusters. These examples also provide a basis for evaluating the learning process, both within and outside entrepreneurial firms in clusters. The systemic view of learning promoted in these two case studies could help both firms and their regions adopt more effective management policies. More specifically these case studies illustrate the two main aspects of the learning process that enables and supports innovation within firms and regions. The UK case study is concerned with the dynamics of 'convergence', paradox and 'uncertainty' that underpin cluster-based growth and development. The Italian case study explores the learning process through the formation, growth and maturity stages of cluster formation and how these promote and sustain innovative firms and regions. These case studies are contextualized in two different industrial environments: a high-technology cluster in the UK and a traditional manufacturing industrial district in Italy. The main emphasis here is on identifying critical features in the learning process that supports innovation in cluster-based firms.

Case study 1: St Asaph, Denbighshire, North Wales
This case study was carried out during 1999–2000 with a view to testing a cluster formation in a small town in North Wales. St Asaph is dominated by small businesses, some of which have benefited from an entrepreneurial

focus on high technology and innovation. From the 1950s onwards, the development of the optical cluster emerged from the vision and drive of Dr Lawrence Pilkington. In 1957, he set up a 'state-of-the-art' factory based on US technology, which became 'Special Glass Ltd'.

The cluster   The optics cluster in St Asaph involves 13 key companies that employ over 1200 individuals, with a total turnover of just over £120m. The Pilkington family still owns (or is a major shareholder in) five of these businesses, employing around 80 per cent of the cluster's workforce. Interestingly, ex-Pilkington employees run all of the other eight businesses. Eighty per cent of the cluster's turnover is derived from the 'high' end of the high-technology optics businesses. The key technology utilized in these firms covers the convergence of glass and optical instruments, generically known as 'optronics'. The global export market is the main target of all these firms and, although overall employment has not grown significantly since the 1970s, the added value of the cluster has more than doubled in the intervening time period. In the 1970s, the two core businesses (Special Glass and Pilkington Optronics) employed around 1000 people. Since then, 500 traditional jobs have been lost and replaced by employment related to high-technology spinoffs. A Wales Opto-Electronics Forum was set up in the 1990s and now has a total membership of about 100 firms. Table 12.1 provides a summary of the nature, scope and distribution of the opto-electronics sector in St Asaph.

Underlying Issues   The optronics cluster in St Asaphs is a sophisticated example of conglomeration based on the visionary ideals of the owners of a leading glass manufacturer. As a large firm-led cluster, its interesting features include its 'family' style make-up, its particular focus on high technology and the manifestation of the convergence factor through two technologies and medium–small firm interaction. In common with other successful clusters, St Asaph attracts well trained, highly paid, quality staff that help boost the skills base of the region. The St Asaph Optronics cluster enjoys a high level of networking, which is institutionally supported by the Optronics Forum and the Welsh Development Agency (WDA). Through its recognition of opto-electronics as a key enabling technology, the WDA has linked strategic economic development policy to the interests of this cluster.

Since Pilkington opened up in St Asaph in 1957, as a single industrial base, the region has seen both the evolution of the company at the cutting edge and the emergence of a cluster of small, high-technology companies around Special Glass. The new firm formation, alongside advances in productivity and convergent technologies, is similar to the evolution of the wool cluster in Prato, albeit on a smaller scale. This also allows for economies of

Table 12.1 The optronics cluster in St Asaph, North Wales

	Date started	Nos. employed	Turnover £m	Technology type	Comments
Pilkington companies					
Special Glass Ltd	1957	230	14	Medium	High export of optical glass, mainly to Japan
Optronics	1967	450	40	High +	Leading world co. in electro & defence optics
Space Technology	1987	80	6	High	Glass covers for space satellites
British Shielding Windows	1988	15	4	Medium	Nuclear industry shields
Micronics	1989	185	15	High+	Ultra-thin glass for displays & data storage
Non-Pilkington companies					
Pinacl	1992	150	38	High	MBO from Optronics, fibre-optics systems for banks, etc
Phoenix	1992	25	2	Medium	Sale to Pilkington employees; processing of optical glass
Omitec	1995	70+	8	High	Gen. manager, ex-Pilkington (only inward investment)
D&R Electronics	1990	6	1	Medium	Distributor of related products and services
Leader Optics	1994	4	0.5	Medium	Consultants to cluster and non-cluster organizations
Others	1968–90	30	3	Various	Various products and services related to similar outputs

Source: Mitra and Murray (1999).

scale (groups of firms cooperating for international markets) and scope (variety of products and services through networks) to be realized, and reflects the convergent factors of combined technologies, growth processes and supportive infrastructure referred to by both Longhi and Keeble (1998) and Porter (1998). The evolution of the St Asaph cluster is closely defined in the sense that specialization in optics and electronics defines the competency base of the member firms and, synergistically, that of the North Wales region.

The spinoff process enables the transition from competency building to competency leveraging more easily than a linear process of development because specific expertise is retained within the nexus of firms and within the region. Specific firms find it easier to deploy addressable assets from the larger network of kindred entrepreneurs and firms. The spatial dimension does not reflect natural resource advantages but the competitive advantage of highly specialized knowledge bases. The regular spinoff process and the inter-firm linkages through technology, people and focused resources also allow for collective efficiency and the development of advanced techniques for customer orientation and cumulative capacity. Innovation, therefore, is more likely to take place in such an environment, with its enhanced skills and knowledge base, its advanced infrastructure and the growing rate of technological spillovers. Thus the management of the innovation process for cluster-based firms is to a great extent tied up with the externalities of networking, the reliance on and use of complementary technologies, the availability of relevant skills and expertise and a focus on similar yet differentiated global markets. The Optronics cluster demonstrates the innovation paradox of growth which is not confined to firms expanding in size but is also manifested through the spinoff process that facilitates small business emergence in a comparatively short time period. The close cluster, regional phenomenon also has a global dimension in that most firms operate in international markets while having a localized, regional network base.

Some general observations: case study 1   In considering the St Asaph case study of clustering and the related learning process, some observations are worth noting:

- different factors and incentives can encourage clustering. The St Asaph model highlights 'visionary leadership' on Pilkington's part. This can be compared to the 'regional high technology excellence' model of Cambridge (Longhi and Keeble, 1998) or to the 'demand factor, large firm–small firm mix' model of West London (Mitra *et al.*, 1999). The way firms in such clusters learn and grow is to some extent dependent on their type;

- organizational forms within a cluster can be dynamic in nature and scope, allowing for different types of firms to emerge and evolve at various times, as with for example the spinoffs in St Asaph. Thus the learning process is concerned with changes in the nature and scope of different organizations, which in turn are dependent upon the collaborative interaction of these organizations;
- technological, organizational and skills convergence is essential to learning systems and to the clustering process, as evinced in the focus on optronics in St Asaph;
- convergence factors lead to the management of paradox, as exemplified in local networking for international markets, the development of internal competencies alongside the management of external interfaces, and increasing returns and economies of scope from upstream activities, especially with small firms, as in the multiple portfolio in St Asaph; the learning process is supported by convergence factors and the emerging set of competencies helps to manage both paradox and complexity;
- the management of externalities, convergence and paradox, coupled with the mix of skills, infrastructure support, new firm formation and technological development, offers the best opportunities for learning, innovation and the realization of sustainable competitive advantage, both at the micro and at the macro levels.

Case study 2: the industrial district of Bari and Matera
The second case study is based on a qualitative survey carried out during 2000–2001 in Italy. The survey was aimed at testing the hypothesis that it is possible to identify different learning mechanisms in different types of cluster formations. The survey focused upon the leather sofa industrial district, localized in the area of Bari and Matera (southern Italy), which has gone through all the main life cycle stages (formation, development and maturity). The survey also explored the role of 'leader' firms in the development of the cluster's innovative capability.

The industrial district (ID) The ID under investigation emerged in the 1950s as a result of an agglomeration of isolated craftsman-like firms which produced leather sofas in small volumes. In the *formation* stage the ID consisted of numerous workshops, each involved in the entire production process and selling their final products to a localized market. The level of labour division among firms was low, so that each of these firms was almost autonomous (inter-firm relationships being scarce). Their products were craftsman-made and were generally characterized by low levels of complexity and innovation. The initial strength of the ID was due to both the technical craftsman-like competencies and the spread of know-how within the area. At this stage the knowledge required to carry out the leather sofa business was not particularly sophisticated. It involved basic, context-specific tacit knowledge, resulting mainly from processes of 'learning by doing' and exchanged through informal, face-to-face relationships (Albino *et al.*, 1999). Mostly skills and tacit knowledge were transferred through lengthy apprenticeships. Apprentices learnt from, and emulated, the expert craftsman, while assimilating a base of tacit knowledge and manufacturing capabilities.

During the 1970s and until the late 1980s, the ID was in the *development* stage, characterized by the entrance of strategic entrepreneurial actors ('terminal firms'). The latter facilitated radical changes in the ID, due mainly to the development of a manufacturing strategy dependent on the externalization of production phases, extensive use of industrial production technologies and the emergence of export quotas. During the second stage, the ID was characterized by the development of labour divisions among highly specialized subcontractors, in accordance with a 'flexible specialization' model. Even if a product was still characterized by a craftsman-like content, marked by a low level of technological automation, 'terminal' firms introduced an important innovation relating to the organization of the production process. This consisted not only of the division of production processes in spatially separable phases, but also of the introduction of a preliminary phase of prototyping and the industrialization of some operations (such as cutting and sewing). Therefore 'terminal firms' developed a new knowledge base and combined it with the tacit competencies accumulated and shared in the local area over many years. This knowledge was transferred in a direct way to subcontractors linked to 'terminal firms', mainly through the use of technical data (design specifications, quality and production standards and technical specifications).

Since the late 1980s, the ID can be said to be in its *maturity* stage. Currently the ID is characterized by the development of a few firms, such as Natuzzi, Nicoletti and Calia, which have acquired 'leader' positions in their specific markets. These firms have undertaken a process of internal growth that involved considerable developments in inter-firm relationships (Carbonara, 2000). Through the definition of more structured relationships, characterized by a higher degree of dependency, the 'leader' firms have achieved a greater control of tangible and intangible resources, activities and knowledge flows to their network of subcontractors. To a large extent, 'leader' firms have increased the degree of 'knowledge sophistication' embedded in the leather sofa production process. This has been made possible through two interrelated processes, one corresponding to tacit knowledge codification and the other related to the transfer of this knowl-

Table 12.2   Main characteristics of cluster development stages

Cluster develop-ment stages	Cluster structure			Nature of knowledge
	Units	Boundary	Network	
Stage 1	Small firms	Closed	Social relationships	Practical knowledge and craftsmanship capabilities
Stage 2	Small–medium specialized firms	Closed	Economic and social relationships	Technical special-ized knowledge, firm-specific
Stage 3	Leader firms / meta-manage-ment structure / highly special-ized firms	Open	More structured economic relationships/social relationships / intersectoral relationships	Market and technological knowledge and strategic capabilities

Source: adapted from Carbonara and Mitra (2001).

edge from the ID's external milieu to the internal environment of the cluster. Such codified knowledge generates new and more complex tacit knowledge after undergoing an acquisition–assimilation process of its own. Therefore 'leader' firms appear to have performed a set of knowledge management processes, endogenous and exogenous to the ID, achieving in this way a stricter control of the innovation process.

As a result of explicit and tacit knowledge processes, the innovative capability of a 'leader' firm has increased and the potential innovative capability of other ID businesses has also grown. The innovative behaviour of the 'leader' firm can be seen to influence directly those firms that have a client–supplier relationship with them, and in an indirect way affect other ID firms that compete with them ('followers'). The former make investments in new technologies as well as in novel managerial tools and techniques, in order to comply with technical specifications defined by 'leader' firms. They also endeavour to satisfy specific requirements concerning, for example, quality standards, lead times, terms of delivery and so on. These firms increase their innovative ability and improve their own knowledge by emulating the strategic behaviour and actions of 'leader' firms. Table 12.2 outlines the main characteristics of cluster-based development stages.

Underlying issues in cluster development
Each learning mechanism that defines different types of cluster development can involve one or more organizational learning processes. Table 12.3 presents a matrix of learning processes characteristic to each stage of cluster development. A summary of the different types of learning and innovation generated by managerial actions taken by the 'leader' firms in the ID is given below.

Table 12.3   Learning processes and cluster development

Cluster	Learning mechanisms in the cluster	Organizational learning processes
Stage 1	Learning by localizing Learning by doing	Empirical learning
Stage 2	Learning by specializing Collective learning	Empirical learning Learning by emulation
Stage 3	Learning by doing/by using Learning by specializing Collective learning Learning by interacting	Empirical learning Learning by emulation Learning by acquisition

Source: adapted from Carbonara and Mitra (2001).

Empirical learning   In the past few years, 'leader' firms have invested considerable resources in R&D activities. Natuzzi, for example, has undertaken a formalized R&D programme (in 1996, the cost of intramural R&D was about three billion lire) and trained/developed its personnel through the Natuzzi Training Centre. Other 'leader' firms, Nicoletti and Calia, have carried out research within the functional areas of design, manufacturing and marketing. In each case, research and development activities were undertaken in an effort to create new production or organizational models. Similar work was also undertaken on new materials for covering and padding as well as innovative production techniques (such as new treatments of leather).

Learning by emulation   Through commitment to, and regular attendance at, international trade fairs and conferences, 'leader' firms acquired new technological and stylistic knowledge from competing firms, which developed within the context of an external marketing orientation that differed significantly from their local focus. Visits to international trade fairs are considered an important source of external knowledge which, once acquired, can be used for learning and development purposes across the whole spectrum of firms in the cluster.

Learning by acquisition Some 'leader' firms endeavour to acquire advanced technical services from external sources. For example, the development of software, business processes re-engineering and quality certification is usually outsourced for expediency and learning purposes. In other cases, 'leader' firms seek financial advice and knowledge from consulting businesses. One instance, for example, referred to quotations on the stock exchange (Natuzzi has been listed on the New York Stock Exchange since 1993). These firms also rely on outside services for strategic advice relating to mergers and acquisitions as well as for the management of international strategic alliances. The knowledge that results from learning acquisition activities, as exemplified above, is discretely disseminated for the benefit of other firms in the cluster.

Leader firms have also established collaboration agreements with public and private research institutes. Calia, for example, is engaged with a local technology and science park (Tecnopolis), in the development of new production technologies. Their research is aimed at creating an advanced prototype for automatic leather cutting. The main objective of this collaboration is the optimization of leather cutting, in terms of significant reductions and savings in manufacturing waste and processing time. Similarly Nicoletti has activated joint research projects with the University of Naples in a drive to develop new production technologies and manufacturing materials aimed at increasing the 'comfort' levels associated with their products (for example, in 1996, the cost of collaborative R&D was about two billion lire). Natuzzi has developed joint research projects with firms operating in the automotive sector, for the purpose of motorcar seat comfort measurement and optimization. Other collaborative projects focused upon inventory management, loading optimization and fast prototyping as well as on the co-design of new production technologies.

Process innovations The effects of learning processes on the innovative capability of 'leader' firms can be best illustrated by analysing some of the most important innovations generated during the same time period. 'Leader' firms have redesigned the layout of their production plants in order to automate most of their manufacturing operations. The process innovations implemented by these firms cover the adoption of the following:

- computer-based systems (CAD, 3CAD and CAM) for the design phase, the sewing process and the polyurethane shaping process;
- automated systems for the cutting process of leather and textile fibres;
- computerised numerical control (CNC) technology for the shaping process of wood components.

Product innovations   The ID's 'leader' firms have introduced stylistic innovations relating to products and their functionality. This type of product innovation is generally based upon continuous research and experimentation with new solutions in product design, materials, colouring and reclining mechanisms. Currently Natuzzi produces over 400 models of modern, traditional and classic furniture, across the whole price range. Every product (sofas, recliners, sofa-beds, sectionals) is available in 480 different coverings, including leather, fabric and micro-fibre. Some 'leader' firms are engaged directly, through intramural R&D, or indirectly, through collaboration agreements with external firms and/or research centres, in research and experimentation activities that focus on new materials. Furthermore 'leader' firms have developed other kinds of innovations, to include the following functional areas:

- *marketing*, by selling in some countries through franchised outlets and chains;
- *organization*, resulting in the formation of new industrial sub-clusters and the creation of inter-firm consortiums, aimed at concentrating their purchasing and distribution activities;
- *supply chain management*, including various techniques of vendor rating and information network linking to strategic suppliers; and
- *operation management*, involving just-in-time techniques, instant inventory analysis, materials requirement planning and revolutionary technical design procedures.

Quality innovations   In recent years, the ID's 'leader' firms have also taken steps towards quality accreditation and certification. For example, Nicoletti's quality system was certified in 1996 to ISO 9001 standard. Similarly, in 1995, Natuzzi's quality system received the ISO 9001 seal of approval and by 1997 this certification was extended to all the economic units within the Natuzzi Group. Recently Calia managed to complete the ISO 9001 certification for its entire production process, including product design activities based on customers' requirements and new product development.

Some general observations: case study 2   The literature on clusters has identified innovative capability as one of the most important competitive factors of cross or pan-organizational productive models (Mitra and Matlay, 2002). In contrast with large firms, where innovations are based essentially on R&D functions, smaller firms operating within IDs tend to acquire the ability to generate innovations through the development and dissemination of a range of specific technical and/or operational competences. The presence of entrepreneurial abilities and the formation of a dense network of relationships among the firms are key elements that facilitate such developments. These innovation mechanisms, known as 'widespread innovative capacity' or 'innovative capability without research', have been the main ingredients of the innovative capability of IDs and clusters in the first phases of their evolutionary process (the phase of 'formation and development'). However, in the context of recent competitive strategies, and as influenced by structural changes that are having an impact on ID operations, new mechanisms of innovation management have emerged. The recent development of firms with a 'leader position' and the emergence of meta-management structures have affected interorganizational relationships and relevant learning processes at both the firm and the ID levels. An analysis of innovation and relevant learning within three different stages of cluster development has identified different performance levels at each stage. Furthermore this approach has also highlighted the key role played by 'leader' firms and meta-management structures in the management of innovation within dynamic IDs. It became obvious from this case study that different learning processes can determine a variety of outcomes related to product, process and organizational aspects of member firms as well as the management of innovation in these firms.

Conclusions and policy considerations
The objective of this chapter was to explore critically the link between collective learning and innovation through clustering, as a management process for both firms and regions that are keen to build on the competitive advantage offered by new technology and innovation. The in-depth analysis of clustering and the adoption of the 'Learning System' research model have generated a number of pertinent findings that could benefit the managers of cluster-based firms as well as policy makers at regional and national levels.

Stakeholders need to consider the learning processes inherent in the management of externalities, convergence issues, paradox, uncertainty and complexity. This is particularly useful in the current economic climate of rapid change and accelerating technological advances. Entrepreneurs and policy makers must take into consideration the global–regional dichotomy, cooperation and competition issues, core competencies and the divergent product base as well as increasing and diminishing returns. This helps to avoid inflexible and counterproductive approaches and strategies that would claim, for example, that only those industries demonstrating increasing returns are likely to survive in the prevailing economic circumstances. Managing paradox also helps to accommodate the differing and occasionally conflicting agendas of stakeholders, especially within an entrepreneurial cluster environment.

Ensuring transversal technological connectivity and the strategic management of know-how and know-where can be successfully achieved through the adoption of a learning system which connects firms, their knowledge base and their competencies with their specific competitive environment. Also, from a policy development point of view, it is critical to identify the evolutionary stages of the firm and indeed of the cluster within which it operates. Of equal value is the acknowledgment that each stage in the evolutionary process offers its own opportunities for managing innovation, both at the level of the firm and at that of the cluster. Finally it is important to stress the critical factors associated with the success of the cluster model. Although clusters can be highly differentiated, it is possible to identify some common factors that affect their success and, in particular, their innovative capability. It emerges that such commonalities are invariably linked with continuous learning, at both firm (learning by specializing) and cluster (collective and interactive learning) level.

References

Albino, V., N. Carbonara and G. Schiuma (1999), 'Knowledge in inter-firm relationships of an industrial district', paper presented at the 44th ICSB World Conference, 20–23 June, Naples.
Albino V., A.C. Garavelli and G. Schiuma (1999), 'Knowledge transfer and inter-firm relationships in industrial districts: the role of the leader firm', *Technovation,* 19, 53–63.
Aldrich H.A. (1999), *Organisations Evolving,* London: Sage.
Audretsch, D. and M.P. Feldman (1994), '*Knowledge Spillovers and the Geography of Innovation and Production*', Schumpeter Society Conference, Munster.
Barney, J. (1991), 'Firm Resources and Competitive Advantage', *Journal of Management,* 17, 99–120
Bellandi M. (1989), 'Capacità innovativa diffusa e sistemi locali di imprese', in G. Becattini (ed.), *Modelli locali di sviluppo,* Bologna: Il Mulino.
Bellini, E., G. Capaldo, M. Raffa and G. Zollo (1997), 'Universities as Resources for Entrepreneurship',working paper, Fredrico II University of Naples, Italy.
Braczyk, H.-J., P. Cooke and M. Heidenreich (1998), *Regional Innovation Systems,* London: UCL Press.
Camagni, R. (1991), 'Introduction: from the local milieu to innovation through cooperation networks', in R. Camagni (ed.), '*Innovation Networks: Spatial Perspectives*', London: Bellhaven Press.
Capello, R. (1998), 'The role of inter-SMEs networking and links in innovative high-tech milieux', proceedings of the international conference 'Networks, Collective Learning and Knowledge Development in Regionally Clustered High-Technology Small and Medium Sized Enterprises in Europe', 7 December, Cambridge.
Carbonara, N. (2000), 'New models of inter-firm networks within industrial districts', proceedings of the RENT XIV Conference on Research in Entrepreneurship and small Business, 23–4 November, Prague.
Carbonara, N. and J. Mitra (2001), 'New Actors For The Competitiveness of Local Clusters and Industrial Districts: a cognitive approach to learning and innovation in Clusters and Industrial Districts', proceedings of the ISBA Small Firms Research and Policy Conference, November, Leicester.
Carlsson, B. and Rikard Stankiewicz (1991), 'On the Nature, Function, and Composition of Technological systems', *Journal of Evolutionary Economics,* 1 (2), 93–118.

Cooke, P. and K. Morgan (1998), 'The Associational Economy: Firms, Regions and Innovation, Oxford: Oxford University Press.

Cullen, J. and H. Matlay (1999), 'Collaborative Learning in Small Firms: Why Skill Standards Don't Work', paper presented at the 22nd Institute of Small Business Affairs Small Firms Policy and Research Conference, 'European Strategies, Growth and Development', 17–19 November, Leeds.

Danson, M. (ed.) (1996), *Small Firm Formation and Regional Economic Development*, London: Routledge.

Enright, M. (1998), 'Regional Clusters and Firm Strategy', in A.D. Chandler, Jr., P. Hagstrom and O. Solvell (eds), *The Dynamic Firm: The Role of Technology, Organisation and Regions*, Oxford: Oxford University Press.

Freeman, C. and L. Soete (1997), *The Economics of Industrial Innovation*, London: Pinter.

Granovetter, M. (1985), 'Economic Action and Social Structure: The Problem of Embeddedness', *American Journal of Sociology*, 91, 349–64.

Keeble, D., C. Lawson, H. Lawton-Smith, B. Moore and F. Wilkinson (1997), 'Internationalisation Processes, Networking and Local Embeddedness *in Technology Intensive Small Firms*', ESRC Centre for Business Research Working Papers, 53, University of Cambridge.

Krugman, P. (1991), *Geography and Trade*, Cambridge, MA: MIT Press.

Leonard, D. (1998), *Wellsprings of knowledge: Building and Sustaining the Sources of Innovation*, HBS Press.

Longhi, C. and D. Keeble (1998), 'European Regional Clusters of High-Technology SMEs: Evolutionary Trajectories in the 1990s', paper presented at the TSER European Network Conference, 7 December, Robinson College, Cambridge.

Lundvall, B.A. (ed.) (1992), *National systems of Innovation: Towards a Theory of Innovation and Active Learning*, London: Pinter.

Malecki, E.J. (1991), *Technology and Economic Development: the Dynamics of Local, Regional and National Change*, New York: Longman.

Marshall, A. (1920), *Principles of Economics,* 8th edn, London: Macmillan.

Marshall, A. (1923), *Industry and Trade*, 3rd edn, London: Macmillan.

Matlay, H. (2000), 'Organisational Learning in Small Learning Organisations: An Empirical Overview', *Education and Training*, 42 (4/5), 202–10.

Mitra J. (1999), 'Managing externalities: integrating technological and organisational change for innovation', proceedings of the 9th International Technology Forum, 4–8 October, Minneapolis.

Mitra J. (2000), 'Making Connections: innovation and collective learning in small businesses', *Education and Training*, 42 (4/5), 228–36.

Mitra, J. and P. Formica (1997), 'Innovative Players in Economic Development in Europe: Learning Companies and Entrepreneurial Universities' in J. Mitra and P. Formica (eds), *Innovation and Economic Development: University–Industry Partnerships in Action*, Dublin: Oak Tree Press.

Mitra, J. and H. Matlay (2000), 'Thematic Clustering: Connecting Organisational Learning in Small and Medium-Sized Businesses', *Industry and Higher Education*, 14 (6), 371–85.

Mitra, J. and H. Matlay (2002), 'Education, Training and Learning in SMEs: A Critical Perspective', paper presented at the 2nd SMEs in a Global Economy Conference, July, Wollongong, Australia.

Mitra, J. and J. Murray (1999), 'Building knowledge-driven clusters: shifting patterns in UK competitiveness policy and practice', workshop paper presented at the 44th ICSB World Conference, 20–23 June, Naples, Italy.

Mitra, J., J. Murray, E. Corti, C. La Storto and P. Formica (1999), 'Cluster-Muster: Cluster-Based Innovation and Growth Management for SMEs', in *Proceedings of the 22nd Institute of Small Business Affairs National Small Firms Policy and Research Conference, 'Small Firms: European Strategies, Growth and Development'*, Leeds, 17–19 November, 1999.

Nachum, L. and D. Keeble (1999), 'Neo-Marshallian nodes, global networks and firm competitiveness: the media cluster of Central London', *ESRC Centre for Business Research*, University of Cambridge, Working Paper 138.

Nadhvi, K. (1998), 'International Competitiveness and Small Firm Clusters – Evidence from Pakistan', *Small Enterprise Development Journal*, 9 (1), March, 12–24.

Nelson, R.R. and Rosenberg, N. (1993), *Technical Innovation and National Systems: A Comparative Analysis*, New York, Oxford University Press.

Piore, M. and C. Sabel (1984), *The second industrial divide: possibilities for prosperity*, New York: Basic Books.

Porter, M. (1998), 'Clusters and Competitiveness', *Harvard Business Review*, 76, Nov.–Dec., 77–99.

Rosenberg, N. (1982), *Inside the Black Box: Technology and Economics*, Cambridge: Cambridge University Press.

Sanchez, R. and A. Heene (1997), 'A competence perspective on Strategic Learning and Knowledge Management' in R. Sanchez and A. Heene (eds) *Strategic Learning and Knowledge Management*, Sussex: John Wiley, 3–15.

Saxenian, A. (1994), *Regional Advantage:Culture and Competition in Silicon Valley and Route 128*, Cambridge, MA: Harvard University Press.

Weber, A. (1929), *The Theory of the Location of Industries* (trans. C. Friedrich), Chicago: University of Chicago Press.

13 Marshalling relations
Hamid Etemad

Introduction

Markets were traditionally segmented: large companies competed in international markets while smaller businesses remained local or regional. However, the global competitive environment is changing dramatically: the drivers of globalization are removing the barriers that segregated the competitive space of the small and the large firms; firms of all sizes have begun to share the same competitive space (Etemad, 1999); it is becoming increasingly difficult for independent small firms to thrive on their own unless they are globally competitive.

As smaller firms are forced to compete in the global markets, they are seeking, and also experimenting with, new arrangements for internationalization, including a rich range of collaborative networks. Some of these arrangements are rival models to multinational enterprises (MNEs). They also put smaller firms in direct competition with these large and integrated firms in the international competitive landscape (Dana, Etemad and Wright, 2001; Etemad, 2003). As these emerging models of international business competition involve both the small and the large enterprises, each relying on different sets of capabilities and skills, and invoke different strategies as a basis of competition in the global environment, the traditional theories of internationalization are rendered impotent. Paramount among these capabilities, especially with smaller firms, is the ability to manage their relations with others.

The primary objective of this chapter is to demonstrate that patterns of growth and international expansion are increasingly dependent on managing an enterprise's commercial, industrial and even political interactions with a host of other firms, associates and stakeholders, often regardless of size and location. The context of these relations changes as firms grow in size and evolve from relatively simple, personal and largely localized relationships in the earlier stages of the enterprise life cycle to those which are more complex and wider in geographic scope during the later stages, requiring a higher degree of institutionalization than before. Managing the multitude of such relations, however, appears to assume greater importance and remains the essence of the entrepreneurial challenge for growth and prosperity in today's globally competitive arena.

This chapter reviews the requirements for growth and expansion of enterprise from three different perspectives: (a) growth and development of the small family enterprise in the recent history of such institutions, (b) growth and development in classical entrepreneurship writings, and (c) growth and expansion of larger MNEs, in order to illustrate that managing relationships, in various forms and context, has been an important requirement for success in entrepreneurship in a wide range of institutions over a long period of time. Stated briefly, the basic premise of this chapter is that the key requisite for success in today's rapidly globalizing business arena is the ability to establish and manage relationships with others exceptionally well. This will ensure higher joint growth and international expansion than those achievable in isolation. These joint developments seek to generate increasingly high synergies (Etemad, 1999; 2003), create deeper dependence or co-dependence (Acs and Yeung, 1999) and stronger symbiosis (Dana, Etemad and Wright, 2000; 2001) between the enterprise, associates and partners.

This chapter consists of five sections. Following this introduction, a review based on an epistemological search for commonalities in the nature and root causes of entrepreneurship, from the early evidence on family enterprise[1] to the early writing on classical entrepreneurship, is presented in the second section. Armed with the insight gained from this review, the chapter proceeds to seek supporting evidence for making a formal case for managing or marshalling relations,[2] as the essence of success in family enterprise and classical entrepreneurship. A review of the theory of internationalization in large firms is presented in the third section in order to illustrate that this essence is equally valid even in large and modern enterprises such as MNEs. The fourth section will argue that well-managed relations between smaller, growth-oriented firms and their larger partners can achieve higher joint outcomes for all parties and that, without these relations, neither party could exploit partnership-based advantages and compete effectively. These incremental efficiencies (Dana and Etemad, 1995) serve as the initial basis for building virtuous cycles of growth and developments based on mutual trust and dependence as envisioned previously by Acs and Yeung (1999), Chamlee-Wright (1997), Etemad, Wright and Dana (2001) and Gulati (1995), among others. Such exceedingly higher temporal dependencies lead to relations portraying symbiotic[3] synergy.[4] The discussion of this new perspective is presented next, followed by conclusions and implications.

A preliminary search for commonalities in early entrepreneurship
From small family enterprise to industrial giants
The concept of family business is as old as the concept of business itself. It has existed for millennia and has been the dominant way of conducting

business nationally and internationally over many centuries. The histories of the Colonna and Orsini families, for example, span centuries, predate Christianity, and go back to the Roman era. As entrepreneurs, family patriarchs may have followed their own entrepreneurial instincts in the relative safety of the family and family enterprise (Brown, 1997; Partridge, 1996). As a part of family affairs, they may have also adhered more to customary family principles, and less to the changing social norms of their time.[5] Historically family enterprises experienced continuous progression and growth for some time. Families such as the Medicis (based in Florence, operating for more than 150 years from the early 1300s), the Della Roveres (based in Urbino, Italy, operating successfully for over 250 years, starting in the early 1470s), and the Farneses (based in Rome, operating for more than 300 years, from 1400 to 1731), accomplished a lot and left long and impressive legacies in Europe. All of these families amassed tremendous wealth, gained commercial and political power, brought much social and political change, and even provided heads of the church in Italy and beyond.[6] Each of the above families succeeded in electing at least one Archbishop of Rome (the Pope) in Italy. Likewise numerous family enterprises started in Great Britain, including the Daltons, Chippendales and Andersons, who became pivotal instruments of change not only in Great Britain but also in the world beyond.

These families were not the exceptional phenomena of their time and location. The Rothschilds, for example, started in Frankfurt from humble beginnings, and eventually revolutionized European banking in the nineteenth century. Similarly, their counterparts in the New World achieved impressive heights and became industrial giants. For example, the Carnegies, Fords, Hearsts, Morgans, Rockefellers and Vanderbilts (mainly based in the eastern United States and operating from the early 1700s), not only played significant roles in creating wealth and power for their families but were also instrumental in creating employment, wealth, growth and development in their regions, if not for the United States as a whole. More significantly, however, these early entrepreneurs contributed to the initial recognition of entrepreneurship as a respectable and legitimate field of managerial practice.

The early writings and documented history of family enterprise provide considerable insight on the actual management practices of the early entrepreneurs and family enterprises (Brown, 1997; Partridge, 1996). These practices were intended mainly to optimize the internal management of the family's enterprises, but were propagated beyond the family enterprise to their immediate regions and beyond the nation, as most social processes inevitably are. Similarly these enterprises were initially intended to create wealth and serve as a power base for their respective families, but they went on to contribute to the prosperity, growth and development of others as well.[7] Most of these enterprises also became internationally successful.

Later, as entrepreneurship evolved into a scholarly field of enquiry, their successful practices[8] – unrelenting innovation, experimentation with entrepreneurial initiatives and even accumulation of a certain know-how, if not principles, in the context of the family enterprise – may have actually influenced their contemporary scholars and helped the initial formation as well as a better understanding of the field. Pioneering scholars, including Richard Cantillon, Richard Ely, Ralph Hess, Jean-Baptist Say and Joseph Schumpeter, must have been inspired by them as they exemplified much of the contemporary entrepreneurial practices of their time. It is also possible that the documented history and the early scholarly writings may have been overly influenced by mostly successful enterprises, especially by those which started from modest beginnings, endured adversity and yet prospered on a sustained basis for decades. These early documentations, however, testify to the strength, the resilience and the type of management practised by these early entrepreneurs in family enterprises.

The twin research questions arising from the above review are how did these family enterprises grow from mostly modest beginnings to become powerful commercial and industrial giants of their time; and what was the key to their growth and prosperity over time? Our initial deduction, derived from the archival research briefly highlighted above, is twofold:

1. that the family patriarchs, and these enterprises by extension, must have managed their commercial, industrial, personal and even political relations (that is, relations with their associates, partners and stakeholders) exceptionally well; and
2. that the context of these relations may have evolved over time from being informal, simpler, more personal, and more of the local family, to more formal, more complex, less personal, more regionalized and even more internationalized than before, requiring an exceedingly higher degree of institutionalization with time.

The true nature of managing (or marshalling) relations appears to have remained the same over the years. We use the above twin insights as our initial working hypothesis. We proceed by examining classical writings on entrepreneurship, which have been mainly confined to the domestic environment, for the first part of the hypothesis (dealing with managing relations) before examining the second part that deals with the international context prevailing currently.

An epistemological search in the early entrepreneurship writings
A search for the origins of scholarly writings on entrepreneurship, Etemad and Lee (2000; 2002) yielded documented evidence for entrepreneurially

oriented developments going as far back as the eighteenth century. Their study shows that there has been a continuous and systematic growth in the literature of entrepreneurship, which has gained a positive momentum and increasing presence with time, especially in the latter part of the twentieth century. The initial writings on entrepreneurships were concentrated on the individual and referred mostly to the entrepreneur himself, who was, for the most part, both the family patriarch and the leader of the family enterprise. Among the early scholarly efforts, the work of Cantillon ([1755] 1931), for example, confirms many aspects of modern entrepreneurship as practised by his contemporary entrepreneurs. He referred to them as a 'special class' of people, who stepped in, 'under-took' charge and controlled the situation. The French word 'entreprendre' means to undertake. He actually called them 'entrepreneurs' (those who both undertake the responsibility and perform their obligation). Of course, the progression of entrepreneurship ideas did not start, nor did it stop, with Cantillon. However, this section must, for the sake of brevity, focus on a selective list of a few and more recent classical contributions.[9]

In the nineteenth century, Jean-Baptiste Say (1803/1830) also examined entrepreneurs as individuals within the context of family enterprise. Following others, he too pointed to entrepreneurs as a special class that created wealth for their families and contributed to their nation's growth and development more than others. Say's observations were anchored in the industrial revolution, which brought change on an unprecedented scale to England and beyond. Say noted that the entrepreneurs of that era, mostly patriarchs of family business, demonstrated unusual skill in 'marshalling'[10] resources to make their dreams possible; and in that process they created wealth, brought growth, nurtured much social change and also displaced numerous businesses, and even industries, of their time.[11] In the industrial revolution era, entrepreneurial initiatives gained momentum, assumed a dynamics of their own, and were propagated beyond their initial and intended boundaries. As the industrial revolution brought much change to Great Britain and extended its reach into the European continent, the entrepreneurial architects of family enterprise found it necessary to expand their formerly family-oriented structure. This transformation could be viewed as an early manifestation of internationalization (or Europeanization) of entrepreneurship in Europe, exposing local entrepreneurs to new and different environments, and requiring further institutionalization in the expanding enterprise.

Entrepreneurial characteristics, attributed to their contemporary entrepreneurs by Ely and Hess (1893), portray the modern concept of 'total managerial action'. Reportedly they managed family enterprises fully and entrepreneurially. Ely and Hess referred to the relationship between risk and reward. Not only was that relation well understood by entrepreneurs, it also appears that their coordinated decisions and executive actions controlled the risk in order to create wealth on a sustained basis. Their entrepreneurial action, in response to market opportunities of the time implicit in these early writings, may have controlled risks through 'total managerial action', including the total management of relations with others, by creating symbiotic synergies in the use of factor inputs (Etemad, 2003). As a precondition for creating increasing wealth at differentially higher rates than those of others, these synergies may have served as the main drivers of higher growth and development at the same time.

Ely and Hess (1893) proposed a four-factor model similar to that of the modern Economic Growth Theory, in which the enterprise and the entrepreneur himself were two of the four factors (in addition to capital and labour). Naturally, the success of their model depended heavily on the pivotal role of the entrepreneur himself for creating the enterprise, acquiring the necessary capital and labour, and 'marshalling' all enterprise-related efficiencies. In the case of family enterprises, both labour and capital were customarily outsourced from their families, which imposed additional family and social obligations on entrepreneurs (owing to the family and social relations). Such obligations must be viewed as an early form of mutual dependence (or interdependence). These co-dependencies[12] may have in turn facilitated, if not led to, the higher synergies in family enterprises.

In the absence of more advanced technologies to account for relatively higher efficiencies (or synergies), these entrepreneurs must have possessed exceptional managerial and social relation skills to establish and then run such wealth-creating institutions. One can easily recognize the enormity of tasks and challenges that these past entrepreneurs faced, and the correspondingly high capabilities they must also have brought to bear in order to deal with them. In Ely and Hess's conceptualization, as pointed out above, entrepreneurs were exceptional people as they embodied every necessary requirement beyond the simple labour and capital to run their enterprises so successfully. They also created the innovative combinations necessary for competing successfully against the prevailing competition, and enhanced them by realizing the higher efficiencies. In comparison with the modern enterprise, these entrepreneurs were the counterparts of knowledge, technology and business intelligence (in the 'knowledge-based' view of the enterprise: Nonaka, 1995; Nonaka and Takauchi, 1996), and enterprise-related resources (in the 'resource-based' view of the enterprise: Barney, 1991; Nelson and Winter, 1982) in addition to total management in the modern sense. This seems to suggest that the entrepreneur and his enterprise were striving to achieve relatively higher efficiencies in the early forms of the modern concept of 'symbiotic synergy' (Etemad, 2003) by honouring their 'mutual dependencies', and meeting their family and social obligations at the same time. Therefore the inevitable conclusion is that entrepreneurs must have skillfully managed their personal relations with the members of their family (for example, as employees), suppliers, customers and other associates and stakeholders – each of which was necessary to the overall 'marshalling' (Say, 1803/1830) of the enterprise as a whole.

The early writings, such as those of Cantillon, Ely and Hess, and Say, exemplify their contemporary entrepreneurs in their respective and prevailing context of the time and environment. These early personifications of entrepreneurs, and characterizations of entrepreneurship, point to entrepreneurs as relation-sensitive, holistic and yet effective managers, as they had to deal with a much smaller circle of local people, mostly family members and close local associates with much deeper personal relations (with the entrepreneur) than the much wider, much more diverse and mostly impersonal counterparts now prevailing in modern, open economies. This is a very plausible conclusion as it is *not* logical to attribute higher productivities or efficiencies to other production factors (capital, labour and technology or even to the enterprise itself).[13] Therefore whatever potential efficiencies may have existed then must necessarily be attributed solely to the impact of superior skills of the classic entrepreneurs in managing their total relations with associates and stakeholders at the time.

The contributions of Joseph Schumpeter, the Austrian economist of the early twentieth century, attribute no less to his contemporary entrepreneurs than to those of his predecessors. Schumpeter (1911/1934) attributed an acute and creative, yet analytical, sense to his contemporary entrepreneurs, where they easily selected 'innovative combinations' to create something new, something with value above all others, something in higher demand by the markets than what had existed before them. Naturally such combinations could be highly 'destructive' to the established businesses and industries, which were offering something relatively less efficient, of less value or in less demand. As the entrepreneurs of the industrial revolution era had done before Schumpter's time, such new creations brought about market disruption, or 'disequilibria', mainly through the process of 'creative destruction' (Schumpeter, 1947) discussed earlier. By definition, Schumpeter's newly introduced innovative combinations used resources relatively more efficiently, performed more optimally and created higher value than the established entities, thereby causing incremental growth for their enterprise, if not for their regions. They naturally diverted demand from the establishment and created incremental employment, wealth and growth for society. Predictably, this process displaced the less efficient and/or less innovative businesses and even industries (Schumpeter, 1928; 1942).

The combination of innovative approaches and incremental efficiencies (or synergies) associated with the entrepreneurial action brought growth and development to the region.

In the terminology of modern economics, Schumpeter's entrepreneurs created circumstances more conducive to obtaining much higher orders of efficiency than those which existed before them. They used the same societal inputs to create differentially higher wealth and value for themselves, their associates, their stakeholders and society as a whole than did their predecessors. Inevitably their associates (including labour and the family) and their respective enterprises benefited, and society experienced growth and development as their more efficient combinations replaced their less efficient counterparts, including enterprises and industries. Again these entrepreneurs must have created much stronger relations and managed them with much higher intensity than was previously known.[14] This rich web of relations may have led to synergies, which deepened mutual dependencies (for example, mutual family relations and obligations to others) and allowed them to leverage family and societal resources to create higher wealth and prosperity, along with newer value chains to replace the older ones.

Although Austrian economics viewed entrepreneurship as an influential factor in economic growth, the Schumpeterian entrepreneur's disruptive impacts did not accord with the mainstream of Austrian economics. Likewise the Scumpeterian idea of *creating* disequilibrium did not receive much support from either Austrian or neoclassical economics. The latter would at best attribute only a 'residual' growth and wealth creation to entrepreneurial activities, which is contrary to the massive evidence from family enterprises highlighted earlier.

As an Austrian economist, Kirzner (1973) did not attribute the same degree of importance to the creation of disequilibria as the precursor for generating opportunities, although he concurred with most of Schumpeter's other observations. Kirznerian entrepreneurs did not have to create the opportunity; the mere identification, '*discovery*', or recognition of such potential 'opportunities' was sufficient. However Kirzner attributed a high degree of 'alertness' to his entrepreneurs for 'discovering' opportunities (Kirzner, 1979: 10–67). They were acutely analytical. In the modern sense, they were highly opportunistic arbitrageurs: they explored opportunities that they, and they alone, identified (or discovered, but did not create) before the others in order to exploit them to create value.[15] This aspect of Kirznerian entrepreneurs is inconsistent with those of classical writers and neoclassical economists. As discussed earlier, classical writers (including Schumpeter) had consistently viewed entrepreneurs as a 'special class' (Cantillon [1755] 1931) and attributed higher analytical and/or 'total managerial' skills (Ely and Hess, 1893) to entrepreneurs than to an 'alert arbitrageur'. Although neoclassical writers, including Adam Smith and Alfred Marshall, may not have agreed with the Kirznerian entrepreneur's higher cognitive abilities (alertness), they would likely support his view of identifying opportunities (as opposed to creating them or their preconditions).

Consider for example a typical case in international trade. A typical international trader is not obliged to, and cannot create (even if he wants to), trade disequilibria to initiate a trade or trade opportunity. The sufficient condition for a trader is to identify such trade opportunities, and to fulfil them in order to create wealth and value through trade, as trade theories have consistently shown. In the prevailing interlinked economies (Ohmae, 1985) now, the case of international traders (such as exporters and importers across country boarders) is similar to that of the Austrian economists' domestic arbitrageur (Kirzner, 1973), taking advantage of a commodity with a lower price in one region (or one country) for sale at a higher price in another region (or another country). In general, opportunities associated with the broader, larger and richer international markets cannot be easily created but do certainly require identification. As in the case of the Kirznerian domestic entrepreneur (or even his 'alert arbitrageur'), international traders can exploit international market opportunities once they have identified and evaluated them (that is, have examined their correspondingly higher risks, challenges or threats). While the true international entrepreneurs 'see' and exploit higher opportunities (that is, perceived benefits higher than corresponding costs), manage the total transaction costs rather well and create value for all concerned in the national and international markets, non-entrepreneurs only see the higher mountains of costs, difficulties, risks and threats, and not the higher potentials for wealth and value creation. The above discussion leads us to conclude that these early classical writings support, and certainly do not contradict, our initial working hypotheses. Therefore we continue to maintain that the essence of entrepreneurship is embodied in *marshalling and managing relations*. However, we recognize that the environmental context of such activities is internationalized, and that our hypothesis must also be examined in this context.

The potential impact of the environmental context
The context within which classical scholars were situated had an inevitable impact on their observations and actions. They were embedded in, and naturally influenced by, their own environmental circumstances (Reynolds, Camp and Hay, 2001; Uzzi, 1999).[16]

Two aspects of context must be considered: the state of resources and the nature of potential opportunities. As for the former, the environmental context of Kirzner's observations, in the latter part of the twentieth century, was much more open and resource- and institution-rich than those of his predecessors in the eighteenth and the nineteenth centuries. Even in Schumpeter's relatively resource-starved, inter-war period of the twentieth century, the mere identification of opportunities was not sufficient for 'marshalling' the required resources for an 'innovative' or a 'creative' action to take hold. Exploitable opportunities had to be created first in most cases. Then the required resources had to be found. The state of personal and social resources (relatively poor in Schumpeter's era as compared with Kirzner's relatively rich era) may have in fact influenced the perceived (or even the actual) degree of importance attached to *creation* as opposed to *identification* of opportunities over time.

Consider, for example, the difference between the cash-rich and forgiving environment of 1998–2000 and the post slow-down environment of 2001. In the former era, most of the new dot-com *ideas* received the first round of financing, which in turn allowed them to utilize capable professionals to manage the venture. Actually these professionals 'created' the necessary conditions for the second round of financing and beyond. In contrast, in the current resource-starved environment, owing to economic slowdown, that is no longer the case. A potential entrepreneur cannot be content with the mere identification of an opportunity. Rather he must shoulder the entire burden. This means identifying the idea, exploring its market viability/feasibility, providing for the necessary resources and managing at least the early stages of the start-ups. Therefore all responsibilities have shifted to the entrepreneurs again.[17] The entrepreneur is expected both to identify and then to give birth to or create opportunities. Using Schumpeter's words, a post slowdown entrepreneur must at least 'create' the necessary conditions for 'disequilibria' to justify the first round of financing. Therefore the discrepancy between 'identification' and 'creation' may be explained in part by the presumed state of an entrepreneur's access to resources, and in part by the societal expectations of the entrepreneur at the time.

As for the latter, however, the difference in opportunities facing entrepreneurs of different eras must also be considered. Actually the physical boundary of potential markets for either identifying or creating opportunities has vastly expanded. It may have been possible for a typical entrepreneur even to 'create a disequilibrium' when the potential market was limited to the smaller and restricted local markets; but it is almost impossible now, as international markets are linked to a typical target market as a result of globalization. These market linkages make it very difficult, if not impossible, to create disequilibria as a basis for opportunity as argued earlier (especially in the case of international trade). 'Identification' appears imminently more achievable than 'creation', especially in integrated international markets. Regardless of the creation–identification controversy, and consistent with our previous observation, the entrepreneurial burden in the prevailing globalized markets has increased substantively.

The impact of knowledge, experimentation and learning
Although the role and form of knowledge, experimentation and learning are not very clear in the classical writings, the success of family businesses suggests that the patriarchs of these family enterprises, or their business leaders, must both have learned over time and also have transferred their know-how to their successors as enterprise knowledge (or even as proprietary secrets) through apprenticeship and other forms of initiation, experimentation, learning and even succession planning within the family enterprise. Family enterprises' practice of providing employment primarily for the members of the family may have facilitated the transfer and may also have been the primary way of transferring such tacit know-how (Kirzner, 1973: 64–9) to other members. This intra-family transfer of knowledge and know-how seems to have endured over time, as it is still an observable hallmark of family enterprises with Chinese heritage (Redding, 1990). This implicit evidence of intergenerational learning (and transfer) in family enterprises points to the possibility of three other potential provisions: (a) that the entrepreneurs themselves must have looked for, and even experimented with, potential solutions over time in order to find the most potent 'innovative combinations', and then discarded the unsuccessful ones while retaining and transferring the promising ones to potential successors (at least within the family enterprise); (b) that at least a part of an entrepreneur's knowledge set may have spilled over and become a public good for others to follow and utilize (entrepreneurial spillover); and (c) that regionally successful (or domestically successful) solutions may have been replicated (that is, with some adjustments through experimentation at the margins) as a basis of growth and expansion into other regions (or international markets). Not only are such learning provisions plausible, as they provide for longitudinal consistency, but they also distinguish entrepreneurs from craftsmen who repeat their craft over time.[18]

The potential scale economies associated with the international context
The mere entrepreneurial 'discovery' (Hayek, 1978; Acs and Yeung, 1999), or even a weak perception of the combined economies of scale and the consequent learning, may have motivated classic entrepreneurs to expand beyond their immediate locale to regional, and then to national, and even international markets to capitalize on the associated scale and learning economies. The process of such expansions may also have affected them in

two distinct, but related, ways: first, it may have transformed their outlook from one of local orientation to one of international orientation; second, it may have forced them to capture the larger-scale economies as well as exposing them to learning from others (and its consequent economies). Simple growth and expansion into international markets would allow for capturing the incremental economies associated with both scale and learning, which in turn could trigger a new wave of scale- and learning-based entrepreneurial discovery. The positive impact of these economies on competitiveness would logically serve as a motivating factor justifying further scale- (and even learning-) based entrepreneurship (one based on the economies of larger scale and the other emanating from increased learning from the diversity of larger and richer international markets for more potent innovative combinations). Given the expanded opportunities of the global markets, the increasing impact of such combined economies may constitute a virtuous cycle feeding on itself (Levitt, 1983) and thus obscuring the distinction between the drivers of growth and expansion.

Knight (1921), McClelland (1961) and Shapero (1975; 1984) have acknowledged the presence of such motivating factors. However they attributed them mainly to the entrepreneur's intrinsic need for a combination of achievement and accomplishments. Although they would have incorporated internationalization to enable their entrepreneurs *to achieve even more* than they would domestically, they might have preferred to see them motivated innately, or intrinsically, to learn more as a natural part of their own entrepreneurial make-up and need for personal growth and achievement (that is, following their own natural journey of 'personal discovery'), rather than driven by the attraction of positive financial impacts or the economic benefits emanating from international expansion. While the former is intrinsic to the entrepreneur and would make the entrepreneur's need for learning and achievement (McClelland, 1961) the enabling motivation for mobilizing factors for further expansion in both the domestic and the international markets, the latter (scale economies) would remain extrinsic to the entrepreneur, and at best constitute only the necessary (but not sufficient) condition for further achievements. This distinction also points to the fundamental difference between the extrinsic and intrinsic drivers of international entrepreneurship. Likewise it points to the difference between the psychologist's and the economist's view of factors motivating the entrepreneur. For the economist, the economic opportunities and benefits (the scale economies, learning economies or even arbitrage opportunities) associated with expansion, as opposed to the entrepreneur's inner needs, attract the entrepreneur to other markets and motivate growth and expansion. The latter case resembles Kirznerian opportunistic arbitrage where an 'alert arbitrageur' (Kirzner, 1973) would contemplate a trade from his local base of operations to other regional, national and even international markets. Stated differently, McClelland, Knight and Shapero would fully support an entrepreneurial response to the change and challenge of environment (globalization of the environment) and opportunities emanating from them through the entrepreneur's basic need for achievement by learning and experimentation. In contrast to an opportunistic or alert arbitrageur (concepts close to Kirzner's articulations), Kirznerian entrepreneurs would naturally consider international opportunities systematically for their higher expansion potentials and profit possibilities. While the allure of broader and larger international markets could easily motivate an economically oriented entrepreneur to internationalize in the economic paradigm, the entrepreneur's innate needs for achievement, as opposed to mere economic opportunism, would have motivated him to expand internationally in the learning and psychological paradigm.

The motivating mechanism notwithstanding, we also maintain that Drucker would fully support internationalization discussion. To Druckerian entrepreneurs, or even managers of smaller and larger enterprises, the 'market orientation' concept would be central to their daily decisions (Drucker, 1974). Market orientation would continually require such entrepreneurs/managers to be alert and responsive not only to their own local markets but also to the broader international markets and true market trends (which continually have an impact on the local and regional markets). Such alertness is necessary for recognition of potential opportunities; and also for potential exposures to risks and threats associated with changing conditions, which could be damaging if undetected. As the latter may erode current opportunities and expose the entrepreneur to unexpected risks and threats, a Druckerian entrepreneur would be required to at least stay abreast of international market developments and perhaps participate in them directly and actively.

The synthesis
The above discussion brings into focus the image of a classical entrepreneur who would embody a complex set of attributes. Such entrepreneurs would, for example, take the following necessary steps:

1. identify a well-considered opportunity as a necessary condition for any consequent transaction (a concept identified by many early scholars but articulated first by Kirzner, 1973);
2. champion their own cause in order to 'marshal' the necessary resources (a concept articulated and used initially by Say (1921),
3. take coordinated action to benefit from calculated risks (a concept articulated and introduced initially by Ely and Hess as early as 1893);

4. create 'innovative combinations' (a concept articulated initially by Schumpeter, 1911/1934) in response to market opportunities 'identified' or 'discovered' (concepts articulatd by Kirzner, 1973);
5. become 'entrepreneurially alert' (a concept articulated by Kirzner, 1973) to take advantage of potential opportunities;
6. benchmark their offerings (that is, innovative combinations) against the true trend in international, open markets[19] (a concept that Drucker, 1974, required from entrepreneurs and managers);
7. learn to accomplish entrepreneurial objectives (a concept that Knight articulated as early as 1921) by deploying potentially successful combinations and to discard others over time to satisfy their intrinsic 'need to achieve' (a concept that McClelland articulated in 1961); and
8. marshal relations with stakeholders and associates based on the concept of symbiotic synergy throughout the entire process of entrepreneurial discovery and accomplishment (a concept introduced by the Etemad in 2003, which is the necessary prerequisite for all of the other steps listed above and for which this chapter is providing support).

The difference of opinion notwithstanding, the underlying enabling forces compelling the entrepreneur to take an action cover a wide range, from intrinsic needs for accomplishment and achievement, motivating learning through experimentation (concepts discussed by Knight, 1921; Hayek 1948: 84–7; McClelland, 1961; Shapero 1975; 1984), to acquiring 'alertness' to opportunities (a concept articulated by Kirzner, 1973, who distinguished 'identification' from 'creation' of opportunities proposed earlier by Schumpeter, 1911/1934, 1947), to managing all the necessary relations for marshalling all required resources. There is, however, a consensus that the consequent action of the entrepreneur would create a new set of dynamics and new synergies in the market associated with the new 'innovative' goods and services. This would in turn disrupt the established market equilibrium in the entrepreneur's favour. Translated into the contemporary terminology, this sequence of actions would allow the entrepreneur to introduce a potent combination of goods and services that others had not recognized before (a concept that Schumpeter saw as pivotal to entrepreneurship), leading to growth, creation of wealth and prosperity following entrepreneurial accomplishments.

The summary highlights of the above discussions are presented in Table 13.1, a brief examination of which points to a varied and complex set of characteristics motivating actions and necessitating reactions in response to different sets of perceived challenges and opportunities. Combined they reaffirm our proposed conceptual construct characterizing and embodying the above characteristics in managing or marshalling relations (with associates and stakeholders) as the essence of entrepreneurship. We have high-lighted two critical dimensions of this construct (synergy and symbiosis) to guide our further examination. The former embodies incremental efficiencies arising from joint actions (of the entrepreneur and his associate), while the latter portrays a sense of mutual dependence (or co-dependence, as opposed to independence) between the entrepreneur and his associates as the necessary condition for sustained and successful joint actions exhibiting continuity, stability, trust and so on. Logically there is no restrictive physical boundary on either of the two concepts that (a) the entrepreneur may rely on mutual relations with associates for joint action in his immediate region, or halfway around the world;[20] and (b) the benefits of incremental efficiencies, resulting from joint actions, may similarly accrue to partners, associates and stakeholders residing in the immediate region or halfway around the world.

The above arguments situate the entrepreneur in a context without boundaries, and compel him to broaden his horizons to global markets regardless of his initial physical presence in a local, national or international market.[21] We combine the two concepts in symbiotic synergy within a global context to capture the above discussion, and to guide our further examination of international entrepreneurship[22] in much larger institutions such as multinational enterprises (MNEs), at the other polar extreme of our examination. This will be discussed in the next section.

The international expansion theories of large firms and managing relations
Managing relations and the theories of MNEs
Theories of the multinational enterprise cover the international expansion of large enterprises. They have evolved along two main streams. One, emanating mainly from the work of Stephen Hymer, posits that a series of internal or proprietary advantages enable the firm to overcome the handicaps of expanding into new, foreign and distant markets. The other theory, known broadly as the 'Scandinavian School' or the 'Stages Model', focuses more on the process of internationalization based on a gradual and careful accumulation of experiential knowledge over time. Both of these approaches view the firm as an essentially self-contained system with few external links and relations. These theories are examined further below.

Managing relations and internationalization of large enterprises
The modern theory of internationalization goes back to the early 1970s, when Hymer (1976) first questioned the reasons for the existence, growth and expansion of multinational enterprises. With the heightened risks of foreign direct investments (FDI) (Dunning, 1973; Buckley, 1989), MNEs face riskier and more costly operating conditions than the national firms

Table 13.1 *Summary highlights of selected aspects of classical entrepreneurship*

Scholar	Emphasis	Means or dominant mechanism	End(s) or impact	Context and/or the point of impact for an action	Distinguishing feature	Primary orientation
Cantillon (1755)	Entreprendre: taking charge and undertaking responsibility for a challenge	Personal control of the situation (or the challenge)	Meeting the challenge (e.g. employment and economic growth)	Family/micro enterprise in eighteenth-century France	The ability to 'take charge'	Enterprise and economic efficiency
Jean-Baptiste Say (1815)	Carrying out initiatives and challenges skillfully	Innate entrepreneurial skills	Change and economic growth	Eighteenth-century Britain and enterprises in midst of industrial revolution	The ability to 'marshal' resources	Economic efficiency
Ely and Hess (1893)	Total managerial action: including decisions on risks, coordination resources, and distributions	Creating integrative synergy between all production factors	Growth of the enterprise for creation of wealth and economic growth in the region	A four-factor model: labour, capital, the enterprise and the entrepreneur (who was the owner–operator)	The ability to take coordinated and integrative actions for the enterprise as a whole	Wealth creation through enterprise growth.
Schumpeter (1911/1934; 1947)	The use of 'innovative combinations' to create disequilibrium	'Creative destruction': innovative use of resources to replace old equilibria	Profitable opportunities that bring about social change and long-term improvement	The socioeconomic environment due for change and causing change by creating/responding to the socioeconomic disequilibria	Creating disequilibria receptive to innovative solutions	Wealth and value creation through innovative change and technological obsolescence

Author						
Knight (1921)	Learning to use economic factors efficiently	Innate or acquired abilities to reduce waste and increase efficiency or effectiveness	Increased production, wealth creation and economic growth	Enterprise production system	Identifying savings and eliminating waste	Economic efficiency, leading to saving to finance growth and wealth creation
Kirzner (1973)	Alertness to identifying market opportunities or disequilibria	Pursuit of fulfilling opportunities through imitative (e.g. arbitrage) and innovative actions	Reduction in socio-economic 'waste' through alertness	Enterprise and the affected socio-economic sectors	Alertness to disequilibria, imperfection (e.g. unfulfilled demand) to which to respond	Profit motive
Drucker (1974)	Focus on market trends and also what they can manifest	Sound marketing: championing of ideas, marshalling resources, marketing results everywhere	Efficient and effective market operations	Market participants primarily, market-related institutions secondarily	Monitoring market(s) to identify and/or create opportunities to fulfil	Marketing and customer orientation: focus on delivering value to customers in open markets through production and marketing
McClelland (1961)	To remove barriers to realizing objectives arising from challenges	Personal need for achievement by meeting challenges	Challenge of personal accomplishments	Internal locus of control to increase the possibility of achievement	High innate drive to achieve	Maximizing self-esteem through success (achieving)
Shapero (1975; 1984)	Judgmental selection and use of attributes: augmenting those with positive impact and avoiding those with negative impact	Selecting and controlling innovative paths with high success probabilities for redirection and reorientation of one's life	Personal success in newly redirected endeavour	Personal challenge primarily, success of enterprise embodying the challenge secondarily	Urge to succeed by learning and retrials even after initial failure	A sense of fulfilling personal challenges (accomplishments)

competing in the same markets. These potentially higher risks combined with the additional costs of 'foreignness', inherent in operating in different foreign host environments (Caves, 1982), situate MNEs in a clearly disadvantageous position as compared to the local firms. Yet they have competed and expanded successfully. Hymer concluded logically that MNEs, and their subsidiaries by extension, must have possessed certain intrinsic advantage(s) not available to their national counterparts in the host country, which compensate for their comparative disadvantage and also put them in at least a level playing field, if not in a competitively advantageous position. Using the insights of the previous sections of this chapter, we suggest that a subsidiary's comparative advantage is in fact its privileged relation with the rest of the MNE's system. Such relations give the subsidiary privileged access to expertise, knowledge and resources of the corporate family. This intrinsic advantage, not available to other local firms, enables the subsidiary to compete initially, and eventually to out-compete the locals. Such privileged access can easily channel potent resources and superior management to the subsidiary, especially in the early stages of its feeble life in the foreign, and possibly hostile, environment, empowering it to stand up to its entrenched national competitors.

Hymer's pioneering work has been extended by recent scholars. Following the original work of Coase (1937), Buckley and Casson (1976) formulated 'Internalization Theory'. This theory focused on the MNE's attempt to create and control an 'internal market' populated by its sister-subsidiaries. This internal market acquired resources from the various members of the MNE's corporate family and then made them available to the sister-subsidiary system at flat prices set by the parent company. This theory was further developed and popularized by Rugman (1979; 1982). Williamson's (1975; 1981) 'Transaction Cost Theory' elaborated on the nature of internal markets and the transaction cost aspects of internalization, viewing such 'internal markets' as an internally controlled hierarchy functioning as, or at times replacing, international markets.

In his 'Eclectic Theory' of MNEs, Dunning (1977; 1980; 1988) proposed ownership- (or firm-) specific advantage (OSA), location-specific advantage (LSA) and internalization (or OLI model for short) as the three principal pillars of this theoretical school of growth through internationalization. A careful re-examination of the OLI theory points to internalization, or the workings of the MNE's internal markets, as the pivotal component of the advantage not available to others: making resources available to the corporate family members at privileged prices based on the nature of their special relationship with the corporate family at the time, reminding us of the inner dynamics of family enterprises, reviewed earlier.

Practically, a typical local subsidiary has access to a pool of technical and financial support available at the MNE's headquarters and other sister-subsidiaries at privileged prices not available to non-members. The technical support may, for example, include access to proprietary R&D results as well as knowledgable technical staff anywhere in the corporate family, all at internally set prices. The financial support may also include access both to the financial resources accumulated in the system and to the supply chain of other sister-subsidiaries. These privileged relations with the rest of the MNE's corporate system (and possibly with their associates) give the local subsidiary access to a host of potentially powerful and proprietary advantages not readily available to national firms, regardless of their size and age. This discussion supports Hymer's argument that it was the impact of such 'advantage(s)' which distinguished MNEs from other firms, thus enabling MNEs to overcome the initial handicap of 'foreignness' in foreign environments, and to survive and prosper in the diverse, if not initially hostile, host market into which they expanded.[23] However Hymer tended to view these advantages in purely economic terms, and as a source of comparative advantage associated with multinational operations. He did not probe the underlying relations enabling the advantage or examine it from other perspectives.

In the absence of such privileged relations in open markets, a subsidiary would be treated identically to the other competitors, which would give the subsidiary no comparative advantage. Those 'privileged relations' of a typical subsidiary with the other members of the same family in the internal market, including the corporate headquarters, provide it with privileged access to the pool of necessary resources for its competitiveness at subsidized prices, which is again analogous to the expansion pattern of family enterprises examined earlier.

From the perspective of special relations, the Eclectic Theory of MNEs decomposed the origin of resources, flowing through the 'internal market', into those derived (or based on) either ownership-specific or location-specific advantages. However the concept of the 'internal market' must be viewed as the arbiter of those relation-based 'advantages'. The privilege of gaining access to the internal market allows each member of the MNE's corporate family to plan for the particular 'innovative combinations' necessary to its respective competitiveness, growth and expansion. The internal market acted as the internal clearing house for resources, both technical and financial, among the MNE's corporate family members at internally set prices, making the faster growth of the family members, and the family fortunes by extension, a real possibility.[24] The headquarters' role in the MNE's internal market resembles the Kirznerian 'alert arbitrageur' (Kirzner, 1973) in open international markets transferring resources from subsidiaries in regions with lower propensities to subsidiaries in regions with higher propensities to create incremental wealth for the entire family.

Retrospectively Hymer, and other scholars following him, could have easily reformulated the 'advantage' in terms of what it actually was and still is: special relations for privileged access to the necessary resources – both economic and non-economic – at privileged prices,[25] which is the essence of marshalling relations. Theoretically subsidiary–MNE relations are governed by the hierarchical powers emanating from the MNE's ownership and control of its subsidiaries. Such powers govern the elaborate and internal system of rights and privileges, including the criteria for access to and redistribution of resources held by the network of the MNE's sister-subsidiaries. With the blessing and cooperation of the corporate parents, each local member (that is, the local subsidiary) can manage its respective part of the network as entrepreneurially as necessary. The position of the parent company at the hub of the network, and the common ownership and centralized control, allow the MNE to further coordinate and manage its collective resources for the optimal growth of the corporate family as a whole (resembling the role of the family patriarch in the family enterprises). Within such a family, a typical subsidiary's relations with the parent company, and the sister-subsidiaries systems, could be managed for incremental mutual efficiencies (added synergies due to complementary cooperations or joint actions) based on the concept of symbiotic synergy enabling virtuous cycles of growth and expansion. Therefore the theory of MNEs is highly consistent with our proposed concept of symbiotic synergy. The management of privileged relations in the MNE's network provides an alternative, yet complementary, explanation for the international growth and expansion of large enterprises.[26]

Managing relations and the Scandinavian theory of internationalization
Scholars in the 'Scandinavian School' or 'Stages Model' have sought to explain internationalization in terms of a *longitudinal process*. Johanson and Vahlne (1977; 1990; 1992), Johanson and Wiedersheim-Paul (1975), Cavusgil (1980; 1982) and Cavusgil, Bilkey and Tesar (1979), among others in this school, advocated a longitudinal progression of internationalization, starting with simple exporting to familiar host markets (Bilkey 1978) with a short 'psychic distance' (Stöttinger and Schlegelmilch, 1998) from home, going on to more involved and fuller 'stages' over time. Each progressively fuller stage of internationalization would expose the firm to higher levels of risk and require more resources (Bilkey and Tesar, 1977; Cavusgil and Nevin, 1981; Cavusgil and Kirpalani, 1993; Cavusgil, 1984). Such stage-wise progression would provide for a gradual accumulation of resources and experiential knowledge (Eriksson, Johanson, Majkgard and

Sharma, 1997), which would in turn empower the internationalizing enterprise to gain a more equal footing over time in the host market that is initially hostile to the enterprise.

Scholars in this school maintained that internationalizing enterprises would begin to expand to less risky markets; less hostile, with shorter psychic distance (Stöttinger and Schlegelmilch, 1998) from home, in the earlier stages of their international expansion. With temporal acquisition of more experience and knowledge, firms learned how to operate in their host environment, enabling them to overcome the disadvantage of foreignness and to accumulate increasingly more resources with time. This also enabled them to utilize more involved options and to expand further and faster into neighbouring markets and beyond. Newer, younger and less experienced operations could also draw on the accumulated knowledge and resources in the enterprise as a whole to expand optimally. As a direct result of privileged access to such an expanding portfolio of expertise, knowledge and know-how, the implication of this theory is that a subsidiary operation, similar to the theory of the MNEs, would leverage network-based resources to defend its initial weak position, and shed its foreignness as fast as possible in order to operate very much like the local firms populating the local market. Beyond the progressive accumulation of experiential knowledge and resources in the system as a whole, and also gaining local expertise with time, this conceptual approach did not attribute a comparative or competitive advantage to MNE operations as Hymer had previously envisioned. In fact it characterized a typical subsidiary operation as one of initial disadvantage (concurring with Hymer on this point), the burden of which had to be (a) controlled carefully in the earlier stages by entry into simpler, more familiar or less hostile markets (for example, those with shortest psychic distance) and more controllable involvements through restricted modes of entry (such as exporting as opposed to FDI) to avoid costly failures; and (b) eventually removed altogether as further experimentation and learning in the later stages enabled the firm to compete more effectively with national firms on an equal footing. Although the limitations of this perspective are pointed out elsewhere (see, for example, Leonidou and Katsikeas, 1996; McDougall, Shane and Oviatt, 1994; Knight and Cavusgil, 1996), we find this family of theories to be complementary to this chapter's thesis, as the path of expansion relies progressively on the prior accumulation of experience and resources by family members for further and future use of other members. The process of internationalization involving progressive stages, each vastly richer in resources, in accumulated experience and in involvement, capable of dealing with higher risks and more complexity, is a logical and pragmatic path for controlled growth and international expansion of an enterprise, especially when facing constrained resources and limited capacity to absorb risk and adversity (which is the case of small growing enterprises).

Unfortunately both of the above theories focus more on intra-firm dynamics for acquisition of resources and experiential knowledge over time and much less on potential inter-firm relations for access to accumulated resources elsewhere for increased competitiveness and faster growth. Although the common ownership and hierarchical controls may have in part excluded the inter-firm relations, the recent developments in non-equity-based arrangements, including networks and strategic alliances, indicate clearly that centralized and unified control is not necessary for mutually beneficial and value adding relations. The intra-firm inner dynamics notwithstanding,[27] we find the insights of the above internationalization theories to be complementary to, if not confirmatory of, the thesis of this chapter based on managing relations for progressively higher levels of symbiotic synergy. We contend that marshalling relations is the necessary prerequisite to the dynamics on which both of the above theories rely to provide their theoretical descriptions. Furthermore marshalling relations is capable of providing a much richer perspective than these theories have provided in the past.

The emerging essence of 'privileged relationships'
The above discussion illustrates that relationships of one form or another have always been at the core of competitiveness. The content of relations, and the process of managing them, may have evolved over time from one that is more personal and simpler (for example, in the family enterprises in their early stages), to one of more complex arrangements (in MNEs). We are, however, in the middle of another evolutionary shift, from the traditional and formal forms of collaboration (in which the locus of relations lies in formal control, hierarchy and common ownership) to newer forms of collaboration in which incremental growth and competitiveness emanate from inter-firm relations based on interdependence and mutuality of benefit with other entities. These new and emerging forms represent a departure from traditional theories, and a move towards a new competitive paradigm in which the unit of competition is no longer the individual firm, but rather networks of firms collaborating for maximum mutual benefit with profound implications for all partners.

In the emerging paradigm, small and medium-sized enterprises (SMEs) face, for example, the choice of slower independent growth and development by relying on their own set of capabilities, competencies, knowledge, and skills (independent of others) over a longer period of time (as in the 'stages theory') for independent operations, or a faster growth through interdependent relations and inter-firm cooperation in the context of networks. In contrast to the former independent and self-contained strategy, the latter will require a different strategy: developing a focused and specialized set of capabilities in support of a common value chain shared with others, each component of which is located in different parts of the world, to generate much larger joint benefits through joint actions, often regardless of size. Although such strategies may require much less developmental time, and thus lead to faster growth in a much more effective and timely fashion, it will also leave the specialized firm highly dependent on other members in the value chain. Such a condition of interdependence (Etemad, Wright and Dana, 2001) or co-dependence (Acs and Yeung, 1999), in exchange for making the focused, specialized and value-adding strategy feasible (within a value chain), appears to be the necessary precondition for effective network-based collaboration, offering much faster growth potentials as well as more competitive presence in international markets than an independent firm can accomplish in isolation.

It seems evident, from the theoretical discussion above, that privileged relationships capture the essence of international growth for both internationalizing SMEs and MNEs. The two words 'privileged' and 'relationships' merit further elaboration. We used a highly formalized and institutionalized MNE–subsidiary relation (which is likely to be a restrictive and conservative case) to examine and illustrate our argument. While the nature of the relationships of a subsidiary with other sister-subsidiaries is generally complementary and synergistic, a typical relationship between a subsidiary and the headquarters is clearly one of dependence and symbiosis, with the headquarters usually dominating. As in typical symbiotic relations, a typical young subsidiary of a multinational enterprise would not survive the competitive onslaught and sustained attacks of the large national firms in its early life if the umbilical cord to the headquarters (the privileged access to the MNE's accumulated resources elsewhere) were to be severed in the earlier stages of a young subsidiary's life in the host country environment.[28] The exact nature of the dependence, and the degree of mutuality in a relationship, would naturally mature with time. For example, early one-way dependence (the subsidiary's dependence on the MNE's system), especially in a subsidiary's early life, can evolve towards interdependence, in which neither party dominates the other, or even into a reverse dependency, as the subsidiary strives to become more focused, and begins to function, for example, as the central hub of its own supply chain network.

Although a rich range of recent developments in non-equity-based collaborations provide the early evidence for special relations (see, for example, Etemad, 2001; 2003), what we have articulated as privileged relations, comprising attributes such as 'symbiosis' (Dana, 2000; Dana, Etemad and Wright, 2000; Etemad, Wright and Dana, 2001) and 'synergy' (Etemad,

1999; 2003), following similar concepts such as 'co-destiny' or 'co-evolution' (Gomes-Casseres 1996: 26) and 'co-dependence' (Acs and Yeung, 1999), capture the true nature of such relations, which for the most part have remained elusive. A comparison of the traditional model, and the emerging paradigm's salient characteristics, are presented in Table 13.2, which shows that the two models exhibit dramatically different characteristics, as discussed earlier.

Discussion and conclusion
In contrast to both international business (dealing mainly with large internationalized enterprises) and entrepreneurship (covering smaller enterprise), international entrepreneurship addresses international growth of smaller firms. It is commonly assumed that international entrepreneurship shares the scholarly foundations, and also the intellectual underpinnings, of both international business and entrepreneurship disciplines (Dana, Etemad and Wright, 2000; 2001; Etemad, Wright and Dana, 2001). The initial working hypothesis of this chapter, however, sought to probe the true nature of what is actually shared by the two fields without prejudice to either one. The research underlying this chapter makes clear that entrepreneurship and international business have *a common essence*, but one which is independent of either field's respective discipline. However their size and scale differentials might initially suggest the contrary. The common essence underlying international entrepreneurship can be simply stated in a few words: managing relations to marshal the necessary resources for generating faster growth through higher synergies and mutual benefits. The earlier articulation of these concepts constituted the working hypothesis of this chapter. The pursuit of this working hypothesis, discussed earlier, uncovered many qualitative commonalities in spite of the quantitative differences between SMEs and MNEs.

Commonalities include the following:

- The process of internationalization is an entrepreneurial act shared by SMEs and MNEs alike, as it exposes both entities to qualitatively different challenges from those at home.
- Both the SMEs and MNEs have historically drawn upon network-based resources (mainly external to SMEs, while internal to the MNE's corporate family) for their respective growth and international expansion.
- Both internationalizing SMEs and MNEs manage their evolving relations within their own networks populated by respective partners, affiliates, associates and stakeholders, often regardless of their size, for mutually beneficial outcomes.

Table 13.2 Selected characteristics of the conventional model versus the emerging partnership-based internationalization paradigm

States / components	Conventional model	Partnership-based paradigm
Basis of value proposition	Differentiation: based on small to moderate scale economies, and possibly scope economies	Higher value: higher quality and lower costs. Based on much larger scale and many specialization and even scope economies
Nature of value	Mostly objective, with market viewed as upper bound	Mostly subjective. Market viewed as lower bound
Firm's strategic value	Close to observed market valuation, e.g. some multiple of revenues (revenue-based)	Based on strategic value of one partner to the partners' collective value chains (e.g. value chain-based and difficult to observe)
Nature of relations of the suppliers in the value chain	Adversarial and independent. Controlled by the dominant firm	Cooperative and collaborative along the value chain (e.g. strategic alliances and other forms of collaborative arrangements)
Competitive scope and orientation	Narrow: local or national	Wide: international or global
Nature of inter-firm competition in the marketplace	Relatively less competitive: Avoidance and segmentation due to low mobility and entry barriers (e.g. legal, geographical and cultural entry barriers)	Highly competitive: Requires participation in free, open international markets (e.g. highly competitive, deregulated, and with lower entry barriers)
Nature of inter-coalition competition	N/A	Highly competitive
Nature of the competitive game	Closer to zero-sum along and across the value chain	Closer to constant (if not increasing) sum along the value chain (intra-coalition). Zero-sum across the value chain (inter-coalition)

Differences include the following:

- Their most obvious difference is one of size rather than one of orientation or intrinsic characteristics.
- The *internal* network of the sister-subsidiary and the parent company, constituting the MNE structure, can provide for temporal cross-subsidization of a subsidiary's initial operations.
- Internationalizing SMEs must create *external* network of their own before capitalizing on the network's growth and expansion potentials.

Our theoretical examination in this chapter further suggests that a new modus operandi, or even a new paradigm, is emerging. This newly emerging paradigm is typified by new strategies centred on partnership, or network-based arrangements, predicated on mutuality of benefits and co-dependence, as opposed to the compelling forces of control by ownership, hierarchy or dominance by virtue of size. Even the dominant and entrenched champions of the traditional model have slowly migrated and embraced the newly emerging model.

Consider IBM, for example. It refused to consider any form of partnership, and withdrew from lucrative markets, such as India (in 1978), as India required IBM to enter into a joint venture with an Indian partner. IBM is now strongly committed to, and is as staunchly entrepreneurial in, managing its relations with its network of partners. It is now involved in a massive number of strategic partnerships with both smaller and larger enterprises. Many of its previously 'internal' processes and operations are entrusted to such 'external' partners. In contrast to its comparatively smaller 'internal' and proprietary network of the past, a pattern of well-managed relations with members of a relatively large 'external' network of partners is gaining stronger currency as time marches on. Other competitors in the same industry, such as Sun Microsystems, who embraced the partnership-based paradigm much earlier, are even more advanced in managing their relations than IBM (Holloway, 1996). For example, the early use of this paradigm allowed Sun Microsystems to avoid a technological upheaval in the industry, due to a major technological shift from CISC-based to RISC-based CPU chips,[29] in the 1980s (Gomes-Casseres, 1996: 98–9).

The implications of the emerging new paradigm
In the old paradigm, SMEs grew systematically, experientially and sequentially over a relatively long time to become larger, multi-product and multi-location operations that progressively resembled MNEs. The concept of 'born globals' – small firms that internationalize at the start, or soon after they are created (Cavusgil, 1994; Knight and Cavusgil, 1996; McDougall

1989 and 1996; McDougall, Shane and Oviatt, 1994; Oviatt and McDougall, 1994 and 1997) – did not exist and could not be easily explained by previous theories. These firms possess neither the accumulated experiential knowledge and the accumulated resources stipulated by the 'Scandinavian School', nor the internal sister-subsidiaries network required by the Hymerian theory of MNEs. Empowered by a network-based growth strategy, and with the assistance of their respective network partners, these entities are internationalizing at unprecedented rates. In fact, internationalizing SMEs can be global enterprises at birth in the emerging paradigm.[30]

Partnership constellations (Gomes-Casseres, 1997) of such younger and smaller firms demonstrate characteristics not anticipated by the extant literature, including a collective desire to learn, grow and act jointly, that enables them to maximize synergies while building trust and dependence in their partnership-based actions. Such constellations also allow for optimizing their relations with partners for increasing 'co-dependence' (Acs and Yeung, 1999), 'co-destiny' (Gomes-Casseres, 1996: 26) and 'symbiosis' (Etemad, Wright and Dana, 2001; Dana, Etemad and Wright, 2000). Their older predecessors were forced to learn such characteristics through setbacks (Etemad, 2003). Previously successful firms, including Xerox, IBM, Honeywell, HP and Motorola, to name but a few, learned experientially how to migrate from the conventional model to the newly emerging paradigm (based on partnership) through many setbacks over a much longer time, and with much higher expenses, than those whose strategy has been based on the essence of the new paradigm from the outset.

This chapter's conclusion is that there is a convincing body of evidence to suggest higher benefits associated with the partnership-based paradigm than with the traditional one. The emerging paradigm is becoming far more potent than the older model as partners learn how to pool resources, amass experiential knowledge, learn from one another and accumulate network-based resources at much faster rates as they evolve. They also learn how to manage their relations for much higher mutual benefits than in the traditional model.

The fundamental implications of this chapter are, first, that internationalization may start with a desire to become globally competitive by adopting a global orientation, and may not initially have a corresponding geographical manifestation. The optimal management of network-based relations does not necessarily require a physical presence in international markets, if the enterprise can achieve and remain globally competitive as a part of a global network. An internationalizing enterprise may, for example, be the local partner of a highly competitive global value chain. Therefore researchers seeking geographical manifestations as a proxy for internationalization may not find them, as the former is no longer the necessary condition for the latter. As an integral part of global value chains in the emerging paradigm, SMEs may 'internationalize' by integrating into the supply chains of large international companies operating principally at home (or at a few locations). Again the traditional measures of internationalization fail to detect such a true state of reality.

At the other polar extreme, an internationally oriented SME may 'outsource' most, if not all, components of its integrated international value chain through symbiotic partnerships, and consequently participate in international markets successfully without relying on, or developing much of, its own production capabilities. Such 'truncated' enterprises may succeed in sustaining themselves if they learn to manage their symbiotic relations with others for mutual benefit, especially if they can reciprocate benefits synergistically to avoid the 'hollow company' syndrome in the long run. Unfortunately the traditional theories have failed to allow for such possibilities and the associated measures to capture such developments. Naturally they are incapable of predicting future partnership-based trends or suggesting potent associative strategies. The challenge facing scholars is to develop proper theories, frameworks, theory essentials and associated measures to capture the prevailing reality based on managing privileged relations, and also to shed light on the incipient patterns of global strategy as they emerge.

As for managers, on the other hand, they must find new entrepreneurial skills, portraying those of the family patriarchs and classical entrepreneurs who managed their relations well. Following these earlier predecessors, they must be able more easily to identify network-based opportunities, to develop the necessary shorter-run capabilities and to acquire specialized resources in order to leverage them for higher mutual benefits in the longer run within the network of associates and partners. Such new strategies may allow them to achieve higher growth and internationalization than those achievable at home and independently. Critical to the future growth of SMEs is the identification and development of strategic strengths (or core competencies), which can be leveraged extensively in the emerging variants of partnership-based internationalization models. This will in turn allow the enterprise to finance the current and next cycle of growth for migration along, if not across, the globally integrated value chains (of both the enterprise and the industry) to achieve multiple objectives including, but not limited to, sustained global competitiveness, international market presence and meaningful participation in incremental value-creation chains globally. Equally critical to managing relations within partners' value chains for international growth and prosperity is the SME's full understanding of its own strategic value as a member of such value chains in the context of networks, in terms of capabilities and limitations, in contrast to independent operations. Managing global relations well will require a full understanding of such evolving strategies and their mutual dependences vis-à-vis network members, and the networks' potentials for joint action as they evolve and grow with time. The emerging theory of internationalization, based on symbiotic synergy, is indeed at the dawn of a new era.

Notes

1. Most family enterprises of the past were mainly locally oriented. We make an allowance for the localized context of these early family enterprises and classical writings on entrepreneurship (that is, an adjustment for the restrictive and closed market of the time to the prevailing open global markets prevailing currently).
2. We use the words 'managing' and 'marshalling' to denote nearly synonymous concepts. However the word 'marshalling' connotes a much more purposeful, forceful and actively directed meaning than the word 'managing'.
3. Symbiosis is defined as the living together, in intimate association or even close union, of two dissimilar organisms. Ordinarily it is used for cases where the association of at least two entities is advantageous, or often necessary, to one or both, and not harmful to either.
4. Synergy is defined as the combined action or operation of at least two entities, such as muscles or nerves, to be more efficient and effective than the sum total of actions of all entities, each acting in isolation. Consider, for example, how the combined effect of two or more drugs is more potent than the action of each separately.
5. It is difficult to assess whether the diverse set of family principles governing family business conformed with or even stringently observed the prevailing rules and regulations of the accepted business principles of the time, as most family enterprises developed a power base of their own. Some of them become the shadow government, if not the de facto government, of the time.
6. These three families gained historical significance as their family's leadership in commercial affairs extended to the seat of Christianity in the Vatican. A member of each family became Pope, in charge of religion and politics during their reign.
7. Although short-lived in most cases, family enterprises associated with the so-called alcohol, oil, rubber and sugar barons were (and some still are) exemplary examples of entrepreneurial successes after the Industrial Revolution.
8. Their progressive entrepreneurial practices may have, in turn, further helped the growth and prosperity of their family enterprise towards commercial/industrial empires, for decades and centuries.
9. For a more detailed discussion of this subject, see Etemad and Lee (1999; 2003).
10. The concept of 'marshalling' resources was introduced for the first time by Jean-Baptiste Say. We extend the concept to relations, which implies that relations are viewed as resources. In fact we contend that managing relations is the prerequisite for getting and marshalling resources.
11. Although what Say observed was renewal based on 'creative destruction', the formal concept (of 'creative destruction') was proposed by Austrian economist, Schumpeter, some 200 years later.
12. Such co-dependencies may have been the counterpart, or the predecessor, of the modern concept of social capital in the nineteenth century.
13. When these four factors are explicitly compared with their counterparts in modern theory, each of whose three factors is more powerful: capital includes knowledge and intellectual capital, labour includes brain power, and technology is much more advanced (both the soft and the hard forms of it) within the context of the modern enterprise (including the complex corporate form of it). Therefore the efficient management of these necessary factors would become an imperative if the enterprise were to sustain growth through competitiveness over time. This may have been the essence of entrepreneurship then, as it still is now.

14. This concept is similar to the modern concept of disruptive technologies that create new value chains and new industries to destroy, and eventually replace, their relatively-ineffective predecessors.

15. Also see Kirzner 1979.

16. We suggest that the explicit absence of an international dimension in the classical conceptualizations of entrepreneurship is mainly due to the constrained environments of their time, which may have narrowed their concept of the market to the limited domestic markets. If international markets had been playing as significant a role then as they do now in the sustained wealth creation and growth (or demise) of the enterprise, classical scholars not only would have incorporated the international dimension explicitly in their conception, but would have substituted international entrepreneurship for their articulation of entrepreneurship. Stated differently, they would have easily incorporated this *catalytic ingredient* into their respective concepts themselves for their contemporary entrepreneurs to conquer the world then and not be content with just their respective domestic markets.

17. While the 1998–2000 era seems much closer to the Kirznerian environment, whereby an identified opportunity would succeed because of the abundant resources enabling even less capable entrepreneurs to succeed, in the currently prevailing environment even highly capable entrepreneurs must prove their potential before they can acquire the resources to start up. Therefore the environment is much closer to the inter-war environment within which Schumpeter was making his observations.

18. The dynamics of learning and its corresponding economies can encourage entrepreneurs to exploit ever larger scale economies associated with progressively larger operations in the national (followed by international) markets and hence lead regional/national entrepreneurs to become international entrepreneurs.

19. Logically there is no good reason to restrict the scope of entrepreneurial action for any potent innovative combinations of goods and services to a limited domestic market. To the contrary, a family of innovative combinations would succeed with even higher likelihood and with larger magnitude in the global markets than in domestic counterparts. Naturally, a globally oriented innovative combination at the outset would stand a higher chance of succeeding, regardless of its origin, as international competitors cannot easily unseat it. This in turn points to global orientation as the critical ingredient of international entrepreneurship, whether the enterprise actually exploits it in the international markets or not.

20. One obvious option is for internationalizing entrepreneurs to seek arrangements between similarly-minded and internationally oriented firms for sustained growth, if not survival, in target international markets, regardless of relative size and bargaining power differentials.

21. By a logical extension, then, whether the orientation to, or a presence in, international markets would have a positive impact on the domestic operations was not a point of contention to many classical writers, including Schumpeter and other Austrian economists, while their potential destructive threats would. The remarkable similarity of implications of classical writings for extending entrepreneurial actions internationally must be viewed as extremely important to entrepreneurship as a whole. In general most classical writers suggest explicitly or imply an acute awareness of the relevant markets affecting the entrepreneur. In light of globalization, an international orientation, if not an explicit presence, is the minimum for defensive purposes.

  One obvious option is for internationalizing entrepreneurs to seek arrangements between like-minded and internationally oriented firms for sustained growth, if not survival, in target international markets, regardless of relative size and bargaining power differentials.

22. Actually this argument internationalizes entrepreneurship. Beyond internationalization of entrepreneurship as the modern replacement for the classical concept of entrepreneurship, the next fundamental question is whether or not the process inherent in entrepreneurship would be similar for international entrepreneurship; or would they be equally applicable to both the smaller and the larger modern firms? This process must

necessarily take into consideration the smaller firm's relatively constrained resources and exceedingly compressed time when facing relatively resource-rich larger firms competing for the same economic space in open international markets. In a parallel fashion, the process must also allow for similar limitations of internationalizing start-ups, as they also face the smallness syndromes at the beginning of their lives.

23. Unfortunately Hymer did not view subsidiary–MNE relations other than as an economic advantage. Could he have seen the relations in terms of the network theory of the firm, resource-based view of the firm, knowledge-based theory of the firm or other rival explanations, the theory of MNEs would have taken a different evolutionary path.

24. We seem to have come to a full circle. The internal market of the modern MNE's corporate family resembles the structure of family enterprises of the past, discussed much earlier in the second section of this paper, with some technical differences: the institution of the MNE has replaced the family structure, and the functions of the family patriarch (or business leader making crucial decisions) are performed by the MNE's headquarters.

25. Resources were examined later by the resource-based view of the firm by Barney (1991), Nelson and Winter (1982) and others. Our view of resources is consistent with their view here. However national firms must acquire their required resources at 'market' prices, while subsidiaries receive them at the internal market prices, thereby making such resources more potent for the subsidiary than for their national counterparts.

26. This alternative explanation may also serve as a basis for an alternative theory of multinational firms. In that theory, the three pillars of the MNE's operations would include Dunning's LSA and OSA, as well as our proposed relationship-specific advantage (RSA).

27. This inner dynamic is further explained in Etemad (2003).

28. The state of a young subsidiary in a host environment is in fact analogous to the state of a child in hostile surroundings. As with the child, the young subsidiary may not survive the onslaught of attacks by large national firms with parental supports. Thus the subsidiary–MNE relation must be viewed as symbiotic at first. However, as the subsidiary learns and grows in the host market, the nature of relations evolves from extreme dependence to one of mutual assistance (synergy) and may even proceed to one of reverse dependence, when a subsidiary becomes a centre of specialized resources, skills and capabilities.

29. The reduced instruction set chip (RISC) was invented by IBM in 1978. However a small start-up, called MIPS, at the hub and within the network of some 140 microelectronic companies, including Sun Microsystems, commercialized the design and caused technological upheaval in the industry.

30. The cases of Siebel Systems and Millennium Pharmaceuticals, to name but two, demonstrate this contention. Siebel's strategy of non-exclusive partnership with Anderson Consulting (later renamed as Accenture) early in its existence gave it an immediate global presence. In a fast progression, Siebel expanded its global reach to more than 700 local partners by providing them with a CRM platform to regenerate, if not revive, their own consulting service, allowing them to grow internationally while emphasizing an extreme co-dependence for its own international growth and expansion. This was a strategic leveraging of its technology platform for mutual growth, synergy and competitiveness. Millennium Pharmaceuticals, on the other hand, grew rapidly by leveraging its high-technology R&D platform in different product lines and industries, using its capabilities to save time and expense for its partners to further leverage its partner-based resources. In a short time, Millennium reached close to full world-scale operations.

References

Acs, Zoltan and Bernard Yeung (1999), 'Entrepreneurial Discovery and the Global Economy', *Global Focus*, 11 (3), 63–72.

Barney, J. (1991), 'Firm Resources and Competitive Advantage', *Journal of Management*, Special Issue on the Resource Based View of the Firm, 17: 99–120.

Bilkey, Warren J. (1978), 'An Attempted Integration of the Literature on the Export Behavior of Firms', *Journal of International Business Studies*, 9 (1), Spring/Summer, 33–46.

Bilkey, Warren J. and George Tesar (1977), 'The Export Behavior of Smaller Sized Wisconsin Manufacturing Firms', *Journal of International Business Studies*, 8 (1), Spring/Summer, 93–8.

Brown, Patricia Fortini (1997), *Art And Life in Renaissance Venice*, Englewood Cliffs, NJ: Prentice-Hall and New York: Perspectives, Harry N. Abraham Publishers.

Buckley, Peter J. (1989), 'Foreign Direct Investment by Small and Medium-Sized Enterprises', *Small Business Economics*, 1, 89–100.

Buckley, Peter J. and Mark Casson (1976), *The Future of the Multinational Enterprise*, London: Macmillan.

Cantillon, Richard (1755), *Essai sur la Nature du Commerce en Général,* London and Paris: R. Gyles; translated (1931), by Henry Higgs, London: Macmillan and Co.

Caves, Richard E. (1982), *Multinational Enterprise and Economic Analysis*, Cambridge: Cambridge University Press.

Cavusgil, S. Tamer (1980), 'On the Internationalisation of Firms', *European Research*, 8.

Cavusgil, S.T. (1982), 'Some observations on the relevance of critical variables for internationalisation stages', in M. Czinkota and G. Tesar (eds), *Export Management: An International Context*, New York: Praeger, pp. 276–85.

Cavusgil, S. Tamer (1984), 'Differences Among Exporting Firms Based on Their Degree of Internationalisation', *Journal of Business Research*, 12 (2), 195–208.

Cavusgil, S. Tamer (1994), 'Born Globals: A Quiet Revolution Among Australian Exporters', *Journal of International Marketing Research*, 2 (3), editorial.

Cavusgil, S. Tamer and V. Kirpalani (1993), 'Introducing Products into Export Markets: Success Factors', *Journal of Business Research*, 27 (1), 1–15.

Cavusgil, S. Tamer and R.J. Nevin (1981), 'International Determinants of Export Marketing Behavior', *Journal of Marketing Research*, 28, 114–19.

Cavusgil, S. Tamer, Warren J. Bilkey and George Tesar (1979), 'A Note on the Export Behavior of Firms', *Journal of International Business Studies*, 10 (1), Spring/Summer, 91–7.

Chamlee-Wright, E. (1997), *The Cultural Foundations of Economic Development*, London and New York: Routledge.

Coase, R.H. (1937), 'The Nature of Firm', *Economica*, 386–405.

Dana, L.P. (2000), 'The Age of Symbiotic Marketing', in H. Etemad and R. Wright (eds), *Proceedings of International Entrepreneurship: Researching Frontiers*, 23–5 September, Montreal: McGill International Entrepreneurship, McGill University.

Dana, L.P. and H. Etemad (1995), 'SMEs Adapting Strategy for NAFTA: A Model for Small and Medium-sized Enterprises', *Journal of Small Business and Entrepreneurship*, 12 (3), July–August, 4–17

Dana, Léo Paul, Hamid Etemad and Richard Wright (2000), 'The Global Reach of Symbiotic Networks', *Journal of European Marketing*, June, 9, No. 2, pp. 1–16.

Dana, Léo Paul, Hamid Etemad and Richard Wright (2001), 'Symbiotic Interdependence', in Dianne Welsh and Ilan Alon (eds), *International Franchising in Emerging Markets*, Chicago: CCH Publishing, pp. 119–29.

Drucker, Peter Ferdinand (1974), *Management, Tasks, Responsibilities, Practices*, New York: Harper and Row.

Dunning, John H. (1973), 'The Determinants of International Production', *Oxford Economic Chapters*, November, 289–336.

Dunning, John H. (1977), 'Trade, Location of Economic Activity and MNE: A Search For An Eclectic Approach', *International Allocation of Economic Activity: Proceedings of A Nobel Symposium Held at Stockholm*, London: Macmillan, pp. 395–418.

Dunning, John H. (1980), 'Toward an Eclectic Theory of International Production: Empirical Tests', *Journal of International Business Studies*, 11 (1), 9–31.

Dunning, John H. (1988), 'The Eclectic Paradigm of International Production: A Restatement and Some Possible Extensions', *Journal of International Business Studies*, 19 (1), 1–31.

Ely, Richard T. and Ralph H. Hess (1893), *Outline of Economics*, New York: Macmillan.

Eriksson, K., J. Johanson, A. Majkgard and D. Sharma (1997), 'Experiential Knowledge and Cost in the Internationalisation Process', *Journal of International Business Studies*, 28 (2), 337–60.

Etemad, H. (1999), 'Globalization and Small and Medium-Sized Enterprises: Search for Potent Strategies', *Global Focus*, 11 (3) Summer, 85–105.

Etemad, H. (2001), 'Globalization of Small Airlines: Contradiction in terms or the newly-emerging Reality?', *Proceedings of the Fourth McGill International Entrepreneurship Conference at the University of Strathclyde*, September, Glasgow: Strathclyde International Business Unit, University of Strathclyde.

Etemad, Hamid (2002), 'Strategies for Internationalisation of Entrepreneurial Firms Facing Different Competitive Environments', in Hamid Etemad (ed.), *The Proceedings of the Third Biennial McGill Conference on International Entrepreneurship: Researching Frontiers*, Volume 1, 13 to16 September, Montreal:

Etemad, Hamid (2003), 'Managing Relations: The Essence of International Entrepreneurship', in Hamid Etemad and Richard Wright (eds), *Globalization and Entrepreneurship: Policy and Strategy Perspectives*, Cheltenham, UK and Northampton, MA: Edward Elgar.

Etemad, Hamid and Yender Lee (2000), 'The Developmental Path of an Emerging Knowledge Network in International Entrepreneurship', *Proceedings of Administrative Sciences Association of Canada, Entrepreneurship Division*, 21 (21), 8–12 July, pp. 72–82.

Etemad, Hamid and Yender Lee (2003), 'The Emerging Knowledge Network of International Entrepreneurship: Theory and Evidence', *Journal of Small Business Economics*, Volume 20, No. 1, pp. 5–23.

Etemad, Hamid, Richard Wright and L.P. Dana. (2001), 'Symbiotic International Business Networks: Collaboration Between Small and large Firms', *Thunderbird International Business Review*, 43 (4), August, 481–500.

Gomes-Casseres, Benjamin (1996), *The Alliance Revolution: The New Shape of Business Rivalry*, Cambridge, MA: Harvard University Press.

Gomes-Casseres, Benjamin (1997), 'Alliance Strategies of Small Firms', *Small Business Economics*, 9 (1), 33–44.

Gulati, R. (1995), 'Does Familiarity Breed Trust? The Implications of Repeated Ties for Contractual Choice in Alliances', *Academy of Management Review*, 38 (1), 85–112

Hayek, F.A. (1948), 'The Use of Knowledge in Society', *Studies in Philosophy, Politics and Economics*, Chicago: University of Chicago Press.

Hayek, F.A. (1978), 'Competition as a Discovery Procedure', *New Studies in Philosophy, Politics, Economics and History of Ideas*, Chicago: University of Chicago Press.

Holloway, Charles A. (1996), 'Supplier Management at Sun Microsystems (A)', Stanford University Graduate School of Business, Palo Alto, CA.

Hymer, Stephan (1976), *International Operations of National Firms: A Study of Direct Foreign Investment*, Cambridge, MA: MIT Press.

Johanson, J. and J.E. Vahlne (1977), 'The Internationalisation Process of the Firm – Four Swedish case studies', *Journal of Management Studies*, 12 (3), 305–322.

Johanson, Jan and Jan-Erik Vahlne (1990), 'The Mechanism of Internationalisation', *International Marketing Review*, 7 (4), 11–24.

Johanson, Jan and Jan-Erik Vahlne (1992), 'Management of Foreign Market Entry', *Scandinavian International Business Review*, 1 (3), 9–27.

Johanson, Jan and Finn Wiedersheim-Paul (1975), 'The Internationalisation of the Firm: Four Swedish Cases', *Journal of International Management Studies*, 12 (3), October, 36–64.

Kirzner, Israel M. (1973), *Competition and Entrepreneurship*, Chicago: University of Chicago Press.

Kirzner, Israel M. (1979), *Perception, Opportunity, and Profit: Studies in the Theory of Entrepreneurship*, Chicago: University of Chicago Press.

Knight, Frank Hyneman (1921), *Risk, Uncertainty and Profit*, Boston and New York: Houghton Mifflin.

Knight, Gary A. and S. Tamer Cavusgil (1996), 'The Born Global Firm', in S. Tamer Cavusgil and Tage Koed Masden (eds), *Advances in International Marketing*, vol. 8, Greenwich: JAI.

Leonidou, Leonidas C. and Constantine S. Katsikeas (1996), 'The Export Development Process', *Journal of International Business Studies*, 27 (3), 517–51.

Levitt, Theodore (1983), 'The Globalization of Markets', *Harvard Business Review*, May–June, 92–102.

McClelland, David Clarence (1961), *The Achieving Society*, Princeton, NJ: D. Van Nostrand.

McDougall, Patricia Phillips (1989), 'International Versus Domestic Entrepreneurship: New Venture Strategic Behavior and Industry Structure', *Journal of Business Venturing*, 5 (4) November, 387–400.

McDougall, Patricia Phillips (1996), 'New Venture Internationalisation, Strategic Change, and Performance: A Follow-Up Study', *Journal of Business Venturing*, 11 (1), 23–40.

McDougall, Patricia Phillips, Scott Shane and Benjamin Milton Oviatt (1994), 'Explaining the Formation of International Joint Ventures: The Limits of Theories from International Business Research', *Journal of Business Venturing*, 9, 469–87.

Nelson, R.R. and S.G. Winter (1982), *An Evolutionary Theory of Economic Change*, Cambridge, MA: Belknap Press.

Nonaka, I. (1995), 'A Theory of Organizational Knowledge Creation', *International Journal of Technology Management*, 11(7/8), 833–45.

Nonaka, I. and H. Takeuchi (1996), *The Knowledge Creating Company: How Japanese Companies Create the Dynamics of Innovation*, New York: Oxford University Press.

Ohmae, Kenichi (1985), *Triad Power: The Coming Shape of Global Competition*, New York: The Free Press, pp. 8–20.

Oviatt, Benjamin Milton and Patricia Phillips McDougall (1994), 'Toward A Theory of International New Ventures', *Journal of International Business Studies*, 25 (1), 45–64.

Oviatt, Benjamin Milton and McDougall, Patricia Phillips (1997), 'Challenges for Internationalisation Process Theory', *Management International Review*, 37 (2), 85–99.

Partridge, Lorne (1996), *The Art of Renaissance: 1400–1600 Rome*, Hong Kong: Calmann and Knight Ltd. and New York: Perspectives, Harry N. Abraham Publishers.

Redding, Gordon (1990), *The Spirit of Chinese Capitalism*, Berlin and New York: Walter de Gruyter.

Reynolds, P., M. Camp and M. Hay (2001), *Global Entrepreneurship Monitor Report*, Kansas City, MO: E.M. Kauffamnn Foundation.

Rugman, A.M. (1979), *International Diversification and the Multinational Enterprise*, Farborough: Lexington.

Rugman, A.M. (1982), *New Theories of Multinationals*, London: Croom Helm.

Say, Jean-Baptiste (1803), *Traite d'économie politique ou simple exposition de la manière dont se forment, se distribuent, et se consomment les richesses*; revised (1819); translated (1830) by C.R. Prinsep, *A Treatise on Political Economy: On Familiar Conversations On the Manner in Which Wealth is Produced, Distributed and Consumed by Society*, Philadelphia: John Grigg and Elliot.

Say, Jean-Baptiste (1815), *Catéchisme d'économie politique*; translated (1821) by John Richter, *Catechism of Political Economy*, London: Sherwood.

Schumpeter, Joseph Allois (1911), *Theorie der wirtschaftlichen Entwicklung*, Munich and Leipzig: Dunker und Humblot; translated (1934) by R. Opie, *The Theory of Economic Development*, Cambridge, MA: Harvard University Press.

Schumpeter, Joseph Allois (1928), 'The Instability of Capitalism', *Economic Journal*, 38, November, 361–86.

Schumpeter, Joseph Allois (1942), *Capitalism, Socialism and Democracy*, New York: Harper and Row.

Schumpeter, Joseph Allois (1947), 'The Creative Response in Economic History', *Journal of Economic History*, 7, November, 149–59.

Shapero, A. (1975), 'The Displaced, Uncomfortable Entrepreneur', *Psychology Today*, 9 (11), 83–133.

Shapero, A. (1984), 'The Entrepreneurial Event', in C. Kent (ed.), *The Environment for Entrepreneurship*, Lexington, MA: DC Heath.

Stöttinger, B. and B. Schlegelmilch (1998), 'Explaining Export Development Through Psychic Distance: Enlightening or Elusive?', *International Marketing Review*, 15 (5), 357–72.

Uzzi, B. (1999), 'Embeddedness in the Making of Financial Capital', *Strategic Management Journal*, 64, 481–505.
Williamson, O.E. (1975), *Markets and Hierarchies: Analysis and Anti-Trust Implications*, New York: Free Press.
Williamson, O.E. (1981), 'The Economics of Organization: The Transaction Cost Approach', *American Journal of Sociology*, 87, 548–77.

14 Entrepreneurial capabilities: a resource-based systemic approach to international entrepreneurship

Jean-Jacques Obrecht

Entrepreneurship is expected to be the fuel of economic development throughout the world. However the grounds for this tribute are contingent. In the parts of the world at the forefront of globalization, the worship of entrepreneurship is linked to the issue of competitiveness which underpins the survival and growth of business firms everywhere. In other significant parts, entrepreneurship development is taken for a necessity to overcome poverty. Here and there entrepreneurs' malfeasance stirs up questions on entrepreneurial captalism with a more or less explicit consideration of ethics. This chapter seeks to address these interconnected issues.

A fresh approach to entrepreneurship is also called for, especially if it has to fit to an international context. After the celebration of the entrepreneurial traits, researchers now emphasize the entrepreneurial process. The latter is viewed in exclusive concert with the market process while overlapping with conventional strategic thought. Insofar as the entrepreneurial process is bound with the competitive behaviours that drive the market process, and to the extent that the core of strategy is winning a market-based competitive advantage, the tuning between entrepreneurial process and market process is perfect. As shown in a multitude of diagrams, the business global environment is set apart precisely because, in mainstream thinking on entrepreneurship, the basic entrepreneurial logic is market-oriented.

The approach of this chapter takes its inspiration from resource-based strategic thinking. It views the entrepreneur as a holder of capabilities, with a special concern for the case of small and medium-sized businesses. It will first specify the concept of entrepreneurial capabilities. In a systemic perspective it will then elaborate on the components of the portfolio of entrepreneurial capabilities. Finally it will present a 'triad model' of those capabilities in which the overall environment of firms is integrated in the entrepreneurship paradigm.

What kind of capabilities peculiar to entrepreneurs are needed in dynamic organizations facing a demanding diverse environment? This question with a view to ethical issues will be the guiding line of this chapter.

It may appear as a plea for an alternative view of the entrepreneur in the 21st century.

The concept of entrepreneurial capabilities

Within the resource-based views on strategy, the concept of 'core competencies' which was worked out originally for the sake of large corporations has developed into a fundamental approach to growth and success in SMEs. 'Core competencies are the collective learning in the organization, especially how to coordinate diverse production skills and integrate multiple streams of technologies . . . competencies that empower individual business to adapt quickly to changing opportunities' (Prahalad and Hamel, 1990). Attaining, enlarging and sustaining a competitive advantage based on 'distinctive competencies' has proved to be within the reach of SMEs (McGee and Peterson, 2000). Moreover, by means of developing a broader resource base including a variety of non-financial resources, such as those obtained by customer or supplier alliances, SMEs operationalize the core competency perspective in their own way (Walsh *et al.*, 1996). SMEs with higher levels of 'entrepreneurial orientation', including such dimensions as propensity to take risks, level of innovation and the ability to recognize opportunities, are reported to possess a wider variety of distinctive competencies and to enjoy higher performance (Smart and Conant, 1994). The 'entrepreneurship core competencies' issue has been viewed, furthermore, in a contingency framework of performance: optimization of resources and strategic formulation depend on whether entrepreneurs act in a precarious situation or in a situation in which they have effective means of action (Aliouat *et al.*, 1999).

As appears from these research positions, competencies as a tool to analyse SMEs are the subject of increasing interest. The main source of advantage as regards methodology is the possible combination of different but converging views on entrepreneurship issues related to SMEs, such as knowledge-based, resource-based and situational approaches (Capaldo *et al.*, 2002). Moreover, in a prospective view related to organizational learning, it has to be emphasized that entrepreneurial competencies should not be limited to consolidating technology and production skills. They should be viewed as a broader range of abilities needed to initiate appropriate actions in specific situations which would not be restricted to organizational performance issues but would extend to the organization's contribution to a 'socially responsible undertaking' (Nijsen, 2002). The recurrence of such initiatives, which in a resourceful way would be applied to a great variety of situations, also leads to organizational learning.

Thereby entrepreneurial capabilites match up to the entrepreneur's capacity to take initiatives within his organization and to take action in an intricate playing field: the entrepreneur as the main driving force on the market has to meet the entrepreneur as a responsible partner in society. They go along with the whole entrepreneurial career of owner-managers in SMEs, from start-up and thereafter. They mean therefore at one and the same time capacities which are needed for an entrepreneurial venturing career and capacities such as those which result from learning.

This integrative approach, however, increases the complexity of the entrepreneurship paradigm since it goes beyond the usual 'dyadic relationship between an individual and an organisation' (Verstraete, 1999). A systemic perspective as a useful tool for dealing with complexity is therefore brought forth in this chapter. It amounts to framing identifiable sets of entrepreneurial capabilites displaying significant interactions. The reference to ontological, phenomenological and genetic points of view allows us to embrace the whole portfolio of capabilities the entrepreneur needs in his playing field to cope with an extensive range of situations.

Thus the systemic triangular view leads up to three types of entrepreneurial capabilities: personal capability, organizational capability and societal capability.

Personal entrepreneurial capability
Personal capability is congruent to the ontological side of entrepreneurial capability. It refers to the abilities that are embedded in the entrepreneur as an individual and whose enactment is dependent on the individual exclusively. Capability meaning the capacity of being used or developed is action-oriented. Therefore, throughout the venturing career of the entrepreneur it is subject to learning by doing. Some concepts developed in entrepreneurship literature serve to back up this point.

The most appealing construct is that referring to 'proactive personality', defined as the extent to which individuals 'take action to influence their environments' (Bateman and Crant, 1993). Proactive individuals are said to 'scan for opportunities, show initiative, take actions and persevere until they reach closure by bringing about change' (ibid.).

According to some findings, a strong association between the 'proactive personality scale' and 'entrepreneurial intentions' has been found (Crant, 1996). Because entrepreneurial intentions form the 'underpinnings of new organizations', they might be viewed as 'the first step in an evolving, long-term process' which allows proactive people 'to capitalise on their personality' (ibid.). Proactive personality disposition has also been directly and significantly related to the entrepreneurial posture of the firm: a more proactive entrepreneur 'creates an organization that scans for opportunities and takes a bold and aggressive approach to the market' (Becherer and Maurer, 1999).

This construct may be compared to Kirzner's theory of alertness (Kirzner, 1973) which assumes that entrepreneurs are more alert to new opportunities and use information differently. The concept of 'entrepreneurial alertness' has been extended in entrepreneurship research to specific searching behaviours focusing on new business ideas. So it has been argued that 'alertness will exhibit itself in a continuous search for information, through broad and undirected scanning that will take place at unconventional times and places, as opposed to a direct, rational search, which takes place in appropriate times . . . and expected places . . . where managerial search is more likely to occur' (Kaish and Gilad, 1991). However these views opposing alertness of entrepreneurs and alertness of managers have seemingly to be settled more firmly, as stated in empirical findings. Furthermore the point is also that Kirzner's concept of alertness is not limited to specific or designated searches for new opportunities. It is a general state of mind inducing entrepreneurs to scan the environment globally and to be responsive to changes at the macro level of the economy as well.

The concept of 'entrepreneurial orientation' also comes close to the substance of entrepreneurial personal capability. It deals with 'willingness to accept risks as necessary antecedents of goal achievements, adoption by the firm of pro-active posture towards its environment, innovativeness in problem solving, especially when it comes to market-oriented applications of technology' (Miles *et al.*, 1993). Research results indicate that a firm's higher entrepreneurial orientation, including such dimensions as propensity to take risks, levels of innovation and the ability to recognize opportunites, reaches a wider variety of distinctive competencies and enjoys higher performance (Smart and Conant, 1994). Other findings support substantive linkage between the resource-based capabilites of a firm and competitive advantage: ability to take action is one of the constructs of distinctive competencies (McGee and Peterson, 2000).

While proactive personality appears in the above-mentioned literature as a personal disposition or orientation, it should be noticed that it goes beyond the usual 'traits' approach, because of its 'action' dimension. On the same grounds its range or scope is greater than that of the 'cognitive' approach. It is indeed a meaningful expression of one's personal capability. Together with the above-mentioned related aspects, it is a substantive constituent of the entrepreneur's 'life world'.

Organizational entrepreneurial capability
Corresponding to the phenomenological aspect of entrepreneurial capability, is the capacity to initiate and to sustain an entrepreneurial dynamism throughout the organization and to stimulate a process of collective learning in view of that.

In the organizational context, proactive behaviour would be constantly asking 'what if' in respect of any inside or outside developments likely to have an effect upon the firm's functioning. In SMEs this vigilance is incumbent on the owner–manager entrepreneur himself, for obvious reasons. The requisite capacities are clearly different from the managerial competencies because they overflow the functional fields, whereas at the same time the entrepreneur, to be effective, has to have empathy with all key managerial tasks. They call for all-purpose sensitivity and contingent problem-solving abilities.

In a systemic view once again, three significant areas where such capacities are needed may be identified: animating organizational potentialities, arranging dependable networks and establishing strategic direction. First, potentialities as possibilities of developing may be found in many parts of an organization and may touch upon ideas, experience, management and so on (Gibb and Scott, 1985). In SMEs the broadest locus of potentialities is undoubtedly 'the' human resource.

The impact of human resource management (HRM) on organizational performance has been brought to light by researchers (Becker and Gerhart, 1996). Human resources in SMEs have been presented as the prime cause of competitive advantage (Aliouat and Nekka, 1999). Tools for SMEs have been elaborated to assess the difficulties and needs of human resource management (D'Amboise and Garand, 1994). Indeed awareness of the crucial part human resources play in development strategies has been said to be lagging behind in the case of SMEs. There is, however, evidence suggesting that small business entrepreneurs are increasingly aware of new management ideas, and a number of organizations in diverse countries have implemented initiatives traditionally identified with larger firms.

The presence of HRM practices in SMEs has proved to be related to characteristics of the organization. Family-controlled SMEs seem to be better off in this respect, because strategic HRM is simpler (Watkins, 1996). In particular a very strong relationship between human resource practices and 'progressive decision-making ideology' (Goll, 1991) has been evidenced. It is worthwhile to note that this concept refers to 'a style of normative decision-making characterized by open communication, participation in management decisions, and a systematic search for opportunities' which is conducive to a variety of HRM programmes. Very small firms, however, are less likely to adopt 'bundles' of HRM practices (Wager, 1998).

In SMEs the entrepreneur's mindset, together with the firm's size, is the major determinant of the variety of HRM practices. Under these circumstances it is up to the owner–manager of a small business to 'invest' in human capital as a locus of potentialities and to animate it to good purpose.

Second, networks provide possible access to alternative resources since conventional resource constraints are a major factor in SME strategy development. They contribute to develop a broader resource base providing reasonable options for gaining, enlarging and sustaining competitive advantage by operationalizing the core competency perspective.

In small organizations, the personal network of the owner–manager determines to a great extent the firm's overall external networks. This involves arranging dependable relationships with the stakeholder environment on a personal basis with a view to building trust and thus reducing uncertainty in business transactions. 'The art, in entrepreneurial management in this respect, is essentially that of managing ambiguity via judgement of people. Perhaps the most important factor underpinning success in this respect is the ability of the manager to see the business through the eyes of the various stakeholders [such as] customers, suppliers, bankers, regulatory authorities, middle men, professionals and competitors' (Gibb, 1998).

The personal part in entrepreneurs' networks has been repeatedly emphasized: 'Personal networks are especially crucial to genuine entrepreneurs who intend to initiate structural change in the market. The original venture as well as subsequent ventures forming the venturing career of the entrepreneur are embedded in the personal network as it organises the entrepreneur's life world' (Johannisson, 1996). Personal networking features the dynamics of 'self-organizing systems' where 'the conditions for interaction between subjects consequently are assumed to include both economic–rational and social–intuitive aspects' (ibid.).

In SMEs the owner–manager's credibility obviously determines the viability of the personal network and thereby the potential advantage a stakeholder network may mean as a possible source for alternative resources.

Finally, strategic direction setting includes both the overall objectives the firm strives to attain and the possible lines leading to operational relevant goals. In SMEs it is a very well documented fact that the personal values and perceptions of the owner–manager entrepreneurs are strong influential factors in this respect.

The main task of the small business entrepreneur is without doubt to develop a purposive business idea, thinking ahead about the future of the firm and taking appropriate initiatives in face of threats and opportunities. But 'high performers are proactive in strategic orientation and exhibit entrepreneurial personal values. In contrast, lower-than-average performers are reactive in strategic orientation and exhibit conservative personal values' (Kotey and Meredith, 1997). Entrepreneurs endowed with a 'progressive decision-making ideology' would also make efforts to obtain the adherence of staff to the possible strategic choices, whereas conservative entrepreneurs would keep to their own way of doing things.

There is, however, the unsettled debate over the level of formalism SMEs should put into practice with a view to increasing the performance of strategic management. Despite a prolific literature on the relationship between planning procedures and organizational performance among small business, limited generalizations have been reached. The reason perhaps lies in the correlative relationship between levels of sophistication and performance: a sophisticated planning process may lead to higher sales, but higher sales may also encourage top management to engage in a more sophisticated planning process (Rue and Ibrahim, 1998). The opposition between supporters of 'vision-based strategy' or 'flexible strategic orientation' and the advocates of 'strategic planning as an institutionalized process' still leaves room for further findings.

One could reasonably assume, however, that formal planning procedures may increase the performance of SMEs insofar as the levels of uncertainty in the business context are not too high or to the extent that they are used above all as a tool for collective learning in view of an uncertain future. Depending on uncertain levels, effective abilities should therefore be a mix of intuitive thinking and careful calculation.

Societal entrepreneurial capability
This set of entrepreneurial capabilities is rooted in the deepest layers of the entrepreneur's genus. Its uniqueness is the outcome of the history common to a people or a country and by this token a crucial vector of its future, since viable human systems are always coming into being.

This genetic point of view emphasizes the reciprocal relationship between entrepreneurship and community. Considering the possible relationships between public and private spheres, there are indeed moves going on, from 'classical steering models' by which 'government endeavours to achieve as great as possible compliance with legislation and regulation by businesses' towards 'new steering relationships' with more 'space for self-regulation' by businesses themselves (Nijsen, 2002). The relationship between entrepreneurship and society can also be regarded in a much broader perspective of dynamical systems theory which says that 'self-organising develops when autonomous units, capable of multiple behavioural choices, operate with individual freedom but within clearly defined frames of reference' (Johannisson, 1996). But, as applied for instance to the case of industrial districts, 'self-organising will only emerge if there is a minimum number of firms and a minimum level of interaction' (ibid.).

In other words, the challenge entrepreneurs have to take up is to be responsive to values of the community whose destiny they share and to enlarge their vision towards the values of other communities within the global business environment. But a small number only of exemplary cases would not be sufficient to bring forth a significant stage in coming into being. Entrepreneurs' collective myopia would lead to non-viable entrepreneurship in practice. In this connection, the entrepreneurs' commitments, which at the present time and increasingly in the near future may become essential, deal with entrepreneurial governance and entrepreneurial finesse. Although these aspects of entrepreneurial societal capability both belong to the 'space for self-regulation', it is worthwhile to give separate emphasis to both.

Entrepreneurial governance raises the question of the entrepreneur's responsiveness to the value system of a community as a whole. It comes down to his readiness to allow for community values and expectations. It questions his willingness to adhere to codes of conduct which are all the more necessary in a civil society as the withdrawal of the boundaries of the state in the regulation of business acitivity is consequential. Only a strong ethical response to self-regulation enables entrepreneurial capitalism to make or break.

An ethical approach in its broadest meaning may embrace indeed the whole space of entrepreneurial possible responsiveness. It finds expression by a responsible relationship towards neighbours in an overriding sense: 'the relationship with the neighbour knits as a responsibilityship' (Levinas, 1982). Ethics leads towards 'a share in universal responsibility . . . and this share in responsibility can only be actively assumed by individuals' (Dherse and Minguet, 1998). Last but not least, putting ethics into practice requires freedom of action. It is freedom individuals enjoy in reality when choosing the kind of life they come to value that defines their capacity for fulfilment and that leads to common welfare in a context of human diversity (Sen, 1992).

This ethical view represents a far-reaching challenge to entrepreneurs as creators of wealth. In the entrepreneurial capability perspective, it calls for the mobilization of 'downstream' as well as 'upstream' capacities. On the one hand, they are connected with the whole set of operations specific to a business organization: this is the field of 'business ethics' that covers the firm's functional areas thoroughly; at the present time, ethics in financial management are seemingly a challenging field worldwide. On the other hand, they are involved in the broader issues of the relationship of business to community. The concepts of 'social responsibility' and 'environmental responsibility' which are currently gaining notoriety give evidence of the prominent role entrepreneurs play or should play as employers of working people and as partners sharing within a community a common destiny.

All firms of any size are called to take part in the development of entrepreneurial governance (Harvey *et al.*, 1991). According to some findings, however, SMEs and large corporations show diverging levels of responsiveness and/or different patterns of ethical behaviour (Longenecker *et al.*, 1989). A number of ways have been suggested to get a better understanding of how small businesses are involved in ethics (Hornsby *et al.*, 1994) or in 'corporate social responsibility' issues (Thompson and Smith, 1991).

The ethical context of entrepreneurship is also recognized as a crucial area. Entrepreneurs were found to differ from non-entrepreneurs in the types of ethical situations they face; entrepreneurs who had previously faced certain situations differed from entrepreneurs lacking prior exposure to ethical dilemmas (Longenecker *et al.*, 1996). Since ethics is obviously also a matter of learning, the ethical dimension brings about a new impulse to the core competency perspective: an increasing number of companies in industry and in service sectors are considering ethics as a resource for uniqueness.

Entrepreneurial finesse takes up the question of the entrepreneur's responsiveness to change of any kind in the business environment and the ability to handle difficult and/or delicate situations in a resourceful way. It emphasizes the entrepreneur's personal sense of what is fitting in complex situations including simultaneously economic and non-economic issues. These days, the capacity to adjust to change in respect to space and/or time in a complex and turbulent environment resulting from globalization is a challenge of major importance and needs a broad range of sensitivity. The present worldwide turbulence and the diversity of its widespread outbreaks adds to uncertainty in the global environment of business but also in the local environment as well.

Owing to the globalization phenomena, moving beyond national borders is an option for SMEs which is becoming more and more a necessity for a large number. Going international implies international networking for global players but, since sustainable networks are based on trust and since trusts depends also on 'visibility', SMEs may come up against more difficulties than large corporations in this respect. This is the reason why local cooperative networks enhance the effective internationalizing process in SMEs (Johannisson, 1994). The importance of local embeddedness, of local access to expertise and technologies, in sustaining firm technological innovation and leadership, including leadership in global markets, has been pointed out (Keeble *et al.*, 1998). Differences in the 'ways of doing things' due to institutional and/or cultural differences may be obstacles to the internationalizing process of SMEs. Overcoming these obstacles entails the extension of entrepreneurial alertness as an ability to master information and knowledge of global scope (Julien and Ramangalahy, 1999).

Moreover the ways small firms internationalize may be different. There is a range of possibilities between 'international-by-stages' (Johanson and

Vahlne, 1977; Cavusgil, 1984) and 'international-at-founding' (Oviatt and McDougall, 1994). As a rule, international involvement by SMEs takes place to a growing degree over time and goes through distinctive stages on the international markets; this, seemingly, is still the general pattern, according to recent findings (Gankema *et al.*, 2000). But due to the pressure of worldwide competition, technology-based firms often have to start their business, from inception, as an 'international new venture' (Oviatt and McDougall, 1994). However, despite the prevalence of the technology-based firms amongst international new ventures (INVs), non-technology-based firms likewise may ground their international competitive pattern on unique resources, so that they may skip or cut down stages in the export development process (Wolff and Pett, 2000).

Finally, as regards the requisites for sustainable international new venturing, the importance of easy access to knowledge flows has been stressed since knowledge is a very special resource whose main characteristic lies in the strength of its 'replication economies'; that is, the economies of scale that can be achieved by reproducing the same information a number of times (Grandinetti and Rullani, 1994). International networks as 'alternative governance structures' for INVs (Oviatt and McDougall, 1994) make access to the international flows of knowledge easier.

On account of the implications of SMEs in internationalization versus globalization, owner–manager entrepreneurs are inevitably involved in a self-regulation versus self-organizing process in which entrepreneurial finesse would operate as a sort of steering device. Arranging local networking in an international perspective and extending alertness to the international arena calls for entrepreneurial finesse indeed. This is equally valid for other aspects like proportioning resource-based and market-based components of international competitive advantage, adapting the international growth path to contingencies with special attention to the international flows of technologies; or, from a more general point of view, recognizing change by its importance and distinguishing between temporary moves and long-term moves. Not surprisingly, managing access to volatile knowledge flows through unstable international networks demands a high level of entrepreneurial finesse.

The ethical side of these issues may also be seen easily, although it may be difficult to deal with. The effective pursuit of an entrepreneurial international career requires thoughtful consideration of differences in culture and institutions. Understanding the meaning of culture, being able to recognize its many manifestations and adapting their business approach to cultural diversity is no small task for small business entrepreneurs, when taking into account the extraordinary variety of 'ways of perceiving things' which are rooted in culture and traditions. They have to be sensitive to a cross-cultural perspective and ready to practise 'intercultural communication' (Harpe and Viviers, 1999). Ethics as a personal disposition towards other people should obviously prevail in this kind of relationship, which is without doubt the most challenging aspect of globalization. Ever since the beginnings of globalization, concepts for interpreting international business ethics have been elaborated, but most of the time to help multinational managers to find compromises between conflicting norms in home and host countries. Entrepreneurs in SMEs also are clearly exposed to the ethics of international business since they show up as increasingly important actors in the international environment.

On the whole, the entrepreneur's position in the community as exhibited by entrepreneurial governance and entrepreneurial finesse gives evidence of the importance of the ethical issues. Acceptance of ethics by entrepreneurs would be a fundamental contribution in making it possible for society to exist as a cooperative venture for mutual advantage. Fortunately there are reasons to believe that non-ethical businesses have no future and that, step by step, a comprehensive ethical awareness is emerging, and not only in the business world. Unfortunately there are less sunny aspects which seem to move further away the time when an alliance between business and ethics can be sealed.

The triad model of entrepreneurial capabilities

The portfolio of entrepreneurial capabilities may be represented by a self-evident triangular construct (see Figure 14.1). Each corner of the triangle corresponds to the preceding identified main types. The circle around the triangle suggests that, when they are mobilized within the playing field of the entrepreneur, they have an interacting relationship. Environment is divided into entrepreneurial environment and general environment.

The model also suggests that the 'ideal' entrepreneur would be endowed with a balanced mix of entrepreneurial capabilities which would be represented by the star in the centre of the triangle and would have the meaning of a goal set for entrepreneurial learning. The ethical part of entrepreneurs' behaviour would appear around this imaginary centre as a common ground interacting with each one of these capabilities. Effective entrepreneurial societal capability depends on proactive personality and entrepreneurial alertness patterns which shape the entrepreneur's personal capability. It is also contingent on organizational potentialities, dependable networks and strategic direction which construct organizational capability. In a reciprocal way, personal and organizational capabilities are influenced by entrepreneurial governance and finesse on account of their ethical content.

Last but not least, this triad model of entrepreneurial capabilites implies that there are two essential constitutive capabilities which form the bottom

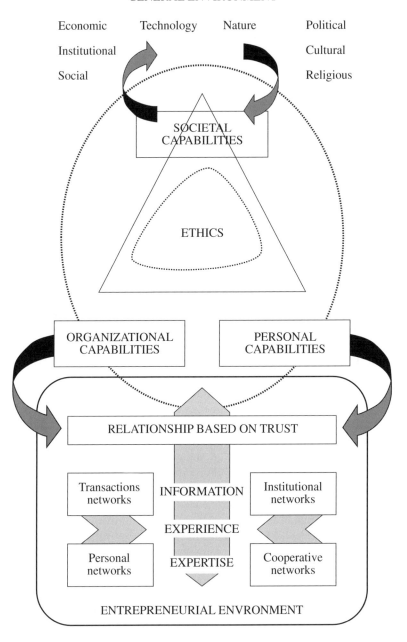

Figure 14.1   Triad model of entrepreneurial capabilities

line: the personal and the organizational capabilities. But the third one which is presented at the top, the societal capability, is the critical one: it determines that kind of entrepreneurship which is sustainable and acceptable in different communitites evolving through time. The triad model is adequate to bring all these aspects to light in a straightforward way and allows for further elaboration. Considering *in fine* the major issues at hand bearing on entrepreneurship worldwide, it is indispensable to make room for cultural aspects, having in mind the differences between individual-based and community-based cultures.

In the western part of the world, where worship of the individual stands for the basic rule of social life and where entrepreneurial malfeasance has been gaining ground for years, the imperative recognition of 'codes of conduct' proper to a civil society is the question at stake.

The 'ethical charts' which have been elaborated in many large corporations, and which are now supposed to be monitored by 'responsibility managers', may be viewed as a 'second-best' tool for entrepreneurial governance, on condition that they are not perverted as a communication trick or a marketing gadget. They may also contribute to a better awareness of worldwide institutional, cultural and social differences and thereby to improving entrepreneurial finesse on a global level insofar as they are not motivated by a kind of hidden ethnocentrism. Nevertheless it should be understood that corporations are not entitled to act as 'moral prescriptors': ethics is not self-interest-minded and rests solely upon individuals.

In a broader perspective however, this is only one side of the problem. The other side concerns the overall weaknesses in civil society: the decay of the social values system itself. Undoubtedly this is a vital global issue for democratic societies. On account of their outstanding role in society, entrepreneurs have to share in this critical issue but with regard to common interests. Then, in this respect, there would be room for ethics again.

In southern and eastern parts of the world, the development of entrepreneurship is often linked to subduing poverty. In these regions, however, collective values which are rooted in community history and traditions are said to stand in the way of entrepreneurial careers. Entrepreneurship development would therefore require a 'process of individualisation in the African way' (Marie, 1997). This means that, owing to the economic pressure imposed by extreme poverty, numbers of people in Africa are induced to rely only on themselves, to broaden the scope of their own initiatives, to make use of their community links for personal goals and to come into 'hybrid compromises' between managing personal projects and attending to community tasks. The enterprising individual is said to be in a 'creative tenseness' between necessary individualism for survival and values based on solidarity. But this is a point of view made by a western commentator.

Instead of focusing on aspects related to individualism, an alternative approach referring to community-based cultures should be given true consideration too. Collective values rooted in history and traditions of African countries, and of other regions with similar cultural configurations, may be seen likewise as useful benchmarks for 'genuine growth' driven by a 'new ethic' and following up 'original bearings' (On'Okundji, 1999). There is an 'ethical exigency in the governance of men in Africa' (Kamto, 1999), meaning that the individual without community is unthinkable.

In some countries collective values regulating social life have a very strong influence within civil society as respected codes of conduct. In Madagascar the so-called 'fihavanana' is a form of 'social pact' relying on mutual respect, tolerance and assistance. Although small business owner-managers seem to give priority to the interests of the firm over the 'fihavanana'-based values, they do not set aside essential values related to the traditions of this country that refer to family, religion, solidarity and mutual support (Rasolofoson, 2001). In point of fact, a large part of the elite in Madagascar worries about the 'everyone for himself' possible outcomes, considering that the abyss between poverty and wealth would become even deeper. Exposure to the ethical perspective of enterprising individuals is therefore all the more important. The imperative to find genuine ways to highlight ethics in the private as well as in the public spheres is absolute.

Concluding remarks
The main argument of this conceptual chapter was to suggest that the challenge entrepreneurs are facing at the beginning of the 21st century cannot be met only by more enterprising behaviour on the part of individuals or business organizations. Much more is needed if one agrees with the idea that common welfare on a global level is the main objective to be reached and that giving attention to this purpose lies not only in the hands of governments or non-profit organizations, although they have an obvious role in bringing about a socially acceptable situation. It has been contended that a resource-based approach that puts forward the entrepreneurial capabilities which are needed in this respect is more enlightening than the prevailing approaches of entrepreneurship. It has been shown how ethics permeate the whole set of entrepreneurial capabilities.

In the face of the dramatic inequalities in the levels of economic development across the world, the dividing line between business and ethics should indeed some day fade away as an archaism. There is no proof that entrepreneurship as it is practised in the utilitarian way is the unique remedy for poverty. Joseph Schumpeter, while not an anarchist, strongly believed that entrepreneurs do help improve society by disrupting current thinking through their creative and innovative abilities. Therefore, as a disruptive activity, entrepreneurship should be able by itself, as a 'self-organizing system', to lead to ethical patterns of innovative behaviour in business.

There is evidence that the educational and vocational training system also has its part to play. The challenge the business schools and/or university faculties have to face is to broaden their views on entrepreneurship. Often they fall into the trap of mainstream thinking in business education which is focused on the segmented traditional functional approach. Above all, failure to participate in the development of an entrepreneurial culture that fits the cultural values of society contingent on the countries and regions of the world would be a serious missed opportunity. Within universities in particular, there is still a virtuous circle to be started in many places.

References

Aliouat, B. and Nekka, H. (1999), 'Human resources as competitive advantage in small-sized firms strategy: core competencies, training and management style' proceedings of the ICSB 44th World Conference, June, Naples.

Aliouat, B., Camion, C. and Gasse, Y. (1999), 'Small-sized firms' managerial practices and entrepreneurship core competencies: a contingency framework of performance', proceedings of the ICSB 44th World Conference, June, Naples.

Bateman, T.S. and Crant, J.M. (1993), 'The proactive component of organizational behavior: a measure and correlates', *Journal of Organizational Behavior*, 14 (2).

Becherer, R.C. and Maurer, J.G. (1999), 'The proactive personality disposition and the entrepreneurial behaviour among small company presidents', *Journal of Small Business Management*, January.

Becker, B. and Gerhart, B. (1996), 'The impact of human resource management on organizational performance: progress and prospects', *Academy of Management Journal*, 39 (4).

Capaldo, G., Iandoli, L., Raffa, M. and Zollo, G. (2002), 'Eliciting small firm's competencies: methodological issues', paper presented to the Rencontres de St Gall 2002, Swiss Research Institute of Small Business and Entrepreneurship, University of St. Gallen.

Cavusgil, T.S. (1984), 'Differences among exporting firms based on their degree of internationalisation', *Journal of Business Research*, 12 (2).

Crant, J.M. (1996), 'The proactive personality scale as a predictor of entrepreneurial intentions', *Journal of Small Business Management*, July.

D'Amboise, G. and Garand, D.J. (1994), 'Proposition de trois grilles d'analyse regroupant les difficultés et besoins de GRH des PME', proceedings of the ICSB 39th World Conference, June, Strasbourg.

Dherse, J.L. and Minguet, H. (1998), 'L'éthique ou le chaos?', Paris: Presses de la Renaissance.

Donaldson, T. (1968), *The Ethics of International Business*, The Ruffin series in Business Ethics, New York, Oxford: Oxford University Press.

Gankema, H.G.J., Snuif, H.R. and Zwart, P.S. (2000), 'The internationalization process of small and medium-sized enterprises: an evaluation of stage theory', *Journal of Small Business Management*, October.

Gibb, A. (1998), 'Entrepreneurial core capacities, competitiveness and management development in the 21st century', paper presentation at IntEnt98 Conference, July, European Business School, Oestrich-Winkel, Germany.

Gibb, A. and Scott, M. (1985), 'Strategic awareness, personal commitment and the process of planning in the small business', *Journal of Management Studies*, 22 (6).

Goll, I. (1991), 'Environment, corporate ideology, and involvement programs', *Industrial Relations*, 30.

Grandinetti, R. and Rullani, E. (1994), 'Sunk internationalisation: small firms and global knowledge', *Revue d'Economie Industrielle*, 67 (1).

Harpe, M. von and Viviers, W. (1999), 'The internationalisation of SMEs: the role of intercultural communication', proceedings of the ICSB 44th World Conference, June, Naples.

Harvey, B., H. van Luijk and Guido Corbetta (eds) (1991), *Market Morality and Company Size*, Dordrecht, Boston, London: Kluwer and Academic Publishers.

Hornsby, J.S., Kuratko, D.F., Naffziger, D.W., Lafollette, W.R. and Hodgetts, R.M. (1994), 'The ethical perceptions of small business owners: a factor analytic study', *Journal of Small Business Management*, October.

Johannisson, B. (1994), 'Building a global strategy. Internationalizing small firms through local networking', proceedings of the ICSB 39th World Conference, June, Strasbourg.

Johannisson, B. (1996), 'Personal networks and emerging interconnecting patterns among small firms as indicators of firm evolution', proceedings of the ICSB 41st World Conference, June, Stockholm.

Johanson, J. and Vahlne, J.E. (1977), 'The internationalization process of the firm. A model of knowledge development and increasing foreign market commitment', *Journal of International Business Studies*, 1st quarter.

Julien, P.-A. and Ramangalahy, C. (1999), 'Competitiveness and performance of small and medium sized exporting firms: an empirical investigation of the impact of their information behaviour', proceedings of the ICSB 44th World Conference, June, Naples.

Kaish, S. and Gilad, B. (1991), 'Characteristics of opportunities search of entrepreneurs versus executives: sources, interests, general alertness', *Journal of Business Venturing*, VI.

Kamto, M. (1999), 'Déchéance de la politique: décrépitude morale et exigence éthique dans le gouvernement des hommes', Yaoundé: Editions Mandara.

Keeble, D., Lawson, C., Smith, H.L., Moore, B. and Wilkinson, F. (1998), 'Internationalisation processes, networking and local embeddedness in technology-intensive small firms', *Small Business Economics*, 2.

Kirzner, I.M. (1973), *Competition and entrepreneurship*, Chicago: University of Chicago Press.

Kotey, B. and Meredith, G.G. (1997), 'Relationship among owner/manager personal values and perceptions, business strategies, and enterprise performance', *Journal of Small Business Management*, April.

Levinas, E. (1982), 'Ethique et infini', Paris: Fayard.

Longenecker, J.G., McKinney, J.A. and Moore, C. (1989), 'Ethics in small business', *Journal of Small Business Management*, January.

Longenecker, J.G., McKinney, J.A. and Moore, C. (1996), 'Ethical issues of entrepreneurs', proceedings of the ICSB 41st World Conference, June, Stockholm.

Marie, A. (1997), 'L'Afrique des individus', Paris: Editions Karthala.

McGee, J.E. and Peterson, M. (2000), 'Toward the development of measures of distinctive competencies among small independent retailers', *Journal of Small Business Management*, April.

Miles, M.P., Arnold, D.R. and Thompson, D.L. (1993), 'The interrelationship between environmental hostility and entrepreneurial orientation', *Journal of Applied Business Research*, 9 (4).

Nijsen, A. (2002), 'New relationships between public and private spheres. Socially responsible undertakings', papers presented to the Rencontres de St Gall 2002, Swiss Research Institute of Small Business and Entrepreneurship, University of St. Gallen.

On'Okundji, O.E. (1999), 'Les entrailles du porc-épic. Une nouvelle éthique pour l'Afrique', Paris: Grasset/Le Monde.

Oviatt, B.M. and McDougall, P.P. (1994), 'Toward a theory of international new ventures', *Journal of International Business Studies*, 1st quarter.

Prahalad, C.K. and Hamel, G. (1990), 'The core competence of the organization', *Harvard Business Review*, May–June.

Rasolofoson, M.T. (2001), 'Logiques culturelles du comportement entrepreneurial à Madagascar', Colloque International I.N.S.C.A.E., November, Antananarivo.

Rue, L.W. and Ibrahim, N.A. (1998), 'The relationship between planning sophistication and performance in small firms', *Journal of Small Business Management*, April.

Sen, A. (1992), 'Inequality re-examined', Oxford: Oxford University Press.

Smart, D.T. and Conant, J.S. (1994), 'Entrepreneurial orientation, distinctive competencies and organizational performance', *Journal of Applied Business Research*, 10 (3).

Thompson, J.K. and Smith, H.L. (1991), 'Social responsibility and small business: suggestions for research', *Journal of Small Business Management*, January.

Verstraete, T. (1999), 'Entrepreneuriat. Connaître l'entrepreneur, comprendre ses actes', Collection Economie et Innovation, Paris: L'Harmattan.

Wager, T.H. (1998), 'Determinants of human resource management practices in small firms: some evidence from Atlantic Canada', *Journal of Small Business Management*, April.

Walsh, S.T., Kirchhoff, B.A. and Boylan, R.L. (1996), 'Core competency strategies for growth in small firms', proceedings of the ICSB 41st World Conference, June, Stockholm.

Watkins, D. (1996), 'How relevant is the HRM literature to management processes in the family firm?', paper presented to the Rencontres de St Gall 1996, Swiss Research Institute of Small Business and Entrepreneurship, University of St. Gallen.

Wolff, J.A. and Pett, T.L. (2000), 'Internationalization of small firms: an examination of export competitive patterns, firm size, and export performance', *Journal of Small Business Management*, April.

PART THREE

GEOGRAPHIC PERSPECTIVES OF INTERNATIONAL ENTREPRENEURSHIP

15 Asia–Pacific perspectives of international entrepreneurship
John Milton-Smith

The role of a technopreneur is to bring together research talent, venture capital, new business concepts and management skill to create commercially successful technological innovations or, alternatively, to leverage innovations effectively through the application of technology. This study sets out to explore whether the Asian crisis of 1997–8 and its aftermath offer any useful insights into the behaviour and practices of Asian SMEs, which might provide a more general understanding of the conditions in which high-technology entrepreneurs are likely to flourish. As a means of examining the same questions from a different perspective, the study also assesses the performance of science and technology parks, evaluating both the Asian and the Australian experience.

There was a widespread view during the 1990s that technological entrepreneurship in Asia had lagged behind Europe and the United States, as opposed to the more traditional areas in which Asian family businesses have excelled, such as property development, retailing and trade, despite considerable effort and urging by governments in the region. A working hypothesis of this chapter is that lack of technopreneurship in most parts of Asia can be attributed to the widespread absence of Strategic Management perspectives, attitudes and skills, especially in the performance of leadership roles. This is largely due to social and cultural factors, rather than to more specific infrastructural weaknesses such as the lack of technological know-how, technology transfer facilities or support systems for training and encouraging technopreneurs.

The case of Singapore provides an interesting illustration because the Singapore government has invested heavily in trying to cultivate technopreneurs (Dana, 1999). In the current environment, however, very few Singaporean entrepreneurs are likely to develop long-term visions, design new business models or conduct radical experiments in any area in which the government plays an active role. There is also a view that technology projects are excessively long-term, extremely high-risk and too capital-intensive. Few Singaporean business people seem to be aware of the upstream and downstream business opportunities for entrepreneurs to work in partnership with technology-based enterprises. But, above all, Singapore's deeply ingrained *kiasu* syndrome, combined with an already heightened fear of failure, acts as a major deterrent to most potential technopreneurs.

At a broad level, Asian entrepreneurs are aware of the threats, opportunities and challenges of internationalization. As Chatterjee and Pearson have pointed out in their recent study of management work goals in Asia, 'the acquisition of new skills and competencies has become of major importance to the contemporary managers in the six countries of this study'. Indeed, according to Chatterjee and Pearson, there is wide recognition of the urgency 'for learning new things' (Chatterjee and Pearson, 2002, pp. 263–4). This level of awareness, however, is not apparent among SME owner-managers. Furthermore, as the research for the present study has revealed, the barriers to entrepreneurship in high technology and value-adding enterprises are related more to the lack of access to Strategic Management know-how and skills training, and perceptions about the intrusive role of government, than to ignorance about the nature of the competitive environment in which they operate. In particular, Asian entrepreneurs need to acquire specific international business knowledge about markets, alliance possibilities and supply chains. They also need to develop new perspectives on stakeholder relationships and cross-cultural communications and, above all, to become more proactive and effective in reaching out to, and connecting with, a much wider and more diverse group of business associates.

Finally, after reviewing the performance of regional science and technology parks around the Asian region, it is concluded that, subject to certain essential conditions, they can be an excellent breeding ground for technopreneurs. However it is essential that they be located and managed so as to create distinct technology clusters, holistic communities of related knowledge workers, and cultures which encourage experimentation, crossing boundaries and collaboration. Even given appropriate resources and facilities, unless the parks are then strongly integrated into the day-to-day work of the neighbouring universities, research institutes and businesses, they will almost certainly fail.

The research design and main findings

As a starting point, it is useful to note that Deloitte Touche Tohmatsu's (DTT) 2001 list of the world's 200 fastest growing companies includes only two Asia–Pacific firms. In the wake of the Asian crisis, it appears that Asian firms have major weaknesses in the areas of business strategy, organizational learning and corporate branding. They have a very limited capacity for coping with the uncertainty, complexity and turbulence inherent in a global economy. Even Singapore's sustained campaign to develop technopreneurs seems to have had only limited success.

Another survey, this one conducted by Andersen Consulting on management responses to the Asian crisis, has shown that most companies have adopted defensive strategies such as cost cutting, postponing new investments, portfolio rationalization and debt restructuring. By contrast, a very small number of companies, including Jollibee Foods (Philippines), Siam Cement (Thailand) and Singapore Airlines, maintained their established commitment to Strategic Management, or what Kotler and Kartajaya call 'the sustainable marketing enterprise (SME) model' (Kotler and Kartajaya, 2000). Continuing to invest in the brand, increasing the value proposition to customers and reinventing the business model, where necessary, are common characteristics of firms which came through the turbulence relatively unscathed. Kartajaya's own management consultancy, MarkPlus & Co., which operates out of Indonesia, is an impressive example of this thesis. His model has become a highly distinctive, widely endorsed product, which gives definition and credibility to the MarkPlus brand. Of course, Kartajaya's own high profile, through his involvement in the marketing professional body and collaboration with Kotler, is another key element in the branding strategy.

Overall, however, the crisis does not appear to have led to significant changes in the way SMEs in Asia operate. Organizational and management learning is particularly slow in Asia, much slower than in other parts of the world. According to a recent PricewaterhouseCoopers (PWC) survey of Asian CEO's, only 47% are prepared to describe their companies as 'very transparent' and the great majority still regard corporate governance and transparency issues – the building blocks of Strategic Management – as major barriers to attracting foreign capital and investment (Pricewaterhouse Coopers, 2002).

From the interviews conducted for this study, there is no sense of the old strategic assumptions being challenged or debated. It is difficult to find evidence of new organizational processes or management systems. Strategic planning, scenario building, competitor analysis, information management and branding continue to be greatly under-utilized tools in the Asian SME sector. Neither from the survey nor from the interviews did evidence emerge of managers who now see the need to create a new vision or a stronger learning culture within their organizations. There has been no sign of task forces being established to analyse changing industry structures, explore new markets, develop new products or even monitor the competitive environment.

Following on from the DTT, Andersen and PWC surveys, the author's own recent research has not only confirmed the general thrust of the findings but also shed more light on underlying problems and possible longer-term solutions. This research is based on 'The Culture Alternative', an instrument developed over the past decade to help organizations adopt a Strategic Management approach. The model is framed around six pairs of interrelated management functions and leadership roles. For example, whereas setting 'goals' is defined as a standard management function, the ability to convert goals into an inspiring, widely shared 'ideology', and into the basis for building a strong corporate brand image in the marketplace, is still quite rare. Nevertheless this ability is undoubtedly a critical business leadership role (see Figure 15.1), which is an essential precondition for enduring corporate success.

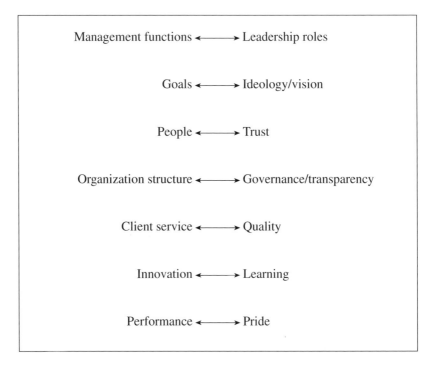

Figure 15.1   The Strategic Management model

Because it has been designed as a Strategic Management tool, 'The Culture Alternative' both facilitates and monitors organizational learning. It helps focus on key issues of strategy, structure and culture (How is strategic intelligence gathered, reviewed and acted upon? To what extent is benchmarking undertaken? Is there a strong commitment to staff development and continuous improvement? What mechanisms are in place to facilitate the flow and exchange of information? How is innovation managed?) When the instrument is administered regularly – on an annual basis, for example – it highlights the extent to which managers have addressed gaps and weaknesses identified in the previous audit and exposes the main areas of leadership challenge. The major elements of the new leadership paradigm are summarized in Figure 15.2.

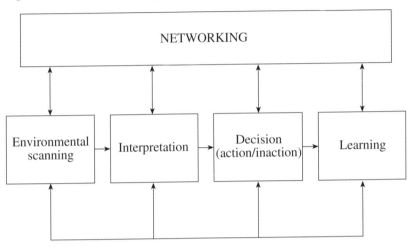

Figure 15.2   The business intelligence system: a networking model

The findings discussed in this chapter are based on feedback obtained during the period 1998–2001 from 40 firms, including 31 high-performing Chinese SMEs, scattered around Asia. They include nine from Singapore, five from each of Malaysia, China and Japan, three from each of Taiwan, Thailand and Hong Kong; two from each of South Korea, Indonesia and the Philippines; and one from Vietnam. The results are compared with previous surveys conducted with public and private sector organizations in Australia over the last 12 years. The main conclusion is that Asian organizations and especially SMEs have significantly weaker strategic frameworks than their western counterparts, even those that regard themselves as 'technopreneurial'. Although there are several notable areas of relative strength, which probably reflect some well-entrenched Asian cultural traditions (in domains such as service, performance and company pride) vision, goal clarity, innovation, organizational learning and governance are major problem areas for most Asian enterprises by international standards, and especially for SMEs.

In the research design and data analysis, the terms 'high technology' and 'technopreneur' are used broadly as a proxy for SMEs which are innovative, expansionist, strategically managed and committed to creating added value through a variety of strategies, such as going international, entering into partnerships, applying intellectual property, developing new systems and processes, exploiting specialized knowledge and know-how and building a strong brand image.

Chinese SMEs

Generational change within traditional overseas Chinese SMEs, still the dominant model in many Asian countries, has been slow. Even younger family members with international qualifications appear to have had only marginal influence on management practices. From the responses to the survey, it becomes clear that overseas Chinese enterprises themselves are still not major sources of business learning, knowledge creation or corporate renewal. On the contrary, the people outside the family and *guanxi* network employed by these enterprises continue to be regarded as foot-soldiers, with virtually no shared sense of longer-term vision or direction, who are brought into service only when the strategy has already been determined. In these companies there is a great reluctance to invest in people, ideas, knowledge creation or intellectual property. And, especially in the case of the overseas Chinese family enterprises, the primary source of tacit strategic knowledge is the *guanxi* network of the owner–manager rather than the processes, systems, competencies and relationships of the business organization.

The pattern of international entrepreneurship has been largely dominated by necessity-driven enterprises. On the whole, the 'refugee mindset' of the overseas Chinese has favoured traditional trading activities and the security of bricks and mortar. Referring specifically to Hong Kong entrepreneurs, but the point has wider application, Fu-Lai Yu reminds us that, 'haunted by the painful experience of their properties being confiscated by the communists', many of them 'took their new home as a temporary haven'. Without access to capital and needing to generate quick and steady cash flows, they have been generally reluctant to commit themselves to major value-adding projects involving investment in consultancy, technology and brand building. This natural business conservatism is perpetuated by their tendency to amass high levels of personal savings and to steer their children towards careers in more prestigious fields such as the professions, corporate management and higher education (Fu-Lai Yu, 2001, p. 39).

Many Chinese owner-managers interviewed in the survey are finding it hard to change their ways. Because of their authoritarian and remote style, it is not easy for them to work with the younger generation of western educated managers. Indeed centralized and secretive decision making makes it difficult for family-controlled conglomerates to innovate, recruit new talent and expand. Despite the Asian crisis, most Chinese owner-managers continue to make decisions in isolation from their staff and to foster a 'yes-man culture'. Surrounded by nervous, insecure sycophants, they rely on trusted associates and their own networks for advice. Many Asian SMEs still retain the characteristics of traditional family organizations. Elders and seniors are respected and deferred to, and subordinates are uncomfortable about floating new ideas, querying directives or offering constructive criticism. There is little room for participation in planning or decision making. Senior managers tend to be aloof, arbitrary and paternalistic and, while accepting a high level of responsibility for the welfare of their employees, they also maintain a high degree of power distance which, as Hofstede and others have pointed out, reinforces and perpetuates the formality of social and organizational hierarchies. Similarly, as Redding and others have pointed out, the lingering residue of Confucian values also means that Chinese family enterprises are suspicious of government and outsiders generally, therefore tending to avoid getting involved in businesses where there is significant state interest (Redding, 1995, pp. 61–9).

The trading and transactional bias of the overseas Chinese family businesses has continued to prevail following the crisis. It is a mindset which is opportunistic rather than creative. The approach is not well suited to creating assets through technopreneurship or brand building. It does not produce an environment which is attractive to knowledge workers or innovators. There is a tendency to regard the business as little more than a convenient receptacle for the owner–manager's own idiosyncratic wheeling and dealing. Indeed Asian firms generally tend to be reactive rather than strategic and this characteristic will increasingly become a handicap, given the complexity, uncertainty and competitiveness of global markets. The owner-managers continue to rely on the old *guanxi* networks, juggling assets, seeking out alternative investment prospects and simply riding out the storm (Cruz, 2001, p. 5). When the turbulence subsides, notwithstanding a modified business profile, it will be business as usual. The owner-managers will continue to focus on their old established networks, exploring possibilities, nurturing projects but still keeping the employees very much in the dark. So-called 'Asian capitalism' still largely prevails, especially among SMEs, which makes it difficult to reform corporate governance practices or introduce a higher level of Strategic Management (Devinney, 1998, pp. 58–9).

With particular reference to South-East Asia, it could hardly be argued that the technopreneurship scene is flourishing. While there are undoubtedly some remarkable success stories, the actual number of genuinely local technopreneurs and creative new enterprises is small and in inverse relationship to the amount of government propaganda, urging and assistance to encourage them. This finding is at odds with Zutshi's conclusion that 'Chinese entrepreneurs have been successful in learning, adapting and moving up the technology ladder more efficiently than the entrepreneurs from many other developing countries' and that they are 'integrating the traditional culture with a global world view' (Zutshi 1997, pp. 183–7). Zutshi acknowledges that research into Chinese business and management practice is very limited, which is true, but on the basis of the small sample of the current study under discussion, it is difficult to share his level of optimism. The subjects of this survey were generally worldly, sophisticated and well-networked but, in varying degrees, they all expressed unease about investing in 'invisible' assets which are not easily tradable, transferable or controllable and which could be exposed to political or bureaucratic interference. The following extracts from interviews conducted for this survey underline these sentiments:

> There's too much politics in the tech business. It's under government control. The Multi-Media Super Corridor, for example, is all government hype to bring in the foreign investors. The MNC's are getting a lot of benefits – there are lot of big names on the Board. But, below the surface, not much is happening. I don't think many locals have pioneered new technology businesses. (Successful Chinese entrepreneur in the services sector, Kuala Lumpur)

> Hsinchu was like an Asian Silicon Valley. It quickly became a high tech city with lots of government research activity, with local universities heavily involved, many US-educated scientists came back and we had many start-ups as well as MNCs. But it's slowing up now. Who knows what will happen? The situation with China is worrying. Both governments have created too much uncertainty. Nothing's safe any more. (Prominent IT consultant, university professor and former senior executive in high tech company, Hsinchu)

> The ruling People's Action Party (PAP) has direct or indirect control over all the high tech areas. There are too many government-linked enterprises – the science parks are full of them. Bio-tech and IT are the priority areas but they're too risky for a businessman like me. Business is tough enough without having politicians and civil servants breathing down your neck. I prefer to keep a low profile . . . I have a few businesses here but I also park assets in Australia just in case and for when I retire. (CEO, diversified business portfolio, primarily involved in project management and construction, Singapore)

In each case, the history of these businesspeople demonstrates, like many others in the survey, the classic characteristics of the entrepreneur: creativity, drive and a willingness to back their judgment. Each one is a product of circumstances which brought out, challenged and realized his natural entrepreneurial qualities. But they also share a deep apprehension about the unmanageable risks associated with the sort of government intrusion and involvement which is common in Asian countries.

In exploring the findings, it becomes clear that there is a need for a shift in focus away from the traditional models of small business education towards a more general emphasis upon cultivating enterprising and innovative behaviour. It is also important to recognize that, as a result of globalization, deregulation and the IT revolution, there are now many more opportunities for innovation and technopreneurship, especially in areas such as outsourcing, partnering, strategic market information, supply chain management, customer service and e-commerce. However, given their traditional aversion to technology businesses, and their recent bitter experience with dot.com investments, it is likely to be some time before Asian entrepreneurs are persuaded that technology is an attractive way to generate new wealth.

Science and technology parks
The main survey was augmented by a complementary review of the performance of science and technology parks in the countries under consideration, with the addition of Australia. This review demonstrated the consistent failure, despite the remarkable proliferation of parks throughout the region, to exploit their potential for becoming innovation hubs, focal points for collaborative knowledge networks and effective incubators of new entrepreneurial enterprises. Given the comprehensiveness of the work done in Australia to evaluate science and technology parks and to examine the variables essential to embedding an innovation culture, the main emphasis will be placed upon Australia as a special case study.

Australia's well-documented failure to convert basic research into commercially successful ventures reflects a widespread problem shared by many countries, including all of those in the survey, with the exception of Taiwan and Japan. In the case of Australia, a recent British study mission surveyed Australian technology parks and carefully examined their linkages with 'associated' universities. As is the case elsewhere, the relationships were somewhat superficial. The final report concluded that, while there are certainly regular joint seminars and meetings, 'Companies only tend to instigate interaction if they are seeking specific expert help from an academic' (Department of Trade and Industry Overseas Study Mission to Australia, 1999). Indeed some Australian technology parks have not succeeded in creating any university spin-offs at all. Subsequently, a government-sponsored 'Innovation Summit' (2000), debated and highlighted the weaknesses in Australia's innovation system. Among the key issues identified were the following:

● the problem of a small domestic market and the lack of economies of scale;
● the high proportion of SMEs, which ensures a low level of R&D investment;

- excessive duplication and fragmentation due to the uncoordinated initiatives of local, state and national governments;
- the need for a national system for selecting, prioritizing and building platform technologies;
- mechanisms, including public policy measures, to counter the low level of investment risk tolerance;
- the importance of clustering strategies to bring researchers, entrepreneurs, venture capitalists and creative people from a wide range of disciplines to work in close proximity;
- inadequate strategic and financial management skills among SME owner-managers, reflected in their tendency to overemphasize profit maximization (Fenton-Jones, 2002, p. 16).

One of the most penetrating criticisms of government initiatives to stimulate innovation and entrepreneurship has been made by a Singapore Member of Parliament who has noted a strong bias 'towards prestige products'. Governments, universities, research funding agencies and incubators certainly have an excessive preference for supporting high-technology projects at the expense of service industry concepts which, on the evidence of growth patterns around the world, frequently lead to better employment generation and higher returns. Skilfully branded service sector enterprises such as Starbucks, McDonalds and CNN provide a valuable precedent which, judging from their track record, innovation policy makers from around the world have tended to ignore.

The leadership challenge ahead: a strategic management perspective
This study has identified very poor leadership and a lack of Strategic Management know-how as major contributing factors to the failure of regional SMEs to become strongly-branded international leaders in technology-related industries. Significant change will depend heavily upon a much greater investment in leadership and management development for SME owner-managers in areas such as business vision, core values and competitive strategy; innovation and learning; leveraging relationships with science parks and universities; and skilfully managing alliances, partnerships and networks. The discussion which follows is designed to provide a basic framework for such initiatives.

Successful leadership is all about inspiring people, developing new business models, focusing goals, defining values, creating added value and managing change. Today's organizations are in a constant state of change and so the effective management of change requires a very particular kind of organizational culture. As a starting point, all the stakeholders need to participate actively in anticipating, conceiving, responding to and implementing change. People's values, priorities, expectations and competencies are the essential determinants of successful organizational change – plans, policies and proclamations are just the beginning. Getting the right balance between continuity and change, creating coherence and commitment in situations where turbulence and uncertainty rule, learning from the past and foreseeing the future – tomorrow's strategic managers will have to be adept at helping people live with paradox and contradiction. But the challenge does not end there. As credibility and confidence become increasingly important factors in international business, business leaders must take responsibility for a much more sophisticated approach to corporate governance, hingeing upon 'the concept of civic virtues, [and] the elemental notion that all of our goals as individuals and groups are bound up in the common good'.

Much more work needs to be done in changing the ingrained mindsets of senior managers, especially in Asia, and modifying a management paradigm which is deeply entrenched. Leadership is still defined in heroic, masculine terms. Personal toughness and physical endurance, exercising authoritarian control and sacrificing the family – these are persistent characteristics of the heroes in the Asian management 'Hall of Fame'. By contrast, so-called 'feminine qualities', which are now increasingly receiving lip-service, are seen as desirable but potentially damaging to the bottom line. However it is now clear that, in the wake of the Asian crisis, managers need to be much more adept in Human Resource Management, crossing cultural boundaries, creating teams based on greater diversity and winning the confidence and trust of a much wider group of stakeholders (Rost, 1993).

Given the speed of technological change, and the competitiveness of the global market, business leadership is the increasingly important ingredient in corporate success and survival. Managing lean, efficient organizations is not enough; simply responding to customer needs and catching up with competitors is not a winning formula. Grasping and shaping the future is what counts in the competitive stakes of the twenty-first century. Asian CEOs must focus on innovation as well as business efficiency. The role of the leader is to interpret market complexity, identify new competitive space, encourage creative people to experiment, develop unique business models and mobilize the company's resources to make it happen (see Box 15.1). These roles will now be explored in greater detail, with particular emphasis on the way successful technopreneurs create and personally shape their own innovation visions, strategies, structures and cultures, as well as making better use of existing innovation seed-beds such as science and technology parks. Consideration will also be given to the way in which the function and performance of science and technology parks could be enhanced to facilitate innovation through knowledge transfer, organizational learning, strategic partnerships and effective networking, making them both a magnet and a catalyst for technopreneurial leadership, innovation and enterprise.

BOX 15.1　UNPACKING THE NEW LEADERSHIP PARADIGM

IDEOLOGY
Pathfinding, communicating a vision, comitting oneself to an ambitious goal, inspiring, energizing stakeholders, providing direction, creating a distinctive corporate 'brand'.

TRUST
Aligning people to goals and strategies, addressing concerns, explaining, communicating openly, reciprocating, being consistent, building partnerships, keeping promises.

QUALITY
Identifying benchmarks, listening, searching, making tough choices, setting high standards, building teams, designing decision-making processes, committing oneself to continuous improvement.

LEARNING
Designing systems, leveraging technology, scanning the environment, gathering information, interpreting data, reviewing performance, developing competencies, constructing models and prototypes.

GOVERNANCE
Emphasizing role clarity, making people accountable, committing oneself to ethical principles, ensuring transparency, managing partnerships, addressing risk factors, designing reporting systems.

PRIDE
Valuing people, upholding ethical standards, creating a sense of collective ownership, motivating people, celebrating achievement, being socially responsible.

Vision, values and strategy

During the coming decade there will be unprecedented opportunities for a new generation of Asian technopreneurs and entrepreneurial SME owner-managers to take advantage of globalization. However this will only happen if they have the foresight and skill to invent businesses which capitalize on emerging paradigm shifts, the analytical sophistication to identify and capture new market niches, the courage to lead organizations with a commitment to continuous innovation and the personal credibility to build a corporate brand which commands both respect and added value in the marketplace.

In a global economy there is already unlimited scope for individual entrepreneurs to invent and brand new business models and open up markets based upon middle-class and aspiring middle-class consumers in every part of the world. The following examples include both visionary founders and second-generation business executives with the foresight to build an international enterprise around a simple but innovative marketing concept. Their common characteristic is a commitment to building new markets. In each case they have quickly transformed a small business into a global empire:

- Howard Schultz (extending the Italian coffee bar culture into a network of nearly 5000 stores worldwide in less than 20 years);
- Andy Grove, Intel (PCs are more important than TVs);
- Bill Gates, Microsoft (the pre-eminence of user-friendly software);
- Rupert Murdoch, News Corp (global information superhighway, integrating telecommunications, media and entertainment capabilities and resources);
- Jan Carlzon, SAS (service that exceeds the customer's expectations);
- Ikio Morita, Sony (continuous innovation in quality consumer electronics);
- Anita Roddick, The Body Shop (ethically and environmentally sensitive cosmetics and personal care products);
- Michael Dell, Dell Computers (direct-to-customer business model of selling and servicing).

While there will be always be opportunities for innovation coming from laboratories, demographics, pressures for process improvement and popular fashion, the most significant source in a global economy arises from rapid changes and disruptions to industry structure and the competitive environment. The recent paradigm shifts that have created, and are still creating, new entrepreneurial business opportunities on an international scale include the following:

- expiry of patents on top-selling drugs and greater involvement of government in healthcare;
- deregulation and integration of financial services;
- the swing away from mainframe computers to PCs and networks of PCs;
- technological convergence and new alliances in communications, consumer electronics, computing and entertainment;
- the power shift from big manufacturers to supermarkets;
- dispersal of control from the centre to the market edge in key technology-based industries such as computers, energy and telephone systems;
- rapid growth of franchising as an expansion strategy in a wide range of industries;
- cosmetics becoming increasingly part of the consumer goods industry;
- collapse of communism and the transformation of command economies;
- worldwide trend towards privatization of state-owned enterprises.

There are also enormous entrepreneurial opportunities for niche players at the local, national and regional levels. Many multinationals are in the process of reinventing themselves in order to achieve a better balance between global efficiency and local responsiveness. Accordingly, sophisticated entrepreneurs have an unprecedented opportunity to distribute, supply, represent, partner and market on behalf of big corporations. Furthermore, as part of this process, there is an exponential growth of licensing and franchising opportunities for small entrepreneurs wishing to shelter under the protection of an established brand name and proven products. Indeed one of biggest emerging entrepreneurial growth markets is to supply people in the less developed countries with reputable, relatively cheap, simple-to-use products (Kripalani and Engardio, 2002, pp. 68–9).

While vision and strategy are important, systematic implementation is equally critical and challenging. The leadership philosophies of CEOs of successful innovative organizations highlight the central importance of a human resource (HR) strategy which brings together highly creative people with widely divergent backgrounds, and then encourages them to experiment, build prototypes and take measured risks. The implementation of such a strategy will include extensive use of project teams, job rotation, spin-offs, strategic alliances and imaginative incentive schemes. Managing corporate creativity is a vital role for entrepreneurial SME owner-managers today. As the editorial of a recent special issue of the *Harvard Business Review* put it, 'promoting innovation is as much about tearing down barriers as blazing trails' (Editors, 2002, p. 6).

Following the scandals which have recently rocked corporate America, with reverberations upon business environments around the world, there has been a renewed recognition of just how delicate and important confidence and trust are in the efficient working of capitalist economies. In the short to medium term, investors and venture capitalists have become extremely cautious and risk-averse and this will have damaging consequences for entrepreneurs. Indeed, following the earlier round of corporate excesses in the 1980s, the very word 'entrepreneur' had already become contaminated in some countries by the image of greedy, flamboyant opportunists, cutting corners and bending the rules, with little regard for ethical principles or the interests of their shareholders. Given the current crisis of confidence, there is now great urgency for SME owner-managers, in particular, to identify critical success factors and to manage them strategically (Ying Fan, 2002, pp. 371–80). In doing so, they will need to recognize the significant differences in the moral dilemmas and business confidence considerations confronting SMEs, as opposed to large corporations. Quite apart from the special ethical dilemmas associated with the practice of *guanxi* in Chinese business cultures, there is more general evidence that 'entrepreneurial settings offer more opportunities for cognitive dissonance than do hierarchical settings' (Solymossy and Masters, 2002, p. 237).

All types of organizations – not just companies – are being forced to redefine and refocus their businesses, in order to create new sources of value, different bases for competitive advantage and greater capacity for innovation. Inevitably this requires them to reconstruct processes, redesign systems, rethink the scope of their activity and rebuild core competencies. In the course of reconceptualizing the enterprise, the spotlight inevitably falls upon key relationships, with suppliers, distributors and customers, upon organizational structures, logistics networks and the roles of the managers. Furthermore, in order to fully capture and convey the benefits of these arrangements, managers are recognizing the need for new strategies for generating and leveraging brand equity. The brand and its logo become the warrant and the symbol for much more customized consumer benefits created by the value chain and, ideally, they take on a life of their own so that they are seen to be much more than the sum of the parts. Brands are an increasingly important aspect of the individual's self-image and vocabulary for social definition.

Innovation and learning
From an international perspective, it may seem almost ironic that many Asian entrepreneurs or would-be entrepreneurs are still plagued by

regressive cultural assumptions and practices. In this connection, the recent work of Deshpande and Farley at Harvard have effectively demolished the notion of a unique 'Asian business model' and confirm that 'successful companies in China or Thailand look a lot like other successful companies regardless of where they are located'. Indeed they show that, 'just as there is no single management model that can be applied unilaterally across cultures, there is no unified Asian style of management' (Silverthorne, 2002, p. 2). However, as the present study demonstrates, although 'country effects' may have little influence in explaining corporate success, international business failure will often result from ignorance of the local culture or, in the case of domestic firms, inhibitions or restrictions imposed by the local environment.

The Asian crisis has clearly demonstrated that the basic principles and practices of Strategic Management are just as critical for SMEs and technopreneurs as for corporate executives and large organizations. Despite differences relating to size and scale, which have implications for the allocation and weighting of management functions, the performance of key leadership roles has general applicability and equal importance. In moving forward from the turmoil of the late 1990s, technopreneurs will need to come to terms with the fact that they must become much more than technologists and adopt a more strategic approach to organizational learning and innovation. Indeed innovation must be seen much less in terms of an occasional product breakthrough and as a reaction to the current competitive environment and much more as a continuous pattern of strategic behaviour, characterizing every aspect of the firm's operations.

Drawing upon the bitter experience of the Asian crisis, there is no more important business leadership role or skill than the ability to facilitate organizational learning as the precondition for developing competitive advantage based on innovation. Perhaps the most important lesson to be learned from the 1997–8 downturn relates to IT. During this period, many would-be technopreneurs allowed themselves to be seduced by the potential of new technology without paying sufficient attention to designing a business strategy for creating value and generating profits. This was certainly the case with the Internet and, as Michael Porter has pointed out, the so-called 'new economy' is not really so new. It is much more 'like an old economy that has access to a new technology'. In most cases, the Internet has not replaced the traditional sources of competitive advantage (Porter 2001, pp. 64–78). Powerful brands, unique products, superior quality and excellent service will continue to be the major sources of business success. However, as Porter rightly argues, 'strategies that integrate the Internet and traditional competitive advantages and ways of competing should win in many industries'. His point applies to technology more generally. Indeed the organizational ability continuously to find ways of integrating various elements, activities and technologies is at the core of a competitive strategy based on innovation.

There is a new considerable body of research, including a celebrated recent study by Christensen at Harvard, which demonstrates that it is virtually impossible to manage both mainstream business activities and sustained innovation from within the same organizational unit (Christensen, 1997). This work shows that successful technopreneurs and organizations which develop competitive advantage around innovation typically have a special innovation group which (a) is close to and strongly supported by the CEO, (b) does not compete with projects in the mainstream organization for resources, (c) is constantly developing networks and partnerships and specializes in building links between academia, government and industry, and (d) operates as a laboratory for bringing ideas and stimuli together from a wide variety of sources to create an environment which is rich in forward thinking and development planning.

At the same time, however, it is vital that organizations in no way depreciate or abandon 'the capabilities, organisational structures and decision-making processes that have made them successful in the mainstreams markets'. Continuity and change, core business and innovation, leadership and management, must be addressed simultaneously, continuously, and be given equal weight. Similarly innovation should not be conceived narrowly in terms of products; innovation is needed in every area of the organization, including customer service, partnerships and even business models. Just as innovation has become the major source of competitive advantage, so strategic partnerships are the key to establishing and maintaining an innovation edge by creating a constant flow of new ideas, organizational learning and market development opportunities. The specific benefits of strategic partnerships include the following (see Doz and Hamel, 1998, pp. 33–56):

- helping the organization to gather relevant market, industry and technological intelligence and to learn how to compete more successfully,
- identifying innovative business opportunities at the earliest possible stage,
- complementing core competency by strengthening skill capabilities and accessing a wider range of strategic resources,
- enabling the organization to customize its products and services by building long-term relationships,
- combining and sharing intellectual property and know-how,
- accessing new customers and larger markets,

- reducing risk by spreading investment, increasing expertise and limiting exposure,
- creating economies of scale by avoiding duplication, sharing resources and exploiting critical mass,
- identifying innovative business opportunities at the earliest possible stage,
- enhancing the organization's image, reputation and brand.

Successful business leaders and technopreneurs use their professional networks to identify opportunities and potential partners. They keep up-to-date with the relevant literature and regularly attend conferences and workshops in their areas of interest. A particularly rich, and increasingly common, source of cutting-edge ideas and technologies is to be found in leading universities of technology. However, many business people still find it difficult to establish and maintain academic linkages. Perhaps the most effective method of tapping into the enormous but underexploited resources of universities, and building a mutual learning alliance, is to make a long-term commitment by joining advisory committees, offering guest lectures and participating in joint research centres.

Science parks and universities
A new generation of more strategically minded technopreneurs will perceive the potential benefits of working within the context of a technology park. Most universities, and especially universities of technology, have active applied research centres and commercial arms which actively market consultancy services and training programmes and which often have strong links with the parks. Serious technopreneurs should closely monitor the activities of these organizations, which frequently provide access to innovative R&D business opportunities, such as exclusive and non-exclusive licensing arrangements, assignments of intellectual property (IP) rights in return for royalty and milestone payments, equity in spin-off and start-up companies, joint venture arrangements and collaborative research agreements incorporating IP arrangements.

An insight into the range of possible university-based opportunities open to proactive technopreneurs is provided by the partnerships currently established by Curtin University of Technology. Like most leading universities of technology, Curtin maintains close links with a wide variety of business, government and industry partners at regional, national and international levels. Examples include the following:

- centres of excellence in industry-focused research and development – relationships with the Western Australia State Government in supporting 12 centres through the provision of research infrastructure support;

- CSIRO – a strategic alliance with Australia's peak scientific research body, with particular focus on mining, minerals and petroleum;
- Woodside Energy Limited and Metasource Limited – a major partnership through the Joint Woodside–Curtin Hydrocarbon Research Facility;
- Cable and Wireless Optus – a strategic alliance supporting the Cable and Wireless Optus chair in e-commerce and the Executive Briefing Centre;
- the biomedical R&D Alliance – sponsorship from industry in an alliance of the biomedical research institutes in Western Australia;
- the Centre for Developmental Health – a collaborative research initiative with support from the TVW Telethon Institute for Child Health Research and the Health department of Western Australia;
- the Centre for Behavioural Research into Cancer – establishment of a significant research focus through partnerships with the Cancer Foundation;
- cooperative research centres (CRCs) – alliances with industries through participation in numerous CRCs.

The processes for establishing, maintaining and developing partnerships are of fundamental importance. To establish a successful partnership, a number of key steps must be taken, including the following:

- undertaking a feasibility study to clarify the scope of the partnership, including areas to be excluded; important issues include ownership of intellectual property rights, databases and non-competitive restrictions;
- jointly agreeing on sharply focused key objectives for the partnership and articulating the roles of each party;
- jointly defining values and behaviours that both partners agree to abide by to underpin the partnership; in doing so, it is important to recognize in a mission statement some of the critical success factors underpinning successful partnerships, such as developing and maintaining two-way trust, commitment and goodwill, ensuring mutual benefit to the parties involved, establishing an environment to support learning and improvement, supporting creativity and innovation, sharing knowledge and learning, enhancing the organization's reputation in key markets, and optimizing community well-being.

Following the establishment phase, careful consideration must be given to the continuity of the relationship. The ongoing management and maintenance of partnerships should be based upon a set of practical guidelines, with provision for:

- the allocation of clear management responsibility and accountability for the partnership;
- maintaining consistent and clear communication;
- embedding the partnership wherever possible into both organizations, without relying solely on one or two originators and risking ending the relationship when one leaves;
- communicating the essence of the partnership in both organizations and the implications for ensuring that the partnership is maintained (for example, there may be a need to appoint a preferred supplier);
- regular monitoring of agreed performance targets/indicators and planned action;
- committing resources to sustain agreed outcomes (managers, skilled staff, linking budgets to priorities, time);
- facilitating and bridging cultural differences;
- developing formal service agreements where appropriate;
- regularly discussing further opportunities to grow the partnership (for example, publicity, joint speaking/network opportunities, existing alliances for benefit of the other partner, preferred supplier status, consultancies, sharing resources for staff development/exchanges, access to supply chains);
- ensuring that both parties are benefiting from the partnership – not 'cherry picking' along the way;
- reviewing disappointments and achievements;
- celebrating and communicating achievements.

In business partnerships, conflicts and disputes are inevitable. It is important to anticipate and address these contingencies by developing agreed governance procedures such as the following:

- clear accountability for managing the partnerships, and providing a central focus (for example, dedicated liaison manager);
- guidelines regarding conflicts of interest;
- potential conflict of interest situations;
- risk assessment and management strategies (for example, communication breakdowns, financial security, resistance to change);
- a well defined process for joint decision making;

- measures of success – what measurement methods and process will be used to identify whether the partnership has met the agreed objectives, such as student satisfaction and retention levels, and who will be involved;
- a conflict resolution process;
- responsibility for and frequency of review processes;
- a clearly articulated exit strategy.

In the light of all these characteristics, criteria and challenges, it is difficult to avoid the conclusion that technology parks, closely collaborating with associated universities, are the key to cultivating dynamic, innovative, technopreneurial partnerships on a significant scale with minimum risk. Of course, they are not the complete answer, as the record clearly shows, and especially so if they are designed primarily as real estate developments. The vital additional element is often a creative intermediary or broker to provide planning support, access to networks and know-how, introductions to potential partners and solutions to financing and marketing requirements.

However, given that new technology is increasingly developed and marketed on a global scale, the rapid growth of a worldwide science and industrial park network is of enormous potential significance. The International Association of Science Parks (IASP) has become a major network and catalyst for learning and innovation by providing a global forum for sharing knowledge, exchanging ideas and stimulating collaboration between entrepreneurial SMEs, research institutes and universities of technology. Apart from bringing the partners together at regular conferences, the IASP arranges specialized consortia in strategic areas such as environmental technology, biotechnology and regional development. It is also currently spearheading a leading-edge project (SMART) to help SMEs gain access to global markets. This involves the creation of a knowledge-based information system for developing, managing and supporting strategic alliances (Editorial, 2001, p. 2).

A business networking approach
In the new economy, the ability to take advantage of knowledge pools and networks will increasingly become the underpinning resource capability which helps identify and sustain partnerships, and stimulate and produce innovation. The concluding section of this chapter will therefore construct a networking model for an innovative learning organization. Strategically managed organizations of the twenty-first century will be open, interactive and continuously networking. Learning will not be a systematic linear exercise; it will be a messy, dynamic process. New information and emerging

concepts will be constantly challenging the status quo and SME managers will need to be extremely resourceful and innovative in designing systems to create, support and leverage their learning networks.

It still involves a huge conceptual leap for traditional SME managers to envisage a global, or even a regional, small business based upon a network of alliances. There is a similar problem in the area of informal networking. Research indicates that SME managers have more difficulty in connecting, communicating and negotiating with foreign counterparts than their peers in large organizations. Lack of management education and cross-cultural communication training are among the major reasons. Given this universal problem, the prominence and wide distribution of overseas Chinese business people throughout Asia gives them a huge potential advantage over their western and Japanese competitors.

Globalization and the enormous business opportunities in Asia make it mandatory for all managers to have highly developed information seeking, business diplomacy and networking skills. These skills are urgently needed by western managers working in Asia as well. It is a region of great diversity, complexity, spread and change. For westerners, the tradition of *guanxi* provides an extra layer of difficulty. So, for all managers everywhere, but especially those operating in the Asian region, it is important to recognize that networking, formal and informal, plays an overarching role in the way organizations interpret, operate in and learn about their environments. At every stage of the decision-making process, networks are drawn upon, both as reference points and as sources of information and advice.

The networking model put forward here, the 'Business Intelligence System' (see Figure 15.2), is embedded within a Strategic Management framework, which identifies decision making as the critical business process, networking as the critical information resource for competing in regional and global markets and learning as the key to sustained competitive advantage (Hamel, 1999, pp. 71–84). It is important to distinguish between formal and informal networks in any group of organizations operating as an alliance to pursue objectives beyond the reach of individual partners working separately. Formal networks come in a wide variety of forms, including consortia joint ventures, partnerships, alliances and a variety of subcontracting and licensing arrangements. An informal network, on the other hand, applies more to individuals than to organizations, but is equally important.

The dominant rationale for establishing a formal network is to obtain the best partners, resources and information with a view to providing optimum service for customers. Examples would include Japanese *keiretsu*, South Korean *chaebols* and the distinctive Indonesian conglomerates, all of which have succumbed to problems arising from inefficiency, collusion and lack of transparency. The main benefits of informal networking are much broader and include monitoring trends, identifying changes in the competitive environment and stimulating new ideas and innovations. An informal network is a much looser configuration of connections, relationships and affiliations, which provides opportunities for exchanging information and ideas, exerting influence and winning support and, above all, raising profile and building reputation. It is important to recognize the significant overlap between formal and informal networking activity. This is reflected in basic international business tasks such as locating an agent, selecting a partner, obtaining information about government policy, monitoring market conditions, identifying customers, establishing an office or plant and recruiting staff. The Internet has created the means to enhance the quality and effectiveness of informal networking by opening up the possibility of virtual alliances through regular on-line communication. According to Deloitte Consulting, only 17% of consumer companies are using the web effectively to link customer management and supply operations. Their research shows that companies establishing 'digital loyalty networks' are much more profitable and enjoy much greater customer loyalty than companies that do not (Deloitte Consulting, 2002). As a guide to SME owner/managers, 12 personal networking protocols have been developed (see Box 15.2) as a framework for conducting business internationally, and especially in Asia. These protocols emphasize the value of regular personal contact and entertaining, the need to maintain a judicious balance between business and non-business conversation, the danger of relying too heavily on networks centred on individual rather than organizational relationships, and the importance of treating networks as vital business investments and assets, and not simply as optional extras.

BOX 15.2 TWELVE PERSONAL NETWORKING
PROTOCOLS FOR SUCCESSFUL
MANAGERS IN ASIA

1. Be aware of the considerable time and hospitality investment in cultivating effective long-term business relationships in Asia.

2. Appreciate the unique features of Asian 'business friendships' which frequently do not extend to the families and may not even include direct business involvement.

3. Give priority to network relationships that are based on mutual interest, complementary resources, regular reciprocity and trust.

4. Ensure that there is a basis for a relationship which is independent of short-term business dealings.

5. Recognize that *guanxi* relationships are intensely personal and rarely transferable.

6. Avoid becoming part of *guanxi* relationships which rely on secrecy, cronyism and collusion.

7. Work through appropriate intermediaries in arranging introductions to potential partners, clients or influential 'helpers'.

8. Assume that networks are dynamic and fluid rather than stable and static, and focus on networks as a whole as well as individual relationships.

9. Accept that, while some relationships may overlap, even partners in the same culture may have little in common and, if brought together, may regard each other with jealousy, suspicion and mistrust.

10. Evaluate business opportunities on the basis of investment risk fundamentals and not simply as a means of sustaining a relationship.

11. Approach networking as a sophisticated management competency which is to be continuously reflected upon, developed and refined.

12. Regard networks as precious, long-term investments which should be valued, nurtured and protected.

References

Chatterjee, Samir R. and Cecil A.L. Pearson (2002), 'Work Goals of Asian Managers. Field Evidence from Singapore, Malaysia, India, Thailand, Brunei and Mongolia', *International Journal of Cross Cultural Management*, 2 (2), 251–68.
Christensen, (1997), *The Innovator's Dilemma: When New Technologies Cause Great Firms to Fail*, Boston: Harvard Business School Press.

Cruz, Elfren Sicango (2001), 'Chinese Family Business: Confucian vs. Global', *BusinessWorld*, 13 March, p. 5.

Dana, Léo-Paul (1999), *Entrepreneurship in Pacific Asia: Past Present & Future*, Singapore, London and Hong Kong: World Scientific.

Deloitte Consulting (2002), 'Bridging the Gap', press release, 20 May.

Department of Trade and Industry Overseas Study Mission to Australia (1999), *Science, Technology, Innovation and Enterprise. Sharing the Australian Experience of Science Parks and Economic Regeneration*, Birmingham: University of Central England Business Schools.

Devinney, Timothy (1998), 'New Models for Asian Capitalism', *Asia Inc.*, October, 58–9.

Doz, Yves L. and Gary Hamel (1998), *Alliance Advantage: The Art of Creating Value through Partnering*, Boston: Harvard Business School Press, pp. 33–56.

Editorial (2001), *IASP News*, July, 5, 2.

Editors (2002), 'The Innovative Enterprise', *Harvard Business Review*, August, 6.

Fenton-Jones, Mark (2002), 'Small Businesses Not Facing Up to Risks', *Australian Financial Review*, 27 August, p. 16.

Fu-Lai Yu, Tony (2001), 'The Role of the Entrepreneur in the Economic Development of Hong Kong', *The Asia–Pacific Journal of Economics and Business*, 5 (2), December, pp. 24–43.

Hamel, G. (1999), 'Bringing Silicon Valley Inside', *Harvard Business Review*, September–October, 71–84.

Kotler, Philip and Hermawan Kartajaya (2000), *Repositioning Asia*, Singapore: John Wiley.

Kripalani, Manjeet and Pete Engardio (2002), 'Small is Profitable', *BusinessWeek*, 28 August, pp. 68–9.

Porter, Michael E. (2001), 'Strategy and the Internet', *Harvard Business Review*, March, 64–78.

PricewaterhouseCoopers (2002), 'Fifth Annual Global CEO Survey', *Financial Times*, London.

Redding, G. (1995), 'Overseas Chinese Networks: Understanding the Enigma', *Long Range Planning*, 28 (1), 61–9.

Rost, Joseph C. (1993), *Leadership for the Twenty-First Century*, Westport CT: Praeger.

Silverthorne, Sean (ed.) (2002), 'The Country Effect: Does Location Matter?', *HBS Working Knowledge*, 18 September, pp. 1–3.

Solymossy, Emeric and John K. Masters (2002), 'Ethics Through an Entrepreneurial Lens: Theory and Observation', *Journal of Business Ethics*, July (I), 38 (3), 237.

Ying Fan (2002), 'Guanxi's Consequences: Personal Gains at Social Cost', *Journal of Business Ethics*, July (II), 38 (4), 371–80.

Zutshi, Ravi K. (1997), 'East Asian SMEs: Learning the Technology', *Journal of Enterprising Culture*, 5 (2), June, 183–7.

16 East Asian perspectives of international entrepreneurship
Chew Soon Beng and Rosalind Chew

The purpose of this chapter is to present an analytical framework to understand the interdependence among foreign investment, international entrepreneurship and domestic entrepreneurship in the new economy. Factors affecting each of these economic activities are analysed for selected countries in East Asia.

The knowledge economy
In the old economy, the law of scarcity prevailed in the sense that, if you can produce goods that others do not and cannot, you enjoy a profit in production because you have a comparative advantage. The same law of scarcity still prevails in the new economy or the knowledge economy, in that you still must have a comparative advantage to profit in business, whether in the production of goods or in services.

One of the main differences between the old economy and the knowledge economy is that there is increasing importance of knowledge, creativity and skills in changing the way firms compete and the sources of comparative advantage between nations (Coates and Warwick, 1999). In the old economy, natural resources were the main factors determining comparative advantage. Next in importance was capital, followed by process technology. Desnoyers and Lirette (1999) document that, in the case of Canada, between 1990 and 1997, high-knowledge industries enjoyed much higher growth in employment than medium-knowledge industries and low-knowledge industries (see Table 16.1). Furthermore medium- and low-knowledge industries are more sensitive to changes in economic conditions than high-knowledge industries. Data on Singapore show the same trend (see Tables 16.2 and 16.3).

Perhaps the most critical difference between the old economy and the knowledge economy is that knowledge is a global public good (Stiglitz, 1999). Hence any comparative advantage will not last long. At the same time, the ability to make use of this public good and the extent of its usefulness will depend in turn on the level of knowledge one possesses. A developed country can utilize a new innovation much better than a developing country. Moreover, in the era of globalization, there is no prize for

Table 16.1   Knowledge-based industries in Canada

High-knowledge industries	Medium-knowledge industries	Low-knowledge industries
Machinery Industry	Mines	Agriculture
Aircraft & Parts	Crude Petroleum & Natural	Forestry
Electrical & Electronic	Gas	Hunting & Fishing
Prods	Food & Beverage	Quarries & Sand Pits
Chemicals & Phar. Prods	Tobacco	Leather
Pipeline Transportation	Rubber & Plastics	Clothing
Electrical Power	Textiles	Wood
Education	Paper & Allied Prods	Furniture & Fixtures
Health & Social Services	Prime Metal Manufacturing	Miscellaneous
Business Service	Printing, Publishing & Allied	Manufacturing
Associations	Metal Fabricating	Transportation
	Motor Vehicles	Storage & Warehousing
	Other Transport Equipment	Retail Trade
	Non-Metallic Mineral	Personal & Domestic
	Products	Services
	Construction	Accommodation, Food
	Communications	& Bevs
	Gas Distribution	Miscellaneous Services
	Other Utilities	
	Wholesale Trade	
	Finance, Insurance & Real	
	Est.	
	Amusement & Recreational	
	Services	

Source: Desnoyers Lirette, (1999).

second place as the winner takes all. The consequence is that we see widening income disparity across nations and within nations. Many countries experience fluctuations in employment level because of the combination of knowledge and globalization, which are not separable.

At the country level, in order to make full use of knowledge, there must be a need to build up the capability to absorb knowledge continuously, to utilize knowledge and to create knowledge just to stay ahead of competition. A country which is more prepared for the knowledge economy will have an advantage, and a national system that is based on decentralization and market signals, rather than administrative decree, will have an edge in competition.

How to excel in the knowledge economy? The consensus in the literature

Table 16.2   Growth rate of employment based on knowledge industries, Singapore 1991–9

Industry major group	Growth rate (%)								Average growth rate (%)
	91–2	92–3	93–4	94–5	95–6	96–7	97–8	98–9	91–9
High-knowledge industries	0.42	−3.20	5.83	3.78	1.06	−0.71	−7.23	−4.68	−0.59
Chem.& Phar. Prods	2.69	3.39	7.83	10.14	7.00	11.94	−0.55	3.88	5.79
Petrol Refineries & Petrol Prods	2.23	2.31	1.64	−6.57	−4.57	−2.46	−4.01	−5.47	−2.11
Machinery	7.65	−2.15	9.87	18.02	6.71	6.40	−0.05	−2.71	5.47
Electrical Machinery & Apparatus	−4.16	−2.62	4.25	−10.67	−13.29	−3.04	−14.36	−15.55	−7.43
Electrical & Electronic Prods	−0.65	−4.04	5.08	2.67	1.23	−3.57	−9.88	−5.19	−1.79
Medical & Optical Prods	3.08	−6.14	7.24	3.74	0.64	−2.01	−1.22	−4.84	0.06
Medium-knowledge industries	2.15	4.66	2.39	1.65	0.75	2.64	−0.58	−2.47	1.40
Food, Beverage & Tobacco	1.84	1.38	−0.18	−5.43	1.56	3.40	1.46	2.03	0.76
Textiles	−1.71	−5.63	−15.74	−14.35	−21.89	−6.46	−2.75	−3.58	−9.01
Paper & Paper Prods	2.03	3.02	5.30	4.96	−4.47	−4.77	−9.11	−0.34	−0.42
Printg & Publishing	2.48	4.22	−1.10	4.88	1.51	0.39	0.57	−10.15	0.35
Rubber & Plastic Prods	0.15	6.91	3.34	6.44	4.86	−1.00	−5.93	0.34	1.89
Non-metallic Mineral Prods	8.35	7.49	4.17	−12.38	18.02	7.64	−5.98	−8.02	2.41
Basic Metals	−2.57	−5.27	5.64	−13.00	−4.97	−9.12	−4.29	−15.84	−6.18
Metal Fabricating	−1.28	7.97	2.60	0.54	3.36	2.68	3.95	2.60	2.80
Transport Equipment	6.60	3.65	5.41	5.73	−4.72	7.18	−0.74	−5.51	2.20
Low-knowledge industries	−7.96	−8.19	−10.02	−15.68	−19.64	−4.85	−6.31	−5.22	−9.73
Wearing Apparel	−9.57	−11.00	−12.53	−19.50	−29.79	−21.00	−4.76	5.70	−12.81
Leather & Leather Prods	−3.79	−6.34	−7.63	−9.35	−7.25	16.63	−9.88	−13.73	−5.17

| Wood & Wood Prods | −4.40 | −11.53 | −9.12 | −4.01 | −10.82 | 18.62 | −2.21 | −6.84 | −3.79 |
| Other Manufacturing | −5.89 | −2.66 | −6.16 | −12.01 | −7.74 | 6.93 | −7.84 | −13.10 | −6.06 |

Note: From 1991 to 1994, industry major groups of processing of jerutong & gum damar, rubber products and plastic products are combined into rubber & plastic products; pottery, china, earthenware & glass products, bricks, tiles & other structural clay products, cement, structural cement & concrete products and non-metallic mineral products are combined into non-metallic products; iron & steel and non-ferrous metal are combined into basic metals. Other manufacturing includes other manufacturing industries listed in the source and granite quarrying.

Source: Report on the *Census of Industrial Production, Singapore 1991–1999.*

lists the following factors (Porter and Stern, 1998, 1999; Stiglitz, 1999; Coates and Warwick, 1999): a stable macroeconomic environment, low inflation, stable exchange rate, no persistent budget deficits, stable investment in human capital, a string of mechanisms to promote training, low direct taxation to encourage work effort and entrepreneurship, tax incentives to promote R&D, availability of venture capital for start-up companies, promotion of competition among business, pro-business legislation, harmonious industrial relations, investment in capability, catalysing collaboration, free flow of foreign talents and, last but far from the least, an efficient public sector which is able to provide a macroeconomic environment and to help the private sector to compete and also to promote innovation and entrepreneurship.

More specifically, each country must invest in manpower in science and technology and in applied research projects that have huge externalities (Stiglitz, 1999). Kay (1999) argues that an important source of knowledge-based competitive advantage is internal architecture, which is the process of trust and knowledge sharing that is developed within organizations. The next important source is referred to as external architecture, which is the kind of knowledge sharing and information processing that takes place between organizations and suppliers, as seen in the Japanese *keiretsu*. We may want to extend Kay's definition to include social architecture, which is the kind of knowledge sharing and information processing and collective action to respond to crisis among business enterprises, national institutions and the labour movement, as in the case of Singapore. It should be highlighted that internal architecture is the basic source of competitive advantage, without which external and social architecture is of marginal consequence. But external and social architecture can induce firms to stay within the boundary, as firms are capable of migrating to other countries.

Taking note that knowledge is a global public good, Kay's definition of competitive advantage in the knowledge economy may be regarded as a public good, but is not easy to emulate. People all over the world know how it works, but to emulate is to change the social relations of a country, which cannot be done overnight. The implication is that the government should aim to build these three levels of architecture such that knowledge will not become a realized public good. A good example is Silicon Valley. We all know how and why it works, but can any country effectively emulate?

Knowledge economy implies that competition is keen and there is no home advantage. Having a huge domestic market has certain advantages but it can be countered by the formation of trade blocs. Both knowledge economy and globalization imply there is no room for inefficient firms, an unproductive workforce, militant trade unions or inefficient government.

Sources of development through investment

Without exception, growth of a country needs investment, especially from foreign countries. With the inflow of foreign capital and the accompanying management and technical expertise, a country can slowly develop and increase both GDP and GDP per capita.

Figure 16.1 shows that foreign capital is normally attracted to a new country by its initial sources of competitive advantages in terms of low wages and natural resources. This type of investment is referred to as resource-based foreign investment (M). When resource-based foreign investment (M) reaches a critical level relative to the productive capacity of the country, wages will rise and the cost of business will also rise.

At this stage of rising wage costs and business costs, the government can continue to attract foreign investment by ensuring an environment that is conducive to business. At the same time, the government must invest substantially in education and find ways to encourage R&D. At the firm level, facing competition from other firms and especially from other countries, firms must create values and also invest in training to stay ahead of competition.

At the next critical stage of development, new sources of competitive advantage come from being in possession of an educated and multiskilled workforce and the emergence of domestic markets. Attracted by this new source of competitive advantage, foreign investment is now more high-tech and knowledge-based. This high-tech foreign investment (W) will push the country to the next stage of economic development, which will further increase wage levels and the cost of doing business.

A country that is able to attract high-tech foreign investment (W) will continue to attract (W) as long as the new source of competitive advantage prevails. At a certain stage of development, owing to the continuing development process and the resultant rise in GDP per capita, a domestic market generated by the increase in local purchasing power begins to emerge. The domestic market will further attract high-tech foreign investment (W). At the same time, local firms will have the resources and expertise to invest. This kind of local investment is referred to as domestic market-based local investment (X). Hence, if domestic entrepreneurship is strong, the local investment will be strong and most will be small and medium enterprises (SMEs).

About 10 to 15 years after the initial source of competitive advantage, some foreign firms may start to reallocate their operations to other countries to gain access to cheaper labour supplies. This relocation of foreign firms (Y) can be damaging to the local economy if not managed properly. This is because, when there is relocation of foreign firms (Y), resource-based foreign investment (M) falls drastically. The country concerned will

Table 16.3 Growth rate of output based on knowledge industries, Singapore, 1991–9

Industry major group	Growth rate (%)								Average growth rate (%)
	91–2	92–3	93–4	94–5	95–6	96–7	97–8	98–9	91–9
High-knowledge industries	3.59	16.42	17.20	15.29	7.99	6.05	−4.00	13.23	9.47
Chemical and Phar. Prods	−7.63	1.88	15.45	18.25	4.34	30.38	8.76	36.56	13.50
Petroleum Refineries & Petroleum Prods	−9.00	9.16	−2.11	−2.94	29.03	6.48	−12.88	6.61	3.04
Machinery	3.71	−3.41	20.37	30.30	10.31	6.89	−9.75	−2.02	7.05
Electrical Machinery & Apparatus	0.28	5.97	15.11	3.59	−7.00	−0.91	−18.10	−5.46	−0.81
Electrical & Electronic Prods	10.66	24.29	23.05	18.09	5.25	3.27	−3.27	12.93	11.78
Medical & Optical Prods	10.00	14.84	4.89	29.21	5.02	9.45	24.56	16.66	14.33
Medium-knowledge industries	5.62	8.02	9.66	7.54	−0.12	4.10	−1.96	−2.79	3.76
Food, Beverage & Tobacco	3.70	4.39	9.19	3.17	1.18	4.07	−8.54	−2.73	1.80
Textiles	−3.33	−5.22	−12.83	−8.23	−19.30	7.52	−0.50	−7.59	−6.19
Paper & Paper Prods	−7.72	6.39	11.10	11.44	−3.31	−6.57	−14.12	0.89	−0.24
Printing & Publishing	10.58	7.94	3.61	11.53	3.55	1.62	−4.00	−0.90	4.24
Rubber & Plastic Prods	−0.47	10.26	12.77	13.61	0.48	2.07	−8.53	9.33	4.94
Non-metallic Mineral Prods	14.24	17.99	9.51	8.66	15.42	10.80	−19.57	−20.26	4.60
Basic Metals	−0.33	4.21	−0.52	−12.70	−3.90	1.47	−17.79	2.83	−3.34
Metal Fabricating	5.65	12.08	14.53	12.74	−0.24	3.15	−1.96	1.37	5.91
Transport Equipment	9.54	4.40	9.74	3.06	−7.01	7.01	20.47	−7.47	4.97
Low-knowledge industries	−6.08	−7.53	1.14	−14.58	−11.59	1.60	−9.73	−3.64	−6.30
Wearing Apparel	−6.18	−18.52	−8.80	−19.69	−17.68	−3.52	1.80	2.45	−8.77

Leather & Leather Prods	7.30	−0.05	−1.73	−4.08	−3.81	36.26	−14.11	24.60	5.55
Wood & Wood Prods	−1.48	−0.90	−5.64	5.67	−6.68	7.56	3.36	−16.97	−1.89
Other Manufacturing	−7.72	2.24	11.01	−14.93	−9.18	0.57	−18.59	−7.70	−5.54

Note: From 1991 to 1994, industry major groups of processing of jerutong & gum damar, rubber products and plastic products are combined into rubber & plastic products; pottery, china, earthenware & glass products, bricks, tiles & others structural clay products, cement, structural cement & concrete products and non-metallic mineral products are combined into non-metallic products; iron & steel and non-ferrous metal are combined into basic metals. Other manufacturing includes other manufacturing industries listed in the source and granite quarrying.

Source: *Census of Industrial Production, Singapore 1991–1999.*

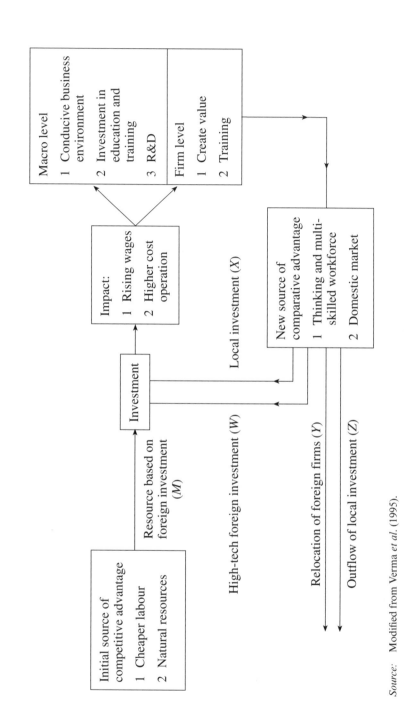

Source: Modified from Verma *et al.* (1995).

Figure 16.1   Development cycle

300

have to depend on high-tech foreign investment (W) and domestic market based local investment (X) for job creation.

A few years after this phase, mature local firms will invest overseas, seeking strategic partners in the region. This outflow of local investment (Z) aims to build the external economy for the country concerned. Hence this international entrepreneurship which helps the local firms to venture aboard must be assisted by the government. For sustainable development, total investment must exceed outflow of funds by the amount required to keep new labour market entrants employed. That is, $M + W + X$ must be greater than $Y + Z$ by the amount necessary to keep the unemployment rate constant.

We use the above theoretical framework to analyse the situation of selected countries in East Asia.

Japan

Japan has no resource-based foreign investment (M). In the 1970s, high-tech foreign investment (W) from developed countries was strong, but local investment (X) was even stronger. Relocation of foreign firms in Japan (Y) was limited. During the 1970s, the outflow of local investment (Z) was on the increase. During the 1970s and 1980s, local investment (X) was greater than the outflow of local investment (Z). But in the 1990s, outflow of local investment (Z) was greater than local investment (X), resulting in a 'hollowing-out' effect in Japan. This contributed to the higher unemployment rate in Japan.

The main reason for Japanese firms investing abroad (Z) is the higher cost of operation in Japan. Since Japan has the highest per capita income in Asia, it is natural that the cost of business will be higher in Japan. However the cause of the hollowing-out effect in Japan is not so much the higher cost of operation but insufficient formation of new companies. That is, new local investment (X) is now too low.

The problem facing Japan therefore is not that there is too much international entrepreneurship, but that there is insufficient domestic entrepreneurship. Japan must slow down the former and find ways to promote the latter.

USA

The USA has experienced a greater outflow of investment to foreign countries than Japan has, yet she has not suffered from a hollowing-out effect. This is because US local investment (X) is as large, if not larger than, the outflow of local investment (Z).

The large local investment (X) in the USA despite her higher per capita income may be explained by three factors: first, the USA is rich in natural resources; second, there has been an inflow of cheap labour into southern USA from South America; third and most importantly, the USA is strong in innovation and in the creation of knowledge. The formation of new companies providing higher value-added is continuous.

Hence, even while international entrepreneurship is strong in the USA, her domestic entrepreneurship is thriving.

Hong Kong and Taiwan

These two economies have suffered the same fate as Japan. Both lack natural resources although they have higher per capita income compared to China. Hence they also have only a small domestic market, and at the same time resource-based foreign investment (M) and high-tech foreign investment (W) are not high. Relocation of foreign firms (Y) has been persistent. Owing to the higher cost of operation, the outflow of local investment (Z) to China is substantial for both economies. At the same time, domestic market local investment (X) is limited because of the high cost of operation. As the outflow of local investment (Z) is greater than domestic market-based local investment (X), both also suffer from the hollowing-out effect.

Thus the problem facing Taiwan and Kong Kong is not that there is too much international entrepreneurship but that there is insufficient domestic entrepreneurship. These two economies must not discourage international entrepreneurship, but need to find ways to promote domestic entrepreneurship.

China

China opened up her economy in 1978. As a result of the transition from the planned economy to a market economy, labour was extremely cheap, but there was practically no purchasing power. Both Hong Kong and Taiwan took advantage of the cheap labour costs and some rather irrational pricing of resources and invested heavily in China. As a result, China received massive investment (M) from these two economies in the 1980s and early 1990s.

By the mid-1990s, although there was a rapid rise in labour costs, especially in the coastal areas, Chinese wages were still low by ASEAN standards. At the same time, the Chinese domestic market emerged. China also invested heavily in education and technology. Hence, in the later half of the 1990s, China continued to receive foreign investment (M) and (W). Local investment (X) in China has also been on the increase. Relocation of foreign firms (Y) has been continuous, but foreign investment has been pouring in because of the promise of the huge domestic market.

While China has been getting a lot of foreign investment, job creation has not been fast enough to cope with the retrenchment of state enterprises because of the reform policy. The rise in unemployment also means that the rise in Chinese labour costs will also be delayed, which will serve as an additional comparative advantage.

For the next five to ten years, China will continue to be the destination of international entrepreneurship from Japan, Taiwan and Hong Kong.

ASEAN
ASEAN comprises many countries, each facing a different situation.

Singapore
Singapore is a city-state with no natural resources. Resource-based foreign investment (M) is zero. Singapore has been relying on both high-tech foreign investment (W) and local investment (X). High-tech foreign investment (W) takes place because of her competitive workforce and conducive business environment. Domestic market-based local investment (X) is largely carried out by government-linked companies. Since the late 1970s, relocation of foreign firms (Y) has been rising as the Singapore economy has started economic restructuring. In the 1990s, as part of her national strategy to develop Singapore's external economy, local investment abroad (Z) was on the increase.

Until the 1997 East Asian currency crisis, Singapore's economy performed quite satisfactorily as high-tech foreign investment (W) plus domestic market-based local investment (X) exceeded relocation of foreign firms (Y) and outflow of local investment (Z).

However, because of the East Asian currency crisis, which badly affected many ASEAN economies, and the rise of China, Singapore has experienced rising unemployment levels as a result of the rapid increase in relocation of foreign firms (Y) and an insufficient increase in foreign investment (W) and domestic market-based local investment (X). Singapore now wants to find ways to increase W by lowering income tax for companies and individuals. At the same time, Singapore is actively promoting SMEs in the hope that domestic market-based local investment (X) can be made larger too. Singapore actively promotes international entrepreneurship. In particular, some statutory bodies such as International Enterprise have a string of programmes encouraging firms in Singapore to invest abroad and expand her market beyond Singapore and the region.

Vietnam, Thailand and Malaysia
For these three countries, foreign investment (M) and (W) has been substantial since the adoption of the open door policy of the respective country. As Malaysian per capita income is higher, relocation of foreign

firms (*Y*) has been rising. For each of these countries to sustain growth, it goes without saying that foreign investment must continue to pour in. Once the per capita income of the respective country reaches a critical level, domestic market-based local investment (*X*) will also increase. Owing to the small population base, the domestic market is not a factor in attracting foreign investment.

Hence these three countries aim to compete with China in attracting foreign investment. International entrepreneurship from these three countries is still not important in their respective economies. The issue facing each of them is how to enhance competitiveness relative to China, which has a huge domestic market, relatively low labour costs, and a hardworking and well educated workforce. In other words, the key issue is how to obtain a fair share of foreign investment. This can be achieved by ensuring the following:

1.   a stable macroeconomic environment in terms of a stable exchange rate, low inflation and no persistent budget deficit;
2.   pro-business culture and practice; greater transparency in government operations and policy, corruption control and improved efficiency of the public sector;
3.   better corporate governance in banks and state enterprises;
4.   improved quality of union officials. The labour movement should help the country to compete for foreign investment rather than aim to improve the standard of living per se as, without jobs, there is no standard of living;
5.   investment in education, which is the easiest to achieve, as most people in ASEAN are eager to learn. However, the government must ensure that tertiary education is affordable;
6.   institution of training programmes for workers in anticipation of the change in economic structure. Most firms would not want to train workers because of labour mobility. This market failure can be removed by the use of macro-based training programmes. The Skills Development Fund scheme in Singapore is a good example of a macro-based training scheme. It goes without saying that only a government with budget surplus can effectively support such a scheme;
7.   if possible, establishment of internal architecture, external architecture and social architecture; a country has to compete as a society to sustain any advantage in competition;
8.   all ASEAN countries should work towards creating a free trade area, which will be discussed below. The worst scenario is for some ASEAN members to squabble among themselves and undermine each other: investors might perceive the region as unstable.

From the preceding discussion, we can see that the domestic market is the key factor. This is why China is in a different league even as a developing country. Mexico and Canada have the North American Free Trade Agreement. The European Union is big and is trying to enlarge by incorporating central and eastern European countries.

ASEAN must establish linkages with the above trade blocs by means of ASEAN–USA, ASEAN–Japan, ASEAN–EU and ASEAN–China agreements. Once these trade linkages are established, ASEAN members will benefit. This will also force ASEAN economies to work more closely with each other. The benefits of FTAs are beyond doubt. Professor Kimura of Keio University estimates that a Japan–ASEAN Comprehensive Economic Partnership would produce the following benefits: ASEAN exports would increase by US$15 billion while Japanese exports would increase by US$10 billion (*Business Times*, 2/5/2002); ASEAN GDP would increase by US$1.7 billion (or as much as 0.5 per cent for some ASEAN members). The benefits would be larger with the formation of a trade bloc that covers ASEAN, China, Korea and Japan.

But ASEAN members have not moved fast enough even within the ASEAN Free Trade Area (AFTA). The idea of AFTA was first launched in 1993 and was supposed to materialize in 2008, but the date was brought forward to 2002, when tariffs were to come down to no more than 5 per cent. However some members have asked for an extra grace period for their key sectors, while other members have threatened to do likewise for their key sectors.

Since the group formation is not moving fast enough, Singapore has taken the initiative to establish her own free trade agreements with the USA, Japan, Australia, New Zealand, Canada and Mexico. The proposed USA–Singapore FTA would be extended to include the Indonesian islands of Batam and Bintan under an agreement called the Integrated Sourcing Initiative (*Business Times*, 2/5/2002). Singapore has repeatedly assured her neighbours that her bilateral FTAs are wholly consistent with AFTA and any member is welcome to sign up.

Conclusion

Singapore is actively promoting international entrepreneurship as part of her strategy to develop the external economy. Taiwan and Hong Kong have a thriving international entrepreneurship in relation to China, which contributes to the hollowing out of these two economies. Owing to political factors, Taiwan has tried to reduce its investment in China.

In the case of ASEAN, the immediate need is not to promote international entrepreneurship but for each ASEAN country to put her house in order. At the same time, ASEAN must move towards AFTA. Increasingly investors and other countries are assessing ASEAN as one identity or as a group. The strength of ASEAN depends on the health of each member, plus the multiplier effect as a grouping.

References

Chew, Soon Beng and Rosalind Chew (1996), *Employment-driven Industrial Relations Regimes: The Singapore Experience*, Aldershot: Avebury.
Chew, Soon Beng and Rosalind Chew (1998), *Economic Development in Singapore: The Next Leap*, New York: Marcel Dekker.
Chew, Soon Beng, Mike Leu and Tan Kim Heng (1998), *Values and Lifestyles of Young Singaporeans*, Singapore: Prentice-Hall.
Chia, Siow Yue (2001), 'Singapore: Towards a Knowledge-Based Economy', in Seiichi Masuyama, Donna Vandenbrink and Siow Yue Chia (eds), *Industrial Restructuring in East Asia: Towards the 21st century*, Singapore: Institute of Southeast Asian Studies, pp. 169–208.
Chng, Meng Kng, Linda Low, Tay Boon Nga and Amina Tyabji (1986), *Technology and Skills in Singapore*, Singapore: Institute of Southeast Asian Studies.
Coates, D. and K. Warwick (1999), 'The Knowledge Driven Economy: Analysis and Background', paper presented at the conference entitled 'The Economics of The Knowledge Driven Economy', 27 January, London.
Desnoyers, A. and Y. Lirette (1999), 'The Knowledge-based Economy and the Labour Market', Human Resources Development, January, Canada.
Goh, Keng Swee (1972), *The Economics of Modernization and Other Essays*, Singapore: Asia Pacific Press.
Goh, Keng Swee (1995), *Wealth of East Asian Nations*, Singapore: Federal Publications.
Kay, M. (1999), 'Internal and External Architecture as sources of Competitive Advantage', paper presented at a conference entitled 'The Economics of the Knowledge Driven Economy', London, 27 January 1999.
Krause, L., Koh Ai Tee and Lee (Tsao) Yuan (1987), *The Singapore Economy Reconsidered*, Singapore: Institute of Southeast Asian Studies.
Lee, Kwan Yew (2002), 'Inaugural Ho Rih Hwa Leadership in Asia Lecture', ST 6/2/2002.
Lim, Chong Yah (1980), *Economic Development in Singapore*, Singapore: Federal Publications.
Lim, Chong Yah (ed.) (1996), *Economic Policy Management in Singapore*, Singapore: Addison-Wesley.
Lim, Chong Yah (1996), 'The Trinity Growth Theory: The Ascendency of Asia and The Decline of the West', *Accounting and Business Review*, 3 (2), July.
Lim, Chong Yah and P. Lloyd (1986), *Singapore: Resources and Growth*, Singapore: Oxford University Press.
Lim, Chong Yah and Associates (1988), *Policy Options for the Singapore Economy*, Singapore: McGraw-Hill.
Low, Aik Meng and Cao Yong (1995), 'The Singapore System Taxation and 1994 Taxation Reform', in Tan, Low and Chew (eds), *Development Experience of Singapore*, Singapore: Hanns Seidel Foundation and Nanyang Business School.
Macleod, G., B. McFarlane and C.H. Davis (1997), 'The Knowledge Economy and the Social Economy', *International Journal of Social Economics*, 24 (11), pp. 1302–24.
Ngiam, Tong Dow (2002), 'Acceptance Speech by Mr Ngiam Tong Dow at EDB Society 12th Annual General Meeting', 25 March 'A Knowledge Based Economy'.
Porter, M.E. (1998), 'Clusters and Competition: New Agendas for Companies, Governments and Institutions', *On Competition*, Boston, MA: Harvard Business School Press.
Porter, M.E. and S. Stern (1999), *The New Challenge to America's Prosperity: Findings from the Innovation Index*, Washington, DC: Council on Competitiveness.
Schein, Edgar (1996), *Strategic Pragmatism: The Culture of Singapore & Economic Development Board*, Cambridge, MA: MIT Press.
Stiglitz, J.E.(1999), 'Knowledge in the Modern Economy', paper presented at the conference entitled 'The Economics of the Knowledge Driven Economy', 27 January, London.

Tan, Chwee Huat (1975), 'The public enterprises as a development strategy: The case of Singapore', *Annals of Public and Cooperative Economy*, January.

Vaitilinhgam, R. (1999), 'Overview: The Economics of the Knowledge Driven Economy', paper presented at the conference entitled 'The Economics of the Knowledge Driven Economy', 27 January, London.

Verma, A., T. Kochan and R. Lansbury (eds) (1995), *Employment Relations in the Growing Asian Economies*, London: Routledge.

17 Two types of self-employed in Canada
Louis Jacques Filion

Introduction

Statistics from many countries show that newly created companies have tended to become smaller since the early 1990s, and that the percentage of self-employed has increased. This is particularly true in Canada, where self-employment has grown by about 1 per cent per year in the last 10 years. In 1999, the self-employed already accounted for more than 18 per cent of Canada's working population (*Small Business Quarterly*, 1999). In 2002, these figures are still true. Although growth is likely to be slower hereafter, it is nevertheless reasonable to think that the self-employed will account for 20 per cent to 25 per cent of the workforce by 2010 – in other words, that their numbers will increase from one in five at the turn of the century to one in four 10 years later. The phenomenon of self-employment is also visible elsewhere in the world, although to a lesser extent. For example, United States statistics place it at slightly over 10 per cent of the total workforce. The Canadian model may therefore be a precursor for other economies in the next millennium, as we evolve towards forms of work organization that are much more fragmented and service-oriented.

It is also relevant to ask what the self-employment phenomenon actually represents: is it an entrepreneurial outgrowth, a defence mechanism developed by a segment of the population in response to radical changes in the labour market, or the result of new, emerging values? Many people view self-employment as a new form of work organization. However, if we look back at the history of mankind, we see that it was actually the most common form of work prior to the 20th century. With the exception of the army, certain religious bodies and a handful of large companies (such as the one responsible for distributing wheat in Rome) large organizations only began to appear during the Industrial Revolution. At the beginning of the 20th century, in almost every country in the world, the working population was concentrated in the farming sector and was largely self-employed. There are, however, significant differences between self-employment as it was then and as it is now. For example, pre-20th century farmers tended to operate micro enterprises employing several family members, whereas today's self-employed work essentially alone, in the service sectors but more and more through peer networks and complementary networks (Filion, 1996a; 1996c).

The economic recession of the early 1990s may have accelerated the development of self-employment. Some people believe the phenomenon of self-employment tends to emerge in difficult periods, when jobs are harder to find. This hypothesis is partly confirmed by the behaviour of the labour market prior to 1990. Stanworth and Gray (1991) showed that self-employment reached a pinnacle in Great Britain in 1936, when it rose to 12.6 per cent of the working population before declining to between 5 per cent and 6 per cent after 1940. However the economic context at the beginning of the new millennium appears to be so favourable to self-employment that the phenomenon is continuing to grow.

Orser and Foster (1992) showed the importance of self-employment, pointing out that nearly 25 per cent of all Canadian families had some form of home-based business activity (usually part-time) by the end of the 1980s. The annual reports of Statistics Canada show that self-employment has grown steadily since 1975 in every region of Canada. Several sources in other countries have also noted its importance (see, for example, OECD, 1996). In 1990, the International Labour Office estimated that more than a billion people throughout the world were self-employed (ILO, 1990), and some authors now suggest that the figure may have doubled over the last decade. One thing appears certain: although cyclical, the place of self-employment in modern society keeps growing overall, to such an extent that the question we should now be asking is just how many self-employed a developed economy can actually absorb. Can Canada go beyond the 25 per cent threshold?

The trend towards self-employment is a result of many different factors, including the following:

- better education,
- increased use of technology in the workplace,
- the need for more flexibility within companies, achieved through subcontracting,
- massive layoffs following corporate closures or restructuring,
- the problems encountered by young people looking for work,
- the emergence of new work-related values,
- a shift in the relative importance of work in overall lifestyles.

The increase in self-employment has altered the entrepreneurial profiles of many countries, by adding a new entrepreneurial category to the existing categories of growth entrepreneurs, technopreneurs, small business owner-managers, family business owners and so on. Self-employment is one of the major labour market transformations of our era, and has a number of consequences for social organization, not least for education. The reason is simple. Most workers in this century have had to find jobs in organizations in order to enter the labour market, and our entire educational system is geared towards this. However, this focus may now have to be revised, owing to the growth in self-employment. Profound changes in the structure of the labour market are transforming our societies. Since most self-employed jobs are in the service sector, our era may well mark the end of the industrial age and its characteristic feature, large-scale salaried manufacturing employment.

It is therefore important to learn more about the self-employed, their motivations, their values, their organization and their methods. This research explores some aspects of the phenomenon. Our initial goal was to understand the relationship between the self-employed and their work. This chapter presents reflections based on exploratory field research carried out in two phases: a questionnaire administered to a focus group and semi-structured interviews with 30 self-employed people. Parts of this chapter have already been published elsewhere (Filion, 2000). Self-employment is a dimension of entrepreneurship that is likely to concern researchers in many countries and may well be of growing interest for international entrepreneurship (Verstraete and Filion, 2001; Wright, 1999).

Although little has been published on the subject of self-employment, the work done generally shows that the phenomenon is growing (Bates, 1995; Bolyle, 1993; Brodie and Stanworth, 1998; Leighton and Felstead, 1992; OECD, 1996; Silvestri, 1991; Vodopivec, 1998). Some authors suggest that the main difficulties encountered by the self-employed are related to marketing and customer development (Hisrich and Peters, 1992; Meredith, 1993), while others focus on methods and tend to emphasize home-based self-employment (Bly and Blake, 1986; Brennan, 1996; Eyler, 1990; Fisher, 1995; Golzen, 1991; Gray and Gray, 1994; Hawkins and Bage, 1990; Kishel and Kishel, 1991; Rice, 1990; Sheedy, 1990).

Definition
Defining self-employment is a complex undertaking that can lead to confusion. This is partly due to the diversity and novelty of the phenomenon. There are hundreds of definitions of the entrepreneur, and each country has its own definition of small business (Filion, 1990a; 1998a; 1998b). Gartner (1990) showed that it was never easy to establish a consensus on definitions in entrepreneurship. In the case of self-employment, the very existence of the prefix 'self' denotes the importance of the individual, and hence of independence, as well as a certain inward focus and solitude (*Oxford English Dictionary*, 1971). Five aspects in particular are often mentioned in discussions of self-employment:

- *independence with regard to customers*:   the self-employed are free to select their customers, and have more than one customer;

- *independence with regard to organization*: the self-employed usually have their own working tools, although they may occasionally use their customers' resources too;
- *solitude at work*: the self-employed basically work alone, although they may interact with others during their work. Many business activities are cyclic. Some self-employed subcontract their surpluses in busy periods, while others hire part-time or full-time staff to help out. The definition of the term 'self-employment' used for this research includes only people who work essentially alone and hire no more than the equivalent of three full-time employees at certain periods of the year;
- *the workplace*: some people feel that self-employment necessarily means working at home, while others do not consider the home-based criterion to be relevant. We did not include this element in our definition of self-employment, since in our view it is concerned more with working conditions than with the nature of the work. We suggest, however, that it may be possible in future research to establish a distinction between the self-employed working at home and those working outside the home. The self-employed can also be divided into many other categories, such as those who travel extensively, those who share services (support, reception, secretarial) with others, those who work alone all day at their business premises, and so on;
- *legal status*: some self-employed form limited companies, while others do not. Although the statistics reveal some differences between the two groups, we did not take this factor into account for this research, although it may be interesting to do so in a future study. There may also be some differences between the full-time and part-time self-employed. This research focused exclusively on full-time self-employed.

Given the above, the term 'self-employed' was defined for this research as a person working for himself or herself, and working basically alone, although possibly interacting with others as part of the work. The self-employed are completely free to choose their customers and to organize themselves as they wish in order to meet the needs of those customers. They are generally completely independent with regard to the way they organize their work.

We use the term *generally* here because some customers prefer or require a self-employed supplier to use their equipment, tools or instruments. This may be the case, for example, of a self-employed trainer who is hired occasionally to give training courses at a customer's training centre, using the equipment on site. A certain amount of judgment is needed in separating the 'true' self-employed from the 'false' self-employed. Society has many 'false' self-employed people who work for only one customer. For the purposes of this research, the term 'self-employed' includes only those who have several customers and who exercise their freedom both to choose their customers and to organize themselves to meet the needs of those customers.

The research
The research was divided into two phases. The first phase involved a focus group, and the second individual interviews with 30 self-employed people. Reports of certain aspects of this research have already been published (Filion, 1996a; 1996b, 1996c; 2000).

The focus group
The focus group was composed of eight people (five women and three men) who had been working for themselves from home for at least a year. They took part in turn in a structured interview comprising 38 questions. The interview lasted six hours, from 9:00 a.m. to 4:00 p.m., with a one-hour break for lunch. The questions were prepared following a survey of the literature on self-employment. The first part of the questionnaire was concerned mainly with the organization of work: for example, 'What do you find most difficult about running a business from home?', 'How do you discipline yourself to work?', 'Do you feel isolated?', 'What led you to choose a home base for your business?', 'Why did you select this particular type of business activity?', 'Can you say if your activities are profitable?', 'What kind of preparation and training would you recommend for people wishing to run a business from home?', 'Is profitability an important element in evaluating the success of a self-employed person?', and so on. The six hours of interviews were recorded and then transcribed. At each response, the respondent's name was noted so that the individual's selection logic and organization could be properly identified. The data and material gathered were used to design the second phase of the research.

The sample, the research methodology and the data analysis
For the second phase, we identified 30 self-employed people who had been in business for at least two years. This was done with the help of a self-employment association. We asked the association to identify 30 successful self-employed people from its bank of 200 members. What we wanted were subjects working in the service sector, since this is where the vast majority of self-employed find their niche. We asked specifically for 10 from the professions, 10 from the trades and 10 from other types of services. The pro-

fessional and trade sectors are currently facing radically different market conditions, but both have a long history. Self-employed professionals and tradespeople have cultures and learning features that are supported by both the education system and the professional corporation networks. However we also decided to focus on a third group of self-employed offering new types of services, including public relations, furniture removals, training, publicity, consulting, tourism, brokerage and sales (computer equipment, printing, drafting, graphic design and so on). All the self-employed in our sample worked in the service sector. Seventeen were men (eight graduates and nine non-graduates) and 13 were women (eight graduates and five non-graduates). None had taken part in the focus group.

The principal researcher ran semi-structured interviews of approximately two to three hours with everyone in the sample, at their place of business in all but three cases (three interviews were held at the researcher's office). The interviews were recorded, 20 were transcribed and 14 were reworked into case studies that are now used in a graduate course for the self-employed. The interviews addressed the issues of background, values, models, career choices and the decision to go into business. They also examined problems related to start-up, organization and management, and discussed the subject's activity system – in other words, organization, marketing, operations, accounting, finance and information. Our goal was to use qualitative analysis to understand the reasons underlying the subject's main choices and chosen working system. This involved tracing the similarities and differences between the patterns of cases studied, in order to identify types. We hoped to establish models that could be used to design venture creation and management courses specifically for the self-employed. The methodology used was a first-level systemic analysis, as described in Filion (1999), which involves exploring professional patterns by referring to typical activities and behavioural patterns.

One of the problems of qualitative research as opposed to quantitative research is the presentation and analysis of the data. In quantitative research, data are presented in summary tables and then discussed in accordance with rules agreed upon by the research community. In qualitative research, the accumulation of data is considerable (almost 100 hours of field interviews and more than 500 pages of word-processed text in this study) and the coding and analysis methods used by researchers vary. The method used for this research was empirical systems modelling methodology, designed by Filion (1999) as a derivative of soft systems methodology (Checkland, 1981; Checkland and Scholes, 1990). It involves looking at the activity system of each subject, superposing the resulting models and trying to identify common emerging patterns. The data were analysed and classified, and this chapter presents a discussion (without citations) based on the data and analysis. Readers with basic training in human systems, system dynamics and soft systems analysis will have an advantage because they will find it easier to understand the approach used to analyse the data. Data analysis is generally longer in qualitative research because the researcher is often exploring areas at the very edge of a field with little or no literature. Qualitative research based on one case can delve very deeply and explore issues that are not quantifiable. In studies involving more than a single case, the researcher often looks for clusters representing common patterns that can be grouped, explained and compared among themselves or with other categories from the same family of organizational actors. It is difficult, in such a short chapter, to report all the observations made in this particular study, but we have tried to present the main elements that reveal the dynamic of the self-employed. We have also presented some comparisons with entrepreneurs. Given the general lack of research on the subject, this exploratory field study contributes some elements to help understand who the self-employed are, what they do and how they organize themselves to do it.

Two separate types of self-employment: involuntary and voluntary
Although we had attempted to build a sample of successful self-employed people, it soon became obvious that self-employment is not easy for anyone. The self-employed have to be constantly on call, customers can never be taken for granted, it is difficult to find replacements to take over during holiday periods and, not least, drawing a line between professional and private life can be a major source of frustration. It is often said that one of the major problems of self-employment is isolation. Only three of our sample (10 per cent) said they really had problems in this area. All those interviewed said they were busy, and more than half said they were so busy that they found it difficult to set time aside for leisure activities. Nine of the people contacted for interviews called several times to postpone, and were removed from the sample after four cancellations. Time is clearly an important resource for the self-employed.

As is often the case with qualitative research, what we found was not necessarily what we were looking for. This happens not only because qualitative research is often used to explore new themes, but also because the researcher and subject can examine a given theme in considerable depth, uncovering previously unsuspected elements. Our past research, much of it in the field of entrepreneurship, has involved several hundred interviews over a period of 30 years. This has allowed the development of an expertise that permits the researcher to go straight to the point right from the beginning of the interview and to explore issues in more depth with the subject. It is often possible to explore emerging patterns with the subject within 45 to 60 minutes of the beginning of the interview.

One of the major observations to emerge from this research is that there were two main types of root definitions at the origin of the decision to become self-employed. An issue-based root definition describes a notional system chosen for its relevance to what the people concerned perceive as matters of contention (Checkland, 1981: 317). Based on this, there appeared to be two separate types of self-employed: the voluntary (VSE) and the involuntary (ISE). Although one of our initial objectives was to identify types, the types identified here were somewhat unexpected. We know that people sometimes become entrepreneurs and go into business because they have no choice, but never in the numbers and to the extent found among our sample of self-employed. Subsequent research, using a random sample of 250 self-employed, confirmed the trend identified in this research, showing that 25 per cent of the subjects fell into the 'involuntary' type (Roy, 1998). Each of these two types has its own, very different, reasons for becoming self-employed. Each has its own activity system, and each needs a different type of training, support and learning.

Involuntary self-employment (ISE)
This type is composed of graduates who became self-employed when they were unable to find jobs, as well as professionals and managers of all ages who lost their jobs following corporate closures or restructuring. Six of our sample of 30 self-employed, that is 20 per cent, were ISEs. They did not choose to become self-employed, but were pushed into it when they were unable to find jobs, after a search that lasted at least one year, and in some cases much longer. They had never considered going into business before, but, when faced with the necessity of earning a living, had no choice but to create their own jobs. The first questions such people had to answer were 'where?' and 'how?' The main problem for would-be ISEs is that they have no model, and generally do not know or frequent business people. All our sample ISEs needed between six and nine months of reflection and between six and ten months of preparation before finally going into business.

An example of involuntary self-employment (ISE)
John had worked for a computer hardware repair shop for nearly 16 years. He was good at his job. Over the years, his employer had asked him to specialize in certain types of hardware. Finally, the firm was bought by a multinational and underwent restructuring. In the new system, the technicians had to have all-round capabilities, because service was offered directly at every point of sale. John was unable to do this. He had worked for years on one particular product line and was not motivated to learn others, even though his line was losing ground on the market every year. He could not repair other products in the time required to offer a competitive price. After

a stressful year, he was laid off. This was no surprise, and in fact he had been looking for another job for several months, without success. Faced with unemployment, he decided to work for himself, in his basement at home. His former employer subcontracted work to him and sent him all its repairs in his speciality line, but this was not enough for John to earn a living, and he had to find other customers too. After two years he was earning approximately 80 per cent of his former salary by working 60 hours a week instead of 40. However he does not have to commute two hours a day, nor does he have to pay for gasoline, parking fees or car maintenance. A friend helps him with his accounting. He still does not know how to market his service or how to set competitive, profitable prices for his work.

Voluntary self-employment (VSE)

The voluntary self-employed had known for many years that they wanted to work for themselves. More than half had a model, someone in their entourage who was self-employed, an entrepreneur or a small business owner–manager. They had prepared for self-employment for some time – more than five years in 20 per cent of cases. Some had even changed jobs to acquire the experience they felt they needed before going into business. For a further 20 per cent, the preparatory stage lasted between three and five years. Twenty-five per cent simply found an idea and launched their business six months later, although they had been considering the possibility for a while (more than a year).

When analysing activity systems (Filion, 1999), it is interesting to look at the way people think and why they do things. It was this process that led us to identify a visionary system among entrepreneurs (Filion, 1990b; 1998c). In the case of the VSEs in the present study, it became clear that the notion of success varied enormously from one individual to another (see Figure 17.1). At the lower end of the range, success is defined on the basis of extrinsic criteria, while at the higher end it is defined on the basis of intrinsic criteria. The extrinsic criteria include elements valued by society, the external signs of success such as status, location of the home, value of the secondary home, type of car, watch, jewellery, clothing, vacation destination and so on: in other words, visible material elements that are considered by society as expressions of success. The intrinsic criteria, on the other hand, are more personal and related to aspects of the self, such as a stimulating cultural life, a serene spiritual life, emotional and mental stability, psychological health, the quality of relationships with family members, and so on. Most of the VSEs interviewed for this research scored between 8 and 10 on the vector. This finding leads us to note an interesting difference between the entrepreneurs studied for previous research (Filion, 1990b; 1998c) and the VSEs studied for this research. In the former case, the key

Figure 17.1   Success vector, self-employed

words would be innovation, vision, and growth, while in the latter case they would be balanced lifestyle and personal ecology.

An example of voluntary self-employment
Peter grew up in a family where almost everyone had a business activity. He had considered going into business when he graduated from college in graphic arts, but decided to acquire some experience first. He worked for four years at different production jobs in a small print business, and then in sales, three years for a medium-sized print business and four years for a multinational. He attended evening classes and seminars on sales and the technical aspects of printing. After 10 years, with a good background in the field, he launched his own printing business. He was 28 years old. He bought a house that was well located for access to transport infrastructures. He had accumulated savings, and was properly prepared financially. He had identified some attractive market segments and potential customers. One year, in June, he resigned from his job. Instead of taking a month's vacation in July, he took a week and used the rest of the time to prepare for full-time operations at the beginning of August. His family was equally enthusiastic and motivated by Peter's career choice. He knew the field and had a good strategy, but the first year was nevertheless difficult. After two years he was earning more than his former salary, even though he had been among the best salesmen in his division. He is very optimistic about the future.

Differences between ISEs and VSEs
In this section we present some general observations on the subjects from our sample, before going on to discuss some more fundamental differences between ISEs and VSEs.

The best growth rates and profitability tended to be reported by VSEs who had prepared well (for between three and five years) before going into business and who had good technical abilities. They also listened to their customers and had set boundaries on their field of competence. They did not hesitate to refer work outside their competence to other people. Generally speaking, they were between 35 and 55 years of age.

Subjects who only just managed to survive financially from their business activities were dynamic, but were either beginning or ending their careers. Those beginning their careers had tended to launch new services. For example, one of our subjects in this type was a tourism consultant, while another did page layouts on a computer, and a third was a freelance journalist in a new sector. They were all under 30 years of age, and still learning their trade. Learning was acquired in two areas: understanding market needs in their field, and technical mastery.

As might be expected, more ISEs than VSEs found themselves in situations of insecurity. One ISE in his fifties had suffered a burnout after a bad business experience with partners. He was unable to find a job and tried his hand at consulting, without success. Another was a former prison inmate and motorcycle gang member who had trained as an electrician and was trying, at 48 years of age, to make a new start in life. He lived in a densely populated area of Montreal, in a small room in the second-floor apartment home of one of his daughters, her husband and their child. He had set up a tiny workshop in the corner of his bedroom.

Yet another ISE had preserved the somewhat inflexible attitude of a unionized employee in the corporate sector, and would not do anything over and above her basic work unless the customer paid overtime. It was two years before she would agree to revise or make minor corrections to her work without charging the customer for overtime. For the past 20 years she had been used to billing her employer for all overtime. Once self-employed, she lost several good customers before finally realizing that, in her new context, the customer is always right. The customer expects to receive the service requested at the price agreed, and feels entitled to ask for minor changes or corrections without having to pay extra. This particular person will certainly need a few more years to acquire the flexibility that will allow her to operate her business successfully, despite the fact that she is highly competent in the technical aspects of her work.

Table 17.1 lists some of the fundamental differences between ISEs and VSEs. VSEs want to work for themselves because they see work as just one of several personal growth elements. They seem to be focused more on self-fulfilment than on possessions. Their emphasis is on 'being' rather than on 'having'. ISEs, on the other hand, consider their work activity as something they have to do to earn a living. For them, it does not seem to be a matter of 'being' or of 'having', but rather of 'doing'. Their activities do not seem to be a source of personal growth.

The culture of self-fulfilment among VSEs suggests that they have a need for independence similar to that observed in entrepreneurs. They want to be their own boss. However the reasons underlying this need differ considerably from those of entrepreneurs. The VSEs select a sector and a business

Table 17.1   Self-employment: differences between voluntary and involuntary self-employed

Voluntary	Involuntary
Emphasis on 'being'	Emphasis on 'doing'
Need for independence	Need for affiliation
Individualist	Sociable
Entrepreneurial culture	Functional culture
Need for achievement	Need to survive
Lifestyle: personal ecology	Lifestyle: regularity
Expertise related to the sector	Expertise not always related to the sector
Systemic thinking	Linear thinking
Flexible, accepts compromise	Rigid, not keen on compromise
Need for freedom	Need for support

activity not only to earn a living, but also to grow as people. They think they can do this best if they control their working environment. For example, they can select the things they do, succeed better without organizational constraints, and grow and learn by focusing on the subjects of most interest to them. The ISEs, on the other hand, exhibit a high need for affiliation. They find it less stressful to work with other people, and as far as possible to work within a framework defined by someone else. Most would make excellent partners for VSEs, since they seem to perform well in a supporting role.

VSEs enjoy working alone. They tend to organize their human contact in the form of sports and leisure activities or volunteer work. In contrast, ISEs enjoy being around people. They seem to suffer more easily from loneliness and seek the company of others both in their work and in their leisure activities.

An interesting observation to emerge from the research is that all the successful self-employed in the sample had someone in their entourage who was also in business for themselves. In some cases this was a spouse, and in others a close relative. Not only did these people serve as models, but they were also a source of discussion and learning, helping to create a business culture. In contrast, none of the self-employed in financial difficulty – they were all ISEs – had a business model in their entourage. Moreover they seemed to receive less support from their spouses, and came from environments where people felt they had no control over what happened. Entrepreneurial models were more common among VSEs. In fact many of the VSEs in our sample would have made excellent entrepreneurs if they had so wished. They often had a remarkable understanding of how their sectors worked, and of the niches and opportunities available to them. They understood what was involved in an entrepreneurial mindset and entrepreneurial action. They were often perfectionists and worked hard on quality. They were perhaps less well-adjusted in interpersonal relationships than entrepreneurs, and may have found it difficult to motivate themselves to influence the behaviour of people around them. The ISEs, however, had very few entrepreneurial models in their environment, and their choice of spouses and friends often reflected this. Their culture was a 'functional' one, where they perceived themselves as cogs in some kind of machine, but not as the motor or the driver. Their attitude can be summed up as follows: tell me what to do and I'll try to do it as well as I can.

The VSEs saw themselves as part of an evolving process within which they could progress, grow and achieve self-fulfilment. Their choice of business activity was one factor among many that allowed them to develop in the direction they wanted. The ISEs, on the other hand, had a more static image of themselves. They often had a strong personal interest in a leisure or sporting activity, but did not appear to have such a strong need for achievement and personal growth as the VSEs in our sample. They simply wanted a business activity that would enable them to earn a living.

The self-perception of the VSEs focused on concepts such as personal balance, and they were well aware that they needed elements outside their work to support their progress in different spheres of their lives. In choosing their activities, they considered factors such as family, relatives, physical and mental exercise, politics and community involvement. The result was a form of personal, self-constructed ecology within which they sought a state of equilibrium for themselves and their families. The ISEs perceived their well-being within a structured and regular framework of work and leisure activities. They looked for forms of work and employment that involved as little change as possible. Differences as well as similarities can be seen here, as both types appear to seek implicit stability and they are not focused on the acquisition of wealth or status. In almost half the cases, this need for a personal ecology among VSEs was a reflex reaction to the fact that, as children, they had missed out on the presence of parents who were professional super-achievers.

When people take the time to prepare themselves before going into business, they usually analyse the sector in order to identify a niche, and subsequently launch a business to occupy that niche. This was the path chosen by most of the VSEs interviewed for this research. They sometimes spent many years methodically studying the sector in which they worked before deciding on the niche they would occupy. The ISEs tended to take a variety of different routes, but can nevertheless be classified under two main headings: those who went into business in a sector they knew because they had relevant expertise, without knowing if a niche existed in that sector, and those who grasped a business opportunity in a sector they did not know well because they thought they could make a living from it. They tended to make more use of mass advertising, while the VSEs relied more on personal contacts and achieved much better results.

The VSEs were able to establish guiding principles for their decisions. They were also able to set boundaries on their activities and learn from what they did. Their desire to learn led them to forge contacts that helped them understand how and why certain things occurred. The ISEs, however, saw their business activities as temporary, even though they might cover a period of several years. They seemed less interested in learning and often did not have a good understanding of the sector as a whole. They appeared to operate simply by doing one task after another, without trying to grasp where they were situated in the general scheme of things and without establishing learning links between what they did and what was happening in their sector.

The VSEs were skilled in their professional activity and in business practice. They had learned that they had to be flexible if they wanted to stay in business. They were particularly flexible in their relations with customers, where they often demonstrated remarkable levels of creativity and adaptability in terms of both the type of service provided and the price charged. They excelled at tailoring their service to the customer's needs. Many saw high customer expectations as a personal challenge, and were motivated by it. Some of the VSEs interviewed had left jobs in organizations because they were the best at what they did, and lacked a challenge to provide motivation. Most were more concerned about their customers' sales than about their own, and were all the more successful because of this. The ISEs, on the other hand, learned to provide a service and tried to do so in as repetitive and regular a way as possible. They usually found it difficult to build a customer base, partly because they did not adjust easily to their customers' individual needs – a capital sin in the service sector. ISEs were usually inflexible when it came to prices and fees, which meant that they lost a lot of good business opportunities. Some would make excellent subcontractors in areas where they could perform repetitive tasks.

The need for freedom was very high among VSEs. Some were ready to compromise, especially by spending more time on their work than they would if they had a regular job, in order to preserve that freedom. The ISEs, however, needed support. Paradoxically, it was the VSEs in our sample that seemed to receive more support from their immediate families, which had a more entrepreneurial mindset than the ISEs' families. The ISEs needed a lot of support, but did not always know what kind, or how or where to find it.

Entrepreneurship and self-employment
It is no easier to situate self-employment within the broader framework of entrepreneurship than it is to situate small business or family business. First, there is very little consensus in the field of entrepreneurship, which could more accurately be described as a field of study in progress rather than as an established discipline (Filion, 1998a; 1998b). Nevertheless, it is possible to make some general comparisons between entrepreneurs and the self-employed. We will also address some of the contributions that a typology of the kind suggested here could make to the field of entrepreneurship. As our research was exploratory in nature, the comments that follow also constitute suggestions for future study.

Entrepreneurs and the self-employed
As there is no general consensus as to what an entrepreneur actually is, we have selected only five points of comparison (Table 17.2) based on some of the elements commonly found in the literature on entrepreneurship and on which a certain number of researchers appear to agree (Filion, 1998a; 1998b). All five are related essentially to what entrepreneurs do rather than to aspects of self-fulfilment. For each of these points, we have established equivalencies from an analysis of the root definitions and activity systems of the self-employed (mainly VSEs) studied in this research.

Table 17.2   Entrepreneurs and self-employed: some comparisons

Entrepreneurs	Self-employed
Innovation	Niche
Wealth creation	Added value
Vision of the enterprise	Personal ecology
Growth	Stability
Detection of opportunities	Challenges

Schumpeter associated entrepreneurs with innovation. The degree of innovation may vary, but entrepreneurs are generally considered to be people who contribute something new. However, the self-employed seem more concerned with identifying a niche than with innovation. Their niche often seems to be temporal, in that companies use them because they offer a quality service adapted to the customer's requirements, at a competitive price and within a time frame that the organization's own personnel cannot match. Some aspects of the service may involve differentiation, but the level of innovation, even among those who believe they have developed a new service, is not as obvious, as is the case in the manufacturing sector, where new products sometimes differ markedly from existing products. For example, a painter interviewed for the research had become skilled at painting special effects on walls. Others were also able to do this, but it nevertheless constituted a competitive advantage that allowed the painter in question to be classified as one of the best in his sector. It is therefore more relevant to associate the self-employed with a niche rather than with innovation, in that they appear to seek unfulfilled needs in a given market segment for services that they are able to provide. This niche appears increasingly to be in the 'time' factor; the self-employed offer a service of equivalent quality but in a shorter time than would be possible in the subcontracting organization.

Some authors have associated entrepreneurs with wealth creation. Say (1996) was probably the first, in the late 1700s, to draw a distinction between the profits of capitalists and those of entrepreneurs. Clearly, however, the self-employed contribute on a much more limited scale in this respect. A more accurate term would perhaps be 'added value', rather than 'wealth', since the organizations and individuals who purchase the services of the self-employed appear to obtain added value in terms of time, money and/or quality.

Entrepreneurs develop visions of the place they would like their products to occupy on the market and of the type of organization they need to achieve this. The vision becomes an anchor point to which the entrepreneurs refer implicitly or explicitly when making decisions and organizing their activity systems. The self-employed, on the other hand, appear to refer to a set of values that allows them to achieve sustained personal growth within a balanced context where the professional activity is not as predominant as is usually the case with entrepreneurs. For example, the VSEs interviewed for this research viewed their spouses and families as important elements in their choice of professional activities. A typical comment was this: 'My father is an entrepreneur who made a lot of money, and was considered successful by society. But I never knew him when I was a child. I set time aside for my family and my children. They are priorities for me.' The term 'personal ecology' seems appropriate to describe the paths chosen by the self-employed and their somewhat smoother progression along those paths.

Entrepreneurs seek innovation and its direct derivative, growth. The self-employed, on the other hand, seek niches in which they can achieve personal fulfilment while earning a living. They want to do something interesting. Personal stability seems to go hand-in-hand with professional stability. Most of the self-employed interviewed were not willing to work as intensely or for such long hours as entrepreneurs, just to obtain growth. Some grow anyway, but elect to do so by means of subcontracting rather than by hiring staff. They design activity systems that allow them to remain free, and do not seem willing to abandon their freedom in exchange for growth.

Entrepreneurs seek business opportunities. The intensity with which they do this varies from year to year, but it is a concern for them. The self-employed, and especially the VSEs, seem to be motivated by challenge – in other words, by obstacles in their field that others have not managed to overcome.

Thus, for many entrepreneurs, the enterprise is an important aspect of their lives, while for the self-employed their business activity is one element among others in their quest for personal growth and fulfilment.

VSEs, ISEs and entrepreneurial typologies

There are many typologies in the field of entrepreneurship (Filion, 1998a). Some of the most frequently cited examples are listed below. Chicha and Julien (1979) classified small businesses into three types: traditional, entrepreneurial and administrative. Collins and Moore (1970) drew a distinction between the 'administrative entrepreneur' and the 'independent entrepreneur'. Glueck (1977) distinguished between three types of self-employed: the entrepreneur, the small business owner–manager and the family business leader. Julien and Marchesnay (1987; 1996) considered the action logic and proposed two types of owner–managers: the PIG type (perpetuation, independence, growth) and the GAP type (growth, autonomy, perpetuation). Lafuente and Salas (1989) established a typology of new entrepreneurs creating businesses in Spain, based on entrepreneurial aspirations and composed of four types: craftsman, risk-oriented, family-oriented and managerial. Laufer (1974) suggested four types of entrepreneur: the manager or innovator, the growth-oriented owner–entrepreneur, the entrepreneur who refuses growth but seeks efficiency, and the craftsman entrepreneur. Smith (1967) identified two types of entrepreneurs: the craftsman and the opportunist or business entrepreneur. He considered the technological entrepreneur to be in a separate type. Smith and Miner (1983) then considered the effects of each type on the type of business that would result. Vesper (1990) identified at least eight types of entrepreneurs: (1) solo self-employed individuals, (2) deal-to-dealers, (3) team builders, (4) independent innovators, (5) pattern multipliers, (6) economy-of-scale exploiters, (7) capital aggregators, and (8) acquirers. Woo *et al.* (1991) addressed and discussed the impact of criteria on the creation of entrepreneurial typologies.

Only one author (Dana, 1997) has looked at the underlying value systems of entrepreneurial actors to explain the roots of their decision to choose entrepreneurship. The research in question is presented as the result of an interdisciplinary literature review, and proposes two types: 'Those from entrepreneurial cultures may be predisposed to self-employment by virtue of cultural conditioning resulting in pro-enterprise values. This results in what has been illustrated as orthodox entrepreneurship . . . When one's reaction to circumstance is to become self-employed, the result may be described as a reactionary enterprise. Unlike orthodox entrepreneurship, this is reactive self-employment' (Dana, 1997). Dana's findings bear some relation to the voluntary/involuntary typology suggested in our research.

What typologies do is provide a basis for understanding the anchor points, value systems and thinking of given groups, along with guidelines for understanding the overall behavioural consistency of the players. None of the typologies studied drew a clear distinction between voluntary and involuntary participants, in any entrepreneurial category. However our research suggests, at least for the self-employed, that the distinction may well be useful when helping prepare future players to launch and manage their business activities.

Comments and discussion
The goal of this research was to understand the self-employment phenomenon. The VSE/ISE distinction helps in understanding the business behaviour of the two groups, and in situating them within the broader framework of entrepreneurship. There have always been people who have gone into business because they were forced to do so, but the numbers of involuntary self-employed appear to have grown significantly over the last decade, at least in Canada. The same trend may well be seen in other entrepreneurial categories in the years to come.

There are a number of reasons for the growth in self-employment. Teleworking appears to have been a factor, as does the increase in the number of better-educated people in our societies. Subcontracting, a significant source of work for the self-employed, provides some companies with much greater flexibility and allows them to cope with fluctuating activity cycles. In some cases, subcontracting actually appears to be a condition for survival.

A further reason for the popularity of self-employment may well be the loss of confidence of many employees in their organizations following the massive layoffs of recent years. Magazines often report stories of people in their forties and fifties who have been laid off by their employers and replaced by someone younger (Munk, 1999). Many of these people had planned long-term careers, but were pressured into early retirement. Some early retirees become self-employed, while many of the others appear to develop a self-preservation reflex after witnessing the individual dramas caused by layoffs. They believe the best way of stabilizing their career is to have more control over their own job security by creating their own business activities. In the medium-term, growing numbers of people, especially the most competent, may well come to the conclusion that their best chance of achieving their lifetime and career goals is to go into business for themselves instead of placing their fate in the hands of an impersonal organization. Many graduates are now considering this radically different approach to career development.

For an entrepreneurship researcher who has done a great deal of work in the field over the last few decades, the strong trend towards fragmentation in the organization of work is very clear. The first half of the 20th century was dominated by large corporations. The 1970s and 1980s saw the arrival of massive numbers of small businesses, which were responsible for creating the vast majority of new jobs. Will the 1990s and 2000s see the creation of even smaller units, and go on to become the era of the self-employed and the micro enterprise?

The number of people living alone is increasing, along with the number of single-parent families and the number of people working alone. As we have seen, this trend appears to reflect rapid changes in values, themselves resulting from the speed of technological change in our societies. The paradigms of the humanities do not appear to be keeping up with progress in the physical sciences. Learning (L) must be greater than change (C) $(L > C)$ if individuals, organizations and societies are to be able to keep up with the rate of change in their environment.

Learning and behaviour seem to adjust more slowly at the organizational level than at the individual level. This explains in part why organizations find it so difficult to keep up. As long as the rate of technological change is faster than the rate of organizational learning and behavioural adjustment, the re-engineering and restructuring process is likely to continue, producing smaller and more flexible labour units both inside and outside organizations. In such a context, many organizations may have to subcontract if they are to remain competitive. There may therefore be a correlation between the speed of change and the growth of self-employment in a society.

This factor partly explains the trend towards smaller working units. However, alongside this, a large proportion of the population, especially university graduates, also seem to be engaged in a profound transformation of values. For a growing percentage of these people, a balanced lifestyle now seems to be more important than any other aspect. We are therefore moving towards separate, personalized value systems with the common denominator of self-fulfilment in a working context as free as possible from the constraints that reduce quality of life. In the self-employment system, what matters is self-fulfilment, on one's own terms and according to one's own criteria.

The major problem currently facing a growing number of people who want (VSE) or are forced (ISE) to become self-employed is the question of acquiring experience. It seems difficult for some young people to find the jobs that will provide them with the type of experience they need to do what they want in life. To help them it would be useful to rethink the concept of school and learning, and to give priority to on-the-job learning of the type that existed traditionally in the craft sectors. Indeed one of the main lessons to be drawn from this research concerns the preparation, education and training systems required by people considering self-employment. Different educational paths are needed for VSEs and ISEs. More resources will have to be invested in the ISEs, for awareness raising and self-assessment among other things, and the ISEs will have to be introduced to self-employment more gradually than the VSEs, since they have more ground to make up and have fewer business models to help them become familiar with business practice.

Generally speaking, VSEs stay in business in their chosen sectors, while ISEs view self-employment as a phase on the way to finding another job. This difference in attitudes is also likely to affect many aspects of the self-employment activity, from the type of client sought (since clients may be perceived as potential employers by ISEs) to the type of training taken. For many ISEs, the best solution may be to find a partner who will fulfil their affiliation needs. The partnership path will also allow younger ISEs to acquire the learning they need to reintegrate the labour market.

Some of the confusion that exists in entrepreneurship may well be due to the fact that the two types identified in this research for the self-employed are in fact present in other entrepreneurial categories too, but to a much greater extent than we may think. It would therefore be interesting, in future research, to explore this in greater depth, using both larger and smaller samples. We also need to enhance our knowledge of the self-employed, clarify the differences between VSEs and ISEs, understand the logic of their choices, and identify the start-up and organizational difficulties faced by each group. At the same time, it is important to situate them with respect to other entrepreneurial actors. In addition to that, models of international entrepreneurship may well have to take the self-employed dimension into account.

References

Bates, T. (1995), 'Self-employment entry across industry groups', *Journal of Business Venturing*, 10, 143–56.

Bly, Robert W. and Gary Blake (1986), *Out on Your Own*, New York: Wiley.

Bolyle, E. (1993), 'The rise of the reluctant entrepreneurs', *International Small Business Journal*, 12 (2), 63–9.

Brennan, G. (1996), *Successfully Self-Employed*, New York: Upstart.

Brodie, S. and J. Stanworth (1998), 'Independent contractors in direct selling: Self-employed but missing from official records', *International Small Business Journal*, 16 (3), 95–101.

Checkland, Peter B. (1981), *Systems Thinking, Systems Practice*, Chichester: Wiley.

Checkland, Peter and Jim Scholes (1990), *Soft Systems Methodology in Action*, Chichester: Wiley.

Chicha, Joseph and Pierre-André Julien (1979), *Les stratégies des P.M.E. et leur adaptation au changement*, Département d'administration et d'économique, Université du Québec à Trois-Rivières, Canada.

Collins, Orvis F. and David G. Moore (1970), *The Organisation Makers: A Behavioral Study of Independent Entrepreneurs*, New York: Appleton-Century-Crofts (Meredith Corp.).

Dana, Léo Paul (1997), 'The origins of self-employment in ethno-cultural communities: Distinguishing between orthodox entrepreneurship and reactionary enterprise', *Canadian Journal of Administrative Science*, 14 (1), 52–68.

Eyler, David R. (1990), *Starting and Operating a Home-Based Business*, New York: Wiley.

Filion, L.J. (1990a), 'Free Trade: The Need for a Definition of Small Business', *Journal of Small Business and Entrepreneurship*, 7 (2), 33–46.

Filion, Louis Jacques (1990b), 'Vision and Relations: Elements for an Entrepreneurial Meta-model', Tenth Annual Babson Entrepreneurship Research Conference, Babson College, MA, 4–6 April, in Neil C. Churchill *et al.* (eds), *Frontiers of Entrepreneurship Research*, pp. 57–71.

Filion, Louis Jacques (1996a), 'A Marketing approach for Micro-Enterprises', UIC/AMA Research Symposium on Marketing and Entrepreneurship, Stockholm, Sweden, 14–15 June, vol. 2, pp. 150–66, reprinted in Gerald E. Hills, Joseph J. Giglierano and Claes M. Hultman (eds) (1997), *Research at the Marketing/Entrepreneurship Interface*, Chicago: The University of Illinois at Chicago, pp. 127–44.

Filion, Louis Jacques (1996b), 'Travail autonome: des volontaires et des involontaires', 13th Annual Conference, Canadian Council for Small Business and Entrepreneurship, Montreal, in Louis Jacques Filion and Dina Lavoie (eds), *Support Systems for Entrepreneurial Societies*, pp. 189–204.

Filion, Louis Jacques (1996c), 'Un système marketing pour le travail autonome : développer des réseaux pairs et complémentaires', 13th Annual Conference, CCSBE/CCPME, Montreal, in Louis Jacques Filion and Dina Lavoie (eds), *Support Systems for Entrepreneurial Societies*, proceedings, vol.1, pp. 205–18.

Filion, Louis Jacques (1998a), 'Entrepreneurship: Entrepreneurs and Small Business Owner–managers', in Pierre-André Julien (ed.) (1998), *The State of the Art in Small Business and Entrepreneurship*, Aldershot: Avebury, pp. 117–49, 428–40.

Filion, L.J. (1998b), 'From Entrepreneurship to Entreprenology: The Emergence of a New Discipline', *Journal of Enterprising Culture*, 6 (1), 1–23.

Filion, Louis Jacques (1998c), 'Two Types of Entrepreneurs: The Operator and the Visionary – Consequences for Education', *Rencontres de St-Gall 1998* (Sept.), in Hans J. Pleitner (ed.), *Renaissance of SMEs in a globalized economy*, pp. 261–70. Swiss Research Institute of Small Business and Entrepreneurship at the University of St.Gallen.

Filion, Louis Jacques (1999), 'Empirical Systems Modelling Methodology: Applications to Entrepreneurial Actors', in John A. Wagner (ed.) (1999), *Advances in Qualitative Organisation Research*, vol.2, Greenwich, CT: JAI Press, pp. 201–20.

Filion, L.J. (2000), 'Travail autonome: des volontaires et des involontaires. Vers de nouvelles formes de pratiques entrepreneuriales', *Gestion, Revue internationale de gestion*, 24 (4), 48–56.

Fisher, Lionel L. (1995), *On Your Own*, Englewood Cliffs, NJ: Prentice-Hall.

Gartner, W.B. (1990), 'What are we talking about when we talk about entrepreneurship?', *Journal of Business Venturing*, 5, 15–29.

Glueck, William F. (1977), *Management*, Hinsdale, IL: The Dryden Press.

Golzen, Godfrey (1991), *The Daily Telegraph Guide to Self-Employment: Working for Yourself*, London: Kogan Page.

Gray, Douglas.A. and Diana L Gray (1994), *Home Inc.: The Canadian Home-Based Business Guide*, Toronto: McGraw-Hill Ryerson.

Hawkins, B. and G. Bage (1990), *Think Up A Business*, London: Rosters.

Hisrich, Robert D. and Michael P. Peters (1992), *On Your Own: How to Start, Develop and Manage a New Business*, Homewood, IL: Irwin.

ILO (1990), *The Promotion of Self-Employment*, International Labour Conference, 77th Session, Geneva: ILO.

Julien, Pierre-André and Michel Marchesnay (1987), *La petite entreprise*, Paris: Vuibert.

Julien, Pierre-André and Michel Marchesnay (1996), *L'entrepreneuriat*, Paris: Economica.

Kishel, Gregory and Patricia Kishel (1991), *Start, Run and Profit From Your Own Home-Based Business*, New York: Wiley.

Lafuente, A. and V. Salas (1989), 'Types of Entrepreneurs and Firms: the Case of New Spanish Firms', *Strategic Management Journal*, 10, 17–30.

Laufer, J. C. (1974), 'Comment on devient entrepreneur', *Revue française de gestion*, 2, 18–29.

Leighton, P. and A. Felstead (1992), *The New Entrepreneurs: Self-Employment and Small Business in Europe*, London: Kogan Page.

Meredith, G.G. (1993), 'Self-employment Survival Strategies in a Recessionary Business Environment', paper presented at the 38th ICSB Conference, 20–23 June.

Munk, N. (1999), 'Finished at Forty', *Fortune*, 139 (2), 50–66.

OECD (1996), *Perspectives de l'emploi*, Paris: OECD.

Orser, Barbara and Mary Foster (1992), *Home Enterprise. Canadians and Home Based Work*, Ottawa, Government of Canada.

Rice, Frederick H. (1990), *Starting a Home-Based Business*, Kansas: Kansas State University.

Roy, Gilles (1998), 'Diagnostic sur le travail autonome: Causes, motivations, problèmes', Maclean Hunter Entrepreneurship Chair, HEC Montreal, Working Paper 98–08.

Say, Jean-Baptiste (1996), *Cours d'économie politique et autres essais*, Paris: Flammarion.

Sheedy, Edna (1990), *Start and Run a Profitable Home-Based Business*, Vancouver: Self-Counsel Press.

Silvestri, G.T. (1991), 'Who Are the Self-Employed? Employment Profiles and Recent Trends', *Occupational Outlook Quarterly*, 35(1), 26–36.

Small Business Quarterly (1999), *Entrepreneurship and Small Business Office*, Ottawa: Industry Canada.

Smith, N.R. (1967), *The Entrepreneur and His Firm: The Relationship between Type of Man and Type of Company*, Bureau of Business Research, East Lansing, Michigan: Michigan State University Press.

Smith, N.R. and J.B. Miner (1983), 'Type of Entrepreneur, Type of Firm, and Managerial Motivation: Implications for Organisational Life Cycle Theory', *Strategic Management Journal*, 4, 325–40.

Statistique Canada (1999), *Report on Self Employment*, Ottawa: Statistique Canada.

Verstraete, T.and L.J. Filion (2001), 'Entrepreneurship: An International Perspective. Letter from the Guest Editors', *International Management*, 6 (1), XV–XIX.

Vesper, Karl H. (1990), *New Venture Strategies*, Englewood Cliffs, NJ: Prentice-Hall.

Vodopivec, M. (1998), 'Turning the unemployed into entrepreneurs: An evaluation of a self-employment program in a transitional economy', *Journal of Developmental Entrepreneurship*, 3 (1), 71–96.

Woo, C. Y., A. C. Cooper and W.C. Dunkelberg (1991), 'The Development and Interpretation of Entrepreneurial Typologies', *Journal of Business Venturing*, 6, 93–114.

Wright, Richard W. (ed.) (1999), *International Entrepreneurship: Globalization for Emerging Businesses*, New York: JAI Press.

18 Canadian perspectives of international entrepreneurship
Martine Spence

The Canadian economy is characterized by its international dependence.* With 30 million inhabitants, the domestic market is limited and Canada relies on trade to fuel employment and growth more than almost any other industrialized country. The figures speak for themselves. Exports of goods and services rose to 468 billion dollars in 2001, or approximately 43 per cent of GDP (compared to an average 17 per cent for G7 countries); 167 000 new jobs were created in the same year, of which a good number are related to international trade. Estimates are that one job in three is tied to international trade. One other notable point to mention is that more than 70 per cent of Canadian exporters are SMEs with annual sales under one million dollars (*www.dfait-maeci.gc.ca*).

The federal government encourages entrepreneurs to expand internationally through the establishment of a large number of services designed to assist SMEs in their export efforts, such as numerous sources of information and export advice, market and sector studies and the services of commercial attachés around the world. The government facilitates services access to entrepreneurs through the creation, in 1997, of a single point of reference: Team Canada Inc (TCI).

TCI is a network of federal departments and agencies, uniting its efforts with those of the regional trade networks established in each province and territory to support the growth of exporters. Its purpose is to rationalize business services. Any business can access the information provided through TCI via the web site (*www.exportsource.gc.ca*) or a special toll-free number.

Whether the entrepreneur is a potential, new or experienced exporter, TCI will be able to respond to its needs and provide guidance, including information on training for international expansion. An executive from a firm wishing to enter the export market, or a professional from a currently exporting firm who wants to develop his knowledge of international trade, will be pointed directly to the appropriate programme.

A question academics have been debating for some time, though, is

* The author would like to kindly thank Caroline Genet for her assistance.

whether entrepreneurs are 'born' or 'made'. Dana (2001) argues that the Schumpeterian entrepreneur who creates an innovation is more likely to be born, while the Kirznerian entrepreneur who simply identifies an opportunity can be taught. A common denominator between these two broad classifications of entrepreneurs is that the innovation, whether created or identified, is exploited for profit.

A substantial body of research suggests that entrepreneurs have personality traits which are not shared by others in society. As a consequence, training has to be tailored to the needs of entrepreneurs. By applying learning style theory to entrepreneurs' characteristics, Ulrich and Cole (1987) demonstrated that entrepreneurs learn through 'active experimentation' to change their skills and attitudes as well as their understanding. Hence Lessem (1986) suggests that the traditional 'apprenticeship' system providing 'a blend of action and learning that results in emotional, mental and physical change' (p. 12) with the help of a mentor and a coach is a more holistic approach than the modern 'training' system. Apprenticeship combines the simultaneous development of the body, mind and spirit in an iterative way until mastery is gained. On the other hand, training delivers a set of standardized directives which may not be totally applicable to the entrepreneur's present situation, and is therefore lacking in the experiential aspect of the development. A survey identifying the training and development methods most adapted to Quebec entrepreneurs showed the need for both lecture and participation (77%), and favoured trade associations working with educational institutions (57%) (Garnier *et al.*, 1985).

Canadian government initiatives in international entrepreneurship training
International entrepreneurship training programmes in Canada vary from the instructor-led type (FITT) at one end of the spectrum, to the 'apprenticeship' type at the other end (NEXPRO). In between these two extremes, NEBS and EXTUS combine theoretical and some experiential knowledge by sending participants to selected markets and facilitating their interaction with potential business partners.

Forum for international trade training (FITT)
FITT is a national and professional not-for-profit organization founded in 1992 by industry and government[1] to develop and deliver international trade training programmes and services, establish country-wide standards and certification, and generally ensure continuing professional development in the practice of international trade (*www.fitt.ca*). FITT programmes are delivered across Canada through community colleges, universities, private organizations and on line.

Specifically FITT is a central body based in Ottawa with seven full-time staff members. Its role is to create and update courses and workshops, to supply material (essentially manuals) to institutions delivering FITT programmes and to ensure the coordination thereof. FITT also warrants the quality of the instructors teaching the programmes.

FITT confers upon international trade professionals, through its FITT*Skills* programme, the nationally recognized Certified International Trade Professional accreditation (CITP). This programme is aimed at individuals with no prior experience but who want to pursue a career in international trade as well as professionals who wish to increase their expertise. Overall, statistics show that FITT*Skills* is utilized primarily by the latter. Fifty three per cent of the trainees were between the ages of 30 and 49 and 55 per cent had three years or more of international trade experience. For the autumn 2002 session 5000 people registered for the programme. The rapid increase in the number of participants in the programme over the past two years is partly due to the recession driving professionals to augment their qualifications, but also demonstrates the success of the programme.

FITT*Skills* consists of a series of eight modules, each 45 hours long: Global Entrepreneurship, International Marketing, International Trade Finance, International Trade Logistics, International Market Entry and Distribution, International Trade Research, Legal Aspects of International Trade, and International Trade Management. The courses were created and developed by professionals belonging to the network of FITT partners and are delivered by international trade professionals who must meet rigorous selection criteria. Different study patterns are available, the more common one being three hours of classroom instruction per week over a 15-week period. Distance learning, using the Internet, is developing as well: over 100 students chose e-learning for the 2002 session. The cost per FITT*Skills* module varies by institution, ranging between $350 and $550 per module.

According to a study sponsored by Human Resources Development Canada and undertaken in April 2002, of 267 students in the FITT*Skills* programme the level of satisfaction was 79 per cent, and 77 per cent of the participants confirmed that FITT*Skills* helps Canadian firms to be more internationally competitive.

In addition to FITT*Skills*, FITT has developed other programmes. *Ag*FITT is an integrated series of workshops in international trade based on the practical aspects of agrofood exports, aimed at the SMEs in this sector. For the moment, as this programme has been delivered only four times, its impact is difficult to assess. In the same vein, FITT*Services* was recently launched to help firms develop export plans through a series of workshops pulling together both theory and practice. The training covers all aspects of exporting services and helps to prepare a business plan suitable for submission to a banker's scrutiny, for either a whole target country or a specific segment in a selected country.

Finally FITT has created and developed, through its network of community colleges and universities, its *Going Global* workshop series. The objective of this series is to help firms, individuals wanting to work in the international trade sector and suppliers of services make the decision of whether or not to enter export markets. The workshops also give them an overview of the advantages and challenges that exporting presents, and guide them through the required steps to expand across borders. For this FITT has allied itself with Team Canada Inc to develop and offer five introductory workshops of three hours each on the following subjects: International Trade, Market Research, International Marketing, International Finance, and International Trade Logistics & Distribution.

Programmes for US-focused Canadian exporters
The United States is, by far, the biggest export target market for Canadian exporters, representing, in 2001, more than 85 per cent of all Canadian exports. Over and above the simple fact of geographic proximity, the North American Free Trade Agreement (NAFTA) has opened the door to significant trading opportunities in the USA and Mexico. As a result, specific programmes have been in place since 1984, such as NEBS (New Exporters to Border States), EXTUS (Exporters to the United States) and Reverse NEBS. Coordinated at the national level by the Department of Foreign Affairs and International Trade, these programmes are organized in each province by the International Trade Centres (*www.strategis.ic.gc.ca*).

These programmes are developed in partnership with the Canadian Consulates in the United States, in particular those in Buffalo and Detroit (*www.infoexport.gc.ca*). They consist of training sessions held in the consulates, often organized in parallel with trade shows, and with the objective of providing participants with deeper insights into a specific commercial sector. NEBS and EXTUS missions vary in size and content, depending upon the area in which they are held (that is, which province or consulate organizes the event) and the industrial sectors which are of interest to the participants.

Each NEBS or EXTUS mission will, in general, last from one to three days and will include an overview of the export process and the supporting programmes and services offered in Canada. At a Consulate General in the USA, mission participants will benefit from activities such as information sessions on border formalities, presentations from American manufacturers' representatives, sales agents and American buyers and distributors, a visit to a trade show of interests to the participants, visits to local wholesalers or retailers, and so on. Cost to the firm of participating in a NEBS or EXTUS mission is in the order of $160 per person, plus travel and subsistence.

Even if NEBS and EXTUS closely match entrepreneurs' needs through their concrete, practical and dynamic structure and by facilitating the exploration and nurturing of potential trade relationships, they do require a relatively important investment in time (approximately an entire week once travel time has been included). For this reason, the vast majority of firms turn to the Reverse NEBS programme. Reverse NEBS is intended for Canadian firms which do not yet export to the United States. It consists of one-day seminars led in Canada by one or several resources persons from the United States. These seminars are generally based upon a particular aspect of trade or a specific sector.

For the financial year 2001–2, 4131 individuals participated in these programmes; 158 chose NEBS, 417 selected EXTUS and the remainder, 3556, Reverse NEBS. Similar programmes also exist for the European and South American markets.

New exporters training and counselling program (NEXPRO)
The New Exporters Training and Counselling Program (NEXPRO) was developed by the Consulting Group of the Business Development Bank of Canada (BDC) in Quebec to respond to the strong demand from local entrepreneurs who wanted to enter the export market (*www.bdc.ca*). This programme, still being piloted by the BDC, was extended in 1993 to all provinces in Canada and support material (essentially course manuals) was developed by FITT.

The distinguishing aspect and the great strength of this programme is the combination of practical group workshops and personalized one-to-one consulting services utilized to coach senior executives. The programme extends over an entire year,[2] and comprises 10 four-hour workshops and 40 hours of consulting. The workshops take place monthly and gather 20 to 25 selected firms, chosen according to specific criteria in order to provide a homogeneous group in terms of sector of activity and level of export experience. These workshops address a specific export-related theme, such as marketing, law or finance, and are led by industry experts from Canada and/or abroad. In addition to the learning experience, the workshops present an opportunity for participating entrepreneurs to develop their networks. Between each group meeting, a BDC consultant visits the firm to verify that the entrepreneur has assimilated the concepts presented at the workshop and has put them into practice within his own company. The programme can also include a visit to the nearest American embassy, where the entrepreneurs meet embassy representatives who can influence the success of their projects. These visits generally include participation in a local trade show or other event of interest to the participants.

Cost to the firm for the NEXPRO programme is $6000, subsidized up to $CAD3000 in Quebec (the subsidy is fully allocated to the company as the BDC Consulting Group takes care of all administrative formalities). In terms of outcome, the clearly stated objective of NEXPRO is that the firm has a fully completed export plan at the end of the programme. In fact, even in the absence of precise statistics, anecdotal evidence from BDC managers suggests that one-third of firms participating in NEXPRO export before the 12-month training–consulting programme has finished, another third develop at the pace of the programme, ending up with a fully-fledged export plan at the end of the year, while the remaining third, for a variety of internal or external reasons, are advised not to proceed with an export programme at the present time.

In terms of results, NEXPRO advertises itself as being particularly profitable and efficient for firms wishing to export, as it includes the sharing of experience with other group members, one-to-one consulting and experiential learning in the target market. Nevertheless impediments to its expansion are recognized. The requirements of the programme in terms of time commitment can be daunting for the entrepreneur as well as for the organizers. For example, putting together a homogeneous group can be time consuming: representatives of the BDC Consulting Group must meet, on average, 150 firms in a given geographic area in order to come up with 20 or 25 which meet the selection criteria for the group. Despite this, NEXPRO continues to function well 14 years on, especially in Quebec where it is subsidized.

Conclusion

The challenge to training entrepreneurs is to be able to address their pragmatic personality, provide easily implementable solutions and recognize their lack of financial resources and time constraints. Although the programmes offered through the different government agencies are aimed at various segments of entrepreneurs, they have been developed with these concerns in mind.

Firstly the programmes being the initiative of either the Canadian federal government or its agencies, they are partly subsidized and hence more affordable to SMEs. Furthermore networking opportunities with other participants, experts in Canada and in the visited countries and potential business partners could provide tangible and intangible future benefits to participating companies.

Secondly the entrepreneurs' pragmatic personality has been taken into account by providing a variety of settings to enhance learning. In a classroom setting, learning happens through the exchange of practical information and experience between the instructors who are experts in their fields and business owners who can share their own experience with the subject matter. Argumentative discussions and real case studies provide context to the subject matter for the entrepreneurs and lead them to possible answers to their concerns.

In the NEBS, EXTUS and NEXPRO programmes, experiential knowledge is gained from visits to selected markets and participation in trade shows. A study by Reid (1984) reported that 91 per cent of respondents who were exporters agreed on the importance of personal visits to foreign markets for gathering relevant and highly valuable information.

The NEXPRO programme goes one step further in the development of international entrepreneurs by providing personal coaching and guidance over a 12-month period. This programme more closely reproduces the 'apprenticeship' environment by focusing on the development of the individual through an iterative process including the acquisition of practical skills until mastery as well as the provision of emotional support. The longevity of the programme and the number of companies involved in export sales as a result of their participation are evidence of the success of such an approach.

Finally time constraints have been addressed by providing a variety of programmes to suit the needs of individual entrepreneurs. The introduction of Reverse NEBS demonstrates the flexibility of Team Canada Inc in adapting to the entrepreneurs' reality.

This chapter has only focused on the national government's initiatives most readily available to develop Canadian international entrepreneurs. Numerous other public and private provincial and regional initiatives exist, especially in the form of seminars on various technical aspects of international expansion for SMEs and organization of trade shows and trade missions to target sectors and markets.

A new national initiative has recently been developed by Export Development Canada (EDC) with a different flavour (*www.edc.ca*). This initiative, however, will not be developed here because of space constraints. It consists of enhancing the awareness of and the taste for international business among young Canadians. Consequently EDC has partnered Canadian universities to increase its visibility among young people and to encourage students' pursuit of international endeavours through competitions, scholarships, and traineeships. Finally individual initiatives by professors (such as the present author) aim to provide future managers with practical export skills through action projects with exporters.

Notes

1.   FITT's founding private sector partners are Canadian Manufacturers and Exporters, The Canadian Chamber of Commerce, The Canadian Federation of Labour, The Canadian

Association of Importers and Exporters, The Canadian Professional Logistics Institute, The Canadian Professional Sales Association and World Trade Centres Canada. Public sector partners are Human Resources Development Canada, the Department of Foreign Affairs and International Trade and Industry Canada.
2. The process has since been shortened to three months for high-tech enterprises, through the initiative of the province of Ontario, and can be adapted according to specific needs.

References

Business Development Bank of Canada (2002) (*http://www.bdc.ca*), accessed 26 September.

Dana, Léo-Paul (2001), 'The education and training of entrepreneurs in Asia', *Education & Training*, 43 (8), 405–16.

Export Development Canada (2002) (*http://www.edc.ca*), accessed 26 September.

Forum International for Trade Training (2002) (*http://www.fitt.ca/links.asp*), accessed 26 September.

Garnier, B., Y. Gasse and P. Cossette (1985), 'The Training needs of owner/managers of small business : an empirical pilot study in Quebec', *Journal of Small Business*, 2 (2), 30–35.

Industry Canada (2002) (*http://strategis.ic.gc.ca/SSG/ig00006e.html*), accessed 26 September.

Lessem, R. (1986), 'Becoming a Metapreneur', *Journal of General Management*, 11 (4), Summer, pp. 5–21.

Ministry of Foreign Affairs and International Trade Canada (2002), (*http://www.dfait-maeci.gc.ca/trade/intl_bus_dev-en.asp*), accessed 26 September.

Reid, R. (1984), 'Information acquisition and export entry decisions in small firms', *Journal of Business Research*, 12, 141–57.

Team Canada Inc. (2002) (*http://exportsource.ca/index_e.cfm*), accessed 26 September.

Ulrich, T.A. and G.S. Cole (1987), 'Toward more Effective Training of Future Entrepreneurs', *Journal of Small Business Management*, 25 (4), October, 32–9.

19 The case of Canadian computer software firms
Rod B. McNaughton and Peter Brown

The concept of 'clustering' is now central to the design of economic development policies in many countries. The belief is that co-located firms experience externalities that improve their performance, and contribute to their innovativeness and international competitiveness. These benefits arise from access to factors of production, and highly localized inter-firm relationships facilitated by place-specific history, economic factors, values and culture (Sabel, 1989; Becattini, 1990). The theory to support this argument comes from a diverse literature including Porter's (1990) work on the creation of competitive advantage, the concepts of both milieu and industrial districts (for example, Camagni, 1991), and research that stresses the role of locally specific knowledge and learning (for example, Malmberg, 1997).

The benefits of co-location are also thought to help firms increase the scope of their markets, and clusters are increasingly seen as a driving force in international trade (Brown and McNaughton, 2002). Clusters are credited with providing an environment in which world-leading technology can be developed, credibility and reputation can be established, and linkages can be developed to gain access to international markets. However there is relatively little empirical evidence to show whether firms located in clusters indeed derive more of their total sales from foreign markets.

This chapter reports research that tests whether co-located firms are more export-intense, using a sample of 537 Canadian software firms drawn from an Industry Canada directory. Firms in the sample include both those specializing in custom computer services and those that produce highly standardized 'shrink wrapped' applications. Thus the relationship between co-location, product standardization and export intensity is explored.

Co-location, product standardization and export intensity
The literature on the externalities experienced in clusters traditionally focused on the supply-side benefits of specialized labour pools, technological spillovers and intermediate input opportunities. However a number of demand-side (or market-related) benefits have also been identified (for example, Prevezer, 1997; Baptista, 1998; Porter, 1998; Saxenian, 1990). Both supply-side and demand-side externalities can contribute to the

competitiveness of a firm and thus its potential to internationalize. This chapter focuses on demand-side benefits as they receive less attention in the literature, and can play a direct role in expanding the scope and intensity of international sales.

In a high-technology market, vendors, their customers and competitors interact in a complex information-rich environment in which there is considerable uncertainty because of the rapid pace of technological change, and a wide variety of technological alternatives (Gatignon and Robertson, 1989; Glazer, 1991; Norton and Bass, 1987). As a result, information costs play a significant role in the exchange process (Eisenhardt, 1989). Location can influence the information costs experienced by both vendors and their customers.

Vendors experience information costs because of the need for environmental monitoring. This refers to information gathering with respect to the actions of competitors, and the needs of existing and potential customers. Buyers experience information costs because of their need to engage in a search process to gather information about vendors that can provide a particular product or service. Rapid technological change means that information acquired about vendors and their products or services rapidly depreciates in value (ibid.). Rapid information turnover may cause buyers to act quickly before their acquired information becomes obsolete.

While it might be assumed that in a high-technology market buyers would engage in extensive search efforts, information obsolescence can curtail the buyer search process (Weiss and Heide, 1993). Furthermore empirical studies of international industrial purchasing behaviour generally show that the search for international suppliers is not systematic, and is often ad hoc (Papadopoulos and Denis, 1988). Information searches often involve limited methods such as using the social networks of existing suppliers (Simon, 1974), conducting searches within existing vendor locations (Liang, 1995) or following others into fashionable regions (Levinthal and March, 1981).

High-technology markets are also characterized by technological heterogeneity, the result of few product standards. This situation is common in emerging markets with numerous competitors who offer a multiplicity of products and technological variations (Lambkin and Day, 1989). Technological heterogeneity is also a source of uncertainty. As the information processing costs of controlling uncertainty by examining all possible alternatives would be high, buyers are likely to perform local restricted searches (Levinthal and March, 1981). Thus buyer search behaviour may be constrained both temporally and spatially.

In an uncertain heterogeneous market it is advantageous for vendors to locate where there is a high density of potential buyers who will include them in their search processes. The traditional literature on clustering points out the advantage of locating near other firms to lever local demand through input–output multipliers (for example, Marshall, 1910). In a dynamic market where the optimal location is difficult to identify, firms choose a location where a large pool of potential customers is likely to exist – an area of dense population or organizational buyers (McCann, 1995). In the case of non-local markets, co-location can still serve this purpose. Local customers and other firms can be conduits to foreign sales. In the Canadian computer software industry, for example, the majority of foreign revenues are generated by sales to Canadian controlled firms in foreign countries (Statistics Canada, 1996). Exports may be initiated when Canadian controlled transnational firms become customers. This pattern is not unique to Canada. Bell (1995) identified client 'followership' as a factor in the internationalization of software firms in Ireland and Finland.

A related point is that location in a cluster can enhance the closeness of vendor–buyer relationships, and strong vertical vendor relationships are often developed that are based on prior purchases. These relationships generate switching costs that act as a disincentive to a wider search (Jackson, 1985). Switching costs can arise because a buyer has invested in equipment or data that are incompatible with new products or systems on the market. Switching costs may also arise because of prior commitments to a particular vendor. This occurs when a buyer has made an investment in a particular vendor relationship that is not easily transferred to another vendor. When specialized services are purchased, buyers and vendors often become linked through a number of people beyond purchasing and sales agents: for example, product developers, application specialists and trainers. To the extent that there are costs associated with establishing a new vendor relationship, there is a disincentive to search outside the existing vendor portfolio (Hakansson, 1982). Thus the existing network of relationships between buyers and vendors also limits searches, even when the customer becomes international.

Locating in a cluster of similar firms also produces potential benefits in terms of discovery and credibility. Discovery refers to the fact that a cluster of similar firms is more identifiable, and can result in more customers searching in the area. This externality was originally identified by Marshall (1910), and is often discussed in the literature on retail store location. Porter (1998) notes the advantage that visiting buyers can see multiple vendors in a single trip, and may perceive less risk if a location provides alternative suppliers. Credibility is the notion that location in a cluster of firms known for their expertise in a sector has a positive effect on reputation. Location in a cluster can provide legitimacy and mediate the liability of newness for small firms (Pouder and St. John, 1996). Both discovery and credibility reduce vendor search costs, and increase the likelihood that a firm in a cluster will be considered as a supplier. Co-located firms also have the opportunity to pursue cooperative actions that will enhance discovery or credibility. For example, firms in clusters can join together in trade promotions such as trade fair participation, trade missions or marketing delegations (Porter, 1998).

Co-location also reduces the environmental search costs for vendors. For example, a new entrant who sees an established firm trading successfully at a particular location will be drawn to locate in the same area because of the apparent market strength of that location (Prevezer, 1997). Similarly there are many instances where infrastructure support for a cluster takes the form of providing information about market trends, competitor activity at home and abroad, prices and availability of products, potential customers, opportunities and technological developments (Humphrey and Schmitz, 1996). This externality makes it possible for a firm to gather information on current and future buyers and their needs, especially where buyers are also part of a cluster. Clustered firms often gain and share information about buyers and their needs, either directly or indirectly through network relationships and informal contact (Porter, 1998). Market information diffuses rapidly among competitors within the region, continually paving the way for new opportunities and enterprises (Saxenian, 1990).

In sum, there are numerous reasons why, all else being equal, co-located firms are likely to have more success internationalizing their sales than firms located outside clusters. In general, clusters reduce the search costs of buyers and the environmental monitoring costs of vendors. These benefits could also attract export-oriented firms to locate in a cluster. Thus:

H_1: the export intensity of a firm is positively associated with location in a cluster.

Considerable variation in mean export intensity is observed within the computer services sector. Firms that sell packaged software have on average much higher export ratios than those that provide custom programming and other services (Cornish, 1996; McNaughton, 1996). The 'tradability' of software is affected by a number of factors, including non-tariff barriers such as language and culture, and regulations that prohibit service firms operating in different jurisdictions or that restrict the flow of service workers. However a key determinant is the extent to which co-production is required because interaction between developers and producers benefits from spatial proximity. The more customized the software, the more product development, sales, production and installation become intertwined processes (O'Farrell and

Hitchens, 1990). In general the more customized a product, the greater the costs and difficulties involved in exporting, and the greater value the offering has to provide to recoup costs and remain competitive compared to local offerings. Thus

> H_2:   the export intensity of a firm is positively related to the
> level of standardization of its products (that is, the propor-
> tion of sales accounted for by software products).

Data on software firm location

To test the hypotheses, information on location and export intensity was obtained for a sample of computer software firms from an online directory of Canadian software firms maintained by Industry Canada. There are 1330 firms listed in the database, of which 537 have export sales, majority Canadian ownership and complete information for the required variables. A typical entry in the directory provides contact names, address(es), total and export sales, number of employees, countries exported to, countries interested in, services or products offered and a description of the firm's strategy.

Identifying the target population of software firms that sell their products and services in foreign markets is not an easy task. There are substantially different estimates of the size of the sector depending on how narrow or broad the definition. Industry Canada (2003a) cites Statistics Canada data that there were approximately 1,700 software firms (NAICS 51121) in 2000, and 46,934 firms in the computer software and services sector (NAICS 51121, 514191, 51421 and 54151 combined). A substantial proportion of computer service firms are self-employed contract programmers. These estimates also include foreign-owned firms and subsidiaries. As the sector has relatively low barriers to entry and exit, there is a high rate of turnover among these small firms. Furthermore, only a small proportion of software firms actually export.

There is little information about the biases that may be reflected in the selection of firms in the directory. Calof (1994) used an earlier version of this directory (the Business Opportunity Sourcing System) in a study of firm size and export propensity among manufacturing firms. He found that the BOSS included 53 per cent of all Canadian manufacturing firms, but that the database is biased towards inclusion of larger firms. This is also likely the case in the present sample. The mean annual revenues of firms in the sample are $CAN750 000 (Table 19.1). The directory is also less likely to include newer firms, as it would take some time for them to be picked up by the directory updating process. The average age of the firms in the sample is 12.6 years (Table 19.1).

Table 19.1   Charactistics of the sample

Variable	Mean	Standard deviation	Minimum	Maximum
INTENSITY – percentage of sales in foreign markets	15.8	28.9	0	100
PRODUCT – Percentage of sales from software products	42.6	32.6	1	100
AGE – age in years	12.6	6.9	5	115
SIZE – revenues in $CAN	750 000	250 000	50 000	50 000 000

Measurement of variables
Export intensity
Export intensity (INTENSITY) is measured by the percentage of sales derived from sales to customers located outside Canada. This variable has an overall mean of 15.8 percent (Table 19.1). The mean for firms located within clusters is 18.8 percent, and for those outside clusters it is 14.4 percent. The F statistic for a test of the difference between these means is 2.72 with an associated p-value of 0.099. This variable is positively skewed, and the median is 0 percent. Thus the natural logarithm of this variable is used in subsequent regression analyses.

Co-location: location in a cluster
The location of sample firms by census metropolitan area (CMA) is given in Table 19.2. Toronto has the largest concentration of firms (23.2 percent), followed by Montreal (17.58 percent), Ottawa (9.3 percent), and Calgary (8.4 percent). At the municipal level, Toronto has only 10.1 percent of the firms, while Montreal has 10.6 percent of the firms, and the remaining firms are distributed among 120 communities. The list of urban areas in Table 19.2, and their relative importance as centres of software specialization is consistent with the geographic pattern of the Canadian software industry described by Industry Canada (2003b).

Canada Post's Forward Sortation Areas (FSA) is used to define intra-urban clusters of firms. Clusters of firms were identified visually by mapping the number of firms in each FSA within a city. This was necessary as clusters can exist that are not evident in a frequency table because of FSA boundaries. A cluster was defined as a focal FSA with at least four firms, and all contiguous FSAs having at least one firm. Only 26 FSAs have more than four firms, and many of these are contiguous. In total there are 177 firms (33 percent of the sample) located within clusters, and 360 firms (67 percent of the sample) located outside clusters in other areas of cities,

Table 19.2   Location of computer software firms, by CMA

CMA	Number of firms	Percentage of total
Montreal	57	10.6
Toronto	54	10.1
Calgary	45	8.4
Ottawa	38	7.1
Edmonton	21	3.9
Vancouver	17	3.2
Winnipeg	14	2.6
Waterloo	12	2.2
120 other centres	279	52.0
Total	537	100.0

and in smaller municipalities. Intra-urban clusters exist only in the Toronto, Montreal, Ottawa and Calgary CMAs. The binary variable CLUSTER has a value of 1 if a firm is located within a cluster, and a value of 0 otherwise.

There are four distinct clusters of firms in the Toronto CMA. The first is located in the downtown Central Business District (CBD), and contains 15 firms in five FSAs. The remaining three are in North York, Markham and Etobicoke. They contain 13 firms in two FSAs, 13 firms in four FSAs and nine firms in two FSAs, respectively. Thus 40 percent of the firms in Toronto lie within a cluster. There are two distinct clusters in Montreal. The first is in the downtown core, and contains 26 firms in seven FSAs. The second is near Dorval and contains 16 firms in four FSAs. Thus 45 percent of the firms in Montreal lie within a cluster. Ottawa has one cluster of 41 firms in only eight FSAs, making it the densest cluster in any city. Further, 81 percent of the firms in that CMA lie within the cluster. Finally there is a single cluster in Calgary, composed of 33 firms in five FSAs. This cluster contains 73 percent of the firms in Calgary.

Product standardization
The extent to which a firm's sales are oriented towards standardized as opposed to customized products is measured by the percentage of gross revenues from software sales (as compared to sales of software services) (PRODUCT). This is an imperfect measure as some types of services can be standardized. However, in the software industry, packaged software is generally seen as synonymous with standardized products, and computer services with customized offerings (Cornish, 1996). The overall mean of PRODUCT is 42.6 percent, and there is a significant difference between the mean of those firms located within clusters (36.6 percent) and the mean of

firms located outside of clusters (45.5 percent) ($F=8.85$, $p=0.003$). Thus, on average, firms located within clusters are more oriented towards software services than are firms located outside clusters. The distribution has a slightly positive skew (the median is 33 percent of sales), but not sufficient to warrant transformation of the variable. For some analyses, a binary indicator of sales orientation is used. Firms are classified as product-oriented if their software sales are above the median, and as service-oriented if their software sales are below the median.

Control variables
Two control variables are included in the analyses. The first is the size of the firm measured by total revenue (SIZE) and the second is the age (AGE) of the firm (number of years rounded to the closest calendar year since the firm was founded). The rationale for including these variables is the substantial literature on incremental export development, which postulates that firms become more export intensive over time as they acquire knowledge and resources (for example, Johanson and Wiedersheim-Paul, 1975; Olson, 1975; Bilkey and Tesar, 1977). Firm size is frequently used as a surrogate for the resources available to expand market scope. However extant empirical studies are equivocal as to the relationship between firm size and export propensity, with some having found a positive relationship, others no significant relationship, and still others thresholds between which size is important (for example, Hirsch and Adar, 1974; Bilkey and Tesar, 1977; Reid, 1982; Cavusgil, 1984a, 1984b; Christensen *et al.*, 1987).

Results
The hypotheses are tested using ordinary least squares regression. The results are shown in Table 19.4. There is statistical support for both H_1 and H_2. Only one of the two control variables (SIZE) is significant. The model explains 15 percent of the variability in export intensity, and about half of the explanatory power is contributed by PRODUCT. Knowing whether a firm is located in a cluster or not explains only 2 percent of the variability in export intensity. The fact that there is a statistically significant association between cluster location and the percentage of sales from software products suggests that there could be an interaction between these variables in their effect on export intensity. The regression model was refitted to include an interaction variable (CLUSTER*PRODUCT), but the interaction term was not found to be statistically significant.

Further analysis of the aggregated data in Table 19.3 provides an explanation. There is no statistically significant difference between the mean export intensity of service-oriented firms located in clusters and those outside clusters, but for product-oriented firms the means are significantly

Table 19.3   Proportion of sales from exports by location and product orientation

Location and orientation	Mean proportion of sales from exports	Standard deviation	Number of firms
Located in a cluster, product-oriented	37.9	39.0	43
Located outside a cluster, product-oriented	23.5	34.0	132
Located in a cluster, service-oriented	12.6	23.9	134
Located outside a cluster, service-oriented	9.1	22.7	228
All locations and orientations	15.8	28.9	537

Note: $F = 17.5$, $p = 0.000$.

different. Thus, while product-oriented firms are more export-intense than service-oriented firms, location in a cluster only influences the export intensity of product-oriented firms. Indeed the mean export intensity of product-oriented firms located in a cluster is 61 percent higher than the mean export intensity of product-oriented firms located outside a cluster, and 316 percent higher than service-oriented firms located outside a cluster. The importance of co-location for product-oriented firms with high export intensity is also emphasized by the fact that only 33 percent of product-oriented firms are located in a cluster, but 59 percent of service-oriented firms are located in a cluster.

Discussion and conclusions
The results of the statistical tests reported in the previous section are generally consistent with the hypotheses linking both co-location and product standardization to export intensity. Specifically a regression model shows that both co-location and product standardization are positively associated with export intensity. However analysis of the data aggregated by cluster location and sales orientation showed that product-oriented firms are less likely to locate in clusters than are service-oriented firms, but those that do are more export-intense. There is a statistically significant difference in the mean export intensity between product-oriented firms located in a cluster and those located outside clusters. There is no association between co-location and export intensity for service-oriented firms. Product-oriented firms, no matter their location, are on average more export-intense than are service-oriented firms.

Table 19.4   Regression of ln(export intensity) with independent variables

Variable	Standardized beta	p-value
CLUSTER – located in a cluster	0.12	0.003
PRODUCT – percentage of sales from		
software products	0.37	0.000
AGE – age of firm	−0.04	0.369
SIZE – total revenues	0.24	0.000

Note: $F = 23.85$, $p = 0.000$; $r = 0.40$, adjusted $r^2 = 0.15$.

In general, standardized products are more readily 'tradable' than are customized services, accounting for the higher export intensity among product-oriented firms. An explanation for the difference in the effect of co-location on export intensity may be found in the different dimensions along which software firms compete. Standardized 'shrink-wrapped' software tends to compete more on the basis of technical features and technological superiority, whereas customized software services tend to compete on the quality of customer service, technical support and/or knowledge of the end-user industry. Thus firms can experience different externalities depending on the extent to which they sell standardized products, and the extent to which their customers are non-local. Firms that provide customized software services have relatively fewer customers, they develop close relationships with those customers and these relationships form the context in which product development takes place. These firms are attracted in greater proportions to clusters, where there is a high density of potential buyers, and increased likelihood of being included in the search processes of potential customers.

In contrast, vendors of packaged software have relatively more customers, and product innovation takes place outside relationships with individual customers. Cornish (1996) evaluated the 'importance of being there' (that is, locating in close proximity to customers to facilitate face-to-face contact) for software firms and concluded that software developers do not need continuous input from all users to acquire market intelligence for product innovation. Access to a core group of advanced users is sufficient, and in the Canadian context these are often not in the local market. Thus vendors of standardized packages do not necessarily need to locate near either customers or their competitors. However the purchasers of packaged software are dependent on vendors for customer service and support, so at least 'perceptual' proximity to customers is required to assuage fears about availability of the vendor for after-sale service and support. When this is not possible through foreign investment, the credibility effect of locating in a cluster may be a partial substitute.

The results with regard to the control variables show that SIZE is significantly associated with export intensity, but AGE is not. The finding with regard to SIZE is consistent with the hypothesis of incremental export development, which postulates that firms become more export-intensive over time as they acquire knowledge and resources (Johanson and Wiedersheim-Paul, 1975). However, the result with regard to AGE is contradictory, and is more consistent with the literature on international new ventures that suggests some firms can enter international markets immediately or soon after founding, and rapidly develop a large and diverse portfolio of export activity (McDougall *et al.*, 1994; Oesterle, 1997; Oviatt and McDougall, 1997). Firm size and age are not closely correlated for this sample of firms. Thus, while considerable resources are necessary to penetrate international markets, these resources do not necessarily take a long time to acquire.

The findings provide some empirical support for the notion that co-location is associated with higher levels of export activity. The literature review provides a rationale for this observation based on the concept of demand-side externalities. The implication is that economic development policies that facilitate clusters may well also influence firms to increase their export intensity. However, for the firms in the sample, co-location accounted for a small proportion of the variability in export intensity, so clustering may be a relatively weak lever for export development. A critical finding is that co-located firms with more standardized products have much higher mean export intensity. Product-oriented firms have higher export intensity on average, but the additional intensity achieved by co-located firms may be related to the particular externalities they experience, for example reductions in customer search costs and uncertainty. Cluster policy needs to be sensitive to the types of externalities different firms may experience from co-location, and to design programmes that help firms to realize benefits from those externalities. For example, a cluster of firms with standardized products benefit more from joint marketing, while a cluster of firms with customized services could benefit more from programmes that help to build one-to-one relationships. Location in a cluster is likely to entail higher office costs as most software clusters are in downtown areas of large cities. Thus managers must consider the trade-off between location costs and the benefit of externalities. Firms can also be active in making sure that benefits are realized from externalities, for example by participating in and helping to co-ordinate joint marketing efforts.

The results suggest that there are advantages in thinking about export benefits of co-location in terms of demand-side externalities. However the study is limited in terms of measurement and the ability to generalize the results. Addressing these issues provides an opportunity for further research. Most market-related externalities relate to information costs, which are not measured directly. The analyses reported in this chapter merely tested whether the observed patterns of export intensity are consistent with the logic of this perspective. Direct measures of information costs need to be developed, and more detailed primary source data collected. Without direct measures it is difficult, for example, to distinguish between the effects of externalities and agglomeration economies. Most surveys of the location decision-making process of producer service firms focus on the characteristics of locations (rent, access, prestige and so on) rather than the utility of a location with respect to market-related externalities (for example, Michalak and Fairbairn, 1993; Matthew, 1993) and performance outcomes such as export intensity. The ideas and empirical test presented in this chapter suggest that additional explanatory variables should be included in studies of location choice.

A final issue is the extent to which the results can be generalized beyond the computer software sector. The results could be different in another sector as the importance of information costs and thus demand-side externalities may vary between sectors. For example, Gad (1979) and Michalak and Fairbairn (1988) show that legal and management service firms rely more often on face-to-face contact than do computer and engineering service firms. Future studies could investigate the influence of co-location on export intensity for a cross-section of industries.

References

Baptista, Rui (1998), 'Clusters, Innovation, and Growth: A survey of the literature', in Peter G.M. Swann, Martha Prevezer and David Stout (eds), *The Dynamics of Industrial Clustering – International Comparisons in Computing and Biotechnology*, Oxford: Oxford University Press.

Becattini, G. (1990), 'The Marshallian Industrial Districts as a Socio-Economic Notion', in F. Pyke, G., Becattini and W. Sengenberger (eds), *Industrial Districts and Inter-firm Co-operation in Italy*, Geneva: International Institute for Labor Studies, pp. 37–51.

Bell, J. (1995), 'The Internationalization of Small Computer Software Firms: A Further Challenge to 'Stage' Theories', *European Journal of Marketing*, 29 (8), 60–75.

Bilkey, W.J. and G. Tesar (1977), 'The Export Behavior of Smaller-Sized Wisconsin Manufacturing Firms', *Journal of International Business Studies*, Spring/Summer, 93–8.

Brown, P. and R.B. McNaughton (2002), 'Global Competitiveness and Local Networks: A Review of the Literature', in R.B. McNaughton and M.B. Green (eds), *Global Competitiveness and Local Networks*, Aldershot: Ashgate Publishing.

Calof, J.L. (1994), 'The Relationship Between Firm Size and Export Behaviour Revisited', *Journal of International Business Studies*, 25 (2), 367–87.

Camagni, R. (1991), *Innovation Networks*, London: Belhaven Press.

Cavusgil, S.T. (1984a), 'Organizational Characteristics Associated with Export Activity', *Journal of Management Studies*, 21 (1), 3–22.

Cavusgil, S.T. (1984b), 'Differences Among Exporting Firms Based on Their Degree of Internationalization', *Journal of Business Research*, 12 (2), 195–208.

Christensen, C.H., A. da Rocha and R.K. Gertner (1987), 'An Empirical Investigation of the Factors Influencing Export Success of Brazilian Firms', *Journal of International Business Studies*, 18 (3), 61–77.

Cornish, S.L. (1996), 'Marketing Software Products: The Importance of 'Being There' and Implications for Business Service Exports', *Environment and Planning, A*, 28, 1661–82.

Eisenhardt, K. (1989), 'Making Fast Strategic Decisions in High Velocity Environments', *Academy of Management Journal*, 33, 543–76.

Gad, G.H.K. (1979), 'Face-to-face Linkages and Office Decentralization Potentials: A Study of Toronto', in P.W. Daniels (ed.), *Studies in Office Growth and Location*, London: Wiley, pp. 277–323.

Gatignon, H. and T. Robertson (1989), 'Technology Diffusion: An Empirical Test of Competitive Effects', *Journal of Marketing*, 53, 35–49.

Glazer, R. (1991), 'Marketing in an Information Intensive Environment: Strategic Implications of Knowledge as an Asset', *Journal of Marketing*, 55, 1–19.

Hakansson, H. (1982), *International Marketing and Purchasing of Industrial Goods*, New York: John Wiley and Sons.

Hirsch, S., and Z. Adar (1974), 'Firm Size and Export Performance', *World Development*, 2 (7), 41–6.

Humphrey, J. and H. Schmitz (1996), 'The Triple C Approach to Local Industrial Policy', *World Development*, 24 (12), 1859–77.

Industry Canada (2003a), Software and Computer Services in Canada. Retrieved August 18 2003 from Industry Canada Strategis Web Site: *http://strategis.ic.gc.ca/epic/internet/inict-tic.nsf/vwGeneratedInterE/it07295e.html*.

Industry Canada (2003b), Information and Communication Technology Clusters – ICT. Retrieved August 18 2003 from Industry Canada Strategis Web Site: *http://strategis.ic.gc.ca/epic/internet/inict c-g tic.nsf/vwGeneratedInterE/h tk00003e.html*.

Jackson, B.B. (1985), *Winning and Keeping Industrial Customers*, Lexington: Lexington Books.

Johanson, J. and F. Wiedersheim-Paul (1975), 'The Internationalization of the Firm: Four Swedish Case Studies', *Journal of Management Studies*, October, 305–22.

Lambkin, M. and G.S. Day (1989), 'Evolutionary Processes in Competitive Markets: Beyond the Product Life Cycle', *Journal of Marketing*, 53, 4–20.

Levinthal, D. and J.G. March (1981), 'A Model of Adaptive Organizational Search', *Journal of Economic Behaviour and Organization*, 2, 307–33.

Liang, Neng, (1995), 'Soliciting Unsolicited Export Orders – Are Recipients Chosen at Random?', *European Journal of Marketing*, 29(8), 37–59.

Malmberg, A. (1997), 'Industrial Geography: Location and Learning', *Progress in Human Geography*, 21(4), 573–82.

Marshall, A. (1910), *Principles of Economics*, 6th edn, London: Macmillan and Co.

Matthew, M.R. (1993), 'The Suburbanization of Toronto Offices', *The Canadian Geographer*, 37 (4), 293–306.

McCann, Philip (1995), 'Rethinking the Economics of Location and Agglomeration', *Urban Studies*, 32 (3), 563–77.

McDougall, Patricia Phillips, Scott Shane and Benjamin M. Oviatt (1994), 'Explaining the Formation of International New Ventures: The Limits of Theories from International Business Research', *Journal of Business Venturing*, 9 (6), 469–87.

McNaughton, Rod B. (1996), 'Foreign Market Channel Integration Decisions of Canadian Computer Software Firms', *International Business Review*, 5 (1), 23–52.

Michalak, W.Z. and K.J. Fairbairn (1988), 'Producer Services in a Peripheral Economy', *Canadian Journal of Regional Studies*, 11, 353–72.

Michalak, W.Z. and K.J. Fairbairn (1993), 'The Location of Producer Services in Edmonton', *The Canadian Geographer*, 37 (1), 2–16.

Norton, J.A. and F.M. Bass (1987), 'Diffusion Theory Model of Adoption and Substitution for Successive Generations of High-Technology Products', *Management Science*, 33, 1069–86.

Oesterle, Michael-Jorg (1997), 'Time-span Until Internationalization: Foreign Market Entry as a Built-in Mechanism of Innovations', *Management International Review*, 37 (2), 125–49.

O'Farrell, P.N. and D.M.W.N. Hitchens (1990), 'Producer Services and Regional Development: Key Conceptual Issues of Taxonomy and Quality Measurement', *Regional Studies*, 24, 163–71.

Olson, H.D. (1975), *Studies in Export Promotion: Attempts to Evaluate Export Stimulation Measures for the Swedish Textile and Clothing Industries*, Uppsala, Sweden: Uppsala University.

Oviatt, Benjamin M. and Patricia Phillips McDougall (1997), 'Challenges for Internationalization Process Theory: The Case of International New Ventures', *Management International Review*, 37, 85–99.

Papadopoulos, N. and J.E. Denis (1988), 'Inventory, Taxonomy and Assessment of Methods for International Market Selection', *International Marketing Review*, Autumn, 38–51.

Porter, M.E. (1990), *The Competitive Advantage of Nations*. London: Macmillan Press.

Porter, M.E. (1998), *On Competition*, Boston: Harvard Business School Press.

Pouder, R. and C.H. St. John (1996), 'Hot Spots and Blind Spots: Geographical Clusters of Firms and Innovation', *Academy of Management Review*, 21 (4), 1192–1225.

Prevezer, M. (1997), 'The Dynamics of Industrial Clustering in Biotechnology', *Small Business Economics*, 9, 255–71.

Reid, S.D. (1982), 'The Impact of Size on Export Behavior in Small Firms', in M.R. Czinkota and G. Tesar (eds), *Export Management: An International Context*, New York: Praeger, pp. 18–38.

Sabel, C. (1989), 'Flexible Specialization and the Reemergence of Regional Economies', in P. Hirst and J. Zeitlin (eds), *Reversing Industrial Decline? Industrial Structure and Policy in Britain and Her Competitors*, Oxford: Berg, pp. 17–70.

Saxenian, A. (1990), 'Regional Networks and the Resurgence of Silicon Valley', *California Management Review*, 33 (1), 89–112.

Simon, H.A. (1974), *Administrative Behavior*, New York: The Free Press.

Statistics Canada (1996), *Canada's International Transactions in Services*, catalogue number 67–203, Ottawa: Government of Canada.

Weiss, A. and J.B. Heide (1993), 'The Nature of Organizational Search in High Technology Markets', *Journal of Marketing Research*, 30, 220–33.

20 Business support for internationalization in England

Leigh Sear and Robert T. Hamilton

This chapter is about the way entrepreneurs in England are supported into and through the process of exporting. We are concerned primarily to document the 'supply side', that is, the nature and coverage of the available support, and then to assess the appropriateness of this against the needs of the internationalizing entrepreneur. It should be noted that the research findings drawn upon in this chapter relate specifically to England, the country that accounted for 87% of all VAT-registered business in Great Britain at the beginning of 2002. In addition, there is a different configuration of provision to support international activity in Wales and Scotland, in terms both of organizations and of the way in which support is delivered. Similarly Ireland has a more distinctive set of initiatives that are covered elsewhere in this volume.

There is a wealth of evidence within the academic literature and government statistics that demonstrate that exporting is the predominant mode by which SMEs engage with international markets and trading. Since the mid-1990s, there has been a great deal of debate around the exporting activities of small and medium-sized enterprises (SMEs), in both a regional and a national context. A brief review of the academic and practitioner literature highlights a number of perceived benefits to firms from exporting. These include exposure to differing ways of doing business (Barclays Bank, 1996), additional demand for the product or service of the business (Julien *et al.*, 1997) and opportunities for modifications of existing products and new product development. The successful development of export markets by SMEs has also been recognized by government as critical to enhancing the competitiveness of these businesses and hence to the strengthening of regional and national economies. It is these public benefits – principally the generation of a larger number of more secure jobs – that provide the basis for the substantial expenditure of government funds in the support of private businesses. This is an issue that we return to later in the chapter. In the next section we report on the overall 'supply-side' provision of advice and information. We follow this with a discussion of the appropriateness of what is being supplied, given the apparent needs of the export-oriented entrepreneur. The chapter then concludes that an improved fit between what is supplied and what is needed is possible and, if achieved, this will raise the effectiveness of the advice and information provided to exporters.

The supply side

The government context

There are conflicting estimates of how many UK SMEs are actively engaged in exporting, ranging from as low as 3% or around 110000 businesses (Bank of England, 1999) to over 40% (Grant Thornton, 1999; Small Business Research Centre, 2000). The government's estimate is 23% (Small Business Service, 2001) which is perceived by policy makers as too low, especially in comparison to rates of exporting activity within other developed market economies such as France and Germany. In response the government has used public monies to provide a range of services and schemes, at a local, regional and national level, to increase the number of businesses engaging with international activities and enhancing the capabilities of existing businesses which are currently engaged with international trade. Indeed British Trade International continues to commit itself to some challenging performance targets as set out in its Corporate Plan 2002–5. These include the following achievements by 2004: a 30% increase in take-up of information services, the development of 5000 new exporters in England, and at least 50% of established exporters assisted improving their business performance by 2004.

Publicly funded business advice and support in England is provided through a network of 45 Business Link offices, managed nationally by the government's Small Business Service (part of the Department of Trade and Industry, or DTI). Each Business Link office is franchised by the Small Business Service to provide a range of support services to local SMEs. The system is designed to be responsive to the needs of local SMEs and facilitate access to other providers of support, particularly private sector organizations such as banks, accountants and specialist consultants. Until April 2001, publicly funded export provision was delivered through the Business Link network, via a network of Export Development Counsellors and DTI secondees. Since April 2001, however, this has been delivered by Trade Partners UK (or TPUK), which is the export development part of British Trade International, the government agency (sponsored by DTI and the Foreign and Commonwealth Office) responsible for promoting different aspects of international trade. In order to promote export provision as part of a holistic business support service, international trade advisers are located in the offices of the majority of Business Link offices.

In addition, a wide array of services are available from private sector organizations such as those of accountants, solicitors, bank managers, freight forwarders and insurance brokers. To this list we could also add the less formal network made up of other exporters, customers and suppliers. There are, then, a wide range of organizations, public and private, providing advice, consultancy, information and training to SMEs wishing to export and those businesses already exporting.

Local and regional contexts: coverage and depth of export provision
In addition to practitioner guides, which provide descriptive insights into the type of organization and support available to SMEs wishing to internationalize, there is an academic literature exploring the availability and configuration of various types of export service and support. At a general level, this literature has focused on evaluating schemes or provision at a national level (for example, National Audit Office, 1996) or different types of support initiative or intervention such as export training (Carrier, 1997). There are relatively few studies which explore the nature of the variation in provision in the different regions of England or the degree of fit between the needs of exporting SMEs and provision (McAuley, 1993). Wilson's *Review of Export Promotion* (1999) did stress, however, that the first step in developing business-driven forms of export provision should be an extensive mapping of provision that highlighted the similarities and differences between regions in the depth and coverage of support, and the extent of any gap between the expectations of the policy makers and the actual needs within the sector.

The available academic literature and insights from a recently completed audit[1] of export provision for Trade Partners UK (Sear *et al.*, 2001) highlight that, at a local and regional level, the support infrastructure for exporting is complex, involving a large number of players in a series of multiple networks and relationships. Amongst this diversity, however, the following eight general types of organization operating as export support providers can be identified:

1. *Government bodies and agencies* incorporating regional and national government bodies and supporting the funding of trade services, such as TPUK. This structure is not fixed. For example, during 1996, responsibility for the delivery of export services was transferred from the Overseas Trade Services to Business Link (National Audit Office, 1996; Atherton and Sear, 1997a). Recently the rebranding of British Trade International as TPUK has created a number of ambiguities, especially in terms of the focus of government support.
2. *Regional agencies* such as Regional Development Agencies (RDAs) that have trade development as one of their strategic activities.
3. The *Business Link network* which bridges, to some extent, the regional–local divide in support configuration, in that it is a sub-

regional provider but operates as an interface between local and regional support programmes.

4. *Local authority* economic development units (EDUs) who focus on trade development and exporting as a means of job and wealth creation.

5. *Chambers of commerce* which operate largely at a sub-regional or local level.

6. *Business federations, associations and institutes* which are generally business-led but with some support and input from the public or quasi-public sector.

7. *Private sector providers* supporting different types of export activity.

8. A broad range of *other providers* of support, such as enterprise agencies and universities, which are involved at a local, regional and national level and offer varied services. Such agencies tend to have somewhat different, and unclear, relationships with the above groupings of providers within and between regions.

The extent to which these different types of organizations are involved in the provision of export services varies between each region, although the role and type of service provided by each grouping of providers is somewhat similar throughout England (Johnson *et al.*, 2000). For example, chambers of commerce tend to provide a plethora of services including advice, information, training and documentation services, while local government economic development units focus on the provision of information and direct financial assistance. There is, however, a degree of flux and interaction between these different organizations, at all levels, that blurs organizational and network boundaries. For example, the development of the Small Business Service franchises has altered the configuration of export services, at a local level, within several of the regions. Such changes and turbulence within support structures create issues to be resolved and present challenges to business support organizations in developing coherence within the configuration of provision that makes sense to the business community (ibid.). For example, since the mid-1990s, there have been three major changes to the nature of central government support for exporting, which has hindered attempts to integrate national schemes, such as market research and language services, into the portfolio of local providers and clarify confusion within the business community as to the accessibility and availability of different schemes (Leonidou and Adams-Florou, 1999).

More specifically four general observations can be made about the coverage and type of exporting support available to SMEs in England. First there are a plethora of advisory, information and 'other' related types of service in each English region. For example, over 40 per cent of organizations in each region provide some form of advisory or information service (see Table 20.1). The majority of such provision is provided by publicly funded agencies such as Business Link, government agencies and other types of providers such as enterprise agencies. In some northern regions, there can be up to 10 different publicly funded and quasi-public agencies, ranging from TPUK to universities and chambers of commerce, providing export advice. Other services tend to be provided by the private sector and include export management, freight forwarding, logistics management and market and product representation services. These services tend to be offered as chargeable services and are aimed at assisting SMEs with the transaction-focused part of international trading activity, whether this be exporting or importing.

Secondly Table 20.1 also highlights that there is a relative lack of financial provision, training and networking services. In five English regions, less than one organization in five provides some form of direct or indirect financial provision. If financial assistance is available at a local, regional or national level, it tends to be provided by two types of provider: private finance providers and/or local government economic development units. The two most common forms of financial assistance are financial subsidies, often in the form of export vouchers, which businesses can use to offset the cost of advice or training from another provider; and grants which are provided to cover the costs of undertaking market research or translating a brochure into a foreign language. In terms of available training offerings, on closer inspection it emerges that the majority of such provision is designed to provide an awareness and develop an understanding of how to complete export documentation, income terms, letters of credit and export procedures. However there are relatively few offerings that help businesses to develop the capabilities and competencies required to manage the different activities and tasks involved in developing a new market and exporting (Atherton and Sear, 1997b).

Thirdly there are a number of differences in the configuration of export provision between northern and southern regions of England.[2] There is a greater propensity for organizations in the northern regions to provide advice, consultancy and information services, whilst providers in the southern regions had a greater propensity to offer other types of service. To an extent, this difference reflects the different configurations of support and interorganizational relationships between the regions. Different regions have different business bases and support infrastructures which tend to influence the point of delivery of assistance (Robson *et al.*, 2000). In the majority of northern regions, for instance, publicly funded agencies can use European monies to underpin a range of export support services that may

Table 20.1 *Percentage of providers in each region offering each type of service*

Service	East	London	South East	South West	East Midlands	West Midlands	North East	North West	Yorkshire & Humber	England
Advice	42.3	51.8	47.5	51.4	58.1	83.9	54.4	75.6	56.8	74.2
Consultancy	38.4	18.5	30.0	48.6	48.4	58.1	54.4	73.1	62.2	35.5
Finance	19.2	11.1	17.5	35.1	29.0	48.3	29.8	14.6	8.1	51.6
Information	50.0	44.4	50.0	67.6	74.2	71.0	42.1	63.4	40.5	74.2
Networking	30.7	14.8	55.0	45.9	51.6	51.6	21.1	46.3	64.7	29.0
Training	34.6	25.9	47.5	37.8	45.2	45.1	22.8	43.9	48.6	12.9
Other	76.9	59.2	62.5	62.2	54.8	61.3	33.3	63.4	45.9	61.3

Note: Percentages add to more than 100 because most providers provide a range of services

357

overlap existing provision. In southern regions, Bennett and Smith (2001) and Sear *et al.* (2001) have noted that there is a more active private sector providing different types of specific service, such as market research consultancy or trade representation service, to SMEs who are willing to pay for niche-focused services.

Finally there is evidence of a qualitative difference in the role that publicly funded and private sector organizations perform in helping SMEs to export. Publicly funded agencies have a greater propensity to adopt process-focused roles, whilst private sector organizations tend to perform more niche focused roles. In part, this difference reflects the type of services provided by private and publicly funded agencies. Private sector providers tend to provide a portfolio of discrete services to exporting SMEs, around one or two areas of expertise, that are used by businesses on a commercial basis. In contrast, in certain northern regions, publicly funded agencies such as Business Link reported providing 12 or 13 services and adopting two or three different delivery roles. This multiplicity of roles is not problematical per se, but does raise an issue in terms of the ability of the organization to match the role required by the business to the role provided by the agency.

These variations in institutional support services can, however, generate a sense of confusion or inconsistency among potential, or actual, business users, particularly if the businesses are located near to an administrative border or have facilities in different areas. This was particularly an issue in regions where agencies have different levels of access to national and European government funding to underpin the design and development of service provision.

Supply and demand: the appropriateness of export support and provision
While the supply side is elaborate and complex, it does remain 'piecemeal' (Stanworth and Gray, 1991, p. 23) and 'fragmented' (Bennett and Robson 1999, p. 177) with a number of differences in the nature of provision both within and between the English regions. Other commentators such as Julien *et al.* (1997) have noted that the availability of significant levels of advice and guidance to support the development of exporting SMEs does not necessarily translate into commensurate levels of usage by small businesses. Atherton and Sear (1997a) and Carrier (1997) suggest that this difference between supply and expressed demand reflects weaknesses in the appropriateness of export offerings.

There have been very few studies that have assessed the needs of SMEs in relation to the supply of support being provided (McAuley, 1993). It is important to highlight this lack of considered insight bearing in mind the current discourse within business support agencies on the need to develop demand-driven forms of support. For example, the Wilson Review (1999,

p. 5) recommends that 'the strategy and objectives of the new operation [TPUK] should be clearly based on business needs'. Gibb (1997) suggests that 'appropriateness' can be measured by the degree to which the support reflects the business development process, as experienced by the business itself. This implies that the role of support interventions is to assist the business in satisfying key 'how to' needs and another factor critical for success is to ensure that the provider understands the distinct culture of the client business and can operate with credibility in that environment. This ability to assimilate with the context of individual SMEs is likely to be most difficult for those coming from careers and training in large formal organizations (Dalley and Hamilton, 2000).

A recent audit of export provision by Sear *et al.* (2001) highlights that the majority of provision within England focuses on the 'front-end' activities of the exporting process such as researching the market and establishing a local presence (see Table 20.2). This reflects a supply-side perception that the relatively low level of exporting activity within the SME community reflects a lack of business awareness of exporting opportunities and how to develop new markets (CBI, 1996). This perception has manifested itself in support organizations providing a range of advisory and information services designed to assist SMEs in finding new customers and understanding conditions in certain markets and sectors. Such provision is premised on a notion that there are available opportunities for businesses to engage with international trade, as opposed to a lack of skills within the business to address and take advantage of these opportunities (Carrier, 1997).

There is, however, a major concern with this support focus on the early stages of the exporting process, which highlights the particular nature of exporting activity in small businesses. Atherton and Sear (1997b) and Chetty and Hamilton (1996) highlight the fact that, during the initial stages of exporting, businesses tend to focus on selling rather than on researching the market and establishing a local presence. This is because 'the development of a new market tended to be transaction-led, i.e. in response to a selling opportunity, rather than planned' (Atherton and Sear, 1997a, p. 1060). As the selling activity is consolidated, however, businesses tend to increase their formal, and purposive, researching of the market and start to develop more considered forms of local presence. Therefore the focus of the majority of publicly funded agencies on helping new and inexperienced exporters to research the market and establish a local presence does not reflect the initial entry point into exporting, via selling.

In addition, Julien *et al.* (1997) suggest that the appropriateness of export offerings can be ascertained by exploring the degree to which services are aimed at different groupings or types of exporting SMEs. Both the Wilson

Table 20.2 Percentage of providers in each region catering for each stage of the exporting process

Service	East	London	South East	South West	East Midlands	West Midlands	North East	North West	Yorkshire & Humber	England
DMC	50.0	51.8	45.0	54.1	64.5	61.3	24.6	56.1	54.1	25.8
RM	57.6	51.8	52.5	64.7	83.9	77.4	59.6	65.9	70.3	54.8
ELP	53.0	44.4	52.5	56.6	67.7	71.0	78.9	61.0	73.0	45.2
Selling	42.3	25.9	55.0	29.7	29.0	64.5	52.6	43.9	32.4	71.0
OF	69.2	44.4	52.5	54.1	38.7	45.2	50.9	65.9	59.5	64.5
S&D	65.3	48.1	55.0	43.2	48.4	51.6	35.1	39.0	32.4	41.9
Strategy	23.0	11.1	22.5	27.0	25.8	35.5	15.8	12.2	24.3	12.9
Financing	3.8	11.1	10.0	8.1	3.2	9.7	8.8	7.3	10.8	58.1

Note: DMC – developing motivation and confidence; RM – researching the market; ELP – establishing a local presence; OF – Order fulfilment; S&D – Shipping and delivery.

Review (1999) and Sear *et al.* (2001) highlight the point that there is a tendency for support organizations throughout England to provide services that can be used by any type of exporting business. In all of the English regions, except one, over 75 per cent of the organizations surveyed by Sear *et al.* (2001) responded that they did not segment service offerings by the key characteristics or needs of the exporter or would-be exporter (see Table 20.3). The lack of segmentation reflects the following:

- The aims and objectives of the organizations required services to be provided to as many SMEs as possible and hence achieve 'visibility' within the market place. This reflects in part the way in which the performance of business support organizations is ascertained and measured. There will be a number of output, as opposed to outcome-related targets for programmes of support and specific initiatives upon which funding is levered (Priest, 1998; Johnson *et al.*, 2000). These will typically include the number of exporters assisted, number of services sold and number of jobs created.
- The role of the agency did not necessitate the segmentation of the market because the agency is largely approached by SMEs to provide a general advisory or information service that negates the need to act in a diagnostic manner.
- There was a lack of appropriate data on the level and nature of exporting activity within the locality which could be used to segment the market and assist in prioritizing which segments of the market to support. The Wilson Review (1999) found that a lack of market intelligence and data was one of the major barriers to being able to develop services that meet the needs of different types of exporting business.

If organizations within the English regions do segment the exporting SME market, they tend to do so by addressing SMEs in certain *sectors* or promoting exporting activity in certain *markets*. The focus on supporting export activity in certain sectors reflects the emphasis placed on sectoral and market development by TPUK, the government offices and the Regional Development Agencies as a strategy for regional development (Robson *et al.*, 2000). On closer inspection, however, there is a degree of tension and overlap between local, regional and national priorities in terms of which sectors are important to local and regional competitiveness. This raises the issue of how these different priorities can be managed into an effective and deliverable programme of support for sector development.

The findings on the lack of segmentation strategies used by agencies in each of the regions is interesting in the context of the emphasis within

Table 20.3 *Percentage of providers using each segmentation strategy*

Service	East	London	South East	South West	East Midlands	West Midlands	North East	North West	Yorkshire & Humber	England
None	92.3	85.1	90.0	78.4	77.4	77.4	94.7	65.9	59.5	67.7
Size	7.6	3.7	2.5	16.2	3.2	9.7	17.5	4.9	–	16.1
Match	7.6	–	7.5	10.8	9.7	16.1	5.3	4.9	21.6	12.9
Sector	19.2	22.2	27.5	24.3	22.6	32.3	19.3	17.1	37.8	41.9
Experience level	11.5	3.7	5.0	5.4	19.4	9.7	5.3	4.9	21.6	–
Geographical area	3.8	3.7	–	2.7	3.2	–	7.0	7.3	–	–

regional international trade plans upon the need for TPUK to work with those businesses new to exporting or inexperienced in managing the exporting process. As noted above, there is a perception within the support network that too few SMEs are engaged with exporting. Interestingly Table 20.3 highlights that, on average, approximately one organization in 10 uses either size or level of experience and expertise in exporting as a criterion for segmenting needs. With the recent introduction of Passport to Export by TPUK, as a gateway into provision for new and inexperienced exporters, there may now be less difference between the rhetoric and practice of government engaging with new exporters.

A clear case can be made for government intervention with new exporters, in that such businesses would either be unwilling or unable to pay for services that may assist them in developing overseas markets or international activity. This has been used as a case for justifying the use of public monies and adding value to the activities of private sector providers. There is, however, both empirical and anecdotal evidence to suggest that export advisers tend to work with more experienced exporters, who may be easier to identify and engage with, and more willing to pay for the provision of specific services. This tension is evident in international trade plans which attempt to balance encouraging greater numbers of businesses to export with greater levels of exporting activity from existing businesses.

Developing effective exporting support in England
The above review of academic and practitioner literature and empirical studies of the nature and configuration of export support highlights the fact that there are a number of key similarities in provision between each region in England, especially in terms of the coverage and depth of provision. Although individual organizations in each of the regions are operating under unique circumstances, because of variations in their internal structure and their external environment, a number of key challenges and opportunities emerge that have implications for local, regional and national support agencies, such as TPUK, in terms of developing effective exporting support and provision.

The first challenge relates to resolving the key gaps and concentrations in provision. Across England, the extensive provision of advice and information and other services suggests that this is considered the most appropriate form of support. However this raises a question concerning whether this configuration of provision reflects a set of particular customer needs and local/regional priorities or represents a lack of differentiation and overlap. Similarly the observed gaps in financial and training provision can be seen as both positive, where services are not being delivered because there is no or minimal demand, and negative, where gaps in provision are problematical in that they indicate a lack of response to market needs or demands. Such concerns can only be resolved by comparing and contrasting audits of supply-side provision against 'audits' of the needs of exporting SMEs. Such a comparison would provide information that could be used by local, regional and national agencies to identify the requirements of exporting SMEs and the responses required to satisfy the 'how to' needs of exporting SMEs. While there are numerous studies of the barriers faced by SMEs in exporting and developing overseas markets (see, for example, Ibeh, 2000), there are few studies that have explicitly explored and assessed the developmental needs and requirements of exporting SMEs. Indeed, even in the 1980s, it was concluded that 'little is known [about] how well demand (firms' need) for support and supply (assistance offered) actually match' (Seringhaus, 1987, p. 27) and, as noted above, the Wilson Review (1999) saw the continuing lack of such information and intelligence as a major barrier to being able to segment effectively the SME market and offering tailored provision.

Another key challenge for support agencies, especially publicly funded agencies, is clarifying what is the most appropriate alignment of support, both geographically and between different types of support provider. In terms of the latter, Sear *et al.* (2001) highlighted that there is a perception amongst providers of export that the private sector is better able to tailor their offerings to different types of exporting SMEs, by addressing the immediate problems and opportunities encountered by the business. Therefore a problem-focused role or opportunity-driven service is provided to meet the 'how to' needs of the business. The lack of targeting and segmentation in the majority of publicly funded offerings, especially advice and information services, would imply that there is a lack of differentiation and hence overlap and competition between publicly funded and private sector provision. To ensure that publicly funded services do not continue to displace and duplicate private sector offerings, there is an issue concerning how publicly funded provision can add value to private sector provision. One key issue here is to deal with the higher level of trust that entrepreneurs have in the advice that they pay for from the private sector providers (Bennett and Robson, 1999).

Previous research on business links and personal business advisers has highlighted that there is a role for publicly funded agencies in providing a process management role (Sear and Agar 1996). Despite the current rhetoric within international trade plans and Small Business Service (SBS) documentation concerning the need for advisers to adopt a process facilitation or management role, as opposed to a more traditional counselling or consultancy role, there is evidence that advisers are encountering a number of difficulties in embedding such a role within the business community (Mole,

2002). In part, this reflects the nature of the targets used by funding agencies to determine the performance of business advisers (Priest, 1998). Unlike a counsellor or consultant, the key aim of a process management role is to develop the skills of the business owner–manager and export managers to manage the export process themselves. In so doing, publicly funded agencies would help the business to manage the risk, uncertainty and complexity associated with exporting and developing new markets (Chetty and Hamilton, 1996).

There are certain key skills or attributes required by a process manager (for example communication and influencing skills and networking abilities) that could be translated into a set of competencies that would underpin the development of a continuing professional programme for export advisers and counsellors. This programme would ensure that export advisers would possess the skills required to perform a process management role, but also develop local and specialist knowledge required to keep up-to-date with businesses who are engaging with and managing the exporting process. Despite TPUK introducing centres to assess the abilities and knowledge possessed by international trade advisers within each region, there is still no national framework by which to accredit continuing professional development for international trade advisers within England. This would be part of a process of ensuring that advisers have the abilities and skills required to work with exporting SMEs to address their needs and requirements (Mole, 2002).

The final challenge for support organizations relates to the mismatch between the focus of support and the exporting process as encountered by SMEs. Most of the providers had no segmentation strategy and those that did tended to favour segmentation by sector. The majority of publicly funded provision is concerned with early stage activities such as locating customers and identifying export opportunities for businesses via market research services. However, when a business starts to move into new export markets, the focus is predominately on more transactional (*developmental*) activities. Therefore there is a difference between the way the support network has conceptualized the process by which a small business starts to sell in an export market and the actual experience of this by the business. Ultimately this difference is one of an emphasis on trade promotion as opposed to trade development. The majority of publicly funded provision is concerned with trade promotion, in particular finding customers and identifying export opportunities for businesses via market research services. As a result the general focus for much of the new market development support is formal and impersonal when the preferred entry point into using support *for the small business* is informal and personalized (Atherton and Sear, 1997b).

How can the interaction between these two approaches be balanced? One starting point is to recognize that small business owner–managers will have vastly different levels of experience in developing export markets and hence different needs in terms of support. For example, the entry point into developing new markets will be different for starter or inexperienced exporters, in comparison to global, or expert, exporters. These different types of business will have different characteristics, encounter different barriers and challenges and hence have different requirements and developmental needs over time. In Table 20.4 we outline a framework that relates a set of areas of 'need to know' for the owner–manager or business to the level of experience in managing the exporting process. Note too that the exporting process is sales-led, as this does seem to be the way in which SME managers actually activate the process.

The implication for support organizations is that support is most effective when it is aimed at assisting businesses with different levels of experience and 'know-how' of the exporting process. The specificity of the support to the emerging challenges facing the owner–manager is crucial and cannot be achieved with a bland undifferentiated service. Segmenting on the basis of experience also serves to focus directly on the needs of the key people involved, the owner and senior managers of the SME. It is the motivation and performance of these individuals that will make or break any foray into a new export market. In addition, Table 20.4 can be used to identify which agencies can address different types of need. For example, while the private sector is best placed to assist more experienced businesses with fulfilling orders and shipping and delivery through the provision of focused services, public agencies could work with the less experienced businesses to develop basic systems to underpin the selling and transaction activity.

Conclusions

We have argued that there is a need to improve the fit between the abundant supply of advice and information and the effectiveness of this in stimulating more exporters and more exports. There are numerous models of internationalization through market development and some consensus on how SME owner–managers experience this process. While there is no shortage of advice and support for potential and active exporters, there is a fairly low uptake of this, particularly from public sector providers, and the overall effectiveness is problematic. The key to effectiveness lies in understanding that people, the owners and key managers, are at the heart of any SME exporting initiative. It seems to follow that the supply of advice needs to reflect the differing needs of these individuals as these are determined and changed by their experiences in international markets. The specificity of the

Table 20.4 *Segmenting support needs by experience level*

Export process	No experience	Inexperienced	Experienced	Expert
Shipping and delivery	Not applicable	Development of basic system	Refining of system internally Search for best external support	Development of closer links with shipping/delivery organizations Consideration of alternate channels of distribution
Fulfilling orders	Not applicable	Based on existing business systems Recognition of need to refine current selling approach/selling	Development of tailored order fulfilment system	Use of order fulfilment/selling systems to gain market/customer knowledge
Selling	Not applicable	Maximize margins Be aware of negotiating and culture differences	More emphasis on generating own sales Improvement of negotiating skills	Shift to marketing and profile development Sensitize to local environment
Establishing a local presence	Not applicable (at this stage)	Develop structure directly related to selling	Expand local presence to wider market development activities	Consider alternative longer-term options
Researching the market	Raise awareness of other markets Identify selling opportunities	Increase understanding of the market and of competitors, agents and partners	Find diversification and new market opportunities	Find optimum marketing and distribution options Transfer 'know-how' between markets

Source: Derived from Atherton and Sear (1997a).

advice provided to the needs of the business is the crucial determinant of effectiveness. This need for specificity, however, stands in some contrast to the generic and impersonal provision from the public sector sources. The real dilemma that these public providers face is the need to be able to claim, in the interests of their accountability, that a large number of businesses have indeed been helped by their offerings. From this point of view, a more selective approach from their standpoint would be seen as much more difficult to justify, given the current scale of their activity. However we do not think that some segmentation along the lines we have indicated need lead to the neglect of a large number of client businesses. We do think that such an approach will lead to much more effective outcomes for the businesses that are involved.

Notes

1. The authors would like to stress that the views expressed in the chapter are their own and do not necessarily reflect the views and attitudes of Trade Partners UK.
2. For the purposes of this paper, the northern regions consist of the East Midlands, North East, North West, West Midlands and Yorkshire and the Humber. The Eastern region, London, South East and South West are classified as southern regions.

References

Atherton, A. and L. Sear (1997a), 'Support for the Exporting SME: Current Configurations of Provision in the North-east of England', paper presented to the 20th National ISBA Small Firms Policy and Research Conference, 19–21 November, Belfast.
Atherton, A. and L. Sear (1997b), 'Working within the Global Economy: Insights into the Internationalisation Process in North-east England', paper presented to the 27th efmd European Small Business Seminar, 17–19 September, Rhodes.
Bank of England (1999), *Smaller Exporters: A Special Report*, London: Bank of England.
Barclays Bank (1996), *Realising Your Export Potential*, Coventry: Barclays Bank.
Bennett, R.J. and P.J.A. Robson (1999), 'The use of external advice by SMEs in Britain', *Entrepreneurship & Regional Development*, 11(2), 155–80.
Bennett, R.J. and C. Smith (2001), 'The influence of location and distance on the supply of business advice', paper presented to the 24th ISBA National Small Firms Policy and Research Conference, November, Leicester.
Carrier, C. (1997), 'The Training and Development Needs of Owner-managers of Small Businesses with Export Potential', paper presented to the 42nd World ICSB Conference, 20–22 June, San Francisco.
CBI (1996), *Trade Secrets: Maximising Export Potential in SMEs*, London: Confederation of British Industry.
Chetty, S.K. and R.T. Hamilton (1996), 'The Process of Exporting in Owner-controlled Firms', *International Small Business Journal*, 14(2), 12–22.
Dalley, J. and R.T. Hamilton (2000), 'Knowledge, context and learning in the small business', *International Small Business Journal*, 18(3), 51–9.
Gibb, A.A. (1997), 'Small Firms Training and Competitiveness: Building Upon the Small Business as a Learning Organisation', *International Small Business Journal*, 15(3), 13–29.
Grant Thornton (1999), *European Business Survey*, London: Grant Thornton.
Ibeh, K. (2000), 'Internationalisation and the small firm', in D. Jones-Evans and S. Carter (eds), *Enterprise and Small Business: Principles, Practice and Policy*, London: Addison Wesley-Longman.

Johnson, S., L. Sear and A. Jenkins (2000), 'Small Business Policy, Support and Governance', in D. Jones-Evans and S. Carter (eds), *Enterprise and Small Business: Principles, Practice and Policy*, London: Addison Wesley-Longman.

Julien, P.A., A. Joyal, L. Deshaies and C. Ramangalahy (1997), 'A Typology of Strategic Behaviour Among Small and Medium-sized Exporting Businesses: A Case Study', *International Small Business Journal*, 15(2), 33–50.

Leonidou, L.C. and A.S. Adams-Florou (1999), 'Types and sources of export information: insights from small business', *International Small Business Journal*, 17(3), 30–48.

McAuley, A. (1993), 'The perceived usefulness of export information sources', *European Journal of Marketing*, 27(10), 52–64.

Mole, K. (2002), 'Business advisers' impact on SMEs', *International Small Business Journal*, 20(2), 139–62.

National Audit Office (1996), *Overseas Trade Services: Assistance to Exporters*, London: HMSO.

Priest, S. (1998), 'Business Link SME Services: Targeting, Innovation and Charging', *Environment and Planning C: Government and Policy*, 6, 177–94.

Robson, B., J. Peck and A. Holden (2000), *Regional Agencies and Area-based Regeneration*, Bristol: The Policy Press.

Sear, L. and J. Agar (1996), *A survey of Business Link personal advisers: are they meeting expectations?*, Durham: Durham University Business School.

Sear, L., M. Dodd and I. Doole (2001), 'An Audit of Export Services in England; Developing Business Focused Support', Small Business and Enterprise Development Conference, University of Leicester, 22–23 March.

Seringhaus, R. (1987), 'The Role of Information Assistance in Small Firms' Export Involvement', *International Small Business Journal*, 5(2), 26–36.

Small Business Research Centre (2000), *British Enterprise in Transition*, Cambridge: Cambridge University Press.

Small Business Service (2001), 'SBS Omnibus Survey', Autumn, London, Department of Trade and Industry (access from www.dti.gov.uk).

Stanworth, J. and C. Gray (eds) (1991), *Bolton 20 Years On*, London: Paul Chapman.

Wilson, R. (1999), *The Review of Export Promotion*, London: Department of Trade and Industry/ Foreign Commonwealth Office.

21 Estonian perspectives of international entrepreneurship
Tiit Elenurm

Main trends in enterprise development in Estonia are influenced by relatively rapid pace of transition to the market economy compared to larger East European transition economies. Policy of Estonian governments in the transition process has been characterized by certain continuity, shaped by liberal economic thinking, abolition of trade barriers and limited application of import tariffs, equal treatment of foreign and local investors, privatizing most large enterprises by the end of 1996, stable currency and restricted public spending during the 1990s. The World Bank country study in 1999 stressed that, since regaining independence in 1991, Estonia has successfully implemented a broad agenda of stabilization and structural reform policies, including introduction of the new national currency under a currency board arrangement. Hard budget constraint was imposed on the public sector and private enterprises, and a 'no bailout' policy for financial institutions was enforced (World Bank, 1999, p. ix). The fact that Estonia was in the first group of transition countries that were engaged in EU accession negotiations on 30 March 1998 can also be seen as a reflection of rapid movement towards the market economy. An EU Commission report on Estonia's progress towards accession as early as 1997 regarded Estonia as a functioning market economy. The accession report for the year 2000 concludes that Estonia should be able to cope with competitive pressure and market forces within the EU in the near term, provided that it stays on its present reform path (European Commission, 2000).

The European Bank for Reconstruction and Development (EBRD) has pointed out that, in 2001, 75% of GDP was contributed by the private sector. Progress with small-scale privatization and the development of a foreign exchange system was assessed by EBRD as meeting the standards and performance norms of advanced industrial countries (EBRD, 2001). That has made Estonia as a small country of only 1.4 million inhabitants a favourite location for foreign investments. Accumulated foreign investments in Estonia were 2050 Euros per capita by the end of 2000, making it one of the highest accumulated foreign direct investment (FDI) levels per capita in Central and Eastern Europe (OECD, 2001). Entrepreneurs from

Sweden and Finland have been especially active in establishing their businesses in Estonia or using services of Estonian SMEs as subcontractors. At the end of the first quarter of 2002, Swedish investments represented 37.3 per cent and Finnish investments 27.7 % of the total FDI stock in Estonia (Bank of Estonia, 2002).

A survey conducted by the Estonian Institute of Future Studies among Estonian entrepreneurs in the northern part of Estonia, Tallinn and Harjumaa county, indicated that 60% of entrepreneurs see Finnish-owned enterprises both as competitors and as co-operation partners, while 28% assess cooperation as the dominating relationship with Finnish companies (Kurik *et al.*, 2002). In 2001, the main destinations of Estonian export were Finland (33.9%), followed by Sweden (14.1%) and Germany (6.9%). Latvia's main export partner was Germany (16.7%) and Lithuania's was the United Kingdom (14.7%) (Statistical Office of Estonia, 2002a, p. 23). Other Baltic countries do not have such dominating foreign trade partners as Finland for Estonia. However 50–60% of Estonian exports to Finland and Sweden in 2001 were based on subcontracting (Statistical Office of Estonia, 2002b).

Estonia was ranked fourth in the 2002 global index of economic freedom calculated on the basis of 10 criteria by the Heritage Foundation and by the *Wall Street Journal* (*http://cf.heritage.org*). This is the same ranking as that of Ireland, Luxembourg and the Netherlands, but higher than that of all other present and potential EU member states. A high degree of openness to the international business environment has resulted in a rapid growth of exports but, on the other hand, an even more rapid increase of import flows. Estonia has become an open market economy and transit trade country, whose share of exports of goods and services in GDP was 91.7% in 2001. The share of the European Union in Estonia's exports was 76.5% in the year 2000 and 69.5% in the year 2001 (Statistical Office of Estonia, 2002a, pp. 19–23).

We will first analyse interconnections between the economic reform process, economic integration with the European Union and development trends of entrepreneurship in Estonia. Our aim is to point out the main challenges of the internationalization process from the point of view of entrepreneurs, who are simultaneously facing the impact of two radical change processes in their business environment: continuing transition towards a more advanced market economy and internationalization in the context of both general globalization trends and accession of Estonia to the European Union. Examples of programmes and initiatives for developing and supporting internationally oriented entrepreneurs are discussed in order to shape the future agenda for developing entrepreneurs which could take into consideration the context of a small open economy.

General development trends of entrepreneurship in Estonia

The classification of small and medium-sized enterprises in Estonia has followed recommendations of the EU Commission (European Commission, 1996) in recent years. In January 2001, the central Commercial Register included 15 577 sole proprietors and 47 335 enterprises. On 1 August 2002, there were 20 259 sole proprietors and 55 737 enterprises on the Commercial Register (Centre of Registers, 2002). The total number of sole proprietors registered at the Tax Board, however, is more than 60 000. At the same time, on the basis of tax returns, the number of active enterprises in the year 2000 was estimated at only 31 346, including 23 429 micro enterprises (0–9 employees), 6106 small enterprises (10–49 employees), 1128 medium-sized enterprises (50–249 employees) and 178 large enterprises (Ministry of Economy, 2002, p. 11). In 2001, most popular types of enterprises by legal forms were private limited companies (58.3% of enterprises) and public limited companies (15.3% of enterprises). General and limited partnerships and commercial associations together represented only 2.3% of enterprises. In 1995, public limited companies represented 70.2% of all enterprises. The Commercial Code which was introduced in 1995 increased founding capital requirements for setting up a public limited company (joint stock company) to 400 000 Estonian crowns (25 565 Euros), resulting in the conversion of public limited companies to private limited companies, where the required founding capital is 10 times lower. Under the regulations of the Commercial Code the number of sole proprietors also increased in recent years.

An important factor influencing entrepreneurial behaviour is abolishing the corporate income tax on reinvested profits starting from the year 2000. This has created incentives for increasing investments by companies already doing business in Estonia. In the first quarter of 2002, the total volume of such investments was 4.4 billion Estonian crowns. The share of investments by enterprises employing 1–19 persons was quite high, at 43%. Enterprises employing more than 99 persons made 37% of investments (Statistical Office of Estonia, 2002c, p. 7). However a lack of external risk capital has in recent years been a constraint on SME development in Estonia. In a Phare-sponsored survey of manufacturing SMEs in 1998, financing was mentioned as the highest-ranking problem area by 28% of respondents, marketing by 22%, and shortage of a qualified labour force by 16% of respondents (Phare, 1999, p. 144). Limited availability of investment loans, low availability of collateral that is acceptable to financial institutions and shortage of loans for working capital have remained problems both for start-up and growing SMEs, although a state agency, Kredex, has offered loan guarantees to SMEs in recent years.

The venture capital market remains weak and fewer than 20 medium and large companies are currently listed on the Tallinn Stock Exchange. Owners of growing SMEs are often forced to consider selling the company to foreign investors and to give up their role as an entrepreneur. This is an especially topical issue for SMEs in these sectors, where the business development logic assumes going international. Preparation for membership of the European Union means harmonization of the Estonian legislation, quality, safety and environment regulations with the EU requirements. Compliance with the new regulatory framework assumes substantial investments, especially in food and retail trade sectors. That may lead many small enterprises into financial difficulties and diminish the number of enterprises in these fields of business activity. Agricultural producers have been exposed to subsidized imports from EU countries but their competitive situation may improve, depending on the results of EU accession negotiations, if Estonia joins the EU common agricultural policy.

Small and medium-sized enterprises in foreign trade and international business

More SMEs are involved in foreign trade operations in a small open economy than in a large economy, where the domestic market is the first growth base for the majority of new ventures. In Estonia export development is a key activity contributing to business growth in sectors where the economy of scale is an important efficiency factor. Estonian liberal foreign trade rules and the stable exchange rate of the Estonian currency against the Euro have simultaneously encouraged SMEs as importers. Estonian legislation has also supported the growth of subcontracting through a customs procedure which allows firms to import components without paying customs duties, thereby reducing their working capital requirements and releasing additional capital. This process is widely used in the clothing and textiles sector and in the metals and machine building industry.

Although large enterprises export a higher proportion of their total output than SMEs, the share of SMEs in total exports increased in the 1990s (Table 21.1). It is medium-sized firms (50–249 employees) that have been increasing their contribution to total exports, in absolute as well as relative terms. One of the potential roles of SMEs in economic development is generation of external income through their foreign trade activities. On the basis of this evidence, OECD exports conclude that the Estonian SME sector is making a growing contribution in this regard (OECD, 2002).

From 1998, the Estonian Export Agency has commissioned surveys on export prospects and barriers that inhibit export development in Estonian companies. The survey conducted in 2001 is based on expert assessments by top managers and export managers representing 338 enterprises. The rate of export growth in the foreseeable future was assessed to be moderate.

Table 21.1   Structure of exports, by size of enterprise

Number of employees	Share of exports from net sales			Share of exports from total exports		
	1997	1998	1999	1997	1998	1999
0–19	13.3	13.9	13.1	18.9	20.0	19.1
20–49	20.8	18.7	20.1	18.3	16.8	15.5
50–99	20.6	23.3	26.3	12.1	14.3	17.7
100–249	27.8	26.9	27.4	16.6	17.5	16.9
>250	37.7	33.2	33.8	34.1	31.4	30.7
Total	22.8	22.0	22.5	100.0	100.0	100.0

Source: Statistical Office of Estonia, Financial statistics of enterprises, 1997–9.

In the year 2002, it is anticipated to remain within 5 to 6%. Finland, Sweden and Latvia are seen as the main destinations of export growth. Respondents see cheap production input and good quality as the main sources of competitive advantage. At the same time 63% of exporters do not use any quality system.

Among main external export barriers, increasing competition in the international marketplace (63% of respondents) and limited information about customs procedures of foreign states (35%) were pointed out. Main barriers for the Estonian business environment also included the customs and taxation policies (56% of respondents). Export barriers inside enterprises were linked to the shortage of finance and working capital (50% of respondents), shortage of qualified labour (38%) and the high level of production costs. Lack of export training was mentioned as an essential barrier by only 13% of respondents and lack of developed products by 17% of respondents. The largest proportion of managers (23%) pointing out the lack of new products as an export barrier can be found in enterprises employing 100–249 employees. Managers in both largest and smallest enterprises stress the new product development barrier less frequently: 14% and 13% of respondents, respectively. In fact the average number of staff in the field of new product development was 1.5 employees per enterprise (Ariko Marketing, 2001). During the period 1998–2000, 44% of enterprises introduced new products to the export market but the share of these products in their sales turnover in the year 2000 was about 9%. Among large enterprises 55% had introduced new export products during the period 1998–2000, but only 36% of small enterprises and 44–5% of medium-sized enterprises had done the same (ibid., p. 18).

The results of this recent export survey support conclusions from earlier research (Elenurm, 2001) that the logic of export development and going international in the SME sector of Estonia as a transition country is different from the logic which has served as the basis of export development programmes in stable market economies. The research on international entrepreneurship has in recent decades been strongly influenced by the stages approach of the Uppsala school (Johanson and Vahlne, 1977, 1990) and approaches that relate stages of entrepreneurial internationalization to product, operation mode and market dimensions (Luostarinen and Welch, 1997).

Over the past few years these approaches have been challenged by the concept of born globals as companies which start exporting and follow internationalization strategies from an early stage of their business activities (Knight and Cavusgil, 1996; Andersson and Wictor, 2001). A paradox of an open emerging market economy is that even a company which does not have an advanced internationalization strategy may be able to move rapidly to the direct export stage by exploiting the cost advantage of low-cost labour and other production resources if by chance it has been identified by a suitable foreign partner. One could label such company 'a born global' if only the formal benchmark of reaching at least 25% share of foreign sales in total sales turnover within three years of their birth is used. However, if the other element of the born global definition ('seeks to derive significant competitive advantage from the use of resources and the sales of outputs in multiple countries': Andersson and Wictor, 2001, p. 43) refers to active strategic efforts, the number of born globals in a transition economy is quite small.

New enterprises or restructured former state enterprises first started to export as opportunistic subcontractors and only later focused on a more strategic approach by comparing different target markets and entry modes and by investing in their own product development and market research. A survey of Baltic clothing exporters (Smallbone and Venesaar 1998) pointed out that, compared with Polish and Bulgarian firms, Baltic clothing exporters, including Estonian enterprises, were more likely to be involved in foreign subcontracting. Although more than half of surveyed clothing firms had subcontract relations with foreign customers, only 10% were acting as subcontractors for domestic customers. Unlike the case of a mature market economy, domestic subcontract chains are a less common feature of the Estonian transition economy. In recent years the strategic challenge of moving from subcontracting to the value-added export of own products has been more clearly perceived by managers of some larger clothing firms after subcontracting-based growth and resource accumulation during the 1990s.

Authors discussing the logic of internationalization stages also point out the importance of learning by experience and feedback from international marketing activities as factors enabling companies to move along the logical path of internationalization (Johanson and Vahlne 1990, Yip *et al.*, 2000). Relevant competence development needs and knowledge gaps should be identified in order to succeed in the international business environment. Entrepreneurs in East European small transition economies face the challenge of intensified learning in the field of international business even if they do not follow explicit and focused internationalization targets in the same way as born globals from advanced market economies.

Experience and challenges of international business learning
The concept of international business learning in an open transition economy has several meanings. Learning needs are not limited to export development and setting up a business abroad. Understanding the international business context is also important to a domestically oriented entrepreneur for forecasting future roles of international players in his domestic marketplace. The entrepreneur has to develop international business negotiation skills in order to make a good deal by setting up a joint venture with a foreign partner or to sell his enterprise to a foreign investor. Training programmes have to match learning by doing experience but also social and political environment factors that have shaped attitudes of entrepreneurs towards international business challenges.

A special international factor that for potential Estonian entrepreneurs created some understanding of the market economy logic and trends in the international business environment was for many Estonians the Finnish mass media of the 1970s and 1980s. It has been quite easy and popular for Estonians in the northern part of the country to follow Finnish TV and radio broadcasts as part of their everyday activities. Decades of such practice have increased Finnish language skills in Estonia. A Finnish employer recruiting an Estonian workforce may find that in the northern part of the country it is quite easy to recruit employees who have some command of the Finnish language. It is not so easy in Tartu or other regions of southern Estonia. Finnish TV broadcasts did not cover these more distant regions. During the Soviet stagnation years it was also possible in Central Russia to find active listeners to the Voice of America or BBC who were able to develop competence in understanding the logic of the market economy. However following and openly discussing in work communities 'enemy propaganda' could not be as widespread a practice there as following and discussing Finnish TV and radio programmes in Estonia. Some elements of American and Nordic management concepts were introduced in Estonian higher education many years before *perestroika* and *glasnost.*

As early as the beginning of *perestroika* in 1986 an experiment giving opportunities to create so-called 'small state enterprises' was initiated in Estonia. These were in fact independent entrepreneurial spin-off companies formally founded by large state-owned enterprises. Small state enterprises were a useful learning-by-doing environment for preparing attitudes and skills to be used in future private entrepreneurship activities. An important initiative in the context of innovative learning was the Estonian economic autonomy (IME) concept first presented in September 1997. Although this concept was never fully implemented in the Soviet system, following public discussion of its principles and action plans was a good learning exercise for large numbers of people, preparing them for the real vision of an independent Estonia and for thinking about the international competitiveness of its economy. A key idea which was discussed in the context of the economic autonomy was introducing Estonia's own convertible currency that could serve as the basis for linking companies to the world market. In fact Estonia's own convertible currency was introduced in June 2002, 10 months after regaining political independence in August 2002.

The first training programmes in the field of export had already started in Estonia during the early stage of disintegration of the Soviet command economy in 1987. Up to the end of the 1980s the key question in foreign trade training was how to understand changing Soviet state regulations on exporting and importing and how to apply skills for running export operations despite bureaucratic rules.

Restoration of the independent Estonian Republic and introduction of the Estonian national currency were accompanied by radical changes in the structure of foreign trade and reorientation to Nordic and other Western markets. Simultaneously the Estonian customs system was created. Contact seminars with Finnish and Swedish companies at this stage gained popularity among Estonian entrepreneurs and managers of still state-owned companies looking for subcontracting opportunities. The partner identification approach during the early 1990s had quite a short time horizon and was not based on long-term export development plans.

In 1994–5, the first Export Development Programme for Growing Companies was conducted by a local training company, EM-International, in cooperation with the Trade Council of Iceland, the University of Vaasa and the Mikkeli Small Entrepreneurship Center of the Helsinki School of Economics. The Nordic Council of Ministers supported the programme. The first version of the programme integrated 10 two-day training sessions and practical work for developing the export marketing plan by each participant. Participating companies had the opportunity to use counsellors and students who collected information about the target market. EM-International later modified the original programme and it has been run under the title Competence Programme for Company Export Managers. Another training company, EMI EWT, had participated in arranging the programme for two years. The next ECP programme was a cooperation project between EM-International and the Estonian Chamber of Commerce and Industry. This version of the Competence Programme for Company Export Managers had nine two-day modules:

I   Foundations of international marketing,
II   Sales contract in foreign trade,
III   Entering foreign markets: customs and transportation,
IV   Banking transactions and finances in foreign trade,
V   Strategic partners and alliances at international markets,
VI   Quality management and new product development for export markets,
VII   Techniques of international business negotiations,
VIII Teamwork in the exporting company,
IX   Assessing and implementing export development programmes.

During feedback sessions at the end of the programme and in interviews conducted after the end of the training cycle, participants in the programme assessed the following as plus factors of this training cycle:

- the systematic basic knowledge and increased competence in export marketing,
- technical aspects of foreign trade operations,
- work for developing the export-oriented business plan,
- a chance to communicate with colleagues.

Aspects which should be improved in such training programmes included the following:

- costing, pricing and financial analysis, banking (especially in Russia),
- more practical examples of successful export strategies,
- practical activity on target markets, visiting target markets,
- how to find investments for export development,
- more group work and practical case studies,
- practical recommendations from sharing experience of practitioners,
- more recommendations about export-related literature,
- too long a training period.

Remarks about the long total period of the programme reflect the busy and turbulent lives of those working in Estonian enterprises in the export field. However nine or 10 two-day sessions over a period of 10 months is not a long period if we follow the original action learning principle of the programme. As a matter of fact, at the present development stage of Estonian entrepreneurship, the majority of small entrepreneurial companies have not yet perceived the need to concentrate their training and development efforts on creating and implementing strategically oriented export plans. They are more ready to deal with knowledge gaps related to technical and legal aspects of export operations and also seek assistance in identifying foreign partners.

A survey of export-related training needs in 94 Estonian companies representing wood and furniture, food processing, electronics, information technology, clothing, mechanical engineering and export logistics sectors which we conducted in the summer and autumn of 1998 deepened our understanding of training needs at the stage of economic transition, when international competitiveness and European Union accession started to become topical issues. The greatest gaps between importance ranking given to the competence area and assessment of the existing level of knowledge were identified in the following areas (Elenurm, 2001):

- the European Union as the target market, entering the market;
- conducting market research in the target market;
- identifying business partners and studying their background;
- legal aspects of foreign trade, the Vienna Convention;
- organizations supporting export development, efficient use of export aid;
- assessing the export potential and competitiveness of the company;
- claims, solving disputes and arbitration;
- composing export–import contracts, the model sales contract form of International Chamber of Commerce (ICC);
- foundations of international marketing;
- intermediaries in foreign trade, model agent contract forms of ICC;
- negotiating techniques.

Listed topics include broader strategically oriented training fields and specific legal and process aspects of foreign trade operations. General strategic analysis of the export potential and competitiveness, market research and different ways to enter EU target markets were considered important training topics mainly by larger companies that had already accumulated export development experience. Entrepreneur–managers of smaller companies were often locked into a subcontracting mode of business and did not see real opportunities for the high-profile strategy of going international even if they acquired relevant know-how. Therefore, at the present stage of transition, differentiated training approaches should take into consideration the resources and life cycles of enterprises.

Customs regulations and procedures related to export and import operations, sales contracts, contracts with brokers and forwarders, Incoterms and techniques of trade negotiations are the main topics of the Foreign Business Basic Course and short courses which are run by EMI EWT. Recently the Competence Programme for Exporters and Importers, aimed at both inward and outward foreign trade operations, has been introduced by EMI EWT.

The contract-based way of thinking has not been deeply rooted in the behaviour model of Estonian new businessmen. Trainees often pay more attention to legal technicalities than to the functions of contracts in the field of expressing the will of business partners and regulating their relations. The Estonian Chamber of Commerce and Industry has arranged information days dealing with the legal aspects of export operations, trade contacts for entering potential markets and other topical export problems. Seminars on international bank transactions, terms and methods of payment were also arranged earlier by ESKO training. Negotiating techniques are taught in workshops arranged by various management training centres.

Several training centres have arranged one or two-day seminars on customs procedures by using representatives of the Estonian State Customs Office as main lecturers. The knowledge base for focusing on customs regulations, procedures and practices of export target countries has been more limited, however. In order to use new opportunities created by Estonian membership in the World Trade Organisation, Estonian exporters should also learn more about import procedures of more distant potential markets.

Training in the field of marketing as an essential concept for export development is arranged by the Finnish Marketing Institute (distance courses), the Executive Training Centre of the Estonian Business School, Helvetia Baltic Partners, Invicta and some other training institutions. A programme for developing consultants in the field of exports was conducted in 1999 as a cooperation project between the Danish Agency for Trade and Industry and the Estonian Export Agency.

This brief overview demonstrates that existing export training practices include multi-module programmes for developing and implementing the export strategy, short seminars on specific fields of export operations and information-sharing events on new trade regulations or international contact opportunities. The Estonian business training sector has become a field of intensive competition. Managers and entrepreneurs have to choose between training programmes promoted by local and foreign-owned training companies and programmes sponsored by foreign aid schemes. Short half-day information events on topical changes in the business environment and regulations from time to time have a high number of participants, but programmes aiming at long-term export development competence often do not have enough committed trainees to run advanced participative training processes. Foreign trainers in internationally sponsored training programmes are sometimes perceived by participants as people 'dealing with ABC knowledge' or 'not knowing our situation and using irrelevant examples'.

International business as an academic subject is taught at Estonian universities and business schools, including the University of Tartu, the Tallinn Technical University and the Estonian Business School. On the entrepreneurship track of the Estonian Business School the export course is focused on preparing students for export operations, searching for information about foreign markets, adapting products to different export markets, choosing entrance modes and distribution channels, and issues related to customs procedures, contracts and export financing. A large majority of masters students but also graduate students participating in distance learning and evening classes already have jobs in enterprises or act as entrepreneurs. Interaction with such students reveals different learning priorities. Some students already have some experience of running small-scale export and import operations. Their main focus is to acquire more detailed know-how about legal and technical issues related to export operations. A learning challenge is to convince them that a long-term export development strategy should also be a priority if they do not identify themselves as foreign trade middlemen but try to assume the role of an entrepreneur in a growing enterprise.

The main gap in the programmes which have been conducted so far has been the limited market survey and counselling input and inability to include in the programme visits to target markets. The reason for this limitation is partly financial and partly lack of trained counsellors having practical experience in branches represented by participants. In advanced market economies one can find large numbers of experienced export managers who, after several decades of export development practice, find a new profession as an export counsellor or trainer. In Estonia, as in other transition economies nobody can claim to have 20 years of local experience in the field of entrepreneurial export development.

References

Andersson, S. and Wictor, I. (2001), 'Innovative International Strategies in New Firms – Born Globals, the Swedish Case', *4th McGill Conference on International Entrepreneurship*, vol. 1, Glasgow: University of Strathclyde, pp. 39–63.
Ariko Marketing (2001), Eksportööride uuring 2001.

382   *Geographic perspectives*

Bank of Estonia (2002), *http://www.ee/EPBE/fdi/4b.html.en*.
Blomstermo, A. and Eriksson, K. (2001), 'Domestic Operations and the Internationalization Process of Firms', *4ᵗʰ McGill Conference on International Entrepreneurship*, vol. 1, Glasgow: University of Strathclyde, pp. 131–58.
Centre of Registers (2002), *http://www.eer.ee/table_eng.phtml*.
EBRD (2001), *Transition Report 2001: Energy in Transition*, London: European Bank for Reconstruction and Development.
Elenurm, T. (2001), 'Development needs of Estonian entrepreneurs and managers for international business', *4ᵗʰ McGill Conference on International Entrepreneurship*, vol. 1, Glasgow: University of Strathclyde, pp. 384–407.
European Commission (1996), *Commission Recommendation 96/28EC of 2 April 1996*.
European Comission (2000), *2000 Regular Report from the Commission on Estonia's Progress Towards Accession* (*http://europa.eu.int/comm/enlargement/estonia*).
Heritage Foundation (2002), *http://cf.heritage.org*.
Johanson, J. and Vahlne, J.-E. (1977), 'The Internationalization Process of the Firm – a Model of Knowledge Development and Increasing Foreign Market Commitments', *Journal of International Business Studies*, 8 (1), 23–32.
Johanson, J. and Vahlne, J.-E.. (1990), 'The Mechanism of Internationalization', *International Marketing Review*, 7 (4), 11–24.
Knight, G. and Cavusgil, S.T. (1996), 'The Born Global Firm: a Challenge to Traditional Internationalization Theory', *Advances in International Marketing*, Stamford: JAI Press, pp. 11–26.
Kurik, S., Terk, E., Kovin, M. and Paling, A. (2002), *Tallinna ja Harjumaa ettevõtjad Eesti-Soome integratsioonist*, Tallinn: Eesti Tuleviku-uuringute Instituut.
Luostarinen, R. and Welch, L. (1997), *International Business Operations*, Helsinki: Kyriiri OY.
Ministry of Economy (2002), *Ettevõtlik Eesti*, Tallinn, Majandusministeerium.
OECD (2001), *OECD Review of Foreign Investments: Estonia*, Paris: OECD.
OECD (2002), *Estonia Country Assessment*, May, Paris: OECD.
Phare (1999), *The State of Small Business in Estonia. Report 1998*, PHARE Support to SME Development in Estonia, Tallinn, 1999.
Smallbone, D. and Venesaar, U. (1998), 'Internationalisation Processes and SME Development in the Baltic States: Some Recent Evidence and Key Policy Issues', *5ᵗʰ Nordic–Baltic Conference in Regional Science*, Estonian Institute of Future Studies, University of Tartu.
Statistical Office of Estonia (2002a), *Estonia, Latvia, Lithuania in Figures 2002*, Tallinn: Statistical Office of Estonia.
Statistical Office of Estonia (2002b), *Statistical Yearbook of Estonia*, Tallinn: Statistical Office of Estonia.
Statistical Office of Estonia (2002c), *Business 2002/1. Quarterly Bulletin*, Tallinn: Statistical Office of Estonia.
World Bank (1999), *Estonia. Implementing the EU Accession Agenda*, Washington, DC: World Bank.
Yip, G., Biscarri and J. and Monti, J. (2000), 'The Role of the Internationalization Process in the Performance of Newly Internationalizing Firms', *Journal of International Marketing*, 8(3), 10–35.

22 Finnish perspectives of international entrepreneurship
Reijo Luostarinen and Mika Gabrielsson

Globalization has become a focus of interest throughout the world.* It is a swearword for some (r)evolutionary communities; it is one of the challenging issues for international organizations; it is also one of the key topics of many national governments; it is an attractive business strategy at the company level; it is a controversial subject for the man in the street; finally it is a growing area of interest in research and teaching in many business schools and universities.

In view of the above, it is understandable that the term 'globalization' can be used in different contexts and can have many different meanings and interpretations. Different societies, such as companies, labour unions, universities, economies and cultures, are globalizing. In this chapter the globalization of firms is under focus. However, even in business, globalization has been studied from different angles. An analysis of the globalization of management thoughts and attitudes has brought an interesting classification à la Perlmutter (1969): ethnocentric, polycentric, regiocentric and geocentric (global). Studies of the globalization of marketing have resulted in two opposite categories: standardization and differentiation (Levitt, 1983). 'Think globally, act locally' has become one of the major slogans in MNCs, indicating the challenging effort involved in searching for a balance. In addition to this, different firms in different countries have globalized at different times and in different ways.

In this chapter the latest globalization phenomenon, the born global company, is studied. Globalization is used in the geographical sense, as a spatial term, to denote the process where the firm extends its operations over the border line of the domestic continent to other continents. These born globals are of special interest as a subject to be studied. Firstly there is a very recent but rapidly growing group of companies of considerable importance for the respective economies. For example, in Australia, 20 per cent of new trade growth in the early 1990s came from born global SMEs (Rennie, 1993). Secondly they seem to behave in very different ways and

* This chapter was originally commissioned by Léo-Paul Dana for the inaugural issue of the *Journal of International Entrepreneurship*.

utilize different strategies than earlier internationalized and globalized companies. Thirdly, owing to the very exceptional visions and strategies from the inception of these firms, the managerial challenges for the entrepreneurs (especially for the many young ones) are also exceptionally large.

In this chapter we try to answer the following questions related to born globals (BGs): what are the characteristics of BGs, where do they exist, when and why did they enter business, how have they done it and what are the major challenges caused by BGs to entrepreneurs, teaching and research.

The BGs are compared with the firms which internationalized and/or globalized earlier, in the traditional way. These comparisons are based on the results of the large empirical studies of Finnish multinationals completed in 1976 (1006 firms), 1983 (1197 firms), 1990 (593) firms and 1997 (390) firms by Luostarinen and his team at the Finland's International Business Operations (FIBO) research programme and on the results of the doctoral and post-doctoral studies at the Centre of International Business Research (CIBR) in the Helsinki School of Economics.

Born Globals as a concept
What BGs are is the first question to be answered. The first empirical studies of the internationalization processes and strategies of the Finnish firms conducted by Luostarinen in 1976–82 within the FIBO programme at the Helsinki School of Economics indicated that, out of 1006 internationalizing industrial firms, 91 per cent started their business first at home in domestic markets before entering foreign markets (Luostarinen, 1979). In addition to this it is interesting to note that the average length of the domestic period based on the results of the studies in 1976, 1983, 1990 and 1997 has become steadily shorter. This development indicates that Finnish firms have entered foreign markets earlier and earlier after the establishment of the firm. The fact that, in the 1997 study, many of the firms entered foreign and domestic markets simultaneously and that a few companies even started foreign business before domestic business indicates that a challenging change in the behaviour of firms has taken place.

Still more interesting is the fact that an increasing number of these companies started to operate on other continents before, simultaneously or soon after entering European markets. These firms are called Born Globals. BGs seem to have come into existence during the last 12 to 17 years; that is, in part since 1985, but mainly since 1990. A clear indication of the very recent and rapidly increasing appearance of the BGs is given in Table 22.1, which is based on our survey of the existence of BGs in Finland. As can be seen, the number of BGs has been steadily increasing annually, leading to the fact that, out of 93 BGs, only 9 per cent were established in 1985–9, 70 per cent in 1990–9, and 22 per cent in 2000–2001.

Table 22.1   Establishment years of born globals

Year	Number	Percent	Number/year
1985–1989	8	9	1.6
1990–1994	25	27	5.0
1995–1999	40	43	8.0
2000–2001	20	22	10.0
Total	93	~100	5.5

However a historical analysis reveals that some, even if only very few, had behaved very similarly much earlier. These so-called 'deviations' from the mainstream pattern of internationalization (Luostarinen, 1979) can be called pioneering or early BGs. Vaisala Corporation, a global market leader in meteorological forecasting systems, is a typical example. It was established in 1936. Its first business was neither in domestic Finnish markets nor in neighbouring or other European markets, but in another continent, the United States. The founder of the Vaisala weather forecasting system company was Doctor Väisälä, who was a globetrotter and an internationally recognized scientist. His basic idea was simple: 'if the US markets accept our products then the rest of the world will also be open for us'. Thanks to a high degree of global experience, excellent foreign language ability, global networking and a strong belief in the excellence and superiority of the product, the perception of risks and uncertainties related to global business were perceived to be exceptionally low in Vaisala, resulting in a very low degree of lateral rigidity towards globalization.

Using our preliminary historical analyses and our pilot studies on BGs, the authors would like to divide born global companies into the two categories: pioneering or early BGs and present-day BGs. Pioneering BGs include firms which started to do business in global markets before 1985, with a very short domestic period, or even without it. There are only seven or eight such companies, such as Vaisala Corporation, totalling about 0.2 per cent of the 4000 Finnish firms which are doing business abroad.

Present-day BGs are firms which were established in or after 1985 and which started to globalize their operations from their very inception, simultaneously with domestic markets or after an exceptionally short domestic period – sometimes they even entered international/global markets first and after that domestic markets. They represent about 4 per cent of 4000 Finnish firms doing business abroad, that is 160 companies, such as Biohit, a Finnish liquid handling and biotech firm and F-secure, a Finnish IT firm.

In order to be able to compare the BG companies with internationaliz-ing/international firms and with globalizing/global firms, corresponding definitions are needed. These definitions are based on the FIBO data banks on the internationalization of Finnish firms.

Internationalizing firms are firms for which domestic business is the largest source of income (over 50 per cent of total sales) but which have also entered other countries on their own continent and which may become international companies in the future (about 2000 firms, or 50 per cent of the 4000 Finnish firms doing business abroad).

International or internationalized firms are firms for which international business is the largest source of sales revenue (over 50 per cent of total sales) and whose major foreign markets are located in their domestic con-tinent (about 1400, or 35 per cent of the 4000 firms).

Globalizing companies are firms which have either started their interna-tionalizing process or are already internationals and have, after that, started to globalize their operations by entering markets outside their domestic continent and which may become global companies in the future (global-izing internationals) (about 400, or 10 per cent of the 4000 firms).

Global companies are companies which have usually first started to inter-nationalize their operations and subsequently have entered global markets, deriving most of their income from non-domestic continents (about 40, or 1 per cent of the 4000 firms).

As to the title of 'born globals', different authors in different countries have named these firms differently. Through the literature analysis we have been able to identify chronologically the following titles for more or less the same phenomenon:

a)   deviations, inconsistencies, variations from the mainstream stages pattern (Luostarinen, 1970, 1979, 1994; Johanson and Vahlne, 1977; Luostarinen and Welch, 1990; Luostarinen and Hellman, 1994; Luostarinen *et al.*, 1994);

b)   new, technology-based firms (Autio *et al.*, 1989; Luostarinen *et. al.*, 1994; Autio, 1995);

c)   high-technology start-ups (Alahuhta, 1990; Jolly *et al.*, 1991);

d)   high value-added exporters/emerging exporters (McKinsey & Co., 1993);

e)   born globals (Rennie, 1993; Knight and Cavusgil, 1996; Madsen and Servais, 1997; Kirpalani and Luostarinen, 1999; Autio *et al.*, 2000; Sasi *et al.*, 2000; Knight *et al.*, 2001);

f)   innovative SMEs with global business idea (Luostarinen *et al.*, 1994);

g)   global start-ups/international new ventures (Oviatt and McDougall, 1994; McDougall *et al.*, 1994);

h)   gazelles (Vahcic, 1995; Birch, 2001);
i)   born internationals (Majkgård and Sharma, 1999);
j)   instant internationals (Preece *et al.*, 1999; Dana, 2001);
k)   global, knowledge-intensive firms (Almor, 2000).

The first authors to pay attention to the deviant behaviour in international business of some firms were the Nordic developers of the stages patterns of internationalization (see point (a) above). In addition to this, the new concepts of de-internationalization and re-internationalization were presented (Luostarinen, 1979). In the 1970s, when the internationalization target country (Luostarinen, 1970; Johanson and Vahlne, 1977) and company-level stage patterns (Luostarinen, 1979, 1994) were presented, the present deviant behaviour of BGs existed only through a very few pioneering BGs.

For the purposes of this chapter, we believe that the title 'born globals' describes best the characteristics of the companies under investigation. In the following the summary is made on the comparison of the way BGs differ from internationalizing/internationalized and/or from globalizing/globalized companies. The review is based on four stages – the establishment stage, domestic stage, internationalization stage and the globalization stage – by analysing the measures taken, strategies followed and structures created in different stages.

Establishment stage
BGs were established after 1985, mainly after 1990; thus, on average, they are much younger than the traditional internationalizing/international firms and globalizing/global companies (traditionals). Owing to the globalization push and pull from inception, the vision or strategic intent of BGs includes global business from the very beginning and the initial growth targets of BGs are much more ambitious than in traditionals. Because BGs have to go abroad and to globalize much earlier and much faster than traditional firms, their need for finance, global market knowledge, R&D know-how and global management skills is much larger from the beginning than in traditionals.

Domestic stage
In traditional companies the domestic stage has been a relatively long, natural and necessary stage of business development, but in BGs the domestic stage has been very short (for one month to two years) or nonexistent. Because of the long domestic stage, the entrepreneurs of the traditionals have had much better opportunities to gather and utilize the experiences and knowledge of the domestic business learning process than is the case for BG entrepreneurs.

Internationalization stage and strategies
BGs' strategies, stages and processes are from their inception based on global business, whereas in traditionals, after the domestic stage, these are based on international business opportunities on the domestic continent. This is why BGs' strategies, stages and processes differ from those of the traditionals as to scale and scope. In consequence of the above, the structures of business portfolios and structures of organization in BGs are also different from those of traditional internationalizing/international firms.

Globalization stage and strategies
Owing to highly specialized niche products, the domestic push forces and foreign pull forces of the lead markets are stronger in BGs than in traditionals. This is why time is a more critical element for BGs and why timing (first in the world markets), speed (rapid penetration and escalation) and rhythm (investments based on availability of resources and on the development of demand) are extremely important for BGs' success. Standardization of product offerings globally as well as marketing strategies in order to gain economies of scale, as well as simultaneous adaptation to the local needs of global lead customers and markets, is a greater challenge than in traditional internationalizing/international firms (see the section 'Strategies of Born Globals' below).

Areas of Born Globals
An interesting question is where these exceptionally behaving BGs are located. This question can be approached from two different angles. What are the countries where the BGs are located and what are the businesses or business areas where they are established? Based on our earlier pilot studies it can be argued that BGs are established mainly in niche business areas. These areas are, as regards product, unique, have high research and development (RD) content and demand high-level management and marketing skills.

According to our pilot studies, the BGs are not only high-tech firms, as usually presented in earlier research, but to be met in all the following five business areas (Kirpalani and Luostarinen, 1999; see also Rennie, 1993): (1) high-tech businesses (Junkkari, 2000), (2) high-design businesses (Rasilainen, 2002), (3) high-service businesses (Rinkinen, 2000), (4) high-know-how businesses (Teimonen, 2001), (5) high-system businesses (Konttinen, 2001).

The results of our survey study of the existence of BGs indicate (Table 22.2) that hi-tech BGs are the largest group (40 per cent), high-system BGs (22 per cent) the second, followed by high-service BGs (21 per cent), high-know-how BGs (12 per cent) and hi-design BGs (4 per cent). It is worth mentioning that biotech companies also are an important sector of BGs.

Table 22.2   Business areas of born globals

Area	Number	Percent	Area total
High-tech	27	30	
High-tech & other	9	10	40
High systems	20	22	22
High service	6	7	
High service & other	13	14	21
High know-how	8	9	
High know-how & other	3	3	12
High design	4	4	4
Total	90	~100	~100

They can be found in all of the above groups, except in high-design businesses.

As to the geographic locations of the corporate headquarters, we may conclude, on the basis of the above, that BGs are certainly to be found in large and rich nations because these offer promising markets with high potential demand for these types of products. In addition, these countries are able to offer good sources of finance and also plenty of global managerial and marketing talents owing to the large number of global companies. However these BGs are also established in small and open economies (SMOPECs). A clear distinction is that, when the BGs of large nations have huge domestic markets and have thus no heavy instant push or pressure to globalize, the BGs of SMOPECs have very open and small, even if sophisticated, markets which are absolutely too small for these businesses and where the demand and competition are getting global very quickly. Thus one could argue that BGs of large countries globalize mainly because of the demand-based pull forces in global markets but BGs of SMOPECs do so also as a result of the push and pressure forces based largely on the smallness and openness of domestic markets and on the fear of expected future competition coming from BGs located in big countries (see Figure 22.1). The latter are equipped not only with better finance and a larger pool of management talent but also with the valuable experiences and scale advantages of doing larger-scale business in the particular niche area in question. The paradox is evident: the small companies with small and open markets and with limited financial and managerial resources have to face the greatest possible managerial challenge: to globalize the firm and to do it soon and fast in order to survive and prosper. This can be seen in the development of international business related slogans used in many SMOPECs. In the 1960s the slogan in Finland was 'Export or die', in the 1970s and 1980s 'Internationalize or die', and in the 1990s and 2000 'Globalize or die'.

It seems that globalization in general and BGs in particular are much more important phenomena for SMOPECs than for large economies. This is one of the major reasons why the Academy of Finland and TEKES, the National Technology Agency, decided to finance a 'mega' project under the 'Finnish Companies and Challenges of Globalization' (LIIKE) research programme. The BG project, as a joint venture between the Helsinki School of Economics and Helsinki University of Technology, is the largest subproject within this programme.

Motives and factors of Born Globals
What have been the major reasons for the recent emergence of BGs? What has happened in the environment? What have been the major motives for the entrepreneurs to start to establish BGs?

As to the global macro business environment, some interesting changes have taken place that facilitate the birth of BGs. Transport connections have become global, wider and more rapid than ever, allowing access to most important business centres on different continents within 24 hours. Information and communication channels have become instant, allowing real-time transfer of data, knowledge, pictures, drawings and other business-related information, and two-way communication. Monetary channels are also allowing more instant transfer of profits, interests, royalties, management fees, technical payments, portfolio and direct investment money and so on globally than in the past. All of these developments are global enablers making it much easier to enter, penetrate and escalate into different continents than has been the case hitherto (see, for example, Rennie 1993; Madsen and Servais, 1997).

As to the environmental macro factors in domestic and foreign markets, the unification and globalization of some consumer tastes, needs and demand patterns have also to be mentioned owing to the globalization development in information, communication, transport and money and knowledge transfer systems described above.

Thanks to these global enablers, competition also has become more and more global. In the past the competitive moves were much more local or regional. Today the reactions and countermeasures are global. Global timing has become important. *Rapids are eating slow ones*. 'Globalize fast or die' has become the major slogan in the businesses of BGs. Integration developments in different markets have led to larger unified markets on different continents, creating larger pull forces to enter.

At the meso or industry level the product development costs in some industries (medicine, biotechnology, ITC) are getting higher. For the firms of SMOPECs this means that the profit contribution received from small domestic markets is not enough. When success rates for new product innovations are still low and life cycles for successful innovations are getting shorter, the pressures to enter global markets have been increasing. This is especially so in the high-tech, high-design, high-service, high-know-how and high-system niche businesses, which are the major areas of BGs.

At the micro or company level the advantages that firms are gaining through globalization, especially in SMOPECs, are so powerful (economies of scale and scope, RD advantages, specialization opportunities and so on) that the basic motives to establish BGs are strong enough to overcome the related risks and uncertainties.

To summarize: enabling global factors have made the globalization of the firm recently much easier in general than ever before. Increasing openness and small size of domestic markets have increased the push forces, particularly in SMOPECs, and reciprocally increased openness and large size of foreign target markets have increased the pull forces, creating a strong macro power field for the development of BGs (see Figure 22.1). When industry-specific factors and company-specific advantages at the meso and micro levels are added to the picture it is no wonder that BGs have come into existence recently.

Strategies of Born Globals

For the review of the major strategies of BGs we use Luostarinen's POM$ICA framework (see Figure 22.2). This consists of two separate but interlinked parts: the globalization strategy and the global marketing strategy. The globalization strategy includes three elements: the product strategy (P), the operation mode strategy (O) and the market strategy (M) (Luostarinen, 1979). In addition to the POM strategy, the global marketing strategy consists of pricing strategy ($), intermediate or distribution channel strategy (I), customer strategy (C) and advertising and promotion strategy (A), forming the $ICA part of the POM$ICA framework (Luostarinen, 2002).

The connecting arrows conditionally indicate that the product strategy has an impact on the selection of pricing strategy, operation strategy affects the selection of intermediate or distribution strategy, and the market strategy influences the determination of customer strategy, and that advertising or promotion strategy is usually dependent on all earlier components.

As mentioned above, the early results of pilot cases of 30 Finnish BGs indicate that these companies may exist in any of the five product categories: high-tech, high-design, high services, high know-how or high systems. They complement their initial product strategy with related product offerings (see Table 22.2) since often the products are new to the world and thus

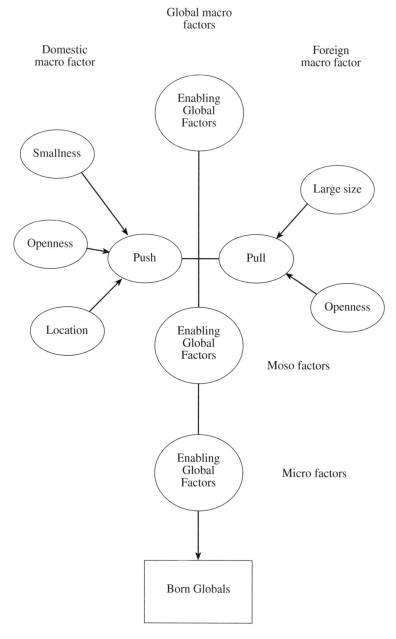

Figure 22.1   Factors influencing the existence of born globals in SMOPECs

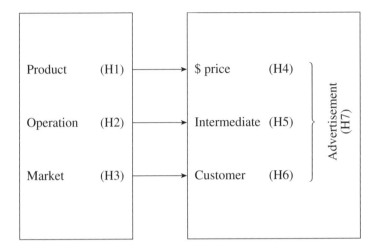

Figure 22.2 POM$ICA impact framework for the planning of global marketing strategy

services are not available from the outset. High-tech companies, for instance, need to offer services for their highly innovative goods on a world-wide basis. The high-service companies package their products into diskettes and manuals, which resemble physical goods in many ways. Also the high-know-how companies complement their product offering with consultation services. Finally, high-system companies by definition offer a combination of products, that is, a mix of goods, services and know-how. Where, traditionally, internationalized firms usually started by selling physical goods abroad and then moved to related services and finally to know-how and systems (Luostarinen, 1979), the BGs deviated from this mainstream pattern by offering high systems very soon after the establishment of the company or even from its inception. (See hypothesis H1.)

H1. *BG companies differ from the product mainstream pattern of the traditionally internationalized companies by using first services, know-how and even systems as their product strategy and by complementing their product strategies with related product offerings in an early stage of their globalization process.*

According to our pilot research findings, BGs have also been found to deviate from the operation mainstream pattern of internationalization in respect of both the holistic operation pattern of the internationalization process (Luostarinen, 1994) and their outward operation strategies

(Luostarinen, 1970, 1979). Traditional firms started their internationalization process first with inward operations, then strengthened the process by moving to outward operations and finally utilized also the cooperation modes (Luostarinen, 1994). As to the outward process, traditionally behaving firms used, first, non-investment marketing modes (indirect, direct or own export), and moved on to direct investment marketing modes (sales or marketing subsidiaries), non-investment production modes (licensing, contract manufacturing, subcontracting, co-production, industrial franchising) and finally to direct investment production modes (assembly and manufacturing units) (Luostarinen, 1970, 1979; see also Svetli *et al.*, 2001). According to our findings based on pilot studies, BGs may rapidly seek strategic alliances (cooperative stage), even as the first step, in order to complement their limited financial and managerial resources. As to the outward process, BGs may proceed at a fast pace through the stages, jumping over certain stages, or even proceeding in the reverse order. Many of the BGs, for instance, have used licensing or have established sales and/or marketing subsidiaries in lead countries before any other operations or, exceptionally, soon after the traditional export entry was initiated.

H2A. BGs deviate from the holistic operation mainstream pattern by proceeding in the reverse order or by moving exceptionally fast/simultaneously through the inward–outward cooperation process.

H2B: BG companies deviate from the outward operation mainstream pattern of internationalization by moving at a fast pace through stages, jumping over stages, or proceeding in the reverse order.

BGs not only deviate from traditional behaviour in respect of products and operations but also in their market expansion process. Traditionally internationalized/globalized firms usually entered countries at a greater and greater business distance (physical, cultural and economic distance; see Luostarinen, 1979). BGs expand simultaneously to such markets that offer high sales potential. Although the business distance between the home and target country may be long, BGs seek sales potential from the main markets from the outset. They can be expected to concentrate on lead markets (Alahuhta, 1990). As these companies have often been financed by venture capitalists with high growth expectations this is seen as only natural. (See hypothesis H3.)

H3. BGs deviate from the market mainstream pattern of internationalization by moving at a fast pace to lead markets, jumping over or even proceeding in the reverse order of what the business distance would indicate.

Our pilot research results indicate that BGs' marketing strategies are highly interdependent on the globalization strategy (Lavikkala, 2001; Mattila, 2001; Ratia, 2001; Viljanen, 2002; Sankari, 2002). The rapid globalization process seems to require that BGs proceed from less advanced marketing strategies to advanced strategies from the outset or at a rapid pace. We will next consider each global marketing mix element separately.

Traditionally internationalizing companies rely heavily on price differentiation on country markets. The accepted wisdom has been that prices should reflect the costs as well as the country market price levels. In the case of BGs it seems that the market pricing is leaking through the country borders. This is due to many factors, which include the influence of increased use of the Internet, the increasing number of global customers and grey market arbitration. Standardized pricing is, however, very difficult to implement across markets and does not capture the full market potential (Sorenson and Wiechmann, 1975). In contrast, getting the first reference customers is of the utmost importance even if it would require selling in the beginning at a lower level than costs. Therefore the preliminary results, that BG companies are using customer value as the basis for pricing across markets, seems logical.

H4. BGs deviate from traditionally internationalized companies in respect of pricing their products according to customer value across markets instead of using cost- based approaches.

Contrary to the traditional impact chain (see Figure 22.2), in BGs marketing channel selections often determine the marketing operation modes to be used. Gaining access to a pan-European or global marketing channel will determine the need for complementary direct marketing investment modes. BGs have limited resources and managerial skills for setting up direct sales channels, especially if the business is not suitable for Internet-based e-commerce. On the other hand, control over marketing channels is crucial owing to high expectations of growth. Gabrielsson's (1999) distribution model indicates that traditionally internationalizing companies advance from either direct or indirect single channels towards more demanding dual or hybrid multiple channels. BGs seem to advance rapidly from single to multiple channels or jump over the single channels and start directly with multiple channels. In connection with direct exporting or marketing subsidiaries, multiple channels may be used. (See hypothesis H5.)

H5. BGs deviate from traditionally internationalizing companies in moving at a fast pace from single channels (indirect, direct) to multiple channels (dual, hybrid) or even starting from the outset with multiple channels.

BGs often base their products on innovations that are highly specialized and tailored to the needs of specific global customer segments. The location of these lead customers often determines the markets to be entered, because the business distance has less importance as an explanatory factor. The global customer (micro) segmentation will first be applied and only as the next step will the customer potential in different world markets be estimated (see Hassan and Samli, 1994). This is contrary to the practice of traditional companies (see Figure 22.2) that are used to conducting their customer segmentation in those countries which have passed through the preliminary screening based on GNP and other macro-level indicators. (See hypothesis H6.)

H6. BGs deviate from traditionally internationalizing companies by selecting, first, lead users through global customer segmentation and, based on that, proceed to the country market selection, which means that the business distance has less explanatory power than earlier.

Building a global brand is essential for BGs in order to create demand that would secure the necessary growth expectations, on the one hand, and safeguard control over marketing activities, on the other (see also Kirpalani and Luostarinen, 1999). Traditional companies may proceed through stages without any brand, private label (PL) or Original Equipment Manager (OEM) brand when the risk of other competitors copying the innovation is low. Due to the high level of pull to globalize, BGs also have a high risk of imitative behaviour from their global competitors and thus a considerable pressure to create a global brand from inception.

H7. BGs deviate from the traditional companies by being subject to high pressure to develop their own global brand from inception.

For the empirical testing of these hypotheses we have defined the BG company as follows:

1. its products should belong either to high-tech, high-service, high-design, high-know-how or high-system category (or combined);
2. it should have been established between 1985 and 2002;
3. its vision or strategic intent should have been from inception to become a globally acting company;
4. to be truly BG the share of sales outside the domestic continent (Europe) should be 50 per cent or more. However lower shares are also accepted for different classification purposes owing to the recent emergence of BGs.

Future challenges
BGs are facing many challenges. Many factors are pushing and pulling them towards rapid globalization, as described earlier. BG companies are much younger than traditional companies and also the entrepreneurs themselves are often young. Therefore it is understandable that BGs are facing many entrepreneurial challenges in respect of management, research and development, purchasing, sales, marketing and finance. Because of the deviant behaviour of the BGs, challenges for the governmental promotional policies are new. These challenges have not been researched in depth, although their importance has been partly recognized. Furthermore there is a need to produce and disseminate this new managerial knowledge to academics, managers and policy makers alike.

Entrepreneurial challenges
As we have shown, the BGs are young firms. Furthermore the founders and employees of the BGs are usually much younger than in traditional internationals. This is especially true in ITC firms in high-tech businesses. In one of the pilot cases examined, the average age of the 35 employed was 25 years.

The above exceptional age characteristics set some extraordinary entrepreneurial challenges. Firstly, because of the young age of management and other personnel there is a real lack of managerial experience and knowledge in almost all the functional areas: global management and global marketing, as well as global sourcing, accounting and finance. The only areas which were in stronger hands were R&D and production owing to the fact that young innovators were mainly technology-oriented experts. It seems that these young entrepreneurs are the first generation which has been living through the development of all PC generations and learned how to use those machines as their slaves. Because of the small size, young age and high level of perceived risks and uncertainties, it is not easy for BGs to hire more globally experienced managers. An additional challenge is caused by the fact that, because of the recent emergence of BGs, there are not that many managers who have knowledge of them. Owing to this state of affairs the vision planning, strategic planning and operative planning may be badly neglected, and earning logics and product portfolios may not be properly considered. These weaknesses in the management are fatal in the eyes of potentially large globalized customer firms, partner firms and financial institutions, causing a strategic problem of trust and credibility.

Secondly, a major entrepreneurial challenge for BGs is to plan and implement proper POM (Product, Operation and Market) strategies for global business. For example, as mentioned, the product strategy of BGs differs from that of traditionally internationalizing firms. Some of the BGs are starting their globalization by introducing complicated systems. The unit price of systems is relatively high. For a customer company, the key question is whether this tiny, young supplier firm with inexperienced managerial and limited financial resources can be reliable and depended upon to deliver such a strategic and sophisticated product.

There are also challenges related to the operation strategies. Quite a lot of BGs reverse the traditional order and start from cooperative modes by trying to sign strategic alliances and cooperative agreements on product development, R&D, sourcing sales or marketing with foreign firms, which often are much larger than the BG in question. This often leads to the problem of imbalance and inequality around the negotiation table. Similarly some BGs step over the first stages and they may start directly from sales subsidiaries or licensing. If BGs proceed in the same stages order as the traditionalists, they do it faster. Again the core challenge for the young entrepreneurs of BGs is to succeed in all of this. It has not been an easy task for the traditionally internationalized firms to proceed step by step from the less risky modes to more demanding, high-investment modes. Now much younger firms should be able to do that straight away, without being able to reduce the risks and uncertainties by proceeding first through less demanding modes and collecting valuable experiences and knowledge through the gradual learning process.

The market strategy of the BGs is also a challenge. Some of them start from lead countries where the number of customers is large and which geographically, culturally and economically are very distant from the SMOPEC country in question. BGs also have to enter and penetrate a larger number of countries within a shorter period of time than traditionally internationalized companies. The key managerial challenge for the BGs is to select the proper target countries for their products and then to enter and penetrate these markets successfully, despite their lack of global market and business knowledge. Especially demanding is the entry to large, sophisticated lead markets where the competition is severe.

Thirdly, the sales and marketing strategy challenges for BGs are also huge. For instance, when the product is ready for introduction onto global markets, a reallocation of resources to sales and marketing is required. How many of the technologically oriented entrepreneurs know how and when to do it and are really ready to do it? In respect of customer strategy it is known that getting the first reference customer is important for BG companies, which lack creditability and trust in the eyes of potential customers. The prices should be low enough to raise customer interest but also high enough to generate adequate profits. In order to get the first reference customer rapidly perhaps penetration pricing is needed, resulting in insufficient income and in unprofitable business. Furthermore BGs should be able to select a segment that is global enough to enable fast growth with their limited resources. Distribution channels are not always easily accessible for small and young BGs, whose product line range is often insufficient for large resellers or retailers. The control of marketing activities should remain in their own hands, but the resources are limited for setting up one's own sales and/or marketing channels. Finally, the development of global brand and marketing campaigns is certainly challenging, given the resources and skills of these young entrepreneurs.

Fourthly, it is crucial for the financial challenges to be overcome in order for the BGs to succeed and survive. The financing needed for product development, the establishment of production and marketing operations and building a presence in global markets usually amounts to much larger amounts than needed traditionally. The entrepreneurs have limited investments of their own and banks hesitate to grant loans because of the lack of guarantees and collaterals and the high risk related to these companies. Therefore different finance alternatives are usually limited to business angels and to public and private venture capitalists, and sometimes to listing on one of the stock exchanges. The former alternatives may require giving up a substantial share of ownership, which entrepreneurs are hesitant to agree upon. Additional problems, especially with venture capital (VC) financing, stem from the fact that there are often differences in objectives and strategies between the entrepreneur and the venture capitalists. The latter alternative is not usually possible before the company has shown its first success on the markets (Sasi and Gabrielsson, 2002).

The recent changes in the business and financial environment have considerable impact on the BGs of today. Whereas it was possible up to June 2000 for them to raise 1.5 to five million Euros and not give up majority of the ownership, this has become much more difficult lately owing to the financial difficulties the venture capitalists have run into and the heavy decline in the demand for, especially, investment and technology-related products. In particular, newly established BGs in ITC and biotechnology fields have had enormous difficulties in getting first round finance (seed money, start-up money) for the RD stage or to get second-round finance for the starting of the commercial stage without clear evidence of rapid and strong future income flows.

The BG entrepreneurs in SMOPECs are facing the greatest managerial challenge of today: that is, the challenge of globalization even at the initial stage when they are just established, being very small, inexperienced in global affairs and with limited financial resources. In our view this and present difficulties in financial markets call for a kind of mixed approach. On one hand, the BGs need to slow down their globalization process in order to be able to manage it in a better way. In addition to this, they have to reduce their huge R&D investments and to have a clearer business focus to match their ability to get enough external finance. Also they ought to start more rapidly the sales and marketing efforts to get sufficient internal finance early enough. On the other hand, they still have to find proper ways to enter, penetrate and escalate rapidly to global markets without taking too great, uncalculated risks, and to be able to satisfy the core needs of their lead customers without losing their focus in the selected niche business. In order to be able to achieve all of this, already established BGs may be forced to deglobalize and, after restructuring their business portfolios and renewing their POM$ICA strategies, to start to reglobalize by utilizing the most rewarding experience of the traditionally internationalized and globalized firms.

Governmental challenges
The major challenges for the governmental organizations responsible for the promotion of cross-border business activities, are caused by the fact that, as a new phenomenon, BGs are relatively unknown to them. However, as mentioned, BGs behave exceptionally, deviating from the behaviour of traditionally internationalizing and internationalized firms.

Taking into account the arguments presented above and the partial evidence on the product, operation and market (POM) strategy based on the pilot projects, the governmental policies should be extended from export promotion to the promotion of all operation modes of international business. In addition to different outward modes, inward and cooperative modes, which traditionally have been left outside the promotional policies, should also be included. This is based on the fact that the success of outward operations is often essentially dependent on the inward operations and on the fact that cooperation modes usually request both inward and outward activities (Luostarinen *et al.*, 1994; Luostarinen and Korhonen, 1998).

Because BGs often utilize multi-product strategies, governments should pay much more attention to the promotion of services, know-how and systems. These product items are not only sold in global markets separately but also combined with the physical goods. Owing to the worldwide sphere of the activities of BGs, the promotional measures of the public agencies should be extended from the international level to the global level, including the growing needs for area-based management systems and organizational solutions.

As earlier emphasized, the founders of the BG firms are usually exceptionally young people with technological skills. They are desperately in need of help in planning for global business. This is where the government can contribute to the sustainable development and survival of this new generation of entrepreneurs.

Research and teaching challenges

Owing to the recent emergence of the BGs the research on them is still in the infant stage, creating challenges for researchers. A lot of theoretical and empirical studies are needed (Knight and Cavusgil, 1996, p. 23). The preliminary hypotheses presented in this chapter are the result of a survey of Finnish BGs, a pilot study on 30 of them and a literature analysis. As mentioned earlier, this study is the largest sub-project of a larger six million Euro LIIKE research programme. The major aim is to contribute to the international body of science on BGs. By testing the hypotheses and by finding solutions and answers to the entrepreneurial, managerial and governmental challenges defined above the authors are trying to do their share in narrowing the broad knowledge gap on BGs.

The results of the three-year BGs research project are to be disseminated to students, academics, business managers and politicians alike. Obviously many challenges are related to this. How best to disseminate the new managerial knowledge on alternative globalization strategies and processes, global marketing strategies and financing of BGs? New skills are to be taught to students related to global and financial management, which may also require new educational methods. Entrepreneurs of BGs need to be reached and consulted in order to avoid severe mistakes. Policy makers need to be advised to broaden governmental support from export and internationalization promotion to the promotion of the globalization of BGs. Finally all of us who are subject to the globalization squeeze and pressure should remember that the slogan really is 'Globalize or die' and not 'Globalize and die'.

References

Alahuhta, Matti (1990), 'Global Growth Strategies for High Technology Challengers', Electrical Engineering Series no. 66, thesis for the degree of Doctor of Technology, Helsinki.

Almor, Tamar (2000), 'Born Global: The Case of Small and Medium Sized, Knowledge-Intensive, Israeli Firms', in Tamar Almor and Niron Hashai (eds), *FDI, International Trade and the Economics of Peacemaking, A tribute to Seev Hirsch*, Rishon LeZion, Israel: School of Business Administration, Academic Division, The College of Management, pp. 119–39.

Autio, Erkko (1995), '*Symplectic and generative impacts of new, technology-based firms in innovation networks: an international comparative study*', doctoral dissertation, Helsinki University of Technology.

Autio, Erkko, Harry J. Sapienza and James G. Almeida (2000), 'Effects of Age at Entry, Knowledge Intensity, and Imitability of International Growth', *Academy of Management Journal*, 43 (5), 909–24.

Autio, Erkko, Martti Kaila, Reima Kanerva and Ilkka Kauranen (1989), *Uudet teknologiayritykset (New Technology Based Companies)*, no. 10, Helsinki: SITRA.

Birch, David (2001), 'The Gazelle Theory', *Small Business*, 23 (7).

Dana, Léo P. (2001), 'Networks, Internationalization and Policy', *Small Business Economics*, 16 (2), March.

Gabrielsson, Mika (1999), S*ales Channel Strategies for International Expansion – The Case of Large Companies in the European PC Industry*, Helsinki: Acta Universitatis Oeconomicae Helsingiensis.

Hassan, Salah S. and A. Cosken Samli, (1994), 'The New Frontiers in Intermarket Segmentation', in S. Salah Hassan and Roger Blackwell (eds), *Global Marketing Perspectives and Cases*, New York: Dryder Press and Harcourt Brace College Publishers.

Johanson, J. and J.-E. Vahlne (1977), 'The Internationalization Process of the Firm', *Journal of International Business Studies*, 8, Spring/Summer.

Jolly, Vijay K., Matti Alahuhta, and Jean-Pierre Jeannet (1991), 'Challenging the Incumbents: How High Technology Start-ups Compete Globally', IMD Working Paper Series WP 91-003, pp. 1–17.

Junkkari, Jasmi (2000), 'The Globalization Strategies of Small and Medium-Sized High Technology Manufacturers', Born Globals Pilot Study/master's thesis, Helsinki School of Economics.

Kirpalani, Manek and Reijo Luostarinen (1999), *Dynamics of Success of SMOPEC Firms in Global Markets*, proceedings of the 25th Annual Meeting of the European International Business Academy, Manchester: EIBA.

Knight, Gary A. and S. Tamer Cavusgil (1996), 'The Born Global Firm: A Challenge to Traditional Internationalization Theory', in S.T. Cavusgil (ed.), *Advances in International Marketing*, 8, 11–26.

Knight, John, Jim Bell and Rod McNaughton (2001), 'The "Born Global" Phenomenon: A Re-birth of an Old Concept?', *Researching New Frontiers*, vol. 2, 4th McGill Conference on International Entrepreneurship, 21–3 September, Glasgow.

Konttinen, Heini (2001), 'Globalisation Strategies of Small and Medium-Sized High-Quality System Companies', Born Globals Pilot Study/master's thesis, Helsinki School of Economics.

Lavikkala, Laura (2001), 'Customer Strategies of Born Globals – Globalization Challenges and Current Practices', Born Globals Pilot Study/master's thesis, Helsinki School of Economics.

Levitt, Theodore (1983), 'The globalization of markets', *Harvard Business Review*, 83 (3), 92–102.

Luostarinen, Reijo (1970), 'Foreign Operations of the Firm', Helsinki School of Economics, licentiate thesis.

Luostarinen, Reijo (1979), 'Internationalization of the Firm', Helsinki School of Economics, doctoral dissertation.

Luostarinen, Reijo (1994), *Internationalization of Finnish Firms and their Response to Global Challenges, Research for Action*, WIDER Report, Forssa: UNU/WIDER.

Luostarinen, Reijo (2002), 'Internationalization and Globalization of the Firms', Lecture Notes, Helsinki School of Economics, Spring.

Luostarinen, Reijo and Harri Hellman (1994), 'The Internationalization Process and Strategies of Finnish Family Firms', CIBR Research Paper Series Y-1, Helsinki School of Economics.

Luostarinen, Reijo and Heli Korhonen (1998), 'Internationalization Stages of the European OECD Countries and their Promotional Policies for Globalization of SMEs', European International Business Academy, proceedings of the 24th Annual Conference, Jerusalem.

Luostarinen, Reijo and Lawrence Welch (1990), *International Business Operations*, Helsinki: Kyriiri Oy.

Luostarinen, Reijo, Heli Korhonen, Jukho Jokinen and Timo Pelkonen (1994), *Globalization and SME*, Ministry of Trade and Industry Reports 59/1994, Helsinki: Ministry of Trade and Industry.

Madsen, Tage and Per Servais (1997), 'The Internationalization of Born Globals – An Evolutionary Process', *International Business Review*, 6 (6), 1–14.

Majkgård, Anders and D. Deo Sharma (1999), 'The Born Internationals', Workshop in International Business and Nordic Workshop on Interorganizational Research, University of Vaasa.

Mattila, Johanna (2001), 'Promotion Strategies of B2C Born Globals', Born Globals Pilot Study/master's thesis, Helsinki School of Economics.

McKinsey & Co. (1993), *Emerging Exporters: Australia's high value-added manufacturing exports*, Melbourne: Australian Manufacturing Council.

McDougall, Patricia Phillips, Scott Shane and Benjamin M. Oviatt (1994), 'Explaining the Formation of International New Ventures: The limits of theories from International Business research', *Journal of Business Venturing*, 9, 469–87.

Oviatt, Benjamin M. and Patricia Phillips McDougall (1994), 'Toward a Theory of International New Ventures', *Journal of International Business Studies*, 25 (1), 45–64.

Perlmutter, Howard V. (1969), 'The Tortuous Evolution of the Multinational Corporation', *Columbia Journal of World Business*, January–February, 9–18.

Preece, Stephen B., G. Miles and M.C. Baetz (1999), 'Explaining the International Intensity and Global Diversity of Early-stage Technology-Based Firms', *Journal of Business Venturing*, 14(3), 259–81.

Rasilainen, Johanna (2002), 'The Globalization Strategies of Small and Medium-Sized High Design Companies', Born Globals Pilot Study, Helsinki School of Economics.

Ratia, Laura (2001), 'Pricing Strategies of Born Global Companies', Born Globals Pilot Study/master's thesis, Helsinki School of Economics.

Rennie, Michael W. (1993), 'Global Competitiveness: Born Global', *The McKinsey Quarterly*, 4, 45–52.

Rinkinen, Laura (2000), 'Globalisation Strategies of Small and Medium-Sized High-Quality Service Companies', Born Globals Pilot Study/master's thesis, Helsinki School of Economics.

Sankari, Petra (2002), 'Distribution Strategies of Born Global Companies', Born Globals Pilot Study/master's thesis, Helsinki School of Economics.

Sasi, Viveca and Mika Gabrielsson (2002), 'Finance Strategies of Globalizing Firms – A Comparison between a Finnish Born International and a Born Global Company', proceedings of the European Academy of Management Conference, 9–11 May, Stockholm.

Sasi, Viveca, Mika Gabrielsson and Matias Myllyrinne (2000), 'Financing and Managing Growth of A Born Global: Case of Mad.Onion', proceedings of the 26th European International Business Academy Annual Conference, Maastricht.

Sorenson, R.Z. and U.E. Wiechmann (1975), 'How Multinationals view Marketing Standardization', *Harvard Business Review*, 53 (3) May–June, 38–54, 166–7.

Svetličič, Marjan, Vitor Corado Simoes and Reijo Luostarinen (2001), 'Selected Theories on Outward Foreign Direct Investment', Phase ACE Project, Outward internationalization facilitating transformation and EU accession; the Case of the Czech Republic, Hungary and Slovenia, Paper no. 1, Ljubljana.

Teimonen, Jenni (2001), 'Globalization Strategies of Small and Medium-Sized High Know-How Companies', master's thesis, Helsinki School of Economics.

Vahcic, A. (1995), 'Entrepreneurship as factor of economic development', *Slovenska ekonomska revija*, 46 (4), 295–312.

Viljanen, Heikki (2002), 'Promotion Strategies of B2B Born Globals', Born Globals Pilot Study, Helsinki School of Economics.

23 Three case studies from Finland
Niina Nummela

The number of small firms operating on international markets has been growing, and simultaneously the process of internationalization has been accelerating. During the last decade, small and medium-sized enterprises (SMEs)[1] have been the object of increasing interest. Politicians, governmental bodies and academics have re-evaluated the significance of this group of firms, and currently regard them as significant sources of wealth and employment. On the other hand, thanks to improved communication systems and the deregulation of tariff barriers, 'the world is getting smaller'. Consequently SMEs are pushed towards and pulled away from international markets. The number of small firms operating internationally has been growing, slowly but steadily. Some researchers have also discovered that the time lag for SME internationalization (that is, the time from the establishment of the firm to the first export delivery) has become shorter (for empirical evidence, see, for example, Hurmerinta-Peltomäki, 2001; Christensen, 1991).[2] This kind of acceleration requires that small firms also acquire the resources and skills needed for international operations more quickly than before.

What does this mean from the perspective of the internationalizing company? At the company level, internationalization seems to be a growth process that is tightly intertwined with the company's other activities (cf. Jones, 1999). Moreover, internationalization at the individual level has become a crucial factor, particularly because experience and learning are considered key features. However it remains unclear how the key business operations change during internationalization, and what kind of resources and skills – at both the organizational and the individual level – are needed to manage the internationalization process successfully.

The objective of this study is to shed some light on this topical issue by describing and analysing change in internationalizing SMEs. A framework based on earlier literature is created and used to analyse the changes due to internationalization in selected case companies. Each case offers a rich description of the changes, and the cross-case analysis reveals the common and differentiating features. The findings indicate that change in internationalization is a more multidimensional and complex concept than anticipated. The framework facilitated the identification and classification of different levels of change. The chapter ends with some propositions, suggestions for further research and a discussion on the limitations of the study.

Change in internationalization
What is change?
This study focuses on change in internationalization, and thus the concept of change has to be defined. There is a vast amount of literature on organizational change and this study does not attempt to review it all. Instead some selected concepts are borrowed from earlier research on organizational change and embedded in the context of small-business internationalization. This follows the tradition in organizational change research in general, as there seem to be no original concepts and most of the research has adopted concepts, metaphors and theories from other disciplines (Van de Ven and Poole, 1995).

The emphasis of earlier research on organizational change has been on the incremental, cumulative change process, which has been used to explain almost everything (Gersick, 1991). The dominant approach – the configuration school – assumes that organizations evolve mainly through periods of stability, which are interrupted by occasional discontinuities (Miller and Friesen, 1984). These revolutionary changes are usually driven by external events, such as changes in technology, in the competitive situation or in the political conditions (Tushman and O'Reilly, 1996), but they may also be a result of internal factors (Gersick, 1991). Organizational changes range from slight adaptations to dramatic shifts in organizational structure, strategy and culture (Schuh, 2001). The theoretical explanation of this development – the punctuated equilibrium paradigm – is based on the assumption that incremental change during the stable periods develops through adjustments to the existing system, with the activity patterns remaining the same, whereas during revolutionary periods the deep underlying structures in the system also change (Gersick, 1991).

However this study is an exception to mainstream research because the focus is not on the process or how and why organizations change. In other words, process theory is not at its core. Instead the interest lies in the *content of change*, that is, what actually changes. Thus change is defined here as the difference in form, quality or state in an organization over a selected time period (cf. Van de Ven and Poole, 1995: 512). This change is studied at the level of one company function, internationalization, when the company extends its activities from domestic to foreign markets (cf. Havnes, 1998). Although changes may be studied at many organizational levels, including those of the individual, group and the organization (Van de Ven and Poole, 1995), in small firms the emphasis should be on the owner–manager, who is often at the core of the change processes. Correspondingly, and following

Hohenthal (2001), the interest of this study is in understanding the individual action and the manager's perception of change.

Change as such can be further classified into various types. For example, Watzlawick *et al.* (1974) distinguished between *first- and second-order* changes in organizations (for a thorough overview on first- and second-order change, see also Chapman, 2002). First-order change indicates an incremental change with gradual modifications within the existing system, whereas second-order change refers to a more fundamental change, which results in differences in the basic governing rules and alterations of the system (Chapman, 2002). Different types of change can be further divided into *alpha*, *beta* and *gamma* change (Golembiewski *et al.*, 1976). According to this classification, a change can be described as an alpha-level change if the actors only extend their current activities, while at the beta level the change can also be observed in the standards by which the behaviour of the actors is assessed, and finally, at the gamma level, a fundamental shift occurs in the system. This classification resembles the earlier description of revolutionary change processes, and it may be assumed that gamma-level changes are the outcomes of these revolutionary development periods. The classification of alpha, beta and gamma changes is applied in this study, alpha and beta changes indicating two levels of a first-order change, and gamma change a second-order change in the company.

Traditionally, organizational change has been studied within frameworks reflecting incremental, first-order change (Chapman, 2002). This system is also valid in reviewing earlier research on small-business internationalization: the traditional approaches follow the path of incremental change, at least implicitly (Havnes, 1998). However, as it seems that the cliché about the increasing pace of change in the globalizing business environment is true (Tushman and O'Reilly, 1996), it could also be assumed that the changes related to internationalization are increasing in number and importance, as well as becoming faster. As a result of this development, success in international business calls for managements and organizations that are able to cope with both incremental and discontinuous change (cf. Tushman and O'Reilly, 1996). Consequently, from the managerial perspective, understanding changes due to internationalization is also crucial.

Change in SME internationalization
It has been argued that change in company internationalization has not been a major area of interest in international business research (Schuh, 2001). This is rather surprising because internationalization is generally understood as an evolutionary process during which a company adapts to the international environment (for example, Calof and Beamish, 1995). The aspect of progressive change in this process has been emphasized by

several researchers. The importance of the strategic perspective has also been underlined: expansion to international markets requires changes in the company strategy in order for it to fit into the novel environment (Schuh, 2001; Lam and White, 1999; McDougall and Oviatt, 1996). Strategic fit is particularly important for rapidly internationalizing companies, which need internationally fit strategies, policies and procedures from inception (McDougall *et al.*, 1994).

As stated earlier, the models for describing and analysing small-business internationalization are dominated by the incremental change paradigm (Lam and White, 1999; Havnes, 1998). These stage models, starting from the Uppsala school (Johanson and Vahlne, 1977), are tempting because of their simplicity and logic. However, despite their popularity, they have also been strongly criticized (for example, Clark *et al.*, 1997; Madsen and Servais, 1997; Petersen and Pedersen, 1997; Andersen, 1993). The majority of internationalization models have followed the most common theory in management literature: the life cycle process theory (for a discussion on process theories, see Van de Ven, 1992). Affected by certain stimuli, a firm will proceed from one stage to another, and all firms will follow a similar pattern. These models are quite deterministic, and are based on an objectivist interpretation of reality and human nature: internationalization is seen as a response to a stimulus, either internal or external to the firm.

As a response to the increasing criticism, researchers with a more subjectivist approach later developed other process models that aim at understanding the internationalization process instead of explaining it. The underlying thought behind these process models is internationalization through increasing experience and learning. However, despite their voluntaristic approach to internationalization, most of them still use the traditional life cycle process theory as their starting point. Only in a few recent studies have researchers applied a more teleological interpretation of the process, according to which a company may take multiple routes in order to achieve the desired end state (for example, Andersen *et al.*, 1997; Madsen and Servais, 1997). To sum up, literature on small-firm internationalization concentrates on describing an evolutionary process of slow-moving change.

Consequently the emphasis in research on small-business internationalization has also been on understanding the process, not on the content. From the perspective of this study it is significant that earlier research neglects the problems companies face during this corporate change process (Lam and White, 1999). This study attempts to fill this gap and focuses on the changes that are due to internationalization. It is assumed that, at the company level, the change related to internationalization is reflected both internally and externally. External changes are those that can be seen from

the outside, such as changes in export strategy (products, markets, operations), whereas internal changes are related to the organizational structure,
finance and personnel (cf. the discussion of dimensions of internationalization in Welch and Luostarinen, 1988). Both internal and external changes
are summarized in the framework below (see Figure 23.1).

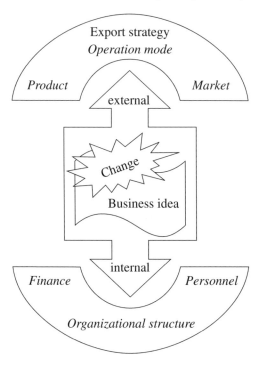

*Figure 23.1   Framework for studying change in the internationalizing small
firm*

The upper part of Figure 23.1 describes the change in the company's
export strategy as internationalization proceeds. In the course of time, a
small firm has to decide whether to adapt the strategy and its key elements:
which products/services it will offer, how and to which markets. These decisions are naturally affected by environmental factors, and they may vary
according to the market. However they are not discussed in detail here
because the extensive literature on international marketing covers most of
these issues.[3] On the other hand, researchers have been less interested in the
internal changes due to internationalization that are illustrated in the lower
part of Figure 23.1. A small firm may have to reassess the company's financial arrangements, reconsider its organizational structure or diversify its

personnel in order to acquire the skills and resources needed for internationalization.

The limited interest in the *financing* of small-business internationalization is surprising for two reasons. First, it is generally assumed that the financial management of small firms is different from that in large firms (LeCornu *et al.*, 1996). If this is the case, it could also be assumed that this difference is even highlighted in the context of internationalization where the contradiction between growth and limited resources is stressed. Second, according to some empirical studies, a significant proportion of the export problems experienced by small firms are somehow finance-related, such as delays in payment, difficulties in setting competitive prices, controlling currency fluctuations and obtaining export finance (for example, Bell, 1995).

Internationalization has an impact on the performance of the firm, and this change can be measured in terms of turnover and/or profit development, as well as by the export share of turnover. However it may take considerable time before the export operations create positive cash flow, and internationalization usually requires substantial financial investments before then. Growth can be financed by reallocating cash flow from other activities, but also otherwise, for example by debt or equity arrangements. In general, small firms find the funding of internationalization rather problematic, mainly for two reasons: either the choice of alternatives is restricted or the manager's preferences for the available alternatives may be biased. It could be argued that, because some small firms do not fully meet the qualifications, the funding available is partly deficient and thus there will always be a gap between supply and demand. (Hamilton and Fox, 1998). On the other hand, it may be a question of pecking order; that is, the manager prefers some forms of funding to others. For some small firms the pecking order may be truncated if managers are unwilling to consider some forms of funding, because of restricted conditions of supply or personal preferences (Howorth, 2001).

Several empirical studies have verified that a pecking order really exists among small firms and that it is often in a truncated form. Financial preferences usually lean towards internally generated funds. Failing this, external debt is preferred, external equity being the last option (Howorth, 2001; Hamilton and Fox, 1998; Barton and Matthews, 1989). Aversion to external finance mainly arises for three reasons: the cost of the funding, the loss of independence and the loss of control (Howorth, 2001; LeCornu *et al.*, 1996; Barton and Matthews, 1989). Desire for independent and autonomous action is one of the key characteristics of entrepreneurship, and in small firms autonomy is often linked with the rights of ownership (Lumpkin and Dess, 1996). Loss of independence seems to be a decisive factor in funding as well, and the comment of Hamilton and Fox (1998:

245) describes it quite well: 'These small-firm owners simply prefer to have all of debt-laden business rather than merely a share in the control of a relatively debt-free operation.'

This study classifies the change related to finance in three types. An *alpha change* implies financing internationalization through internal funding, by increasing its efficiency and reallocating the cash flow from other activities. A *beta change* is when internationalization is at least partly financed with debt from external institutions, such as banks. Finally, a *gamma change* means that internationalization is financed through external equity, for example by introducing a venture capitalist as a minority owner in the company.

Internal changes are naturally tightly intertwined, and a change related to finance may also have effects on the organizational structure (as in the case of minority ownership) and vice versa. It could be argued that, as the company internationalizes, the administrative and organizational demands increase and the company needs to respond to this by making organizational rearrangements (Welch and Luostarinen, 1988). From the perspective of change and internationalization, there are two key questions: the first concerns what export-related activities are carried out inside the firm and which ones are left for selected partners, and the second how the internal activities are organized.

An increasing number of partnerships and alliances has been considered one of the distinctive characteristics of globalization, and has been a way for companies to match their capabilities to the changing environment (Sachwald, 1998). The shortened time span in business operations probably requires even more effective and concise utilization of the network, particularly as far as entering foreign markets is concerned. This, in turn, leads to variety in governance structures. Parker (1996) suggests that, because of globalization, organizations use more hybrid forms instead of traditional governance structures. Miles and Snow (1986: 63) argued back in the 1980s that the rising new organizational forms were both causes and effects of the changing nature of the new environment. According to them, strategies and structures are based on managers' attempts to match companies' capabilities to the environment.

It is possible to achieve this matching by developing the company's external relationships either vertically or horizontally. Vertical cooperation is based on the idea that the management redefines the boundaries of the firm by making contracts with other organizations. This means that some activities are considered core competences[4] that are kept inside the company boundaries, whereas others may be assigned to reliable partners in order to improve the efficiency of the firm. Horizontal cooperation, on the other hand, refers to partnerships and alliances with other companies on the same level of the value chain. In this case, cooperation is based on a common goal, which the partners aim to achieve through joint activities. Internationalization may require both types of cooperation in order to be as competitive as possible. Competitive advantage may be obtained, for example, through the creation of a well-functioning supplier network, or through alliances with other firms (small or large) to acquire the resources needed on international markets.

It is not only in the development of external relationships of the company that change due to internationalization is reflected, but also in its internal arrangements. The key question is how to organize its international activities. The existing organizational structure may be sufficient for the domestic market or even for managing an international dealer network, but sometimes more fundamental structural changes are required to ensure control and presence on the target market (Lam and White, 1999). One additional motive for organizational change may be the desire to demonstrate commitment to international markets in general, or to some target market in particular (Welch and Luostarinen, 1988).

It is proposed here that internationalization may result in various changes in organizational structure. At the *alpha* level, these changes may mean a move towards short-term cooperation, either vertical or horizontal, in order to improve the efficiency of the company on international markets. A *beta*-level change might be an attempt to create long-term alliances with reliable partners in order to remain internationally competitive. A *gamma*-level change indicates a permanent internal change in which the company creates subsidiaries or joint ventures abroad in order to monitor the target markets.

As Welch and Luostarinen (1988) have accurately pointed out, internationalization depends heavily on the people initiating and carrying out the activities related to it. Therefore it may be assumed that it probably has an effect on the *personnel* of the company. Earlier research on internationalization assumes that it is based on experiential knowledge, which the personnel collect from foreign operations (for example Johanson and Vahlne, 1990). The manager as a decision maker is in a key role as a voluntary, individual actor in the process. Experiential learning by key decision makers and other personnel will occur as they recognize the opportunities and problems, seek solutions to these problems and then put the solutions into practice. However, in addition to learning about external elements, such as foreign markets and institutions, this also includes learning about the internal resources of a firm, and its capabilities in new and unfamiliar conditions (Eriksson *et al.*, 1997). Theories of individual learning also take into account the personal experience and knowledge that is stored in the firm from its birth. This also means that, when people move from one company to another, they carry the experience with them, which also partly explains the accelerating internationalization of SMEs and the 'leapfrogging' of stages in the process.

From the perspective of the company, it is a question of maintaining and developing the collective memory. Imitation, reflection and learning-by-doing result in experiences that are stored in the collective memory of the firm. Internationalization may require changes in this collective memory, and it could be argued that long-term success in international business depends on the company's ability to change and develop (Hohenthal, 2001). Such change and development may be supported by the acquisition of supplementary knowledge and experience, in terms of training existing employees, buying expertise from professionals or recruiting new people.

It is proposed here that the personnel of a small firm will encounter some changes due to internationalization. These changes arise from the development of the collective memory of the company. An example of an *alpha*-level change would be incremental learning by the existing personnel through familiarizing themselves with the activities and collecting experience. This may be complemented by occasional 'shopping', that is, acquiring assistance from professional service providers, such as translation offices and forwarding agents. A *beta*-level change may involve training the existing personnel and thus offering them the additional skills and knowledge needed to carry out the activities related to internationalization. This may also include the creation of more permanent relationships with professional service providers. Finally a *gamma*-level change would be the recruitment of new personnel for international activities, thus importing their experience into the company.

Changes in a company do not occur in a vacuum, but are strongly intertwined with the core of the business. A firm's international operations are based on its business idea, which lies behind any changes. It may be argued that a reciprocal relationship exists between change due to internationalization and the business idea of the company. All changes have to be in accordance with the business idea, and it may be that some changes occur because the business idea has been reassessed. On the other hand, the business idea is sometimes modified because of internationalization. From the perspective of a company, a change in the business idea could be described as a revolutionary change, which alters the deep structures of the firm. This kind of change could be classified as a second-order change, which would lead to different ways of operating. These kinds of fundamental changes are bound to have an effect on the company's internationalization as well.

To sum up, at the company level this study describes change due to internationalization according to the framework illustrated in Figure 28.1. The changes are classified into first- (alpha, beta) and second-order (gamma) changes in each of the dimensions. This analysis will result in a classification of the companies according to the changes due to internationalization.

Research design
Change as a study object requires special attention to be given to the research design because of the retrospective and longitudinal perspective needed. Particularly when the focus is on change processes, longitudinal research is recommended, as it permits the identification and observation of processes (Kimberly, 1976). As stated earlier, the number of empirical studies on change and internationalization is limited, and only a few of them have taken a longitudinal research approach. Among the few exceptions are the studies by Schuh (2001), Havnes (1998) and McDougall and Oviatt (1996). Schuh examined the evolution of the international marketing strategies of eight companies by using a longitudinal case study method.[5] Havnes (1998) analysed first- and second-order changes in internationalization and used the data from the international Interstratos research project in his study.[6] McDougall and Oviatt (1996) did a follow-up study analysing the internationalization of new-venture manufacturers in the computer and communications equipment industries.[7] In most cases the analysis of change seems to be based on stage models of internationalization.

The reasons for the lack of longitudinal studies are obvious: they require a lot of work and take a considerable time compared with traditional research designs. However, although they are laborious, they do offer the possibility of obtaining very rich descriptions of the internationalization of the companies concerned. For this reason, this study also takes a retrospective perspective, although the research design is not necessarily longitudinal, as the data were collected at only one point in time from three case companies that are at different stages in their internationalization. The case companies are all manufacturing companies located in south-western Finland.

One of the key questions to be solved in the research design was the question of timing (on the importance of timing in research design, see Mitchell and James, 2001). What is the time period during which the respondents reflect on the changes related to internationalization? In order to make this evaluation frame as stable as possible, the first export delivery was selected as the starting point (t^0) in the analysis (Figure 23.2). When this starting point is fixed for all of the companies, the findings from each one may be compared in cross-case analysis. The time period in question is the time from the first export delivery (t^0) to the time of the data collection (t^1). The study comprises companies that were in different stages of internationalization at the time of the data collection (t_). Company representatives were

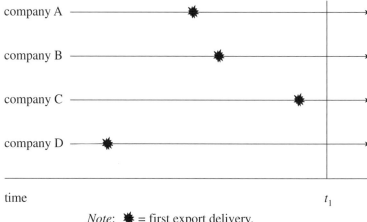

Note: ✳ = first export delivery.

Figure 23.2   Comparison of cases

asked to look back and describe the changes during the time period in question. In analyses of change, the key interests are the triggers – deadlines, milestones and crisis situations (Gersick, 1991) – which could also be called critical events or incidents (for example, Halinen *et al.*, 1999). Following the critical incidents enables the researcher to observe mechanisms and processes through which changes are created (Schuh, 2001). However the definition of a critical event is a subjective one, as the actors themselves determine which events are critical and which are not (Halinen *et al.*, 1999). This study concerns the critical events related to internationalization. Some less notable and less conscious changes were also brought to light by comparing the interview data with the documents. If available, the documents were also helpful for checking details such as numerical information.

One representative from each company was interviewed face-to-face. The person interviewed was the managing director, or in one case the chairman of the board, as the owner and founder of the company had recently withdrawn from the day-to-day management. The interviews were semi-structured and followed a loose pattern based on the theoretical framework. Data triangulation was used to complement the personal interviews, and other, particularly secondary, data were collected. Memos, annual reports, brochures, Internet pages and other material, as well as newspaper articles, were used as additional sources of information.

Another question related to the research design was the selection of the case companies. In order to get as broad an overview of the phenomenon as possible, no industry or other background limitations were imposed. The case companies include firms with different internationalization histories, born globals, born-again globals and 'traditional' firms[8] among them. This variety was considered to increase the richness of the data and the diversity of the cross-case analysis as the time period in focus varied considerably. Some details of the case companies are summarized in Table 23.1 below, while a more detailed description of each company follows in the next chapter.

Table 23.1   Summary of the case firms' selected characteristics

	Company M	Company N	Company O
Turnover in 2001	euro 2mn	euro 4mn	euro 5.5mn
Personnel in 2001	38	13	45
Exports (%) in 2001	70	73	10
Founded	1967	1986	1984

Change in the case companies

Company M

Company M is a small garment manufacturer, specializing in sport and leisurewear. In 2001 the turnover was approximately two million euro and the company employed 38 persons. It is family-owned by five brothers, three of whom are actively involved in the business. The company was established in 1967 when the founder (the father of the current owners) bought the facilities of a dressmaker's shop. It originally continued with the earlier activities of making tailor-made dresses, skirts and trousers. However, quite soon, the owners realized that the business was not profitable and they moved into more lucrative products. Since that time the company has manufactured high-quality sports and leisurewear, particularly for professionals. However the major product lines have varied considerably during the company's history.

In the 1970s, the major product line was sports outfits. This business started with an inquiry from a local football team and expanded quite rapidly to other sports and cities. Not only local and Finnish sports groups, but also national teams, for example in ice hockey, have used their products as the official team outfit. At the same time, the company also manufactured sponsored clothing for companies (such as car dealers and rally teams). These products became more important during the 1980s and gradually turned into the major product line. A totally new product line started in 1991 as the company began manufacturing harness clothing. This business started quite accidentally, when a friend of the managing director suggested it to him. This friend owned trotters and knew that the drivers needed high-quality clothing. This has continued as the major product line of the company until today. However special garments, such as official, certified clothing for naval pilots and policemen, have been produced as a sideline during the last few years, and have become an important product group. The managing director anticipates that the demand for these products will grow in the future.

The company started exporting in 1970, when they received an unsolicited order from France. The Finnish importer of Peugeot cars was a key customer and had ordered a considerable number of their sponsored jackets from company M. As it happened, their French principal also needed similar products and they decided to order them from company M, too. However, this was a one-off transaction, which did not lead to any further business. At the same time, the first contacts were made with a Swedish businessman who sold sports outfits to Swedish teams. Through his contacts with Finnish sportsmen he had received information about company M and got in touch with them. Gradually he ordered more and more of the company's products and this contact led to a business relationship which is still intact. At the moment this person acts as M's representative in Scandinavia. From Sweden the company expanded to Norway, which became a major market for its sponsored clothing in the 1980s, and then to Denmark. However 'true internationalization', as the managing director described it, started with its harness clothing in the 1990s.

With the help of friends who had lived for some time in the Netherlands, the company established business contacts there. After getting a foothold on the Dutch market in the early 1990s, it started its expansion to the Central European market. The next markets were France, Austria, Germany, Italy, Switzerland and Spain, and gradually the company covered all major harness racing countries in Europe. Expansion to other markets was discussed, and the same friends suggested a contact in the United States. This contact initiated the dealer relationship there, and a dealership was established later with a Canadian company through a connection at a trade fair. Entry to the North American market was facilitated by the exchange rates, because at that time the US dollar was very strong.

Currently the proportion of exports exceeds 70 per cent of the turnover, and in harness clothing it is almost 95 per cent. The company is very committed to internationalization. One sign of this commitment is naturally the significance of exports for its business. However the attitudinal component of commitment is also clearly visible at all levels of the organization. Export orders are considered important and the personnel are aware of the high quality requirements on international markets.

At the moment, the company has dealers in Austria, the Benelux countries (located in the Netherlands), Canada, two in France, two in Germany,

Scandinavia (located in Sweden), Switzerland and the United States. A Finnish dealer also has a shop at a racing centre in the Helsinki area. All the dealers are independent companies, although two of them use the brand name in their company name, by mutual agreement. Most of the dealers are small distributors and the representatives have some background, either professional or leisure, in harness racing or horses in general. This is considered a very important issue, as most of the business in that field seems to be created through personal networks. Company M does not sell directly to any customers and always directs unsolicited orders to the nearest dealer.

The company has specifically decided to concentrate on specialized high-quality clothing, as it cannot compete with the mass production in countries with lower labour costs. It aims at manufacturing products that can stand the higher price level. It has never considered moving even a small part of the production to countries with lower labour costs. On the contrary, it also prefers Finnish manufacturers in its purchasing of raw materials. The main supplier is the Finnish fabric producer Finlayson, and, if needed, its range is complemented by material from smaller Finnish suppliers.

Because of the strong focus on special products, price has become a secondary issue in exports; the managing director even claims that price has never been a problem. Customers seem to be prepared to pay more for a high-quality product. Still, success on international markets has required strong investment in quality, as foreign customers demand top product quality and punctual deliveries. The high price level is also sustainable because of the creation of the strong brand. The key idea behind the development of this brand has been cooperation with the best trainers and drivers. Sponsoring has guaranteed visibility and a growing reputation on international markets, and also growing demand as amateurs and second-rank professionals wish to identify themselves with the top drivers. Gradually the company has become one of the leading brands in harness clothing in Europe.

A look back shows that there have been remarkable changes in the company's operations in recent years. The changing importance of different product lines was mentioned earlier, and it can be concluded that, although there have been significant changes in the products, these changes have not been due to internationalization. The main triggers have been economic fluctuations: during periods of economic downturn the company has searched for new routes to survival. In fact changes in the products have had an effect on the internationalization of the company as they have 'opened doors' to new markets. As far as the product is concerned, the company history seems to be characterized by relatively stable periods during which any changes have been mainly due to continuous product development, that is, first-order changes. However these periods have been interrupted by radical developments which have also had an impact on the business idea of the company, and vice versa. Following these second-order changes, the business has again evolved in a steady manner.

The change in product lines seems to be partly intertwined with the question of markets. This is quite natural, as the product determines its potential customer groups. The number of markets covered through the dealer network is considerable for a small firm, and the company has also extended its business overseas. However market selection has not been very thoroughly planned: on the contrary, most of the markets have been entered quite accidentally, through personal contacts. Because of its limited resources, the company has selected the operation mode that requires the least effort, that is, a network of local distributors. This operation mode has remained the same on all markets, in spite of the radical changes in product lines. To sum up, the externally visible change in company M due to internationalization is considerable if the current situation is compared with the time of the first export delivery in the early 1970s. Although change has often been incremental, the end result is that the product today is totally different and the markets more diverse than at that time. The only thing that has remained the same is the operation mode.

The internal changes are also analysed here. During its 30 years of operation on international markets, the company has always *financed* activities from cash flow. The managing director clearly prefers this source of funding and he has a strong aversion to external capital. The main reason for this aversion is the fear of loss of control. There also seems to be a strong mentality of 'not needed here, we have always been able to take care of ourselves'. It could be concluded that, from this perspective, the changes due to internationalization are *alpha*-level changes. As far as the *personnel* are concerned, the situation is one of status quo. International operations have always been the responsibility of the managing director and his brother, the production manager. There is also a clerk who is responsible for the paperwork related to the export deliveries. According to the managing director, the employees have not been trained in international business: learning has happened 'the hard way' and is merely based on collected experience. In other words, from the perspective of the personnel, too, the changes are at the *alpha* level.

The internal *organization structure* of company M has not changed significantly since the first export delivery. However external relationships have diversified considerably since the company started exporting harness clothing in the 1990s. The main product in this group is an overall, or a combination of a jacket and trousers. Potential customers need additional apparel to go with this product, and because of the substantial demand the company has complemented its own product with several types of accessories. At the moment the product range includes thermal underwear, turtleneck sweaters, quilted jackets and vests, socks, racing gloves, winter caps, driver's bags and helmets. The company manufactures none of these products, but orders them from reliable Finnish and foreign suppliers. Close relationships with their five key suppliers are of crucial importance to the company as nowadays they are jointly responsible for the positive image of the brand on international markets. In conclusion, the changes in the organization structure can be defined as *beta*-level changes.

Company N
Company N is a small company developing, manufacturing and marketing hand-held radio terminals for wireless communications and auto identification. The turnover in 2001 was approximately four million euros and the company employed 13 people. The products are sold under its own trademark. The main selling points are high quality, design and ergonomics. The company received the Innofinland prize for its products and business concepts in 2001.

The company was established in 1986 as an engineering office designing telecommunications-related products, such as mobile-phone accessories, cellular-network accessories, wireless phone boxes and digital voice-messaging products. At that time the company invented and designed products to order, and the managing director described them as the 'Gyro Gearlooses' of the field. The managing director had worked for Nokia-Mobira (currently Nokia Mobile Phones), and he brought the majority of his customer contacts with him. The customers were mainly mobile-phone manufacturers, such as Alcatel, Ericsson and Benefon. The business was very profitable for some years, but in the early 1990s the company encountered severe financial setbacks because of the liquidity problems of their largest customer. As a result, the operations were driven down to a minimal level and the company focused on auto identification and radio-frequency data collection.

The development of the current product started in 1993 with a suggestion from a customer. This customer had a problem: the sophisticated computer systems in administration, management and marketing were not compatible with the systems used in their logistical activities. As a solution to this problem, the company created their own product, a wireless data-collection system. It consists of hand-held radio handsets, which are used to communicate with the host system via base station(s) using an efficient communication protocol. The host system may be a PC or a more complex computer system. The system aims at improving customers' logistics operations with real-time data capture and communication. The product family was introduced on the market in 1997 after considerable investment in product development and, particularly, design. There are two customer groups for the products: retailers and industrial and service companies. The products are already in use in Finland in the major retailing chains as well as in several service firms (for example pharmacies and automobile inspectors). Internationally the company is attempting to reach potential customers through the dealers, but also directly by contacting either the customers or the system integrators responsible for systems development (such as Wincur Nixdorf).

The company has had occasional export deliveries since its birth, but more regular and planned operations started first with their own product family. Internationalization was a natural strategy as the domestic markets for the product were quite limited. The company started exporting these products in 1997, and in 2001 the proportion of exports exceeded 70 per cent of the turnover. The main market area is Europe, particularly the Nordic countries (40 per cent of the sales), the United Kingdom (20 per cent) and Germany (15 per cent). The decision to enter international markets was based on an explicit decision-making process. The first step was to build an international dealer network. For this purpose, a person with experience of international business was recruited in 1999. The first targets were the professional magazines, in which they put advertisements for dealers. These advertisements produced an overwhelming number of contacts, and the company had to choose the best candidates in each country. Later, contacts with dealers were also established through the grapevine. At the moment the company has a broad dealer network in Europe (including Austria, the Czech Republic, Denmark, France, Ireland, Italy, Latvia, Lithuania, the Netherlands, Norway, Poland, Portugal, Slovakia, Spain, Sweden and Switzerland). It also has dealers in Brazil, Israel and South Africa.

After a smooth beginning the company decided not to rush to several markets, but to concentrate investments on a few specific areas. It directed its first efforts to the British market, chosen because it was well developed, with an existing demand, and it was also competitive. In order to improve its presence on that market the company established a sales subsidiary in 2001. From here the company moved its main interest to the German market, which is considerable in size but less developed than the British market. It therefore required a lot of support and promotion at first. 'The work of a missionary,' as the managing director described it. Nevertheless he anticipates that this will be their most important European market in the future. In order to monitor market developments more closely, the company established a sales subsidiary in Germany in spring 2002.

The company is clearly committed to internationalization, not least because of the significance of its exports. However there is a clear attitudinal commitment too. Although there are specified responsibilities, there is no specific export department or export manager. On the contrary, all employees are responsible for export-related questions. The managing director himself has a strong background in international business, and he has recruited people with similar, but complementary, experience.

Analysing change in Company N is slightly problematic as the definition of its export start is not unequivocal. There are two alternative starting points: the miscellaneous deliveries to international markets in the 1980s and the exports of their own system that started in 1997. The change in internationalization has been considerable since the 1980s as the product is completely different, the number of markets has increased considerably and the operation modes are more complex than the direct deliveries of the time. However the first export deal of their own system is also justifiable as the starting point because this was the start of regular and systematic international operations. In this case, the external changes due to internationalization are not as notable, although not non-existent. The product has remained the same, although improvements have been made in the course of product development. An increase in the number of target markets has also occurred during this time in addition to the change in operation modes. Consequently the latter time (1997) is taken as the point of comparison in this study.

Internally the changes are analysed from the perspective of *finance*, personnel and organization structure. The international operations have been financed both from cash flow and through venture capital. One business partner has been involved in the company since the early 1990s, and a Finnish professional investor has recently acquired a minority ownership (33 per cent). The latter investment is particularly directed towards international expansion. Accordingly, the finance-related changes can be defined as *gamma*-level changes. The company has also invested considerably in the training of its *personnel,* and experienced people have been recruited for international operations during the internationalization process. One person was recruited because of her competence in the creation of international dealer networks, one because of his knowledge of the main market areas and one because of his experience in the products. Consequently the changes related to personnel are also *gamma*-level changes. Finally the company has decided to concentrate on its core competence, marketing and designing the products, and it has created a network of subcontractors to which all other activities are outsourced. Additionally, it has set up two sales subsidiaries on the two major markets. Thus the changes related to the *organization structure* are also *gamma*-level changes.

Company O

Company O is a small subcontractor for technical plastic components, and a manufacturer of plastic rollers. In 2001, the turnover of the company was approximately 5.5 million euros and it employed 45 people. More than half of its production is exported indirectly, and in 2001 the proportion of direct exports was approximately 10 per cent of the turnover. The owner–manager, his son and three other key people own the company, which was established in 1984 as an offshoot of another company operating since 1977. The owners first had a company which specialized in products for concrete reinforcement and casting. Our case company was established to respond to the increasing demand for plastic components in the construction industry. In the beginning it operated exclusively in contract manufacturing, acquiring the roller product in 1987 from another company, which had gone bankrupt.

In contract manufacturing the company takes responsibility, from planning and design to the manufacture of the prototype and production tools. Its areas of specialization in subcontracting are injection moulding and vacuum forming. The company's own product is a plastic multidirectional roller allowing simultaneous movement of uniform products in all directions. The rollers are mainly used in industrial conveyors and they are suitable for all industries where material or packages need to be smoothly and easily transferred, sorted or turned in any direction. Customers include companies in the metal and electronics industries, bakeries and other parts of the food industry, furniture and other wood processing, packaging and the glass, rubber and printing industries. One roller costs approximately one euro. The main export product has been the roller, but during the last few years the company has also followed its customers abroad in contract manufacturing. At the moment, for example, it is delivering subcontracted products to Canada, Mexico and the United Kingdom.

The company started regular exports in 1987 by selling its rollers on German markets. The first export contact was made at a trade fair in Hanover and this business has continued since. The first foreign customer is still one of the company's biggest. After Germany, the company went on to the Nordic countries and started actively looking for a representative. The first distributor proved to be inefficient and was replaced by another. The current distributor is a consultant who is covering Sweden, but is also looking for projects in Norway and Denmark, although these countries have their own distributors.

At the moment, company O has distributors or agents in 22 countries all around the world. Its European agents are in Austria, Denmark, Belgium, the Czech Republic, France, Germany, Iceland, Italy, Norway, Poland, Portugal, Spain, Sweden, Switzerland and the UK. Outside Europe it has dealers in South Korea, the USA, Mexico, Argentina, Brazil, Australia and New Zealand. The main export market is central Europe (Germany, France, Switzerland, the Czech Republic and Poland) and these together cover approximately 30 per cent of the exports. The majority of the distributors are dealers in components and conveyor systems, and the rollers are marketed in their product catalogues to companies manufacturing materials-handling systems. The distributors are independent companies who buy the rollers and stock them in their own stores. Most of the dealers market their products in catalogues directed to professional buyers.

The company is relatively committed to internationalization, but at the company level it has made a strategic decision to concentrate on contract manufacturing. The main export product, the roller, will remain a significant product line on the side, but it will not be the main focus of company development. However attitudinal commitment to internationalization is strong, as the managing director has had strong international connections from birth. His mother was born in the United States, and from an early age he was interested in languages and in other countries. He worked as a trainee in Sweden and Switzerland during his engineering studies, and he started his working career as a technical planner in Germany. This kind of international background could be considered exceptional for a Finnish entrepreneur of his age, as he has already celebrated his sixtieth birthday.

If the situations in company O now and at the time of the first export delivery are compared, it can be concluded that no external changes due to internationalization are noticeable. The main export product has remained the same, although it has been developed to meet customer feedback. However the company has recently also entered a new field by exporting subcontracted products. These introductory deliveries may indicate an incremental external change, but as the deliveries are quite recent and so far also irregular, it is as yet impossible to draw any conclusions. The company started exporting indirectly through large Finnish customers. Thereafter it started direct exports via a local dealer on the German market, and this operation mode has been repeated in other markets as well. Externally the only dimension that has changed during the internationalization process is the market: the number of markets on which the company operates is considerable and the dealers are scattered around the world. However the company has spread to these markets gradually, starting from physically and psychologically close countries and moving to more distant ones. The company has thus been a good example of the traditional internationalization process. In sum, the externally visible changes due to internationalization in company O are clearly first-order changes, and there have been no radical changes interrupting this stable development.

The internal changes have also been incremental. The internationalization process has been financed totally by cash flow from other activities. Consequently the changes in *finance* are at the *alpha* level. On the other hand, the tasks and responsibilities related to exporting have rested with the same people the whole time. The export manager takes care of sales and routines, and the owner–manager (nowadays the chairman of the board) assists with technical matters and sales to the German-speaking countries. Occasionally they have been able to decrease their workload with the help of a clerk in the office. The export manager and sometimes the owner–manager have actively participated in diverse training programmes in order to improve their skills in international business, and particularly in languages. It can thus be concluded that the changes related to *personnel* seem to be *beta*-level changes. From the perspective of *organizational structure*, the company is very well linked to other companies. This is due to the fact that, since its founding, it has strictly focused on its core competence and has outsourced all major activities. For example, roller assembly takes place at local sheltered works, logistics and storage are the responsibility of an independent entrepreneur, and the company has long-term business relationships with raw materials, tool and mould suppliers. This organization structure has evolved progressively over the lifetime of the company in an attempt to maintain competitiveness. However, as this development process has had nothing to do with internationalization, it can be concluded that there have been *no changes* due to internationalization from this perspective.

To sum up, the development of company O has been very stable during its lifetime, and this development process has not been interrupted by any significant changes. The original business idea has remained the same over the years. However the owner–manager has recently stepped down from the position of managing director to become full-time chairman of the board. This change of management does not indicate any changes in the core business, but it does imply that strategy development is continuous.

Cross-case analysis

The three case companies have clear similarities and differences. First, they all are experienced exporters and relatively committed to internationalization. Although company O is less dependent on export operations than the others, the management of the company is attitudinally very committed. Second, they all operate on numerous markets dispersed all over the world, which means that they have acquired multifaceted experience of international business. However, from the perspective of change due to internationalization, they also differ significantly from each other. The major changes in the case companies are summarized in Table 23.2.

Table 23.2   A summary of the changes in the case companies

	Company M	Company N	Company O
Business idea	Several second-order changes	One second-order change	Unchanged
External change Product Operation mode Market	Continuous first-order change between several second-order changes based on changes in business idea	Continuous first-order change and one second-order change due to change in business idea	Continuous first-order changes
Internal change Finance Personnel Organization	First-order changes (*alpha* in two and *beta* in one dimension)	Second-order changes (*gamma* changes in all dimensions)	First-order changes (*alpha* and *beta*) in two dimensions, no changes in one

The external changes in the case companies vary, ranging from only first-order changes in company O to the several second-order changes of company M. Additionally the underlying reasons for external and internal changes diverge. It seems that there is a link between changes in the business idea and external changes, whereas internal changes are less dependent on the development of business idea. Furthermore the extent of change differs in the case companies. Nevertheless, when the extent of change is evaluated, it should be kept in mind that the number of changes is not always decisive. The triggers of change are also of importance. The external changes in company M were mostly triggered by environmental forces or persons outside the company; that is, they were the outcomes of a reactive adaptation process. In contrast, the changes in company N were planned beforehand inside the company, which demonstrated more proactive behaviour and advanced strategic planning.

Internal changes due to internationalization vary between no changes at all to significant *gamma*-level changes. All the changes in companies M and O can be classified as first-order changes, whereas those in company N were all second-order changes. The changes in company N were naturally partly due to the radical change in the core of the business, but the impact of internationalization has also been considerable. These changes were unavoidable given the need to implement the growth strategy of the company. It is possible that these strategic choices also explain at least some of the differences between the companies. The management in company N made some clear strategic decisions in connection with the radical change in the company in the 1990s, and the changes due to internationalization could be considered logical consequences of these decisions. On the other hand, it seems that the management in companies M and O have not made any clear strategic choices, and the companies have more or less 'drifted' into their current position. It may be assumed that strategic decisions are a necessary requirement for second-order internal changes, whereas incremental first-order changes probably occur without any definite decisions being made.

Changes in the different dimensions do not seem to be related to each other, but vary independently in the given context. Changes in finance, for example, are moderated by the entrepreneur's subjective preferences and their pecking order for potential funding. Subjective preferences seem to be related to other types of change as well. It could be expected, for instance, that a manager with a global mindset, as in company O, appreciates formal education and training and recommends it to other personnel as well. Additionally, if the manager has previous experience in international business and adequate language skills, additional personnel with these capabilities are not needed.

The cases also indicate that changes in organization structure are often brought about by pressure from customers. For example, company N established sales subsidiaries in its main markets in order to respond to the need there. On the other hand, company M created a network of suppliers in order to offer the complementary products the customers required. This is quite natural, as a change in organization structure, particularly a permanent one, requires considerable investment, and a positive impact on company performance has to be assured before any action is taken.

Conclusions

Findings from the case companies support the argument that small firms take diverse routes to internationalization. Thus the level of changes due to internationalization also varies considerably. The cases showed that the framework used in this study is a well-functioning tool for analysing such changes, as all relevant issues seem to be covered. It was not only the internal and external changes, but also the role of the business idea, that was highlighted in the companies.

It seems that change in SME internationalization is more multidimensional than assumed. Various types of change could be identified and the phenomenon itself was analysed at diverse levels. The complexity of the concept is also demonstrated through the fact that the changes in the different dimensions are not necessarily connected, but they are very context dependent. This sets substantial managerial challenges as it complicates the identification of weak signals from the environment and thus the prediction of future changes. This multidimensionality also presents considerable requirements for research, as operationalization has to be carefully managed. An explicit definition is essential if reliable and comparable results are to be obtained.

Theoretically it is interesting that the cases indicate different levels of change, but also various triggers and sources of change. It was rather surprising that the case companies' commitment to internationalization was not always connected with the changes. It could have been anticipated that a strong dependence on exports and additional commitment to internationalization would have encouraged more noticeable changes. However, in our case company M, the changes due to internationalization were quite limited despite its high commitment. On the other hand, a connection between the strategy and particularly strategic decision making and change could be observed: strategic decisions seem to lead to more visible changes. This could also be linked to the internationalization process of the firm: traditional, incremental internationalization may often proceed without any radical turning points, and as a result the changes in the company are also mainly first-order changes. In contrast, 'born-again-global' firms are typically firms in which there has been at least one critical incident during their history: the decision to start exporting. This radical change touches the company as a whole and may also lead to more fundamental changes due to internationalization.

Despite the interesting findings, this study also has some limitations. First the findings are based on only three cases and thus the results can only be considered tentative. Nevertheless they open up new avenues for further research and point out topics that need more elaboration. It would be worthwhile, for example, to study sources of radical change in detail. When do they actually occur and why? Another fascinating area would be the study of born global companies and changes in them. It has been argued that these companies should have been created to fit the international business environment from inception (McDougall *et al.*, 1994). In other words, it could be assumed that there would be fewer changes due to internationalization in these companies. An empirical study would be required to verify the justification of this argument. Additionally the study could be extended to companies whose internationalization has proceeded from exporting to more demanding operation modes. McDougall and Oviatt (1996) have argued that operation modes that require more resource commitment also call for more strategic changes, and it would no doubt be rewarding to examine whether this is really so.

A second limitation of the study is the problem related to the identification of change. A retrospective research design is always challenging as it depends heavily on the time perspective and on the memory of the respondents. Additionally, for the respondents, it is sometimes difficult to recognize change because, from their perspective, it may be considered as a part of normal business development. However a more significant issue is the fact that it is sometimes difficult to separate change related to internationalization from other change happening in the company. Although the relationship between change and internationalization was emphasized during the interviews, there is the possibility that the managers were describing change at the company level, and thus the changes related to internationalization were given more weight than they should have been. Nevertheless this does not seem to have been a problem in this study – rather the reverse, because the changes identified were mostly first-order changes.

This study is an attempt to respond to increasing criticism of the existing theory of internationalization and it offers a novel perspective on SME internationalization. According to the findings, SMEs might be able to anticipate future changes in the environment and to adapt to them. This will also be reflected in their strategic planning. Additionally the information can be utilized in organizing public support for internationalizing SMEs, particularly from the viewpoint of the support systems.

Notes

1. Defining small and medium-sized enterprises has proved to be very complicated. This chapter uses the European Union definition: SMEs employ fewer than 250 persons, their annual sales do not exceed 20 million ECU and they are independent (that is, other companies' share of ownership does not exceed 25 per cent). The terms 'SME', 'small firm' and 'small business' are used interchangeably throughout the chapter.
2. Although internationalization includes both the inward and outward operations of a firm (Welch and Luostarinen, 1988), this article focuses on the outward operations of SMEs, particularly on direct exporting, as this is the most common form of international operations among small firms.
3. The debate on whether to standardize or adapt the product on foreign markets started as early as in the late 1960s (Buzzell, 1968) and since that time it has been a standard topic in international marketing textbooks. Diverse operational modes are also well covered in the literature, although the change aspect has often been neglected (for recent discussion on the change of operation mode, see for example, Pedersen *et al.*, 2002; Petersen and Welch, 2002; Petersen *et al.*, 2000; Calof and Beamish, 1995). Additionally, internationalization inherently includes a change of market, so from the viewpoint of this study the interest lies in the extent of that change, measured according to the number and geographic location of the target markets, for example.
4. A core competence is a competitively unique bundle of skills and technologies that contributes substantially to customer value and forms the basis for entry into new markets (Hamel and Prahalad, 1994).
5. The companies included the large multinationals Procter & Gamble Europe, Nestlé and Heineken, as well as five business units of three Austrian companies. The companies were analysed within a framework consisting of four stages: early internationalization, local market expansion, regionalization and globalization.
6. These panel data included information on 1700 firms from seven European countries during the period 1991–5.
7. A follow-up questionnaire was sent to companies who had participated in a related study two years earlier, and the findings of these two studies were compared.
8. Bell *et al.* (2001) have classified internationally operating firms into three categories: Born Globals, Born-again Globals and traditional firms. Traditional firms follow the

incremental internationalization process, Born Globals are international from inception and Born-again Globals are well-established firms which focus on domestic markets at start-up, but which later start a rapid internationalization process (ibid.: 174).

References

Andersen, Otto (1993), 'On the internationalization process of firms: A critical analysis', *Journal of International Business Studies*, 24 (2), 209–31.

Andersen, Poul Houman, Per Blenker and Poul Rind Christensen (1997), 'Generic Routes to Subcontractors' Internationalisation', in I. Björkman and M. Forsgren (eds), *The Nature of the International Firm*, Copenhagen: Copenhagen Business School Press, pp. 231–55.

Barton, Sidney L. and Charles H. Matthews (1989), 'Small firm financing: Implications from a strategic management perspective', *Journal of Small Business Management*, 27 (1), 1–7.

Bell, Jim (1995), 'A Comparative Study of the Export Problems of Small Computer Software Exporters in Finland, Ireland and Norway', *International Business Review*, 6 (6), 585–604.

Bell, Jim, Rod McNaughton and Steve Young (2001), '"Born-again global" firms. An extension to the "born global" phenomenon', *Journal of International Management*, 7 (3), 173–89.

Buzzell, Robert D. (1968), 'Can you standardize multinational marketing?', *Harvard Business Review*, 46 (6), 102–13.

Calof, Jonathan L. and Paul W. Beamish (1995), 'Adapting to Foreign Markets: Explaining Internationalization', *International Business Review*, 4 (2), 115–31.

Chapman, Judith Ann (2002), 'A framework for transformational change in organisations', *Leadership & Organization Development Journal*, 23 (1), 16–25.

Christensen, Poul Rind (1991), 'The small and medium-sized exporter's squeeze: empirical evidence and model reflections', *Entrepreneurship & Regional Development*, 3 (1), 49–65.

Clark, Timothy, Derek S. Pugh and Geoff Mallory (1997), 'The Process of Internationalization in the Operating Firm', *International Business Review*, 6 (6), 605–23.

Eriksson, Kent, Jan Johanson, Anders Majkgård and D. Deo Sharma (1997), 'Experiential knowledge and cost in the internationalization process', *Journal of International Business Studies*, 28 (2), 337–59.

Gersick, Connie J.G. (1991), 'Revolutionary change theories: A multilevel exploration of the punctuated equilibrium paradigm', *Academy of Management Review*, 16 (1), 10–36.

Golembiewski, R.T., K. Billingsley and S. Yeager (1976), 'Measuring change and persistence in human affairs: Types of change generated by OD designs', *Journal of Applied Behavioral Science*, 12 (2), 133–55.

Halinen, Aino, Asta Salmi and Virpi Havila (1999), 'From dyadic change to changing business networks: An analytical framework', *Journal of Management Studies*, 36 (6), 779–94.

Hamel, Gary and C.K. Prahalad (1994), *Competing for the future*, Boston, MA: Harvard Business School Press.

Hamilton, Robert T. and Mark A. Fox (1998), 'The financing preferences of small firm owners', *International Journal of Entrepreneurial Behaviour & Research*, 4 (3), 239–48.

Havnes, Per-Anders (1998), 'Dynamics of small business internationalisation. A European panel study', PhD dissertation, University of Stirling, Stirling, UK.

Hohenthal, Jukka (2001), 'The creation of international business relationships. Experience and performance in the internationalisation process of SMEs', doctoral thesis no.90, Department of Business Studies, Uppsala University, Uppsala.

Howorth, Carole A. (2001), 'Small Firms' Demand for Finance: A Research Note', *International Small Business Journal*, 19 (4), 78–86.

Hurmerinta-Peltomäki, Leila (2001), 'Time and internationalisation. The shortened adoption lag in small business internationalisation', *Publications of the Turku School of Economics and Business Administration*, Series A-7:2001, Turku, Finland.

Johanson, Jan and Jan-Erik Vahlne (1977), 'The internationalisation process of the firm – a model of knowledge development and increasing foreign market commitments', *Journal of International Business*, 8 (1), 23–32.

Johanson, Jan and Jan-Erik Vahlne (1990), 'The Mechanism of Internationalisation', *International Marketing Review*, 7 (4), 11–24.
Jones, Marian V. (1999), 'The Internationalization of Small High-Technology Firms', *Journal of International Marketing*, 7 (4), 15–41.
Katsikeas, C.S. and L.C. Leonidou (2000), 'Firm-level export performance assessment: Review, evaluation and development', *Academy of Marketing Science*, 28 (4), 493–511.
Kimberly, John R. (1976), 'Issues in the Design of Longitudinal Organizational Research', *Sociological Methods & Research*, 4 (3), 321–47.
Lam, Long W. and Louis P. White (1999), 'An adaptive choice model of the internationalisation process', *International Journal of Organizational Analysis*, 7 (2), 105–34.
LeCornu, Mark R., Richard G.P. McMahon, David M. Forsaith and Anthony M.J. Stanger (1996), 'The Small Enterprise Financial Objective Function', *Journal of Small Business Management*, 34 (3), 1–14.
Lumpkin, G.T. and Gregory G. Dess (1996), 'Clarifying the entrepreneurial orientation construct and linking it to performance', *Academy of Management Review*, 21 (1), 135–72.
Madsen, Tage K. and Per Servais (1997), 'The internationalization of born globals: an evolutionary process?', *International Business Review*, 6 (6), 561–83.
McDougall, Patricia Phillips and Benjamin M. Oviatt (1996), 'New venture internationalization, strategic change and performance: A follow-up study', *Journal of Business Venturing*, 11 (1), 23–40.
McDougall, P.P., S. Shane and B.M. Oviatt (1994), 'Explaining the formation of international new ventures: The limits of theories from international business research', *Journal of Business Venturing*, 9 (6), 469–87.
Miles, R.E. and C.C. Snow (1986), 'Organizations: New Concepts for New Forms', *California Management Review*, 28 (3), 62–73.
Miller, Danny and Peter H. Friesen (1984), *Organizations: A quantum view*, Englewood Cliffs, NJ: Prentice-Hall.
Mitchell, Terence R. and Lawrence, R. James (2001), 'Building better theory: Time and the specification of when things happen', *Academy of Management Review*, 26 (4), 530–47.
Parker, Barbara (1996), 'Evolution and Revolution: from International Business to Globalization', in R. Stewart, C.H. Clegg and R.N. Walter (eds), *Handbook of Organization Studies*, London: Sage, pp. 484–506.
Pedersen, T., B. Petersen and G.R.G. Benito (2002), 'Change of foreign operation method: impetus and switching costs', *International Business Review*, 11 (3), 325–45.
Petersen, Bent and Torben Pedersen (1997), 'Twenty Years After – Support and Critique of the Uppsala Internationalisation Model', in I. Björkman and M. Forsgren (eds), *The Nature of the International Firm*, Copenhagen: Copenhagen Business School Press, pp. 117–34.
Petersen, Bent and Lawrence S. Welch (2002), 'Foreign operation mode combinations and internationalisation', *Journal of Business Research*, 55 (2), 157–62.
Petersen, Bent, Denice Ellen Welch and Lawrence Stephenson Welch (2000), 'Creating Meaningful Switching Options in International Operations', *Long Range Planning*, 33 (5), 688–705.
Sachwald, Frédérique (1998), 'Co-operative agreements and the theory of the firm: Focusing on barriers to change', *Journal of Economic Behavior & Organization*, 35 (2), 203–25.
Schuh, Arnold (2001), 'Strategic change during the internationalisation of the firm', Proceedings of the 27th EIBA Conference, 13–15 December, Paris.
Tushman, Michael L. and Charles A. O'Reilly (1996), 'Ambidextrous Organizations: Managing Evolutionary and Revolutionary Change', *California Management Review*, 38 (4), 8–30.
Van de Ven, Andrew H. (1992), 'Suggestions for studying strategy process: A research note', *Strategic Management Journal*, 13 (13), Special Issue, 169–88.
Van de Ven, Andrew H. and Marshall Scott Poole (1995), 'Explaining development and change in organizations', *Academy of Management Review*, 20 (3), 510–40.
Watzlawick, P., J.H. Weakland and R. Fisch (1974), *Change: Principles of Problem Formation and Problem Resolution*, New York: Norton.
Welch, L.S. and R. Luostarinen (1988), 'Internationalization: Evolution of a concept', *Journal of General Management*, 14 (2), 34–55.

24 French perspectives of international entrepreneurship
Alain Fayolle

In France, conflicting information is circulating concerning student and graduate business start-ups.* The specialist press regularly publishes articles detailing the entrepreneurial character of the younger generations. The 'new French entrepreneurs' seem to be getting younger and younger and 'no longer wait to leave school to launch their entrepreneurial projects'.[1] Communication technologies and the Internet appear to attract them and to catalyse the entrepreneurial process. Each day sees students and young graduates starting out on their international business ventures. Some cases of start-ups by students from the French 'Grandes Ecoles' are analysed in the press and experts are beginning to talk about an important change in mentalities and behaviour. A study made of 900 business and engineering school final year students (KORELAT, 1999), suggested that as many as 45% of those concerned were strongly attracted, in the short term, by the idea of setting up their own business, mainly in an international context.

However, although some enterprising students have received media coverage, this new interest in start-ups shown by 'Grandes Ecoles' and university students, does not, for the moment, mean the entrepreneurial revolution has begun in France. Firstly, it must be remembered that, over the past five years, the number of *ex nihilo* company start-ups per year in France has steadily decreased, from 183764 in 1994 to 166190 in 1998 (APCE, 1998). As this concerns primarily students and young graduates, it presents no reason to rejoice. In a recent survey of 1000 start-ups created between June 1997 and May 1998, only 6% were by young entrepreneurs (EUROPME, 1999). These 'beginners', are, for the most part, students who begin their professional career by realizing their entrepreneurial projects. However, the survey does not indicate how many are students or young graduates of French higher education. In an analysis based on age groups, excluding the agricultural and the 'liberal' professions, official INSEE

* The author would like to kindly thank Allen Vernier, Benjamin Lepesant and Benjamin Djiane for their research assistance and involvement with the data collection and analysis, and also Professor Daniel Evans of EM Lyon for his assistance in completing a first version of this work.

431

statistics show that young people and young graduates rarely create their own companies (INSEE, 1997).

Another recent survey of 10 000 people, all of whom graduated in 1996 and were chosen at random from the French metropolitan higher educational establishments, gives a low number of those who have set up on their own in the three years following their graduation (CEREQ, 1999): barely 1% of engineering school graduates and 2% of business school graduates. As regards business schools recognized by the state, the figure is close to zero. Thus we can say that the start-up phenomenon remains fairly marginal among students and young graduates in France despite the apparent trend towards entrepreneurship in the French education system (Fayolle, 2000a).

In an earlier paper, the impact of entrepreneurial training programmes on the entrepreneurial behaviour of students and graduates was analysed (Fayolle, 2000b). In the present chapter, we will look at the students and young graduates who have created their companies to understand better their principal characteristics and the logic process that led them to create their own businesses. We will approach the phenomenon from a new angle, our main aim being to offer more knowledge about such entrepreneurs. Then we will try to promote this career path for students and help those, and the institutions, who are involved in the company start-up processes. It is of primordial interest for academies and for French society, because, very often, the companies created by this type of entrepreneur have a high growth potential and also have a great propensity to develop international activities quickly.

The bulk of the research is centred upon a sample of 16 student/graduate entrepreneurs followed during the second term in 1999. Before presenting our results and their analysis, we develop the synthesis we made of the existing research surrounding this phenomenon, as well as the theoretical framework and methodological approach we used.

The relation between students and graduates and business start-ups

To understand better the motivation and logic which lead students and graduates to start their own businesses, we feel it is necessary to position the phenomenon in the global problem of career choice and to analyse the entrepreneurial paths chosen by French students and young graduates.

Concerning the careers of young French graduates

Students and graduates can be considered as a specific social group. As such, numerous studies have been made of them. The graduate is a product of a structured education system which is divided into many heterogeneous tracks. Each organization proposes its own logic, representations and career models. Thus, at the beginning of the twentieth century, the engineer's identity was primarily based on technical and professional values (Veblen, 1971). Today graduates are moving away from such technical values towards relational and social ones (Lojkine, 1992). An engineering or business school is a place for professional socialization, and the graduate leaves with a number of possible professional representations of his/her future.

These representations are based on a career model, to which the graduate must conform if he or she wishes to succeed (Bouffartigue, 1994). The career models offered to engineers and managers generally combine a double development, both hierarchical and professional. The first is characterized by the succession of three statuses: beginner, expert, director. The second identifies three steps: technical, managerial, strategic (Robin, 1994). A successful manager is one who, when middle-aged, is a senior manager. Obviously, these 'ideal' career models are subject to economic and contextual changes. Changes in organizational structures and labour market tensions can raise new questions concerning the careers of young graduates (Dany, 1991).

Career models also depend on the particularities of the educational systems the degrees are obtained from. The role and importance of the degree in the careers of young managers who have graduated from the top management schools has also been mentioned (Safavian-Martinon, 1998). The author's theory is that there is a relation between the degree held and some career decisions (preferences, possibilities, beliefs). Having different degrees reflects the logic of partially different actors which in turn can help us to understand why 'Grandes Ecoles' graduates choose different career paths from other, notably university, graduates. One interesting result from this work is the lack of 'entrepreneurial spirit' among HEC graduates,[2] few of whom decided to create their own company or actively participate in small companies, in contrast to university students.

The influence of the degree or the school has also been studied previously. Bourdieu (1989) states that, in a society of privileges, the degree, particularly when awarded by a highly reputable institution, replaces privilege related to birth, and that one of the functions of the education system is that of creating an elite. Ribeil (1984) suggests a graduate engineer's entrepreneurial propensity is inversely proportional to the 'value' of the degree. Bauer (1988) and other sociologists (Maurice *et al.*, 1982) show how the access to certain positions and other prestigious jobs is reserved for graduates from just a few schools. The 'royal way' and the career paths presented to graduates would seem to favour top positions in the civil service and the major companies, while ignoring the small and medium-sized companies and all entrepreneurial situations. Fayolle and Livian (1995) suggest that engineering schools minimize any entrepreneurial propensity and propose the setting up of programmes to make people more aware of entrepreneurship in order to develop 'an entrepreneurial wakening' among engineering school students.

Having reached this point in our development, we feel it is necessary to look more closely at the entrepreneurial paths chosen by students and young graduates.

Concerning the entrepreneurial paths chosen by students and young graduates

By entrepreneurial path we mean, on the one hand, the development of an entrepreneurial propensity or an entrepreneurial intention and, on the other hand, the behaviour or entrepreneurial act itself, in other words the creation of a start-up. The two notions (intention and behaviour) are not equivalent and to have, at a given time, an entrepreneurial intention does not mean it will actually happen. Some research (Katz, 1990 ; Tkachev and Kolvereid, 1999) have underlined the complexity of the relation between intention and behaviour.

Many studies have been devoted to the measuring or the modelling of what we have chosen to call 'entrepreneurial intention'. Fewer have looked at 'entrepreneurial behaviour', which is obviously pertinent to the social group which is at the centre of our work. In order to deal with the entrepreneurial path chosen by the students and young graduates, we now look at their entrepreneurial intention and behaviour.

The entrepreneurial intention of students

At a quantitative level, previous research which has tried to measure the entrepreneurial intentions or preferences of students has generally led to a double conclusion: first, that levels of intention appear high, even very high; second, that there would appear to be differences and gaps between countries, particularly between the USA and France.

In the United States, research has revealed a strong attraction to entrepreneurial careers. Hills and Welsch (1986) identified a high level of entrepreneurial intention (52%) among a sample of around 2000 students from two business schools. A national survey indicated that 46% of college students consider working for their own businesses an excellent professional move (Brenner *et al.*, 1991, p. 62). The same authors present the results of a survey concerning 1000 students following the best American MBA programmes. The most surprising finding is that 44% of those interviewed expressed an intention, in the mid-term, to work independently. An international survey shows that the interest of American students in working independently is extremely high (57.1%), while it is much lower in France

(28.3%) (Weihe and Reich, 1991). Moreover, the latter have a relatively negative image of entrepreneurs. Another survey, this time conducted in France on a sample of 2400 students, showed contrasting intentions according to the programmes followed and the institution attended (ZELIG, 1998). Thus 21% of university management students wished to create their own company, 16% in the science and technical universities, 13% in the business schools and 9% in the engineering schools. Whatever the track, entrepreneurial intentions were relatively low.

At a qualitative level, entrepreneurial intentions appear to be influenced by a number of factors. Preferences in terms of career develop around such values as the feeling of fulfilment, job security or the opportunity to acquire new skills and techniques (Brenner *et al.*, 1991). The different professional paths may be appealing, depending on social situations, personal experiences, educational background and dominant mental representations. As the choice is between being an entrepreneur and being an employee, some research has been able to highlight the influence of different variables. For example, Scott and Twomey (1988) demonstrated that students whose parents are entrepreneurs prefer by far business ventures, and recoil from employee status positions in major companies. Those students with some 'professional' experience also opt for entrepreneurship (Hills and Welsch, 1986). Fayolle (1996) shows that engineering school students who are heavily involved in student associations or creating associations during their studies are more inclined to choose the entrepreneurial track as a professional path. Moreover, the desire to create is even higher among students who have combined scientific studies with management studies, for example.

The part played by the education system in one's desire to create and the development of entrepreneurial skills has frequently been mentioned in previous research. Some authors believe that university and school are places where a student's entrepreneurial potential can be identified, assessed and developed (Gasse, 1985; Aurifeille and Hernandez, 1991; Filion, 1994). Entrepreneurship must be presented carefully, taught and shown to be a possible career option (Gasse, 1985, p. 555). The importance of the university environment has also been underlined by Johannisson (1991).

The entrepreneurial behavior of students
In our introduction, we showed that, in France, at a quantitative level, entrepreneurship among students and graduates was low. At a qualitative level, some works seem to support the idea of the existence of significant differences in attitude between entrepreneur students and those who are not (Robinson *et al.*, 1991). In France, working with two student samples from Dauphine University in Paris, Leger (1994, 1996) demonstrates that enterprising students, following an entrepreneurship programme, are different

from other students. They appear more active, ready to take risks, adaptable and solid. Family backgrounds are varied and, in particular, more entrepreneurial. They declare their autonomy, their need for independence, self-assurance and a taste for competition. Other research concerning entrepreneurship graduates underlines the role played by the university. This role is clearly highlighted in research which tried to link entrepreneurship and education (Schuman *et al.*, 1987). The authors found significant differences between the four schools they studied. Babson College, which is known for its entrepreneurship courses, has a high percentage of independent entrepreneurs and company creators among the 1311 people interviewed. From the research, Babson has the image of an institution which specializes in the teaching of business.

In a survey of 25 French business schools, Fayolle (2000b) concludes that the entrepreneurial behaviour of the students and graduates varies according to the competitive positioning of the schools and the direction taken in the entrepreneurship programmes. To sum up, social, contextual and psychological variables would seem to determine the entrepreneurial behaviour of students and young graduates.

The theoretical framework of our research
The different theoretical models which exist, and which come from the fields of sociology and psychology, attempt to explain why an individual chooses to be an employee or to be 'self-employed'. Some models consider that personality is a determining factor and that it is possible to identify psychological characteristics and distinct personality profiles between those who work as self-employed and those who work as employees (Begley and Boyd, 1987). The 'role models' school of thought considers that 'exemplarity', particularly when coming from the parents, is an important determining factor in entrepreneurial action (Brockhaus and Horowitz, 1986; Scott and Twomey, 1988; Katz, 1992; Mathews and Moser, 1995, 1996). Dyer (1994) uses an integrated model which is relative to the concept of 'entrepreneurial career'. In such a theoretical approach, three families of factors can explain career choices: those which are related to the psychological and demographic data, those which take social aspects into consideration (role models, culture, parental support and so on) and finally those which concern the more economic criteria (available resources, job market, professional opportunities and so on).

For a number of years now, the theory of planned behaviour has been used to shape entrepreneurial intention. Here career intentions depend on the attitude in relation to target behaviour, social standards and the level of perceived control (Ajzen, 1991). Krueger and Carsrud (1993) applied the theory of planned behaviour to the study of entrepreneurial intention.

Using their work, researchers created models designed to understand the development of entrepreneurial intention among students (Kolvereid, 1996 ; Autio *et al.*, 1997; Tkachev and Kolvereid, 1999). The model developed by Autio *et al.* is, for example, designed to explain the entrepreneurial intention of students from four different countries. According to the authors, it depends on numerous variables which are linked to the university environment, career preferences, values, the image of entrepreneurship, the individual's situation and educational and professional background.

Alongside the psychological and sociological perspectives, which have been widely studied already, other positions have sometimes been adopted. The economic outlook in particular has made it possible to elaborate many contributions. We will not develop such models here as they do not necessarily fit into our way of thinking. Nevertheless, we feel it important to mention how some economists have used the theory of human capital to predict the choice of work status (Tucker, 1990; Pesteau and Possen, 1992) or of the approaches based on the maximizing of the usefulness of the action (Douglas and Shepherd, 2000).

The theoretical framework we have used is based on sociological and psychological perspectives. The model is similar to that used by other researchers (Autio *et al.*, 1997; Davidsson, 1995); however we have integrated the action component that integrates the action plan of the entrepreneur after intent has been established. Our aim was not to test a new model based on existing models but to have a solid reference framework designed to direct and facilitate our field study.

'Opportunities are seized by those who are prepared to seize them'. In this simple quotation, Krueger and Brazeal (1994) underscore the importance of creating an environment that encourages entrepreneurial potential. Once a potential has been developed, changes, a series of events or 'trigger events' are required to induce intent as well as to move from intent to action (Learned, 1992). As has been seen, these events can be linked to a random occurrence or the results of a planned behaviour within the educational environment.

Probably one of the most important contributory factors to entrepreneurial intent is perceived self-efficacy[3] (Davidsson, 1995; Krueger and Brazeal, 1994). The educational setting appears to be a fertile ground for development of this quality: participation in student associations; evaluation of work in and out of class; peer evaluation. All of these elements can contribute to the way one sees oneself and whether one believes one is capable of being a successful entrepreneur.

The concept of 'action logic' comes from sociology and has been recently explicated (Amblard *et al.*, 1996). The theory proposed to justify the concept is linked to the need to federate and to articulate different autonomized sociological notions. An 'action logic' can be defined, and is created, by the meeting of an historically and culturally formed strategic actor (Crozier and Friedberg, 1977) and an action situation. This actor–situation dialectic and the subsequent interactions allow the action logic to take shape and to determine individual behaviour.

In this light, and by immediately basing our approach on the hypothesis of the existence of specific motivations and action logic which take students and graduates towards the creation of new businesses, we have decided to retain four groups of variables in our model. The first group is the personal variables: motivations, preferences, beliefs and values. The second is the variables linked to personal and/or professional experience. Here we felt it was important to investigate the in-company training periods and the level of involvement in student and/or other associations. The third group includes the contextual and social variables, including factors from the university and the educational or economic environment. The final group offers a series of variables linked to the personal environment (influence of parents, encouragement and support given at the time of the business creation).

The theoretical model which helped us in our research can be presented as in Figure 24.1.

Methodological approach
We now present our sample and explain how the survey and data analysis were carried out.

The sample
Owing to the difficulty in contacting recently graduated entrepreneurs (the information in the directories being rather limited), we decided to concentrate on three French specialized entrepreneurship programmes, 'HEC Entrepreneurs', the 'Entrepreneurship Track' at the university of Paris-Dauphine and the 'Entrepreneurship Programmes for Students' offered at EM Lyon. Our sample population includes 16 recently graduated entrepreneurs (male only). The principal characteristics are presented in Table 24.1.

All company start-ups, the oldest dating back to the beginning of the 1990s, concern service activities. Roughly 50% can be considered as particularly innovative. All of them have a high propensity to develop international businesses. Half of the entrepreneurs in our sample created their companies before graduating, the others a short time after, giving priority to their degree course or needing more time before starting.

Survey and analysis methods
Semi-directive interviews were conducted for about two hours. These were led by teams of two researchers, the first to take notes, the second to analyse

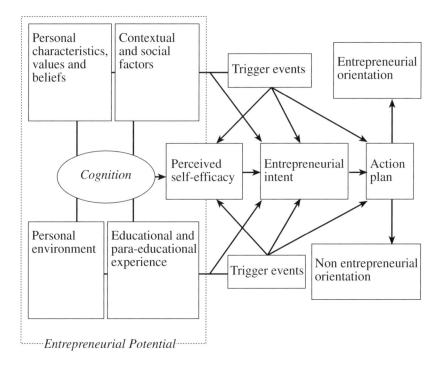

Figure 24.1   From entrepreneurial potential to action: the business creation phenomenon for French students and graduates

Table 24.1   Sample population

Total	16
Start-ups less than one year old	9
Average creation age	23
Institutions	
EM LYON	8
HEC Entrepreneurs	2
Université Dauphine	5
ICN*	1

Note: * This person is the partner of one of the EM Lyon graduates.

what was said in order to reformulate the key points and to direct the interview. To analyse the information, content analysis techniques were used.

The themes of the interviews were derived from the model. The initial grid included the following themes :

- personal environment,
- training and education,
- experiences and responsibilities (training periods, sandwich courses, association work, class delegate and so on),
- career orientation and planning,
- feeling of being different,
- problem of choice between an employee, independent or start-up position,
- awareness period at the outset,
- going for it: opportunity and choice of partners, influence of reason and passion,
- type and level of parental support (financial, moral),
- motivation and 'action logic',
- image of entrepreneurship and self-portrait (creator, entrepreneur, organizer, leader),
- perception and acceptance of risk.

Findings

Below is a presentation of the principal results around some themes or questions which are, for us, particularly important. They concern the personal environment, training and education, work for associations, experience, hobbies, desire to create, support, the decision, perception of risk, partners, motivation, representation and image of the entrepreneur and the entrepreneurial process.

An entrepreneurial familial environment

Fourteen people of the sample have parents who are 'self-employed': three fathers and one mother are doctors in medicine, one father and three mothers are artists, nine fathers are entrepreneurs, and one father is a craftsman. There have even been cases of internal mobility within these different categories (two doctors in medicine became entrepreneurs).

We were not interested in grandparents or brothers and sisters, however several people spontaneously said that their grandparents or brothers were directors or company creators. Also we did not check to see whether the people interviewed were the eldest in the family or not.

Those interviewed are generally aware of the impact their environment has had on their decision during, or at the end of, their studies. One person told us his decision was made in order to be different from his father and not to be compared to him.

Table 24.2   Educational experience

Single post-secondary level degree	11
Multiple post-secondary level degrees	5
University studies	8
'Grandes Ecoles' studies	8
University and 'Grandes Ecoles' studies	4
Business and sales education	12
Engineering education	4

School or university: a place for meeting people and opportunities

As shown in Table 24.2, our sample is composed of people who were graduated in the French higher education system. Almost 50% of those interviewed have followed entrepreneurship programmes and 30% chose their studies with the intention of creating their own businesses. Creation opportunities generally appear during the educational experience (encountering future partners, discovering ideas for start-ups) and are backed up by academic support programmes or tutoring. However, even if acquaintances are made during one's education, this does not seem to be a determining factor in the act itself. Some of those interviewed acknowledged having felt there was a gap between themselves and the course content, or other students: generally speaking this could be translated as a greater maturity and awareness of their difference from others.

A strong commitment in the student associations

Nine interviewees worked for a student association (or several): five of them were presidents. In most cases the associations in question are the most important in their institution in terms of budget and fame. These include the 'Bureau des Elèves', the 'Junior Entreprise' and the 'Petit Paumé' (EM Lyon). These associations are project-based and require a lot of commitment. Those who were presidents said they had worked on the projects they had initiated and developed them from start to finish. Seven (including the previous five) also had solid experience in other fields too: organizing events, belonging to musical groups, political events.

We noticed that few of them mentioned any such activities before entering further education. At least three interviewees discovered their entrepreneurial qualities while presiding over or organizing the associations. They also felt this kind of experience gave more credit to their projects, as far as they and their partners were concerned.

A strong relationship between professional experiences and starting a business

Six interviewees had 'odd jobs' during their studies: one of them in order to pay back a loan for a party which had been a flop, most of the others to have some kind of financial independence from their parents. As for in-company training:

- 12 had done classical training periods of less than six months;
- three had done slightly longer ones (nine to 12 months);
- three had followed a sandwich course;
- one had never done a training period but had worked throughout his studies on a part-time contract;
- seven had done their training periods in a field close to that in which they went on to create their business.

Some collected experience and types of experience (one did odd jobs, training periods and a sandwich course) but, overall, they all had more experience than their average classmates. As for the type of company, 14 had at least some experience of a major company, and some were able to compare this to a small and medium-sized firm and even a start-up. Two only had experience of small and medium-sized firms or start-ups.

It is rare to feel the desire to create one's own business during a training period. There is instead a negative thought process which leads to not wanting to work for a major company in the future. All those interviewed linked their desire to create their own business to their initial professional experience (particularly in reaction to major companies) and they all stressed their taste for practical work and operational aspects.

Passion

Seven interviewees confessed to having a passion: for three it was music, for two computers, for one sport and for the other the media. Of these seven people, five went on to create in a field related to their passion. However most of them said they could have started up in another field, although creating in the field of one's passion could be an advantage as one already knows the activity fairly well.

The desire to become an entrepreneur: family and education

As far as the desire to create is concerned, nine wanted to create before even entering their school or university, and the most precocious said they wanted to create before the age of 18. Seven said they got the desire while following an entrepreneurship course at school or university. For seven of them, the feeling came at a precise moment: following a 'création d'entreprise' programme at EM Lyon for one of them, following a training period for another; after their student association experience for two of them; having met his future partner for another; for another, it was following an MBA project assignment; and for the last it developed because of a focus of interest from his childhood.

A very helpful close environment

Most felt supported and encouraged by their friends and family. The professors also have a role to play. They support and advise during the creation process. All underlined the need for and importance of support during this difficult creation process. This suggests that the support of social networks (Reynolds, 1991) has a direct impact on entrepreneurial intent and action.

Five entrepreneurs also spoke of the influence of their parents' professions. Generally speaking, all were aware of the impact of their environment on the creation process.

To be or not to be an entrepreneur

We wanted to know here what had played a major role in the entrepreneurial decision. For nine of those interviewed, this was encountering their future partners. For six others, it was encountering future partners, plus the idea of creating. For three others, they were the initiators themselves.

Four interviewees also mentioned an openness to opportunities, which should not be confused with opportunism, but more a logic related to business opportunity. Finally, six interviewees started up in fields they already knew and had experience of. Most of those interviewed see the entrepreneurial decision as logical, a natural phenomenon, which they are not always aware of. One, however, considered a new business start-up as a means or a step in his career plan.

A weak perception of risk

Many spoke to us of the notion of failure in France. Indeed, compared to other countries, it is much harder to create in France: there are a number of obstacles and failure is seen in a bad light. However, a business creation is often looked upon positively even if it fails, as it is relatively easy to be hired as a consultant or in a company in the same sector. Moreover, interviewees also added that success is also seen in a bad light in France.

Most interviewees said that the end of one's studies was probably the best time to begin because responsibilities are low: they are single, there are no children, no mortgage payments and so on. At least four of our sample said, 'the most we can lose is one year'. Only one borrowed a lot of money to start up, but this did not reduce his desire to create.

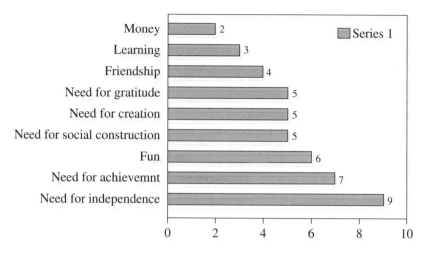

Figure 24.2   Entrepreneurial motivation

A collective phenomenon through partnership
Only one from the sample went it alone. Another said that, even if he had a partner, his project was his and his alone. All, however, spoke of the need to have a partner as a complement, in terms of skills, advice and financial and moral support. Of the 16 people in our sample, nine started up with two or more partners, seven with a single partner. For more than half of them, the partners were extremely good friends. However, if having a partner is a determining factor, seven admitted that they felt they could have gone it alone.

Seven underlined the fact that having a partner is not a commitment for life, as they had either lost or separated from their partner somewhere along the way. Four out of the seven who had set up more than 18 months earlier had found themselves alone for their first creation, and the others had lost their partners at some other point along the way.

Five of the 16 interviewees benefited from their partners' previous experience. Generally this means a network of connections, experience of directing or managing, or past business start-up experience.

Need for independence and achievement, but also the importance of fun
We counted the number of times different forms of motivation were mentioned by the interviewees (Figure 24.2). These findings are consistent with other studies conducted on entrepreneurial motivations for both young and old (see, for example, Brenner *et al.*, 1991).

Contrasted views on entrepreneurs and entrepreneurship
Seven interviewees considered themselves entrepreneurs. However, the term itself is fairly vague. For some this meant an adventurer, for others a creator who builds and develops his business internationally (which is already quite a full definition). Four felt they were creators, meaning they enjoyed building a project but not necessarily seeing it grow. Two used the term 'builders'. Others used more unusual terms such as 'project leader' or 'manager'.

Some entrepreneurs, often the oldest in our sample entrepreneurs, explained that there had been a natural evolution in their profile and function, from creator to builder. Moreover, some also spoke of the qualities or profile of an entrepreneur, while others believe there is no one profile of an entrepreneur, the only point in common being possibly in the way of thinking. Finally, others admitted that the image they had at the start was slightly glorified and that you have to 'create to learn to create'.

Discussion and interpretations of the results

We have organized our development around two axes of unequal importance. The first presents the general and not very original results, inasmuch as they have already been dealt with in previous research. The second highlights a more original dimension to the creation of start-ups by students and young graduates. This is the play dimension.

Not surprisingly, the results of this study are consistent with studies and observations of young entrepreneurs in other countries. As suggested by other research, entrepreneurs have more in common with their counterparts in other cultures than they do with non-entrepreneurs in the same culture. This section presents a brief overview of the results of the study and similarities to other work. Overall, all those interviewed spontaneously recognized or accepted that there was a period in the process leading towards the creation during which they became more aware of the phenomenon. The personal environment plays a part in this period (even those whose parents are not entrepreneurs themselves admitted that this 'could help, it's obvious').

On the other hand, what was found during the interviews was that most young graduates, even though they were aware of some kind of process, did not know how it works and had not necessarily even thought about it. Many things would thus appear to happen subconsciously. Students dive 'head first' into the entrepreneurial process. Again this behaviour is consistent with that of young entrepreneurs in other cultures. Cowe (1998, p. 74) quotes a young entrepreneur as saying, 'If I knew then what I know now, I would probably have done it differently. But one of the benefits of youth is, at times, you don't realize how vulnerable the business is – if you did you probably wouldn't have done it in the first place. Naivety is useful – and quite necessary for the entrepreneur.' According to a young American entrepreneur, 'I felt no fear . . . If you overanalyze everything, you see how difficult it could be. It holds people back from (acting on) the wonderful ideas within them' (Stern, 1996, p. 49). Finally, it seems obvious that a certain maturity is required, although this does not become obvious until later.

One other element they all recognized is the importance of opportunity, usually related to an encounter. When asked, 'Where does this desire to create come from?', a common response was, 'I met M.X, my partner. . . .'. Some responded along the lines of 'when we were young, me and my partners would play at creating companies.'

If one considers that just over half of the students questioned had entrepreneurial intentions before their studies, it becomes apparent that, during the educational experience, intent was either established or reinforced. As various factors that have been shown to determine entrepreneurial intent can be considered fixed over the pre- and post-academic period, one needs to focus on the contextual factors, personal experience and factors leading to changes in perceived self-efficacy during the academic experience.

A recent study of an MBA cohort (Erikson, 1998) using an intention-based model suggests that, of the three primary determinants of self-efficacy (mastery experience, vicarious experience and social influence), only social influence was statistically significant. Operationalized as 'respondents' perceptions about what others think they ought to do', it suggests that societal values, and how these values are perceived, has a strong impact on students' entrepreneurial intentions.

The results of our study confirm this approach. Societal values regarding the 'appropriate' role of business school graduates is in contradiction with entrepreneurial intent. As students move from one communal environment to another, not only are perceptions modified, but the relevant societal value concerning entrepreneurial careers changes. In a pro-entrepreneurial environment, perceived self-efficacy can be directed towards entrepreneurship as the potential entrepreneur's perception of him/herself is reinforced by the communal values. As suggested by Walstad and Kourlisky (1998, p. 2), 'education should improve the perceived feasibility for entrepreneurship by increasing the knowledge of students, building confidence and promoting self-efficacy. It should improve the perceived desirability for entrepreneurship by showing students that this activity is highly regarded and socially accepted by the community'.

An interesting point for reflection here is that the potential entrepreneur may be faced with conflicting perceptions. As is often the case with young people, the values of their immediate environment may be more influential in decision making than the perceived values of others. This places the entrepreneur as a 'rebel'. As can be seen in other cultures, young people are more oriented towards 'freestyling' or 'going with the flow'. The degree of uncertainty in certain sectors makes it necessary for people to be flexible in their career planning. There is a need to 'break away from the traditional mould'.

The entrepreneur agrees to play a game, possibly taking on a different persona. In her book, Kushell (1999) clearly makes reference to the idea that young entrepreneurs are acting: playing a role (dress, schedule, office and so on). The environment also plays a decisive role, whether this is the family, friends who are often used as advisors, specialists, 'free consultants' or 'kind profs', but in particular, 'fantastic advisors'. The environment also permanently supplies ideas. However, looking back, the economic and legislative environment often has a negative impact: 'If I had to do it again, I would never do it in France' or 'It's disgusting, you just pay, pay, pay. Even if the Post Office is on strike and payment arrives late, you have to pay your employment insurance policies . . . it's ridiculous.' The importance of the environment is consistent with that identified by previous studies concerning entrepreneurship by students.

The French students' and graduates' start-up process has some similarities and differences when compared with other known entrepreneurial processes. In a way, it is like an original and clear 'construction' for those involved. Some identified motivations (need for independence, need for achievement) are widely dealt with in research on entrepreneurs. Others are more original, such as the fun, the friendship, the learning or the dynamics of the creation/construction. Whatever the case, such entrepreneurs do not give any negative motivations and the failure or abandonment phenomena do not really concern them.

Going for it seems 'logical', 'obvious' or 'normal', in a process where everything happens fast as soon as a number of requirements are met (meeting potential partners, the idea, working on a creation idea at school, positive feedback from the environment and so on). Together this takes the students from a stage of intellectual curiosity or a desire to start up to the belief that it is possible and worth trying. It thus becomes a game in which 'there is not a lot to lose, and a lot to win'.

This sentiment is also expressed in other cultures. As recently suggested in a Canadian on-line magazine oriented towards young entrepreneurs, 'People are realizing that entrepreneurs are as diverse as people in general, and for many, entrepreneurship is the place where business mingles with pleasure; where fun, freedom, creativity and imagination run wild.' It is worth noting that there is some evidence to suggest that the problems faced by young entrepreneurs (under 30 years of age) are quite similar to those of older entrepreneurs; however, the decision process for starting businesses is of longer duration for older entrepreneurs (Lorrain and Raymond, 1994).

The idea that young entrepreneurs often set out on a journey to start up a business but also to learn is also confirmed. Becoming an entrepreneur is part of the journey. Focus is on becoming an entrepreneur, not on the business itself. Also confirmed is the importance of networking for young entrepreneurs. Various authors and researchers suggest that networking is an essential element for young entrepreneurs. This compensates for their lack of experience. As suggested by Cowe (1998), 'Complete inexperience is an unlikely starting point for success but the basics of running a business can be picked up in a few years after leaving school or university. And additional expertise can be garnered from advisers or non-executive directors.' Recognizing what one does not master is essential.

The relevance of the play dimension

For young graduates, starting up a business is like a game. The rules are the same: a break from the real world, individual and collective learning, creating groups through affinities, and finally the element of uncertainty and no turning back. It is also through the aims (sensations, passion, seeking pleasure) that the process can be likened to a game.

The use of the term 'play' may be surprising in such a serious context, where efficacy, rationality and use are a must. A game belongs to the non-essential, the unreasonable and the irrational. However, if we look further at the structural elements, similarities can be found between a game and entrepreneurial experience. We now demonstrate the existence of similarities between a game and creating a business by developing four basic elements of a game: the break from reality, the learning process, the group and notions of uncertainty and irreversibility. We will also see that a game has to be included in a temporal framework and never lasts forever, just as the entrepreneurs do not play throughout their lives.

The game and escaping reality

A game is a means to distance oneself from reality. It is beyond the constraints of everyday life which restrict the individual's movements. To talk of an escape from reality when dealing with young graduate business creations may seem surprising. However, many legitimize their will to create by a strong desire, almost a need, to escape from the career possibilities presented to them. Their wish is to create their own reality, rather than be confined to a world which in no way corresponds to their personality and hopes. This does not mean they wish to be free from any form of structure. On the contrary, the action is like a game, with its own rules and not those of a reality which is not theirs. For Caillois (1958) a game is nothing more than an activity which is regulated, obeying normal laws, which briefly sets up a new legislation which takes over, but also fictional as it is accompanied by an awareness of a second reality or clear unreality in relation to everyday life. The creation of rules and a personal reality puts players in 'control': they have the final decision and make the ultimate judgment.

However, this does not mask the other reality, which does not offer such decision-making powers and the responsibilities they seek. This raises the problem of going beyond this apparent incompatibility. And this is where an element of the game comes into play which allows us to imagine a relation which is different from that which is usually found in everyday life: an element which allows the individual to become another person, which Caillois calls 'mimicry'. One of the aspects of this false reality is the need to play a role, to disguise oneself. Those interviewed often said that, in order to make up for their lack of experience, they had to 'bluff' or to pretend that their project, despite their age, was credible. Indeed, whether inside or outside the company, the young graduate has to adopt behaviour which is not his and acquire new skills when dealing with clients or financial partners, for example. This is his learning to 'be' a treasurer, the communications expert or the marketer. Concerning his attitude, he has to appear sure of himself, mature and be able to convince others about the viability and profitability of his venture. To conclude, he must often 'disguise' himself and play different roles.

In her book, *The Young Entrepreneur's Edge*, Jennifer Kushell dedicates an entire chapter to creating a professional image. Appearance, business meetings, dealing with questions about age, all are part of a role – the role of the entrepreneur.

The game as a learning process

A game does not simply take the actor into another world. It is also an instrument. Etymologically speaking, the noun play comes from the latin '*ludus*' meaning game but also learning: the *ludi magister* was none other than the schoolmaster.

A game is a learning tool or instrument which is what young graduate entrepreneurs are after. They want to be confronted by situations which are new and yet real from which to learn. You make mistakes which can be learnt from, because, although they may be irreversible, you can do better the next time or even get your revenge. This is the opinion of young business creators. Many consider themselves as students still and see their entrepreneurial life as an experiment where they have little to lose and a lot to learn. This learning process via confrontation and immersion in real situations is similar to a game where one is up against a sort of artificial intelligence. By touching different objects you learn about them and learn to avoid them. For Piaget, (1936, 1964) the predominance of this play aspect happens in children somewhere between birth and the age of two. The link with the entrepreneur is attractive as the entrepreneur is just beginning to discover and understand a new world. Moreover, during the interviews, one young creator referred to the kind of construction games young children play with. The learning process should not be limited simply to the interaction between an individual and an environment. There are other elements, other actors, other partners who can share their skills and knowledge with others.

The game and the importance of the group
We rarely play alone and, if we do, the idea of the game is to attract other players. One steadfast element in the creation process is that most business creators never create alone. Indeed there are more likely to be three rather than two initial partners involved. Hence our association with a game. Players want to be part of the same adventure, or to play with people they appreciate. The more players there are, the more interesting the game becomes. Communication, exchanges and mutual interests become key elements. You learn to socialize. It is the same for entrepreneurs. There is a similar state of mind, you are brought together by strong common values, a desire to experience something unique. Added to this, the choice of partners is based on criteria which are similar to those for games and are apparently strictly non-professional. Many young business creators in our sample mentioned 'friendship' as a reason for joining forces. Over and above the need to have partners (few felt like going it alone), it was meeting future partners while at school or outside school that led most of them to begin their projects. Clearly, partnerships are based more on friendship than on professional values.

When creating a business, the young graduate extends the game period initially experienced with his partners, when the notion of fun was omnipresent.

Uncertainty
The final play-related element is uncertainty. For Caillois (1958), 'playing, is not knowing where you are going even if the route has been planned'; the outcome of a game is unknown. Our young creators have launched themselves into an adventure whose benefits are unknown, all the more so as this is governed by time, unlike joining an existing business with clear objectives, a fixed salary and possibilities for promotion from the outset.

The uncertainty of this particular game is recognized and accepted by our sample of post-adolescents. For some of them, accepting the risks linked to the level of uncertainty is just 'part of the game'.

The temporal dimension of the game

The young business creator stands out through his play logic. This does not mean we question the profile of entrepreneurs in general as such, but we can position it in a time dimension. Indeed, just as the business is expected to evolve, so is the entrepreneur. This became apparent following a longitudinal analysis of our sample. We were able to highlight the progressive disappearance of some play characteristics as experience increases.

The longer the experience, in years, the closer the profile of the young business creator is to the more 'classical' entrepreneur profile. Indeed, the elements which we found to describe the entrepreneur as an actor anchored in a play dimension are altered: friends, experience, the break from reality and pleasure. The observation of the challenges changes dramatically and priorities alter, the risks become more difficult to accept, and being involved in the future of the business all appear much less attractive. Also some past entrepreneurial experience can lead to frustration: if, for example, the entrepreneurs have had to quit a project they have been working on full time. Once freed from this initial experience, their only desire is to begin again.

The foregoing clearly demonstrates the play dimension of business creation for young entrepreneurs. However, time will progressively calm and reduce the specificity and intensity of this dimension.

Conclusion

We feel it is important to mention the limits of our work before underlining some of our results. Firstly, the sample was small, all male, with a low diversity of institutions and programmes. Another limitation was due to our approach during the interviews and the problems encountered during them to obtain reliable and qualified information from the perceptions and impressions of those interviewed. However, despite these limits, some results must be taken as hypotheses which are both fundamental and original.

The business creation phenomenon among young French students and graduates is the result of a particular construction and action logic which is specific to this group of individuals. They have no negative motivations , they are not breaking away from anything, but tend to include some characteristics of their lives as young adults in their business creation process: first, the child–rebel in them which reflects a rejection of the system and its rules, particularly in relation to established career paths which are promoted by their educational background; secondly, the playful child element which means they take decisions without really thinking beforehand and which are affective and make way for pleasure and game logics by giving greater importance to the play dimension.

452   *Geographic perspectives*

Finally, we hope these initial results will encourage others to look more closely at this phenomenon and to extend and test the hypotheses presented.

Notes

1. Quotations in this first paragraph come from French newspapers such as *Le Monde*, *Les Echos* and *Le Nouvel Observateur*.
2. HEC is probably the most famous Business School in France.
3. This concept seeks to measure the degree of control that an individual is perceiving about his/her capability to perform a behaviour. In our case: the entre.

References

Ajzen, I. (1991), 'The theory of planned behavior', *Organizational Behavior and Human Decision Processes*, 50, 1–63.
Amblard, H., P. Bernoux, G. Herreros and Y.F. Livian (1996), *Les nouvelles approches sociologiques des organisations*, Paris: Editions du Seuil.
APCE (1998), *Rapport Annuel*, Paris : APCE.
Aurifeille, J.M. and E.M. Hernandez (1991), 'Détection du potentiel entrepreneurial d'une population étudiante', *Economies et Sociétés, série Sciences de gestion* (17), 39–55.
Autio, E., R.H. Keeley, M. Klofsten and T. Ulfstedt (1997), 'Entrepreneurial intent among students: testing an intent model in Asia, Scandinavia and USA', *Frontiers of Entrepreneurship Research*, 133–47.
Bauer, M. (1988), 'Grands patrons, Capital Etat et Entreprise: les 200 révèlent . . .', *Sociologie du travail*, (4), 567–84.
Begley, T.M. and D.P. Boyd (1987), 'Psychological characteristics associated with performance in entrepreneurial firms and smaller businesses', *Journal of Business Venturing*, 2 (1), 79–93.
Bouffartigue, P. (1994), 'Les ingénieurs débutants', *Revue Française de Sociologie*, 35 (1), 69–100.
Bourdieu, P. (1989), *La noblesse d'Etat, Grandes Ecoles et esprit de corps*, Paris : Les Editions de Minuit.
Brenner, O.C, C. Pringle and J. Greenhaus (1991), 'Perceived fulfillment of organizational employment versus entrepreneurship: work values and career intentions of business college graduates', *Journal of Small Business Management*, July, 62–80.
Brockhaus, R.H. and P.S. Horowitz (1986), 'The psychology of the entrepreneur', in D.L. Sexton and A.W. Smilor (eds), *The Art and Science of Entrepreneurship*, Cambridge, MA: Ballinger, pp. 25–48.
Caillois, R. (1958), *Les jeux et les hommes, le masque et le vertige*, Paris : Editions Gallimard.
CEREQ (1999), 'Diplômés de l'enseignement supérieur. La reprise de l'emploi ne profite pas à toutes les filières', Bref 156, CEREQ.
Cowe, R. (1998), 'Are you ever too young?', *Management Today*, December, London.
Crozier, M. and E. Friedberg (1977), *L'acteur et le système*, Paris: Editions du Seuil, Points, Politique.
Dany, F. and Y.F. Livian (1991), 'Quelles carrières pour les jeunes diplômés?', *Futuribles*, June, 3–16.
Davidsson, P. (1995), 'Determinants of Entrepreneurial Intentions', paper presented at the RENT IX Conference, Placenza, Italy.
Douglas, E.J. and D.A. Shepherd (2000), 'Entrepreneurship as a utility maximizing response', *Journal of Business Venturing*, (15), 231–51.
Dyer, W.G. (1994), 'Toward a theory of entrepreneurial careers', *Entrepreneurship Theory and Practice*, Winter, 7–21.
Erikson, T. (1998), '*A study of entrepreneurial intentions among a cohort MBAs – the extended Bird model*', paper presented at the 43rd ICSB World Conference.
EUROPME (1999), 'Portrait–robot et socio-styles des créateurs d'entreprise en 1998', Study Report, Groupe ESC Rennes.

Fayolle, A. (1996), 'Contribution à l'étude des comportements entrepreneuriaux des ingénieurs français', these de doctorat en sciences de gestion, Université Jean Moulin Lyon 3.

Fayolle, A. (2000a), 'L'enseignement de l'entrepreneuriat dans le système éducatif supérieur français: un regard sur la situation actuelle', *Gestion 2000*, (3), 77–95.

Fayolle, A. (2000b), 'Exploratory study to assess the effects of entrepreneurship programs on student entrepreneurial behaviors', *Journal of Enterprising Culture*, 8 (2), 169–84.

Fayolle, A. and Y.F. Livian (1995), 'Entrepreneurial Behavior of French Engineers. An exploratory Study', in S. Birley and I. MacMillan (eds), *International Entrepreneurship*, London: Routledge, pp. 202–28.

Filion, L.J. (1994), 'Ten Steps to Entrepreneurial Teaching', *Journal of Small Business and Entrepreneurship*, 11 (3), 68–78.

Gasse, Y. (1985), 'A strategy for the promotion and identification of potential entrepreneurs at the secondary school level', *Frontiers of Entrepreneurship Research*, Wellesley, MA: Babson College, pp. 538–559.

Hills, G.E. and H. Welsch (1986), 'Entrepreneurship behavioral intentions and student independence characteristics and experiences', *Frontiers of Entrepreneurship Research*, Wellesley, MA: Babson College, pp. 173–86.

INSEE (1997), Enquête emploi, Paris: INSEE.

Johannisson, B. (1991), 'University training for entrepreneurship: Swedish approaches', *Entrepreneurship and Regional Development* (3), 67–82.

Katz, J.A. (1990), 'Longitudinal analysis of self employment follow-through', *Entrepreneurship Regional Development*, 2 (1), 15–25.

Katz, J.A. (1992), 'Secondary analysis in entrepreneurship: an introduction to databases and data management', *Journal of Small Business Management*, 30 (20), 74–86.

Kolvereid L. (1996), 'Organizational employment versus self-employment : reasons for career choice intentions', *Entrepreneurship Theory and Practice*, Spring, 23–31.

KORELAT (1999), 'Les jeunes diplômés et la création d'entreprise', Study Report Summary.

Krueger, N. and D. Brazeal (1994), 'Entrepreneurial potential and potential entrepreneurs', *Entrepreneurship Theory and Practice*, Spring.

Krueger, N.F. and A.L. Carsrud (1993), 'Entrepreneurial intentions: applying the theory of planned behaviour', *Entrepreneurship and Regional Development*, 5 (1), 315–30.

Kushell, J. (1999), *The Young Entrepreneur's Edge*, New York: Random House.

Learned, K. (1992), 'What Happened Before the Organization? A Model of Organizational Formation', *Entrepreneurship Theory and Practice*, Fall.

Leger, C. (1994), *'Les étudiants créateurs: un exemple à l'Université Paris–Dauphine'*, Paris: Editions ANCE.

Leger, C. (1996), 'Dynasties d'entreprise et dynasties d'entreprendre', *Entreprises et histoire* (12), 89–100.

Lojkine, J. (1992), *'Les jeunes diplômés – un groupe social en quête d'identité*, Paris: P.U.F.

Lorrain, J. and L. Raymond (1994), 'Young Entrepreneurs: Beliefs and Reality', *Frontiers of Entrepreneurship Research*, Wellesley, MA: Babson College.

Mathews, C.H. and S.B. Moser (1995), 'Family background and gender: implications for interest in small firm ownership', *Entrepreneurship and Regional Development* (7), 365–77.

Mathews, C.H. and S.B. Moser (1996), 'A longitudinal investigation of the impact of family background and gender on interest in small firm ownership', *Journal of Small Business Management*, 34 (2), 29–43.

Maurice, M., F. Sellier and J.J. Silvestre (1982), *Politique d'éducation et organisation industrielle en France et en Allemagne*, Paris: P.U.F.

Naffziger, D., J. Hornsby and D. Kuratko (1994), 'A proposed research model of entrepreneurial motivation', *Entrepreneurship Theory and Practice*, Spring.

Pesteau, P. and U. Possen (1992), 'How do taxes affect occupational choice', *Public Finance*, 47 (1), 108–119.

Piaget, J. (1936), *La naissance de l'intelligence chez l'enfant*, Paris : Editions Delachaux et Niestlé.

Piaget, J. (1964), *Six études de psychologie*, Paris : Editions de Noël.

Reynolds, P. (1991), 'Sociology and Entrepreneurship: Concepts and Contributions', *Entrepreneurship Theory and Practice*, Winter.

Ribeil, G. (1984), 'Entreprendre hier et aujourd'hui: la contribution des ingénieurs', *Culture Technique* (12), 77–92.

Robin, J.Y. (1994), *Radioscopie de cadres – Itinéraire professionnel et biographie éducative*, Paris : L'Harmattan.

Robinson, P.B., J.C. Huefner and H.K. Hunt (1991), 'Entrepreneurial research on student subjects does not generalize to real world entrepreneurs', *Journal of Small Business Management*, 29 (2), 42–50.

Safavian-Martinon, M. (1998), 'Le lien entre le diplôme et la logique d'acteur relative à la carrière: une explication du rôle du diplôme dans la carrière des jeunes cadres issus des grandes écoles de gestion', thèse pour le doctorat en sciences de gestion, Université Paris I.

Scott, M.G. and D.F. Twomey (1988), 'The Long-term Supply of Entrepreneurs: Students' career aspirations in relation to entrepreneurship', *Journal of Small Business Management*, 26 (4), 5–13.

Shuman, J.C., J.A. Seeger and N.C. Teebagy (1987), 'Entrepreneurial activity and educational background', *Frontiers of Entrepreneurship Research*, Wellesley, MA: Babson College, pp. 590–99.

Stern, G. (1996), 'Young entrepreneurs make their mark', Nation's Business, Washington.

Tkachev, A. and L. Kolvereid (1999), 'Self-employment intentions among Russian students', *Entrepreneurship and Regional Development*, 11 (3) 269–80.

Tucker, I.B. (1990), 'Employer seniority discrimination: evidence from entrepreneurial occupational choice', *Economic Letters*, 32 (2), 85–9.

Veblen, T. (1971), *Les ingénieurs et le capitalisme*, Paris: Gordon and Breach.

Walstad, W. and M. Kourlisky (1998), 'Entrepreneurial attitudes and knowledge of black youth', *Entrepreneurship Theory and Practice*, Winter.

Weihe, H.J., and F.R. Reich (1991), 'Entrepreneurial interest among business students: Results of an international study', pp. 179–98.

ZELIG (1998), 'Enquête sur les intentions entrepreneuriales des étudiants français'.

25 Greek perspectives of international entrepreneurship
Pavlos Dimitratos and Spyros Lioukas

Should firms concentrate their international operations on established or emerging markets? This chapter addresses this theme by examining internationalization ventures of small and medium-sized manufacturing firms based in a smaller EU country in south-east Europe with an advancing economy, namely Greece.* Preliminary evidence, from a study that includes both quantitative and qualitative aspects, suggests that investigated firms tend to achieve superior performance in established rather than in emerging markets. However, it may still be premature to make such a performance comparison between the two country categories.

In established markets, implementation of foreign direct investment modes, that is joint ventures and subsidiaries, and enterprise experience in the foreign market can have a positive influence on performance; uncertainty about the foreign country may have a negative influence on performance. In emerging markets, adoption of low, 'penetration' prices and strategic significance of the country to the international growth of the firm can have a positive influence on performance. Interestingly, firms which operate in both market categories seem to achieve poorer performance than firms which operate in only one of them.

The evidence of this study also suggests that particular organizational variables, such as entrepreneurial style, do not apply to operations in specific countries but rather to foreign operations or even the whole range of operations of the firm. This fact implies that 'international' entrepreneurship may be an inappropriate term to use for the ventures of firms at a specific foreign country level.

As the number of firms which cross their national borders increases, business managers have to make strategic choices with regard to the selection of foreign destination markets. Should firms focus on developed countries with established markets or on less developed countries with emerging markets? There are two questions associated with this dilemma: which strategic, organizational and environmental variables are associated with

* The authors would like to kindly thank Stephen Young, Neil Hood and Michael McDermott for their constructive suggestions and comments on earlier versions of this chapter.

superior performance in each of the two categories, and do firms which operate in both market categories achieve any 'synergies' leading to improved performance? Research on these issues is scant and, hence, this chapter seeks to provide some preliminary empirical evidence from small manufacturing firms based in south-east Europe (SEE), notably Greece.

The theme of strategy–performance association in an international context is very important for firms and researchers alike (cf. Capon *et al.*, 1990; Gopinath and Hoffman, 1995; Hambrick, 1980). It is of fundamental significance to business managers and researchers to understand which strategic choices, organizational parameters and environmental conditions may be conducive to superior performance abroad. The present research seeks to provide some evidence on this theme.

The proposition that this research adopts is that the internationalization ventures of the firm represent an entrepreneurial act (Ibeh and Young, 2001; Lumpkin and Dess, 1996). This appears to apply especially to the international operations of small firms which face a liability of smallness (Stinchcombe, 1965) in the competitive foreign markets due to the limited extent of human, financial and production resources that they possess. Management of those international entrepreneurial firms would be interested to know which of the two country groups would be associated with superior performance.

Having implemented one of the most intensive macroeconomic adjustment programmes in the EU, Greece currently scores notably well in terms of inflation, budget deficit and GNP growth rate. The organization of the Olympic Games in Athens in 2004 will further boost the vibrant Greek economy and project worldwide the image of a fast developing country. Greece's customary trading partners consist of EU countries, with Germany absorbing about one-quarter of its exports. Greece is isolated geographically from the rest of the EU nations since it is the only EU country that does not have borders with any other member state.

The developments in SEE, the ongoing integration of this region's countries into the international system (EU, WTO and so on) and the opening of these markets highlight Greece's strategic location vis-à-vis the new-market economies of this region. Greece can effectively serve as a major gateway to the emerging markets of SEE. This explains the interest of European and international investors, who increasingly establish operations in Greece in order to gain access to SEE countries (OECD, 2001).

The dissolution of the former Soviet bloc in the late 1980s and early 1990s, and the developments in the former Yugoslav Federation in the 1990s, provided opportunities for many Greek enterprises to expand trade with SEE countries. Between 1990 and 2000, Greek exports to Balkan countries more than tripled, and exports to countries of Central Europe and the former

Soviet Union more than doubled. Moreover, unpublished evidence from the Greek authorities suggests that around 3000 Greek firms have recently begun foreign direct investment (FDI) operations, that is joint ventures and subsidiaries, in the new-market economies of SEE. Thus the examination of Greek small firms which seek to select international destination markets is of major importance owing to, on the one hand, Greece's long-standing trade and FDI operations in EU countries and, on the other, its geographic location and the recent opening of the emerging markets of SEE.

The chapter is organized as follows. In the first section the theoretical background of the study is discussed. In the second section the methodological aspects of the study, along with its conceptual model, are presented. In the third section the findings of the research are analysed while the fourth section discusses their importance and how they fit into previous studies. The chapter concludes with the implications of the study for management and theory.

Research background
Researchers contend that strategic choices and organizational characteristics can be influenced by environmental conditions of the foreign market (Aulakh *et al.*, 2000; Buckley, 1990; Dunning, 1988; Erramilli *et al.*, 1997). This chapter builds on this contention by contrasting business operations in established and emerging markets. It appears that there is a dearth of research on this issue: few empirical studies have examined differences of business practices, environmental perceptions and performances between these two country groups.

In one of the most comprehensive studies, Erramilli *et al.* (1997) present evidence from Korean firms showing that in less developed countries the sources of competitive advantage tend to be related to low-cost strategy, high labour intensity and high technological intensity. By contrast, in developed countries the sources of competitive advantage are associated with high product differentiation and low labour intensity. The authors also find that, if the firm possesses these sources of competitive advantage, it will tend to exploit them by seeking a high percentage of ownership in its foreign subsidiaries. Therefore this research implies that the state of development of the host country may influence the strategic choices that render competitive advantage in this country. Nevertheless no performance comparison for business operations between the two country categories is attempted in this study.

In another comprehensive study, Aulakh *et al.* (2000) find that exporting firms based in Brazil, Chile and Mexico improve their performances when they implement low-cost strategies in developed countries and differentiation strategies in developing countries. The same study presents evidence that, in developed countries, unlike in developing ones, implementation of marketing mix adaptation strategies leads to superior performance. Overall, the findings of this research, along with that by Erramilli *et al.* (1997), suggest that effective strategies of internationalized firms can vary across foreign markets, depending on the stage of development of the destination country. However, no answer is provided with regard to whether operations in developed as opposed to developing countries are associated with higher performance of the entering firms.

On this last theme, Denis and Depelteau (1985), in their research on Canadian firms, provide evidence in favour of concentrating international business operations on established markets, because of higher performance achieved. Yet Collins (1990) and Merchant (2000) find that performances of US firms with international operations in developed and developing countries do not significantly differ.

This theme has also been researched to some extent for firms based in economies with an intermediate level of development. These firms may have to overcome a possible adverse country of origin effect. This is because, when consumers have a choice between a product from a developed country and another from a less developed country, with little knowledge of the characteristics of both, they are likely to choose the one from the developed country (Johanson *et al.*, 1985). Taking this into consideration, it appears reasonable that aggressive Brazilian manufacturers export to a greater percentage in underdeveloped countries than passive Brazilian exporters do (Da Rocha *et al.*, 1990).

However, research evidence is not conclusive. Christensen *et al.* (1987) find that successful Brazilian exporters rely more on established markets. Similar conclusions are provided by studies of firms based in Central America (Dominguez and Sequeira, 1993), India (Das, 1994) and Peru (Douglas, 1996). How can this be the case? Porter (1990) argues in favour of aiming at established markets by proposing that, in order for the firm to remain innovative, it must seek to serve demanding buyers with the most exacting needs. It is legitimate to assume that these buyers will be customers in established markets, whose marketplaces involve intense competition levels, rather than in emerging markets. In effect, demanding customers motivate the firm to become more innovative and competitive, and eventually successful, notwithstanding the high level of competition encountered.

Another related theme for which inadequate empirical evidence exists refers to whether there are potential synergies for firms that operate in both developed and less developed countries. Experiential knowledge gained and business methods applied to one country may be effectively transferred to others (Welch and Welch, 1996). However, other researchers disagree, suggesting that such experience may not be easy to transfer to other countries (Evans *et al.*, 1992; Hilton, 1992; O'Grady and Lane, 1996). This is because other factors, such as industry-specific knowledge, may act as potential barriers (O' Grady and Lane, 1996). In addition, it appears that no empirical findings exist concerning potential 'performance synergies' between developed and less developed countries.

Overall, it seems that past research findings provide mixed evidence on whether operations in established as opposed to emerging markets are associated with higher business performance or not. Moreover, only the studies by Erramilli *et al.* (1997) and Aulakh *et al.* (2000) offer comparative evidence for enterprise strategic and organizational parameters in the two country categories. The theme of possible synergies in terms of performance between the two categories is practically unexplored. Such a dearth of studies also appears to exist in the international entrepreneurship literature which customarily investigates the ventures of younger or smaller firms (Burgel and Murray, 2000; Dana *et al.*, 1999). It is imperative for managers of small firms to find out which of the two country categories offer more attractive market opportunities, a theme which should lie at the heart of the international entrepreneurship research.

Research method
Sample and data collection
The present study draws upon a sample of Greek manufacturing firms that are small or medium in size. The survey focused on four sectors which have exhibited traditionally strong export intensity, while recently they have shown increased FDI involvement. Each of the four sectors constituted a subset of the population. Thus the population was split into four mutually exclusive subsets, and a random sample was drawn following a stratified sampling procedure. In particular, the firms selected belong to the food, beverages, garments or footwear sectors of the Greek industry, are independent Greek firms, employ between 10 and 250 employees, and exhibit outward international activities through either exporting or FDI modes.

The methodology employed has both quantitative and qualitative aspects. With regard to its quantitative aspect, a structured questionnaire was used and answers were solicited through personal interviews with business managers. Variables expressed in either interval (Likert) or ratio scales were employed to facilitate subsequent statistical quantitative analysis. A pre-testing of the questionnaire by academics and six business managers in order to check its lucidity and clarity had taken place before the launch of the survey. Prior to conducting the personal interview in each firm, the most knowledgable manager in charge of the firm's international operations was sought.

With regard to the methodology's qualitative aspect, notes involving quotations from the respondents were taken during the interview process. These data were content analysed in order to discover recurring themes or patterns (cf. Krippendorff, 1980) regarding the strategies, organizational characteristics, environmental conditions and performances in both established and emerging markets of the firm. The evidence obtained from the qualitative part of the research adds insights to the evidence from the quantitative part and increases the validity of the empirical findings. Such a synergy between the two methodological approaches can illuminate the phenomenon under investigation (Jick, 1979). In the following section of this chapter, selected quotations from the respondents are offered to support the results of the qualitative part of the research, a practice which increases the methodological trustworthiness of a study's findings (Healy and Perry, 2000).

Overall, 343 firms were qualified to be part of the sample, while 114 cooperated in the survey by providing all required answers, yielding a response rate of 33%. The unit of analysis in this study is the internationalization venture, viz. the international operations of the firm in a particular (established or emerging) market. Queries were focused on the country in which the firm managed to achieve the highest level of sales among the developed countries. Likewise the same procedure was followed for the country among the less developed countries. This means that, if the firm had international operations in both country groups, two observations were recorded in two respective countries, something which pertained to the operations of 51 firms of the sample. Hence 165 observations are included in the analysis for both the quantitative and the qualitative parts of the study.

In total, 89 internationalization ventures relate to established markets and 76 to emerging markets. The grouping of Hoskisson *et al.* (2000), which is largely based on that of International Finance Corporation (IFC, 1999), was employed to classify countries into developed and less developed ones. In the former category, mainly the countries of the Triad market and Oceania are included. All remaining countries fall into the category of less developed countries.

Conceptual framework and variables employed
Firm-specific and host country-specific variables are hypothesized to affect performance in that country. The conceptual framework of the study incorporating these variables appears in Figure 25.1. Although domestic country parameters also influence performance in the foreign country, they are not employed since the emphasis is on identifying possible differences between the two destination country categories. Therefore the findings of

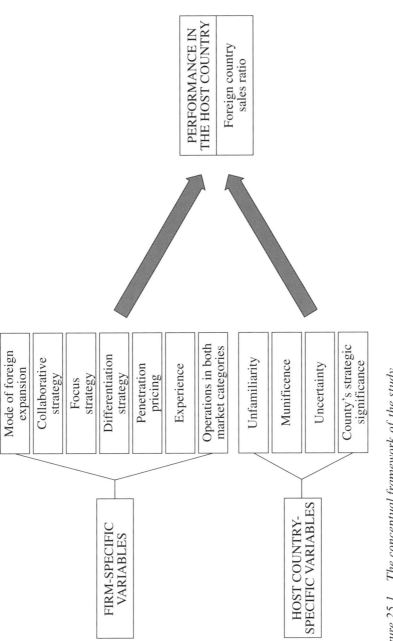

Figure 25.1   The conceptual framework of the study

this study should be viewed as being conditional on domestic country (Greek) variables.

The Appendix presents the employed questionnaire items, Cronbach's alphas and key references for the study's variables. In the firm-specific variables set, the *mode of foreign expansion* is a major strategic choice that the firm has to decide upon in the foreign country. The increased use of cooperative forms in international business (Contractor, 1990; Dunning, 1995) calls for inclusion of the *collaborative strategy* variable also. In addition, firm-specific variables include competitive strategies, viz. *focus strategy*, *differentiation strategy* and *penetration pricing*, which the firm pursues in order to attain competitive advantage in the foreign country. Another parameter is *experience* of the firm in the foreign country, which is accepted to be a major determinant of the firm's international operations and performance, especially by scholars espousing the incremental school of enterprise international expansion (Bilkey and Tesar, 1977; Johanson and Vahlne, 1977, 1990; Johanson and Wiedersheim-Paul, 1975). Whether the firm has *operations in both market categories* or not is also captured in the firm-specific variables set.

In the host country-specific variables set, *unfamiliarity* measures the perceived cultural dissimilarity between the domestic and the foreign country. *Munificence* and *uncertainty* are also included since they are regularly employed to capture environmental perceptions in studies of strategic management. Perceived *strategic significance of the country* to the international growth of the firm constitutes the fourth variable in the host country-specific variables group.

Performance in the host country is captured through the *foreign country sales ratio*. Apart from this ratio's use in previous studies (for example, Moon and Lee, 1990; Sullivan, 1994), the pre-testing of the questionnaire revealed that managers of the firms often measure performance in the host country mainly through the level of sales in that country or the contribution of these sales to the overall enterprise sales. The latter performance indicator was employed in this study since it takes into consideration and accounts for differences of firm size. This research does not use any profit measures to capture performance in the host country, because firms were either unable or reluctant to provide relevant information on how they scored in their international operations in specific foreign markets.

Findings of the study
The quantitative aspect of the study
Table 25.1 provides percentage frequencies for the mode of foreign expansion in the whole sample and each of the two country categories. The frequencies show that for both country categories the most frequent expan-

Table 25.1   Frequencies of the mode of foreign expansion (per cent)

Foreign expansion mode	Whole sample (*n*=165)	Established markets (*n*=89)	Emerging markets (*n*=76)
Exports through offices or organizations in the home country	6.1	6.7	5.3
Exports through agents in the foreign country	11.5	9.0	14.5
Exports through intermediaries in the foreign market	45.5	47.2	43.4
Direct exports to customers in the foreign country	28.5	29.2	27.6
Foreign direct investment modes	8.4	7.9	9.2

sion mode is exporting through wholesalers/retailers located in the foreign market. It is noteworthy that less than 10% of the internationalization ventures in both groups take place through joint ventures or subsidiaries.

The low implementation of FDI modes in both country categories may be due to the fact that the majority of Greek firms have been undertaking international activities for a relatively short time, less than nine years, as the results in Table 25.2 suggest. Table 25.2 presents mean scores and standard deviations for the numerical variables of the study. The evidence that Greek firms tend to choose exporting modes of expansion in their international operations appears to strengthen the proposition of the incremental method of enterprise international expansion: firms are likely to commit higher levels of resources gradually as understanding of the foreign market and business environment is acquired (Bilkey and Tesar, 1977; Johanson and Vahlne, 1977, 1990; Johanson and Wiedersheim-Paul, 1975).

Table 25.2 presents notable results concerning the implementation of collaborative and competitive strategies. In both country categories firms pursue collaborative strategies to a very low extent. Cooperation arrangements between Greek firms may be in their early stages (Bourantas and Mandes, 1987; Makridakis *et al.*, 1997). Implementation of all competitive strategies (focus strategy, differentiation strategy and penetration pricing) takes place to a higher extent than to that of collaborative strategy. The country's strategic significance to the international growth of the firm appears relatively high, a result which is expected inasmuch as the 'best-selling' countries of the firm in the two market categories were investigated.

A *t*-test was employed to determine whether the mean scores of the study's numerical variables differ significantly between established and emerging markets, and Table 25.2 presents these results also. With reference to experience in the foreign country, it appears that it is significantly higher

Table 25.2 Descriptive statistics of the study's numerical variables

Variable	Mean (standard deviation)		
	Whole sample ($n=165$)	Established markets ($n=89$)	Emerging markets ($n=76$)
Collaborative strategy (1–7 scale)	1.67 (0.60)	1.73 (0.57)	1.59 (0.62)
Focus strategy (1–7 scale)	3.83 (2.03)	4.04 (2.04)	3.58 (2.00)
Differentiation strategy (1–7 scale)	3.91 (1.31)	3.98 (1.24)	3.84 (1.39)
Penetration pricing (1–7 scale)	3.06 (1.93)	2.99 (1.89)	3.14 (1.98)
Experience (years)	8.71 (10.12)	10.80* (12.18)	6.26* (6.23)
Unfamiliarity (1–7 scale)	4.36 (1.77)	4.78* (1.56)	3.88* (1.88)
Munificence (1–7 scale)	4.01 (1.10)	3.95 (1.12)	4.09 (1.07)
Uncertainty (1–7 scale)	3.97 (1.55)	3.87 (1.58)	4.09 (1.52)
Country's strategic significance (1–7 scale)	5.22 (1.64)	5.33 (1.65)	5.11 (1.63)
Foreign country sales ratio (%)	15.14 (20.26)	19.89* (22.51)	9.58* (15.66)

Note: * The sample means differ significantly ($p < 0.01$).

for the internationalization ventures in developed than in less developed countries. This finding is not surprising, inasmuch as Greece's traditional target destinations have been EU countries. Most emerging markets, and especially those of the SEE region, which appear repeatedly as destination countries in this research, have been serviced lately.

The results in Table 25.2 show that Greek business managers consider aspects of their own culture, norms and mentality to be more similar to those of neighbouring SEE countries than those of their traditional EU trading partners. It may be that cultural proximity to SEE countries makes their uncertainty seem lower than it actually is and, in effect, may bring uncertainty down to levels comparable to those of EU countries. Moreover, on average, an internationalized Greek small firm earns about 20% of its sales from operations in its 'best-seller' established market and about 10% in its 'best-seller' emerging market. According to the difference of means test, performance of the investigated firms in developed countries is significantly higher than that in less developed countries.

In order to discover which variables are related to superior performance in foreign countries, three regression sets were run: for the whole sample and for each of the two country categories. Table 25.3 presents Pearson correlation coefficients for the variables of the regression involving the whole sample. There are no strong correlation patterns among the study's variables, with the highest correlation coefficient being -0.58 between two modes of expansion (direct exports to customers and exports through intermediaries) and all others below ±0.33. A similar pattern of no strong correlation is also encountered among the variables involving the datasets of the two market groups.

Table 25.4 presents the results of the three regressions. Multicollinearity did not appear to be a source of bias. The R^2 values in all three regression sets are above 30%, which is acceptable given the cross-sectional and cross-national nature of the sample. All three F ratios are large and their related significance levels very small (less than 5%).

The results for the regression involving the whole sample indicate that a negative, yet weak, effect is obtained for operations in emerging markets. This negative effect is compatible with the finding obtained from the difference of means test: compared to operations in emerging markets, operations in established markets can be associated with higher levels of performance. Moreover, the results for the whole sample show a negative effect on foreign country performance for business operations in both market categories. Interestingly, this last statistical finding suggests that operations in both country categories can be detrimental to the performance of the small firm in the foreign market.

In the dataset consisting of established markets, implementation of FDI

Table 25.3   Correlation matrix of the variables in the whole sample (n = 165)

Variable	Pearson correlation coefficient														
	(1)	(2)	(3)	(4)	(5)	(6)	(7)	(8)	(9)	(10)	(11)	(12)	(13)	(14)	(15)
1. Exports through agents	1.00														
2. Exports through intermediaries	-0.33a	1.00													
3. Direct exports	-0.23a	-0.58a	1.00												
4. FDI modes	-0.11	-0.28a	-0.19b	1.00											
5. Collaborative strategy	-0.05	-0.10	-0.08	0.29a	1.00										
6. Focus strategy	0.04	-0.21a	0.10	0.11	0.15	1.00									
7. Differentiation strategy	-0.23a	-0.01	0.08	0.19b	0.20a	-0.01	1.00								
8. Penetration pricing	-0.10	0.06	0.04	0.07	-0.01	-0.01	0.21a	1.00							
9. Log of experience	-0.11	0.22a	-0.11	-0.07	0.07	-0.09	0.15	0.09	1.00						
10. Operations in both market categories	0.17b	-0.01	-0.08	-0.03	-0.07	-0.12	0.16b	-0.09	-0.13	1.00					
11. Unfamiliarity	-0.02	-0.11	-0.02	0.14	0.09	0.02	-0.05	-0.10	-0.11	0.01	1.00				
12. Munificence	-0.07	-0.06	0.05	0.12	-0.01	-0.03	0.17b	0.09	0.09	0.19b	-0.04	1.00			
13. Uncertainty	0.02	0.04	-0.03	0.09	0.09	-0.08	0.17b	0.08	-0.07	0.15b	-0.03	0.12	1.00		
14. Country's strategic significance	-0.04	-0.03	0.02	0.02	0.15	0.01	0.33a	0.09	0.21a	0.12	0.01	0.15	0.15b	1.00	
15. Operations in emerging markets	0.09	-0.04	-0.02	0.02	-0.15	-0.12	-0.06	0.04	-0.24a	0.10	-0.25a	0.06	0.08	-0.05	1.00
16. Log of foreign country sales ratio	-0.04	0.03	-0.05	0.11	0.22a	-0.01	0.19b	0.17b	0.32a	-0.25a	0.03	-0.07	-0.14	0.24a	-0.24a

Notes: $^{a}p < 0.01$; $^{b}p < 0.05$.

Table 25.4 Regression with log of foreign country sales ratio as the dependent variable

Variable	Standardized beta (t statistic)		
	Whole sample ($n=165$)	Established markets ($n=89$)	Emerging markets ($n=76$)
Exports through agents (dummy)	0.174 (1.535)	0.243[c] (1.678)	−0.032 (−0.155)
Exports through intermediaries (dummy)	0.144 (0.930)	0.276 (1.383)	−0.179 (−0.641)
Direct exports (dummy)	0.095 (0.664)	0.250 (1.344)	−0.251 (−1.006)
FDI modes (dummy)	0.153 (1.442)	0.311[b] (2.261)	−0.186 (−1.006)
Collaborative strategy	0.129[c] (1.710)	0.119 (1.146)	0.166 (1.368)
Focus strategy	−0.069 (−0.963)	−0.121 (−1.197)	−0.002 (−0.015)
Differentiation strategy	0.135[c] (1.683)	0.133 (1.199)	0.065 (0.506)
Penetration pricing	0.107 (1.493)	0.069 (0.705)	0.293[b] (2.340)
Log of experience	0.173[b] (2.238)	0.212[b] (2.069)	0.072 (0.565)
Operations in both market categories (dummy)	−0.224[a] (−2.960)	−0.346[a] (−3.347)	0.013 (0.095)
Unfamiliarity	0.011 (0.153)	0.042 (0.405)	−0.145 (−1.187)
Munificence	−0.075 (−1.033)	−0.110 (−1.071)	−0.089 (−0.692)
Uncertainty	−0.167[b] (−2.301)	−0.213[b] (−2.096)	−0.052 (−0.429)
Country's strategic significance	0.186[b] (2.475)	0.142 (1.349)	0.304[b] (2.267)
Operations in emerging markets (dummy)	−0.147[c] (−1.941)		
R square	0.303	0.359	0.313
F test	4.326[a]	2.961[a]	1.984[b]

Note: [a] $p<0.01$; [b] $p<0.05$; [c] $p<0.10$.

467

modes of expansion and experience of the firm in the foreign market may be positively related to performance,[1] whereas uncertainty of the foreign country and business operations in both market categories may be negatively related. As far as the last finding is concerned, it seems that investigated firms which have business operations in developed countries can achieve superior performance if they limit their presence in the established market category.

In the dataset consisting of emerging markets, adoption of penetration pricing and strategic significance of the country to the international growth of the small firm appear significantly and positively linked to performance. The positive effect of the strategic significance of a less developed country on international operations is fully understood after taking into consideration the evidence from the qualitative part of this research.

The qualitative aspect of the study
Five patterns emerged from the content analysis of the field notes. The first pattern is associated with the fact that some organizational variables, such as entrepreneurial style, management resources for internationalization and international management systems of planning and control, relate to the foreign or even the whole range of operations of the firm rather than its ventures at a specific foreign country level. In other words, as the pre-testing of the questionnaire and the analysis of the field notes reveal, these organizational variables are not country-specific, and thus do not appear in Figure 25.1. This may be largely due to the liabilities of 'smallness' and 'newness' of the investigated firms in the international marketplace. In particular, international entrepreneurship does not relate to operations in specific foreign countries. The statement by the international operations manager of a beverages firm concerning the entrepreneurial style of his firm is illustrative:

> The average Greek firm is tiny in the foreign markets according to international standards and went abroad lately after the country's entry into the European Economic Community in 1981 and, especially, the opening of SEE markets in the 1990s. Most Greek firms still emphasize operations in their domestic market and view foreign markets as secondary to their targets and goals. Therefore it may be an overstatement to argue that the entrepreneurial mode differs between the domestic and the foreign countries, and across foreign countries. The ways we approach our competitors, our risk orientations and our innovativeness methods mostly depend on the stimuli present in the Greek market. We do not have the know-how or the means to modify them across countries, at least in the present stage of our international development.

The second pattern of the qualitative part of this research casts some doubts on the statement that Greek small firms should aim at established markets because of higher performance achieved in these markets. Firms have entered the emerging markets relatively more recently. Thus managers may expect their investments in the less developed countries to render profitable outcomes further in the future. Expectations about pay-back periods can differ between the two market groups, and so the comparison concerning performance may be premature at present. The statement of the owner of a food firm is illuminating:

> I know that initially my investment in Bulgaria is likely not to make any money. Somehow I expect this, given that I do not know exactly what these consumers want, what distributors require, what competitors offer. Nevertheless, I perceive the first three to five years in Bulgaria as a period in which I have to learn all these. After this time, I will be in a much better position in terms of sales and profits. Hey, do you expect to have profits even in your local market from the very start?

The third pattern refers to the importance of FDI expansion modes for performance in established markets. The content analysis of the field notes suggests that even firms which currently employ export agents or intermediaries abroad to expand in developed countries hope for establishment of an FDI mode at a later stage. It appears that firms often employ such FDI modes in established markets in order to satisfy the customer needs better. The expansion through joint ventures or subsidiaries may substantially facilitate the growth of the firm and increase the chances of superior performance in these markets. The corollary of this argument is the statement by the managing director of a food firm which has formed a joint venture in Italy:

> It is essential to establish sooner or later an advanced non-exporting mode in order to service the Italian market efficiently. The customers, suppliers, competitors and government there perceive such modes as moves signifying major commitment, and the respective entering of small firms as determined players in the competitive Italian industry. Our joint venture with our Italian competitor provides us with significant market leverage and is a must for success in Italy.

The fourth pattern is linked to another factor associated with improved performance in less developed markets. The evidence from the qualitative part of this study leads to a better understanding of the weight that an emerging market can have for the international operations of the firm. It appears that many investigated firms attach substantial importance to countries of SEE when examined in the context of their broader strategic international market portfolios, as the remark by the export manager of a footwear firm illustrates:

The firm's operations in Romania are of key importance to its international expansion in the whole SEE region. We perceive this country to be our strategic distribution centre not only for Romania but also its adjacent countries. Our Romanian export agent already supplies products to Bulgarian, Hungarian, Ukrainian and Czech customers. Romania serves as our strategic hub for expansion into other SEE markets.

The fifth pattern emerging from the qualitative aspect of the study is connected with the dilemma of sole or combined presence in both market categories. The evidence from the qualitative part of the research suggests that, owing to the fierce competitive environment of many foreign countries, and especially that of the developed ones, firms regard business operations in one rather than two market categories as a contributor to enhanced performance abroad. The statement of an international operations manager of a garments firm with foreign activities only in Germany is characteristic:

I see many businesses, which have cooperated with German clients for many years, look for market opportunities in Balkans ardently. I am not saying that these neighbouring markets should be discarded. But, if you are satisfied with your long-standing client, why should you squander money elsewhere? Can you manage to be everywhere there is opportunity, especially if you are a small player? Obviously not.

Discussion of the findings

Should Greek small firms pursue international operations primarily in the established markets of their traditional trading partners, such as Germany, USA, Italy, UK and France, or should they shift their interest to the new and emerging neighbouring SEE markets, such as Bulgaria, Former Yugoslav Republic of Macedonia, Albania, Russia and New Yugoslavia? This dilemma is of major significance in view of the challenges of EU enlargement in SEE and the opportunities this offers to enterprise development.

On the strength of the statistical evidence, performance in developed countries is significantly higher than that in less developed countries. This may be due to Porter's (1990) aforementioned assertion: demanding customers in established markets can induce firms to become competitive and successful. However, when examined along with the other predictors, the effect of operations in emerging markets on performance, although still negative, loses much of its statistical significance. The additional evidence obtained from the qualitative part of the study further questions the argument that business operations in developed markets lead to enhanced performance. In fact, *the relatively recent enterprise entry and the different expectations concerning pay-back horizons in emerging markets can lead to the conclusion that the statistical evidence, which suggests that small firms perform better in developed countries, should be viewed with caution.*

Influence of firm- and country-specific variables on performance
With reference to the first theme of the study, which variables of the study's conceptual model are associated with enhanced performance in each of the two market groups, six variables seem to be of especial importance: in established markets, implementation of FDI modes and enterprise experience appear positively associated with performance, while uncertainty of the foreign country and operations in both market categories appear negatively associated with performance; in emerging markets, adoption of penetration pricing and strategic significance of the host country to the international growth of the firm seem positively associated with performance.

It appears that strategic, organizational and environmental variables affect the performance of the firm in foreign markets. This result validates the comprehensive conceptual framework that has been adopted in this study and corroborates the argument that the firm's performance should be explained by such holistic frameworks (Lenz, 1980). Nevertheless, the results from the regressions in the two datasets have to be viewed with caution owing to the small ratio of observations to independent variables. Although this ratio is higher than the suggested five to one minimum figure (Hair *et al.* 1995), a higher number of observations would have provided more generalizable results, especially for the dataset consisting of emerging markets.

Established markets   Implementation of FDI modes, that is joint ventures and subsidiaries, appears to be linked to enhanced performance in established markets, a finding which emerges particularly from the qualitative part of the study. This association has been observed for operations in developed countries, possibly because of the higher level of competition encountered in their markets. As the content analysis of the field notes reveals, use of FDI modes of expansion in developed countries may signal to all market participants that the entering small firm possesses the strength and determination to become a serious player in its industry, something which can lead to an increase in performance abroad.

Firms should also acquire experience in established markets in order to achieve superior performance. This finding is compatible with the proposition of the incremental school: experience is of major significance and the driving force behind an enterprise's international operations and performance (Bilkey and Tesar, 1977; Johanson and Vahlne, 1977, 1990; Johanson and Wiedersheim-Paul, 1975). This association is established for the developed countries in which it is likely that the level of market sophistication and complexity requires a high degree of experience and familiarity with the modus operandi of their markets.

Firms appear to achieve improved performance in environmental contexts of developed countries that are distinguished by low uncertainty. This is not unexpected since an uncertain environment urges firms to devote significant resources to adaptation (Carlsson, 1989), something which is more likely to apply to small firms which possess a limited amount of human, financial and production resources. Such an adaptation has to occur in constantly changing and uncertain environmental contexts and can exert a detrimental impact on performance (Haveman, 1993; Slater and Narver, 1994).

Emerging markets   The finding regarding the positive association between penetration pricing and performance in the less developed countries group implies that firms in these countries would better price their products at the lowest possible level. This result corroborates findings of export studies which suggest that penetration pricing is positively associated with performance (Christensen *et al.*, 1987; Kirpalani and Macintosh, 1980; Moon and Lee, 1990). It appears that it may still be too early to pursue sophisticated differentiation strategies in the currently formed new-market economies.

The positive effect of strategic significance of the less developed country to the international growth of the firm suggests that firms are likely to consider SEE countries as vital to their business operations in this neighbouring region. The evidence provided by the qualitative part of this study suggests that firms can regard these countries as key centres of their strategic international market portfolios. Business operations in SEE markets may lead to opportunities for expansion into other adjacent markets. This behaviour is in accord with evidence which suggests that strategic motivations can exist when firms enter a foreign country that offers international market interconnectedness possibilities (Douglas and Craig, 1996; Hill *et al.* 1990; Kim and Hwang, 1992).

'Performance synergies' between the two market categories
With reference to the second theme of the study (whether firms which operate in both market categories achieve any 'synergies' leading to improved performance), the existing evidence seems to negate this proposition. To the best of our knowledge, this is the first study that provides some empirical evidence on this issue. A negative effect of operations in both market categories on performance abroad is observed from the evidence obtained by both the quantitative and qualitative parts of this research. This appears to be the case especially for firms which currently have business operations in developed countries, perhaps owing to the higher level of competition in these countries and the subsequent higher level of consideration that they deserve. There are not any noticeable effects

of knowledge or experience transfer between the two country groups, and this can be associated with observations of researchers presented in the literature review (Evans *et al.*, 1992; Hilton, 1992; O'Grady and Lane, 1996).

However, *the evidence from this study suggesting that the presence in both country categories is detrimental to the firm's performance in foreign markets should be viewed as preliminary*, for two reasons. First, small firms were investigated which may not possess the resources to compete effectively in both country categories simultaneously. Second, and more important, the performance indicator employed, viz. foreign country sales ratio, appears to capture only a snapshot of accomplishments in the host country, lacking aspects which could provide a more long-run appreciation of the impact of internationalization on the firm's performance.

Conclusions and implications
The selection of foreign destination markets is of major importance to business managers. The present study presents some empirical evidence on this issue from 114 small and medium-sized Greek manufacturing firms with 165 internationalization ventures. The international activities of these firms constitute an entrepreneurial act, given their small size and relatively little experience in the international marketplace. Employing a methodology which had both quantitative and qualitative aspects, the research used a performance measurement analysis to draw implications for international business and international entrepreneurship. The key findings of this research provide the following suggestions.

Emphasis on established markets
Provisional evidence suggests that it may be to Greek small firms' advantage to concentrate on established rather than emerging markets. This is because internationalization ventures in developed countries are likely to be associated with higher levels of performance. The findings suggest that enterprises operating in developed countries benefit if they employ joint ventures and subsidiaries, gain as much experience as possible and try to reduce uncertainty.

Joint ventures and subsidiaries   Although FDI modes of expansion require substantial resource commitments, they seem likely to affect performance in the foreign market positively. FDI modes appear to indicate to all market participants that entering firms are serious players in the competitive developed countries, something which can increase the firm's leverage and performance abroad. It is also likely that, through these FDI modes, intimate knowledge of the foreign market is acquired. This may facilitate smooth operations of the firm and improve performance in host markets.

Experience   The greater the experience of the firm in a developed country, the higher the possibility of enhanced performance in that country. Firms have to become acquainted with the customer buying preferences, the competitive practices, and the economic and political system of a developed country. Greek small firms have to become responsive to the idiosyncrasies of the German, US, Italian, UK or French markets, and this involves persistence and long-run commitment. An opportunistic strategy focusing on short-term presence and consequent gains appears problematic in established markets.

Reducing uncertainty   The lower the uncertainty of a country owing to economic, political, legal, social and market-specific factors, the higher the likelihood of firms' improved performance in this country. Not all developed countries present the same degree of uncertainty and, thus, prior examination of country risk factors for destination foreign markets seems advisable. With regard to the selected destination foreign countries, use of export guarantees, foreign exchange rate management techniques and foreign investment insurance plans to hedge against uncertainty appears to be a prudent strategy to follow.

Less emphasis on emerging markets?
There is tentative evidence in this study that Greek small firms may achieve poorer performance in emerging rather than established markets. Nevertheless, this statement should be viewed with caution because investments in less developed countries, particularly those of SEE, have taken place recently. Consequently, the pay-off period may not have come yet. Entering firms still learn how to operate in the new-market economies of SEE. The emerging market opportunities in these countries, and the small geographic and cultural proximity with most of them, constitute appealing grounds for many Greek firms to advance international operations in their markets. Therefore countries of the SEE region are likely to continue to serve as attractive targets for many Greek small businesses. The findings suggest that enterprises operating in less developed countries perform better if they follow penetration pricing and select markets that are crucial to the firms' international operations.

Penetration pricing   The lower the price of the products in a less developed country, the higher the probability of enhanced performance in that country. Customers in the Balkan and East European countries have low purchasing power and assign primary importance to the low cost of the product. Thus penetration pricing is likely to make the product known to them and lead to superior performance. Sophisticated differentiation strategies may not be currently appropriate for the emerging markets.

Key markets The SEE region offers significant challenges and opportunities for growth, and it appears that synergies in terms of market interconnectedness exist in this region. Small firms seem to perform better when they operate in countries which provide opportunities for current or future expansion into other SEE markets. This finding asks for examination of strategic international market portfolios in the SEE region.

Focus on one of the two country zones
The evidence from this study suggests that, compared to firms with international operations in only one of the two country categories, firms with operations in both country categories achieve poorer performance. In particular, firms that currently operate in established markets appear to be better off if they 'stick to their knitting', avoiding diversifying their international efforts into emerging markets also. While this proposition may be subject to the constraining factor that performance and enterprise accomplishments in the two market categories may not be comparable currently, it appears that Greek small firms can achieve improved performance if they specialize in the market category that they know best. No learning synergies seem to take place between the two country zones. Perhaps this occurs because the new-market economies of SEE still undergo dramatic political, social and economic changes. Because of this, it might be rather costly for firms with operations in both country groups to monitor and comprehend the market developments taking place in the emerging SEE markets.

With regard to the implications of the study for research, an important conclusion is that particular organizational parameters of the small firm may not be specific to the internationalization ventures of the firm abroad. The findings of this study reveal that this can be the case for the entrepreneurial style of the firm because it appears to be unchanged across foreign countries. Not only that but also the evidence suggests that managers of the firms do not differentiate entrepreneurial style between domestic and foreign markets. This seems to suggest that, for the investigated firms, one 'universal' entrepreneurial mode exists and cannot be distinguished between domestic and international business.

These findings are specific to smaller firms in low-technology industries which, by and large, have entered the international marketplace lately. Therefore more research is needed in order to come up with additional evidence on whether these propositions hold for firms in high-technology industries and firms which possess greater levels of international experience. This is necessary in order to define appropriately and draw up the boundaries of international entrepreneurship. Also further examinations for entrepreneurial firms based in smaller countries with dynamic economies are particularly welcome. This theme is very important to other countries with advancing economies, such as Ireland, Korea, Portugal and Spain.

Note

1. The fact that FDI modes of expansion present a statistically significant regression coefficient suggests that, controlling for other independent variables, the implementation of these modes yields higher performance than exports through offices or organizations located in the home country (the 'reference group' in the regression). This statistical finding does not mean that returns from FDI modes are higher than those from all exporting modes. In fact, a *t*-test for differences in the regression coefficients was employed following Hardy (1993): no statistically significant differences were found between the performance effects of FDI and each of the other exporting modes in the regression for the dataset consisting of established markets.

Appendix: operationalization of the variables

Variable	Questionnaire items	Alpha	References
Mode of foreign expansion	Four dummy variables capturing (a) exports through offices or organizations in the home country (this mode is the 'reference group' in the regressions); (b) exports through agents in the foreign country; (c) exports through intermediaries (wholesalers or retailers) in the foreign country; (d) direct exports to customers in the foreign country; (e) foreign direct investment modes (joint ventures or subsidiaries)	—	Root (1987), Young *et al.* (1989)
Collaborative strategy	Composite variable of twelve 7-point scales measuring the degree to which the firm in the foreign country participates in cooperative activities: (1) joint production, (2) joint R&D, (3) joint distribution, (4) joint advertising and promotion (activities 1 to 4 with competitors), (5–8) (activities 1 to 4 with non-competitors), (9) pricing from industry-wide lists, (10) producing industry-wide standard items, (11) member of the confederation of producers of the same sector, (12) networking with universities and other research institutions	0.82	Dollinger (1990), Dollinger and Golden (1992)

Appendix (continued)

Variable	Questionnaire items	Alpha	References
Focus strategy	Composite variable of two 7-point scales measuring the degree to which the firm in the foreign country fulfils the needs of (1) specific categories of customers, (2) particular market segments	0.71	Porter (1980)
Differentiation strategy	Composite variable of five 7-point scales measuring the degree to which the firm in the foreign country differentiates its products from the competing ones, based on (1) the products' quality, (2) the products' design, (3) the products' technological superiority, (4) the products' pre- and after- sales service, (5) advertising and promotional techniques	0.75	Mintzberg (1988), Porter (1980)
Penetration pricing	Composite variable of two 7-point scales measuring the degree to which the firm in the foreign country prices its products: (1) at the lowest possible level which is below the average market price in the foreign country, (2) at a level lower than that of the domestic market	0.64	Leontiades (1985), Mintzberg (1988)
Experience	Number of years the firm has had operations in the foreign country	—	Bilkey and Tesar (1977)
Operations in both market categories	Dummy variable capturing whether the firm has business operations in both market categories	—	Welch and Welch (1996)
Unfamiliarity	Composite variable of three 7-point scales measuring the degree to which the firm perceives the domestic country to be dissimilar to the foreign country with respect to (1) mentality, (2) sociocultural norms, (3) values	0.76	Johanson and Vahlne (1977), Root (1987)
Munificence	Composite variable of three 7-point scales measuring the degree to which the firm perceives the environment of the foreign country to be (1) safe, (2) rich in opportunities, (3) controllable and manipulable by the firm	0.66	Khandwalla (1977)

Appendix (continued)

Variable	Questionnaire items	Alpha	References
Uncertainty	Composite variable of nine 7-point scales measuring the degree to which it is difficult to forecast the expected sales of the firm in the foreign country owing to this country's (1) inflation rate, (2) exchange rate with the main foreign currency, (3) tax policy, (4) ability through the party in power to maintain control of the government, (5) national laws affecting international business, (6) legal regulations affecting businesses, (7) threat of social unrest, (8) competitive market strategies, (9) customer preferences	0.86	Achrol and Stern (1988), Miller (1993), Miller and Dröge (1986)
Country's strategic significance	One 7-point scale measuring the degree to which the country is strategically significant to the international growth of the firm	—	Hill *et al.* (1990); Kim and Hwang (1992)
Foreign country sales ratio	Ratio of sales in the foreign country over total enterprise sales for a fiscal year	—	Moon and Lee (1990), Sullivan (1994)

References

Achrol, R.S. and L.W. Stern (1988), 'Environmental determinants of decision-making uncertainty in marketing channels', *Journal of Marketing Research*, 25, 36–50.

Aulakh, P.S., M. Kotabe and H. Teegan (2000), 'Export strategies and performance of firms from emerging economies: evidence from Brazil, Chile and Mexico', *Academy of Management Journal*, 43, 342–61.

Bilkey, W.J. and G. Tesar (1977), 'The export behavior of smaller-sized Wisconsin manufacturing firms', *Journal of International Business Studies*, 8(1), 93–8.

Bourantas, D. and G. Mandes (1987), 'A profile of the Greek manager – a survey', *European Management Journal*, 5, 57–61.

Buckley, P.J. (1990), 'Problems and developments in the core theory of international business', *Journal of International Business Studies*, 21, 657–66.

Burgel, O. and G.C. Murray (2000), 'The international market entry choices of start-up companies in high-technology industries', *Journal of International Marketing*, 8(2), 33–62.

Capon, N., J.U. Farley and S. Hoenig (1990), 'Determinants of financial performance: a meta analysis', *Management Science*, 36, 1143–59.

Carlsson, B. (1989), 'Small-scale industry at a crossroads: U.S. machine tools in global perspective', *Small Business Economics*, 1, 245–61.

Christensen, C.H., A. Da Rocha and R.K. Gertner (1987), 'An empirical investigation of the factors influencing exporting success of Brazilian firms', *Journal of International Business Studies*, 18(3), 61–77.

Collins, J.M. (1990), 'A market performance comparison of US firms active in domestic developed and developing countries', *Journal of International Business Studies*, 21, 271–87.

Contractor, F.J. (1990), 'Contractual and cooperative forms of international business: towards a unified theory of modal choice', *Management International Review*, 30(1), 31–54.

Dana, L.P., H. Etemad and R. Wright (1999), 'The impact of globalisation on SMEs', *Global Focus*, 11(4), 93–105.

Da Rocha, A., C.H. Christensen and C.E. Da Cunha (1990), 'Aggressive and passive exporters: a study in the Brazilian furniture industry', *International Marketing Review*, 7(5), 6–15.

Das, M. (1994), 'Successful and unsuccessful exporters from developing countries: some preliminary findings', *European Journal of Marketing*, 28(12), 19–33.

Denis, J.-E. and D. Depelteau (1985), 'Market knowledge, diversification and export expansion', *Journal of International Business Studies*, 16(3), 77–89.

Dollinger, M.J. (1990), 'The evolution of collective strategies in fragmented industries', *Academy of Management Review*, 15, 266–85.

Dollinger, M.J. and P.A. Golden (1992), 'Interorganizational and collective strategies in small firms', *Journal of Management*, 18, 695–715.

Dominguez, L.V. and C.G. Sequeira (1993), 'Determinants of LDC exporters' performance: a cross-national study', *Journal of International Business Studies*, 24, 19–40.

Douglas, M. (1996), 'The strategies and characteristics of exporting SMEs: a study of Peruvian firms', *Journal of Global Marketing*, 28(12), 19–33.

Douglas, S.P. and C.S. Craig (1996), 'Global portfolio planning and market interconnectedness', *Journal of International Marketing*, 4(1), 93–110.

Dunning, J.H. (1988), 'The eclectic paradigm of international production: a restatement and some possible extensions', *Journal of International Business Studies*, 19, 1–31.

Dunning, J.H. (1995), 'Reappraising the eclectic paradigm in an age of alliance capitalism', *Journal of International Business Studies*, 26, 461–91.

Erramilli, M.K., S. Agarwal and S.-S. Kim (1997), 'Are firm-specific advantages location-specific too?', *Journal of International Business Studies*, 28, 479–502.

Evans, W., H. Lane and S. O'Grady (1992), *Border Crossings: Doing Business in the U.S.*, Scarborough, Ontario, Canada: Prentice-Hall.

Gopinath, C. and R.C. Hoffman (1995), 'The relevance of strategy research: practitioner and academic viewpoints', *Journal of Management Studies*, 32, 575–94.

Hair, J.F., R.E. Anderson, R.L. Tatham and W.C. Black (1995), *Multivariate Data Analysis with Readings*, 4th edn, Englewood Cliffs, NJ: Prentice-Hall.

Hambrick, D.C. (1980), 'Operationalizing the concept of business-level strategy in research', *Academy of Management Review*, 5, 567–75.

Hardy, M.A. (1993), *Regression with Dummy Variables – a Sage University Paper*, 93, Newbury Park, CA: Sage.

Haveman, H. (1993), 'Organizational size and change: diversification in the savings and loan industry after deregulation', *Administrative Science Quarterly*, 38, 20–50.

Healy, M. and C. Perry (2000), 'Comprehensive criteria to judge validity and reliability of qualitative research within the realism paradigm', *Qualitative Market Research*, 3(3), 118–26.

Hill, C.W.L., P. Hwang and W.C. Kim (1990), 'An eclectic theory of the choice of international entry mode', *Strategic Management Journal*, 11, 117–28.

Hilton, A. (1992), 'Mythology, markets, and the emerging Europe', *Harvard Business Review*, 70(6), 50–54.

Hoskisson, R.E., L. Eden, C.M. Lau and M. Wright (2000), 'Strategy in emerging economies', *Academy of Management Journal*, 43, 249–67.

Ibeh, K.I.N. and S. Young (2001), 'Exporting as an entrepreneurial act – an empirical study of Nigerian firms', *European Journal of Marketing*, 35, 566–86.

IFC (International Finance Corporation) (1999), database available (*http://www.ifc.org/EMDB/SLIDES/sld009.htm*).

Jick, T.D. (1979), 'Mixing qualitative and quantitative methods: triangulation in action', *Administrative Science Quarterly*, 24, 603–11.

Johanson, J. and J.-E. Vahlne (1977), 'The internationalization process of the firm: a model of knowledge development and increasing foreign market commitments', *Journal of International Business Studies*, 8(1), 23–32.

Johanson, J. and J.-E. Vahlne (1990), 'The mechanism of internationalisation', *International Marketing Review*, 7(4), 11–24.

Johanson, J. and F. Wiedersheim-Paul (1975), 'The internationalization of the firm: four Swedish cases', *Journal of Management Studies*, 12, 305–22.

Johanson, J., S.P. Douglas and I. Nonaka (1985), 'Asserting the impact of country of origin on product evaluations: a new methodological perspective', *Journal of Marketing Research*, 22, 388–96.

Khandwalla, P.N. (1977), *The Design of Organizations*, New York: Hartcourt Bruce Jovanovich.

Kim, W.C. and P. Hwang (1992), 'Global strategy and multinationals' entry mode choice', *Journal of International Business Studies*, 23(1), 29–53.

Kirpalani, V.H. and N.B. Macintosh (1980), 'Internal marketing effectiveness of technology-oriented small firms', *Journal of International Business Studies*, 11(3), 81–90.

Krippendorff, K. (1980), *Content Analysis: An Introduction to its Methodology*, Newbury Park, CA: Sage.

Lenz, R.T. (1980), 'Environment, strategy, organization structure and performance: patterns in one industry', *Strategic Management Journal*, 1, 209–26.

Leontiades, J.C. (1985), *Multinational Corporate Strategy – Planning for World Markets*, Lexington, MA: Lexington Books.

Lumpkin, G.T. and G.G. Dess (1996), 'Clarifying the entrepreneurial construct and linking it to performance', *Academy of Management Review*, 21, 135–72.

Makridakis, S., Y. Caloghirou, L. Papagiannakis and P. Trivellas (1997), 'The dualism of Greek firms and management: present state and future implications', *European Management Journal*, 15, 381–402.

Merchant, H. (2000), 'Configurations of international joint ventures', *Management International Review*, 40(2), 107–40.

Miller, D. and C. Dröge (1986), 'Psychological and traditional determinants of structure', *Administrative Science Quarterly*, 31, 539–60.

Miller, K.D. (1993), 'Industry and country effects on managers' perceptions of environmental uncertainties', *Journal of International Business Studies*, 24, 693–714.

Mintzberg, H. (1988), 'Generic strategies: toward a comprehensive framework', in R. Lamb and P. Shrivastava (eds), *Advances in Strategic Management*, 5, Greenwich, CT: JAI Press, pp. 1–67.

Moon, J. and H. Lee (1990), 'On the internal correlates of export stage development: an empirical investigation in the Korean electronics industry', *International Marketing Review*, 7(5), 16–26.

O'Grady, S. and H.W. Lane (1996), 'The psychic distance paradox', *Journal of International Business Studies*, 27, 309–33.

OECD (Organisation for Economic Cooperation and Development) (2001), *Regulatory Review of Greece*, Paris: OECD.

Porter, M.E. (1980), *Competitive Strategy – Techniques for Analyzing Industries and Competitors*, New York: Free Press.

Porter, M.E. (1990), *The Competitive Advantage of Nations*, New York: Free Press.

Root, F.R. (1987), *Entry Strategies for International Markets*, Lexington, MA: Lexington Books.

Slater, S.F. and J.C. Narver (1994), 'Does competitive environment moderate the market orientation–performance relationship?', *Journal of Marketing*, 58, 46–55.

Stinchcombe, A.L. (1965), 'Social structures and organizations', in J.G. March (ed.), *Handbook of Organizations*, Chicago, IL: Rand McNally, pp. 142–93.

Sullivan, D. (1994), 'Measuring the degree of internationalization of a firm', *Journal of International Business Studies*, 25, 325–42.

Welch, D.E. and L.S. Welch (1996), 'The internationalization process and networks: a strategic management perspective', *Journal of International Marketing*, 4(3), 11–28.

Young, S., J. Hamill, C. Wheeler and J.R. Davies (1989), *International Market Entry and Development*, Englewood Cliffs, NJ: Prentice-Hall.

26 Indian perspectives of international entrepreneurship
Shameen Prashantham

Internationalization among small firms, and notably small knowledge-intensive firms (SKIFs), can be unusually rapid, and is often influenced by three aspects of the international entrepreneur: knowledge, intent and networks. However both internationalization-related and other entrepreneurial activities – and therefore international entrepreneurship – can be hampered by macroeconomic disincentives or a hostile environment. This often tends to be the case in developing economies such as India, given which, the success story of the Indian software industry acquires great significance as a notable exception to the rule. It has emerged as an exemplar for developing economy entrepreneurs seeking their fortune in the software and other industries. Drawing on the literature relevant to international entrepreneurship, as well as secondary and some primary data on the Indian software industry, this chapter points out that international entrepreneurs in a developing economy can be successful through their own entrepreneurial efforts, especially when encouraged and facilitated by favourable policy measures. There still are, however, key challenges that they have to deal with.

Most studies of small firm internationalization have taken place in developed economy contexts (Bell and Young, 1998), thus depriving aspiring business people in developing economies of rigorous research-based inputs on international entrepreneurship. Even as more empirical work in this area needs to be done, this chapter seeks to offer some insight into ways in which international entrepreneurs in developing contexts can achieve success, by drawing on literature relevant to internationalization and citing the example of the Indian software industry.

It is hoped that some of the issues dealt with in this discussion of the Indian software industry will be insightful and inspirational to international entrepreneurs in a developing economy context. The following sections deal with

- small firm internationalization, especially for knowledge-intensive firms,
- entrepreneurship and the role of entrepreneurs in small firm internationalization,

- incentives and disincentives for international entrepreneurs in developing economies,
- the Indian context in terms of fostering entrepreneurship,
- the development and growth of the Indian software industry,
- examples of four Indian software entrepreneurs who were drawn to found firms,
- implications of the preceding sections for theory, entrepreneurship and policy.

Small firm internationalization

Bell and Young (1998) point out that there is no unanimity in the definition of the term 'internationalization'. Welch and Luostarinen (1988) have defined it as 'the process of increasing involvement in international operations'. They suggest that internationalization can involve both inward and outward activities. A different perspective is provided by Naidu *et al.* (1997, p. 115): 'Internationalization is a gradual process whereby a firm develops a network of global trade relationships.'

Jones (1999) comments that surprisingly little is known about internationalization in relation to small firms, and blames this on assumptions pertaining to the resource limitations of small firms and literature that is skewed towards the area of export, in part because of the relatively low risk and commitment involved. The focus on a single entry mode, viz. exporting, has contributed to major shortcomings in internationalization theory (Leonidou and Katsikeas, 1996). However, several other entry modes exist, which include exporting, licensing, franchising, management contracts, turnkey contracts, international subcontracting, industrial cooperation agreements, contractual joint ventures, equity joint ventures, wholly owned subsidiaries, mergers and acquisitions, and strategic alliances. These various modes vary according to the commitment, cost efficiency, control and risk involved (Anderson and Gatignon, 1986, Erramilli and Rao, 1993; Young *et al.*, 1989).

Some of the early thinking on internationalization emanated from work in the 1970s, such as that of Johanson and Wiedersheim-Paul (1975), Johanson and Vahlne (1977) and Bilkey and Tesar (1977), which have come to be known collectively as 'stage' theories or incremental frameworks. These continue to be the dominant theories in the field (Welch and Luostarinen, 1988; Johanson and Vahlne, 1990; Coviello and McAuley, 1999) although they have received much criticism (Turnbull, 1987; Andersen, 1993; Bell 1995; O'Farrell *et al.*, 1998). Among the stage models, distinction has been made between the work of Nordic authors such as Johanson and Vahlne (1977) and American authors such as Bilkey and Tesar (1977); the former is referred to as the Uppsala Model and the latter as the Innovation Model (Andersen, 1993). The overall thrust of both models is similar to the extent that they suggest that firms internationalize in incremental steps. They differ, however, in their emphasis; the Uppsala Model views the internationalization process as a result of firms' commitment and knowledge, while the Innovation Model views the internationalization process as the consequence of innovation, where firms respond to, for example, unsolicited orders.

Some authors take a resource-based view of the firm and suggest that small firm internationalization, at least initially, is largely a function of the firm's resources and competencies. The competencies of the management team, in particular, has been recognized (Aaby and Slater, 1989; Chetty and Hamilton, 1993). The resource issue also has a bearing on another theme mentioned in the internationalization literature, strategy, which follows, in part, from a firm's resource base. Young *et al.* (1989) rejected existing theories of internationalization and presented one of their own, based on the firm's objectives (short- or long-term) within the overall scope of the firm's corporate strategy.

An alternative perspective on internationalization has been the so-called 'networks' approach, which can, however, be seen as complementary rather than contradictory to the 'stage' theories (Coviello and McAuley, 1999). Johanson and Mattsson (1988) argued that industrial networks involving other players such as customers and suppliers influence internationalization decisions of firms. Even Johanson and Vahlne (1990, 1992) have acknowledged the role of other actors in the internationalization process, while other scholars suggest that the network perspective is a contingency model to existing 'stage' theories (Bell and Young, 1998).

Network relationships are 'stable and changing' (Johanson and Mattsson, 1988, p. 291) and may exist across borders (ibid.) or be spatially bound in 'clusters' (Porter, 1990; Enright, 1999). Clusters may influence the internationalization of SKIFs through *marketing externalities* such as, for example, intra-cluster referrals, credibility and reputation, informational spillovers, and active joint marketing (Brown and Bell, 2000). Brown and McNaughton (2000) suggest that, while the original location of a cluster may have been accidental rather than rational, younger firms often locate in such clusters to benefit from the ensuing externalities.

Network relationships have been found to accelerate the internationalization of small firms (Bell, 1995; Coviello and Munro, 1997), which is not altogether surprising given that small firms, in general, are renowned for their networking ability (Jones, 1999). Indeed, some small firms have been deemed to be international from inception and variously referred to as 'born globals', 'new international ventures' and 'global start-ups' (Rennie, 1993; Oviatt and McDougall, 1994, 1997; McDougall *et al.* 1994; Knight and Cavusgil, 1996; Madsen and Servais, 1997; Johnson, 1999; Rasmussen and Madsen, 1999).

As with the literature on management strategy, individual theories of small firm internationalization at best proffer a partial view of the subject, and there is merit in taking an eclectic view (Dunning, 1988; Mintzberg and Lampel, 1999). The total incompatibility of the various views on internationalization is debatable. For instance, although sharp differences exist between an objective-led approach where quantitative, fact-based methodology guides decision making and a process-based approach with incremental steps, it is quite conceivable that knowledge (as presented by Johanson and Vahlne, 1977, 1990) can inform a firm's strategy process.

Entrepreneurship
While no particular personality trait is 'truly' entrepreneurial (Bhide, 1994), the business-related characteristics of the entrepreneur have a strong bearing on the internationalization of small firms (Aaby and Slater, 1989; Chetty and Hamilton, 1993; Leonidou and Katsikeas, 1996; Welch and Luostarinen, 1988); this is particularly true in relation to firms that are international from inception (Madsen and Servais, 1997; Rasmussen and Madsen, 1999). A synthesis of the literature on entrepreneurship, small firms and knowledge-intensive firms (given this chapter's reference to software firms) suggests that three interdependent factors, which are mostly brought to the table by the entrepreneur himself or herself, play an important role in the development of small entrepreneurial firms, including their internationalization: knowledge, intent and networks.

Knowledge
Innovation is a key goal for small entrepreneurial firms (Acs *et al.*, 1999; Almeida, 1999; Audretsch, 1999; Carlsson, 1999; Hagel and Singer, 1999; Hamel, 1996; Lerner, 1999) and knowledge is the chief preoccupation of knowledge-intensive firms (Alvesson, 1993, 1995; Autio *et al.*, 2000; Elkjaer, 2000; Nurmi, 1998; Tenkasi and Boland, 1996). Domains of specialized knowledge of the entrepreneur often determine the firm's main offerings and therefore the prior *experience* (including education) of the entrepreneur is crucial in the context of SKIFs, and may have a bearing on his or her strategic and international orientation, innovativeness and network relationships (Berry, 1998; Crick and Jones, 2000; Ibeh and Young, 2001; Madhok, 1996; McDougall and Oviatt, 2000; Young, 1987). Related to knowledge is *innovativeness* or innovative behaviour of the entrepreneur (Baker, 1979), which can have a positive impact on the firm's performance in international markets (Kundu and Katz, 2000). Although some studies have failed to demonstrate this conclusively, the literature still maintains

the importance of innovativeness alongside other characteristics such as autonomy, risk taking and competitive aggressiveness (Lumpkin and Dess, 1996). Innovation is crucial to SKIFs' coping with their competitive environments (Zahra and Neubaum, 1998).

Intent

An entrepreneur's *strategic orientation* has a bearing on how well the technology strategy of the firm is integrated with the overall corporate strategy of the firm (Berry, 1996; Kundu and Katz, 2000) and also has a bearing on the type of planning style adopted. An important factor in the internationalization of SKIFs is the *international orientation* or vision of the entrepreneur (Aaby and Slater, 1989). Reference has also been made to the importance of a 'global mindset' on the part of the technology entrepreneur, as a pre-state requirement for success in the global marketplace (Berry, 1998). These notions refer to the entrepreneur's philosophy (Becherer and Maurer, 1997) or attitude, which may have a bearing on decisions such as changes in entry mode (Calof and Beamish, 1995). There is apparently a tension in the literature in terms of whether successful small entrepreneurial firms adopt – or ought to adopt – a formal or informal approach to their strategy formulation, as captured in the debate between marketing orientation (MO) and entrepreneurial orientation (EO), respectively (Tzokas *et al.*, 2001). The ideal situation for a small firm is when both an entrepreneurial and a marketing orientation coexist, notwithstanding the contradictory skill sets that they entail. Becherer and Maurer (1997) found support for their hypothesis that the EO of an entrepreneur-led firm is directly related to its MO, and concluded that EO and MO are part of the same underlying philosophy.

Networks

Network relationships with players such as suppliers, customers, universities and even competitors have a great influence on small firms' (and especially SKIFs') business activities. Small firms are resource-poor (Hadjimanolis, 2000a; McNamee *et al.*, 2000) and external network relationships can be vital to a small firm's viability, compensate for resources it lacks (McNamee *et al.*, 2000) and facilitate knowledge building (Almeida, 1999) and, therefore, innovation since resource-rich small firms innovate better than resource-poor ones (Hadjimanolis, 2000b). These relationships may be available through regional networks (Saxenien, 1990), and smaller firms have been seen to be more adept at integrating into local regional networks than larger firms (Almeida, 1999); these subnational regions' climate may however be supportive, detrimental or neutral (Goetz and Freshwater, 2001). The role of networks acquires significance when knowledge-intensive and high-technology firms (typically small ones) specialize (Carlsson, 1999). As discussed earlier, network relationships are significant, both facilitating and constraining, for competitive advantage in general and internationalization in particular (Bell, 1995; Coviello and Munro, 1995). Strategic alliances may be entered into (Rao and Klein, 1994) or the lead may be taken from key clients (Bell, 1995; O'Farrell *et al.*, 1998). Alvesson (1993) also mentions the importance of inter-firm networks in creating reputation for knowledge-intensive firms.

International entrepreneurship in a developing economy context
The macro environment in which a firm operates may have certain disincentives with respect to international marketing. Das (1994) has suggested that two distinct problems can be identified that face exporters from developing economies: government policies and interventions, and market-related problems. She suggests that policy makers need to focus promotion activities on key industries, motivate managers to export, encourage the diversification of exporters' product mix (that is, shift to high-value offerings) and liberalize the economy. Policies generally reflect the politicoeconomic philosophy of a particular nation, which for example may have socialist leanings, as in the case of India (Vachani, 1997). Calof and Vivier's (1995) study of South African small and medium-sized enterprises found that problems that exporters faced pertained to, among other factors, domestic and international politics (including the dismantling of sanctions) and trade policy (including the implications of GATT).

Disincentives may take the form of institutional barriers or a lack of 'soft infrastructure' (Khanna and Palepu, 1999, p. 126) such as efficient product, capital and labour markets as well as regulatory mechanisms. These often exist in developing economies and may be a disincentive both for host country firms and for international ones. Other disincentives include elaborate procedures (Jain and Kapoor, 1996) and complex bureaucracy (Naidu *et al.*, 1997). Ibeh and Young (2001) have identified the following disincentives among Nigerian firms: unstable political climate, low technology level, poor local infrastructure, unstable exchange rate and inconsistent implementation of government policy.

Given that internationalization – notably export development – is seen as a source of economic advancement (Naidu *et al.*, 1997), incentives may also be available to firms as part of the local government policy. Government policy in terms of infrastructure provision and positive attitude to entrepreneurs can have a very beneficial impact, especially when concentrated in a geographic cluster, and is particularly beneficial where the national system of innovation is weak, such as in less advanced countries (Fontes and Coombs, 1995).

Clearly, operating in a developing economy context can be challenging for a SKIF, and requires tenacity, patience and capital resources. Maddy (2000), an African technology entrepreneur, distinguishes between two sources of capital for entrepreneurial firms in a developing economy: 'do-gooders' (for example, quasi-government agencies) and 'do-wellers' (such as private investors). Disincentives in dealing with them are a lack of trust in the entrepreneur and highly demanding expectations of success, respectively. She warns prospective entrepreneurs that the going can be very, very tough. 'The fact is, only 2% of the world's 6 billion people have access to the Internet. The revolution has hardly begun. Yes, change may come to emerging-market countries thanks to technology. But it will take time. Entrepreneurs can change the world as long as they don't try – as I did – to do it on a shoe string' (ibid., p. 62).

International entrepreneurship in India

It has been suggested that, owing to cultural factors such as the caste system, Indians have generally not been entrepreneurially minded (Dana, 2000), although certain communities among Indians are noted for their business acumen both in India and in foreign lands where they have settled (Bhagwathi, 1966). Furthermore restrictive government policy has not been encouraging of international entrepreneurship. As Naidu *et al.* (1997, p. 119) say, 'high levels of government interface has effectively inhibited international entrepreneurship'.

The underlying philosophy of the initial economic development activities after India gained independence from the British in 1947 was that the government knew best and therefore had to be the key driver of business activities. As a consequence, Indian entrepreneurs had to become adept at playing the 'game' of obtaining requisite licences, which involved a combination of lobbying strength and political connections, which often came at the cost of funding political parties or bribing officials. This, in turn, meant that it was mainly large business houses who had the financial and political clout to succeed over the long haul; small firms, despite the Gandhian sanction bestowed on them – Gandhi was a great believer in encouraging small firms through reserving certain products for their exclusive production – were often hampered by government control (Mahibala, 1997; Ramu, 1997; Sundarajan, 1997). In relation to exports, the Indian government was not very encouraging, especially after an acute balance of payments (BoP) crisis in the 1970s. Public policy at the time tended to be inward-looking, with the emphasis being on import substitution, rather than exports. A key objective was to limit the use of valuable foreign exchange by Indian firms (Naidu *et al.*, 1997; Vachani, 1997).

The position today is a lot different, especially after the liberalization efforts initiated from 1991 onwards (Vachani, 1997). Studies have demonstrated innovative abilities among Indian entrepreneurs (Manimala, 1992a, 1992b, 1992c, 1992d). While competing in international markets is highly challenging for family-run businesses in India (Murthy, 1999), Indian exporters seem to be upbeat, going by Jain and Kapoor's (1994) survey of the attitudes of Delhi-based entrepreneurs. According to them (ibid., pp. 80–81), 'On the whole, though the surveyed Indian firms viewed exporting as a more challenging and arduous task, they considered it as an activity worth the efforts as it enhances firm stability and entails greater growth and profit potential.' Most exporters had begun international marketing activity as a consequence of internal stimuli, which is different from American exporters discussed by Bilkey and Tesar (1977).

The optimism among Indian exporters detected by Jain and Kapoor is echoed by authors such as Naidu *et al.* (1997, p. 124), according to whom 'India has the potential of being a major player in world exports. It has the ingredients for success – entrepreneurial spirit of business people, ingenuity and motivation, and a wealth of resources. Nevertheless, the export sector has been stifled in the past through bureaucracy and disincentives. Recent liberalization of the Indian economy creates opportunities for Indian enterprises to successfully break into foreign markets. However, a proactive export assistance and promotion policy is required for achieving this objective.' While certain initiatives have been undertaken to foster entrepreneurship in India (as documented by Dana, 2000), such as the National Institute for Entrepreneurship and Small Business Development and Entrepreneurship Development Institute of India, arguably the greatest impetus for international entrepreneurship has come from the much-publicized success of the Indian software industry, which has become an exemplar to budding Indian entrepreneurs, especially those dreaming of success in international markets.

The software industry in India: an exception and exemplar
The case of the Indian software industry is significant in that it has transcended difficulties associated with entrepreneurship in India such as unfavourable cultural biases (Dana, 2000) and restrictive policy (Naidu *et al.*, 1997; Vachani, 1997). According to Correa (1996, p. 177), 'India is the most successful software exporter among developing economies.'

The origins of the Indian software industry, notable particularly because of its strong export focus, can be seen in the early 1970s when the government promoted software exports (Correa, 1996). This was also a period when stringent regulations saw international IT majors such as IBM pulling out of the country, thus creating a void that domestic hardware vendors rushed in to fill. The early 1980s saw the PC revolution enhancing the international demand for software, as well as the beginnings of liberal-ization policies in the Indian economy. Software exports from India began to grow.

The game plan followed by most Indian software companies was remark-ably simple and uniform. It entailed exploiting the low labour costs for soft-ware programming talent in India, compared to the west and especially the USA, through the provision of software developers for on-site work at client sites (often referred to as 'body-shopping'), supplemented by off-shore software development in India.

While the historical basis for the emergence of a pool of technical talent lies in the setting up of educational institutions and public sector under-takings (PSUs) in fields such as aeronautics, especially in the southern Indian city of Bangalore (referred to as the Silicon Valley of India), a unique impetus to the Indian software industry came from multinational corporations (MNCs) that set up shop there after the liberalization initia-tives of 1991 (Heitzman, 1997). Notable in this regard are Motorola and Texas Instruments, who were instrumental in raising labour wages and offering professionals interesting (as opposed to low-end and tedious coding work) projects, with a view to attracting the best talent available locally. Today, several other IT majors such as Microsoft and Sun Microsystems have development centres, many of which deal with state-of-the-art design.

However, these developments have seen wages rise and, as a consequence, the cost advantage of Indian firms, especially reputable ones, is slipping in comparison to rivals in China and the Philippines. Therefore some of the better Indian firms are aggressively seeking to graduate to higher levels of the value chain. Some firms are seeking profitable forays into Information Technology Enabled Services (ITES) such as call centres (Merchant, 2001d). The vast majority of Indian software firms, however, remain focused on low-level coding work; their viability in the long term is in serious doubt (Daniel, 2001; Merchant, 2001a, 2001b; Sadagopan, 1999).

It has been said in recent times that India has produced many successful software firms and beauty queens because the government was not involved. That may be somewhat unfair as government policy since the 1970s has justifiably encouraged software exports (Correa, 1996). More recently, apart from the tax holiday that software firms enjoy, the govern-ment upgraded the Department of Electronics (DoE) into the Ministry of Information Technology (MIT), which has been entrusted to a prominent Cabinet minister. One of the key challenges of this ministry remains the creation of suitable infrastructure (Donald, 2001).

What are the factors that have led to the success of the Indian industry? Kundu and Katz (2000) have determined that managerial characteristics such as entrepreneurs' educational background, technological innovativeness and strategic orientation have played a vital role. According to Correa (1996), factors such as the widespread use of the English language, apart from programmers' skill and quick response to demand, have contributed to success; he warns other developing economies that some of these factors (such as the use of the English language) have a historical basis that other countries (such as, for example, Latin American countries) will find difficult to easily emulate. Although the widespread availability of technical education in India is often mentioned, Merchant (2001c) points out that supply of such education still falls well short of demand. The competencies of software professionals, stemming from their training and experience (Ram and Jagadish, 1999), professional treatment of employees in the better software firms (Agarwal, 1999) and network relationships with Indian software entrepreneurs in Silicon Valley, USA (Luce, 2001; Murdoch, 2000) have been other success factors.

Indian software international entrepreneurs: four examples
As mentioned, the success of Indian software entrepreneurs has led to young entrepreneurs being encouraged to launch their own software start-ups. The following is a brief account of four such entrepreneurs, who were interviewed in Bangalore recently, in terms of their background, knowledge, intent, networks and view of policy. It gives an indication of diverse routes that entrepreneurs take to end up founding and leading a software firm in India. Names have been withheld to protect their identity.

Firm VGS
Firm VGS was started by an engineer upon his graduation in 1995 because of the 'fire in [his] belly', despite pressure from his parents to study further and become the first postgraduate in the family. He is neither from a prestigious Indian university nor foreign-trained, yet his passion 'to do something innovative' led him to pursue aggressively his entrepreneurial dreams.

His knowledge base is constantly evolving, guided by market trends; having begun in software services he is leading the company into a diversification into Information Technology Enabled Services (ITES), such as call centres. His intent, in terms of internationalization, has been to avoid popular and highly competitive markets such as the USA. Instead, he has focused on Australia, recently setting up a one-man marketing team there; his next targets are the 'virgin territories' of South Africa and Zimbabwe. His networks have mainly been domestic, with only recently proactive measures being taken to acquire and cultivate network relationships overseas.

The government, he says, has failed to make life easier for entrepreneurs and he has experienced many instances of running from pillar to post in order to get things done for the business. Policy measures are often half-baked according to him; for instance, the government may improve roads but 'forget that power also is essential'.

Firm NC

Firm NC was started by a computer professional trained at Rutgers University, after spending 10 years in the USA. Although he harboured the occasional desire to become an entrepreneur at some point, his decision to start NC was precipitated by a family crisis which forced him to return to his home town of Bangalore in 2000. He was given a project to work on by a former American client.

His knowledge base is a function of his more recent work in the USA and deals primarily with e-commerce. His intent appears to be to remain fully focused on international business, as he feels he has a long way to go before establishing himself in India. Towards this end, he relies heavily on the Internet – through B2B portals such as that of *The Economist* magazine and NeoIT – for international business in non-American markets. His networks primarily stem from professional contacts in the USA, and he is trying to expand these by engaging business development contractors who, for a commission, canvass the wares of Indian firms in foreign markets.

In his experience, the government, specifically the Software Technology Parks of India (STPI), can be very bureaucratic. While seeking to move premises, he found the paperwork and formalities to be cumbersome and unnecessarily multiple; a single-window mechanism would make things a lot easier, he feels.

Firm E

Firm E was started by a computer professional who studied at the University of Texas in Austin and stayed on in the USA for a brief professional stint. At Austin he had also attended entrepreneurship classes at the business school, clearly indicating an interest in starting up his own firm, which he did upon his return to India in 1996, after calculating that that could be more remunerative than a salaried job at an IT firm.

His knowledge was chiefly Internet-oriented, based on his training and professional experience in the USA. Accordingly, his firm's chief mandate has been 'to help firms get onto the Net'. However, his knowledge base has evolved over time, expanding with client needs, especially those of loyal customers. To that extent he feels that he has ceased to be a specialist and has become more of a generalist. His intent in terms of geographic focus has been flexible and it took three years before he received his first international contract – an unsolicited order from a British firm who located him through Firm E's Web site and were impressed thereafter by his speed of response to requests for information and proposals. His networks today seem to comprise primarily existing clients, although a few orders did come as a consequence of professional contacts in the USA.

In terms of government-related bodies, he has mainly dealt with the Software Technology Parks of India (STPI), and has found his association with them beneficial, although he finds certain rules pertaining to customs bonding to be obsolete. Furthermore, he feels that small firms in general do not have much of a voice in industry associations.

Firm M

Firm M was spun off from Motorola's Indian operations and is unique in terms of its focus on being a 'pure product player'; in other words, it offers packaged solutions rather than the customary software services offered by most Indian software firms (including the three discussed above). The directors of Firm M are graduates of prestigious business and engineering schools in India and abroad; the CEO is an alumnus of the Indian Institute of Managament in Ahmedabad, India's premier business school. The timing of the directors' decision to propose the spin-off successfully coincides, rather significantly, with the craze for Internet start-ups. Not surprisingly, the company offers a software product for software companies that it describes as 'Web-native'. Nonetheless, the relevance of the offering has remained undiminished even after the collapse of most dot-coms.

The knowledge of the CEO and his core team follows from the work carried out initially at Motorola and from prior education. The intent has been to aim at software firms across the world in a cluster-by-cluster approach after initially operating in India, with a view to refining the product before launching overseas. It is envisaged, however, that in less than five years the vast majority of business will be from abroad. The networks, to which much attention is paid, emanate from Motorola and business school contacts, as well as venture capitalists and senior IT and business professionals who have been formally inducted as company 'advisors'.

While the CEO of Firm M did not voice any strong reservation about government policy, he felt that product-oriented firms did not receive quite the impetus or supportive industry forums that they needed – and even deserved.

Conclusion: implications for theory building, entrepreneurship and policy

In terms of theory building, the foregoing discussion has brought out the inadequacy of research in developing economy contexts and would suggest that greater collaborative research among scholars in developed and developing economies will bridge the knowledge gap that seems to exist in terms of theory building. A related issue is the need for forums and publications (such as this book) where insights about various economy contexts can be disseminated to wide audiences of international entrepreneurs. Such efforts, it is suggested, will be of mutual benefit and international entrepreneurs based in developed economies may well find that they have useful lessons to learn, especially in relation to innovative behaviour, from their counterparts in developing economies who often have to make do with fewer resources and therefore are forced to devise ingenious ways of succeeding.

In terms of managerial practice, software entrepreneurs in India and, indeed, elsewhere in developing economies, would do well to address at least three issues that are emerging. First is the issue of *services versus products*; in other words, firms are having to face competitive pressure to cease being mere low-level code providers and upgrade their offerings to packaged solutions or products. Second is the issue of *software versus Information Technology Enabled Services (ITES)*; in other words, software firms are faced with the question of whether or not to diversify in light of emerging opportunities such as ITES, of which call centres constitute a prominent example. Long-term success will need to be balanced with short-term revenue goals. Third is the issue of *small versus large firms*; in other words, small firms are finding it increasingly hard to survive as large players strive to gain business in a very sluggish world economy, and achieving greater knowledge intensity in specialized domains appears to be fast becoming mandatory for SKIFs. This in turn will enhance – and make even more challenging – their scope for and efforts towards internationalization. Indeed, it is a matter of survival.

In terms of policy making, governments in developing economies should seek to provide international entrepreneurs with advanced training inputs and enhance their network relationships through mentoring programmes; useful insight can be obtained from the Irish experience discussed elsewhere in this book (see Chapter 27). In the specific case of India, serious attention must be paid to various policy issues including definition of small firms, financing, rules and procedures, technology applications, cluster formation and strategy formulation (Gulati, 1997; Krishnan, 1997; Mahibala, 1997; Prabhu, 1997; Ramu, 1997; Sundarajan, 1997; Thampy and Kulkarni, 1997). From the interviews it is evident that infrastructure in terms of power, communication facilities and transportation needs to be improved and common interest groups facilitated for international entrepreneurs. In relation to exports, areas that require improvement include access to marketing information, international promotion, and procedures and documentation (Jain and Kapoor, 1994).

494   *Geographic perspectives*

References

Aaby, N.-E. and Slater, S.F. (1989), 'Management Influences on Export Performance: A Review of the Empirical Literature 1978–88', *International Marketing Review*, 6 (4), 7–26.

Acs, Z.J., Morck, R. and Yeung, B. (1999), 'Evolution, Community, and the Global Economy', in Z.J. Acs (ed.), *Are Small Firms Important?: Their Role and Impact*, Norwell, MA: Kluwer Academic Publishers, pp. 147–58.

Agarwal, N.M. (1999), 'Managing Knowledge Workers: Benchmarking Indian IT Organisations', *Management Review*, June, 81–92.

Almeida, P. (1999), 'Semiconductor Startups and the Exploration of New Technological Territory', in Z.J. Acs (ed.), *Are Small Firms Important?: Their Role and Impact*, Norwell, MA: Kluwer Academic Publishers, pp. 39–50.

Alvesson, M. (1993), 'Organizations as Rhetoric: Knowledge-Intensive Firms and the Struggle with Ambiguity', *Journal of Management Studies*, 30 (6), 997–1015.

Alvesson, M. (1995), *Management of Knowledge-Intensive Firms*, Berlin: De Grutyer.

Andersen, O. (1993), 'On the Internationalisation Process of Firms: A Critical Analysis', *Journal of International Business Studies*, 24 (2), 209–31.

Anderson, E. and Gatignon, H. (1986), 'Modes of Foreign Entry', *Journal of International Business Studies*, 17 (3), 1–26.

Audretsch, D.B. (1999), 'Small Firms and Efficiency', in Z.J. Acs (ed.), *Are Small Firms Important?: Their Role and Impact*, Norwell, MA: Kluwer Academic Publishers, pp. 21–38.

Autio, E., Sapienza, H.J. and Almeida, J.G. (2000), 'Effects of age at entry, knowledge intensity, and imitability on international growth', *Academy of Management Journal*, 43 (5), 909–24.

Baker, M.J. (1979), 'Export Myopia', *The Quarterly Review of Marketing*, Spring, 1–10.

Becherer, R.C. and Maurer, J.G. (1997), 'The moderating effect of environmental variables on the entrepreneurial and marketing orientation of entrepreneur-led firms', *Entrepreneurship Theory and Practice*, 22 (1), 47–58.

Bell, J. (1995), 'The internationalization of small computer software firms', *European Journal of Marketing*, 29 (8), 60–75.

Bell, J. and Young, S. (1998), 'Towards an Integrative Framework of the Internationalization of the Firm', in G. Hooley, R. Loveridge and D. Wilson (eds), *Internationalization: Process, Context and Markets*, London: Macmillan, pp. 5–28.

Berry, M.M.J. (1998), 'Strategic Planning in Small Tech Firms', *Long Range Planning*, 31 (3), 455–66.

Bhagwathi, J. (1966), *The Economics of Underdeveloped Countries*, New York: World University Library (McGraw-Hill).

Bhide, A. (1994), 'How Entrepreneurs Craft Strategies That Work', *Harvard Business Review*, 72 (2) (March–April), 150–61.

Bilkey, W.J. and Tesar, G. (1977), 'The Export Behavior of Smaller Sized Wisconsin Manufacturing Firms', *Journal of International Business Studies*, 8 (1), 93–8.

Brown, P. and Bell, J. (2000), 'Industrial Clusters and Small Firm Internationalisation', in S. Young and N. Hood (eds), *27th Annual Conference UK Chapter Academy of International Business: The Multinational in the Millennium: Companies and Countries, Changes and Choices*, volume 1, Glasgow: University of Strathclyde, pp. 73–96

Brown, P. and McNaughton, R. (2000), 'Cluster development programmes: Panacea or placebo for promoting SME growth and internationalisation?', paper presented at the Conference on International Entrepreneurship: Researching New Frontiers, 23–5 September, Montreal, Canada.

Calof, J.L. and Beamish, P.W. (1995), 'Adapting to Foreign Markets: Explaining Internationalization', *International Business Review*, 4 (2), 115–31.

Calof, J.L. and Viviers, W. (1995), 'Internationalization Behaviour of Small- and Medium-sized South African Enterprises', *Journal of Small Business Management*, 33 (4), 71–79.

Carlsson, B. (1999), 'Small Business, Entrepreneurship, and Industrial Dynamics', in Z.J. Acs (ed.), *Are Small Firms Important?: Their Role and Impact*, Norwell, MA: Kluwer Academic Publishers, pp. 99–110.

Chetty, S.K. and Hamilton, R.T. (1993), 'Firm-level Determinants of Export Performance: A Meta-analysis', *International Marketing Review*, 10 (3), 26–34.

Correa, C.M. (1996), 'Strategies for Software Exports from Developing Countries', *World Development*, 24 (1), 171–82.

Coviello, N. and Munro, H. (1995), 'Growing the Entrepreneurial Firm: Networking for International Market Development', *European Journal of Marketing*, 29 (7), 49–61.

Coviello, N. and Munro, H. (1997), 'Network Relationships and the Internationalization Process of Small Software Firms', *International Business Review*, 6, (4), 361–86.

Coviello, N.E. and McAuley, A. (1999), 'Internationalisation and the Smaller Firm: A Review of the Contemporary Empirical Research', *Management International Review*, 39 (3), 223–56.

Crick, D. and Jones, M.V. (2000), 'Small high-technology firms and international high-technology markets', *Journal of International Marketing*, 8 (2), 63–85.

Dana, L.P. (2000), 'Creating Entrepreneurs in India', *Journal of Small Business Management*, 38 (1), 86–91.

Daniel, C. (2001), 'Confident mood persists as challenge gathers pace', *FT-IT Review (with Financial Times)*, 21 February, p.XV.

Das, M. (1994), 'Successful and Unsuccessful Exporters from Developing Countries: Some Preliminary Findings', *European Journal of Marketing*, 28 (12), 19–33.

Donald, A. (2001), 'Infrastructure bottlenecks hinder IT expansion', *FT-IT Review (with Financial Times)*, 21 February, p.XVI.

Dunning, J.H. (1988), 'The Eclectic Paradigm of International Production: A Restatement and Some Possible Extensions', *Journal of International Business Studies*, 18 (1), 1–30.

Elkjaer, B. (2000), 'Learning and getting to know: the case of knowledge workers', *Human Resource Development International*, 3 (3), 343–59.

Enright, M.J. (1999), 'The Globalization of Competition and the Localization of Competitive Advantage: Policies Towards Regional Clustering', in N. Hood and S. Young (eds), *The Globalization of Multinational Enterprise Activity and Economic Development*, London: Macmillan, pp. 303–32.

Erramilli, M.K. and Rao, C.P. (1993), 'Service Firms' International Entry Mode Choice: A Modified Transaction Cost Analysis Approach', *Journal of Marketing*, 57 (3) (July), 19–38.

Fontes, M. and Coombs, R. (1995), 'New technology-based firms and technology acquisition in Portugal: firms' adaptive responses to a less favourable environment', *Technovation*, 15 (8), 497–510.

Goetz, S.J. and Freshwater, D. (2001), 'State-Level Determinants of Entrepreneurship and a Preliminary Measure of Entrepreneurial Climate', *Economic Development Quarterly*, 15 (1), 58–70.

Gulati, M. (1997), 'Industrial Clusters and SSI Development', *Management Review*, October–December, 97–103.

Hadjimanolis, A. (2000a), 'A Resource-based View of Innovativeness in Small Firms', *Technology Analysis & Strategic Management*, 12 (2), 262–81.

Hadjimanolis, A. (2000b), 'An investigation of innovation antecedents in small firms in the context of a small developing country', *R&D Management*, 30 (3), 235–45.

Hagel, J. and Singer, M. (1999), 'Unbundling the Corporation', *Harvard Business Review*, 77 (2) (March–April), 133–41.

Hamel, G. (1996), 'Strategy as Revolution', *Harvard Business Review*, 74 (4) (July–August), 69–82.

Heitzman, J. (1997), 'High Technology Entrepreneurship and Development in Bangalore', *Management Review*, October–December, 85–96.

Ibeh, K.I.N. and Young, S. (2001), 'Exporting as an entrepreneurial act: An empirical study of Nigerian firms', *European Journal of Marketing*, 35 (5/6), 566–86.

Jain, S.K. and Kapoor, M.C. (1996), 'Export Attitudes and Behaviour in India: A Pilot Study', *Journal of Global Marketing*, 10 (2), 75–95.

Johanson, J. and Mattsson, L-G. (1988), 'Internationalization in Industrial Systems – A Network Approach', in N. Hood and J.-E. Vahlne (eds), *Strategies in Global Competition*, London: Croom Helm, pp. 287–314.

Johanson, J. and Vahlne, J-E. (1977), 'The Internationalization Process of the Firm – A Model of Knowledge Development and Increasing Foreign Market Commitment', *Journal of International Business Studies*, 8 (Spring/Summer), 23–32.

Johanson, J. and Vahlne, J-E. (1990), 'The Mechanism of Internationalization', *International Marketing Review*, 7 (4), 11–24.

Johanson, J. and Vahlne, J-E. (1992), 'Management of Foreign Market Entry', *Scandinavian International Business Review*, 1 (3), 9–27.

Johanson, J. and Wiedersheim-Paul, F. (1975), 'The Internationalization of the Firm – Four Swedish Cases', *Journal of Management Studies*, 12, 305–22.

Johnson, J.E. (1999), 'Towards a success factor framework for global start-ups', *Global Focus*, 11 (3), 73–84.

Jones, M.V. (1999), 'The internationalization of small high-technology firms', *Journal of International Marketing*, 7 (4), 15–41.

Khanna, T. and Palepu, K. (1999), 'The Right Way to Restructure Conglomerates in Emerging Markets', *Harvard Business Review* (July–August), 125–34.

Knight, G.A. and Cavusgil, S.T. (1996), 'The born global firm: a challenge to traditional internationalisation theory, *Advances in International Marketing*, 8, 11–26.

Krishnan, R.T. (1997), 'Is Strategy Important for Small Companies', *Management Review*, October–December, 105–11.

Kundu, S.K. and Katz, J.A. (2000), 'The Internationalization of Small Firms: An Empirical Study of the Indian Software Industry', paper presented at the Conference on International Entrepreneurship: Researching New Frontiers, 23–5 September, Montreal, Canada.

Leonidou, L. and Katsikeas, C.S. (1996), 'The Export Development Process: An Integrative Review of Empirical Models', *Journal of International Business Studies*, 27 (3), 517–51.

Lerner, J. (1999), 'Small Business, Innovation, and Public Policy', in Z.J. Acs (ed.), *Are Small Firms Important?: Their Role and Impact*, Norwell, MA: Kluwer Academic Publishers, pp. 159–68.

Luce, E. (2001), 'India lures the expat dollar', *Financial Times*, 28 February, p. 17.

Lumpkin, G.T. and Dess, G.G. (1996), 'Clarifying the entrepreneurial orientation construct and linking it to performance', *The Academy of Management Review*, 21 (1), 135–172.

Maddy, M. (2000), 'Dream Deferred: The Story of a High-Tech Entrepreneur in a Low-Tech World', *Harvard Business Review*, 78 (3) (May–June), 56–69.

Madhok, A. (1996), 'Know-how-, Experience-, and Competition-related Considerations in Foreign Market Entry: an Exploratory Investigation', *International Business Review*, 5 (4), 339–60.

Madsen, T.K. and Servais, P. (1997), 'The Internationalization of Born Globals: an Evolutionary Process?', *International Marketing Review*, 6 (6), 561–83.

Mahibala, M. (1997), 'SSIs: Simplifying Rules and Procedures', *Management Review*, October–December, 69–70.

Manimala, M.J. (1992a), 'Entrepreneurial Heuristics: A Comparison Between High PI (Pioneering-Innovative) and Low PI Ventures', *Journal of Business Venturing*, 7 (6), 477–504.

Manimala, M.J. (1992b), 'Innovative Entrepreneurship: Testing the Theory of Environmental Determinism', in B.L. Maheshwari (ed.), *Innovations in Management for Development*, New Delhi: Tata McGraw-Hill Publishing Co., pp. 100–118.

Manimala, M.J. (1992c), 'Entrepreneurial Innovation: Beyond Schumpeter', *Creativity and Innovation Management*, 1 (1) (March), 46–55.

Manimala, M.J. (1992d), 'New Venture Strategies: The Innovators' Choice', *The Journal of Social and Economic Studies*, 3–21.

McDougall, P.P. and Oviatt, B.M. (2000), 'International Entrepreneurship: The Intersection of Two Research Paths', *Academy of Management Journal*, 43 (5), 902–6.

McDougall, P.P., Shane, S., and Oviatt, B.M. (1994), 'Explaining the Formation of International New Ventures: The Limits of Theories from International Business Research', *Journal of Business Venturing*, 9, 469–87.

McNamee, P., Greenan, K. and McFerran, B. (2000), 'Shifting the predominant cultural paradigm in small businesses through active competitive benchmarking', *Journal of Strategic Marketing*, 8, 241–55.

Merchant, K. (2001a), 'Sector hopes it can turn problems into solutions/India's software exporters serve an increasingly global market', *FT-IT Review (with Financial Times)*, 21 February, pp.XIII–XIV.

Merchant, K. (2001b), 'Defining the Indian software brand in a competitive world', *FT-IT Review (with Financial Times)*, 21 February, p.XIV.

Merchant, K. (2001c), 'Supply fails to meet demand', *FT-IT Review (with Financial Times)*, 21 February, p.XVI.

Merchant, K. (2001d), 'India learns language of customer service', *Financial Times*, 4 April, p. 14.

Mintzberg, H. and Lampel, J. (1999), 'Reflecting on the Strategy Process', *Sloan Management Review*, 40 (Spring), 21–30.

Murdoch, A. (2000), 'India: A Software Giant Awakens', *Scotland on Sunday*, 5 December, p. 5.

Murthy, K.R.S. (1999), 'The Challenge of Globalisation for Indian Family Business', *Management Review*, March, 95–102.

Naidu, G.M., Cavusgil, S.T., Murthy, B.K. and Sarkar, M. (1997), 'An Export Promotion Model for India: Implications for Public Policy', *International Business Review*, 6 (2), 113–25.

Nurmi, R. 1998), 'Knowledge-Intensive Firms', *Business Horizons*, May–June, 26–32.

O'Farrell, P.N., Wood, P.A. and Zheng, J. (1998), 'Regional Influences on Foreign Market Development by Business Service Companies: Elements of a Strategic Context Explanation', *Regional Studies*, 32 (1), 31–48.

Oviatt, B.M. and McDougall, P.P. (1994), 'Toward a Theory of New International Ventures', *Journal of International Business Studies*, 25, (1), 45–64.

Oviatt, B.M. and McDougall, P.P. (1997), 'Challenges for internationalization process theory', *Management International Review*, 37 (2), 85–99.

Porter, M.E. (1990), 'The Competitive Advantage of Nations', *Harvard Business Review*, 58 (2) (March–April).

Prabhu, G.N. (1997), 'SSIs and Technology Management', *Management Review*, October–December, 75–8.

Ram, V.A. and Jagadish, S. (1999), 'Project Managers in the Software Industry – A Competency Profile', *Management Review*, June, 67–74.

Ramu, S.S. (1997), 'Small Industries Policy', *Management Review*, October–December, pp. 51–6.

Rao, P.M. and Klein, J.A. (1994) 'Growing Importance of Marketing Strategies for the Software Industry', *Industrial Marketing Management*, 23, 29–37.

Rasmussen, E.S. and Madsen, T.K. (1999), 'The Founding of the Born Global Company in Denmark and Australia', paper presented at the 7th Cross Cultural Consumer and Business Studies Research Conference, 12–15 December, Canun, Mexico.

Rennie, M.W. (1993), 'Global competitiveness: Born global', *The McKinsey Quarterly* (4), 45–54.

Sadagopan, S. (1999), 'Information Technology: Redefining Boundaries', *Management Review*, June, 49–66.

Saxenien, A. (1990), 'Regional Networks and the Resurgence of Silicon Valley', *California Management Review*, Fall, 89–112.

Sundarajan, S. (1997), 'Promoting Entrepreneurship: Future Policy Directions', *Management Review*, October–December, 49–50.

Tenkasi, R.V. and Boland, R.J. (1996), 'Exploring knowledge diversity in knowledge intensive firms: a new role for information systems', *Journal of Organizational Change*, 9 (1), 79–91.

Thampy, A. and Kulkarni, P.S. (1997), 'Financing SSIs: Two Perspectives', *Management Review*, October–December, 57–64.

Turnbull, P.W. (1987), 'A Challenge to the Stages Theory of the Internationalization Process', in S. Reid and P. Rosson (eds), *Managing Export Entry and Expansion*, New York: Praeger.

Tzokas, N., Carter, S. and Kyriazopoulos, P. (2001), 'Marketing and Entrepreneurial Orientation in Small Firms', *Enterprise and Innovation Management Studies*, 2 (1), 19–33.
Vachani, S. (1997), 'Economic Liberalization's Effect on Sources of Competitive Advantage of Different Groups of Companies: The Case of India', *International Business Review*, 6 (2), 165–84.
Welch, L.S., and Luostarinen, R. (1988), 'Internationalization: Evolution of a Concept', *Journal of General Management*, 14 (2), 36–64.
Young, S. (1987), 'Business Strategy and the Internationalization of Business: Recent Approaches', *Managerial and Decision Economics*, 8, 31–40.
Young, S., Hamill, J., Wheeler, C. and Davies, J.R. (1989), *International Market Entry and Development*, Hemel Hempstead: Harvester Wheatsheaf.
Zahra, S.A. and Neubaum, D.O. (1998), 'Environmental adversity and the entrepreneurial activities of new ventures', *Journal of Developmental Entrepreneurship*, 3 (2), 123–40.

27 Irish perspectives on developing international entrepreneurs

Jim Bell, David Demick, Ian Callaghan and Aidan O'Reilly

Despite growing policy and research interest in small firm internationalization (Coviello and McAuley, 1999), little attention has been focused on the international dimensions of entrepreneurship (Oviatt and McDougall, 1994; Mostafa and Wheeler, 2001) and even less on the personal and professional development of international entrepreneurs. The need to address these issues is particularly important in light of the emergence of smaller entrepreneurial 'born global' firms that have been able to take advantage of technological advances to internationalize rapidly (McKinsey & Co., 1993; Coviello, 1994; McDougall *et al.*, 1994; Knight and Cavusgil, 1996).

Much has been written on the topic of entrepreneurship and enterprise development (Cromie *et al.*, 1992; Gibb, 1993, 1996; Carson *et al.*, 1995; Westhead and Storey, 1997; Carter and Jones-Evans, 2000; Kurato and Welsch, 2001). Indeed the importance of developing practical skills to support entrepreneurial activities is a central theme in the extant literature. However, Mumford (1993) also contends that 'individuals can learn but are unlikely to be taught' and Vickerstaff and Parker (1995) observe that 'informal on-the-job training is the mainstay of training activities' in smaller enterprise. To foster these skills in international entrepreneurs, development programmes should focus upon 'learning experiences' (Gibb, 1997), rather than formal training content, building on on-the-job learning opportunities. This can be achieved through the involvement of experienced mentors working with groups of small firms on the 'hands-on' application of relevant concepts.

In addition to these mentoring activities, Dubini and Aldrich (1991) contend that networks have a major role to play in the development of entrepreneurial skills, given that 'personal contact networks are a useful tool for entrepreneurs who wish to enlarge their spans of action and save time'. Butler and Hansen (1981) suggest that these personal networks are a decision support mechanism that can play a significant role in introducing a more disciplined approach to entrepreneurial decision making. Carson (1993) also argues the need for personal contact networks to be formalized.

The importance of these entrepreneurial networks is widely recognized in the literature (Birley, 1985; Szarka, 1990; Axelsson and Easton, 1992; Saxenian, 1992; Grotz and Braun, 1993; Malecki and Veldhoen, 1993; Human and Provan, 1997). Also evident is growing policy maker enthusiasm for their role in regional and national economic development (Cooke and Morgan, 1993; Ferland *et al.*, 1994, Todtling, 1994; Rosenfeld, 1996; White *et al.*, 1996). Business support agencies and academic institutions can play a valuable role in fostering the formation, development and 'formalization' of such networks.

Collectively the present authors have accumulated extensive experience in international business education, have been involved in various initiatives to internationalize Irish entrepreneurial firms and have undertaken export-focused small-firm development assignations elsewhere (Bell and Brown, 1990; Demick, 1997; Demick and O'Reilly, 2000). This chapter describes, discusses and evaluates academic and public policy involvement in four specific initiatives that seek to develop international entrepreneurial competencies within Irish SMEs. These include the Explorers Programme, an internationally focused Teaching Company scheme, the Small Business Export Development Programme and the Accelerated Export Development Programme. We contend that each of these offerings has interesting international entrepreneurship and network development features that are eminently transferable to other locations.

Irish initiatives
Explorers
This offering has its origins in an Export Market Development Programme (EMDP) that was first introduced in Ireland in 1988. In its original format the programme involved academics, firms and development agencies in both parts of Ireland and offered two programmes, one focusing on the EU and the other on North America. (For a detailed description of the modus operandi of the EMDP, together with a comprehensive evaluation of programme outcomes, see Bell *et al.*, 1992). In its present form, it involves Northern Ireland firms, focuses primarily on Europe and North America but also includes other international markets. *Explorers* is delivered by Edge, a Northern Ireland consulting firm with offices in Amsterdam, Boston, Singapore and Sydney (see *www.edge.plc*). Invest Northern Ireland, the government body responsible for economic development, provides assistance for participating firms and graduates.

In summary, every year *Explorers* attaches some 80 recent graduates to a similar number of exporting firms. The majority of these firms are small entrepreneurial SMEs that, typically, employ 50–100 staff and have an annual turnover of $5–10 million. After a ten-week period of in-company training, the graduate spends approximately six months in the target foreign market conducting research and undertaking specific tasks to secure business for their host company in the international market.

The benefits derived by both parties are self-evident. The young graduate gains excellent practical experience in an international environment and in over 75% of cases is actually offered permanent employment by the company in an overseas position. Companies obtain additional human capital in the form of well-educated graduates with specialization in areas such as business, engineering, information technology or modern languages. Very often these resources address very specific resource gaps for the firm.

Companies are expected to contribute approximately US$15–20 thousand in order to take part in an *Explorers* programme. This amount varies according to the particular market under investigation, the specific nature of the project and the pre-agreed travel budget required for the graduate to accomplish the necessary tasks. However, the actual cost involved is significantly more, but is subsidized on a 50/50 basis by Invest Northern Ireland, the sponsoring government agency. Graduates taking part in the programme receive a training allowance and have their living expenses met while abroad. By participating in *Explorers*, they are eligible to sit examinations for the Advanced Certificate in International Trade, an internationally recognized qualification.

In terms of specific outcomes, a recent independent evaluation of the programme estimated that over US$60 million of additional export sales have been generated by some 500 *Explorers* projects undertaken since 1993. In addition:

- 90% of firms indicated it had improved their export performance/ capability,
- 60% of firms repeat the programme after one or two years for other markets,
- 70% of firms stated that their projects either fully met or exceeded expectations,
- 69% of projects also develop into further business opportunities.

From the graduates' perspective, some 50% accepted positions within the host firm and over 90% found employment within six months of completing *Explorers*. Most of these posts were in Irish exporting firms, but some were with international companies.

Explorers has recently been awarded ISO9001 status and Edge received a UK National Training Award in 2000. It is highly regarded by all the economic development bodies in Northern Ireland and also by the Northern Ireland Chamber of Commerce, the NI branch of the Confederation of

British Industry and the Institute of Export. In addition, the programme has attracted policy-maker interest in other countries. Edge has recently piloted a similar programme in Singapore and intends to roll it out in a number of other locations.

Teaching company schemes (TCS)
These involve a tripartite partnership between academia, industry and government agencies and are intended to facilitate technology transfer from universities to firms, utilizing a graduate 'associate' as a conduit (see *www.tcd.co.uk*). The Teaching Company programme is available throughout the UK, Northern Ireland being one of the best performing regions, with 19 current schemes and over 200 previous collaborations. In the main, these schemes involve engineering, science and technology projects, where the 'associate' works on some aspect of product development under the supervision of an academic mentor.

However, they can also be used to help firms to develop new domestic or international markets. In these cases the 'knowledge transfer' dimension from the academic institution is marketing knowledge. Such schemes quite often also involve a scientific and business dimension, where the firm is seeking new export markets, but where existing product offerings need to be adapted or new products need to be developed to meet different conditions or consumer requirements.

Typically a Teaching Company scheme will last for two years, but it may involve several associates over a three-year period. During the scheme the associate is on the university payroll, but he/she works for the company. The university receives funding to pay the associate's salary, 'buy out' a proportion of the supervising academic's time, provide administrative support and contribute to overheads. Built into the funding is a training and development budget to enable the associate to attend courses or address identified skill deficits. Often the associate will register with the university partner for postgraduate studies or a higher degree. The participating firm and the Teaching Company directorate finance the total cost of the scheme in a 40/60 ratio. The cost of a two-year project is usually in the region of US$100–120 thousand and the net cost to the firm is some US$20–25 thousand per annum.

Bell and Demick (1996), describe one such scheme. This involved Valpar Industrial, an Irish SME seeking to develop the market in Australasia for beverage dispensing products used in the soft drinks and beer industry (see *http://www.valpar.co.uk*). The project involved a detailed investigation of the Australasian region, including the Australian, New Zealand, Japanese and Singaporean markets. The associate then developed appropriate market entry modes for each market and identified key channel partners before implementing the product and market development strategy.

As an outcome of the programme the firm has established significant business in all major markets in the region and has since expanded its activities into China. When the firm received the Queen's Award for Export Achievement, it generously recognized the support it had received from the university through the Teaching Company scheme. The associate was offered and accepted employment within the company as export sales and marketing manager. After a number of years in this position, she was appointed as European marketing manager for another Irish SME.

A new initiative in a similar vein and modus operandi is the *Fusion* programme offered by Inter*trade* Ireland, the recently formed Irish cross-border trade organization (see *http://www.intertradeireland.com*). The main difference from the TCS scheme is that *Fusion* requires the academic partner to be located in Northern Ireland and the participating firm in the Republic of Ireland, or vice versa, thus encouraging cross-border collaboration. Funding mechanisms are also slightly different, but the technology-transfer dimension of the *Fusion* programme is very comparable to that of the Teaching Company scheme.

At present a pilot programme is operating with approximately 20 firms in the Irish border regions, but there are very strong indications that, once this initial offering has been formally evaluated, a full-scale programme will be rolled out within the next 18–24 months.

The Export Development Programme
During the early 1990s it was increasingly recognized that the survival, growth and competitiveness of many small businesses in Northern Ireland would depend on their determination and ability to source business in external markets, primarily because the domestic market is too small. As a result, the government-funded agency was charged with developing SMEs and the Local Enterprise Development Unit (LEDU) launched an Export Development Programme (EDP) in 1995.

Through this programme LEDU seeks to provide participating companies with the confidence and knowledge required to enable them to identify, enter and develop new export markets. Specifically, the objectives of the EDP are the following:

- to develop greater export market awareness and orientation among participating firms;
- to increase awareness of the issues involved in exporting;
- to generate export sales outside the British Isles, with a target that such business should account for 10% of total sales within 12 months and 15% within two years;

- to facilitate the development of practical and realistic export marketing plans;
- to facilitate the successful implementation of these export marketing plans.

Overall, the desired programme outputs are the removal of barriers to export growth among small entrepreneurial firms and the development and adoption of more strategic approaches to international markets, with firms entering and remaining in at least one new export market. In the process of seeking to meet these objectives and outcomes, it was envisaged that the export management competencies and skills of each participating firm would be enhanced.

The overall EDP process consists of eight months of planned activities based on residential events, workshop inputs and mentoring from a local consultant. The mentoring meetings with firms are designed to stimulate, plan and track the progress of their export development activities. Specifically, mentoring involves a combination of (a) diagnosing the company's exporting needs, (b) identifying practical solutions to address export needs, (c) assisting in developing a practical export plan, and (d) helping prepare for a visit to an export market. In addition to the mentoring from the local consultant, participants benefit from the assistance of a consultant based in the target export market. He or she provides the company with market intelligence, useful contacts and logistic support for the market visit.

Formal inputs are designed for both training and interactive activity (such as export selling techniques) and to provide an opportunity for networking with other participants, guest speakers and trainers. To date, in excess of 250 companies have taken part in a series of EDP programmes. The cost to firms is minimal, typically less than US$2000, and is supported by the sponsoring agency that meets up to 50% of the programme costs.

The Accelerated Export Development Programme (AEDP)
Industrial regeneration and job creation in the border regions of Ireland have been highlighted as an important priority by policy makers in both parts of Ireland. This emphasis reflects the need to provide additional non-agricultural employment in rural areas and to support the development of existing local SMEs that are facing greater competitive challenges due to locational disadvantages.

A more specific programme than the EDP reported above is the Accelerated Export Development Programme. This initiative is supported by An Bord Trachtala and Invest Northern Ireland and funded by the European Union, the Peace and Reconciliation Fund and government sources. Additionally, firms pay a fee of about US$5000.

The key objective of the programme is to assist SMEs from Northern Ireland and the Republic of Ireland to accelerate their export development. Specifically, it is anticipated that, on average, the SMEs will double their annual export sales or achieve an additional £500000 (c. US$750000) in annual export turnover, whichever is the larger, within two years of project completion. In the process of seeking to meet these objectives, it is envisaged that the export management competencies and skills of each participating firm will be enhanced. The outcomes are achieved through the firms gaining confidence, knowledge and skills to enter at least one new export market. In order to provide firms with a planning framework and encourage them to adopt more structured approaches, a central element of the programme is the development and implementation of an export-marketing plan covering a three-year period.

The AEDP project management team consists of a project director and two senior advisors (both academics at the University of Ulster, with extensive prior industrial experience). The overall AEDP process consists of 15 days of activities per annum (including three overnight residential workshops of two days each). These involve all participating SMEs and enable the CEO/manager and management team to network and share market information on focused export markets in a self-help peer group learning situation. The in-company project days take the form of a monthly mentoring meeting with the management team designed to stimulate, plan and track the progress of the export development activities. An agreed agenda for each meeting ensures a discipline so often missing in SME management.

Specifically, mentoring meetings involve a combination of the following activities:

- strategic capability analysis,
- export opportunity investigations,
- analysis of technology transfer potential,
- export strategic plan and priorities from present product portfolio and technology transfer plans,
- export human resource capability,
- management information systems strengthening plan,
- export buyer network management,
- export product quality, adaptation and packaging,
- export promotion plan,
- export finance plan,
- export logistics and delivery systems,
- export monitoring system design and review.

An innovation in the current programme involves company 'hosting', where firms take it in turn to invite the other participants to their premises to showcase their premises, organize a presentation on the firm's activities and business strategy and provide a luncheon or reception.

To date some 20 Irish SMEs have taken part in the pilot and current programme. They are drawn from a variety of sectors including the agri-food industry, construction, consumer products, furniture, giftware and industrial plastics and information technology. The rationale for a cross-industry programme is to ensure good representation from important Irish sectors and to avoid a situation where the programme is overly focused on any given sector. This approach also helps to prevent any difficulties that may arise owing to commercial confidentiality or sensitivity.

Participant firms on both the pilot and current programme were carefully selected using the following criteria:

- firms already selling into Republic of Ireland (or Great Britain in the case of companies from the Republic);
- owners/key decision makers who were highly motivated to expand exports;
- a product range or potential new product(s) capable of being exported;
- specific target market(s) and a timetable of entry in mind;
- financial and production capability for export expansion;
- a commitment that the CEO or owner manager would participate.

In terms of the demographic profiles, all firms had an annual turnover of less than £5 million and export revenues below £2.5 million at the start of the programme. None of the participating firms employed more than 150 staff.

In all, eight firms took part in the pilot programme and for most the outcomes were very positive. In six cases, firms increased exports by 100% and several achieved levels of export growth of between 200 and 400%. Significantly, these results were attained in spite of difficult trading conditions in international markets and unfavourable exchange rates. Only two firms failed to meet the stated 100% export growth objective owing to unprecedented domestic market demand. All firms improved their performance in key export markets and accessed at least one new international market, with higher performers establishing new business in three or four countries. A number of firms also initiated new product development programmes to address opportunities identified in these markets.

In most cases, employment within the firms also rose as a result of increased export activity. In total, some 150 new export-related jobs were created as a direct result of the pilot programme. A summary of actual and anticipated outcomes for each firm, as reported in an independent evaluation conducted in late 2000, is shown in Table 27.1.

Table 27.1   Actual and anticipated programme outcomes

Company	Increased export capability/ competence	Improved export profitability	Increased penetration of key export markets	Increased number of export products	Increased number of export markets
A	♦	∇	♦	♦	♦
B	♦	∇	♦	♦	♦
C	♦	♦	∇	∇	♦
D	♦	♦	♦	♦	♦
E	♦	♦	∇	∇	♦
G	♦	∇	♦	♦	♦
H	♦	∇	♦	∇	♦
I	♦	♦	♦	♦	♦

Note: ♦ Achieved by July 2000; ∇ Anticipated in the future.

Another valuable feature of the AEDP as a whole is the opportunity for firms to extend their networks of contacts in terms of support services (for example, potential suppliers and freight forwarders), prospective channel partners or clients and external sources of assistance. These were accessed via the project teams' extensive networks as well as those of the guest speakers and other participant firms. In several cases, business was negotiated between firms on the programme. In addition, by taking part in a formal programme, firms were able to gain better access to funding and support agencies and to their networks of contacts.

Ten firms are participating in the current programme that was launched in early 2001, five each from Northern Ireland and the Republic of Ireland. Their profiles are similar to those involved in the pilot scheme, in terms of size and prior export experience. As with the pilot programme, they come from a diverse range of sectors. While the programme still has some 18 months to run before a comprehensive evaluation can take place, there are already positive indicators in terms of growth of sales in key export markets, entry into additional destinations, new product development for these countries and improved levels of international competitiveness. There is also clear evidence of rising employment and improved profitability.

Taken in conjunction with the objective performance measures for the pilot programme and for each of the participating firms thereon, these outcomes provide significant evidence regarding the benefits of the programme. In particular, they demonstrate an improvement in the fabric, planning horizons and strategic directions of the firms.

Several developments are planned for the future in terms of variants of the AEDP programme. The first is an initiative directed at non-exporters wishing to initiate international activities. The second is an advanced programme aimed at experienced companies seeking to develop partnerships such as joint ventures or strategic alliances in overseas markets. These potential offerings are currently in an early design phase, but are likely to attract policy interest and support in light of a stated Irish government objective of increasing the stock of exporting firms and improving the competitiveness of indigenous firms operating internationally.

Discussion
While each of the described programmes had a different and unique modus operandi all involve tripartite collaboration between academia, government and industry. In the case of *Explorers*, much of the academic collaboration took place during the development of the offering that preceded it, where academic staff were responsible for recruitment of companies and candidates, matching them and providing initial training for the graduates. While these functions are now undertaken by Edge, academics retain linkages into the firms and continue actively to promote the programme to final year students. The firms can also access other business and management development packages offered by Edge or utilize their extensive networks of overseas contacts and mentors.

In the case of Teaching Company schemes, there is close collaboration over a two to three year period, but often the long-term relationship between supervising academic, associate and company continues in a mentoring capacity after the scheme is finished. Similarly, with AEDP, collaboration between academic partners and firms often continues as relationships become embedded in wider contact and support networks. While the involvement of academics in the EDP is generally restricted to an advisory and evaluation role for the local government development agency, participant firms tend to be known to university staff and deeper relationships often ensue.

Collectively and individually, these Irish initiatives address many of the support needs of entrepreneurial firms as identified in the extant literature. These include guidance on addressing human, financial and managerial resource gaps, assistance in developing international market research skills, encouraging technology transfer from academia to industry and supporting management development. Facilitating the development of networks with clients, suppliers, government support agencies and financial institutions is also a common feature of the programmes (see Table 27.2). These local and global networks are crucial to improving the international competitiveness and performance of small entrepreneurial firms. Furthermore, firms often receive additional support from the university via student consulting projects, or *pro bono* advice and consultancy.

Table 27.2   Enterprise development outcomes

	Explorers	TCS	EDP	AEDP
Knowledge acquisition	♦	♦	♦	♦
Skills development	♦	♦	♦	♦
Network development	♦	♦	♦	♦
Management development	♦	♦	♦	♦
Strategic planning	♦	♦	♦	♦
Resource acquisition	♦	♦	♦	♦

Given first-hand knowledge of the programmes and experience of supporting these Irish offerings, the present authors are convinced of their merit in assisting in the development of international entrepreneurs. We would also contend that they could easily be transferred to other locations with similar positive benefits and outcomes. In fact, such initiatives are particularly pertinent in an era when the potential international contributions of small entrepreneurial firms are finally receiving the research recognition and policy maker attention they deserve. Clearly, the availability of government financial support may be an issue that needs to be addressed at a local or national level, and assistance as generous as that provided for Irish firms may not be available to the same extent elsewhere. Nevertheless, we would conclude that such offerings represent an excellent investment of time and effort for firms, even in the absence of such assistance. Moreover, they provide useful models for support agencies in other countries to emulate, adapt and adopt.

References

Axelsson, B. and G. Easton (eds) (1992), *Industrial Networks a New View of Reality*, London: Routledge.

Bell, J. and S. Brown (1990), 'Pragmatic Perspectives in International Marketing Education', *Journal of Management Development*, 9 (1), 39–50.

Bell, J. and D. Demick (1996), 'Valpar Pythons: Improving Export Marketing Intelligence and Planning with the Aid of a Teaching Company Scheme', *Marketing Intelligence and Planning*, 14 (5), 31–8.

Bell, J., M. Murray and K. Madden (1992), 'Developing Exportise: An Irish Perspective', *International Small Business Journal*, 10 (2), 37–53.

Birley, S. (1985), 'The Role of Networks in the Entrepreneurial Process', *Journal of Business Venturing*, 1, 107–17.

Butler, J.E. and S. Hansen (1981), 'Network evolution, entrepreneurial success and regional development', *Entrepreneurship and Regional Development*, 3, 1–16.

Carson, D., S. Cromie, P. McGowan and J. Hill (1995), *Marketing and Entrepreneurship in SMEs: An Innovative Approach*, London: Prentice-Hall International.

Carson, D.J. (1993), 'A philosophy for marketing education in small firms', *Journal of Marketing Management*, 9, 189–204.

Carter, S. and D. Jones-Evans (2000), *Enterprise and Small Business Principles, Practice and Policy*, London: Financial Times/Prentice-Hall.

Cooke, P. and K. Morgan (1993), 'The Network Paradigm: New Departures in Corporate and Regional Development', *Environment and Planning D: Society and Space*, 11, 543–64.

Coviello, N.E. (1994), 'Internationalizing the entrepreneurial high technology, knowledge-intensive firm', Unpublished PhD dissertation, University of Auckland, Auckland, New Zealand.

Coviello, N.E. and A. McAuley (1999), 'Internationalisation and the Smaller Firm: A Review of Contemporary Empirical Research', *Management International Review*, 39 (3), 223–56.

Cromie, S., I. Callaghan and M. Jansen (1992), 'The Entrepreneurial Tendencies of Managers: A research note', *British Journal of Management*, 3, 1–5.

Demick, D. (1997), 'Developing Entrepreneurial Support Networks within Academia: A Hungarian Experience', in G.E. Hills, J.J. Giglierano and G.M. Hultman (eds), *Research at the Marketing/Entrepreneurship Interface*, University of Illinois at Chicago, pp. 491–502.

Demick, D. and A.J. O'Reilly (2000), 'Supporting SME Internationalisation: A collaborative Project for Accelerated Export Development', *Irish Marketing Review*, 13 (1), 34–45.

Dubini, P. and H. Aldrich (1991), 'Personal and extended networks are central to the entrepreneurial process', *Journal of Business Venturing*, 6, 305–13.

Ferland, M., B. Montreuil, D. Poulin and S. Gauvin (1994), 'Quebec's Strategy to Foster Value-Adding Interfirm Cooperation: A Dual Focus on Clustering and Networking', Université Laval, Quebec.

Gibb, A.A. (1993), 'Key factors in the design of policy support for SME development process', *Entrepreneurship and Regional Development*, 5, 1–24.

Gibb, A.A. (1996), 'Entrepreneurship and small business management: can we afford to neglect them in the twenty-first century business school?', *British Journal of Management*, 7, 309–21.

Gibb, A.A. (1997), 'Small firms' training and industrial competitiveness; building on the small firm as a learning organisation', *International Small Business Journal*, 15 (3), 13–29.

Grotz, R. and B. Braun (1993), 'Networks, Milieux and Individual Firm Strategies: Empirical Evidence of an Innovative SME Environment', *Geografiska Annaler B*, 75 (3), 149–62.

Human, S.E. and K.G. Provan (1997), 'An Emergent Theory of Structure and Outcomes in Small-Firm Strategic Manufacturing Networks', *Academy of Management Journal*, 40 (2), 368–403.

Knight, G. and S. Tamer Cavusgil (1996), 'The born global firm: a challenge to traditional internationalization theory', *Advances in International Marketing*, New York: JAI Press, pp. 11–26.

Kurato, D.F. and H.P. Welsch (2001), *Strategic Entrepreneurial Growth*, Orlando, FL: Harcourt College Publishers.

Malecki, E.J. and M.E. Veldhoen (1993), 'Network Activities, Information and Competitiveness in Small Firms', *Geografiska Annaler B*, 75(3), 131–47.

McDougall, P.P., S. Shane and B.M. Oviatt (1994), 'Explaining the formation of international new ventures: the limits of theories from international business research', *Journal of Business Venturing*, 9, 469–87.

McKinsey & Co. (1993), 'Emerging exporters: Australia's high value-added manufacturing exporters', Australian Manufacturing Council, Melbourne.

Mostafa, R. and C. Wheeler (2001), 'Internet Enabled International Entrepreneurship', in M. Jones and P. Dimitratos (eds), *Researching New Frontiers* (4th McGill Conference on International Entrepreneurship), vol. 2, 294–303.

Mumford, A. (1993), *Management development – strategies for action*, 2nd edn, Exeter: SRP Ltd.

Oviatt, B.M. and P.P. McDougall (1994), 'Toward a theory of international new ventures', *Journal of International Business Studies*, 25(1), 45–64.

Rosenfeld, S.A. (1996), 'Does cooperation enhance competitiveness? Assessing the impacts of Interim Collaboration', *Research Policy*, 25, 247–63.

Saxenian, A. (1992), 'The Origins and Dynamics of Production Networks in Silicon Valley', *Research Policy*, 20, 423–37.

Szarka, J. (1990), 'Networking and Small Firms', *International Small Business Journal*, 8(2), 10–22.

Todtling, F. (1994), 'Regional Networks of High-Technology Firms – The Case of the Greater Boston Region', *Technovation*, 14(5), 323–43.

Vickerstaff, S. and K.T. Parker (1995), 'Helping small firms: The contribution of TECs and LECs', *International Small Business Journal*, 13 (4), 56–72.

Westhead, P. and D. Storey (1997), Training Provision and Development of Small and Medium-Sized Enterprises, Research Report No. 26, London: HMSO.

White, J.E., M.J. Gorton and I. Chaston (1996), 'Facilitating Co-operative Networks of High-Technology Small Firms: Problems and Strategies', *Small Business and Enterprise Development*, 3, 34–47.

28 Japanese perspectives of international entrepreneurship

Paul W. Beamish and Jane W. Lu

Japanese small and medium sized firms (SMEs) are internationalizing at an accelerating rate.* Using a longitudinal dataset, this research provides a comprehensive analysis of this phenomenon in terms of Japanese SMEs' foreign direct investments (FDIs), a most entrepreneurial form of internationalization.

The analysis in this research answers questions concerning how Japanese SMEs have made foreign direct investment in terms of the timing of entry, and of the sectors and locations of these investments. The analysis also explores the differences in subsidiary characteristics across sectors and regions, and it links these differences in characteristics to the performance of Japanese SMEs' international subsidiaries. Japanese SMEs' joint ventures outperformed their wholly-owned subsidiaries, while subsidiary performance is positively correlated with subsidiary age and investment size but negatively correlated with the level of Japanese control.

With the decline in trade barriers and the advance in technology, SMEs are playing an increasingly important role in international markets (Oviatt and McDougall, 1994, 1999). As a consequence of this surge, the internationalization of SMEs began to attract greater levels of attention in both the entrepreneurship literature and the international business literature. This increased attention led to the birth of a new academic field: international entrepreneurship, which is at the intersection of the two literatures (McDougall and Oviatt, 2000).

Within this new yet fast-growing field, studies have looked at the internationalization of SMEs from a variety of countries. However, to the best of our knowledge, there is little systematic investigation on the internationalization of Japanese SMEs. Given the importance of Japan in the world economy and the dominance of SMEs in Japanese economy (Dana, 1998), such a study is much needed. In addition, most studies on the internationalization of SMEs tend to use cross-sectional data, probably owing to the

* The research presented in this chapter was supported by a research grant from the National University of Singapore (#R-313–000–045–112), by a Social Sciences and Humanities Research Council of Canada Grant (#410–2001–0143) and by the Asian Management Institute at the University of Western Ontario.

difficulties in locating the necessary data. As one of the first steps towards addressing these issues, this study examined 1118 foreign direct investments made by 221 Japanese SMEs over the 1964–9 period. These longitudinal data allowed us to provide both a historical account and a detailed analysis of the internationalization process of SMEs. Specifically we explore the characteristics and performance of Japanese SMEs' worldwide investments. We focus on Japanese SMEs' FDI activities because Japan has been the second leading source of FDI flows, behind only the United States (UNCTAD, 2000) and because FDI entails higher risk and hence is more entrepreneurial in nature (Lu and Beamish, 2001).

In this examination we answer questions concerning the form that Japanese SMEs' FDIs have taken, including such features as entry mode, investment size, control strategies and the sectors and regions in which investments have been made. Furthermore we explore questions concerning the organizational implications of these investments by looking at relationships between the characteristics of the investments and the performance of foreign subsidiaries.

We initiate our study with a description of the data and methodology for this research. We then proceed to an overview of the internationalization of Japanese SMEs in terms of the timing, the sectoral pattern and the location of Japanese SMEs' FDIs, followed by an examination of their foreign subsidiary characteristics (entry mode, subsidiary age, investment size and control) across major sectors and regions. Furthermore, by attempting to link aspects of subsidiaries with performance, the conclusions of this study should have appeal to SME managers who have invested or are interested in making foreign investments.

Methodology
Data
We collected information on both Japanese SMEs and their international subsidiaries. The main source of Japanese parent company information is *Nikkei NEEDS* tapes, an electronic database compiled by Nihon Keizai Shinbun-sha. This database provides financial information on all Japanese firms listed on the Tokyo stock exchange. The *Nikkei NEEDS* tapes report detailed firm-level information compiled from the firm's balance sheet and income statement and includes other supplementary data (for example, number of employees). Annual information can be traced since 1964 from this database. For this study we used information up to the 2000 edition which provided information on more than 3000 publicly listed Japanese firms. Where required, additional parent company information was gathered from the *Analysts' Guide,* a publication by Daiwa Institute of Research, the *GlobalVantage* database and various editions of the *Japan*

Company Handbook, all of which have a coverage of parent firms similar to that in the *Nikkei NEEDS* tapes.

The source of information for the foreign direct investment of Japanese firms is *Kaigai Shinshutsu Kigyou Souran, Kuni-Betsu*. This source is published by Toyo Keizai Inc., a large Japanese compiler and publisher of business-level, statistical and economic information. The data reported in *Kaigai Shinshutsu Kigyou Souran* was based on responses to questionnaires sent to all firms listed on Japanese stock exchanges, as well as to major unlisted firms. Researchers at Toyo Keizai used press releases, annual reports and telephone interviews to supplement the questionnaire data and to increase the comprehensiveness of the information reported in *Kaigai Shinshutsu Kigyou Souran*. The coverage is close to the population of foreign subsidiaries for firms that responded to the survey (Yamawaki, 1991). In terms of the data, it provides information on the date of establishment, the entry mode, the equity position and identity of the subsidiary's parents. It also reports the subsidiary's industry, its equity capital, sales and total employment, the identity of joint venture partners, local and expatriate employment levels and subsidiary performance. For this study, the 1986, 1989, 1992, 1994, 1997, 1999 and 2001 editions were used to develop a relatively complete, longitudinal profile of Japanese SMEs' internationalization process. The 2001 edition of this data source provides information on more than 19 000 subsidiaries (both SMEs and large) of Japanese firms established in more than 100 countries around the world.

Sample

There is no generally accepted definition of SMEs. The most widely used one in the entrepreneurship literature is the definition provided by the American Small Business Administration (SBA). The SBA defines SMEs as stand-alone enterprises with fewer than 500 employees (for example, Wolff and Pett, 2000; Lu and Beamish, 2001). As we use longitudinal data on Japanese firms and firm size changes over time, we need to define an SME at a specific time. We included a Japanese firm in the sample if its number of employees met the SBA's SME definition at the time of its first FDI. Please note that, as number of employees can only be traced back as far as 1964, for firms who made FDIs prior to 1964 we used employee information of the first data year. In this way, we could make sure that our sample firms were SMEs when they started internationalizing. Using these criteria, we identified 221 Japanese SMEs with 1118 overseas subsidiaries. In the analyses that follow, some of the 1118 subsidiaries were removed from the sample because of incomplete data on individual variables. On average, in the full sample, the response rate was 30 per cent for the performance measure and 90 per cent or higher for all other variables.

The data description that follows is primarily descriptive, utilizing figures and tables to portray a general picture of the internationalization of Japanese SMEs. The form of analysis on subsidiary characteristics and their association with performance in later sections is exploratory, and is supplemented by statistical tests to substantiate differences and relationships.

An overview of the internationalization of Japanese firms
Timing of internationalization
All foreign investments by listed Japanese SMEs in our sample were made after the Second World War. The earliest were made in 1952 as a holding company in France. The second one was in 1954 in the industrial machinery industry in Australia. The third was in 1955 in the real estate industry in the United Sates. Figure 28.1 depicts the timing and the flow of Japanese SMEs' FDIs since 1964, when the flow became continuous. It shows both the number of Japanese SMEs who made their first FDIs and the number of FDIs established by Japanese SMEs in each year. The pattern of these two lines are qualitatively consistent.

The overall pattern of these two lines shows an accelerating rate of internationalization of Japanese SMEs over time, consistent with findings in studies using non-Japanese samples (Hisrich *et al.*, 1996; Zahra *et al.*, 2000; Oviatt and McDougall, 1994, 1999). Within this general pattern, however, there were two setbacks in the flow of Japanese firms which established their first FDIs. The rate of newly internationalizing Japanese SMEs and the number of newly established FDIs by Japanese SMEs increased slowly but steadily in the 1970s, accelerated in the 1980s and reached its first peak

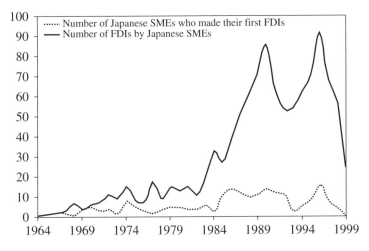

Figure 28.1   Timing of the internationalization of Japanese SMEs

in 1990, when 14 Japanese SMEs made their initial FDIs and 85 FDIs were established by Japanese SMEs. The onset of the 1990s saw a rapid decline in the rate of internationalization by Japanese SMEs. This was followed by an increase in the number of internationalizing Japanese SMEs and the number of FDIs by Japanese SMEs which reached its second peak in 1996, when 16 Japanese SMEs initiated their FDI activities and 91 FDIs were made by Japanese SMEs. This second upward trend was short, as it was followed by another sharp decline in the late 1990s.

The overall pattern of the timing of Japanese SMEs' overseas investment is closely related to the development of the Japanese economy. After 1950, the Japanese economy recovered from the Second World War and experienced a period of fast economic growth. Being the backbone of the industrial sector in Japan, Japanese SMEs were encouraged to expand into foreign countries (Bird, 2002). The surge in the number of newly internationalizing Japanese SMEs and the number of FDIs by Japanese SMEs during the second half of the 1980s was reflective of the 'bubble economy' in Japan where firms were influenced by an over-heated economy and easy money. Some firms pursued expansion without much regard for their resources and capabilities. The sharp decline in investment in the first half of the 1990s showed the effects of the bursting of the 'bubble economy' on Japanese firms in terms of their internationalization. There was another sharp investment surge in the mid-1990s, which was followed by a rapid decline with the onset of the 1997 Asian financial crisis.

Sectoral pattern

The Japanese SMEs' international subsidiaries in the sample were classified into one of ten broad industry categories. Table 28.1 provides a breakdown of Japanese SMEs' FDIs by industry and by time periods. The sectoral pattern in Table 28.1 shows that investments have been made in all 9 broad SIC industry categories. While Japanese SMEs' FDI had wide industry coverage, it was not evenly distributed across all sectors. Japanese SMEs' FDIs were concentrated in the manufacturing industry and wholesale trade, which respectively accounted for 45% and 31% of all Japanese SMEs' overseas subsidiaries. This pattern is consistent across different time periods. The motivations behind overseas production are well documented. For example, the establishment of production-oriented subsidiaries in foreign countries helped to circumvent trade barriers erected by the foreign governments. Japanese SMEs could also take advantage of location-specific resources, such as competitively priced labour forces, in China and Southeast Asia. The nature of the wholesale trade sector meant that the firms in this industry were at the forefront of internationalization because they had the most extensive exposure and connections to foreign markets.

Table 28.1   Sector of Japanese SMEs' international subsidiaries

Sector	Before 1970	1970–79	1980–89	1990–99	Total
Agriculture, forestry & fishing	0	2	7	5	14
Mining	0	0	3	2	5
Construction	0	0	3	4	7
Manufacturing	14	48	149	290	501
Transport	0	3	4	12	19
Wholesale trade	9	41	114	177	341
Retail trade	0	3	8	25	36
Finance, insurance & real estate	3	4	25	67	99
Services	0	5	27	62	94
Total	26	106	340	644	1116

Table 28.2   Region of Japanese SMEs' international subsidiaries

Region	Before 1970	1970–79	1980–89	1990–99	Total
Asia	15	46	128	355	544
North America	9	33	116	139	297
Europe	1	11	72	120	204
South / Latin America	0	8	8	17	33
Oceania	1	7	15	11	34
Africa / Middle East	0	1	1	4	6
Total	26	106	340	646	1118

Location pattern

Table 28.2 decomposes the number of entries by region over different time periods. The six regions specified in this table conform to the breakdown of regions provided in Toyo Keizai (2001), in which seven regions were specified; however, because of the small numbers of entries made into Africa and the Middle East, these categories were combined in the table. When assigning countries to regions, the categorization procedure used in Toyo Keizai (2001) was followed.

A comparison across different columns in Table 28.2 indicates that, overall, the most popular investment region among Japanese SMEs was Asia, which was home to 49 per cent of the subsidiaries in this study's database. North America and Europe were the next two most popular regions, respectively receiving 26 per cent and 18 per cent of cumulative investment from Japanese SMEs by the end of 2000. Three other regions, South and Latin America, Oceania and Africa/Middle East accounted for the remaining 7 per cent of Japanese SMEs' direct investment.

Another observation from Table 28.2 is that the regional preference of Japanese investors changes over time. Although Asia has been the major destination of Japanese SMEs' FDI throughout all time periods, the gap in terms of the number of FDIs between Asia and North America was minimal before the 1990s. In the 1990s, Asia attracted increasingly larger shares of Japanese SMEs' FDIs and the gap between Asia and North America as host regions for Japanese SMEs' international subsidiaries widened significantly. The change in Japanese SMEs' FDI location preference is consistent with Asia's growing prominence as a major recipient region of worldwide FDI (UNCTAD, 2000).

At the country level, the 10 most popular host countries to Japanese SMEs' FDIs (cumulatively) are the USA, China, Hong Kong, Singapore, Taiwan, the UK, Thailand, Malaysia, Korea and Germany. The total number of subsidiaries in these 10 host countries accounted for more than 78 per cent of all Japanese SMEs' international subsidiaries. Table 28.3 presents data on the top six host countries for Japanese SMEs' international subsidiaries by time period.

Table 28.3   Top 6 host countries of Japanese SMEs' international subsidiaries

Before 1970	1970–79	1980–89	1990–99	Total
Taiwan	USA	USA	USA	USA
USA	Singapore	Taiwan	China	China
Hong Kong	Korea	United Kingdom	Hong Kong	Hong Kong
	Hong Kong	Hong Kong	Singapore	Singapore
	Brazil	Singapore	Thailand	Taiwan
	Germany	Germany	Malaysia	United Kingdom

As can be seen from Table 28.3, Taiwan was the most popular investment location for Japanese SMEs before 1970. Although Taiwan's position was replaced by the USA after 1970, it remained a popular investment location for Japanese SMEs along with other emerging markets in Asia. After the 1980s, China became the second most popular investment location for Japanese SMEs, just behind the USA. The popularity of China as a host country is in general a reflection of the successful institution of the 'open door policy' initiated by the Chinese government in 1979. Given its huge market growth potential and low production costs, China has been one of the most popular investment locations for foreign investors, especially

Japanese investors. In a survey by Japan External Trade Organization (Jetro) in 2001, 95.7% of the respondents (Japanese firms) named China as the primary location for their FDIs within the next three years (Lugo, 2001).

To have a better understanding of the sectoral and location patterns of FDIs by Japanese SMEs, we decomposed 2001 data by sector and by region in Table 28.4. It is clear that there were significant differences ($p < 0.01$) in location choices across sectors. The FDIs in the manufacturing sector were heavily concentrated in Asia while other sectors such as wholesale trade, finance, insurance and real estate and services were more evenly distributed across all regions. The heavy concentration of manufacturing in Asia confirms the investment motivations of Japanese SMEs, that is to capture the untapped market potential of Asian countries and/or to take advantage of competitively priced labour in Asian countries.

Characteristics of Japanese SMEs' international subsidiaries
This section examines the characteristics of individual subsidiaries of Japanese SMEs. It begins by examining the entry mode and then moves to three other subsidiary characteristics (subsidiary age, subsidiary size and Japanese control), which are in turn measured by four variables. In looking at these characteristics, a comparison is made across industrial sectors and regions to identify any differences.

Entry mode
The entry mode decision is one of the most important decisions made when undertaking a foreign investment. This is because the choice of mode can affect both the likelihood of survival of the foreign subsidiary (Li, 1995) and its performance, such as profitability and market share (Pan *et al.*, 1999). Four entry modes are evident in our sample. These modes include both shared and solely-owned subsidiaries, as well as newly established and acquired subsidiaries (or greenfield and brownfield subsidiaries). Using these two dimensions (full or shared ownership, and acquired or new subsidiary), four mutually exclusive entry modes can be identified (see Table 28.5):

1. wholly-owned – greenfield operation in which 95 percent or more of the equity is possessed by one Japanese firm;
2. joint venture – greenfield operation in which two or more firms possess at least 5 percent of the subsidiary's equity;
3. acquisition – the purchase of a controlling interest in an existing enterprise; and
4. capital participation – the purchase (via an equity infusion from a Japanese firm) of a partial interest in an existing domestic firm.

Table 28.4   Distribution of Japanese SMEs' international subsidiaries (by sector and by region), 2001

Sector	Asia	North America	Europe	South/ Latin America	Oceania	Africa/ Middle East	Total
Agriculture, forestry & fishing	4	6	1	1	2	0	14
Mining	1	1	0	0	3	0	5
Construction	6	1	0	0	0	0	7
Manufacturing	318	99	61	9	13	1	501
Transport	10	3	4	0	1	1	19
Wholesale trade	125	110	85	10	8	3	341
Retail trade	25	5	4	0	2	0	36
Finance, insurance & real estate	21	44	21	11	2	0	99
Services	32	28	28	2	3	1	94
Total	542	297	204	33	34	6	1116

Note: Pearson *chi*-square = 221.909, $p = 0.000$.

520

Table 28.5   Entry mode of Japanese SMEs' international subsidiaries

Mode	Before 1970	1970–79	1980–89	1990–99	Total
Wholly-owned	16	60	188	310	574
Joint venture	8	41	111	243	403
Acquisition	0	2	17	48	67
Capital participation	2	2	23	36	63
Total	26	105	339	637	1 107

As displayed in Table 28.5, the two modes that involved the acquisition (partial or full) of an existing domestic operation were rarely implemented, while 88 per cent of all Japanese SMEs' subsidiaries were established as greenfield operations (52% wholly-owned and 36% joint venture). This strong preference for greenfield operations is consistent across all time periods. The prominence of greenfield operations among all entry modes in Japanese SMEs' subsidiaries is consistent with the general conclusion of previous research that Japanese investors have a distinct preference for new start-ups (greenfield) over acquisitions (Beamish *et al.*, 1997).

We also examined the impact of using a more stringent definition of joint venture, as advocated by Delios and Beamish (2002), which requires the possession of at least 20 per cent of the subsidiary's equity. This alternative definition reduced the number of JVs from 403 to 394. In the subsequent analyses related to entry mode, we employed both JV definitions and found qualitatively similar results. We report the results by the 5 per cent or more equity level JV definition, but the discussions are applicable to the alternative JV definition.

Tables 28.6 and 28.7 provide breakdown of entry modes using 2001 data by sector and by region. Table 28.6 shows that entry mode differs significantly ($p < 0.01$) by region. Joint venture is the preferred mode in Asia, while wholly-owned is more dominant in North America and Europe. Table 28.7 shows that entry mode differs significantly ($p < 0.01$) by sector. In the manufacturing sector, joint venture is the preferred mode; while in the wholesale trade, finance, insurance & real estate and services sectors, wholly-owned is a more dominant entry mode. This partly reflects the need for control in these sectors.

Given most investments in Asia by Japanese SMEs are in the manufacturing sector, this regional pattern of entry mode is actually consistent with the sectoral pattern in Table 28.7. In addition, this pattern can be partially attributed to the general trend in which joint ventures are preferred for foreign

Table 28.6   Entry mode of Japanese SMEs' international subsidiaries (by region), 2001

Region	Wholly-owned	Joint venture	Acquisition	Capital participation	Total
Asia	200	302	11	22	535
North America	209	47	24	17	297
Europe	120	35	30	18	203
South / Latin America	19	11	0	2	32
Oceania	23	5	2	4	34
Africa / Middle East	3	3	0	0	6
Total	574	403	67	63	1 107

Note: Pearson *chi*-square = 216.587, $p = 0.000$.

Table 28.7   Entry mode of Japanese SMEs' international subsidiaries (by sector), 2001

Sector	Wholly-owned	Joint venture	Acquisition	Capital participation	Total
Agriculture, forestry & fishing	3	9	2	0	14
Mining	3	2	0	0	5
Construction	3	3	0	1	7
Manufacturing	166	252	39	38	495
Transport	11	5	1	2	19
Wholesale trade	248	64	15	10	337
Retail trade	18	15	1	2	36
Finance, insurance & real estate	68	20	4	7	99
Services	54	32	5	3	94
Total	574	402	67	63	1 106

Note: Pearson *chi*-square = 160.959, $p = 0.000$.

entries in developing countries in which foreign investors have little experience. On the other hand, the 'choice' of joint venture over wholly-owned may not be a reflection of preference but rather the lack of availability of alternatives. Investment regulations were stringent on the ownership and control of foreign-owned enterprises, and wholly-owned foreign subsidiaries were rare before 1990 in Asia.

Table 28.8   Characteristics of Japanese SMEs' international subsidiaries (by sector), 2001

Sector	Subsidiary age (year)	Number of employees (count)	Japanese equity ownership (per cent)	Japanese expatriate (per cent)
Agriculture, forestry and fishing	12.59	30.67	74.75	2.22
Mining	12.77	107.00	100.00	12.98
Construction	8.25	76.40	85.00	10.60
Manufacturing	10.01	203.61	79.70	4.89
Transport	8.67	16.29	81.09	36.96
Wholesale trade	10.57	34.40	93.36	19.55
Retail trade	8.87	65.30	70.12	7.05
Finance, insurance & real estate	8.48	32.81	93.59	30.80
Services	7.60	72.07	88.91	32.00
Mean	9.81	121.99	85.69	12.74

Note: All differences significant at $p < 0.01$.

Subsidiary age

Subsidiary age is the first of the latter three subsidiary characteristics examined in this section (see Tables 28.8 and 28.9). Subsidiary age is defined as the operation time period of the subsidiary in the host country from the declared date of subsidiary formation. As expected, subsidiaries in the services, construction and finance, insurance and real estate sectors have the lowest age because the majority of investments by Japanese SMEs in the these sectors were made in the 1990s. In terms of region, subsidiaries established in Asia, Europe and Africa/Middle East have the lowest age because the majority of investments by Japanese SMEs in these regions were made in the 1990s. Overall, the differences in subsidiary age across sectors and regions are a reflection of the timing of entry (see Figure 28.1 and Tables 28.1 and 28.2).

Subsidiary size

Subsidiary size reflects the level of commitment that foreign investor(s) have made to their international subsidiaries. It can be measured by sales, capitalization and employment. In this study we use the number of employees because the other two measures, sales and capitalization, were infrequently reported.

*Table 28.9   Characteristics of Japanese SMEs' international subsidiaries
(by region), 2001*

Region	Subsidiary age (year)	Number of employees (count)	Japanese equity ownership (per cent)	Japanese expatriate (per cent)
Asia	9.51	161.65	79.20	8.22
North America	10.44	65.21	93.33	24.99
Europe	9.12	63.59	93.98	10.77
South / Latin America	10.21	125.50	90.86	16.72
Oceania	12.85	62.64	100.00	17.73
Africa / Middle East	9.49	21.40	80.00	26.47
Mean	9.81	121.99	85.69	12.74

Note: Differences in subsidiary age significant at $p<0.10$, all other differences significant at $p<0.01$.

Again, as might be expected, subsidiaries in the manufacturing sector appear to be the largest, as these have the highest mean number of employees. Meanwhile, subsidiaries in the transportation, finance, insurance and real estate and wholesale trade sector had the lowest number of employees. The differences in subsidiary size are quite dramatic. For example, the ratio of mean number of employees in Japanese SMEs' international subsidiaries in the manufacturing, wholesale trade and transport sectors is approximately 12:2:1. In terms of region, subsidiaries in Asia have the highest mean number of employees because the majority of Japanese SMEs' investment in Asia is in the manufacturing sector.

Japanese control
Parent control in a subsidiary refers to the influence the parent has over the operation and the output of the subsidiary. The control of foreign subsidiaries is a critical issue within multinational enterprises because the parent's ability to influence systems and decisions has ramifications for both the foreign affiliate's likelihood of success (Stopford and Wells, 1972; Root, 1987; Woodcock *et al.*, 1994) and its probability of survival (Li, 1995). There are a variety of control mechanisms that can be used by a foreign investing firm. Two of the more prominent and commonly used are control through equity ownership and control through assigning parent company employees (expatriates) to overseas subsidiaries. We measured the extent of Japanese SMEs' control by looking at these two mechanisms; that is, the percentage equity ownership of Japanese investor(s) and the percentage of Japanese expatriates in total employment. The use of ratios

rather than absolute numbers helps to control for the biasing effects of subsidiary size.

When we look at the extent of Japanese control across sectors, we find that the percent equity holdings of Japanese SMEs are the highest in the wholesale trade and finance, insurance and real estate sectors. The higher percentage equity holdings reflect a greater prevalence of wholly-owned subsidiaries in these two sectors. As shown in Table 28.7, nearly 74% and 69% of Japanese SMEs' subsidiaries in the wholesale trade and finance, insurance and real estate sectors, respectively, are wholly-owned subsidiaries. Furthermore, as evidence of substantive differences in control, we find that in 49 of the 64 joint ventures in the wholesale trade sector and 17 of the 20 joint ventures in the finance, insurance and real estate sector, the Japanese SMEs' equity holding is greater than 50 per cent. Consistent with high Japanese equity holdings, these two sectors also have a higher percentage of Japanese expatriates, compared to the manufacturing sector.

This observation is consistent with previous observations on Japanese investment in other host countries. For example, Beamish and Delios (1999) studied Japanese investment in a variety of transitional economies and found that the mean equity possessed by Japanese firms in the trading sector was almost 20 per cent higher than the mean for manufacturing sector subsidiaries. The use of a higher percentage of expatriates and the holding of higher equity levels in subsidiaries in the wholesale trade and finance, insurance and real estate sectors are indicative of the need to have more direct control over the operations of subsidiaries in these two sectors. This need stems from the high value-added activities that are performed in these subsidiaries. Direct control of the subsidiaries in these two sectors helps the parent firm to integrate better these high value-added activities into its global strategy (Anand and Delios, 1996).

Compared to the manufacturing sector, the service sector has a much higher percentage of Japanese expatriates. This reflects the non-standardized and skilled labour that goes into the production of the services rendered by subsidiaries in the service sector. Hence the need for control is greater. In the manufacturing sector, activities tend to be more routine and, once operations are established, the need for control is less intense.

In addition, we observe (Table 28.8) that in most of the sectors where the percentage of Japanese expatriates is high, the total average number of employees in the subsidiary is relatively low. This is because a higher proportion of those subsidiaries tend to be sales offices.

In terms of region, the Japanese SMEs' equity holdings were the highest in North America and Europe, consistent with the prevalence of wholly-owned mode in these two regions (see Table 28.7). In contrast, the percentages of Japanese SMEs' equity holdings and Japanese expatriates were the lowest in Asia, the most popular location for subsidiaries in the manufacturing sector.

Characteristics and performance of Japanese SMEs' FDIs
This section attempts to establish links between the above subsidiary characteristics and performance. As reported earlier, subsidiary performance is given as a managerial report: subsidiary general managers reported whether the subsidiary made a loss, break-even or gain in the year of the survey (Toyo Keizai, 2001). Among the 1118 subsidiaries in our sample, there are 378 responses to the performance variable. Among these, 223 subsidiaries reported profitable operations, 82 break-even and 73 identified their subsidiary as making a loss in 2000. This section provides a general picture of the performance of Japanese SMEs' FDIs by sector, by region, by entry mode, and by subsidiary characteristics.

Sector and performance
We compare the performance of Japanese subsidiaries across sectors by comparing the percentage of profitable, break-even and loss-making subsidiaries. As shown in Table 28.10, there seem to be differences across sectors. Among the two major sectors, manufacturing and wholesale trade, the manufacturing sector had more profitable subsidiaries in absolute numbers. However, the overall differences across sectors were not statistically significant.

Table 28.10   Performance of Japanese SMEs' international subsidiaries (by sector), 2001

Sector	Loss	Break-even	Profitable	Total
Agriculture, forestry & fishing	0	0	2	2
Mining	0	1	1	2
Construction	0	1	2	3
Manufacturing	37	45	132	214
Transport	1	1	2	4
Wholesale trade	24	26	71	121
Retail trade	2	0	3	5
Finance, insurance & real estate	7	4	7	18
Services	2	4	3	9
Total	73	82	223	378

Note: Pearson *chi*-square $= 14.455$, $p = 0.565$.

Table 28.11 *Performance of Japanese SMEs' international subsidiaries (by region), 2001*

Region	Loss	Break-even	Profitable	Total
Asia	34	48	133	215
North America	18	21	50	89
Europe	13	8	26	47
South / Latin America	2	2	7	11
Oceania	5	1	6	12
Africa / Middle East	1	2	1	4
Total	73	82	223	378

Note: Pearson *chi*-square $= 10.979$, $p = 0.359$.

Region and performance

Table 28.11 compares the performance of Japanese SMEs' subsidiaries across regions. Among the three major regions, Asia, North America and Europe, subsidiaries in Asia are the most profitable. This is consistent with the performance differences across sectors (see Table 28.10) because the majority of Japanese SMEs' manufacturing subsidiaries are located in Asia. However, as with the results in Table 28.10, the results in Table 28.11 were statistically insignificant.

Entry mode and performance

The relationship between entry mode and performance has been a central focus in a number of studies of foreign direct investment. Within the present study, performance differences across entry modes were significant (see Table 28.12). Among the two most popular entry modes, wholly-owned and joint venture, joint venture has a higher percentage of profitable subsidiaries. The result is a little surprising, because it contradicts the findings by Nitsch *et al.* (1995), who found that wholly-owned Japanese subsidiaries in Europe performed best.

There are two explanations for this. First, each entry mode has its own advantages and disadvantages. On one hand, the wholly-owned mode enables the foreign investor to have complete control of the subsidiary. This eliminates the potential for conflicts between partners that exists in the case of joint ventures. However, making investments solely by themselves, foreign investors often do not have access to the potential help that local partners in joint ventures can provide, such as local knowledge. On the other hand, it is well known that joint ventures can sometimes be difficult to manage because of the potential conflicts among partners. However, when

Table 28.12   Performance of Japanese SMEs' international subsidiaries
(by entry mode), 2001

Mode	Loss	Break-even	Profitable	Total
Wholly-owned	41	44	92	177
Joint venture	29	34	98	161
Acquisition	2	3	14	19
Capital participation	1	1	19	21
Total	73	82	223	378

Note: Pearson *chi*-square = 14.281, $p = 0.027$.

well-managed, joint ventures can be effective forms of foreign entry, with partners pooling complementary resources. Thus the mixed results on the relationship between entry mode and performance demonstrate that both modes have viable rationales for their implementation, and that other considerations may interact to tip the balance towards one mode or another.

Second, there are differences in sample characteristics. While the sample for the study by Nitsch *et al.* (1995) was made up mainly of large Japanese firms, our study focused exclusively on Japanese SMEs. By definition, SMEs face constraints in resources and capabilities (Jarillo, 1989; Beamish, 1999). Such constraints become more prominent when SMEs start to internationalize (Zacharakis, 1997). One way to overcome this difficulty is to form joint ventures so as to have access to partners' resources (Jarillo, 1989; Zacharakis, 1997; Beamish, 1999). Taking the differences in sample characteristics into consideration, our findings actually suggest that a contingency approach (Shaver, 1998) may be required to distinguish how the performance of these two modes differs.

Subsidiary age, size, Japanese control and performance
Table 28.13 explores the basic relationships between subsidiary age, size, Japanese control and performance. It shows that subsidiary age is positively related to subsidiary performance. If we take subsidiary age to be a proxy for the foreign investor's experience in the host country, it is not surprising that more experienced foreign investors have higher performing subsidiaries. The fact that subsidiary experience is positively associated with subsidiary performance is supportive of the theories and results of prior studies (for example, Johanson and Vahlne, 1977; Delios and Beamish, 1999). In our sample of Japanese SMEs, profitable subsidiaries have operated an average of 14 years, while unprofitable subsidiaries have operated an average of about 11 years.

Table 28.13 *Characteristics of Japanese SMEs' international subsidiaries (by performance), 2001*

Region	Subsidiary age (year)	Number of employees (count)	Japanese equity ownership (per cent)	Japanese expatriate (per cent)
Loss	11.50	118.47	87.07	9
Break-even	10.98	71.20	86.96	19
Profitable	14.07	171.47	83.95	9
Total	12.90	138.12	85.20	11

Note: Differences in Japanese expatriates not significant, all other differences significant at $p < 0.01$.

The size of the investment was likewise expected to have a relationship to performance. It is clear from Table 28.13 that profitable subsidiaries had the largest investment size in terms of the total number of employees. Investment size reflects parent firms' commitment to the subsidiaries as well as the resources available to the subsidiaries. The positive association between investment size and subsidiary performance highlights the importance of resources in undertaking foreign investments, especially for SMEs.

As shown in Table 28.13, both measures of Japanese control display observational differences across subsidiary performance categories. The percentage of Japanese equity holdings has a consistently negative relationship with subsidiary performance, while the percentage of Japanese expatriates shows a less consistent pattern. The negative relationship between Japanese equity holdings and subsidiary performance is consistent with our findings that, on average, Japanese SMEs' joint ventures outperformed their wholly-owned subsidiaries (Table 28.12).

The result contradicts the findings of Killing (1983), who used a small sample of joint ventures established only in developed countries, and the findings by Ding (1997), who used a sample of Sino-US joint ventures in China. However, the result provides support for Tomlinson's (1970) argument that the sharing of responsibility with local associates will lead to a greater contribution from them and, in turn, a greater return on investment. More importantly, if we consider the concentration of Japanese SMEs' international subsidiaries in Asia, our findings are consistent with Beamish's (1985) observation of a strong correlation between unsatisfactory performance and dominant foreign control in subsidiaries in less developed countries.

Discussions and conclusions

Before offering our final thoughts on these results, we suggest that interpretations of the results from this study should be tempered by limitations in our analysis. First, our sample consisted of only Japanese SMEs. Caution should be taken in generalizing the results of this study beyond the Japanese context. Furthermore, owing to the problem of data availability, this study only included publicly listed SMEs. Future studies could include unlisted SMEs to provide a more complete picture of the internationalization of SMEs.

Despite these limitations, this illustration and analysis of the characteristics and performance of Japanese SMEs' internationalization adds to the body of international business literature and entrepreneurship literature in two ways. First, it presents an overview of Japanese SMEs' internationalization, which has received sparse attention in the literature. Second, it provides insight into the links between subsidiary characteristics and performance.

Japanese SMEs' internationalization after the Second World War had a steady but slow increase through the 1970s and the first half of the 1980s, followed by a rapid surge in the late 1980s. The investments were mainly in the manufacturing and wholesale trade sectors, clustering in Asia, North America and Europe. Greenfield operations were the dominant entry mode, within which joint ventures were implemented with the greatest frequency.

Our analysis of subsidiary characteristics reveals significant differences across sectors and investment regions. Consistent with the timing pattern of Japanese SMEs' FDIs, the subsidiary age was the lowest in the services, construction and finance, insurance and real estate sectors, and in Asia, Europe and Africa/Middle East where the majority of entries were made in the 1990s. Reflecting the nature of the sectors, manufacturing had the highest mean number of employees. Control by the Japanese in terms of both equity ownership and percentage of Japanese expatriates was highest in the wholesale trade and finance, insurance and real estate sectors, suggesting that more control was desired when high value-added activities were conducted in the foreign subsidiaries.

The associations of subsidiary performance with subsidiary characteristics were also examined. Contrary to previous findings on the relationships between sector, location and performance, there was no significant relationship between either sector and performance or location and performance. This suggests that the sector and investment location are not by themselves related to subsidiary profitability, at least for Japanese SMEs' investments.

More importantly, we observed a positive relationship between subsidiary age and performance, a positive relationship between subsidiary size and performance, and a negative relationship between Japanese control and performance. The positive relationship between subsidiary age and performance reflects the positive host country experience effect on Japanese SMEs' subsidiary performance. It also demonstrates the importance of entry timing to capture the investment opportunities at an early stage and to achieve first-mover advantages. It suggests that Japanese SMEs should internationalize as soon as they are ready.

The positive relationship between subsidiary size and performance shows the importance of resources in international expansion. Combined with the observation that Japanese SMEs' joint ventures outperformed their wholly-owned subsidiaries, this suggests that Japanese SMEs use joint ventures in their international expansion to overcome their resource constraints.

Finally, the negative association of the Japanese equity holdings with subsidiary performance illustrates the importance of the participation of local partners in the management of international subsidiaries. Local partners contribute to better subsidiary performance by providing local knowledge about government regulations and about local market conditions and by helping build local networks to circumvent the barriers which are often impenetrable to foreign investor(s). Our findings suggest that Japanese SMEs should structure their joint ventures in a way that can maximize the participation of local partners.

References

Anand, Jaideep and Delios, Andrew (1996), 'Competing Globally: How Japanese MNEs have matched Goals and Strategies in India and China', *Columbia Journal of World Business,* 31(3): 50–62.

Beamish, Paul W. (1985), 'The Characteristics of Joint Ventures in Developed and Developing Countries', *Columbia Journal of World Business,* 20(3): 13–19.

Beamish, Paul W. (1999), 'The Role of Alliances in International Entrepreneurship', *Research in Global Strategic Management,* Greenwich: JAI Press, pp. 43–61.

Beamish, Paul W. and Delios, Andrew (1999), 'Japanese Investment in Transitional Economies: Characteristics and Performance', in D. Denison (ed.), *Organizational Change in Transitional Economies,* Ann Arbor: University of Michigan Press.

Beamish, Paul W., Delios, Andrew and Lecraw, D.J. (1997), *Japanese Multinationals in the Global Economy,* Cheltenham, UK and Lyme, USA: Edward Elgar.

Bird, Allan (2002), *Encyclopedia of Japanese Business and Management,* London and New York: Routledge.

Dana, Léo Paul (1998), 'Small but not independent: SMEs in Japan', *Journal of Small Business Management,* 36 (4): 73–6.

Delios, Andrew and Beamish, Paul W. (1999), 'Ownership Strategy of Japanese Firms: Transactional, Institutional and Experience Influences', *Strategic Management Journal,* 20 (10): 915–33.

Delios, Andrew and Beamish, Paul W. (2004), 'Revisiting IJV Performance', *Management International Review,* forthcoming.

Ding, D.Z. (1997), Control, Conflict, and Performance: A Study of U.S.–Chinese Joint Ventures', *Journal of International Marketing,* 5(3): 31–45.

Hisrich, Robert D., Honig-Haftel, Sandra, McDougall, P.P. and Oviatt, B.M. (1996), 'International Entrepreneurship: Past, Present, and Future', *Entrepreneurship Theory and Practice,* 20(4): 5–11.

Jarillo, J.C. (1989), 'Entrepreneurship and Growth: The Strategic Use of External Resources', *Journal of Business Venturing*, 4: 133–47.

Johanson, J. and Vahlne, J. (1977), 'The Internationalisation Process of the Firm – A Model of Knowledge Development and Increasing Market Commitments', *Journal of International Business Studies*, 8(1): 23–32.

Killing, J.P. (1983), *Strategies For Joint Venture Success*, New York: Praeger.

Li, J.T. (1995), 'Foreign Entry and Survival: Effects of Strategic Choices on Performance in International Markets', *Strategic Management Journal*, 16(5): 333–51.

Lu, Jane W. and Beamish, Paul W. (2001), 'The Internationalisation and Performance of SMEs', *Strategic Management Journal*, 22: 565–86.

Lugo, Letotes Marie T. (2001), 'Japan Firms Seen to Pour More FDIs', *BusinessWorld*, 13 Dec., Manila.

McDougall, P.P. and Oviatt, B.M. (2000), 'International Entrepreneurship: The Intersection of Two Research Paths', *Academy of Management Journal*, 43(5): 902–8.

Nitsch, D., Beamish Paul W. and Makino, S. (1995), 'Characteristics and Performance of Japanese Foreign Direct Investment in Europe', *European Management Journal,* 13(3): 276–85.

Oviatt, B.M. and McDougall, P.P. (1994), 'Toward a Theory of International New Ventures', *Journal of International Business Studies*, 25(1): 45–61.

Oviatt, B.M. and McDougall, P.P. (1999), 'Accelerated Internationalisation: Why Are New and Small Ventures Internationalizing in Greater Numbers and with Increasing Speed?', in Richard Wright (ed.), *Research in Global Strategic Management*, Stamford, CT: JAI Press.

Pan, Y., Li, S. and Tse, David K. (1999), 'The Impact of Order and Mode of Market Entry on Profitability and Market Share', *Journal of International Business Studies*, 30(1): 81–103.

Root, F.R. (1987), *Entry Strategies for International Markets*, Lexington, MA: D.C.Heath.

Shaver, J.M. (1998), 'Accounting for Endogeneity When Assessing Strategy Performance: Does Entry Mode Choice Affect FDI Survival?', *Management Science*, 44(4): 571–87.

Stopford, J.M. and Wells, Jr., L.T. (1972), *Managing the Multinational Enterprise*, New York: Basic Books.

Tomlinson, J.W.C. (1970), *The Joint Venture Process in International Business: India and Pakistan*, Cambridge, MA: MIT Press.

Toyo Keizai (2001), *Kaigai Shinshutsu Kigyo Soran (Japanese Overseas Investment)*, Tokyo: Toyo Kauai Shinposha.

UNCTAD (2000), *World Investment Report 2000: Transnational Corporations, Market Structure and Competition Policy*, New York and Geneva: United Nations.

Wolff, A. James and Pett, Timothy L. (2000), 'Internationalisation of Small Firms: An Examination of Export Competitive Patterns, Firm Size, and Export Performance', *Journal of Small Business Management*, 38(2): 34–47.

Woodcock, C.P., Beamish, Paul W. and Makino, S. (1994), 'Ownership-Based Entry Mode Strategies and International Performance', *Journal of International Business Studies*, 25(2): 253–73.

Yamawaki, Hideki (1991), 'Exports and Foreign Distributional Activities: Evidence on Japanese Firms in the United States', *Review of Economics and Statistics*, 73: 294–300.

Zacharakis, Andrew L. (1997), 'Entrepreneurial Entry into Foreign Markets: A Transaction Cost Perspective', *Entrepreneurship Theory and Practice*, 21(3): 23–39.

Zahra, Shaker A., Ireland, R. Duane and Hitt, Michael A. (2000), 'International Expansion by New Venture Firms: International Diversity, Mode of Market Entry, Technological Learning and Performance', *Academy of Management Journal*, 43(5): 925–50.

29 New Zealand perspectives of international entrepreneurship

Howard H. Frederick, John Thompson and Peter J. Mellalieu

World's most isolated country

Slightly bigger than the United Kingdom, New Zealand is the world's most isolated country. Its closest eastern neighbour is Chile, more than 6000 miles away. To the west, it takes more than three hours' flight to reach Sydney or Melbourne. To the north one travels through 45 degrees of the earth's circumference to reach Siberia. New Zealand is the closest warm airport to Antarctica, eight hours to the south.

On the face of it, you would imagine that New Zealand, with its 2.4 million adults, could hardly survive on the domestic market alone and that its entrepreneurs would immediate become globalized. New Zealand has a competitive and open microeconomic environment that is reasonably free of distortion, but its relative income has declined over much of the last 50 years. Its real per capita income fell, from among the highest in the world in the 1950s to just under the OECD average in 1970, to twentieth in the OECD by 1999. Although the New Zealand economy grew, other developed countries grew more rapidly.

To build a vibrant economy and to retain OECD rank, New Zealand must quickly adapt to the changing international environment. It needs to be innovative in everything it does so that the disadvantages of size and distance from markets are more than compensated for by the difference it brings to products and processes. To earn first-world incomes, the New Zealand economy needs to have global reach and not be constrained to being a small country at the bottom of the South Pacific. One often compares New Zealand, particularly its innovative character, to such countries as Ireland and Finland. But draw two circles of radius 2200km: while the one centred on New Zealand's Wellington captures 3.8 million New Zealanders, the one centred on Helsinki captures 300 million people from 39 countries.

New Zealand's need for international entrepreneurship

It is evident that New Zealand has a clear need to develop international entrepreneurs who can capture global markets. The point of departure for this article is McDougall and Oviatt's (2000) definition of international entrepreneurship as 'a combination of innovative, proactive, and risk-seeking behavior that crosses or is compared across national borders and is intended to create value in business organizations'.[1] Clearly, the ideal type of Kiwi international entrepreneur would be an e-commerce venture that goes international at birth. To do so requires prodigious amounts of innovation, risk-taking behaviour and entrepreneurial talent. Do New Zealanders have those capabilities? These matters will be the subject of the present chapter.

Innovation in spades

New Zealanders take pride in their innovation. All New Zealanders originally came to this country as migrants, travellers or pioneers, or are the descendants of migrants. The ancestors of the Māori, New Zealand's indigenous people, came here about 800 years ago as migrants from Eastern Polynesia. Over the last 200 years, successive waves of migrants have arrived from Western Europe, the Pacific and Asia. The pioneering spirit endures today, having spawned many original thinkers and achievers who are internationally known and respected. A New Zealander, Ernest Rutherford, won a Nobel Prize for discovering the structure of the atom. A New Zealander, William H. Pickering, ran NASA's Jet Propulsion Laboratory while the Apollo rockets were developed for their manned lunar excursions. A New Zealander, Edmund Hillary, was the first man to drive a modified farm tractor to the South Pole, having earlier, with Sherpa Tenzing, been first to reach the summit of Mount Everest. A New Zealander and Information Age pioneer, Alan MacDiarmid, discovered that plastics could conduct electricity and won the 2000 Nobel Prize for Chemistry.

Compared with many other countries, innovation and ingenuity are an integral part of the Kiwi national culture. Blokes in sheds, agricultural Field Days, backyard contraptions: the conditions of New Zealand life have promoted a certain kind of eccentric experimentation that has led to Kiwis often being world-class in the fields they choose to enter. Call it what you will: Kiwi ingenuity, that can-do attitude, give it a go, No. 8 wire or Black Magic – New Zealanders are filled with it. The problem is, innovation and entrepreneurship are not the same thing. An innovation is something new that has the potential of changing relationships. New Zealanders are great innovators. But an innovation uncommercialized is an innovation wasted. If entrepreneurship is the commercialization or exploitation of innovation, the New Zealanders are poor at translating innovation into commercial products and into wealth. To achieve economic progress, innovation and entrepreneurship need to go hand in hand.

Small, innovative companies in New Zealand face particular challenges that restrict their ability to grow internationally and to remain based in New Zealand. These include restricted access to venture capital, lack of funds to invest in research and development, and insufficiently skilled management. The New Zealand market is small, and international markets do not perceive New Zealand as a credible source of high-tech products. Aspiring high-tech companies must focus on the USA and European markets to make an impact on any aspect of the global industry, but there are major challenges for New Zealand companies intent on achieving and sustaining success in those markets. They are highly diverse, expensive to reach, and competition is intense.

Yet New Zealanders have always shown a remarkable ability to respond creatively and positively to challenges. Just as the first shipment of refrigerated meat aboard the *Dunedin* in February 1882 opened up new overseas markets for its primary products, so the Internet opens up new markets for New Zealand's knowledge exports. These include such products as software, technology, education, film, television, Web design, telecommunications, financial services, call centres and others, all of which can travel down the information superhighways to the world at the speed of light. For New Zealand, one of the single most important aspects of the Information Age is the 'death of distance'.[2] That distance will no longer determine the cost of communications will be one of the most dynamic shaping forces for New Zealand. It will alter, in ways that are only dimly imaginable, patterns of international trade, concepts of national borders and the basis of decisions about where people live and work.

New Zealand's policy development over the past two decades has focused on creating a modern, open, competitive economy and on shifting an increasing part of our productive capacity to the knowledge-based industries that are delivering the fastest growth rates worldwide. Our own Global Entrepreneurship Monitor New Zealand 2002 endeavour, followed in the footsteps (albeit outside the government) of other important policy initiatives, including The Foresight Project; Information Technology Advisory Group's *Knowledge Economy* report; The Knowledge Wave conference; the Science and Innovation Advisory Council; the Tertiary Education Advisory Commission; the Prime Minister's *Growing an Innovative New Zealand*; and the Social Entrepreneurship Conference 2001.[3]

World-rank starters-up

In mid-year 2002 we carried out a population survey of 2836 adult New Zealanders to measure the entrepreneurial behaviour and the attitudes of the working-age population.[4] This sample made up the New Zealand portion of the 113 286 individuals surveyed in the *Global Entrepreneurship*

Monitor (GEM) 2002 by 25 respected polling firms in 37 countries (representing 2.4 billion adults between ages 18 and 64).[5] The age and gender structure of all samples was compared to the US Census International Database projections for 2002 and all weights were adjusted so each national sample matched this standardized source.

With a total entrepreneurial activity (TEA) of 14%, our data show that New Zealand is one of the world's most entrepreneurial countries and it has retained its high ranking from 2001. Of the 14% of New Zealanders who are entrepreneurs, 83% are opportunity entrepreneurs and 16% are necessity entrepreneurs. That means New Zealand has the highest proportion of opportunity entrepreneurs in the OECD and developed countries, and ranks significantly higher than the USA.

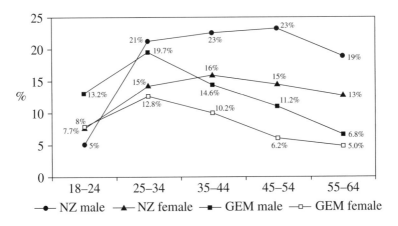

Figure 29.1   Total entrepreneurial activity by age and gender in New Zealand

In Figure 29.1 we see the age and gender distribution of New Zealand entrepreneurs compared to the global average.[6] New Zealanders experience a sharp increase in entrepreneurial behaviour from ages 18 to 34 to surpass the global averages. Throughout the mid-ages (34–54) the number of male and females entrepreneurs is fairly constant in New Zealand, compared to sharp declines elsewhere. Young New Zealand women aged 18–24 are more entrepreneurial than young men, but males overtake females throughout the rest of life with the biggest gender discrepancy coming during the most productive years of ages 45–54.

Our data show that Māori[7] have an 11.9% rate of total entrepreneurial activity, compared to 14% for New Zealand as a whole, 14.5% non-Māori, and 8% for the other 36 GEM countries. Ranked on their own, Māori in

New Zealand would be the world's seventh most entrepreneurial, exceeding the USA, Ireland, Canada and Australia. There are other significant findings. About 75% of new small businesses in New Zealand have one or more family members, including those related by blood, marriage, or adoption, together owning and controlling more than 50% of the business. This is on a par with the global picture. New Zealand ranks well back in the availability of venture capital. Only 18 companies in New Zealand received venture capital in 2001, down from 25 in 2000. This means that only an extremely small proportion of the most promising firms, perhaps one in ten thousand, will receive financial support from venture capital. The primary source of initial financial support for start-ups in New Zealand remains informal funds from friends, family and associates. Yet New Zealand is once again in the top ranks in terms of 'business angel' activity. We estimate that 4.3% of New Zealand adults made informal investments in business start-ups in the 2000–2002 period, with a median amount invested of NZ$20000. As a percentage of GDP, the role of business angels in New Zealand is in the top five countries globally.

The paradox of low wealth creation
We can point to New Zealand's considerable achievements in entrepreneurship, but we are left asking why our high entrepreneurial rate does not translate into the wealth creation that is needed to grow a bigger economic cake for us all. The blunt truth is that most of our entrepreneurs typically aim quite low. At most, they want to start a six-person business in the inward-looking service industry focused on the Auckland market. We have a huge start-up rate, but our wealth creation rate is poor.

When asked, we usually roll out three answers as to why New Zealand falls short:

- our overall start-up rate is very high, but our success rate is low-to-moderate;
- New Zealand entrepreneurs have low horizons and aspirations; they are not the growth-driven dynamic companies that are needed to bring New Zealand into the top OECD ranks that it once occupied;
- New Zealand entrepreneurs tend to create lifestyle-oriented rather than growth-oriented businesses.

This results in an 'entrepreneurial gap' between a high start-up rate and a low-to-moderate success rate.

When we look at the types of businesses these entrepreneurs are starting, the aspirations of today's Kiwi entrepreneurs are modest and their aims are low. We have identified some of the types of new businesses that New

Table 29.1   Types of entrepreneurial businesses being started by New Zealander entrepreneurs (June 2001)

Percentage	Type of business	Examples
63	Services	Accountancy, antiques, architectural, automobile repair, boarding, business consultancy, cafe, cleaning, computers consultancy, contracting, courier, decorating, dental, diving, education, electrical, engineering, environmental, export, finance, food, gardening, hairdressing, health, hospitality, importing, insurance, Internet, landscaping, lawn mowing, marketing, media, medical, merchandising, painting, panel beating, personal training, photography, plumbing, publishing, real estate, restaurant, retail, risk management, secretarial, security, sky diving, software engineering, taxi, teaching, telecommunications, tourism, transport, waste disposal, watch repair
19	Extractive industries	Agricultural, dairy, farm, fish, fishing, forestry, honey, horticulture, orchard, seed
18	Products/ manufacturing	Aluminium, boats, bricklaying, building, butchering, carpets, clothing, concrete, construction, fencing, fibreglass, forklifts, furniture, grocery, heavy machinery, homecare products, industrial supplies, jewellery, manufacturing, petrol stations, stationery, trading, yachts
10	'New Economy' oriented	Artificial insemination, film production, advertising, mentoring, computers, education, information, technical sales, support, software, networking, web hosting, servers, environmental, policy consultant, finance, investment services, foreign exchange, technology, electronics, IT, media, project management, risk management, software engineering, research & development, telecommunications

Note: The first three categories total 100%; the 'new economy' category spreads across all three.

Zealanders are starting (Table 29.1).[8] Only about 10 percent of our entrepreneurs could be classified loosely as 'New Economy / Value-Added' entrepreneurs. In other words, New Zealand's entrepreneurs are not the dynamic, export- and growth-driven companies that the country needs to raise itself back into the top ranks of the OECD.

Why are New Zealand entrepreneurs not necessarily international wealth creators?

As a country we are obviously extraordinary opportunity takers, and this translates into a high start-up rate. But are these people who are starting up a new business necessarily the right people to go on to become international entrepreneurs and create wealth, especially working alone or in very small firms?

The TEA index that we are using measures start-up behaviour, but it does not analyse some of those elusive concepts that might answer our question.[9] Possibly not everyone who starts a new business is an entrepreneur: 'starters-up' may be enterprising, but there is a subtle difference. *True entrepreneurs are people who habitually create and innovate to build something of recognized value around perceived opportunities.* The key words here are 'build' and 'create value'. Do New Zealanders actually build (or grow) their businesses and do they create value?

We wanted to go beyond the population survey to explore some of these subtleties because this may help us understand why New Zealanders, with all of their apparent excellence in starting new businesses, often fail to grow, expand and create new wealth.[10]

The basic dilemma is that many start-ups may never achieve anything new, or create any wealth; they merely optimize supply and demand in established markets and add nothing of value. An apparently good idea may never find customers. The business struggles at best and then disappears. It may be inadequately financed or badly managed, but more likely the person starting it is the wrong person and he or she fails to recognize the vital importance of building an entrepreneurial team with complementary abilities. The ability to identify a good potential opportunity does not automatically guarantee a successful business, let alone a value-creating business, however committed the person might be.

It is important to point out here that the other side of the coin is also true. Many people sitting comfortably with managerial jobs often have more entrepreneurial talents than they realize. They do not appreciate what wealth they could create if they only took the first step. They need a trigger event to set them off on their journey. For many, it is spotting a market opportunity or niche. For some, it is a redundancy pay-out. For others, it comes from job loss accompanied by the need to feed the family. The motivations are complex, but *if the wrong people spot the good opportunity, if they set off unprepared and then fail to build an entrepreneurial team, their chances of creating wealth are low.* In contrast, people who set off on their entrepreneurial journey 'by necessity' may find themselves successful because they are actually entrepreneurs waiting to let pent-up energies explode.

The key to understanding the character and potential of any person lies in those behaviours that are habitual, ones that come naturally and are done well. Each of us has a particular set of character themes that makes us the way we are. We excel in some roles but not in others. A character theme is a personality attribute or characteristic that defines our normal, expected behaviour. Our individual set of themes forms our inner psychological core and defines the things we do most readily and instinctively. In all aspects of our lives we demonstrate our particular set of character themes in the ways we behave – we cannot help it.

We called back 242 of the people whom we had identified in the adult population survey as starting up a new business in order to ask them 20 further questions indicating the presence of particular character themes (Table 29.2). Some relate to those characteristics specifically associated with the entrepreneur, while others relate to other personality types such as the 'inventor', the 'leader' and the 'non-entrepreneur' (character themes are often shared amongst different personality types.) Respondents gave a score from 1 to 10 indicating the extent to which they believed a particular characteristic described them, and these scores were averaged across the entire sample. The strongest character theme we found in our New Zealand sample is *opportunity taking*. This certainly validates New Zealand's ranking as having the highest proportion of opportunity entrepreneurs in the OECD. This is a vital theme for the entrepreneur, and it would also explain why, as a country, New Zealand has one of the world's highest rates of start-up activity.

In our sample, *performance orientation*, the ability to set milestones and to measure progress, ranks twelfth. A sense of urgency is very low as well. What is worse, the lowest character theme in our survey is *ego*, defined as wanting to make a recognised difference. Around the world, recognition is one temperament that has been identified as fundamentally underpinning entrepreneurial motivation. But ego is very low in New Zealand. Does this low ego score explain the *tall poppy syndrome*, where Kiwis cut down their achievers? Partially offsetting the low ego score is the tenth position for *courage*. Courage is closely linked to ego and relates to the ability to deal with setbacks. Kiwi entrepreneurs suffer the slings and arrows of outrageous intolerance but they display courage to persevere amidst this adversity.

Interestingly, the second-, third- and fifth-most mentioned character themes in our sample of business starters-up are all non-entrepreneur themes (or rather, they are shared with non-entrepreneurs). These character themes have a strong people and relationship element, but they are not about selecting and leading. They are important in managing staff and customer relations, but these character themes do not overcome the absence of

Table 29.2 Character themes of high start-up individuals

Character theme	Definition	Most often associated with:	New Zealand ranking (frequency of mention)
Opportunity taking	Engaging and taking on perceived opportunities	Entrepreneur	1
Developer	Seeing and encouraging potential in others	Entrepreneur enabler	2
Woo	Winning others over and enjoying their approval	Non-entrepreneur	3
Time focus	Setting, engaging and meeting deadlines	Entrepreneur and leader	4
Relator	Preferring to work with trusted colleagues	Non-entrepreneur	5
Focus	Concentrating on the task in hand and staying on course	Entrepreneur and leader	6
Creativity	Constantly buzzing with ideas	Inventor and entrepreneur	7
Team	Getting the right people together	Entrepreneur and leader	8
Systematic	Enjoying detail, systems and procedures	Non-entrepreneur	9
Courage	Determination in the face of setbacks	Entrepreneur and leader	10
Mastery	Basking in expertise others don't have	Inventor	11
Performance orientation	Setting milestones and measuring progress	Entrepreneur	12
Networking	Developing a set of potentially valuable contacts	Entrepreneur	13
Influencing	Getting people to take things on and to provide resources	Leader	14
Envisioning	Communicating a strategy to others	Leader	15
Strategic	Seeing a clear route forward	Leader	16
Empowering	Getting people to accept responsibility for things	Leader	17
Urgency	Real drive to get on with things now	Entrepreneur	18
Disciplined	Enjoying structure and organization	Non-entrepreneur	19
Ego	Wanting to make a recognized difference	Entrepreneur and leader	20

other themes, unless the team includes a more entrepreneurial partner in the business.

Those themes which specifically relate to *focus*, also vital for the successful entrepreneur, were ranked fourth and sixth, which is positive, but *urgency*, also related to focus, is down in eighteenth position in the rankings. New Zealanders simply have no urgency to expand. We often hear, 'More customers? Why should I grow when I've got my weekend home and boat?'

Other findings in this survey of character themes include the following:

- creativity, the starting point for (entrepreneurial) ideas, was ranked seventh;
- networking, something which is natural and instinctive for successful entrepreneurs, was ranked thirteenth;
- those themes which characterize the leader specifically – linked to strategy, envisioning, empowering and influencing – all came in the mid-teens in the rankings;
- when comparing the entrepreneur themes with the leader themes, the respondents are more entrepreneurs than leaders;
- inventor themes (partly but not wholly incorporated within the entrepreneur themes) are higher than the entrepreneur theme overall;
- the 'enabling' theme, so critical for those who help and support entrepreneurs, came out with one of the highest average scores.

If we step back and examine these themes more holistically, we see a split in character themes that should be found in entrepreneurs: some themes ranked high whilst others ranked low. Those relating to the 'team' element (critical for growth) were generally higher than the basic entrepreneur themes. This may suggest an intention to grow, despite the underpinning entrepreneur talents not being as strong as one might wish. Linking this to the relatively high rankings for *woo* and *relator,* we might also conclude that our respondents like working in teams but perhaps see the team as an end in itself rather than as a means to an end, which is more the entrepreneurial perspective. This could also help explain the low placement of *ego*, which is by nature an individual character theme.

Significantly, the average score for the non-entrepreneur themes is higher than the average for the ones that we usually classify as entrepreneur themes. Does this mean that our sample is not made up of true entrepreneurs? Does it mean that people are pursuing self-employment without having the basic talents? Does it mean that starters-up are not necessarily true entrepreneurs? This analysis may suggest that we have identified a set of opportunity takers rather than entrepreneurs. Their survival and wealth creation potential may depend on their ability to put together entrepreneurial teams that compensate for missing characteristics. The starter-up needs the performance orientation and ego from other individuals to make a truly prosperous company.

How to overcome the 'entrepreneurial gap'?

There is obviously an 'entrepreneurial gap' between a high start-up rate and a low wealth-creation rate. This is the gap that can be filled with smart policies and programmes, particularly in the areas of education and training, finance and venture capital, R&D transfer, and cultural and social norms. We have to raise our game and stimulate more dynamic, export-oriented firms.

Taking this one step forward, if through policy we could encourage these qualities and abilities, we could increase New Zealand's *supply of entrepreneurship*, in turn a catalyst for market transformation, economic growth, employment and increased per capita income. From a policy perspective, what affects the supply of this market-transforming entrepreneurship? There are three factors that can increase the supply of entrepreneurship:

- *Motivation* to become an entrepreneur is largely affected by education and training, the availability of start-up capital, ease of entry into the market and whether a person is an immigrant, but also by age, gender, regional location, employment, income level, wealth, prevalence of small firms, infrastructure endowment and history. How do we create national, regional and local supportive and opportunistic environments to enable potential entrepreneurs to gain access to the resources they need to get started?
- *Skills* to become an entrepreneur become available to a person through entrepreneurship education in the schools, start-up training, mentoring and networking initiatives. How do we impart the knowledge and skills people need to be effective as entrepreneurs?
- *Opportunity* to become an entrepreneur is based upon an individual decision as to whether self-employment is the best available career option. It is affected by incentives such as profit and economic benefits; cultural support or sanctions; whether one comes from an entrepreneurial family; the social recognition of the entrepreneur; the relative security of the social safety net; and the security of being a 'manager' instead of an 'employer'. How do we work at the individual level to motivate people to start and grow their own businesses?[11]

To date, most discussions in New Zealand have focused on small business policy, not entrepreneurship policy. We maintain that it is equally important to focus on motivating more new entrepreneurs, encouraging more people (particularly youth, Māori and women) to start their own businesses, and creating an entrepreneurial culture. Nascent and new entrepreneurs have different needs from small business owners. We have proposed various policy initiatives that involve governmental actions, entrepreneurship benchmarking, access to capital, taxation, administrative and legislative burden, business support and market incentives for entrepreneurs.

How we train international entrepreneurs
The number one concern of experts in New Zealand is education and training. According to GEM, New Zealand rates top in the world (with the USA and Canada) for the excellence with which primary and secondary schools teach creativity, self-sufficiency and personal initiative. Most countries, including New Zealand, do poorly in teaching the principles of the market economy in primary and secondary schools. New Zealand ranks poorly with most of the rest of the world in terms of whether primary and secondary schools provide adequate attention to entrepreneurship and new venture creation. Only the USA and Canada stand out in teaching entrepreneurship to young students. Turning to the tertiary sector, our experts feel that New Zealand universities and polytechnics are not giving adequate attention to entrepreneurship courses and programmes. When asked whether 'the level of business and management education is truly world-class', our experts ranked New Zealand in the lower third of all countries.

This is the nut that we have been trying to crack at Institute of Technology (UNITEC): creating a a Kiwi-style, world-class professional masters programme focused on the needs of those people who intend to lead the creation and growth of new businesses, new products, new services or new processes. To this end, the Master of Business Innovation & Entrepreneurship (MBIE) was accredited in November 2000.

The design of the programme was informed by the Master of Entrepreneurship and Innovation (MEI) programme offered since the early 1980s by Swinburne University of Technology (Melbourne) and through UNITEC's extensive consultation with many other academics, entrepreneurs and institutions throughout the UK, the USA and Australia. The programme is distinctive in adopting a cohort-based teaching approach, an emphasis on both personal and professional development, and a focus on creating globally-focused 'serial entrepreneurs' – those people (or organizations) who habitually create and innovate to build something of recognized value around perceived opportunities. The formal aim of the MBIE programme is to produce graduates who are likely to work as innovators, entrepreneurs, corporate new venture developers, venture investors or professional consultants who are able (a) to: generate and evaluate new business ideas, (b) to establish and develop innovative businesses, both national and global, (c) to give new life, direction and growth to their own or their clients' businesses, (d) to analyse alternative approaches to implementing business opportunities, and (e) to assist financial, service or government agencies on business development strategies

The programme is intended for three classes of participants. First, there are practising innovators and entrepreneurs who wish to enhance their ability to create, develop and grow high-growth new ventures (whether from a 'greenfields' start-up situation, from an existing small-medium enterprise, or from a corporate context). Second, there are aspiring innovators and entrepreneurs who are keen to 'make the leap' into establishing and growing a new venture under their own leadership. The third class are co-preneurs who work with, advise or support the endeavours of innovators and entrepreneurs: administrators and operations managers, functional specialists, and those engaged in consulting, advising, training, business coaching, entrepreneurship research, teaching and policy advice.

Students come from a very broad range of professions, including research scientist, project manager, teacher, nurse, general manager, consultant, business development manager and marine officer. The age of students ranges from 22 to 55. The programme is offered in part-time and full-time mode. It requires about 2400 hours of work that the student can spread over two years in full-time mode, or three years in a part-time programme. Students can move flexibly between full-time and part-time modes. The basic structure for each course is pre-readings, a full-time attendance block, post study and an assignment, another block including assignment presentations, more study and final assignment. Extensive use is made of guest entrepreneurs and visiting professors from both New Zealand and internationally.

The programme philosophy is informed by two key pedagogies. The pedagogy of action learning guides students to apply their learning to business development issues of concern to themselves or their employing organizations. The pedagogy of 'talent, temperament, technique' encourages students to recognize the strengths and weaknesses of their own talents and temperaments (whether entrepreneurial, innovatorial or co-preneurial), and to develop their personal techniques (or skills) of leading (or working with) innovation and entrepreneurial projects and teams.

The programme is structured around three phases. Phase 1, 'Foundations', focuses on understanding the requirements for managing innovation and establishing entrepreneurial ventures, whether inside an existing company or as a stand-alone enterprise. This phase allows students to explore and debate the theories of entrepreneurship, and to explore the features of their own entrepreneurial life themes. The phase also introduces a selection of the key capabilities needed to identify and evaluate new ventures, which include environmental analysis, creative thinking, opportunity screening, strategy and business research. The phase concludes with a reported evaluation of the commercial feasibility of new venture opportunities proposed by course participants. Students also develop a professional learning agenda, their personal guide to developing and practising key entrepreneurial techniques and capabilities. Students wishing to exit after this phase receive a Postgraduate Certificate in Business Innovation & Entrepreneurship.

Phase 2, 'Global Growth', extends understanding of entrepreneurship and the entrepreneurial spirit with particular reference to the challenge of managing the growth of a business opportunity and operating in a global environment. Financial planning capabilities are extended beyond those established in Phase 1. The phase concludes with the student producing a comprehensive business plan capable of being used as a platform to attract venture funding and guiding the implementation of a new venture or a new process. Students wishing to exit after this phase receive a Postgraduate Diploma in Business Innovation & Entrepreneurship.

Phase 3, 'Mastery', extends both the theory and practice of innovation and entrepreneurship, with particular attention to research, legal, social, ethical and implementation issues. The phase concludes with the student completing an industry-based research project that may include critical reflection on the establishment of an entrepreneurial business, a new process or a new corporate venture.

Conclusions

New Zealand desperately needs international entrepreneurs but, owing to its isolation and other historical, social and economic conditions, Kiwi entrepreneurs have low horizons and aspirations. They are great at starting a business but not in using that business to grow and create wealth ('to grow the cake for all New Zealanders'). We have identified deficiencies in both character traits and in skills that inhibit the rise of an internationally entrepreneurial class of New Zealand wealth creators. We have also implemented an education and research programme that aims to correct these deficiencies. It is clear that New Zealand can never return to the top half of OECD rankings unless it learns to use its obvious innovative talents and prodigious start-up behaviour in ways that translate these activities into wealth creation for these individuals and for the nation.

Notes

1.   P.P. McDougall and B.M. Oviatt (2000), 'International entrepreneurship: The intersection of two paths. Guest Editor's Introduction', *Academy of Management Journal*, 43(5): 902–8.

2. Frances Cairncross, 'Economist Telecommunications survey: The death of distance', *Economist*, 30 September 1995.
3. Ministry of Research, Science and Technology (1999), 'Blueprint for Change: Government's Policies and Procedures for Its Research, Science and Technology Investments', Wellington: Ministry of Research, Science and Technology (*http://www.morst.govt.nz/publications/blueprint/index.htm*);

   Information Technology Advisory Committee (1999), chaired by Minister of Information Technology Maurice Williamson; 'Foreword' by Ralph Norris, in Howard H. Frederick and Donald J. McIlroy, *New Zealand's Knowledge Economy*, Wellington: Ministry of Commerce, 1999 (*http://www.med.govt.nz/pbt/infotech/knowledge_economy/*);

   The Knowledge Wave Trust (*www.knowledgewave.org.nz*);

   Science and Innovation Advisory Council (2001), *New Zealanders: Innovators To The World. Turning Great Ideas Into Great Ventures. A Proposed Innovation Framework for New Zealand*, Wellington: Science and Innovation Advisory Council;

   Tertiary Education Advisory Committee (2001–2), *Shaping the System*, Wellington: Tertiary Education Advisory Committee, 2001; *Shaping the Strategy*, Wellington: Tertiary Education Advisory Committee, 2001; *Shaping the Funding Framework*, Wellington: Tertiary Education Advisory Committee, 2001; *Shaping a Shared Vision*, Wellington: Tertiary Education Advisory Committee, July 2000;

   Prime Minister Helen Clark (2002), *Growing an Innovative New Zealand* (*http://www.executive.govt.nz/minister/clark/innovate/*);

   Proceedings from the Social Entrepreneurship Conference 2001, Community Employment Group, Department of Labour, Wellington, July 2002 (*www.ceg.govt.nz*).
4. Howard H. Frederick, Peter J. Carswell, Ella Henry, Ian Chaston, John Thompson, Judi Campbell and Andy Pivac (2002), *Bartercard New Zealand Global Entrepreneurship Monitor 2002*, Auckland: New Zealand Centre for Innovation & Entrepreneurship
5. See Paul D. Reynolds, William D. Bygrave, Erkko Autio and Michael Hay (2002), *Global Entrepreneurship Monitor 2002 Summary Report*, Babson College, Ewing Marion Kauffman Foundation and London Business School. (*www.gemconsortium.org*).
6. This scale should be read, for example, '5% of male New Zealanders aged 18–24 are entrepreneurs', '21% of male New Zealanders aged 25–34 are entrepreneurs', and so on.
7. For our international readers: Polynesian settlers arrived in Aotearoa ('Land of the Long White Cloud') about the tenth century. Aotearoa was visited briefly by the Dutch navigator Abel Tasman in 1642. However, it was not until 1769 that the British naval captain James Cook and his crew became the first Europeans to explore New Zealand's coastline thoroughly. The word Māori meant 'usual or ordinary' as opposed to the 'different', European settlers. Before the arrival of Europeans, Māori had no name for themselves as a nation, only a number of tribal names. The Māori language (te reo) is one of two officially recognized languages in New Zealand, the other being English. Long vowels in the Māori language are marked with a macron.
8. Howard H. Frederick and Peter J. Carswell (2001), *Global Entrepreneurship Monitor New Zealand 2001*, Auckland: New Zealand Centre for Innovation & Entrepreneurship (*www.unitec.ac.nz/gem*).
9. How we calculate the TEA index: these surveys produced a measure we call the Total Entrepreneurial Activity Index (TEA). We divided start-ups into nascent and new firms. To qualify as a *nascent* entrepreneur, an individual had to satisfy three conditions: they had done something (taken some action) to create a new business in the past year; second, they had to expect to share ownership of the new firm; third, the firm must not have paid salaries or wages for more than three months. If the new firm had paid salaries and wages for more than three months but less than 42 months it was classified as a *new* firm. The TEA measure is the sum of (1) those individuals involved in the start-up process (nascent entrepreneurs) and (2) individuals active as owner–managers of firms less than 42 months old. Those 5% that qualified for both are counted only once.
10. Special thanks for this section to John Thompson, Huddersfield University Business School, United Kingdom, who wishes to acknowledge discussions with Dr Bill Bolton

and ideas developed out of discussions with Gallup Inc., Lincoln, Nebraska, USA. The underpinning themes are taken from: W.K. Bolton and J.L. Thompson (2000), *Entrepreneurs: Talent, Temperament, Technique*, Butterworth Heinemann; and W.K. Bolton and J.L. Thompson (2002), *The Entrepreneur in Focus – Achieve Your Potential*, Thomson Learning.

11.   Adapted from David Burnett, Founder, Technopreneurial.com, 'Hunting for Heffalumps – The Supply of Entrepreneurship and Economic Development' (Web Page), available at *http://www.technopreneurial.com/articles/heffalump.asp*; and C. Mirijam van Praag and Hans Van Ophem, 'Determinants of Willingness and Opportunity to Start as an Entrepreneur', *Kyklos*, 1995, 48:4, 513–40; also Lundstrom *et al.*

30 International expansion of New Zealand firms

Heather I. M. Wilson, Sylvie K. Chetty and Gurvinder S. Shergill

This chapter is based on a study of 117 small to medium-sized New Zealand exporting firms across all industries.* Our objective was to investigate the relevance of previous knowledge to the assessment of current international assignments. The results confirm the existence of three types of experiential knowledge that appear to accord with Eriksson *et al.*'s foreign business knowledge, foreign institutional knowledge and internationalization knowledge constructs (1997). However, these elements combined only explain 48 per cent of the variance in our data. Additional experiential knowledge constructs are identified relating to compliance and development/adaptation issues, which when combined with the other constructs explain 69 per cent of the variance in our data. Our contribution lies in the further development and refinement of the experiential knowledge constructs for use in future studies on internationalization.

With increasing globalization and worldwide trade liberalization, research on learning and internationalization has become an important issue in the international business literature. As firms increase their international involvement by conducting business in countries that have different business customs, business institutions and infrastructure they have to widen their internationalization knowledge. One perspective on learning is that firms which have previous experience have an advantage as they can learn from these experiences and add their new knowledge to these accumulated experiences (Madhok, 1997; Cohen and Levinthal, 1990; Eriksson *et al.*, 1997). Previous experiences determine routines, which are fundamental to the firm's future actions, and these routines have to be relevant to those needed in a particular market (Madhok, 1997). As a firm internationalizes it acquires, evaluates, assimilates, integrates and diffuses knowledge, which Madhok (ibid.) refers to as 'capability accumulation'.

* All of the authors contributed equally to this chapter and order of authorship was determined by a stochastic process. The authors are indebted to Kent Eriksson, Jan Johanson, Jukka Hohenthal and Anders Majkgård of Uppsala University and D. Deo Sharma of Copenhagen Business School for the questionnaire design applied in this study.

In addition, a firm's learning is seen as the ability of a firm to use its prior related knowledge and diverse background to identify the value of new information and to develop this into something creative. Cohen and Levinthal (1990: 128) use the term 'absorptive capacity' to refer to a firm's ability to 'recognise the value of new, external information, assimilate it, and apply it to commercial ends'. This concept of absorptive capacity highlights the importance of previous knowledge for learning new tasks. As a firm accumulates absorptive capacity in one task it becomes more experienced in accumulating it in subsequent tasks. In the context of internationalization this could mean that, as a firm learns in one international market, its learning and performance in another market will be influenced by this previous experience and the chances of successful performance will be improved.

The purpose of this chapter is to identify which aspects of prior knowledge and routines play an important role in conducting a current international assignment. We develop and test three hypotheses based on three types of international experiential knowledge, which Eriksson *et al.* (1997) categorize as 'foreign business knowledge', 'foreign institutional knowledge' and 'internationalization knowledge'. This approach allows us to ascertain whether the three knowledge constructs identified by Eriksson *et al.* capture the full extent of relevant experiential knowledge in the internationalization process. The resulting conclusions and implications refine Eriksson *et al.*'s knowledge constructs while highlighting the relevance of the additional knowledge constructs relating to compliance and development/adaptation. Meanwhile, the following section provides a review of the literature informing the development of the hypotheses that we test in this chapter. This is followed by a discussion of the method and measures employed to test the hypotheses and the presentation of the results.

Review of the literature
The internationalization process
We use Calof and Beamish's definition of internationalization, which is 'the process of adapting firms' operations (strategy, structure, resources, etc.) to international environments' (1995: 116). The term 'internationalization' has been frequently used to describe the growth in a firm's international operations (Cavusgil and Nevin, 1981; Johanson and Vahlne, 1977; Johanson and Wiedersheim-Paul, 1975; Luostarinen, 1980). These studies considered internationalization to be a gradual, sequential process through different stages, with the firm increasing its commitment to international operations as it proceeded through each stage. This pattern-oriented approach, because it uses stages as its central concept, is often referred to as the stages model. Various stages models of internationalization have been described:

first, the Uppsala process model (Johanson and Vahlne, 1977, 1990; Johanson and Wiedersheim Paul, 1975; Welch and Luostarinen, 1988); second, the innovation–adoption internationalization models (Andersen, 1993; Bilkey and Tesar, 1977), and third, the management decision-making process towards internationalization model (Reid, 1981).

The most frequently used of these stages models is the Uppsala process model (Johanson and Vahlne, 1977). Put simply, experientially based market specific knowledge leads to the identification of market opportunities to which the firm decides to commit resources. In turn, market interaction and integration lead to reduced uncertainty and risk perception resulting in current activities being increased in scale and an increasing commitment to the foreign market. Two types of market knowledge are important in understanding the model. One is objective knowledge, which can be taught, is easily acquired and is explicit in nature. However, the more critical knowledge is experiential, and this is context-specific and more implicit in nature; that is, firms acquire important market information mainly from their experience in that market. Experiential knowledge is a vital resource as it is difficult to acquire knowledge in new markets (Barkema *et al.*, 1996). It is this experiential knowledge that reduces the firm's perception of market uncertainty or risk that, in turn, have an impact on its market commitment decisions. Increased market commitment occurs in the following stages: (1) no regular export activities, (2) export via independent agents, (3) creation of an offshore sales subsidiary, and (4) overseas production facilities (Johanson and Wiedersheim-Paul, 1975).

It is important to note that the focus is on the experience of the firm in the international market rather than the experience of the individual, and that the current activities of the firm are its main source of experience. Although the firm may be able to recruit people with experience in the target markets, until they are able to generate experiential knowledge of the firm they will not have a significant impact on the firm's internationalization efforts. Essentially, market and firm experience are both required. The delay in generating experiential knowledge, either at the firm to market level or at the experienced individual to firm level, will mean that internationalization progresses slowly and incrementally. This approach to internationalization has come under criticism as other studies (for example, Millington and Bayliss, 1990; Hedlund and Kverneland, 1985) have found that firms in fact leapfrog stages of internationalization rather than proceeding gradually as suggested by the stages approach. Eriksson *et al.* (1997) however support the incremental approach to internationalization as it allows a firm to learn more realistically from small incremental steps to internationalization than from huge mistakes made from the leapfrog approach. They conclude that managers gain important experiential knowledge from the mistakes they make in the gradual approach, with the result that firms are successively in a better position to realize what information is required and where to go to find it. In a later study, Eriksson *et al.* (2000: 39) reinforce this position by illustrating that current experiential knowledge is more readily applied to 'closer' foreign markets when compared with 'more novel' foreign markets.

Experiential knowledge in internationalization
Firms that expand internationally gain experiential knowledge about foreign markets, foreign cultures, foreign institutions and other market-specific knowledge (Barkema *et al.*, 1996). Using Nelson and Winter's (1982) evolutionary theory, Madhok (1997) argues that firm capabilities are the consequence of consolidating individual skills, organization and technology through routines, which evolve gradually through time and experience. Denis and Depelteau (1985) found that firms place a greater emphasis on acquiring knowledge through interacting with the market environment compared with information obtained through public or private information services. It is experiential knowledge that offers such advantages as 'direct knowing, immediate understanding, learning without the conscious use of reasoning, or making a choice without formal analysis' (Brockman and Anthony, 1998: 455),

Despite the clear focus on experiential knowledge in the process model of internationalization, there is an absence of studies empirically investigating the concept of experiential knowledge as it relates to internationalization. A notable exception to this is the work of Eriksson *et al.* (1997) pertaining to experiential knowledge and the perceived cost of internationalization. The authors find a strong relationship between the lack of foreign business and foreign institutional knowledge and the perceived cost of internationalization. In turn, foreign business knowledge and foreign institutional knowledge are found to be dependent on internationalization knowledge. Through the development and testing of these three experiential knowledge constructs, Eriksson *et al.* reinforce the notion that experiential knowledge reduces perceptions of difficulty concerning internationalization. Eriksson *et al.*, in a later study employing their knowledge constructs in relation to the geographical scope of the firm's operations, call for a more in-depth examination of their internationalization construct in particular, given that it 'captures a firm's ability to apply and to develop its accumulated unique knowledge as it gains foreign business experience in a way that supports further internationalization' (2000: 40). We use Eriksson *et al.*'s three types of experiential knowledge in internationalization as points of reference for this study, namely foreign 'business knowledge', 'foreign institutional knowledge' and 'internationalization knowledge'. In particular, we attempt to ascertain whether these three constructs capture the full extent of relevant prior experiential knowledge in conducting a current international assignment.

Foreign business knowledge

Eriksson *et al.* (1997: 343) define foreign business knowledge as 'experiential knowledge of clients, the market, and competitors'. They argue that if the firm lacks knowledge of how its customers operate then this is a disadvantage for the firm. A firm can acquire this knowledge by working closely with its customers to gain knowledge about the market and how local businesses operate. When firms conduct business with foreign counterparts they acquire knowledge from each other (Hamel, 1991). A large amount of internationalization activity is associated with networking as it involves building relationships with foreign intermediaries, customers, suppliers and alliance partners. Firms benefit from collaboration as it gives them the opportunity to overcome limitations in their capabilities and resources to conduct business in a particular market (Madhok, 1996). Several studies have been done on the dynamics of cooperation in international joint ventures (Beamish and Banks, 1987; Makino and Delios, 1996) and cooperative alliances (Aulakh *et al.*, 1996; Johnson *et al.*, 1996). Hallen *et al.* (1991) state that much knowledge is generated as business partners commit themselves to the relationship by adapting to each other. The adaptations may be small-scale, and will therefore have smaller learning effects, or major, for example in a situation where a new product is developed for a specific customer (von Hippel, 1978).

In the current study, we explore a number of variables that are taken into consideration by a firm as it undertakes an international assignment. If we take the position that foreign business knowledge is a meaningful construct, then we would expect to see relationships between variables pertaining to 'clients, the market and competitors' (Eriksson *et al.*, 1997: 343). Therefore we predict:

> H1 variables pertaining to clients, the market and competitors will load on one factor that we can term 'foreign business knowledge'.

Internationalization knowledge

Eriksson *et al.* (1997: 345) maintain that internationalization knowledge stems from 'A firm's experience of organizing internationalization' and 'knowing what knowledge is required in different situations and different settings connected with internationalization, and where to seek this knowledge'. As a firm internationalizes it accumulates knowledge, which becomes part of the organization's knowledge and routines (Eriksson *et al.*, 1997; Nelson and Winter, 1982). The firm has to be able to match its existing resources with those needed in a specific market so it has to focus on developing knowledge at the level of both the market and the firm (Johanson and Vahlne, 1977; Madhok, 1996, 1997; Eriksson *et al.*, 1997). A firm operating in diverse foreign markets could be accumulating a wide range of knowledge that provides it with the capabilities to recognize which new opportunities to exploit (Cohen and Levinthal, 1990; Miller and Chen, 1996). When the firm becomes involved in more diverse markets it needs to increase investment to acquire capability in each of these foreign markets. A firm has to be capable of collecting information, coordinating activities and identifying trends in these foreign markets (Barkema *et al.*, 1997).

Again, if we take the position that internationalization knowledge is a meaningful construct in the conduct of an international assignment, we would expect to see relationships between variables pertaining to 'A firm's experience of organizing internationalization' (Eriksson *et al.*, 1997: 345). Therefore we predict:

> H2   variables pertaining to a firm's experience of organizing internationalization will load on one factor that we can term 'internationalization knowledge'.

Foreign institutional knowledge

Eriksson *et al.* (1997: 343) define foreign institutional knowledge as 'experiential knowledge of government, institutional framework, rules, norms, and values'. They maintain that, if a firm lacks experiential institutional knowledge, it has difficulty understanding the technical and commercial laws in a particular market. Foreign institutional knowledge refers to knowledge about the local economy, politics, culture and business customs of a region, consumer demand, infrastructure and other factors on doing business in a particular market (Makino and Delios, 1996). A lack of knowledge of social, political and economic conditions of a particular market are a disadvantage to the firm (Beamish, 1984).

As with Hypotheses 1 and 2, we take the position that, if foreign institutional knowledge is a meaningful construct as firms undertake international assignments, we will see relationships between variables concerning the target country's 'government, institutional framework, rules, norms, and values' (Eriksson *et al.*, 1997: 343). Therefore we predict:

> H3   variables pertaining to government, institutional frameworks, rules, norms and values will load on one factor that we can term 'foreign institutional knowledge'.

Method of research

This study was conducted in New Zealand in 1999 using a mail question-naire. The sampling frame was 'Kompass', which provided a list of New Zealand exporting firms. A total of 706 small to medium-sized firms across industries were chosen randomly from this database. Before the main survey was conducted the questionnaire was tested by making a pilot survey of 50 of these firms. In the main survey there were three mail-outs of the questionnaire, covering letter and stamped addressed envelope. A covering letter sent with the questionnaire suggested that the person in charge of international business operations be responsible for filling in the questionnaire. After each mail-out respondents were given a month to return the completed questionnaire. If they did not respond then a ques-tionnaire with the covering letter and stamped addressed envelope was sent to them in the second and third mail-outs.

Various incentives were used to encourage respondents to fill in the ques-tionnaire. First, the covering letter explained the importance of the study and that it was part of an international study. Second, respondents were offered copies of the completed report. Third, for every questionnaire com-pleted NZ$5.00 would be donated to a children's charitable organization. Fourth, a stamped addressed envelope was posted with the questionnaire and covering letter. Fifth, the covering letter guaranteed confidentiality and anonymity of the data gathered. In the first mail-out there were 52 useable questionnaires and 22 respondents said they were non-exporters. In the second mail-out there were 51 useable questionnaires and 30 said that they were non-exporters. In the third mail out there were 14 useable questionnaires and five said they were non-exporters. This resulted in an effective response rate of 20 per cent or 117 useable questionnaires from 599 firms (706 original firms less the 50 pilot firms and less the 57 non-exporters). Although the sampling frame used was the most up-to-date on exporting firms in New Zealand, 8 per cent responded that they were non-exporters.

Data analysis and results

The questionnaire comprised 23 items consisting of seven-point Likert scales to ascertain the extent to which the respondent fully agreed or fully disagreed with statements pertaining to the usefulness of different aspects of their prior business experience in relation to their current international assignment. The internal consistency measure, coefficient alpha (Cronbach, 1951), was equal to 0.89, indicating that the questionnaire was reliable. We used factor analysis with varimax rotation in order to understand the underlying structure of our data. The Kaiser–Meyer–Olkin measure of sampling adequacy was 0.78 and Bartlett's test of sphericity was significant, indicating that it was appropriate to apply the factor analytical technique to this data set.

The initial factor solution identified six factors from our data, based on the pattern of the scree plot and the decision rule that eigenvalues should be greater than or equal to one. Three criteria were applied to determine whether the factors were of practical value: individual item factor loadings had to exceed 0.55 (Hair *et al.*, 1998), the loading of the item on the primary factor had to exceed the loading on other factors by at least 0.20 (Kerlinger, 1986) and at least two items had to load on an individual factor (Golen, 1980). These stringent retention criteria were met with the third factor solution, with two items being dropped for the second factor solution and a further three for the third factor solution. The final factor solution consisted of 18 items and five factors (see Table 30.1) and these factors were assessed for scale reliability using Cronbach's alpha measure.

Hypothesis 1
The variables comprising Factor 1 in Table 30.1 relate to experience with customers and suppliers in New Zealand, overseas suppliers, customer's customers, customer's suppliers of supplementary products and/or services, and competing suppliers (bold type). These relationships broadly define the competitive market in which a firm operates, as predicted by Hypothesis 1, and this factor explains 17.5 per cent of the variance in the data. The high Cronbach's alpha of 0.82 indicates that these variables combine into a reliable measure that can be termed 'foreign business knowledge', as indicated by the literature.

It is interesting to note, however, that one of the variables that we expected to relate to this factor, namely overseas customers, was deleted from the solution. Although it loaded on Factor 1, we were unable to clearly differentiate it from Factor 2, internationalization knowledge; that is, there was not a clear 0.20 separation from the loading on Factor 1 versus the loading on Factor 2 (Kerlinger, 1986). Likewise, the item experience with foreign and international authorities and organizations loaded on Factor 1 but was deleted because we could not clearly differentiate it from Factor 3, foreign institutional knowledge. This will be discussed further in the Conclusions and Implications section of the chapter.

Hypothesis 2
Hypothesis 2 predicted that variables concerning a firm's experience of organizing internationalization would group together as one discernible factor that might be termed 'internationalization knowledge'. According to Table 30.1, Factor 2 consists of variables relating to the management and support of personnel abroad, the practice of financing overseas assign-

ments, experience relating to doing business with new customers, and experience relating to doing business in new markets. These variables are all concerned with the nuts and bolts of organizing an international assignment and can conceivably be grouped together under the construct 'internationalization knowledge', as predicted by Hypothesis 2. This factor alone explains 17 per cent of the variance in the data and the individual elements combine into a reliable scale with a Cronbach's alpha of 0.780.

Although the item pertaining to management practice of cooperating with other organizations also loaded on Factor 2, it was deleted from the solution because we were unable to differentiate it clearly from Factor 3, foreign institutional knowledge. Again, this implication will be considered in the final section of this chapter.

Hypothesis 3
Our final hypothesis relating to foreign institutional knowledge accords with Factor 3 in Table 30.1. The variables grouping under this factor consist of matters of business culture, language experience, country infrastructure and industry structure. These elements can be taken to represent the idiosyncrasies relating to business conduct in a particular country and can be termed 'foreign institutional knowledge', as predicted by Hypothesis 3. Together these variables explain 14 per cent of the variance in the data and combine into a reliable measure as measured by the Cronbach's alpha of 0.786.

Factors 1 to 3, representing foreign business knowledge, internationalization knowledge and foreign institutional knowledge, explain a total of 48 per cent of the variance in the data of this study. Two additional factors fell out of the data analysis. Factor 4 contains variables relating to business laws and laws concerning technology, product and quality standards, issues we originally believed would be part of the foreign institutional knowledge construct. These elements relate to compliance issues and it may be the case that we have captured another experiential knowledge construct that might be termed 'foreign compliance knowledge'. Together they explain an additional 10.5 per cent of the variance in our data and the scale has acceptable reliability, given the Cronbach's alpha of 0.758. Interestingly, another variable pertaining to financial practice and currency laws loaded on Factor 3, foreign institutional knowledge, but was dropped from the factor solution because we could not clearly differentiate it from Factor 4.

Although foreign business knowledge appears to capture the nuts and bolts of conducting international assignments, Factor 5 seems to be picking up an additional element relating to the technical aspects of managing international expansion. Variables pertaining to issues of product and process development and adaptation combine to explain an additional 10.5

Table 30.1 Rotated factor matrix of variables on assignment execution and previous business exerience

Variables	Factor 1	Factor 2	Factor 3	Factor 4	Factor 5
1. Customers in New Zealand	**0.592**	0.363	−0.208	−0.218	0.009
2. Suppliers in New Zealand	**0.735**	−0.137	−0.003	0.178	0.240
3. Suppliers abroad	**0.784**	−0.174	0.189	0.249	0.124
4. Customer's customers	**0.727**	0.178	0.199	0.004	0.080
5. Customer's suppliers of products and services that supplement yours	**0.748**	0.032	0.139	0.330	−0.309
6. Competing suppliers	**0.654**	0.238	0.189	−0.154	−0.237
7. Laws on technology, product and quality standards	0.136	0.130	0.092	**0.851**	0.184
8. Business laws	0.105	0.155	0.271	**0.799**	0.017
9. Business culture	0.028	−0.019	0.193	0.090	0.193
10. Language	−0.004	0.413	**0.625**	−0.078	0.382
11. Infrastructure	0.137	0.009	**0.752**	0.288	0.123
12. Industry structure	0.128	0.037	**0.813**	0.254	−0.109
13. Management and support of personnel abroad	0.078	**0.578**	**0.675**	0.153	0.053
14. Practice of financing assignments abroad	0.043	**0.710**	0.308	−0.036	0.002
15. Product development and adaptation	0.029	0.431	0.124	0.085	**0.765**
16. Production process development and adaptation	0.005	0.161	0.172	0.138	**0.850**
17. Doing business with new customers	0.030	**0.850**	0.235	0.169	0.208
18. Doing business in new markets	0.067	**0.849**	0.052	0.104	0.235
			0.047		
Percentage of variation explained	17.5	16.9	14.0	10.5	10.5
Cumulative percentage of variation explained	17.5	34.4	48.4	58.9	69.4
Cronbach's alpha:	0.820	0.780	0.786	0.758	0.876

Variables dropped after first factor solution

	Reason
1. Practice on technology, product and quality standards	Factor loading at $0.405 < 0.55$ threshold; loaded on Factor 5
2. Financial practices and currency laws	Loading on Factor 3 at $0.597 = 0.2$ from loading of 0.436 on Factor 4
3. Management practice of cooperating	Loading on Factor 2 at $0.552 = 0.2$ from loading of 0.391 on Factor 3

Variables dropped after first factor solution

	Reason
1. Customers abroad	Loading on Factor 1 at $0.545 = 0.2$ from loading of 0.374 on Factor 2
2. Foreign and international authorities and organizations	Loading on Factor 1 at $0.556 = 0.2$ from loading of 0.423 on Factor 3

per cent of the variance in our data with a reliable Cronbach's alpha of 0.876. Again it may be the case that we have captured another experiential knowledge construct that we might term 'foreign development/adaptation knowledge'. The variable concerned with practical experience of technology, product and quality standards also loaded on Factor 5 but was dropped from the analysis because the factor loading of 0.41 failed to meet the threshold 0.55 factor loading (Hair *et al.*, 1998) for incorporation in to the final factor solution.

Conclusions and implications

This chapter aimed to identify variables relating to previous experience that managers find valuable in conducting a current international business assignment and to relate these to the experiential knowledge constructs of Eriksson *et al.* (1997, 2000). The data illustrate that prior knowledge of clients, the market and competitors, or foreign business knowledge, the firm's experience of organizing international efforts, or internationalization knowledge, and experience of foreign governments, institutional frameworks, rules, norms and values, or foreign institutional knowledge, are key considerations in the conduct of current international assignments. Our results reinforce the 'Uppsala model' showing that experiential knowledge is an important explanatory variable in international developments. In addition, this study was able to identify and refine the constructs of internationalization knowledge, foreign business knowledge and foreign institutional knowledge as originally proposed by Eriksson *et al.* (1997). More importantly, perhaps, two additional and meaningful constructs were identified, namely foreign compliance knowledge and foreign development/ adaptation knowledge.

First, foreign compliance knowledge represents a meaningful construct since prior studies on exporting impediments have highlighted how firms struggle to come to terms with the administration and customs procedures of different countries (for a review, see Aaby and Slater, 1989). Indeed, while Styles and Ambler (1994) found few exporting problems relating to infrastructure issues in industrialized markets, difficult legal problems were highlighted as an exception. We expected these items to load on the foreign institutional knowledge construct in our study, but our data highlight that legal concerns about doing business in the target nation and about product, technology and quality standards are important and distinct issues. Refinement of this foreign compliance knowledge construct might involve the addition of concern for financial laws, which in the original data set was grouped with financial practice and which we had to drop from the analysis because of the high loading on the two factors of foreign compliance knowledge and foreign institutional knowledge. Financial practice may then separately and more strongly load on the foreign institutional knowledge construct.

Second, our finding concerning the importance of previous foreign development/adaptation knowledge may help to shed light on contradictory findings on product adaptation and export success; for example, Cavusgil and Zou (1994) found in favour of adaptation, while Christensen *et al.* (1987) found in favour of standardization. Rather than a direct relationship existing between adaptation and export success, perhaps there is an indirect relationship with prior adaptation experience acting as a moderating effect. In addition, in terms of the development focus, Nassimbeni (2001) found that, to enter and be successful in foreign markets, firms were both compelled and stimulated to extend their product range, innovate and improve the customization techniques. He concluded that, since many of the marketing mix elements become delegated to market intermediaries as firms enter new markets, innovation of the product is one area where firms are able to 'act with greater effect and autonomy' (ibid.: 260). Issues of product and process development and adaptation were originally expected to load on the internationalization knowledge construct, and this clear distinction indicates that prior experience in this area is an important and separate consideration in the international development of the firm. Refinement of this construct might involve changing the item, practice of technology, product and quality standards, which failed to meet the loading threshold, to experience with product extension, innovation and customization following the findings of Nassimbeni (2001).

In terms of future research, we have identified some variables that require further development and refinement in the context of Eriksson *et al.*'s original experiential knowledge constructs (1997). Where we have one variable loading on two separate constructs, there may be scope for unbundling these aspects of international experiential knowledge. For example, experience with overseas customers loaded on both the foreign business knowledge and internationalization knowledge constructs. It may be more meaningful to ask separate questions pertaining to the situational learning from relations with overseas customers (foreign business knowledge) and to the processual learning picked up from interactions with overseas customers (internationalization knowledge). Likewise experience with foreign and international authorities and organizations loaded on both foreign business knowledge and foreign institutional knowledge. It may be more appropriate to separate these foreign international authorities and organizations on the basis of whether they have direct relations with the study firms (foreign business knowledge) or more indirect relations (foreign institutional knowledge). Finally, with management practice of cooperating loading on both internationalization knowledge and foreign institutional knowledge, it may be better to separate this item on the basis of task-driven cooperation (internationalization knowledge) from environmentally driven cooperation (foreign institutional knowledge).

References

Aaby, N.-E. and Slater, S.F., 'Management Influences on Export Performance: A Review of the Empirical Literature 1978–88', *Int. Mktg. Review* 6 (1989): 7–26.

Andersen, Otto, 'On the Internationalisation Process of Firms: A Critical Analysis', *J. of Int. Bus. Studies* 24 (1993): 209–32.

Aulakh, Preet S., Kotabe, Masaaki and Sahay, Arvind, 'Trust and Performance in Cross-border Marketing Partnerships: a Behavioural Approach', *J. of Int. Bus. Studies*, special issue (1996): 1005–29.

Barkema, Harry G., Bell, John H.G. and Pennings, Johannes M., 'Foreign Entry, Cultural Barriers, and Learning', *Strat. Mgt. J.* 17 (1996): 151–66.

Barkema Harry G., Shenkar, Oded, Vermeulen, Freek and Bell, John H.G., 'Working Abroad, Working With Others: How Firms Learn to Operate International Joint Ventures', *Acad. of Mgt. J.* 40 (1997): 426–42.

Beamish, Paul W., 'Joint Venture Performance in Developing Countries', Unpublished PhD dissertation (1984), The University of Western Ontario, London, Ontario, Canada.

Beamish, Paul W. and Banks, John C., 'Equity Joint Ventures and the Theory of the Multinational Enterprise', *J. of Int. Bus. Studies* 19 (1987): 1–16.

Bilkey, Warren J. and Tesar, George, 'The Export Behaviour of Smaller Wisconsin Manufacturing Firms', *J. of Int. Bus. Studies* 9 (Spring/Summer 1977): 93–8.

Brockman, E. and Anthony, W., 'The Influence of Tacit Knowledge and Collective Mind on Strategic Planning', *J. of Mgt. Issues* 10 (1998): 204–22.

Calof, Jonathan L. and Beamish, Paul W., 'Adapting to Foreign Markets: Explaining Internationalisation', *Int. Bus. Review* 4 (1995): 115–31.

Cavusgil, S. Tamer and Nevin, John R., 'Internal Determinants of Export Marketing Behaviour: an Empirical Investigation', *J. of Mktg. Res.* (February 1981): 114–19.

Cavusgil, S. Tamer and Zou, S., 'Marketing Strategy–Performance Relationship: An Investigation of the Empirical Link in Export Market Ventures', *J. of Mktg.* 58 (January 1994): 1–21.

Christensen, C.H., Rocha, A. and Gertner, R.K., 'An Empirical Investigation of the Factors Influencing Export Success of Brazilian Firms', *J. of Bus. Studies* (Fall 1987): 61–77.

Cohen, Wesley M. and Levinthal, Daniel A., 'Absorptive Capacity: A New Perspective on Learning and Innovation', *Admin. Science Quarterly* 35 (1990): 128–52.

Cronbach, L.J., 'Coefficient Alpha and the Internal Structure of Tests', *Psychometrika* 16 (1951): 297–334.

Denis, J. and Depelteau, D., 'Market Knowledge, Diversification and Export Expansion', *J. of Int. Bus. Studies* 16 (1985): 77–89.

Eriksson, Kent, Johanson, Jan, Majkgård, Anders and Sharma, D. Deo, 'Experiential Knowledge and Cost in the Internationalisation Process', *J. of Int. Bus. Studies* 28 (1997): 337–60.

Eriksson, Kent, Johanson, Jan, Majkgård, Anders and Sharma, D. Deo, 'Effect of Variation on Knowledge Accumulation in the Internationalisation Process', *Int. Studies of Mgt. and Org.* 30 (2000): 26–44.

Golen, S., 'An Analysis of Communication Barriers in Public Accounting Firms', *The J. of Bus. Communication* 17 (1980): 39–49.

Hair, Joseph F., Anderson, Rolph, Tatham, Ronald L. and Black, William C., *Multivariate Data Analysis*, Sydney: Prentice-Hall International, 1998.

Hallen Lars, Johanson Jan and Seyed-Mohamed, Nazim, 'Interfirm Adaptation in Business Relationships', *J. of Mktg.* 55 (April 1991): 29–37.

Hamel, Gary, 'Competition for Competence and Interpartner Learning Within International Strategic Alliances', *Strat. Mgt. J.* 12 (1991): 83–103.

Hedlund, Gunnar and Kverneland, Arne, 'Are Strategies for Foreign Markets Changing? The Case of Swedish Investment in Japan', *Int. Studies of Mgt. and Org.* 15 (1985): 41–59.

Johanson, Jan and Vahlne, Jan-Erik, 'The Internationalisation Process of the Firm – A Model of Knowledge Development and Increasing Foreign Market Commitments', *J. of Int. Bus. Studies* 8 (Spring/Summer 1977): 23–32.

Johanson, Jan and Vahlne, Jan-Erik, 'The Mechanism of Internationalisation', *Int. Mktg. Review* 7 (1990): 11–24.

Johanson, Jan and Wiedersheim-Paul, Finn, 'The Internationalisation of the Firm – Four Swedish Cases', *J. of Mgt. Studies* 12 (1975): 305–22.

Johnson, Jean L., Cullen, John B., Sakano, Tomoaki and Takenouchi, Hideyuki, 'Setting the Stage for Trust and Strategic Integration in Japanese–U.S. Cooperative Alliances', *J. of Int. Bus. Studies* 27 (1996): 981–1004.

Kerlinger, Fred N., *Foundations of Behavioral Research*, New York: Holt, Rinehart and Winston, 1986.

Luostarinen, Reijo, *Internationalisation of the Firm*, Helsinki: Helsinki School of Economics, 1980.

Madhok, Anoop, 'Know-how-, Experience- and Competition-related Considerations in Foreign Market Entry: an Exploratory Investigation', *Int. Bus. Review* 5 (1996): 339–66.

Madhok, Anoop, 'Cost, Value and Foreign Market Entry Mode: The Transaction and the Firm', *Strat. Mgt. J.* 18 (1997): 39–61.

Makino, Shige and Delios, Andrew (1996), 'Local Knowledge Transfer and Performance: Implications for Alliance Formation in Asia', *J. of Int. Bus. Studies* 27 (1996): 905–27.

Miller, D. and Chen, Ming-Jer, 'The Simplicity of Competitive Repertoires: An Empirical Analysis', *Strat. Mgt. J.* 17 (1996): 419–39.

Millington, Andrew I. and Bayliss, Brian T., 'The Process of Internationalisation: UK Companies in the EC', *Mgt. Int. Review* 30 (1990): 151–61.

Nassimbeni, Guido, 'Technology, Innovation Capacity, and the Export Attitude of Small Manufacturing Firms: a Logit/Tobit Model', *Res. Policy* 30 (2001): 245–62.

Nelson, Richard R. and Winter, Sidney G., *An Evolutionary Theory of Economic Change*, Cambridge, MA: Harvard University Press, 1982.

Reid, Stan, 'The Decision-Maker and Export Entry and Expansion', *J. of Int. Bus. Studies* 12 (1981): 101–12.

Styles, Chris and Ambler, Tim, 'Successful Export Practice: the UK Experience', *Int. Mktg. Review* 11 (1994): 23–47.

Von Hippel, E., 'Successful Industrial Products from Customer Ideas', *J. of Mktg.* 42 (1978): 39–49.

Welch, Lawrence and Luostarinen, Reijo, 'Internationalisation: Evolution of a Concept', *J. of General Mgt.* 14 (1988): 34–55.

31 Swedish perspectives of international entrepreneurship

Anders Blomstermo, Kent Eriksson and D. Deo Sharma

The internationalization process research (Welch and Wiedersheim-Paul, 1980a,b), as well as research in business strategy (Porter, 1985) have acknowledged the importance of domestic operations for the international operations of firms. It is concluded that firms start operations in domestic markets, and, thereafter, enter international markets. Porter's (1980) framework 'five forces', 'generic strategies' and 'value chain' have their roots in the domestic market of the firm. He argues that the firms should implement its strategy by managing well in the domestic market. Superior performance can result from competitive advantage of a firm being perceived as having a focus on one particular market segment. Research on born globals, on the other hand, questions the impact of domestic experience on international operations (McDougall *et al.*, 1994; Knight and Cavusgil, 1996). To the best of our knowledge, the effects of domestic operations on learning and knowledge accumulation in the internationalization process of firms is controversial and remains largely uninvestigated.

We investigate the effects of the duration of domestic operations on the accumulation of knowledge in internationalizing firms. This is important since firms often start their operations in the domestic market. An important research issue is how the duration of domestic operations influences the accumulation of knowledge in firms.

Internationalization process studies that use a behavioural approach emphasize the importance of knowledge and learning in the internationalization of firms. Based on the work by Aharoni (1966), Cyert and March (1963) and Penrose (1959), it is stated that the internationalization process of firms is path-dependent, based on experience, sequential, local, and relies upon feedback (Autio et al., 2000; Eriksson et al., 2000, 2001). The authors also emphasize that firms initially operate in their domestic markets and that any knowledge accumulated reflects operations in these domestic contexts (Bilkey, 1978; Johanson and Vahlne, 1977; Perlmutter, 1969; Vernon, 1966). Firms collect knowledge on markets abroad through operations in the market. As firms operate abroad they learn about their clients, their needs, resources and limitations. Operations abroad are a source of knowledge on new business options, opportunities as well as threats, abroad (Chang, 1995; Kogut, 1983). The current stock of knowledge thus drives the future course of internationalization decisions in firms. Accumulating knowledge on foreign markets is costly (Eriksson et al., 1997). Studies show that in the process of going abroad firms gradually increase resource commitment abroad. Firms start internationalizing from countries at a short psychic distance from their domestic market. Initially firms export. Thereafter, resource commitment abroad is increased and firms establish sales subsidiaries abroad. Finally, foreign production starts (Johanson and Wiedersheim-Paul, 1975). Three interrelated components of knowledge, critical to internationalization, are identified: internationalization knowledge, foreign business knowledge and foreign institutional knowledge (Eriksson et al. 1997). Institutional knowledge is defined as knowledge of government and institutional framework, rules, norms and values that apply in the markets where firms operate. Internationalization knowledge concerns knowledge of the firm's capability and resources for engaging in international operations. Internationalization knowledge operates as a repository in which knowledge may be stored for some time (Yu, 1990). It is firm-specific, and integrates and coordinates all internationalization activities of a firm, including the search for and transmission of business and institutional knowledge. This knowledge is embedded in the routines, norms and structure of a firm, and is neither country-specific nor specific to the foreign market entry mode. A critical consideration in internationalization is the compatibility of the firm's existing resources and those needed for a particular foreign market (Johanson and Vahlne, 1977; Madhok, 1997). Business knowledge is defined as knowledge about customers, competitors and market conditions in particular foreign markets. In overseas markets, a lack of knowledge about clients and the manner in which they do business creates problems. The three components of knowledge are related, and thus a lack of internationalization knowledge influences lack of business knowledge and institutional knowledge about foreign markets. The number of countries in which a firm is operating abroad, as well as the length of operations abroad, affect the knowledge accumulation in internationalizing firms (Eriksson et al., 2000a, 2001; Luo, 1999).

We begin with a discussion of learning in the internationalization process of firms. Then, we present our structural model, in which three different types of knowledge in the internationalization process of the firm are identified. This leads to the formation of five hypotheses on the relationship between the duration of domestic operations and knowledge development in a firm's internationalization process. Thereafter, a presentation of the method and data employed is given, followed by an LISREL analysis. The results are then discussed and some implications examined in more detail.

Learning in the internationalization process
The internationalization process of firms implies accumulating new knowledge and making sense of an unknown and unfamiliar situation. In this sense-making process, internationalizing firms first extract cues from a situation that they are unfamiliar with. These cues form the seeds from which managers develop a larger sense of institutional and business knowledge abroad (Weick, 1991). In this sense-making, the current theory-in-use in a firm plays a dominant role. Based on a firm's theory-in-use, information is filtered and adjusted to the firm's own information-processing capacity. The current theory-in-use in firms influences the sense-making process through (1) determining what cues are extracted, and (2) interpreting the extracted cues. In the context of the internationalization of firms, domestic operations influence both steps in the sense-making process. The existing theory-in-use restricts what new knowledge firms can accumulate. In turbulent environments internationalizing firms need to unlearn some of the old and established knowledge. Learning is dynamic and involves making sense out of past histories; it is linked to current and past knowledge. Knowledge is embedded in the organizational routines, administrative structure (Senge, 1990) or theory in use (Argyris and Schön, 1978) developed to manage operations of firms. When going abroad, firms base their activities on this domestically accumulated knowledge.

We distinguish between lower and higher orders of learning in the internationalization process of firms. These are embedded in a firm's routines and theory-in-use, as well as the strategies of the firm. In the context of going abroad, internationalization knowledge forms the theory-in-use in firms, with regard to their international business strategy. Lack of internationalization knowledge is perceived when the theory-in-use is vague or irrelevant. A lack of internationalization knowledge leads to lack of business and institutional knowledge about overseas markets. Higher order learning implies a restructuring of the existing theory-in-use in firms (Argyris and Schön, 1978). When the theory-in-use is applied to international operations, similarities and differences between the domestic and foreign operations are detected and cues are collected. Deviations and errors are recorded, leading to modifications and restructuring of the theories-in-use in firms. If such errors are compatible with the existing mental models, corrections are made without altering the current mental models and theory-in-use. Such lower order learning may result in differentiation, specification and extension of the theory-in-use or marginal modification of strategies and structures.

Higher order learning in the internationalization process occurs when (a) experience concerns areas that are fundamental to the firm, (b) repeated error corrections do not lead to the expected outcomes, and (c) there is an accumulation of a number of errors that together question the assumptions of the received theory-in-use. A restructuring of the theory-in-use and the corresponding mental models may take place when the received theory-in-use no longer seems workable. Higher order learning is based on lower order learning, so the accumulated knowledge of a firm contains elements of both lower and higher order. Restructuring of the theory-in-use and corresponding mental models is for the most part gradual and expensive.

Three hypotheses

Several internationalization models and export studies emphasize the importance of domestic operations. In the product life-cycle model the importance of domestic operations is explicit (Vernon, 1966). Such models state that initially (that is, in phase 1) products are innovated and produced in the domestic (in this case, the US) market and that domestic operations act as a source of advantage for these firms. In later phases, as the market potential abroad builds, production moves abroad. Thus, in phase 2, foreign production starts. In phase 3, foreign producers become just as competitive in their export markets and, in phase 4, import competition within the US market begins. The U-model by Johanson and Vahlne (1977) postulates, though only implicitly, a connection between domestic operations and the internationalization of firms. In a related work, Welch and Wiedersheim-Paul (1980a) and Wiedersheim-Paul et al. (1978) are explicit in their emphasis on the importance of domestic operations for the internationalization process of firms, and state that internationalization starts at home.

Several other researchers emphasize the importance of domestic operations: the eclectic approach (Dunning, 1977), the transaction cost approach (Williamson, 1975) and the internalization theory (Buckley and Casson, 1976). None of these studies, however, explicitly analyses the effects of domestic operations on knowledge accumulation in firms. In these theories, a precondition for successful internationalization of firms is a firm-specific advantage. This firm-specific advantage is then used abroad to compensate for the disadvantages of being a foreigner on the market (Hymer, 1976). Finally Porter (1985) argues in favour of a direct correlation between domestic operations and a firm's international competitiveness. Ghosal (1994) states that firms that internationalize early develop fewer routines, which may inhibit their internationalization.

In a number of empirically based export studies, a measure of the duration of domestic operations of firms is frequently included. In an early study, Bilkey and Tesar (1977) identify six stages in the export expansion of firms, followed by Cavusgil (1984) who identifies five stages, Czinkota (1982) and Barret and Wilkinson (1985) with six, Moon and Lee (1990) with three, Lim, Sharkey and Kim (1991) with four and, most recently, Rao and Naidu (1992) and Crick (1995) with six stages of export expansion. Although the above studies do differ, they all adopt the duration of domestic operations as one of the stages in the export development process of firms. And although implicit, a direct correlation between the duration of domestic operations and the knowledge accumulated in firms is presumed. However, as stated by Leonidou and Katsikeas (1996), none of the studies operationalize the effects of domestic operations explicitly. In a similar study, Ursic and Czinkota (1984) examine the attitude of firms towards exporting, finding a more favourable attitude towards exporting in firms that have been in business for less than 20 years than in firms that have been in business for more than 20 years. The effect of domestic operations is, however, not analysed. In his studies of US firms, Davidson (1980, 1983) does not explicitly analyse the effects of domestic market operations.

In a study on manufacturing firms, Brush (1992) found that longer domestic operations prior to initiating foreign sales did not positively affect foreign sales. In their study of Canadian firms entering the US market, O'Grady and Lane (1996) found that prior experience in the domestic market actually inhibited firms from learning about the differences between Canadian and US customers, as well as the level of competition in the US market. Brush (1992), McDougall et al. (1994) and Oviatt and McDougall (1994) show that many firms entered overseas markets early in their lifetime. McDougall et al. (1994), Jolly, Alahuta, and Jeannet (1992) and McKinsey & Co. (1993) found several firms who served the world market from the very start, concluding, that from inception, firms have the necessary mental models and organizational routines to combine resources from the different national markets. Similarly, Bell (1995) found a number of firms that did not establish domestic sales before going international, more important factors being relationships, both foreign and domestic, industry-specific factors and the nature of the niche in the target market. Reid (1981) states that, in newer, smaller firms, the competence and experience of top management is more likely to influence internationalization.

The effect of domestic operations on knowledge accumulation in internationalizing firms is thus unclear. Though none of the above-mentioned studies differentiates between the different components of knowledge, an overwhelming volume of the empirical research in the field supports the view that accumulating knowledge in domestic markets may actually have a negative effect on a firm's accumulation of foreign business knowledge. This may happen as going abroad implies operations in a new environment and this may require unlearning some old knowledge and practices developed in the domestic market. The firm's procedural knowledge may thus be domestic knowledge that is applied to an international situation, and there is a need for the firm to unlearn the domestically generated procedural knowledge and develop procedural internationalization knowledge. Such an unlearning is, however, difficult to achieve. The knowledge accumulated in domestic markets may develop as a barrier to internationalizing. The longer a firm operates in the domestic market the more institutionalized the domestic market based knowledge and business practices in the firm and the more difficult it is to unlearn them. In combination with the literature on learning reviewed earlier, we therefore formulate the following hypothesis:

> H1   The longer a firm operates in its domestic market, the more
> it lacks foreign business knowledge.

Researchers on internationalization processes of firms recognize the importance of knowledge about foreign culture, governments, rules and regulations (Lenway and Murtha, 1994; Jansson, Saqib and Sharma, 1995). Research shows that new exporters are less aware of foreign institutions. New exporters frequently perceive a lack of knowledge about institutional aspects such as the international transfer of funds, documentation requirements (Yang, Leione, and Alden, 1992) and foreign business practices (Czinkota and Johnston, 1981) as problematic. In addition, managers of firms with long domestic market experience may not be aware of the underlying assumptions of their own culture, which, in turn, may inhibit them from learning about the foreign institutional environment. In the process of internationalization, misinterpretations may occur (O'Grady and Lane, 1996). Therefore our second hypothesis is formulated:

> H2   The longer a firm operates in the domestic market, the
> more it lacks foreign institutional knowledge.

Cohen and Levinthal (1990), show that existing theory-in-use and the associated routines exert a determining effect on future accumulation of knowledge in internationalizing firms. In the context of internationalization, this implies that the theory-in-use in firms that is based on their domestic operations, may inhibit an internationalizing firm from picking up and interpreting cues from abroad. This in turn may inhibit accumulation of knowledge on foreign markets. If the firm has been operating in the domestic market for a long time, its current theory-in-use is likely to be strong. Replacing the current theory-in-use in a firm may require radical redefinition of the firm's strategies and operations. This is cumbersome, expensive and time-consuming. Research on national culture shows that 'how things are done' varies across nations (Hofstede, 2001). Buckley (1993) argues that firms may become dependent on national traits and these may be non-transferable to foreign markets. The internationalization knowledge and the theory-in-use of firms are 'automatically' and 'unconsciously' accessible to the internationalizing firms. This inhibits adaptation to foreign markets and the ability to learn. A higher order learning is hard to achieve. We therefore propose:

> H3   The longer a firm operates in its domestic market, the more
> it lacks internationalization knowledge.

Methodology
A questionnaire-based statistical survey was conducted. We used three secondary sources: trade registers, branch registers and business publications. The sample size, by industry, was as follows: legal services 16 (4.5%), engineering and architecture firms 119 (32.9%), computer software and data processing 36 (9.9%), advertising 54 (14.9%), accounting 17 (4.7%), education firms 19 (5.2%), management consulting 78 (21.5%), and miscellaneous services 23 (6.4%). Altogether, 774 companies were included in the mail survey. The questionnaires were addressed to the company presidents engaged in the firms' foreign operations. In all, 329 presidents and 33 vice-presidents of foreign operations, finance and other, answered the questions. A five-point Likert scale (ranging from 'not at all important' to 'very important') was used. The response rate was 62.7%, and 47 of the 409 responding firms were excluded from the analysis for reasons of insufficient information on a number of variables. The remaining 362 firms provided data on most key variables. However the amount of time (duration) since the company's first step abroad was provided by 206 firms, which is our sample. A standard test of non-response bias shows no differences between early and late respondents (Armstrong and Overton, 1977). Consequently non-response bias is not a problem.

In order to analyze the general knowledge development process in the internationalization process of firms, we used a measure that did not relate to any specific internationalization decision. Incremental market commitment has been measured as the execution of an additional client order abroad. 'Additional' implies receiving a new assignment from customers or an additional assignment for an existing customer. The respondents were not asked to consider any specific market or any specific foreign market entry mode.

The overall fit of the LISREL models is assessed by χ^2, degree of freedom measures, and a probability estimate (p-value) (Jöreskog and Sörbom, 1993: 121). The R^2 value is a measure of the strength of a linear relationship estimate. To test significance, the t-values are studied. Pairwise deletion is used to take into consideration missing values. We also checked by listwise deletion and received more or less the same result.

The structural model

The construct 'lack of business knowledge' is meant to capture the lack of knowledge about such things as foreign firms, clients and markets abroad. The construct consists of two indicators (Figure 31.1), which concern important ways of gaining foreign business knowledge. They concern the respondents' evaluation of the lack of foreign subsidiaries or representative companies outside the domestic market, or the lack of cooperative agreements with foreign firms. The construct 'lack of institutional knowledge' reflects knowledge about the institutional conditions and the culture and language of foreign markets. The construct consists of two indicators, which are specific, and concern a lack of knowledge about the language, laws, norms and standards in foreign business. The construct 'lack of internationalization knowledge' concerns the international experience in general. This type of experience is gained from operating in an international environment and is not a country-specific experience. The construct consists of two indicators: lack of foreign experience and lack of unique knowledge and competence. The construct 'perceived cost' consists of one indicator based on the perception of the overall cost of an additional assignment abroad. This indicator captures the overall cost judgement made by managers. Finally, the construct 'domestic duration' consists of one indicator based on the difference between a firm's year of establishment and its first operations abroad. This objective indicator was coded as a 7-point log scale.

Results

The first empirical test is to investigate whether domestic duration has an effect on knowledge development for these firms. For this purpose, domestic duration was coded as a seven-point log scale, where 1 represents a duration of less than five years, including also 'born globals'. The subsequent scale points are log transformations of the length of domestic duration of less than five years. The distribution is skewed, with most firms having less than five years' experience before internationalization commences. The effect of domestic duration on the knowledge development model for all firms is displayed in figure 31.1. The results show that a longer domestic duration leads to a greater perceived lack of internationalization knowledge. The direct effect on business and institutional knowledge is positive but insignificant. Apparently there is a need to develop internationalization knowledge before specific business and institutional conditions in local markets can be understood. However the clarity of these results is muddled by the fact that domestic duration does not explain much of the variation in internationalization knowledge ($R^2 = 0.02$). This issue is further investigated by dividing the sample into two groups, those with less than five years domestic duration, and those with five years or more domestic duration.

Firms with domestic durations longer than five years differ from the total sample. First, they exhibit no significant effect of domestic duration on lack of internationalization knowledge (coefficient = 0.13, $t = 1.32$). In this group, internationalization knowledge seems not to play the fundamental role it plays for all firms, taken together. Also domestic duration increases the perceived lack of institutional knowledge. Institutional knowledge is more fundamental in knowledge development since increasing lack of institutional knowledge also increases the perceived cost of an additional step abroad. The effect on business knowledge is insignificant. The results show that business knowledge is of less significance and does not play a fundamental role in internationalization for firms with domestic operations before internationalization. Firms with previous domestic duration have developed a way of learning about market expansion that is not sensitive to issues specific to internationalization, but that this is still the basis for their international expansion. They experience difficulties in attaining knowledge about institutional conditions in foreign markets. This can be explained in that such firms follow their clients abroad, or that they, for other reasons, are not confronted with the task of developing business relationships in foreign markets.

The group of firms with little or no domestic duration is made up of firms with domestic durations of less than five years and those that are born global. They are grouped into one category in the previous analysis of all firms in the sample. But, in order to assess the effect of domestic duration, this analysis attempts to recode this one category into a scale. There is a positive significant (coefficient = 0.24, $t = 2.35$) effect on internationalization knowledge, suggesting that even limited domestic business is formative for the routines developed in a firm. The effect of domestic duration on institutional knowledge is negative and insignificant, suggesting that managers perceive that even a little domestic duration reduces the lack of business knowledge in international market expansion. One explanation for this may be that firms have not realized just how difficult it is to acquire institutional knowledge. The direct effect of domestic duration on business knowledge is significant and positive (coefficient = 0.63, $t = 4.03$). This can be interpreted as indicating that, the longer domestic duration the firm has, the more important is business knowledge in the internationalization process of firms.

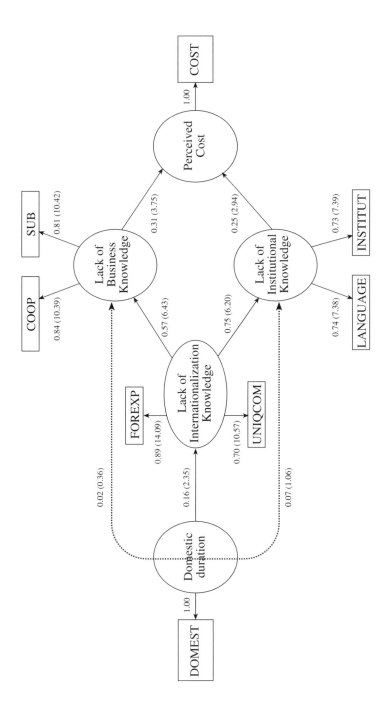

Note: Figures given are coefficients (t-values in parentheses). Model χ^2 is 22.20 (14 d.f.), p-value 0.08. Dotted lines represent insignificant relations. Complete questions for each indicator given in Appendix.

Figure 31.1 Effect of domestic duration on experiential knowledge model for all firms

Conclusion

Compared with other research, this chapter has the advantage that it relates domestic duration to knowledge development in the internationalizing firms. This is in line with the recent research that explains the internationalization process of firms in terms of experiential knowledge development and learning (Eriksson et al., 1997). This chapter has the advantage that it contributes to the developing research interest on Born Global firms and their learning processes in the internationalization process. Our results neither support or contradict the findings by Oviatt and McDougall (1994); on the other hand, this chapter raises many questions for future research.

The LISREL analysis supports the thesis that the length of domestic operations affects the accumulation of knowledge in the internationalizing firm. On a closer look we identified different patterns for firms with domestic duration shorter than five years and for those with five years' or more domestic duration before the first foreign assignment. Furthermore, H1 and H2 are not fully supported. H1 stated that the longer firms operate in the domestic market the more they lack foreign business knowledge. H2 stipulated a similar relationship for institutional knowledge. In both cases the direction of the correlation is as hypothesized, but the strength of the correlation is weak. These results do not contradict our theoretical approach, but we need more research. H3 stated that the longer a firm operates in the domestic market prior to going abroad the more it lacks internationalization knowledge. H3 is supported. Internationalization knowledge is a mediating construct in the model and all the effects of domestic duration are mediated by it. This construct captures a firm's ability to apply and develop its unique knowledge as it gains business knowledge from abroad. Our study indicates that born globals' show another structure of absorptive capacity than firms which have five years' or more domestic duration before the first foreign assignment. These findings support the earlier research on born globals by McDougall et al. (1994) and Oviatt and McDougall (1994). However, more research is required into early internationalization with particular emphasis on internationalization knowledge.

This chapter demonstrates that the duration of domestic business activities prior to the inception of internationalization is fundamental to knowledge development in a firm. The contribution of this result is to point out the importance of the formation of routines for subsequent knowledge development. Therefore internationalization is multifaceted, and firm learning about business problems is complex. The adolescence of the internationalizing firm contains many clues to future learning from continued expansion. A particular effect of the formation of routines is that business knowledge seems not to be a part of knowledge development for firms that have spent time domestically before going international. A likely explanation for this is that those firms follow their clients abroad, and do not seek new business relationships in the foreign market.

Managerial implications and future research
Our findings indicate that it is easier for firms – in terms of absorptive capacity – to go abroad soon after their inception. It is much harder for firms with long domestic experience to change their mental models and processes. Autio *et al.* (2000) found that, the earlier firms go abroad, the greater their knowledge intensity and the faster they grow internationally. As firms get older they develop mental models that hamper their ability to grow in new environments (Cohen and Levinthal, 1990). Second, in line with Hofstede (2001) our results point out that institutional knowledge is an important managerial issue for firms with five years' or more domestic operations before the first foreign assignment. Business knowledge and knowledge about the product are more easily transferred from the domestic market to the foreign market in comparison with institutional knowledge. At home, institutional matters are taken for granted by these firms and they often underestimate the problems in entering a new foreign market (O'Grady and Lane, 1996). The longer these firms work at home, the more processes and routines are developed. This implies that it is more difficult to unlearn and accumulate new knowledge. It requires new mental models and higher-order-learning in the internationalization process.

Our findings are based on a sample of service firms. Can those findings be generalized to manufacturing firms? Research based on samples of both can help us answer such questions. Moreover in-depth case studies can provide us with more detailed knowledge about the learning mechanisms in born globals. Finally, we suggest that there is reason to be cautious in assuming that long domestic operations are a fundamental prerequisite in the internationalization process of firms.

References

Aharoni, Y. (1966), *The foreign investment decision process.* Boston, Mass.: Division of Research, Graduate School of Business Administration, Harvard University.
Anderson, E. and Gatignon, H. (1986), Modes of entry: A transactions cost analysis and propositions. *Journal of International Business Studies*, 17 (3): 1–26.
Anderson, J.C. and Gerbing, D.W. (1988), Structural equation modeling in practice: A review and recommended two-step approach. *Psychological Bulletin*, 103 (3): 411–423.
Argyris, C. and Schön, D.A. (1978), *Organizational Learning: A theory of action perspective.* Addison-Wesley: Reading, Mass.
Armstrong, J.S. and Overton, T.S. (1977), Estimating non-response bias in mail surveys. *Journal of Marketing Research*, 1(3): 396–402.
Autio, E., Sapienza H.J. and Almeida J.G. (2000), Effects of age at entry, knowledge intensity, and imitability on international growth. *Academy of Management Journal,* 4(5): 909–924.

Ball, C.A. and Tschoegl, A.E. (1982), The decision to establish a foreign bank branch or sub-sidiary: An application of binary classification procedures. *Journal of Financial and Quantitative Analysis*, 17: 411–424

Barkema, H.G., Bell, J.H.J. and Pennings, J.M. (1996), Foreign entry, cultural barriers, and learning. *Strategic Management Journal*, 17: 151–166.

Barkema, H.G. and Vermeulen, F. (1998), International expansion through start-up or acqui-sition: A learning perspective. *Academy of Management Journal*, 41 (1): 7–27.

Barret, N.I. and Wilkinson, I.F. (1985), Export stimulation: A segmentation study of the exporting problems of Australian manufacturing firms. *European Journal of Marketing*, 19 (2): 53–72.

Beamish, P.W. and Banks, J.C. (1987), Equity joint ventures and the theory of the multina-tional enterprise. *Journal of International Business Studies*, 19 (2): 1–16.

Bell, J. (1995), The internationalization of small computer software firms: A further challenge to 'stage' theories. *European Journal of Marketing*, 29: 60–75.

Bilkey, W.J. (1978), An attempted integration of the literature on the export behavior of firms. *Journal of International Business Studies*, 13 (Fall): 39–55.

Bilkey, W.J. and Tesar, G. (1977), The export behaviour of smaller sized Wisconsin manufac-turing firms. *Journal of International Business Studies*, 8 (1): 93–98.

Bollen, K.A. (1989), *Structural equations with latent variables.* New York: John Wiley & Sons.

Bollen, K.A. and Long, S.J. (eds) (1993), *Testing Structural Equation Models.* Newbury Park: Sage.

Brush, C. (1992), *Factors motivating small firms to internationalize: The effect of firm age.* Doctoral dissertation, Boston University.

Buckley, P.J. (1993), The role of management in internalisation theory. *Management International Review*, 33 (3): 197–207.

Buckley, P.J. and Casson, M. (1976), *The future of the multinational enterprise.* London: Macmillan.

Burenstam-Linder, S. (1961), *An essay on trade and transformation.* New York: Wiley.

Calof, L.J. and Beamish, P.W. (1995), Adapting to foreign markets: Explaining international-ization. *International Business Review*, 4 (2): 115–131.

Cavusgil, S.T. (1980), On the internationalization process of firms. *European Research*, 8(November): 273–281.

Cavusgil, S.T. (1984), Organizational characteristics associated with export activity. *Journal of Management Studies*, 21 (1): 3–22.

Chang, S.J. (1995), International expansion strategy of Japanese firms: Capability building through sequential entry. *Academy of Management Journal*, 38 (2): 383–407.

Cohen, W. and Levinthal, D. (1990), Absorptive capacity: A new perspective on learning and innovation. *Administration Science Quarterly*, 35: 128–152.

Corsini, R. (1987), *Concise encyclopedia of psychology.* New York: Wiley.

Crick, D. (1995), An investigation into the targeting of U.K. export assistance. *European Journal of Marketing*, 29 (8): 76–94.

Cyert, R.M. and March, J.G. (1963), *A behavioural theory of the firm.* New York: Prentice-Hall.

Czinkota, M. (1982), *Export development strategies: US promotion policies.* New York: Praeger Publishers.

Czinkota, M. and Johnston, W.J. (1981), Segmenting US firms for export development. *Journal of Business Research*, 9 (4): 353–366.

Davenport, T.H. and Prusak, L. (1998), *Working knowledge.* Harvard Business School Press: Boston, MA.

Davidson, W.H. (1980), The location of foreign direct investment activity: country character-istics and experience effects. *Journal of International Business Studies*, 11 (2): 9–22.

Davidson, W.H. (1983), Market similarity and market selection: Implications of international marketing strategy. *Journal of Business Research*, 11: 439–456.

Duncan, R. and Weiss, A. (1979), Organizational learning: Implications for organizational design. In B. Staw *et al.* (eds), *Research in Organizational Behavior*, 1: 75–132, Greenwich, CT: JAI Press.

Dunning, J.H. (1977), Trade, location of economic activity and the MNE: A search for an eclectic approach. In B. Ohlin *et al.* (eds), *The international allocation of economic activity.* New York: Holmes & Meier.

Dunning, J.H. (1980), Towards an eclectic theory of international production: some empirical tests. *Journal of International Business Studies*, 11 (1): 9–31.

Dunning, J.H. (1988), The eclectic paradigm of international production: A restatement and some possible extensions. *Journal of International Business Studies*, 19 (1): 1–31.

Eriksson, K., Johanson, J., Majkgård, A. and Sharma, D.D. (1997), Experiential knowledge and cost in the internationalization process, *Journal of International Business Studies*, 28 (2): 337–360.

Eriksson, K., Johanson, J., Majkgård, A. and Sharma, D.D. (2001), Time and experience in the internationalization process. *Zeitschrift Für Betriebswirtschaft*, 71 (1): 21–44.

Eriksson, K., Johanson, J., Majkgård, A. and Sharma, D.D. (2000a), Effect of variation on knowledge accumulation in the internationalization process. *International Studies of Management & Organization*, 30 (1): 26–44.

Eriksson, K., Majkgård, A. and Sharma, D.D. (2000b), Path dependence in the internationalization process. *Management International Review*, 40 (4): 307–328.

Fiol, C.M. and Lyles, M.A. (1985), Organizational learning. *Academy of Management Review*, 1 (4): 803–813.

Garvin, D., A. (1993), Building a learning organization. *Harvard Business Review*, 71 (4): 78–91.

Gatignon, H. and Anderson, E. (1988), The multinational corporation's degree of control over foreign subsidiaries: An empirical test of a transaction cost explanation. *Journal of Law, Economics, and Organization*, 4 (2): 305–335.

Ghosal, S. (1994), Diversification and diversifact. *California Management Review*, 37 (1), 8–28.

Hayduk, L.A. (1987), *Structural equation modeling with LISREL: Essentials and advances.* Baltimore: John Hopkins University Press.

Hofstede, G. (2001), *Culture's Consequences: Comparing values, behaviors, institutions, and organizations across nations.* Thousand Oaks, California: Sage Publications.

Hymer, S.H. (1976), The international operations of national firms: A study of direct foreign investment. Doctoral dissertation, MIT, Cambridge, MA: MIT Press.

Jansson, H., Saqib, M. and Sharma, D.D. (1995), *The state and transnational corporations: A network approach to industrial policy in India.* London: Edward Elgar Publishing.

Johanson, J. and Vahlne, J.-E. (1977), The internationalization process of the firm – A model of knowledge development and increasing foreign market commitments. *Journal of International Business Studies*, 8 (1): 23–32.

Johanson, J. and Wiedersheim-Paul, F. (1975), The internationalization of the firm – Four Swedish cases. *Journal of Management Studies*, 12 (3): 305–322.

Jolly, V.K., Alahuta, M. and Jeannet, J.-P. (1992), Challenging the incumbents: How high technology start-ups compete globally. *Journal of Strategic Change*, 1: 71–82.

Jöreskog, K.-G. and Sörbom, D. (1993), *LISREL 8: Structural equation modeling with the SIMPLIS command language.* Chicago: Scientific Software International.

Knight, G.A. and Cavusgil, S.T. (1996), The born global firm: A challenge to traditional internationalization theory. *Advances in International Marketing*, 8: 11–26.

Kogut, B. (1983), Foreign direct investment as a sequential process, In C. P. Kindleberger *et al.* (eds), *The multinational corporation in the 1980s:* 36–56, Cambridge, MA: MIT Press.

Kogut, B. and Chang. S.J. (1991), Technological capabilities and Japanese foreign direct investment in the United States. *The Review of Economics and Statistics*, 73 (3): 401–413.

Kogut, B. and Singh, H. (1988), The effect of national culture on the choice of entry mode. *Journal of International Business Studies*, 19 (3): 411–432.

Leonidou, L.C. and Katsikeas, C.S. (1996), The export development process: An integrative review of empirical models. *Journal of International Business Studies*, 3: 625–646.

Lenway, S.A. and Murtha, T.P. (1994), Country capabilities and the strategic state: How national political institutions affect multinational corporations' strategies. *Strategic Management Journal*, 15: 113–130.

Lim, J.-S., Sharkey, W. and Kim, K.I. (1991), An empirical test of an export adoption model. *Management International Review*, 31 (1): 51–62.

Lord, F.C. and Novick, M.R. (1968), *Statistical Theories of Mental Test Scores*, Reading, MA: Addison-Wesley.

Luo, Y. (1999), Time based experience and international expansion: The case of an emerging economy. *Journal of Management Studies*, 36 (4): 505–534.

Madhok, A. (1997), Cost, value and foreign market entry mode: The transaction and the firm, *Strategic Management Journal*, 18 (1): 39–61.

March, J.G. (1991), Exploration and exploitation in organizational learning. *Organization Science*, 2 (1): 71–87.

McDougall, P.P., Shane, S. and Oviatt, B.M. (1994), Explaining the formation of international new ventures: The limits of theories from international business research. *Journal of Business venturing*, 9: 469–487.

McKinsey & Co. (1993), *Emerging exporters. Australia's high value-added manufacturing exporters*. Melbourne: McKinsey & Company and the Australian Manufacturing Council.

Moon, J. and Lee, H. (1990), On the internal correlates of export stage development: An empirical investigation in the Korean electronics industry. *International Marketing Review*, 7 (5): 16–26.

O'Grady, S. and Lane, H.W. (1996), The psychic distance paradox. *Journal of International Business Studies*, 27 (2): 309–333.

Oviatt, B.M. and McDougall, P.P. (1994), Toward a theory of international new ventures. *Journal of International Business Studies*, 25 (1): 45–64.

Penrose, E.T. (1959), *The Theory of the Growth of the Firm.* Oxford, England: Basil Blackwell.

Perlmutter, H. V. (1969), The tortuous evolution of the multinational corporation, *Columbia Journal of World Business*, 4 (1): 9–18.

Porter, M.E. (1980), *Competitive Advantage.* New York: The Free Press.

Porter, M.E. (1985), *Competitive Strategy.* New York: Free Press.

Rao,T.R. and Naidu, G.M. (1992), Are the stages of internationalization empirically supportable? *Journal of Global Marketing*, 6 (1/2): 147–170.

Reid, S.D. (1981), The decision-maker and export entry and expansion. *Journal of International Business Studies*, 12 (2): 101–112.

Senge, P.M. (1990), The leader's new work: Building learning organizations. *Sloan Management Review*, 32 (1): 7–24.

Simonin, B.L. (1999a), Ambiguity and the process of knowledge transfer in strategic alliances. *Strategic Management Journal*, 20 (7): 595–623.

Simonin, B.L. (1999b), Transfer of marketing know-how in international strategic alliances: An empirical investigation of the role and antecedents of knowledge ambiguity. *Journal of International Business Studies*, 30 (3): 463–490.

Ursic, M.L. and Czinkota, M.R. (1984), An experience curve explanation of export expansion. *Journal of Business Research*, 12: 159–168.

Vernon, R. (1966), International investment and international trade in the product cycle. *Quarterly Journal of Economics*, 80 (2): 190–207.

Weick, K.E. (1991), The traditional quality of organizational learning. *Organization Science*, 2 (1): 116–124.

Weinstein, A.K. (1977), Foreign investment by service firms: The case of multinational advertising agencies. *Journal of International Business Studies*, 8 (1): 83–91.

Welch, L.W. and Wiedersheim-Paul, F. (1980a), Initial exports – A marketing failure? *Journal of Management Studies*, 17 (3): 333–344.

Welch, L.W. and Wiedersheim-Paul, F. (1980b), Domestic expansion: Internationalization at home. *Essays in International Business*, 2, December, College of Business Administration, The University of South Carolina.

Wiedersheim-Paul, F., Olson, H.C. and Welch, L.S. (1978), Pre-export activity: The first step in internationalization. *Journal of International Business Studies*, 8 (1): 47–58.

Williamson, O.E. (1975), *Markets and hierarchies: Analysis and antitrust implications.* New York: The Free Press.

Yang, Y.S., Leione, R.P. and Alden, D.L. (1992), A market expansion ability approach to identify potential exporters. *Journal of Marketing*, 56: 84–96.

Yu, C.-M.J. (1990), The experience effect and foreign direct investment. *Weltwirtschaftliches Archiv*, 126: 561–579.

32 The internationalization process of firms in the United Kingdom
Dave Crick

This chapter discusses the findings from a longitudinal study involving the internationalization process of firms and focuses on the activities of a group of firms that had, at the start of the investigation, discontinued export activities. It contributes to the growing body of knowledge in the field of international entrepreneurship by identifying their internationalization strategies over a period of three years. Its objective is to supplement existing work on internationalization theory that has tended to report on the activities of firms at one point in time rather than map these over a certain period. In discussing this study, the chapter starts by defining what is meant by internationalization and explains why this might be viewed as an entrepreneurial act. After contextualizing the work, the literature on internationalization theory is reviewed. The research focus and methodological approach undertaken in this investigation are subsequently outlined before the findings are reported upon. The chapter ends with a discussion on the conclusions that are drawn from the study.

Background: internationalization as an entrepreneurial act
In this study, the term 'internationalization' is used in the same context as that defined by Welch and Luostarinen (1988), as 'the process of increasing involvement in international markets'. If the decision to engage and increase involvement in overseas business is to be seen as an entrepreneurial act, it appears reasonable to commence with a brief discussion of what is meant by 'entrepreneurship' in order to contextualize our subject. While much has been written about this topic area and no single agreed definition exists, recent work by Shane and Venkataraman (2000) suggests that 'entrepreneurship is concerned with the discovery and exploitation of profitable opportunities'. If this is accepted, it could be argued that opportunity recognition and exploitation might be undertaken in either the domestic market, overseas, or in fact both. The purpose of this chapter is to review studies involving internationalization theory and to incorporate recent entrepreneurial literature with the view to developing our understanding of the decision making process.

Within the working definition used in this chapter, it is evident that entrepreneurship is a process, a way of undertaking business activities within a certain mindset, rather than a means by which to categorize firms. This is important since many of the papers that review the internationalization literature concentrate on smaller firms (Andersen, 1993; Leonidou and Katsikeas, 1996; Coviello and McAuley, 1999). Arguably, managers of larger firms that seek to recognize and exploit opportunities either at home or abroad may equally be seen as taking an entrepreneurial stance.

Even so, from a resource-based view, it may also be argued that larger firms are usually subject to different circumstances that make them distinct from small and medium-sized enterprises (SMEs). Specifically, these different circumstances refer to more than the number of employees, often used as a means of categorizing various sizes of businesses (Storey, 1994). For example, this includes the financial resources at their disposal to seek out opportunities and the more specialist staff employed in various functions to manage activities. This is pertinent in the case of this chapter, given that managers of SMEs are more likely to manage a number of functions within their businesses owing to their limited staff base in comparison to their larger counterparts. Consequently, they will tend to have less specialized knowledge in areas such as international business activities as they will be balancing time spent between domestic and overseas sales. Indeed, this also has methodological implications since it will have an impact on identifying who needs to be contacted in research studies.

Internationalization behaviour: a review of the literature
A wide body of literature exists on the export behaviour of firms (Bilkey, 1978; Miesenbock, 1988; Aaby and Slater, 1989). A number of models have been proposed to categorize firms' internationalization processes but, arguably, similar characteristics are shared between them (Andersen, 1993; Leonidou and Katsikeas, 1996; Coviello and McAuley, 1999). These essentially classify firms' activities from the pre-export stage through to more committed stages of exporting and international business involvement such as subsidiaries. The basis of early work in this field suggests that managers start the internationalization process by serving markets that are psychologically (culturally) close to their own. They are often established in their domestic market before commencing overseas activities. Subsequently, they incrementally commit increasing resources to the foreign market(s) and usually concentrate on countries that are increasingly 'psychically' distant, that is, less culturally similar (Bilkey and Tesar, 1977; Johanson and Vahlne, 1977; Cavusgil, 1980; Czinkota, 1982).

Although the stage theories have received some degree of support, criticisms have been put forward; this is important in the context of policy makers' support for firms at various stages of internationalization (Crick, 1995; Korhonen et al., 1996). For example, at the time of Crick's (1995) study, the UK government used a three-stage classification of firms in their provision of export assistance: non-exporter, passive and active exporter. Andersen (1993) highlighted limitations in the theories' ability to delineate boundaries between stages or adequately explain the processes that lead to movement between stages. Trade sector and country factors have also been highlighted as important (Bell, 1995; Boter and Holmquist, 1996; Bell *et al.*, 1998; Jones, 1999). For example, Bell *et al.* (1998) found some degree of support for the stage theories in mature sectors with less support in knowledge-intensive sectors. Moreover, differences have been found in the internationalization processes of manufacturing and service firms (Erramilli and Rao, 1991; Edvardsson *et al.*, 1993; Chadee and Mattsson, 1998; Knight, 1999), with the applicability of stage theories to the latter being questionable. However, as differences between products and services become more blurred, arguably the explanatory powers of these frameworks diminish.

Recent literature has led to the identification of firms that have been termed 'born global' or 'international new ventures' (McKinsey & Co., 1993; McDougall *et al.*, 1994; Oviatt and McDougall, 1994, 1995; McDougall and Oviatt, 1996; Madsen and Servais, 1997). These tend to be firms formed as a result of a significant breakthrough in some process or technology (McKinsey & Co., 1993), where managers adopt a global focus from the outset and embark on rapid and dedicated internationalization. Knight and Cavusgil (1996) suggest that the emergence of these firms can be explained by recent trends such as advances in information and communication technologies, the increasing role of niche markets, and the growth of global networks, which are facilitating the development of mutually beneficial relationships with international partners.

The gradual move from culturally close markets to those further away (assumed in the stage models) has in some cases therefore been replaced by rapid internationalization, for example, involving a strategy of concentrating on lead markets. For example, Bell *et al.* (1998) found that this strategy was seen as an opportunity for some firms as this allowed sales to grow more rapidly than if they exploited other market opportunities. Even so, recent studies have identified firms in low-tech sectors that share characteristics with their high-tech counterparts. McAuley (1999) found entrepreneurial firms in the Scottish arts and crafts sector that internationalized rapidly for a number of reasons, such as orders derived from craft fairs and exhibitions. Knight *et al.* (2002) found that a number of New Zealand seafood firms had internationalized rapidly after business set-up owing to trading ties with the UK that existed at that time. Studies have indicated that it would therefore be wrong to associate rapid internationalization with only high-tech firms.

Studies have questioned the presumed forward movement of firms throughout the stages of internationalization. Crick and Jones (2000) used case study research to identify high-tech firms that internationalized through a variety of modes of market entry and at different paces. Sometimes commitment to international activities would be reduced to concentrate on the domestic market, while the effort in serving individual overseas markets also varied, depending on a variety of conditions. For example, in some cases, subsidiaries were set up to serve key markets, while in other cases firms would allocate resources in serving markets deemed less important as orders arrived. In this latter case, some markets would not be served for periods of time as managers exploited more profitable opportunities for a variety of reasons, such as the introduction of a new product suitable for a particular market. In other words, some managers were found to concentrate on key markets while others spread efforts over a number of markets to gain advantages such as 'first mover status'.

Bell *et al.* (1998) also used case study research involving a combination of high- and low-tech firms, and found different patterns in their internationalization processes. The low-tech firms were found to be more likely to adopt a staged, incremental, internationalization process similar to that advocated in existing models. Internationalization behaviour was affected by both internal and external conditions that varied on a case-by-case basis. For example, issues influencing overseas activities ranged from management buy-outs or other changes in the managerial teams to competitive conditions. In comparison, high-tech firms were likely to internationalize more rapidly, using different modes of market entry in line with recent work involving 'born global' firms. Bell *et al.* (1998) point out that much of the internationalization literature, to date, has been formulated as a result of a positivist methodological approach, for example, using aggregated statistical data. They suggest that a holistic approach may be more useful in explaining internationalization and this may require a qualitative methodology – an implication for researchers addressing this complex subject area, such as the study in this chapter.

Crick (2002) argued that the presumed forward motion of models was potentially misleading since the broad term 'non-exporter' at the first stage of internationalization did not adequately account for firms with different degrees of prior overseas experience. For example, this included those firms with no prior experience, some with aspirations to commence exporting and some with no desire to do so. It also involved those with prior experience but with no current export involvement. Within these, some firms might not want to recommence overseas activities, while others might want to. This is important given that the level of assistance is likely to vary between firms with varying degrees of prior experience and commitment to engage in overseas activities.

Once firms internationalize, Bell and Young (1998) suggest that the nature and pace of internationalization is conditioned by product, industry and other external environmental variables, as well as by firm-specific factors. These factors are important as particular 'critical incidents', either internal or external to the firm, may have an impact on firms' overall business strategies and market focus. As a result, firms may also experience 'epochs' of internationalization, followed by periods of consolidation or retrenchment, or they may be involved in particular 'episodes' that lead to rapid international expansion or de-internationalization (Oesterle, 1997). Bell and Young (1998) proceed to suggest that firms should be viewed as being in 'states' rather than 'stages' of internationalization. This reflects strategies that result in both forward and backward movement within the traditional 'stage' typology. This seems appropriate in terms of an international entrepreneurial perspective, given that firms are likely to be identifying and exploiting different opportunities in particular markets at given points in time.

The resources of SMEs and the link with internationalization strategy should not be overlooked. Indeed, Andersen and Kheam (1998) used a resource-based framework to explore the international growth strategies of SMEs. Moreover, the resource base of firms and the link with the wider business strategy is important. For example, Coviello and Munro (1997) identify issues such as product diversification and acquisition as influences in international development. Welch and Welch (1996) highlight the significance of the 'strategic foundations' (knowledge, skills and experience, networks and so on) of the business and its external environment and identify planned and unplanned routes to internationalization, with networking important in both. Internationalization strategies are affected by multiple influences from an internal and external perspective and identifying these factors within a sample of SMEs forms the focus of this study.

Research focus

This chapter focuses on one specific group of firms that has to date received very little attention within the literature, namely firms that have discontinued exporting (Pauwels and Matthyssens, 1999; Crick, 2002). Their entrepreneurial activities are studied over a period of three years. Since entrepreneurship has been viewed by Shane and Venkataraman (2000) as the discovery and exploitation of profitable opportunities, Seringhaus's (1987) observation that the literature has viewed a firm's export withdrawal largely as a failure needs to be reviewed. Indeed, in some cases, executives might concentrate on the domestic market for strategic reasons (Crick and Jones, 2000) whereas in other cases 'failure' might be a quite accurate term to describe the result of poor preparation in planning and information gathering (Welch and Wiedersheim-Paul, 1980). Furthermore, export withdrawal may be viewed as advantageous in the event that alternative modes of market entry can be used to serve the needs of foreign buyers (Crick and Jones, 2000). This consideration becomes important when determining the support that might be required by managers, and available to them, to help avoid export withdrawal.

The contribution of this chapter is to supplement existing work on internationalization theory that has tended to report on the activities of firms at one point in time and offer a longitudinal perspective to the field of international entrepreneurship. It extends the work of Bell and Young (1998) and investigates the proposition that firms are in 'states' rather than 'stages' of internationalization, reacting to both internal and external factors. The practical relevance of this study relates to the fact that policy makers may need to offer specific assistance to managers of these different types of non-exporting firms, based on issues such as commitment to overseas markets, in order to encourage them to recommence international activities.

Methodology
Original study
This study reports on a longitudinal investigation and therefore it is important to summarize the methodological approach undertaken in the original study that led to the identification of the firms that participated in the research for this chapter. No sampling frame was known to exist at the time of the original study that contained SMEs that had discontinued export activities. Consequently, one had to be constructed in the course of that investigation. A maximum of 100 employees was used in that study to minimize the potential effect of resource bias and all firms selected were independent and indigenously owned to avoid potential bias from parental control. Only firms in a single sector were chosen to avoid potential trade sectoral bias. The electronics sector was chosen because of the existence of a sampling frame; also the proximity of a number of firms to the author's institution would facilitate the conducting of interviews based on time and cost considerations.

An existing sampling frame was available that had been formulated for a previous study and this was originally drawn from businesses in the FAME database (a database that is widely available and allows firms to be selected by 'fields' such as trade sector). This database allowed the identification of firms with recent export experience and whose decision to discontinue exporting was quite new rather than having taken place some while back (within the previous year). The database allowed the identification of firms that had totally withdrawn from all overseas markets, rather than simply from particular countries while still selling to certain others. Firms had been asked to indicate their stage of internationalization by marking the appropriate category on a list provided in a postal questionnaire (building on the model used by Campbell, 1987). Two groups of firms were identified at that stage of the project: first, 'our firm has exported in the past but is not currently engaged in exporting and does not plan to export in the future' (termed 'disinterested firms'); second, 'our firm has exported in the past, but is not currently engaged in exporting; however, it plans to do so in the future' (termed 'disappointed firms').

A questionnaire was mailed to all 141 disinterested and disappointed firms in the database. It was asked that, in the event of responsibility for exporting being handled by someone other than the contact person, for example with a turnover of staff, the questionnaire be passed to the executive with responsibility in this area. Despite potential key informant bias (Phillips, 1981), respondents were asked to indicate whether they were responsible for the decision to discontinue exporting. This was the case in the vast majority of cases, the exceptions being where respondents viewed it as a joint decision with other executives. Although potential bias could have been introduced by managers answering with hindsight, the effect of this was anticipated to be compensated for, since the reasons for making the decision were still relatively clear in the executives' minds.

Firms whose questionnaires were returned because they had ceased trading were removed from the database. This left 60 usable questionnaires and this was considered to be an acceptable response rate. The responses from the two groups under investigation were skewed (34 firms that had stopped exporting as a short-term measure, compared with 26 that had decided to discontinue exporting as a longer-term strategy). In-depth interviews were subsequently undertaken with 24 firms, that is, 12 in each group (based on time and cost constraints).

Follow-up study
In the course of this follow-up study, in-depth interviews were subsequently undertaken with the 21 of the same 24 firms after a period of 18 months and three years, the results from the latter interviews being the focus of this chapter. Three firms had ceased trading over the period. The same interviewees participated in all but two of the interviews in the follow-up study, since most had fortunately not changed roles. The exceptions involved changes in the managerial teams resulting from takeovers (see Figure 32.1). The bias in response resulting from these changes in staff was considered relevant given that these executives were not knowledgable about the decision to discontinue exporting. However, interviews had taken place with staff in post at earlier stages of the study and this had provided the relevant data concerning the decision to discontinue exporting. The new incum-

bents were still relevant to the study at this stage since they were in a position to say what changes had occurred since taking on the roles.

As with earlier stages of this study, the use of interviews enabled managers to provide rationales to account for the way events unfolded over time (Denzin and Lincoln, 1998), although several potential weaknesses were also noted. These were the possibility of misinterpretation of collected data, potential researcher bias and the degree of honesty of the interviewee (Marshall and Rossman, 1995). The criteria proposed by Guba and Lincoln (1998) were observed, namely to take due account of the nature, the trustworthiness (credibility, confirmability and so on) and the authenticity of the research.

Findings
The richness of data generated by the interviews indicated that the most appropriate way to present the findings from the study was to summarize the way in which firms varied in their internationalization strategies rather than to provide case studies in their own right. The latter was considered inappropriate because of space restrictions. To aid understanding, a summary of the way in which internationalization varied between the firms over the three time periods of the study is shown diagrammatically in Figure 32.1. The findings in this chapter concentrate on the latter period but do make reference to earlier ones for comparative purposes, that is, to show developmental strategies.

Figure 32.1 indicates that, in the first period, that is, at the start of the study, disappointed firms had made a decision to discontinue exporting as a short-term measure while disinterested firms considered the decision to be longer-term. Particular differences between the firms are worth mentioning here. Disinterested firms had, in the main, experienced basic procedural problems internally, such as locating representatives, and this was found to have influenced the decision to discontinue exporting. This was in contrast to disappointed firms who, in the main, were experienced exporters that knew the mechanics of overseas trade, but had faced environmental problems, notably competition issues largely resulting from the high rate of sterling.

It can be seen in Figure 32.1 that, in the second period, that is, after 18 months, the two groups of firms started to vary in their strategies. In the disinterested firms, it was not surprising that eight served only the domestic market, since executives had previously indicated that the decision to discontinue exporting was a long-term strategy. Four disinterested firms were reacting to a few occasional orders from overseas, as a result of prior agency contracts, but international commitment was still marginal. They preferred to concentrate on opportunities in the domestic market.

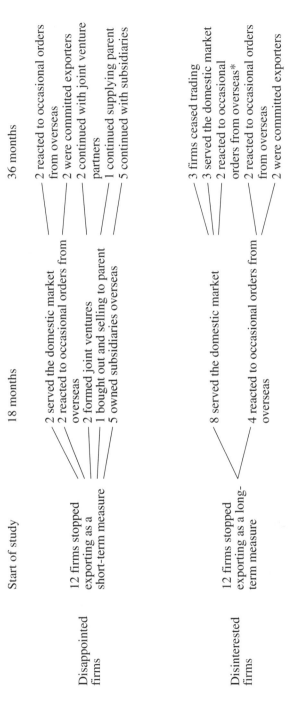

Start of study

18 months

36 months

Disappointed firms

12 firms stopped exporting as a short-term measure

2 served the domestic market
2 reacted to occasional orders from overseas
2 formed joint ventures
1 bought out and selling to parent
5 owned subsidiaries overseas

2 reacted to occasional orders from overseas
2 were committed exporters
2 continued with joint venture partners
1 continued supplying parent
5 continued with subsidiaries

Disinterested firms

12 firms stopped exporting as a long-term measure

8 served the domestic market
4 reacted to occasional orders from overseas

3 firms ceased trading
3 served the domestic market
2 reacted to occasional orders from overseas*
2 reacted to occasional orders from overseas
2 were committed exporters

Note: *A change of managerial team resulted from takeovers.

Figure 32.1 An overview of the sample firms' internationalization strategies over the three-year period

In contrast, the disappointed firms had a variety of strategies under way. Two firms concentrated on the domestic market since competitive issues indicated that opportunities were better, at least in the short term. Another two firms adopted much the same approach, but did react to a few occasional orders from overseas that stemmed from previous agency agreements. Two firms were more committed to international activities and saw the way forward to be via joint venture agreements with overseas firms, since export competitiveness was hampered by the high rate of sterling. One firm had been bought by an overseas business and was selling almost all of its output to the parent. The last five firms saw the best way forward to be via opening subsidiaries in key markets overseas to exploit cost advantages and offset problems of competitiveness in a way similar to the firms that had signed joint ventures. It is now important to turn to the focus of this study, namely the findings after three years, where interesting contrasts were found between the firms.

Disinterested firms three years after the export withdrawal decision
It was interesting that three of the disinterested firms that had concentrated on the domestic market 18 months after the investigation commenced had ceased trading. From maintaining contact with the firms over the period, it was evident that the domestic market had become too small and competitive as a result of rivalry (not least from foreign firms) and they could no longer compete. Two of the three executives conceded that they should have looked for new markets, potentially overseas, but specifically with respect to differentiating their product base so that even new customers in the domestic market could be served. The remaining executive claimed the firm could not compete either domestically or overseas, blaming in part the UK government for the strength of sterling. Whether they may be viewed as having 'failed' because of discontinuing exporting, or whether the reason was a combination of factors, remains questionable.

Three of the eight disinterested firms that had decided to concentrate on the domestic market 18 months after the study commenced were still doing so. They claimed to have met objectives since orders were steady if not growing in the UK market. Competitiveness had been maintained in two firms by scaling down operations to specialize in the core areas of the firms' product portfolios, whereas the other had differentiated the product to meet the demands of customers in the UK. It might be argued that they had thus taken an entrepreneurial stance by identifying and exploiting new opportunities domestically. It would be inappropriate to suggest they were 'failed exporters'.

The remaining two firms that were concentrating on the UK market 18 months after discontinuing exporting were now reacting to occasional orders from overseas while still focusing on the domestic market. These orders typically arrived from old customers. Objectives had been met since order books were fairly steady, given the perceived competitive environment that they were operating in. These two firms were anticipating increasing their commitment to overseas markets in the near future since the UK market was seen as too small and competitive to sustain the firms in the long term. It should be remembered that executives stated at the start of the study that exporting was halted as a long-term strategy. The fact that, after three years, they were reacting to occasional orders from overseas and looking to increase them highlights the relatively fluid 'state' of internationalization they were operating within. However, care should be taken with this observation as both firms had new members of their management team as a result of takeovers. Consequently, the importance of new management that includes 'committed internationalists' should not be overlooked in reshaping firms' overseas strategies.

Four disinterested firms had started to react to occasional orders from overseas 18 months after discontinuing exporting. Of these, two were still doing so but were hoping to increase activities in the future since it was believed that the relatively small, competitive UK market could not sustain them in the long term. After three years, they were essentially serving repeat customer orders. In contrast, the other two had now become what might be termed 'committed' exporters, given that export turnover was back to the levels three years earlier. They had exploited both old and new market opportunities, the latter with the help of government assistance. Interestingly, both firms had hired new managers for the very purpose of assisting growth, not least through international market development.

Disappointed firms three years after the export withdrawal decision
The disappointed firms, for the most part, were operating in a similar manner to what they had been doing when they were interviewed 18 months after the start of the study. Two firms that were only serving the domestic market after 18 months were now reacting to occasional orders from overseas, but were essentially passive exporters with a domestic focus. The change in activities resulted from the realization that the domestic market could not sustain long-term growth and there was a need to obtain international sales. A view had been taken to recommence exporting cautiously by contacting prior agents overseas while researching other opportunities. For example, executives from both firms had taken part in trade missions overseas to identify opportunities.

Two firms that were reacting to the receipt of occasional orders after 18 months were now 'committed' exporters and seeking to increase overseas sales further. Export orders had passed levels achieved prior to the decision to withdraw from overseas markets. The firms had gone through a period of revising their product portfolios and were now concentrating on key growth segments where they could enter markets early to obtain a competitive advantage. Research had been undertaken and firms felt ready to address the needs of the identified market opportunities. Entrepreneurial learning had therefore taken place over the period of study and executives felt they were better placed to compete overseas.

The remaining eight firms had not fundamentally changed their internationalization strategies since they were interviewed at the 18-month mark. Two were still working with joint venture partners in key markets, but were also exporting to markets deemed of lower priority. This was, in the main, via agency agreements. The same approach was true for the five firms that owned subsidiaries overseas after 18 months. These were serving key markets via subsidiaries and low priority markets via exports arising largely from agency agreements. The final firm, the one that was bought by an overseas business, was still shipping the vast majority of its output to the parent, as had been agreed at the takeover stage.

Discussion

The contribution of this chapter to the growing body of work in the area of international entrepreneurship was to build on existing work involving internationalization theory. It offers a longitudinal perspective and extends the work of Bell and Young (1998), investigating the proposition that firms are in 'states' rather than 'stages' of internationalization, reacting to both internal and external factors. Two groups of firms were studied over a period of three years, namely those that viewed the export withdrawal decision as short-term and those that considered it to be a longer-term decision.

It was evident that entrepreneurial learning took place to varying degrees within the firms under investigation. Some firms had learnt from earlier decisions and developed strategies to assist future competitiveness. The 'stages' models of internationalization suggested a forward-moving process for firms with increasing levels of overseas commitment. The findings from the present study indicate that the 'stages' models may not adequately address the dynamic nature of internationalization processes whereby firms are faced with varying degrees of risks and opportunities on a continuing basis. Both internal and external issues fed into decision making and consequently firms were in 'states' rather than 'stages' of internationalization, as Bell and Young (1998) suggest.

Internally, managerial perceptions of risk, resources available (both human and financial) and commitment to international activities as opposed to opportunities domestically provided key issues in this study.

Externally, the competitive environment (broadly speaking) provided a whole host of potential opportunities and threats that affected the decision to undertake international activities. While it was evident that the single most important issue related to competitiveness (being a function of many things, such as competitors' prices, the strength of sterling and ability to offer credit), firms were able to learn from experience and spot new opportunities. For example, several firms exploited modes of market entry other than the exporting route to maintain competitiveness, some via joint ventures and others through subsidiaries, typically in low cost countries.

Another interesting feature from the study related to entrepreneurial learning (including that of the managerial team) with respect to managing the product portfolio and exploiting new markets. Ansoff's (1965) growth strategies have been well documented in the marketing literature and appear relevant to a number of firms in this study. Penetration of existing market niches appeared a practical proposition to some, whereas others were developing new products, markets or both to remain competitive. The decision was affected in some firms by the change in managerial teams, sometimes via takeover and in others by the owner/manager hiring specialist managers. Some firms set out to exploit new markets quickly by developing new products before the competitors moved in.

The issue of entrepreneurial learning and decision making should therefore be seen alongside the need to change teams in some cases; that is, to bring in expertise or simply new ideas. However, this is not always practicable, with some owner–managers preferring to run what is known as a 'lifestyle' business and being unable or unwilling to delegate. Arguably, this had affected some firms in this study, with three ceasing trading. While the exact cause could not be fully determined, such an attitude did appear to be a contributing factor.

In contrast, some firms took a more gradual approach to exploiting new markets. Previous markets were selected, usually via renegotiating prior agency agreements, in order to develop revenue to go after new markets. This strategy was more consistent with the stage models, except that firms had discontinued exporting and recommenced activities, an issue not recognized in existing models. Clearly, some markets were dropped completely by some firms while others were only dropped temporarily. Issues ranging from market potential to competitive rivalry affected the nature of this decision. Interestingly, some markets were dropped in relation to the export mode, but still served via other modes of market entry such as joint ventures and subsidiaries. Therefore care must be taken in describing firms as making an export withdrawal decision if they are to re-enter a market subsequently, perhaps using an alternative form of market entry. To be technical, perhaps a timescale needs to be proposed to describe such firms as having 'de-internationalized', but pragmatically the issue is less important. More important is the need for policy makers to better understand small firms' approaches to internationalization so that effective assistance can be offered.

It appears from the results of this study that firms internationalize at different paces, through different routes and as a result of different learning experiences. Some firms may well have a forward motion from the pre-export stage to a more committed approach. Others, such as the firms in this study, may have to stop overseas activities and start again once conditions are more favourable. Consequently, it is perhaps more difficult to model internationalization strategy than the existing stage models may have suggested. Indeed, it may be unhelpful to do so, since entrepreneurs will seek and exploit opportunities in different ways and it is important that policy makers are on hand to support these activities. While broad, generic assistance may be useful to new exporters, those with experience will know the basics and require more tailored support.

Findings from this study suggested firms are likely to be willing to pay for tailored support if they believe it is 'value for money'. For example, some firms actively participated in subsidized overseas trade missions. The notion of 'value for money' is in reality difficult to measure since some orders may be received some time after support is offered, depending on the assistance in question. In the case of trade missions, firms may develop contacts but receive an order quite some time afterwards. Consequently, more intensive assistance in locating viable market opportunities may be the way forward, with the benefits being shared between the firm and the support provider, perhaps via a commission, but this an area of debate in its own right. In the meantime, this study has contributed to the sum of knowledge in the area of international entrepreneurship by providing results from a longitudinal investigation into internationalization processes and offered a basis on which future work can build.

References

Aaby, N.-E. and S.F. Slater (1989), 'Management influences on export performance: a review of the empirical literature 1978–88', *International Marketing Review*, 6 (4), 7–26.

Andersen, O. (1993), 'On the internationalisation process of firms: a critical analysis', *Journal of International Business Studies*, 24 (2), 209–31.

Andersen, O. and L.S. Kheam (1998), 'Resource-based theory and international growth strategies: an exploratory study', *International Business Review*, 7, 163–84.

Ansoff, I. (1965), 'Strategies for growth', *Harvard Business Review*, September–October, 113–24.

Bell, J. (1995), 'The internationalisation of small computer software firms', *European Journal of Marketing*, 29 (8), 60–75.

Bell, J. and S. Young (1998), 'Towards an integrative framework of the internationalisation of the firm', in G. Hooley, R. Loveridge and D. Wilson (eds), *Internationalisation: Process, Context and Markets*, London: Macmillan, pp. 3–28.

Bell, J., D. Crick and S. Young (1998), 'A holistic perspective on small firm growth and internationalisation', paper presented at the Academy of International Business Conference, City University Business School, London.

Bilkey, W.J. (1978), 'An attempted integration of the literature on the export behaviour of firms', *Journal of International Business Studies*, 9 (1), 33–46.

Bilkey, W.J. and G. Tesar (1977), 'The export behavior of smaller-sized Wisconsin manufacturing firms', *Journal of International Business Studies*, 8, 93–8.

Boter, H. and C. Holmquist (1996), 'Industry characteristics and internationalisation processes in small firms', *Journal of Business Venturing*, 11 (6), 471–87.

Campbell, D. (1987), 'An Empirical Examination of Selected Target Firms' Perceptions of U.S. Department of Commerce Export Promotion Programs, unpublished doctoral dissertation, University of Arkansas.

Cavusgil, S.T. (1980), 'On the internationalisation process of the firm', *European Research*, 6, 273–81.

Chadee, D. and J. Mattsson (1998), 'Do service and merchandise exporters behave and perform differently?', *European Journal of Marketing*, 32 (9/10), 830–42.

Coviello, N.E. and A. McAuley (1999), 'Internationalisation and the smaller firm: a review of contemporary empirical research', *Management International Review*, 39 (2), 223–57.

Coviello, N.E. and H. Munro (1997), 'Network relationships and the internationalisation process of small software firms', *International Business Review*, 6 (4), 361–86.

Crick, D. (1995), 'An investigation into the targeting of U.K. export assistance', *European Journal of Marketing*, 29 (8), 76–94.

Crick, D. (2002), 'The decision to discontinue exporting: SMEs in two U.K. trade sectors', *Journal of Small Business Management*, 40 (1), 66–77.

Crick, D. and M. Jones (2000), 'Small high technology firms and international high technology markets', *Journal of International Marketing*, 8 (2), 63–85.

Czinkota, M.R. (1982), *Export Development Strategies*, New York: Praeger.

Denzin, N.S. and Y.S. Lincoln (eds) (1998), *The Landscape of Qualitative Research: Theories and Issues*, London: Sage Publications.

Edvardsson, B., L. Edvinsson and H. Nystrom (1993), 'Internationalisation in service companies', *The Service Industries Journal*, 13 (1), 80–97.

Erramilli, M.K. and C.P. Rao (1991), 'The experience factor in foreign market entry behaviour of service firms', *Journal of International Business Studies*, Fall, 479–501.

Guba, E.G. and Y.S. Lincoln (1998), 'Competing paradigms in qualitative research', in N.S. Denzin and Y.S. Lincoln (eds), *The Landscape of Qualitative Research: Theories and Issues*, London: Sage Publications.

Johanson, J. and J-E. Vahlne (1977), 'The internationalisation process of the firm – a model of knowledge development and increasing foreign market commitment', *Journal of International Business Studies*, Spring–Summer, 23–32.

Jones, M. (1999), 'The internationalisation of small high-technology firms', *Journal of International Marketing*, 7 (4), 15–41.

Knight, G. (1999), 'International services marketing: review of research, 1980–1998', *Journal of Services Marketing*, 13 (4/5), 347–60.

Knight, G. and S.T. Cavusgil (1996), 'The born global firm: a challenge to traditional internationalization theory', *Advances in International Marketing*, New York: JAI Press, pp. 11–26.

Knight, J., J. Bell and R. McNaughton (2002), 'Satisfaction with paying for government export assistance', paper presented at the AIB Conference, Preston.

Korhonen, H., R. Luostarinen and L. Welch (1996), 'Internationalisation of SMEs: inward–outward patterns and government policy', *Management International Review*, 36, 315–29.

Leonidou, L.C. and C.S. Katsikeas (1996), 'The export development process: an integrative review of empirical models', *Journal of International Business Studies*, 27 (3), 517–51.

Madsen, T. and P. Servais (1997), 'The internationalization of born globals: an evolutionary process?', *International Business Review*, 6 (6), 561–83.

Marshall, C. and G.B. Rossman (1995), *Designing Qualitative Research*, London: Sage Publications.

McAuley, A. (1999), 'Entrepreneurial instant exporters in the Scottish arts and crafts sector', *Journal of International Marketing*, 7 (4), 67–82.

McDougall, P.P. and B.M. Oviatt (1996), 'New venture internationalisation, strategic change, and performance: a follow-up study', *Journal of Business Venturing*, 11, 23–40.

McDougall, P.P., S. Shane and B.M. Oviatt (1994), 'Explaining the formation of international new ventures: the limits of theories from international business research', *Journal of Business Venturing*, 9, 469–87.

McKinsey & Co. (1993), *Emerging Exporters: Australia's High Value-Added Manufacturing Exporters*, Melbourne: Australian Manufacturing Council.

Miesenbock, K.J. (1988), 'Small businesses and exporting: a literature review', *International Small Business Journal*, 6 (2), 42–61.

Oesterle, M-J. (1997), 'Time span until internationalization: foreign market entry as a built-in mechanism of innovation', *Management International Review*, 37 (2), 125–49.

Oviatt, B.M. and P.P. McDougall (1994), 'Toward a theory of international new ventures', *Journal of International Business Studies*, 25 (1), 45–64.

Oviatt, B.M. and P.P. McDougall (1995), 'Global start-ups: entrepreneurs on a world-wide stage', *Academy of Management Executive*, 9 (2), 30–44.

Pauwels, P. and P. Matthyssens (1999), 'A strategy process perspective on export withdrawal', *Journal of International Marketing*, 7 (3), 10–37

Phillips, L.W. (1981), 'Assessing measurement error in key informant reports: a methodological note on organisational analysis in marketing', *Journal of Marketing Research*, 18, 395–415.

Seringhaus, R.F.H. (1987), 'Do experienced exporters have market entry problems?', *The Finnish Journal of Management*, 4, 376–88.

Shane, S. and S. Venkataraman (2000), 'The promise of entrepreneurship as a field of research', *Academy of Management Review*, 25 (1), 217–26.

Storey, D. J. (1994), *Understanding the Small Business Sector*, London: Routledge.

Welch, L.S. and R.K. Luostarinen (1988), 'Internationalization: evolution of a concept', *Journal of General Management*, 14 (2), 34–55.

Welch, D.E. and L.S. Welch (1996), 'The internationalization process and networks: a strategic management perspective', *Journal of International Marketing*, 4 (3), 11–28.

Welch, L.S. and F. Wiedersheim-Paul (1980), 'Initial exports – a marketing failure', *Journal of Management Studies*, October, 333–44.

33 Internationalization and size, age and profitability in the United Kingdom
Graham Hall and Ciwen Tu

Exports represent about 30 per cent of the Gross Domestic Product of the United Kingdom. Hardly surprisingly, improving export performance has been regarded as important by successive governments, a sentiment exemplified by Lord Clinton Davis (1998), then Minister of Trade:

> The importance of exporting to Britain's economy cannot be overstated. Not only does it contribute to our economy, earning the revenue that helps to pay for the standard of living and quality of life we all want, exporting is also the best way of sharpening our competitive edge.

The factors associated with the degree of export activity are clearly of relevance to the formulation of industrial policy. Here we consider three candidates: size, age and profitability. We are concerned to establish whether they are related to the proportion of a company's sales that it exports, the export ratio or the decision to export at all, the export propensity. Our study encompasses firms of all sizes but particular attention is devoted to small firms. All models and tests are carried out at sector level because of the strong possibility that industry characteristics could influence the strength of relationships.

The first section of this chapter will briefly justify our choice of relationships; the second will describe our data and methodology; the third will report our results on the strength of the relationship between the explanatory variables and the export ratio; the fourth the relationship between the explanatory variables and the export propensity. The fifth section provides concluding remarks.

Choice of relationships
Size and export performance
Whether size is related to either the export ratio or export propensity or to both is a popular topic of research (Aaby and Slater, 1989; Bannock and Partners, 1987; Bilkey and Tesar, 1977; Bonaccorsi, 1992; Caughey and Chetty, 1994; Cavusgil *et al.*, 1979; Cavusgil, 1980; Cavusgil, 1984a, 1984b; Cooper and Kleinschmidt, 1985; Crookell and Graham, 1979; Czinkota and Johnston, 1983; Daniels and Goyburo, 1976; Gemünden, 1991; Johanson

and Vahlne, 1977; Katsikeas, 1994; Kaynak, 1985; Keng and Jiuan, 1989; Kirpalani and MacIntosh, 1980; Leonidou *et al.*, 1998; Madsen, 1987; Malekzadeh and Nahavandi, 1984; Miesenbock, 1988; Moen, 1999; Naidu and Prasad, 1994; Ogram, 1982; Ong and Pearson, 1982; Piercy, 1981; Reid, 1982; Seringhaus, 1986/7; Stening and McDougall, 1975; Tyebjee, 1994; Ursic and Czinkota, 1984; Welch and Wiedersheim-Paul, 1980; Westhead, 1994; Withey, 1980; Yaprak, 1985).

Whilst Aaby and Slater (1989) conclude: 'For all the attention that this variable has received, there is little agreement regarding the impact that organization size has on either propensity to export or export success.' Our own interpretation of the evidence is that it is weighted in favour of a positive relationship between size and both measures of export behaviour.

Theoretically the arguments for size being correlated with the export ratio are less compelling than the ones with export propensity. The most obvious barrier around export markets that face small firms is the fixed costs of entry, for instance those associated with gaining an understanding of overseas laws, regulations, business practices and market conditions.

Once this hurdle has been jumped, size will only provide an advantage if there are economies of scale in variable costs. Sources of falling average variable costs in overseas search and marketing are not as readily identifiable as fixed costs in these activities. In their absence it is not at all obvious why small firms that do export should earn a smaller proportion than large firms of their income from non-domestic markets.

A second reason why decision makers within firms may not consider seeking business overseas is that they do not perceive that they possess any competitive advantages. This modesty is most likely to be found amongst small firm owner–managers. If they are serving local or regional markets there may not be any significant differences between the products or services they are offering from those of their counterparts in other parts of the country. If their markets are national they may hold a similar view about lack of advantages over products or services provided by overseas producers. If firms enter overseas markets in spite of not enjoying competitive advantage they may earn lower returns, depending on the costs of entry, but, as argued above, it is not unambiguous that this will affect the export ratio. In the alternative scenario, where small firms do, indeed, possess some sort of advantage over overseas producers, there would be even less reason to suppose their export ratio to be lower than those of larger firms.

Age of company
It is common for researchers on company performances and behaviour to include age in their set of explanatory variables and this is especially true when their samples are drawn from the small firm sector. Writers on export

performance are no exception (Bilkey, 1978; Cavusgil, 1980; Cavusgil, 1984a, 1984b; Daniels and Goyburo, 1976; Johanson and Vahlne, 1977; Keng and Jiuan, 1989; Kirpalani and MacIntosh, 1980; Miesenbock, 1988; Ogram, 1982; Ong and Pearson, 1982; Reid, 1982; Tyebjee, 1994; Ursic and Czinkota, 1984; Welch and Wiedersheim-Paul, 1980). Age is usually employed as a surrogate for organizational knowledge which it is assumed is built up through experience which, in turn, increases with the length of time that a firm is in operation. Age is given added emphasis within the literature on internationalization because of the popularity of various versions of theories depicting the process of internationalization as consisting of stages (Bell, 1995; Bilkey and Tesar, 1977; Cavusgil, 1980; Gankema *et al.*, 2000; McDougall *et al.*, 1994; Moini, 1997; Reid, 1981; Reuber and Fischer, 1997; Yaprak, 1985).

In some, a certain degree of inevitability is implied as firms gain in experience and confidence and move through stages of increasing commitment and proactivity. In others, greater stress is put on the stochastic nature of a movement between stages, especially as regarding whether any business is conducted overseas at all. Whatever the case, it is commonly assumed that, the longer a firm has been in operation, the more likely that it will have internationalized and, if so, that its degree of internationalization will have increased.

Profitability
While it is crucial to the health of the UK economy that earnings be derived from overseas, it is by no means certain that it is in the interest of individual firms that they should attempt to achieve this; the 'competitive edge' that Clinton Davis extols above can cut both ways. Not only will there be costs from selling overseas but there is no reason for supposing that the resulting profit margins will be higher than would be earned in domestic markets. Writers on this topic sometimes give the impression that they are assuming higher margins accompany exporting because otherwise the decision to export would not have been taken. At the risk of being accused of creating a straw man, it should not be forgotten that ex ante expectations need not be realized ex post, or that the implicit assumption about the motivation for exporting may be unfounded. Push factors, originating from within domestic materials, represent credible alternatives to the pull of the foreign. Even if the motivation for exporting is to achieve a growth denied by domestic markets, increased rates of return need not follow from increased sales; indeed, in worst-case scenarios, the volume of profits can fall. The theoretical ambiguity on the relationship between export performance and profitability is reflected in the lack of consensus empirically (Axinn *et al.*, 1995; Bell *et al.*, 1996; Cavusgil, 1984a; Christensen *et al.*, 1987; Tyebjee, 1994).

Sample and methodology

Our sample was drawn from FAME (Financial Analyses Made Easy), jointly developed and promoted by Jordans and Bureau Van Dijk. Though this is vast, gaps in the data meant that the most companies we could employ was 42721, of which about 53% had workforces of 50 or less and 32% between 51 and 250. The smallest category accounted for just under 4% of the total exported by the sample, the medium 8.6% and firms with over 250 about 87%. All data refer to 1999 and are disaggregated into 19 sectors of activity. Disaggregation was necessitated by the possibility that sector characteristics, either domestically or overseas, could influence the strength of any of the relationships encompassed by this study.

Our methodology consists of

a) ordinary least squares (OLS) regressions of exports/sales on size, measured alternatively by number in workforce and turnover, age of company and return on investment (ROI), of exporters within our sample, firstly with respect to the full sample and then to companies with workforces of a hundred or less. Companies not exporting were omitted to avoid the obvious bias that would result from including cases with zero value of the dependent variable;

b) logit regressions, similarly specified but run on a sample including non-exporters. These were assigned the value of 'O' as the dependent variable and 'I' was assigned to exporters;

c) the arithmetic means of exporters and non-exporters was compared with respect to each variable.

Influences on the export ratio

Table 33.1 shows that, in the full sample of exporters, the explanatory power of age, size and ROI is generally low. Focusing on (A) (the results are not markedly different whichever measure of size is selected) shows that in only the model drawing its sample from utilities is the R^2 in double figures. This of course does not imply that coefficients are not significant. However, in only seven sector models is the coefficient on age statistically significant at 10% in six on size, and in seven on ROI. On the full sample the coefficients are statistically significant but of negligible value.

Table 33.2 shows that when the models are tested on the sample of small firms, and when size is measured by number employed, their explanatory power generally increases. In the case of utilities, 'hotels and restaurants' and 'public administration and defence' the explanation could lie with their limited degrees of freedom but this cannot be the case with the six other sector models displaying definite improvement in explanatory power. It would seem that it is the increased importance in the number of employees

Table 33.1 Exporters among all industries (1999): linear regression model

Industry	(A) ratio = $a + b_1$Age $+ b_2$Employee $+ b_3$ROI $+ e$							(B) ratio = $a + b_1$Age $+ b_2$Turnover $+ b_3$ROI $+ e$						
	b_1	Sig.	b_2	Sig.	b_3	Sig.	R^2	b_1	Sig.	b_2	Sig.	b_3	Sig.	R^2
1. Primary sector (agriculture, mining, etc)	2.57E-03	0.013	1.44E-06	0.655	-7.00E-05	0.829	0.030	2.47E-03	0.017	-8.90E-08	0.092	-6.10E-05	0.850	0.042
2. Food, beverages, tobacco	3.79E-04	0.437	9.37E-07	0.709	-6.90E-06	0.970	0.002	4.17E-04	0.393	3.38E-08	0.187	2.77E-05	0.881	0.006
3. Textiles, wearing apparel, leather	-2.80E-04	0.514	7.83E-06	0.028	-7.10E-06	0.901	0.010	-2.70E-04	0.520	2.17E-07	0.038	-6.20E-06	0.966	0.009
4. Wood, cork, paper	5.51E-04	0.253	3.38E-05	0.001	2.37E-04	0.322	0.051	5.47E-04	0.254	2.75E-07	0.000	2.31E-04	0.332	0.059
5. Publishing, printing	-1.00E-03	0.061	1.20E-05	0.056	1.32E-04	0.218	0.018	-1.00E-03	0.058	1.18E-07	0.018	1.31E-07	0.220	0.022
6. Chemicals, rubber, plastics, non-metallic products	-4.40E-04	0.148	1.14E-05	0.000	-6.40E-05	0.616	0.014	-3.30E-04	0.283	1.08E-08	0.039	-6.60E-05	0.605	0.004
7. Metals & metal products	3.14E-04	0.323	1.61E-05	0.000	1.36E-06	0.988	0.012	3.39E-04	0.285	1.98E-07	0.000	-1.22E-06	0.990	0.016
8. Machinery, equipment, furniture, recycling	-4.60E-04	0.070	8.39E-06	0.000	-1.00E-04	0.061	0.011	-4.33E-04	0.087	6.80E-08	0.000	-1.10E-04	0.057	0.010
9. Gas, water, electricity	8.44E-03	0.046	-3.80E-06	0.712	-1.90E-03	0.191	0.238	7.98E-03	0.056	-3.10E-08	0.465	-1.80E-03	0.217	0.252
10. Construction	1.01E-03	0.230	3.35E-07	0.972	4.87E-06	0.974	0.005	1.15E-03	0.174	-6.00E-08	0.438	7.80E-06	0.958	0.006
11. Wholesale & retail trade	-6.50E-04	0.024	-2.30E-07	0.865	-1.40E-04	0.046	0.003	-3.20E-04	0.889	6.02E-08	0.262	-4.40E-04	0.829	0.036
12. Hotels & restaurants	-1.30E-04	0.953	2.37E-06	0.171	-6.40E-04	0.755	0.053	9.70E-04	0.343	4.02E-08	0.201	-3.20E-04	0.161	0.015
13. Transport	9.79E-04	0.339	3.63E-06	0.349	-3.10E-04	-0.164	0.013	-2.70E-03	0.399	2.14E-09	0.892	-6.50E-04	0.380	0.063
14. Post and telecommunication	-2.40E-03	0.437	-3.20E-07	0.892	-6.50E-04	0.038	0.063	-7.20E-03	0.000	-1.80E-07	0.045	3.56E-04	0.101	0.090
15. Banks	-7.20E-03	0.000	-1.40E-05	0.250	3.52E-04	0.107	0.078	-8.00E-05	0.969	3.87E-07	0.578	5.41E-04	0.069	0.034
16. Insurance companies	6.77E-04	0.742	-3.10E-05	0.598	5.23E-04	0.079	0.034	6.77E-04	0.742	-3.10E-05	0.598	5.23E-04	0.079	0.034
17. Other services	-7.60E-04	0.052	-1.10E-06	0.655	-1.40E-04	0.005	0.004	-7.60E-04	0.052	-1.10E-06	0.655	-1.40E-04	0.005	0.004
18. Public administration and defence	-4.60E-03	0.718	4.63E-05	0.853	9.90E-06	0.995	0.029	-4.60E-03	4.718	4.63E-05	0.853	9.90E-06	0.995	0.029
19. Education, health	3.19E-03	0.270	-1.20E-04	0.448	3.10E-05	0.949	0.035	3.19E-03	0.270	-1.20E-04	0.448	3.10E-05	0.949	0.035
All Industries	-6.10E-04	0.000	3.04E-06	0.000	-9.40E-05	0.000	0.004	-6.00E-04	0.000	1.69E-08	0.000	-9.40E-05	0.000	0.003

Table 33.2 Small exporters among all industries (1999): linear regression model

Industry	(A) ratio = a + b1Age + b2Employee + b3ROI + e							(B) ratio = a + b1Age + b2Turnover + b3ROI + e						
	b_1	Sig.	b_2	Sig.	b_3	Sig.	R^2	b_1	Sig.	b_2	Sig.	b_3	Sig.	R^2
1. Primary sector (agriculture, mining, etc)	3.00E-03	0.154	-4.00E-03	0.004	-6.50E-04	0.161	0.120	1.56E-03	0.466	1.45E-06	0.541	-7.30E-04	0.137	0.033
2. Food, beverages, tobacco	1.37E-03	0.159	-1.60E-03	0.065	2.90E-04	0.343	0.047	1.20E-03	0.212	2.71E-06	0.025	2.63E-04	0.388	0.059
3. Textiles, wearing apparel, leather	-2.90E-04	0.714	-1.20E-03	0.092	1.86E-05	0.934	0.015	-3.90E-04	0.626	2.20E-06	-0.507	6.00E-05	0.790	0.004
4. Wood, cork, paper	-8.00E-05	0.938	-2.10E-03	0.025	1.97E-04	0.527	0.059	-6.30E-04	0.535	3.96E-06	0.389	2.33E-04	0.466	0.018
5. Publishing, printing	-6.00E-04	0.503	-2.60E-03	0.000	6.93E-05	0.530	0.074	-1.10E-03	0.219	-1.30E-07	0.929	7.60E-05	0.511	0.008
6. Chemicals, rubber, plastics, non-metallic products	-2.00E-03	0.000	-1.30E-04	0.765	4.18E-05	0.812	0.024	-2.00E-03	0.000	-1.50E-07	0.895	4.38E-05	0.803	0.023
7. Metals & metal products	-4.10E-04	0.448	-6.40E-04	0.117	1.17E-04	0.303	0.007	-5.00E-04	0.361	-7.50E-07	0.699	1.11E-04	0.329	0.003
8. Machinery, equipment, furniture, recycling	-1.10E-03	0.018	-7.40E-04	0.012	-4.00E-05	0.568	0.010	-1.20E-03	0.007	6.42E-07	0.378	-4.30E-05	0.547	0.006
9. Gas, water, electricity	-1.80E-03	0.913	-1.40E-02	0.503	1.59E-03	0.785	0.351	4.93E-03	0.650	-2.60E-05	0.615	-1.30E-04	0.977	0.300
10. Construction	4.07E-03	0.006	-4.90E-03	0.000	1.43E-04	0.475	0.180	4.08E-03	0.009	-1.10E-04	0.051	1.71E-04	0.427	0.066
11. Wholesale & retail trade	-1.20E-04	0.755	-2.30E-03	0.000	-6.80E-05	0.357	0.039	-5.40E-04	0.154	1.41E-06	0.000	-1.00E-04	0.175	0.015
12. Hotels & restaurants	5.94E-03	0.330	-7.10E-03	0.250	-7.60E-03	0.356	0.404	6.45E-03	0.257	-1.30E-04	0.146	-8.60E-03	0.007	0.499
13. Transport	3.65E-03	0.024	-4.80E-03	0.000	-1.40E-04	0.615	0.152	3.07E-03	0.078	-1.40E-06	0.468	-8.60E-05	0.781	0.018
14. Post and telecommunication	-1.90E-02	0.015	-3.80E-03	0.052	-1.40E-03	0.030	0.298	-1.80E-02	0.033	4.87E-06	0.388	-1.10E-03	0.071	0.247
15. Banks	-8.10E-03	0.010	-3.70E-03	0.003	4.55E-04	0.027	0.146	-8.40E-03	0.010	-1.90E-06	0.136	4.80E-04	0.023	0.104
16. Insurance companies	-1.30E-03	0.687	1.63E-04	0.937	3.49E-04	0.302	0.018	-1.70E-03	0.597	1.49E-05	0.419	3.49E-04	0.296	0.028
17. Other services	7.85E-05	0.887	-2.50E-03	0.000	-1.40E-04	0.021	0.038	-2.20E-04	0.699	1.40E-07	0.512	-1.30E-04	0.026	0.002
18. Public administration and defence	-5.80E-05	0.997	7.42E-04	0.924	1.36E-03	0.497	0.237	4.83E-03	0.779	2.35E-05	0.385	1.37E-03	0.434	0.382
19. Education, health	5.60E-03	0.180	-3.60E-03	0.202	2.36E-04	0.686	0.107	6.34E-03	0.123	-4.30E-05	0.088	1.78E-04	0.751	0.144
All Industries	-9.00E-04	0.000	-1.90E-03	0.000	-5.90E-05	0.072	0.032	-1.30E-03	0.000	3.29E-07	0.032	-5.90E-05	0.079	0.006

that is driving the change in R^2. The coefficients on age continue to have generally low statistical significance and the coefficients on ROI are hardly ever statistically significant.

What is very curious because of its counter-intuitiveness is the generally negative sign of b_2, implying that, as the size of the labour force is increased, the proportion of sales earned overseas decreases. The same negative relationship does not generally hold for the alternative measure of size and turnover, but of the four sector models with coefficients that were statistically significant at 10% two had positive signs.

The lack of any marked relationship between the export ratio and size, age and ROI may reflect misspecification, in particular the assumption of linearity. Various non-linear relationships were tested, indeed until the process veered into data mining, but without success. Figures 33A.1 to 33A.3 in the Appendix demonstrate through bar charts why we were not successful with respect both to measures of size and to age. The bar chart depicting the relationship between the export ratio and ROI has been included in the main body of the text (Figure 33.1) because of its interest-

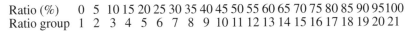

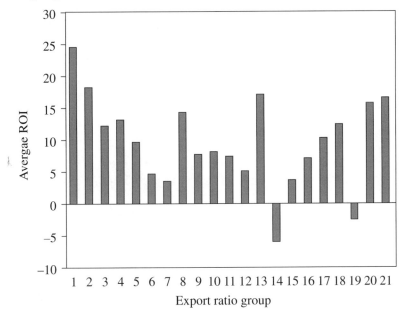

Figure 33.1   Relationship between export ratio and ROI

ing revelations. Not only is there clearly no relationship between ROI and the export ratio but the export ratios associated with the highest ROIs are respectively zero and one. It is beyond the scope of this study to explore the reason for this but it would seem a question that might usefully be answered in future work.

Influences on export propensity
Focusing on the Nagelkerke measure in Table 33.3(A), only three sector models have R^2 in double figures and that for the total sample is very low. Table 33.3(B) has about the same degree of explanatory power overall with even less at sector level, though it should be borne in mind that measures of explanatory power in cross-sectional qualitative response models are usually lower than what would usually be regarded as an acceptable level for R^2 in OLS regression.

The coefficient on age is significant at 10% or higher in eight sector models in Table 33.3(A), that on number of employees highly significant in 14 and that on ROI at 10% or above in five. Substituting turnover for labour force in Table 33.3(B) serves to underline the importance of size as a discriminator between exporters and non-exporters. Indeed, in only 'Post and telecommunication' and 'Public administration and defence' does there appear to be no relationship.

Tables 33.4(A) and 33.4(B) indicate that the discriminatory power of our models is no higher when tested on a sample of small firms alone. The coefficient on age is significant in seven sector models but not necessarily the same set as in Table 33.3. In two of the sectors age becomes a significant discriminator only when firms with over a hundred employees are included in the sample and, in two, when they are omitted. The coefficient on number of employees is significant, usually highly, in 13 sector models, that on turnover in all but three. In only six sectors is the coefficient on ROI significant at 10% or above and these are included in the 13 with coefficients negatively signed.

Comparison of means
As a further test of the strength of size, age and ROI as discriminators their mean values were compared between exporters and non-exporters. While such a simple methodology lacks the elegance of qualitative response models, especially in their potential for prediction, it is arguably more straightforward to interpret and is more robust.

Size served as a powerful discriminator across the full sample. In all but two sectors exporters have higher levels of turnover than non-exporters and usually at levels of significance that would be regarded as high. In 'Chemicals etc' the difference is not significantly different at 10% and in

Table 33.3(A) All companies: logistic regression model

| Industry | | $logp = a + b1Age + b2\,Employee + b3\,ROI + E$ | | | | | | | | |
	-2 Log Likelihood	Cox&Snell R_2	Nagelkerke $-R_2$	constant	b1	Sig.	b2	Sig.	b3	Sig.
1. Primary sector (agriculture, mining, etc)	765.012	0.111	0.156	−0.926	−0.006	0.139	0.001	0.000	−0.001	0.431
2. Food, beverages, tobacco	1087.388	0.013	0.017	−0.289	0.008	0.007	0.000	0.200	0.001	0.429
3. Textiles, wearing apparel, leather	709.089	0.056	0.084	0.628	0.004	0.345	0.002	0.000	0.000	0.872
4. Wood, cork, paper	678.252	0.138	0.184	−0.683	0.001	0.758	0.004	0.000	−0.002	0.306
5. Publishing, printing	1660.583	0.040	0.055	−0.849	0.003	0.321	0.001	0.000	0.000	0.920
6. Chemicals, rubber, plastics, non-metallic products	1646.580	0.030	0.047	0.971	0.008	0.006	0.001	0.000	−0.002	0.009
7. Metals & metal products	2071.248	0.046	0.066	0.434	0.007	0.011	0.002	0.000	−0.001	0.070
8. Machinery, equipment, furniture, recycling	3972.200	0.025	0.038	0.827	0.011	0.000	0.001	0.000	0.000	0.256
9. Gas, water, electricity	120.198	0.095	0.149	−1.988	0.021	0.167	0.000	0.003	−0.003	0.372
10. Construction	1924.096	0.039	0.074	−2.196	0.004	0.274	0.001	0.000	−0.002	0.006
11. Wholesale & retail trade	9710.760	0.001	0.001	−0.526	−0.002	0.067	0.000	0.474	0.000	0.530
12. Hotels & restaurants	318.557	0.015	0.055	−3.647	0.016	0.046	0.000	0.010	−0.001	0.669
13. Transport	1566.447	0.012	0.019	−1.653	0.006	0.078	0.000	0.001	0.001	0.324
14. Post and telecommunication	329.028	0.021	0.029	−0.783	0.012	0.398	0.000	0.297	−0.001	0.328
15. Banks	1074.432	0.037	0.057	−1.296	−0.006	0.274	0.001	0.000	−0.002	0.001
16. Insurance companies	627.094	0.039	0.077	−2.060	−0.006	0.359	0.002	0.000	−0.001	0.141
17. Other services	14105.778	0.010	0.014	−0.839	−0.004	0.005	0.000	0.000	−0.001	0.000
18. Public administration and defence	44.954	0.060	0.081	−0.862	0.030	0.409	0.000	0.712	0.000	0.940
19. Education, health	350.862	0.007	0.017	−2.349	0.007	0.497	−0.001	0.209	0.001	0.520
All Industries	51093.302	0.014	0.019	−0.683	0.009	0.000	0.000	0.000	−0.001	0.000

Table 33.3 (B)

Industry	−2 Log Likelihood	Cox&Snell R_2	Nagelkerke −R_2	logp = a + b1 Age + b2 Employee + b3 ROI + E						
				constant	b1	Sig.	b2	Sig.	b3	Sig.
1. Primary sector (agriculture, mining, etc)	807.41	0.054	0.075	−0.867	−0.002	0.591	0.000	0.000	−0.001	0.277
2. Food, beverages, tobacco	1085.946	0.015	0.020	−0.306	0.008	0.006	0.000	0.073	0.001	0.379
3. Textiles, wearing apparel, leather	698.168	0.071	0.107	0.506	0.004	0.300	0.000	0.000	0.000	0.776
4. Wood, cork, paper	691.194	0.117	0.157	−0.550	0.002	0.500	0.000	0.000	−0.002	0.159
5. Publishing, printing	1656.17	0.043	0.059	−0.835	0.003	0.308	0.000	0.000	0.000	0.885
6. Chemicals, rubber, plastics, non-metallic products	1635.14	0.037	0.057	0.956	0.007	0.012	0.000	0.000	−0.002	0.007
7. Metals & metal products	2059.421	0.052	0.075	0.418	0.007	0.008	0.000	0.000	−0.001	0.059
8. Machinery, equipment, furniture, recycling	4003.785	0.017	0.026	0.900	0.012	0.000	0.000	0.000	−0.001	0.220
9. Gas, water, electricity	126.625	0.050	0.078	−1.783	0.017	0.241	0.000	0.019	−0.002	0.423
10. Construction	1943.189	0.033	0.062	−2.174	0.004	0.181	0.000	0.000	−0.002	0.005
11. Wholesale & retail trade	9708.363	0.001	0.001	−0.527	−0.002	0.056	0.000	0.106	0.000	0.543
12. Hotels & restaurants	315.913	0.017	0.064	−3.642	0.015	0.058	0.000	0.061	−0.001	0.677
13. Transport	1564.582	0.013	0.021	−1.653	0.006	0.008	0.000	0.001	0.001	0.346
14. Post and telecommunication	328.277	0.024	0.033	−0.786	0.011	0.422	0.000	0.210	−0.001	0.330
15. Banks	1091.099	0.022	0.034	−1.257	−0.005	0.424	0.000	0.006	−0.002	0.000
16. Insurance companies	626.796	0.040	0.078	−2.008	−0.008	0.288	0.000	0.000	−0.020	0.063
17. Other services	14034.424	0.016	0.023	−0.863	−0.004	0.004	0.000	0.000	−0.001	0.000
18. Public administration and defence	44.582	0.070	0.094	−0.930	0.028	0.471	0.000	0.535	−0.001	0.805
19. Education, health	353.54	0.003	0.007	−2.433	0.007	0.459	0.000	0.416	0.001	0.506
All Industries	51034.101	0.015	0.021	−0.688	0.009	0.000	0.000	0.000	−0.001	0.000

Table 33.4(A) Small companies: logistic regression model

logp = a + b1Age + b2 Employee + b3 ROI + E

Industry	−2 Log Likelihood	Cox&Snell R$_2$	Nagelkerke −R$_2$	constant	b1	Sig.	b2	Sig.	b3	Sig.
1. Primary sector (agriculture, mining, etc)	412.403	0.087	0.138	−1.546	−0.023	0.001	0.024	0.000	−0.001	0.488
2. Food, beverages, tobacco	393.443	0.061	0.090	−1.251	0.014	0.011	0.012	0.004	0.004	0.038
3. Textiles, wearing apparel, leather	389.062	0.061	0.085	−0.208	0.008	0.189	0.018	0.000	−0.001	0.665
4. Wood, cork, paper	377.552	0.051	0.070	−1.349	−0.002	0.748	0.017	0.000	−0.003	0.199
5. Publishing, printing	1043.958	0.017	0.025	−1.396	0.004	0.397	0.010	0.000	0.001	0.308
6. Chemicals, rubber, plastics, non-metallic products	922.872	0.072	0.101	−0.143	0.007	0.094	0.021	0.000	−0.002	0.057
7. Metals & metal products	1271.720	0.088	0.120	−0.541	0.004	0.308	0.023	0.000	−0.001	0.197
8. Machinery, equipment, furniture, recycling	2337.992	0.063	0.088	−0.088	0.004	0.170	0.020	0.000	−0.001	0.107
9. Gas, water, electricity	40.340	0.044	0.085	−2.927	0.027	0.165	0.017	0.307	−0.003	0.346
10. Construction	1067.591	0.010	0.023	−2.790	0.004	0.385	0.010	0.001	−0.002	0.015
11. Wholesale & retail trade	7189.452	0.001	0.002	−0.531	−0.004	0.019	0.002	0.096	0.000	0.835
12. Hotels & restaurants	88.971	0.005	0.033	−4.499	0.027	0.059	−0.003	0.785	0.000	0.962
13. Transport	998.397	0.004	0.007	−1.537	−0.006	0.237	0.005	0.089	0.001	0.423
14. Post and telecommunication	180.685	0.023	0.033	−0.725	0.009	0.725	0.001	0.922	−0.004	0.080
15. Banks	767.874	0.023	0.040	−1.486	−0.021	0.022	0.009	0.012	−0.002	0.003
16. Insurance companies	479.801	0.005	0.012	−2.250	−0.013	0.181	0.007	0.214	−0.001	0.461
17. Other services	9608.186	0.046	0.069	−1.459	−0.006	0.000	0.018	0.000	−0.001	0.000
18. Public administration and defence	28.436	0.054	0.075	−1.397	0.046	0.323	0.006	0.004	−0.001	0.867
19. Education, health	224.997	0.013	0.027	−1.777	−0.010	0.507	−0.011	0.116	0.002	0.248
All Industries	31629.058	0.040	0.056	−1.293	0.002	0.003	0.015	0.000	−0.001	0.000

Table 33.4(B)

Industry	-2 Log Likelihood	Cox&Snell R_2	Nagelkerke $-R_2$	constant	b1	Sig.	b2	Sig.	b3	Sig.
				logp = a + b1Age + b2 Employee + b3 ROI + E						
1. Primary sector (agriculture, mining, etc)	440.774	0.028	0.045	-0.975	-0.021	0.004	0.000	0.079	-0.001	0.595
2. Food, beverages, tobacco	392.899	0.069	0.092	-0.910	0.014	0.011	0.000	0.015	0.003	0.089
3. Textiles, wearing apparel, leather	392.628	0.051	0.071	0.041	0.010	0.086	0.000	0.002	-0.001	0.439
4. Wood, cork, paper	371.187	0.071	0.097	-1.186	0.001	0.866	0.000	0.000	-0.005	0.047
5. Publishing, printing	1053.118	0.007	0.010	-1.089	0.005	0.246	0.000	0.078	0.000	0.485
6. Chemicals, rubber, plastics, non-metallic products	943.660	0.047	0.067	0.229	0.009	0.034	0.000	0.000	-0.002	0.038
7. Metals & metal products	1312.772	0.051	0.069	-0.138	0.007	0.043	0.000	0.000	-0.001	0.117
8. Machinery, equipment, furniture, recycling	2392.127	0.037	0.052	0.230	0.008	0.010	0.000	0.000	-0.001	0.019
9. Gas, water, electricity	39.045	0.064	0.125	-1.855	0.016	0.345	0.000	0.382	-0.002	0.497
10. Construction	1078.694	0.004	0.010	-2.511	0.007	0.163	0.000	0.592	-0.002	0.018
11. Wholesale & retail trade	7144.065	0.010	0.013	-0.592	-0.003	0.037	0.000	0.000	0.000	0.783
12. Hotels & restaurants	88.253	0.006	0.042	-4.761	0.027	0.060	0.000	0.252	0.000	0.967
13. Transport	999.205	0.004	0.006	-1.427	-0.005	0.302	0.000	0.136	0.001	0.449
14. Post and telecommunication	178.291	0.039	0.055	-1.003	0.019	0.498	0.000	0.133	-0.004	0.090
15. Banks	773.805	0.017	0.028	-1.313	-0.002	0.030	0.000	0.964	-0.002	0.002
16. Insurance companies	478.143	0.007	0.016	-2.158	-0.013	0.166	0.000	0.051	-0.001	-0.337
17. Other services	9914.991	0.013	0.019	-1.039	-0.007	0.000	0.000	0.000	-0.001	0.000
18. Public administration and defence	25.500	0.168	0.231	-2.049	0.065	0.197	0.000	0.107	-0.001	0.795
19. Education, health	226.473	0.009	0.019	-2.240	-0.008	0.565	0.000	0.232	0.002	0.234
All Industries	32439.358	0.010	0.013	-0.910	0.005	0.000	0.000	0.000	-0.001	0.000

'Education, health' non-exporters are actually larger. Size of labour force does not discriminate quite as well at sector level, with four demonstrating differences that are not statistically different at 10%.

Within the sample of small firms exporters have on average higher levels of turnover but in seven sectors differences are not significant. Across all sectors, with one exception, exporters have larger labour forces, but in four sectors differences are not statistically significant at practically any level. In the exception 'Education, health', non-exporters employed on average six more people.

In the total sample exporters were on average older than non-exporters. The differences were statistically significant at high levels in 12 sectors. In 'Banks', however, exporters are on average two years younger. In the sample of small firms, exporters were on average two and a half years older than non-exporters. Differences are statistically significant in nine sectors, the only exception being 'Wholesale and retail trade' where exporters were younger by a year.

The comparison of ROI does not provide very much ground for extolling the benefits to companies from exporting. On the full sample, whilst exporters earned on average 13% ROI, non-exporters enjoyed 27.4%. There were only three sectors in which non-exporters did not earn more, but differences were not statistically different at the levels of significance normally applied. In seven sectors the lower earnings were statistically significant at 5% or above. In the sample of small firms the pattern is continued. Non-exporters earned on average 24% ROI, more than twice that of exporters. Differences were statistically significant in five sectors at 5% or above. In the remainder success was not correlated in either direction with whether constituent companies conducted business overseas.

Concluding remarks
It would appear that the influences on the level of the export ratio are quite different from those on export propensity. Size is strongly associated with the latter, implying fixed costs in exporting, but is not related to the proportion of sales earned from overseas, perhaps reflecting an absence of economies of scale in variable costs.

Older companies are more likely to take the decision to seek business overseas, providing some support for stage theories of internationalization, but are not more likely to export a higher proportion of their sales than younger companies, a prediction from most versions of stage theory.

Profitability is not correlated with the sales ratio. Indeed the highest returns are earned by firms focusing entirely either on the domestic market or on overseas. There is, however, a very strong negative relationship between export propensity and profitability. There are several possible explanations for this, for instance that firms are forced by low domestic returns to look for business overseas, or that low returns are evidence of the costs of exporting. Clearly, this is an area ripe for further work; equally clearly, decision makers within firms should think carefully before acting on the advice of the government minister quoted at the beginning of this chapter.

Appendix

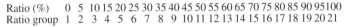

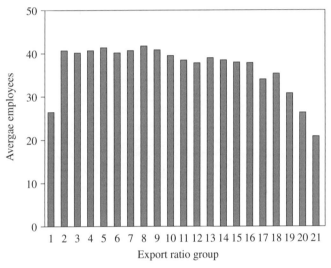

Figure 33A.1   *Relationship between export ratio and number of employees*

Ratio (%)   0   5   10 15 20 25 30 35 40 45 50 55 60 65 70 75 80 85 90 95 100
Ratio group   1   2   3   4   5   6   7   8   9 10 11 12 13 14 15 16 17 18 19 20 21

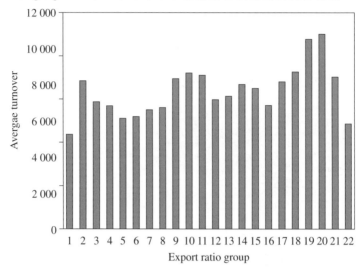

Figure 33A.2   Relationship between export ratio and turnover

Ratio (%)   0   5   10 15 20 25 30 35 40 45 50 55 60 65 70 75 80 85 90 95 100
Ratio group   1   2   3   4   5   6   7   8   9 10 11 12 13 14 15 16 17 18 19 20 21

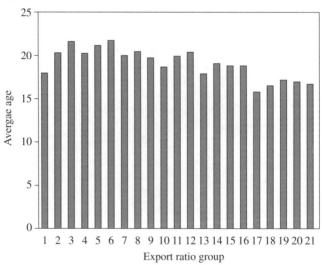

Figure 33A.3   Relationship between export ratio and age

References

Aaby, N.E. and Slater, S.F. (1989), 'Management Influences on Export Performance: A Review of the Empirical Literature, 1978–88', *International Marketing Review*, 6 (4), 7–23.

Axinn, C.N., Savitt, R., Sinkula, J.M. and Thach, S.V. (1995), 'Export Intention, Beliefs, and Behaviors in Smaller Industrial Firms', *Journal of Business Research*, 32, 49–55.

Bannock, G. & Partners (1987), 'Into Active Exporting', in Department of Trade & Industry (ed.), *SME Research Database*, pp. 276–7.

Bell, J. (1995), 'The Internationalization of Small Computer Software Firms – A Further Challenge to "Stage" Theories', *European Journal of Marketing*, 29 (8), 60–75.

Bell, P., Franchino, F., Perks, K. and Stevens, G.R. (1996), 'The Process of Internationalisation – Realities and Myths of Small Firm Growth in European and World Markets', Working Paper, University of Brighton Business School.

Bilkey, W.J. (1978), 'An Attempted Integration of the Literature on the Export Behaviour of Firms', *Journal of International Business Studies*, 9 (1), 33–46.

Bilkey, W.J. (1982), 'Variables Associated with Export Profitability', *Journal of International Business Studies*, 13 (2), 39–55.

Bilkey, W.J. and Tesar, G. (1977), 'The Export Behavior of Smaller-sized Wisconsin Manufacturing Firms', *Journal of International Business Studies*, 8 (1), 93–8.

Bonaccorsi, A. (1992), 'On the Relationship Between Firm Size and Export Intensity', *Journal of International Business Studies*, 23 (4), 605–36.

Burpitt, W.J. and Rondinelli, D.A. (2000), 'Small Firms' Motivations for Exporting: To Earn and Learn?', *Journal of Small Business Management*, 38 (4), October, 1–14.

Caughey, M. and Chetty, S. (1994), 'Pre-export Behaviour of Small Manufacturing Firms in New Zealand', *International Small Business Journal*, 12 (3), 62–8.

Cavusgil, S.T. (1980), 'On the internationalisation process of firms', *European Research*, 8, November, 273–81.

Cavusgil, S.T. (1982), 'Some Observations on the Relevance of Critical Variables for Internationalization Stages', in M.R. Czinkota and G. Tesar (eds), *Export Management: An International Context*, New York: Praeger, pp. 276–85.

Cavusgil, S.T. (1984a), 'Organizational Characteristics Associated with Export Activity', *Journal of Management Studies*, 21 (1), 3–22.

Cavusgil, S.T. (1984b), 'Differences Among Exporting Firms Based on Their Degree of Internationalisation', *Journal of Business Research*, 12 (2), 195–208.

Cavusgil, S.T., Bilkey, W.J. and Tesar, G. (1979), 'A Note on the Export Behaviour of Firms: Exporter Profiles', *Journal of International Business Studies*, 10 (1), 91–7.

Chetty, S.K. and Hamilton, R.T. (1996), 'The Process of Exporting in Owner-controlled Firms', *International Small Business Journal*, 14 (2), 12–25.

Christensen, C.H., da Rocha A. and Gertner, R.K. (1987), 'An Empirical Investigation of the Factors Influencing Exporting Success of Brazilian Firms', *Journal of International Business Studies*, 18 (3), 61–77.

Cooper, R.G. and Kleinschmidt, E.J. (1985), 'The Impact of Export Strategy on Export Sales Performance', *Journal of International Business Studies*, 16 (1), 37–55.

Crookell, H. and Graham, I. (1979), 'Internal Determinants of Export Marketing Behaviour: An Empirical Investigation', *Journal of Marketing Research*, 18 (1), 114–19.

Culpan, R. (1989), 'An Investigation of Export Behaviour of Firms: The Relevance of Firm Size', *Journal of Business Research*, 18, 207–18.

Czinkota, M.R. and Johnston, W.J. (1983), 'Export: Does Sales Volume Make a Difference?', *Journal of International Business Studies*, 14 (1), 147–53.

Daniels, J.D. and Goyburo, J. (1976), 'The Exporter–Non-Exporter Interface: A Search for Variables', *Foreign Trade Review*, 3, 258–82.

Gankema, H.G.J., Snuif, H.R. and Zwart, P.S. (2000), 'The Internationalization Process of Small and Medium-sized Enterprises: An Evaluation of Stage Theory', *Journal of Small Business Management*, 38 (4), October, 15–27.

Gemünden, H.G. (1991), 'Success Factors of Exporting Marketing: A Meta-analytic Critique of the Empirical Studies', in S.J. Palivoda (ed.), *New Perspectives on International Marketing*, New York: Routledge, pp. 36–62.

Holmlund, M. and Kock, S. (1998), 'Relationships and the Internationalisation of Finnish Small and Medium-sized Companies', *International Small Business Journal*, 16 (4), July–September, 46–64.

Johanson, J. and Vahlne, J.E. (1977), 'The Internationalisation Process of the Firm: A Model of Knowledge Development and Increasing Commitments', *Journal of International Business Studies*, 8 (1), 23–32.

Julien, P.A., Joyal, A., Deshaies, L. and Ramangalahy, C. (1997), 'A Typology of Strategic Behaviour Among Small and Medium-sized Export Businesses: A Case Study', *International Small Business Journal*, 15 (2), 33–49.

Katsikeas, C. (1994), 'Export Competitive Advantages: The Relevance of Firm Characteristic', *International Marketing Review*, 3 (11), 33–53.

Kaynak, E. (1985), 'Correlates of Export Performance in Resource-based Industries', *Global Perspectives in Marketing*, New York: Greenwood Press.

Keng, K.A. and Jiuan, T.S. (1989), 'Differences Between Small and Medium Sized Export and Non-export Firms: Nature or Nurture', *International Marketing Review*, 6 (4), 27–40.

Kirpalani, V.H. and Maclntosh, N.B. (1980), 'Internal Marketing Effectiveness of Technology-oriented Small Firms', *Journal of International Business Studies*, 11 (3), 81–90.

Leonidou, L.C., Katsikeas, C.S. and Piercy, N. (1998), 'Identifying Managerial Influences on Exporting: Past Research and Future Directions', *Journal of International Marketing*, 6 (2), 74–102.

Madsen, T.K. (1987), 'Empirical Export Performance Studies: A Review of Conceptualisations and Findings', *Advances in International Marketing*, 2, 177–98.

Malekzadeh, A.R. and Nahavandi, A. (1984), 'Small Business Exporting: Misconceptions Are Abundant', *American Journal of Small Business*, 9 (4), 7–14.

McDougall, P.P. and Oviatt, B.M. (1996), 'New Venture Internationalization, Strategic Change, and Performance: A Follow-up Study', *Journal of Business Venturing*, 11: 23–40.

McDougall, P.P., Shane, S. and Oviatt, B.M. (1994), 'Explaining the Formation of International New Ventures: The Limits of Theories from International Business Research', *Journal of Business Venturing*, 9, 469–87.

Miesenbock, K.J. (1988), 'Small Business and Export: A Literature Review', *International Small Business Journal*, 6 (2), 42–61.

Moen, O. (1999), 'The Relationship Between Firm Size, Competitive Advantages and Export Performance Revisited', *International Small Business Journal*, 18 (1), 53–72.

Moini, A.H. (1997), 'Barriers Inhibiting Export Performance of Small and Medium-Sized Manufacturing Firms', *Journal of Global Marketing*, 10 (4), 67–93.

Naidu, G.M. and Prasad, V.K. (1994), 'Predictors of Export Strategy and Performance of Small- and Medium-Sized Firms', *Journal of Business Research*, 31 (1), 107–15.

Ogram, E.W., Jr. (1982), 'Exporters and Non-exporters: A Profile of Small Manufacturing Firms in Georgia', in M.R. Czinkota and G. Tesar (eds), *Export Management: An International Context*, New York: Praeger, pp. 70–84.

Ong, C.H. and Pearson, A.W. (1982), 'The Impact of Technical Characteristics on Export Activity: A Study of Small and Medium-sized UK Electronic Firms', *R&D Management*, 12 (4), 189–96.

Oviatt, B.M. and McDougall, P.P. (1994), 'Toward a Theory of International New Ventures', *Journal of International Business Studies*, 25 (1), 45–64.

Piercy, N. (1981), 'Company Internationalisation: Active and Reactive Exporting', *Journal of Marketing*, 15 (3), 26–40.

Reid, S.D. (1981), 'The Decision Maker and Export Entry and Expansion', *Journal of International Business Studies*, 12 (2), 101–12.

Reid, S.D. (1982), 'The Impact of Size on Export Behaviour in Small Firms', in M.R. Czinkota and G. Tesar (eds), *Export Management: An International Context*, New York: Praeger, pp. 18–38.

Reid, S.D. (1985), 'Exporting: Does Volume Make A Difference? – Comment', *Journal of International Business Studies*, 16 (2), 153–5.

Reuber, A.R. and Fischer, E. (1997), 'The Influence of the Management Team's International Experience on the Internationalization Behaviour of SMEs', *Journal of International Business Studies*, 28 (4), pp. 807–25.

Seringhaus, R. (1986/7), 'The Role of Information Assistance in Small Firms' Export Involvement', *International Small Business Journal*, 5 (2), 26–36.

Stening, B.W. and McDougall, G.H.G. (1975), 'Something to Think About: Identifying the High Performance Exporter', *Canada Commerce*, December, 12–15.

Styles, C. and Ambler, T. (1994), 'Successful Export Practice: The UK Experience', *International Marketing Review*, 11 (6), 23–47.

Tyebjee, T.T. (1994), 'Internationalisation of High Tech Firms: Initial vs. Extended Involvement', *Journal of Global Marketing*, 7 (4), 59–81.

Ursic, M.L. and Czinkota, M.R. (1984), 'An Experience Curve Explanation of Export Expansion', *Journal of Business Research*, 12 (2), 159–68.

Welch, L.S. and Wiedersheim-Paul, F. (1980), 'Initial Exports – A Marketing Failure?', *The Journal of Management Studies*, 17 (4), 334–44.

Westhead, P. (1994), 'A Matched Pair Comparison of Exporting and Non-exporting Small Firms in Great Britain', Working paper no.19, Centre for Small and Medium-sized Enterprises, Warwick Business School.

Withey, J.J. (1980), 'Difference Between Exporters and Non-Exporters: Some Hypotheses Concerning Small Manufacturing Business', *American Journal of Small Business*, 4 (3), Winter, 29–37.

Yaprak, A. (1985), 'An Empirical Study of the Differences Between Small Exporting and Non-Exporting US Firms', *International Marketing Review*, 2, 72–83.

34 United States perspectives of international entrepreneurship
Bella L. Galperin

> Wealth is created by Americans – by creativity and enterprise and risk-taking.
> But government can create an environment where businesses and entrepreneurs
> and families can dream and flourish. (President George W. Bush)

In his address on small businesses, George W. Bush noted that the role of
government is not to generate wealth but to create an environment in which
entrepreneurs can flourish.* The president stated that low taxes and clear
and sensible regulations are necessary in helping small businesses in the
United States. In his agenda, he recognized the importance of providing
new tax incentives to make it easier for small businesses to make important
job-creating investments. With new tax incentives, most entrepreneurs will
have more income needed to expand, buy more equipment and hire more
employees (Small Business Administration, 2002, 26 March).

Given that entrepreneurship and small businesses are the backbone of
the American economy, it is not surprising that issues relating to entrepreneurs
and small business owners are part of the president's agenda.
According to the US Small Business Administration (SBA), there are
approximately 25 million small businesses in the United States (Small
Business Administration, 2002, July 30). Small businesses represent 99.7%
of all employers, employ 53% of the private workforce, provide 47% of all
sales in the country and 55% of innovations. In addition, small businesses
account for 35% of federal contract dollars, 38% of jobs in high-technology
sectors, 51% of private sector output and represent 96% of all US exporters
(ibid.).

The recent technological and policy developments, such as the increased
use of the Internet and a reduction of trade barriers, have generated new
opportunities for American entrepreneurs and small businesses to sell their
products and services overseas. According to the U.S. Department of
Commerce, the growth of many American companies is undoubtedly
coming from sales abroad. US exports of goods and services have increased
from $852 billion in 1996 to $1 trillion in 2000 (Arnold, 2001). The findings

---

* The author would like to kindly thank Casey Barnes, Sharon Benoit, Misty Kane, Gloria
Le-Quang-Wong, Phil Ouzts, Guru Prasad, Marcia Sergent and Bob Taft, for their asistance.

of the SBA suggest that small businesses accounted for a significant amount of these exports.

More specifically, US exports to Mexico and European Union countries have significantly increased over the years. US exports to Mexico grew by 141.3% from 1995 to 2000 (ibid.). American exports to European countries have also steadily increased, by 266% from 1983 to 2000, reaching approximately $165 billion in 2000. According to the U.S. Department of Commerce, small and medium-sized firms have played a large role in these exports. For example, more than 20 000 small and medium-sized firms exported goods worth $6.5 billion to Germany (U.S. Department of Commerce, 2002, January 2).

Despite the central role of entrepreneurs and small businesses in the global economy, much of the literature has examined entrepreneurship in a domestic context (for example, Dale, 2000; Jones, 1995; Simon *et al.*, 2002). For example, researchers have focused on the development of small business management skills and the cultivation of entrepreneurial skills in order to prepare individuals to become successful entrepreneurs in their local communities (Dale, 2000; Jones, 1995). Less attention has been given to the development of American entrepreneurs who wish to expand internationally and become leading global citizens.

This chapter presents an overview of the initiatives and support available to American entrepreneurs and small business owners who are interested in expanding internationally. Specifically, the programs and services offered by government agencies, academia and professional industry associations are examined. Qualitative data from semi-structured interviews were used to complement the findings. The interviews were primarily conducted with individuals who work for organizations in the state of Florida. Finally, future directions in the development of international entrepreneurs in the United States are discussed.

Exploring American initiatives and programs

In the United States, there are a number of initiatives and programs available to entrepreneurs and small business owners who are interested in internationalizing their businesses. While there are several organizations which offer assistance to entrepreneurs who wish to expand overseas, this chapter will focus on the major initiatives and programs that are offered by (1) the US Commercial Service; (2) state-level organizations; (3) US Small Business Administration; (4) the World Trade Centers Association; (5) Centers for International Business Education and Research; (6) International Business 2000 Consortium; and (7) professional industry associations. The programs offered by each these organizations will be discussed below.

US Commercial Service

The US Commercial Service is one of several federal government agencies which promote American exports. The U.S. Commercial Service was founded in 1980 (U.S. Department of Commerce, 2002). The US Commercial Service is a unit of the International Trade Administration and part of the U.S. Department of Commerce. The US Commercial Service offers a wide variety of programs and services to entrepreneurs and small and medium-sized business owners who are interested in entering and succeeding in global markets. It has 105 Export Assistance Centers in the United States and 151 offices located around the world, with a total network of 1800 employees (US Department of Commerce, 2002). The mission of the US Commercial Service is to support commercial interests in the United States and help businesses, especially small and medium-sized enterprises, to increase sales and market share around the world.

The US Commercial Service currently serves a client base of 88 100 American companies and counseled 17 855 companies in 2000, a 21% increase on 1999. Nearly all of its clients were small and medium-sized companies (U.S. Department of Commerce, 2002). Phil Ouzts, manager of the Export Assistance Program for the U.S. Department of Commerce in Orlando, Florida, noted, 'Our clients are typically smaller businesses. It is amazing to me how many clients there are in Central Florida who are successful exporters and who have less than 100 employees. A product in demand, determination to succeed overseas and commitment from top management can more than compensate for not having hundreds of employees.'

In particular, the purpose of the US Commercial Service is (1) to promote the export of US goods and services to support the American economy, preserve job security and create jobs; (2) to protect and advocate for American business interests overseas; (3) to help US firms export by providing counseling and advice, information on overseas markets and international contacts; and (4) to support the export promotion efforts of other public and private organizations (U.S. Department of Commerce, n.d.).

With a team of highly trained professionals, the US Commercial Service helps entrepreneurs and small business owners expand their global network by offering commercial centers, which offer meeting space, computers, fax and phone facilities. In addition, through its website (*www.USATrade.gov*), it offers access to export professionals in more than 200 cites worldwide, free market research on 85 countries, programs to promote American products and services, services to locate international buyers, and e-commerce services. Specifically, through its BuyUSA.com program, it can locate foreign buyers for US suppliers by combining the power of the Internet with the Service's worldwide network. Given that these services are customized to meet the needs of the clients and will help reduce the risk in entering new markets, the services can be very useful for entrepreneurs and small business owners.

Additionally, the US Commercial Service promotes the products and services of its clients by organizing and/or participating in trade event shows around the world (U.S. Department of Commerce, n.d.). These events include more than 30 industry-focused domestic trade events that attract foreign buyers from throughout the world. These events have helped entrepreneurs initiate and expand export sales around the world.

Finally, the US Commercial Service offers several services to help its clients find future international partners. These services include (1) Matchmaker Trade Delegations, which offer participants the opportunity of face-to-face meetings with pre-screened, qualified business prospects in key target markets; (2) International Partner Searchers, which enable clients to obtain detailed company information on pre-screened potential partners that have expressed an interest in their companies; (3) the Gold Key Service, a program that provides US companies with on-site appointments with prospective business partners in more than 80 markets; (4) *Commercial News USA*, the US Commercial Service's informative magazine that introduces US products and services to more than 160000 buyers throughout the world; and (5) Video Connect USA, an e-commerce program that enables US companies to participate in four to five appointments through the use of video conferencing technology (U.S. Department of Commerce, 2001, March; U.S. Department of Commerce, 2002, 6 June).

When asked about the various services offered by the US Commercial Service, Ouzts noted, 'While we have a lot of stand-in-shelf item products, such as the Gold Key Service and the International Partner Search, they may fit the needs of some of the clients some of the time. They never fit the needs of all the clients all the time. A lot of what we do is becoming more and more tailor-made to facilitate the client needs.' The US Commercial Service makes great efforts to adapt its services to its customers. When asked about the Gold Key Service in particular, Ouzts stated, 'The Gold Key is totally customized to meet the needs of the client and to also correspond to the market situation. Since it is necessary for the client to travel to these markets in order to participate in the Gold Key, the commercial officer at the embassy makes great efforts to evaluate the client's product and/or service to determine the feasibility of using the Gold Key. The US Commercial Service wants to ensure that if a client travels half way around the world for a Gold Key, the results will be positive. Incidentally, the level of customer satisfaction with the Gold Key Service is very high with multiple usages by major clients.'

The services offered by the US Commercial Service have been invaluable for many small business owners and entrepreneurs who have been interested in expanding their businesses overseas. For example, Da Vinci Gourmet Ltd, a small Seattle company of 85 employees, which was established in 1989, expanded its sales to more than 50 countries with the assistance of the Seattle U.S. Export Assistance Center's market research and overseas trade missions (U.S. Department of Commerce, 2002, June 18). The export sales of Da Vinci Gourmet Ltd, a company that provides speciality syrups, confections and gourmet sauces, rose from 8% of total sales in 1997 to more than 22% in 2001. Secretary of Commerce Don Evans, whose offices assisted Da Vinci Gourmet Ltd to expand internationally, said, 'It is the American dream. Being an entrepreneur means being innovative and creative. By partnering with the U.S. government, small businesses can be successful' (U.S Department of Commerce, 2001, May 17).

The strong customer orientation of the US Commercial Service has caught the attention of many entrepreneurs and small business owners. According to annual reports, the US Commercial Service domestic offices conducted 44 156 export counseling sessions in 2000, a 37% increase on 1999. Their domestic offices generated 4627 verifiable export sales, worth $5.1 billion in 2000. Furthermore, the US Commercial Service international offices conducted 189 867 export counseling sessions in 2000. Their international offices generated 4628 verifiable export sales, worth $16.2 billion in 2000 (U.S. Department of Commerce, 2002). Seventy per cent of these sales were from small and medium-sized companies.

Moreover, there are state-level organizations that offer a number of programs and services that may help entrepreneurs and small business owners to develop the necessary skills to conduct business overseas. These initiatives and programs are discussed below.

State-level organizations
Entrepreneurs and small business owners who are interested in expanding internationally may also seek assistance from state-level organizations. These organizations help companies in their respective states to explore international business opportunities. For example, the Virginia Economic Development Partnership helps companies in the state of Virginia to expand into international markets. More specifically, the mission of the International Trade Development, a division of the Virginia Economic Development Partnership, is to 'increase sales for Virginia companies by assisting their entry to foreign markets' (Virginia Economic Development Partnership, 2001). The International Trade division offers a variety of programs and services, such as trade missions, trade shows, market research reports and educational seminars statewide, in order to help Virginia companies to expand internationally.

Similarly, the International Business Development, a program of the Arkansas Department of Economic Development, promotes exports and helps companies in the state of Arkansas to develop globally. The Department offers services such as market research, agent/distributor searches, consulting, workshops and trade missions in order to provide Arkansas companies with the necessary assistance in promoting their products and/or service in the global marketplace (Arkansas Department of Economic Development, 2001).

Entrepreneurs and small business owners in the state of Florida can receive assistance from Enterprise Florida Inc. (EFI). Headquartered in Orlando, EFI is a not-for-profit, private–public partnership established to develop the economy of the state of Florida (Enterprise Florida Inc, 2002). When asked whether Enterprise Florida Inc. was a state-level organization, Casey Barnes, International Marketing representative for the International Trade and Business Development Unit, said, 'EFI is the economic development organization for the state of Florida. We, partners with economic development organizations on the local level, provide companies with a multitude of services, ranging from assistance with corporate expansions to export counseling for international trade. EFI is mostly funded by the state of Florida, but also raises a certain amount of capital from private companies.'

The mission of EFI is clear: Barnes continued, 'Enterprise Florida's job is jobs. EFI's mission is to increase economic opportunities for all Floridians through the creation and retention of quality jobs and the active support of strong and growing businesses.' While the mission does not specify whether EFI is aimed at entrepreneurs and small businesses, Barnes noted, 'EFI is designed to work with small and medium-sized firms. Some larger firms may have entire international departments devoted to researching markets and getting the right products to the right places. Many smaller companies cannot afford that luxury, and that's where EFI can help.'

Specifically, the International Trade and Business Development Unit of EFI offers a wide variety of services, such as (1) export counseling to Florida companies; (2) overseas trade missions and shows; (3) export financing assistance through the Florida Export Finance Corporation (among other sources); and (4) a free trade lead program that provides Florida manufacturers and service providers with leads from companies around the world. EFI is also actively involved in recruiting companies overseas to invest in Florida (Enterprise Florida Inc., 2002).

When asked about the initiatives offered by EFI, Barnes stated, 'One of the most important services EFI provides is one-to-one counseling to Florida exporters. However, EFI also conducts market research, forwards international partner referrals and assists Florida exports in inbound and outbound missions and shows. On a typical outbound mission, Enterprise Florida will arrange transportation, lodging, market briefings and, most importantly, schedule one-on-one appointments with qualified overseas buyers. This service is especially valuable to small exporters who typically have trouble getting top-level appointments with overseas companies.'

In order to assess the success of the trade missions, EFI distributes annual customer satisfaction surveys and keeps summary statistics of actual sales and expected sales of their trade missions and shows. Barnes stated, 'We conduct a customer satisfaction survey of companies we assisted in the past year. We also capture the amount of sales that were generated by a company through an EFI-related event or service. The sales figures, kept strictly confidential, are used to determine the impact that EFI has on creating jobs in the state of Florida.' Barnes further stressed the importance of obtaining customer feedback. He noted, 'We closely track the satisfaction [of our clients]. It is in our best interest to do that. Our success is only generated by the people that we serve.'

In line with Barnes' remarks, the 2002 customer satisfaction survey results for EFI indicated that export and trade assistance services led to very high levels of satisfaction. The services ranked most highly by clients were international trade shows/missions, overall project assistance, export assistance and information resources (Ernest & Young LLP, 2002).

In addition, the US SBA has played a central role in the development of international entrepreneurs. Through its various offices, it provides a number of programs and initiatives for entrepreneurs. These initiatives will be outlined in the section below.

US Small Business Administration
The US SBA was specifically created by Congress in 1953 to help America's entrepreneurs develop small enterprises. Currently, there are SBA offices in every state. The SBA offers a wide variety of programs, such as financial and federal contract procurement assistance; management assistance; specialized outreach programs for women, minorities and armed forces veterans; and loans to victims of natural disasters (Small Business Administration, 2001, 3 March). The SBA also has an Office of International Trade, which focuses on specialized advice in international trade; an Office of Entrepreneurial Development; and Small Business Development Centers which counsel entrepreneurs on issues relating to domestic and international trade issues. The programs offered by these offices will be discussed in greater detail.

Office of International Trade   The SBA Office of International Trade provides export information and development assistance, such as trade counseling, training, legal assistance and publications to entrepreneurs and small business owners who are interested in expanding overseas. It has US Export Assistance Centers or 'one stop shops' which provide small and medium-sized businesses with local export assistance. These centers are located in major metropolitan areas throughout the United States, such as Atlanta, Georgia; Baltimore, Maryland; Boston, Massachusetts; Long Beach, California; Miami, Florida and New York City (Small Business Administration, 2002, 24 June).

In addition, small business owners and entrepreneurs who are currently exporting or plan to export in the future will find that SBA's loan products are very helpful. The SBA offers three different loan products: SBA Export*Express*, the Export Working Capital Loan and the International Trade Loan. First, SBA Export*Express* includes lending and technical assistance to help small business owners who have difficulty in obtaining sufficient export funding. Second, the Export Working Capital Loan offers loans with a 90% guarantee up to $1 million, low fees and flexible terms to small companies who need credit to close a sale after they have invested the time, money and resources to develop export leads. Finally, the International Trade Loan program can guarantee up to $1.25 million in combined working capital and facilities and equipment loans. In order to obtain the loan, applicants must establish that the loan proceeds will expand an existing export market or develop new export markets, or that their business is negatively affected by import competition (Small Business Administration, 2001, October).

The SBA Office of International Trade offers other services such as Trade Mission (TM) OnLine, a database of US small businesses that are currently seeking to export. Since TM OnLine is also used as a search engine for foreign firms and US companies who are looking for a business partner or supplier, this service can help small businesses expand internationally (Small Business Administration, 2001, 8 May). The Office of International Trade also provides business education and training programs at the various US Export Assistance Centers. These programs are offered in conjunction with the U.S. Department of Commerce, the Export–Import Bank, and state and local economic groups.

Office of Entrepreneurial Development The SBA also has an Office of Entrepreneurial Development, which specializes in business counseling and training. This office is primarily interested in 'helping small businesses start, grow and be competitive in the global markets by providing quality, counseling and other forms of management technical assistance' (Small Business Administration, 2002, 11 June). While the programs and services directly relate to issues in the domestic context, such as Native American

Affairs and Women's Business Ownership, the website provides a link to international trade under the section, 'Other Highlighted SBA Services'.

Small Business Development Centers   Small Business Development Centers (SBDCs) provide management assistance to current and prospective small business owners (Small Business Administration, 2002, 11 February). SBDCs are a network of services designed to 'make a significant, strategic investment in building and enhancing local economies in the United States, Puerto Rico, US Virgin Islands, Guam and American Samoa' (Small Business Administration, 2002, 4 April). The services offered by SBDCs are designed to provide counseling, training and technical assistance in all aspects of small business management such as financial, marketing, production, organization and engineering. Other programs include technical assistance, venture capital formation, rural development and international trade assistance.

SBDCs cooperate with the private sector, the educational community and federal, state and local governments to increase the economic development in the United States by providing management and technical assistance to entrepreneurs and small business owners. Since 1980, over 8 million entrepreneurs have received services from SBDCs (Small Business Administration, 2002, 4 April). In 2001, SBDCs counseled and trained approximately 610000 clients.

Currently there are 58 SBDCs, one in each state, except for Texas which has four, the District of Columbia, Guam, Puerto Rico, Samoa and the US Virgin Islands, with a network of approximately 1000 service locations (Small Business Administration, 2002, 11 February). In each state, a lead organization sponsors the SBDC and manages the program. The lead organization coordinates programs, which are offered to small businesses through a network of subcenters and satellite locations in each state. Subcenters are located in colleges, universities, community colleges, vocational schools, chambers of commerce and economic development corporations. For example, New York State Small Business Development Center is administered by the State University of New York and has offices throughout the state. The Howard University SBDC operates out of Howard University School of Business and provides assistance to entrepreneurs and small businesses in the Washington, DC area. The SBDC in the state of Maryland has a partnership with the University of Maryland. The Florida Small Business Development Center Network, administered by the Florida Network State Director's Office, is located at the University of West Florida in Pensacola, Florida.

More specifically, the Florida SBDC Network has a statewide network of 29 regional centers and sub-centers located in the state of Florida as well as partner locations (for example, chambers of commerce, economic councils and banks). The Florida SBDC network has advised over 250000 entrepreneurs and small business owners with over 1000000 hours of one-on-one counseling, over 20000 business training events for more than 450000 participants and has provided answers to over 1425000 requests for information (Florida Small Business Development Center Network, 2002a).

While the Florida SBDC network helps entrepreneurs to start and grow their businesses in the state of Florida by providing counseling, training and information to help them make important business decisions in general, the Office of International Programs is a special program that is designed to provide entrepreneurs with the necessary information on developing the international aspect of their business strategy. The Office of International Programs is also part of Team Florida, a network including Enterprise Florida Inc. and the US Commercial Service, a strategy designed to increase Florida's visibility in the international marketplace. In order to increase trade between different countries, the Office also works with overseas partner countries in Argentina, Australia, Curacao, France, Japan and Mexico (Florida Small Business Development Center Network, 2002a).

The Office of International Programs provides counseling on issues relating to international trade, and offers training courses such as the Trade Florida Series, a program that consists of the Trade Florida Primer; Business of Exporting; and the Export Florida Training Program. The Trade Florida Primer is an introduction to international trade and the Business of Exporting course is a three-hour seminar that covers the basics of trade and resource partners. The Export Florida course offers training certification in small business exporting. The program consists of six sessions, covering export fundamentals, market selection, partner selection, pricing, financing the transaction and completing the transaction. Marcia Sergent, Director of the Office of International Programs, further noted that SBDCs offer trade programs customized for their client base in topics such as Doing Business with the USA and Exporting with the Experts (Marcia Sergent, personal communication, 30 July 2002).

The Florida SBDC Network has been credited with providing the necessary professional resources for a number of entrepreneurs in Florida, such as Lori Bitar, owner of Tutors Unlimited Inc.; Lisa Strickland, owner of Xtremely Board; Rod Vargas and Chris Parent, owners of Apex Environmental Engineering & Compliance, Inc.; and Scott Bartkowski and Debra Atkinson of Artificial Reefs Inc. More specifically, after receiving assistance in marketing issues and business planning assistance in 1999, Artificial Reefs Inc. was interested in expanding into foreign markets. With the assistance of the SBDC, an international expansion plan was formulated which has resulted in several potential business opportunities in Mexico and the Pacific Rim (Florida Small Business Development Center Network, 2002b).

Unlike the US SBA, the World Trade Centers Association (WTCA), a non-governmental association, provides its members with a number of programs and services to facilitate international trade. The trade initiatives and programs offered by the WTCA are discussed below.

World Trade Centers Association
The World Trade Centers Association (WTCA) was incorporated in 1970, as a not-for-profit, non-political, global membership association that provides its members with international trade services and tools to conduct business. More than a building or an organisation, a World Trade Center (WTC) brings together business and government agencies that are involved in international trade, provides essential trade services and stimulates the economy in its region.

The mission of the WTCA is 'to promote world peace through trade and commerce' (World Trade Center Orlando, 2002a). WTCA, headquartered in New York, has 338 World Trade Centers in 101 countries. WTCs offer trade information, business leads and an array of business services to help member companies in their international business endeavours. Since the WTC services are reciprocal, members can use the services at the various WTCs around the world.

World Trade Centers offer their members and tenants a wide variety of services and facilities, such as (1) Individual Import and Export Counseling, which helps companies prepare an initial export strategy and provides companies with advice on financial assistance; (2) Trade Information Services, which offer companies up-to-date information about specific regions, including market research which can be tailored to a company's specific needs (for example, country analysis and industry research), profiles on business contacts, governmental regulations, business culture and customs, and information on products and services; (3) Trade Education Services, consisting of trade educational workshops, seminars and courses on key global business issues; (4) Business Services, including support facilities, such as video conferencing, secretarial services, temporary office space, meeting rooms, translation and interpretation capabilities; (5) WTCA Online, an internet website that is an international trade information hub for accessing valuable databases of information, posting and reviewing trade leads and obtaining credit reports and company profiles; (6) Intern Program, providing college-level students with the opportunity to learn and experience many facets of international business while earning school credit; (7) Inbound Mission Programs, such as Business Matchmaking Programs where appointments between buyers, sellers, joint venture partnerships and governmental officials are arranged; (8) Group Trade Missions, which help businesses explore new markets by working together with other WTCs and governmental agencies to promote products and services; and (9) WTC clubs which offer comfortable lounge and dining services for members. In addition, the World Trade Center University offers certificate courses in international trade and on-line accredited degrees in international business (World Trade Center Orlando, n.d.a).

Specifically, WTC Orlando regularly coordinates training classes on topics such as 'Marketing Your Company's Products Overseas', 'Finding Overseas Partners', 'Financial Aspects', 'Legal Aspects' and 'Shipping and Logistics'. When asked about the initiatives of the World Trade Center, Misty Kane, Vice-President of WTC Orlando, stated, 'If you are pursuing or doing international business you should become a member of a World Trade Center. By being a member of a World Trade Center you have many resources, tools and assistance offered to you. We find at times that many of our very small-sized member businesses utilize us as their international arm, so that they can concentrate on sales. When many of the members travel they like to take advantage of dining in the private World Trade Center clubs and staying in the hotels of the World Trade Centers. All of the services and resources are available in one location, making it easier for you to conduct business in a cost effective and efficient manner. It is considered by many as a one-stop facility.'

WTCs serve a million members worldwide (World Trade Center Orlando, n.d.b). When asked about the composition of the WTCA membership, Kane responded, 'The majority of World Trade Center Orlando's membership is small and medium-sized companies.' Although the WTCA provides assistance to small and medium-sized enterprises as well as large organizations, its programs and services can serve as important tools for entrepreneurs and small business owners. Since entrepreneurs and small business owners have a limited amount of resources, the wide variety of services and training offered by WTCs can provide them with the necessary resources and training. Kane specifically noted how WTCs would benefit entrepreneurs and small business owners. She stated, 'small enterprises find the services World Trade Centers offer help them to be prepared when venturing overseas and thus it helps them to avoid costly mistakes'.

The services and programs offered by WTC Orlando have successfully helped entrepreneurs to export internationally. For example, a member of WTC Orlando, Joseph Durek, president and chief executive officer of Lentek International, a company that develops chemical-free pest control products, started his business out of his home in the early 1990s and has grown it to a company with over 100 employees. Having used the services of WTC Orlando to expand internationally, Joseph Durek now exports to more than 65 countries worldwide (World Trade Center Orlando, 2002b). In fact, he was selected by a committee of the WTC Orlando to appear in the WTCA Book of Honor. The WTCA Book of Honor is an award that recognizes individuals who strive to enhance world peace and economic stability through international business.

There are also academic organizations that can help entrepreneurs and small business owners to develop the necessary skills to excel in the global marketplace. The Centers for International Business Education and Research (CIBERs) and the International Business (IB) 2000 Consortium are discussed below.

Centers for International Business Education and Research
CIBERs were created by Congress under the Omnibus Trade and Competitiveness Act of 1988 to enhance the capacity for international understanding and competitiveness in the United States. CIBERs, administered by the US Department of Education, link the manpower and technological needs of the American business community, and state and local agencies with the international education, language training and research capabilities of the universities across the nation. In essence, the 30 centers can be considered as the regional and national resources of practitioners, students and teachers (Centers for International Business Education and Research, 2001a).

While CIBERs engage in a variety of activities to increase the national competitiveness of the United States, such as faculty development and funding research projects, they also provide support for small and medium-sized businesses that are interested in expanding overseas. Educational programs for businesses include export training, market information, management reviews and response strategies to increased competitiveness (Centers for International Business Education and Research, 2001a). Organized events and discussions about international business, evening and summer courses in modern languages, and the consulting and marketing research services offered by CIBERs may be especially helpful to the entrepreneur who is interested in expanding overseas.

The CIBERs that provide outreach programs for the local business community are located throughout the United States (Centers for International Business Education and Research, 2001b). Examples of the programs available at the various locations include the Export Academy and Global Interact Network at Michigan State University; the NAFTA Center and the Institute for International Business Ethics at Thunderbird; and the International Practica at the University of North Carolina.

International Business 2000 Consortium

The collaboration among American educational institutions has resulted in the development of initiatives to establish linkages between business practitioners and students in order to advance international business. For example, cooperation among the University of Florida, the University of Tampa, Florida Atlantic University and the University of Central Florida, known as the IB 2000 Consortium, offers the IB 2000 Program.

The IB 2000 Program provides students with the opportunity to work with local entrepreneurs to develop strategies to expand internationally and then travel overseas to select qualified business partners. Upon successful completion of the program, the students are certified as company representatives by the Small Business Development Center.

Students must enroll in the program for two semesters. In the spring semester, the students learn about exporting, recruit companies to participate in the program and then work with the companies to develop approaches to enter overseas markets. Once the preliminary research has been conducted, teams of two students travel overseas on behalf of the companies to conduct product-specific market research, identify, interview and generate a list of potential business partners. Every student team has at least one member who is fluent in the language of the host country. In order to make the contacts efficiently and effectively, the students work out of the offices of overseas sponsors. Past sponsors include the U.S. Department of Commerce, World Trade Centers, American chambers of commerce, and Walt Disney World.

More specifically, students are required to develop premium leads. A premium lead occurs when, first, the students provide company information to the potential overseas business partner. Second, the potential business partner shows sincere interest in the product or service. Third, the students visit the facilities of the potential partner overseas and interview the person to determine the level of interest and under what terms the partner would be willing to enter into a business relationship. Once the team has generated the premium lead, the American company is immediately contacted in order for the two firms to meet.

Many entrepreneurs have benefited from the IB 2000 Program. Over 60 companies have participated in the program and over 1500 premium leads for companies have been generated from the IB 2000 Program. For example, Jim Sherry from Dearborn Electronics stated, 'IB 2000 is A-One. Over the past three years this program has been an effective tool in identifying and more importantly qualifying foreign sales contacts for Dearborn. Look for us to be a repeat player.'

Bob Taft, founder and director of the IB 2000 Program at the University of Central Florida, noted that firms must pay $4000 to participate in the program (Bob Taft, personal communication, 6 August 2002). The fees charged to the participating companies for the services, as well as the support of the sponsoring organizations, has helped fund the IB 2000 Program.

Finally, there are a number of professional industry organizations, which can provide counseling and mentoring for entrepreneurs who are interested in expanding overseas. Below, the initiatives offered by a couple of professional industry organizations are outlined.

Professional industry organizations
There are a number of professional organizations, largely consisting of business practitioners, that may help in the development of international entrepreneurs. The Service Corps of Retired Executives (SCORE) and The Indus Entrepreneurs (TiE), two professional industry organizations, are discussed below.

Service Corps of Retired Executives   SCORE is a not-for-profit organization of retired executives who are dedicated to facilitating the formation, growth and success of small businesses nationwide. The SCORE Association was founded in 1964 by the SBA in order to help American small businesses prosper (Small Business Administration, 2002, 16 October). SCORE consists of working and retired executives and business owners who donate their time and expertise, providing confidential counseling and mentoring free of charge. In addition, SCORE offers low-cost workshops in various areas such as marketing and sales and financial management techniques, as well as international trade at one of their 700 locations in the United States.

Although SCORE's primary mission is not to provide entrepreneurs with the skills to expand internationally, volunteers who have experience in this area can counsel entrepreneurs who are interested in conducting business internationally. According to the 2001 statistics, SCORE has 900 counselors with foreign trade experience. Currently there are 11 500 SCORE volunteers and over 800 cyber-counselors with 600 skills (Small Business Administration, 2002, 16 October).

Since 1964, SCORE has served more than 4.5 million clients and has assisted approximately 300 000 entrepreneurs annually. In 2001, SCORE provided 387 938 services for the small business community through counseling, educational training workshops and on-line assistance. In the same year, 59 118 entrepreneurs participated in SCORE e-mail counseling, which is available 24 hours a day, 7 days a week (SCORE, n.d).

The Indus Entrepreneurs   The Indus Entrepreneurs (TiE), chartered in 1992, is a unique not-for-profit volunteer global organization that strives to advance all aspects of entrepreneurship and professionalism. Although TiE stands for 'The Indus Entrepreneurs', connoting the ethnic background of the individuals who chartered the organization, TiE now represents 'Talent, ideas, and Enterprise'. TiE's primary objective is to 'provide a platform on which people with entrepreneurial spirit and all others interested in economic value creation can come together to share their ideas' (TiE, 2002a). In other words, TiE's important mission is to offer mentorship and counseling to its members in several areas relating to entrepreneurship (TiE, 2002b). It also holds regular programs and events that include monthly company presentations, panels on contemporary issues, networking, workshops and special interest group events, which focus on specific issues and opportunities.

While TiE's primary goal is not to help entrepreneurs to expand internationally, the various activities can provide its members with the learning opportunity needed to become successful international entrepreneurs. First, the special interest group events can provide entrepreneurs with the necessary knowledge to expand overseas. Second, the mentoring and counseling offered by established international entrepreneurs can significantly help less experienced entrepreneurs who wish to engage in international business. Finally, the membership can provide entrepreneurs with a mechanism to meet potential business partners. Since there are 38 TiE chapters in nine countries, including the USA, Canada, India, the UK, Pakistan, Singapore, Dubai, Australia and Malaysia (TiE, 2002a), international entrepreneurs may take advantage of a wide range of networking opportunities.

Discussion

Entrepreneurship has played a major role in American culture since the nineteenth-century industrial revolution. Entrepreneurs have been responsible for approximately one third of the difference between the economic growth in the United States and other nations. According to the National Commission on Entrepreneurship (2002), the United States is one of the most 'entrepreneurial' nations in the world because Americans believe that they have opportunities to start businesses and live in a culture that respects entrepreneurship as an occupation.

Given the importance of entrepreneurship in the American economy, there are several programs available to entrepreneurs who wish to develop their skills to succeed in both the domestic and international marketplace. This chapter has focused on the initiatives offered by various governmental, academic and professional industry organizations that may help entrepreneurs and small business owners to expand their businesses overseas. Despite their slightly different perspectives, these organizations collectively provide entrepreneurs with various forms of support, such as assistance in organising trade missions, the development of management and exporting skills and the opportunity to network and meet various business contacts around the globe. These organizations give entrepreneurs and small business owners the necessary knowledge and skills to succeed in the global marketplace.

For example, Florida entrepreneurs who wish to expand in foreign markets may seek assistance from the US Commercial Service, part of the U.S. Department of Commerce; Enterprise Florida, a public–private partnership at the state level; Florida SBDC Network, a state-wide network of centers and sub-centers in the state of Florida; and regional economic development commissions, such as the Metro Orlando International Affairs Commission (MOIAC), a not-for-profit, public–private partnership that enhances the international investment and export opportunities for Metro Orlando (Sharon Benoit, personal communication, 30 July 2002).

In addition, entrepreneurs may also visit World Trade Centers of Florida, the five centers located in the state of Florida; the Florida Export District Council, which helps local small and medium-sized businesses to export overseas (District Export Councils, n.d.). The CIBERs in the state of Florida (for example The University of Florida and Florida International University) and members of the IB 2000 Consortium may also provide Florida entrepreneurs with the necessary training and development to export abroad. Finally, chapters of SCORE and TiE in the state of Florida as well as local entrepreneurial not-for-profit organizations, such as the Team of Professional Innovators and Entrepreneurs (TOPIE), may provide Florida entrepreneurs with networking and mentoring opportunities, an essential aspect in international entrepreneurship. TOPIE is a not-for-profit organization, founded by Guru Prasad, which promotes entrepreneur networking in Central Florida (Guru Prasad, personal communication, 1 August 2002; TOPIE, 2002).

The various organizations within the state of Florida cooperate with each other in order to facilitate the internationalization of American entrepreneurs and small business owners. One of the interviewees summarized the collaboration between the various organizations as follows: 'These organizations are pooling their resources and assistance to offer companies. We only have so much manpower. All of us can pool our resources, tools, and information together to help that one company achieve success.' In other words, organizations complement each other and work as a network to ensure the success of the international entrepreneur.

Specifically, the successful international expansion and the entrepreneurial efforts of Durek, president and CEO of Lentek International Inc.

into more than 65 countries provides a good illustration of the synergy between these various organizations. As noted above, Durek, a client of WTC Orlando, was selected to be in the WTCA Book of Honor. While WTC Orlando contributed to the accomplishments of Lentek International Inc., Durek was also part of the IB 2000 Program, offered by the IB 2000 Consortium. Durek noted, 'I am a huge fan of the program not only because of the professional results the students generated for my company and others, but also because of the experience it provides the students.' Durek continued, 'Any company that is serious about doing business internationally should definitely apply for the IB 2000 Program.' In addition, MOIAC helped Lentek International Inc. to expand internationally (Gloria LeQuang-Wong, personal communication, 31 July 2002). In recognition of the company's export growth, Lentek International Inc., an Orange County-based company, was awarded the Exporter of the Year award (Metro Orlando International Affairs Commission, 2002).

In the future, it is likely that the cooperation among the various agencies will continue. Linkages between various federal, state and local organizations can further ensure the development and success of international entrepreneurs. A recent press release by the US Commercial Service announced a unique partnership between the Connecticut Department of Economic and Community Development and the U.S. Department of Commerce. Connecticut will be the first state in the nation to collaborate with the federal government in order to make it easier for small and medium-sized Connecticut companies to export worldwide (U.S. Department of Commerce, 2002, March, 4). The innovative program will help qualified Connecticut businesses to have 'export-ready' products so that they are able to compete overseas promptly.

Furthermore, newly developed Internet websites and information technologies will provide American entrepreneurs with more information regarding the opportunities to expand overseas. President George W. Bush acknowledged the need to provide entrepreneurs and small business owners with necessary information to ensure the continual growth of their businesses. In an attempt to address this issue, he has plans to develop an accessible Internet site, called 'Business Compliance Self-Service One-Stop', by 2003 (Small Business Administration, 2002, 26 March). This site will be an important resource in providing compliance assistance as well as information on permitting and licensing.

The U.S. Department of Commerce also launched an innovative website to help small and medium-sized businesses keep informed of the potential increases in US import duties. The website, Section 301 Alert (*www.ita.gov/301Alert*) provides entrepreneurs and small-business owners with the latest information on unfair restrictions on US exports (U.S. Department of Commerce, 2001, June 7). More recently, the U.S. Department of Commerce announced a new technological tool that can provide American entrepreneurs with information on exporting to Mexico. *Beyond the Basics: Exporting to Mexico* is a reference desktop tool that can guide entrepreneurs on ways to export successfully to the Mexican market, one of the largest markets for American exports (U.S. Department of Commerce, 2002, 22 January).

In sum, there are numerous initiatives available to American entrepreneurs and small business owners who are interested in internationalizing their businesses. These initiatives have played a central role in the development and cultivation of successful entrepreneurs in the United States. With the growth of partnerships among organizations that provide assistance to international entrepreneurs and new information technologies, it is expected that entrepreneurs will receive greater assistance, further facilitating their success in the global marketplace.

References

Arkansas Department of Economic Development (2001), 'International business', retrieved 21 September 2002 (*http://aedc.state.ar.us/International*).

Arnold, P.A. (2001), *International marketing resource guide*, Herdon, VA: Braddock Communications Inc.

Centers for International Business Education and Research (2001a), 'What is a CIBER?', retrieved 30 July 2002 (*http://ciber.centers.purdue.edu/definition.html*).

Centers for International Business Education and Research (2001b), 'Outreach to the local business community', retrieved 30 July 2002 (*http://ciber.centers.purdue.edu/business-main.html*).

Dale, L.R. (2000), 'Leadership training programs: A five year impact', *Academy of Entrepreneurship Journal, 6*, 84–92.

District Export Councils (n.d.), 'What is a DEC?', District Export Councils.

Enterprise Florida Inc. (2002), 'International trade & business development unit', Coral Gables, Florida.

Ernest & Young LLP (2002), *2002 Customer satisfaction survey results for Enterprise Florida Inc.*, Washington, DC: Ernest & Young LLP.

Florida Small Business Development Center Network (2002a), 'Over 20 years helping entrepreneurs form, sustain and grow successful businesses', retrieved 30 July 2002 (*http://www.floridasbdc.com/AboutUs/WhoWeAre.asp*).

Florida Small Business Development Center Network (2002b), 'Over 20 years helping entrepreneurs form, sustain and grow successful businesses. Client Profile of the Month', retrieved 30 July 2002 (*http://www.floridasbdc.com/ClientProfile/clientprofile.asp*).

Jones, K. (1995), 'An investigation of the psychodynamics associated with ethnic entrepreneurship', *Academy of Entrepreneurship Journal, 1*, 53–64.

Metro Orlando International Affairs Commission (2002), 'MOIAC presents exporter of the year award to Lentek International Inc.', immediate release 15 May 2002, Metro Orlando International Affairs Commission, Orlando, Florida.

National Commission on Entrepreneurship (2002), 'The critical role entrepreneurship plays in our economy', retrieved 18 October 2002 (*http://www.ncoe.org/entrepreneurship/who_are.html*).

SCORE (n.d.), 'SCORE Association Profile', retrieved 18 October 2002 (*http://www.score.org/association/profile.html*).

Simon, M., B. Elango, S.M. Houghton and S. Savelli (2002), 'The successful product pioneer: Manintaining commitment while adapting to change', *Journal of Small Business Management*, 40, 187–203.

Small Business Administration (3 March 2001), '47 years of service to America's small businesses: The U.S. Small Business Administration, 1953–2000', retrieved 30 July 2002 (*http://www.sba.gov/aboutsba.html*).

Small Business Administration (8 May 2001), 'What is TM OnLine?' retrieved 30 July 2002 (*http://www.sba.gov/tmonline/whatis.html*).

Small Business Administration (October 2001), 'Export financing for small businesses', Small Business Administration no. CO-0111 (10/01).

Small Business Administration (11 February 2002), 'SBDC mission and overview', retrieved 30 July 2002 (*http://www.sba.gov/sbdc/mission.html*).

Small Business Administration (26 March 2002), 'American small business: Driving innovation and creating jobs', retrieved 30 July 2002 (*http://www.sba.gov/news/smallbusinessagenda.html*).

Small Business Administration (4 April 2002), 'Small Business Development Centers', retrieved 30 July 2002 (*http://www.sba.gov/SBDC.html*).

Small Business Administration (11 June 2002), 'Office of entrepreneurial development', retrieved 30 July 2002 (*http://www.sba.gov/ed.html*).

Small Business Administration (24 June 2002), 'American small business: Office of international trade. Network of U.S. Export assistance centers', retrieved 21 September 2002 (*http://www.sba.gov/news/smallbusinessagenda.html*).

Small Business Administration (30 July 2002), 'Learn about SBA', retrieved 21 September 2002 (*http://www.sba.gov/aboutsba.html*).

Small Business Administration (16 October 2002), 'SCORE', retrieved 18 October 2002 (*http://www.sba.gov/starting/aboutscore.html*).

TiE (2002a), 'Frequently asked questions', retrieved 18 October 2002 (*http://www.tie.org/library/faqs.asp*).

TiE (2002b), 'Mentoring at TiE', retrieved 18 October 2002 (*http://www.tie.org/library/mentoring.asp*).

TOPIE (2002), 'Team of Professional Internet Entrepreneurs: It's all about you', retrieved 7 August 2002 (*http://www.topie.net*).

U.S. Department of Commerce (n.d.), 'Where you are and where you want to go', The Commercial Service, Department of Commerce, United States of America.

U.S. Department of Commerce (March 2001), 'U.S. Commercial Service: Your global business partner. Get to global markets faster and more profitably', The Commercial Service, Department of Commerce, United States of America.

U.S. Department of Commerce (17 May 2001), 'Center helps deal with exports. With global market expanding for specialty syrup maker, assistance project flavors success of its international sales. Press room release 051701', retrieved 1 August 2002 (*http://www.usatrade.gov/website\website.nsf*).

U.S. Department of Commerce (7 June 2001), 'New Commerce website alerts small and medium-sized businesses of pending government actions under Section 301. Press release 060701', retrieved 1 August 2002 (*http://www.usatrade.gov/website/website.nsf*).

U.S. Department of Commerce (2002), 'About Us: The U.S. Commercial Service – Your Global Business Partner', retrieved 1 August 2002 (*http://www.usatrade.gov/website/website.nsf/WebBySubj/Main_AboutUS*).

U.S. Department of Commerce (2 January 2002), 'U.S. Exporters may gain from switch to Euro after January 1. Press release 010202', retrieved 30 July 2002 (*http://www.usatrade.gov/website/website.nsf*).

U.S Department of Commerce (22 January 2002), 'Beyond Basics. Press release 012202', retrieved 1 August 2002 (*http://www.usatrade.gov/website/website.nsf*).

U.S. Department of Commerce (4 March 2002), 'Lieutenant Governor Rell announces help for export-ready companies. Success Story 030402', retrieved 30 July 2002 (*http://www.usatrade.gov/website\website.nsf*).

U.S. Department of Commerce (6 June 2002), 'A Secure place in global markets for Ampro Electronics. Success Story 06/26', retrieved 30 July 2002 (*http://www.usatrade.gov/ website\website.nsf*).

U.S. Department of Commerce (18 June 2002), 'Commerce secretary Evans honors Washington Business for export achievement. Da Vinci Gourmet of Seattle cited for pursuit of export markets', retrieved 1 August 2002 (*http://www.usatrade.gov/website\website.nsf/ WebBySubj/Main_WhatsNew061802*).

Virginia Economic Development Partnership (2001), 'International Business Development', retrieved 21 September 2002 (*http://yesvirginia.org/trade dev.asp*).

World Trade Center Orlando (n.d.a), 'Benefits of Membership', World Trade Center Orlando.

World Trade Center Orlando (n.d.b), 'Concept: A Fact Sheet', World Trade Center Orlando.

World Trade Center Orlando (2002a), 'World Trade Center Incident', World Trade Center Orlando.

World Trade Center Orlando (2002b), '*Joseph Durek, President of Lentek International, Inc. is Recipient of the Prestigious WTCA Book of Honor!*', retrieved 31 July 2002 (*http:// www.worldtradecenterorlando.org/main.shtml*).

35 Internationalizing European IPOs in the United States
Boyd D. Cohen

Initial public offerings (IPOs) have become a fertile ground of research for entrepreneurship scholars in recent years.* At the same time, there is a growing interest among entrepreneurship scholars in the intersection between entrepreneurship and international business. This study seeks to link these two emerging research themes by examining Europe-based firms' IPOs in the USA. The intuitive benefit of launching an IPO in the USA is that the firms are seeking to tap into the large capital base in the USA and gain access to US markets. However, this study found that, following a US IPO, European firms gained legitimacy and increased their internationalization efforts, with much of the growth in European markets.

During the 1990s we observed a significant transition from domestic and regional commerce to one of global trade, where traditional boundaries to cross-border economic activity have declined rapidly. The most common explanation for this shift towards a global economy was the pace of technological change which, among other things, significantly reduced prior communication barriers. Entrepreneurs have been among the most affected (both positively and negatively) by the increasing globalization of commerce. This has coincided with a heightened interest in international entrepreneurship research which, until 1989, was non-existent. Now, only a decade later, it is considered one of the most rapidly growing and important areas of research for entrepreneurship and international business scholars (Wright and Ricks, 1994, p. 699).

The generally agreed upon definition of international entrepreneurship applied to this chapter is 'a combination of innovative, proactive, and risk-seeking behavior that crosses or is compared across national borders and is intended to create value in business organization' (McDougall and Oviatt 2000, p. 903). Therefore the two broad categories of current research can be considered as comparisons of entrepreneurship activity, governmental policies and culture towards entrepreneurship across countries, and as research which examines the internationalization process of entrepreneurial firms. This chapter focuses on the internationalization of European ventures.

---

* A previous version of this chapter was presented at the Babson Kauffman Entrepreneurship Conference in June 2002.

At the beginning of the 21st century, the European Union seems poised to take on a critical role in the member nations' economies, as well as the global economy. The continued political and economic integration through a common currency and the EU's expansion eastward point to an increasingly powerful, global union. Most of the research regarding cross-border entrepreneurship has been conducted with a North American focus. However, given the distinct nature of the member nations of the EU (for example, smaller size and population, disparate cultures, single currency), there is a need for further research regarding the cross-border activities of entrepreneurial firms in the EU. This chapter seeks to close some critical gaps in our collective knowledge of the internationalization of EU firms.

Initial public offerings (IPOs)

Management scholars in the 1990s and first part of the 21st century increasingly focused their studies on initial public offerings (IPOs) (Welbourne and Andrews, 1996; Deeds *et al.*, 1997; Kim and Ritter 1999; Certo *et al.*, 2001). The growing interest among entrepreneurship scholars in IPOs was partially affected by the use of the IPO as a preferred exit strategy for early inside investors (Carter and Van Auken, 1994, p. 69). Among the exit strategies available to entrepreneurs, venture capitalists and other inside investors, an initial public offering provides the highest degree of 'upside' potential (Prasad *et al.*, 1995, p. 31). The amount of money raised in an IPO enables entrepreneurial firms to pursue growth and expansion strategies, increase their research and development efforts and gain acquisition currency (Deeds *et al.*, 1997, p. 33). Another, perhaps more profound, reason for the increased attention to IPOs related to the exponentially increasing amount of equity raised in IPOs throughout the 1990s and the early 21st century. In 2001, considered a bad year for IPOs, 10 offerings raised more than $1 billion and the average proceeds raised in the 87 IPOs for the year was $448.4 million (*www.ipocentral.com*). By contrast, the average proceeds in 1988 were only $12 million (Welbourne and Andrews, 1996, p. 904).

Not only does it provide the opportunities for creating wealth among the inside investors, but the act of going public may be considered the ultimate measure of success for the growing entrepreneurial firm (Champion 1999, p. 685). The cachet associated with 'going public' is something that excites employees (especially those holding options), entrepreneurs, investors (who often see the IPO as the ideal exit) and alliance partners.

Historically, research on IPOs has focused on the financial implications of the IPO. Finance scholars focus on issues such as underpricing (for example, Beatty and Ritter, 1986) and underwriter reputation (Carter *et al.*, 1998), while strategic management and entrepreneurship scholars in the 1990s began examining management issues affecting IPO valuation (Welbourne and Andrews, 1996; Cohen and Dean 2001). However, there has been a void in research pertaining to non-financial benefits of IPOs. While IPOs provide firms with large amounts of capital, there are also many drawbacks, such as the amount of time required to prepare for the IPO, the high costs (compared with private offerings), requirements of transparency of operations and financial performance and increased pressure for short-term performance (Allen, 1999, p. 307). The numerous challenges associated with going public lend support to the notion that the IPO may be perceived to provide more benefits than purely a large cash injection. The non-financial motivations and benefits of going public represent a potential untapped area for scholarly study and may help to provide an explanation for the seemingly high value placed upon going public among investors and managers of young and growing firms.

This study begins to address the gap by examining IPOs in the USA from European firms. While it may seem obvious that access to capital represents the primary benefit for European firms launching IPOs in the USA, European firms experience benefits well beyond the proceeds raised by the IPO. Specifically, this study has two primary research questions: do European firms experience non-financial benefits from a US IPO, and, among European IPOs in the USA, is there a relationship between the non-financial post-IPO gains and firm performance after issuing an IPO?

Theoretical foundation
While the majority of studies grounded in financial theories assume that access to capital is the primary driver for and benefit of going public (see Ibbotson *et al.*, 1988), this study intends to expand our understanding of the benefits of going public. Specifically, this chapter explores pre- and post-IPO values for both legitimacy and level of internationalization among firms issuing European IPOs in the USA. The following discussion lays out the theoretical justification for these constructs and concludes with the associated hypotheses.

Legitimacy
Besides the potentially lucrative exit for inside investors and the large cash infusion provided by the IPO, a US public offering also enables a firm to gain almost instant legitimacy among critical stakeholders (Deeds *et al.*, 1997, p. 32). Legitimacy provides a firm with access to a variety of resources, such as capital, suppliers, customers, clients, governmental support, knowledge and alliance partners (Hannan and Freeman, 1977; Meyer and Rowan, 1977; Oliver, 1990; Aldrich and Fiol, 1994; Deeds *et al.*, 1997). Legitimacy is 'a generalized perception or assumption that the

actions of an entity are desirable, proper or appropriate within some socially constructed system of norms, values, beliefs and definitions' (Suchman, 1995, p. 571). Of the more than 5 million active businesses in the USA fewer than 20 000 are actually publicly traded (Aldrich, 1999, p. 8). Given that far less than one-half of 1 per cent of US firms reach publicly traded status, those few that do, from the USA or abroad, obtain a certain amount of legitimacy among the various stakeholders by demonstrating their ability to meet the strict performance and size criteria required of the major US exchanges.

Legitimacy management

Suchman (1995, p. 586) identified three challenges for legitimacy management: gaining legitimacy, maintaining legitimacy and repairing legitimacy. Gaining legitimacy is the responsibility of new and young ventures who have to build legitimacy in the eyes of potential stakeholders. This research is focused on initial public offerings. While the firms may not be just out of the box, they are relatively young at IPO (Cohen and Dean, 2001). Therefore this research is primarily focused on indicators associated with gaining legitimacy.

Cognitive v. sociopolitical legitimacy

Aldrich and Fiol (1994, p. 648) identified two primary categories of new venture legitimacy: cognitive and sociopolitical. Both types of legitimacy are continuous constructs, as opposed to dichotomous. Cognitive legitimacy represents the proliferation of knowledge about a new venture (ibid.). A firm has attained the upper range of cognitive legitimacy when it has become taken for granted in the relevant population. This is the strongest form of legitimacy because rival organizations would have an almost insurmountable task of challenging the taken-for-granted organization. Sociopolitical legitimacy, according to Aldrich and Fiol (ibid.), represents the 'process by which key stakeholders, the general public, key opinion leaders, or government officials accept a venture as appropriate and right, given existing norms and laws'.

The current study will focus on the cognitive legitimacy construct. Given this study's focus on US initial public offerings of European firms, the author's primary objective is to examine how the IPO provides a potential instantaneous boost to the firm's legitimacy. In this environment, it is appropriate to concentrate on the cognitive legitimacy gains accrued.

Strategic versus institutional legitimacy

Previous research on organizational legitimacy has taken two divergent perspectives: strategic or institutional (Suchman, 1995, p. 575). Strategic approaches to legitimacy suggest that legitimacy is a resource which can be managed, as in the strategic choice perspective (Child, 1972). Institutional approaches to legitimacy suggest that the external environment confers legitimacy on organizations and that there is little that managers can do to gain legitimacy for their firm, as in the population ecology perspective (DiMaggio and Powell, 1983; Oliver, 1991). This distinction has clear implications for the study of legitimacy. If we accept the strategic approach, scholarly work could be conducted to provide normative guidance to practitioners on the ways in which they could attain increased legitimacy and thus enhance their survival chances. However, an institutional approach would encourage scholars to identify environmental conditions which enhance legitimacy, but would leave little room for normative advice. This chapter focuses primarily on the strategic form of legitimacy by suggesting that European firms launch IPOs in the USA not only to gain access to capital and US markets, but to enhance their legitimacy. This suggests a strategic intent on the part of the senior management and inside investors to acquire legitimacy.

Internationalization

Traditional international business theory suggests that firms gradually internationalize (over several years) through a process of incremental steps, including establishing a comfort level in the domestic market, followed by export via independent representatives (agents), then the establishment of a sales subsidiary and finally production/manufacturing facilities abroad. This theoretical lens has been applied (and subsequently altered) to international business research since the 1970s (Johanson and Valhne, 1977).

Entrepreneurship scholars have argued that this gradual, incrementalist approach to internationalization does not accurately predict the internationalization activities of many young high-growth entrepreneurial ventures of today. Instead they argue that increasing industry pressure (Ghoshal and Nohria, 1993, p. 31), globalizing market conditions (Cavusgil and Zhau, 1994, p. 4) and increased environmental uncertainty (Harveston and Davis, 2001, p. 18), have led to entrepreneurial firms which engage in accelerated internationalization or are 'born global' (Oviatt and McDougall 1995, p. 31).

A more dynamic and flexible internationalization model, known as the eclectic paradigm (Dunning and McQueen, 1981) took hold in the 1980s. The model, primarily a triangulation of economic theories, attempts to provide descriptive explanations of internationalization activity. However, the eclectic paradigm falls short on many counts and, by its own author's admission, is too broad to be used for predictive purposes (Dunning, 1988,

p. 1). Therefore the eclectic model also is limited in its applicability to entrepreneurship research.

In the latter part of the 1990s, entrepreneurship scholars began suggesting a need for new theory to address the 'born global' and early internationalization activity of many young firms in the new economy (Bloodgood *et al.*, 1996; Oviatt and McDougall, 1997). This chapter seeks to extend this evolving theory of internationalization activity by focusing on the internationalizing activity of European firm IPOs in the USA, both prior to and following the IPO.

Foreign IPOs

> The deal [Scandinavian Broadcast System's IPO in the USA] illustrates an escalating trend of small foreign growth companies, located largely in Europe, that are turning to the U.S. equities market to raise capital. Many are doing so without first listing or issuing stock at home or in the international euromarket. The U.S. has a well-established market for taking small companies public. (Leanard, 1993, p. 19)

This study represents one of the first empirical examinations of Europe-based firms who launched IPOs in the USA. In recent years, there has been a significant increase in the number of foreign IPOs in the USA with a large percentage of them coming from Europe (Cifrino *et al.*, 2001, p. 38). These IPOs are commonly referred to as American Depository Receipts (ADR) in the financial community. There are many reasons to launch a foreign IPO in the USA, including (Shearer 2001, p. 7) a desire to enhance operations or sales in the USA, to improve analyst coverage and of course to gain access to larger amounts of capital to pursue growth and acquisition strategies. However, an ADR may also boost the company's international profile by increasing name recognition among potential customers and alliance partners (Cifrino *et al.*, 2001, p. 38).

In order to be listed on a US exchange, firms are required to meet very rigorous disclosure and performance standards. The mere presence on a US exchange can boost a foreign firm's legitimacy in international markets owing to the market's knowledge of the requirements for listing and to the increased analyst attention (Shearer, 2001, p. 7): 'Now that we are listed on the NYSE, we are viewed more positively by investors. The increased transparency, due to compliance with U.S. GAAP and the SEC's financial reporting requirements, are very welcomed by them [investors]' (Doris Schurdack, Sulzer Medica investor relations in Darby, 1997, p. 19).

In a survey of 57 Italian IPOs (Ravasi and Marchisio, forthcoming), two of the most frequently cited reasons for going public were 'to improve the image and the prestige of the company' and 'to increase the visibility of the company'. While the current study does not measure motivations for going public it does seek to measure non-financial outcomes of going public in the USA. The Ravasi and Marchisio study only examined domestic IPOs in Italy. Given the widely accepted leadership in equity markets in the USA (Leanard, 1993, p. 19), coupled with the stringent performance and reporting requirements, a European firm's IPO in the USA should have a positive impact on the firm's legitimacy in the USA and abroad.

> Hypothesis 1a   a European firm's legitimacy in the USA will increase following a US IPO.
>
> Hypothesis 1b   a European firm's legitimacy in Europe will increase following a US IPO.

Internationalization

While many IPO firms are not entrepreneurial by definition, a large percentage of them are young and are seeking to continue their growth phase (Cohen and Dean, 2001). Regardless of their entrepreneurial classification, European firms face big challenges in trying to cross their own home country borders. While American firms are more likely to be able to utilize the incrementalist approach (Johanson and Vahlne, 1977), European firms have much smaller domestic markets, and therefore are often forced to internationalize more quickly than their American counterparts. This poses an added challenge to European firms, as crossing borders in Europe is not the same as crossing from New York to Massachusetts. The need for internationalizing is particularly strong in technology-based firms who often have small product niches and large capital expenditures in research and development (Preece *et al.*, 1999, p. 260). In order to attain a scale large enough to support product development costs, technology firms are often forced to pursue early internationalization.

> The highly fragmented nature of the European market has always presented a huge barrier to European technology companies; the costs of expanding internationally, setting multiple subsidiaries in place in order to do business across Europe, is often cripplingly high, especially for young companies. The cultural and language differences are also significant, as are the diversity of fiscal systems, social policies and working practices and, needless to say, the currencies of each country. (Anonymous, 1997)

The act of issuing an ADR in and of itself represents an international activity, as the firm is choosing to be placed on equity markets abroad. ADRs are often used as a tool to attract attention from international investors and to enhance their international prestige (Johnson, 2000, p. 7). The enhanced international legitimacy, coupled with the international intent of launching a foreign IPO (Cifrino *et al.*, 2001, p. 39), is hypothesized to lead to increased international activity subsequent to the US IPO.

Hypothesis 2   the internationalization activity of European firms will increase following their US IPO.

Performance
While there is a vast amount of extant literature on predictors of firm performance for domestic and international firms, and for domestic IPO firms, researchers have yet to address the post-IPO performance of foreign-based firms. This chapter seeks to expand our understanding of the way an ADR affects a firm's legitimacy and international activity. However, to understand the importance of the measures studied here, it is also important to examine their impact on the firm's performance post-IPO.

Prior research has found relationships between the levels of internationalization activity and firm performance (Juha-Pekka *et al.*, 2001; Lenn and Ramaswamy, 1999). However, little research has explored the internationalization–performance relationship among newly public, European firms. An IPO enhances a firm's cognitive legitimacy among various stakeholders by increasing the quantity of publicly available information regarding the firm's activities. This is particularly true in the case of foreign IPOs in the USA because of the heavy reporting requirements to be listed and the increased availability of in-depth analyst reports (Shearer, 2001, p. 8).

As discussed above, improvements in legitimacy can result in several benefits, such as increased access to suppliers, clients and government organizations (Hannan and Freeman, 1977; Meyer and Rowan, 1977; Oliver, 1990; Aldrich and Fiol, 1994; Deeds *et al.*, 1997). Given the many benefits accrued to legitimate firms, it is reasonable to assert that increases in legitimacy could have a positive impact on a firm's performance. Prior research has shown a relationship between firm and industry legitimacy and the amount of proceeds obtained in the IPO (Deeds *et al.*, 1997; Cohen and Dean, 2001). There is a gap, however, in our knowledge of the existence of an empirical relationship between legitimacy and performance.

Hypothesis 3   the changes in internationalization activity and legitimacy for European firms following a US IPO will be related to firm performance post-IPO.

Methods
Sample and design
The 120 firms from the current 15 EU member states that launched IPOs in the USA between 1995 and 2000 constitute the sample frame for this

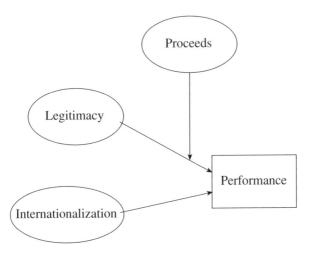

Figure 35.1   Hypothesis 3

study. Firms were eliminated from the sample if they did not have one year of operating history prior to the IPO (owing to their recent formation as a joint venture or spin-off from existing firms). These firms were removed because the hypotheses require information for the year prior to the firm's IPO, and because these firms do not represent the intended IPO sample frame for this study. Additionally, privatizations of state-owned enterprises were also removed since they represent anomalies vis-à-vis traditional IPOs (they have operated as monopolies since inception, have few if any competitors and are typically extremely large and old). This led to a sample size of 94 (*n*=94), which was used to test hypotheses 1a, 1b and 2. Of the 95 firms in the sample, 56 (60 per cent) are technology-based firms. The highest occurrence of IPOs comes from the United Kingdom, which was represented by 38 firms, followed by France (14), Germany (9) and Ireland (9). Three EU countries were not represented (Austria, Denmark and Portugal). The sample size was further reduced to test hypothesis 3 empirically owing to missing performance data.

Independent variables

Legitimacy   For the purpose of this study legitimacy was operationalized as the number of articles published in the year prior to and the year following IPO. Individual judgments are enhanced through increased access to information (Tverssky and Kahneman, 1981). Therefore a firm receiving increased attention in the business and industry press should yield increasing firm legitimacy. The data were gathered from the Business and Industry (B&I) database. B&I contains over 2 million articles published since 1994 in 'leading trade magazines and newsletters, the general business press, regional newspapers and international business dailies' focused primarily on North America and Europe. B&I has a search function which enables the distinction between US specific articles and non-US (primarily European) articles. The majority of the articles in B&I not published in the USA are from the European press. Therefore European legitimacy was identified as the number of articles pre- and post-IPO, subtracted by the number of US specific articles (US legitimacy). For hypothesis 3, US legitimacy and European legitimacy were collapsed into one variable (legitimacy).

Internationalization activity   The use of acquisitions and cooperative agreements as a means of rapid entry into international markets has been clearly identified in prior research (Lu and Beamish, 2001; Andersson *et al.*, 1997). Cooperative agreements and acquisitions can be an integral part of a small and medium-sized enterprise' (SME) international growth strategy, given that SMEs typically have fewer resources (Welch, 1992) and have difficulties achieving scale efficiencies (Etemad *et al.*, 2001) sufficient to pursue aggressive international growth.

The amount of internationalization activity was operationalized as the number of acquisitions and cooperative agreements among sample firms which involved at least one firm from a foreign country. The number of cooperative agreements engaged in by sample firms prior to and after IPO was collected using the TFSD Joint Ventures & Alliances database. This database includes data on joint ventures, strategic alliances, sales and marketing arrangements and licensing and distribution agreements among firms around the world. The database contains over 85 000 records dating back to 1990. Acquisition data were gathered from the TFSD Worldwide Mergers & Acquisitions database which reports mergers and acquisitions among public and private firms throughout the world. The database contains nearly 400 000 transactions dating back to 1981.

Dependent variable

Firm performance   Firm performance for this study was operationalized as the change in stock price from the opening day of the IPO to one year after IPO. Stock price has been used as a dependent variable in studies of first-mover advantages (Lee *et al.*, 2000), cooperative agreements (Park and Kim, 1997; Somnath, 1998) and the role of industry membership in post-IPO performance (Young and Zaima, 1988). The stock price of the firm on the opening day (offer price) was derived from the ipodata.com's company profiles, and the one-year post-IPO price was derived from bigcharts.com's historical quotes section.

Control variable

Proceeds   The amount of proceeds obtained in the IPO was used as a control variable in all of the hypotheses testing. IPO proceeds have often been used as the dependent variable in IPO studies (Deeds *et al.*, 1997, Welbourne and Andrews, 1996) in order to assess the performance of the IPO. The current research seeks to extend the notion of IPO performance beyond the amount of capital raised in the IPO, and thus uses proceeds as a control variable, as opposed to the dependent variable. Controlling for proceeds assists in minimizing a counter-argument to significant findings that firms acquiring relatively more cash from an IPO would intuitively have more opportunities to engage in acquisitions and cooperative agreements, and would probably receive more press attention as well. The amount of proceeds generated by the IPO was identified through the ipodata.com company profile pages. This variable was highly skewed (skewness=4.39; kurtosis=20.85). Therefore a natural log of proceeds was created, resulting in a more normalized distribution (skewness=1.81; kurtosis=5.35).

Descriptive statistics for the independent, dependent and control variables are presented in Table 35.1.

Table 35.1   Descriptive statistics and correlations for relevant variables

Variable	Mean	s.d.
Independent variables		
1. US articles before IPO	10.26	17.16
2. US articles after IPO	16.24	28.59
3. World articles ($-$US) before IPO	18.01	29.37
4. World Articles ($-$US) after IPO	35.97	55.04
5. International activity before IPO	1.00	1.96
6. International activity after IPO	2.35	3.39
Dependent variable		
7. 1 Year change in stock Price	6.56	31.26
Control variable		
8. IPO proceeds (millions	361.3	793.2
IPO proceeds (natural log)	6.56	31.25

Note: Correlations greater than 0.11 indicate $p < 0.05$

Methodology

In order to test hypotheses 1a, 1b and 2, repeated measures analysis was undertaken. Owing to the desire to compare the increases (or decreases) in each of the discussed measures prior to and following IPO, a repeated measures test is most appropriate. In order to test hypothesis 3, hierarchical regression was performed.

Analysis and results

Hypotheses 1a, 1b and 2 were all tested using repeated measures (Table 35.2) and supported with the descriptive statistics (Table 35.3). While the repeated measures test only reports whether or not a significant difference exists between pre- and post-IPO, directionality can be inferred from the descriptive statistics.

Table 35.2   Repeated measures results

Variable	F	Sig.
US legitimacy	6.81	0.011
European legitimacy	37.34	0.000
Internationalization	5.53	0.021

Hypothesis 1a suggested that a European firm's IPO in the USA would be related to an increase in the firm's legitimacy in the USA. This hypothesis was supported ($p<0.05$). The mean for pre-IPO articles was 10.26 and 16.24 for post-IPO articles. Of the 95 firms in the sample, only 20 experienced a reduction in articles in the year following the IPO, with four firms experiencing a reduction of 10 or more. Of the remaining 75 firms, 13 experienced no change in articles following the IPO and 62 experienced increases in articles, with 16 experiencing gains of 10 or more.

Hypothesis 1b suggested that a European firm's IPO in the USA would be related to an increase of legitimacy in Europe. This hypothesis was also supported ($p<0.001$). The mean for number of articles prior to the IPO (18.01) was half of the mean for post-IPO articles (35.97). Of the 95 firms in the sample, only 14 experienced fewer European articles post-IPO (with only three experiencing a decrease of 10 or more), while 70 firms experienced increases (43 experiencing increases of 10 or more).

Hypothesis 2 suggested that internationalization activity of European IPO firms would increase following the US IPO. This hypothesis was also supported ($p<0.05$). Only 10 of the firms decreased their international activity post-IPO, while 49 increased their international activity. An additional examination of the international activity was also performed through a variable entitled 'supranational'. This required an analysis of the details of the cooperative agreements identified through the TFSD Joint Ventures & Alliances database. If the cooperative agreement involved firms from at least two foreign countries, or the agreement was designed to exploit more than two foreign countries, the agreement was considered supranational. Only six firms prior to the IPO engaged in supranational agreements, while 23 firms engaged in supranational activity post-IPO.

Hypothesis 3 suggested that increases in internationalization activity and legitimacy would be positively related to firm performance post-IPO. The internationalization variable was derived from data on cooperative agreements and acquisitions (see below). Hypothesis 3 was tested using multiple regression (Table 35.3). Support was found for the relationship between the increase in internationalization activity and stock price change. While controlling for amount of proceeds obtained in the IPO, the change in internationalization activity (r^2 change=11.6%, $p=0.009$) was significantly related to stock price performance. However, change in legitimacy was not significantly related (r^2 change=1.4%, $p=0.334$) to post-IPO performance.

Table 35.3   Regression results

	Model 1	Model 2	Model 3
Proceeds	0.075	−0.003	−0.076
Internationalization activity		0.341**	0.297*
Legitimacy			0.152
N = 61			
R2		0.116*	0.130*
Adjusted R2		0.086*	0.085*
R2 Change		0.11**	0.014

Note: *pc = 0.05, **pc = 0.01.

Discussion

This chapter has applied legitimacy and internationalization lenses towards the study of European IPOs in the USA (ADRs). The present study involved two unique research questions. The first examined the non-financial benefits of issuing an ADR for European firms, by examining the pre- and post-IPO change in legitimacy, number of cooperative agreements and internationalization activity.

As was expected, legitimacy in the United States improved following the US IPO. Many firms operating in European markets struggle to gain access to US investors and consumers. The US IPO creates an awareness of these firms in the USA and therefore may enhance the firms' ability to penetrate

US markets. While finding enhanced US legitimacy for the European ADRs is not very surprising, a more intriguing finding is that a US IPO for a foreign firm may actually enhance the firm's legitimacy in its own country and region. This possibility is supported by the following statement from Michael Cawley, Director of Finance for Ryanair, a low-cost air carrier based in Ireland. In referring to the benefits accrued to Ryanair in Ireland of the US IPO (Darby, 1997, p. 21), Cawley states: 'The American investment community, which is well regarded as being ahead in terms of airline investing, thought our company was a good one, and that certainly helped with the home market.'

Further in-depth analysis of the internationalization activity found that supranational agreements increased significantly among the firms in this sample following the US IPO. In terms of their internationalization process, it appears that the ADR enables firms not only to increase their internationalization activity, but also to expand their regional and global reach. There were 23 companies involved in 31 supranational agreements after the IPO (as opposed to only seven firms prior to the IPO). Interestingly, of the 31 supranational agreements post IPO, 14 agreements involved Europe-specific activity. This suggests that an ADR may not only help firms improve legitimacy in their home regions but also assist their geographic expansion within their home region.

Finally, the increase in internationalization activity in the year following the IPO was significantly related to stock price performance. This is in line with previous research which has found evidence to support the internationalization–performance relationship among multinational firms. This study, however, is one of the first to examine and establish the existence of an internationalization–performance relationship among newly public, European firms. Future research should seek to examine this finding further. For example, does the market also value internationalization activities for newly public US firms? What types of alliances and acquisitions are most valued by the market? Technology-based firms in Europe are clearly at a disadvantage in that their home markets are often too small to support the R&D activities of a niche product. Therefore the need, and perhaps realization, to internationalize is more prominent than for young American firms.

As the European Union continues its integration (including the adoption of the Euro as of 1 January 2001), the member nations and the entrepreneurial firms within them are beginning to compete collectively with US entrepreneurs for capital and market share in the USA, in Europe and globally. We have witnessed an increase in European firms crossing into the USA to tap US equity markets. The intuitive explanation for foreign firms to issue an IPO in the USA is that they are seeking to tap into the large capital base in the USA. But this study found support for the existence of several other potential benefits.

This chapter expands our limited knowledge of foreign-based IPOs. As entrepreneurship scholars continue to challenge the applicability of traditional theories of internationalization, findings from this study may contribute towards our continued efforts to build theory regarding 'born global' and 'gradually globalizing' firms. Additionally the results may help top management teams and inside investors of foreign firms to improve their understanding of the potential benefits of launching IPOs in the USA as an exit strategy or as a means to execute growth strategies.

References

Aldrich, H.E. (1999), *Organizations Evolving*, London: Sage Publications.
Aldrich, H.E. and M. Fiol (1994), '"Fools rush in?" Conditions affecting entrepreneurial strategies in new organizations', *Academy of Management Review*, 19 (4), 645–70.
Allen, K. (1999), *Launching New Ventures*, Boston: Houghton Mifflin.
Andersson, U., J. Johanson and J.E. Vahlne (1997), 'Organic acquisitions in the internationalization process of the business firm', *Management International Review*, 37 (2), 67–84.
Anonymous (1997), 'The state of Europe', *Computer Business Review*, 5 (156).
Beatty, R. and J. Ritter (1986), 'Investment banking, reputation and the underpricing of initial public offerings', *Journal of Financial Economics*, 15, 213–32.
Bloodgood, J., H. Sapienza and J. Almeida (1996), 'The internationalization of new high-potential U.S. ventures: Antecedents and outcomes', *Entrepreneurship Theory and Practice*, 20 (2), 43–57.
Carter, R.B. and H.E. Van Auken (1994), 'Venture capital firms' preferences for projects in particular stages of development', *Journal of Small Business Management*, 32 (1), 60–73.
Carter, R.B., F.H. Dark and A.K. Singh (1998), 'Underwriter reputation, initial returns, and the long-run performance of IPO stocks', *Journal of Finance*, 53 (1), 285–311.
Cavusgil, S.T. and S. Zhau (1994), 'Marketing strategy–performance relationship: an investigation of the empirical link in export market ventures', *Journal of Marketing*, 58, 1–21.
Certo, S., J. Covin, C. Daily and D. Dalton (2001), 'Wealth and the effects of founder management among IPO-stage new ventures', *Strategic Management Journal*, 22, 641–58.
Champion, D. (1999), 'Entrepreneurship', *Harvard Business Review*, 77 (1), 17–20.
Child, J. (1972), 'Organization structure, environment, and performance: The role of strategic choice', *Sociology*, 6 (1), 1–22.
Cifrino, D., M. Stein and C. Moss (2001), 'Foreign deals offer possible cure for domestic IPO blues', *Venture Capital Journal*, 38–40.
Cohen, B., and T. Dean (2001), 'Top management teams and investors' valuation of initial public offerings: An examination of web-based and non-web-based new ventures', *Frontiers of Entrepreneurship Research*, Boston, Massachusetts: Boston College.
Darby, R. (1997), 'U.S. stock exchanges seek a foreign flair', *Investment Dealers' Digest*, 63 (32), 18–23.
Deeds, D.L., D. Decarolis and J.E. Coombs (1997), 'The impact of firm-specific capabilities on the amount of capital raised in an initial public offering: Evidence from the biotechnology industry', *Journal of Business Venturing*, 12 (1), 31–46.
DiMaggio, P.J. and W.W. Powell (1983), 'The iron cage revisited: Institutional isomorphism and collective rationality in organizational fields', *American Sociological Review*, 48 (2), 147–60.
Dunning, J. (1988), 'The eclectic paradigm of international production: A restatement and some possible extensions', *Journal of International Business Studies*, 19 (1), 1–30.
Dunning, J. and M. McQueen (1981), 'The eclectic theory of international production: A case study of the international hotel industry', *Managerial and Decision Economics*, 2, 197–210.

Etemad, H., R.W. Wright and L.P. Dana (2001), 'Symbiotic international business networks: Collaboration between small and large firms', *Thunderbird International Business Review*, 43 (4), 481–99.

Ghoshal, S. and N. Nohria (1993), 'Horses for courses: Organizational forms for multinational corporations', *Sloan Management Review*, 34 (2), 23–35.

Hannan, M.T. and J.H. Freeman (1977), 'The population ecology of organizations', *American Journal of Sociology*, 82 (5), 929–64.

Harveston, P.D. and P.S. Davis (2001), 'Entrepreneurship and the Born Global Phenomenon: Theoretical foundations and a research agenda', in John Butler (ed.), *E-Commerce and Entrepreneurship: Research in Entrepreneurship and Management*, Greenwich: Information Age Publishing, pp. 1–30.

Ibbotson, R., J. Sindelar and J. Ritter (1988), 'Initial public offerings', *Journal of Applied Corporate Finance*, 1, 37–45.

Johanson, J. and J. Vahlne (1977), 'The internationalization process of the firm – A model of knowledge development and increasing foreign market commitment', *Journal of International Business Studies,* 8 (1), 23–32.

Johnson, M. (2000), 'The rise of the ADR', *Corporate Finance*, 193, 6–8.

Juha-Pekka, K., J. Larimo and S. Pynnonen (2001), 'Value creation in foreign direct investments', *Management International Review*, 41 (4), 357–76.

Kim, M. and J. Ritter (1999), 'Valuing Epos', *Journal of Financial Economics*, 53, 409–37.

Leanard, R. (1993), 'Foreign IPOs leave home to woo US investors', *Global Finance*, 7 (5), 19–20.

Lee, H., K.G. Smith, C.M. Grimm and A. Schomburg (2000), 'Timing, order and durability of new product advantages with imitation', *Strategic Management Journal*, 21 (1), 23–30.

Lenn, G. and K. Ramaswamy (1999), 'An empirical examination of the form of the relationship between multinationality and performance', *Journal of International Business Studies*, 30 (1), 173–88.

Lu, J.W. and P. Beamish (2001), 'The internationalization and performance of SMEs', *Strategic Management Journal*, 22 (6), 565–86.

McDougall, P. and B. Oviatt (2000), 'International entrepreneurship: the intersection of two research paths', *Academy of Management Journal*, 43, 902–908.

Meyer, J.W. and B. Rowan (1977), 'Institutionalized organizations: Formal structure as myth and ceremony', *American Journal of Sociology*, 83 (2), 340–63.

Oliver, C. (1990), 'Determinants of interorganizational relationships: Integration and future directions', *Academy of Management Review*, 15 (2), 241–65.

Oliver, C. (1991), 'Strategic responses to institutional process', *Academy of Management Review*, 16 (1), 145–79.

Oviatt, B. and P. McDougall (1995), 'Global start-ups: Entrepreneurs on a worldwide stage', *Academy of Management Executive*, 9 (2), 30–43.

Oviatt, B. and P. McDougall (1997), 'Challenges for internationalization process theory: The case of international new ventures', *Management International Review*, 37 (2), 85–99.

Park, S.H. and D. Kim (1997), 'Market valuation of joint ventures: Joint venture characteristics and wealth gains', *Journal of Business Venturing*, 12 (2), 83–108.

Prasad, D., G. Vozikis, G. Bruton and A. Merikas (1995), '"Harvesting" through initial public offerings (IPOs): The implications of underpricing for the small firm', *Entrepreneurship Theory and Practice,* 20 (2), 31–41.

Preece, S., G. Miles and M. Baetz (1999), 'Explaining the international intensity and global diversity of early-stage technology-based firms', *Journal of Business Venturing*, 14 (3), 259–81.

Ravasi, D. and G. Marchisio (forthcoming), 'Going public and the enrichment of a supportive network: Some evidence from Italian initial public offerings', *Small Business Economics*.

Shearer, B. (2001), 'Vive la différence: ADRs grow as an acquisition strategy', *Mergers and Acquisitions*, 36 (4), 6–10.

Somnath, D. (1998), 'Impact of strategic alliances on firm valuation', *Academy of Management Journal*, 41 (1), 27–41.

Suchman, M.C. (1995), 'Managing legitimacy: Strategic and institutional approaches', *Academy of Management Review*, 20 (3), 571–610.

Tverssky, A. and D. Kahneman (1981), 'The framing of decisions and the psychology of choice', *Science*, 211, 453–8.

Welbourne, T.M. and A.O. Andrews (1996), 'Predicting the performance of initial public offerings: Should human resource management be in the equation?', *Academy of Management Journal*, 39 (4), 891–919.

Welch, L. (1992), 'The use of alliances by small firms in achieving internationalization', *Scandinavian International Business Review*, 1 (2), 21–37.

Wright, R.W. and D.A. Ricks (1994), 'Trends in international business research: Twenty-five years later', *Journal of International Business Studies*, 25, 687–701.

Young, J.E. and J.K. Zaima (1988), 'The aftermarket performance of small firm initial public offerings', *Journal of Business Venturing*, 3(1), 77–87.

PART FOUR

FRANCHISING PERSPECTIVES

36 The internationalization of franchising systems into industrialized economies
Dianne H. B. Welsh and Ilan Alon

Franchising began in the United States in the 1850s with the Singer Sewing Machine Company. One of the most famous beginning franchisors was Henry Ford, who figured out that the value of franchise systems was to distribute cars quickly to yearning first-time car buyers, while not being encumbered with the cost of inventory. Today, franchising encompasses a system that is used around the world to sell over 1 trillion dollars' worth of goods and services from Tokyo to New York (Reynolds, 2002). Franchising is powerful. Franchising is here to stay. This chapter summarizes the preeminent research in the field of international franchising, concentrating on North America, the Pacific Rim and other industrialized countries. These countries can be considered to have the most advanced forms of franchising with the most market penetration. It is worth noting that North America is the home of the most franchisors' headquarters. The two other countries that are experiencing phenomenal growth in franchising that we will cover in this chapter are Israel and South Africa.

North America
Dianne Welsh (2002) looks at franchising from a futuristic perspective, examining where franchising has been in the 1970s, 1980s and 1990s in the United States and Canada and where it is headed. Currently, franchising is 40 percent of retail trade in the USA and 25 percent in Canada (Fenwick, 2001; Scrivener, 2001). In her article, Welsh covers the definitions of franchising, regulations, survival rates, recent developments and future trends. One trend identified is the focus on self-reliance. Young people want higher income, job security and self-satisfaction that come with owning their own business or franchise. This will affect franchising growth positively, especially for women and minorities internationally. Additionally, she defines the term, 'transgenerational franchising' (Welsh, 2002).

John Clarkin (2002) examines the differences in expansion strategies among more than 1200 North American franchises. International market development is continuing to be increasingly important. The study examines two major issues: the differences in size, age and other characteristics between those pursuing international expansion and those not, and the possible motivations for international expansion. Clarkin's study (2002) found similar results to a study done 27 years earlier that found opportunity recognition to be a more important motivator for international expansion than market saturation. He explains the reasons for the findings and their implications.

Multi-unit and master franchising
Marko Grunhagen and Robert Mittelstaedt (2002), one of the founders of the International Society of Franchising, give us a historical synopsis of franchising, and then look at the state of the franchise industry and recent developments that have spurred its growth and expansion. They describe new industry segments that have emerged, including franchisees' mini-chains that cross states and regions. They also discuss the reasons behind the astronomical growth of multi-unit franchising from the franchisor as well as the franchisee perspectives. The major advantages usually cited to franchise are covered, with the authors giving some new reasons not previously considered.

Grunhagen and Mittelstaedt also look at the motivations of multi-unit franchisees, which may be different from the usual explanations given for franchising. The literature gives three reasons why individuals franchise: single unit franchisees are so eager to get into business for themselves that they become risk-indifferent; multi-unit operators believe they can 'beat the system' by the advantages of a larger and more geographically dispersed locations; and franchisees are not entrepreneurs so they need the system franchising has built in. The authors argue that entrepreneurship is an important motivator for multi-unit franchisee ownership. The article adds to the body of literature by addressing franchisee motivations and concluding that entrepreneurship is a reasonable explanation for the growth of multi-unit franchising.

In his article, 'The organisational determinants of master international franchising', Ilan Alon (2000) first defines and explains why master franchising is such a popular form for global expansion. He then goes on to develop a group of propositions concerning the impact of certain organizational variables on the use of master franchise agreements overseas. These types of agreements are primarily used for business format franchisors. He divides the factors into three explanations: resource-based, knowledge-based and strategy-based. The resource-based explanation looks at size, age and brand name asset specificity. The knowledge-based explanations include know-how and experience in managing global operations. Price, product and strategies are given as strategy-based reasons. These explanations should be examined before a franchisor enters a host country and decides the level of risk that he or she is able to tolerate. Alon gives a theoretical framework for global expansion that can be added to and is sorely needed in the field.

Somchanok Coompanthu and Kendall Roth's (2002) article focuses on international services and explores the various organizational forms that are possible and their impact on profitability. In particular, the article focuses on the use of plural management. Plural management can be defined as using a combination of company-owned or company-operated and franchised forms. Unit growth, uniformity, local responsiveness and system-wide adaptation are all affected by the use of plural management. It was found that, when there is high performance ambiguity or when it is difficult to determine employee job performance, firms are more likely to use franchised forms for international expansion. When there is a great deal of outcome uncertainty, company-owned and company-operated forms are more likely. The authors urge franchisors to look at the nature of the industry and the organizational forms that have worked best to achieve a higher performance level in the future. Plural management is offered as a strategic solution to the problems of achieving tight control if there is high performance ambiguity and the need to respond effectively to local markets.

Erramilli *et al.* (2002) also look at global entry modes in the service industry. However, their article focuses on non-equity modes of entry that feature minimal or no investment requirements. In particular, these non-equity modes are popular among consumer services firms, such as hotels and restaurants. Professional services firms, for example consulting businesses, rarely use this form. The study looks at the reasons for choosing between two non-equity modes: franchising and management service contracts. It takes the perspective that the form that most effectively transfers organizational capabilities is the form that should be adopted, rather than the one that provides the most effective control over the subsidiary. The latter is the form most recommended by international business theories. An international sample of hotel firms was used to find that capabilities that are difficult to imitate cannot be effectively transferred through franchising. In such cases, a management service contract was preferable. Infrastructure was found to be critical to the type of mode chosen and the success of the franchise. Additionally, the level of development of the country had an effect. In countries where customers are more service-conscious, and there is an ample supply of talented managers and investors, franchising works better. The authors warn that the firms focus mostly on the transfer characteristics of their business when making these modal decisions. If they are not perfectly imitable, there will be problems with franchising and more frequent calling for management service contracts.

Global franchise relationships
Jorg Sydow (2002) examines the service sector also, but looks at network leadership. He argues that, strategically, franchise systems need to link to interorganizational networks and be more relationship oriented. He also covers the management practices that are necessary for this to happen and anchors his recommendations in the theories that have been developed on structure. He illustrates the application of this theory with six business format franchise networks in Germany: McDonald's ® (fast food restaurants), OBI (retail superstores), Aufina (real estate agencies), Schulerhilfe (tutoring providers), ComputerLand (retail sales and computer services) and Hyper Services (service providers). Sydow offers concrete suggestions for the industry to follow as well as implications for management that have global applications.

Charles Keith Hawkes and Soumava Bandyopadhyay (2002) build a framework that examines the cultural and legal barriers that American franchisors could face as they expand globally. Their framework is built on two dimensions: the cultural distance (more versus less) of the market from the United States, and the extent of legal barriers (few versus many) in the market compared to the United States. Strategies that should be taken by the franchisor in view of these barriers are explicated. For example, if the countries are culturally close to the US but have more legal barriers, such as Italy and Spain, product or trade name franchising may be a better operating choice than business format franchising. In countries that are culturally distant from the US but have relatively fewer legal barriers, such as Japan, the opposite should be true. In the Gulf Region (Middle East), a great deal of adaptation of the product and the business format would be necessary because many legal barriers exist in these countries and they are culturally distant. In all, this article offers practical advice that is easily understood and implemented.

The United States
Fred DeLuca created the second largest franchise operation in the world when he created Subway. In North America, Subway just surpassed McDonald's with the greatest number of locations. Fred tells his story of how Subway conquered America and then spread worldwide. It all began in 1965 with the help of a family friend who loaned him $1000 to help pay for college tuition. In 2002, the business had more than 16000 franchised restaurants in 74 countries. The DeLuca *et al.* article covers the management challenges facing the franchise as it has expanded globally as well as a summary of its growth in certain counties, including Australia, Venezuela, India, and China. The article concludes with a summary of future endeavors on the horizon.

Ilan Alon (2002) analyzes how these industries have expanded globally through the number of outlets, including size and scale, the growth rate, the pricing strategy and the geographical dispersion. These factors aid in explaining why franchisors have gone global. However, there are differences between the three industries that are discussed. For instance, the age of the franchise was an insignificant factor for the hotel and professional business service categories, and had a negative relationship to internationalization in the retailing sector. One of the most interesting findings of the study involved the fact that younger franchisors in the retail sector were more likely to franchise. Alon provides clear evidence that the decision to go international should be studied at the industry level. This study clears the way for the development of a complete model of internationalization that is sorely needed by the franchise industry to make better decisions on where, when and why to go global.

Canada
With a population of 30 million and its close proximity and culture, Canada is often the first stop for US franchisors to expand internationally. Paul Jones and Michelle Wong (2002) describe the current state of the Canadian market, including currency, banking, legislation at the federal and province levels, and regulations. Additionally, the authors discuss the numerous factors to consider in adapting franchise agreements to the Canadian market, in particular the enforcement of contracts from one province to the next. Two provinces which have their own franchise legislation (Alberta and Ontario) are covered in detail in the article. Canada has followed the lead of the European Union and enacted the Personal Information Protection and Electronic Documents Act which protects all personal information in the private sector collected in the course of commercial activities by companies. Quebec has had such legislation in place since 1994, while Ontario has prepared a draft of its own privacy legislation and two other provinces are in the process of doing the same. In 2004, the federal legislation will extend to the provinces that have not passed their own legislation concerning privacy. In all, Jones and Wong's article comprehensively covers all basic aspects of what a franchisor needs to know to enter the market. It would benefit potential and existing franchisees to read the article in order to gain complete understanding of the entire franchise system in Canada.

The Pacific Rim
This vast area of the world is an open door to franchisors looking for densely populated consumer markets that are receptive to new opportunities. Despite the critics' misgivings, western fast food chains first entered

East Asian markets with a great deal of success. Kentucky Fried Chicken (KFC) average sales per store in Asia are US $1.2 million per year, compared to per store revenues in the United States of $750000 per year. Stephen Choo (2002) chose three franchisors with different capabilities and levels of internationalization to illustrate the critical success factors needed to enter the East Asian market. Dome Coffees from Australia, The Coffee Bean & Tea Leaf Company from the United States and Royal Copenhagen Ice Cream from Australia are qualitatively analyzed using the techniques of Yin (1994) and Miles and Huberman (1994). Results showed that there were six main key success factors in the East Asian market: distance management, contract enforcement, cultural adaptability, host country risk management, marketing approach and partnership management. The greater the cultural differences between the franchisor and franchisees in East Asia, the more important these success factors become in transferring a profitable franchise system. Choo makes a significant contribution in providing any potential or current franchisor with a useful insight into approaching and competing successfully in this market.

Japan
Nitin Sanghavi (2002) reviews the opportunities and challenges for companies to use franchising as a growth strategy in the Japanese market. He covers the recent developments in the Japanese and retail consumer markets, the effect of the stock market and what it will take to be profitable in this densely populated country. Compared to other industries, franchising has done relatively well, maintaining a growth rate of 6 to 8 percent. In terms of number of stores, service-related franchises showed the most growth, although sales per store were not as significant as food services or retail commerce franchises. Some 70 percent of the total increase in sales of the franchise industry as a whole was in retail commerce franchises. The author helps the reader to understand the effect of various business customs and lifestyle trends on franchise success in Japan and explains how the franchise should include these factors in its overall business strategy and structure to be successful.

New Zealand
Franchising in New Zealand has grown exponentially in the past five years. John Paynter (2002) summarizes the history of franchising and the results of the annual survey of the Franchise Association of New Zealand since its inception. A total of 111 systems is analyzed in terms of the number currently operating in the country, the number of people employed, the number of franchised and company-owned units, the percentage increase in sales growth, the industry groupings by percentage, the number of native

franchise operations and the median start-up costs, among other statistics. Of particular interest are his results on the number of systems that have websites (84 percent) and the failure rate data. Over a three-year period, only 6 percent failed and a miniscule 16 percent of franchisors (6 percent of franchisees) considered franchising not to be a good return on their investment. A hardy 77 percent rated their system excellent or above average. These results are good news for the industry.

Léo Paul Dana (2002a) encapsulates the New Zealand franchise market, which has the highest number of franchises per capita. Additionally, three-quarters of these involve New Zealand-based franchisors. Foreign franchisors are primarily from Australia. Dana gives us a detailed description of both, as well as possible legislation that may be enacted in the future. New Zealand currently does not have any franchise legislation but may enact similar legislation in the future to that passed in July 1998 in Australia.

He also discusses initiatives that the government should consider to aid in franchise development as well as future challenges to the industry. In particular, Dana indicates that future research should explore why New Zealand franchisors tend not to expand globally.

Other countries
Israel
Dana (2002b) analyzes the current state of franchising in Israel, explains why franchising has gained popularity quickly and explores the reasons for its accelerated growth. He gives two basic reasons for this phenomenon. First, Israel is a country composed of many immigrants. In the 1990s, there were a million new immigrants. Secondly, thousands of defense military personnel retired in their early forties with a lump sum payment from the government of $250 000 and were looking for investment opportunities. Many bought franchises. That has fueled the growth of home-grown franchises in banking, financial services, fashion and fast food. Interestingly enough, Israeli franchisors have not ventured abroad to a great extent, with a couple of notable exceptions. Burger Ranch has done well, entering the Hungarian and Romanian markets, while Reliable Rent a Car has done well in expanding into the Mediterranean region: Cyprus, Egypt, Italy, Malta, Portugal, Spain and Turkey. Dana also summarizes the legal environment in Israel and what he sees as possible franchise legislation and protection in the future.

South Africa
Anita du Toit's (2002) study of franchising in South Africa focuses on the issue of encroachment in multi-brand franchises with the use of in-depth

interviews of franchisors who had operated a business format franchise and had two or more franchised brands. About 10 percent of the franchisors in South Africa met the criteria. Qualitative analysis with the use of themes to give a larger, consolidated picture was utilized following the suggestions of Creswell (1994). Eight themes emerged and are described in detail in the article: brand management systems, achieving economies of scale, brand positioning, cultural divergence, conflict between stakeholders, policies on geographical proximity, failure of acquisitions and separation of brands. Du Toit concludes by making recommendations for future research based on her results and theorizes that perhaps multi-brand franchises may not be able to be managed successfully to avoid encroachment. She also includes some great recommendations that, if incorporated, would improve brand management of multi-brand franchises and assist in avoiding encroachment problems, good suggestions wherever the franchise is located worldwide.

Conclusions

The advent of franchising is a worldwide phenomenon. The importance of franchising cannot be overlooked. In countries around the globe, franchising affects the economy substantially, with its percentage of the retail trade increasing daily. It accounts for $1 trillion in retail spending per year and employs one in 16 workers in the United States (Reynolds, 2002). In some countries, franchising is approaching half their total retail sales. Although franchising has its critics, and there are franchises to definitely avoid, it is here to stay. The more we know about franchising, the better off the public and the industry will be. We have attempted to answer the call for additional research to understand international franchising by starting where it began, in North America, then covering its growth and development in the industrialized countries of the world. In 2001, we edited two companion volumes that were also published by Commerce Clearing House, now CCH, Inc., *International franchising in emerging markets: Central and Eastern Europe and Latin America* (Welsh and Alon, 2001) and *International franchising in emerging markets: China, India, and other Asian countries* (Alon and Welsh, 2001). Another volume was published in 2002, *International franchising in industrialized markets: North America, the Pacific Rim, and other countries* (Welsh and Alon, 2002). The fourth volume was *International franchising in industrialized markets: Western and Northern Europe* (Alon and Welsh, 2003). To our knowledge, this is the first attempt to summarize the research on a global basis, from a practitioner as well as an academic viewpoint. Franchisors, franchisees, those studying franchising, the governments of countries interested in furthering economic development and employment, and the massive populations who desire the opportunity to try franchising themselves through purchasing a franchising, starting their own franchise or tasting its fare, all need this information. This chapter offers final reflections as to the state of research in the field and what future research needs to take place. We hope to increase the knowledge level of franchising worldwide and spur increased exploration and research in the field.

In the last chapter of our first book, *International franchising in emerging markets: Central and Eastern Europe and Latin America* (Welsh and Alon, 2001), we identified areas ripe for future research. Forms of franchising and the ability to adapt to the ever-changing global marketplace were mentioned as two areas that needed exploration. We answered the call in our second volume. Four of the articles in this volume discuss various forms of franchising, including multi-unit franchising, master franchising, form choice and plural management, and non-equity modes of entry. In our third volume two of the articles look at adaptation. Jorg Sydow (Welsh and Alon, 2002) discusses network leadership and Charles Keith Hawkes and Soumava Bandyopadhyay (Welsh and Alon, 2002) discuss culture and legal barriers from an international entry perspective.

These papers all point to the same fact: it is becoming more complex for franchising to adapt to a world marketplace that is increasingly accessible with technological advances. There are more forms of franchising, and there is an increasing symbiotic relationship among the various stakeholders of franchising: franchisors, franchisees, host markets and consumers. What has not been addressed is the addition of franchisee associations in these symbiotic relationships and the fact that they are becoming at least as powerful, if not more powerful in some spheres, as associations worldwide that have been traditionally composed of franchisors. We predict that these influential organizations will continue to wield an increasing share of power in the future. Furthermore, it is likely that such franchisor and franchisee organizations, respectively, will join in associations of their counterparts by region or to mirror political associations, such as the European Franchise Federation (EFF) has formed as the European Union (EU) has become a reality. In larger part, these organizations will eventually exert a major influence on supplier networks, legislation, regulatory standards and safeguards, and shared technology and communication. They will transcend language and cultural barriers to create networks that are user-friendly. As John Reynolds, President of the International Franchising Foundation mentions in his foreword, John Naisbitt, author of *Megatrends* (1982), predicted that the future of franchising would benefit from an increasingly service-based economy, an increasingly convenience-oriented society, a more specialized workforce, more participation by women and minorities, and an increasingly globally based marketing strategy. The articles in these volumes reveal that his future trend analysis is coming true sooner than originally predicted. Research will make us understand where these trends are and where the industry is going.

Family business franchises are now entering their second generation, and a small number are even third-generation franchises. This is particularly true of franchises in the United States, as it has the longest history of franchising. However, other parts of the world that particular franchises first developed, such as hotel and restaurant industries, are also experiencing 'transgenerational franchising'. Transgenerational franchising, as defined by Dianne Welsh, is the continuing operation of a franchise or franchises that have gone from the original franchisee(s) to another generation of franchisee(s) that are connected either by family membership or ownership. When the international component is added to a transgenerational franchise or network of franchises, a more complex form of franchising emerges. This has major implications for the franchisor who is trying to maintain positive relationships with franchisees. Additionally, the franchisor may be transgenerational. Welsh calls this the 'blind date' phenomenon in franchising. The ability of the franchise system to sustain these long-term relationships could have a major impact on the future of franchising.

The Raymond Institute is in the process of conducting a survey on US family businesses and is requesting that family business franchises take part (Markins, 2002). Dianne Welsh is working with the Raymond Institute to understand the impact of family businesses on franchising and the actual size of this population that is predicted to keep growing in the future. Since franchising accounts for 5 percent of the 8 million small businesses in the USA, and two-thirds of these small businesses are considered family businesses, the impact of this combination is profound in real terms today. In some parts of the globe, such as the Pacific Rim, the percentage of family businesses is even higher, up to 90 percent or more. Tomorrow, the way we do business from a management, marketing and legal standpoint may be very different as a consequence of these changing demographics. This area is ripe for research and methodologically should be studied using longitudinal data analyses.

Internationalization of the franchise systems in developed countries has increased the importance of organizational management and learning issues in the global context. That is why Cecilia Falbe and Dianne Welsh composed panels on leadership, vision, strategic decision making and the Internet at the 2001 International Society of Franchising Conference (Welsh, Adler, Falbe, Gardner and Rennick, 2001). Ilan Alon and Dianne Welsh also organized a panel on international franchising in emerging markets to address such issues as they relate to global franchising (Alon and Welsh, 2002) that featured leading experts on global franchising such as Marcel Portman, Rajiv Dant, Skip Swerdlow, John Stanworth, Audesh Paswan and Cecilia Falbe. If the industry is to continue to grow, it needs to transform itself into a 21st-century learning organization. Technology can be compared to a moving treadmill, with the speed of information continually moving up to the next level. Communication is of utmost importance in this age. The environment must be continually scanned for relevant information on the market and its customers. The franchisor and the headquarters staff must provide leadership to communicate their vision to the franchise community. In turn, the franchisees, customers and associations must communicate their vision of the future to the franchisor. Strategic decision making must evolve from this interaction. It is important that the vision is clear to all stakeholders. The world marketplace demands it.

References

Alon, Ilan (2000), 'The organisational determinants of master international franchising', *Journal of Business & Entrepreneurship*, 12 (2), 1–18.

—— (2002), 'Organisational factors of U.S. international franchising: A comparative study of retailing, hotels, and professional business services', in Dianne H.B. Welsh and Ilan Alon (eds), *International franchising in industrialized markets: North America, the Pacific Rim, and other countries*, Riverwoods, IL: CCH.

Alon, Ilan and Dianne H.B. Welsh (eds) (2001), *International franchising in emerging markets: China, India, and other Asian countries*, Riverwoods, IL: CCH.

Alon, Ilan and Diane H.B. Welsh (2003), *International Franchising in industrial markets: Western and Northern Europe*, Riverwoods, IL: CCH.

Choo, Stephen (2002), 'Valuable lessons for international franchisors when expanding into East Asia', in Dianne H.B. Welsh and Ilan Alon (eds), *International franchising in industrialized markets: North America, the Pacific Rim, and other countries*, Riverwoods, IL: CCH.

Clarkin, John E. (2002), 'Market maturation or opportunity recognition? An examination of international expansion by U.S. and Canadian franchise systems', in Dianne H.B. Welsh and Ilan Alon (eds), *International franchising in industrialized markets: North America, the Pacific Rim, and other countries*, Riverwoods, IL: CCH.

Coompanthu, Somchanok and Kendall Roth (2002), 'International services: The choice of organisational forms and plural management', in Dianne H.B. Welsh and Ilan Alon (eds), *International franchising in industrialized markets: North America, the Pacific Rim, and other countries*, Riverwoods, IL: CCH.

Creswell, J.W. (1994), *Research design: Qualitative and quantitative approaches*, Thousand Oaks, CA: Sage Publications.

Dana, Léo-Paul (2002a), 'Franchising in New Zealand', in Dianne H.B. Welsh and Ilan Alon (eds), *International franchising in industrialized markets: North America, the Pacific Rim, and other countries*, Riverwoods, IL: CCH.

Dana, Léo-Paul. (2002b), 'Israel's experience with franchising', in Dianne H.B. Welsh and Ilan Alon (eds), *International franchising in industrialized markets: North America, the Pacific Rim, and other countries,* Riverwoods, IL: CCH.

DeLuca, Fred, Annie Smith and Les Winograd (2002), 'The Subway story: Making North American franchising history', in Dianne H.B. Welsh and Ilan Alon (eds), *International franchising in industrialized markets: North America, the Pacific Rim, and other countries,* Riverwoods, IL: CCH.

Erramilli, M. Krishna, Sanjeev Agarwal and Chekitan S. Dev (2002), 'Choice between non-equity entry modes: An organisational capability perspective', in Dianne H.B. Welsh and Ilan Alon (eds), *International franchising in industrialized markets: North America, the Pacific Rim, and other countries*, Riverwoods, IL: CCH.

Fenwick, L. (2001), 'Emerging markets: Defining global opportunities', *Franchising World*, 33 (4), 54–55.

Grunhagen, Marko and Robert A. Mittelstaedt (2002), 'Multi-unit franchising: An opportunity for franchisees globally?', in Dianne H.B. Welsh and Ilan Alon (eds), *International franchising in industrialized markets: North America, the Pacific Rim, and other countries*, Riverwoods, IL: CCH.

Hawkes, Charles Keith and Soumava Bandyopadhyay (2002), 'International growth of U.S. Franchising: Cultural and legal barriers', in Dianne H.B. Welsh and Ilan Alon (eds), *International franchising in industrialized markets: North America, the Pacific Rim, and other countries*, Riverwoods, IL: CCH.

Jones, Paul and Michelle Wong (2002), 'Franchising in Canada', in Dianne H.B. Welsh and Ilan Alon (eds), *International franchising in industrialized markets: North America, the Pacific Rim, and other countries*, Riverwoods, IL: CCH.

Markins, Carol (2002), 'Businesses needed for national survey', *IFA Insider*, 7 (15):4.

Miles, Matthew B. and Michael A. Huberman (1994), *Qualitative data Analysis*, 2nd edn, Beverly Hills, CA: Sage Publications.

Naisbitt, John (1982), *Megatrends*, New York: Warner Books.

Paynter, John (2002), 'Franchising in New Zealand: History and current status', in Dianne H.B. Welsh and Ilan Alon (eds), *International franchising in industrialized markets: North America, the Pacific Rim, and other countries*, Riverwoods, IL: CCH.

Reynolds, John (2002), 'Foreword', in Dianne H.B. Welsh and Ilan Alon (eds), *International franchising in industrialized markets: North America, the Pacific Rim, and other countries*, Riverwoods, IL: CCH.

Sanghavi, Nitin (2002), 'Franchising as a growth strategy in the Japanese retail market', in Dianne H.B. Welsh and Ilan Alon (eds), *International franchising in industrialized markets: North America, the Pacific Rim, and other countries*, Riverwoods, IL: CCH.

Scrivener, C. (2001), 'Franchise finance in Canada', *Franchising World*, 33 (4), 53.

Sydow, Jorg (2002), 'Franchise systems as strategic networks: Studying network leadership in the service sector', in Dianne H.B. Welsh and Ilan Alon (eds), *International franchising in industrialized markets: North America, the Pacific Rim, and other countries*, Riverwoods, IL: CCH.

Toit, Anita du (2002), 'An exploratory study of encroachment in multi-brand franchise Organisations', in Dianne H.B. Welsh and Ilan Alon (eds), *International franchising in industrialized markets: North America, the Pacific Rim, and other countries,* Riverwoods, IL: CCH.

Welsh, Dianne H.B. (2002), 'Franchising: A 21st century perspective', in Dianne H.B. Welsh and Ilan Alon (eds), *International franchising in industrialized markets: North America, the Pacific Rim, and other countries*, Riverwoods, IL: CCH.

Welsh, Dianne H.B., Michael F. Adler, Cecilia M. Falbe, Regina O. Gardner and Lori A. Rennick (2001), 'Multiple uses of the internet in franchising'. Moderated the Symposium at the International Society of Franchising, February, Las Vegas, NV.

Welsh, Diane H.B. and Ilan Alon (eds) (2002), *International franchising in industrialized markets: North America, the Pacific Rim, and other countries*, Riverwoods, IL: CCH.

Welsh, Dianne H.B. and Ilan Alon (eds) (2001), *International franchising in emerging markets: Central and Eastern Europe and Latin America*, Riverwoods, IL: CCH.

Yin, Robert K. (1994), *Case study research design and methods*, 2nd edn, Beverly Hills, CA: Sage Publications.

37 The internationalization of franchise systems into emerging and transitional economies
Dianne H. B. Welsh and Ilan Alon

This chapter answers the urgent call from both the franchise industry and the academic community for research on world franchising markets. It summarizes the main research that has been conducted on international franchising in emerging markets. First, the chapter answers the relevant question of what is an emerging market from a franchisor perspective. The level of economic development that is needed for a franchiser to consider entering a particular country for expansion is explored. Next, economic growth is discussed, along with market governance.

The chapter then examines specific, practical franchising research that has been conducted in various parts of the globe. Much of the research that has been conducted thus far in the franchising field is descriptive. In other words, the state of franchising in a particular country is described. This is usual when the field being studied is so new. Initially, the chapter explores the practice and theory development of international franchising that currently exists: comprehensive theory development is sorely needed. The chapter goes on to divide the research into areas of the emerging world market: Central and Eastern Europe, Mexico and South America, China, India other Asian countries and other areas of promise that include Kuwait and South Africa. Specific cases of franchises that have entered these markets and their experiences are given. The chapter concludes by discussing the next step: to develop a research base and understanding of emerging markets in addition to the opportunities and challenges for franchising.

Franchising has experienced phenomenal growth both in the USA and abroad in recent years. Figures vary, but it is estimated that US franchising generates $800 billion worth of business in gross sales and represents 40 percent of the retail trade (Swartz, 2001). While in the United States, Canada and parts of Western Europe franchising has reached domestic market saturation, emerging markets remain relatively untapped. Emerging markets, accounting for 80% of the world's population and 60% of the world's natural resources, present the most dynamic potential for long-term growth to businesses, in general, and to franchisors, in particular. The U.S. Department of Commerce estimated that over 75% of the expected growth in world trade over the next two decades will come from emerging countries, particularly big emerging countries, which account for over half the world's population but only 25% of its GDP. Emerging markets are among the fastest growing markets for international franchisors. Several surveys conducted by the International Franchising Association show that more and more franchisors are seeking opportunities in emerging markets. An article in *Franchising World* (Amies, 1999, pp. 27–8) stated, 'Franchises are springing up in the most unlikely and for many of us unheard-of, places . . . Those franchisors who can establish a beach-head on these wilder shores could do very well, but the risks are great.'

What is an emerging market?
While there is no consensus definition of the term 'emerging market', Czinkota and Ronkainen (1997) identified three characteristics associated with an emerging economy: level of economic development, economic growth and market governance. The level of economic development is commonly used to delineate emerging markets. It is associated with the anachronisms of the World Bank and the United Nations, which include terms such as 'less developed countries' (LDCs), 'third world countries' and 'developing countries'. The level of economic development is typically measured in terms of GDP per capita. GDP per capita is a useful measure of economic development because it is related to the population's wealth, extent of a middle class and level of industrial and service sector development (Alon and McKee, 1999). The World Bank divides countries on the basis of GDP per capita into four classes. Three of the big emerging countries (India, China and Vietnam) fall into the lowest income class. According to the United Nations, only about 15% of the world's population resides in developed market economy countries (Czinkota and Ronkainen, 1997). When analyzing emerging markets, it is important to adjust GDP per capita to purchasing power parity in order to gauge income in relation to the 'real' cost of living (Arnold and Quelch, 1998).

Economic growth is usually measured in terms of the country's GDP growth rate. The usage of economic growth is consistent with the concept of 'emerging'. Most of the countries referred to as emerging markets enjoyed GDP growth rates exceeding 5 percent from 1990 to 1997, with some markets, particularly in East Asia, displaying double-digit growth rates (Czinkota and Ronkainen, 1997). From 1997 to 1999, East Asia, Brazil and Russia encountered financial crises that set back their economies' growth. Such crises demonstrate that the often-touted high growth rates of emerging markets may not be sustainable over a long period of time. The level of economic growth is among the most important considerations for international franchising expansion (Alon and McKee,

1999). When examining an emerging market's GDP growth, one must contrast it to the growth in population. If population growth rates exceed GDP growth rates, the standard of living in those countries will actually drop over time. One useful measure that captures both growth rates is GDP per capita growth rate.

The third criterion for judging emerging markets is the country's market governance. Market governance includes the level of free markets, government control of key resources, stability of the market system and the regulatory environment. Countries that are liberalizing their economic institutions and democratizing their political structures are often referred to as 'transitional economies/countries'. These transitions have been welcomed by the west and regarded as opportunities for international franchise expansion. International investors weigh the risks that are introduced by the reorganization of economic and political units in the particular emerging marketplace (Czinkota and Ronkainen, 1997). Such risks are systematically evaluated by western institutions such as the Economist Intelligence Unit, Institutional Investors and the International Country Risk Guide (ICRG). Market governance influences a wide array of country risk elements, such as government regulation and red tape, political stability, bribery, ownership restrictions, controls of capital flows and import restrictions. All these factors affect international franchisors' evaluations of foreign market potential (Alon and McKee, 1999).

Review of the literature
A number of authors, both industry analysts and academics, have identified emerging markets as a topic that needs further research for the franchise industry. In 1988, Kaufmann and Leibenstein wrote an article for the United Nations when franchising in developing countries was just beginning. In 1990, Welsh conducted the first survey on Russian soil on franchising, at a time when the word 'franchising' had no meaning to the population, except when it was coupled with McDonald's. That was the same year the franchise opened in Moscow, to a tremendous welcoming by the Russian people and the press (Welsh and Swerdlow, 1991). Since that time, franchising in emerging markets has grown dramatically. For example, by 1995, there were 26 more franchisors in Brazil alone than there were in all of South America in 1985 (International Franchise Research Centre, 2000).

Academics and practitioners have answered the call for more research and evaluation of franchising in these new markets around the globe. Young *et al.* (2000) examined the content of articles that had been published in the *International Society of Franchising Proceedings*. Out of almost 70 articles between 1987 and 1999, nine dealt with economies in transition and 14 others dealt with developing economies. The book includes a useful table that looks at international franchise articles by country/region. Practitioners have also published articles on the topic. For example, Leonard Swartz (2001) examined the state of franchising in Asia – China, Indonesia, Singapore and Malaysia – and Eastern Europe – Russia, Poland, Hungary and Greece – as well as the Middle East – United Arab Emirates, Israel, Saudi Arabia, Kuwait and Egypt – and South America – Chile, Uruguay, Brazil, Argentina, Colombia and Peru.

This chapter summarizes the research that has been conducted in emerging economies. We have searched the Proceedings of the International Society of Franchising of 1986, the first year the proceedings were published, and all others from 1988 to 2000. The International Society of Franchising, formerly known as the Society of Franchising, is the premier academic organization that focuses on franchise research. It has traditionally held its conference annually in conjunction with the International Franchising Association (IFA) Convention. The IFA Educational Foundation donated $5000 to found the Society of Franchising Conference in 1986. No conference was held in 1987. We also searched the only journal exclusively devoted to franchising research that has existed in recent years, *Franchising Research: An International Journal*, published by MCB University Press. It was published in 1986–8, before being merged with the *Journal of Consumer Marketing*. The Franchising Research section was discontinued in 2000 for lack of submissions in the narrow area of franchising and consumer marketing studies. A number of years ago the International Franchising Association published a franchising research journal, which, however, was short-lived. The American Bar Association (ABA) publishes a journal focusing solely on legal issues in franchising that is published quarterly. A summary of the articles in the *Proceedings of the International Society of Franchising* and *Franchising Research: An International Journal* solely focusing on franchising in emerging markets appears in Table 37.1.

Practice and theory development
Authors have examined why franchising has had such an impact internationally and what forms franchising has taken in different parts of the world. Grimaldi (1992) analyzed the opportunities for franchising in free trade zones. Kaufmann (2001) looked at the issues of cultural and legal differences in the age of the Internet and the impact of franchising on host country development. Specifically, he examined the modes of entry, cultural differences and proven concepts, cultural differences and technology, legal differences and host country development. Stanworth *et al.* (2001) looked at franchising as a means of technology transfer for developing

economies. Their article explored the background to the internationalization of franchising, factors favorable to the growth of franchising, benefits to developing economies, other consequences for developing economies, advantages and risks to franchisors, as well as government actions to encourage franchising. The authors gave special insights into Indonesia, China and Brazil.

Models are beginning to be developed in international franchising. However, they are scarce. Thompson and Merrilees (2001) examined marketing through a modular approach to branding and operations for international retail franchising systems. Examples of Australian firms extending their franchise systems into Eastern Europe, Asia and Latin America demonstrated the applicability of this approach to branding in their study. Other authors indicate that new symbiotic relationships are created when franchising expands into developing countries. Franchising allows firms to achieve the expanded reach and efficiencies associated with internationalization more rapidly and effectively than the firms could achieve on their own. Dana *et al.* (2001) developed an Interdependence Paradigm to explain these franchising market networks using examples of firms in South Korea and the Philippines.

Central and Eastern Europe
Nitin Sanghavi (2001) gives his personal perspective on the use of franchising as an economic development tool from his numerous experiences with these countries. He summarized the current state of franchising in Eastern Europe as compared to 1997 when he first looked at the topic (Sanghavi, 1997).

Swerdlow *et al.* (2001) and Alon and Banai (2001) in their respective entries give us an historical review of franchise development in Russia as well as a current and future look at the prospects for franchise development in an area of the world that is barely realizing its full potential as an economic power. Both studies examined the post-communist economy with a focus on environmental factors associated with international franchise development and entry strategies those potential franchisors would find successful. The studies included some practical suggestions for those entering and maneuvering through this huge market. Skip Swerdlow and Dianne Welsh, along with co-authors, published a number of articles in the early 1990s examining franchising in the former USSR that are summarized in Swerdlow and Bushmarin (1994) and Welsh and Swerdlow (1991,1993). Christy and Haftel also summarized the early Russian marketplace in a 1992 article. In 1993, the same authors published the only case study on franchising in Russia in an earlier era when Pizza Hut opened in Moscow.

Table 37.1   Summary of US published articles on franchising

Year	Title	Author(s)
1988	Franchising in Asia	Justis, Neilson and Yoo
1988	International business format franchising and retail entrepreneurship: A possible source of retail know-how for developing countries	Kaufmann and Leibenstein
1990	Franchise management in East Asia	Chan and Justis
1991	Opportunities and challenges for franchisors in the U.S.S.R.: Preliminary results of a survey of Soviet university students	Welsh and Swerdlow
1992	The future of franchising in the U.S.S.R.: A statistical analysis of the opinions of Soviet university students	Swerdlow and Welsh
1992	Franchising opportunities in the free trade zones of developing countries	Grimaldi
1992	Pizzas in Mexico? Si!	Willems, English and Ito
1992	Franchising entry and developmental strategies in the former Soviet Union	Christy and Haftel
1993	Pizza Hut in Moscow: Post-coup system development and expansion	Christy and Haftel
1993	A cross-cultural study of American and Russian hotel employees: A preliminary review and its implications for franchisors	Welsh and Swerdlow
1994	A survey of franchising in Singapore	Chan, Foo, Quek and Justis
1994	Franchising in China: A look at KFC and McDonalds	English and Xau
1994	Does business format management master Marxism in post-coup Russia?	Swerdlow and Bushmarin
1995	Franchising in Brazil	Josias and McIntyre
1995	Franchising in India: An introduction	Paswan and Dant
1995	Franchising in Indonesia	Chan and Justis
1996	Franchising in South Africa	Scholtz
1996	Franchising into Asia: An overview of selected target markets	McCosker
1996	Local franchising development in Singapore	Goh and Lee
1996	The case of the elegant shoplifter, Shuwaikh, Kuwait	Welsh, Raven and Al-Bisher
1997	Franchising as a tool for SME development in transitional economies: The case of Central European countries	Sanghavi
1997	An overview of South African franchising	Scholtz

Table 37.1 (continued)

Year	Title	Author(s)
1998	NAFTA and franchising: A comparison of franchisor perceptions of characteristics associated with franchisee success and failure in Canada, Mexico and the United States	Falbe and Welsh
1998	Franchising in Slovenia: Support to the development of franchise systems in Central Europe	Pavlin
1998	Case Study: Strategic alliances in international franchising – the entry of Silver Streak Restaurant Corporation into Mexico	Hadjimarcou and Barnes
2000	New trends in Slovenian franchising	Pavlin
2000	International franchising: Evidence from US and Canadian franchisors in Mexico	Lafontaine and Oxley

Note: The authors do not intend this list to be comprehensive; for full details see References.

Aneta Nedialkova (2001) specifically examined franchising opportunities in Bulgaria, with a focus on the macroeconomic factors. International investors have been developing franchises in Bulgaria for more than 25 years. However, the market has remained sluggish because of the highly bureaucratic government system. The study described a number of positive elements and success stories that gave reasons to be optimistic concerning the future of franchise development in Bulgaria.

Ljiljana Viducic (2001) described the two types of franchise arrangements that are prevalent in Croatia, using the examples of McDonald's and Diner's Club. Primarily, franchising has taken the form of several corporate facilities in operation, where local interaction with the store is limited to employment, not ownership, and the second form where an entrepreneur is taken on as a franchise holder with the understanding that his capital involvement will increase over time as well as his ownership interest as a full franchisee. Additionally, the study elaborated on the current state of Croatian franchise activity and other forms of market expansion that have been successful in Croatia.

The current condition of Slovenian franchising is analyzed empirically in an article by Pavlin (2001). Using the definition of franchising adopted by the European Franchise Federation, there are currently over 40 operating franchise systems in Slovenia. Pavelin compared these results to studies he conducted on Slovenian franchising that were published in 1998 and

2000. In 1998, there were 40 franchises operating in his country, of which 20 participated in his survey on the current state of franchising. The study included results from a recent survey of prospective Slovenian franchisees identifying their core attributes and offered a framework for profitable future development of the industry in Slovenia that might be useful for franchisors and franchisees.

Mexico and South America

Three studies have focused on different aspects of Mexican franchising. Teegan (2001) examined foreign expansion and market entry from three different perspectives. The first perspective is that of the Mexican franchisee that might purchase the rights to a US-based franchise; the second perspective is that of the US franchisor that might sell the rights to their business format; the third perspective is that of the host government, namely Mexico, in terms of the economic impact and development within their country. The author shared the results of a survey of over 70 Mexican franchisees of US-based franchise systems. Results showed that the commonly held belief within both the United States and Mexico concerning the desirability of franchising as a mode of market entry and caution on the part of franchisees, franchisors and the host governments is warranted. Teegan gives a realistic view of the risks and rewards of franchising and a generous amount of information for those contemplating franchising in Mexico.

Hadjimarcou and Barnes (2001) explained the expansion process of a relatively new and small franchisor, Silver Streak Restaurant Corporation, into Mexico in a case study. The authors explained the cultural challenges of entering Mexico, the company's efforts to identify a suitable partner in the host country, the adaptation of the concept to address differences in the new market and the multitude of crucial decisions that need to be made when going international. The authors discussed the recent changes in the law that favor franchising, as well as the role that strategic alliances played in the success of their international franchise efforts. Implications for both research and practitioners are explicated. Silver Streak Restaurant Corporation originally opened their first franchised restaurant in 1996 in Juarez, a city of 1.5 million on the border of the United States (Hadjimarcou and Barnes, 1998).

In 2001, Welsh updated the 1998 study with Falbe that was the first to examine the effect, if any, of the North American Free Trade Agreement (NAFTA) on franchisor perceptions of characteristics associated with franchisee success and failure in Canada, Mexico and the United States (Falbe & Welsh, 1998, 2001; Welsh, 2001). The original research addressed two key issues in franchising. The first question addressed was the extent of franchisee success and failure. This question was answered by analyzing franchise executives' perceptions of the importance of a number of characteristics associated with franchisee success and failure. The second issue was addressed by examining if there were any differences among the executives' perceptions of these characteristics based on the location of the franchisor. Their 1998 study found that the respondents' perceptions of the importance of system quality, brand name, local environment and communication and other scales of franchisor and franchisee activities differed by country of origin. Additionally, results of the study showed that neither business type nor franchise size had any effect on perceptions of success or failure. The authors examined the research that has been conducted since the study appeared in 1998 and what we know in 2001. In a similar study, Lafontaine and Oxley (2000) found that the majority of US and Canadian franchisors employed the same contract terms in Mexico as in their home market. Their study reported the operations of more than 200 US and Canadian franchisors in Mexico.

Josias and McIntyre published the first article examining franchising in Brazil in 1995. In 2001, McIntyre gave us an update on what is now the third largest franchising market in the world. Only the United States and Canada have more franchises than Brazil. The author covers the history of franchising in Brazil, describes what is unique about Brazilian franchising and gives her view of the country's prospects for the future franchise market. She views Brazilian franchising as ripe for development, as evidenced by the size of the domestic franchise industry, demographics of the population and current economic conditions.

China

China has been explored from a franchise perspective in many industries since the country opened up to foreign investment. We will cover these major areas of research, most of which would fall under descriptive research.

The hotel industry

China is looked at by three professors from the Department of Hotel and Tourism Management at the Hong Kong Polytechnic University – Ray Pine, Hanqin Qiu Zhang, and Pingshu Qi (2001). They discussed the rapid expansion of the franchised hotel industry in China and the opportunities that exist for further development. Additionally, they expanded on the creation and growth of indigenous hotel chains. From 1979 to 1999, the number of hotels in China grew from the ground up, so to speak. There are now 7035 hotels where there previously were none (China National Tourism Administration, 1993–2000). The profit rate was only 1% in 1997 (ibid.), but since that time they have become comparably profitable as a result of diversification and decentralization of the industry.

Additionally, the authors examined how many of the top hotel chains have entered China: about 10% of the world's top 300 corporate hotel chains, according to *Hotel* magazine in 1999 (Cruz, 1999), have done so. Holiday Inn is the biggest hotel chain there, with 18 hotels and 10 more under negotiation. Three key aspects of the hotel industry are covered in the study and discussed thoroughly: the existing small share of franchised and chain-operated hotels, the rapid growth of hotels and the concomitant drop in hotel profits, and the country's economy and infrastructure. The authors related their understanding of China's cultural, economic and political background that are essential for success in this market, as well as completing a SWOT (Strengths, Weaknesses, Opportunities and Threats) analysis of the Chinese hotel industry.

The fast food industry
Wilke English, from the United States, teamed up with one of his Chinese students, Chin Xau (2001) to look at two prominent franchises that entered China early on: KFC and McDonalds. The authors gave us an update from the early beginning of franchising in 1994, when these franchises were in a joint venture arrangement, with the Chinese government basically as the 'franchisee'. Their study covered the challenges faced by these early franchising pioneers, such as political uncertainty and government control, and the quickfire success they have experienced. They also cited cultural considerations that make franchising a viable business strategy in China. The authors' step-by-step guide to cultural awareness and sensitivity is particularly useful in China today, as it was when the original article was written. Topics such as how to develop good relationships, coordination with joint venture partners, negotiation tactics and problem-solving strategies are covered in detail. They compared and contrasted the experience of KFC in China, the first major US-based fast food franchise to enter Mainland China, to that of McDonalds. Despite spending four and a half years in negotiations with the government before they were able to open their first location, the 650-seat Beijing restaurant has been extremely successful, breaking all KFC world sales records (*Almanac of China's Foreign Economic Relations and Trade*, 1991). The article described how KFC took a direct approach with the government, while McDonalds pursued a cautious strategy and opened its first restaurant in Shenzhen, a city adjacent to Hong Kong. However, it changed its strategy on its second restaurant to mirror KFC's tactics. It opened the world's largest McDonalds in Beijing, with seating for 702 (English and Xau, 2001). English and Xau gave a useful summary table of franchising investment particulars in China and other Asian countries to compare entry and investment strategies (see Chan and Justis, 1990; *Investment Guide*, 1991; English and Xau, 2001).

Wilke English's 'Y2K Update' looked at these two franchised fast food systems, which now have about 650 total outlets in China. They own all but 5–15% of the fast food restaurants in that country. Of the 720 fast food franchise units listed in a recent report, 90% were either KFC or McDonald's (English, 2001). The author pointed out the lack of competition these two chains have encountered in China. A useful table is included of the fast food restaurant chains currently in China, including the number in China as a whole, Beijing, other parts of China, and Japan (English, 2001). The author also covered the recent legislation passed in China that contains a similar legal structure to franchising in the United States. In 1997, the Ministry of Internal Trade passed regulations that appear to have created a business format similar to US franchising. The franchisee is no longer the government, as it was in the early 1990s, but a Chinese citizen. This makes franchising much more inviting for potential franchisors seeking to enter this vast and expansive market (English, 2001; Nair, 2001). With the help of Ilan Alon, Rollins Graduate School of Management, who collected the Y2K data, Wilke English compiled price comparisons in dollars and in yuan between the McDonald's menu items of 1993 and 2000 in China and those in Belton, Texas (the author's place of residence) (English, 2001).

Legal issues
Anna Han in her 2001 study expanded on these legal issues affecting franchising in China. She pointed out the many market segments and diverse populations in China that make the market interesting as well as challenging for the franchisor. She examined China's 1997 franchising measures, how they are defined and what must be included in franchise agreements to be in full compliance with China's Contract Law (Ninth National People's Congress, 1999). Intellectual property rights and how they are protected are covered. Han pointed out that particular care must be given to the selection of Chinese trade names and marks that accompany patents, trademarks, trade names, copyrights, trade secrets and domain names. She also examined in detail all the laws that franchisors must comply with, including labor laws, land use regulations and tax laws that are in addition to specific laws governing franchising. Dispute resolution, arbitration and litigation alternatives in franchise agreements and how they are enforced in the Chinese Court of Law are explicated. Han also examined the enforcement of laws, particularly arbitrated and judicial awards that are still problematic for those entering the Chinese market. The author indicated precisely what this market consists of, highly segmented sub-markets and franchise operations that must pay attention to local preferences, differences between generations and the rural versus urban population mix if they are to be

successful. She also touched on what types of franchises have been and could be successful in this market with a growing urban population and increasingly affluent consumer base.

Cases

The beauty business　Three studies are written by actual practicing franchisees in the Chinese market. The first is an interview with a Chinese beauty parlor franchisor in Shanghai that took place in July 2000. Ilan Alon (2001) used a standardized interview instrument that consisted of 23 questions concerning ownership, franchising and strategic marketing that is a modified version of an instrument by Dahlstrom and Nygaard (1999). Six major findings that are helpful to understanding the state of franchising and business development in China emerged and are summarized in the study. The findings include, for example, that 38% of the franchisor's outlets are in Shanghai (all located in the downtown area) and 56% of the Shanghai outlets are owned by the franchisor (Alon, 2001). Additionally, the study found that start-up costs run at about $20000, and that the franchisor primarily relies on tie-in sales rather than royalties for his revenue base (ibid.).

Consulting　S.R. Nair (2001), who owns a US-based company engaged in joint ventures in China, as well as being a consultant on the topic, gave us an overview of franchising in China from the perspective of a franchisee. The author gave a historical picture of the country from an economic perspective, as it exists today, and how it has been transformed. He noted that the government's decision to close inefficient, state-owned enterprises left millions laid off to fend for themselves. Nair sees franchising as part of the solution to China's huge unemployment problems and a vehicle for partially closing the gap between the growing populations that are very wealthy or very poor (Overholt, 1993). Nair also explored the advantages and disadvantages of franchising in China, the pros and cons of direct and indirect franchising, and the types of opportunities available for foreign firms to invest and establish a foothold in this gigantic market (Nair, 2001). The six variations for entering the market are described in detail. These are equity joint ventures, cooperative joint ventures, wholly foreign-owned enterprises, representative offices, processing and compensation trade, and technology licensing. These forms are described with examples of successful businesses in each, including ITN, McDonald's, KFC, Chem-Dry, Starbucks, Hard Rock Café, TGIF and Subway, among others (ibid.).

Management recruiting　Richard Hoon (2001), who is responsible for 17 countries in Asia with Management Recruiters International (MRI), discussed the history of business development since 1992, when the Chinese government announced the decision to reform the economy through decentralization efforts. This was the beginning of many reforms aimed at privatizing state enterprises. Hoon discussed the problems these early franchise pioneers encountered, the state of business today and his personal experiences opening professional service franchises in this new marketplace. He is one of the 'Tiananmen Generation', the best and brightest, lured home by the open economy, which he sees as the future driving force behind the government reforms, propelling China into the status of a world economic power. With a population of 1.2 billion, it is easy to imagine all the possibilities for business development. Many have already succeeded. By 1990, over 400 foreign enterprises had begun businesses in China, and 70% were profitable (ibid.). However, as the author points out, business in China is as much about relationships as it is about profits.

Hoon (2001) described his personal strategy for opening locations in China for MRI in the three most promising commercial hubs: Beijing, Guangzhou and Shanghai. He also described his formula for success and future plans for MRI Asia – strategies the reader can learn from.

India
India is a country with a huge potential for franchising growth. Paswan, Dant and Young (2001) wrote a descriptive study of the evolving contemporary franchising industry. It is estimated that the current market in India totals approximately one billion US dollars, and has a growth rate per annum of 30 percent (US Dept. of Commerce, 2000). The United States government has designated India as a big emerging market (BEM). While many franchises have already opened here, the country is still in the early stages of franchise development.

There are 800 franchisors operating in Indian market (Kumarkaushalam, 2000). Some of the well known names include Pepsi, Coca-Cola, Baskin Robbins, Wimpy, McDonald's, KFC, Holiday Inn, Quality Inns, Marriott, Hyatt Regency, Best Western, Sheraton and Ramada. There are also many home-grown franchises. The authors described the characteristics of both the multinational franchise organizations and the home-grown franchise systems. The key business sectors include, but are not limited to, soft drinks, ice creams, fast foods, health care, computer education, beauty/fitness clinics, hotel/tourism and the retail sector (US Dept. of Commerce, 2000). The fastest growing sector appears to be information technology education. Paswan, Dant and Young (2001) covered some prospects and caveats for entering this market as a franchisor. The distinguishing feature of franchising, as the authors related, is the creative modes of entry franchisors have utilized. This created definitional issues such as whether a business can legitimately claim to be a franchise. The authors re-examined seven key dimensions that are crucial to a business being considered a franchise (Winsor and Quinonee, 1994). From these, four core principles were derived that apply for an Indian franchise to be considered a legitimate franchise. The authors related that all four must be present: the principle of conformity and standardization, the principle of formalized revenue sharing, the principal of operational control and the principle of continuity (Paswan, Dant and Young, 2001). Finally, the study also named several contractual elements that have been identified as important by the Indian franchise community, that will eventually define what is meant by a franchise in India. These elements are extremely helpful for identifying opportunities in this market (Dheer and Gupta, 1999).

Franchisor survey

In a second study, by Dant and Kaufmann (2001), a descriptive account was given from a 2000 survey of franchisors in the Delhi area of approximately 250 franchisors. There was estimated to be around 800 franchisors in all of India, primarily operating in Delhi, Mumbai (formerly Bombay), Bangalore and Chennai (formerly Madras). The pilot survey was aimed at developing a descriptive document for the industry similar to *Franchising in the Economy*, published by the U.S. Department of Commerce until 1988. The data were divided into six major categories of findings: distribution by sectors, scope and ownership patterns, system age and size, franchisee selection, financial arrangements and operating procedures. Dant and Kaufmann (ibid.), compared and contrasted these findings to the technology-based franchise systems that are prevalent in the Delhi area and are considered by some as the future of franchising in India. The authors cited the fact that India currently ranks as the twelfth largest economy in the world, based on nominal GNP (Pal, 2000; US Dept. of Commerce, 2000). The middle classes, which are the most likely to be franchise customers, constitute about 20% of the total population, which equates to between 200 and 250 million consumers (US Dept. of Commerce, 2000). The study ends with advice for franchisors worldwide who are considering the Indian market.

Consumer survey

Paswan, Young and Kantamneni (2001) developed a 32-question survey based upon the public's perception of franchising. The perceptions identified were socioeconomic effects, social well-being, employment opportunity and consumer benefits. The authors developed dimensions based on these perceptions. They encompassed people's concern for their society, a sense of well-being at the individual and social level, cultural preservation, potential for business growth, infrastructure development, employment opportunities, employment sources, product quality-enhancing mechanism, fear of exploitation, quality of life and overall social benefits, among other items. The convenience sample of 385 included middle- to upper-class men and women from the state of Andhra Pradesh (including Hyderabad). The results indicated that there are six major dimensions potential customers use to evaluate a franchise: macro- and socioeconomic concerns, social well-being, individual well-being, consumer benefits, quality improvement and localized development. Paswan, Young and Kantamneni (2001) urged further research in emerging markets to look also at the customer side, as well as the franchisor and franchisee sides of the equation, when evaluating potential markets.

Other parts of Asia
Researchers began publishing articles on franchising in Asia in 1995. Chan and Justis (1995) looked at franchising in Indonesia by investigating the climate for franchising and the perceptions of the Indonesian people regarding franchising. McCosker (1996) reported on a survey of foreign franchises that wanted to enter the Asian markets of Singapore, Malaysia, Hong Kong and Indonesia. He gathered information from the existing literature as well as from franchisors that had already entered these markets, and from interviews conducted during visits to those countries. Chan *et al.* (1994) published an article that reported on a survey that identified the major franchises that existed, the different types of franchises and the nature and characteristics of franchise agreements in Singapore. Subsequent to this study, Chan and Justis published an earlier study examining franchising in East Asia, in general (1990).

Goh and Lee (1996) surveyed 62 franchisors in Singapore to assess the state of franchise development as well as franchise fee structures, the prevalence of home-grown franchises and the effect of the government's efforts to promote franchising. Mark Goh (2001) again assessed Singapore's franchise industry. He presented the results from two surveys: one was conducted in 1995 on 62 local franchisors and another in 1999 by the applicable government agency, the Singapore Trade and Development Board (1999) on 140 existing and potential local franchisors. The first survey found that most franchisors were engaged in mass market franchising. The second survey, covering 140 existing and potential franchisors, found that high start-up costs and overly high expectations concerning income levels posed significant challenges in recruiting franchises. However, the survey also showed that 80% of the franchisors believed their franchises had been successful and profitable. At least half of those responding already had franchises operating in other countries, particularly in Southeast Asia, but also in the Middle East and Africa. Goh (2001) summarized the opportunities and difficulties a franchisor may face when entering Singapore. This study is essential reading for anyone considering the Singapore market.

The Gulf region
The restaurant industry
Khan and Khan (2001) specifically analyzed the restaurant industry in the Middle East, concentrating on the major trends and success factors related to franchising. The authors emphasized the political and legal considerations, language, culture and traditions, menu items and service, demographic and economic changes, and availability of resources that must be taken into consideration when entering this market. The authors included a table of 22 countries that is differentiated by area, population, annual population growth and GDP (*http://plasma.nationalgeographic.com/mapmachine/ facts_fs.html*). Additionally, handy assessment checklists are included that can be utilized by franchisors considering entering a new market. The authors also included checklists for assessing political, sociocultural, and franchising-related factors that would be particularly helpful for those that are less than familiar with the Middle East. It should be noted that each country is unique and these checklists could be used to compare differences between countries and their markets in terms of assessment.

Cases: coffee and cars
Welsh, Raven and two former students presented cases on Starbucks Coffee International (Raven *et al.*, 2001) and on Mercedes Benz in Kuwait (Welsh *et al.*, 2001). The latter is a real event that occurred while the Kuwaiti student worked at his family's dealership. It deals with fundamental issues such as religion, culture and legal regulations that bind all three. There is not a separation of church and state in these countries, so the case is important for those entering these markets to understand how they are inextricably intertwined and the effect it has on business development.

Starbucks Coffee began in 1971 as one small shop in Seattle, Washington's Pike Place Market. It expanded from 11 stores in 1987 to over 500 today. Starbucks currently has retail locations in the Republic of Korea, Japan, Singapore, the Philippines, Taiwan, Thailand, the United Kingdom, New Zealand, Malaysia, Beijing, Kuwait, Lebanon, the United Arab Emirates (Dubai), Qatar, Hong Kong, Shanghai, Australia, Saudi Arabia and Bahrain (Cuevas and Johnson, 2001). The Starbucks article was written in 1996 and published in 2001 before Starbucks actually entered this market and is quite forward thinking. Interestingly, as predicted in the original article, Starbucks opened its first outlet in Sharq, Kuwait in 1999 (Seattle Post, 1999), and it has become one of its most profitable stores in the entire region (Business Wire, 2000). Its licensing partner, M.H. Alshaya Co. W.L.L., has opened Starbucks in six Gulf Region countries – Qatar, Kuwait, Lebanon, the United Arab Emirates, Saudi Arabia and Bahrain – with more outlets planned (Alshaya Company News, 2001; Alshaya Home Page, 2001). Both articles gave excellent insights into the country, the region, the culture and its people, thanks to the collaboration between the academic authors and the native Kuwaitis.

Kazakhstan
The Central Asian country, Kazakhstan, had approximately 35000 franchised outlets by 1998 (Aimanbetova *et al.*, 1998). Franchising is categorized by industry to better understand the level of franchise development and market penetration. Akhmetov and Raiskhanova (2001) described franchising from an institutional context and a development perspective, then went on to discuss the economic condition of the country and the reforms that have been established by the government that will enhance business development. Finally, the authors gave their viewpoint on particular franchise industries that they believed would thrive, with a discussion of future research that needs to be conducted, including an analysis of the potential for success of different franchises.

South Africa
Scholtz, in his 1996 and 1997 articles, described the state and penetration of franchising as a form of business in South Africa. He included an overview of the environment for franchising, the population and the legal regulations concerning franchising. In 1997, he reported that there were 170 franchise systems and 600 outlets operating in the country and that the market was ripe for further entry of international franchises.

Conclusion
We have attempted to answer the call for additional research in the area of emerging franchise markets worldwide, first by defining what an emerging market is, then summarizing the research from both a theoretical and a practical development perspective and by discussing specific franchise studies by world region. In doing this, we hope to have raised the level of understanding among franchisors, franchisees, franchise associations, consultants and academics concerning franchising around the globe. To our knowledge, this is the first attempt at summarizing the research on a global basis, from both a practitioner and an academic viewpoint. We hope this furthers the discussion of franchising in emerging markets and leads to a more comprehensive development of the international field of franchising.

References

Aimanbetova, G., B. Konurbaeva and D. Akishev (1998), 'The financial market of Kazakhstan in 1998', *Economic Trends*, October/November, 28–35.

Akhmetov, A. and R. Raiskhanova (2001), 'Franchising in Kazakhstan', in I. Alon and D.H.B. Welsh (eds), *International franchising in emerging markets: China, India, and other Asian countries*, Riverwoods, IL, US: CCH.

Alon, I. (2001), 'An interview with a Chinese franchisor in Shanghai: XiangShanShouShen – A beautification parlor', in I. Alon and D.H.B. Welsh (eds), *International franchising in emerging markets: China, India, and other Asian countries*, Riverwoods, IL, US: CCH.

Alon, I. and M. Banai (2001), 'Franchising opportunities and threats in Russia', in D.H.B. Welsh and I. Alon (eds), *International Franchising in Emerging Markets: Central and Eastern Europe and Latin America*, Riverwoods, IL, US: CCH.

Alon, I. and D.I. McKee (1999), 'Towards a macro-environmental model of international franchising', *Multinational Business Review*, 7 (1), 76–82.

Alshaya Company News, *http://www.alshaya.com/news.htm*, accessed 18/3/2001.

Alshaya Home Page, *http://www.alshaya.com/leader.htm*, accessed 18/3/2001.

Amies, M. (1999), 'The wilder shores of franchising', *Franchising World*, 31 (1), 27–28.

Arnold, D.J. and J.A. Quelch (1998), 'New strategies in emerging markets', *Sloan Management Review*, Fall, 7–20.

Business Wire (2000), 'Starbucks opens first retail store in Dubai, plans to expand into Qatar, Saudi Arabia and Bahrain by the end of the year', *http://www.businesswire.com/cnn/sbux.htm*.

Chan, P.S. and R. Justis (1990), 'Franchise management in East Asia', *Academy of Management Executive*, May, 75–85.

Chan, P.S. and R.T. Justis (1995), 'Franchising in Indonesia', *Proceedings of the International Society of Franchising*, San Juan, Puerto Rico/Minneapolis, MN: University of St. Thomas.

Chan, P.S., J.K.S. Foo, G. Quek and R.T. Justis (1994), 'A survey of franchising in Singapore', *Proceedings of the International Society of Franchising*, Las Vegas, NV/Minneapolis, MN: University of St. Thomas.

China National Tourism Administration (1993–2000), *The Yearbook of China Tourism Statistics*, Beijing: China Travel and Tourism Press.

Christy, R.L. and S.M. Haftel (1992), 'Franchising entry and developmental strategies in the former Soviet Union', *Proceedings of the International Society of Franchising*, Palm Springs, CA/Minneapolis, MN: University of St. Thomas.

Christy, R.L. and S.M. Haftel (1993), 'Pizza Hut in Moscow: Post-coup system development and expansion', *Proceedings of the International Society of Franchising*, San Francisco, CA/Minneapolis, MN: University of St. Thomas.

Cruz, T.D. (1999), 'Brand loyalty', *Hotels*, Feb. 51–4.

Cuevas, L. and D. Johnson (2001), 'Methods to build international business: Starbucks demonstrates successful expansion methods', *Signs of the Times*, *http://www.signweb.com/management/cont/management0900.html*.

Czinkota M.R. and I.A. Ronkainen (1997), 'International business and trade in the next decade: Report from a Delphi study', Georgetown University Working Paper, 1777–25–297, Washington, DC.

Dahlstrom, R. and A. Nygaard (1999), 'Ownership decisions in plural contractual systems: Twelve networks from the quick service restaurant industry', *European Journal of Marketing*, 33 (1/2), 59–87.

Dana, L.P., H. Etemad and R.W. Wright (2001), 'Franchising in Emerging Markets: Symbiotic interdependence within marketing networks', in D.H.B. Welsh and I. Alon (eds), *International Franchising in Emerging Markets: Central and Eastern Europe and Latin America*, Riverwoods, IL, US: CCH.

Dant, R.P. and P.J. Kaufmann (2001), 'The emerging empirical patterns of franchising in India', in I. Alon and D.H.B. Welsh (eds), *International franchising in emerging markets: China, India, and other Asian countries*, Riverwoods, IL, US: CCH.

Dheer, R. and S.L. Gupta (1999), *Franchising Workshop in Mumbai IM1990302*, US and Foreign Commercial Service and US Dept. of State: Washington, DC.

English, W. (2001), 'Franchising in China: Y2K update', in I. Alon and D.H.B. Welsh (eds), *International Franchising in Emerging Markets: China, India and other Asian Countries*, Riverwoods, IL, US: CCH.

English, W. and C. Xau (1994), 'Franchising in China: A look at KFC and McDonald's', *Proceedings of the International Society of Franchising*, Las Vegas, NV.

English, W. and C. Xau (2001), 'Franchising in China: A look at KFC and McDonald's', in D.H.B. Welsh and I. Alon (eds), *International Franchising in Emerging Markets: Central and Eastern Europe and Latin America*, Riverwoods, IL, US: CCH.

Falbe, C.M. and D.H.B. Welsh (1998), 'NAFTA and franchising: A comparison of franchisor perceptions of characteristics associated with franchisee success and failure in Canada, Mexico and the United States', *Journal of Business Venturing*, 13 (2),151–71.

Falbe, C.M. and D.H.B. Welsh (2001), 'NAFTA and franchising: A comparison of franchisor perceptions of characteristics associated with franchisee success and failure in Canada, Mexico and the United States', in D.H.B. Welsh and I. Alon (eds), *International Franchising in Emerging Markets: Central and Eastern Europe and Latin America*, Riverwoods, IL, US: CCH.

Goh, M. (2001), 'Singapore's local franchise industry: An assessment', in I. Alon and D.H.B. Welsh (eds), *International franchising in emerging economies: China, India, and other Asian countries*, Riverwoods, IL, US: CCH.

Goh, M. and H. Lee (1996), 'Local franchising development in Singapore', *Franchising Research: An International Journal*, 1 (3), 8–20.

Grimaldi, A. (1992), 'Franchising opportunities in the free trade zones of developing countries', *Proceedings of the International Society of Franchising*, Palm Springs, CA. Minneapolis, MN: University of St. Thomas.

Hadjimarcou, J. and J.W. Barnes (1998), 'Case study: Strategic alliances in international franchising – the entry of Silver Streak Restaurant Corporation into Mexico', *Journal of Consumer Marketing*, 15 (6), 598–607.

Hadjimarcou, J. and J.W. Barnes (2001), 'Strategic alliances in international franchising – The entry of Silver Streak restaurant corporation into Mexico', in D.H.B. Welsh and I. Alon (eds), *International Franchising in Emerging Markets: Central and Eastern Europe and Latin America*, Riverwoods, IL, US: CCH.

Han, A. (2001), 'Legal aspects of franchising in China', in I. Alon and D.H.B. Welsh (eds), *International franchising in emerging markets: China, India, and other Asian countries*, Riverwoods, IL, US: CCH.

Hoon, R.T.W. (2001), 'Entering China: The experience of the MRI franchise in the new market', in I.Alon and D.H.B. Welsh (eds), *International franchising in emerging markets: China, India, and other Asian countries*, Riverwoods, IL, US: CCH.

International Franchise Research Centre (2000), 'World wide franchising statistics', IFRC Web Site (*www.wmin.ac.uk/~purdydl*).

Josias, A. and F.S. McIntyre (1995), 'Franchising in Brazil', *Proceedings of the International Society of Franchising*, San Juan, Puerto Rico/Minneapolis, MN: University of St. Thomas.

Justis, R.T., W. Nielson and S.J. Yoo (1988), 'Franchising in Asia', *Proceedings of the International Society of Franchising*, San Francisco, CA.

Khan, M.A. and M.M. Khan (2001), 'Emerging markets for restaurant franchising in Middle Eastern countries', in I. Alon and D.H.B. Welsh (eds), *International franchising in emerging markets: China, India, and other Asian countries*, Riverwoods, IL, US: CCH.

Kaufmann, P.J. (2001), 'International business format franchising and retail entrepreneurship: A possible source of retail know-how for developing countries – post-script', in D.H.B. Welsh and I. Alon (eds), *International Franchising in Emerging Markets: Central and Eastern Europe and Latin America*, Riverwoods, IL: CCH.

Kaufmann, P.J. and H. Leibenstein (1988), 'International business format franchising and retail entrepreneurship: A possible source of retail know-how for developing countries', *Journal of Development Planning*, 18, 165–79.

Kumarkaushalam (2000), 'There's money in franchising and this dotcom wants a share', *Financial Express*, August 4.

Lafontaine, F. and J. Oxley (2000), 'International franchising: Evidence from US and Canadian franchisors in Mexico', *Proceedings of the International Society of Franchising*, San Diego, CA/Minneapolis, MN: University of St. Thomas.

McCosker, C.F. (1996), 'Franchising into Asia: An overview of selected target markets', *Proceedings of the International Society of Franchising*, Honolulu, HI/Minneapolis, MN: University of St. Thomas.

McIntyre, F. (2001), 'Franchising in Brazil', in D.H.B. Welsh and I. Alon (eds), *International Franchising in Emerging Markets: Central and Eastern Europe and Latin America*, Riverwoods, IL, US: CCH.

Nair, S.R. (2001), 'Franchising opportunities in China from the perspective of a franchisee', in I. Alon and D.H.B. Welsh (eds), *International franchising in emerging markets: China, India, and other Asian countries*, Riverwoods, IL, US: CCH.

Nedialkova, A.A. (2001), 'Bulgaria – economic development and franchising', in D.H.B. Welsh and I. Alon (eds), *International Franchising in Emerging Markets: Central and Eastern Europe and Latin America*, Riverwoods, IL, US: CCH.

Overholt, W.H. (1993), *China, the Next Economic Superpower*, London: Weidenfeld and Nicolson.

Pal, C.Y. (2001), 'India's "big emerging market" opporunity', *Franchising World*, 32 (May/June), 63.

Paswan, A.K. and R.P. Dant (1995), 'Franchising in India: An introduction', *Proceedings of the International Society of Franchising*, San Juan, Puerto Rico/Minneapolis, MN: University of St. Thomas.

Paswan, A.K., R.P. Dant and J.A. Young (2001), 'The evolution of franchising in India: Prospects and caveats', in I. Alon and D.H.B. Welsh (eds), *International franchising in emerging markets: China, India, and other Asian countries*, Riverwoods, IL, US: CCH.

Paswan, A.K., J.A. Young and S.P. Kantamneni (2001), 'Public opinion about franchising in an emerging market: An exploratory investigation involving Indian consumers', in I. Alon and D.H.B. Welsh (eds), *International franchising in emerging markets: China, India, and other Asian countries*, Riverwoods, IL, US: CCH.

Pavlin, I. (1998), 'Franchising in Slovenia: Support to the development of franchise systems in Central Europe', *Proceedings of the International Society of Franchising*, Las Vegas, NV/Minneapolis, MN: University of St. Thomas.

Pavlin, I. (2000), 'New trends in Slovenian franchising', *Proceedings of the International Society of Franchising*, San Diego, CA/Minneapolis, MN: University of St. Thomas.

Pavlin, I. (2001), 'New trends in Slovenian franchising', in D.H.B. Welsh and I. Alon (eds), *International Franchising in Emerging Markets: Central and Eastern Europe and Latin America*, Riverwoods, IL, US: CCH.

Pine, R., H.Q. Zhang and P. Qi (2001), 'The challenges and opportunities of franchising in China's hotel industry', in I. Alon and D.H.B. Welsh (eds), *International franchising in emerging markets: China, India, and other Asian countries*, Riverwoods, IL, US: CCH.

Raven, P.V., D.H.B. Welsh and N. Al-Mutair (2001), 'Starbucks international coffee in Kuwait: Gateway to the Persian Gulf', in I. Alon and D.H.B. Welsh (eds), *International franchising in emerging markets: China, India, and other Asian countries*, Riverwoods, IL, US: CCH.

Sanghavi, N. (1997), 'Franchising as a tool for SME development in transitional economies: The case of Central European countries', *Proceedings of the International Society of Franchising*, Orlando, FL/Minneapolis, MN: University of St. Thomas.

Sanghavi, N. (2001), 'The use of franchising as a tool in SME development in developing economies: The case of Central European countries', in D.H.B. Welsh and I. Alon (eds), *International Franchising in Emerging Markets: Central and Eastern Europe and Latin America*, Riverwoods, IL: CCH.

Scholtz, G.J. (1996), 'Franchising in South Africa', *Proceedings of the International Society of Franchising*, Honolulu, HI/Minneapolis, MN: University of St. Thomas.

Scholtz, G.J. (1997), 'An overview of South African franchising', *Franchising Research: An International Journal*, 2 (4), 145–51.

Singapore Trade and Development Board (1999), *Singapore Franchise Industry Survey 1999*, Singapore: Singapore Trade and Development Board.

Seattle Post – Intelligencer (1999), 'Starbucks opens another store abroad – in Kuwait', Seattle, WA, February 15.

Stanworth, J., S. Price and D. Purdy (2001), 'Franchising as a source of technology transfer to developing countries', in D.H.B. Welsh and I. Alon (eds), *International Franchising in Emerging Markets: Central and Eastern Europe and Latin America*, Riverwoods, IL, US: CCH.

Swartz, L.N. (2001), 'Franchising successfully circles the globe', in D.H.B. Welsh and I. Alon (eds), *International Franchising in Emerging Markets: Central and Eastern Europe and Latin America*, Riverwoods, IL: CCH.

Swerdlow, S. and N. Bushmarin (1994), 'Does format management master Marxism in post-coup Russia? Franchise system mentality creeps into the lodging industry', *Proceedings of the International Society of Franchising*, Las Vegas, NV/Minneapolis, MN: University of St. Thomas.

Swerdlow, S. and D.H.B. Welsh (1992), 'The future of franchising in the U.S.S.R.: A statistical analysis of the opinions of Soviet university students', *Proceedings of the International Society of Franchising*, Palm Springs, CA/Minneapolis, MN: University of St. Thomas.

Swerdlow, S., W.S. Roehl and D.H.B. Welsh (2001), 'Hospitality franchising in Russia for the 21st century: Issues, strategies and challenges', in D.H.B. Welsh and I. Alon (eds), *International Franchising in Emerging markets: Central and Eastern Europe and Latin America*, Riverwoods, IL, US: CCH.

Teegan, H. (2001), 'Franchising in Mexico', in D.H.B.Welsh and I. Alon (eds), *International Franchising in Emerging Markets: Central and Eastern Europe and Latin America*, Riverwoods, IL, US: CCH.

Thompson, M. and B. Merrilees (2001), 'A modular approach to branding and operations for international franchising systems in emerging markets', in D.H.B. Welsh and I. Alon (eds), *International Franchising in Emerging Markets: Central and Eastern Europe and Latin America*, Riverwoods, IL, US: CCH.

Viducic, L. (2001), 'The role of franchising in establishing and internationalization of business with special reference to Croatia', in D.H.B. Welsh and I. Alon (eds), *International Franchising in Emerging Markets: Central and Eastern Europe and Latin America*, Riverwoods, IL, US: CCH.

Welsh, D.H.B. (2001). 'NAFTA and franchising: A post-script', in D.H.B. Welsh and I. Alon (eds), *International Franchising in Emerging Markets: Central and Eastern Europe and Latin America,* Riverwoods, IL, US: CCH.

Welsh, D.H.B. and S. Swerdlow, (1991), 'Opportunities and challenges for franchisors in the U.S.S.R.: Preliminary results of a survey of Soviet university students', *Proceedings of the International Society of Franchising*, Miami Beach, FL.

Welsh, D.H.B. and S. Swerdlow (1993), 'A cross-cultural study of American and Russian hotel employees: A preliminary review and its implications for franchisors', *Proceedings of the International Society of Franchising*, San Francisco, CA.

Welsh, D.H.B., P. Raven and F.Al-Bisher (1996), 'The case of the elegant shoplifter, Shuwaikh, Kuwait', *Franchising Research: An International Journal*, 1 (3), 43–5.

Welsh, D.H.B., P.V. Raven and F. Al-Bisher (2001), 'Franchise relations in the Gulf Region: The case of the elegant shoplifter', in I. Alon and D.H.B. Welsh (eds), *International franchising in emerging markets: China, India, and other Asian countries*, Riverwoods, IL, US: CCH.

Willems, J., W. English and V. Ito (1992), 'Pizzas in Mexico? Si!', *Proceedings of the International Society of Franchising*, Palm Springs, CA.

Winsor, R.D. and R.L. Quinonee (1994), 'The nature and scope of franchising: A review of functional and legal definitions', in Skip Swerdlow (ed.), *Understanding and Accepting Different Perspectives: Empowering Relationships in 1994 and Beyond*, Las Vegas, NV: paper no. 12.

Young, J.A., F.S. McIntyre and R.D. Green (2000), 'The International Society of Franchising: A thirteen-year review', *Proceedings of the International Society of Franchising*, San Diego, CA.

38 A model for the choice of organizational form in international franchising

V. Nilakant, Callum J. Floyd and Mary Ellen Gordon

Franchising has become ubiquitous, not only locally but also globally (Quinn, 1999). Over one-third of all retail sales in the United States pass through franchises, making franchising a dominant mode of retail entrepreneurship in the United States (Bradach, 1997; Shane, 1998). The growth rate of franchising is comparable to that of the US economy as a whole since 1986, with more than 200 new franchises appearing each year (Lafontaine and Shaw, 1998; Shane and Spell, 1998). As the franchise business arrangement is also a government-supported form of international involvement, business format franchising is becoming a preferred method of entry into foreign markets (Alon and McKee, 1999; Eroglu, 1992; Welch, 1989).

Despite its increased use, franchising is a complex phenomenon (Bradach and Eccles, 1989). It can be simultaneously viewed as an organizational arrangement, a governance mechanism or a resource exchange process. Outwardly, the franchise chain may seem like a simple organizational form seeking to provide a standardized product or service. McDonald's exemplifies this replication of a simple business concept, providing stringent selection, training, operating and monitoring practices, so that customers receive a similar experience at over 8000 restaurants in the United States and 26000 worldwide. While units of this franchise system and many others appear strikingly similar, beneath may reside complex strata of heterogeneous organizational arrangements. Franchise systems often comprise both company-owned and franchised units (Brickley and Dark, 1987; Caves and Murphy, 1976; Lafontaine and Kaufmann, 1994; Rubin, 1978; Shane, 1996). More importantly, franchised units can be linked to the franchiser through two arrangements called single-unit and multi-unit franchising (Bradach, 1998; Kaufmann, 1992; Kaufmann & Dant, 1996; Kaufmann & Kim, 1995; Lowell, 1991). To add to this complexity, multi-unit forms consist of a variety of organizational designs that can be categorized as direct and indirect forms. Despite its ubiquity and complexity, franchising is scarcely mentioned in books that survey the literature in organization theory (Bradach, 1997).

International franchisers face a bewildering array of choices with respect to franchising form. While there is growing interest in studying internationalization of franchising, there is little research in the choice of franchising form that is appropriate for a given foreign market. This chapter seeks to fill this gap by providing a conceptual model that can help international franchisers choose an appropriate franchising form. The model is based on an integration of franchising with extant organization theory and is motivated by a view of franchising primarily as an organizational arrangement. We address the issue of diversity of organizational forms in franchising, which despite its prevalence, is poorly understood (Bradach, 1995, 1998; Kaufmann and Dant, 1996; Kaufmann and Kim, 1995). We build on a structural contingency perspective to argue that environmental and task contingencies shape organizational forms by influencing organizational design criteria. We specify these criteria and show how each design criterion is associated with ex ante and ex post transaction costs. In doing so, we seek to shed light on the organizational design decisions in international franchising by elucidating the role of transaction costs in influencing the choice of organizational form. Analysing the phenomenon of franchising as an organizational arrangement, we seek to contribute to organization theory by unbundling the concept of fit in terms of transaction costs and by showing how these costs are embedded in specific environmental and task contexts.

The chapter is arranged as follows. First, we present basic aspects of business format franchising and describe the five organizational forms in franchising. Second, we survey the literature on franchising and propose a framework to theorize about organizational design choices in franchising. Third, we discuss the influence of environmental uncertainty. Fourth, we examine the influence of task uncertainty on organizational form. We also present specific propositions relating dimensions of environmental and task uncertainty to choice of franchising forms. We conclude by summarizing the chapter's contribution to international franchising and to extant organization theory.

Business format franchising

The focus of this paper is business format franchising (BFF), which accounts for nearly three-quarters of all franchise arrangements in the United States (Combs and Castrogiovanni, 1994). Typically, BFF involves the franchiser providing franchisees with a comprehensive business package including a product or service, trademark, methods of operations and continuing guidance (Hoffman and Preble, 1991). Well-recognized subsectors utilizing BFF include fast-food restaurants, domestic cleaners, business services, computer equipment, real estate, convenience food stores, car repairs and a variety of other products and services (Justis and Judd, 1986). This can be distinguished from product and trade name franchising which uses franchisees to distribute a product under a franchiser's trademark, and is common in car sales, retail petrol and soft drink distribution (Preble, 1995).

A franchise relationship involves a franchiser granting franchisees the right to operate a business format, comprising a product or service for sale to the market through satellite enterprises (Stern and Stanworth, 1994), often in particular locations (Norton, 1988b). The franchiser normally charges franchisees an initial fee for this right as well as royalties, typically a percentage of sales (Falbe and Dandridge, 1992; Norton, 1988a, 1988b; Shane, 1996; Rubin, 1978). Some also require franchisees to contribute an advertising fee to be used solely for advertising expenses (Desai, 1997). The essence of the franchise relationship is formalized in a franchise agreement, a legal document that provides legally binding obligations and duties on both franchiser and franchisee (Felstead, 1993). The franchiser's control may extend over a variety of aspects. These may include products sold, price, quality, hours of operation, conditions of the plant, inventory, insurance, personnel and accounting and auditing (Felstead, 1993; Rubin, 1978; Shane, 1996). Furthermore, the franchisee may be compelled to purchase inputs from the franchiser or from a list of approved suppliers (Norton, 1988a, 1988b; Rubin, 1978). The franchiser normally provides managerial assistance to the franchisee in areas such as site selection, store layout, promotions, an advice hotline, bookkeeping and so on, though the actual extent of continuing support among franchisers varies (Rubin, 1978).

Multi-unit franchising
Franchise systems can consist of a variety of franchising arrangements that may be grouped into two types of organizational arrangements. In *single-unit franchising,* franchisees operate a single franchise outlet (Kaufmann and Dant, 1996). This is consistent with a historical image of franchising (Caves and Murphy, 1976; Curran and Stanworth, 1983; Norton, 1988b, Oxenfeldt and Kelly, 1969; Rubin, 1978). Frequently, a franchisee may own more than one outlet, leading to *multi-unit franchising* forms (Baucus *et al.*, 1993; Bradach, 1995, 1998; Kaufmann, 1992; Kaufmann and Dant, 1996; Kaufmann and Kim, 1995; Lafontaine and Kaufmann, 1994). For example, in the study reported by Bradach (1997), 17 people owned half of KFC's 3592 franchise units. Multi-unit franchising is a pervasive phenomenon and offers an attractive business entry and growth option to international franchisers.

Broadly, multi-unit franchising forms can be further categorized into two groups, the *direct* and the *indirect* form. In the direct form, a high performing franchisee may be permitted to expand and purchase additional franchises on an incremental basis. This is called *sequential franchising* (Kaufmann, 1992; Kaufmann and Dant, 1996; Kaufmann and Kim, 1995). An important implication of sequential franchising is the necessity to hire employees as managers as it becomes increasingly difficult for the franchisee to maintain a direct operating role with each additional unit (Kaufmann, 1992). *Area development* involves the franchiser granting the franchisee the rights and obligation to establish and operate more than one franchised unit within a specific territory. Frequently, a development schedule will be agreed upon specifying a minimum rate of expansion and the area developer must have the financial and managerial capacity to develop the units (Lowell, 1991). As with sequential franchising, area development franchisees recruit employees to manage units. Both sequential franchising and area development constitute the direct form. However, the franchiser may still retain the right to establish new units through company outlets or single-unit franchising.

In the indirect form, the franchisee is granted the right to provide franchises to other parties (Lowell, 1991). This form is called *sub-franchising*. A sub-franchiser is responsible for regional or local issues affecting sub-franchisees such as site selection, training, operating assistance and monitoring – tasks normally performed by a franchiser in the direct form (ibid.). In addition, units are more likely to be owner-operated compared to the direct forms, although in some instances sub-franchisers may also be granted the right to own and operate franchises themselves (Justis and Judd, 1986; Kaufmann and Kim, 1995; Lowell, 1991). Typically, a development schedule may be specified. *Area representation* is a variation of sub-franchising in which the agreement also normally involves an exclusive territory and a development schedule (Lowell, 1991). Under an area representation agreement the franchiser grants an area representative the right to solicit prospective franchisees. The area representative furnishes franchisees with supporting services but does not recruit sub-franchisees. The type and extent of services provided by the area representative also varies and is frequently less than what is provided under sub-franchising agreements (ibid.). The indirect form comprises both sub-franchising and area representation agreements. Again, the franchiser will often reserve the right to establish company-owned operations or franchises within the territory offered to sub-franchisees and area representatives (ibid.).

Direct and indirect forms differ on two important aspects. First, in the indirect form, owners are more likely to manage units under sub-franchising and area representation agreements. In contrast, the direct forms may have more employee–managers. Second, in the indirect form, there is an additional layer of hierarchy and control between the franchiser and unit-level management. While, in the indirect forms, contracts exist between the franchiser and the area/area representatives, on the one hand, and between the franchisees and the area/area representatives, on the other, the franchiser still retains a non-contractual interest in the behaviour of the franchisees as it can influence consumer perceptions of the entire chain and, therefore, the franchiser's brand equity. Figure 38.1 illustrates the direct and indirect forms. Franchise systems may comprise more than one franchising form. For example, well-known fast-food systems Pizza Hut and McDonald's combine area developers, sequential multi-unit holders and company-owned units within their franchise systems (Kaufmann, 1993; Kroc, 1977; Love, 1985).

Theoretical issues in franchising
The franchising literature has mostly focused attention on two theoretical issues: why do firms choose to franchise and why do firms operate both company-owned and franchised outlets? There are two alternative explanations for firms choosing to franchise rather than expand through company ownership. The 'capital scarcity' or 'resource allocation theory' argues that firms choose franchising because they lack the necessary capital or managerial resources for expansion (Oxenfeldt and Kelly, 1969; Hunt, 1972). The second perspective, 'agency theory' (Baiman, 1982, 1990; Eisenhardt, 1985, 1988, 1989; Levinthal, 1988; Moore, 1981; Scapens, 1985) views organizational forms as arising out of the relationship between principals (franchisers) and agents (franchisees/managers). The theory invokes the principle of utility maximization to argue that the agent will not always act in the best interests of the principal (Jensen and Meckling, 1976). Agency theory identifies two impediments to effective contractual performance: moral hazard or the lack of effort on the part of the agent and adverse selection or the misrepresentation of ability by the agent (Fama and Jensen, 1983). While agency theory has been criticized for its underlying assumptions about human behaviour and organizational processes (Donaldson, 1990), it does offer a useful framework for examining franchising relationships. It is argued that franchising facilitates the reduction of the problems associated with adverse selection and moral hazard by making the franchisee the residual claimant on the proceeds of a franchised outlet (Combs and Ketchen, 1999).

The capital scarcity theory has been criticized on two counts. First, it is argued that franchisees are a costly source of capital compared to passive investors. This is because franchisees have a limited number of outlets and face greater risks. They are likely, therefore, to demand greater returns (Norton, 1995; Rubin, 1990). Second, it is argued that agency theory provides a more robust explanation precluding the necessity to invoke capital

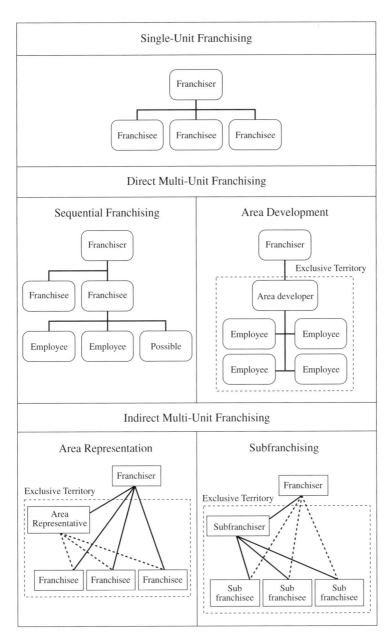

Source: Adapted from Kaufmann and Kim (1995).

Figure 38.1   Franchising forms

scarcity arguments (Shane, 1998). However, there is indirect support for the capital scarcity theory. In one study, access to capital was cited as a reason for franchising by 60 per cent of managers surveyed (Dant, 1995). There is evidence that franchising increases and falls in response to interest rate increases (Martin and Justis, 1993). This is seen as a support for the capital scarcity theory since interest rates influence the number of capital-scarce firms in an economy. Agency theory has also received empirical support. Brickley and Dark (1987) found that franchising was favoured over company ownership under conditions of high monitoring costs, low initial investment cost per unit and high frequency of repeat customers per unit. Thompson (1992) found that company ownership is favoured in urban areas and in areas where there are large numbers of units. Studies by Thomas *et al.* (1990) and Combs and Castrogiovanni (1994) also support agency theory arguments. While each theory has received modest empirical support, it is likely that together they may explain why firms choose to franchise.

Based on a study of 152 franchisers in the fast-food restaurant industry, Kaufmann and Dant (1996) found that the use of multi-unit franchising is positively related to growth rates. They argue that such an effect indicates that capital scarcity may be the reason for franchisers to use multi-unit franchising. This is because multi-unit franchising arrangements cannot control for shirking at the unit level. They also found that the level of commitment franchisers feel towards continuing to franchise is negatively related to the average number of units per franchisee and negatively related to their ability to obtain capital elsewhere. They conclude that this is 'consistent with the idea that agency and capital reasons are working in concert to explain franchising' (ibid.: 355). Combs and Ketchen (1999) tested predictions related to firms' franchising decisions based on agency theory and capital scarcity hypothesis on a sample of 91 restaurant chains. The study found that, while the agency variables were significant predictors of franchising, the capital scarcity variables explained additional variance. They concluded: 'Such a finding not only sheds light on a long-disputed aspect of franchising research but also points to the need for the application of multiple theories in studies of franchising literature' (ibid.: 205). While both these studies are based on the fast-food industry, making generalization to all franchise relationships somewhat problematic, the findings do indicate the need for the use of multiple perspectives for studying organizational arrangements such as franchising. Another study (Shane and Foo, 1999) supports the use of multiple perspectives in franchising research. The authors examined the survival of 1292 new franchisers established in the USA from 1979 to 1996. Their study supports the use of institutional explanations in addition to economic explanations for the survival of new franchisers.

The second issue that is both puzzling and contentious in franchising is the simultaneous operation of both company-owned and franchised outlets in franchise chains. This has not received a great deal of attention. Bradach (1997) refers to this simultaneous use of company-owned and franchised outlets as the plural form. Why do franchise chains prefer the plural form, given that they manifest contrasting economic and managerial characteristics? Again there are competing explanations for this puzzling phenomenon. The economic explanation is based on the use of the promotion-based incentive systems to motivate managers. It is argued that in some organizations the economies of scale associated with production are such that the corporate hierarchy is not large enough to provide promotion-based incentive systems for all lower-level managers (Brown, 1998). Therefore these organizations decide to franchise, since franchising provides an alternative incentive system. However, complete franchising is less optimal since the promotion-based system is more efficient. Thus the economic model argues that dual distribution or the plural form and franchising is a long-run equilibrium solution for organization.

Bradach (1997) offers an alternative organizational explanation. Using an ethnographic field study of five large US restaurant chains, he argues that the plural form enhances the performance of the chain overall by rectifying some of the weaknesses and elevating some of the strengths of the company-owned and franchise units. Specifically, he discusses four processes – modelling, ratcheting, socialization and mutual learning – that promote uniformity and system-wide adaptation. In his study, franchisees modelled the structure and practices of company-owned units to manage their multiple units. Ratcheting involved 'having each arrangement serve as a benchmark for the other on a variety of performance measures' (Bradach, 1998: 8). The socialization process involved using company people as franchisees. Mutual learning refers to the process where the franchisees and company-owned units complemented each other in generating, testing, selecting and implementing new ideas. In the absence of any empirical support for the economic model, Bradach's study offers a richer explanation for the prevalence of the plural form. The most important contribution of his study is the need to view organizational design choices in franchising in terms of a balance between conflicting demands of standardization and adaptation.

Organizational design issues in franchising
In theorizing about the diversity of organizational forms in franchising, we address two specific questions: what factors influence the choice between single-unit and multi-unit franchising, and what factors influence the choice between direct and indirect forms within multi-unit franchising? We build on the structural contingency notion that organizational design choices are

driven by the need to reduce environmental and task uncertainty (Burns and Stalker, 1961; Donaldson, 1987, 1995a, 1995b; Galbraith, 1973; Lawrence and Lorsch, 1967; Thompson, 1967). Therefore alternative organizational designs represent the decision makers' choices in managing different aspects of environmental and task uncertainties (Stinchcombe, 1990). In other words, environmental and task dimensions or contingencies influence the choice of organizational form. In order to map the nature of this influence, the environmental and task contingencies need to be identified and linked to specific organizational design criteria. Therefore we first operationalize the dimensions of environmental and task uncertainty based on the extant literature in structural contingency theory. Second, we propose four design criteria based on the extant literature on franchising forms (Bradach, 1998; Kaufmann and Eroglu, 1999) and link each criterion to specific dimensions of the environment and task uncertainty.

Structural contingency theory has paid a great deal of attention to the concept of environmental uncertainty. There is a well-established literature that conceptualizes environmental uncertainty in terms of three dimensions. These are *munificence*, or capacity of the environment, *dynamism*, or turbulence in the environment, and *complexity*, in terms of heterogeneity and dispersion (Aldrich, 1979; Child, 1972; Duncan, 1972; Mintzberg, 1979; Scott, 1981; Dess and Beard, 1984). We operationalize munificence as the size and growth of the market. We define demand size as total market sales for a particular product/service within a domestic economy. Demand growth refers to the change in total market sales for a particular product/ service sector within a domestic economy. Accordingly, we propose demand size and demand growth as the two variables associated with munificence. We propose intensity of rivalry as a measure of environmental dynamism. Intense rivalry leads to the introduction of new products and services, calls for flexibility and adaptation and heightens uncertainty for rival organizations. Managerial efficiency becomes paramount in administering chain units. Intensity of rivalry calls for system-wide efficiency, more diligent unit managers, clear communication, and power to make adaptations and monitor effectively on a system-wide basis. We propose demand heterogeneity and demand dispersion as measures of environmental complexity. Apart from size, growth and heterogeneity, demand may also be geographically dispersed.

Finally, in structural contingency theory, task uncertainty has been operationalized in terms of diversity of outputs, number of different input resources utilized and the level of goal difficulty (Galbraith, 1973). We argue that task uncertainty is related to the product/service features of a franchise and operationalize it in terms of product-line breadth, number of suppliers and inputs and product complexity.

Organizational design criteria in franchising
We contend that a franchising form must provide for four design criteria:
(a) growth by adding units, (b) standardization by ensuring uniformity,
consistency and system-wide implementation of new ideas, (c) local responsiveness by responding to variations in local demand, and (d) management of task complexity.

The importance of growth as a design criterion is well established in the
franchising literature. It has been shown that the use of franchising not only
overcomes managerial limits to growth but also enhances firm growth and
survival (Lafontaine, 1992; Kaufmann and Dant, 1996; Shane, 1996). In
franchise chains, typically growth is associated with addition of new units,
since existing units are unable to grow beyond a certain limit imposed by
their location (Bradach, 1998). Demand size and demand growth are the
two key environmental variables associated with growth. The size of the
total market influences the feasibility of growth. Establishing chain unit
and sales growth at a rate commensurate with increases in demand is
important as any lag means missed opportunities, which may result in the
creation of new and/or larger competitors.

The second design criterion is standardization. Standardization not only
reduces costs by achieving economies of scale but also reduces the cost of
monitoring quality across units (Kaufmann and Eroglu, 1999). While franchising may convert franchisees into residual claimants and take care of the
problem of suboptimal effort, it is unable to deal with the problem of misdirected effort (Shane, 1996). Hence monitoring is still needed to minimize
misdirected effort. Standardization reduces the cost of monitoring by quan-
tifying subjective properties such as quality or convenience (Kaufmann and
Eroglu, 1999). Standardization also reduces costs by minimizing duplication of systems and practices. Therefore it is directly associated with a strategy of cost minimization. However, standardization also affords benefits
other than cost minimization. It permits consistency of image and service
(ibid.). Uniformity in terms of image and service is critical in establishing a
favourable market position. Standardization also facilitates the introduction of new products and services by providing the franchiser with better
information about changes to the system and by facilitating system-wide
implementation (ibid.). Intensity of rivalry is the environmental driver for
standardization. This is because competition reduces profit margins and
pushes franchisers towards greater cost savings. As markets get saturated
and rivalry intensifies, cost minimization becomes an attractive option.
Standardization helps franchisers to reduce costs.

The third design criterion is local adaptation. Local adaptation is critical when a franchise chain operates in diverse or changing markets.
Meeting local requirements becomes paramount for the unit operator.

However, the need for local adaptation may conflict with the franchise chain's requirement for uniformity and standardization (Bradach, 1998). Therefore local adaptation needs to be balanced by standardization. This conflict between adaptation at the local level and standardization at the system level increases the importance of four areas of franchise system management. First, chain unit managers must be diligent in order to identify and respond to customer wants and be motivated to communicate important market information to the franchiser. Second, there must be clear communication paths for accurate and timely flows of information. Third, the franchiser must maintain bargaining power over franchisees to assist adaptation at the chain-unit level. Finally, bargaining power is also required for effective monitoring, to ensure conformity with standardized practices. Local adaptation is related to both diversity in markets and the dispersed nature of demand (Kaufmann and Eroglu, 1999). Heterogeneous demand requires unit operators to be locally responsive. Dispersed demand means chain units must be established in locations geographically removed from their franchiser. We expect demand heterogeneity to be associated with local adaptation and demand dispersion to be associated with both local adaptation and growth.

The fourth design criterion is managing task complexity. In a franchise, four features of the product/service offerings contribute to task complexity. *Product-line breadth* (PLB) refers to the number of different product types or services that chain units offer to customers; accordingly, some businesses may have a narrow PLB while others have a broad PLB. For example, a specialist retailer may carry a smaller range of stock compared to a general retailer. *Number of suppliers* refers to the number of separate entities from whom a franchise sources products that are offered to customers. *The number of inputs* refers to the number of product inputs involved in the product/service offering. Finally, *product complexity* refers to the relative simplicity/complexity of preparing the product/service mix for customers. PLB, the number of suppliers and the number of inputs also affect product complexity. We propose that product/service features of a franchise drive the need to manage task complexity.

These four structural requirements with their associated environmental/task dimensions are summarized in Table 38.1. Environmental and task contingencies influence the choice of design criteria in franchising. Given specific environmental and task contingencies, franchisers must choose an organizational form that is superior in meeting the design criterion associated with the specific environmental or task dimension. The notion of 'fit' or alignment in structural contingency theory captures this idea of linking environmental/task drivers with organizational design attributes of fit (Van de Ven and Drazin, 1985). However, in this chapter we have adopted a

Table 38.1   *Environmental/task dimensions and organizational design
criteria in franchising*

Environmental/task dimensions based on structural contingency theory	Organizational design criteria based on franchising literature
Munificence operationalized as demand size & demand growth	Growth
Dynamism operationalized as intensity of rivalry	Standardization
Complexity operationalized as demand heterogeneity & demand dispersion	Local adaptation
Task complexity operationalized as product-line breadth, number of suppliers, number of inputs and product complexity	Management of task complexity

different approach. We depart from contingency theory by including two other sources of uncertainty that are ignored by the theory.

Choice of organizational form in franchising
The central idea in contingency theory is that environmental and task uncertainties influence the design of organizational forms. However, these two sources of uncertainty do not exhaust all the sources of uncertainty that impinge on an organization. There are other significant sources of uncertainty that have an impact on organizational design choices. As Stinchcombe (1990) notes, one of the most complex uncertainties facing organizations concerns the ability and willingness of people to do the work. This is particularly significant in the franchising context. Franchisers face two types of uncertainty relating to the ability and willingness of people. First, they face uncertainty while recruiting potential franchisees. They may be unsure about the franchisee's ability to manage the unit in the overall interest of the chain. They need to be able to attract the right people, select the most competent, and train them adequately to ensure overall effectiveness. Second, franchisers face uncertainty with regard to franchisees' performance. They may be unsure whether the franchisees have made the optimal effort in the overall interest of the chain. They need to motivate, monitor and manage the franchisees to ensure the overall effectiveness of the chain.

These uncertainties impose significant costs on the franchiser. Using transaction costs economics terminology, we refer to them as ex ante and ex post costs. Ex ante costs refer to the costs associated with attracting, selecting, training and establishing franchisees. Ex post costs refer to the costs associated with motivating, managing, monitoring franchisees and also ensuring conformity of franchisees with standardized practices. Alternatively, the two types of uncertainties can also be conceptualized within an agency theory framework. The first type of uncertainty that relates to franchisee recruitment and ability is a problem of adverse selection or hidden information, while the second type of uncertainty relating to franchisee willingness is a problem of moral hazard or hidden effort (Arrow, 1985; Bergen *et al.*, 1992).

Agency theory and transaction costs economics have both commonalties and differences. They both emphasize a managerial discretion set-up and efficient contracting, but differ with respect to unit of analysis, focal cost concern and contractual focus (Williamson, 1988). We contend that ex ante and ex post costs can be analysed using an agency theory framework. We support this argument by showing how ex post costs can be viewed in agency theory terms. Ex post costs are made up of two components: motivational costs, that is, the costs of motivating unit managers, and standardization costs, which are costs associated with ensuring uniformity and adaptation of standardized practices. The motivational problems are reduced to a great extent by making franchisees residual claimants. In accordance with agency theory, we expect franchisees or owner–operators to be more motivated than employee–managers in ensuring optimal performance of their units. Therefore we expect franchisers to incur lower costs in motivating owner–operators compared to employee–managers. Indirect forms have more owner–operators than employee–managers in comparison with the direct forms. Therefore we expect indirect forms to be associated with lower motivational costs. On the other hand, centralization of decisions about uniform practices tends to reduce standardization costs. When decision making is delegated, as in indirect forms, we expect standardization costs to be higher owing to duplication of systems and procedures. Therefore we expect indirect forms to have relatively higher standardization costs compared to the direct forms.

Each design criterion emphasizes one type of cost over the other. In the following section, we show that ex ante costs are associated with growth. Standardization and local responsiveness require greater attention to ex post costs. Task complexity is associated with both ex ante and ex post costs. Figure 38.2 summarizes our arguments. Franchising forms differ in their ability to mitigate these costs. Therefore comparison of costs offers a way to choose an optimal structure. More importantly, analysing these two uncertainties in terms of transaction costs is a useful way to unpack the concept of fit that is central to structural contingency theory. We analyse fit in terms of transaction costs and choose the form that minimizes these

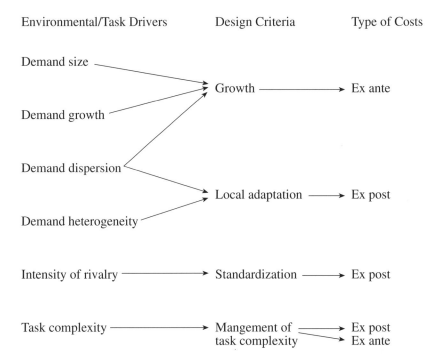

Environmental/Task Drivers   Design Criteria   Type of Costs

Figure 38.2   Relationship between environmental/task factors, design criteria and transaction costs

costs. In the following sections, we consider each of the environmental and task contingencies and analyse their impact on single- and multi-unit franchising in the first instance in terms of transaction costs. Subsequently, we compare direct and indirect forms within multi-unit franchising in terms of ex ante and ex post costs.

Influence of environmental uncertainty
Munificence
Demand size and demand growth constitute munificence. Both demand size and demand growth require the design to emphasize growth. Ex ante costs are crucial in assessing designs for growth. Higher demand size requires more units to be established and managed, imposing significant capital requirements and managerial burden on the franchiser. While the single-unit form provides the franchiser with direct control and, therefore, lowers ex post costs, multi-unit franchising enables the franchiser to economize on ex ante costs. This is not without disadvantages: owner involvement in units is reduced (Kaufmann, 1992) and franchisees acquire

bargaining power with additional units (Lowell, 1991). However, franchisers may be willing to trade control for lower ex ante costs. Therefore we propose:

> Proposition 1   When demand size is high, multi-unit franchising forms will be more prevalent compared to the single-unit form.

Given that multi-unit forms will be more prevalent, how does a franchiser choose between a direct and an indirect form? Both forms will lower ex ante costs compared to the single-unit franchising form; therefore we need to compare the motivational and standardization cost components of the ex post costs. A direct form will have more employee–managers compared to an indirect form. Therefore indirect forms with owner–operators will minimize motivational costs, but will compromise standardization costs by duplicating the franchisers' role through master franchisees. On the other hand, direct forms minimize standardization costs by providing franchiser support directly but jeopardize motivational costs through having more employee–managers. The franchiser is left to choose between faster growth through lower motivational costs in the indirect forms and advantages of greater standardization in the direct forms. Therefore the choice between direct and indirect forms is influenced by the franchiser's preference for standardization as opposed to rapid growth. Therefore we propose:

> Proposition 2   When demand size is high, the choice between direct and indirect forms will be mediated by the franchiser's strategic choice.

Single-unit franchising has lower growth potential because franchisers recruit, train and socialize new franchisees for each additional franchised unit. In other words, the ex ante costs of this form are high. Through enabling existing franchisees to expand, we anticipate multi-unit forms to yield greater growth prospects, while also economizing on franchiser resources. In terms of sales growth at the outlet level, however, we expect single-unit franchising to perform best. Direct multi-unit forms involve decreasing owner involvement, and hence productivity, in individual units. We expect that while sales growth per individual unit is compromised, these multi-unit forms provide greater potential for growth in the number of units, leading to larger overall growth. Indirect forms are also likely to enable faster growth in units as franchisers focus scarce resources on recruiting and training master franchisees that, in turn, establish and support multiple units within specified territories. Thus, with the recruitment of several master franchisees, these forms enable the simultaneous development of units in multiple markets/territories. In terms of sales growth at the unit level, these forms should perform similarly to the single-unit form since they preserve owner involvement at the unit level. In summary, we propose the following:

> Proposition 3   When demand growth is high, multi-unit franchising form will be more prevalent than the single-unit form.

The strategic choice between standardization and faster growth will mediate the choice between direct and indirect multi-unit forms. Sequential franchising and area development attempt to achieve growth while preserving cost efficiencies through centralizing franchiser support. However, they compromise unit-level growth by reducing owner involvement in unit-level operations. Conversely, area representation and sub-franchising preserve owner involvement to maximize output at the unit level. However, by duplicating the franchiser's role in different markets using master franchisees, they compromise standardization costs. Hence we propose the following:

> Proposition 4   When demand growth is high, the choice between direct and indirect forms will be mediated by the franchiser's strategic choice.

Complexity
We operationalize complexity as demand heterogeneity and demand dispersion. Demand heterogeneity imposes conflicting demands on the franchiser. On the one hand, units need to be responsive to local demand. This may require units to adopt different practices and will, therefore, be in conflict with the system's requirement for standardized practices. The franchiser needs to balance the conflicting demands of standardization and local responsiveness. Both standardization and local adaptation are related to ex post costs. Therefore, under conditions of heterogeneous demand, ex post costs become crucial. In keeping with agency theory, we expect that owner–managers will be more diligent and therefore more motivated than employee–managers to identify and respond to different customer requirements and pass information on to the franchiser. Accordingly, we propose that single-unit franchising will perform well in this regard. This receives some empirical support from Bradach's (1998) five-chain study, where he notes multi-unit franchisees providing fewer ideas than 'hands-on' owner–operators. The power with which each form provides the franchiser to

make adaptations and monitor chain units effectively becomes increasingly important with heterogeneous demand. Single-unit franchising provides the most appropriate form because the franchiser's power to make changes is reduced in multi-unit forms (Lowell, 1991). In indirect forms such as area representation and sub-franchising, unit management diligence should be similar to single-unit franchising, as each form is likely to have owner–managers. However, area representation and sub-franchising are likely to reduce the effectiveness of adaptations and monitoring since they compromise standardization costs. Therefore we suggest:

> Proposition 5   When demand heterogeneity is high, the single-unit franchising forms will be more prevalent than multi-unit forms.

Demand dispersion requires the establishment and management of geographically isolated outlets. Therefore both ex ante and ex post costs may be important. Ex ante costs are highest with single-unit franchising where new franchisees are recruited for each unit. Direct multi-unit forms economize on these costs. Sequential franchising enables the franchiser to economize on these costs through expanding existing high-performing, established and experienced franchisees. Granting an exclusive territory for multiple units from the outset, as in area development, lowers ex ante costs further.

When demand is dispersed, ex post costs are also crucial. Brickley and Dark (1987) proposed and found that the proportion of franchisee-owned units to company-owned units was greater with distance from franchiser headquarters. They concluded that employee–managers need more monitoring for suboptimal effort than franchisees because they do not have residual claims tied to the performance of their unit. Following this, we expect that sequential franchising and area development will incur greater ex post costs, since they have employee–managers who require supervision for suboptimal and misdirected effort. In terms of ex post costs, we expect the prevalence of single-unit franchising to be higher with high demand dispersion.

Compared to single-unit franchising, indirect forms such as area representation and sub-franchising reduce ex ante franchising costs as master franchisees under each arrangement undertake activities normally performed by the franchiser. Sub-franchising reduces these costs most since franchisers delegate more responsibilities with this form. They also reduce ex post costs. An area representative may, and a sub-franchiser almost certainly will, be granted tasks associated with monitoring franchisees within their territory. These forms, and especially sub-franchising, are also likely to reduce costs normally associated with the franchiser performing such tasks. Therefore we expect that area representation and sub-franchising will be more likely to be adopted with dispersed demand.

In summary, with high dispersion of demand, both ex ante and ex post costs point to increased prevalence of indirect forms such as area representation and sub-franchising. In terms of ex ante costs, we expect the increased prevalence of direct forms such as sequential franchising and area development. However, the opposite appears to be true in terms of ex post costs. We expect that the savings from ex ante costs will be greater than additional costs of monitoring that will increase the ex post costs. Thus, we propose the following:

Proposition 6   When demand dispersion is high, multi-unit forms will be more prevalent than the single-unit form.

Proposition 7   When demand dispersion is high, indirect multi-unit forms will be more prevalent than direct multi-unit forms.

Dynamism

We operationalize dynamism as intensity of rivalry. Intensity of rivalry requires the structure to be competitive in terms of maintaining uniformity, introducing new products and services and facilitating system-wide adaptation. Therefore standardization is the crucial structural requirement associated with rivalry. Standardization is directly related to ex post costs. Therefore intense rivalry increases the importance of ex post costs. We expect single-unit franchising to provide more diligent management than direct forms such as sequential franchising and area development since owners are more likely to be managers. We also expect sequential franchising to be better than area development since area development is likely to result in a greater prevalence of employee–managers. Single-unit franchising is also less likely to result in delay, distortion, exclusion or loss of important market information than sequential franchising and area development. This is because franchisees are more likely to report directly to the franchiser. Multi-unit forms such as sequential franchising and area development are likely to be less effective in communicating as employee–managers first communicate with the franchisee, who passes the information to the franchiser. Thus potential for delay, distortion, exclusion or loss of important information is increased (Stern and El Ansary, 1977). Therefore the single-unit franchising form has lower ex post franchising costs compared to the direct forms such as sequential franchising and area development. Inefficiencies are likely to be greatest in area development with a higher proportion of employee–managers.

Like single-unit franchising, indirect forms such as area representation and sub-franchising are likely to provide diligent owners as managers. Franchiser power for influencing and monitoring system-wide adaptations, however, is likely to be lower with area representation and sub-franchising, and we expect sub-franchising to reduce this power the most. Thus these two are likely to impede the speed and quality of chain unit adaptations. Compared to single-unit franchising, standardization costs are higher in area representation and sub-franchising through their additional hierarchy. Inefficiencies in this area are likely to be greatest with sub-franchising because sub-franchisers are delegated higher levels of responsibility than area representatives. In conclusion, we propose the following:

> Proposition 8   When intensity of rivalry is high, single-unit franchising will be more prevalent than the multi-unit forms.[1]

Influence of task uncertainty

The remaining four factors that can influence the choice of a franchise form are product-line breadth, number of suppliers, number of inputs and product complexity. Different levels of each factor affect the complexity of unit management. The more complex the task, the harder it is to find competent operators for the units. High task complexity requires greater emphasis on recruiting unit managers, unit management decision making, ensuring the quality of training and support, providing clear communication and monitoring quality. Therefore task complexity requires attention to both ex ante and ex post costs. With increasing task complexity, the quality of decision making, of training and support and of monitoring the franchise holders and unit managers becomes paramount. Ex ante costs will be higher because of the difficulties associated with attracting and selecting high-quality unit managers. However, hiring high-quality unit managers will reduce ex post costs because they are likely to make high quality decisions, and need less training, monitoring and support.

Ex ante costs will be lowest with single-unit franchising. The quality of individuals recruited will also be highest with single-unit franchising because the franchiser individually recruits and forms contracts with owner–managers. In contrast, in direct multi-unit forms, sequential franchisees and area developers are more likely to recruit employees as managers, increasing the risks of poor selection. This risk is greater with area development owing to the exclusive rights to multiple outlet units from the outset. Also single-unit franchising is less likely to result in the delay, distortion, exclusion or loss of important market information compared to both sequential franchising and area development.

Compared to single-unit franchising, we also expect indirect forms such as area representation and sub-franchising to have higher ex post costs, owing to the relative levels of responsibilities delegated to intermediaries. We expect recruitment quality to be poorest with sub-franchising, since the franchiser has less involvement in this process. Compared to single-unit franchising, we expect area representation and sub-franchising to compromise the quality of training and support. This is, again, due to the increasing responsibilities delegated to area representatives and sub-franchisers. The quality of monitoring is also likely to decrease with area representation and sub-franchising as monitoring is delegated to master franchisees. Our analysis suggests the following proposition:

Proposition 9   When task complexity is high, the single-unit franchising form will be more prevalent than the multi-unit forms.

Conclusion

The focus of this chapter is on the organizational design choices international franchisers face in choosing between single-unit and multi-unit forms first, and in selecting between direct and indirect forms within multi-unit franchising next. We propose that franchisers must choose organizational forms that reduce transaction costs within specific environmental and task contexts. A feature of franchise systems that is puzzling is that they may consist of more than one franchising form. For example, well-known fast-food systems Pizza Hut and McDonald's combine area developers, sequential multi-unit holders and company-owned units within their franchise systems (Kaufmann, 1993; Kroc, 1977; Love, 1985). How can this phenomenon be explained using our framework?

We propose that franchisers face changing environmental contingencies over a period of time. Multiple forms could be a result of choices made at different periods in response to specific contingencies. For example, in the initial phases of a product's life cycle, the growth in demand may be slow, resulting in the choice of single-unit franchising. As the product or service is established, demand may grow rapidly, resulting in multi-unit franchising forms. As the market becomes mature, the franchiser may again opt for either single-unit franchising or company-owned outlets. For instance, Pizza Hut has not offered any new franchise areas to the public, except for minority opportunity programmes, since 1971 (Kaufmann, 1993). The phenomenon also highlights two limitations in our framework. First, our framework does not address the choice of organizational arrangement within direct and indirect forms. Second, it does not include institutional factors such as sociopolitical approval that may influence transaction costs and, therefore, choice of organizational form (Shane and Foo, 1999).

Despite these limitations, this study contributes to extant organization theory in three ways. First, it seeks to integrate franchising with extant theory by adopting a structural contingency perspective to show how organizational design criteria are shaped by specific environmental and task contexts. We dimensionalize these environmental and task contingencies in terms of market and product features that are amenable to operationalization and measurement.

Second, it extends structural contingency theory by unpacking the concept of fit in terms of transaction costs. We show how each design criterion, and the environmental or task contingency that influences it, is associated with ex ante and ex post transaction costs. We argue that organizational forms that reduce transaction costs within specific environmental and task contexts will fit these environmental and task contingencies. Our comparison of alternative designs on these transaction costs is motivated by agency theory arguments.

Third, the study contributes to integrating transaction cost economics with extant organization theory. There has been a long-standing debate regarding the proliferation of perspectives within organization theory (Donaldson, 1995a; Pfeffer, 1993, 1997; Van Maanen, 1995a, 1995b). This debate has been accompanied by a concern over the dominance of economic theories of organization such as transaction cost economics and agency theory (Donaldson, 1990; Pfeffer, 1993). Both transaction cost economics and agency theory have been criticized on several counts. Transaction cost theory has been particularly criticized for lacking realism and balance in its analysis of organizational forms (Ghoshal and Moran, 1996; Moran and Ghoshal, 1996). We concur with this criticism and propose that transaction costs exist within a broader environmental context (Granovetter, 1985). In this study, we view transaction costs as being embedded in specific environmental and task contexts and operationalize these costs in terms of ex ante and ex post costs. Thus the study also seeks to illuminate how transaction cost contingencies shape organizational forms.

On a practical level, the chapter helps international franchisers to choose between alternative organizational designs in specific environmental or task contexts. We believe that this chapter is particularly relevant for franchisers seeking to enter or expand into emerging economies. With the gradual saturation of the US market, most growth for existing franchisers is likely to occur through international expansion. This chapter offers a framework to make new and appropriate choices about franchising forms in new markets.

Note

1. The empirical evidence may seem to contradict this proposition since fast-food chains such as McDonald's, Burger King and KFC all use multi-unit franchising. We argue that both demand size and demand growth may have initially led to the adoption of multi-unit forms in this industry. As markets become saturated, however, the intensity of rivalry increases. Once this happens, franchisers are more likely to prefer single-unit franchising. This preference is likely to influence the structure used for incremental units and may result in a restructuring of the existing franchise form.

References

Aldrich, H.E. (1979), *Organizations and environments*, Englewood Cliffs, NJ: Prentice-Hall.

Alon, Ilan and McKee, David L. (1999), 'The internationalisation of professional service franchises', *The Journal of Consumer Marketing*, 16 (1): 74–85.

Arrow, K.J. (1985), 'The economics of agency', in J.W. Pratt and R.J. Zeckhauser (eds), *Principles and agents: The structure of business*, Boston, MA: Harvard University Press, pp. 37–51.

Baiman, S. (1982), 'Agency research in managerial accounting: A survey', *Journal of Accounting Literature*, 1: 154–213.

Baiman, S. (1990), 'Agency research in managerial accounting: A second look', *Accounting, Organizations and Society*, 15(4): 341–71.

Baucus, D.A., Baucus, M.S. and Human, S.E. (1993), 'Choosing a franchise: How base fees and royalties relate to the value of the franchise', *Journal of Small Business Management*, 31: 91–104.

Bergen, M., Dutta, S. and Walker, O.C. Jr. (1992), 'Agency relationships in marketing: A review of the implications and applications of agency and related theories', *Journal of Marketing*, 56(3): 1–24.

Bradach, J.L. (1995), 'Chains within chains: The role of multi-unit franchisees', *Journal of Marketing Channels*, 4: 65–81.

Bradach, J.L. (1997), 'Using the plural form in the management of restaurant chains', *Administrative Science Quarterly*, 42: 276–303.

Bradach, J.L. (1998), *Franchise organizations*, Boston: Harvard Business School Press.

Bradach, J.L. and Eccles, R. (1989), 'Price, authority, and trust', *Annual Review of Sociology*, 15: 97–118.

Brickley, J.A. and Dark, F.H. (1987), 'The choice of organisational form: The case of franchising', *Journal of Financial Economics*, 18: 401–20.

Brown, W.O. (1998), 'Transaction costs, corporate hierarchies, and the theory of franchising', *Journal of Economic Behavior and Organization*, 36(3): 319–29.

Burns, T. and Stalker, G.M. (1961), *The management of innovation*, London: Tavistock.

Caves, R.E. and Murphy, W.F. (1976), 'Franchising firms, markets and intangible assets', *Southern Economic Journal*, 42: 572–86.

Child, J. (1972), 'Organisational structure, environment and performance: The role of strategic choice', *Sociology*, 6: 1–22.

Combs, J.G. and Castrogiovanni, G.J. (1994), 'Franchiser strategy: A proposed model and empirical test of franchise versus company ownership', *Journal of Small Business Management*, 32: 37–48.

Combs, J.G. and Ketchen, D.J. (1999), 'Can capital scarcity help agency theory explain franchising? Revisiting the capital scarcity hypothesis', *Academy of Management Journal*, 42(2): 196–207.

Curran, J. and Stanworth, J. (1983), 'Franchising in the modern economy – towards a theoretical understanding', *International Small Business Journal*, 2(1): 8–26.

Dant, R.P. (1995), 'Motivations for franchising: Rhetoric vs. reality', *International Small Business Journal*, 14: 10–32.

Desai, P.S. (1997), 'Advertising fee in business-format franchising', *Management Science*, 43: 1401–19.

Dess, G.G. and Beard, D.W. (1984), 'Dimensions of organisational task environments', *Administrative Science Quarterly*, 29: 52–71.

Donaldson, L. (1987), 'Strategy and structural adjustment to regain fit and performance: In defense of contingency theory', *Journal of Management Studies*, 24(1): 33–48.

Donaldson, L. (1990), 'The ethereal hand: Organisational economics and management theory', *Academy of Management Review*, 15(3): 369–81.

Donaldson, L. (1995a), *American anti-management theories of organization: A critique of paradigm proliferation*, Cambridge: Cambridge University Press.

Donaldson, L. (ed.) (1995b), *Contingency theory*, Brookefield, VT: Dartmouth.

Duncan, R.B. (1972), 'Characteristics of organisational environments and contingency theory', *Administrative Science Quarterly*, 17: 313–27.

Eisenhardt, K.M. (1985), 'Control: Organisational and economic approaches', *Management Science*, 31: 134–49.

Eisenhardt, K.M. (1988), 'Agency and institutional explanations of compensation in retail sales', *Academy of Management Journal*, 31: 488–511.

Eisenhardt, K.M. (1989), 'Agency theory: An assessment and review', *Academy of Management Review*, 14(1): 57–74.

Eroglu, Sevgin, (1992), 'The internationalisation process of franchise systems: A conceptual model', *International Marketing Review*, 9(5): 19–30.

Falbe, C.M. and Dandridge, T.C. (1992), 'Franchising as a strategic partnership: Issues of co-operation and conflict in a global market', *International Small Business Journal*, 10(3): 40–51.

Fama, E.F. and Jensen, M.C. (1983), 'Agency problems and residual claims', *Journal of Law and Economics*, 26: 327–49.

Felstead, A. (1993), *The corporate paradox: Power and control in the business franchise*, London: Routledge.

Galbraith, J. (1973), *Designing complex organizations*, Reading: Addison-Wesley.

Ghoshal, S. and Moran, P. (1996), 'Bad for practice: A critique of the transaction cost theory', *Academy of Management Review*, 21(1): 13–47.

Granovetter, M. (1985), 'Economic action and social structure: The problem of embeddedness', *American Journal of Sociology*, 91: 481–510.

Hoffman, R.C. and Preble, J.F. (1991), 'Franchising: Selecting a strategy for rapid growth', *Long Range Planning*, 24: 74–85.

Hunt, S.D. (1972), 'The socioeconomic consequences of the franchise system of distribution', *Journal of Marketing,* 2: 32–8.

Jensen, M.C. and Meckling, W.H. (1976), 'Theory of the firm: Managerial behavior, agency costs and ownership structure', *Journal of Financial Economics*, 3: 305–60.

Justis, R.T. and Judd, R. (1986), 'Master franchising: A new look', *Journal of Small Business Management*, 24(3): 16–21.

Kaufmann, P.J. (1992), 'The impact of managerial performance decay on franchisers' store allocation strategies', *Journal of Marketing Channels*, 1(4): 51–79.

Kaufmann, P.J. (1993), *Pizza Hut: Home delivery*, Boston: Harvard Case Services.

Kaufmann, P.J. and Dant, R.P. (1996), 'Multi-unit franchising: Growth and management issues', *Journal of Business Venturing*, 11: 343–58.

Kaufmann, P.J. and Ergolu, S. (1999), 'Standardization and adaptation in business format franchising', *Journal of Business Venturing*, 14(1): 69–85.

Kaufmann, P.J. and Kim, S.H.M. (1995), 'Master franchising and system growth rates', *Journal of Marketing Channels*, 4 (1 and 2), 49–64.

Kroc, R. (1977), *Grinding it out: The making of McDonald's*, Chicago: Contemporary Books.

Lafontaine, F. (1992), 'Agency theory and franchising: Some empirical results', *RAND Journal of Economics*, 23: 263–83.

Lafontaine, F. and Kaufmann, P.J. (1994), 'The evolution of ownership patterns in franchise systems', *Journal of Retailing*, 70(2): 97–113.

Lafontaine, F. and Shaw, K.L. (1998), 'Franchiser growth and franchiser entry and exit in the U.S. market: myth and reality', *Journal of Business Venturing*, 13(2): 95–112.

Lawrence, P.R. and Lorsch, J.W. (1967), *Organization and environment: Managing differentia-tion and integration*, Boston: Division of Research, Graduate School of Business Administration, Harvard University.

Levinthal, D. (1988), 'A survey of agency models of organizations', *Journal of Economic Behaviour and Organization*, 9: 153–85.

Love, J.F. (1985), *McDonald's: Behind the arches*, New York: Bantam.

Lowell, H.B. (1991), *Multiple-unit franchising: The key to rapid system growth*, Washington, DC: International Franchise Association.

Martin, R.E. and Justis, R.T. (1993), 'Franchising, liquidity constraints and entry', *Applied Economics*, 25(9): 1269–77.

Mintzberg, H. (1979), *The structuring of organizations. A synthesis of the research*, Englewood Cliffs, NJ: Prentice-Hall.

Moore, John H. (1981), 'Agency costs, technical change and Soviet central planning', *Journal of Law and Economics*, 24: 189–214.

Moran, P. and Ghoshal, S. (1996), 'Theories of economic organization: The case for realism and balance', *Academy of Management Review*, 21(1): 58–72.

Norton, S.W. (1988a), 'Franchising, brand name capital, and the entrepreneurial capacity problem', *Strategic Management Journal*, 9: 105–14.

Norton, S.W. (1988b), 'An empirical look at franchising as an organisational form', *Journal of Business*, 61(2): 197–218.

Norton, S.W. (1995), 'Is franchising a capital structure issue?', *Journal of Corporate Finance*, 2: 75–101.

Oxenfeldt, A.R. and Kelly, A.O. (1969), 'Will successful franchise systems ultimately become wholly-owned chains?', *Journal of Retailing*, 44(4): 69–83.

Pfeffer, J. (1993), 'Barriers to the advance of organization science: Paradigm development as a dependent variable', *Academy of Management Review*, 18: 599–620.

Pfeffer, J. (1997), *New directions for organization theory: Problems and prospects*, New York: Oxford University Press.

Preble, J.F. (1995), 'Franchising systems around the globe: A status report', *Journal of Small Business Management*, 33(2): 80–88.

Quinn, Barry (1999), 'Control and support in an international franchise network', *International Marketing Review*, 16(4/5), 345–62.

Rubin, P.H. (1978), 'The theory of the firm and the structure of the franchise contract', *The Journal of Law and Economics*, 21: 223–33.

Rubin, P.H. (1990), *Managing business transactions*, New York: Free Press.

Scapens, R.W. (1985), *Management accounting: a review of contemporary developments*, London: Macmillan.

Scott, W.R. (1981), *Organizations: Rational, natural and open systems*, Englewood Cliffs, NJ: Prentice-Hall.

Shane, S.A. (1996), 'Hybrid organisational arrangements and their implications for firm growth and survival: A study of new franchisers', *Academy of Management Journal*, 39(1): 216–34.

Shane, S. (1998), 'Research notes and communications: Making new franchise systems work', *Strategic Management Journal*, 19(7): 697–707.

Shane, S. and Foo, M. (1999), 'New firm survival: Institutional explanations for new fran-chiser mortality', *Management Science*, 45(2): 142–59.

Shane, S. and Spell, C. (1998), 'Factors for new franchise success', *Sloan Management Review*, Spring: 43–50.

Stern, L.W. and El Ansary, A.I. (1977), *Marketing channels*, Englewood Cliffs, NJ: Prentice-Hall.

Stern, P. and Stanworth, J. (1994), 'Improving small business survival rates via franchising – The role of the banks in Europe', *International Small Business Journal*, 12: 15–25.

Stinchcombe, Arthur L. (1990), *Information and Organizations*, Berkeley: University of California Press.

Thomas, W.L., O'Hara, M.J. and Musgrave, F.W. (1990), 'The effects of ownership and invest-ment upon the performance of franchise systems', *American–Economist*, 34(1): 54–61.

Thompson, J.D. (1967), *Organizations in action*, New York: McGraw-Hill.
Thompson, R.S. (1992), 'Company ownership versus franchising: Issues and evidence', *Journal of Economic Studies*, 19(4): 31–42.
Van de Ven, A.H. and Drazin, R. (1985), 'The concept of fit in contingency theory', *Research in Organisational Behavior*, 7: 333–65.
Van Maanen, J. (1995a), 'Fear and loathing in organization studies', *Organization Science,* 6: 687–92.
Van Maanen, J. (1995b), 'Style as organization theory', *Organization Science,* 1: 209–64.
Welch, Lawrence S. (1989), 'Diffusion of franchise system use in international operations', *International Marketing Review,* 6(5): 7–19.
Williamson, O.E. (1988), 'Corporate finance and corporate governance', *The Journal of Finance*, XLIII(3): 567–91.

PART FIVE

TOWARDS FUTURE RESEARCH IN INTERNATIONAL ENTREPRENEURSHIP

39 A network perspective of international entrepreneurship
Susanna Hinttu, Maria Forsman and Soren Kock

The purpose of this study is to develop the understanding of how social networks affect the internationalization processes of firms. Of particular interest is how social networks make a difference in terms of business partner selection. First we present a traditional theoretical framework to the internationalization process and focus more deeply on the network approach within the internationalization process. We continue by describing the social network approach and in more detail the impact of social networks on the internationalization of firms. Excerpts from empirical findings of different studies illustrate the theoretical discussion. Finally we conclude the discussion with implications and suggestions for further research.

Methods
When adopting a relationship approach some methodological difficulties need to be pointed out. An outsider may get a somewhat superficial comprehension of the relationship and the network the actor is involved in as a whole, since the actors may have different perceptions of the network. We do not consider networks as set structures but as subjectively perceived contexts more or less planned for activities having an impact on the internationalization process. Each actor has a network position in a specified network. Actors can be positively connected, implying a synergetic, cooperative relation, or negatively connected when they compete to develop exchange relationships with a third party (Bengtsson and Kock, 1999). Relationships are here assumed to be positive.

Our methodological approach is qualitative in the sense that we have conducted semi-structured interviews with key actors in selected firms. Some of the cases quoted are based on secondary data. The aim of the interviews was to try to pinpoint and describe the existing networks that the studied key actors are in. Since international integration is an important aspect of internationalization, strategic objectives to establish positive connections to other actors involve developing relationships with several different geographical regions (Hertz and Mattsson, 2002). Two dimensions of social networks may be recognized, actors embedded in a psychically closer national network and actors in a more distant international network. However, we draw attention to the importance of the international social network, consisting of considerable significant relationships when deciding on the partner selection.

The internationalization process
The conception of firms expanding into international markets in an incremental stepwise manner is well documented. Johanson and Vahlne (1977) probably provide the most commonly cited conceptual and empirical base for this notion, known as the Uppsala model. Their research stresses that managerial learning takes place during the internationalization process and shows that a series of stages of internationalization occurs as commitment and investments in foreign markets increase. According to the model, firms are often predicted to start the internationalization process by moving to markets psychically close to the domestic market and entering more distant markets at a later stage. After the initial expansion with low risk, indirect exporting to similar markets, firms will improve their foreign market knowledge and gain more experience. This leads to a greater increase in foreign market commitment and to expansion into more distant markets over time. The model also shows how managerial learning drives internationalization (Coviello and Munro 1997).

> Today, Firm C has agents in both Sweden and Australia, and also direct contacts established by the entrepreneur himself. In the future, the role of agents will be very limited. Direct contacts and probably also joint ventures will come in [to] the picture. The entrepreneur has become friends with other managers he has met at fairs abroad or via clients, from whom he has learned a lot, and vice versa. They know the business in the country concerned, and have operated for a long time there; the entrepreneur believes that, in the long run, they will act as godfathers, to help them to get into the markets. (Hurmerinta-Peltomaki, 2001)

Christensen and Lindmark (1993) claim that the present models of internationalization take into account only problems more characteristic of large firms and that these models do not consider the importance of the network context or the case of social networks. Findings suggesting that the model of internationalization is somewhat different for small firms from larger corporations, and thus results particularly interesting for this study, are presented by Lindqvist (1988) and Bell (1995). They suggest that the pattern of internationalization and the entry mode choice of small firms may be influenced by, among other factors, close relationships with customers (Lindqvist, 1988) and that inter-firm relationships (with clients, suppliers and so on) appear influential in both market selection and mode of entry for small firms (Bell 1995).

Johanson and Vahlne (1992) found foreign market entry to be a gradual process, resulting from interaction between parties that are developing and maintaining relationships over time. A sequential search process is likely to be undertaken, first by contacting actors the firm has direct relationships with and, later, actors with whom the firm has indirect relationships. Using the social network as an information source and also as a potential partner search area is common. Researchers within the area of internationalization have started to examine the important role of personal relationships in promoting business (Agndal and Axelsson, 2002) but so far research is modest when it comes to the development of business relationships. 'The last few years we could have sold more boats than we can build. We haven't had to do any marketing at all, with old contacts . . . we have easily sold everything the firm has produced' (personal interview with Marketing Director Johansson, Baltic Yachts); 'Information about the competitors and new opportunities are obtained from personal relationships as well as from the customers, Internet and agents' (personal interview with Managing Director Staffans, Baltic Yachts).

The conclusions from studies made by Holmlund and Kock (1998) is that firms are not able to increase their rate of international business beyond a certain level in accordance with the stage model. The authors, however, do not elaborate on the reason why some firms are able to extend their business abroad quite rapidly when others get stuck at one of the first stages in the stage model described.

The network perspective further develops the models of incremental internationalization by suggesting that a strategy of a firm emerges as a pattern of behaviour influenced by a variety of network relationships (Coviello and Munro, 1997).

Internationalization and the network model

Based on the degree of internationalization of the market and the firm, respectively, a model has been developed by Johanson and Mattsson (1988) (see Figure 39.1). As demonstrated by the model, firms have access to and need for different resources during different market conditions.

A firm with few international business relationships and whose competitors and suppliers are in the same position can be categorized as 'The Early Starter'. The firm has little knowledge of foreign markets and has little opportunity to acquire knowledge from its relationships in the home market. An agent can, however, provide information about ways to enter a market abroad. Consequently, the agent will reduce the risk and costs. Early starters can be encouraged to internationalize by distributors or buyers abroad.

'The Lonely International' is a firm that is highly internationalized but

	Degree of Internationalization of the Market		
		Low	High
Degree of Internationalization of the Firm	Low	The Early Starter	The Late Starter
	High	The Lonely International	The International Among Others

Figure 39.1   Internationalization and the network model

embedded in the domestic market with few international actors. Commonly it is the lonely international that alone has the possibility of internationalizing the domestic market. The firm has knowledge and experience from foreign markets; that is, it has been exposed to various ideas and experience which advance the firm's knowledge development (Chetty and Blankenburg-Holm, 2000; Barkema and Vermeulen, 1998). The lonely international is a forerunner in the domestic market and thereby has a strategic advantage.

'The Late Starter' is embedded in relationships in a domestic market that is already highly internationalized. Through these direct or indirect relationships the firm will gain access to international actors. The firm will more or less be forced to internationalize. The late starter has been left behind and has a disadvantage as competitors have already entered foreign markets.

'The International Among Others' is a highly internationalized firm operating on an internationalized market. The firm has knowledge about international actors and markets and can commit itself to international activities. The firm also has easy access to the resources required both domestically and internationally.

However, the model has also been criticized for certain weaknesses. Chetty and Blankenburg-Holm (2000) found some irregularities where the model did not distinctively describe every matrix. In addition, they claim that no attempts were made to describe how firms move from one position to another, nor were different problems or i.e. the importance of decision makers or firm characteristics, discussed. Despite a stimulus for internationalization, the manager might not respond out of fear of losing control over the firm, unwillingness to internationalize or on other personal grounds.

The nature of the relationships established between various parties will influence strategic decisions since the network involves resource exchange among its different members (Sharma, 1993). Through these network resources firms can gain a lot of useful new information at the right time. Information exchange takes place not only within the direct network. Also referrals through a third party can be useful in the long run. Burt (1992) states that the above-mentioned information benefits are maximized in a large diverse network of trusted contacts. Thus firms operate in networks where the relationships function as bridges to unfamiliar markets; the opportunities and motivation for internationalization are obtained through these bridges (Sharma and Johanson, 1987).

Sometimes the internationalization may also follow a somewhat unpredictable pattern, related to the opportunities and threats of the external environment (Benito and Welch, 1994). Opportunities and threats may be presented to the firm by partners in the same network, as in our example below, and may therefore influence the firm's future actions. These external ties may drive, ease or prevent firms' choice of actions in their international process (Coviello and Munro, 1997).

> Having this Swedish client is very important for us; because of them we find out what happens outside the borders, what is the price level and how our competitors are acting. It gives us a totally different picture than if we were operating only in Finland, alone. (Hurmerinta-Peltomaki, 2001)

The social network perspective

Galaskiewicz and Zaheer (1999) point out that missing from the discussions of organizational fields are the social networks which exist among natural persons. These people have contacts, which extend far beyond the walls of the organizations they are working in. Networks by definition are constantly evolving and changing. The critical elements in a firm's strategic success are the ability of the firms in the network to influence these changes over time and thus create and maintain the most advantageous membership. The composition of the network and the degree to which the actors of the network are rich in information, skills, referrals and other resources a firm needs are significantly important for the firm's future success (ibid.).

> It doesn't matter if people around here would start producing identical boats as us tomorrow. They would not be able to sell one single boat. They would be too expensive. It's all built on social relations with the company after many, many

years in the business . . . we have a lot of personal relationships out there which we can use and are using. . . . We are much more known internationally than we are on the domestic market, our exports are a hundred per cent. (Personal interview with Marketing Director Johansson, Baltic Yachts)

In spite of the fact that there is a growing consensus that networks do matter, a debate has arisen over whether it is the closed network with many strong ties or the more open network with the brokerage opportunities that is the more important. Clarifying the implications of cohesive versus disconnected networks for various organizational outcomes is therefore of great importance. A cohesive network, as explained by Coleman (1988), is important for the development of social capital. It ensures that actors behave in a trustworthy manner because it allows proliferation of obligations and expectations. It is also the source, where reliable information is exchanged and where norms that put collective interests ahead of individual self-interest can be observed. Some benefits of the cohesive network can only be captured by those who invest in them (ibid.).

> By employing Chinese persons from the industry in question – often from organizations with which they had been negotiating – the export company obtained employees in China with guanxi to buyers and/or governmental organizations. The highly specialized educational system in China also resulted in extensive social networks among those who had worked together. These persons occupied central positions and had quite strong ties with centrally placed actors in the social networks that often were found within an industry. (Bjorkman and Kock, 1995)

A central actor in a disconnected network, as Burt (1992) explains it, gains additional advantages such as more valuable information received early and, through more referrals, serving as a positive force for future opportunities. The disconnected network works most efficiently if those with whom the central actor has direct and indirect relationships have no direct or indirect ties to one another; that is, the network is rich in structural holes (Burt, 1992).

Granovetter (1973) states that relationships based on weak ties are of greater importance when considering distribution of new information flowing in the network, since people moving in circles distant from our own will have access to different information. It is suggested that close relationships reflect the concept of embeddedness. These relationships are distinguished by the personal nature of the business relationship and their effect on economic processes.

Strong ties are even more emphasized by Uzzi (1997), stating that embedded relationships have three main components that regulate the expectations and behaviour of the exchange partners: trust, fine-grained information transfer and joint problem-solving arrangements. The relationships are managed by trust, which promotes access to privileged resources and extra efforts. Furthermore, the information transfer in the embedded network is more fine-grained, tacit and holistic compared to pure price exchange data of market relations. Finally the joint problem-solving arrangements deepen the relationship and promote useful learning and innovation.

> Several respondents noted that the development of personal trust was more important in China than in other locations where they had been working. The trust that exists between actors in a social network was seen as particularly important concerning transactions which involved illegal elements such as 'extra commissions' paid to foreign bank accounts or lavish gifts. (Bjorkman and Kock, 1995)

Figure 39.2 presents the various dimensions of social relationships. The *atomistic* manager has few and weak social relationships. The manager can be considered as lonely and is often left outside. In an international context this type of manager has problems as every new decision follows a trial-and-error pattern.

The *collective* manager aims at collecting information from different sources in order to minimize the risk involved when taking decisions concerning international business. The major drawback is that, since the information comes from weak ties, its trustworthiness can sometimes be questioned. If the collective manager does not give information back, the others will soon regard him as a 'black hole', consuming information and giving nothing back.

	Number of social relationships	
	Few	Many
Weak	Atomistic	Collective
Strong	Safe	Hub

(Strength of social relationships)

Figure 39.2   Dimensions of social relationships

The *safe* manager uses few but strong relationships in his decision process in international business. That the relationships are strong indicates that he can trust the information received and has developed a more comprehensive contract, which might also include problem solving. A disadvantage is that the other individuals have the same norms and the information is therefore very similar and can become a burden in some cases, as mentioned earlier. This manager deals with long-lasting social relationships.

The *hub* manager has gained a very strong and central position as he has many strong relationships. He is connected to different networks and can consequently receive a lot of new information at an early stage, which he can use for connecting different parties and creating new opportunities. His major problem is that the time invested in all the relationships needs to be reduced and therefore he only keeps in touch with the most central actors in each cluster in his network.

The influence of social networks on the internationalization process of SMEs

Much of the small firm network research focuses on general network influences on firm behaviour, but certain studies, as mentioned before, have highlighted the potential role of networks in small firm internationalization (Lindqvist, 1988; Bell, 1995). However, these studies have not looked specifically at social networks, formal as well as informal, and their impact on the internationalization process. Coviello and Munro (1997) state that literature on the potential influence of network relationships on the internationalization process is increasing, but that research providing detailed information about specific network and relationship influence is non-existent. Their findings indicate that, in small software firms, the internationalization decisions and growth patterns are very much shaped by their network of formal and informal relationships.

Having experienced market success, each firm also began to desire greater control in the network and looked forward to furthering their international expansion through development of additional relationships (ibid.). Just as skilled managers are important to the growth of the firm (Penrose, 1959), they are significant in internationalization.

Agndal and Axelsson (2002) point out that a new person in a firm will always bring with him a personal network consisting of family, friends and earlier business relationships, which they call the 'relationship sediment'. These contacts can be used for either company or private purposes, depending on that particular person's willingness to share and ability to use them.

Galaskiewicz and Zaheer (1999) claim that several aspects of interpersonal ties distinguish them from interorganizational ties. The contents of interpersonal ties may often be either expressive or emotional, but do also usually include an instrumental aspect. They are also generally invested with meaning, which makes them central to a person's identity. They can also be inherently positive or negative, meaning that a person may enjoy or dislike engaging in relationships with others. These ties can play an important part in a firm's strategy to gain control over its environment. The social networks between individuals are largely invisible and mostly unknown to others outside the network, which gives the firms involved a competitive advantage. Certain problems may, however, occur, according to Galaskiewicz and Zaheer (1999) on different levels such as the micro behavioural level, the relational level and the field level.

The first problem on the micro behavioural level is the expression problem. As interpersonal ties are likely to present a more salient expressive aspect and contain more emotions than interorganizational ties, the reaction of employees to certain features can be emotional, and consequently perhaps not serve the interest of the employer. The second problem is the hierarchy problem. A direct proportional impact has been established between the results of personal ties on interorganizational strategy and the status of the individuals involved (Zaheer, Lofstrom and George, 1998, cited in Galaskiewicz and Zaheer, 1999). An organization is divided into different hierarchical levels, and the social networks of actors at different levels are likely to bring different benefits to the organization. Owing to the homogeneity of social networks, actors further up in the hierarchy have more useful network contacts and consequently the power to effect changes in the organization to a greater extent. The third problem on the micro level is the agency problem: 'individual members of the organization are likely to pursue their own interests at the expense of the organization' (Jensen and Meckling, 1976, cited in Galaskiewicz and Zaheer, 1999).

On the relational level the problem appears if a firm becomes too dependent on a specific network tie and thus vulnerable. Negative sides of having too strong relationships are identified in the extract below. Uzzi (1997) also warns of the problem that firms situated in a network of strong personal relationships run the risk of adapting too slowly to changes. As investments are made in long-term relationships, particularly where personal relations and organizational relationships are mixed, it becomes harder to take an unemotional and coldly calculating view of the members in the network (Galaskiewicz and Zaheer, 1999).

> And we must admit that long-term relationships have their drawbacks, if the social bonds become too strong. When this happens the persons involved will put security and friendship before a good deal. Hence, we are convinced that relationships are beneficial as long as they do not go too far [down] the line and become more important than the business. (Kock, 1991)

At the third level, the field level, social networks can more easily be used to cement collaborative relationships and have a limitless competitive potential when the number of connected others is low. Under conditions of uncertainty, the trustworthy information received from your close network becomes very attractive and therefore the investment in social relationships is never a waste (Galaskiewicz and Zaheer, 1999)

As there are not so many different hierarchy levels in smaller firms, one can assume that different personal ties in a small firm can have a greater impact than in larger companies. According to Holmlund and Kock (1998), and as the selected example below shows, individuals in small and medium-sized firm have a substantial impact on the internationalization process as close social relationships with other individuals affect the motivation to start internationalizing. In the Finnish SMEs studied by Holmlund and Kock (ibid.) the social networks of the management in the home country as well as abroad affect the internationalization process significantly. Coviello and Munro's (1997) findings indicate that small firms show a pattern externalizing their international market development activities through investment in network relationships.

> In 1964 the CEO of the company received the first order from the U.S.A. The order was placed by an agent in New York City interested in importing abrasive paper to the U.S.A. The contact was established through a social relationship between the CEO of the agency and a lady living in Helsinki. The agent wanted to work on commission. The order gave boost to the company's turnover but resulted in a considerable loss. In 1967 the new CEO, who had studied in New York City, decided to try again to enter the market in the U.S.A. He approached one of the buyers he knew from the earlier attempt. Later on the single largest buyer in the U.S.A. was reached through a social relationship between one of the company's salesmen and the owner of the buying company. (Grahn, 1996, translation by the authors)

Benassi (1993) draws research attention to the role of personal ties in making formalized relationships possible, since his sample shows that personal relationships were the starting point for several strategic alliances. Bjorkman and Kock (1995) state that it may be difficult empirically to distinguish between social, information and business exchanges when actors interact. Studies using the network approach have commonly treated social networks as an outcome of business networks. Consequently, a business network consists of three dimensions: activities, resources and actors (Hakansson and Johanson, 1992). The actor dimension makes up the social network in the business network. Which comes first, the social or the business relationship, is difficult to decide as it varies according to the context. An important question is when a business relationship develops to also include a social dimension, and vice versa. In international business it is common for a manager to activate 'sleeping' social relationships when entering a new market in order to decrease the involved risk.

> I called my friend in Sweden and said that I'd established a firm that produces moulds. Then he just said, 'Okay, send me one'. And I did. There wasn't any bargaining. He just bought a mould. (Hurmerinta-Peltomaki, 2001)

Also the position of an actor in a network is of great importance, whether the actor is in a central position or not. The centrality can be divided into a global and local centrality. A position is locally central if it has a great number of connections in its immediate environment (Nieminen, 1974) while it is globally central if it is strategically significant in the overall structure of the network (Freeman, 1979). A central position indicates that an individual has access to more information through stronger relationships with key decision makers and informants. In other terms, investments in social relationships to centrally positioned individuals are extremely important.

> The general perception was, however, that if you manage to develop a good personal relationship with the central decision maker you have a good chance of winning business deals controlled by this person. (Bjorkman and Kock, 1995)

Many interactions in predominantly social relationships may have an impact on business relations regardless of whether monetary values are exchanged or not. It might also be the other way around, that strong business relations deepen into becoming also personal relations. Bjorkman and Kock (ibid.) and Salmi and Backman (1999) come to the conclusion that in some markets, such as the Chinese and Russian markets, social bonds typically precede business bonds. In China, social relations are of high significance both in order to obtain important information but also to influence Chinese decision makers (Bjorkman and Kock, 1995).

> . . . that's a long story. It takes you several years to really build up a good relationship with them. In the beginning you have to pay visits there, and you can invite them to your office. And gradually you know who is the decision maker. Then you build up a very good relationship with them. You should know what they like, what kind of topic they like to talk about, what is their background, even what kind of food they like. (Bjorkman and Kock, 1995)

Burt (1992) argues that firms as well as individuals purposefully work towards structuring their networks in order to receive higher rates of return on their investments. The more non-redundant contacts you have, the more efficient your network is, providing you with more benefits, such as information and control. Hakansson and Johanson (1993) on the other hand comment that networks are cognitive constructions, and individuals within an organization may have different perceptions about the membership of the network, its structure and modalities governing various transactions. In accordance with the findings of Uzzi (1997), we also believe that the most efficient network would be one consisting of several weak ties providing the focal actor with new information, but also of strong ties, which consist of a deeper long-lasting cooperation where parties can develop and jointly solve problems.

Freeman (1979) adds yet another concept of centrality, which he terms 'the betweenness'. Betweenness measures the extent to which a particular actor lies 'between' other actors in a network and to what extent this actor or firm can play the part of a 'broker' or 'gatekeeper' in a network. In our example below, the Swedish firm has an intermediary role as a 'gatekeeper' and therefore becomes very central to the network because of the potential control the firm has over others.

> A French firm, a supplier of abrasive papers to RENAULT and specialized in delivering both small and large quantities in different sizes of the product at short notice. The firms have been involved in a long-term relationship for about 15 years. The French firm employs a Swedish company producing abrasives as a supplier. Some years ago the owner of the French firm bought a major share of the Swedish company. After the takeover the Swedish company implemented outsourcing as an important part of their strategy. In 1999 the Swedes had to decide if they should invest in a new production line for a special quality of abrasive paper needed to supply RENAULT's after-sales products. Instead the Swedish firm got in contact with a Finnish competitor, knowing that the Finnish company had recently invested in a new production line and had at this point an overcapacity. The Finnish firm had for a long time been interested in supplying abrasive paper to RENAULT but had noticed that the relationship between the French supplier and RENAULT consisted of very strong ties. The cooperation that started between the Swedish and the Finnish firms made it possible for the Finns to indirectly come into contact with a new and important buyer, RENAULT, which in the long run can be seen as a potential very fruitful investment in a new customer relationship. (Personal interview with Klaus Erbismann, Non-label Manager at KWH/Mirka)

Andersen and Buvik (2002) describe the assessment of potential international exchange partners as a screening process, which involves gathering information about potential partners. A useful information source when seeking potential partners is the social network of the focal firm. The process is likely to go on, after first using actors that the firm has direct relations with, to indirect ties of the firm (cf. Blankenburg *et al.*, 1999).

Conclusions
From the theoretical discussion and the illustrative cases we can conclude that social relationships are very important in the internationalization

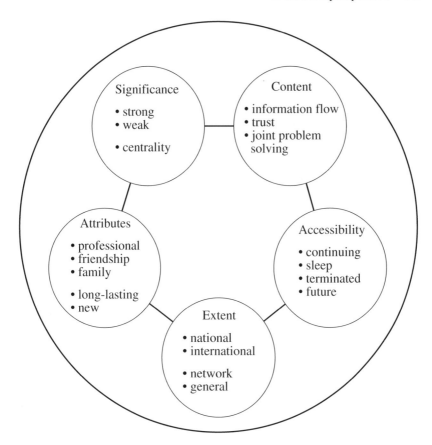

Figure 39.3   Dimensions of the social relationship in internationalization

process. The social relationships of the managers in the SMEs have helped them to gain access to information and new customers, and to expand their business.

In Figure 39.3, the factors that have an impact on the social relationship in internationalization are depicted. The figure is inspired by Agndal and Axelsson (2002) but is here further developed and improved. The five main factors are classified into a first category consisting of significance and content and a secondary category of accessibility, extent and attributes.

As regards the first category, the *significance* of the relationship depends on the usefulness of the connection compared to the time spent on nurturing the relationship. It is often hard to ensure the potential of every link and different types of connections are therefore of great importance. In order to get information about, for example, potential partners or foreign buyers, the manager needs to make use of both strong and weak relationships. From the strong relationships the manager will receive more trustworthy information. From the weak relationships the manager gets more new information faster, but this information has not necessarily passed through the same norm filter as that of strong relationships. It is, however, difficult to determine whether a strong cohesive network or a more open network with weak relationships is more significant. We argue that, in the internationalization process, both are crucial. The strong relationships are, however, more essential as they can act as a context for problem solving and innovations and thus bring more quality into the relationship for the partners involved. In certain geographical areas, access to specific relationships are even a question of staying in business or not.

Other important issues concern how central and valuable the actors are in their present social network. A central actor with the right information sees new opportunities sooner and will be able to coordinate action between different partners when needed. A central actor is also attractive as a new network contact for others and will thus easily be able to expand his own network.

The *content* of the relationship is a question of how the relationship between the actors in the social relationship functions. The expectations and behaviour are regulated by fine-grained information transfer, joint problem-solving arrangements and trust. The information of strong relationships is more tacit and holistic. Trust is the basis for mutual social relationships and gives the actors access to privileged resources when unforeseen extra efforts are put into the relationship. Finally, joint problem solving based on a high degree of trust will strengthen the social relationship and simultaneously promote useful learning and innovation.

The second category of our dimensions of the social relationship consists of the availability, reach and type of relationship. The *accessibility* of the relationship indicates whether it is a continuing relationship, a sleeping, terminated or maybe a future relationship. The continuing relationship is an active social relationship based on mutuality, no matter if it is a strong or weak relationship. The stronger the relationship, the more intense it will be. Sleeping relationships are former relationships that are now put on hold. These relationships can, with some effort, be activated when needed. Terminated relationships are difficult to activate, since they usually are no longer mutual or, even worse, lack the trust that once was there. Future relationships are perhaps still undiscovered or might be in the initial screening phase, representing a potential for coming opportunities.

The *extent* of the relationship is national and/or international, depending on the focal actor. Nowadays customers, suppliers and partners are usually spread over a wide geographical area. An actor who has worked or studied abroad has a deeper international knowledge. The actor's national and international experience can be compared with the internationalization process of the firm elaborated earlier on in this chapter. Strong international social connections are an advantage for actors in their international business activities. The reach of the link can be divided into two additional categories, network reach or general reach. This is dependant on whether the relationship is part of a larger network or can be seen as just a momentary general connection.

We have divided the *attributes* of the relationship into two sub-groups, namely professional, friendship or family, on one hand, and long-lasting or new, on the other. The borderlines between the ones in the first group might be fuzzy, as relationships that are based on friendship can also be used for business purposes and therefore develop into a relationship consisting of both types. The relationship can also begin with business but later on deepen into including both friendship and business. All categories in the first group can also be divided, depending on whether the relationship has just started or is one that has lasted for a long time.

Suggestions for further research

Figure 39.3 can be seen as a source for many different directions of research in this field. The impact of social relationships on the internationalization process is important. A problematic question is the extent to which they do have an impact. Some of our cases illustrate that it is not possible to complete the mission of internationalization without the use of social relationships. An aim for further research would consequently be to analyse the interaction between the impact of social relationships and goal-oriented actions undertaken by the managers in the internationalization process. To what extent can social relationships of the manager support him in achieving the strategic goals of the internationalization?

In order to better understand the social networks and how they evolve and are used over time, longitudinal studies are needed. In such studies the dynamics of social networks would become more visible.

Perhaps the most important research challenge, however, is to develop a deeper understanding of the ways in which strong and weak relationships differ in the internationalization process. Which combination of strong and weak relationships would be the most fruitful, and which kind of relationship should be developed with whom? These are key questions in SMEs with often limited resources, which need to be used in the most efficient way. Should the manager of the SME go for strong or weak relationships in his attempts to build social relationships that can be useful in his business performance?

References

Agndal, H. and B. Axelsson (2002) 'Internationalisation of the Firm – The Influence of Relationship Sediments', in V. Havila, M. Forsgren and H. Hakansson (eds), *Critical Perspectives on Internationalisation*, Oxford: Pergamon Press.

Andersen, O. and A. Buvik (2002), 'Firms' Internationalisation and Alternative Approaches to the International Customer/Market Selection', *International Business Review*, 11 (3), 347–63.

Barkema, H.G. and F. Vermeulen (1998), 'International expansion through start-up or aquisition: A learning perspective', *Academy of Management Journal*, 41 (1), 7–26.

Bell, J. (1995), 'The Internationalisation of Small Computer Software Firms – a Further Challenge to "Stage" Theories', *European Journal of Marketing*, 29 (8), 60–75.

Benassi, M. (1993), 'External Growth in the Computer Industry', in G. Grabher (ed.), *The Embedded Firm*, London: Routledge, pp. 95–115.

Bengtsson, M. and S. Kock (1999), 'Cooperation and Competition in Relationships among Competitors in Business Networks', *The Journal of Business and Industrial Marketing*, 14 (3), 178–94.

Benito, G.R.G. and L.S. Welch (1994), 'Foreign Market Servicing: Beyond Choice of Entry Mode', *Journal of International Marketing*, 2 (2), 7–27.

Bjorkman, I. and S. Kock (1995), 'Social Relationships and Business Networks: The Case of Western Companies in China', *International Business Review*, 4 (4), 519–35.

Blankenburg, H.D., K. Eriksson and J. Johanson (1999), 'Creating value through mutual commitment to business network relationships', *Strategic Management Journal*, 20, 467–86.

Burt, B.S. (1992), *Structural Holes. The Social Structure of Competition*, Cambridge, MA: Harvard University Press

Chetty, S. and D. Blankenburg-Holm (2000), 'Internationalisation of Small to Medium-sized Manufacturing Firms: a Network Approach', *International Business Review*, 9, 77–93.

Christensen, P.R. and L. Lindmark (1993), 'Location and Internationalisation of Small Firms', in L. Lundqvist and L.O. Persson (eds), *Visions and Strategies in European Integration*, Berlin/Heidelberg: Springer-Verlag, pp. 131–51.

Coleman, J.S. (1988), 'Social Capital in the Creation of Human Capital', *American Journal of Sociology*, 94, Supplement, S95–S120.

Coviello, N. and H. Munro (1997), 'Network Relationships and the Internationalisation Process of Small Software Firms', *International Business Review*, 6 (4), 361–86.

Freeman, L.C. (1979), 'Centrality in Social Networks: I. Conceptual Clarification', *Social Networks*, 1.

Galaskiewicz, J. and A. Zaheer (1999), 'Networks of Competitive Advantage', in S.B. Andrews and D. Knoke (eds), *Research in the Sociology of Organizations*, vol. 16, Greenwich, CT: JAI Press, pp. 237–61.

Grahn, J. (1996), 'Internationaliseringsprocessen i foretag exemplefierat med en fallstudie av KWH Mirka' (The Internationalisation Process in Firms, exemplified by the KWH Mirka Case), Swedish School of Economics and Business Administration, Vasa, Finland.

Granovetter, M.S. (1973), 'The Strength of Weak Ties', *American Journal of Sociology*, 78, 1360–80.

Hakansson, H. and J. Johanson (1992), 'A Model of Industrial Networks', in B. Axelsson and G. Easton (eds), *Industrial Networks: A New View of Reality*, London: Routledge, pp. 28–34.

Hakansson, H. and J. Johanson (1993), 'The Network as Governance Structure: Interfirm Cooperation Beyond Markets and Hierarchies', in G. Grabher (ed.), *The Embedded Firm*, London: Routledge, pp. 35–51.

Hertz, S. and L.-G. Mattsson (2002), 'Collective competition and the dynamics of market restructuring – local vs global perspectives', paper presented at the conference on 'Different Perspectives on Competition and Cooperation', Umea, Sweden, May.

Holmlund, M. and S. Kock (1998), 'Relationships and the Internationalisation of the Finnish Small and Medium-sized Companies', *International Small Business Journal*, 16 (4), 46–61.

Hurmerinta-Peltomaki, L. (2001), 'Time and Internationalisation – The Shortened Adoption Lag in Small Business Internationalisation', publication of the Turku School of Economics and Business Administration, series A-7:2001, Turku.

Johanson, J. and L-G. Mattsson (1988), 'Internationalisation in Industrial Systems – a Network Approach', in P.J. Buckley and P.N. Ghauri (eds), *The Internationalisation of the Firm: a Reader*, London: Academic Press, pp. 303–21.

Johanson, J. and J-E. Vahlne (1977), 'The Internationalisation Process of the Firm – a Model of Knowledge Development and Increasing Foreign Market Commitment', *Journal of International Business Studies*, Spring/Summer, 23–32.

Johanson, J. and J.-E. Vahlne (1992), 'Management of Foreign Market Entry', *Scandinavian International Business Review*, 1 (3), 9–27.

Kock, S. (1991), '*A Strategic Process for Gaining External Resources Through Long-Lasting Relationships. Examples from two Finnish and two Swedish Industrial Firms,*' Publication of the Swedish School of Economics and Business Administration, 47.

Lindqvist, M. (1988), 'Internationalisation of Small Technology-Based Firms: Three Illustrative Case Studies on Swedish Firms', Stockholm School of Economics Research Paper 88/15.

Nieminen, V. (1974), 'On Centrality in a Graph', *Scandinavian Journal of Psychology*, 15.

Penrose, E.T. (1959), *The Theory of the Growth of the Firm*, Oxford: Basil Blackwell.

Salmi, A. and J. Backman (1999), 'Personal Relations in Russian Business: Two Circles', in R. Kosonen and A. Salmi (eds), *Institutions and Post-Socialist Transition*, Helsinki: Helsinki School of Economics and Business Administration, pp. 139–68.

Sharma, D. (1993), 'Introduction: Industrial Networks in Marketing', in S.T. Cavusgil and D. Sharma (eds), *Advances in International Marketing*, Greenwich: JAI Press: pp. 1–9.

Sharma, D. and J. Johanson (1987), 'Technical Consultancy in Internationalisation', *International Marketing Review*, winter, 20–29.

Uzzi, B. (1997), 'Social Structure and Competition in Interfirm Networks: The Paradox of Embeddedness', *Administrative Science Quarterly*, 42 (1), 35–67.

Personal communications

Erbismann, Klaus, Non-label Manager at KWH/Mirka, Finland, 27.7.2002, 10.00–11.30, conducted by Susanna Hinttu and Soren Kock.

Johansson, Per-Goran, Marketing Director at Baltic Yachts, Bosund, Finland, 23.4.2002, 9.00–10.15, conducted by Maria Forsman.

Staffans, Lisbeth, Managing Director at Baltic Yachts, Bosund, Finland, 25.4.2002, 9.15–11.00, conducted by Maria Forsman.

40 Emerging research issues in international entrepreneurship

Shaker A. Zahra, Peggy Cloninger, Ji Feng Yu and Youngjun Choi

Research on international entrepreneurship (IE) has drawn worldwide attention.* This chapter identifies six emerging areas in IE research, examines the progress in research on each to date, and outlines the theoretical and empirical foundations of this research. The chapter also identifies issues that require attention in future research and the methodological innovations necessary to address them. The discussion highlights bountiful opportunities for interesting and insightful IE research.

The study of IE has grown rapidly over the past decade, reflecting the increasing globalization of business activities and the rising importance of entrepreneurship in gaining a competitive advantage in global markets. While the growth of this scholarship has been a welcome development, IE research has taken different directions and past findings have been noncumulative (Zahra and George, 2002). Therefore it is important to assess the progress made to date and to outline effective strategies to improve future research. One way to achieve this purpose is to focus on key emerging research issues, establish their theoretical relevance and propose an effective research strategy to pursue them. This chapter presents such an effort, hoping to give future research greater focus and to improve the quality of its findings.

The six issues covered in this chapter are the effect of mode of entry on learning and subsequent organizational performance; the effect of industry characteristics on new ventures' internationalization; internationalization of service industries; conducting comparative IE studies; the effect of the Internet on the internationalization of new firms; and building new theories in IE. These issues have received some interest in the literature but we believe that a qualitative shift in the thrust of future research is necessary. Besides grounding future IE research in good theory, researchers should go

* The authors of this chapter have benefited from discussions with colleagues at Helsinki University of Technology, Jönköping International Business School and the University of Minnesota. This research was funded in part by the Kauffman Center for Entrepreneurial Leadership at the Ewing Marion Kauffman Foundation.

beyond traditional paradigms and develop new theories that define the boundaries of the IE field and give meaning to its findings.

To develop our analysis, we look back and examine the progress made to date in studying each of the six issues analysed in this chapter. We then look forward and outline key research questions that deserve special attention and how to study them. With efforts such as these, our review and analysis are necessarily selective and may not capture every issue of potential interest to readers; however, we will draw attention to our six key issues in the hope of stimulating creative and productive scholarship that will enrich our understanding of IE.

IE, mode of entry, knowledge and performance

In examining the internationalization of new ventures, IE researchers have studied the modes of entry that these firms use (Zahra *et al.*, 2000). Researchers have sought to document the frequency with which new ventures use different modes of entry to penetrate new foreign markets, giving special attention to the differences between established and younger new ventures in their choices of these modes. This research has been guided by a belief that established firms often have goals and resource bases that differ markedly from those of new ventures. Limited in their foreign market experience and resources, new ventures have to show a great amount of creativity in selecting the 'right' mode of foreign entry.

Past IE research has also explored the implications of the mode of entry for the acquisition of new skills, especially those related to knowledge and learning (ibid.). While some IE studies have linked the mode of entry to future performance (ibid.), the sources of variability in organizational performance are not well understood. This is especially the case when new ventures diversify their international operations.

There is a considerable body of research on the implications of diversification for company performance. Zahra and Garvis (2000) review this extensive literature, concluding that empirical evidence is mixed at best. Past findings show serious measurement and theory deficiencies, leading to contradictory findings. Of concern, however, is that this young field of IE does not appear to heed the advice of prior researchers from the international business (IB) and strategy disciplines. For example, few IE researchers separate related from unrelated diversification as they seek to document the performance implications of foreign venturing activities.

The merits and limitations of related and unrelated diversification have been debated in the literature for decades (for a review, see Zahra and Garvis, 2000). Most prior discussions have examined the strategic and financial benefits of using related as opposed to unrelated diversification. One of the key benefits of diversification is learning, especially by acquiring new knowledge. This knowledge can fuel product and process innovations that can give new ventures a competitive advantage in their international operations.

Related diversification allows the new venture to bring in related knowledge that can be used to quickly revamp operations, increase innovation and stimulate growth. This process can enrich the venture's knowledge base. The fact that knowledge is somewhat related enables the new venture to absorb the knowledge being imported from outside. Commonality of knowledge is also important for its successful absorption and exploitation (Zahra and George, 2002). By combining such related knowledge, new ventures can proceed to innovate and differentiate their products from those offered by the competition. Combinative knowledge can also fuel radical innovations that improve new ventures' competitive positions and enhance their financial and non-financial performance.

Unrelated diversification takes new ventures into new fields, venturing beyond their traditional knowledge bases. This process can be taxing to the new firm and its executives who have to decipher and understand incoming knowledge. This task is complicated by the fact that much of the incoming knowledge is tacit in nature, thus slowing down the process by which the new venture assimilates new knowledge. Managers also have to combine different types of knowledge, which is a demanding process. Combining knowledge requires new venture managers to find common building blocks among different knowledge bases and then consider ways in which this knowledge can be integrated. Knowledge integration is also a complex social process where multiple actors have to come together and determine the best approach to achieve this goal. Organizational political realities can impede this integration. Still, integration can generate entirely new knowledge that can spur innovation while expanding the cognitive map of the new venture as it diversifies its international operations.

IE researchers have yet to explore the implications of various modes of entry into foreign markets (such as diversification) for knowledge integration, synthesis and creation within new ventures. This gap in the IE literature is puzzling because of the widespread interest today in understanding the antecedents of organizational learning, particularly among international new ventures. Autio *et al.* (2000) highlight the various sources of learning advantages of newness. They propose that international new ventures might have advantages over their well-established rivals in acquiring and learning new skills through international expansion. These advantages, which may vary significantly among high- and low-technology industries, have profound effects on company performance.

It is clear from the above discussion that there are many opportunities for IE researchers to explore the effect of modes of entry on organizational learning. Notably the factors that affect the choice of these modes should be documented, especially because most research has studied well-established companies, not new ventures. It is also important to explore how firm, industry and macro conditions interact to influence new ventures' choices of entry modes. There is also a need to understand how international new ventures achieve 'strategic coherence' in their choice and implementation of different modes of entry. Strategic coherence arises from the relatedness that exists in new ventures' market choices. While many new ventures might compete as niche players in their domestic markets, it is not clear from the IE literature whether this strategy is also used as these firms expand internationally. If new ventures specialize as they internationalize their operations, the limitations of this strategy for organizational learning should be better documented. If these new ventures diversify their operations, IE researchers should be aware of the extent of the relatedness of the firm's strategic choices and how it affects organizational learning.

New ventures might also learn different skills and capabilities from their international expansion. Zahra *et al.* (2000) highlight technological learning as one such outcome. New ventures that internationalize their operations might also learn about their new markets and competition. Dealing with liabilities of foreignness and newness can also improve an international new venture's social learning about new national cultures and groups of customers. IE researchers would benefit from examining these different types of learning and how they might be combined to improve the firm's knowledge base and its strategic repertoire.

Future IE research would also benefit from exploring potential shifts in new ventures' use of different modes of foreign entry. Understanding these shifts can also help to explain the risk preferences of new ventures, shifts in industry conditions, changes in resource bases and variations in the composition of top management. Understanding path dependencies, if any, in new ventures' selection of various modes of foreign entry is also important.

IE, industry environments and performance
Even though the industries that some new ventures enter are similar across the world, many vary considerably from one region or country to another. Industries develop at different rates and the basic technologies that undergird these industries also diffuse at different rates across the globe. Social, cultural, technological, political and historical conditions also influence the pace of industry evolution, organization and structure. For example, the fashion industry in Italy, France and the USA, though among the most developed worldwide, reflects significantly different economic, social, cultural and historical factors. Future IE researchers, therefore, would benefit

from considering the various industry environments across countries or world regions. This can guide managerial thinking about effective strategies new ventures should (or can) use in each country (Birley and Westhead, 1990).

Industry environments also change over time but often evolve in a relatively predictable cycle. Broadly, this cycle has four stages: emerging, transitional, mature and declining. Different industries lie at different stages of development and even the same industry might exhibit different stages of growth across countries. New ventures going international might seek to capitalize on these differences in industry evolution by diffusing new technologies and applying managerial systems that lead to efficiency. Yet the IE literature does not provide compelling evidence on the extent to which new ventures might benefit from these differences across countries in the stage of industry evolution. Traditional trade theories (Oviatt and McDougall, 1994) often indicate that companies from advanced countries seek to diffuse their established products and technologies in newer markets. Some international new ventures play a key role in this regard, while challenging the traditional assumption that firms go abroad once their technologies (products) have reached maturity. Some new ventures internationalize their operations early, using innovative technologies.

A recent review of IE research highlights the paucity of studies that examine the effect of industry characteristics on new ventures' internationalization (Zahra and George, 2002). While acknowledging the importance of these variables, the IE literature is limited in this regard to a few case studies. We believe the time has come to link industry characteristics directly to the extent, scope and speed of internationalization among new ventures. The extent of internationalization refers to the percentage of a firm's various value chain activities that are conducted across international borders. Scope refers to the number of markets, industries and countries in which the new venture conducts its international operations. Speed refers to the extent to which the new venture quickly internationalizes its operations.

Examining industry characteristics also provides an important opportunity for IE researchers to document how new ventures compete internationally across the various stages of the industry life cycle. In turn, this makes it possible for IE scholars to study the dynamics of strategic change among different types of international new ventures (for example, diversified versus niche players). Strategic changes that accompany internationalization have not been examined in depth in the IE literature, yet these changes define new ventures' identity and determine their boundaries. By examining industry transitions from one phase to another, IE researchers can document shifts in international new ventures' goals and strategies. IE researchers can also observe changes in the nature of international new ventures' resource bases (whether tangible or intangible) and how they influence the way new ventures compete and develop a competitive advantage. Further, by incorporating the characteristics of the environment into their analyses, IE researchers can also improve our understanding of the payoff from international new ventures' diversification (or other modes of foreign entry) for organizational learning and subsequent growth and profitability. Industry variables may also have important implications for the relationship between the mode of foreign entry and company performance.

The motivations for internationalization may vary among new ventures according to industry characteristics and changes in these characteristics. These motivations have strategic components (such as building networks), organizational components (such as defining firm boundaries) and financial components (such as profitability and growth). IE researchers would benefit from examining these motivations and how they might influence the outcomes of internationalization. Changes in these motivations over time are another worthwhile issue to explore.

It is also important to highlight the need for greater consistency in future IE research on industry characteristics. Zahra and George's (2002) review shows that several variables have been examined in prior IE research. These variables include the intensity of domestic competition, rates of domestic growth, government policies, economies of scale, type of industry, industry profitability and growth rates, and institutional environments, among others. While these variables are relevant, IE researchers appear to ignore decades of research in strategic management and industrial organizational economics that suggest different classifications of industry types (Grant, 2002) and different sets of industry characteristics (Porter, 1980, 1986). Future IE scholars would benefit from exploring and using these classifications in their studies.

IE in Service New Ventures

Services, typically defined as deeds, performances and efforts that provide benefits to customers (Clark *et al.*, 1996; Dunning, 1989), now account for over half the gross domestic product in all developed countries and in most developing economies (UN, 1994b). Employment, production, trade and investment in services have also exceeded those in the manufacturing sector for several years (Hilsenrath, 2002; UN, 1994b). Though service industries have been more heavily regulated than goods, today's decreasing trade barriers have encouraged the internationalization of many service industries (Campbell and Verbeke, 1994).

The number of service new ventures that have gone international has increased over the past decade (OECD, 1997). For example, a sample of young US-based firms in the environmental industry yielded 42 international firms out of a usable sample of 190 firms, and 34 of these 42 firms were service firms (Cloninger, 2000). Yet, to date, little attention has been given to examining the internationalization of services or to new service firms entering international markets. Given the important role of service industries in today's global economy, IE researchers should examine these industries.

Most business theories have been developed within manufacturing firms (Boddewyn *et al.*, 1986). Empirical studies have also sometimes failed to distinguish between service and manufacturing activities (for example, Chattopadhyay *et al.*, 2001). This raises a question about the generalizability of prior research findings. Several factors may have contributed to the fact that researchers have ignored the distinction between service and manufacturing industries. Manufacturing industries have a major portion of their operations in services. This trend persists (and sometimes grows) as industries become knowledge-intensive. Also some studies show considerable similarities in the internationalization of service and manufacturing industries (for example, Erramilli, 1991), indicating that existing theories can be adapted to accommodate services as well as manufactured goods (Boddewyn *et al.*, 1986; Erramilli, 1993). For example, although the eclectic paradigm seeks to explain international production, some claim that it is also applicable to service firms (Dunning and Kundu, 1995). Thus some scholars suggest that separating services and goods may be too simplistic, or a 'false' dichotomy (Dunning, 1989). The distinction between physical goods and services is more a matter of degree.

Other studies that have considered service and manufacturing activities, or that have drawn comparisons, have found major differences between these industry types. One study concludes that executives believe that firms that pioneer the creation of innovative manufactured products assume greater risks but enjoy superior performance in comparison to those firms that pioneer new services (Song *et al.*, 1999). Similarly, Fladmoe-Lindquist and Jacque (1993) find that the propensity to franchise in service firms, unlike manufacturing, increases a firm's international experience. Edgett and Egan (1995) also find that specific characteristics of services, such as customer participation, play a significant role in determining performance. These findings have led Edgett and Parkinson (1993) to call upon researchers not to combine goods and services in their analyses and instead, to focus specifically on services.

When services are examined, they are frequently analyzed in the context of a single industry. Consequently potential differences among disparate service industries are ignored (Aharoni, 1993) and therefore direct comparisons between service and manufacturing activities become difficult. For example, Sharma and Johanson (1987) report that the majority of Swedish technical consulting firms they surveyed entered developing, rather than advanced, countries first. These authors surmise that risk was not an issue because the skills of professional technical consultants can easily be transferred to other markets. However these researchers did not include manufacturers in their study, making a direct comparison impossible.

The recent research by Cloninger (2000) overcomes some of the methodological and conceptual issues that have handicapped some earlier IE research on service industries. Cloninger focuses directly on the influence of service characteristics (for example, intangibility, simultaneity and perishability) on various dimensions of a new venture's internationalization. Though her sample is restricted to a single industry (environmental technology), both service and manufacturing firms are included in the analyses. Also her study measures the various characteristics exhibited in a firm's outputs, concluding that service characteristics significantly influence special dimensions of internationalization (foreign revenues, entry mode or location).

Whether or not researchers should focus exclusively on services, or combine goods and services for the purpose of drawing comparisons, empirically exploring the internationalization of service new ventures is complex. One problem is that the boundaries between goods and services have blurred, as noted previously. Thus it is increasingly difficult to find examples of either pure goods or pure services (Dunning, 1989). Instead, firms' outputs are likely to involve combinations of goods and services (Hirsch, 1993), as reported earlier. For instance, manufactured goods, such as complex communication equipment, are accompanied by essential services like design, marketing and assistance on how to use and maintain the equipment (OECD, 1997).

Service industries also vary in the degree to which they exhibit various characteristics. These services can range from highly capital-intensive to highly human capital-intensive (Aharoni, 1993). Services such as banking are often accompanied by, or embedded in, a physical good when delivered. Banking services may be delivered via an automatic teller, and the output may be highly tangible, such as cash, or highly intangible, such as information about an account temporarily flashed on a computer monitor. For instance, some researchers categorize services as hard or soft services, where hard services are activities such as software support or design, and soft services are activities like advertising or fast food franchises (Dunning, 1993).

When the 'degree' of service is considered in IE research, however, its measurement remains arbitrary. Services may be categorized as human capital-intensive or not, as hard or soft, or by some other ranking system. For example, one study of the banking industry simply ranks the transportability of each possible banking output such as credit cards, prepayment cards and financial loans, using a multi-point scale (UN, 1994a). While such single item proxies of service content may facilitate replication, they do not establish reliable measures or support the validity of the findings.

Even though some studies have attempted to clarify the concept of 'service' and to measure it (for example, deBretani and Ragot, 1996; Edgett and Egan, 1995; Parasuraman *et al.*, 1988), only two studies, by Hartman and Lindgren (1994) and Cloninger (2000), have explored multiple characteristics commonly attributed to services: intangibility, perishability, simultaneity (inseparability) and heterogeneity. Hartman and Lindgren's study is limited, however, by its use of a sample of parents at one elementary school, and by the minimal attention given to the development of items. Still, their findings suggest that services can be categorized by multiple factors.

The study by Cloninger (2000) examined four service characteristics. The first was intangibility, defined as the non-material aspects of a service, including atmosphere, ideas, performance and attitude (Clark *et al.*, 1996). The second was simultaneity, which referred to the condition that services must be produced and consumed at the same time. The third was perishability, which indicated that a good or a service loses value if delivery is delayed (for example, handbooks to assist in environmental audits become outdated). The fourth and final characteristic was heterogeneity, which indicated the degree to which a good or service was customized to meet customers' expectations.

Clearly research examining the internationalization of service firms remains notably sparse (Dunning, 1993; OECD, 1997). With the exceptions of banking and financial services, few sectors have been closely examined (Dunning, 1993). Most studies on the internationalization of service new ventures do not consider the key characteristics commonly attributed to services.

Even though some researchers believe that the internationalization of services is not entirely unlike the internationalization of manufacturing, future IE researchers should examine the characteristics of service firms' outputs when designing their studies. Firms whose outputs have a high degree of simultaneity may encourage a firm to adopt a more focused, specialized competitive strategy (Campbell and Verbeke, 1994; Dunning, 1993). This might actually enhance the ability of a service new venture to compete internationally, since older and more diversified competitors may have less of an advantage internationally. Theory building can no longer neglect the importance of service characteristics and IE researchers should begin to address the influence of service content on new ventures' international strategies and performance. IE researchers should also examine the influence of service characteristics in multiple sectors and across countries.

Comparative studies and IE

Most prior research has examined companies that have gone international from inception, which is consistent with earlier definitions of the IE field (for example, Oviatt and McDougall, 1994). This focus is understandable in view of the growing role new ventures play in today's global economy. However this narrow focus excludes established companies' efforts aimed at internationalizing their operations (Zahra and George, 2002). Established companies have strong resource bases, including formal and informal networks that can expedite their internationalization efforts. Established companies also benefit from their name recognition, well-established brands and experienced managers. These factors can promote and expedite the internationalization of their operations. Established companies may also have different goals and aspirations that differ significantly from those of new ventures that seek to internationalize their operations. Yet limited IE research has explored the potential differences that exist between new ventures and established companies as they venture abroad. Also potential differences between new ventures and established companies in the mode of foreign entry, scope and speed of expansion and success rates in internationalization have not been well documented.

Clearly future research opportunities abound for examining the antecedents, patterns and effects of internationalization, comparing established companies and new ventures. This research could fill a gap in the literature about the relative advantages of these two firm types. For instance, Autio *et al.* (2000) observe that new firms might enjoy unique advantages over their established companies in terms of learning. It would be useful to test this proposition more directly by comparing new firms and established companies. Similarly, Zahra *et al.* (2000) suggest that new ventures can and do learn a great deal about technology by internationalizing their operations. Research on multinational companies reaches a similar conclusion and, therefore, it would be beneficial if these two research streams (established companies and new ventures) were integrated. This would permit a direct test of the similarities and differences that might exist between these firms.

There is also a need to conduct comparative studies of new ventures and established companies from different countries. A recent review of past IE research highlights the paucity of such studies (Zahra and George, 2002). Comparative studies that use multiple countries would help to refine and extend our understanding of the unique social, economic, technological and governmental institutional forces that influence the international activities of companies of different sizes and ages. These factors might explain how and why international new ventures come into existence in the first place. Finally, understanding the social, economic, technological and governmental institutional forces can explain the survival rates of those ventures that go abroad and the competitive strategies they employ to achieve success in their international markets.

IE and the Internet

Since the early 1990s, the accelerated internationalization of new ventures has attracted the attention of IB scholars. Several IB studies have attempted to explain why new ventures go abroad so early in their life cycles. These studies highlight the learning advantages of newness (Autio *et al.*, 2000), alertness of entrepreneurs (McDougall *et al.*, 1994), technological learning promoted by international expansion (Zahra *et al.*, 2000) and the complementarity of large and small multinational companies. Yet none of the existing theories explains why accelerated internationalization has occurred only recently among new ventures. Changes in the global economy may be one reason for this phenomenon. The advent of digital technology also may have increased new ventures' internationalization.

Digital technology, especially the Internet, has improved rapidly since the early 1990s. The number of Internet users has soared, from only tens of thousands at the beginning of the last decade to 300 million at the end of 1990s. Using the Internet, new ventures can now obtain foreign market information cheaply, more easily gain access to foreign buyers and sellers, and more efficiently develop alliances with foreign partners. These factors might enable new ventures to enter foreign markets early in their life cycles, even when they lack significant foreign market experience.

Our understanding of the relationship between new ventures' accelerated internationalization and the Internet technology is limited. In one of the few studies published to date, Zaheer and Manrakhan (2001) propose that gaining remote access through the Internet might increase the number of countries from which a firm can obtain resources or customers. The introduction of business-to-business (B2B) trading networks also increases the global market participation of younger firms from peripheral countries. Thus the development of Internet technology can promote new ventures' increase in internationalization business.

To date, few IE studies have investigated the influence of the Internet technology on new ventures' internationalization. This provides an excellent opportunity to develop an influential research programme within IE. This programme of research can determine whether, indeed, the use of the Internet enhances foreign growth and whether any such effect varies from one industry to the next. IE researchers can also establish whether the Internet becomes an effective substitute for 'vertical integration'. If so, this information can serve as a foundation for examining the various strategic and financial effects of the Internet for new ventures' internationalization.

Theory building in IE

Many of the shortcomings of the IE literature discussed in this chapter stem from ineffective theoretical grounding. We are also concerned that some earlier studies suffer from serious methodological and analytical problems that preclude a compelling empirical test of well known theories in the context of the IE phenomenon. This problem is not unique to IE research, however: research on emerging issues often exhibits similar short-comings. Nevertheless, with the widespread attention given to IE, the time has come to focus theory building and testing.

Oviatt and McDougall (1994) have argued that traditional theories do not fully or efficiently explain new ventures' early internationalization. McDougall *et al.* (1994) have also shown that some well-known theories are limited in their explanatory powers regarding the IE phenomenon. These are important insights, ones that have improved our understanding of the limits of our knowledge. While our search for new theories continues, it is necessary to reflect on some of the key variables that handicap theory building in IE. A major part of the problem is that the boundaries of IE remain poorly defined. These boundaries appear to be loosely defined across studies and time (for a review, see Zahra and George, 2002). Like other phenomena, IE research has evolved over time, making it imperative to revise and question our assumptions about the boundaries that define the field. A good theory should help IE researchers in mapping research issues to be explored, added or discarded.

Theory building is also a complex process and few are gifted in this regard. Theories emerge as flashes of insight or as efforts aimed at imposing order on empirical observations. Theories also emerge as a consequence of empirical findings. Theory building and testing are closely intertwined, and are also iterative processes that require patience, insight, creativity and multiple skills. These activities also take time. Clearly there is a need to go beyond criticizing existing theories for failing to explain IE. Instead it is necessary to develop theories that provide greater guidance on the boundaries of this phenomenon, to decide what makes IE research questions distinct and important, and how IE research enriches the literature.

An effective IE theory would also bring greater clarity about the relationships being examined in future research. This could be achieved by articulating the causal chain among variables of interest. It can also be accomplished by questioning the assumptions that underlie the models being examined in IE research. Some researchers ground their work in economic cost–benefit paradigms. While this approach has important merits, it

Table 40.1   Emerging research issues in international entrepreneurship (IE)

Research issues	Key future research perspectives
Mode of entry, knowledge and performance	Factors affecting new ventures' choices of entry modes
	'Strategic coherence' of new ventures and the effective implementation of different modes of foreign entry
	Different types of learning and their impact upon new ventures' knowledge base
	Shifts in new ventures' different modes of entry
	Path dependencies in new firms' modes of entry
IE, industry environments and performance	Relationship between industry characteristics and the scope, depth and speed of internationalization among new ventures
	The effect of industry characteristics upon the outcomes of new ventures' internationalization
	Competitive strategies new ventures employ across various stages of the industry life cycle
	Motivations for internationalization and their influence on new venture performance across different stages of the industry life cycle
IE and inter-nationalization of services	Comparison studies about firms from multiple service industries
	The influence of service content on international new ventures' strategies and performance
	The influence of service characteristics in multiple sectors, settings and countries
Comparative studies and IE	Differences between new ventures and established companies in mode of entry, pattern and speed of foreign expansion, and success rates in international markets
	The relative advantages of new ventures and established companies
	Comparative studies of new ventures and established companies from different countries
The Internet and internationalization	Connection between specific uses of the Internet, such as marketing, sales and communication, and firm internationalization
	Impact of use of the Internet on the scope, depth and speed of new venture internationalization
	The contingent influence of the Internet on new venture internationalization, by industry characteristics
Theory building in IE	New theories to define the boundary of IE area
	Research studies based on economic versus relational exchange model

overlooks the non-financial factors that influence new ventures' internationalization and its outcomes. Traditional analyses have usually explored economic, rather than relational, exchanges. IE researchers might also benefit from examining relational exchange models that explain the choice of the mode of entry and its effect on performance. Oviatt and McDougall (1994) suggest that such exchanges are important in explaining the internationalization of new ventures. Zahra *et al.* (2002) show empirically that such relationships matter in explaining the speed and scope of new ventures' internationalization. Sohn (1995) also suggests that relationships often serve as a substitute for economic norms of exchange, particularly in the choice of new firms' mode of entry into a foreign market.

Conclusion

IE is a fast growing area of scholarly inquiry, one that has attracted global attention. In this chapter we have suggested that new theories and methods are needed to study IE and ensure that future findings are cumulative. We are thrilled by the widespread recognition of IE as an important area of scholarly inquiry but fear that past research has been fragmented in its focus and findings. By grounding IE research in good theory and using innovative methods, future researchers can add significantly to the literature. The six issues chosen for analysis in this chapter offer a wide range of options for future research in this area. They highlight the importance of restoring the 'entrepreneurial' dimension of IE. We are concerned that some researchers have accepted (or rejected) theories developed in other disciplines on a wholesale basis, ignoring the distinctiveness of the IE field. We hope that this chapter encourages future researchers to capitalize on this distinctiveness in conducting future studies.

References

Aharoni, Y. (1993), 'Globalisation of professional business services', in Y. Aharoni (ed.), *Coalitions and competition: The globalisation of professional business services*, London: Routledge, pp. 1–19.

Autio, E., Sapienza, H.J. and Almeida, J.G. (2000), 'Effects of age at entry, knowledge intensity, and imitability on international growth', *Academy of Management Journal*, 43(5): 909–24.

Birley, S. and Westhead, P. (1990), 'Growth and performance contrasts between types of small firms', *Strategic Management Journal*, 11(7): 535–57.

Boddewyn, J.J., Halbrich, M.B. and Perry, A.C. (1986), 'Service multinationals: Conceptualization, measurement and theory', *Journal of International Business Studies*, 17(3): 41–57.

Chattopadhyay, P., Glick, W. and Huber, G.P. (2001), 'Organizational actions in response to threats and opportunities', *Academy of Management Journal*, 44(5): 937–55.

Clark, T., Rajaratnam, D. and Smith, T. (1996), 'Toward a theory of international services: Marketing intangibles in a world of nations', *Journal of International Marketing*, 4(2): 9–28.

Cloninger, P.A. (2000), 'The influence of service characteristics on internationalisation: Extending the eclectic paradigm', PhD thesis, Georgia State University.

de Bretani, U. and Ragot, E. (1996), 'Developing new business-to-business professional services: What factors impact performance?', *Industrial Marketing Management*, 25(6): 517–30.

Dollinger, M. (1999), *Entrepreneurship: strategies and resources*, Upper Saddle River: Prentice-Hall.

Dunning, J.H. (1988), 'The eclectic paradigm of international production: A restatement and some possible extensions', *Journal of International Business Studies*, 19(1): 1–31.

Dunning, J.H. (1989), *Transnational corporations and the growth of services: Some conceptual and theoretical issues*, New York: UN.

Dunning, J.H. (1993), *The globalisation of business: The challenge of the 1990s*, London: Routledge.

Dunning, J.H. and Kundu, S.K. (1995), 'The internationalisation of the hotel industry – Some findings from a field study', *Management International Review*, 35(2): 101–33.

Edgett, S. and Egan, C. (1995), 'Competitive orientations in professional services', *Journal of Professional Services Marketing*, 12(2): 31–47.

Edgett, S. and Parkinson, S. (1993), 'Marketing for service industries – A review', *Service Industries Journal*, 13(3): 19–39.

Erramilli, M.K. (1991), 'The experience factor in foreign market entry behavior of service firms', *Journal of International Business Studies*, 22(3): 479–501.

Erramilli, M.K. (1993), 'Service firms' international entry-mode choice: A modified transaction-cost analysis approach', *Journal of Marketing*, 57(3): 19–38.

Fladmoe-Lindquist, K. and Jacque, L.L. (1993), 'Control modes in international service operations: The propensity to franchise', *Management Science*, 41(7): 1238–49.

Hartman, D. and Lindgren, J. (1994), 'Consumer evaluations of goods and services: Implications for services marketing', *Journal of Services Marketing*, 7(2): 4–15.

Hilsenrath, J.E. (2002), 'Big U.S. service sectors boosted late 1990s surge in productivity', *Wall Street Journal*, Monday 22 April: A2–A4.

Hirsch, S. (1993), 'The globalisation of services and service-intensive goods industries', in Y. Aharoni (ed.) *Coalitions and competition: The globalisation of professional services*, London: Routledge, pp. 66–78.

McDougall, P.P., Shane, S. and Oviatt, B.M. (1994), 'Explaining the formation of international new ventures: The limits of theories from international business research', *Journal of Business Venturing*, 9(6): 469–87.

Organisation for Economic Co-operation and Development (OECD) (1997), *Globalisation and Small and Medium Enterprises*, vol 1., Paris: OECD.

Oviatt, B.M. and McDougall, P.P. (1994), 'Toward a theory of international new ventures', *Journal of International Business Studies*, 25(1): 45–61.

Parasuraman, A., Zeithaml, V.A. and Berry, L.L. (1988), 'SERVQUAL: A multiple-item scale for measuring consumer perceptions of service quality', *Journal of Retailing*, 64(1), 12–40.

Porter, M. (1980), *Competitive Strategy*, New York: Free Press.

Porter (ed.) (1986), *Competition in Global Industries*, Boston, MA: Harvard Business School Press, pp. 15–60.

Sharma, D. D. and Johanson J. (1987), 'Technical consultancy internationalisation', *International Marketing Review*, 4(4): 20–29.

Sohn, J.H.D. (1994), 'Social knowledge as a control system: A proposition and evidence from the Japanese FDI behavior', *Journal of International Business Studies*, 25(2): 295–324.

Song, X. M., Di Benedetto, C.A. and Zhao, Y.L. (1999), 'Pioneering advantages in manufacturing and service industries: empirical evidence from nine countries', *Strategic Management Journal*, 20(9): 811–36.

UN (1994a), *The tradability of banking services, impact and implications*, New York: UN.

UN (1994b), *Liberalizing international transactions in services: A handbook*, New York: UN.

Zaheer, S. and Manrakhan, S. (200), 'Concentration and dispersion in global industries: remote electronic access and the location of economic activities', *Journal of International Business Studies*, 32(4): 667–86.

Zahra, S. and Garvis, S. (2000), 'International Corporate Entrepreneurship and Company Performance: The Moderating Effect of International Environmental Hostility', *Journal of Business Venturing*, 15 (5,6): 469–92.

Zahra, S. and George, G. (2002), 'International Entrepreneurship: Research Contributions and Future Directions', in M. Hitt, D.R. Ireland, M. Camp and D.L. Sexton (eds), *Strategic Entrepreneurship: Entrepreneurial Strategies for Wealth Creation*, New York: Blackwell, pp. 255–88.

Zahra, S.A., Ireland, D.R. and Hitt, M.A. (2000a), 'International expansion by new venture firms: International diversity, mode of market entry, technological learning and performance', *Academy of Management Journal*, 43(5): 925–50.

Zahra, S., Matherne, B. and Carleton, J. (2002), 'Technological Resource Leveraging and the Internationalisation of New Ventures', *Journal of International Entrepreneurship*.

41 An action research approach for internationalization

Claudio Vignali

In the tradition of Reg Revans, the guru of action learning, common sense is always the best approach to any management process. It is vital that management learn during the process, helping themselves from comments made by all stakeholders. A rational decision during this process, with a rational conclusion, must be the paramount aim: 'There can be no action without learning and no learning without action' (Revans, 1998, p. 14). Without application all research is artificial. However, some argue that the process of managerial decision making, a major aspect of the strategic planning procedure of small and medium-size enterprises (SMEs), has become more problematic because modern management, more than ever before, is faced with an immense complexity of tasks in an increasingly volatile business enviroment. For many years writers have been suggesting that organizations should focus and rely on the fundamental formal models and techniques of strategic planning.

On the other hand, we must acknowledge the problem that there has been a lack of agreed academic tools to facilitate practical understanding about the nature of management research. Heuristic devices, commonly known as management tools, are usually misconceived and misunderstood. A clear understanding and their regular use can only benefit the management process. This chapter develops the methodology used in operationalizing heuristic devices as practitioners extend their use of the marketing mix in developing their strategic process. In this process they always face problems and the answers always cause concern. This chapter develops a model which defines the use of the heuristic devices and allows action and review. The qualitative approach in action research was analysed in a series of case studies, which formed the basis of the research materials used in SMEs.

Planning systems were expected to produce the best strategies as well as step-by-step instructions for carrying out those strategies so that the doers, the managers of business, could not get them wrong. As we now know, planning has not exactly worked out that way (Mintzberg, 1994a, p. 107). Mintzberg's view on marketing planning, although articulated in a 'certain cynicism of tone' (Mintzberg 1994b, p. 4), reflects existing critical discussions concerning the marketing theory in general, and strategic planning and marketing models in particular.

There seems to exist doubt about the effects of the nuisances of marketing theory and planning. These are reflected in McDonald's statement: 'it is necessary to reiterate that marketing theory is not practised in industry' (1992, p. 8). However, one major part of the strategic planning process is the application of marketing models, especially in non-mathematical form as heuristic devices. These models have been widely discussed and analysed in theory and were frequently included in management education. It is argued that the power of these devices as managerial tools is high and well known (Vignali, Schmidt and Davies, 1994, p. 965). Therefore not the models themselves but rather the process of applying them is seen as the major stumbling block for successful planning.

The research method adopted in this chapter is likely to be tied to certain assumptions about how to observe and understand people's behaviour and ideas. Currently, there are two dominant paradigms striving for dominance in the social sciences. The first, older one, is positivism. The basic belief of this paradigm is the existence of a truth or objective reality waiting to be discovered by social scientists. The discovery of this reality and the general causal laws that govern behaviour is characterized by a detached, neutral and objective approach to research. Positivism is derived from the natural sciences and therefore reflects the assumptions and methodologies prevalent in this area: for example the quantitative analysis of data. However, it is argued that positivistic methods were mainly developed for the verification and not the generation of new theory (Easterby-Smith *et al.*, 1999, p. 32). Susman and Evered (1978, p. 584) present four elements to support this argument. Firstly, organizations are artefacts, created by human beings to serve their ends, and they obey laws that are affected by human purposes and actions. Secondly, organizations are systems of human action in which the means and ends are guided by values. Thirdly, empirical observation and logical reconstruction of organizational activities are not sufficient for a science of organization because organizations are planned according to their members' conceptions of the future. These conceptions do not have a truth value in the positivistic sense. Furthermore, organizations can be understood experientially by organizational researchers and need not be supported empirically or validated logically to find the truth of many propositions. Fourthly, organizations can be legitimate objects of scientific inquiry only as single cases without considering whether such cases are subsumable under general laws. Knowledge about what actions are appropriate for problem solving need not be derived by reference to a general category of similar organizations from which we know what the best action to take is on average.

The second school of thought to consider is phenomenology. The starting point is the idea that reality is socially constructed and given meaning by people rather than objectively determined. Hence the task of the researcher should not be to gather facts and measure how often certain patterns occur, but to appreciate the different constructions and meanings that people place upon their experience. This could be aligned to a process more associated with action research.

The objective of this chapter is to test the appropriateness of the current heuristic marketing devices process and the development of a new model based on these findings. Therefore, derived from the preceding discussion, one section of the chapter includes positivistic aspects in order to evaluate and test existing theory. The second section, the generation of a new model, follows a phenomenological methodology in order to be able to establish new aspects, a more defined action research approach with SMEs in mind.

Literature on action research

Action research, 'research into practice, done by practitioners, for practitioners', is seen as a way of investigating professional practice via continuously developing sequences of 'action' and reflection (Zuber-Skerrit, 1996, pp. 5, 13). Action research is an approach which aims at both taking action and creating knowledge or theory about the actions.

A majority of authors trace the invention and introduction of the term 'action research' back to Kurt Lewin, a social scientist, who first developed the action research concept in the 1940s to respond to the increasing problems he perceived in the social sciences (Coghlan and Brannick, 2001, p. 4; Revans, 1998). However, some authors claim that the practice of action research is a good deal older than the actual term noted by Lewin. Warmington (1979, p. 1), for instance, illustrates research projects in the late 1920s and early 1930s which, in his view, had most of the traits that are said to be characteristic of present-day action research.

In reflecting on Lewin's work, Argyris (1993) identifies and summarizes four 'core themes' of his particular approach to social inquiry:

1. Lewin took an approach to integrate theory with practice and connected all real life problems with theory.
2. He designed research by framing the whole and then differentiating the parts.
3. He saw the researcher as an inventor and emphasized that one could only understand something when one tried to change it.
4. He changed the role of those being studied from subjects to clients that help to produce more valid knowledge.

Action research, in the traditional (Lewinian) sense, can be seen as an approach to research that is based on a collaborative problem-solving relationship between researcher and client, which simultaneously aims at the solution of a perceived problem and the generation of new knowledge. Probably best known and most cited is Rapoport's (1990, p. 499) definition of action research, which also emphasizes action research being a practical and collaborative undertaking within an acceptable ethical framework: Action research aims to contribute both to the *practical concerns of people in an immediate problematic situation* and to the goals of social science by *joint collaboration* within a mutually *acceptable ethical framework*.

Within the attempts to characterize action research, some academics make claims that go well beyond those made by Lewin himself (Peters and Robinson, 1984, p. 116). Figure 41.1 illustrates the key features listed by 11 significant authors writing about action research.

	General												Idiosyncratic		
	Problem focused	Action oriented	Organic process (i.e. cyclical)	Collaborative/participatory	Ethically based	Experimental	Scientific	Naturalistic	Normative	Reeducative	Emancipatory	Stresses group dynamic	Concretely critical	Low a priori precision With high accuracy	Unconstrained dialogue
Argyris (1980)	[✓]*	✓**[✓]	[✓]	[✓]	[✓]	✓	✓	✓	✓	✓				✓	
Corey (1983)	✓	[✓]	✓	✓			✓								
Cunningham (1976)	✓	✓	✓	✓					[✓]	[✓]		✓			
Elliot (1979)	✓	✓		✓	✓			✓		✓					✓
Foster (1972)	✓	[✓]		✓	✓										
French & Bell (1973)	✓	✓	✓	✓			✓	✓				✓			
Kemmis (1981)	[✓]	✓	✓	✓	[✓]	[✓]	[✓]	[✓]		[✓]	✓		✓		
Ketterer et. al. (1980)	✓	✓	✓	✓				✓							
Rapoport (1970)	✓	[✓]		✓	✓		✓								
Smith (1977)	[✓]	[✓]	[✓]	✓	✓	✓	✓								
Lewin (1948)	✓	✓	✓	✓		✓	✓			✓	✓	[✓]	✓		

Notes:
* A tick in brackets [✓] indicates that the author has mentioned this characteristic, but has not highlighted it.
** A tick indicates that the author has explicitly highlighted this character.

Source: Peters and Robinson (1984, p. 119).

Figure 41.1   Characteristics of action research

The action research process adopted in the SME sector

In Lewin's original contribution, he suggested a scheme for performing an action research project. His idea of action research implied several cycles of analysis, fact finding, conceptualization, reconceptualization, planning and evaluation to be carried out simultaneously to generate knowledge and find practical (workable) solutions (Dickens and Watkins, 1999, p. 133). Lewin emphasized the necessity of continuous research activities to unravel the problem gradually as new data are gathered and interpreted and the understanding of the problem is enhanced during the research process (Gronhaug and Olson, 1999, p. 9).

In compliance with the Lewinian model of action research authors like Zuber-Skerrit (1996, p. 96) or Coghlan and Brannick (2001, p. 16) argue that action research projects in organizational contexts typically move through several distinct stages within a cycle, from the initial problem identification to its final solution. Coghlan and Brannick (2001, p. 17) furthermore suggest pursuing a 'pre-step' which has to be undertaken in order to understand the external and internal driving forces relating to the project. The three main stages, diagnosing, planning, and action taking and evaluation, follow this initial 'pre-step'.

A multitude of definitions of action research exist and various authors combine different attributes and characteristics with it. There is, in addition, a controversy about the recognition of action research as a scientific method. This discrepancy stems partly from the insufficient definition in Lewin's seminal work. Furthermore, differing underlying meta-theoretical views on the world and the nature and purpose of science, manifested in differing worldviews, paradigms or orientations, exist. These ideas strongly influence perceptions concerning the nature of science, the subjective–objective dimension and the explicitness of long-term conflicts in society. In other words, the assessment of the scientific nature of action research strongly depends on the worldview or paradigm the assessor supports.

Subsequently, a brief overview about the two major, and extreme, paradigms in social sciences, positivism and phenomenology, is displayed and action research is located in this theoretical framework. Thereby, the designation 'positivism' will be used vicariously for all terminologies pertinent to this worldview or orientation (for example, all approaches to science that consider scientific knowledge to be obtainable only from sense data that can be directly experienced and verified between independent observer: see Susman and Evered, 1978, p. 583). The same applies to the term 'phenomenology'.

Positivism has a long intellectual history dating back to the late 15th and early 16th century, when a strong faith in rationality existed (Deshpande, 1983, p. 102), and is connected to the work of Bacon (1561–1626) and

Descartes (1596–1650), (McLaughlin, 1993, p. 182). The perception of everyday scientific reality was in terms of human senses: if a phenomenon could not be seen, heard, touched, smelled or tasted, it could not exist. Under the extreme positivism point of view, man is a passive responder and reality is conceived as a concrete structure. In this perspective, knowledge can be created 'at a distance' (Gronhaug and Olson, 1999, p. 7). This positivist conception of science dominated the physical, biological and social sciences for more than a hundred years and at a later stage was linked to the work of the French mathematician and philosopher Auguste Comte (1798–1857). He used the term 'positive' to refer to the actual in comparison to the imaginary (Susman and Evered, 1978, p. 582) and argued that society could be studied by using the same logic of enquiry as that employed by the natural sciences (McLaughlin, 1993, p. 182). Two assumptions underlie this paradigm: firstly, that reality is external and objective, and secondly, that knowledge is only of significance if it is based on observations of this external reality (Easterby-Smith *et al.*, 1999, p. 22). They follow from implications, partly put forward by Comte.

1. Independence: the observer is independent of what is being observed.
2. Value-freedom: the choice of what to study, and how to study it, can be determined by objective criteria rather than by human beliefs and interests.
3. Causality: the aim of social science should be to identify causal explanations and fundamental laws that explain regularities in human social behaviour.
4. Hypothetical–deductive: science proceeds through a process of hypothesizing fundamental laws and then deducing what kinds of observations will demonstrate the truth or falsity of these hypotheses.
5. Operational: concepts need to be operationalized in a way which enables facts to be measured quantitatively.
6. Reductionism: problems as a whole are better understood if they are reduced to their simplest possible elements.
7. Generalization: in order to be able to generalize about regularities in human and social behaviour it is necessary to select samples of sufficient size.
8. Cross-sectional analysis: making comparisons of variations across samples can most easily identify such regularities (ibid., p. 23).

Furthermore, the positivist view in the social sciences is the primary discipline and, although the philosophy is recognized as a separate discipline, it is seen as parasitic upon the findings of science. In addition, there is a fundamental distinction between fact and value: fact being the product of science, whilst value represents an entirely different and inferior order of phenomenon. This reflects the underlying assumptions displayed above. There exist, however, various nuances represented by the many schools of positivistic thought, and the short description given in this chapter does not do justice to all of them.

Largely in reaction to the application of positivism to social sciences, another paradigm has arisen. The primary objective of this worldview, termed phenomenology,[1] is the direct investigation and description of phenomena as consciously experienced without theories about their causal explanation and as free as possible from unexamined preconceptions and presuppositions. Vico (1668–1744), for instance, argued that one could not study man and society in the same way as one studied inanimate nature (McLaughlin, 1993, p. 191). This paradigm therefore stems from the view that the world and 'reality' are not objective and exterior, but are socially constructed and given meaning by people. This so called 'phenomenology' or 'idealism' was strongly influenced by authors like Husserl, Brentano, Hegel, Schleiermacher and Weber in the 19th century. Weber, for example, was more concerned with the mind as the creator of reality (Deshpande, 1983, p. 102). One should therefore try to understand why people have different experiences, rather than search for fundamental laws and external causes to explain their behaviour (Easterby-Smith *et al.*, 1999, p. 24).

The differences between the phenomenological paradigm, which incorporates qualitative methods, and positivism, which follows a quantitative approach, are discussed later. Reichardt and Cook state:

> The quantitative paradigm is said to have a positivistic, hypothetical–deductive, particularistic, objective, outcome-oriented, and natural science world view. In contrast, the qualitative paradigm is said to subscribe to a phenomenological, inductive, holistic, subjective, process-oriented, and social anthropological worldview. (1979, pp. 9, 10, cited in Deshpande, 1983, p. 102)

Denzin and Lincoln(1994, p. 11) indicate that there are five interpretive paradigms that structure qualitative research: positivist/postpositivist, constructive, feminist, ethnic, marxist, and cultural. Each interpretive paradigm makes particular demands on the researcher, determining the questions posed and influencing the decisions made. The authors further argue that qualitative research involves the collection of a variety of empirical materials and the application of a wide range of methods (ibid., p. 2). The qualitative researcher is therefore like to a *bricoleur*, being multimethodoligical in focus and putting together a series of practices that provide solutions.

Table 41.1 reflects major differences between the positivistic and the phenomenological paradigm.

Table 41.1 *Differences between positivism and phenomenology*

Positivist paradigm	Phenomenological paradigm
Basic beliefs:	
The world is external and objective	The world is socially constructed and subjective
Observer is independent	Observer is part of what is observed
Science is value-free	Science is driven by human interest
Researcher should:	
Focus on facts	Focus on meanings
Look for causality and fundamental laws	Try to understand what is happening
Reduce phenomena to simplest elements	Look at the totality of each situation
Formulate hypotheses and then test them	Develop ideas through induction from data
Practice outcome-oriented work	Practice process-oriented work
Analyse – particularistic approach	Synthesize – holistic approach
Preferred methods include:	
Quantitative methods	Qualitative methods
Operationalizing concepts so that they can be measured	Using multiple methods to establish different views of phenomena
Taking large samples	Small samples investigated in depth or over time
Uncontrolled, naturalistic observational measurement	Subjective 'insider's' perspective, close to the data
Objective, 'outsider's' perspective, distanced from the data	
Question of validity	
Does an instrument measure what it is supposed to measure?	Has the researcher gained full access to the knowledge and meanings of informants?
Question of reliability	
Will the measure yield the same results on different occasions (assuming no real change in what is to be measured)?	Will similar observations be made by different researchers on different occasions?
Question of generalizability	
What is the probability that patterns observed in a sample will also be present in the wider population from which the sample was drawn?	How likely is it that ideas and theories generated in one setting will also apply in other settings?

Source: Easterby-Smith *et al.* (1999, pp. 27, 41); Deshpande (1983, pp. 103).

This table displays the 'pure' versions of each paradigm. Although the basic beliefs may be incompatible in theory, when it comes to actual research techniques often a middle way between the two approaches is applied (Easterby-Smith *et al.*, 1999, p. 26; McLaughlin, 1993, p. 181). Deshpande (1983, p. 107) states that several scholars have noted that quantitative methodologies (therefore following the positivistic paradigm) emphasize reliability (frequently to the exclusion of validity), while qualitative methodologies emphasize validity while playing down reliability.

Authors with a phenomenological background have published several attacks on positivism. One of the strongest has been on its assumptions of value freedom. Authors like Habermas have pointed out that any form of knowledge is an instrument of self-preservation. Human interests condition the way we enquire into, and construct our knowledge of, the world. The positivistic claim for independence of values and interests can therefore be questioned in practice. Another aspect, important for the further discussion about action research, is the ability of the paradigms to generate and test theories. We could argue that probably the most telling and fundamental distinction between the paradigms is with regard to the dimension of verification versus discovery. Habermas states furthermore that quantitative methods, and therefore the positivist paradigm, have been developed most directly for the task of verifying or confirming theories, and qualitative methods (the phenomenological approach) were purposely developed for the task of discovering or generating theories (Deshpande, 1983, p. 105). Mintzberg (1979, p. 584) emphasizes the importance of theory development and the application of exploratory research in contrast to a focus on 'rigorous research methodologies'. He states that 'there would be no interesting hypothesis to test if no one ever generalized beyond his or her data' and that 'the field of organization theory has . . . paid dearly for the obsession with *rigour* in the choice of methodology' (1979, pp. 584, 583).

Another point of criticism is the increasing discrepancy between theory and practice. The often cited 'ivory tower' (for example, Byrne, 1990, p. 50; Rapoport, 1990, p. 506; Simon, 1994, p. 1) describes this 'estrangement of academic research from business practice' (Simon, 1994, p. 5) over recent years. Byrne (1990, p. 1) cites the dean of a business school arguing that 80 per cent of management research may be irrelevant. The BAIN Commission on Management Research, as an answer to ensure research's distinctive contribution, demanded an increased collaborative dialogue between researchers and practitioners and emphasized the development of research on topics of critical importance to organizations and the practice of management (McLaughlin and Thorpe, 2000, pp. 6f).

Literature on heuristic devices
As the literature examines the strategic marketing management and planning process, emphasis will be put on the limitations connected to this work. Next, the use of heuristic devices to support strategic decision making will be analysed. This chapter is written for the marketing scholar, therefore it is assumed that readers will be familiar with the strategic management process. Owing to the constraints of space, emphasis has been placed on the analysis of action research, as this is seen as a fairly 'new' topic in marketing. Consequently, the following discussion will only briefly reflect the existing literature on strategic planning and the use of heuristic devices.

Strategic marketing management and planning
Strategic marketing management[2] is widely reflected in the current literature and there are various differing descriptions of this topic. Greenley (1984, p. 46) summarizes several descriptions ranging from 'broad means of achieving given aims', 'fundamental means or schemes', 'crucial and central issues to the use of the marketing function' to 'the grand design to achieve objectives'. Proctor and Kitchen give a rather broad definition: 'Strategic management is about steering an organization so that it avoids the various threats that can exist in its environment while allowing it to take advantage of any opportunities that present themselves' (Proctor and Kitchen, 1990 , p. 4).

Decision making is at the heart of strategic management (Wilson and Gilligan, 1997, p. 6). Detailed descriptions of the nature and different modes of strategic decisions are intensively discussed elsewhere (McDonald, 1996, pp. 12ff). It is suggested that strategic planning is superior to an unplanned approach to strategy definition. The paramount aim of strategic planning is the maximization of success, in the form of increased and sustainable competitive advantage (Easton, 1988, p. 31), by systemically analysing possible futures. However, it is unlikely that one single idea has a long-standing impact on a firm's fortunes since ideas are soon copied and the competitive advantage is soon eroded (Proctor and Ruocco, 1992, p. 50). This counts especially because the marketing environment in which the company manoeuvres is becoming increasingly complex in terms of competition and fuzzy market boundaries.

The process of strategic marketing planning follows the steps of analysis, planning, decision making (or implementation) and control. Several sub-steps by different authors have expanded these steps. However, there are various critical voices, probably culminating in Mintzberg's (1994a), '*The Rise and Fall of Strategic Planning*' (Nicholls, 1995, p. 4). Marketing theory has been criticized as being of little use for practitioners. There is a wide discussion about the 'ivory tower' of academia (Byrne, 1990, p. 50) which is concerned with the estrangement of theory from practice. It is furthermore argued that many non-academic voices, for example senior business people, consultants and journalists, are listened to in preference to marketing academics. Hence the theoretical underpinnings of marketing thoughts are coming under an increasing threat and often they are being perceived as lacking any relevance to the modern business world (Hill and McGowan, 1998, p. 70).

The use of heuristic devices to support strategic decision making used in the SME sector

Procedures for deriving solutions from models are either deductive or inductive. A deductive process describes the movement from the model to a solution in either symbolic or numerical form. Such procedures are supplied by mathematics, for example the calculus. An explicit analytical procedure for finding the solution is called an algorithm. Even if a mathematical model cannot be established or solved, and many are too complex for solution, it can be used to compare alternative solutions. It is sometimes possible to conduct a sequence of comparisons, each suggested by the previous one and each likely to contain a better alternative than given in any previous comparison. Such a solution-seeking procedure is called 'heuristic'. Inductive procedures involve trying and comparing different values of the controlled variables. This can happen in iterative steps, reaching successively improved solutions until either an optimal solution is reached or further progress cannot be justified in iterative steps.

Heuristic marketing devices, therefore, are models which can be used by the practitioner in order to obtain comparably quick solutions to a complex marketing problem. The results do not need to be mathematically correct; the strength of these models lies in their simplicity and their ability to model complex, sometimes even dynamic, situations.

Greenley (1989, p. 46) presents four major bases that are used in the literature to explain the detail of marketing strategy. These are the marketing mixes, the product life cycle, market share and competition, and positioning. In addition, special strategies for both international and industrial markets are proposed. Vignali *et al.* argue that the power of simple devices as managerial tools is well known (Vignali and Davies, 1994, p. 965). The authors highlight the example of the 4Ps, developed by McCarthy, and the Boston Consulting Group Matrix. In addition, McDonald highlights the Ansoff Matrix, Market Segmentation, Product Life Cycle Analysis, Portfolio Management and 'a host of techniques' revolving around the four basic elements of the marketing mix, the 4Ps (product, price, promotion, place) (McDonald, 1992, p. 9).

These models are widely explained and analysed in the existing literature (see, for example, Kotler, 2000; Baker, 1990; Wilson and Gilligan, 1997). Furthermore, the advantages and limitations of these models are frequently discussed elsewhere, so no deeper analysis of the existing models will be conducted here.

The combination of action research and heuristic devices
Although on both topics, action research and heuristic marketing devices, a voluminous literature is available, no concept of the combination of the two approaches exists. This is partly determined by the different worldviews, which are prevalent in both approaches. Whereas action research is similar to the phenomenological paradigm, the marketing scholar very much reflects the positivistic philosophy. The marketing scholar has derived knowledge from the social sciences and is therefore devoted to reductionism, objectivism and rigour (McDonald, 1992, p. 8), and mainly quantitative methods are applied (Hunt, 1994, p. 13). The limitations of this paradigm have been extensively discussed in the literature and there has been a call for the use of phenomenological methods in marketing (see, for instance, Hunt, 1994, p. 13; McDonald, 1992, p. 8). The limitations of current marketing practice have an impact on both academics and practitioners, one being the inability of positivistic approaches to generate new theories. Hunt argues that, currently, there are no original contributions of marketing to the strategy dialogue; rather concepts developed in the 1950s and 1960s are borrowed (Hunt, 1994, p. 14). Furthermore it is seen that 'marketing's job' is to apply the theories of other disciplines to marketing phenomena, according to the 'applied science' notion. This results in a lack of new theory which reflects more recent developments and an increasingly dynamic, volatile and aggressive environment. Therefore practitioners are unable to rely on the academic developments of marketing in order to facilitate their strategic and tactical decision making.

In addition, it is argued that the use of existing models by practitioners is only limited. McDonald argues that the application of marketing theory in practice is practically non-existent. He gives three reasons for this: companies have never heard of the theory, companies have heard of it but do not understand it, or companies have heard of it, have tried it and found that it is largely irrelevant (McDonald, 1992, p. 8f). Nevertheless, the existing heuristic marketing devices can offer practitioners powerful tools when applied adequately, as can be seen by various case studies in which these models were applied under supervision of academics or consultants.

Action research, on the other hand, is being increasingly applied in various business areas and has proved to offer several advantageous characteristics, which are superior to traditionally applied methods. However, action research also has limitations, which have to be considered. This leads to the challenging question whether it is possible to merge the two approaches and utilize the advantages and existing expertise of both principles while trying to compensate the individual limitations of each. The result could be an advanced model, exploiting the benefits of positivism and phenomenology, with synergistic effects exceeding the benefits of a basic model.

Conclusion

As outlined above, heuristic marketing devices are often applied following a process of analysis, planning and control; a real-world problem usually exists and triggers off the research process. However, as concluded above, not all application processes of marketing models encompass the control aspect. The main steps beginning with the existence of a real-world problem are analysis/diagnosing, planning the action, taking action and finally reflecting on and evaluating the action taken. One signpost for the solution of this problem could be the development of another approach to problem solving on the practical level and theory generation in an academic sense. This is paramount for the management of SMEs.

The procedure described below is believed to offer an appropriate way of researching the main questions this article is concerned with. It guides the reader and shows what steps will be followed to investigate the possibility of combining heuristic devices and action research in one integrative model.

Basically, action should be divided into three major parts, theoretical analysis, practical analysis and model integration, which are depicted in Figure 41.2. These steps are carried out repeatedly, until a 'best' solution is found. After researching a large number of companies, the author distinguishes and combines two different processes followed by action researchers and practitioners utilizing heuristic devices (Figure 41.3). Finally this model clearly identifies the importance of both heuristic devices and the action research cycle. The extended heuristic/action model integrates both the practical application and phenomenology approaches, to create a commonsense approach to the management process of decision making.

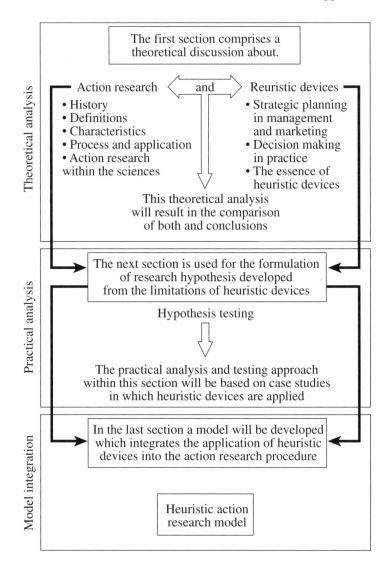

The first section comprises a
theoretical discussion about.

Theoretical analysis

Action research ⟨ and ⟩ Reuristic devices

• History
• Definitions
• Characteristics
• Process and application
• Action research
within the sciences

• Strategic planning
  in management
  and marketing
• Decision making
  in practice
• The essence of
  heuristic devices

This theoretical analysis
will result in the comparison
of both and conclusions

Practical analysis

The next section is used for the formulation
of research hypothesis developed
from the limitations of heuristic devices

Hypothesis testing

The practical analysis and testing approach
within this section will be based on case studies
in which heuristic devices are applied

Model integration

In the last section a model will be developed
which integrates the application of heuristic
devices into the action research procedure

Heuristic action
research model

Figure 41.2   The action research/heuristic device process

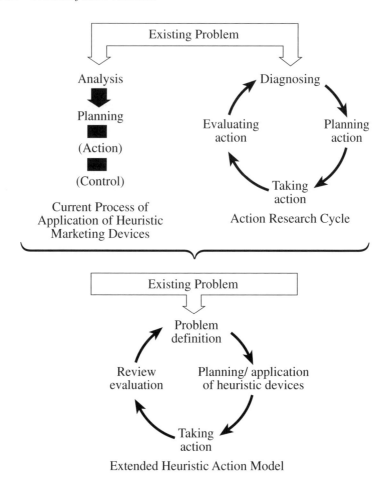

Figure 41.3   Process of the heuristic action model

Notes

1. Heidegger, for instance, questioned the word 'phenomenology' and traced it back to the meanings of the Greek concepts of *phainomenon* and *logos*. *Phenomenon* is 'that which shows itself from itself' but, together with the concept of *logos*, it means 'to let that which shows itself be seen from itself in the very way in which it shows itself from itself'. This definition is based on Aristotle's work. (*http://www.britannica.com/eb/article?eu=115435& tocid=68556#68556.toc*).
2. The integration of marketing as part of a market-oriented business philosophy has led simultaneously to a greater proximity of marketing and management concepts. Furthermore, by organizing and integrating all of the company's outside-oriented activities, strategic marketing supports the strategic management process (Jüttner and Wehrli, 1994, p. 42). Therefore, in this chapter, strategic marketing management and strategic management will not be distinct.

References

Argyris, C. (1993), *Knowledge for Action, A Guide to Overcoming Barriers to Organizational Change*, San Francisco: Jossey-Bass.

Baker, M. (1990), *Marketing Strategy*, Basingstoke: Macmillan.

Byrne, J.A. (1990), 'Is Research in the Ivory Tower "fuzzy, irrelevant, pretentious"' 29 Oct., *Business Week*, p. 50.

Coghlan, D. and Brannick, T. (2001), *Doing Action Research: In your own organisation*, London: Sage Publications.

Denzin, N.K. and Lincoln, Y.S. (1994), *Handbook of Qualitative Research*, London: Sage Publications, pp. 1–19.

Deshpande, R. (1983), ' "Paradigms Lost": on theory and method in research in marketing', *Journal of Marketing*, 47, Fall, 91–110.

Dickens, L. and Watkins, K. (1999), *'Action Research: Rethinking Lewin'*, *Management Learning*, 30 (2), 127–40.

Easterby-Smith, M., Thorpe, R. and Lowe, A. (1999), *Management Research, An Introduction*, London: Sage Publications.

Easton, G. (1988), 'Competition and Marketing Strategy', *European Journal of Marketing*, 18 (6), 90–103.

Greenley, G.E. (1984), 'An Understanding of Marketing Strategy', *European Journal of Marketing*, 18 (6), 60–103

Gronhaug, K. and Olson, O. (1999), 'Action research and knowledge creation: merits and challenges', *Qualitative market research: An International Journal*, 2 (1), 6–14.

Hill, J. and McGowan, P. (1998), 'Developing a Marketing Plan', *Journal of Marketing Practice*, 5 (1), 29–38.

Hunt, S.D. (1994), 'On Rethinking Marketing: Our Discipline, Our Practice, Our Methods', *European Journal of Marketing*, 28 (3), 13–25.

Juttner, U. and Wehrli, H.P. (1989), 'Competitive Advantage', *Journal of Business and Industrial Marketing*, 9 (4), 42–63.

Kotler, P. (2000), *Marketing Management*, Englewood Cliffs, NJ: Prentice-Hall.

McDonald, M. (1996), 'Strategic Marketing Planning: Theory, Practice and Research Agendas', *Journal of Marketing Management*, 12, 5–27.

McDonald, M.H.B. (1992), 'Strategic Marketing Planning: A State-of-the-art Review', *Marketing Intelligence and Planning*, 10 (4), 4–22.

McLaughlin, H. (1993), 'Silences in Management Research: Challenges From the "Margins"', unpublished thesis, Manchester Metropolitan University.

McLaughlin, H. and Thorpe, R. (2000), 'All in Bain: lost voices in the development of management research', Manchester Metropolitan University.

Mintzberg, H. (1979), 'An Emerging Strategy of "Direct Research"', *Administrative Science Quarterly*, 24, 582– .

Mintzberg, H. (1994a), 'The Fall and Rise of Strategic Planning', *Harvard Business Review*, January, 582–9.

Mintzberg, H. (1994b), *Rise and Fall of Strategic Planning*, New York: Prentice-Hall.

Nicholls, J. (1995), 'The MCC decision matrix: a tool for applying strategic logic to everyday activity', *Management Decision*, 33 (6), 4–10.

Peters, M. and Robinson, V. (1984), 'The Origins and Status of Action Research', *The Journal of Applied Behavioural Science*, 2 (2), 113–24.

Proctor, R.A. and Kitchen, P.J. (1990), 'Strategic Planning: An Overview of Product Portfolio Models', *Marketing Intelligence and Planning*, 8 (7), 4–11.

Proctor, T. and Ruocco, P. (1992), 'Generating Marketing Strategies: A Structured Creative Decision Support Model', *Management Decision*, 30 (5), 50–53.

Rapoport, R.N. (1990), 'Three Dilemmas in Action Research', *Human Relations*, 23 (6), 499–513.

Revans, R. (1998), 'ABC of Action learning', lemons crane.

Saker, J. and Smith, G. (1995), 'Use of Participating Action Research', *Journal of Strategic Marketing*, 4 (3), 69–84.

Simon, H. (1994), 'Marketing Science in the Ivory Tower', *Business Strategic Review*, 5 (1), 29–38.

Susman, G.I. and Evered, R.D. (1978), 'An Assessment of the Scientific Merits of Action Research', Administrative Science Quarterly, 23, 582–603.

Vignali, C., Shmidt, R. and Davies, B.J. (1994), 'The Marketing Mix Redefined and Mapped: Introducing the MIXMAP Model', *Management Decision*, 32 (8), 11–16.

Warmington, A. (1979), 'Action research: its methods and implications', Manchester Business School and Centre for Business Research.

Wilson, R.M.S. and Gilligan, C. (1997), *Strategic Marketing Management: Planning, implementation and control*, Oxford: Butterworth-Heinemann.

Zuber-Skerritt, O. (ed.) (1996), *New Directions in Action Research*, London: The Falmer Press.

42 Family business successions: toward future research
Robert H. Brockhaus Sr.

Succession of management is a significant moment in a family business's life. Indeed, Ward (1987) defines a family business as a business that will be passed from one generation to another. Because of the importance of a successful transfer of management, much has been written about succession issues (Sharma *et al.*, 1996). Succession is one issue that requires analysis from the perspectives of family, management and ownership systems in order to understand adequately the perspectives of the different stakeholders. Lansberg (1988) describes how succession planning is a topic that is approached with ambivalence because it 'imposes a wide variety of significant changes on the family firm: family relationships need to be realigned, traditional patterns of influence are redistributed, and long-standing management and ownership structures must give way to new structures'. Lansberg's studies suggest how succession affects the founder, the successor, the family, the managers, the owners and other stakeholders. This chapter will attempt to summarize the key issues and what past research has discovered. Its review of research will be structured along a sequence of activities related to succession. The order of topics to be presented is industry strategic analysis; family business analysis; selection of successor; development of successor and relationship issues. Because much of what has been written is not based upon well-designed empirical research studies, suggestions for improved research methodologies will be made.

Industry strategic analysis
The question of 'business first' or 'family first' is usually answered by family business consultants to the effect that the business's strategic needs should take precedence over benefits to individual family members. The literature in the field of business strategy maintains that, before a business strategic plan can be developed, an understanding of the industry needs to be determined.

Issues such as growth of demand, technological impacts, financial requirements, competitive environment, personnel required, governmental regulations and economic strength of customers, suppliers and competitors are all important industry factors that have a direct impact on the strategic plan of a family business.

Drozdow (1989) stresses that often the senior generation will provide experiences that help the junior generation learn how the business works, but fails to provide them with the skills to recognize new opportunities and to develop new strategies to take advantage of these opportunities. Drozdow (1990) suggested that, in family businesses in industries undergoing significant change, successors should be selected who can restructure the business or establish a new business. Levinson (1971) suggested that businesses with significant growth should professionalize the business by eliminating family members and hiring non-family managers. There have been no studies that have examined these factors and related them to succession issues. Are certain industry conditions better for family management than for non-family management, or vice versa? Is the development program for successors different under different industry conditions? Are there conditions that would suggest selling the business? No research has attempted to examine these questions or suggestions.

Family business analysis
Barnes and Hershon (1976) wrote that family transitions and company transitions usually occur together. They believe that, while the stress might be higher at these times, the combination of both transitions usually results in a smooth transition from relationship perspectives. Drozdow (1990) suggests that, before a family business selects a successor, it must answer some basic questions. Is it a source of employment, an investment or a vehicle to bring the family together? Is the business operating efficiently and profitably? She proposes that answers to these questions will determine what type of leader is needed to achieve the goals.

Malone (1989) found that strategic planning and continuity planning are related. Rosenblatt *et al.* (1985) pointed out that there is often tension because of conflict between the family system and the business system. Ward (1987) stated that strategic planning needs to incorporate the strategic plans of the family as well as of the business. Rutigliano (1986) suggested that there is a tendency to put the needs of the family before those of the business.

Davis (1982) suggested that family businesses tend to have a relatively high degree of intentionality of commitment to achievement and perseverance which derives from individual pride, family pride and family tradition. The frequency with which family businesses stress the positive value of family ownership of the business to their customers suggests that a relationship does exist. There is a vast amount of research needed about the impact of family business succession on its marketing approaches.

Financing is almost always a key concern of businesses, and family businesses are not exceptions. It is typical for the junior generation initially to assume the senior management position and, at a later date, to assume the ownership. The assumption of ownership can be by inheritance at the death of the senior generation, by purchase from the senior generation or by gifting of the ownership by the senior generation. All three scenarios are fraught with financial and legal issues related to taxation. These issues are compounded by fairness issues within the family. Although many families hope to continue family ownership, there are other families who decide that the sale of the business is in the family's best interest. Malone (1989) addresses leverage buyouts as a means of transition of ownership. Hoffmire and Gilbert (1992) discussed the applicability of employee stock ownership plans (ESOP) for family firms. Dreux (1990) suggested additional alternatives for obtaining cash from the business. Another form of taking capital out of the business is with a public offering. Bygrave and Timmons (1992) summarized the research done on initial public offerings and offered suggestions for future research needs. Although much has been written on the transfer of ownership, there is virtually no comparative research that has examined this critical topic.

The logic of these recommendations appears sound, but there has been no empirical testing of them. Do the results of succession vary according to the family's perception of the role of the business for the family? How do the steps of succession vary with the level of disconnection between the family systems and business systems and strategic plans? How is what happens when the family transition occurs at a different time than business transition different from the outcomes when they occur at the same time?

Selection of successor
Among the important conditions affecting management succession are the attitudes of the families (Birley, 1986). If the family does not support a specific family member assuming the leadership role, it is unlikely to occur. Davis (1986) stated that 'personal relations among relatives often take precedence over maximum profit' in family firms. Therefore a number of writers believe that a potential successor must have the trust of family members actively involved in the business (Goldberg and Woolridge, 1992; Horton, 1982; Lansberg and Astrachan, 1994). Of particular concern is the level of interest of members of the junior generation (Longenecker and Schoen, 1978; Ward, 1987; Churchill and Hatten, 1987; Handler, 1989).

Stavrou (1996), in a study of university students, reported finding that offspring intentions to join and not join the family business were significantly related to individual needs, goals, skills and abilities. She further found that the decision to not enter the business is related to family issues and not to business issues.

Increasingly, the selection criteria have become more objective. The following criteria are often used in evaluating potential successor's abilities to meet the strategic plans of the family business: education, technological skills, managerial skills and financial management skills. Of lesser importance are age, sex and birth order. Drozdow (1989) pointed out that there has been an ever-increasing tendency by family businesses to select a successor who was not the eldest son, thereby setting aside a long-established norm. A daughter or youngest son is increasingly selected as the person best able to be the new leader of the family business. Chrisman *et al.* (1998) found integrity and commitment to business more important than gender and birth order. It is frequently acknowledged that the eldest may not always be the best and sons may not necessarily be better than daughters (Ayres, 1990; Kaye, 1992). Barnes (1988) suggested that one reason for this persistence in choosing the eldest is that incongruity develops between the successor's standing in the business and the family when a younger son or a daughter takes over the business, which thus leads to ambiguity and rivalry within the family. As a result, incumbents, in order to preserve family harmony, may be discouraged from choosing a younger son or a daughter as successor.

Once again, the research needed to confirm these opinions is sparse and strongly designed empirical studies are needed. Controlling for other variables, research could examine the impact on business success and family relations of younger sons' and daughters' succession to that of older sons. Research could attempt to determine whether forms of education/counseling can reduce the family conflicts over the selection of a successor.

Development of successor
Longenecker and Schoen (1978) stated that the transfer of management is a long one, beginning in childhood, with the two primary points in time being when the successor enters the business on a full-time basis and when the leadership role is transferred. Peter Davis (1986) believes that personal skills and organizational development are needed for a family firm to develop through various stages. Similarly, Handler (1990) found that succession is a multiple stage process. This finding is similar to the findings of corporate executive succession (Farquhar, 1989; Friedman, 1987; Gabarro, 1979; Gilmore and McCann, 1983; Gordon and Rosen, 1981; Vancil, 1987).

Gaining experience outside the business has been recommended by Nelton (1986) and Danco (1982). Many consultants recommend at least three to five years in another business. Others suggest that at least one promotion should occur, thereby demonstrating the individual's ability. Experience outside the company helps the successor develop an identity and prepare for a wider range of problems that may confront the organization (Barnes, 1988; Correll, 1989).

There is a strong belief that the junior generation needs ever-increasing management responsibilities and breadth and diversity of experiences in the family business. This includes contacts with key suppliers, customers, lenders and others. Experience in the family business enables the successor to develop relationships within the company and understand the culture and intricacies of the business (Danco, 1982; Lansberg and Astrachan, 1994). Lansberg (1986) supports the importance of the junior generation family member's skills and overall ability to do the job. Danco (1982) urged that performance review should be part of the development process.

A tool to improve succession success is academic courses for family business members. Family business courses have grown rapidly in number over the last decade, but there has been little research conducted on the effectiveness of these courses. Family business courses were discussed at the first Family Business Educators Conference held in 1992, just prior to the Family Firm Institute annual meeting. In 1993, the Family Business Educators Conference that was held in conjunction with Saint Louis University's Gateway Series on Entrepreneurship Research yielded the first formal recommendations for research of family business courses. These recommendations were very similar to those suggested by Block (1981) who reported on the status of research on this aspect of entrepreneurship. They were encouraged by the quantity of work that has been done, given that entrepreneurship education is a relatively new development. They listed several challenges for future research: the development of appropriate research methodologies; the determination of needs of different student audiences; the qualifications of the instructor; and the most effective pedagogical methods.

Will this trend increase the success rate of second generation management as more qualified individuals lead the business rather than a family member who just happens to be the eldest son? Does experience in other companies improve success rates? Does such experience decrease the likelihood of the junior generation returning to the family business? No studies have attempted to examine these questions.

Relationship issues
More research and other writings have addressed the relationship issues than any other aspect of succession. Peter Davis (1986) indicated the importance of personal skills and organizational development in order for a family firm to progress successfully from an early stage to a later stage in its growth. Churchill and Hatten (1987) developed a life cycle approach to describe the succession process between father and son in a family firm. They distinguish four stages: (1) a stage of owner-management, where the owner is the only member of the family directly involved in the business; (2)

a training and development stage, where the offspring learns the business; (3) a partnership stage between father and son; and (4) a power transfer stage, where responsibilities shift to the successor.

Literature on both family business and executive succession emphasizes the importance of the relationship between the successor and the incumbent in determining the process, timing and effectiveness of the succession. A smooth succession requires the cooperation of the incumbent and the successor (Handler, 1992; Hollander and Elman, 1988). A good personal relationship between these individuals will contribute to the training and development of the successors (Lansberg, 1988, Chrisman *et al.*, 1998).

Similarly, Handler (1990) found that succession represents a mutual role adjustment process between the founder and next-generation family members during which the predecessor lessens his or her involvement in the firm over time. Davis & Haverston (1998) found similar results. Matthews *et al.* (1996) concluded from their research that the evaluation of the junior member's perception of the parents, the parents' perception of the junior member and each one's self-assessment will have a major impact on the succession process. Gomez-Mejia *et al.* (2001) also found the role of family ties to be important.

Many writers (Churchill and Lewis, 1983; Dyer, 1986; Greiner, 1972; Kaplan, 1987; Kets de Vries, 1985; Levinson, 1971; Schein, 1983, 1985) or CEOs (Sonnenfeld, 1987) have concluded that it is in the nature of founders/entrepreneurs to have difficulty giving up what they have created and/or run. They are capable of acting out this difficulty in a variety of nonproductive ways. Danco (1982) faults the founder for committing 'corporeuthanasia' which he defines as 'the owner's act of willfully killing off the business he loves by failing to provide in his lifetime for a viable organization with clear continuity'.

According to Lansberg (1988), the founder fears losing control and is concerned that retiring from the firm will mean a demotion in his role within the family. Loss of identity and power in the firm may mean loss of stature in the community as well. The spouse too may conspire not to do succession planning because the firm has played an important role in her identity (K. Danco, 1981; Rosenblatt *et al.*, 1985). Goldberg and Woolridge's (1992) research suggested that the successor must take control of the succession process. Shepherd and Zacharakis (2000) also stressed the decision-making process of the successor.

Several possibilities have been offered as ways of overcoming the founder's resistance to change through succession. One is through helping the founder to become more self-aware (Hall, 1986; Kaplan, 1987; Zaleznik and Kets de Vries, 1985). Another approach is to encourage the senior member to leave the old venture and start another. 'Instead of trying to change himself, he can continue to be a pioneer, but on a new frontier' (Zaleznik and Kets de Vries, 1985, p. 229). The quality of the relationship between the leader and the successor is a critical determinant of the succession process.

Siblings' conflicts are frequently an issue when succession is being considered or executed. Bowen (1976) developed the concept of the degree of differentiation in a family being along a continuum from enmeshed to autonomous. Swogger (1991) based his recommendations on Bowen's work. He suggested that bonding versus rivalry, autonomy versus dependency and leadership versus paralysis are key issues. He believed that, to the extent that emotional individuation occurs between the members of the junior generation, the succession issues are more easily resolved.

Consultants often recommend that a board of directors composed of some non-family members can provide a more impartial evaluation of business succession. Even though much more research has been carried out on this aspect of succession, there still are many opportunities to investigate. Does emotional individuation play a significant role in resolving succession issues? Is it linear or non-linear? If the senior member establishes a 'second career', are succession results improved?

Research methodologies
The level of research interest in family business succession issues has increased greatly in the last decade. However, many of the published articles are based upon casual observations rather than well-designed empirical studies. To improve the quality of the research methodology, past family business research methodology will be reviewed and critiqued. Finally, some specific recommendations will be presented that can enhance the quality and value of family business research.

Researchers
The initial writers on the subject of family business were consultants to family businesses. Frequently they were financial advisors or family therapists (Lansberg *et al.*, 1988). They wrote of their observations and suggested ways in which family businesses could avoid some of the pitfalls that the authors had observed confronting their clients. The majority of family business articles are currently of this type (Swartz, 1989). Similarly, there are many articles that have stated the contributions of family businesses to the GNP and to employment, much as entrepreneurship and small business writers have done and continue to do.

Problems include a lack of secondary data sources, forcing researchers to conduct field research studies. Field studies, in turn, are difficult to achieve because of the family business owners' lack of interest in participating in such studies, the wide spectrum of 'family businesses', the lack of theories for hypothesis testing, and the lack of commonly accepted definitions of an entrepreneur or a family business.

Comparative studies

Family business researchers have seldom done studies in which family businesses are contrasted with non-family businesses (Daily and Dollinger, 1992). Nor have there been attempts to compare family businesses with one another on the basis of such factors as size, number of family members, mothers versus fathers as founders, daughters versus sons as second generation and so on (Dumans, 1990; Salaganicoff, 1990). Family business researchers would be well advised to consider comparative studies for the possible causal relationships that they may be able to introduce into the knowledge base (Brown, 1991).

Longitudinal studies

Research has suffered from a lack of longitudinal studies (Van de Ven and Garud, 1989). This lack is understandable. First, family businesses are seldom willing to take part in a study that requires a single response from them, and one that requires several periods of interaction is even more difficult. Also the discontinuance rate is high for small businesses, thereby making follow-up difficult. Another factor is that younger researchers need to produce refereed journal articles in a relatively short period of time to obtain tenure and promotion. This need acts as a deterrent to conducting longitudinal studies.

Research methodologies

Two common weaknesses of all of the types of efforts described above are the failure of the researchers to enunciate appropriate research designs and the absence of sophisticated statistical techniques (Aldrich, 1992). Many of the first family business researchers came from a consulting background and had never been schooled in sound research practices. As a younger group of better trained investigators began to study family business topics, the quality of research design and use of statistical tools greatly improved (Handler, 1989).

There is also a growing source of data banks that will enable researchers with sound research design and statistical skills to vigorously probe more these secondary sources for new perspectives (Katz, 1992).

Relevancy of issues

Family business research has tended to focus more on issues of practical value to family businesses (Lansberg, 1988). However, this positive condition will become more threatened as the current family business researchers, who have consulting relationships with family businesses, are supplemented by those with a more theoretical background. These newcomers will probably bring better research skills but can be expected to be more interested in research topics that are less relevant to issues facing family business owners.

Definitions

Family business researchers are confronted by a definitional dilemma (Lansberg, 1988). Some researchers argue that family business is any in which more than one member of the family is affected by business decisions. Under this definition, a proprietorship is a family business if the single owner discusses the business with his or her spouse at dinner. Others require that at least two members of the family are active in the management and/or ownership of the business. Still others consider a family business as one with family members from different generations active in the business. Some expect the family to be owners of at least 51% of the stock, while others believe the family simply needs to be able to exert its desires normally on major decisions. A number of definitions which have been listed by Handler (1989) appear in Table 42.1. Because of this wide difference of opinions, it is unlikely that a definition will be agreed upon in the near future. Therefore it is very important that family business researchers describe fully the subset of family business that is being studied.

Entrepreneurship researchers in the 1970s and 1980s devoted a significant amount of effort in attempting to obtain a definition for the term 'entrepreneur'. By 1990, most researchers had come to the realization that a single definition of the term was not going to be widely accepted. The importance of fully describing the subjects in any specific study became more fully recognized (Katz and Brockhaus, 1993). The descriptive variables that they recommend are listed in Table 42.2. Many of these are equally important for family business researchers to include in the descriptions of the family businesses they study.

International research

Another form of boundary is international borders. Until the late 1980s, North American entrepreneurship researchers seldom referenced work done in other parts of the world, despite the fact that significant research was being conducted elsewhere (Brockhaus, 1992). Attendance at North American family business conferences by researchers living outside North America has tended to make American researchers more aware of the work done elsewhere and there is continued improvement in the inclusion of the work done outside North America (Lank, 1991). Perhaps one reason is the recognition of significant differences in family cultures in different areas of

Table 42.1   Alternative definitions of family business

Ownership–management

Alcorn (1982) A profit-making concern that is either a proprietorship, a partnership, or a corporation. . . If part of the stock is publicly owned, the family must also operate the business (p. 23)

Barry (1975) An enterprise which, in practice, is controlled by the members of a single family (p. 42)

Barnes & Hershon (1976) Controlling ownership [is] rested in the hands of an individual or of the members of a single family (p. 106)

Dyer (1986) A family firm is an organization in which decisions regarding its ownership or management are influenced by a relationship to a family (or families) (p. xiv)

Lansberg (1988) A business in which the members of a family have legal control over ownership (p. 2)

Stern (1986) [A business] owned and run by members of one or two families (p.xxi)

Interdependent subsystems (family involvement in the business)

Beckhard & Dyer (1983) The subsystems in the family firm system . . . include (1) the business as an entity, (2) the family as an entity, (3) the founder as an entity, and (4) such linking organizations as the board of directors (p. 6)

Davis (1986) It is the interaction between two sets of organization, family and business, that establishes the basic character of the family business and defines its uniqueness (p. 47)

Generational transfer

Churchill & Hatten (1987) What is usually meant by 'family business' . . . is either the occurrence or the anticipation that a younger family member has or will assume control of the business from an elder (p. 52)

Ward (1987) [A business] that will be passed on for the family's next generation to manage and control (p. 252)

Multiple conditions

Donnelley (1988) A company is considered a family business when it has been closely identified with at least two generations of a family and when this link has had a mutual influence on company policy and on the interests and objectives of the family (p. 94)

Rosenblatt et al. (1985) Any business in which the majority ownership or control lies within a single family and in which two or more family members are or at some time were directly involved in the business (pp. 4–5)

Source: W.C. Handler (1989), 'Methodological issues and considerations in studying family businesses', *Family Business Review*, 2(3).

Table 42.2   Demographic variables in entrepreneurial research

---

1) How did you become the owner or principal manger of this business?
2) How many businesses have you started?
3) What was your primary reason for starting this business?
4) When you started this business, what did you primarily plan to do?
5) What is your highest level of education completed?
6) What is your sex?
7) How many years of experience did you have in this field or industry when you started or joined this business?
8) What was your age at your last birthday?
9) What is your marital status?
10) What is your position in the business?
11) To what degree are you involved in the business?
12) What was the dollar volume of your business in the last fiscal year?
13) What was the dollar volume of your business in the previous fiscal year?
14) What was the number of full-time employees (or full-time equivalents if you have part-time employees) in your organization at the end of the last fiscal year?
15) What was the number of full-time employees in your organization at the end of the previous fiscal year?
16) What is the breadth of your organization's operations?
17) What year did your firm begin operation?
18) What year did the current management assume control of the firm?
19) Classify your major business activities.
20) What percentage of the business is owned by you?
21) What is the total number of owners (either stockholders or partners)?
22) What is your form of organization?
23) What percentage of management in your business are family members?
24) What percentage of your company is owned by management?
25) What was the value of the total assets of the company at the end of its last fiscal year?
26) What is the total owner's equity in the firm?
27) What is your business's long-term debt?
28) How many products do you sell?
29) How many services do you sell?
30) How many of your leading products and services go to generating 80% of your dollar volume?
31) How complex technologically is your product/service?
32) How complex technologically is your production/operation?
33) Does your business have one or more unique strengths in the market-place relative to your competitors?
34) Do you have a written business plan?
35) What are your major business goals?
36) What is your preferred strategy for fostering business growth?

Table 42.2 (continued)

---

37) What is your preferred strategy for financing business growth?
38) What kinds of individuals or groups are available in your community to help you evaluate your business ideas?
39) What is the availability of start-up capital for a new business in your community?
40) Give the location of your business. Given a zip code, the following community data can be obtained from federal government statistics: Age distribution, Education distribution, Occupation by Industry, Household Income, Per Capita Income.

Source: This abbreviated version is taken from J.A. Katz, R.H. Brockhaus Sr. and G.E. Hills (1983), *Demographics variables in entrepreneurship research. Advances in entrepreneurship, firm emergence and growth*, vol. 1, Greenwich, CT: JAI Press, pp. 229–234.

the world. Another is the general increased level of awareness of the international aspects of business in general.

Ethics and values
Ethics is about standards of behaviour which society demands for people to live together in an agreeable manner. Although each person develops his or her own standard, there need to be commonly accepted rules. These rules exist at many different levels in society: there are rules that are supported in principle by people throughout the world; there are others that exist within specific cultures; and there are still others that are industry standards.

Of interest is how an individual reacts when faced by a dilemma that forces a choice between two conflicting sets of ethical principles or values. It is this area in which many family business owners find themselves. Forced to choose between what might be the best decision for the business and what might be the best decision for the family or an individual member of the family is a very difficult yet common ethical decision facing many family businesses and their owners. There is virtually no research on the way family business owners and others in their families arrive at these crucial decisions (Handler, 1992).

In addition to the normal methodological care that a researcher must exercise, research such as this requires extra attention to ethical issues confronting the researchers (Seashore *et al.*, 1982). As Dees and Starr (1992) suggest, the questions in need of answering are those that are not easily discussed. To obtain answers the researcher much obtain the trust of the family business members. This, in turn, requires the researcher to avoid the use of deception and to strive to eliminate personal biases in the collection of the information and in the reporting of the findings.

The researcher must fully disclose the purpose of the study, how the information will be compiled, the guarantee of confidentiality, and the benefits of the research to society, and still elicit complete and honest responses. The examination of personal biases is equally difficult: the researcher may be unaware of his or her own personal biases. A team approach can help to overcome this problem. Taped interviews (with the knowledge and approval of the subjects) can allow for others to review the conclusions of the researcher to determine whether any inaccuracies have occurred.

Well-thought-out research methodologies, research questions and careful attention to personal ethics by the researcher could provide both the academic community and the family business owners with greatly improved insight into this most difficult aspect of conflicting ethical values.

Towards the future

Family business research has increased greatly in quality and quantity in the last decade. However, as this review has demonstrated, there are many topics that have not been adequately studied and others that have not been examined with sound research methodologies. As globalization spreads families across the globe, family businesses are likely to have increasingly international issues to consider. It is hoped that future research into family business succession issues will be conducted in a more vigorous methodological manner, but will maintain the thrust of much of the previous research that has served to provide direct benefit to family business owners, their families and the other stakeholders.

References

Alcorn, P.B. (1982), *Success and Survival in the Family-Owned Firm*, New York: McGraw-Hill.

Ayres, G.R. (1990), 'Rough Family Justice: Equity in Family Business Succession Planning', *Family Business Review*, 3(1), 3–22.

Barnes, L.B. (1998), 'Incongruent Hierarchies: Daughters and Younger Sons as Company CEOs', *Family Business Review*, 1(1), 9–21.

Barnes, L.B. and Hershon, S.A. (1976), 'Transferring Power in the Family Business', *Harvard Business Review*, 54(4), 105–14.

Birley, S. (1986), 'Succession in the Family Firm: The Inheritor's View', *Journal of Small Business Management*, July, 36–43.

Block, P. (1981), *Flawless Consulting: A Guide to Getting Your Expertise Used*, Pfeiffer and Co.

Bowen, M. (1976), 'Theory in the Practice of Psychotherapy', in P.J. Geurin, Jr. (ed.), *Family Therapy: Theory and Practice*, New York: Gardner Press.

Brockhaus, R.H. (1992), 'Entrepreneurship Education and Research in Europe', *The State of the Art of Entrepreneurship*, 560–78.

Brown, F.H. (1991), *Reweaving the Family Tapestry: A Multigenerational Approach to Families*, New York: Norton.

Bygrave, W. and Timmons, J. (1992), *Venture Capital at the Crossroads*, McGraw-Hill Professional.

Chrisman, J.J., Chua, J.H, and Sharma, P. (1998), 'Important Attributes of Successors in Family Businesses', *Family Business Review*, 10(2), 19–34.

Churchhill, N.C. and Hatten, K.J. (1987), 'Non-Market-Based Transfers of Wealth and

Power: A Research Framework for Family Businesses', *American Journal of Small Business*, 11(3), 51–64.

Churchhill, N.C. and Lewis, V.L. (1983), 'The Five Stages of Small Growth', *Harvard Business Review*, May–June, 30–51.

Correll, R.W. (1989), 'Facing up to Moving Forward: A Third-Generation Successor's Reflections', *Family Business Review*, 2(1), 17–29.

Daily, C.M. and Dollinger, M.J. (1992), 'An empirical examination of ownership structure in family and professionally managed firms', *Family Business Review*, 5(2), 117–36.

Danco, K. (1981), *From the Other Side of the Bed: A Woman Looks at Life in the Family Business*, Cleveland: The University Press.

Danco, L. (1982), *Beyond Survival: A Guide for the Business Owner and His Family*, Cleveland: The University Press.

Davis, J.A. (1982), 'The Influence of Life Stage on Father–Son Work Relationships in Family Companies', doctoral dissertation, Harvard Business School.

Davis, P. (1986), 'Family Business: Perspectives on Change', *Agency Sales Magazine*, June, pp. 9–16.

Davis, P.S. and Haverston, P.D. (1998), 'The influence of the family on the family business succession process: A multi-generational perspective', *Entrepreneurship Theory and Practice*, Spring, 31–53.

Dees, J.G. and Starr, J.A. (1992), 'Entrepreneurship Through an Ethical Lens', in Donald L. Sexton and John D. Kasarda (eds), *The State of the Art of Entrepreneurship*, Boston, MA: PWS-Kent.

Donnelley, Robert G. (1988), 'The Family Business', *Family Business Review*, 1(4), 427–45.

Dreux, D.R. (1990), 'Financing Family Business: Alternatives to Selling out and Going Public', *Family Business Review*, 3, 225–243.

Drozdow, N. (1989), 'Thinking That is Intuitive to the Boss Must be Chartered for the Next Generation', *The Business Week Newsletter for Family-Owned Businesses*, 1(19), 11 August.

Drozdow, N. (1990), 'Revenues and Relationships: Consulting That Links Business Strategy to Family process', presentation to the Family Firm Institute Conference, Atlanta, Georgia, 18 Oct.

Dumans, C.A. (1990), 'Preparing the new CEO: managing the father–daughter succession process in family businesses', *Family Business Review*, 169–81.

Dyer, W.G. Jr. (1986), *Cultural Change in Family Firms: Anticipating and Managing Business and Family Transitions*, San Francisco: Jossey Bass.

Farquhar, K.A. (1989), 'Employee Responses to External Executive Succession: Attributions and the Emergence of Leadership', doctoral dissertation, Boston University, Department of Psychology.

Friedman, S. (1987), 'The Succession Process: Theoretical Considerations', paper presented at the Annual Meeting of the Academy of Management, New Orleans.

Gabarro, J. (1979), 'Socialization at the Top: How CEO's and Subordinates Evolve Interpersonal Contracts', *Organizational Dynamics*, 7(3), 3–23.

Gilmore, R.N. and McCann, J.E. (1983), 'Designing Effective Transitions for New Correctional Leaders', in J.W. Doig (ed.), *Criminal Corrections: Ideals and Realities*, Lexington: Lexington Books.

Goldberg, Steven D. and Woolridge, Bill (1992), 'Succession: From the Other End of the Telescope', paper presented at the Academy of Management Meeting in Las Vegas, Nevada.

Gomez-Mejia, L., Nunez-Nickel, M. and Gutierrez, I. (2001), 'The role of family ties in agency contract', *Academy of Management Journal*, 44, 81–95.

Gordon, G.E. and Rosen, N. (1981), 'Critical Factors in Leadership Succession', *Organizational Behavior and Human Performance*, 27, 227–54.

Greiner, L.W. (1972), 'Evolutions and Revolutions as Organizations Grow', *Harvard Business Review*, July–August, 37–46.

Hall, D.T. (1986), 'Dilemmas in Linking Succession Planning to Individual Executive Learning', *Human Resource Management*, Summer, 25(2), 235–65.

Handler, W.C. (1989), 'Managing the Family Firm Succession Process: The Next-Generation Family Member's Experience', doctoral dissertation, Boston University School of Management.

Handler, W.C. (1990), 'Succession in Family Firms; A Mutual Role Adjustment Between Entrepreneur and Next-Generation Family Members', *Entrepreneurship: Theory and Practice*, 15(1), 37–51.

Handler, W.C. (1992), 'The Succession Experience of the Next-Generation', *Family Business Review*, 5(3), 283–307.

Hoffmire, J.S. and Gilbert, R.J. (1992), 'Questions and Answers Regarding ESOPs for Family Businesses', *Family Business Review*, 5(2), 173–80.

Hollander, B.S. and Elman, N.S. (1988), 'Family-Owned Businesses: An Emerging Field of Inquiry', *Family Business Review*, 1(2), 145–64.

Horton, T.P. (1982), 'The Baton of Succession', *Management Review*, 71, 2–3.

Kaplan, R. (1987), 'Helping Succession Succeed – With High-Powered Development', paper presented at Meetings of the Academy of Management, New Orleans, Louisiana.

Katz, J.A. (1992), 'Secondary analysis in entrepreneurship: an introduction to data bases and data management', *Journal of Small Business Management*, 30 (20), 74–86.

Katz, J.A. and Brockhaus, R.H. (1993), *Advances in the study of entrepreneurship firm emergence and growth – Volume 1*, Greenwich, CT: JAI Press.

Kaye, K. (1992), 'The Kid Brother', *Family Business Review*, 5(3), 237–56.

Kelly, G. (1955), *The Psychology of Personal Constructs*, vol. 1, New York: Norton.

Kets de Vries, M.F.R. (1985), 'The Dark Side of Entrepreneurship', *Harvard Business Review*, November–December, 160–7.

Lank, A.G. (1991), 'Challenging Times for European Family Enterprises', *Family Business Review*, 121–25.

Lansberg, I.S. (1983), 'Conversation with Richard Beckhard', *Organizational Dynamics*, Summer, 12, 29–38.

Lansberg, I.S. (1986), 'Program for the Study of Family Firms: Survey on Succession and Continuity', Yale University School of Organization and Management.

Lansberg, I.S. (1988), 'The Succession Conspiracy', *Family Business Review*, 1(2), 119–43.

Lansberg, I. and Astrachan, J.H. (1994), 'Influence of Family Relationships on Succession Planning and Training: The Importance of Mediating Factors', *Family Business Review*, 7(1), 39–59.

Levinson, H. (1971), 'Conflicts the Plague the Family Business', *Harvard Business Review*, March–April, 53–62.

Longenecker, J.G. and Schoen, J.E. (1978), 'An Empirical Investigation of Pre-Entry Socialization of Successors for Leadership in Family-Controlled Business', *Management Perspectives on Organizational Effectiveness*, Southern Management Association Meetings.

Longenecker, J.G. and Schoen, J.E. (1978), 'Management Succession in the Family Business', *Journal of Small Business Management*, July, 1–6.

Malone, S.C. (1989), 'Selected Correlates of Business Continuity Planning in the Family Business', *Family Business Review*, 2(4), 341–53.

Matthews, C.H., Moore, T.W. and Fialko, A.S. (1996), 'A Theory of Leadership Succession in the Family Firm', presented at the 10th Annual Conference of the United States Association for Small Business and Entrepreneurship, Atlanta, Georgia.

Nelton, S. (1986), 'Making Sure Your Business Outlasts You', *Nations Business*, January, 32–8.

Rosenblatt, P., Mik, L., Anderson, R. and Johnson, P. (1985), *The Family in Business*, San Francisco: Jossey Bass.

Rutigliano, A. (1986), 'When Worlds Collide: Problems in Family-Owned Businesses', *Management Review*, American Management Association, 22–9 February.

Salaganicoff, M. (1990), 'Women in family business: challenges and opportunities', *Family Business Review*, 125–37.

Schein, E.H. (1983), 'The Role of the Founder in the Creation of Organizational Culture', *Organizational Dynamics*, Summer, 12, 13–28.

Schein, E.H. (1985), *Organizational Culture and Leadership*, San Francisco: Jossey Bass.

Seashore, S., Lawler, E. Mirvis, P. and Cammann, C. (1982), *Observing and Measuring Organizational Change: A Guide to Field Practice*, New York: Wiley.

Sharma, P., Chrisman, J.J. and Chua, J.H. (1996), *A review and annotated bibliography of family business studies*, Boston: Kluwer Academic Publishers.

Shepherd, D.A. and Zacharakis, A.L. (2000), 'Structuring family business succession: An analysis of the future leader's decision making', *Entrepreneurship Theory and Practice*, 24(4), 25–39.

Sonnenfeld, J. (1987), 'Chief Executives as the Heroes or Villains of the Executive Process', paper presented at the Meetings of the Academy of Management, New Orleans, Louisiana.

Stavrou, Eleni (1996), 'Intergenerational Transitions in Family Enterprise: Factors Influencing Offspring Intentions to Seek Employment in the Family Business'.

Stern, M.H. (1986), *Inside the Family-held Business*, New York: Harcourt Brace Jovanovich.

Swartz, S. (1989), 'The Challenges of Multidisciplinary Consulting to Family-Owned Businesses', *Family Business Review*, 2(4).

Swogger, G. (1991), 'Assessing the Successor Generation in Family Business', *Family Business Review*, 4(4), 397–411.

Van de Ven, A.H. and Garud, R. (1989), 'A framework for understanding the emergence of new industries', in Rosenbloom, R. and Burgelman, R. (eds) *Research on technological innovation and management policy*, 4, Greenwich, CT: JAI Press, 195–226.

Vancil, R.F. (1987), *Passing the Baton: Managing the Process of CEO Succession*, Boston: Harvard Business School Press.

Ward, J.L. (1987), *Keeping the Family Business Healthy*, San Francisco: Jossey Bass.

Zaleznik, A. and Kets de Vries, M.F.R. (1985), *Power and The Corporate Mind*, Chicago, IL: Bonus.

43 On field research methods for theory building and testing
Thierry Volery

This chapter discusses the different standpoints from which the entrepreneurship phenomenon can be analysed. Four main units of analysis are identified: the individual, the environment, the project and the newly created organization. Conducting research in an international environment is particularly challenging because of cultural, economic and technical differences which affect the entrepreneurial process. This chapter further presents a typology of field research methods and discusses their contribution to theory building and testing. The overall conclusion is that field research methods will continue to be used heavily to develop entrepreneurship research. These conditions include a balanced research agenda, multifaceted research approaches and innovative data-gathering techniques. The chapter also recommends new methodological inputs from other academic disciplines that are more experienced with human interaction research.

In recent years, the field of entrepreneurship has experienced increased criticism, for several reasons. Firstly, the phenomenon of entrepreneurship has lacked a conceptual framework that explains and predicts a set of empirical phenomena. Much of this has stemmed from the absence of a broadly accepted definition of entrepreneurship. Secondly, and as a consequence, scholars in entrepreneurship have been at pains to explain how their field differs from others such as strategic management, small business management or economics. Thirdly, much of the criticism relates to the research methods used to investigate the phenomenon of entrepreneurship. The criticism spans researchers' descriptive orientation, lack of conceptual adequacy, the commonsense nature of findings, reductionism at the expense of complexity and lack of scientific rigour (Shane and Venkataraman, 2000). These critics call for more rigorous research methods to describe, explain and predict the entrepreneurship phenomenon.

Following Venkataraman (1997, p. 120), we define entrepreneurship as the process brought about by individuals of identifying new opportunities and converting them into marketable products or services. Therefore the field of entrepreneurship involves the study of sources of opportunities; the processes of discovery, evaluation and exploitation of opportunities; and the set of individuals who discover, evaluate and exploit them.

The purpose of this chapter is threefold. Firstly, we identify the different units of analysis possible in entrepreneurship. To achieve this, a model of new venture formation is presented and discussed. Secondly, we show the difficulties and potential pitfalls in conducting international research in entrepreneurship based on a practical example. Thirdly, we discuss the contributions made by field research methods to the development of theory in entrepreneurship. This is done by presenting a framework for classifying field studies by their data collection technique. We outline the capacity of field methods to make a further contribution to theory development, particularly at the level of theory building using a triangulation approach.

What unit of analysis to choose?
As suggested by Gartner (1989), it may be useful for scholars to shift their focus from the characteristics and functions of the entrepreneur, and the myriad of definitions of what constitutes an entrepreneur, and focus instead on the nature and characteristics of the entrepreneurial process. As Figure 43.1 shows, this process involves all the functions, activities and actions associated with the discovery, evaluation and exploitation of opportunities. Central to the process of new venture formation is the founding individual. Whether the entrepreneur is perceived as a 'captain of industry', a hard-headed risk bearer, a man apart or a visionary, he or she is overwhelmingly perceived to be different in important ways from the non-entrepreneur (for example the manager). Many researchers believe these differences lie in the psychological traits and background of the entrepreneur.

However, entrepreneurs do not operate in a vacuum; they respond to their environments. A conducive political, economic, social and infrastructure environment facilitates the emergence of new business ventures. Figure 43.1 shows that the initiation of new ventures requires the combination of the right individual at the right place. The typical would-be entrepreneur is constantly attuned to environmental changes that may suggest an opportunity. The literature makes it clear, however, that opportunities do not drop from the sky. They are created within and among organizations as a product of networks of relationships and exchanges (Low and MacMillan, 1988). Opportunities come most frequently to people located in advantageous positions within networks.

Individuals may have the propensity to found and evolve in a conducive entrepreneurial environment; they may even have identified a promising opportunity, but the actual decision to attempt to launch the venture arises from a clear intention and this implies action. In new venture formation, intention is a conscious state of mind that directs attention towards the goal of establishing the new organization (Bird, 1989). With the expression of

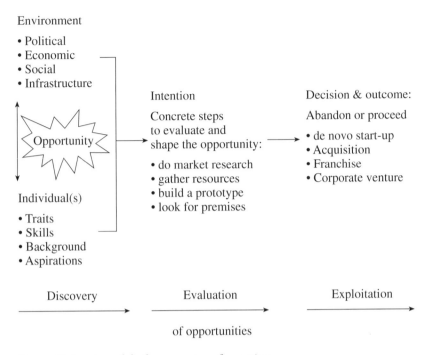

Figure 43.1   A model of new venture formation

intention ('I am going to try to start a business') the nascent entrepreneur takes concrete steps to evaluate the business opportunity and to gather resources in order to launch the venture. Such steps can include the formulation of strategy, the development of a prototype, the first market research, the identification of potential partners and the drafting of a business plan.

Having assessed the opportunity, nascent entrepreneurs must decide whether they want to proceed and exploit the opportunity, or to abandon it. There are several types of potential outcome at the end of the entrepreneurial process because different organizational arrangements for the exploitation of opportunities exist. Although most of the research in entrepreneurship has focused on new independent start-ups as the principal type of outcome, we must also consider other entrepreneurial outcomes, such as corporate ventures, franchises, joint ventures and business acquisitions. No matter what the type of outcome is, the key issue is that the organizational form which seems the most suitable to pursue the opportunity will ultimately commercialize a new product or service in the marketplace.

Following the model presented in Figure 43.1, we suggest that research in entrepreneurship essentially revolves around the stages of discovery, evaluation and exploitation of opportunities. For each stage, the following units of analysis may be considered: the individual, the environment, the opportunity or project and the organization set up by the entrepreneur.

The difficulties of conducting research at the international level

While research is being conducted in an international context, the environment dimension can change considerably. The cultural, legal, economic and technological environments influencing entrepreneurship vary significantly amongst and even, sometimes, within countries. Conducting a research project at the international level therefore increases this complexity. The Global Entrepreneurship Monitor (GEM) (see Reynolds *et al.*, 2001) is a good example of such a project. GEM aims to bring together the world's best scholars in entrepreneurship to study the complex relationship between entrepreneurship and economic growth. From its inception in 1997, the project was designed to be a long-term, multinational study, and in 2002 it encompassed 40 countries. Data were assembled from three principal sources: surveys of the adult population, in-depth interviews with national experts in entrepreneurship in each country, and a wide selection of standardized national data from various international organizations.

Researchers in the GEM consortium frequently face a series of difficulties because of the international nature of the project. These difficulties can be divided into three broad categories.

- *Translation and understanding of questions* Some items in the survey instrument are particularly difficult to translate and they can be interpreted differently across countries. For example, the item 'You are, alone or with others, currently trying to start a new business'. It is particularly difficult to assess the level of commitment of the nascent entrepreneur to the emerging venture. In certain countries (such as China, Brazil, Mexico or India) many people are constantly looking for better opportunities and consequently 'trying to set up a business'. However, this might not be a serious attempt and these individuals devote little time to the evaluation of the opportunity. Hence this question, which measures entrepreneurial intention across countries, is not always easy to interpret.
- *Various sampling and data collection methods* In certain countries, it is not possible to obtain a random sample of the adult population (individuals aged between 18 and 65). There are for example no or incomplete phone registries in China, India and Brazil. Moreover, only a fraction of the population in these countries has a telephone. As a consequence, survey firms which collect the data have to send investigators in the field to conduct face-to-face interviews.

- *Quality monitoring of local survey firms* Adult population surveys are outsourced to survey firms selected by the GEM coordination team based in London. While national coordinators in each participating country can make suggestions regarding the survey firm, the overall coordination and final choice of survey firms is made by the GEM coordination team. The advantage of this organization is that the coordination team can sometimes negotiate better prices if one international survey company (such as ACNielsen, MORI or Ipsos) conducts the survey in several countries. However, it is often difficult to monitor the quality of the work of survey firms and the data collected must be carefully edited to ensure their completeness, consistency and reliability. Despite all these efforts, mistakes, albeit rare, have existed in the data set and in yearly reports since the project was launched.

Field research methods

Entrepreneurship is intertwined with a complex set of contiguous and overlapping constructs such as the management of change, innovation, uncertainty, new product development and industry revolution. Furthermore, the phenomenon has been investigated from disciplines as varied as marketing, industrial economics, economics, sociology, psychology, history and anthropology. Each of these disciplines has its own paradigm, units of analysis, assumptions and research biases. Given this disciplinary diversity, it is not surprising that theory development in entrepreneurship relies on a broad array of research methods. As an organizational science, entrepreneurship research has tools available which include field methods (such as surveys, case studies and action research), computer data bases, simulations and combinations of various approaches (Snow and Thomas, 1994). Field studies are those which involve real entrepreneurs and new ventures as contrasted with ad hoc groups or events that are created and studied in the laboratory.

As shown in Table 43.1, field research methods can, perhaps more than any other method, realistically examine entrepreneurial processes and outcomes; that is, they provide mechanisms for observing individuals and their entrepreneurial project in their natural settings. In entrepreneurship, field studies have taken many forms, including single and multiple case studies, questionnaire surveys, action research and field experiments. Sample sizes have ranged from the single case to several thousands of observations, and the unit of analysis has spanned the would-be entrepreneur, the 'successful' entrepreneur and the institutional outcome of the entrepreneurial process (for example de novo start-up, franchise, corporate venture, spin off).

Table 43.1   Types of organizational research methods and techniques

Features	Methods	Data collection techniques or principles
Natural environment, uncontrolled	Field methods (e.g. surveys, case surveys, case studies, action research, grounded and ethnographic research)	Structured observations Unstructured or semi-structured interviews Questionnaires Archival analysis
	Computer data bases	Researcher accesses information collected by others
	Experimental simulations	Researcher tries to create a realistic facsimile of a situation, sets it in motion and observes its behaviour
	Laboratory experiments	Researcher examines organizational processes under tightly controlled conditions
Artificial environment, controlled	Computer simulation	Researcher uses mathematical modelling to construct a complete and closed model of the phenomenon of interest

Entrepreneurship field studies can be categorized into six major types, based primarily on the data-collection technique:

- *Observations*   Scientific observation is the systematic process of recording the behavioural patterns of people, objects and occurrences without communicating with them (Zikmund, 1997, p. 263). Field studies require direct observations, a straightforward attempt to observe and record what naturally occurs; the investigator does not create an artificial situation.

- *Interviews*   Interviews are a technique for collecting data in which selected participants are asked questions in order to find out what they do, think or feel. Interviews make it easy to compare answers and may be face-to-face, voice-to-voice or screen-to-screen, conducted with individuals or with a group of individuals (Hussey and Hussey, 1997). A positivistic approach suggests structured, closed questions which have been prepared beforehand. A phenomenological approach, in contrast, usually adopts semi-structured interviews and in-depth interviews to produce 'rich' information about a particular topic.

- *Questionnaires*   A questionnaire is a list of carefully structured questions, chosen after considerable testing, with a view to eliciting reliable responses from a chosen sample. The aim is to find out what a selected group of participants do, think or feel. Under a positivistic paradigm, questionnaires can be used for large-scale surveys. Each question can be coded at the design stage and completed questionnaires can be computer processed. A positivistic approach suggests that closed questions should be used, whereas a phenomenological approach suggests open-ended questions. Questionnaires can be administrated in different ways: face-to-face, over the phone, via video-conference or via e-mail.

- *Archival analysis*   This technique focuses upon the examination of documents created and kept by the entrepreneur and/or the organization. Examples are business plans, patent application, official minutes and records, diaries and contracts. Field research is primarily concerned with the analysis of primary documents (those written by the entrepreneur and other actors in the start-up process).

- *Field experiments*   In contrast to the four previous categories, this type of field technique involves the researcher imposing a substantial degree of structure on the situation. Field experiments are a research investigation in which conditions are controlled so that one or more variables can be manipulated in order to test a hypothesis. Business experiments hold the greatest potential for establishing cause-and-effect relationships. Although field experiments offer the advantage that they are conducted in real situations, and thus avoid many of the drawbacks of the laboratory experiment, there may be problems establishing and conducting the research. In particular, it is not always possible to exclude outside influences affecting the experiment.

- *Muti-method study*   This type of field study is a composite of two or more of the techniques discussed above. For example, Larsson (1993) remarked that the case survey is a potentially powerful method of identifying and statistically testing patterns across studies. The basic procedure of the case survey is (a) to select a group of existing case studies relevant to the chosen research questions, (b) to design a coding scheme for systematic conversion of the qualitative case descriptions into quantified variables, (c) to use multiple raters to code the cases and measure their inter-rater reliability, and (d) to analyse the coded data statistically. Another example of multi-method studies is focus groups which combine interviews and observations. Under the guidance of a group leader, selected participants are prompted to discuss their opinions, reactions and feelings about a product, service, type of situation or concept. The researcher should try to create a relaxed atmosphere and record what is said while also observing how participants react.

Contributions of field methods to theory development and testing

Before a theory can be tested, it must be constructed. The process of theory construction typically includes steps such as the delimitation of the phenomenon to be studied, the identification of relevant constructs and the development of hypotheses (Eisenhardt, 1989; Yin, 1984). Theory building essentially draws on inductive logic, which is the hallmark of the subjectivist or phenomenological approach. This approach emphasizes qualitative data-gathering methods such as in-depth study techniques, interpretive data analysis and intuitive inferences.

After a theory has been assembled, it can be tested. Here, it is usually the objectivist approach which is predominant. This approach uses natural science as a model for research, stressing methodological rigour and the internal validity of its studies. Research within this perspective aims to create lawlike generalizations that are empirically testable. Because of statistical requirements, theory testing usually requires studies of a larger size and a quantitative perspective as compared with theory building.

Research in entrepreneurship is still in is early stages compared with almost all the physical and most of the social sciences (Brazeal and Herbert, 1999). Therefore theoretical agreement would ideally precede empirical agreement. This suggests that research efforts should be primarily directed at theory building rather than theory testing. Indeed, entrepreneurship will gain in credibility and become a discipline only if it is built on a solid theoretical framework. Development of theory is a central activity in organizational research, and authors have traditionally developed theory by combining observations from previous literature, common sense and experience. However, the tie to actual data has often been tenuous (Shane and Venkataraman, 2000). Yet, as Glaser and Strauss (1967) argue, it is the intimate connection with empirical reality that permits the development of a testable, relevant and valid theory.

Similarly, Bygrave (1989, p. 20) asserted:

> What we need at this stage are more empirical models that describe observed phenomena as accurately as possible. But we should be careful not to get caught up in Laplace's dream that all phenomena could be described by formulas. Even in the physical sciences, a model is at best a mathematical metaphor of reality; in the social sciences, it may be nothing more than a caricature.

This suggests that there is a need for theories to guide the selection of the key variables in entrepreneurship. A variety of methodologies and data collection techniques should be considered to explore the entrepreneurial actors, process and events. Moreover, qualitative rather than quantitative methodologies may be appropriate to explore particular research questions. Along these lines, Eisenhardt (1989) proposed a process of inducting theory using case studies. Overall, such a process is highly interactive and tightly linked to data. This research approach is especially appropriate in new topic areas such as entrepreneurship.

To explore or test present theories, research questions and/or hypotheses, several methodological issues need to be considered when focusing upon entrepreneurs as well the entrepreneurial event and process. Hofer and Bygrave (1992) have highlighted the stages that should be considered. They suggested that studies in entrepreneurship need to justify the research design. The research design is the fundamental plan for carrying out the empirical data gathering necessary to corroborate or refute the basic conceptual frameworks, models or theories being studied. Bygrave (1989) remarked that researchers should collect their own data to get at the heart of the entrepreneurship process. A slow, methodical process of careful observation and description is required. Once good description is achieved, good comparisons and contrasts can be made, and subsets of similar ventures can be studied.

In recent years, a considerable growth in field studies focusing upon entrepreneurs and entrepreneurial events and processes has become apparent. Savage and Black (1995) provided a two-dimensional framework to categorize the crucial methodological choices. They suggested that researchers must consider epistemological choices along one dimension and teleological choices along the other. Epistemological categories focus on three techniques of gathering data: experiencing (that is, observation, participation), enquiring (that is, interviews) and examining (that is, archival items). The teleological dimension emphasizes the purposes of a researcher enquiry. These can range from the objective (for example, the characteristics of language used as a form of communication in entrepreneurship and the discovery of regularities) to the more subjective (for example, the meaning of actions and reflection). Each of these approaches may be associated with different types of field data. For example, attempts to discover regularities may be based on grounded theory and event analysis. Comprehension of the meaning of actions may, however, be approached using phenomenology. Savage and Black noted that future research in entrepreneurship might usefully analyse the meaning of entrepreneurial action utilizing an 'experiencing' technique of data collection.

At this early stage of theory development, the purpose of a theory can vary to encompass description, explanation or prediction. To achieve this goal, we suggest considering the use of different approaches, methods and techniques in the same study to overcome the potential bias and sterility of a single-method approach. This calls for triangulation (Easterby-Smith *et al.*, Thorpe and Lowe, 1991). By combining multiple observers, methods and empirical materials, researchers in entrepreneurship can also hope to overcome the weakness or intrinsic biases and problems that come from single-method, single-observer, single-theory studies. For example, Denzin and Lincoln (1994) argue that the use of different methods by a number of researchers studying the same phenomenon should, if their conclusions are the same, lead to greater validity and reliability than a single methodological approach. We can identify four basic types of triangulation:

- data triangulation, involving time, space and individuals;
- investigator triangulation, which consists of the use of multiple, rather than single observers;
- theory triangulation, which consists of using more than one theoretical scheme in the interpretation of the phenomenon;
- methodological triangulation, which involves using more than one method and may consist of within-method or between-method strategies.

Triangulation implies, in Larsson's words (1993), that a third line of research should be proposed, whereby quantitative methods are included with qualitative research to avoid antagonism between the ojectivist and subjectivist schools of thought. This approach allows for the blended methods such as case survey analysis, case meta-analysis and structured content analysis of cases. The focus is on the use of case study methodology as a mediator between the subjectivist and objectivist approach. The suggestion is that case studies should develop through implementing ideas from the objectivist tradition, stressing rigour and comparative logic.

Conclusion
Given the nature of entrepreneurship and the fact that it is still an emerging field, we should, at this stage of research, emphasize interpretation and understanding, not purposive–rational explanation and prediction. Understanding may be achieved through better conceptualizations, formulation of central questions for future actions, or simply through reporting relevant action patterns during the opportunity identification–evaluation–exploitation stages of the entrepreneurial process. At the same time, a better understanding of the nascent entrepreneur–new venture dialogic is also needed. Instead of aiming at 'grand' theories with testable hypotheses, we may also focus on developing medium-range theories that are less broad in scope and at a lower level of abstraction.

This calls for (a) a balanced research agenda, (b) more sophisticated, multifaceted research approaches, and (c) more innovative data-gathering techniques. Until now, many studies have attempted to test theories borrowed from other fields of research, before establishing a solid theoretical framework for entrepreneurship. More efforts should be directed at theory building at this early stage. Theory generation in complex and dynamic settings like emerging organizations calls for a variety and a combination of approaches, methods and data-collection techniques. Such a triangulation could find a deeper understanding of forces affecting the entrepreneurship phenomenon, through highlighting the 'what, who, how and why' of organizational and individual action. New data-collection techniques could also be used. Most studies in entrepreneurship in the past have relied solely on interviews or questionnaires as the primary technique to gather data. Observations, archival analysis and simulations have been too often neglected as potential sources of information.

Ultimately however, the research approaches, methods and data-collection techniques discussed here do not prescribe how analysis should be undertaken, in order to have valuable and robust research findings. Open-ended or semi-structured interviews, for example, can be analysed using a host of different methods, ranging from traditional textual content analysis to sophisticated computer-based statistical packages. In this sense, it is important to recognize that it is not necessarily the selection of field method that accounts for the value of the research, but the wider research design and the analysis technique(s) employed.

References

Bird, B.J (1989), *Entrepreneurial Behavior*, Glenview, IL: Scott, Foresman and Co.

Brazeal, D. and Herbert,T. (1999), 'The genesis of entrepreneurship', *Entrepreneurship Theory and Practice*, 23, 29–45.

Bygrave, W.D. (1989), 'The entrepreneurship paradigm: A philosophical look at its research methologies', *Entrepreneurship Theory and Practice*, 14, 7–26.

Denzin, N.K. and Lincoln, Y.S. (eds) (1994), *Handbook of Qualitative Research*, Thousand Oaks: Sage.

Easterby-Smith, M., Thorpe, R. and Lowe, A. (1991), *Management Research: An Introduction*, London: Sage.

Eisenhardt, K.M. (1989), 'Building theories from case study research', *Academy of Management Review*, 14(4), 532–50.

Gartner, W.B. (1989), 'Who is the entrepreneur? is the wrong question', *Entrepreneurship Theory and Practice*, 13, 47–68.

Glaser, B. and Strauss, A. (1967), *The Discovery of Grounded Theory: Strategies of Qualitative Research*, London: Weidenfeld and Nicolson.

Hofer, C. and Bygrave, W.D. (1992), 'Researching entrepreneurship', *Entrepreneurship Theory and Practice*,16, 91–100

Hussey, J. and Hussey, R. (1997), *Business Research*, London: Macmillan.

Larsson, R. (1993), 'Case survey methodology : Quantitative analysis of patterns across case studies', *Academy of Management Journal*, 36(6), 1515–46.

Low, M.B. and MacMillan, I.C. (1988), 'Entrepreneurship: Past Research and Future Challenges', *Journal of Management*, 14(2), 139–61.

Reynold, P.D., Camp, S.M., Bygrave, W.D., Autio, E. and Hay, M. (2001), *Global Entrepreneurship – Monitor, Executive Report*, Kansas City: Kaufman Center for Entrepreneurial Leadership.

Savage, G.T. and Black, J.A. (1995), 'Firms-level entrepreneurship and field research, The studies and their methodological context', *Entrepreneurship Theory and Practice*, 19, 25–34.

Shane, S. and Venkataraman, S. (2000), 'The promise of entrepreneurship as a field of research', *Academy of Management Review*, 25(1), 217–26.

Snow, C. and Thomas, J.B. (1994), 'Field research methods in strategic management: Contributions to theory building and testing', *Journal of Management*, 31, 458–79.

Venkataraman, S. (1997), 'The Distinctive Domain of Entrepreneurship Research', in J. Katz (ed.), *Advances in Entrepreneurship, Firm Emergence and Growth*, Greenwich, CT: JAI Press, pp. 119–38.

Yin, R.K. (1984), *Case Study Research: Design and Methods*, Beverly Hills: Sage.

Zikmund, W.G. (1997), *Business Research Methods*, 5th edn, Forth Worth: The Dryden Press.

Index